CALIFORNIA
FISHING

TOM STIENSTRA

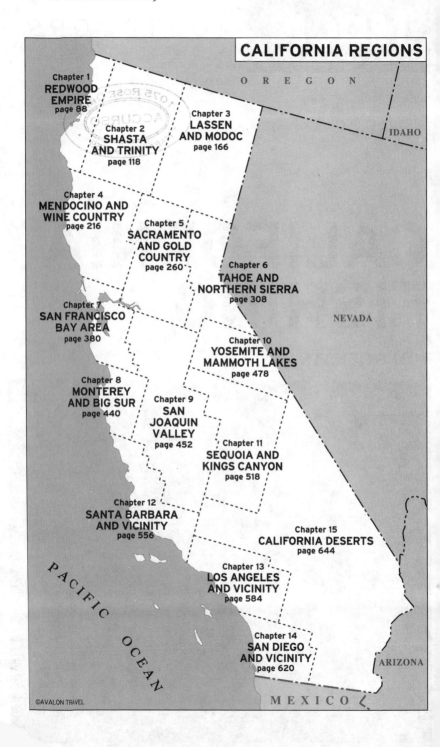

CALIFORNIA REGIONS

OREGON

IDAHO

NEVADA

ARIZONA

PACIFIC OCEAN

MEXICO

©AVALON TRAVEL

Contents

How to Use This Book

ABOUT THE FISHING PROFILES

The sites are listed in a consistent, easy-to-read format to help you choose the ideal fishing spot. If you already know the name of the specific site you want to visit, or the name of the surrounding geological area or nearby feature (town, national or state park, forest, mountain, lake, river, etc.), look it up in the index and turn to the corresponding page. Here is a sample profile:

Site name and number →

Map the site can be found on and page number the map can be found on →

1 SOMEWHERE USA FISHING

General location of the site in relation to the nearest major town or landmark

Rating: 8

at the mouth of the Somewhere River on Lake Someplace

Map 1.2, page 4 **BEST (**

Symbol indicating that the site is listed among the author's top picks

Each fishing location in this book begins with a brief overview of its setting. The description typically addresses the best spots and approaches for catching fish, seasonal variations in species availability (including information on hatchery plants), special regulations, and the average size of fish caught at that location. This section also includes information on other activities popular at the site.

Facilities, fees: This section notes the presence of boat ramps and access areas, as well as the facilities available at or near the site, such as restrooms, picnic areas, snack bars, restaurants, lodges, marinas, boat rental outlets, campgrounds, and where to buy supplies, such as groceries and gas. Information on launch and access fees is also noted here.

Directions: This section provides mile-by-mile driving directions to the fishing spot from the nearest major town or highway.

Contact: This section provides contact information for the site as well as nearby boat rentals, bait and tackle shops, and other related services. It also notes whether maps are available for purchase; see *Resources* at the back of the book for additional contact information.

ABOUT THE RATINGS

Every fishing spot in this book has been rated on a scale of 1 through 10. The ratings are based on three elements: (1) number of fish, (2) size of fish, and (3) scenic beauty.

10	Can't be improved!
9	Has all three of the elements.
8	Has two of the elements, almost three.
7	Has two of the elements.
6	Has one of the elements, almost two.
5	Has one of the elements, parts of the others.
4	Has one of the elements.
3	Almost has one of the elements.
2	Has none of the elements.
1	Hopeless.

Keep in mind that several factors influence a successful fishing trip. Many waters rated a 4 or 5 can provide good fishing and a quality adventure when conditions are ideal. Similarly, even at the highest-rated waters, the fish can go off the bite (no kidding).

MAP SYMBOLS

Expressway	80	Interstate Freeway	✗	Airfield
Primary Road	101	U.S. Highway	✈	Airport
Secondary Road	21	State Highway	○	City/Town
Unpaved Road	66	County Highway	▲	Mountain
Ferry		Lake	♠	Park
National Border		Dry Lake	ノ(	Pass
State Border		Seasonal Lake	◉	State Capital

ABOUT THE MAPS

This book is divided into chapters based on major regions in the state; an overview map of these regions precedes the table of contents. Each chapter begins with a map of the region, which is further broken down into detail maps. Sites are noted on the detail maps by number.

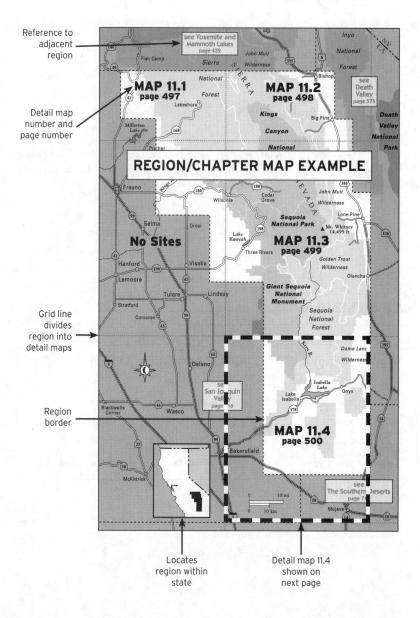

Reference to adjacent region

Detail map number and page number

Grid line divides region into detail maps

Region border

REGION/CHAPTER MAP EXAMPLE

No Sites

Locates region within state

Detail map 11.4 shown on next page

Indicates adjacent detail maps within region

Locates detail map within region

Map number → **Map 11.4**

Sites shown on detail map and the page range where those sites are listed → **Sites 105-117 Pages 564-570**

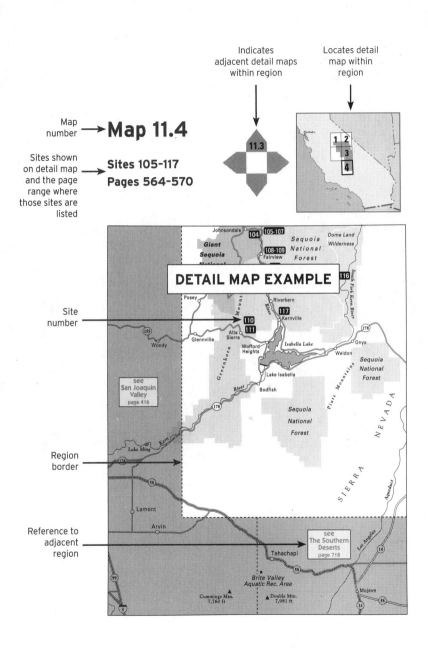

11.3

1 2
3
4

Johnsondale 104 105-107
Giant Sequoia National 108-109 Fairview

Sequoia National Forest

Dome Land Wilderness

DETAIL MAP EXAMPLE

116

Posey

Riverkern

Site number 110 117 Kernville
111
Alta Sierra
Glennville Wofford Heights *Isabella Lake*

155

Woody

178

Onyx

Weldon

Sequoia National Forest

see San Joaquin Valley page 416

Lake Isabella

Bodfish

Sequoia National Forest

178

Region border

Lake Ming

Lamont

Reference to adjacent region

Arvin

see The Southern Deserts page 718

Tehachapi

58

Los Angeles

14

99

Brite Valley Aquatic Rec. Area

Cummings Mtn. 7,760 ft

Double Mtn. 7,981 ft

Mojave

58

5

INTRODUCTION

© RAMBOB STIENSTRA

Author's Note

California has roughly 400 drive-to lakes, 500 hike-in lakes, 175 major streams, and 1,200 miles of coastline. That means there are enough places covered in this book to fish a different spot every weekend for 22 years. My dream is to capture all of this and to give you the best guide to fishing in California.

To merit your faith, I have personally ventured to all 58 counties in California, searching for every hidden spot, as well as for the secrets at the better-known ones. I, along with senior research editor Kathie Morgan, have checked and reviewed every listing in this book. And while hundreds of people were involved in polishing the final product, the book you hold in your hands right now was personally worked over on my keyboard.

Even though *Moon California Camping* is my bestselling title, *Moon California Fishing* is my life work, and it involves 30 years of roaming around California, looking for every spot to cast to.

Each spot has its expert—and when I visit, I try to fish with them. It's like parting the curtains on a window to a secret world where wonderful things are possible each and every moment. Some 40 fishing experts, each of whom I fished with, were involved in the creation of the how-to section of the book. Now you're fishing with them too. Each is listed—and thanked—in my *Acknowledgments*.

I fish, hike, and camp 365 days a year. It's my full-time job, and has been my career for more than 30 years. If there is one book I want you to have on the seat of your car as you venture out to find California's best fishing, this is it.

Look for my boat out on the water, the custom-designed 18-footer with the words *The Stienstra Navy* on the big Honda outboard. See you out there.

—Tom Stienstra

Best Fishing Spots

Can't decide where to fish? The following lists provide the top California fishing spots in several categories:

◖ Best Freshwater Fisheries

Sacramento River: Redding to Anderson, trout in stream, Shasta and Trinity, page 158.
Clear Lake, catfish, Mendocino and Wine Country, page 234.
San Joaquin Delta, largemouth bass, Sacramento and Gold Country, page 292.
Lake Tahoe, Mackinaw trout, Tahoe and Northern Sierra, page 341.
Ansel Adams Wilderness, lake trout, Yosemite and Mammoth Lakes, page 494.

◖ Best Saltwater Fisheries

Crescent City Deep Sea, rockfish and lingcod on Point George Reef,
    Redwood Empire, page 98.
Ventura Deep Sea/Channel Islands, halibut on Santa Rosa Island, Santa Barbara
    and Vicinity, page 573.
Catalina Island, yellowtail, Los Angeles and Vicinity, page 588.
Santa Monica/Redondo Deep Sea, bonito, Los Angeles and Vicinity, page 589.
San Diego Deep Sea, albacore, San Diego and Vicinity, page 626.

◖ Best Hike-In Fisheries

Marble Mountain Wilderness, Shasta and Trinity, page 123.
Trinity Alps Wilderness, Shasta and Trinity, page 141.
Middle Fork Feather River, Sacramento and Gold Country, page 268.
Henry W. Coe State Park, San Francisco Bay Area, page 434.
Ansel Adams Wilderness, Yosemite and Mammoth Lakes, page 494.
Golden Trout Wilderness, Sequoia and Kings Canyon, page 549.

Steve Griffin with a Mackinaw trout

◖ Best Places to Teach Kids to Fish

Iron Gate Reservoir/Copco Lake, Shasta and Trinity, page 128.
Lake Siskiyou, Shasta and Trinity, page 136.
Shasta Lake, Shasta and Trinity, page 152.
Clear Lake, Mendocino and Wine Country, page 234.
Lake Berryessa, Mendocino and Wine Country, page 247.
San Pablo Reservoir, San Francisco Bay Area, page 399.
Lake Chabot, San Francisco Bay Area, page 403.
Del Valle Reservoir, San Francisco Bay Area, page 410.
Pinecrest Lake, Yosemite and Mammoth Lakes, page 481.
Convict Lake, Yosemite and Mammoth Lakes, page 508.
Pine Flat Lake, Sequoia and Kings Canyon, page 540.
Santa Ana River Lakes, Los Angeles and Vicinity, page 606.
Lake Perris, Los Angeles and Vicinity, page 607.
Irvine Lake, Los Angeles and Vicinity, page 608.

◖ Most Unusual Fisheries

Trinity Alps Wilderness, Shasta and Trinity, page 141.
Independence Lake, Tahoe and Northern Sierra, page 322.
Martis Creek Reservoir, Tahoe and Northern Sierra, page 336.
Hell Hole Reservoir, Tahoe and Northern Sierra, page 340.
Kirman Lake, Tahoe and Northern Sierra, page 371.
Dixon Lake, San Diego and Vicinity, page 628.
Salton Sea, California Deserts, page 659.

Fishing Tips

STARTING OUT

Brother Rambob creeps up on the mountain stream as quiet as a scout in a Zane Grey western. For fishing in the wilderness, he wears moccasins, stalks as much as walks, and is careful to keep his shadow off the water. With his little spinning rod, he'll zip his lure within an inch or two of its desired mark. He probes along rocks, the edges of riffles, pocket water, or wherever he can find a change in river habitat. Rambob is trout fishing, and he's a master at it.

In most cases he'll catch a trout on his first or second cast. After that it's time to move up the river, giving no spot much more than five minutes' due. Stick and move, stick and move, stalking the stream like a bobcat that homes in on an unsuspecting rabbit. He might keep a few trout for dinner, but mostly he releases what he catches. Rambob doesn't necessarily fish for food. It's the feeling that comes with it.

You don't need a million dollars' worth of fancy gear to catch fish. What you need is the right outlook—like Rambob's—no matter what you fish for, and that can be learned. That goes regardless of whether you are fishing for trout or bass, the two most popular fish in the United States, or most any other fish. Though you might buy and try everything imaginable, your fishing tackle selection at your grasp should be as simple and clutter-free as possible.

At home I've got every piece of fishing tackle you might imagine, and many tackle boxes, racks, and cabinets filled with all kinds of stuff. I've got one lure that looks like a chipmunk and another that resembles a miniature can of beer with hooks. If I hear of something

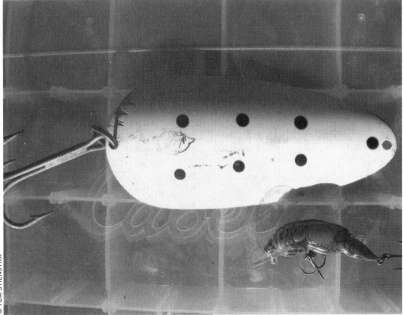

© TOM STIENSTRA

Note the teeth marks on this big Dardevle.

all spooled up for spring

new, I want to try it and usually do. It's a result of my lifelong fascination with the sport.

But if you just want to catch fish, there's an easier way to go. And when I go fishing, I take that path. I don't try to bring everything; it would be impossible. Instead I bring a relatively small amount of gear. At home I will scan my tackle boxes for equipment and lures, make my selections, and bring just the essentials. Rod, reel, and tackle will fit into a side pocket of my backpack or a small carrying bag.

So what kind of rod should be used on an outdoor trip? For most freshwater anglers, I suggest the use of a light, multipiece spinning rod for trout that will break down to a small size. One of the best quality pack rods is a four-piece Daiwa 6.5-foot, number SMC 664ULFS. Other major rod manufacturers offer similar premium rods. It's tough to miss with any of them.

The use of graphite/glass composites in fishing rods has made them lighter and more

sensitive, yet stronger. The only downside to graphite as a rod material is that it can be brittle. If you rap your rod against something, it can crack or cause a weak spot. That weak spot can eventually snap under even light pressure, like setting a hook or casting. Of course, a bit of care will prevent that from ever occurring.

If you haven't bought a fishing reel in some time, you will be surprised at the quality and price of micro spinning reels on the market. The reels come tiny and strong, with rear-control drag systems. Daiwa, Shimano, Cabela's, BassPro, and others all make premium reels. They're worth it. With your purchase, you've just bought a reel that will last for years and years.

The one downside to spinning reels is that after long-term use, the bail spring will weaken. The result is that after casting and beginning to reel, the bail will sometimes not flip over and allow the reel to retrieve the line. Then you have to do it by hand. This can be incredibly frustrating, particularly when stream fishing, where instant line pickup is essential. The solution is to have a new bail spring installed every few years. This is a cheap, quick operation for a tackle expert.

You might own a giant tackle box filled with lures, but on a fishing trip you are better off to fit just the essentials into a small container. One of the best ways to do that is to use the Plano Micro-Magnum 3414, a tiny two-sided tackle box for trout anglers that fits into a shirt pocket. In mine, I can fit 20 lures in one side of the box and 20 flies, split shot, and snap swivels in the other. For bass lures, which are bigger, you need a slightly larger box, but the same principle applies.

There are more fishing lures on the market than you can imagine, but a few special ones can do the job. I make sure these are in my box on every trip. For trout, I carry a small black Panther Martin spinner with yellow spots, a small gold Kastmaster, a yellow Roostertail, a gold Z-Ray with red spots, a Super Duper, and a Mepps Lightning spinner.

You can take it a step further using insider's wisdom. My old pal Ed "the Dunk" showed me his trick of taking a tiny Dardevle spoon, spray painting it flat black, and dabbing five tiny red dots on it. It's a real killer, particularly in tiny streams where the trout are spooky.

The best trout catcher I've ever used on rivers is a small metal lure called a Met-L Fly. On days when nothing else works, it can be like going to a shooting gallery. The problem is that the lure is nearly impossible to find. Rambob and I consider the few we have remaining

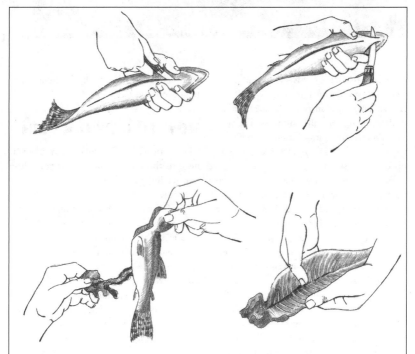

Basic Steps to Cleaning a Fish: First, slit belly from anal vent to gills. Then sever lower junctions of gills. Next, pull out innards and gills. And last but not least, run thumbnail along cavity to clean out dark matter.

small spoons

so valuable that if the lure is snagged on a rock, a cold swim is deemed mandatory for its retrieval. These lures in vintage shape from the mid-1960s are very difficult to find (a poor imitation failed an introduction in the 1990s), but I still have a stash. In fact, I keep one on my computer stand.

For bass, you can also fit all you need into a small plastic tackle box. I have fished with many bass pros, and all of them actually use just a few lures: a white spinner bait, a small jig called a Gits-It, a surface plug called a Zara Spook, and plastic worms. At times, as when the bass move into shoreline areas during the spring, shad minnow imitations like those made by Rebel or Rapala can be dynamite. My favorite is the one-inch, blue-silver Rapala. Every spring as the lakes begin to warm and the fish snap out of their winter doldrums, I like to float and paddle around in my small raft. I'll cast that little Rapala along the shoreline and catch and release hundreds of bass, bluegill, and sunfish. The fish

are usually sitting close to the shoreline, awaiting my offering.

HOW TO CATCH A FISH

There's an old angler's joke about how you need to think like a fish. But if you're the one getting zilched, you may not think it's so funny.

The irony is that it is your mental approach, what you see and what you miss, that often determines your fishing luck. Some people will spend a lot of money on tackle, lures, and fishing clothes, and that done, just saunter up to a stream or lake, cast out, and wonder why they are not catching fish. The answer is their mental outlook. They are not attuning themselves to their surroundings.

You must live on nature's level, not your own. Try this and you will become aware of things you never believed even existed. Soon you will see things that will allow you to catch fish. You can get a head start by reading about fishing, but to get your degree in fishing, you must attend the University of Nature.

On every fishing trip, regardless of what you fish for, try to follow three hard-and-fast rules:

1. Always approach the fishing spot so you will be undetected.
2. Present your lure, fly, or bait in a manner so it appears completely natural, as if no line were attached.
3. Stick and move, hitting one spot, working it the best you can, then moving to the next.

Approach

No one can just walk up to a stream or lake, cast out, and start catching fish as if someone had waved a magic wand. Instead, give the fish credit for being smart. After all, they live there.

Your approach must be completely undetected by the fish. Fish can sense your presence through sight and sound, though this is misinterpreted by most people. By sight, this rarely means the fish actually see you; more likely they will see your shadow on the water or the movement of your arm or rod while casting. By sound, it doesn't mean they hear you talking, but that they will detect the vibrations of your footsteps along the shore, kicking a rock, or the unnatural plunking sound of a heavy cast hitting the water. Any of these elements can spook them off the bite. To fish undetected, you must walk softly, keep your shadow off the water, and keep your casting motion low. All of these keys become easier at sunrise or sunset, when shadows are on the water. At midday a high sun causes a high level of light penetration in the water, which can make the fish skittish to any foreign presence.

As when hunting, you must stalk the spots. When my brother Rambob sneaks up on a fishing spot, he is like a burglar sneaking through an unlocked window.

Presentation

Your lure, fly, or bait must appear in the water as if no line were attached, so it looks

as natural as possible. My pal Mo Furniss has skin-dived in rivers to watch what the fish see when somebody is fishing.

"You wouldn't believe it," he said. "When the lure hits the water, every trout within 40 feet, like 15, 20 trout, will do a little zigzag. They all see the lure and are aware something is going on. Meanwhile, onshore the guy casting doesn't get a bite and thinks there aren't any fish in the river."

If your offering is aimed at fooling a fish into striking, it must appear as part of its natural habitat, like an insect just hatched or a small fish looking for a spot to hide. That's where you come in.

After you have sneaked up on a fishing spot, you should zip your cast upstream and start your retrieval as soon as it hits the water. If you let the lure sink to the bottom and then start the retrieval, you have no chance. A minnow, for instance, does not sink to the bottom, then start swimming. On rivers, the retrieval should be more of a drift, as if the "minnow" is in trouble and the current is sweeping it downstream.

When fishing on trout streams, always hike and cast upriver and retrieve as the offering drifts downstream in the current. This is effective because trout will sit almost motionless, pointed upstream, finning against the current. This way they can see anything coming their direction, and if a potential food morsel arrives, all they need to do is move over a few inches, open their mouths, and they've got an easy lunch. Thus you must cast upstream.

Conversely, if you cast downstream, your retrieval will bring the lure from behind the fish, where he cannot see it approaching. And I've never seen a trout that had eyes in its tail. In addition, when you're retrieving a downstream lure, the river current tends to sweep your lure inshore to the rocks.

Finding Spots

A lot of anglers don't catch fish. The key is where they are looking. The rule of the wild is that fish (and other wildlife) congregate

The rule of the wild is that wildlife will congregate wherever there is a distinct change in habitat. To find where fish are hiding, look where a riffle pours into a small pond, where a rapid plunges into a deep hole and flattens, and around submerged trees, rock piles, and boulders in the middle of a long riffle.

© TOM STIENSTRA

big lures

wherever there is a distinct change in the habitat. This is where you should begin your search.

In a river, it can be where a riffle pours into a small pool, a rapid that plunges into a deep hole and flattens, a big boulder in the middle of a long riffle, a shoreline point, a rock pile, a submerged tree. Look for the changes. Conversely, long, straight stretches of shoreline do not hold fish—the habitat is lousy.

On rivers, the most productive areas are often where short riffles tumble into small oxygenated pools. After sneaking up from the downstream side and staying low, you should zip your cast so the lure plops gently into the white water just above the pool. Start your retrieval instantly; the lure will drift downstream and plunk into the pool. Bang! That's where the trout will hit. Take a few more casts and then head upstream to the next spot.

With a careful approach and lure presentation and by fishing in the right spots, you have the ticket to many exciting days on the water.

FISHING PRIVATE PONDS

An astute few know of California's nonpublic paradises—some 6,000 lakes and ponds located on private property, where you have a chance to create your own personal haven for hiking or fishing.

Private ponds and lakes are perfect destinations for people who don't mind making the significant effort to find them and then finagle permission to fish them. In exchange for some work, you can be rewarded with being able to fish and hike in great places with nobody else around.

Many of these lakes and adjoining wild country are on privately owned ranches in the foothills. You might figure I would be the last person in the world that ranchers would let on their private property—after all, a guy who is liable to write about it? But guess again, because by using a relatively simple system, I have gained access to ranches with more than 25 private lakes.

These include ranches on the coast where short hikes take me to lookouts with astounding views of the Pacific Ocean, and ranches with lakes in the foothills where I have caught as many as 50 bass weighing up to six pounds in a few hours. The surrounding habitat is often home to rabbits and deer that are not only abundant but seem more curious than cautious about the rare sight of a human.

First, to imagine what is possible, consider a new perspective. I wish I could take every person who complains about California being too crowded for a ride in my airplane. Looking down, you'll discover that about 90 percent of the state consists of wild, unsettled country in the hills, while the remaining 10 percent in the flatlands is jammed with clogged roads and towns and cities. In the country, you can look down from an airplane and discover that lakes seem to be hidden away almost everywhere, and this is where your search for a personal paradise starts.

Well, you don't need a ride in an airplane to discover this; just make a trip to the county assessor's office of your choice.

The key piece of knowledge is that at every county assessor's office in California, each acre of land has been mapped and cataloged, allowing anybody with a spare hour to find secret, private lakes and learn who owns them.

The walls of many assessor's offices are covered with giant maps that show the county in great detail. You can scan these maps to locate hidden lakes on private property. I've done it many times. In almost all cases, the maps are split into numbered parcels or grids, and by following a simple numbering system, you are directed to more detailed map books. Eventually you are led to a property owner's name and address. It's like connecting the dots—easy detective work—and completing the chain takes about 10–15 minutes per property. If you are new to tracking the paper trail, employees at the assessor's offices are usually extremely helpful.

So by simply scanning maps and tracking through parcel books, you can find three or four large ranch properties with lakes, as well as the identities and addresses of their owners. This information is available to the public primarily for real estate investors, who track dates and prices of all purchases, and for county officials, who record transactions and levy property taxes for each parcel.

Once you know the identity of a rancher,

ANGLER ETHICS

- Always keep only the fish you will eat. Never waste a fish.

- Always bring a plastic bag to pick up any litter you come across. Never litter.

- Always check state fishing regulations prior to fishing any water. Never guess.

- Always take personal responsibility for practicing safe boating skills. Never hope.

- Always have a map before venturing to hike-in streams. Never trespass.

- Always conduct yourself quietly in campgrounds. Never disturb your neighbor.

- Always be absolutely fire-safe. Never figure, "It'll be okay."

- Always call the Department of Fish and Game's toll-free poacher hotline at 888/334-2258 (888/ DFG-CAL-TIP) if you see illegal activity. Never ignore it.

- Always share information with children, particularly those new to the sport. Never be rude; you will be repaid in kind.

- Always give financial support to the conservation organization that best protects your favorite fishery. Never expect somebody else to protect it.

you need to make a direct, friendly approach, attempting to gain permission for access. A word of warning: Ranch owners are private people, and they do not want to be your friend. Instead of glad-handing, be direct but courteous, get to the point, and don't waste their time.

I usually start by phoning if I can obtain the number, then explain right away why I am calling: "Captain Picard, just once or twice a year it would be of great value to me to be able to hike on your ranch and maybe fish a little in your lake. I would be happy to visit in a way that would never even let you know I was there."

If they haven't hung up yet, I might follow with: "To visit it, even rarely, would be like a dream."

If they're still listening, make your pitch: "I would like to obtain permission to fish, catch-and-release?"

The rancher usually responds without a direct no, but rather by explaining the potential problems of opening a private ranch to visitors, so make a note of every problem cited, then respond: "I got it—gates must be kept closed, stay clear of the cows, no swimming in the lake, no hunting, and throw the fish back. That sounds great to me."

The call usually takes less than five minutes. Believe it or not, ranchers are almost never asked directly for permission for access, and while some will say no straight off, others are beguiled, even surprised, at the lengths some will go "just to go fishing." Sometimes it can take two or three calls and a short private meeting, but one way or another, it is often possible to gain access to these private ranchlands. I usually arrange access to each property just once or twice a year. After all, you never want to be considered a pain in the neck.

Detective work and persistence are required. Is it worth it? Yes! The first time I hiked on a private ranch near the coast, I spotted 12 rabbits and three deer, and after hiking up to a ridge, I witnessed one of the most gorgeous

© TOM STIENSTRA

medium spoons

sunsets imaginable, the sun dipping into the ocean. The first time I fished a private pond, I caught 38 bass and bluegill, with 20 of the bass ranging 14–18 inches.

Not only that, but after learning that others were interested in their ponds, some ranchers planted bass, catfish, and bluegill for the first time, turning fishless ponds into great fishing holes in just a few years. At one of these ponds, four years after the first bass was planted, I caught a six-pounder that towed my little raft around just like in *The Old Man and the Sea*.

Of course, there is no guarantee of great fishing. Take the rancher I met at Duarte's Tavern, in Pescadero. After I explained my intentions, he got this excited look in his eye and said, "Do you mind if I fish with you?"

Are you kidding? I thought, and we were off to his lake. In no time, we were tying on our lures. The guy appeared so excited that it looked like he might explode.

"This is great!" he said. "Why, until you called, I didn't even know there were any fish in my lake!"

Turned out (heh, heh), there weren't.

GETTING KIDS HOOKED ON THE OUTDOORS

How do you get a boy or girl excited about the outdoors? How do you compete with a remote control and a television? How do you prove to a kid that success comes from persistence, spirit, and logic—and not from pushing buttons?

The answer lies in these 10 Commandments for Kids. These lessons will get youngsters excited about the outdoors and make sure adults help foster their interest, not kill it. Some are obvious, some are not, but all are important:

1. Children should be taken on trips to places where there is a guarantee of action without the need for complicated techniques. A good example is camping in a park where large numbers of wildlife can be viewed, such as squirrels, chipmunks, deer, and even a bear.

Other good choices are fishing at a small pond loaded with bluegill or going hunting and letting a kid shoot a 0.22 at pinecones all day. Boys and girls want action, not solitude.

2. Enthusiasm is contagious. If you are not excited about an adventure, you can't expect a child to be. Show a genuine zest for life in the outdoors and point out everything as if it were the first time you had ever seen it.

3. Always, always, always be seated when talking to someone small. This allows the adult and the child to be on the same level. That is why fishing in a small boat is perfect. Nothing is worse for youngsters than having a big person look down at them and give orders. What fun is that?

4. Always demonstrate how to do something, whether gathering sticks for a campfire, cleaning a trout, or tying a knot. Never tell. Always show. When a kid is lectured, the buttons often click to "off." Instead, children learn most behavior patterns and outdoor skills by watching adults—even when the adults are not aware they are being watched.

5. Let kids be kids. Allow the adventure to happen, rather than trying to force it to conform to some preconceived plan. If kids get sidetracked watching pollywogs, chasing butterflies, or sneaking up on chipmunks, let them be. A youngster can have more fun turning over rocks and examining different kinds of bugs than sitting in one spot waiting for a fish to bite.

6. Expect the attention span of a young person to be short. Instead of getting frustrated, use it to your advantage. How? By bringing along a bag of candy and snacks. When there is a lull in the camp activity, out comes the bag. Don't let them know what goodies await, so each one becomes a surprise. I always do this with my boys. We call these "bonus items."

7. Make absolutely certain the child's sleeping bag is clean, dry, and warm. Nothing is worse than discomfort when trying to sleep, and a refreshing sleep makes for a positive attitude the next day. In addition, kids can become quite

© TOM STIENSTRA

scared of animals at night. A parent should not wait for signs of fear, but always play the part of the outdoor guardian, the one who will "take care of everything."

8. Kids quickly relate to outdoor ethics. They will enjoy eating everything they catch, building a safe campfire, and picking up their litter, and from that they will develop a sense of pride. Bringing extra plastic garbage bags to pick up any trash you come across is a good idea. Kids long remember when they make right what somebody else has done wrong.

9. If you want youngsters hooked on the outdoors for life, take a close-up photograph of them holding up fish they have caught, blowing on the campfire, or completing other camp tasks. Young children can forget how much fun they had, but they'll never forget if they have a picture to remind them.

10. The least important word you can ever say to a kid is "I." Keep track of how often you are saying "Thank you," and "What do you think?" Not very often? Then you'll lose out. The most important words of all are: "I am proud of you."

Sport Fish

BLUEGILL, SUNFISH, AND CRAPPIE

BEST FISHING SPOTS

1. Private ranch ponds
2. Lake Hodges
3. Lake Cuyamaca
4. Lake Berryessa
5. Irvine Lake
6. Lake Perris
7. Lake Amador
8. Clear Lake
9. El Capitan Lake
10. Shasta Lake

bluegill

BOB RACE

Tackle

Use ultra-light spinning rod-and-reel combinations when fishing for bluegill, sunfish, or crappie.

Rods: Fenwick HMG: 4.5-foot UL spinning (GS46UL), 5-foot UL spinning (GS50UL); Berkley Series One: 5-foot UL spinning (SOS501UL).

Reels: Abu Garcia Cardinal 801 (C801); Mitchell 310XGe (310XGe); Daiwa Spinmatic Z500T, Pinnacle TC2 (one of the world's smallest spinning reels), or the Fin-Nor Mega-Lite 1000.

Line: Use 4-pound test line, though highly skilled anglers should consider 2-pound line. (Warning: You can break it with bare hands!)

Fly-fishing: Try 5-weight rods (8 or 8.5 feet long), floating line, and 9-foot leaders; if short casts are acceptable, such as at a farm pond, use a 4-weight rod.

Rigging

BLUEGILL, SUNFISH, AND PERCH

There are many rigging options, of course. I prefer catch-and-release with lures and flies,

while others would rather die than use anything but a worm under a bobber.

When a fly fisher finds a school of bluegill, a fish can be caught on nearly every cast by using a black or olive-green woolly worm and a strip retrieve. Small frog poppers also work.

Many small lures, such as the Rebel series of micro lures (Teeny Wee Crawfish or Froggy), Rapala floating minnow (one inch long, best in blue/silver or black/gold), and Norman Crappie Crankbait, are excellent for pan fish, especially bluegill and redear. Others love nothing more than dunking a worm under a bobber, then watching that bobber dance on the surface. To use bait, follow these directions: tie a No. 8 or No. 10 baitholder hook on the end of your line, then clamp a single, very small split shot 18 inches above the hook for weight (at times, such as in windless conditions, no weight is necessary). Use a red worm for bait, placing it on the hook with a worm threader, then add a small bobber a few feet above that.

To take it a step further, instead of a simple bare hook, use a Colorado Spinner rigged with a No. 8 or No. 10 hook baited with a small worm. A Colorado Spinner is simply a hook with a small spinner blade on the shank. The spinner puts out a small flash to help attract fish to your bait. It flashes whenever the bobber is moved, either by a light breeze, a tug by you, or a nibbling fish.

When using a bobber, there is more excitement because you are "sight-fishing"—that is, every nibble, tug, and bite on your bait is telegraphed through that little dancing bobber.

For perch, add a short piece of red yarn as a teaser at the shank of the hook before baiting it with a worm. During the best bites, you can even catch perch on nothing more than the yarn.

CRAPPIE

There are two species of crappie: White crappie are often abundant but small; black crappie are less common but larger. Either way, they are among the best-tasting fish available in freshwater. When you get into a school, you can catch dozens of them.

Crappie prefer eating minnows instead of worms. Therefore, use a live minnow for bait, or a jig that simulates a minnow. Rig as if for bluegill, but instead of using a worm for bait, hook a live minnow gently through the mouth. When you get a pickup, that bobber will dance just the same.

If you prefer to use lures that simulate minnows, simply tie the lure directly to your line. In this application, do not use a snap swivel. Use a crappie jig, which are best in white, yellow, yellow/red, or white/red. Other lures that work well include a Beetle Spin (a small spinner bait, best in white with red streak), EPS Grubhead, and a tiny silver Johnson's Minnow (a spoon).

If you are new to a lake or not sure where to fish, another trick is to use a crappie jig under a bobber, then drift along the shore. With the two-rod stamp available for California anglers at warm-water lakes, three people in a small boat can circle the boat with six jigs under bobbers, then let the breeze push them gently along the shore. If you get too far from shore, stop the boat and reset the drift—crappie are almost never found in open water.

Time and Place

First you must identify a pond or lake that has pan fish. Small ponds are the best for bluegill and sunfish, especially ponds with many tules along the shoreline and weed beds in shallow corners. Crappie usually require a larger water base to expand to large populations, and Sacramento and yellow perch are always abundant wherever they are introduced, such as Lake Crowley (in the eastern Sierra) and Copco Lake (near the Oregon border).

STATE RECORDS

Bluegill:
3 lb. 14 oz.	Rancho Murrieta Res.	Michael Holoubek	June 22, 2008

Redear sunfish:
5 lb. 3 oz.	Folsom South Canal	Anthony White Jr.	June 27, 1994

White crappie:
4 lb. 8 oz.	Clear Lake	Carol Carlton	April 26, 1971

Black crappie:
4 lb. 1 oz.	New Hogan Reservoir	Wilma Honey	March 29, 1975

Sacramento perch:
3 lb. 10 oz.	Crowley Lake	Jack Johnson	May 22, 1979

Once on the water, the best spots for bluegill, sunfish, and perch are on the edges of tule berms or weed beds, in the vicinity of submerged trees, or in shady areas during very hot weather. Crappie prefer underwater structures such as trees, old dock pilings, and submerged rock piles. If you don't start getting nibbles within 10 or 15 minutes, then it's time to move. These fish like to school up together, often in groups of 50 or more, and you should keep exploring new spots until you find them.

If you fish from a float tube, small raft, or boat, you can catch bluegill like crazy during the beginning of summer with lures, casting them right along the shoreline, tules, and trees.

The best technique for crappie in midsummer is often to fish at night, right under an intense, bright light at a dock, such as at Clear Lake. Cabela's and Bass Pro, the mail-order specialists, sell an attractor light that can be placed in the water. The light attracts gnats, which in turn attract minnows, which in turn attract crappie. When fishing at night with a bright light, you can either offer a live minnow for bait, hooking it gently through the back, or cast small white crappie jigs across the path of the light.

During the day, instead of letting the fish come to you, you have to go to the fish. They tend to roam some 15–20 feet deep, amid submerged trees with lots of branches or near areas with rock piles. The technique is very simple: using a white or yellow crappie jig, you let it down straight below the boat, then simply pull on your line with the rod and let the jig settle again. Up and down, that's all there is to it. When you get a bite, stick to the spot, because crappie always hang out in schools, even the big ones.

Tricks

A good fish finder can really help in locating crappie. In addition, crappie are often discovered by accident while bass fishing, because a big crappie will often hit a bass lure, especially around docks and submerged trees or brush piles. I always keep a rod ready, prerigged with a crappie jig. Then while bass fishing, if I catch a crappie by accident, I grab my crappie rod, get right over the fish, and start jigging straight up and down.

Some people will try anything to find a school of fish. Here's the craziest technique I've ever heard: start by blowing up a small balloon, then tie 15 feet of fishing line to a hook. After catching a bluegill or crappie, put a hook through the back of the fish and toss the fish and the balloon back into the lake. The logic is that the bluegill will swim back to the school, tugging the balloon along the surface as an indicator of where all the fish are. The theory is that if you cast to the balloon, then you are casting to the school of fish. Alas, it doesn't seem to work as well in practice as it does in theory.

Personal Note

This is one of my favorite stories.

Dad baited his hook with a worm, clipped on a little red-and-white bobber a few feet above it, and tossed it out along a patch of tules. Before long he had done so for all five of his kids—three girls and two boys—and they sat along the shore transfixed by the sight of the bobbers floating on the surface.

"Let's count to 25," said Dad.

"One… two… three… four," started Mom, leading the family chant.

Suddenly, when the family had counted to 12, one of the bobbers started popping around, dancing a bit from side to side, then was pulled under the surface a few inches. The oldest boy, Bobby, grabbed his rod, and his eyes looked as if they were going to pop out of his head.

"I've got one! I've got one!" he shouted. He tussled away with the fish, and after a few moments proudly brought a four-inch bluegill to the shore.

"It's a beauty," said Mom.

"Let's put it in a bucket," added Dad.

He dipped a big bucket in the lake, filled it with water, and the bluegill was dropped in.

The two younger children, Susan and Tommy, immediately stopped fishing to watch the bluegill in the bucket. But in the next hour, Bobby caught another, Dad caught two, and Mom and the two older girls, Nancy and Janet, shared a catch.

So after an hour, there were five bluegill swimming around in the big bucket, which fascinated the kids—the little boy in particular. He picked up his rod and reeled in the line, then put his bait in the bucket, dangling it amid the fish.

"I don't know why you're fishing over in the lake," he announced. "The fish are here, right in the bucket. You can see them."

I remember the episode well because that little kid was me at age four, right about when I started to grow my beard.

CATFISH

BEST FISHING SPOTS

1. Clear Lake
2. Lake Casitas
3. Lower Otay Lake
4. Lake Amador
5. Lake Cuyamaca
6. Colorado River, Parker Valley area
7. Back San Joaquin Delta
8. Lake Berryessa
9. San Pablo Reservoir

white catfish

PAUL B. JOHNSON

Tackle

With catfish more than any other fish, you must first identify the size you hope to catch and then select the appropriate tackle for it.

CATFISH UNDER 12 INCHES

Rod: Fenwick HMG 6.5-foot M spinning (GS66M); Berkley Series One 6-foot M spinning (SOS601M).
Reel: Abu Garcia Cardinal 804 (C804); Mitchell 300XGe (300XGe).
Line: 10-pound Berkley Trilene MAXX (TMFS10-15); 10-pound Stren Original (SKRB-A0100). Use a 6- or 6.5-foot rod, medium action, with a spinning reel with 8- or 10-pound test line. Most people simply pick the rod they use for trout or bass, and it works just fine.

CATFISH 12 INCHES TO 10 POUNDS

Rod: Berkley Air IM7 9-foot MH (A94-9-MH) or a 6.5-foot Pflueger PX66M; Fenwick Inshore 8-foot Livebait casting (FINLB80-2540).
Reel: Abu Garcia Cardinal 807 (C807); Abu Garcia REVO Inshore (REVOINS); Pflueger Supreme SP30 (eight ball bearings).
Line: 12-pound Berkley Trilene Big Cat (BCFS30-81); 30-pound Berkley Big Game (BGQS30C-SB).

CATFISH 10 POUNDS AND UP

Rod: Berkley Air IM7 9-foot MH (A94-9-MH); Fenwick Inshore 8-foot Livebait casting (FINLB80-2540); 7-foot fiberglass CalStar 196 (rated at 12- to 20-pound line).
Reel: Abu Garcia Cardinal 807 (C807); Abu

CATFISH STATE RECORDS

Blue catfish:
113 lb. 5 oz. San Vicente Lake   Steve Oudomsouk   July 24, 2008

Channel catfish:
53 lb. 8 oz.   San Joaquin River   Randall Gilgert, Jr. September 22, 2008

Flathead catfish:
72 lb. 14 oz. Colorado River   Billy Potter   April 22, 2003

White catfish:
22 lb. 0 oz.   William Land Park Pond James Robinson   March 21, 1994

Garcia REVO Inshore (REVOINS); Ambassadeur 6500C3.

Line: 30-pound Berkley Trilene Big Cat (BCFS30-81); 30-pound Berkley Big Game (BGQS30C-SB). Use 12-pound line unless you have prospects for a catfish over 25 pounds; in that case, use 30-pound line.

Rigging

The best approach for most locations is to rig with a sliding barrel sinker setup. Start by putting your fishing line through a barrel sinker. Then tie a snap swivel to your line, which acts as a stop for the sinker. From the snap swivel, tie on 18–24 inches of leader, and then tie a Size 1 bait holder hook to the end of the leader.

Many people who fish for catfish use standard surf leaders with two snelled hooks and a sinker. Most people use far too heavy of a sinker, often so heavy that when a catfish picks up the bait, it detects the weight of the sinker and then drops the bait.

There is a little-known alternative that was taught to me by George "Mr. Catfish" Powers, who caught 5,000–6,000 catfish a year at Clear Lake. With light spinning tackle, he would place two small No. 10 Kahle hooks on a loop knot, with the hooks opposed to each other. Then he would clamp a 1/32-ounce split shot onto the line 12 inches above the hooks. Next he put on his bait, two dead minnows with slit stomachs that were hooked through

their backs, opposite each other. This method tends to catch catfish in the two- to five-pound class.

For extremely large catfish, you must upsize everything, including hooks and bait. Some of the biggest catfish have been caught with whole bluegills for bait (see Department of Fish and Game regulations to make certain this is legal in the water you have chosen).

Time and Place

Catfish are most active when feeding on warm summer nights under bright moons. They prefer warm water and will seek out sloughs and protected coves far up lake arms to find it.

In daytime, they hunker down in holes or on the shaded sides of small hills on the lake bottom, and will stay there until evening shade takes over a lake.

In winter, with cold temperatures, catfish go into a deep slowdown. But even when water temperatures are cold, three consecutive days of clear, warm weather in the spring will set off their first feeding of the year, and some of the best catfishing imaginable is during this period.

Catfish live in warm-water lakes, ponds, reservoirs, sloughs, deltas, and backwater eddies, as well as in the slow-moving water of the Colorado River.

Tricks

Use clams, anchovies, sardines, chicken livers,

crawdads, or night crawlers for bait. With a two-rod stamp, two anglers can have four rods and try a variety of baits.

Catfish become active feeders once shade takes over a lake and then more so as dusk turns to night. They are scavengers, feeding on whatever they can find, using their whiskers to sense their way even in very murky water. The mouths of sloughs, inlets, and outlets, as well as edges of tule berms, are good spots.

In the daytime, catfish will hold to shaded ledges and holes. Some anglers find one good catfish hole at a lake and catch fish there for years—and it would take the Jaws of Life to get their mouths open before they'd tell you where it was.

The habitat that will hold catfish is where the bottom has natural ledges, hills, and holes—these places are best found at natural lakes, at ponds, and well up the arms of reservoirs.

The Mr. Catfish Method

On bright, sunny days, scuba divers in lakes have discovered that catfish will be lying perfectly still on the shaded side of the little mud dobs (that is, the little hills on the lake bottoms). You will never see a catfish on the sunny side of those mud dobs. It's as if the fish are locked in jail.

To take advantage of this knowledge when fishing during the day, start by always casting directly into the sun. Never cast with your back to the sun.

After the line has sunk to the bottom, take the fishing line between your thumb and forefinger and pull it toward you at the rate of about seven or eight inches per minute. After three minutes, for instance, you will have retrieved about two feet of line. Eventually, the tip of your rod will pull down about an inch.

As you take in another inch or two of line, the rod tip will pull down a bit more. That's because the bait is being dragged uphill on one of those mud dobs. Because you cast right into the sun, it's now on the sunny side.

You then pull the line a bit more, and the rod tip will spring straight, the pressure relieved. That's because the bait just tumbled toward you on the shady side of that mud dob.

This is the moment of truth. Watch where your line enters the water. If it moves two or three inches, then you are getting a catfish bite. Set the hook and you're on.

Personal Note

The first time I went fishing with George Powers, the legendary "Mr. Catfish," we caught 27 catfish between noon and 2 P.M., when catfishing is supposed to be at its ultimate worst, and then went home because George made a cast and didn't catch a fish. Over the several years that I fished with him, it always went like this.

One time, as an experiment during a day when we were catching a catfish on every cast, I attempted to do the exact opposite—casting with my back to the sun. My beloved companion shook his head in exasperation, wondering how I could possibly try anything different from what had been proven.

In this unscientific test, I didn't get a bite for 30 minutes, while "Mr. Catfish," casting directly into the sun, continued to fill the stringer. I finally turned around, started casting into the sun again, letting the bait tumble into the shady side of those mud dobs, and immediately began catching fish.

"You're a stubborn one," said George, a bit irked. "A lot of people are like that. Dang it, I try. A lot of people listen, but they don't practice what they're listenin' to."

LARGEMOUTH BASS

BEST FISHING SPOTS

1. South San Joaquin Delta
2. Clear Lake
3. Bullards Bar Reservoir
4. Cachuma Lake
5. Lake San Antonio
6. Castaic Lake
7. Lake Hodges
8. Lake Oroville
9. Camanche Lake
10. Lake Morena

largemouth bass

PAUL B. JOHNSON

Tackle

Many anglers keep several rods ready rigged with spinnerbaits, plastic worms, rip baits, and one for flipping, so they can be switched at a moment's notice. Many matched combination rod-and-reel setups are available.

Following are some examples of perfect setups:

Surface Zara Spook Rig: Lure: 3 1/2-inch Zara Super Spook Junior in light blue/silver (bleeding shad); Rod: Loomis 7-foot medium CBR843; Reel: Pflueger Supreme LP; Line: 10-pound Yozuri clear.

Senko Worm Rig: Lure: 4-inch Yamamoto Senko in watermelon green (other dark colors okay); Rod: Loomis 6 1/2-foot medium GLXSJR782; Reel: Pflueger Medalist 6030; Line: 8-pound Yozuri clear.

The following are also excellent setups:

Rods

Spinnerbait rod (conventional): 6 1/2-foot Loomis MBR783C or 6 1/2-foot Shimano (Jimmy Houston) JHC66MH; Fenwick Elite Tech 6-3 Target/Spinnerbait Casting (ECT/SB63M-MF); Berkley Tactix 6-0 Spinnerbait casting (TXC601MF).

Plastic worm rod (spinning): 6 1/2-foot Loomis SJR782 or 6 1/2-foot Shimano (Jimmy Houston) JHS66M.

Flippin' stick (conventional): 7 1/2-foot Loomis FR904X or 7-foot, 10-inch St. Croix Avid AC710HS; Fenwick Elite Tech 7-6 Flippin' Stik Casting (ECFP76H-F); Berkley Tactix 7-6 Flippin' Stik (TXC761H-T).

Dropshotting (spinning): 7-foot Loomis SJR841; Fenwick Elite Tech 6-7 Drop Shot Spinning (ESDS67M-XF); Berkley Tactix 6-6 Drop Shot/Finesse Spinning (TXS661M).

Crankbaits: Fenwick Elite Tech 6-6 Crankshaft Casting (ECC66M-MF); Berkley Tactix 7-0 Cranking (Glass) Casting (TXCG701M).

Carolina Rig: Fenwick Elite Tech 7-0 Riggin' Stik Casting (ECR70MH-F); Berkley Tactix 6-6 Jigging & Worming Casting (TXC661MF).

Reels

Conventional: Abu Garcia REVO Premier (REVO PRM); Abu Garcia REVO Inshore (REVO INS); Abu Garcia EXT (5600EXT); Abu Garcia Ambassadeur Record (RCN51) Shimano CU200B or Daiwa ProCaster X 103HA.

Spinning: Abu Garcia Cardinal 804 (C804); Abu Garcia Cardinal 802 (C802); Abu Garcia

Cardinal 704LX (C704LX) Shimano Sahara 2000F or Daiwa TDS2500.

Flippin': Castaic CA200 (use 15- to 30-pound test line).

Downshotting: Shimano Stradic ST 2000 FG (use 6- to 10-pound test line).

LINE

In most cases, 10-pound test is ideal for most applications. Some anglers who use spinning tackle drop down to 8-pound test, and when catching bass in the foot-long class or in crowded lake conditions, they drop down to 6-pound test. Some people using conventional gear and casting large spinnerbaits, Castaic Trout, or heavy jigs will use as high as 20-pound test. Many pro bassers use braided Fire Line that tests out 60 pounds or 80 pounds.

Two Great Tricks

The only thing frustrating when the bass are biting like crazy is that you can go through 75 plastic grubs and plastic worms in a long three-day weekend. But there are two secret tricks to make your plastic worms and grubs last longer.

The key is that they tear right where the hook exits the plastic body. The tears happen with the bass strikes.

Insider's trick No. 1: With a "Wacky Senko Tool," place a quarter-inch O-ring on the tool, then fit the O-ring on the neck of a Senko worm. Tie a No. 1 hook on your line, and set the hook on the O-ring rather than in the Senko. For weight, if necessary, embed a small pencil sinker in the center of the Senko. This allows you to use the same Senko for 15 or 20 fish, rather than having to replace the worm every two or three fish. For more information, contact Hi's Tackle, San Francisco, 415/221-3825.

Insider's trick No. 2: McDonald's fast-food joints have the best plastic straws for this trick. Take a straw and cut a quarter-inch section off it. Take that quarter-inch section of plastic straw and fit it over your plastic grub or worm right where the hook will exit. When you rig, run the hook through the piece of plastic straw. When you get a strike, the hook will not tear the plastic worm because that small piece of plastic straw acts like armor.

BASS STATE RECORDS

Largemouth bass:

22 lb. 0 oz.	Castaic Lake	Bob Crupi	March 15, 1991*

Largemouth bass:

21 lb. 12 oz.	Castaic Lake	Michael Arujo	March 5, 1991 *(recognized by DFG)*

Smallmouth bass:

9 lb. 13 oz.	Pardee Lake	Harold Hardin	July 3, 2007

Spotted bass:

10 lb. 4 oz.	Pine Flat Lake	Brian Shishido	May 3, 2001

White bass:

5 lb. 5 oz.	Colorado River (Ferguson Lake)	Milton Mize	May 8, 1972

* This fish was weighed on a certified scale on land, photographed repeatedly, then released. It is recognized as a line-class world record by the International Game Fish Association, but not as a state record by the State Department of Fish and Game (DFG), since the fish was released. That decision by DFG is universally criticized by sport anglers.

Record Bass

One magic spring day at Otay Lake, Jack Neu caught five largemouth bass that weighed a total of 53 pounds, 12 ounces, probably the largest five-fish bass limit ever caught. I was with Jack on that special day, and as it evolved, it was as if everyone at Otay had been launched into a different orbit from the rest of the world. In a two-hour span at the dock scale, 30 bass weighing eight pounds or more were checked in. Out on the water, though, Jack and I were still at it. He'd caught four that weighed a total of 45 pounds, topped by a 16-pounder. One more and he'd earn a place in history. He got it: it weighed an even 8 pounds.

The secret to catching giant bass, I learned from Jack, is to search for giant bass, then mark, anchor, and fish for that single bass.

Start by motoring your boat around a cove or off a point at the pace of a slow walk, and while doing so, study the marks on your fish finder or graph. When you see a big bass, you feel like a safecracker who has just heard the right click on the dial. At that point, toss out a small buoy to mark the spot. Then motor the boat off to the side, throw out an anchor, and turn off the engine.

LIVE BAIT

For bait, use crawdads, jumbo minnows, or shiners. For crawdads, keep them on a cardboard flat. Wave your hands over the top of the crawdads as if you were a sorcerer casting a magic spell—first one that moves gets elected for the job of bait.

Hold the winner on its side with a thumb and forefinger, positioned so the little bugger can't nail you with a pincher, then hook it right between the eyes with the No. 8 hook tied to your fishing line.

Use no sinker, no leader. Just a small hook. That way the crawdad will swim around most naturally. When a big bass starts to chase it, the crawdad will swim off trying to escape. Nothing gets a big bass more excited than what appears to be a good meal about to escape.

Toss the bait out toward the buoy, then let the crawdad swim to the bottom. Wait and watch, staring at where your line enters the lake.

When your line twitches a bit, get ready. Stand with your rod, being careful not to pull or twitch (if you move the bait, it will spook the bass), and point the rod at the water. Often nothing happens. Five seconds, ten seconds. It will drive you crazy. But think of the logic: You know a big bass is down there (you marked it), you know your crawdad is down there, and you know that something made it move.

When the slack line begins to draw tight, it means the big bass is picking it up. Get in the set position, and when the line tightens a lot, set the hook hard.

Note that big bass never jump but instead bulldog in short thrusts of power near the lake bottom.

Never think that all you have to do is show up, use electronics to find a big bass, and then toss your bait out to catch it. It sure doesn't work that way most of the time. Electronics provide an edge, not a guarantee.

HARD BAITS

The reward of using lures is that instead of waiting for the fish, you are pursuing them. Doing it, though, requires the approach of a detective.

Hard baits, such as the Zara Spook (a surface lure) and the Husky Jerk (which you fish 10–20 feet deep), work best at dawn and dusk. That is when the bass are most apt to be aggressive feeders, including on the surface. When sun hits the water, bass are less aggressive and hard baits do not work as well.

Bass anglers who use only lures get more action, try more strategies, and cover a lot more water than anglers who use bait. The trade-off, however, is a trend toward smaller fish. But it's an attractive deal.

You have to take several factors into consideration: water temperature, water clarity, weather, depth of fish, and whether they are in pre-spawn, spawn, or post-spawn periods. Any of these can have a tremendous influence on your approach at any lake or reservoir. Then there is the lake itself, and you must have the ability to find habitat that will hold bass.

One of the first orders of business is to determine how deep the bass are and what seasonal influences are affecting them. The year is divided into periods: pre-spawn, spawn, post-spawn, and winter. You recognize these periods by coordinating time of year with water temperature and recent weather trends.

My favorite surface hard baits are Zara Spook, Jitterbug, and poppers. My choices for subsurface are: Shad Rap, Husky Jerk Rapala, Rogue Thunderstick, Rebel-series of Crickhoppers (for ponds), Countdown Rapala, and Rat-L-Trap series.

PLASTICS

Question: When does a quarter beat a $5 bill in the great outdoors?

Answer: When you go bass fishing at one of California's reservoirs.

Let me explain. At a fishing show, I overheard two fishermen arguing over the merit of buying high-end "hard baits"—that is, Rapala, Rebel, Bomber, Rogue, or other similar fishing lures that simulate a small fish. After all, they can cost $5 apiece.

But you can often get more mileage out of $0.25. A "plastic", is a grub, worm or lizardlike or crawdadlike replica. They sell in packs of 10 for about $2.50, or about $0.25 apiece, and can catch a lot more bass in reservoirs.

The reason is that California reservoirs are very steep-sided; 40 feet from the bank it can be 40 feet deep, or in some cases, 100 feet deep. At these steep-banked reservoirs, the bass stage along the bottom, then move vertically, or up and down, according to water temperature and feed on crawdads, worms, and threadfin shad.

As a result, you must fish vertically. If you use a lead darthead jig or bullet-style sinker on your line, and then rig a plastic, you can catch the bass because you are fishing vertically. You can also dropshot literally straight down from the boat, just 10–20 feet from shore.

Crankbaits work great at shallow lakes and ponds because the fish feed horizontally.

From my boat, I usually cast toward the shore and let the jig sink down along the bottom. In sequence, at 5, 10, 20, 30, 40, and 50 feet deep, I stop the sink with a crank of the reel and a jerk of the rod, and will locate how deep the bass are.

At Oroville, Berryessa, and Shasta, I fully expect to catch and release 100 fish per day using this method, from mid-March through mid-May. So can you!

My favorite plastics include: 4-inch Yamamoto Senko in watermelon green (other dark colors okay); Zoom 3 1/2-inch Salty Fat Albert in single tail and double, in clear/silver/black, watermelon; Zoom fluke; Berkley Power Grub with Gulp (best in bucket with juice); Zoom Brush Hog; Mann's Hard Nose lizard. There are many more (because they work so well, I've got a dozen tackle boxes of just plastics).

I use big gap 3/0 and 4/0 Gamakatsu hooks, and also dartheads: 1/16-ounce, 1/8-ounce, 3/16-ounce and 1/4-ounce. I prefer dartheads with smaller weights and ballheads with heavier weights.

THE BIG SWIM BAITS

Swim baits are giant plastic worms designed to catch bass that weigh 10 pounds or more. You need special persistence with spirit to get your bite. You also need heavy gear to fish the deep structure. This is a specialized form of bass fishing that appeals only to experts. You can go many hours before bites, and because the baits are so big, often 10 inches, you can blow the set if you don't have the exact right sense of feel and timing.

The best swim baits are: Huddleston, AC Plug, Castaic Trout, and several others that are similar. These lures are expensive.

Time and Place
THE PRE-SPAWN BITE

With the arrival of spring, when the weather is just starting to warm up and the water temperature climbs from the high 40s to the low 60s, the bass change their behavior. They begin to emerge from the winter slowdown and start to think about eating something. This is called pre-spawn, and during this period most of the bass are 15–25 feet deep—deeper if the water is cold; shallower if it is warm. The best way to entice them is to use quarter-ounce jigs with a pork-rind trailer (called "pig-and-jig"), salt-and-pepper grubs, Gitzits, large spinnerbaits, and diving plugs.

Each lake has a different set of factors, of course, but as the water starts to warm up, the bass usually go from being very deep and suspended (often along underwater drop-offs) to moving up a bit off submerged rock piles, near creek inlets, and off shoreline points. During the pre-spawn period, the water temperature can fluctuate for months, just as the weather in early spring seems to have trouble making up its mind whether to be hot or cold, dry or wet, windy or calm. In turn, that affects the depth of the fish.

As winter starts its transition to spring, the larger fish will be on the secondary points. A few bass will be in the coves, but these are usually only the dinks. Forget 'em. Work the secondary points with grubs, often 15–30 feet deep.

THE SPAWN BITE

As spring arrives in force, the steady warm weather comes, and the water temperature rises to 62–66°F. This is when the bass change their behavior for a second time. They rise up to the shallows, in the backs of coves, and along stretches of shoreline with tules, submerged trees, or overhanging bushes. The bass are getting ready to spawn, marking out their territory. This can provide some of the most exciting fishing of the year. All fish should be released so they can spawn successfully, of course.

You approach the coves quietly, then make precise casts right along the shoreline in as little as two inches of water. One trick when using a mouse (imitation), spinnerbait, or plastic worm is to cast right on the shoreline, then twitch it so that it plops in the water. It looks alive, and the bass, now territorial and defending the nest, will attack like a police dog biting a burglar's butt.

Many lures are effective during this period. Plastic lures that imitate shad are called "hard baits" or "crankbaits," and many work well, since to the bass they resemble invading minnows wanting to nibble on the nest. The following are worth using: Rattlin' Rogue, Shad Rap, Rattletrap, Countdown Rapala, Fat Rap, Hula Popper, Jitterbug, Rebel minnow, Crawdad, Rebel Pop-R, and Chugger. Spinnerbaits (Terminator is a great one), buzzbaits, and even plastic worms fished shallow can also entice strikes. When the water is a bit murky, use spinnerbaits or even the Blue Fox minnow spinner.

Just after the spawn, the bass stay near the bed to guard the mass of tiny fry. You can cast into the fry and get a strike as the bass defends them.

THE POST-SPAWN BITE

After the spawn, usually in early summer, the fish move "off the beds," leaving the shallows and moving into areas where there is good underwater structure, usually 8–15 feet deep. By this time, the water temperature is usually 68–74°F. The post-spawn period extends from early summer through fall.

This is where knowing a lake pays off. You can spend a lot of time looking for the fish and not finding them if you don't know where to find traditional structures that will hold the bass during the summer. Shade becomes very important. Cast right along boat docks, because the fish often hang under the dock to catch some shade.

In addition to docks, other excellent places for bass during the post-spawn period are submerged trees (stickups) and bushes, areas around old dock pilings, deep coves where shoreline vegetation provides shade, large rock piles, and edges of tule berms.

Although some surface action occurs at dawn and dusk, the best results come when fishing deeper. And while some hard baits can attract bass (Shad Rap and Rat-L-Trap are good examples), the best results are on plastic worms and grubs.

The best are the Senko, Brush Hog, Zoom Fluke, lizard, frog, rat, and plastic worms, such as Green Weenie, especially the small one with the red head. The best colors are motor oil, purple, and black, or the salt-and-pepper flecked grubs.

Summer Worming

Worming in the hot months takes a lot of skill to do right. Most people cast the worm out and reel it back in way too fast. Consider how it looks to the bass. It needs to appear as natural as possible, and that means working it very slowly. The favored technique with a worm is walking it down shoreline ledges into structure. This simply means retrieving it slowly enough along the lake bottom so it slithers right into the intended destination, where a bass is hanging out for the day.

As the summer progresses and the water temperature continues to climb, the bass become more and more difficult to catch. This difficulty is compounded at reservoirs with dropping water levels that force the bass to move to different areas. The combination is rough on anglers, who must now approach a familiar lake that has had a dropping water level as if it were a completely new water. Add intense waterskiing pressure (where the wake from speeding boats slaps against the shoreline) and you can face a very challenging scenario. One thing that happens is that the bass will be scattered vertically, from 25 feet deep to 100 feet deep, or in some cases, deeper. Though almost nobody does it, what actually works best is trolling bass plugs off a downrigger line to get down deep. It may sound like sacrilege to troll for bass, but if the only thing that counts is getting the fish, this is the best way to do it in late summer.

Winter Jigging

In winter the cold weather finally returns, the metabolism of the bass slows down, and they head deep to find the warmest water in the lake. Few anglers try for bass during this period because conventional methods rarely work. It can seem as if there isn't a single bass in the entire lake. What to do? The answer is to drift your boat over an underwater ledge, drop-off, or hole that is 35–50 feet deep, then simply jig straight up and down. This technique also can take fish during the pre-spawn period, when a cold-weather snap returns the fish to winter tendencies. Dropshotting can be very effective in winter as well. Using live bait, such as the jumbo minnow, also can take very large fish during this period.

Dropshotting

You practically need the Jaws of Life to get a bass to open its mouth once the rain and cold temperatures arrive in California, right? Well, anglers have found their Jaws of Life with a technique brought in from Japan that solves the annual winter-fishing slow-up. It is called "downshotting" or "dropshotting." This is how the great Skeet Reese showed me how to set up: tie a No. 2 hook to your line with a Palomar knot, and leave the tag end to your knot, anywhere from a foot to two feet (depending exactly how far off the bottom you want your bait to be). On the tag, affix a bell-shaped sinker (3/16- to 1/4-ounce) with a plastic clip, where you just slide the tag end of your line into the clip to affix it. What works best dropshotting—and spare me the outrage letters, please—is live bait, a live minnow or a full night crawler threaded on the hook. For plastics, a three-inch Keeper leech worm (best color is oxblood), hooked right through the nose (as if minnow fishing), can be excellent, or your favorite plastic grub, Senko or crawdad imitation.

It works during the cold winter months because the bass are deep, often right on the bottom. The secret is to cast out, let the plastic worm sink to the bottom, then let the boat drift so the bait is trailed slowly, just above the bottom. When you get a pickup, do not set the hook, which will pull the worm away from the bass, but instead reel down to the fish.

One trick with this system is to use a sinker made out of tungsten, which is harder than lead and can make a tapping sound on rocky bottoms that attracts the bass. Another trick is to use 8- or 10-pound line on your reel, tie on a small barrel swivel, and from there drop down to a 6-pound leader. That way, if you get snagged, the 6-pound will break off and all you have to do is tie on another leader.

Ponds

One of the best ways to introduce newcomers to bass fishing is to take them to a small lake or farm pond in the spring, when the first warm weather of the year gets the bass hungry, active, and inspired to move into the shallows and carve out spawning territory. From bank or boat, you cast out small lures along the shore, and there are times when the bass seem to smack the lure almost as soon as it hits the water.

Every spring from March through May, I take my two boys, Jeremy and Kris, on a trip to farm ponds, and we fish out of our little rafts. We paddle around, then cast along the shoreline, using either spinning gear or fly tackle. Floating or shallow diving lures (such as the one-inch Rapala) or small poppers can attract large numbers of surface strikes. We've had many days when we've caught 50–100 fish, although only rarely will one be larger than 14 or 15 inches.

As summer arrives, using plastics such as the Green Weenie will inspire bite after bite, while the bass will snub hard baits. I've had 50-fish days with double twist-tail Fat Albert grubs rigged on ¼-ounce darthead jig.

Insider's Note

A high-quality electronic fish finder is a must. It shows bottom contour, depth, and water temperature, and it marks fish. But those who are very serious about bass fishing are better off with the paper graphs. Even though they are more expensive because you have to keep buying paper scrolls for them, they are more detailed, even showing the size of individual fish; and because the information is all recorded on paper, you can take it home, lay it out on a table, and study the lake bottom. After doing this for a while, you can get to know the bottom of a lake as well as the layout of your own home.

Personal Note

When it comes to bass, history is being made in the present in California, not just looked up in record books. There have been several line-class world records for largemouth bass, including the most famous of all, the 22-pound bass caught and released at Castaic Lake by Bob Crupi, which was just four ounces shy of the all-time world record. Because so many anglers spend so much effort searching for big bass, the world record has become a legend among legends. It weighed 22 pounds, 4 ounces, and was caught in 1932 in Georgia by a postal worker named George Perry, who, after documenting the fish's weight, took it home, cut it up, cooked it, and (with the help of his family) ate it. That legendary record was tied in 2009 in Japan at Lake Biwa by Kurita Manabu. Many expect a new record in the 24-pound class, likely coming from a lake in California. A nine-month growing season, plants of trout, and most pros releasing the big ones means a chance for something special in the future.

TROUT

BEST FISHING SPOTS FOR LOTS OF TROUT

1. Sacramento River, Redding to Anderson
2. Lake Davis
3. John Muir Wilderness
4. Convict Lake
5. San Pablo Reservoir
6. Blue Lake, Alpine County
7. Big Bear Lake
8. Frenchman Lake
9. Del Valle Reservoir
10. Lake Amador

BEST FISHING SPOTS FOR BIG TROUT

1. Lower Twin Lake
2. Bridgeport Reservoir
3. Independence Lake
4. Eagle Lake
5. Kirman Lake
6. Crowley Lake
7. Collins Lake
8. San Pablo Reservoir
9. East Walker River
10. Shasta Lake

BEST FLY-FISHING SPOTS FOR LOTS OF TROUT

1. Sacramento River, Redding to Anderson (by boat)
2. East Walker River
3. Middle Fork Feather River (hike-in)
4. Fall River
5. Kirman Lake
6. Owens River, Big Springs to Crowley
7. Pit River
8. Crowley Lake
9. Matterhorn Canyon, Yosemite Wilderness
10. Lake Davis

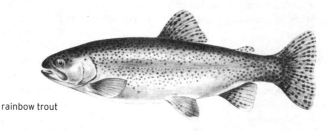

rainbow trout

PAUL B. JOHNSON

Tackle and Rigging

SPINNING

Try a 6 1/2-foot Loomis SR781 rod matched with a Shimano Stradic ST2000FG reel. Other options:

Rod: Fenwick Techna AV 6-6 M Spinning (AVS66MF); Berkley Tactix 6-0 L Trout-Spinning (TXTS60-2L).

Reel: Abu Garcia Cardinal 802 (C802).

Combo: Mitchell 300Xe (300Xe/662M). Many excellent factory-ready combo rigs are available from every major manufacturer, including Shakespeare, Pflueger, Abu, Daiwa, and others.

TROLLING

A 7-foot Loomis PR8400C (rated for 6- to 12-pound line) matched with a Shimano Calcutta CT50 is a stellar setup. Or try:

Rod: Berkley Tactix 7-0 ML Kowanee Trout-Casting (TXTC70-2M); Fenwick Techna AV 7-0 M Triggerstik (AVC70MF).

Reel: Abu Garcia Ambassadeur Line Counter (5500LC).

Line: 8-pound Berkley Trilene XT (XTVS8-15) paired with 6-pound Vanish Fluorocarbon leader (VLM6-15); 6-pound Berkley Trilene Sensation (SNSF6-15) for light-line trolling near surface. For deep-water trolling with a downrigger or using leadcore line, switch to a larger capacity reel, such as the Abu Garcia Royal Extreme RXT 6600C reel; this works a lot better than spinning rod-and-reel setups—you don't get the line twist you sometimes get with spinning reels, and with a 7-foot rod (instead of a standard 6 1/2-foot spinning rod), it is a lot easier to set the hook quickly.

Fly Rod

My personal favorite is the Sage 5-weight, 9-foot XP 590-4, with a Galvan reel and Simms waders. Fenwick also makes an outstanding introductory package based on its 8 1/2-foot 6-weight. Use either 3X or 4X leaders, 7 1/2 feet long for newcomers to the sport, 9 feet long for most conditions, or 12 feet long for still, clear water. The more advanced fly fisher can try the 8 1/2- or 9-foot Loomis 6-weight or the Sage 6-weight, matched with an Abel, Galvan, or Loomis Adventurer reel.

Line

The standard line for trout is 6-pound test. In lakes with high water clarity use 4-pound test or no higher than 6-pound test. In lakes with low water clarity you can get away with 8-pound test. A solution to the problem of line-shy big fish has been solved with fluorocarbon leader material. Fluorocarbon line is very strong yet virtually invisible. It allows anglers to use strong line in all applications for line-shy big fish, from saltwater fly-fishing for bonefish to trolling for trout in crystal-clear lakes. When reeling the backing on, be sure to leave enough room for your fly line.

Backpacking

Take a four-piece Daiwa pack rod matched with a Daiwa Spinmatic 500Z reel or a six-piece Daiwa SMC 66ULFS rod (at times difficult to locate) matched with a Fin-Nor MegaLite ML-1000 spinning reel. Both rods come with hard plastic tubes that will fit in a backpack.

Getting the Big Ones

This is exactly what I do to catch the big ones: **Methods:** 1) Troll using downriggers to reach precise depths on the edge of underwater ledges and channels, near submerged boulder fields, springs, or weed beds, or the old river channels. 2) Jig, straight up and down at ledges or springs. 3) Flycast with sink-tip lines and leeches, with strip retrieve, on the edges of weed beds. 4) Baitfish with night crawler under slip bobber at springs.

Rod, reel, line: My favorite for trolling is a 7-foot Loomis PR8400C matched with an Abu-5 Ambassadeur level-wind, with 250 yards of fresh 10-pound Maxima Ultra-Green.

Leader, swivels: Tie on black barrel swivel to fishing line, add 27 inches of 6-pound test Flourocarbon leader, and snap swivel for lure.

Lures, flies: 2 1/4- or 2 1/2-inch Needlefish lure in rainbow, black/silver, red/white/black or brown trout, with red eye added to head of lure; 2 1/2-inch Z-Ray, yellow with red spots; 2 3/4-inch jointed Rapala (floating), gold/black; marabou trolling flies (no snap swivel); 4 1/2-inch rat lure with double treble hooks.

Cat-and-mouse: Off a downrigger on the deep line, run a jointed Rebel. On the shallow line, run a Needlefish. It will look like a small trout is chasing a small fish. I've got most of my big trout this way.

Must-do trick: I always keep a pack of the stick-on red eyes available. If a lure does not have an eye, I stick one on near the head of the lure.

Time and Place

Any time there is a dramatic change in habitat, you will find fish along the edge of that border. Long, straight, bare stretches of shoreline do not hold fish. On the other hand, jagged points, coves, rock piles, drop-offs, submerged boulders, and trees do. Look for the change. It

TROUT STATE RECORDS

Rainbow trout:
23 lb. 0 oz. Lake Natoma Jeremy Brucklacher January 17, 2000

Hatchery rainbow trout:
28 lb. 5 oz. Butte County Pond James Harrold January 3, 2006

Brown trout:
26 lb. 8 oz. Upper Twin Lake Danny Stearman April 30, 1987

Cutthroat trout:
31 lb. 8 oz. Lake Tahoe William Pomin 1911

Brook trout:
9 lb. 12 oz. Silver Lake, Texas Haynes September 9, 1932
Amador County

might be where a tiny feeder stream is trickling into the lake or where the late-afternoon shade line crosses the water. You must locate and fish these areas. In many rivers, trout will point themselves upstream and sit motionlessly in pocket water waiting for insects to float by. They move just a few inches from side to side when they pick off the insects.

In many lakes—particularly those with little underwater structure, reefs, or drop-offs—a lot of people think the central purpose of electronic fish finders lies in finding the little blips that indicate fish. Actually they are best used to examine the bottom contours of the lake. Remember: 10 percent of the water will hold 90 percent of the trout. This is true not only horizontally (at key habitat areas), but vertically as well. You must troll at the precise depth, especially if you want to catch big trout.

In spring, trout are often near the surface, roaming around in the top 10–15 feet of water, picking off the first insect hatches of the year and snaring misled minnows. As summer arrives, the warm water on top drives the trout deeper to a layer known as the thermocline. The thermocline is cool and rich in oxygen and food. In the summer the trout will always be in the thermocline. In the fall, usually around the third week of October, lakes

will "turn over," as the stratified temperature zones do a flip-flop, bringing the trout again to the surface for several weeks. When winter sets in, the trout go deep, this time seeking warmer water.

So right off, the spring and fall are the best times to troll for trout, because the fish are near the surface and no specialized deep-water techniques are required. In the summer, when most people fish, the trout are buried in the thermocline, except for brief periods at dawn and dusk, when they come up to the surface for the evening rise. By that time, however, many people have already left without getting a bite. The problem is that summer anglers troll too shallow, right over the top of the trout.

Fly-Fishing a River

The No. 1 advantage of fly-fishing is that you have the opportunity to fish more, not less, than with other methods. The fact that fly-fishing qualifies as an art form for many is a bonus.

Remember that 90 percent of trout feeding is subsurface. That is why nymphing—short lining weighted nymphs in pocket water—is an outstanding way to catch trout in freestone streams. A freestone stream is one that flows over rocks and boulders.

COLOR UNDER WATER

As sunlight penetration in the water diminishes, so does the vividness of colors. In fact, as you go deeper, all colors eventually turn black, but at incredibly different rates.

Bright red turns black underwater faster than any other color. That makes it effective only in shallow water, where light penetration is highest. If you fish deeper than 40 feet during typical ocean-water clarity, red can lose its powers as an attractant. To the fish, it will actually appear black. The best time to use red for salmon is during the fall, when the salmon's spawning mode kicks into overdrive and when the fish school outside the entrances to major rivers just 25-35 feet deep.

In the middle of the color spectrum is lime green or chartreuse, which shows up very well between 25 and 45 feet deep – exactly where most salmon are during the summer months, when the plankton is thick and salmon are corralling schools of anchovies. When in doubt, go with chartreuse.

At the end of the spectrum, blue is capable of reflecting the smallest glimmers of light. That is why blue-sided lures or baits are the most effective color when fishing deep or in ocean water that is thick with plankton or otherwise has low water clarity. Some anglers have told me that blue should never be used, since it is disguised by the water and fish can't see it. According to a series of tests, the opposite is true. Blue shows up in deep water better than any other color.

The following fly patterns will make a good fly box for most any stream: Pheasant Tail, Prince Nymph, Copper John, Hare's Ear, Z-Wing caddis, Elk Hair caddis, Adams, Light Cahill, Yellow Humpy, Royal Wulff, woolly bugger, and Zonker.

With chest waders and a wading staff, wade near the center of a fair-running stream. Next, zip short casts to the little spots that hold trout. The fly should land just upstream of the spot and be allowed to drift past the spot. Then, pick the fly up, backcast once to dry it off, and zip the cast to the next spot on the river. With a spinning rod you have to retrieve the lure all the way back through unproductive water. That is why you spend much more time actually fishing promising spots by wading and fly-fishing than by using a spinning rod.

After delivering your fly, "mend" the line (flipping it to the outside), so that the fly will drift straight with the current as if no line were attached. If the fly skids instead of drifts, not only will no trout hit it, but you may even spook the hole.

Follow the fly with your fly rod; that is, keep your rod pointed in the direction of the fly, and then watch your line carefully on the drift. Often the trout are just sitting in the pockets, moving just an inch or two either way to pick off insects as they float past. Remember, you don't need much line out. If you are fishing a nymph (wet), all you will see when a trout grabs it is the downstream flow of your line stopping. You have to strike right now. You'll never feel a thing. It's all in the watching.

If you have difficulty mastering this, a great trick when fishing wet flies or nymphs is to use a strike indicator, which is attached just above where the leader and fly line are connected. A strike indicator floats, providing an exciting visual tip-off to every strike. Shops sell Styrofoam strike indicators in different colors. Another trick is to use the sleeve of a colored floating line and thread it on the head of your leader. When fishing deep water, use a Corky, held in place with a small piece of toothpick. I've used this trick to catch 10-pound rainbow trout on a fly rod.

In fishing cold, freestone streams, Ted Fay designed a system using two flies simultaneously, usually both weighted nymphs, a Stonefly and a Bomber, and fishing pocket water with short casts. It was a fantastic display one early summer day when he caught 10 trout on his first five casts and then just grinned at me as if he did it all the time.

Remember that 90 percent of the time, trout will be feeding subsurface. That is why nymphing is a very effective way to catch trout in California.

The other 10 percent of the time is when there is a surface hatch of insects, which in turn inspires a surface feed. This usually occurs at dawn and dusk in summer for 30 minutes to two hours. In the fall it can occur for hours during a good caddis hatch. It is exciting fishing because it is so visual to see the hatches, cast to rising fish, see the strike, and see the set. This is when long casts, accuracy, and soft deliveries can make all the difference. If you slap the line on the water in your delivery, you will spook the fish off the bite. So start with short casts at each spot, mastering the soft presentation, and then extend your casts out to work the entire spot.

Gene St. Denis with a big Tahoe brown trout

© TOM STIENSTRA

Fly-fishing is not only productive, it teaches you tremendous lessons about insects, water temperature, feed patterns, and seasonal cycles. Fly-fishing is a fun, exciting sport that provides the maximum intimacy with your river surroundings. You get more than fishing; you get an experience that touches all of the senses.

Trolling a Lake

More people troll for trout than try any other method across California's hundreds of lakes and reservoirs, and the Dunckel method can help any of them catch more and larger fish. The key is getting the depth, trolling speed, and rigging exact.

LURES

Here's what you might look for: Humdinger (purple, blue/purple, or gold with red stripe), Cripplure (gold or gold with red stripe), Needlefish (rainbow, gold with flecked dots, cop car, red/black with silver flash), Triple Teaser (white with red head), Z-Ray (gold or white with red dots), Roostertail (black/yellow with silver spinner), Kastmaster (gold or rainbow trout), Mepps Lightning, Little Cleo (gold), Bingo Bug, Speedy Shiner (gold), Rapala (fire tiger, black/gold), Rebel Froggy, F-7 Flatfish (frog), Wee Wart, Koke-A-Nut, and Super Duper (gold/red).

For some, all they know is trolling a night crawler behind flashers, but even that can be given a twist. A good trick is to troll a black or dark-green woolly worm fly behind Cousin Carl's Half-Fast flashers. Another excellent trick is to use a small dodger, such as a Sling Blade, and then add 18 inches of leader to your lure.

When using lures, always test them with and without snap swivels. The lures must look perfect as they are trolled. In addition, when selecting a lure for size, be sure to add the length of the snap swivel as if it were part of the lure. For instance, a one-inch lure with a 1/4-inch-long snap swivel would be seen by the fish as a 1 1/4-inch minnow. This is important when matching the size lure to the size forage in a lake.

Flashers and night crawlers: Use Cousin Carl's Half-Fast flashers with the two half-brass and half-silver blades in the flat (not dimpled) finish (the exception is in high wind, when I also use the hammered/dimpled finish. I also like the Sep's Mini Flashers because of their minimal drag. Many other types can work, and the most famous are the Luhr Jensen Ford Fenders. In any case, be sure you follow the directions on the back of the container and have the exact amount of leader that the manufacturer recommends. You just plain have to get it right.

Use half a night crawler and work it onto the hook so it lies perfectly straight in the water, with a small piece running free behind the hook. This can be done quickly with a worm threader. You skewer the night crawler with the threader, a small-diameter piece of metal tubing, and place your hook on one end of the tubing. Then work the night crawler from the tubing to your hook and line. Thus the worm lies perfectly flat in the water.

If you keep getting short strikes, with the trout consistently biting off the ends of your night crawlers, resist the urge to shorten the night crawler, as this will reduce its action in the water. Instead add a stinger hook. To accomplish this, when you tie on a hook, do not trim off the excess line. Tie on an additional hook to the line, then hook the end of the night crawler with it as a trailer or stinger.

Depth

In summer, trout will be locked in the thermocline as if they are locked in jail. This depth can vary a great deal from lake to lake, but without a way to troll deep and test different depths, you will likely be fishing right over the top of all the trout.

Many methods are available to help you troll deeper, including using downriggers, plastic planers, or leadcore line, or just by adding weight. With downriggers, no heavy weight is required on your line, so using very light tackle is possible even when fishing deep.

With leadcore in small lakes, a trick is to tie on 30 feet of leader and then troll a Triple Teaser. I have always used Scotty downriggers. My personal choice is the Scotty Depthpower, two of which are mounted on my boat. Whatever you choose, just make sure you do it.

Always test different depths starting deep and ending shallow until you find the fish. Downriggers and leadcore trolling line are excellent for testing, because downriggers provide exact readouts of how deep the line is, while leadcore line is color coded. Therefore, when you find the fish, you can return to the same depth at every drop. Trout will stay in an ideal temperature zone as if in lockdown.

The exceptions are short periods at dawn and dusk, when the trout often feed on the surface. In spring and fall, when the water is cool, the trout are often in the top 10 feet of water as well.

Speed

The natural way to select trolling speed with lures is to trail the lure alongside the boat and watch to see if the action is exactly right. A tip is to let the lure trail about 10 feet behind the boat, then check it out, because many lures behave differently with more line in the water.

When using metal lures, you can go a bit faster. When using Rapalas or Rebel-style bass lures for brown trout, it is important to troll slower than when using flashy metal lures for rainbow trout. When you are trolling with flashers and a night crawler, you want the blades to just barely tumble, not spin crazily.

Most boats troll way too fast. Add a trolling plate to any motor larger than two horsepower in order to be able to slow the boat. In small lakes, a trick I sometimes use on my boat is to sometimes use a high-thrust Minnkota electric trolling motor (to keep it from draining the batteries for my engine, it is wired to two separate batteries). You have to be able to control your trolling speed perfectly. At times, fast can work just fine. At most other times, slow is better. At big lakes, the rule of thumb is 2.5 miles per hour for rainbow trout. But when in doubt, go slower.

If you are renting a boat at a lake, be prepared to get one with a motor that doesn't have a trolling plate by bringing along a five-gallon bucket with a rope. You can tie the bucket to the side or drag it behind to slow the boat.

Never run your boat straight down a lake unless you are following the edge of the old river channel. Instead troll so you follow the contours of the shoreline. If the shoreline is straight, then try zigzags and figure eights over a hot spot, or stop the boat completely, then give it a surge. Why? Each of these actions makes the lure drop in the water, fluttering as it goes down as if wounded. Then, when the lure gets straightened out by the line, it will swim as if trying to escape. My dad and I discovered this by accident years ago when my engine ran out of gas one day, stopping the boat and causing the lure to drop in the water. When we both started to reel in, big trout immediately hammered both of our lures—a big double, both were 19-inchers.

Another great trick is to take advantage of windy days. A breeze can often help by creating a riffle on the water, which attracts the trout to come up shallower. If the wind blows enough, it can provide the perfect trolling speed. I will turn my engine off and let the late-afternoon breeze push my boat over the best spots while the lures trail behind the boat.

Drift Jigging

This is a wild-card option that can produce large fish at lakes. Instead of trolling, you turn the engine off and let the boat drift slowly over prime areas that have been identified as holding trout. You let a lure descend straight down from the boat; when satisfied with the depth (often best right off the bottom), you simply jerk the rod up, then let the lure settle back down. You repeat this over and over. Crazy? Give it a try, especially in late winter. Many huge trout can be caught with this method when nothing else will work. The best lures for drift-jigging for trout are a white crappie jig, Gitzit, and Krocodile spoon.

Fishing a Lake from Shore

When fishing a lake from the shore, use very light spinning gear: an ultralight graphite rod with a micro spinning reel and light line. Never use anything heavier than 4-pound test.

The most simple is a single-hook rig. You start by slipping a small barrel sinker (for casting weight) over your line, then tying a snap swivel to the line. Add 14 inches of leader and a No. 8 hook. A key with this setup is making sure your bait floats up off the bottom a few inches. That can be done by using Power Bait, Zeke's Floating Cheese, or a marshmallow. If you use a night crawler for bait, you can use a worm inflator to pump it up like a little balloon to make it float. A worm inflator is actually just a small empty plastic bottle with a hollow needle. You jab the needle into the night crawler, give the bottle a squeeze, and the little guy looks like a tiny brown balloon.

A more advanced two-hook rig is very popular. Take your fishing line in hand and slip on a small, clear red bead, then tie on a snap swivel. Tie on a Lyons Leader (developed by Dave Lyons), which consists of a loop (which is attached to the snap swivel) with 18 inches of leader, to a No. 8 bait hook on one side, then eight inches of leader to a No. 8 egg hook on the other side.

To bait up, place half a night crawler on the bait hook, using a worm threader (see *Lures*) so it will lie straight. Then place a salmon egg on the other hook, working it up to the eye of the hook, and then mold a small piece of Power Bait (chartreuse or rainbow sparkle) over the shank and hook.

With a careful flip, toss it out 35 or 40 feet. What happens is that the night crawler will sink to the bottom, but the Power Bait and egg float up a bit, just above any weeds down there, right where the trout are swimming.

The trick is to put your rod down, leaving the bail of the spinning reel open, then take the line from the reel and place it under the light plastic lid of a worm tub. There's virtually no resistance, so when a fish picks up the bait, it doesn't get spooked. But when the line gets pulled out from under that lid, you know darn well there's something going on down there. Heh, heh.

When your line moves a bit in the water, then tightens, flip the bail over on your reel and set the hook.

Fishing Wilderness Lakes and Streams

Whether fishing at a lake or a stream in the wilderness, identify the promising spots, make five casts, then move on to the next spot. Stick and move and keep on. That's the key in the wilderness. If you ever take a look at the underwater world, you see that after five or six casts, the fish even start to get used to your lure. The lesson? If you haven't caught one by then, you are not going to—time to move on.

Keep your tackle simple. To keep our backpacks as light as possible, we often keep a half dozen lures in a 35-mm film canister—that's it.

The lure that works best is the gold Met-L Fly. Other lures that work well are the Panther Martin spinner (black body and yellow spots, gold blade), Z-Ray (black with red spots, or gold with red spots), yellow Roostertail (with yellow/black body, yellow backtail, gold blade), or Kastmaster (in gold, rainbow trout, or blue/silver).

We have another one we call "The Mr. Dunckel Special," after the man who invented it. It is a 1/16-ounce Dardevle spoon that is painted flat black and dabbed with five tiny spots of red paint. It works well in clear-water conditions, when many lures frighten the fish instead of attracting them. The fly-and-bubble combination can work great in high mountain lakes, especially in the southern Sierra.

To fish the wilderness, you must be willing to hike, and hike a lot. You have to hike into remote areas, then hike some more up and down the stream or around the lake, then hike back to camp. The best I've ever seen at this is my older brother, Bob Stienstra Jr., the best wilderness trout angler around—so good that we call him Rambob. When stalking the evening rise, he's a mix of Davy Crockett and a Miwok chief. He wears moccasins and walks softly but doesn't carry a big stick—it's more like a magic wand.

In the wilderness he does not wait around for the fish to bite. Instead he chases them down like a river hunter who would fit right into a Louis L'Amour western.

He sneaks up along the stream, walking softly and low, keeping his shadow off the water, then zips short casts into the headwaters of pools, the edges of riffles, tail-outs, and the pockets along boulders.

Rambob doesn't wait long for an answer. He either gets his bite or moves on, making only a few casts at each hole, and therein lies his secret. He covers a tremendous amount of water in a short time.

Rambob has the stamina to carry out this strategy. He covers about a mile of river per hour, walking almost as much as fishing, but in the process he gets a fresh look at a new hole every few minutes. Wearing those trademark moccasins, he moves quickly and silently, stopping at the good-looking spots to make short but precise casts, then moving on to the next. I've never seen him so happy as when he's in his moccasins in the wilderness, then comes around a bend and spots a deep river hole, the kind where the water flows through a chute at the head of it like a miniature waterfall. He knows what's ahead, and the vision is enough to compel him onward.

It's like you've used a time machine to return to the days of Joe Walker, the greatest trailblazer of them all, and Liver-Eatin' Johnson, the legendary woodsman who inspired the movie *Jeremiah Johnson*.

Insider's Notes

• If you are not catching fish, drop to a lighter line size. In tests I've done, 4-pound line can outcatch 6-pound line 10 to 1 in areas with high water clarity. Always use fluorocarbon leaders, which are almost invisible.

• If you get a strike yet no hookup, immediately let out 15 feet of line, then let it tighten.

This is a great trick. The fish will believe it has struck and wounded the bait, and will then come back to eat it.

• During periods of water drawdowns at reservoirs, take a hard look at the dry lakebed and memorize the areas that will attract trout during high water. At the end of summer, if you beach your boat and hunt the obvious snags, you can find dozens of lures and flashers.

Personal Note

Trout fishing in California is like religion: many paths, one truth. Trout are found in more habitats than any other fish—from lonely creeks in the South Warner Mountains of Modoc County to urban ponds in the San Francisco Bay Area and the L.A. basin, and from large reservoirs in the foothills to gemlike lakes in high wilderness country. They come in a variety of sizes and species, and the methods used to entice them vary just as much. You can troll or bait-dunk, sneak up on a pool in a stream like a Miwok, or spend an evening wading hip-deep with a fly rod.

Many paths, one truth. No fish inspires more dreams, fulfills more good times, or lures people to more adventures than the trout.

MACKINAW TROUT

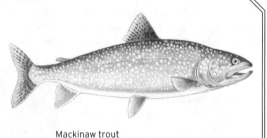

BEST FISHING SPOTS

1. Lake Tahoe
2. Donner Lake
3. Bucks Lake
4. Hell Hole Reservoir
5. Bear River Reservoir
6. Gold Lake
7. Stampede Reservoir
8. Fallen Leaf Lake
9. Caples Lake
10. Union Valley Reservoir

Mackinaw trout

PAUL B. JOHNSON

Tackle

Use a 6.5- to 8-foot graphite composite rod rated for 15-pound line and a level-wind reel that will hold at least 250 yards of line, filled with fresh 10- to 15-pound line. Some commercial charter boats use wire line and heavy rods, then try to rack up large scores of small fish that hardly fight at all. For the most fun, resist using heavy tackle and instead use downriggers for trolling, which allows the use of lighter tackle.

Rod: Berkley Tactix 7-0 ML Kowanee Trout-Casting (TXTC70-2M); Fenwick Techna AV 7-0 M Triggerstik (AVC70MF); 8-foot Shimano TDR1802.

Reel: Abu Garcia Ambassadeur Line Counter (5500LC); Shimano Triton TRN200.

Line: 12-pound Berkley 100 Fluorocarbon; Berkley Vanish (TFFS12-15) or (VFS12-15); 12-pound test green DuPont Magna-Thin or Maxima Ultra-Green. Note that line can be critical for Mackinaw trout, since they usually live in deep, very clear waters. That is why you must use a line that is nearly invisible and very small in diameter, so that it cuts through the water instead of creating a large bow.

MACKINAW TROUT STATE RECORD

| 37 lb. 6 oz. | Lake Tahoe | Robert Aronsen | June 21, 1974 |

Rigging

The most productive setup is a dodger-and-minnow combination. For bait, use a large minnow (at Tahoe, use a Tahoe redside minnow, the only legal minnow there). Thread a treble hook through the minnow. To do that, take a six-inch taxidermy needle and your line and start it through the anal opening. Pass the needle through the minnow's mouth, then tie the treble hook to the line so that the shaft of the hook is entering the fish. It looks just like a lure but is better because when the big Mackinaws come up to nibble, they taste fish, not plastic.

To make it even better, the minnow is best trolled 18 inches behind a No. 00 solid chrome dodger made by Luhr Jensen. The dodger-and-minnow combo provides perfect action, attraction, and smell, especially during the summer months, when the Mackinaws sometimes have to be teased into striking. When the bite is tougher, a shorter leader (12–14 inches), which can provide more back-and-forth action, is a good insurance policy.

In the cold months from November through May, you can get a hookup by trolling an ivory-colored M-2 Flatfish lure—your line clipped to the downrigger line to reach the proper depth, of course. J Plugs also can work very well. I have also used giant spoons, such as the six-inch Five of Diamonds and Dardevles, in red and white or chartreuse with red spots. Some people will hover over a spot and jig straight up and down with Krocodiles or Gitzits. This is called vertical jigging.

If you are fishing a lake the first time for Mackinaws, you need a good depthfinder to locate the deep bottom ledges. The fish are often suspended just off the deep underwater ledges. With a depthfinder, search for sudden drop-offs, then troll just off them. The converse is also true: long, sloping bottoms will not hold Mackinaw trout.

By using electric downriggers that provide precise depth counts, we are able to troll precise depths. A downrigger is a separate reel of wire line that is heavily weighted—your fishing line is attached to the wire line by a clip. When a fish strikes, your fishing line pops free and you fight only the fish, not any weight. That is why downriggers are so perfect for trolling deep.

Even though the fish come big and often go deep, you don't need particularly heavy tackle when using downriggers. Most of the prime Mackinaw water is not loaded with bottom structure, so you usually don't have to fear the fish will wind the line around a submerged tree stump or other snag, breaking it. In addition,

big Mackinaw trout

it is the downrigger that takes the strain of the lead needed to get deep, not the rod.

Time and Place

Mackinaw trout inhabit only cold water, preferring temperatures no warmer than 50°F. They often roam hundreds of feet deep during the summer months, but emerge in shallower areas during the coldest days of the year in late winter. They are also especially light sensitive and can be driven to darker and deeper depths during days with flat water and bright sun and during nights with a bright moon. So your best bet is to fish during a new moon, overcast weather, or right at dawn. There is often a bite from dawn to 7:30 A.M.; then it gets spotty until about 9 A.M. After that, on blue-sky days you might as well quit.

Tricks

A real key to landing Mackinaw is "learning the lake." Every lake has habitat that will hold fish. With Mackinaw, 90 percent will be in about 10 percent of the water. So with a depthfinder, learn these spots and fish them exclusively.

Often the best fishing is in cold, overcast weather with a wind chop on the water. The reason these conditions are good for catching big Mackinaw trout is that the fish are less likely to get spooked off the bite, which is common during clear, calm, warm days, especially following full moons.

Some people swear by vertical jigging, but your arm can wear out far before a Mackinaw decides to bite.

Personal Note

Mackinaws can get big and strong, and when they do, they can provide a fight that is like being grabbed by the hair on your head and lifted right off the ground.

The big Mackinaws are called "lakers," as in lake trout, and are better known in the Arctic as the king of lakes. Although the state record is a 38-pounder at Tahoe, there are legends of 50- and 60-pounders roaming even now.

One of my favorite spots for big Mackinaw trout is called the Dome, at Lake Tahoe. Beneath the flat, dark-blue surface of Tahoe, this dome rises high above the surrounding lake bottom like an underwater mountaintop. It is offshore of the south-shore casinos. In the space of about 100 yards, the lake bottom of Tahoe rises from 750 feet deep to only 160 feet deep; then, moving inshore, it falls off again to 265 feet. The Dome is about 50 yards across and has about 10 feet of grass growing on top of it, and the big trout lie in there, swimming around and feeding. Not many fish are caught here, but there is a short bite that starts at first light. I won a Tahoe fishing tournament here once with Dan Hannum by catching 11- and 9-pounders in 45 minutes, losing one that was bigger, releasing several 3-pounders—and then just like that, the bite was over.

Since the fish hang out in the grass that grows on top of the dome, by trolling your lures right across the top of the grass, you can entice them to come up and take a look—and perhaps take a bite.

On a trip in the Northwest Territories at Great Bear Lake, my pal Trevor Slaymaker and I spent two days and 20 straight hours on the water, not fishing, but searching for the perfect Mackinaw habitat, camping out along the shore for a few hours while en route. We finally found it in a large bay, where an 8-foot bottom was cut by a 15- to 25-foot canyon down the center of the bay. We then trolled that canyon and in four hours caught six huge Mackinaws—42, 38, 32, 26, 22, and 20 pounds—one of the most remarkable sessions of fishing I have ever had. I mounted the 42-pounder (which is 47 inches long) and released all of the others.

STEELHEAD

BEST FISHING SPOTS

1. Smith River, Main Stem, forks to U.S. 101 bridge (by boat)
2. Smith River, Middle Fork along U.S. 199 (by shore)
3. Klamath River
4. South Fork Eel River
5. Feather River
6. Mad River
7. Mattole River
8. American River
9. Trinity River
10. Redwood Creek

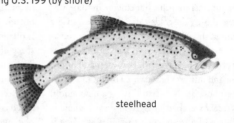

steelhead

PAUL B. JOHNSON

Tackle

Conventional: Try an 8 1/4-foot Fenwick HMG rod with an Ambassadeur 4500 or 5500 reel, or an 8 1/2-foot Loomis STR1024C rod matched with a Calcutta 250 reel. Other options: Berkley Air IM7 8-6 MH (A92-8-6MH); Fenwick HMX 8-6 MH or Salmon/Steelhead casting (HMXT86MH-2) with Abu Garcia EXT Pro (5600EXT-PRO) or Abu Garcia REVO Premiere (REVOPRM).

Spinning: The Berkley Air IM7 8-6 M (A94-8-6M) and the Fenwick HMX 8-3 ML Salmon/Steelhead Spinning (HMXS83ML-2S) rods are good. For reel, go with Abu Garcia Cardinal 804 (C804) or Abu Garcia Cardinal 704LX (C704LX). Good combos include the Loomis STR1024S rod matched with a Shimano Stradic ST 4000FG reel, and the 7-foot Shakespeare Ugly Stik with a rear-drag spinning reel (SPA040R).

Line: Use 10-pound test if water clarity is fair, 8-pound test if it's clear, and 6-pound test if it's very clear or being used by an extremely

skilled angler. On the Smith River in Northern California, virtually everybody uses Maxima Ultra-Green. Another good choice is Berkley Trilene 100 percent fluorocarbon 8/10-pound test (depending on water clarity).

Fly-fishing: Use a 9-foot Sage 8-weight rod, an Abel saltwater fly reel with spools loaded with sink-tip, and floating lines, each backed with 300 yards of 30-pound Spectra. I use a 10-foot Sage 8-weight SP 8100-3 with an Abel saltwater fly reel. Use a 10-pound leader and knots with 100 percent strength. For juvenile steelhead, or "half-pounders" as they are called (actually, they can be as long as 15–20 inches), a 6- or 6/7-weight rod suited for rainbow trout is acceptable. A good match is an 8 1/2-foot Fenwick 8-weight IronFeather IF 866 with a Pflueger single-action reel.

Rigging

Wear a fishing vest or jacket that is set up in advance with key tackle elements in separate pockets. Readily accessible should be a small

STEELHEAD STATE RECORD

27 lb. 4 oz.	Smith River	Robert Halley	December 22, 1976

spool of leader material (usually 8-pound Maxima), pencil lead, hooks, and a pair of clippers and pliers hanging from plastic ties. A covered tub of roe for bait should be ready in another pocket. It is advisable to have pre-tied leaders readily accessible so you can spend your time fishing, not tying rigs after snags and break-offs. A large net is required to land steelhead, even from shore, usually with an opening about three feet across; small trout nets will not work, especially if you try to land California's first 30-pound steelhead.

Use the three-way swivel concept. You tie on three feet of leader and your steelhead hook to one swivel (available pre-tied at tackle shops) and four or five inches of leader with a dropper loop to another swivel. From the dropper loop, clamp on a pencil sinker. Use roe for bait.

Another option for weight is to use a Slinky, which is a special sinker less apt to get snagged in shallow, rocky areas. Attach the Slinky on a snap swivel, then slip your line through the eye of the snap swivel. From the end of your line, tie on a barrel sinker. From the barrel sinker, add three feet of leader to your steelhead hook.

Other options include putting a little Styrofoam Glo Ball or plastic Corky on the line at the eye of the hook as an attractor, or using Puff Balls instead of bait.

Some shoreliners use lures, such as the gold Little Cleo, Kastmaster, or artificial egg clusters, but this can get expensive; snags are quite common because it is absolutely necessary that you drift your offering for steelhead near the stream bottom.

By boat you can rig the same when using bait. However, another good system is using Hot Shot or Wee Wart plugs. Let them flutter in the current behind the boat while the guide uses the oars to keep the boat almost motionless. Another system is to use a Hot 'N' Tot plug, remove the hook, and add two feet of leader and a hook with a threaded night crawler or a fly for bait.

Fly fishers have their best success using the Brindle Bug, Silver Hilton, Assassin, or even a dark woolly worm.

Time and Place

Early in the winter, when the seasonal rains are just starting and river levels are beginning to come up, steelhead often wait for a storm (and higher stream levels) or higher tides before leaving the ocean. In small coastal streams, the steelhead shoot through the mouth of the river during a high tide, then hole up in the lower river lagoon until stream flows are high enough upstream for them to venture onward. The recipe for steelhead is simple: just add water. The ideal situation is enough rain to freshen up the river and attract the steelhead upstream, but not so much rain that the river is muddied up or the stream is flowing too high and fast to fish.

If the stream is "greened up, freshened up," then you are in business. Steelhead will enter the river system and head upstream, stopping in the slicks just upstream of white water, in the holes just downstream of white water, occasionally along the edges of riffles, in holes on sharp bends in the river, aside large boulders, and in tail-outs (especially on major rivers early in the season).

The type of water that holds steelhead in a river is similar to that which holds trout in a mountain stream—projected on a larger scale,

THE 1 PERCENT CLUB

If you catch a 15-pound steelhead, you have joined California's 1 Percent Club. That is because 97 percent of California's anglers have never caught a steelhead, according to a survey conducted by Fish and Game. Out of the 3 percent who have, just one-third have caught a 15-pounder. If you are an honorary member of the 1 Percent Club, you are probably both lucky and good.

of course. Steelhead use the river as a highway, then spawn in the tributaries. They don't like to stop moving, but they will at certain areas to rest a bit, especially after swimming through some rough water. This is when you get your chance. I like to fish the holes, especially above white water. After a steelhead charges through that white water, it is bound to hole up for a while to rest before heading on upstream.

Tricks

You simply cannot saunter up to the riverbank and start casting. That is like throwing bricks in the river and expecting the fish to bite. If the river is clear, particularly in canyons, stop 15–20 feet short of the shoreline and make your initial casts from there. When the water is clear, any sight of casting motion, even the shadow of the rod on the water, can spook the fish.

Get up early and be on the water before first light. Never spend much more than 20 or 30 minutes at a spot. Then, when you're on a spot, fish the entire hole: the head, the middle, and the tail. Always keep moving. Most steelhead streams in California are bordered by two-lane highways with dirt pullouts alongside many of the best spots, which allow anglers to park and then hike down to the river.

The first few casts should not be long casts across the river. You could scare off the ones closer to the bank by casting right over their heads if you cast long. Instead, the first few casts should be along your side of the shore, then gradually reaching farther out. Work the entire hole, not just the head, tail, or middle, and if you don't catch anything, get the heck out of there and try another spot.

After the cast, the bait must drift downstream as if no line is attached, as if the drift of the roe is completely natural. The steelhead has to think this is for real. I remember that with every single cast. It is absolutely essential to get a good drift.

A big error many anglers make is "skidding" their bait. This happens when the line is tight and the bait is pulled across the current instead of drifting with it. You'll never get a bite with skidding bait.

When a steelhead bites, it's an exciting moment, one you'll never forget. Like so many fish that are tremendous fighters, their bite is often quite light. The reason is that the fish are often resting, finning in place, head pointed upstream, when along comes this chunk of roe drifting downstream. Instead of a savage attack, they usually just move over a few feet in the stream to stop the passing bait.

Another reason for a light bite is that steelhead are often just mouthing the roe; that is, stopping it and then burying it in the gravel river bottom. Like salmon, steelhead bury their eggs in river gravel, where they hatch after six weeks.

It takes time on the water to develop a "touch," to be able to discern the difference between a steelhead stopping the bait and a sinker hitting a rock on the river bottom.

You must be able to feel your sinker hitting the bottom. After getting the hang of a good drift out of each cast, feeling the sinker drifting down along the river bottom, you suddenly become so tuned in that whenever you feel anything weird, you know it's a fish and not a rock. The bite of a big steelhead usually feels more like a suction than a jolt, and when you're on top of your game, you can tell the difference every time.

Insider's Notes

• When big steelhead are first hooked, they make a tremendous run downstream, one of the most exciting moments in all fishing. If they get into white water, it's good-bye. So the challenge is to turn the fish before it "can get downstream on you," as we say. A great trick from shore is to kneel on a rock and point the butt of the fishing rod at the steelhead, in the process putting a huge bend in the rod and tremendous pressure on the fish. We call this "giving them the butt." Often you can remain at a stalemate for many minutes with a big fish in this position, where the fish is unable to head downstream and escape into the rapids, but at the same time is too powerful for you to gain any line. Once a big steelhead starts swimming cross-stream, instead of up and down the stream, you are on your way to landing it.

• When steelhead are easily spooked, such as in clear, slow-moving water, sometimes the bites are so light you will feel nothing at all. If you wait for a big yank, you might as well hire yourself out as a statue. Instead, watch the fishing line as it trails out across the river during these periods. When the bow in it tightens a bit—bang!—set the hook, because that is often the only discernible sign that a steelhead has stopped the downstream flow of the bait.

• When you get a hookup while fishing from a boat, always anchor the boat in an eddy to fight the fish, or jump out (with hip waders) and fight the fish from shore. If you stay in a boat during the fight, when the fish makes its power runs downstream, all the boatman has to do is let the boat drift down the river with the fish, and much of the excitement of the run is lost.

• A big steelhead is the fastest freshwater fish in California, capable of covering 27 feet per second.

• The steelhead is special because it is spawned in a coastal freshwater stream and then swims out to sea, where it spends much of its life. The steelhead, unlike salmon, does not die after spawning. In shorter streams where the swim is not long or hazardous, many return to spawn for a second or third time. Steelhead that have been in freshwater for a time develop a broad red stripe on their sides and look like a large stream rainbow; this is most common on the Klamath River. In the ocean, both salmon and steelhead are steel blue on the back and silvery on the sides.

Personal Note

If you are new to the game, the first thing to remember is that a steelhead is a trout, a rainbow trout that lives most of its life in the ocean, getting big and strong before returning to rivers during the winter to spawn. This is important, because if you want to catch steelhead from the shoreline, you must use skills very similar to those necessary for fishing mountain trout streams during the summer. The difference between a summer trout stream in the mountains and a winter steelhead stream near the coast is size: Everything is bigger. The water is bigger, the fish are bigger, and the tackle is bigger.

I once went 500 casts without a bite, then caught 14- and 16-pounders on back-to-back casts. My personal best day was catching and releasing 13 steelhead ranging 12–17 pounds.

The guy who taught me how to catch them is Jim Csutoras of Crescent City. On one trip long ago with Jim, he taught me the most important part of this art.

On my first cast and drift, I snagged up, then broke off. I quickly retrieved, tied on another dropper loop, and clamped on a sinker. I was just about to cast again when I saw the bow in Csutoras's line tighten just a bit, not more than six inches, and before I could shout to him, Csutoras saw it himself and set the hook. His rod bent down like a croquet hoop.

"A good one, a good one," he said. The fish flashed upstream, then jumped, landing with a tremendous splash, like a bowling ball dropped from a helicopter, then flashed across the stream and jumped again. Csutoras gave it the butt (see *Insider's Notes*) and managed to stop a long power run at a pool just above a big rapid. After a 15-minute standoff with neither party gaining an inch, suddenly the steelhead ripped cross-stream right at Csutoras, the line went limp, and Jimmy reeled like crazy to catch up to the fish. Before he could, the steelhead jumped again, right in front of us, its shiny silver sides flashing in the sunlight, and then shot away back to the other side of the river.

In the next 10 minutes, the battle settled down to a give-and-take, with Csutoras kneeling and pointing the butt of the rod at the fish whenever it threatened to go downstream. Finally, after a 25-minute fight, the steelhead was persuaded to the shore, played out. It was huge, about three feet long and an honest 18 or 19 pounds, maybe even 20.

Csutoras gazed fondly at the fish, then unhooked it, grabbed it near the tail, and worked the fish back and forth in the stream, forcing water through its mouth and gills to revive it. In a few minutes, the steelhead regained its strength and with a flip of its tail was free, darting back into the depths of the river.

That is the lesson: to release these magnificent fish to fight again another day.

STURGEON

BEST FISHING SPOTS

1. San Pablo Bay, "Sturgeon Triangle," bordered by China Camp, Buoy 5, and the Pumphouse
2. Suisun Bay, Mothball Fleet
3. San Francisco Bay, Richmond Bridge
4. Lower Delta, Middlegrounds, between Roe and Ryer Islands
5. Sacramento River, southern tip of Decker Island
6. South San Francisco Bay, Alameda Rock Wall
7. South San Francisco Bay, Dumbarton Bridge
8. Cache Slough, Sacramento River Delta
9. Carquinez Strait, Mare Island Rock Wall
10. Sacramento River, Knights Landing/Colusa

white sturgeon

BOB RACE

Tackle and Rigging

Rods: A great rod is the 7-foot Shakespeare Tiger BWC2201; Berkley Power Pole; Berkley Air IM7 8-6 MH (A92-8-6MH); Fenwick HMX 8-6 MH Salmon/Steelhead casting (HMXT86MH-2).

Reels: Try the Shimano TLD Star 20/40S; Abu Garcia EXT Pro (5600EXT-PRO); Abu Garcia REVO Premiere (REVOPRM); Penn 3/0.

Line: 30-pound Berkley Big Game (BSQS30C-15). Most anglers use 30-pound line. Some prefer 20-pound line to make casting easier; others like to go heavier, to 40- and even 60-pound line, in case they hook one of those elusive 300-pounders.

Terminal rigging: Start by placing a slider over your fishing line. A slider is a tube with a snap swivel connected to it, a cheap piece of tackle available at shops near places where sturgeon are caught. With the line going through your slider, tie a strong snap swivel to the end of the fishing line. Clip on a pre-tied sturgeon rig to the snap swivel on your line, and then clip your sinker to the snap swivel on the slider.

Sturgeon rigs: Use plastic-coated wire line with a single 6/0 hook, or two 4/0 hooks opposed to each other. Use the single-hook rigs

STURGEON STATE RECORD

468 lb. 0 oz.	San Pablo Bay	Joey Pallotta	July 9, 1983

when using mud shrimp, ghost shrimp, eel, herring, smelt, or shad for bait; use the two-hook rigs when using grass shrimp.

Bait for sturgeon: Match the bait for the salinity of the area you are fishing, For saltwater, use grass shrimp, mud shrimp, herring roe during a herring spawn, herring fillet, or whole herring when herring are in the vicinity but not spawning. For brackish water, use ghost shrimp or mud shrimp. For freshwater, use ghost shrimp or fresh shad.

Time and Place

Sturgeon have always fascinated me. My life-best, a 9-foot, 400-pounder, was an amazing spectacle with many full jumps—an hour-long battle royale that covered more than a mile of water, and ended when I unhooked the behemoth and he swam away happy. Your next cast, as my mentor Keith Fraser notes, might be a 40-incher, or it might be a 400-pounder. You never know. The only sure thing is you won't catch one unless your bait is in the water.

The season, tides, and water flows are critical to sturgeon.

While sturgeon live much of their lives in the ocean, they will enter estuaries in larger numbers from Thanksgiving through early summer, when there are new opportunities for feeding or a significant push of freshwater through the estuary.

Fast-moving tides, especially minus low outgoing tides, kick up feed on the bottom, which can get the sturgeon on the prowl. Slow tides often mean terrible fishing, especially during periods of little rain and slow water flows.

A slow tide in the San Francisco Bay Area is when there is little difference between a high tide and the following low tide. For instance, a high tide of 4.1 feet followed by a low tide of 3.6 feet has a differential of only 0.5 feet of

moving water. That is very slow. In comparison, a high tide of 7.8 feet followed by a low tide of -.2 feet has a differential of 8.0 feet of moving water—a fast tide.

During periods of high rainfall, when the push of outgoing freshwater is quite high, tides don't make much difference. But since heavy rain periods occur only rarely, sturgeon anglers must instead attune themselves to how tides affect the fishery.

The best fishing in the San Francisco Bay system is during outgoing tides just before (very good) and during (good) a cycle of minus low tides. More specifically, the best period is during the latter part of an outgoing tide, such as on a Thursday afternoon just before a weekend of minus low tides. Many sturgeon anglers talk about "big minus tides," but the best fishing is usually just before these big minuses and almost never just after the big minus tides have arrived.

Since minus tides occur late in the day during winter, the sturgeon fishing is often best in the winter, in the late afternoon. To fine-tune it a step more, the best fishing is often during the two days prior to when the minus low tides begin, 3:30–5:30 P.M. Tide books identify these periods. They phase in and out in two-week cycles throughout the winter and spring.

You do not need to be a slave to fishing to catch sturgeon—that is, staying on the water for many hours in order to hook this fish. Often we fish just two or three hours, and many times we have just started fishing at 3:30 P.M., right when others are returning home, skunked from slaving away on the water all day, frustrated.

Tricks

One key is to use a Sturgeon Board. It not only works as a rod holder when the boat is rocking around (it also can be used from shore or on a pier), but also it can raise your rate of successful hook-sets. It was invented by Keith Fraser, the Bay Area's sturgeon wizard.

The Sturgeon Board measures 58 inches long and 2.5 inches wide. At the top is a 0.75-inch piece with a slot in the center where the rod is placed. There are also two three-inch-high vertical pieces on each side of the board, located 16 inches from the bottom. Those vertical pieces keep the reel upright, and the pieces at the top of the board with the slot keep the rod in place.

The board, with the rod sitting in it, is rested at a 45-degree angle against the boat rail. The rod is left untouched until a fish bite is registered.

Fraser will cast out, reel in the slack, put the rod in place, and stare at the rod tip. His focus is so intense that sometimes he resembles the Sphinx. Should there come a bite, Fraser will carefully lift the butt of the rod, which tips the rod forward, using the slotted piece at the end of the Sturgeon Board as an axis point. If the rod tip is pulled down again—and often it can be less than an inch—he slams the hook home.

"Mistakes are easily made," Fraser explained. "The thing to remember is that even though sturgeon are huge, their bite is often very delicate. It is more of a soft pump than anything else. Also, the fish are very sensitive to anything unusual. If they feel any movement or agitation with the bait, it can spook them. If you jiggle the rod at all, they're gone."

That explains why sturgeon fishing can be so difficult for so many. By moving the rod around, even just a few inches, you can scare off the fish.

"Whether anglers are holding their rod or not, what usually happens with most guys is that when they get a bite, they immediately pick up the rod or get excited and move it around a bit," Fraser said. "Sometimes they will even stand up, getting ready to set the hook, waiting for another pumper. But sturgeon are so sensitive that just by sensing

the moving of the rod like that, the fish get spooked off the bait. The sturgeon never comes back, and the guy doesn't catch anything. It happens over and over."

A similar system is used by delta guide Barry Canevaro (see the *Striped Bass* section), but instead of a Sturgeon Board, he uses what are called Balance Wedges for each rod. A Balance Wedge is a simple V-cut wedge, in which the rod rests like a balancing teeter-totter. When a fish bites, the rod tips forward. Canevaro then gently picks up the rod, points it toward the sturgeon, and stares hard at where the line enters the water. When the line moves a bit, sometimes just an inch or two as the fish tightens any slack, Canevaro sets the hook. That tightening line indicates that the fish has the bait in its mouth.

Using the Balance Wedge is also very effective when fishing in deep water channels in the delta or in the San Francisco Bay during times when sturgeon are feeding on the roe of spawning herring. When a herring spawn occurs, you can gather roe from seaweed, pilings, or rocks and use it for bait. The roe is only effective for bait during a herring spawn, however. During nonspawn periods, using whole herring for bait can be more effective.

Insider's Notes
• A variety of bait robbers can knock the bait off the hook, particularly when you are using mud shrimp for bait. I wind elastic thread around the mud shrimp a few times to secure it more firmly to the hook.
• During strong tides, your bait can float up off the bottom, away from where the sturgeon are using their round, vacuum-cleaner mouths to filter feed through the mud. The solution is to place a rubber-core sinker about eight inches up from the bait, which will keep the bait right on the bottom.
• To get proper hook penetration on the set, tighten the drag 100 percent to ensure there is no line slippage. Once the fish is hooked, immediately back down on the drag for the fight.

• The white sturgeon is the largest freshwater fish in North America. In the past century, there are records of sturgeon reaching 20 feet and 1,900 pounds. Sturgeon grow slowly and live for many years, some reaching 100 years of age. They do not spawn every year, as do most other fish, but they can spawn once every six or seven years. Because the fish may live at sea for periods of time, even up to eight years in rare cases, the variation in their numbers in bay waters can give the appearance of great population fluctuations.

• Commercial netting in the Carquinez Strait nearly wiped out the sturgeon. In 1917 a complete closure was put into effect until 1954, when sportfishing for sturgeon again became legal. To protect juvenile sturgeon and large adult spawners, it is illegal to keep sturgeon under 46 inches or over 72 inches. Sport anglers now regard the sturgeon as a world-class fishery, with many encouraging catch-and-release fishing to help ensure future successful spawns, many large fish, and a productive future.

Personal Note

The good old days weren't always as good as they seemed. I remember how it was trying to catch a sturgeon back then—I felt more like a prisoner of prayer than anything else. It was hour after hour of waiting for a bite, and when a nibble would finally come, I never seemed to have a chance to set the hook.

"Oh, that's normal," I was told by an old curmudgeon at a boat ramp. "The average is about 40 hours per sturgeon."

Then after a one-day lesson by a tall, bold gent named Keith Fraser, everything changed. I caught a 100-pounder and a 150-pounder on back-to-back days, then I went five years in which I averaged nearly a sturgeon per hour of fishing—and during that span never got skunked on a trip.

After having fished with Fraser many times, I asked him to start documenting his fishing trips. In 41 trips over the winter season, he hooked 86 sturgeon (keepers over 46 inches) and had only 10 missed sets. In one period he hooked 26 straight without a missed set. All but one of the fish were released, including two weighing more than 200 pounds. In three of the trips I took part in, we fished a total of 11 hours and caught and released eight sturgeon.

On a trip that year with Fraser and John Beuttler, of United Anglers of California, I had a potential world record on my line for two hours—a 90-pound sturgeon on 8-pound test line. I finally had persuaded the fish within 30 feet of the boat, and with a swift outgoing tide running past, I needed the help of my companions to back the boat to the fish in order to land it (the tide was too strong to drag the fish the last 30 feet). But right then, both Fraser and Beuttler hooked up and had their hands full with their own big sturgeons. After five minutes, my fish revived, went hurtling off on a 150-yard run, then finally jumped and landed on the line, snapping it, and was gone forever. I never really got over that fish until I landed and released the 400-pounder.

SALMON

BEST FISHING SPOTS

1. Fort Bragg
2. Golden Gate/Duxbury Reef
3. Monterey/Santa Cruz
4. Sacramento River, Anderson
5. Half Moon Bay/Pacifica
6. Klamath River
7. American River
8. Feather River
9. Crescent City
10. Sacramento River, Sacramento to Isleton

chinook, also known as king salmon

PAUL B. JOHNSON

Tackle

Mooching: Try the 8-foot Loomis HSR981 rod matched with a Shimano Calcutta 400 CT400 reel. Another great mooching rod is the 8-foot Daiwa CG 785M, designed by Chuck Louie, who has designed and tied several custom rods for me.

Trolling: Try the 7 1/2-foot Seeker Classic SC800 rod matched with a Penn 113HL reel.

Back-trolling on the river: 7-foot, 9-inch Loomis HSR930 rod with a Penn 965 reel.

Line: 14- to 20-pound test for mooching, 20-pound test for trolling, 20-pound test for back-trolling.

Downrigger: When trolling in your own boat for salmon in the ocean, use a Scotty Depthpower, an electric downrigger.

Time and Place

Salmon prefer water that is 52–54°F and will tolerate between 48°F and 59°F. If you don't have a temperature gauge, you are missing out on a major clue, and I never go on a fishing trip without one. Off the Southern California coast, where salmon roam during the spring, trolling 100–300 feet deep may be required to find the preferred cooler water.

The ideal condition for salmon fishing in the ocean is water that is cool and nutrient-rich, with relatively low water clarity. This will occur on a gray-sky day when the wind is causing a light chop on the water and plankton production is high. It is ideal because salmon are most apt to be shallow, rarely deeper than 40 feet. The opposite holds true on a blue-sky day with no wind and no plankton, when the salmon must go deep to avoid bright sunlight penetration.

Another factor for determining the best depths to find salmon in the ocean is baitfish concentrations. When salmon are feeding on juvenile rockfish at reef areas, which they often do when no schools of anchovies are in the area, they are usually 240–300 feet deep. When salmon are feeding on squid or shrimp, as they commonly do in early spring, the best depth is usually 70–90 feet. When salmon are feeding on large schools of anchovies or herring, they are often just 25–40 feet deep. Remember this and get it right.

In the spring, salmon often roam within boating range of Oxnard, Hueneme Canyon, and Morro Bay. In April, Monterey Bay, Santa Cruz, and Half Moon Bay often attract large schools of fish. In late spring and early summer, the salmon tend to be off the Bay Area coast, feeding on shrimp, squid, and juvenile rockfish at offshore reefs, often in the vicinity of the Farallon Islands, Point Reyes, and Deep Reef (out of Half Moon Bay). In July, anchovies arrive at inshore waters, and the salmon follow them right in, typically at Pedro Point, off Pacifica; Duxbury, off Marin; and the Whistle Buoy, off Bodega Bay. At the same time, Fort Bragg, Shelter Cove, Eureka, Trinidad, and Crescent City can have salmon within just a few miles of the harbor.

By August the salmon begin schooling in preparation for their spawning migration, and by late August that migration starts in the Klamath River to the north, and to the south, in San Francisco Bay on up into the Sacramento River system. By September salmon arrive to all the major rivers in the Central Valley and continue at full force through late October. Often there is a secondary run of extremely large fish in late November from Red Bluff up to the Anderson area of the Sacramento River.

So what should you do, troll or mooch? According to my logs of the Golden Gate fleet, trolling produces higher numbers of fish, while mooching produces larger fish. Trolling is best in spring and fall; mooching is best when the baitfish and salmon are tightly schooled, as in midsummer.

Mooching

Mooching is best from midsummer through fall, when the fish are no longer traveling great distances but are holding in schools, feeding on hordes of anchovies. You turn your engine off and let the boat drift, keeping your rod in hand to sense every bite, set every hook.

RIGGING

If you are not familiar with how to hook your bait with a mooching rig, board a party boat and have the deckhand show you exactly how. Most slip a sinker slider on their line, then tie a snap swivel on the end of the line to act as a stop for the slider. From the clip on the slider, you then attach your sinker. From the snap swivel, you add your leader and bait. The hook is threaded through the anal opening of the fish, with a rubber band wound around the head to keep it in place. The bait should have a bend in it, so it bobs and weaves as the boat drifts in the current.

HOOK SETTING

The key with mooching is knowing how to set the hook. With circle hooks, when you get a bite, you must let the fish turn and swim sideways with the bait. The hook will slide across the inside of the mouth of the fish, then hook it in the corner of the mouth.

Since salmon strike from the underside, their forward motion toward the boat can create some immediate slack in the line. As a result, you react by reeling the line taut, as in "reeling down to the fish." If you don't, you will rarely get the hook set. If the tip of your rod is too soft, this can also cause some missed sets.

Because the use of circle hooks when mooching is now law, anyone who loves to

SALMON STATE RECORDS

King salmon/freshwater:

88 lb. 0 oz.	Sacramento River, in Tehama County	Lindy Lindberg	November 21, 1979

King salmon/saltwater:

65 lb. 4 oz.	Crescent City	Frank Cox	August 21, 2002

Silver salmon:

22 lb. 0 oz.	Papermill Creek (Lagunitas)	Milton Hain	January 3, 1959

rear back and set the hook hard can have great difficulty hooking a salmon. What happens instead is that you simply yank the hook out of the mouth of the fish. So remember: never yank or tug when you get a bite. Instead, let the bite happen, enjoy the excitement of the moment, then reel down to the fish.

Trolling

PARTY-BOAT TROLLING

The most common trolling technique on party boats is using a sinker release, into which a two- or three-pound sinker is placed. When the salmon strikes, the sinker is released to the bottom, and you fight the fish, not the weight.

Regardless of what you choose, the position of your rod on the party boat is important. I always fish in one of three places: on the bow, so my bait is the first one seen by a school of fish; right next to the window looking into the cabin, so I can see the fish finder and always be aware of baitfish concentrations and their depth; or on the stern, so I can let out more line and fish deep if necessary (from 10 A.M. on) without tangling other lines on the boat.

PRIVATE-BOAT TROLLING

If you have your own boat, you would be wise to get it set up with downriggers, which allow trolling at precise depths to 200 feet without putting strain on your rod. A downrigger has a separate spool filled with wire line, and a metal arm to withstand the heavy weight on the downrigger line. The fishing line is clipped to the downrigger line, which releases when a fish strikes. So not only can you fish precise depths, but you can also use light fishing rods. I use Scotty Depthpower electronic downriggers.

TROLLING OPTIONS

Some anglers use plastic trolling planers, such as the Deep Six or Pink Lady, in order to get deep enough. The darting action of a lure and the pinwheel motion imparted by a Rotary Killer aren't effective because they look good. In fact, salmon in the ocean do not rely primarily on their sight and smell to feed. What is much

WHY FISH GET AWAY

Part I: One phobia shared by salmon anglers is losing big fish. Some people make up for it by losing the small ones, too. The reason for so many lost fish is simple: failure to keep the rod bent while fighting the fish. Keeping your rod bent during a fight guarantees a tight line; slack line allows salmon to throw the barbless hook.

Part II: If anything nicks or crosses the line, such as another fishing line, a weight, or a net, it can cause a moment of slack line. In that moment, many fish are lost.

Part III: When a salmon takes off, keep your thumb off the spool. The moment you thumb the reel to add pressure to slow down a run, you can pop the fish off just like that. Never thumb your reel for any saltwater fish.

more important is that salmon detect the vibrations of baitfish through their lateral line sensors, which run the length of their bodies. It is like built-in sonar, allowing the salmon to detect sound and vibrations through the water.

USING DODGERS

I always troll with at least one or two dodgers, but only occasionally with a flasher. A dodger shakes back and forth in the water, emitting a signal that acts like a homing beeper for a salmon's built-in radar. The salmon can "hear" the action of the dodger and are then attracted to the area. A dodger simulates the back-and-forth action of the tail of an attacking salmon. Other salmon pick up the vibrations through the water and figure one of their buddies has found some food, so they race to the scene. It is very important when using dodgers to use them exactly as detailed in the directions. If it says to use 24 inches of leader between the dodger and your bait, then use exactly 24 inches. The best dodger on the market for salmon is the No. 0 brass/silver model made by Luhr Jensen. Some tricks:

• Troll a dodger from the rod that is farthest forward on the boat, and troll a few baits without a dodger from the other rods fished from the stern. The dodger at the front will get the salmon's attention, and the rods behind it will get the fish.

• If you have downriggers, run a dodger off the downrigger weight. To give it the correct action, add 24 inches of leader and a Krocodile or Apex spoon from which the hooks have been removed. It is illegal to have a lure with a hook or a baited hook from a downrigger weight. But for the purpose of attraction, this system will attract salmon, which then have your trolled baits, spoons, or hoochies (a plastic skirt on a hook) to pick from.

USING FLASHERS

Flashers are longer than dodgers, measuring up to two feet, and are built to turn slowly and wobble in large loops as they are trolled. When light catches the sides, it reflects flashes similar to the shiny scales of a school of baitfish. I don't like them much for two reasons. One is that they travel in large circles and often tangle with other lines. The other is that relying on flash instead of action to attract salmon is a mistake. Dick Pool's studies with underwater cameras prove this.

Troll deeper as the sun gets high: you can often fish shallow at daybreak, but as the sun gets high in the sky, causing more light to penetrate the water, you have to go deeper to reach the fish.

Pier Fishing
RIGGING

There are two good systems to catch salmon from a pier. The first is called a Pacifica Pier "trolley rig." You start with a four- to eight-ounce pier sinker (which looks like a four-legged spider), tying it to your line, then make a short underhand cast, with the sinker grabbing the bottom and holding tight despite the ocean

surge. You then attach a pier bobber, which is about the size of an apple, to the line with a snap swivel, along with six feet of leader and a size 5/0 hook. After hooking a whole anchovy for bait, you let the bobber and bait "trolley" down the line to the water. You end up with that giant bobber floating on the surface, a whole anchovy for bait below it, and you wait for that bobber to get tugged under, perhaps when a giant salmon has taken the bait.

Another option is to rig an anchovy mooching-style, attach a rubber-core sinker on the line, and then attach a large Styrofoam float. This setup also can be effective in the tidal lagoons of the Smith, Eel, and Klamath Rivers when the salmon first enter the lower river during the fall.

One last thing: If you try to catch salmon from a pier, remember to bring a crab trap to hoist the fish with when it is played out. Otherwise you will find landing the fish an impossible task.

River Fishing

Salmon start moving upriver during late summer and fall on California's major river systems, with the best fishing in September and October, fair prospects in August and November. The major rivers are the Sacramento, Feather, American, Klamath, Trinity, and Smith. In big rain years, the San Joaquin system also can attract salmon. As the fish swim upstream, they stop in deep river holes, often in schools, before continuing their upstream migration.

RUNNING THE BOAT

Boats are positioned at the head of a river hole, the boat headed upriver with the engine still running. The motor is given just enough gas so the boat remains almost motionless in the water. The driver of the boat then eases up a touch on the motor, allowing the boat to drift slowly downriver, a foot at a time. Those aboard fish the hole downstream of the boat, as the boat is eased very slowly over it, backwards. That is why it is called back-bouncing or back-trolling. *Note:* When the rivers are low, many switch from propellers to jet drives on their engines to keep from hitting rocks with propellers.

Rigging

Whether back-bouncing or back-trolling, use a three-way rig. That is a three-way swivel. On one swivel you tie your fishing line. On another you tie a short dropper and tie on your weight (which can vary from 1–12 ounces, depending on the depth of the hole and the strength of the river current). From the third swivel, you tie on your leader and attach your lure or your hook. The best lures are the Kwikfish or the T-50 or M-2 Flatfish. In either case, tie a sardine fillet, which is called a "sardine wrapper," onto the underside of the lure. When using roe, use a 2/0 or 3/0 hook rigged with a loop to help hold the roe.

Back-Bouncing

Use roe for bait. The technique when using roe is to keep the sinker along the bottom, "walking" it down the river holes. It takes a developed touch to detect bites and a ramrod strike to set the hook. Don't just bounce the sinker on the bottom, but actually try to "walk" it along the river bottom. As you lift the rod and reposition the sinker, over and over, you will develop a fine touch for exactly how it should feel at all times. When this occurs, you will be right on top of every bite. You will discover that often the salmon simply mouth the roe, the theory being they are mouthing the bait in order to rebury it. Set the hook!

Back-Trolling

With rod in hand, anglers allow their bait, roe, or Flatfish lure (with a sardine fillet tied with thread to the underside) to trail off the bottom about 40 or 50 feet behind the boat. With a Kwikfish or Flatfish lure, the constant wobbling of the lure makes it easier for newcomers to set the hook. Sometimes the fish just smash the lure, and you're on. Other times the fish stop the lure—the moment you feel the lure

stop wobbling—that is, when you feel nothing, set the hook.

Shore Fishing

Salmon rest on the bottom of deep river holes in the course of their upriver journey, and getting a bait or lure to drift properly and deep enough through these holes can be very difficult from land. The exceptions are on the Trinity and Smith Rivers, where nature has placed many a shoreline rock adjacent to some of the best deep river holes, and also at the mouth of the Klamath River, where shoreliners can wade the prime lower river near the U.S. 101 bridge.

Personal Note

It takes someone who's a bit of a detective, mariner, and athlete to chase down California's big salmon. Dick Pool is all three of these, and I often think how this became obvious on one July trip out of Bodega Bay. Dick taught me how to use downriggers to catch big salmon on the ocean, even when everybody else is getting zilched.

An armada of boats was trolling just outside the harbor at a spot called the Whistle Buoy. Nobody was catching anything. And after two hours, neither were we. It was time to test different depths and try a few tricks.

First we added dodgers off our downrigger weights as attractors. Then we went deep, trolling 60–100 feet deep with two lines clipped to each downrigger. At 85 feet down, we connected. In a three-hour span, the three of us landed 12 salmon, including a 30-pounder, keeping just a few for the barbecue.

Mysteriously, other boats began following us around, the skippers watching with binoculars, including some captains on commercial boats. When Dick released a 10-pounder—and no other boat in the armada had even raised a net—the radio waves went wild. Everybody figured we had a secret lure. Nope. We had a secret depth. Everybody else was too shallow, trolling right over the top of the fish.

It allowed a rare glimpse into a wonderful world of more and bigger salmon.

STRIPED BASS

BEST FISHING SPOTS

1. Sacramento River, Colusa area
2. San Francisco Bay
3. San Pablo Bay
4. O'Neill Forebay
5. Sacramento River, Rio Vista
6. San Luis Reservoir
7. Deadman's Rock, San Francisco
8. San Joaquin Delta
9. South San Francisco Bay
10. Feather River

striped bass

PAUL B. JOHNSON

Tackle and Rigging

Live-bait drifting: For your rod use a 7-foot Penn Pro Sabre A270C, rated 12- to 30-test line; a 7 1/2-foot Loomis PSR90-25C, rated 20- to 30-pound test; or an 8-foot Daiwa Sealine VIP 1968L. Matching reels include Pro Gear 251, Penn 2/0 Jigmaster, Penn LD225 Lever Drag, and Daiwa HV30. Use 20-pound line.

Trolling: Try a 7-foot Penn 196 rod matched with a Calcutta 400 reel; 14- to 20-pound test line.

Plugging (conventional): Use a 6 1/2-foot Loomis MBR783C rod with a Daiwa Pro-Caster X 103HA reel.

Spinning: Pair a 6 1/2-foot Shimano JHS66M rod with a Shimano Sahara 2000F reel. Use 12- or 14-pound test line.

Time and Place

Stripers are anadromous, living a part of their lives in the sea and returning each season to spawn in the waters of the delta and the Sacramento and San Joaquin Rivers. Striped bass spawn in April, May, and June in the Sacramento Delta and Sacramento River, roughly from Colusa on downstream. After spawning, they migrate to San Francisco Bay. In the spring, the smaller "scout fish" are the first to arrive—four- to six-pounders, roaming the rocky shoreline areas of San Pablo Bay, San Francisco Bay (from Albany to Berkeley), and in the South Bay from Candlestick to San Mateo. As summer arrives and anchovies migrate into the bay en masse, the bulk of the striper run follows down from the delta. Late June through mid-July provides outstanding fishing in San Francisco Bay. The stripers then migrate to the ocean in July, providing prospects from San Francisco on south to Pacifica, and often in Half Moon Bay. In August and September the fish roam the ocean along the shore, from Marin to Monterey, before schooling and returning to San Francisco Bay in late September and early October. In October and November, adult fish migrate up to San Pablo Bay, Suisun Bay, and the lower Delta. As the early rains arrive, the fish are inspired to swim farther upstream, and by December the bulk of the

STRIPED BASS STATE RECORD

67 lb. 8 oz.	O'Neill Forebay	Hank Ferguson	May 7, 1992

run moves up into the delta. They spend the winter in the lower delta, and then at the first sign of spring, as water temperatures warm, they begin to cycle into spawning mode. Again, they have come full circle.

Much of the fishing luck for striped bass is dependent on tides. Large, fast-moving tides are ideal for anchoring and using bait. Small, slow-moving tides are good for trolling or plugging, but best at the top of the tide and the beginning of the outgoing tide, when the water clarity is best. Moderate-strength incoming tides are best for live-bait drifting. At the beach, stripers bite best right when either tide turns.

In other waters, particularly reservoirs, lakes, and canals, the best time is usually right at dawn, particularly during a period when the moon is dark. That early-morning bite can be excellent, but instead of bait fishing, it is usually better to try either trolling or plugging.

Live-Bait Drifting

The rocks and reefs of San Francisco Bay are home for the striped bass. When you bounce a sinker on his house, it's like knocking on his door. They like to come out and see who's there. That's the story—and there is science to explain it. Most of the reefs are actually sloping ledges, where baitfish get trapped and pinned during good tidal movement. That is why they are such good places to fish.

The boat drifts with the tide over the prime reef areas. Meanwhile, you dangle your live bait, usually anchovies, near the bay bottom.

For terminal tackle, use the three-way swivel concept. From one of the swivels, you just tie on your fishing line. From another you tie off your sinker with about eight inches of leaders. From the remaining swivel you tie on a short-shanked live-bait hook to three-foot leaders. Pre-tied rigs are available for $1. Anchovies should be hooked vertically through the nose or in the upper gill collar. Shiner perch should be hooked horizontally through the nose. Mud

suckers should be hooked vertically through the upper lip.

As you drift over the reefs, you will learn to sense the sinker bouncing along the bottom, and you will develop a touch that allows you to "walk" the bait right up the side of an upsloping reef, instead of merely bouncing it on the bottom. This way your bait can be presented in a lifelike manner. It takes some experience to tell the rocks from the bites, but after a few hours, you will suddenly realize the difference and start hooking striped bass and other fish. Some people get it right off. Having the correct tackle helps plenty.

Another great adventure is to "use chromies" and to try "pumping the Tower." Oh yeah? Let me explain: "Chromies" are three-ounce, chrome-plated, cigar-shaped sinkers. You tie one to your line and add 24 inches of leader and a 2/0 or 3/0 live-bait hook, on which you hook an anchovy or shiner perch. It is called "pumping the Tower" because you let the bait down about 15 or 20 feet, then pump your rod up and reel down to retrieve it. Since 9/11, the U.S. Coast Guard does not allow boats to get up tight to the South Tower, where schools of fish usually congregate.

Fishing live bait from boats along the beach can be just as exciting, with striped bass corralling schools of anchovies against the back of the surf line. The water is quite shallow, often just 7–10 feet deep, and you use very little weight. After tying on a No. 1 or 2/0 live-bait hook, add a half-ounce or one-ounce rubber-core sinker 15 inches above the hook. Use live anchovies for bait, hooking them through the gill cover, allowing them to roam near the bottom, and keeping your reel on free spool as they go.

All hell can break loose during a good beach bite, with diving birds, surf casters tossing lures out toward the boats, and 5 or 10 people aboard hooked up simultaneously.

Trolling

In the delta, the first thing anybody should do is take a water temperature reading. The magic number is 56. If it's 56°F or warmer, then it is excellent for trolling. If it's cooler than 56°F, it is better for bait fishing. As the water gets colder, the trolling bite tapers off.

At high tide and slack water, troll using two lures with a spreader: a No. 17 Bomber off a seven-foot leader, the other a two-ounce leaded jig with a Fish Trap off a three-foot leader (then during moving tide action, anchor and use shad for bait). Two other good combinations are a Rebel and a Worm-Tail jig, and also a Creek Cub Pike and a Pet Spoon.

Excellent trolling lures include the big Rebel minnow (both solid and jointed), Rapala, Bomber, Worm-Tail jig (in green or chartreuse), Striper Razor, Hair Raiser, Bug-Eye, Krocodile (chrome or chrome with lime-green strip), Hopkins, Miki, and Kastmaster (gold).

Striper trolling can be productive in lakes and bays because the fish tend to be scattered, rather than tightly schooled as in the ocean. With trolling, you cover the maximum amount of water in the minimum amount of time. But when you find the fish while trolling, particularly in the vicinity of a known underwater structure, it is often better to stop the boat and cast to the fish. This is called plugging.

Plugging

Plugging allows the opportunity to use lighter gear, spinning rods, and even fly rods. The one-ounce Hair Raiser, Striper Razor, and Worm-Tail jigs are very effective because that twisty tail does a little dance as it is retrieved. Or you might use a darthead jig and put on a grub with twist-tail. At lakes, casting deep-diving plugs such as the Big Mac also can take stripers, particularly at first light. Regardless of the reservoir, the best spots are often near the dam. As for fly patterns, the shad streamer tied by Ralph Kana of Oakland is a beautiful and effective pattern for stripers; it won a national competition for the best-tied saltwater fly.

Water clarity is important when tossing out a lure or fly. If water clarity is not good, you are better off anchoring and using bait.

One trick we often do is to troll until we get a hookup. If it's a 4- to 10-pounder, a school fish, we then stop and cast to the school. This is how you can have sieges of 20 and 30 fish in a few hours. It will last as long as the tide does, about two or three hours.

In late winter and spring, the Sacramento River (in the vicinity of Colusa) can provide some of the best plugging for stripers imaginable—a 50-fish day or better. Anchor above the river hole, then cast jigs rigged with plastic twist-tail grubs and work them along the bottom of the hole. The stripers will stack up on the upstream side of the hole, pointed upstream, waiting for food to come tumbling down to them. It's the easiest fishing you've ever seen—like "shooting fish in a barrel." Hah!

Anchoring and Bait Fishing

The first time I used Barry Canevaro's system of placing the rod in a balance wedge and using shad for bait, I caught 13 striped bass in three hours, keeping one for a photo and releasing the rest, including a 25-pounder. It was quite an introduction. On trips with Master Canevaro, we have averaged about one striper per hour, although most of the fish are caught in two- and three-hour periods, when a school moves into the hole.

The wedge system for balancing fishing rods is at the center of his success. It looks crazy. You will swear your rod will be pulled into the water when you get a bite. Instead, it tips forward like a teeter-totter, with the wedge as the axis point. But no matter how big the bass, the rod doesn't get pulled into the water. No matter how light the bite, you will never miss one.

When your rod teeters forward, that means you are getting a bite. Pick up the rod gently, careful not to raise it, and point it toward the water. Keep your reel on free spool and thumb on the line, and when your line tightens a bit, allow it to unroll from the reel. When it spools off more quickly, flip the brake on the reel, put your thumb on the line, and set the hook.

When the water is 50°F and warmer, the fish take the bait readily and swim off with it quickly. When the water is colder, they are apt to play with it and swim off with it very slowly. For the latter, you need a lighter touch to convert these bites into hookups.

The terminal rigging is straightforward. First, slip a slider tube onto your line (that is, that little tube with the snap swivel attached), and attach a sinker. Tie a snap swivel to the end of the line, and from that, clasp on a three-foot striper leader with a 9/0 hook.

Shad is the best bait for the delta. Bullheads, mud suckers, and ghost shrimp can also be good baits for striped bass. If you are unfamiliar with how to rig them on the hook, ask for a demonstration at the bait shop. When using shad, for instance, Canevaro will fillet one side, poke the hook through three times—through the fillet, through the fish, and then back through the fillet—and then, with the line, put a half hitch around the tail of the bait. It works, and not only in the delta, but also when still-fishing for striped bass in reservoirs or in the access points along the California Aqueduct.

Surf Fishing

Few things can match the sheer excitement of catching a big bass in the high surf, especially when the prospects of working over a school are imminent. Most newcomers to the sport start by surf fishing from a beach. What you discover quickly is that all the hoopla about "birds, bait, and bass" doesn't seem to happen too often. So you end up casting away with scarcely a sign of life and nary a bite, and wondering what it takes to get in on all the great beach fishing you've heard about.

It takes a lot of time. After a while you will start recognizing the signs of the presence of fish, and you'll then start cutting the odds down to your favor. Look for hovering birds, rippled surface water from schools of bait, or even small flashes from a fish feeding frenzy.

When fishing from the beach, long casts are critical to reach the feeding bass. The longest casts are made with revolving spool reels, or the Australian Alvey reel, with low-diameter 20-pound line and an 11-foot surf rod. From the beach, the best success is with metal lures and live anchovy baits that have been snagged. The best lures are the 3 3/4-ounce Krocodile (chrome with lime green strip), Hopkins, and Miki.

When there are large amounts of anchovies in the area, a snag rig provides the opportunity to fish with live bait. A snag rig consists of tying a barrel swivel to the end of your line, then adding four feet of 50-pound test leader, tying on a snap swivel, and clipping on a five-ounce sinker. Midway on the leader, tie a dropper loop and add a 4/0 treble hook. When birds are diving, cast the rig, snag an anchovy, and then let it sit there. The stripers often can't resist wounded bait.

An exciting prospect is to abandon the beach areas and clamber out to rocky points. This is often where the larger bass are caught. Instead of heavy metal jigs, use giant plugs, such as a 10-inch Pencil Popper, Striper Strike, Giant Pikie Minnow, and the largest Rebel minnow. Because these plugs are lighter than metal jigs, for casting ease you are better off using a spinning reel than a revolving spool reel. This is also true when fishing the access points on the California Aqueduct.

Should a bass continue to follow, use a hesitating retrieve, then allow it to rest briefly on the surface. Jig it, dance it, try anything that might induce a fish to strike.

Insider's Note

When chasing striped bass up and down the coast of the Bay Area, by boat or on the beach, you must make a special note of ocean surge conditions. When the surge is down between late June and early September, the stripers are apt to corral anchovies against the surf line, providing a chance for fantastic fishing, plugging or using live bait by boat or making long casts from the beach. When days of 20-knot winds create a large inshore surge, the inshore hydraulics of the waves push the baitfish offshore, and the striped bass will follow them right off. When this happens, there is no hope.

Personal Note

You can chase striped bass across thousands of miles of waterways, try all manner of strategies, and after years end up being just what you were when you started: a prisoner of hope. Why do people keep at it? Ah, for those special periods when you find the fish and then start catching them as fast as if they were hungry bluegill.

Striped bass not only get big, they are also school fish, so when you hit it right, you have the chance to catch a lot of big fish in a short period of time. This experience can change your perspective on the world—it suddenly becomes a place where greatness is possible. To recapture the feeling, you may even start chasing the fish on their migratory pathway in the ocean, through the bays and delta, maybe even to reservoirs, canals, and Colorado River lakes.

I have had a taste of both the best and the worst. Imagine catching 13 striped bass of up to 25 pounds in three hours of bait fishing in the delta. Or 11 stripers of up to 28 pounds

in two hours right under the Golden Gate Bridge. Or getting nearly a fish per cast in a 20-minute siege at O'Neill Forebay. Or taking a 30-pounder right off Pacifica by beach surf casting. Then there are the other times—not a nibble, not a strike, nothing at all for days. You might swear there isn't a striped bass left on the planet.

I remember when I'd been tipped off about an evening surf bite. I drove to the scene and saw dozens of diving gulls and pelicans, with about a dozen anglers all fighting stripers at once. I grabbed my rod and started sprinting down the beach, along with several other anglers. It took me about five minutes to reach the spot, and all in one motion, without stopping, I cast out, then hooked up almost immediately. Another angler was right behind me and attempted the same thing, but he was running so fast that when he cast out, the rod slipped from his hands and went flying into the surf. Twenty minutes later, everybody on the scene had limited but this one poor guy, who was on his hands and knees in the water looking for his rod. He never did find it.

Things like this just seem to happen.

HALIBUT

BEST FISHING SPOTS

1. Santa Rosa Island
2. Catalina Island
3. San Miguel Island
4. San Francisco Bay
5. Morro Bay
6. Carpenteria
7. Offshore Mission Bay (between La Jolla kelp beds and Point Loma kelp beds)
8. Gaviota Beach
9. Humboldt Bay
10. Monterey Bay

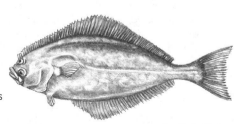

Pacific halibut

BOB RACE

HALIBUT STATE RECORD

67 lb. 4 oz. Santa Rosa Island Francisco Rivera July 1, 2011

Tackle

Several choices are ideal for halibut. In general, it's good to use a 6- to 7-foot rod rated for 12- to 25-test line, with a revolving spool reel, usually without a level-wind.

Rods: 6-foot Sturdy Stick No. JBSS3080-L (available only at www.halibut.net), 7-foot Penn Pro Sabre A270C, rated 12- to 30-pound test line, 7 1/2-foot Loomis PSR90-25C, rated 20- to 30-pound test, 8-foot Daiwa Sealine VIP 1968L.

Reels: Matching reels include Accurate BX-500, Pro Gear 251, Penn 2/0 Jigmaster, Penn LD225 lever Drag, and Daiwa HV30.

Line: Use fresh 20- or 30-pound line.

Rigging

USING LIVE BAIT

The rigging depends on the depth. In shallow areas, tie on a 2/0 live-bait hook and add on—depending on tidal surge—a one-half ounce or two-ounce rubber-core sinker. In water 20 feet or deeper, or where more weight is needed to get the bait on the bottom, rig with a three-way swivel. Tie your line off one swivel, a one- or two-inch dropper and a sinker off another swivel, and 24 inches of leader and a hook on the remaining swivel. With a three-way rig, the most common mistake is using too much line on the dropper where your sinker is tied. When fishing rocky areas with live bait, an eight-inch dropper is ideal, but when fishing sandy areas for halibut, a very short dropper is necessary to ensure that the bait is right at the bottom. Some anglers use almost no dropper at all with sinkers on sand bottoms.

JIGGING

The best jigs for halibut are the FAT Squid (see *UV Light for Halibut and Lingcod*), Worm-Tail, Striper Razor, and Shim. Because of the placement of the hook—at the tail, where the halibut starts his bite, jigs can work when bait does not. But halibut are more apt to bite a bait than a jig. For this reason, bait the jig with a fillet of anchovy, best prepared by cutting a fillet off one side of a bait, starting midway on the anchovy and including the tail in the fillet. The little anchovy fillet gives the jig some taste and smell. I then spray the jig with a fish attractant.

TROLLING

Use lures such as the four-inch Rapala, Rebel, or Bang-O B, or chrome spoons such as the 3 3/4-ounce Krocodile or Hopkins. It is often necessary to add weight ahead of the lure to get it down to the bottom. This is best done with a three-way swivel, rigging it as when using live bait, except that instead of tying on a hook, you tie on the lure.

PIER OR SHORE FISHING

Use the sliding sinker system. Start by placing a slider over your fishing line. (A slider is a tube, a cheap, common item sold at tackle shops.) With the line going through your slider, tie a strong snap swivel to the end of the fishing line. Tie 24 inches of leader onto the snap swivel, and to the end of the leader, tie on a 2/0 live-bait hook. For bait, use a whole anchovy, live if available, hooking it through the lower jaw and nose. Cast it out and wait; from a pier, you must wait for the fish to come to you, but often enough they do just that. In addition, you may catch many other desirable species of fish while you wait. Always have a crab net available, which is necessary to hoist a big, played-out fish up to the pier deck.

Time and Place

Halibut often feed according to tide activity.

The best tidal period for halibut is at the beginning of a moderate outgoing tide—that is, just after a high tide has topped out (what is called "the top of the tide") and at the start of the outgoing tide. Slow to moderate tides are best for halibut.

On the other hand, strong moving tides, particularly after a minus low tide, will kill the halibut bite. So avoid tide cycles that include minus tides. Avoid large differentials between high and low tides, which can be figured by subtracting the difference between back-to-back tides. Halibut prefer clear water, and the best time to get it is just after the top of the tide.

Halibut do not hang out at rocky areas but prefer expanses of sand bottom, often staying very close to the bottom, whether feeding or not. One September day I saw 500 halibut just off the docks at Catalina, just hanging out on the bottom as if it were a parking lot.

That is why the boat is allowed to drift in the tide along these sandy spots while the anglers aboard dangle live bait along the bottom. If the tide is too strong or the water too muddy, the halibut often move out or go off the bite. If the tide is too weak, concentrations of baitfish can be in short supply. That is when it can be necessary to run the boat in gear at very slow speeds, as if you were motor mooching, in order to simulate a drift.

Tricks

After rigging up, always use a lively anchovy for bait, selecting one that is neither scraped nor missing any scales. Hook the anchovy vertically, starting the hook through the lower jaw and running it through the nose. Drop the bait over the side, let it spool down to the bottom, and then get ready.

Even though halibut are equipped with a sharp set of chompers designed to slice up anchovies, they rarely slam into a bait, lure, or jig with much ferocity. Rather, they frustrate most anglers, nibbling, nibbling, and nibbling, like a wary dog sneaking licks from his master's dinner plate.

When getting a bite, some anglers believe the proper technique is to bow the rod down to the fish; some put the reel on free spool and thumb off some line; some do nothing but wait. My preference is to bow the rod down a bit, count to three, then set the hook. When I feel I'm really on the fish, I'll rely on touch alone, free-spooling the bait until there is just the right tension spooling off the reel before setting the hook.

Once you hook a halibut, you will discover you have a decent fighter on your hands, more bulldog than greyhound, with a few surprises up its sleeve. During the initial critical transition from bite and hookup to fight, confusion sets in as to whether you are indeed hooked up, because the fish never simply takes the bait and runs. In fact, during the first 20 or 30 seconds, it can seem as though you are just reeling in a heavy weight. Then suddenly something sparks in that pea-sized fish brain. Realizing it has been hooked, the halibut is likely to roar right back down to the bottom where you first hooked it. The bigger the fish, the more powerful the runs, of course; the

© BOB ROBERTS

Tom Stienstra with life-best halibut

latter half of the fight can really wear down an angler as the fish hovers and circles in the water like a spacecraft.

Trolling can be a preferred alternative in the spring and early summer, when the fish are scattered and just arriving at inshore areas and bays. The best catch rates for trollers are not gained from using the most sporting method, but rather from using wire line with a heavy cannonball sinker on the end, a series of green hoochies baited with squid, and a hoochie placed every two feet. Used by commercial hook-and-line halibut anglers who fish out of small boats, this system can provide tremendous results when other methods are just hit-and-miss.

Trolling speed is critical, and you should always let the lure "swim" alongside the boat to check for proper action before letting it down to the bottom.

UV LIGHT FOR HALIBUT AND LINGCOD

The plastic contraption on the inventor's fishing line looked like nothing I've ever seen—maybe something you'd put on your Christmas tree. He dropped it from his fishing rod into the briny green and the plastic hunk seemed to come alive. It was a squid, glowing in effervescence, its tentacles undulating in the current. A separate wire arm, called a spreader bar, glowed and extended to the side to keep the sinker clear of the lure. John Beath, the creator of this new lure as well as rigging for halibut, lingcod, and just about anything that swims in the sea, set up another and inserted a tubelike light inside the squid body.

"The light is why it glows, so it looks alive," said Beath, who then squirted a fish scent into a small container in the lure and added a half of herring on a big hook hidden in the tentacles. "The scent and bait is why it smells and tastes alive, too."

Our sinkers hit the bottom and within seconds we both hooked up with 20-pound halibut. That was only the start. After several more halibut in the next hour, a huge fish grabbed Beath's lure with a violent surge.

Beath set the hook and when he reared back on the rod and tried to reel, the halibut powered off with such force that it hauled the tip of Beath's fishing rod into the water—then surged off with 40 yards of line. Beath fought the fish for a half hour, taking in line, then losing it right back. At one point, he used the rod holder as a fulcrum to help leverage the fish. But when the fish made a bulldog power dive, the pressure pulled the screws of the rod holder right out of the side of the boat. He caught sight of the fish about 20 feet below the boat; it was a big halibut that resembled a spacecraft in *Star Wars*. The drama finally ended when Beath hand-gaffed the fish and dragged it over the side and into the boat, where it proceeded to flip-flop and knock the hell out of everything in range. It was huge—about 4.5 feet long and 82 pounds, and was the biggest fish anybody had seen around these parts for weeks.

In the world of fishing, Beath is becoming a prodigy. He has a line-class world record for salmon, where he landed a 51-pound salmon on 6-pound line. His inventions for saltwater fishing are just starting to take hold along the Pacific coast, from California to Alaska, with the introduction of the 9-inch Super Squid, 5-inch FAT Squid, to go with Ultra-Violet technology in spreader bars, lighting, and spray-on scents.

In networking with other outdoors writers, I heard about a guy who was testing new theories and lures in Alaska and caught a 7-foot, 325-pound halibut. It turned out to be Beath. I then learned that Beath's specialty is using ultra-violet lights and scents in deep water, and we arranged a trip to test his latest inventions.

"My secret is that I'm really curious and want to try everything and go everywhere," Beath said. "I'm always having people say to me, 'But I've always done it this way, and it works.' I don't argue with them. I just keep trying new things, new places, until I hit on something that's really special."

He's one of a handful of guys who can keep

up with me when it comes to fishing—too much is not enough. At a kelp bed tucked inside an island point, in just 30 feet of water, the air was still, the water calm, and we pulled out our light tackle. For an hour, we tested a variety of FAT Squids and Point Wilson Darts and rarely went more than 10 seconds without a fish—catch-and-release, lingcod, yelloweye, blacks, and more… you never knew what might bite next.

We turned our backs on them to try for something big, and offshore we went, about 10 miles out, in 350 feet of water, stopping the boat when the fish finder marked a big school of baitfish, likely herring, near the bottom. Beath pulled out his inventions: an ultraviolet spreader bar with a UV-painted 12-ounce sinker on one side and, on the other side, an ultraviolet FAT Squid with the built-in scent ball, saturated with a liquid called Fool-a-Fish. Down went our lines. Again, in seconds, the fish started biting. Only this time they were big lingcod with a 300-yard head start. The biggest ling went more than 30 pounds; it came up with its bowling ball–size mouth wide open, full of spiked teeth. After a photo, Beath released it, along with many others. "Got to provide a resource for the future." Over the course of two hours, they wore us out. "The one thing I do that nobody else is doing is use UV light in everything, the spreader bar, squid, and the scent. That's the secret. Fish see your bait down there like it's a thousand tiny mirrors."

For more information and to contact John Beath, visit his product online at www.halibut.net.

Insider's Notes

• I've tried the trick of adding a stinger hook on the tail of an anchovy to catch these tail-striking halibut, but it never seems to work. If the fish are consistently scraping the tails of my bait and never getting hooked, I switch over to jigs.

• Once a halibut is landed, the fight is far from over. A halibut can appear to be within seconds of its last gill flap when finally brought aboard, only to go bonkers upon hitting the deck, flipping and flopping high and wide. Some anglers attempt to whack the fish in the head with a billy club, but this just seems to make them angrier—and maybe even gets those teeth snapping more. The answer is to give a good whack in the back, not the head, and it'll settle down soon enough.

• Of the 60 or so piers detailed in this book, more than 20 offer a chance to catch halibut. It is a long shot, to be sure, but long shots can come in.

Personal Note

If you catch a large, flat fish that's brown on one side and white on the other, and you're not exactly sure what it is, heed this advice: do not stick your finger in its mouth!

A confused angler holding a fish he'd just caught walked into a bait shop, looked at the owner with a mystified expression, then asked innocently: "How can you tell the difference between a flounder and a halibut?"

The shop owner gave him a curious glance, then said, "Put your finger in its mouth. If your finger gets bit off, it's a halibut."

Well, as the story goes, the fellow responded by sticking his finger in the fish's mouth, whereupon the fish immediately bit it off. The guy pulled his hand away and stared at the little red stub.

"Guess it's a halibut," said the owner.

ROCKFISH AND LINGCOD

BEST FISHING SPOTS

1. Point St. George Reef, Crescent City
2. Cordell Bank/Fanny Shoal, Bodega Bay
3. San Simeon/Morro Bay
4. Farallon Islands
5. Cleone Reef, Fort Bragg
6. Año Nuevo Island, Santa Cruz
7. San Miguel Island
8. Brockway Point, Santa Rosa Island
9. San Gregorio/Pescadero reefs, Half Moon Bay
10. Point Sur, Monterey

lingcod

BOB RACE

Tackle

The tackle that's available for rent aboard party boats and the personal gear that anglers bring along can vary dramatically. Rental rods are often overgunned for the job. I always bring two or three rods: a light rod for casting jigs for smaller schoolfish, a medium-weight jigging rod, and a heavy rod for deep-water lingcod. I've burned up four reels on rockfish by using reels designed for bass at freshwater lakes, but the fun has been well worth it.

Light gear: For schoolfish such as blues, yellows, and yellowtail rockfish, use a light but stiff-action 7-foot graphite rod. A good one is the Loomis SWR844C matched with the Daiwa Millionaire level-wind CV-Z300A. Pflueger, Daiwa, BassPro, Quantam, Shimano, and others make similar style reels. Fill it with 12- or 14-pound Maxima, or 30-pound test Spider Wire (casts like 14-pound), which allows underhand flip casts of great distances. When using Spider Wire, double the line up when tying knots.

Medium gear: For medium-weight rods, the 7-foot Penn Pro Sabre A270C is one of the best all-around saltwater rods available, well matched with the Daiwa HV30 reel or Penn 3/0 Jigmaster.

Heavy gear: For deep-water heavy gear, short, stout rods are necessary to persuade the big lingcod out of their rocky haunts. A good deep-

water lingcod rod is the Penn 670 matched with a Penn 4/0 113HL and 40-pound P-line.

Rigging

Light tackle: For midwater schoolfish and shallow reef fish, the rigging is very simple. You just tie on the jig of your choice. The preferred setup is a three-ounce jig head rigged with a split-tail Scampi, which is considered a "swim bait." Other outstanding jigs are the Tady, Gibbs Minnow, and Fish Trap. My personal favorite is a metal jig, a Point Wilson Dart, purple and silver, five or six inches, which simulates a live anchovy. This works great at inshore reefs, around kelp beds, and at shallow offshore reefs near islands.

Medium tackle for bottomfish: For the two-hook maximum, the best setup is a single, large leadhead jig with a FAT Squid or a Scampi tail, where you also set up a "cheater" jig about 18 inches up from the Scampi. The best cheater jigs are a shrimpfly, Live-Action Shrimp (very difficult to locate, but sensational), Hair Raiser, and Worm-Tail jigs. This works great at medium-depth reefs, generally 180–240 feet deep. Using shrimpfly rigs was once standard up and down the coast. Hook restrictions have ended that.

Heavy tackle for lingcod: 16-ounce chrome-plated Hex Bars rigged with shrimpfly cheaters

(18 inches up from the Hex Bar) are the best way to get big lings. A 7.5-inch FAT Squid works great. Another big-time winner is dark blue or purple Banana Bars with a phosphorescent Hair Raiser tied as a cheater. Diamond jigs are also popular. In all cases, snags are a real pain for the unlucky or inattentive. This works best at deep-water (280–400 feet) reefs and in Southern California reefs, sometimes much deeper.

Time and Place

Note that fishing regulations often change from year to year, for seasons, depth restrictions, bag limits, size limits, and even annual quotas for the fleet. Always check current regulations with Fish and Game or with a marina or party-boat operator before planning a trip.

That aside, sea conditions are often key to rockfish success. Note that sea condition and buoy reports are available on the Internet for the entire California coast through the National Oceanic Atmospheric Administration's weather site, updated on the hour, at www.noaa.gov.

When swells are deeper than five feet and spaced less than eight or nine seconds apart, it can be difficult for smaller sport boats, 18–24 feet, to navigate comfortably on the ocean. If swells are larger than six feet or spaced shorter than eight seconds apart, it can be dangerous for small boats and uncomfortable even aboard the 50- to 65-foot party boats. In addition, a large swell can cause an inshore surge, pushing rockfish out of shallow-water reef areas.

When seas are calm, such as three feet every 12 seconds, boaters can fish at all the spots in comfort and ease, as well as under safe conditions for smaller boats of 18–24 feet. Generally, conditions are safe when swells are less than six feet, though the skill and experience of each boater will determine the safety of every trip.

Note that rockfish are not "rockcod." There is no such thing as a "rockcod," though many people call them that.

In winter, spring, and early summer, rockfish live at offshore reefs in water 180–400 feet deep, and even deeper at reefs off Southern

STATE RECORDS

Lingcod:

56 lb. 0 oz.	Crescent City/ Point St. George Reef (near Crescent City)	Carey Mitchell	July 12, 1992

Cabezon:

23 lb. 4 oz.	Los Angeles	Bruce Kuhn	April 20, 1958

Black rockfish:

9 lb. 2 oz.	San Francisco Mile Light/ Light Station	Trent Wilcox	September 3, 1988

Bocaccio rockfish:

17 lb. 8 oz.	Crescent City/ Point St. George Reef	Sam Strait	October 25, 1987

Vermilion rockfish:

14 lb. 9 oz.	Morro Bay	Bobby Cruce	July 31, 1996

Yellowtail rockfish:

5 lb. 8 oz.	off Alder Creek (near Monterey)	Alberto Cortez	August 4, 1991

Kelp bass:

14 lb. 7 oz.	San Clemente Island	C. O. Taylor	July 30, 1958

© TOM STIENSTRA

my bud John Beath with a big lingcod

California. As sea conditions calm in early summer, rockfish and lingcod emerge from these very deep haunts and proliferate at shallower reefs, even as shallow as 10 feet during very calm conditions along the rocky coastal areas. The best fishing is often in late summer and fall, when sea conditions are often the calmest of the year, making not only for a good bite, but also for safe boating.

In addition, the arrival of midwater schoolfish, such as blues and yellows, usually occurs in midsummer and continues until the ocean gets turned upside down by winter storms. This is when light-tackle fishing with swim baits can be extraordinary, providing dozens of hookups without your having to worry about snags on the bottom.

Tricks

• For using light tackle for maximum fun, become an expert at underhand casting from the side of a boat. On a typical drift over a reef, the boat will be drifting sideways, getting pushed by the wind and current. Cast in the same direction as the drift; the boat will go toward the jig, typically a bar, instead of away from it. That makes it a lot easier to get deep

and gives you more fishing time on the drift. If there is no wind, cast in the same direction that the swells are running. Often a rockfish will take the jig on the way down, not on the way back up. Most of the time the jig goes right down to the bottom, and you should work it just off of the bottom.

• For big lings, the moment there is a light sensation in the weight of the bar, set up the hook and crank up a few turns as fast as possible. That can get those big lings off the bottom, so that they won't get into the rocks.

• Remember that a lure with a single flat side, like a Tady lure, sinks slower than a cylindrical or bullet-shaped lure. When getting to the bottom fast is important, as when the water is really deep or when the current is running fast, the rounded lures are the best bet. When the drift is slow and the water is no deeper than 300 feet, a flat-sided lure allows the angler a much better chance to catch fish "on the sink." Often lingcod and large bocaccio rockfish can be taken this way. Another advantage besides the fast action is that the lure never has a chance to snag up on the bottom.

• If you go two or three drops without a hookup, either move the boat to a new spot or switch to a different lure. There are no rewards in this sport for persistence with something that isn't working. Constantly experiment.

• Rockfish often go off the bite during a full moon. They also have daily migrant habits, much like a herd of cows that go out to the field to graze, then return to the barn to get milked. If you fish enough, you will recognize these reef-specific movements, and you'll be in the right spot at the right time to intercept them.

• Care should be taken when removing rockfish from the hook, particularly those with the large scales and sharp spines—species like vermilion, yellow-eyes, canaries, coppers, and cows. Each of those spines is tipped with toxins that can give you a nasty sting in whatever part of the anatomy that gets nailed, the kind of pain that gives a person goosebumps even to remember it afterward.

Personal Note

For 25 years now, anglers, wildlife lovers, and hard-core environmentalists alike have protested how commercial anglers have tried to clean out the ocean. The commercial boats often drag nets that are like vacuum cleaners, hang gill nets that are miles long, and set miles-long lines with thousands of hooks. In the process, they have killed marine birds, sea otters, marine mammals, juvenile fish, and nontarget fish species in their mission to kill every rockfish they can get their mitts on.

In recent years the Pacific Fisheries Management Council (PFMC) and the California Fish and Game Commission have ordered cutbacks on sportfishing for rockfish and lingcod in order to "share the pain," the absurd government mantra. Each year, commercial anglers take 85–90 percent of the catch, and sport anglers take roughly 10–15 percent.

Share the pain? Your worst enemy has caused a train wreck, and yet you—the healthy one—are scheduled to have your legs amputated.

BONITO

BEST FISHING SPOTS

1. Redondo Harbor
2. Santa Monica Bay
3. Newport Beach
4. Point Loma kelp beds
5. Long Beach Horseshoe Kelp
6. Long Beach oil rigs
7. Point Dume
8. Oceanside Barn kelp beds
9. Catalina Island
10. Coronado Island

bonito

BOB RACE

Tackle and Rigging

Gear: 7-foot Seeker BCSW (3/8- to 3/4-ounce lures) rod, Shimano Baitrunner 3500 reel, filled with 8- or 10-pound line; gear for largemouth bass can be used effectively for bonito as well.

Hooks: No. 2, 4, or 6 hook on the end of your line. You must match the size of the hook to the size of the bait. Most people use live anchovies and bring along a large collection of hooks, gill-hooking the anchovy in its collarbone.

BONITO STATE RECORD

| 21 lb. 5 oz. | 181 Spot | Kim Larson | October 19, 2003 |

Weights: None in shallow water or where there is very little current and the anchovy is "fly-lined" out.

Sinkers: Split shot or rubber-core sinker, added 18 inches up from the bait to get the bait deeper if necessary.

Sight-cast jigging: Twin-tailed plastics such as Scampi or Mojo jigs, best with three- or four-ounce leadheads.

Special tackle note: Bonito can be very line-shy. When fish are abundant but will not bite, drop down in line size. Some anglers even drop down to spinning rods designed for trout, using 4-pound test. Though it is nearly impossible to land a bonito with this gear, you can often get the fish to bite.

Time and Place

Bonito are not usually difficult to locate. If there is no sign of fish, troll a feather jig to locate them. When you get a strike, stop the boat and either fish with live bait or cast jigs. At other times, you can see them crashing bait and boiling on the surface, and you cast to them. Sometimes they school around kelp areas.

The best fishing is from early summer to early fall, and it's often best in late summer.

Tricks

Be certain the bait is fresh and try not to squeeze it when you hook it.

With a conventional reel, keep your reel on free spool, thumb the line out, and be ready at all times for a strike. Boom! When it happens, let the fish run off for just a second, no more, no less; put the reel in gear, set the hook, and get ready to run around the boat chasing the fish. When using a spinner reel, keep the bail open and control the line with your forefinger.

Fly fishers can have tremendous excitement when the bonito are on the surface. Use a No. 6/7- or 8-weight rod with a saltwater fly reel that can take plenty of pressure. Cast bonito feathers, see the strike, then hang on for the ride. When schools of three- and four-pound bonito are marauding anchovies, fly-fishing for them is as fun as for any fish in California.

Bonito become inedible if they are not bled immediately and are allowed to sit uncleaned for long periods. For this reason many people release all the bonito they catch. But if you are going to keep them, bleed each fish immediately and store them on ice. Never waste the life of a fish. Either release them or eat them. There is no middle ground.

Personal Note

If you were to try to conduct a brain scan of a bonito, the machine would probably short-circuit. These fish are just plain nuts. They are vicious attackers, and when hooked, they zigzag all over the place. Pound for pound, this little tuna may be the best fighting fish around. They typically range 3–5 pounds, with a few 7- or 8-pounders in the mix; they are rarely more than 10 pounds.

On all kinds of tackle, even fly-fishing gear, they provide great sport. Bonito are often not picky eaters. Find them and you'll catch them.

At other times they can be very line-shy. At Redondo, the bonito often cruise around for months, driving everybody crazy. That includes anglers who are hooking them and anglers who are not. If you are not, it is particularly frustrating, because you know the fish are there. That is when it is time to try something different, right? After all, if you keep doing what you've always done, you'll keep getting what you've always got.

When the bonito go into a line-shy mode, I discovered that what works is to use 4-pound

Maxima Ultra-Green with a No. 6 gold hook. I even switch over to trout gear. Sure, I don't land hardly anything, but I get bites, and then I have one wild ride after another. Bonito go absolutely crazy, zigging, zagging, sprinting off, and even spooling me. I keep a big supply of line in the boat, just in case, and refill the reels quickly to do it all again.

YELLOWTAIL

BEST FISHING SPOTS

1. Catalina Island
2. Coronado Island
3. Long Beach oil rigs
4. La Jolla kelp beds
5. Long Beach Horseshoe Kelp
6. Point Dume Big Kelp
7. Santa Barbara Island
8. Point Loma kelp beds
9. Point Vicente
10. Rocky Point (Long Beach)

yellowtail

PAUL B. JOHNSON

Tackle

High-quality tackle is essential, but an advantage is that what works for albacore can also work well for yellowtail. Rods must be powerful and yet have sensitive tips. Reels must be strong, high-speed, revolving-spool saltwater reels—that is, with retrieve ratios of six to one, or at least five to one.

Rods: 7-foot Sabre 270 (rated at 12- to 30-pound test line), 7-foot CalStar Graphiter 700XL (12–30), 7-foot Loomis Pelagic PSR84-20C (15–25). Note that while long rods (a personal preference) are necessary for casting, short rods do fine for jigging straight up and down.

Reels: Pro Gear 251, Penn 501, Penn 525 Mag., Penn 12T, Accurate TDR 50.

Line: 20- or 30-pound test.

Rigging

Anglers use three methods for yellowtail: free-spooling live squid, trolling, and jigging. The ideal situation comes in the fall, when squid become abundant. Skippers and deckhands often chum yellowtail right up to the surface. But when the situation is less than ideal, which is most of the time, other strategies need to be employed.

Free-spooling live squid: For the standard rigging, tie on a 2/0 to 4/0 hook, then double-hook the tail of the squid. Bring the hook through once, then bring it through again. That secures the bait. If the yellowtail are near the surface, no weight is necessary. If you need to get down 20 or 30 feet, a split shot will do the trick. Should you need to go much deeper, add a rubber-core sinker. Anchovies, sardines, and jacksmelt also can make a live bait.

Trolling: If you don't have chum, and there is no sign of yellowtail breaking, troll a large Rapala, the one that is painted to look like a mackerel. When you are not sure where specifically to start, trolling is the only way to cover a lot of water in a short time. In the process, you should continually scan the surface water to spot the fish boiling. If you get a hookup,

YELLOWTAIL STATE RECORD

63 lb. 1 oz.	Santa Barbara Island	Kwang Nam Lee	June 18, 2000

circle the area trolling, or stop and either try to chum the yellowtail up or cast jigs.

Casting jigs: The six-ounce Tady jigs and Yo-Yo jigs are mainstays, with either a single or treble hook, but various other jigs will work. The best colors are blue and white, mackerel, solid chrome, and what is called scrambled eggs (brown and yellow). In the early summer, a common practice is to chum lots of anchovies to attract the fish, then "throw iron" (cast metal jigs to them).

Time and Place

Yellowtail are along the Southern California coast all summer and into fall. When the bait (that is, squid, anchovies, sardines, and jacksmelt) shows up, you can bet that the yellowtail won't be far behind. It seems that as the ocean calms, the bait school, and the yellowtail school as well. This often peaks in late summer and early fall, when the sea conditions are often the calmest of the year.

My favorite spot for yellowtail is Catalina Island. I fish the southwest shore and start by catching jacksmelt on small jigs. I then put those smelt on hooks, let them down, and start catching yellowtail.

Tricks

Line weight can be critical at this point, both in the odds of getting a bite and the odds of landing the fish. When the yellowtail are picky, and lord knows they can be, use 30-pound line to minimize its visibility in the water. During a wide-open bite, when that is a moot point, use 40- or 60-pound line.

To catch live squid, you use small jigs, let them down near the bottom, then catch squid that are 8–10 inches long. The same trick can work for jacksmelt.

If you see yellowtail breaking the surface, you can be on the verge of some of California's most exciting fishing. Approach the school cautiously, being sure not to spook them, then stop short and cast to them. Party boats will often anchor near an undersea pinnacle, and the deckhands chum away with anchovies to attract the yellowtail toward the boat.

You can't wait for the fish to reach the boat. If you want to get the most bites, get a longer rod with a reel that can really cast, and cast that squid as far back to them as you can. Get that bait in front of them.

After a hookup, the ability to stop a yellowtail from a long run is critical not only in the rocks, but around the oil rigs stationed along the coast. The metal legs of the oil rigs are sharp and protrude to create a more stable base. When the yellowtail hits, it can break you off on those legs every time.

Insider's Note

When you have to use light line to get bit, yellowtail can really rock you. It's nothing for them to run 60 or 70 yards and get into the rocks. A trick with light line is that if the fish gets into the rocks, just free-spool it until it comes out, then you can play it again. When you're fishing over a pinnacle, the yellowtail get picky, and everybody onboard has to drop down to lighter line. A boat can get 100 pickups and catch only four fish.

The big boys—the 30- and 40-pounders known as Homeguards—are usually caught right near the bottom, often so deep that landing one requires the kind of work that can make you feel as if your arm is going to fall off.

Personal Note

The best advice I've received about yellowtail came from Pat McDonell, editor of *Western Outdoor News:* "No matter how much you know, the fish always seem to know more."

This is the kind of fish that can get inside your mind and realign your senses. Becoming afflicted takes only one wide-open surface bite; you use no weight, a live squid for bait, and get near-instant hookups of big yellowtail that immediately burn 40, 50, even 60 yards of line before you can figure out what's happening.

Yellowtail are among the fightingest fish in California (as well as one of the tastiest). They can get big—30–40 pounds—and fishing them is demanding yet rewarding. My life-best is a 38-pounder.

On one trip to Catalina, my compadre Jim Klinger caught a beauty and filleted the fish right on the spot, cutting the meat into three-inch chunks. We dipped the chunks into a mix of soy sauce and wasabi in a bowl, then ate the fish raw. At sashimi restaurants, yellowtail is called *hamachi,* is considered to be the sweetest of all sushi, and costs a fortune—and here we were in the middle of nowhere, eating all we could hold of fish we had just caught. At one point Klinger took a bite, absorbing the succulent tastes like a king, then said with a laugh, "I wonder what the rest of the world is doing right now?"

ALBACORE

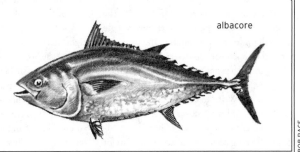

BEST FISHING SPOTS

1. San Diego
2. Oceanside
3. Oxnard
4. Los Angeles
5. Monterey Bay
6. Morro Bay
7. Ventura
8. Bodega Bay
9. Half Moon Bay
10. Fort Bragg

albacore

BOB RACE

Tackle and Rigging

Rods must be powerful and yet have sensitive tips. Reels must be strong, high-speed, revolving-spool saltwater reels; that is, with retrieve ratios of six to one, or at least five to one. The tackle suggested for yellowtail will also work well.

Rods: 7-foot Sabre 270 (rated at 12- to 30-pound test line), 7-foot CalStar Graphiter 700XL (12–30), 7-foot Loomis Pelagic PSR84-20C (15–25).

Reels: Pro Gear 251, Penn Jigmaster 500, Penn 525 Mag.

Line: 20- or 30-pound test.

Hooks: You must match the size of hook to the size of bait: size 3/0 hook when using live anchovies; size 1/0 hook when using live sardines. Tie the hook using a Palomar knot, which helps the bait swim naturally as if no line were attached. Hook the bait vertically through the nose or in the upper gill collar.

Jigging: Keep a second rod set up with a Fish Trap jig. Use a 1 1/2-ounce or 2-ounce lead-head, then keep an assortment of Fish Traps available.

Fly-fishing: Dan Blanton squid fly with a fluorocarbon leader, 10-weight rod, Abel reel, lead-core fly line, 30-pound Spectra backing.

ALBACORE STATE RECORD

90 lb. 0 oz.   Santa Cruz   Don Giberson   October 21, 1997

Time and Place

The Pacific Ocean is the largest body of water in the world (10,700 miles wide and covering 64 million square miles), and at one time or another, albacore migrate across most of it, chasing saury and other baitfish and following the warm offshore currents from Japan to California. They show along California every year in wide variation, typically arriving with the warm currents that swing within 35–75 miles off the coast from summer through early fall.

"Albacore water" is clear, cobalt blue, and typically 61–66°F. Skippers often study sea-surface temperature reports, look for gradients where warm water meets cold, then fish the warm-water side. Albacore sometimes migrate through underwater seamounts and canyons. Once the general area is determined, the boat will head to the spot and then start trolling.

But every year is different. When? Where? How many? Will the ocean be too rough to reach them? These wild-card variables turn every angler into a prisoner of hope.

The first big counts of albacore come in for San Diego boats in early summer. By midsummer they have usually migrated up along Los Angeles, Oxnard, and Santa Barbara. By August, boats out of Morro and Monterey Bays often have them within easy range, and by the end of August, so do boats out of Half Moon Bay, ports in San Francisco Bay, and Bodega Bay. During an Indian summer of late September, there is often a sensational run within close range of Shelter Cove.

In good years, they can be reached within 5 or 10 miles of the coast. In bad years, albacore can be well over 100 miles offshore, a terrible boat ride. When the albacore are feeding near the surface around the boat, hooking one on a fly rod can be the wildest ride imaginable.

Tricks

It is essential to have a global positioning system (GPS) and electronic charts, which allow anglers to pinpoint every spot across the sea. As the fish are discovered, anglers will exchange exact GPS coordinates to locate the fish again.

When fishing for albacore, you practically troll your little petunia off looking for fish. It's like lighting a long fuse to a stick of dynamite. You troll, troll, troll, searching for the fish—an unpredictable, time-consuming, and sometimes frustrating affair. But when you connect, you can connect big-time. A wide-open albacore bite is one of the biggest jackpots of ocean fishing.

Troll Zuker jigs and feather tuna jigs (six to eight inches long) with 60 feet of line trailed behind the boat at six knots. The jigs will skip across the sea surface in the wake, with four rods across the back of the boat. Anglers alternate in sequence as to who is credited with what rod. If you are assigned a jig rod, then get an outside rod and let a little bit of extra line out. Since the albacore come up at an angle, if your feather jig is on the outside and out a little bit farther than the others, you can catch the first albacore that comes up to take a look.

When a troll rod gets a fish on, the boat immediately circles, then stops. Deckhands chum scoops of anchovies overboard, trying to attract the entire school of albacore to the surface and turn the scene into a wide-open melee. Meanwhile, the anglers grab their rods and either use live anchovies for bait or cast jigs. It's a wild affair, with everybody rushing to the bait tank and the railing simultaneously.

When the albacore are chummed right up to the surface, casting Fish Trap jigs can result in instant hookups.

Your bait is absolutely critical. If it doesn't swim right, you don't have a chance. Pick out a green bait and handle it very carefully, hook it quickly through the collar, and start fishing. If you drop it, kick it overboard. If any scales come off, it's worthless. You don't want a bait with a red nose, sore from banging away at the side of the bait tank. If you haven't been bit by an albacore after one minute, bring it up, snap it off, and put on another. You just plain must have quality live bait.

Insider's Notes

• When fighting an albacore, keep your thumb off the spool. The moment you thumb the line, the albacore will pop right off. Instead, let it run and enjoy the ride. Do not try to stop it by thumbing the line.

• When several fish are hooked simultaneously, do not call for the gaff for landing the fish. Instead, wait until you see the first silver-blue flash through the azure water. At that point, shout "Color! Color!" It is likely that when the albacore sees the boat, it will vault off in another laserlike burst, maybe 30 yards in a second. The deckhand will usually have plenty of time to be ready to gaff your fish.

• Usually a few big tuna run amid the school of albacore. This includes bigeyes in Southern California and bluefin in Central and Northern California waters. These fish can be line-shy but are the awesome line-burners of the California coast. Get one and you will never forget it.

Pat McDonell, editor of *Western Outdoor News,* provided the following trick for catching them: "When the boat stops, everybody is crazy going after the albacore," he said. "Drop a jig or a heavily weighted Scampi down 50–60 yards, then reel up. That's how you can get in on the bigeye or large albacore, which are underneath the school. The bait is on top, the schoolfish are under the bait, and the big guys are on the bottom."

Personal Note

With no land in sight when albacore fishing, it can feel as if you are among the last people on the planet.

The truth is that you never know quite what is in store. If the fish go deep, or the wind is up, or the bait disappears, you can end up with just a handful of catches; or worse, nothing but exhaustion. Or you can get lucky when all in the cosmos is aligned. I was aboard one trip like this where five of us caught 80 or 90 albacore—then finally turned our backs on them when we were just plain worn out.

When you hook albacore, you just kind of hang on for the ride. It seems as if the fish are trying to swim to China. They are strong, fast, and have incredible burst speeds. All it takes is one great trip and you will never look at this world quite the same way again.

In the vast expanse of the Pacific off the Bay Area coast, the albacore is one of the hottest fish out there.

REDWOOD EMPIRE

© ANGIE WILLIAMS/123RF.COM

BEST FISHING SPOTS

◖ Saltwater Fisheries
Crescent City Deep Sea, **page 98.**

The Del Norte coast, Smith River canyons, and

the groves of giant redwood trees at Jedediah Smith Redwoods State Park make this area one of the most beautiful spots in America. It is also one of California's most outstanding fishing areas. In addition to its excellent boat and shoreline access, the Smith River provides the opportunity for the state's biggest steelhead all winter long, and in the fall it attracts a run of giant-sized salmon.

Along the Crescent City coast, fishing for rockfish and lingcod is excellent in summer and fall, as is limit fishing for salmon. To the nearby south, the Klamath River gets an excellent run of salmon in September and early October. The lower reaches of the river are often filled with fish and anglers alike.

The Humboldt coast and its environs can sometimes provide the best of fishing, but at other times, well ... The centerpiece is Humboldt Bay, heading "out the jaws" and into the ocean. Here you'll find salmon, rockfish, lingcod, big halibut, and seven-gill sharks. In the fall and winter, there are good prospects from shore for redtail perch.

At Trinidad Harbor, there are additional opportunities for excellent inshore fishing and crabbing by boat (launching via a hoist). In Six Rivers National Forest and near Orick, you'll find a handful of small lakes that are great for small rainbow trout. Stone Lagoon and Lake Earl have large sea-run cutthroat trout, and one little-known lake, Dead Lake, has bass.

Humboldt County's streams attract big salmon and steelhead during their respective spawning migrations. The Eel, Van Duzen, Redwood Creek, Mad, Mattole, and Smith Rivers are California's best steelhead rivers. The Mattole, a remote steelhead stream on the Lost Coast, is always an intriguing option and is often best in late winter and early spring. In addition, the South Fork Eel provides excellent access for bank fishing.

So what's the beef? The winds can howl in the spring here, in summer the fog is heavy and low, and in the winter the Eel, Van Duzen, and Mad Rivers quickly become muddy after rains.

Visitors come from around the world to the Redwood Empire for one reason: to see the groves of giant redwoods, the tallest trees in the world. On a perfect day, refracted sunlight beams through the forest canopy, creating a solemn, cathedral-like effect. It feels as if you are standing in the center of the earth's pure magic. But the redwood forests are only one of the attractions to this area. The Smith River canyon, the Del Norte and Humboldt coasts, and the remote edge of the Siskiyou Wilderness in Six Rivers National Forest all make this region like none other in the world.

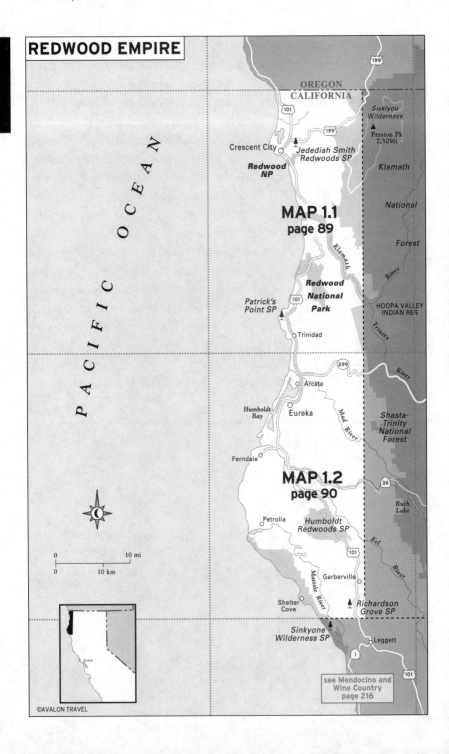

REDWOOD EMPIRE

PACIFIC OCEAN

OREGON
CALIFORNIA

199

101

199

Crescent City

Jedediah Smith
Redwoods SP

Redwood
NP

Siskiyou
Wilderness

▲ Preston Pk
7,309ft

Klamath

National

MAP 1.1
page 89

Forest

Klamath River

Redwood
National
Park

HOOPA VALLEY
INDIAN RES

Patrick's
Point SP

101

Trinidad

Trinity River

299

Arcata

Humboldt
Bay

Eureka

Mad River

Shasta-
Trinity
National
Forest

Ferndale

MAP 1.2
page 90

36

Ruth
Lake

Petrolia

Humboldt
Redwoods SP

Eel River

101

Mattole River

Garberville

Shelter
Cove

↑ Richardson
Grove SP

0   10 mi
0   10 km

Sinkyone
Wilderness SP

Leggett

1

see Mendocino and
Wine Country
page 216

101

©AVALON TRAVEL

Map 1.1

**Sites 1-16
Pages 91-103**

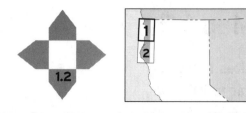

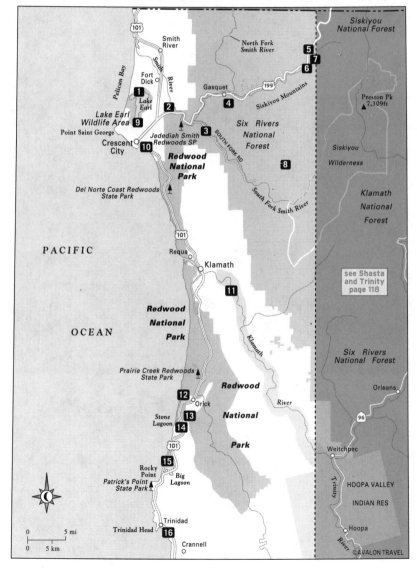

Map 1.2

Sites 17-26
Pages 105-114

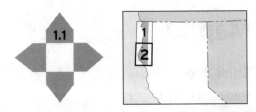

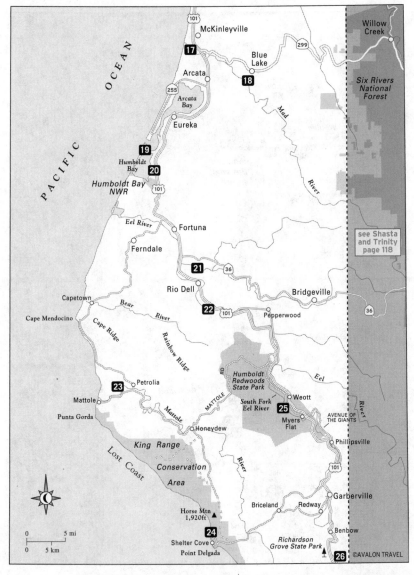

1 LAKE EARL/TOLOWA DUNES STATE PARK

Rating: 3

near Crescent City
Map 1.1, page 89

Lake Earl is the largest lake in Del Norte County, but because tourists can't see it from U.S. 101—and because it provides only mediocre fishing—the lake gets very little attention. It is in a unique setting though, near sea level and less than a mile from the Pacific Ocean. Lake Tolowa, its neighbor to the west, is connected to Lake Earl by a short, narrow, curving piece of water. It borders coastal sand dunes and sometimes overflows into the ocean after heavy rainfall.

The lake is large and shallow, and no trout are stocked. There are no bass, bluegill, catfish, or other typical lake sport fish either. Instead, a few sea-run cutthroat trout enter adjoining Lake Tolowa from the ocean in the winter and then spend the rest of their lives roaming both Tolowa and Earl. Occasionally, some escape to the ocean when the sandbar is breached. Some of the cutthroat trout are good size, 15 or 16 inches, but they are few and elusive. Flounder also live in the lake and tend to congregate in the narrow connector section between Tolowa and Earl. If you try fishing here, that is where to start—at the narrows, typically the entrances to the narrows.

In any event, the fishing is usually poor, and unless you get into a batch of cutthroat or flounder, you might swear there are no fish at all. Adding to recent problems here is the fact that rising lake levels have begun to cover private property. There has been a local uproar over this, and some residents even breach the sandy dam to allow water to pour out to the ocean, thus lowering the level of the lake. More than likely, when that occurs, fish go out with the water.

Arriving in spring adds a great sideshow to this adventure. That is when 25,000 Aleutian Canada geese fly over the area. There are also some excellent walk-in campgrounds that most people are clueless about.

Facilities, fees: Six environmental walk-in campsites are provided. Drinking water is not available. Fishing access is free.

Directions: In Crescent City on U.S. 101, drive to Northcrest Drive. Turn northwest on Northcrest Drive and drive about 3.5 miles to Lake View Road. At Lake View Road, turn left and drive a mile to the road's end to the Lake Earl boat launch.

Contact: Tolowa Dunes State Park, North Coast Redwoods District, 707/465-2145, www.parks.ca.gov (click on Visit a Park).

2 SMITH RIVER

Rating: 9

east of Crescent City in
Six Rivers National Forest
Map 1.1, page 89

The Smith River is the crown jewel of the nation's streams: a fountain of pure water, undammed and unbridled, running sapphire-blue and free through granite canyons. The river grows California's biggest salmon and steelhead, which arrive at the Smith every fall and winter (respectively) and beguile and excite anglers. During summer months, a decent fishery for sea-run cutthroat trout (in the lower river) is also provided.

When you see the Smith, the first thing you will say is, "Look how beautiful the water is." Even after heavy winter rains (which can turn most rivers into brown muck), the Smith generally runs blue and clear because of its hard granite base and because its water supply is drained from a huge mountain acreage. This combination gives the river the ability to cleanse itself.

The most favored run with a drift boat is to put in at the Forks and then make the trip down to the county park or to the popular takeout below the U.S. 101 bridge. A dozen good spots hold steelhead in this stretch of river. Some of the best are adjacent to Jedediah

Smith Redwoods State Park, including White Horse and Covered Bridge. Covered Bridge can also be accessed from the bank. In addition, the area near Jedediah Smith Redwoods State Park has many of the area's biggest redwood trees, an awesome reminder of how special this country is.

Timing is very important, especially for bank fishing. Above the forks of the main stem, the going can be rugged, but fish can be caught—especially as the water is rising during the beginning of a rainstorm, or as the water is dropping.

When the river is very high from sustained rain and ensuing runoff, a lot of locals do well on large steelhead with what is called plunking. That's where you set up with a heavy weight off a three-way rig and a Spin 'N Glo. In fact, these plunkers often just sit in their trucks and watch their rods while it rains. Some of the biggest fish—such as steelhead over 20 pounds—are caught this way. The best spots for plunking during high water are at the county park ("Ruby"), the water tower ("Water Tower"), and the Bailey Hole (see *Directions*), all in the lower river.

Alas, there are some drawbacks. The fish are very difficult to catch, especially when you compare the Smith River with nearby Chetco River to the north, which enters the sea at Brookings, in southern Oregon. Some people you'll encounter might spend an hour talking about how beautiful the Smith River is without mentioning that they haven't caught a fish in a week. It takes years to learn how to fish this river. But once that process is underway, you may feel as if the magical secrets of nature are being revealed to you.

The best way to start the learning process is to hire a guide, get in the guide's drift boat, and fish the lower river. Most drift boat trips average a fish or two per day. In the process, you will get an excellent fishing lesson and will experience the excitement of tangling with a Smith River–bred salmon or steelhead. I also advise taking an onshore lesson from a guide who specializes in bank fishing so that you

can make many return trips in future years and fish by yourself.

One of the great rewards of this experience is the size of the fish. In the fall and early winter, the ratio of 25- to 40-pound salmon to those that are smaller is better than on any other river in the western United States. In fact, salmon in the 50- and 60-pound class are caught each year, and 70- and 80-pounders are occasionally landed. The river just grows big fish. The same is true with steelhead. A 10-pounder is an average-size fish, 15-pounders are common, and more 20-pounders are caught here than on any other river in California. The state-record steelhead, 27 pounds, 4 ounces, was taken from the Smith, and several weighing in at over 30 pounds have been hooked and lost.

But they just don't come easy. I once went 2,000 casts on the Smith without a bite. Then, I caught 15-pound steelhead in back-to-back casts, both near-instant hookups when the bait hit the water. Another time, I didn't catch a fish for four days. The next day, I caught 11 steelhead all over 10 pounds. It was the best day I have ever had with steelhead anywhere in the world. It doesn't take luck—I know that. It takes persistence and spirit.

Fishing on the Smith requires line the fish cannot see. If your reel has anything but Maxima Ultra-Green or its equivalent, some guides will immediately strip off your line and replace it. Because the Smith's water is so clear, fish will avoid any line that is more visible, as if you were throwing large boulders into the river. When the river is low and clear, I use 6-pound test. I know that sounds crazy, but that is what it takes; 10-pound test tends to be standard, 8-pound test as the water clears, and 12-pound test when the river turns murky.

In addition, because the fish are big, you must have a big net with you. A lot of out-of-towners don't have big enough nets; they figure, "I'll be okay with what I've got," and then they spend years howling at the moon over how they lost a 45-pound salmon with their little net.

Timing is always a critical factor when you are angling for migratory fish. In October, salmon start stacking up in river holes in the lower river, and they only venture far upriver after a few rains. The best spot is the Sand Hole. You can launch from Ship Ashore and row upriver to the spot, or hike in less than a mile. There is another dirt boat ramp upstream, but in low tides, you must get out of your boat in the river and drag it through the shallow spot. At the Sand Hole, fly fishers in prams will anchor and then fly-cast with streamers and hope to hook a 30- or 40-pounder. On one trip, I had 42- and 35-pounders on back-to-back casts. Use 10-weight rods, high D lines, and expect wind. One problem at the Sand Hole is the illegal snagging that occurs by poachers from shore. It's very frustrating to see the abuse.

During the winter, steelhead use the river as a highway; they head straight through the lower river and then spawn in the tributaries. Almost every year there is a weeklong period in January and often again in March when it doesn't rain. During these times, the steelhead will slow their journey, and anglers have the opportunity for hookups at the prime holes.

You can make a lot of casts and spend a lot of days here before you are finally rewarded. But in the process you will refine your craft and have the pleasure of spending your days learning along one of America's most beautiful rivers.

Note that Department of Fish and Game (DFG) regulations have become more complex. Closure dates and hook rules can vary. But one clear rule that's had a beneficial effect on the Smith River is the ban on motors in the lower river. That has prevented guides from Oregon fishing over and over again the spots that are holding lots of steelhead. California guides traditionally have oared their boats, so if they want to fish the same stretch of water, they have to row upstream along shore to do it.

Note: The Smith River is subject to emergency closures starting on October 1 if flows are below the prescribed levels needed to protect migrating salmon and steelhead. Call to get details on the status of coastal streams: rivers subject to low-flow closures (recording) 707/822-3164; river flows at Jed Smith (recording) 707/458-3659 (sometimes inoperable, listen after tone); river flows at U.S. 101 bridge (recording) 707/487-6321 (reliable, listen after tone).

Facilities, fees: Several campgrounds are available, including sites at Jedediah Smith Redwoods State Park and a few Forest Service camps. These camps are along U.S. 199 and provide streamside access. Motels in the area include the Hiouchi Motel, 707/458-3041, and Patrick's Creek Lodge, 707/457-3323. Camping, lodging, and supplies can be obtained in Crescent City and along the Smith River. Fishing access is free.

Directions: To lower river (Bailey Hole): From Crescent City, drive north on U.S. 101 for about 10 miles to Smith River Bridge. Cross over bridge and take the first left at Fred Haight Drive. Drive to the sign for the county boat ramp on the left. Park and walk 400 yards to river.

To Jedediah Smith Redwoods State Park: From Crescent City, take U.S. 101 north for four miles to the junction with U.S. 199. Bear right at U.S. 199 and drive five miles to the park entrance on the right.

To Middle Fork Smith: From Crescent City, take U.S. 101 north for four miles to the junction with U.S. 199. Bear right at U.S. 199 and drive six miles to Hiouchi. Continue east on U.S. 199 with pullouts along river at fishing spots for 20 miles.

To South Fork Smith: From Crescent City, take U.S. 101 north for four miles to the junction with U.S. 199. Bear right at U.S. 199 and drive six miles to Hiouchi, then continue one mile to South Fork Road. Turn right, cross two bridges to a Y with South Fork Road, and turn left. There are pullouts along the river at fishing spots for 15 miles.

Contact: Jedediah Smith Redwoods State Park, 707/464-6101, or ranger kiosk at 707/458-3018, www.parks.ca.gov (click on Visit a Park); Six Rivers National Forest, Gasquet Ranger District, 707/457-3131, www.fs.fed.us/r5—click on Forest Offices.

Supplies: Englund Marine, Crescent City, 707/464-1650, www.englundmarine.com; Hiouchi Hamlet, 707/458-3321 or 800/722-9468, www.hiouchirv.com.

Guides: Albert Kutzkey, 530/941-3474, www.kutzkeyfishing.com; Wally Johnson, 530/496-3291, www.steelheadguides.com; Kevin Brock, 800/995-5543, www.fishkevin brock.com.

❸ SOUTH FORK SMITH RIVER

Rating: 8

east of Crescent City in
Six Rivers National Forest
Map 1.1, page 89

This stream seems to have been placed on earth for lone-wolf types who love to hunt steelhead. You will find many small dirt turnouts along South Fork Road, although they generally have room for only one or two vehicles. Steelheaders will park in these turnouts, scramble down to the river, and then find a streamside perch where they can make casts for the elusive Smith River steelhead. The best fishing for steelhead on the South Fork Smith is in January and February, with December and March considered the shoulder seasons. October and November can attract salmon. Upstream on the South Fork, there is a fair trout fishery during the summer months.

If a vehicle is already parked in the turnout, you must drive on to the next one. It is considered steelhead sacrilege to crowd a lone wolf on his spot. But if you're way out here on the South Fork Smith, you're probably already aware of that rule. No matter. There are a dozen or so spots along the South Fork where a shoreliner can cast away in seclusion, hoping the next cast invites a big steelhead. These fish don't come often or easy.

The ideal way to approach the river is to get up before dawn (already fully rigged, so you don't have to tie any knots in darkness), then get on the river at first light. Hit a spot, drive on to the next one, then hit again. In a day you should

fish 6–10 spots. This approach can be a problem on weekends, when more anglers are on the river and the few available spots are taken.

When the South Fork is green and fishable, park your car or pickup truck at the pullouts along the river, make the tromp down to the hole, and then make your casts. Some of the better spots for shoreline fishing on the entire Smith system are on the South Fork, including the mouth of Goose Creek, the mouth of Hurdy Gurdy Creek, Steel Bridge, and on downstream to the falls at the gorge.

The Lower South Fork is also difficult to access for two reasons: one is that there often seems an impenetrable jungle of brush set on steep slopes, and the other reason is that just upstream from the forks is the South Fork Gorge, where access is largely impossible.

As a result, some of the best bank fishing in California for big fish has largely been taken out of circulation after heavy rains, which are common here. The only solution on the South Fork Smith is to head far upstream, all the way to the point of demarcation at the mouth of Goose Creek, and to fish from here all the way down, hitting and moving.

If you have the idea that this experience isn't for everybody, you are right. Fishing the South Fork Smith is highly specialized, and it requires that you master difficult skills. There are long odds for the uninitiated. But this is Man versus Nature. It's you against the river, with no help provided and no crowd watching, which is exactly what some anglers want.

Note: The South Fork Smith is subject to emergency closures starting October 1 if flows are below the prescribed levels needed to protect the migrating salmon and steelhead. The Department of Fish and Game has a recorded message that details the status of coastal streams (707/822-3164), or check out www.dfg.ca.gov.

Facilities, fees: Several campgrounds are available, including Big Flat Camp, a primitive Forest Service campground adjacent to Hurdy Gurdy Creek's entrance into the South Fork Smith River; there's no drinking water, so bring your own. The nearest facilities are in Hiouchi. Motels in the area include the Hiouchi Motel, 707/458-3041, and Patrick's Creek Lodge, 707/457-3323. Camping, lodging, and supplies can be obtained in Crescent City and along the Smith River. Fishing access is free.

Directions: From Crescent City, drive north on U.S. 101 for four miles to the junction with U.S. 199, turn east on U.S. 199, and drive five miles to Hiouchi. Continue just past Hiouchi, turn right at South Fork Road, and cross two bridges. At the Y, turn left on South Fork Road and drive along South Fork Smith River for 5–14 miles. Direct access is available at the pullouts along the road.

Contact: For camping information and general information: Six Rivers National Forest, Gasquet Ranger District, 707/457-3131, www .fs.fed.us/r5—click on Forest Offices; Jedediah Smith Redwoods State Park, 707/458-3018, www.parks.ca.gov (click on Visit a Park).

Information: Lunker Fish Trips, Hiouchi, 707/458-4704 or 800/248-4704.

◢ DRY LAKE

Rating: 3

near Crescent City in
Six Rivers National Forest
Map 1.1, page 89

Just as guys who are nicknamed "Tiny" are usually huge, "Dry" Lake is anything but dry. It is a little water hole that can look like a mud hole in early spring. Dry Lake is a tiny, bowl-shaped lake that's just over three acres and set at 1,500 feet; it is so obscure that even the locals don't visit it. Yet the Department of Fish and Game occasionally stocks trout here, but not all years. In addition, there is the opportunity for eastern brook trout and catfish. Once the rain stops and the lake settles, it is a pretty spot, found near the headwaters of Hurdy Gurdy Creek.

If you continue north on the Forest Service road over Gordon Mountain (4,153 feet) and down the other side to Camp Six—about a 10-mile drive from the lake—you will reach

the rainiest place in the lower 48 states. It rained 256 inches there in 1983, the highest amount ever recorded in the contiguous United States. Dry? Just remember the last guy you met named Tiny.

Facilities, fees: The lake has one small, primitive campsite with a vault toilet that is available in summer months. No drinking water or other facilities are provided. Big Flat Camp, a primitive Forest Service campground (without drinking water), is adjacent to Hurdy Gurdy Creek's entrance into the South Fork Smith River. There is also a developed state park campground at Jedediah Smith Redwoods on U.S. 199. Fishing access is free.

Directions: From Crescent City, take U.S. 101 north for four miles to U.S. 199. Bear right on U.S. 199 and drive about seven miles (just past the entrance to Jedediah Smith Redwoods State Park) to the town of Hiouchi. In Hiouchi, continue for one mile to South Fork Road. Turn right and drive 0.5 mile to a junction with South Fork Road. Turn left on South Fork Road and drive 14 miles to Big Flat Ranger Station and County Road 405/French Hill Road. Turn left on County Road 405/French Hill Road, then drive five miles to Dry Lake.

Contact: Smith River National Recreation Area, P.O. Box 228, Gasquet, CA 95543, 707/457-3131, www.fs.fed.us/r5—click on Forest Offices.

◢ UPPER MIDDLE FORK SMITH RIVER

Rating: 7

northeast of Crescent City in
Six Rivers National Forest
Map 1.1, page 89

This grid map charts only a small piece of the Smith River, but it is one of my favorite sections. The Middle Fork Smith is right along U.S. 199, and streamside camps and good fishing spots are easily accessible from the road.

Access is good along U.S. 199, and while driving you can see many of the better spots, the pullouts for parking, and the trails leading down to the river. Because many of these spots have pullouts along the highway, if you see a vehicle parked there, you know that somebody is already fishing that spot—so you can head on to the next spot rather than taking 20 minutes to park, rig, and head down, just to find somebody already standing on the best rock.

In addition, there are several campgrounds operated by the Forest Service along this stretch of river. They provide walk-to access to good stretches of steelhead water.

The Upper Smith is narrow, similar to a mountain trout stream. Instead of angling for dink-sized trout, however, you are fishing for 20-pound steelhead. You must approach this portion of the river with complete stealth lest you tip off the fish to your presence. On this stretch of river, do not walk right down the river and begin casting. Instead, stop 30 feet short of the stream and start casting from there. That way the steelhead cannot see your casting motion or even the shadow of your fishing rod on the water. Light lines, such as 6- or 8-pound test Maxima, are essential in such clear water with these cautious fish.

When these fish fight, though, they're anything but cautious. The steelhead run hellbent for leather, and if they get downriver into fast water, it's "Good-bye, Mabeline." You'll lose 'em for sure.

This section of the Smith is particularly pristine. It is so pretty that even if you don't come away with a catch, just watching the river go by can be pleasure enough.

Because it is such a distant drive for most to reach the Upper Smith River along U.S. 199, most out-of-towners never see it and never fish it. But it's a beautiful piece of water and well worth exploring.

Note: The Smith River is subject to emergency closures starting October 1 if flows are below the prescribed levels needed to protect the migrating salmon and steelhead. The Department of Fish and Game has a recorded message that details the status of coastal streams: 707/822-3164.

Facilities, fees: There are three campgrounds east of Gasquet: Patrick Creek (seven miles), Grassy Flat (four miles), and Panther Flat (two miles). Lodging is available at Patrick Creek Lodge (a quarter-mile wheelchair-accessible trail and fishing platform are between Patrick Creek Campground and Patrick Creek Lodge). Limited supplies can be obtained in Gasquet, and fishing licenses and supplies are available in Hiouchi. Fishing access is free.

Directions: From Crescent City, take U.S. 101 north for four miles to U.S. 199. Bear right on U.S. 199 and go 14 miles to the small town of Gasquet. Continue northeast on U.S. 199. Direct river access is available off the highway over the next 1–7 miles; look for pullouts on the side of the road and at campgrounds.

Contact: Camping and general information: Smith River National Recreation Area, P.O. Box 228, Gasquet, CA 95543, 707/457-3131, www.fs.fed.us/r5—click on Forest Offices.

Information and supplies: Hiouchi Hamlet, 707/458-3114; Patrick Creek Lodge, 707/457-3323; Lunker Fish Trips, Hiouchi, 707/458-4704 or 800/248-4704.

6 SIX RIVERS NATIONAL FOREST

Rating: 5

east of Crescent City (off U.S. 199)

Map 1.1, page 89

Six Rivers National Forest is among the lesser-traveled areas within California's 20 million acres of national forest. It contains big trees and many streams but relatively few lakes. And even though this forest has been cut extensively by loggers, untouched land in the Siskiyou Wilderness makes for prime backpacking.

Only a few lakes within the forest provide viable fisheries, including Buck Lake (just outside the Six Rivers National Forest boundary) and Island Lake (accessible by way of a four-mile, gut-thumping, straight-up climb of a hike). Of the two, Buck Lake offers better fishing, particularly early in the season, following

Memorial Day weekend. Island Lake, with an area of just three acres, is at an elevation of 5,000 feet and has a maximum depth of just 14 feet. It always seems to be loaded with the inevitable dinkers, which makes sense, since it is stocked with fingerling trout. If you don't get turned on by the fishing, the climb to the top of Jedediah Mountain, on the backside of the lake, is not too difficult and provides wondrous views of the Siskiyou backbone.

Don't be too quick to bypass this area as a hike-in retreat. Devils Punchbowl (in the Siskiyou Wilderness) and Bear Mountain Lake (at 6,424 feet) are premium destinations. The ambitious can head into the adjoining Klamath National Forest. The Kelsey Trail, which begins at a signed spur road off the South Fork Smith Road, goes all the way to the Marble Mountains and beyond to the east. The trout in Island Lake are dinkers to be sure, but there are times when the size of the trout becomes almost irrelevant. Almost.

Facilities, fees: Several campgrounds are available, including Big Flat and Patrick Creek Campgrounds. Fishing access is free.

Directions: Several Forest Service access roads off U.S. 199 lead into the park.

Contact: Smith River National Recreation Area, P.O. Box 228, Gasquet, CA 95543, 707/457-3131, www.fs.fed.us/r5—click on Forest Offices; Six Rivers National Forest, 707/442-1721.

7 SANGER LAKE

Rating: 4
east of Gasquet in Six Rivers National Forest
Map 1.1, page 89

Sanger Lake, a small, out-of-the-way, cold-water pond, provides peace, quiet, and a chance to catch little brook trout. It is just six acres, set at 5,100 feet just below Sanger Peak (5,862 feet) to the north, with a maximum depth of 25 feet. The long, circuitous drive, mainly on gravel and dirt roads in national forest, is enough to keep most folks far away.

Sanger Lake's inaccessibility makes it a better fishing location, provided that you don't mind the dink-sized brook trout and rainbow trout. Fish and Game plants these small fish using airplanes to drop in the pint-sized variety. They theorize that the fish will eventually grow to larger sizes, although that doesn't seem to happen too often. That's okay. With the tranquility available here, any fish you catch is a bonus.

Many people see Sanger Lake for the first time in the course of driving to the Young's Valley Trailhead, which provides trailhead hiking access to the headwater of Clear Creek and the Siskiyou Wilderness. The road to the trailhead is closed near Sanger Lake.

Facilities, fees: There are no on-site facilities. There is a small, primitive campsite. No restroom or drinking water is available. Trash must be packed out. Fishing access is free.

Directions: From Crescent City drive north on U.S. 101 for four miles to U.S. 199. Bear right (east) on U.S. 199 and drive 32 miles to Forest Road 18N07/Knopki Road. Turn right and drive five miles to Forest Road 18N07. Continue on Forest Road 18N07 for 10 miles (it's twisty) to where it dead-ends at Forest Road 4803. Turn left and drive 0.5 mile to a pullout area for parking. Sanger Lake is not visible from the parking area but is just over the adjacent berm.

Contact: Smith River National Recreation Area, P.O. Box 228, Gasquet, CA 95543, 707/457-3131, www.fs.fed.us/r5—click on Forest Offices; Klamath National Forest, Happy Camp Ranger District, 530/493-2243.

8 MUSLATT LAKE

Rating: 3
near Crescent City in
Six Rivers National Forest
Map 1.1, page 89

Little Muslatt Lake is not much more than a puddle, just one acre in size. It is at 1,200 feet, at the foot of Muslatt Mountain, and has a small outlet stream that eventually winds all over the mountains and pours into the Smith River. It provides fishing for small rainbow trout and catfish. In some years, the DFG stocks the lake with trout by airplane.

If you arrive after a recent stock, you will see and catch only four- and five-inch-class trout. The bigger fellows are in there, but they're usually deeper and more wary since they've lived through a summer or two. Find out when the stocks take place, and then steer clear of the lake for a while; wait for when those little trout have had a chance to grow a few inches and make for a decent evening fish fry.

Facilities, fees: No facilities are provided. Big Flat Camp is off South Fork Road near Hurdy Gurdy Creek, and the more developed Jedediah Smith Redwoods State Park offers sites on U.S. 199. Fishing access is free.

Directions: From Crescent City, drive north on U.S. 101 for four miles to the junction with U.S. 199. Bear right on U.S. 199 and drive five miles to Hiouchi. Continue just past Hiouchi, turn right at South Fork Road, and cross two bridges. At the Y, turn left on South Fork Road and drive along South Fork Smith River for 14 miles to Big Flat. In Big Flat, the road becomes Forest Service Road 16N02. Continue for five miles and turn right at the sign for Muslatt Lake.

Contact: Smith River National Recreation Area, P.O. Box 228, Gasquet, CA 95543, 707/457-3131, www.fs.fed.us/r5—click on Forest Offices.

9 DEAD LAKE

Rating: 5

near Crescent City
Map 1.1, page 89

File this spot away in the back of your mind, then make sure you try it out when you are in the area. This little lake provides good bass fishing, is easy to reach, and is missed by virtually every angler who passes through the area.

Dead Lake's name was appropriate at one time, because it did seem like a dead lake, but an experimental plant of largemouth bass took hold, and the lake has come alive. The fishing here can be quite good, especially on spring evenings, if you cast floating lures or spinnerbaits along the shoreline. Dead Lake's long and narrow shape helps make it good for bass because it provides good shoreline bass habitat.

As the years have gone by, Dead Lake has somehow remained a great secret for Del Norte County and the few out-of-town visitors who know of it.

Facilities, fees: No facilities are provided at the lake; all services and lodging are two miles away, in Crescent City. Fishing access is free.

Directions: From U.S. 101 in Crescent City, turn west on Washington Boulevard and drive 1.5 miles (almost to the airport) to Riverside Road. Turn right (north) on Riverside Road and drive to the lake.

Contact: Englund Marine, Crescent City, 707/464-1650, www.englundmarine.com.

10 CRESCENT CITY DEEP SEA

Rating: 9

at Crescent City Harbor
Map 1.1, page 89   BEST (

Redwoods meet the sea in Crescent City, and a lot of out-of-towners meet fish here, too. Salmon fishing is best in July and August and decent in June and September, while rockfish and lingcod are large and abundant year-round. In the fall, rockfishing at Crescent City Deep Sea is among the best anywhere on the Pacific coast.

If you arrive from the south, especially at night, you'll catch a lovely glimpse of the harbor from the lookout on U.S. 101. This half moon–shaped natural harbor provides refuge from the terrible northwest spring winds. Accordingly, the most important part of your trip (whether you own a boat or plan to get a charter) is calling ahead for wind and sea projections. Winter storms can be nasty and frequent. Between fronts, however, the ocean is often in its calmest state of the year.

A calm ocean means it's time to go. Most summer salmon boats take a 260-degree heading out of the harbor. Frequently they encounter fish after an hour's run. In the fall, boats head north and troll outside the mouth of the Smith River. Catch rates are not as high during this period, but your chances of catching a 40-pounder here are better than anyplace else in California.

For a near guarantee of fish, take a deep-sea trip to the St. George Reef, which is just northwest of Point St. George. The reef near Star Rock, Whale Rock, and Long Rock provides an outstanding habitat for abundant and big rockfish and lingcod. Lingcod in the 20- and 30-pound class are common; every fall, anglers even catch a few 40-pounders.

Note that fishing regulations often change here from year to year, for seasons, depth restrictions, bag limits, size limits, and even annual quotas for the fleet. Always check current regulations with Fish and Game or with a marina or party-boat operator before planning a trip.

If this sounds good, that's because it is. There are a few drawbacks, however. It rains a lot up here, and when it doesn't rain, it's often foggy. Private boaters should venture out only in seaworthy vessels equipped with competent navigation equipment. Late summer and fall—when the skies are clear and warm, the ocean usually calm, and the fish eager—are the exceptions to this rule. If you make the trip at that time, you might just spot me at the boat launch.

During the summer and fall months, shallow-water rockfishing at Crescent City Deep Sea can also be outstanding. The rocky reefs just behind Pebble Beach Drive are particularly good; anglers fishing in 15–60 feet of water can do well on lingcod and a host of other bottomfish species.

One bonus is in early winter, when the Dungeness crab fishing can be among the best anywhere along the California coast. A word of warning, though: The seas can be extremely hazardous. However, the irony is that between storm fronts, some of the calmest seas of the year can arrive. That is your time to jump.

Another bonus is that fishing surf perch can also be very good off Kellogg, South, and Endert Beaches—dig up some live sand crabs for bait, and you're in business.

I was at this harbor during the tsunami of 2011, and it was an amazing spectacle to see the water pour in and create a giant whirlpool in the harbor. The forces tore up docks and pilings, which then poked holes in boats and sank them. The resilience of the people and the old sea comes to mind when I look at the place now, and watch boats heading out to catch fish as if the event never occurred.

Facilities, fees: A boat ramp, tackle shop, small marina, and restaurants are at the harbor. Lodging and campgrounds are nearby. The U.S. Coast Guard is stationed in the harbor, but only seldom can you pry information from anybody there.

Directions: From Crescent City, drive one mile south on U.S. 101 and turn west on Anchor Way.

Contact: Crescent City Harbor District, 707/464-6174; Crescent City–Del Norte County Chamber of Commerce (general information and a free travel packet), 800/343-8300, www.delnorte.org; Englund Marine, Crescent City, 707/464-1650, www.englundmarine.com; The Chart Room, 707/464-5993; Golden Bear Fishing Charters, 707/951-0119, www.goldenbearfishingcharters.com; Tally Ho II Ocean Charters, 707/464-1236.

11 KLAMATH RIVER

Rating: 8

near the town of Klamath and
Redwood National Park

Map 1.1, page 89

On Labor Day the Lower Klamath River looks like the salmon capital of the western world. Maybe it is.

The annual fall salmon run on the Lower Klamath peaks in September, and in the best years, the river can be lined elbow-to-elbow with wading anglers casting spinners or bait, sitting in oared drift boats or high-powered jet sleds. Every campground—public or private—will be full or close to it; the same goes for lodges and hotels. From all the hoopla, you'd probably figure that everybody is catching huge salmon, right? Well, the reality is that the catch rates are only fair, especially for shoreliners, although a few know-hows have learned how to get an edge on the masses.

The best fishing is occasionally upstream from the mouth, both at Terwer Riffle and farther upstream at the mouth of Blue Creek. Other popular spots are at Glen, Waukell, Blake, and Johnson's Riffles and at the mouth of the Trinity River. Most of the salmon here are in the 10-pound class, and a few range to 20 pounds. It is very rare to find larger salmon on the Klamath.

The season begins with a run of "springers," that is, salmon that arrive in late May and June. These salmon are quick-moving fish, and it is difficult to intercept them, but it can be done. The fall-run salmon begin arriving by mid-July, and most people try to catch them in the tidal zone. The salmon run peaks in the Lower Klamath between mid-August and mid-September. Afterward, the fish head upstream. (For details, trace the Klamath River using this book's maps.)

By September, half-pounders begin to arrive at the mouth and head upstream. Half-pounders are actually juvenile steelhead ranging in size 12–18 inches. They often arrive in big schools and can provide exciting fishing.

The key to the future success of this river is the number of fish that return to swim upstream and spawn. Because of the high numbers of salmon caught by commercial fishers and in Indian gill nets, the salmon population has suffered. Meanwhile, sport anglers pay the freight and have their seasons and limits

reduced, despite the fact that they take less than 10 percent of the overall catch. Anglers hope that a Klamath River Power Troika, a committee made up of commercial, Native American, and sporting interests, can agree on harvest quotas and an equitable split that would ensure that the salmon return to this stream in large numbers.

The habitat is in place. The Klamath River is capable of supporting runs of more than 100,000 salmon every fall. With proper management techniques, salmon could return in those numbers again. The Iron Gate Dam must be taken out so the river again provides spawning habitat and cool flows in late summer and early fall.

If so, all those people out on Labor Day weekend will do more than just cast into the light fall breeze. They will have a realistic chance of catching a salmon, the king of the Klamath, and the excellence of this once-great river will be reclaimed.

Facilities, fees: Several motels, public campgrounds, private campgrounds, and RV parks are available. Steelhead Lodge offers RV spaces, a motel, a restaurant, and a bar, 707/482-8145. Klamath Camper Corral, 800/701-7275, and Panther Creek RV Resort, 707/482-5105, are other options. Fishing access is free.

Directions: From Eureka, drive north on U.S. 101 to Klamath and the junction with Highway 169. Turn east on Highway 169 and drive 3.2 miles to Terwer Riffle Road. Turn right (south) on Terwer Riffle Road and drive one block to Steelhead Lodge and access to the Klamath River. Additional river access is available along Highway 169.

Contact: Klamath National Forest, Orleans Ranger District, 530/627-3291; Happy Camp Ranger District, 530/493-2243, www.fs.fed.us/r5—click on Forest Offices.

Guides and outfitters: Somes Bar Store, 530/469-3350, www.salmonriveroutpost.com; Klamath River Outfitters, 530/469-3349 or 800/748-3735, www.klamathriveroutfitters.com; Kevin Brock, 800/995-5543, www.fishkevinbrock.com.

1 2 REDWOOD CREEK

Rating: 5

near Orick in Redwood National Park
Map 1.1, page 89

Sometimes all you want in this world is woods and water. Redwood Creek at Orick provides both, along with a chance to catch some fresh-run steelhead every winter.

Redwood Creek is one of the small coastal streams that attract a modest steelhead run. Access is very easy, and fishing spots are similarly obvious. The best approach is to wear hip waders, then make casts in the slow-moving riffles upstream of the U.S. 101 bridge.

Note that on the north side of the bridge is an access road that heads down to the mouth of the river. That provides an option to fish for steelhead arriving fresh from the ocean. Often your only competition here is a group of sea lions.

As with all small coastal streams, timing is absolutely critical. If you arrive during a drought, the river will be closed to angling to protect the fish. If you arrive while it's raining, the stream will be too high and muddy for you to make a cast. You have to time your arrival just right, a few days after a fair rain. Infusions of freshwater attract steelhead into the stream; if water clarity is at least 2–3 feet, you can wade and cast with the hope of hooking a sea-run migrant.

For a handful of anglers, Redwood Creek is their favorite steelhead river. It is small, intimate, and beautiful, yet it is a paradox: there are periods when there is a fantastic chance to catch a 10-pound fish, and at other times there can be no fish at all. So when the fish are in, a lot of people are quick on the telephone to the Orick Market, and given the word, off they go to fish this river.

Redwood Creek's catch rates are not high. Fishing success generally goes to know-how locals who jump on the stream when they notice that the steelhead are moving through. Your telephone and car may be the most important pieces of fishing equipment in this location.

This beautiful area is close to both Redwood National and State Parks and Prairie Creek Redwoods State Park. Some of the biggest trees in the world are in this region, and when the filtered sunlight cascades down, being in the woods can make you feel as if you're inside a cathedral. An angler can find some religion by spending time here.

Facilities, fees: Tackle and supplies are available in Orick at the Orick Market, 707/488-3225. Campgrounds are provided a few miles north in Prairie Creek Redwoods State Park. Fishing access is free.

Directions: From Eureka, take U.S. 101 north for 45 miles to the town of Orick. Continue north 0.5 mile to Redwood Creek, where access is available.

Contact: Prairie Creek Redwoods State Park (camping information), 707/465-7347, www.parks.ca.gov.

1 3 FRESHWATER LAGOON

Rating: 7

north of Trinidad in
Humboldt Lagoons State Park
Map 1.1, page 89

The name Freshwater Lagoon gives it away. All the vacationers cruising U.S. 101 figure out from the name alone that this lagoon is freshwater, not saltwater. Of the three lagoons in the immediate area, Freshwater is the only one on the east side of the highway (right, another tip-off).

All of which explains why visitor traffic pours into this spot, while Stone Lagoon and Big Lagoon to the south receive relative trickles of anglers. The shoreline fishing is good for rainbow trout—abundant stocks of trout from the Department of Fish and Game make sure of that. These fish make nice stringers for shoreline bait dunkers. If you don't mind the company, Freshwater Lagoon often provides the best catch rates of any freshwater spot in the area.

Most of the trout are planted into Freshwater Lagoon at the northwest corner, which is where the best fishing generally takes place. Most of the planters run 10–12 inches in length. In the winter, however, some beautiful holdover rainbows in the three- to five-pound class are taken. Typically, the female holdovers have chrome sides and dark-blue backs and look a lot like miniature steelhead. The bucks caught at this time of year are often dark in color. The first day or two after a plant is the best time to catch these larger trout. The big guys seem to be attracted by thousands of freshly planted fish milling around in the shallows, and they move in for a closer look. In addition, largemouth bass have taken hold in the lake. Only a handful of locals seem to know the bass are in here.

Always check current regulations before planning your trip for any of the lagoons in the area.

In the summer, the Freshwater Lagoon's surface becomes infested with moss; shore casting for trout can be difficult at that time. Anglers with float tubes, however, do well fishing for the lagoon's secret population of largemouth bass by casting to the open-water patches in the weeds.

This has been one of the most popular RV parking spots in the entire North Coast of California. RV parking and camping in the huge unpaved area along the highway is now technically prohibited, but when 400 RVs show up on Memorial Day weekend and park anyway, there's not much rangers can do. If this prohibition does begin to lessen use at Freshwater Lagoon, that can only mean one thing for the fishing: it is bound to get better. Same number of fish, fewer anglers.

Facilities, fees: A visitors center, restrooms with flush toilets, and boat ramp are available. Three campgrounds are nearby at Stone Lagoon. Two tackle shops are in Trinidad. Fishing access is free.

Directions: From Eureka, take U.S. 101 north for 22 miles north to Trinidad. At Trinidad, continue north on U.S. 101 for eight miles to Big Lagoon Park Road. From there, continue eight miles to Freshwater Lagoon, on the right.

Contact: Humboldt Lagoons State Park, Visitors Center, 707/488-2169, www.parks

.ca.gov (click on Visit a Park); Humboldt County Parks, 707/445-7651, co.humboldt. ca.us/portal.

■4 STONE LAGOON

Rating: 6

north of Trinidad in
Humboldt Lagoons State Park
Map 1.1, page 89

The fishing for cutthroat trout at Stone Lagoon fluctuates from year to year as much as any fishery in California—anywhere from terrible to sensational.

Set on a 10-mile section of Del Norte County coast, this is my favorite of the three freshwater lagoons. You get a boat-in shoreline campsite set in a cove just out of sight of the highway, prime canoeing water, and decent trout fishing. It is also overlooked by many out-of-towners. As with Big Lagoon to the south, most folks believe this lagoon is saltwater, not freshwater, and that it doesn't have any fish or campsites. Wrong again.

Stone Lagoon can be one of the brightest spots on the entire North Coast. A program implemented by the local private sector, the DFG, and the fisheries department at Humboldt State University is intended to rebuild the lagoon's native population of coastal cutthroat trout. At times the lagoon can seem loaded with 12- to 15-inch cutthroat. I love paddling my canoe around here, casting Jake's spinners, gold with red spots, for cutthroat, and who knows, you might just see an elk along the shore. The herd here continues to flourish.

Regulations governing steelhead and cutthroat specify catch-and-release only and barbless lures. Check current regulations before planning your trip.

Even if the fish decide not to bite, the pleasure of the adventure is worth the energy spent to get here. After all, how many other campsites allow you to park your canoe near your campsite, then go out for an evening paddle? In this part of California, the answer is none. This is it.

Facilities, fees: A visitors center, drinking water, restroom, and flush toilets are available. There are three campgrounds: Dry Lagoon, a walk-in camp; Big Lagoon; and the best, Stone Lagoon, a boat-in at Ryan's Cove, on the western shoreline across the lagoon. Supplies can be obtained in Trinidad. A fee is charged for camping. Day-use is free. Fishing access is free.

Directions: From Eureka, take U.S. 101 north for 41 miles (15 miles north of Trinidad) to Stone Lagoon. At Stone Lagoon, turn left at the visitors center and boat access. The boat-in campground is in a cove directly across the lagoon from the visitors center. The campsites are dispersed in an area covering about 300 yards in the landing area.

Contact: Stone Lagoon Visitors Center, 707/488-2169; Humboldt Lagoons State Park, Visitors Center, 707/488-2169, www .parks.ca.gov (click on Visit a Park); Humboldt County Parks, 707/445-7651, co.humboldt .ca.us/portal; Salty's Surf 'n Tackle, 707/677-0300.

15 BIG LAGOON

Rating: 5

north of Trinidad in Big Lagoon County Park

Map 1.1, page 89

Of the three lagoons along this stretch of U.S. 101, Big Lagoon gets the least amount of fishing pressure. A lot of out-of-towners cruising by on U.S. 101 think (at first glance) that Big Lagoon is filled with saltwater, not freshwater. They probably have this misconception because Big Lagoon is west of U.S. 101, and it's barely separated from the ocean by a long, thin sand dune. But freshwater it is; Big Lagoon provides trout fishing in this unusual coastal setting.

A chance for steelhead is available here when winter storms raise the level of the lagoon enough to breach the sandbar that separates it from the ocean. The fish don't spend too much time in the lagoon proper. They tend to make tracks for the creek that feeds it. Trollers

pulling plugs such as Wiggle Warts and Hot Shots intercept a few bright steelhead each season as the fish head toward their natal stream. Some sea-run cutthroat trout also inhabit Big Lagoon; they will smack chartreuse/orange Little Cleo spoons or inflated night crawlers fished in the extreme northern corner of the lake.

This is a fun place to plunk in a canoe, paddle around, and catch a few trout in the process. Access is easy, and campsites are available nearby. Regardless, it is rare that anybody paddles around on the lagoon. They just keep on driving by, day after day, on U.S. 101. After all, they think it's saltwater.

Facilities, fees: A boat ramp, drinking water, and restrooms with flush toilets are available. Trinidad has two tackle shops: Salty's and Bob's Boat Basin. Campgrounds are at Patrick's Point State Park in Trinidad and at Stone Lagoon, to the immediate north. There is a camping fee. Access is free. Pets are permitted. There is a parking fee.

Directions: From Eureka, take U.S. 101 north for 22 miles to Trinidad. At Trinidad, continue north on U.S. 101 for eight miles to Big Lagoon Park Road. Turn left (west) at Big Lagoon Park Road and drive two miles to the park.

Contact: Humboldt Lagoons State Park, Visitors Center, 707/488-2169, www.parks.ca.gov (click on Visit a Park); Humboldt County Parks, 707/445-7651, co.humboldt.ca.us/portal; Salty's Surf 'n Tackle, 707/677-0300.

16 TRINIDAD HARBOR

Rating: 9

in Trinidad

Map 1.1, page 89

In the fishing industry, Trinidad Harbor used to be a little brother to Eureka and Crescent City. No longer so. Trinidad now offers charter boats and boat rentals. Local Native Americans have bought this operation—the wharf, restaurant, gift shop, and fishing business—and have committed to long-term improvements.

So many people miss out on Trinidad. One good trip here, however, will keep you coming back for the rest of your life. This is a beautiful chunk of coast made up of a protected bay sprinkled with rock-tipped islands and prime fishing grounds just off Trinidad Head. Patrick's Point State Park—one of the prettiest small parks in California, with Sitka spruce, heavy fern undergrowth, and trails that tunnel through vegetation—is immediately north of the harbor.

Every July the salmon here move inshore in a tremendous horde. These large schools of fish swim within five miles of land, an easy trip even for small boats. Show up at the boat hoist at dawn, drop into the water, and quickly cruise around Trinidad Head to the fish. When the salmon move in, they are usually quite easy to find—just join the flotilla of boats trolling for them. Fishing here can be exciting, with fast hookups and a generous number of 15- and 20-pounders. Schools of silver salmon (which must be released and are identifiable by their white mouths) sometimes arrive and monopolize the fishery. These fish are more apt to jump than their big brothers, the king salmon. As fall approaches, anglers tend to catch quality fish rather than great quantities of fish. It's common to hook a few large king salmon but not very many silver salmon or schoolie-sized kings (salmon in the two-foot class). It takes more time to catch fish during the fall, but the sky is clear, the days are warm, and the ocean is in its calmest state of the year. All of these conditions make for very good rockfishing at various inshore reefs, a bonus taken for granted by most locals. Whenever you fish here, always check salmon regulations beforehand.

A word of caution for summer visitors: Hone your boat navigation skills. Trinidad Harbor is often quite foggy in the summer, particularly in July and August, when the fishing is at its best. Boaters who are unfamiliar with the area may find themselves cloaked in the stuff—hence the popularity of GPS navigation devices and professional charter-boat services. Late winter and spring can be quite windy, so your timing must be right when entering the water.

During the summer, anglers generally catch a few huge lingcod, with some weighing more than 40 pounds, around the numerous reefs between the harbor and Agate Beach, to the north. Anglers also hook, usually by accident, some large Pacific halibut (up to 100 pounds). If you're visiting without a boat, all is not lost; Seascape rents 15-foot rowboats. On calm summer days the rockfish and lingcod action is surprisingly good around the harbor's boat moorings. I suggest you try using purple or root beer–colored Scampis on one-ounce leadhead jigs.

On good days, crabbing is also possible. This area is a natural habitat for Dungeness crabs. Set a series of traps, spend the day rock-fishing, then return to your traps and add a few big Dungeness crabs to your bag. What a feast for the wise!

Note that fishing regulations often change here from year to year, for seasons, depth restrictions, bag limits, size limits, and even annual quotas for the fleet. Always check current regulations with Fish and Game or with a marina or party-boat operator before planning a trip.

Facilities, fees: Seascape has a tackle shop and restaurant. Party-boat charters are also available. A nearby campground is at Patrick's Point State Park, and several motels provide good, low-cost lodging. There is no boat launch, but a boat hoist is provided at the pier. There is a boat-launch fee for using the hoist. There is a fee for party boats.

Directions: From Eureka, drive north on U.S. 101 for 28 miles to Trinidad. Take the Trinidad exit, turn left at the stop sign, and drive under the U.S. 101 overpass to Main Street. Continue on Main Street to Trinity Street. Turn left and drive a short distance to Edwards Street. Turn right on Edwards Street and drive to the parking area at the foot of the harbor, adjacent to the Seascape Restaurant, Trinidad Pier.

Contact: Trinidad Chamber of Commerce

(free travel packet), 707/677-0223, www
.trinidad.ca.gov.

Fishing and party-boat information: Seascape Pier, 707/677-3625; Salty's Surf 'n
Tackle, 707/677-0300; Trinidad Bay Charters,
707/839-4743 or 800/839-4744 (California
only), www.trinidadbaycharters.net; Patrick's
Point Charters, 707/445-4106, www.patricks
pointcharters.com.

17 MOUTH OF THE MAD RIVER

Rating: 5

near Arcata on the Pacific Ocean
Map 1.2, page 90

When anglers assess the Mad River, they usually think of salmon and steelhead. In the late
fall and winter (respectively), these fish run
upstream to the town of Blue Lake. But don't
think about salmon and steelhead when you're
fishing the mouth of the Mad. In fact, it is
illegal to fish within a 200-yard radius of the
mouth of the river from January 1 through
July 31, a restriction designed to protect sea-
run migrants. The mouth of the Mad comes
alive with perch (not steelhead) during the
summer and fall, especially in August and
September.

This is one of the best summer shoreline
fishing spots anywhere on the North Coast.
The adjacent surf zone, near the mouth of
the river, is also loaded with perch. You can
reach the mouth of the river by using a four-
wheel drive on Clam Beach. The perch here
are good-sized, clean, and healthy; they taste
great when they're battered up home-style
and fried.

Tides and bait selection will greatly influence your prospects. I suggest fishing after
a minus tide has bottomed out, during the
first three hours of the incoming tide. Sand
crabs are the preferred bait. Make sure the
sand crab's mouth is fully intact; perch seem
to know the difference. If you like tossing
out line from the beach and catching a batch

of fish, the mouth of the Mad River is your
place.

The Department of Fish and Game has a
recorded message that details the status of
coastal streams (707/822-3164), or check out
www.dfg.ca.gov.

Facilities, fees: A boat ramp is provided.
You can camp at Mad River Rapids RV Park
in Arcata, 800/822-7776, www.madriverrv
.com, or at nearby Clam Beach County Park,
707/445-7652, co.humboldt.ca.us/portal. Fishing access is free.

Directions: From Eureka, drive north on U.S.
101 to the Giuntoli Lane exit. Turn west and
drive 0.5 mile on Janes Road to Heindon
Road. Turn right (north) on Heindon Road
and drive one mile to Miller. Turn left on
Miller Lane and drive one mile west to Mad
River Road. Turn north on Mad River Road
and drive to the river mouth.

Contact: Pacific Outfitters, Eureka, 707/443-
6328; Mad River Fish Hatchery, 707/822-
0592; Arcata Chamber of Commerce,
707/822-3619, www.arcatachamber.com;
Eureka Fly Shop, 707/444-2000, www.eureka
flyshop.com.

18 MAD RIVER

Rating: 6

near Arcata
Map 1.2, page 90

One of Northern California's biggest enigmas
is the Mad River. Lord, this river can tease you
and please you with some of the best catch
rates for steelhead—if you hit it right, during
the winter. The steelhead run is best from late
December into February.

But if you hit the river during periods of heavy
rain, it can frustrate and humiliate you. In heavy-
rain seasons, some people call the Mad River
the "Mud River," since it often runs brown for
weeks on end. But hit it right and your prayers
may be answered. It is one of the few rivers where
you still have a chance to catch steelhead in the
winter, even when water clarity is not the best.

The reason the river turns brown so fast during a rain is that the hillsides bordering the Mad and its tributaries have been heavily logged. If you stand atop any of the hills above the town of Blue Lake, it looks as if somebody took a gigantic lawn mower and cleared the trees for as far as you can see. Silt, which rushes into the river every time it rains, choking out most natural spawning, is the result of this logging.

At times, the Mad River can seem one of California's most productive steelhead rivers. That is largely because the Department of Fish and Game operates a hatchery just upstream from the town of Blue Lake. Since this hatchery is only eight miles from the ocean, winter steelhead return rates are often very high. From fall's first rains through March, as many as 15,000 steelhead (in the 6- to 15-plus-pound range) return to the Mad. The majority of the fish congregate right around the hatchery. During the run, anglers swarm the riffles just above and below the hatchery.

The best fishing takes place downstream of the hatchery, in the town of Blue Lake, where steelhead can stack up like firewood. It can provide excellent shoreline fishing.

Don't expect to catch many salmon in the Mad River—they simply don't return here in large numbers. Local anglers who fish every day all season long may catch only one or two of these fish per year. Head for the Klamath River if you want to catch salmon.

One of the legendary fishing records in California, the state-record steelhead, 27 pounds and 4 ounces (from the Smith River), was likely broken in 2003 on the Mad River near Arcata by an anonymous soul who reportedly ate the fish. A steelhead that had already been gutted and cleaned was weighed at 26 pounds at a certified scale at Long's Drugs in Eureka. That means, had the fish been kept intact, it would likely have weighed several more pounds. In addition, a Fish and Game employee conducting a creel census also witnessed the steelhead, measured it at 48 inches, and told the angler he likely had a state-record fish.

Note: The Mad River is subject to emergency closures starting October 1 if flows are below the prescribed levels needed to protect migrating salmon and steelhead. The river is also subject to special regulations that can change from week to week. Check current status before planning your trip. The Department of Fish and Game has a recorded message that details the status of coastal streams: call 707/822-3164 or check out www.dfg.ca.gov.

Facilities, fees: A picnic area and public restrooms are provided at the hatchery. RV camping is available in Arcata at Mad River Rapids RV Park in Arcata, 800/822-7776, www.madriverrv.com, and Widow White Creek RV Park, 707/839-1137. Fishing access is free.

Directions: From Eureka, drive north on U.S. 101 for 12 miles to Highway 299. Turn east on Highway 299 and drive six miles to the town of Blue Lake and Blue Lake Boulevard. Take Blue Lake Boulevard to Greenwood Boulevard. Turn right on Greenwood Boulevard and drive to the four-way stop with Hatcher Road. Bear right on Hatchery Road (Greenwood turns into Hatchery Road) and drive 1.5 miles to the Mad River Fish Hatchery. Most fishing is done between the hatchery and the nearby bridge.

Contact: Pacific Outfitters, Eureka, 707/443-6328; Bucksport Sporting Goods, Eureka, 707/442-1832; Mad River Fish Hatchery, 707/822-0592.

19 HUMBOLDT BAY

Rating: 8

in Eureka

Map 1.2, page 90

Humboldt is a long, narrow bay bordered by wetlands on its northern flats, near Arcata, and on its southern flats as well. People often overlook this vast body of water as a viable fishing spot, but the fishing can be superior near the quite narrow mouth of the bay, where big halibut, seven-gill sharks, and (in the fall) salmon hang out. Other good spots include areas near the PG&E plant and along the southern shoreline, which is best for perch.

Most folks know that California halibut inhabit Humboldt Bay, but it wasn't until recent years that anglers really started taking good numbers of these fish. Captain Phil Glenn was one of the bay's halibut pioneers. Glenn turned to Humboldt Bay's halibut population when heavy restrictions were placed on salmon anglers. He found a virtually untapped resource right under his nose. The bay is full of halibut (weighing 6–30 pounds), and Glenn discovered that he could catch them by drifting live anchovies in areas such as the Arcata and Breacut channels.

Large sharks are the big surprise in Humboldt Bay. Seven-gill sharks, also called cow sharks, often roam just north of King Salmon. Many grow to seven feet in length and weigh close to 200 pounds, but very few people fish for them. These sharks have tremendous strength; the power of their first run always surprises the inexperienced. Use wire line, 16/0 hooks, and sufficient weight to take your bait right to the bottom of the bay. Seven-gill sharks are scavengers; they generally stay at the bottom of the bay rather than cruise around looking for a surfer's dangling legs. Still, the big ones are dangerous if they are brought aboard alive. For safety reasons, they should be dispatched with a bang stick—unless you release them, as you should with anything you don't plan on eating. While the fish is still in the water, cut its spinal column at the tail to bleed the shark out. Because of a shark's unique circulatory system, the meat can be ruined if it is not bled.

Perch fishing is a less specialized sport. Redtail perch are particularly abundant in Humboldt Bay, especially during the winter. Consistently, shore casters using sand crabs for bait find the area adjacent to the old PG&E plant to be quite productive. The area around South Bay is also fruitful. If you are new to the Humboldt Bay area, Bucksport Sporting Goods can put you on the fish.

In the fall, small-boat owners who may fear venturing out into the ocean get the unique opportunity to troll for salmon in the calm waters of Humboldt Bay. Just pretend that you're in the ocean and troll along; instead of moving through potentially turbulent seas, you will find yourself in flat, calm water. Catch rates are not high during this fall run, but when you have the opportunity to tie up with a salmon in a small aluminum boat, it's worth a shot.

Spring lingcod fishing off the north and south jetties can also be productive. To catch small greenling, fish during slack tide and use bloodworms for bait. Once you catch one, hook it through the upper lip and toss it out around the riprap. Attach a softball-sized balloon six feet up your line; this will keep your baitfish from swimming into the rocks. You'll know you have a fish on when your bobber goes under.

Note that fishing regulations often change here from year to year for seasons, depth restrictions, bag limits, size limits, and even annual quotas for the fleet. Always check current regulations with Fish and Game or with a marina or party-boat operator before planning a trip.

Facilities, fees: Camping, lodging, food, bait, and tackle can be found in Eureka. Boat ramps are available. Fishing access is free.

Directions: To Eureka boat ramp: From U.S. 101, take Washington Street and drive west 0.75 mile to Waterfront Drive. Turn right and drive to the marina on the right.

To Arcata boat ramp: In Arcata on U.S. 101, take the Arcata/Samoa exit and drive west on Samoa Boulevard (look for the sign for Arcata Marsh and boat ramp). At the sign turn left and drive to the boat ramp.

To Samoa boat ramp: In Eureka on U.S. 101, take the Highway 255 exit and drive west (over Indian Island) to Samoa Boulevard (also called Navy Base Road). Turn south and drive four miles to the signed turnoff for the boat ramp (near Fairhaven).

Contact: For general information and a free travel packet, contact Eureka Chamber of Commerce, 707/442-3738 or 800/356-6381, www.eurekachamber.com.

Information: Bucksport Sporting Goods, Eureka, 707/442-1832; Pacific Outfitters, Eureka, 707/443-6328; Eureka Public Marina, 707/268-1973, www.ci.eureka.ca.gov.

Party boats: Celtic Charter Service, 707/442-7843, www.shellbacksportfishing .com.

20 EUREKA COASTAL SALMON

Rating: 8

in Eureka on Humboldt Bay

Map 1.2, page 90

Established in 1850, Eureka is one of the oldest towns in the state. Logging and fishing have long been the two primary industries, and when you talk fishing in these parts, you are talking salmon. A bonus comes in the fall with fishing for rockfish and lingcod.

By July, the salmon can practically jump into boats here. Most of the salmon are kings, usually weighing 6–10 pounds, with a light sprinkling of bigger fellows in the 15- to 25-pound class. The mix often includes a few pods of silver salmon (identified by their white mouth), which must be released if caught.

Windy weather and choppy seas often hamper prospects early in the season, and while the late season brings the opportunity to catch the biggest fish of the year, there are fewer of them. In between, during the magic months of July and August, anglers come from near and far to chase the roaming coastal schools of wild fish.

The prime fishing zone is almost always between the mouth of the Eel River (just south of Humboldt Bay) and the mouth of the Mad River (just north of Humboldt Bay). From the bay, skippers will head straight "out front," or "out the jaws," and troll in the vicinity of this zone, which usually ranges from just offshore to five or six miles out. In any case, it's within reach of private boats in the 18- to 24-foot class, as well as larger charters. Before salmon fishing here, always check the current regulations. They change yearly.

In the fall or after the quota of sport-caught salmon has been reached, many anglers switch over to deep-sea fishing for rockfish. The average rockfish and lingcod are very large, but getting to the best fishing grounds offshore Cape Mendocino requires quite a long trip. No matter. The sea is calmest in the fall, and on many days the boat ride turns into a celebration.

Note that fishing regulations often change here from year to year for seasons, depth restrictions, bag limits, size limits, and even annual quotas for the fleet. Always check current regulations with Fish and Game or with a marina or party-boat operator before planning a trip.

Facilities, fees: RVers can camp at Johnnie's Marina and RV Park, 707/442-2284, or E-Z Landing RV Park and Marina, 707/442-1118. A boat ramp is available nearby. Supplies can be obtained in Eureka. Fishing access is free.

Directions: To Eureka boat ramp: From U.S. 101, take Washington Street and drive west 0.75 mile to Waterfront Drive. Turn right and drive to the marina on the right.

To Arcata boat ramp: In Arcata on U.S. 101, take the Arcata/Samoa exit and drive west on Samoa Boulevard (look for the sign for Arcata Marsh and boat ramp). At the sign turn left and drive to the boat ramp.

To Samoa boat ramp: In Eureka on U.S. 101, take the Highway 255 exit and drive west (over Indian Island) to Samoa Boulevard (also called Navy Base Road). Turn south and drive four miles to the signed turnoff for the boat ramp (near Fairhaven).

Contact: General information and a free travel packet are available from the Eureka Chamber of Commerce, 707/442-3738 or 800/356-6381, www.eurekachamber.com.

Information and supplies: Bucksport Sporting Goods, Eureka, 707/442-1832; Pacific Outfitters, Eureka, 707/443-6328; Eureka Public Marina, 707/268-1973, www.ci.eureka .ca.gov.

21 VAN DUZEN RIVER

Rating: 4

near Eureka

Map 1.2, page 90

A lot of out-of-towners miss out on the Van Duzen, but not the locals. They don't like to talk about it much lest the word leak out, but Van Duzen regulations continue to permit angling for resident trout in waters upstream of Eaton Falls. Note that fishing is prohibited year-round on the Van Duzen and its tributaries—including the South Fork Van Duzen—from the Highway 36 bridge at Bridgeville to Eaton Falls. This closure was initiated to protect the population of summer steelhead, which has been low in recent years due to the disappearance of critical holding pools. Summer steelhead arrive in the spring and need deep pools to escape high summer temperatures and to spawn in the fall.

During the fall, anglers fly-fishing from small car-top prams just downstream from the mouth of the Van Duzen can do quite well on salmon. When steelhead are in the area, bank anglers fish the hole right where the Van enters the Eel, using a method that seems better suited to planted trout at an inland reservoir than for big ocean-fresh steelhead. They pin cocktail shrimp on a hook along with a mini marshmallow and cast out with a sliding sinker rig. Once the weight settles to the bottom, the angler pops the rod into a holder, breaks out a lawn chair, and waits for a passing steelhead to bite. Sounds strange, but it works.

Although access to the Van Duzen is easy, very few steelhead anglers utilize this river. If you catch it right, it will surprise you.

Note: The Van Duzen River is subject to emergency closures starting October 1 if flows are below the prescribed levels needed to protect migrating salmon and steelhead. The river is also subject to special regulations that can change from week to week. The Department of Fish and Game has a recorded message that details the status of coastal streams: call 707/822-3164 or check www.dfg.ca.gov.

Facilities, fees: Van Duzen County Park provides a campground. You can camp at Grizzly Creek Redwoods State Park. Supplies can be obtained in Bridgeville or Carlotta. There is a day-use fee at Grizzly Creek Park. There is a cost for fishing access within the state park. There is no charge if you park outside of the park.

Directions: From Eureka, drive south on U.S. 101 to the junction of Highway 36 at Alton. Turn east on Highway 36 and drive about 17 miles to Grizzly Creek Redwoods. River access points are located along Highway 36. Check DFG regulations for closures.

Contact: Grizzly Creek Redwoods State Park, 707/777-3683, www.parks.ca.gov; Van Duzen County Park, 707/445-7651, co.humboldt.ca.us/portal; Eureka Fly Shop, 707/444-2000, www.eurekaflyshop.com; Bucksport Sporting Goods, Eureka, 707/442-1832.

22 EEL RIVER

Rating: 7

near Eureka

Map 1.2, page 90

The Eel River flows through some of the West's most easily accessible and beautiful country. U.S. 101 runs right alongside the river, bordered by redwoods, firs, and other conifers. In some years, the quality of the scenery is matched by that of the fishing, both for salmon and steelhead.

Tight restrictions on salmon catches in the Pacific Ocean have led to higher runs of fish on the Eel. In October, prior to heavy rains, the salmon will enter the Eel during high tides and start stacking up in the river between Fernbridge and Fortuna. As the rains come, the salmon are sprung, heading upstream, which in the case of this river is actually south. Since the highway traces much of the main stem of the Eel, there are many access roads that put good spots within easy reach.

For salmon, always search out the deeper holes with slow-moving river currents. These are the perfect spots for salmon to rest in during the course of their upriver journey. At times, if you have a high enough vantage point, you can even see them milling about near the stream bottom. Now get this: the best bait for salmon on this river is a cocktail shrimp topped off with a small white marshmallow. Some guides swear by fresh roe, of course, but even they will try the sweet stuff now and then. The key here is to fish on the drift, always keeping a close watch on your line. Often the only indication that you are getting a strike is when the steady downstream bow in your line straightens a bit. That means a salmon has stopped the drift of your bait. If you wait for a tremendous strike, you are apt to turn into a statue.

Come winter, the rains and the steelhead arrive simultaneously. The combination of past logging damage in watersheds, erosion, silt runoff, and heavy rains has resulted in a river that can muddy up quicker than any other in California. If the rains continue, it can stay muddy for weeks on end. When that happens, the only solution is to head upstream to the South Fork, where water clarity and fishable water are more reliable. During moderate rainy seasons, however, the main Eel will stay "greened up" and provide a tremendous steelhead fishery. When these conditions prevail, many guides with drift boats will put in at the South Fork, then work their way downriver on the main Eel. The lighter the rains, the more apt this section of river is to provide the best fishing. And the resident steelhead can get big. The Eel is second only to the Smith River in the number of 20-pounders it produces, and the catch rates are much, much higher than on the Smith. The best opportunity is with a drift boat, either bumping roe or running Hot Shot or Wee Wart plugs downstream of the boat while the guide oars to keep you almost motionless on the water. You'll typically start early and fish late, and in the process you can hope to catch two or three bright-run steelies.

A few things to remember: In the summer,

there is virtually no fishing. The river turns into a trickle, and those "little trout" that you might spot in the small pools are actually juvenile steelhead that should be left alone—or they're Sacramento squawfish, which will eat trout if they can. In addition, hordes of out-of-staters clog the highway around these parts in the summer. In the winter, however, it is a completely different scene. Tourists are few, anglers are excited, and in every store and gas station you could post a sign that says "Fishing spoken here."

Note: The Eel River is subject to emergency closures starting October 1 if flows are below the prescribed levels needed to protect migrating salmon and steelhead. The river is also subject to special regulations that can change from week to week. Check current status before planning your trip. The Department of Fish and Game has a recorded message that details the status of coastal streams: call 707/822-3164 or check www.dfg.ca.gov.

Facilities, fees: Several campgrounds with drinking water, restrooms, flush toilets, and RV dump stations are available. State parks charge day-use fees. Riverwalk RV Park, Fortuna, 800/705-5359, www.riverwalkrv park.com, is another option. Fishing access is free.

Directions: From Eureka, drive south on U.S. 101. The river largely parallels the highway, and access is available off almost every spur road, as well as through several small towns along the river, including Fortuna, Rio Dell, Shively, and Holmes.

Contact: Bureau of Land Management, Arcata Field Office, 707/825-2300, www.blm .gov/ca.

Information and supplies: Bucksport Sporting Goods, Eureka, 707/442-1832; Pacific Outfitters, Eureka, 707/443-6328; Brown's Sporting Goods, Garberville, 707/923-2533; Eureka Fly Shop, 707/444-2000, www.eureka flyshop.com.

Guides: Frank Humphrey, Garberville, 707/923-3643; Kevin Brock, 800/995-5543, www.fishkevinbrock.com.

23 MATTOLE RIVER

Rating: 7

near Eureka

Map 1.2, page 90

Almost everybody overlooks the Honeydew Valley, one of Northern California's little paradises. This place is so out of the way that nobody gets here by accident. It takes only one visit to figure out why this stretch of land is known as the Lost Coast.

The Mattole is one of the most remote steelhead rivers in California. But if you can hit it right, it offers the second-biggest steelhead in the state (second only to the Smith River). The steelhead on the Mattole are beautiful, bright fish, fresh from the ocean and full of fight. And these fish aren't midgets either, often ranging 8–14 pounds, with a few bigger and a few smaller.

One spot to consider is near the mouth of the river, well below the Petrolia Bridge. A parking area is available here, from which you can walk out to the end of a sandbar. You cast to fresh-run steelhead, just as they emerge from the ocean to enter the river.

In the Honeydew Valley, many of the prime spots for shoreliners are off-limits because reaching them requires crossing over private land. What to do? Stop in at the Honeydew Store or Petrolia Store, and the folks there will keep you out of trouble by detailing the best public-access spots.

The Mattole River cuts a charmed path down the center of the valley. This beautiful stream handles a lot of water. The steelhead usually start entering the river in good numbers in late December, but the fishing is often best much later in the season. With the county campground near the mouth, this river can be an ideal winter camping/fishing destination, provided you bring a rainproof tent and plenty of spare clothing.

The biggest problem here is the rain. It downright pours. It can rain an inch an hour here during winter squalls, as much as anywhere in the lower 48 states, but that is the magic stuff that makes for big steelhead. Locals wear rubber boots throughout the winter as a matter of course. Because the rain can come fast and hard, the fishability of the river is often questionable. So it's absolutely essential to call the Honeydew Store to get the latest river conditions before heading out.

A great bonus on the Mattole is fishing for perch right at the mouth of the river—that is, where it flows into the ocean. This can provide excellent fishing, best on sand crabs, at the bottom of low tides (minus tides are the best here) and during the first two hours of incoming tides. Note that the mouth of the Mattole, like other small coastal streams, is closed to fishing in the winter, spring, and early summer to protect migrating steelhead. But the area near the mouth attracts good numbers of perch even when the mouth of the river is blocked by the sandbar, which happens at various times.

For a river that handles such a large volume of water, the one disappointment is the relatively low number of salmon. They just aren't there. Local conservationists are making a great push to enhance the Mattole's salmon populations, however, and that's just what's needed to complete the picture of this fine river.

Note: The Mattole River is subject to emergency closures starting October 1 if flows are below the prescribed levels needed to protect migrating salmon and steelhead. The river is also subject to special regulations that can change from week to week. Check current status before planning your trip. The Department of Fish and Game has a recorded message that details the status of coastal streams: call 707/822-3164 or check www.dfg.ca.gov.

Facilities, fees: Campgrounds with restrooms, showers, flush toilets, and drinking water are nearby, south of Petrolia and near the mouth of the Mattole. Nearby A.W. Way County Park also offers camping options. Fishing access is free.

Directions: From U.S. 101 north of Garberville, take the South Fork–Honeydew exit and drive west to Honeydew. At Honeydew, turn right on Mattole Road and drive toward Petrolia. At the second bridge over the Mattole River, one mile before Petrolia, turn west on Lighthouse Road and drive five miles to the campground at the end of the road. The road runs parallel to the river, with the best public access closest to the mouth of the river.

Contact: Camping on the adjacent lands: Bureau of Land Management, Arcata Field Office, 707/825-2300, www.blm.gov/ca; A.W. Way County Park, 707/445-7651, co.humboldt.ca.us/portal.

Information: Honeydew Store, 707/629-3310; Petrolia Store, 707/629-3455; Eureka Fly Shop, 707/444-2000, www.eurekafly shop.com.

Guide: Frank Humphrey, Garberville, 707/923-3643.

24 SHELTER COVE

Rating: 9

south of Eureka

Map 1.2, page 90

One of the great advantages to salmon fishing at Shelter Cove is that you can launch a small aluminum boat and then catch salmon within a mile or two of the ramp.

Though remote, Shelter Cove offers the ideal base camp for the traveling salmon angler with an oceangoing skiff or cruiser on a trailer. The new boat launch is outstanding, and the stocks of Klamath-run salmon are apparently on the upswing. Point Delgada provides a natural shelter for the boat launch, reducing surge from offshore swells and making launching and loading easier.

Most of the fishing for salmon is done by trolling, not mooching. A lot of people use plastic planer-divers to get the bait down, instead of cannonball sinkers on releases; I prefer a Scotty downrigger. The salmon average in the 5- to 8-pound range, with a light mix of kings in the 10- to 15-pound class, rarely bigger. A few schools of silver salmon

also migrate through this area every summer, usually in July.

Another bonus is good inshore rockfishing. Just get over any reef, drop a jig down to the bottom, and you will start catching fish. As long as you are over rocks, you will be in business.

The newest fishery off Shelter Cove is for Pacific halibut, giving anglers a chance to experience a bit of Alaska in Northern California. The halibut average 30–60 pounds but can get bigger. A 112-pounder is the biggest documented here, caught by Darren Brown of Garberville. The top spot for halibut is the Mattole Canyon north of Punta Gorda, a 25-mile trip from Shelter Cove. A calm day is required to reach this spot; the season runs May 1 through September 30.

Some huge lingcod and rockfish can also be taken on the local reefs. The best success can come drifting whole herring and mackerel at 220–260 feet deep.

Note: If you'll be staying here a few days, check with the DFG on the salmon-possession limit. In recent years an increased enforcement effort has resulted in some vacationers being busted with coolers full of salmon from a week of limit fishing.

Facilities, fees: A campground (Shelter Cove Campground, 707/986-7474), six-lane boat ramp, gas station, restaurant, lodging, tackle shop, and supplies are available. Fishing access is free. There is a fee for party boats.

Directions: From Eureka, drive south on U.S. 101 for 60 miles to the Redway/Shelter Cove exit. Take that exit and drive north on Redwood Road for 2.5 miles to Briceland-Shelter Cove Road. Turn right (west) and drive 18 miles (following the truck/RV route signs) to Upper Pacific Drive. Turn left (south) on Upper Pacific Drive and proceed (it becomes Machi Road) 0.5 mile to Shelter Cove Campground. A boat ramp is nearby.

Contact: Fishing information and tackle: Mario's Marina, 707/986-7595, www.shelter coveca.info.

Party boats: Shelter Cove Sportfishing,

707/923-1668, www.codking.com; Outcast Sportfishing, 707/986-9842, www.outcast sportfish.com.

25 SOUTH FORK EEL RIVER (GARBERVILLE TO FORTUNA)

Rating: 8

near Garberville

Map 1.2, page 90

Wanted: Big steelhead, a stream that can be fished effectively from shore, reliable reports on river conditions, and good choices for camping and/or lodging.

On the South Fork Eel, you get all that. The catch is the weather, which is always a chancy proposition here, with heavy rains quickly turning the river's emerald-green flows to chocolate brown. When that happens, it takes several days without rain before the waters clear enough to become fishable—and by that time, it is bound to rain again. After all, that's why the trees are so tall up here. So what to do?

You must get to know this river in its up-stream (southerly) portions, which clear most quickly and offer the best shoreline fishing. This is particularly true around Benbow, Cooks Valley, Piercy, and as far upstream as Smithe Redwoods and sometimes even Leggett. There you'll find many obvious areas that are prime for shoreliners, with steelhead in the 6- to 15-pound class offering both challenges and rewards.

River conditions are critical here. The higher the clarity, the farther downriver (north) you will fish; either that, or you will be forced to switch over to lighter, less visible line. Conversely, the lower the water clarity, the farther upstream (south) you must fish. It's that simple, and this is one place where you can get a reliable report on fishing conditions. Just phone Brown's Sporting Goods in Garberville, and they will get you up to speed. I've been calling them for many years prior to my trips to the South Fork Eel.

Even though many guides fish this river when water clarity is decent, the majority of the fish in the South Fork of the Eel River are caught by bank anglers using fresh roe. The preferred entreaty is called Killer Roe and it is available at Brown's. Virtually all of the shore-caught steelhead are taken on roe, fished with care and persistence in pockets at the tail ends of runs. At high water, the best put-ins for those with drift boats are near Leggett and at Smithe Redwoods.

One frustrating element about the South Fork Eel is that it can be difficult to make long-range plans that will stick. Because of frequent rains, you need to be flexible. If you expect the fish to fit into your rigid schedule, you stand the chance of getting the big zilch. But if you try to work with the fish's schedule, well, then you are on your way.

Another bonus is the number of choices for camping and lodging. Quality camps are at Richardson Grove State Park, Standish-Hickey State Recreation Area, and several privately run parks. There are hotels in Garberville.

Note: The South Fork Eel River is subject to emergency closures starting October 1 if flows are below the prescribed levels needed to protect migrating salmon and steelhead. The river is also subject to special regulations that can change from week to week. Check current status before planning your trip. The Department of Fish and Game has a recorded message that details the status of coastal streams: call 707/822-3164 or check out www.dfg.ca.gov.

Facilities, fees: Several campgrounds are nearby and have restrooms with flush toilets and drinking water. The most famous is at Richardson Grove State Park, between Cooks Valley and Benbow. Supplies can be obtained in Leggett, Laytonville, and Piercy. Tackle and supplies can be obtained in Garberville at Brown's Sporting Goods. Fishing access is free.

Directions: U.S. 101 parallels much of the South Fork Eel, starting in Leggett (84 miles south of Eureka) and running downstream (north) past Benbow, Garberville, Miranda, and Myers Flat on to its confluence with the main stem of the Eel.

Contact: Richardson Grove State Park, 707/247-3318, reservations 800/444-7275, www.parks.ca.gov; Standish-Hickey State Recreation Area, 707/925-6482; Big Bend Lodge, 707/925-2440, www.riversrunlodge .com; Redwoods River Resort, 707/925-6249, www.redwoodriverresort.com; Brown's Sporting Goods, Garberville, 707/923-2533; Eureka Fly Shop, 707/444-2000, www.eurekafly shop.com.

Guide: Frank Humphrey, Garberville, 707/923-3643; Wayne "Sierra" Hansen, 530/222-2840, www.norcalsteelhead.com.

26 SOUTH FORK EEL RIVER (LEGGETT TO GARBERVILLE)

Rating: 8

north of Leggett

Map 1.2, page 90

Steelhead anglers know all about how muddy the Eel River can get. They say that after a good winter rain, you could plant a crop of potatoes in the river, it's so muddy. As for the fishing, that's zilch until the river starts to green up, which can take from a week to 10 days.

So what's an angler to do? Sit on your keister praying for sun? Not when you have access to the South Fork Eel. You see, heavy rains and the corresponding high stream flows allow the steelhead to swim upriver, way upriver; the section of the South Fork Eel just downstream of Leggett can provide fishable water a few days after a gully washer, when the rest of the Eel system is a brownout.

There are several good spots between Leggett and Piercy. The best are at the deep bend in the river just south of Piercy, accessible from Highway 271; at a deep bend west of Standish-Hickey State Recreation Area (within walking distance); and just west of U.S. 101 at Leggett. At the latter, a small road off adjacent Highway 1 leads down to the stream.

Other advantages are offered on this section of river. One is the number of campgrounds in the area, which provide several options for base camps. This is also the closest major steelhead stream to the San Francisco Bay Area and can easily be done in a weekend trip if you leave for the river Friday evening.

Note: This is a winter-only fishery. In the summer, this section of the river dwindles to a trickle and has no trout. In addition, the South Fork Eel may be closed starting October 1 if flows are below the prescribed levels needed to protect migrating salmon and steelhead. The Department of Fish and Game has a recorded message that details the status of coastal streams: call 707/822-3164 or check out www.dfg.ca.gov.

Facilities, fees: Several campgrounds can be found along the river on U.S. 101, including Rock Creek, Standish Hickey, and Redwoods River Resort. Cabins and lodging are also available. Supplies can be obtained in Leggett and Piercy. Fishing access is free.

Directions: From the junction of U.S. 101 and Highway 1 in Leggett, drive north on U.S. 101. Access points are excellent near the Smithe Redwoods State Reserve at Bridges Creek and Dora Creek, and near Standish-Hickey State Recreation Area, off the South Leggett exit. Access is also available off the Highway 271 exit (four-wheel drive is advised).

Contact: Brown's Sporting Goods, Garberville, 707/923-2533; Redwoods River Resort, 707/925-6249, www.redwoodriverresort.com; The Peg House, Leggett, 707/925-6444; Standish-Hickey State Recreation Area, 707/925-6482, www.parks.ca.gov.

Guide: Frank Humphrey, Garberville, 707/923-3643; Wayne "Sierra" Hansen, 530/222-2840, www.norcalsteelhead.com.

SHASTA
AND TRINITY

© TOM STIENSTRA

BEST FISHING SPOTS

(Freshwater Fisheries
Sacramento River: Redding to Anderson,
  page 158.

(Hike-In Fisheries
Marble Mountain Wilderness, **page 123.**
Trinity Alps Wilderness, **page 141.**

(Places to Teach Kids to Fish
Iron Gate Reservoir/Copco Lake, **page 128.**
Lake Siskiyou, **page 136.**
Shasta Lake, **page 152.**

(Most Unusual Fisheries
Trinity Alps Wilderness, **page 141.**

This is one of California's most beautiful regions.

The heart is 14,162-foot Mount Shasta. The mountain's sphere of influence spans a radius of 125 miles, and its shadow is felt everywhere. The opportunities seem boundless – giant Shasta Lake, the Sacramento River above and below the lake, and several wilderness areas and national forests all provide excellent fishing. This is one of the best regions anywhere for an outdoor adventure – especially fishing, boating, camping, and exploring.

Shasta Lake is one of America's top recreation lakes. It is the one destination that is big enough to handle all who love it. The massive reservoir boasts 370 miles of shoreline, 1,200 campsites, 21 boat launches, 11 marinas, 35 resorts, and numerous houseboat and cabin rentals. A remarkable 22 species of fish live in the lake. For catch rates, it is one of the West's best lakes for bass.

The Trinity Alps Wilderness is vast and charmed; lakes are sprinkled everywhere. It's also home to the headwaters for feeder streams to the Trinity River, Klamath River, New River, Wooley Creek, and others. To the nearby north is the Russian Wilderness and the Marble Mountain Wilderness. The beautiful Marble Mountain Wilderness provides lots of fish, and its Ukonom Basin is home to more bears than any place outside Yosemite.

The Upper Klamath River features one of the best accessible portions of the entire 200 miles of river, from just below Iron Gate Dam on downstream, past I-5 and the Tree of Heaven Campground. It is an easy trip in a drift boat, raft, or canoe, with many good spots for steelhead along the way, as well as some other spots that you can park and walk to.

This remote region of California features 100 miles of the Klamath River (and a major tributary, the Salmon River). Shore access is good along the Klamath, and there are obvious pullouts along Highway 96 for the best fishing spots.

Trinity Lake provides outstanding boating and fishing, including excellent fishing for smallmouth bass, and just downstream, smaller Lewiston Lake offers a quiet alternative for trout. One advantage to Lewiston Lake is that it is always full of water, making for a very pretty scene. Downstream of Lewiston, the Trinity River provides low-cost rafting and outstanding shoreline access along Highway 299 for salmon and steelhead. Some of the best catch rates in California are on the Trinity River for salmon in October.

The rest of the region is little traveled, sparsely populated, and home to a few lakes. Those include Copco Lake, where you'll have a chance to catch yellow perch by the bucketful, and Iron Gate, a top spot for bass fishing in the region.

The Klamath Mountains are also well known as Bigfoot country. If you drive up the Forest Service road at Bluff Creek, just off Highway 96 upstream of Weitchpec, you can even find the spot where the famous Bigfoot home film footage was shot in the 1960s. Well, I haven't seen Bigfoot, but I have discovered fantastic opportunities for outdoor recreation.

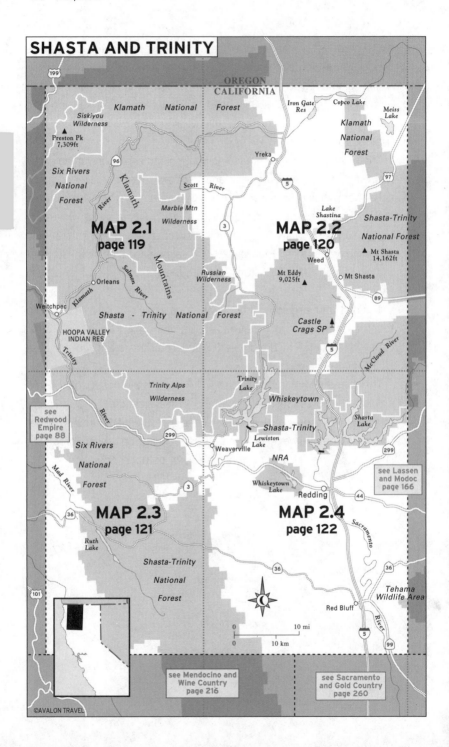

SHASTA AND TRINITY

MAP 2.1
page 119

MAP 2.2
page 120

MAP 2.3
page 121

MAP 2.4
page 122

OREGON
CALIFORNIA

Klamath   National   Forest

Siskiyou
Wilderness

Preston Pk
7,309ft

Six Rivers
National
Forest

Marble Mtn
Wilderness

Scott   River

Russian
Wilderness

Klamath

Mountains

Orleans

Salmon River

Weitchpec

Shasta - Trinity National Forest

HOOPA VALLEY
INDIAN RES

Trinity

Iron Gate
Res

Copco Lake

Meiss
Lake

Yreka

Klamath
National
Forest

Lake
Shastina

Weed

Mt Eddy
9,025ft

Shasta-Trinity
National Forest

Mt Shasta
14,162ft

Mt Shasta

Castle
Crags SP

McCloud River

see
Redwood
Empire
page 88

Trinity Alps
Wilderness

River

Trinity
Lake

Whiskeytown

Shasta-Trinity

Shasta
Lake

Six Rivers
National

Forest

Mad River

Weaverville

Lewiston
Lake

NRA

see Lassen
and Modoc
page 166

Ruth
Lake

Whiskeytown
Lake

Redding

Sacramento

Shasta-Trinity
National
Forest

Red Bluff

Tehama
Wildlife
Area

River

0   10 mi

0   10 km

©AVALON TRAVEL

see Mendocino and
Wine Country
page 216

see Sacramento
and Gold Country
page 260

Map 2.1

Sites 1-5
Pages 123-127

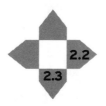

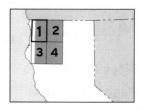

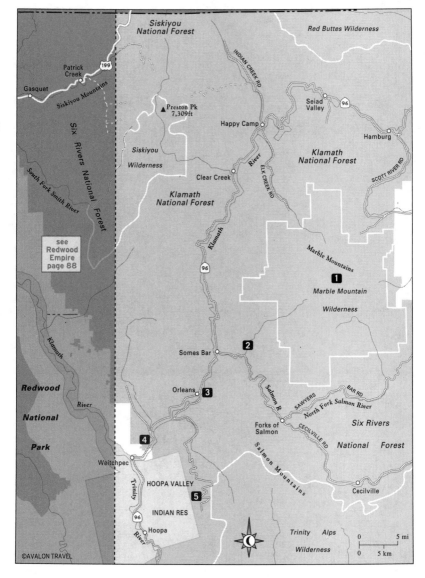

Map 2.2

Sites 6-25
Pages 128-144

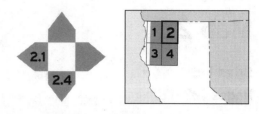

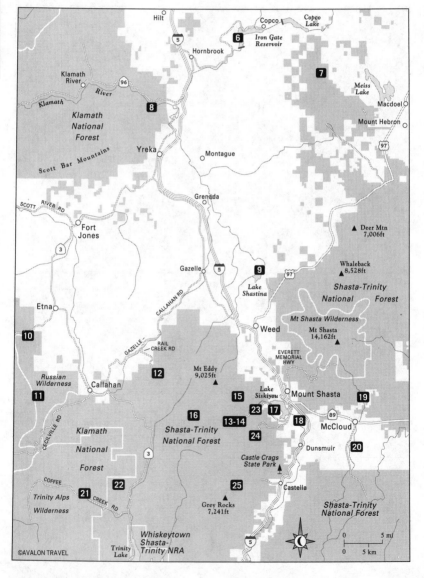

Map 2.3

Sites 26-31
Pages 145-149

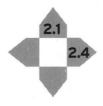

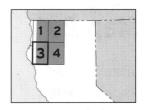

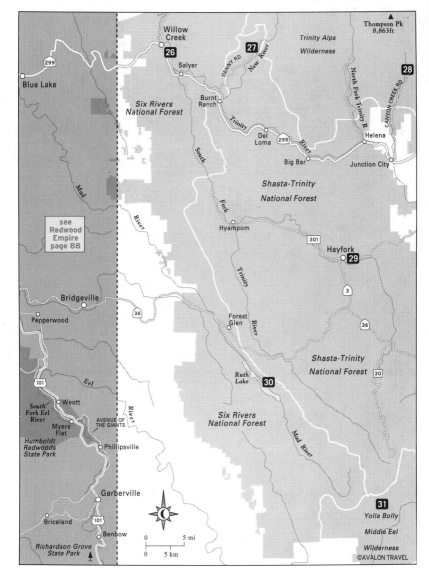

Map 2.4

Sites 32-39
Pages 149-160

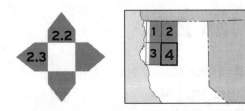

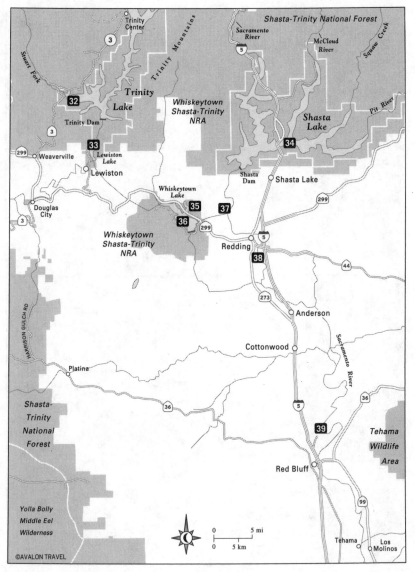

1 MARBLE MOUNTAIN WILDERNESS

Rating: 9

northeast of Eureka near
Klamath National Forest

Map 2.1, page 119   **BEST (**

Bay Area backpackers like Yosemite and Tahoe. Los Angeles backpackers like Kings Canyon and Mount Whitney. Eureka and Redding backpackers like the Trinity Alps and Mount Shasta. With all of these popular favorites, Marble Mountain is one of the great overlooked wilderness areas of the West. It is a large wilderness offering more than a hundred lakes, several outstanding peaks, and (that's right) good fishing. Though aerial stocks in the Sierra have largely been halted, many of these lakes still provide good fishing.

Because of the large number of lakes within this wilderness, you can plan a weeklong trip during which you camp at a different lake each evening. Of course the deeper you get into the wilderness, the better the fishing is. That's always the law of the land.

Spirit Lake is such a place. Ringed by conifers and always full, it is one of the prettiest lakes I have ever seen and has plenty of brook trout and rainbow trout that are up to 10 and 11 inches in length. In the evening, when the local osprey takes a dive, he never goes away empty-taloned.

There are many good lakes within Marble Mountain Wilderness, most with a mix of rainbow trout and brook trout. My favorites are Spirit Lake, Big Hancock Lake, Cuddihy Lakes 1 and 3 (forget 2 and 4), Ukonom Lake, Lower Wright Lake.

At some point in the past, these occasionally have provided fair catches: Abbott Lake, Bear Lake, Buckhorn Lake, Campbell Lake, Clear Lake, Deadman Lake, Deep Lake, Dogwood Lake, Lower English Lake, Fisher Lake, Gate Lake, Granite Lakes, Katherine Lake, Kidder Lake, Long High Lake, Marten Lake, Monument Lake, Onemile Lake, Paradise Lake, Pine Lake, Pleasant Lake, Rainy Lake, Secret Lake, Shadow Lake, Sky High Lake, and Lower Wright Lake.

I often hike to the lakes that are not accessible by trails. The trout at such lakes have never heard of hooks, and many of them have never even heard of people. At one such lake, my friend Michael Furniss tossed in a large boulder that made a tremendous splash. The trout actually swam toward it, rather than away from it; they were curious about all the commotion.

The Marble Mountain Wilderness is a real beauty, and many side trips are possible from within it. Take a day pack and scramble up Marble Mountain (6,880 feet), King's Castle (7,405 feet), Buckhorn Mountain (6,908 feet), or one of the many shorter peaks. Lush growth and big trees surround the trail that runs along Wooley Creek.

Facilities, fees: Facilities are not available in the wilderness area. Primitive campsites can be found at trailheads off various Forest Service roads; these roads join with Highway 96 to the north and Salmon River Road to the south. Fishing access is free.

Directions: There are many access points for the Marble Mountain Wilderness. Here are two of the primary trailheads:

• Paradise Lake Trailhead: From I-5 at Yreka take the Highway 3/Fort Jones exit and drive 16.5 miles to Fort Jones. Turn right on Scott River Road, and drive 16.8 miles to the turn-off for Indian Scotty Campground. Cross the concrete bridge, bear left on Forest Service Road 44N45, and drive about five miles. Turn right on an unmarked Forest Service road and drive six miles (signed Paradise Lake) to the trailhead near the wilderness border.

• Haypress Meadows Trailhead: From Highway 299 at Willow Creek, turn north on Highway 96 and drive 42 miles to Orleans. Continue eight miles to Somes Bar and Salmon River Road. Turn right on Salmon River Road (Highway 93) and drive 100 feet to a "Camp 3/Haypress Trailhead" sign and Forest Service Road 15N17 (Offield Mountain Road). Turn left and drive 14.6 miles to

Forest Service Road 15N17E. Turn left and drive 1.5 miles to the access road for Haypress Trailhead. Turn left and drive one mile to the trailhead.

Contact: Klamath National Forest, Salmon and Scott River Ranger District, 11263 North Highway 3, Fort Jones, CA 96032-9702, 530/468-5351, www.fs.fed.us/r5—click on Forest Offices.

❷ SALMON RIVER

Rating: 6

near Orleans in Klamath National Forest

Map 2.1, page 119

The payoff on this getaway is a river that looks like a trout stream where the fish are six pounds instead of six inches. There's a catch, of course. It's out in the middle of friggin' nowhere. You've heard about drives that seem endless. This one really is. It's a brain-grinding 401 miles from San Francisco, and once you get there, you drive some more to find the best spots. Rules require catch-and-release; always check Department of Fish and Game (DFG) regulations before steelhead fishing anywhere, of course.

This is the Salmon River in Northern California, set in a cold, deep canyon in Klamath National Forest. It is the prettiest of the dozens of tributaries and feeder creeks on the 200-mile Klamath River and also provides the best bank fishing access for winter steelhead, the fastest of the state's freshwater fish with a burst speed of 27 feet per second. It is open to fishing through February, catch-and-release.

The canyon is a work of art. The river's pool-and-drop composition makes it a perfect canvas for an angler to create a masterpiece, using a fishing rod as a brush. Steelhead in the four- to eight-pound class are sprinkled throughout the river in February and March, best from Forks of the Salmon on downstream to the mouth of Wooley Creek. A logging road at the bottom of the canyon provides access to dozens of good spots, with turnouts and faint trails leading to the river. When ready to cast, remember this rule of thumb: look for bubbles floating on the river surface. These are often the runs that hold steelhead, typically the edge of riffles at the entry points of rapids, tail-outs, and the upper and lower ends of pools amid many bowling ball–size boulders.

Most anglers use traditional steelhead set-ups, three-way rigs with roe for bait. Others will cast Little Cleos, and a handful will fly-fish with Assassins, Silver Hiltons, or weighted nymphs with a copper head. One of my all-time prize catches was on the Cal Salmon, a seven-pound steelhead that went berserk when hooked with a 5-weight fly rod more suitable for small rainbow trout.

A few words of warning: Because the canyon walls loom so high, the river gets very little direct sunlight. While that is good for fishing (steelhead turn shy in bright sun), it makes temperatures frigid, often 15–25°F on clear winter days. In addition, the most direct route to the river is over a logging road at Etna Summit (5,970 feet), which can get buried by snow, requiring an even more circuitous drive on Highway 96, the Klamath River Highway. When the Etna Summit is open, the nearest lodging is 37 miles away (in Etna).

Yet these problems become solutions for the ambitious few. Because it is so remote, cold, and difficult to reach, you can often have much of the canyon to yourself.

While the Salmon River is known for its adult steelhead, good runs of half-pounders do enter the lower section below Lily Creek. You can catch them here using conventional methods, including spinning gear, and also fly-fishing. Through November, most techniques can work on the Lower Salmon River, including night crawlers. Once the water gets cold, Glo Bugs will be your best offering.

Once you reach the tributary of Lily Creek, the road starts to separate from the river and then climbs to the Forks of Salmon. There is still access in this section, but it is far more difficult. Even with good access, the Salmon River is very lightly fished. Most people traveling to this region fish the nearby Klamath instead.

This is a place dear to my heart, with many special memories with my old friend, the late Ted Fay. The first time I fished the Salmon River, I witnessed one of the most amazing fishing episodes of my life. I was with Ted, a legendary fly fisher and storyteller who invented the dropper system of nymphing with two flies. We were sitting in my pickup truck, watching a black bear try to catch a steelhead in the river. After a half hour the bear gave up and left, still hungry, probably to see if he could find a camper visiting from the Bay Area, or maybe an outdoors writer.

Later that day, Ted and I had not caught anything either. As we drove out, I pulled over to the same spot where we had watched the bear make his fruitless attempt.

"If the bear knew a steelhead was in there, then we know there's a fish there, too," said Ted.

We approached the spot quietly, walking lightly. Then Ted performed the kind of feat that creates legends: he caught the steelhead that had eluded the bear. His cast was delivered so lightly that the fly, a customized Silver Hilton, drifted from riffle to hole as if no line were attached. An instant later, it was a hookup, and Fay—an older man—was taken to the limit to land the fish. After 15 minutes, he succeeded.

For a young outdoors writer, it was a baptismal indoctrination to the Salmon River.

Facilities, fees: The main stem and both forks of the river are open to fishing November through February only. Campgrounds are available nearby, off Highway 96 on the Klamath River. Camps are also upstream on the Salmon. Supplies can be obtained in Orleans and Somes Bar. Fishing access is free. Open through February 28, catch-and-release.

Directions: From Sacramento, take I-5 north to Redding and continue 103 miles to the exit for Yreka and Highway 3. Take that exit, turn left at the stop sign, and drive a short distance to Highway 3. Turn left and go 38 miles to Etna. Turn right through town (it becomes Sawyers Bar Road) and go 37 miles to Sawyers Bar (legal fishing starts here) and continue 16 miles to Forks of Salmon. Legal water is from Sawyer's Bar Bridge on downstream on North Fork Salmon, and from the confluence of East Fork at Cecilville on downstream on South Fork Salmon.

Lodging: Motel Etna, 317 Collier Way, Etna, CA 96027, 530/467-5338; Six Rivers National Forest, Orleans Ranger District, 530/627-3291, www.fs.fed.us/r5—click on Forest Offices.

Information and supplies: Somes Bar General Store, 530/469-3350, www.salmon riveroutpost.com; Orleans Market, 530/627-3326.

Guide: Klamath River Outfitters, 800/748-3735, www.klamathriveroutfitters.com.

3 KLAMATH RIVER

Rating: 8
near Orleans in Six Rivers National Forest
Map 2.1, page 119

The Klamath is one place where nature's artwork often seems perfect. This river tumbles around boulders and into gorges, and then flattens into slicks. From start to finish, the Klamath is framed by a high, tree-lined canyon rim and an azure sky.

Abundant wildlife and easy access to prime fishing spots make the central Klamath one of California's best fishing rivers. The steelhead start arriving in August and keep on arriving all the way through April, although the peak period is from mid-September through early November. The Klamath has one of the longest steelhead runs in America: it spans nine months and is ideal for shoreliners or guides with drift boats and jet boats.

The best bites occur in the fall, before the water temperature drops below 46°F. The steelhead and the half-pounders (juvenile steelhead in the 12- to 18-inch class) are most active when the water temperature is 52–58°F;

they strike flies, Glo Bugs, Brindlebugs, Silver Hiltons, and night crawlers. When the water temperature drops below 46°F, the steelhead stop hitting flies, and their grabs on night crawlers become a lot more subtle.

A key to the mid-Klamath's appeal consists of its many premium shoreline fishing spots. All you have to do is cruise Highway 96; when you spot heads of riffles, tail-outs, and deep bends, stop and make a few casts. In a day of hitting and moving, you can fish almost as many spots as if you were using a drift boat. Many pullouts along Highway 96 (a winding, two-lane road) connect to short trails that lead down to the river. My favorite spots are at the mouth of the Shasta River, the mouth of the Scott River, along a five-mile stretch through Seiad Valley just upstream from the town of Happy Camp, and from T Bar on downstream to Somes Bar.

This area is the heart of steelhead fishing on the Klamath River in October, November, and December. Expect there to be good numbers of steelhead in this stretch of river. Access is excellent.

Because the Klamath has a tendency to muddy up quickly during a winter storm, not many people target it for late winter steelhead fishing. However, when the weather holds off, some of the best winter steelhead fishing can occur in this section of the Klamath.

Steelhead on the Klamath are not as large as those on the Smith River, but they are available in good numbers. Klamath steelhead are generally in the two- to six-pound class. The average fish is about 20–21 inches. On a good day you might catch a dozen half-pounders, with a possible pair of three- to four-pounders in the mix and a chance at one bigger, perhaps weighing five or six pounds.

A lot of anglers do not realize that the steelhead hold in different areas on the Klamath according to time of day.

Even though the Klamath's clarity is typically poor, which helps hide anglers, the bite can shut off during midday if bright sunlight and hot weather are present. Under such conditions, it is vital to fish in shaded areas and be on the water at both dawn and dusk.

One trick I learned from guide Dale Lackey was never to fish an area where the fish are looking upstream into the sun. The fish simply will not hold in large numbers in these areas, and the few that do tend not to bite. Yet these same riffles can hold large numbers of fish at dawn or dusk. One of my favorite techniques here is to fish not only the riffles and tail-outs that look like good steelhead water, but also the shoreline edges—always on the shaded side of the river and avoiding water where there is direct sunlight.

One year I rafted the entire river (at flood stage), from its headwaters in Oregon all the way to the Pacific Ocean. This waterway is vibrant with life, not only fish, but many species of birds and other wildlife.

Facilities, fees: Several Forest Service campgrounds are along Highway 96. Lodging is available at Sandy Bar Ranch in Orleans, 530/627-3379. Supplies can be obtained in the towns of Klamath River, Weitchpec, Somes Bar, Happy Camp, Seiad Valley, Horse Creek, and Orleans. Fishing access is free.

Directions: From Eureka, drive north on U.S. 101 past Arcata to Highway 299. Turn east on Highway 299 and drive 42 miles to Highway 96. Turn left (north) and drive 40 miles to the town of Orleans. Continue northeast on Highway 96, which runs parallel to the river. Direct river access is available off turnouts along Highway 96, as well as from short spur roads that lead to the river.

Contact: Six Rivers National Forest, Orleans Ranger District, 530/627-3291, www.fs.fed .us/r5—click on Forest Offices.

Information: Somes Bar General Store, 530/469-3350, www.salmonriveroutpost.com.

Guides: Wally Johnson, Seiad Valley, 530/496-3291, www.steelheadguides.com; J&J Guide Service, 530/222-6253; Klamath River Outfitters, 800/748-3735, www.klamath riveroutfitters.com; Three Rivers Guide Service, 530/925-7990, www.threeriversguide service.com.

4 FISH LAKE

Rating: 5

southwest of Orleans in
Six Rivers National Forest
Map 2.1, page 119

In many ways, this lake provides the ideal summer camping/fishing destination. It is just far enough out of the way that most people miss it, but it isn't that difficult to reach.

Fish Lake is quite pretty, set in the woods and with a Forest Service road encircling it. The lakeside camp is practically a cast's distance from the water. The lake usually provides its best fishing in June, when the weather is just starting to warm up from a long winter, but the water is still cold.

Fish Lake is well suited to anglers who like to fish from a pram, raft, or float tube, because motors are not allowed on the lake. Since almost everybody sticks to the shoreline, they are limited to spots where the vegetation is broken and the lake is accessible. With a small raft or something similar, you can explore the entire lake quite easily.

Note that this is classic Bigfoot country, set near the mouth of Bluff Creek, where one of the most famous pieces of Bigfoot footage was taken. However, I always thought the Sasquatch had a zipper running down his back.

Facilities, fees: A concrete boat ramp is available. There are 10 sites for tents and 14 sites for tents or RVs up to 35 feet long. Picnic tables and fire grills are provided. Drinking water, vault toilets, and a camp host are available. Leashed pets are permitted. Fishing access is free.

Directions: From Sacramento, take I-5 north to Redding and the exit for Highway 299 West. Take that exit and drive west on Highway 299 Willow Creek and Highway 96. Turn north (right) on Highway 96 and drive to Weitchpec, and continue seven miles to Fish Lake Road. Turn left on Fish Lake Road and drive five miles (stay to the right at the Y) to Fish Lake.

Contact: Six Rivers National Forest, Orleans Ranger District, 530/627-3291, www.fs.fed.us/r5—click on Forest Offices; Early Bird Market, Willow Creek, 530/629-4431.

5 SIX RIVERS NATIONAL FOREST

Rating: 4

northeast of Eureka (off Highway 96)
Map 2.1, page 119

This portion of the national forest does not contain a large number of lakes and it does not receive much pressure from hike-in anglers.

Six Rivers' best fishing prospects can be found at Lower Mill Creek Lake, east of Hoopa, near north Trinity Mountain. This lake is stocked from an airplane each spring with 1,000 small rainbow trout.

The national forest encompasses myriad small streams, all of which eventually feed into some of California's wildest rivers. It seems as if a small creek flows through the wedge at the bottom of every canyon. These streams are among the features that make this area popular with a handful of backpackers. In terms of trout fishing, however, you'll find pretty slim pickings.

Facilities, fees: Nine campgrounds with drinking water, fire rings, vault toilets, and garbage service are available. Fishing access is free.

Directions: From Eureka, take U.S. 101 north for 10 miles to Highway 299. Turn east on Highway 299 and drive to Willow Creek. Turn north on Highway 96 and drive to Hoopa Valley.

From Redding, drive west on Highway 299 to Willow Creek and the junction with Highway 96. Turn right (north) on Highway 96 to Hoopa Valley.

Fishing access is available off roads that intersect Highway 96 in Hoopa Valley and lead east to Trinity Mountain. A Forest Service map is required.

Contact: Six Rivers National Forest, 707/442-1721, www.fs.fed.us/r5—click on Forest Offices.

6 IRON GATE RESERVOIR/ COPCO LAKE

Rating: 7

near Yreka and Klamath National Forest

Map 2.2, page 120   BEST ◖

If you want loads of fish, you'll love Iron Gate Reservoir and Copco Lake, which have trout, crappie, bass, and channel cat. If you simply want big fish, you'll hate 'em; except for the rare large bass or catfish, you tend to get small fish here. People, especially kids, generally love to catch lots of anything, however, so they learn to appreciate these lakes.

Iron Gate is downstream of Copco and is faster to reach from I-5. It has developed into a good bass lake for know-hows. Iron Gate not only provides good catch rates for bass from March through June, but if you stick with it, you will eventually hook a 3- to 5-pounder. It is one of the most improved fisheries in the north state.

Copco is the upper lake. It is loaded with yellow perch, the smallish fellows that often turn uninspired kids into enthusiastic lifelong anglers. Because there are so many yellow perch here, they are not subject to a catch limit. These fish go on an excellent bite every summer. All you need are warm water and a few tips. Yellow perch are only about five to seven inches in length and they fight like a tug-of-war between Goldie Hawn and Arnold Schwarzenegger, but they taste as good as any other fish, so let the kids catch them.

Talk about easy: use a little piece of red yarn on a hook, a small piece of red worm on a hook, or a little red lure. If you decide to use yarn or a piece of worm, just plunk it out in front of you. The pier next to Copco Lake's boat ramp is the best spot for this kind of fishing. I also suggest getting out a little farther in a small raft or boat. If you use a lure, jig it straight up and down. Test different depths; when you get a strike, start filling your stringer. No kidding. After a few hours of a good bite, you will wish you hadn't kept them all. It's common to catch 30 or 35 of the little buggers. On a summer day, a person can literally catch a hundred yellow perch. You'll get home and spend a couple hours cleaning them all.

If you have never experienced this kind of success or believe you are jinxed, consider making a trip here.

The dams at both Iron Gate and Copco Lakes block the migration of salmon and have led to poor water quality in the Klamath River. In one plan, both dams would be removed, the lakes eliminated and the canyon returned to Klamath River. In an attempt to placate anglers, Pacific Power has developed several fishing access and recreation sites at both lakes. At Iron Gate, ramps are available at Fall Creek Park, Mirror Cove Camp, and Long Gulch Park. Piers or docks are offered at Wanaka Spring Park, Camp Creek, and Mirror Cove Camp.

Upstream at Copco Lake, Mallard Cove and Copco Cove boat ramps and picnic areas · are available.

Facilities, fees: Three boat launches, four campgrounds, and three picnic areas are available at Iron Gate Reservoir. There are two boat launches and two picnic areas at adjoining Copco Lake. Fishing access is free.

Directions to Iron Gate: From Redding, drive north on I-5 to Yreka and continue past the Klamathon Bridge and to the exit for Henley/Hornbrook. Take that exit, turn east, and drive 1.5 miles through Henley to Hornbrook and Roy Jones Road. Turn right and continue (it becomes Copco Road) along the Klamath River to the Iron Gate Dam. Bear left (still on Copco Road) and drive 3–4 miles to turnoffs on the right to the boat ramps and Iron Gate Reservoir.

Directions to Copco Lake: From Redding, drive north on I-5 to the exit for Grenada. Take that exit, turn right on County Road A12, and drive 0.5 mile to Montague–Grenada Road. Turn left and drive north, through Montague (the road becomes Montague–Ager Road) and continue to Ager–Beswick Road. Turn right and drive (curving at times) to a fork at Copco Lake. Turn right and drive a short distance to a boat ramp on the left. To get to the best fishing spot, turn right at the fork and drive two miles to Copco Road. Turn left and drive to a boat ramp adjacent to the dam at the west end of the lake.

Contact: Pacific Power, www.pacificorp.com/about/or/california, 503/813-6666.

Information and supplies: Hornbrook Chevron, 530/475-3448.

7 JUANITA LAKE

Rating: 4

near Macdoel in Klamath National Forest
Map 2.2, page 120

This lake is overlooked by many Californians who hunger for exactly the kind of fishing experience it offers: Juanita is small, out-of-the-way, reachable by car, and set at 5,100 feet in a little-known area of Klamath National Forest. It provides lakeside camping and decent trout fishing, as well as an opportunity in summer months for bass and catfish. Few folks know about this spot or about the hundreds of similar lakes in California's more remote areas.

The Department of Fish and Game stocks Juanita Lake with fingerling rainbow trout. The water isn't exactly plugged with fish, but the DFG does plant trout here—a plant that provides the lake's few visitors with fair prospects. Fish and Game also stocks Juanita with brown trout in the six- to eight-inch class. If you want sizzle, you're in the wrong place. But if you're looking for a quiet campsite along a lake and a chance to catch some brook trout, the shoe just might fit. Juanita Lake has had a problem with golden shiners; perhaps the bass will help keep them under control. A bonus here is a paved route around the lake that is wheelchair-accessible. It is about 1.25 miles long.

Facilities, fees: There are 12 tent sites, 11 sites for RVs up to 32 feet, and a group site that can accommodate 50 people. Picnic tables and fire grills are provided. Drinking water and vault toilets are available. Boating is allowed, but no motorboats are permitted on the lake. Many facilities are wheelchair-accessible. Leashed pets are permitted.

Directions: From Redding, drive north on I-5 to Weed. Take the Central Weed/Highway 97 exit. Turn right at the stop sign and drive one mile through town to Highway 97. Bear right on Highway 97 and drive 37 miles to Ball Mountain Road (if you pass the Goosenest Ranger Station, you have gone too far). Turn left on Ball Mountain Road and drive 2.5 miles to a fork with Forest Road 46N04/Juanita Lake Road. Bear right at the fork (Juanita Lake access road) and drive three miles to the lake.

Contact: Klamath National Forest, Goosenest Ranger District, 530/398-4391, www.fs.fed.us/r5—click on Forest Offices.

8 UPPER KLAMATH RIVER

Rating: 9

near Yreka in Klamath National Forest
Map 2.2, page 120

The uppermost stretches often provide some of this river's best winter steelhead prospects. From November through February, thousands of steelhead swim in the river's pockets from Iron Gate Dam on downstream, under the I-5 bridge, to Tree of Heaven Campground. Salmon arrive in October; when a good school moves in, this stretch of water is frequently loaded with drift boats:

There's one catch: you need a boat to fish properly here, because shoreline access is quite poor. I suggest hiring a guide for a trip down the river. Let the guide hold the oars while you hold the rod; drift a night crawler or a Hot Shot lure in the downstream current. Over the course of a morning, you might get 10 or 15 strikes. Even if you think you are hexed with a cataclysmic jinx, you are bound to luck into a few fish.

Alternatively, you can wade into the river where it pours into the Klamath, which is just a few miles west of I-5 via Highway 96. The water can be cold, especially in mid-December, when the ice will freeze in your line guides; this is the time, however, when the fish arrive. Because of the low winter water temperatures, you don't need to be on the river early. In fact, during colder periods, fish often refuse to bite until the sun warms the surface waters by a degree or two.

Guide Ron Denardi finds the top action back-trolling with crawdad crankbaits and Wee Warts and fly-fishing with leech pattern flies and casting spinners. These are strong, bright fish, many weighing 2–5 pounds.

Facilities, fees: A gravel boat launch is just downstream of Iron Gate Reservoir. From I-5, take the Henley–Hornbrook exit. Turn east on Copco Road and drive seven miles to the ramp. Several campgrounds can be found along the river; Tree of Heaven, on Highway 96 about five miles west of I-5, is a good choice. Fishing access is free.

Directions: From Redding, drive north on I-5 to Yreka and continue past the Klamathon Bridge and to the exit for Henley/Hornbrook. Take that exit, turn east, and drive 1.5 miles through Henley to Hornbrook and Roy Jones Road. Turn right and continue (it becomes Copco Road) along the Klamath River to the Iron Gate Dam. A boat launch area is on the right.

For shore-fishing access: From Redding, drive north on I-5 to Yreka and continue to the Klamathon Bridge and Highway 96. Take that exit. Fishing access is available along the river upstream of the Klamathon Bridge. Or turn west on Highway 96. Fishing access is available along Highway 96 seven miles at Tree of Heaven Campground.

Contact: Pacific Power, www.pacificorp.com/about/or/california, 503/813-6666; Klamath River RV Park, 707/482-2091, www.klamathriverrv.com; Hornbrook Chevron, 530/475-3448; Quigley's General Store, Klamath River, 530/465-2224.

Guides: Jack Trout Guide Service, 530/926-4540, www.jacktrout.com or www.mtshasta

.com; Wally Johnson, Seiad Valley, 530/496-3291, www.steelheadguides.com; J&J Guide Service, 530/222-6253; Three Rivers Guide Service, 530/925-7990, www.threeriversguideservice.com.

9 LAKE SHASTINA

Rating: 5

near Weed and Klamath National Forest

Map 2.2, page 120

Most people don't know this, but Lake Shastina is a decent bass lake in foothills of the mountain country of Mount Shasta. What? A bass lake in the mountains of Northern California? Is this possible? Yes, yes, and yes.

As spring turns to summer, you'll find bass at Lake Shastina. People often catch bass here in the 12- to 15-inch range, sometimes even larger. The first time you hook a big one, you'll swear you have a big trout, but you don't. It's a bass, the kind of fish that makes this place special.

Lake Shastina's view is attractive, too. The lake is set on the northern slopes of Mount Shasta, the giant volcano that rises like a diamond out of a field of coal. Because of the lake's proximity to the mountain, however, spring weather can be cold and windy. There are times it can be blowing 25 mph at Shastina, and yet it can be calm just over the Black Butte Summit at Lake Siskiyou. It's vital to track the weather up here. During the first five-day binge of warm weather, it's time to hit Shastina and fish for those bass. Shastina is also good in spring and early summer for trout, and in late summer for catfish. The lake also contains some redear sunfish and bluegill.

The lake occasionally provides good trolling for trout, including a chance at brown trout in the five-pound class. The best bet for trout is trolling Needlefish in the river channel at the upper end of the lake in April.

Shastina is one of the few lakes in California offering lakeside housing, including several small developments. Local weather is generally cold in winter and windy in spring; these conditions keep housing prices quite low compared to rates on other vacation lakes. Lake levels can also shrink in midsummer, when Shastina's water is sent via the Shasta River to the valley to the north, to promote hay growth. During some years, locals call the lake "River Shastina," because it reaches such low levels before the rains come. But they're just joking. They hope to scare people off so nobody else will find out about the big crappie.

Facilities, fees: A boat launch is provided, along with a primitive campground with chemical toilets. There is no drinking water. Supplies can be obtained in Weed. Fishing access is free.

Directions: From Redding, take I-5 north to Weed and continue three miles to the Edgewood exit. Take that exit to the stop sign, bear right (north) on Edgewood Road, and drive through Edgewood (slow when passing the elementary school) for two miles to Jackson Ranch Road. Turn right and drive about four miles to Emerald Isle Road/Lake Shastina on the left. Turn left and drive two miles to the lake and a T junction. Turn right and drive a short distance to a boat ramp.

Contact: Siskiyou County Visitors Bureau, www.visitsiskiyou.org.

Lodging: Lake Shastina Golf Resort, 800/358-4653, www.lakeshastinagolf.com.

10 TAYLOR LAKE

Rating: 7

southwest of the town of Etna
in the Russian Wilderness
Map 2.2, page 120

If you want a wilderness experience without the grunt of a serious overnight hike, you've come to the right place. The fishing is good here, too. Rainbow trout and, more rarely, brown trout are eager to take a fly or a Panther Martin spinner during the evening rise.

Because this lake is set just a quarter-mile inside the wilderness boundary, many people who spot it on a map mistakenly believe it is very difficult to reach. It isn't. The walk to Taylor Lake is a short stroll. None of the lakes in the Russian Wilderness are very large, but this ranks as one of the biggest. It is shaped like a kidney bean, and an outlet creek is set along the access trail.

This lake provides an ideal setting and conditions (a remote area, a short hike, and good trout fishing) for many people on their first overnight trip in a wild area.

Facilities, fees: A primitive campground is provided, but there are no facilities. There is a wheelchair-accessible path to the lake. Fishing access is free.

Directions: From Redding, take I-5 north to Yreka and the exit for Highway 3/Fort Jones. Take that exit to the stop sign, turn left, and drive a short distance to the stoplight and Highway 3. Turn left and drive 28 miles to Etna and Main Street. Bear right and take Main Street through Etna and drive 10.25 miles (it becomes Somes Bar Road) over Etna Summit to Forest Road 41N18 (signed for Taylor Lake). Turn left and continue to the parking area. Park and walk a short distance to the lake. The trail is wheelchair-accessible.

Contact: Klamath National Forest, Salmon and Scott River Ranger District, 11263 North Highway 3, Fort Jones, CA 96032-9702, 530/468-5351, www.fs.fed.us/r5—click on Forest Offices.

11 RUSSIAN WILDERNESS

Rating: 6

northwest of Weaverville near
Klamath National Forest
Map 2.2, page 120

Have you ever known a place that's so pristine, yet so small that it can't handle many visitors at a time? The Russian Wilderness falls into this category. If you go, please walk softly, take only pictures, and leave only footprints.

The Russian is the smallest wilderness in

California's Forest Service system. It is only about two miles wide and six miles long, and it is best known for encompassing a prime stretch of the Pacific Crest Trail (PCT). The ambitious and skilled mountaineer can take off from the PCT and visit lakes that attract few visitors. But then again, the area can bear few people.

Like so many wilderness areas, the lakes that are the easiest to reach are naturally the ones to get the highest number of backpackers and fishing pressure—and in turn, it can be difficult to catch fish at such places. In the Russian Wilderness, the more difficult lakes to reach can provide outstanding fishing, especially for good-sized brook trout.

Big Blue Lake is a good example. Reaching this lake is a fairly rough task, but individuals able to read contour maps and the lay of the land can succeed. A campsite is available near the outlet of the lake, and fishing during the evening rise is quite good. I once saw a 20-incher slurping bugs on the surface, so I crept up and delivered a perfect cast, but a 4-inch dinker grabbed the lure before the big guy had a chance.

There are several good lakes to fish in the area, although some, as I said, are not accessible by trail. The best are Big Blue Lake, Paynes Lake, and Big Duck Lake.

Facilities, fees: No facilities are available. Fishing access is free.

Directions to PCT Trailhead/Etna Summit: From Redding, take I-5 north to Yreka and the exit for Highway 3/Fort Jones. Take that exit to the stop sign, turn left, and drive a short distance to the stoplight and Highway 3. Turn left and drive 28 miles to Etna and Main Street. Bear right and take Main Street through Etna and drive eight miles (it becomes Somes Bar Road) to Etna Summit. Parking and trailhead are on the left.

Directions to PCT/Russian Peak area Trailhead: From Redding, take I-5 north to Weed and continue five miles to the Edgewood exit. Take that exit to the stop sign. Turn left and drive through the underpass to another stop sign with Old Highway 99. Turn right and

drive six miles to Gazelle. Turn left at Gazelle on Gazelle–Callahan Road and drive about 20 miles to the junction with Highway 3. Continue straight and drive through Callahan to Cecilville Road (County Road 402). Turn left and drive about 12 miles to the signed turnoff to the PCT trailhead. Turn right and drive to the end of the road (high-clearance vehicle recommended) to the PCT trailhead.

Contact: Klamath National Forest, Salmon and Scott River Ranger District, 11263 North Highway 3, Fort Jones, CA 96032-9702, 530/468-5351, www.fs.fed.us/r5—click on Forest Offices.

12 KANGAROO LAKE

Rating: 7

near Callahan in Klamath National Forest

Map 2.2, page 120

Nestled in the Scott Mountains at 6,050 feet, little Kangaroo Lake is the perfect hideaway for campers and anglers who want to get away from it all. The road in is quite pretty, especially below Scott Mountain, in the pristine, unpeopled valleys. This small (25 acres) but deep (100 feet) alpine water is situated in a mountain bowl. The campsites are reached via a short walk from the parking area, and the lake is just a few minutes from the campground. There's good shoreline fishing for large brook trout and decent-sized rainbow trout. No motors are allowed in the lake, so it can be ideal for a kayak, canoe, pram, or other hand-carried boat.

The fishing is good here. Kangaroo is one of the few lakes in the region that the Department of Fish and Game stocks with yearlings as well as fingerlings. The prime attraction is the brook trout, averaging 12–14 inches, which can be caught from the shore. Rainbow trout provide a steady fishery as well.

Of all lakes in the Scott Mountains, Kangaroo is my favorite, providing good camping, good hiking, and best of all, often excellent fishing. It is an ideal lake for a float tube, a rubber raft, or even for a youngster fishing from shore with Power Bait. Another plus is that visitors can access a trailhead for the Pacific Crest Trail.

Facilities, fees: There are 18 campsites at the lake. Picnic tables and fire grills are provided. Drinking water and vault toilets are available. Some facilities are wheelchair-accessible, including a nearby fishing pier. Supplies can be obtained in Callahan. Fishing access is free. There is a fee for camping.

Directions: From Redding, drive north on I-5 just past Weed and take the Edgewood turnoff. At the stop sign, turn left and drive a short distance to the stop sign at Old Stage Road. Turn right on Old Stage Road and drive six miles to Gazelle. In Gazelle, turn left at Gazelle–Callahan Road and drive over the summit. From the summit, continue about five miles to Rail Creek Road. Turn left at Rail Creek Road and drive approximately five miles to where the road dead-ends at Kangaroo Lake Walk-In.

Contact: Klamath National Forest, Scott and Salmon River Ranger District, 530/468-5351, www.fs.fed.us/r5—click on Forest Offices; Siskiyou County Visitors Bureau, www.visit siskiyou.org.

13 PICAYUNE LAKE

Rating: 5

near Mount Shasta
Map 2.2, page 120

Of all the pretty lakes in the Trinity Divide country, this is one of the prettiest. Picayune, which is almost always full, is lined by firs, pines, and cedars and is bordered on the western side by a steep face. The surrounding land is owned by the Roseburg Lumber Company, not the U.S. Forest Service, and that's where the controversy starts.

Some at Roseburg will tell you that access to the lake is prohibited, and then they point to the locked pipe gate on the access road, and their private cabin on the lake. But I've been told that that's just to discourage access. Walk-in access is okay; it's about a half-mile hike to reach the lake. That keeps the numbers to about zero. Camping is prohibited. Roseburg constructed a cabin and a dock at the lake, but they are strictly off-limits to visitors.

The truth is that the fishing at Gumboot Lake, which you pass on the way in, is better, even if it isn't planted anymore. So few have reason to venture on to Picayune.

Facilities, fees: There are no on-site facilities. You can camp nearby at Gumboot Lake. Supplies can be obtained in Mount Shasta. Fishing access is free.

Directions: From Redding, take I-5 north to the town of Mount Shasta and the exit for Central Mount Shasta. Take that exit and drive to the stop sign. Turn left and continue a short distance to Old Stage Road. Turn left and drive 0.25 mile to a Y at W. A. Barr Road. Bear right on W. A. Barr Road and drive past Box Canyon Dam and the Lake Siskiyou Campground entrance. Continue 10 miles to a fork with Gumboot Lake. Stay right at the fork (left goes to Gumboot) and continue one mile to Bear Creek Road/Forest Road 40N45. Turn right and drive along the ridge (the lake will be below you to the left) for one mile to an unsigned junction. Turn left and drive to the gate. Park and hike the last 0.5 mile to the lake.

Contact: Shasta-Trinity National Forest, Mount Shasta Ranger District, 530/926-4511, www.fs.fed.us/r5—click on Forest Offices.

14 GUMBOOT LAKE

Rating: 8

near Mount Shasta in
Shasta-Trinity National Forest
Map 2.2, page 120

Gumboot is quite pretty, bordered by a meadow and a steep face on the far side and well treed on the other. It also provides good trout fishing, best from a float tube, canoe, pram, or raft (motors are neither permitted nor needed), or from the shoreline using a fly-and-bubble combination. Fly fishers can have sensational evening bites here, using sink-tip lines, black leech, and strip retrieve.

The key here is water temperature. In the summer, when the water temperature is warmest, you must fish the shaded parts of the lake. But in the fall, when the water is cooler, you must fish the areas that get sun.

The lake is so small it doesn't need sizable trout stocks to provide good fishing—and when you hook 12- and 13-inchers instead of those little Sierra slim-jims, things can get quite exciting.

A lot of local folks have discovered this, and Gumboot has been getting increased fishing pressure in recent years. On most summer and fall weekends, there are as many as a dozen rods on this little lake, and the campsites are usually filled. Several outstanding hikes are available in the area. Many will trek 10 minutes through forest to find Upper Gumboot Lake, which is not much more than a pond with small trout. My favorite hike here is to scramble up the mountain behind the Upper Gumboot to the ridgeline, hit the Pacific Crest Trail, then turn left and claim the peak that is just above the lake. This is a great vantage point with stellar views of Mount Shasta and provides quite an afternoon adventure as you wait for the evening bite.

Note: As part of the settlement to the Citizens of Biological Diversity lawsuit, the DFG stopped planting in Gumboot—even though the Diversity folks have never even been to this lake. (I know because I asked them.)

Facilities, fees: A few primitive campsites with vault toilets are available, but there is no drinking water. Motorized boats are not permitted on the lake. Fishing access is free.

Directions: From Redding, take I-5 north to the town of Mount Shasta and the exit for Central Mount Shasta. Take that exit and drive to the stop sign. Turn left and continue a short distance to Old Stage Road. Turn left and drive 0.25 mile to a Y at W. A. Barr Road. Bear right on W. A. Barr Road and drive past Box Canyon Dam and the Lake Siskiyou

Campground entrance. Continue 10 miles to a fork with Gumboot Lake. Bear left and drive 0.5 mile to the lake.

Contact: Shasta-Trinity National Forest, Mount Shasta Ranger District, 530/926-4511, www.fs.fed.us/r5—click on Forest Offices; Siskiyou County Visitors Bureau, www.visit siskiyou.org; Sportsmen's Den, Mount Shasta, 530/926-2295, www.mtshastasports.com.

Guides: Jack Trout Guide Service, 530/926-4540, www.jacktrout.com or www.mtshasta .com.

15 TOAD LAKE

Rating: 5

near Mount Shasta in
Shasta-Trinity National Forest

Map 2.2, page 120

You'll get just about everything at this classic fishing spot. Everything, that is, except good-sized trout.

A lot of people steer clear of Toad Lake because the access road is rough, particularly a terribly bumpy spot about a half mile from the parking area. That's a plus. And it's a pretty lake, set in a rock bowl carved by glacial action and filled each spring by snowmelt. Another plus.

It is excellent for swimming, another plus. And hiking? A half-hour hike will take you above the rock bowl and onto the Pacific Crest Trail, and in another 15 minutes you'll arrive at Porcupine Lake (stocked with fingerling rainbow trout), which has an absolutely pristine setting. If you're looking for a mountain to climb, a six-mile grunt will get you to the top of Mount Eddy (9,025 feet), the highest mountain in the local range, for an eye-popping view of Mount Shasta.

Add that up and put it in your mental cash register: Right, quite a place. And Toad Lake is ideal for camping, provided you don't mind carrying your gear on the 10-minute walk to the lake.

If only the trout were bigger?... If only...

well, you can dream. People swear that now and again somebody actually catches one that is longer than six or seven inches. However, I have yet to see such a catch here with my own eyes.

Facilities, fees: There are six walk-in campsites available with vault toilets, but there is no drinking water. Garbage must be packed out. Supplies can be obtained in Mount Shasta. Fishing access is free.

Directions: From Redding, take I-5 north to the town of Mount Shasta and the exit for Central Mount Shasta. Take that exit and drive to the stop sign. Turn left and continue a short distance to Old Stage Road. Turn left and drive 0.25 mile to a Y at W. A. Barr Road. Bear right on W. A. Barr Road and drive past Box Canyon Dam and the Lake Siskiyou Campground entrance. Continue up the mountain (the road becomes Forest Road 26) and continue just past a concrete bridge to Forest Road 41N53. Turn right and drive 0.2 mile to a fork with Forest Road 40N64. Bear left at the fork (paved road) and drive for 11 miles to the parking area. At times, the road is extremely bumpy and twisty, turns to dirt, and the final 0.5 mile to the trailhead is rocky and rough. High-clearance, four-wheel-drive vehicles are recommended. From the trailhead, walk in about 0.5 mile to the lake and campsites.

Contact: Shasta-Trinity National Forest, Mount Shasta Ranger District, 530/926-4511, www.fs.fed.us/r5—click on Forest Offices; Siskiyou County Visitors Bureau, www.visit siskiyou.org; Sportsmen's Den, Mount Shasta, 530/926-2295, www.mtshastasports.com.

16 SHASTA-TRINITY NATIONAL FOREST

Rating: 8

near Mount Shasta

Map 2.2, page 120

This must be God's country, because nobody else could be clever enough to have created it. You get miles of wild land, good access via Forest Service roads, and dozens of lakes that are accessible on short hikes. The Department of Fish and Game stocks the lakes with fingerlings, which stand a decent chance of reaching the pan-size range. For people who don't feel like hiking to the ends of the earth, Shasta-Trinity National Forest makes the ideal fishing/camping destination.

The forestland covers a large amount of land, so the first step is to get a Forest Service map, pinpoint the lakes on the following list, and start planning your trip.

The following hike-in lakes provide the best fishing around: Bluff Lake, Bull Lake, Cabin Meadow Lake, Caldwell Lakes, Cliff Lake, Crater Lakes, Deadfall Lakes, Devil's Lake, Dobkins Lake, Echo Lake/the Seven Lakes Basin, Gray Rock Lake, Grouse Lake, Helen Lake, Highland Lake, Horseshoe Lake, Little Castle Lake, Lost Lake, Masterson Meadow Lake, Mumbo Lake, Rock Fence Lake, Scott Lake, Slide Lake, Terrace Lake, Timber Lake, Twin Lakes, and West Park Lakes.

Yes, that's quite a lot of choices. The best advice for newcomers is to pick the largest lakes possible, then head to some of the smaller nearby lakes on side trips.

Because many of these lakes require a hike of an hour or less, they attract a lot of locals on weekends. So if you're planning a multi-day camping trip, it's a good idea to hit those easier-to-access lakes during the week; if you'll be there on a weekend, pick a destination that requires a little more effort to reach. You see, there is a lesson to be learned here: the harder a lake is to reach, the fewer the people who will go there. Ultimately, that translates to better fishing.

Facilities, fees: Campgrounds are provided throughout the forest; a few primitive campsites are available at higher elevations. Fishing access is free.

Directions: Access roads for Shasta-Trinity National Forest are off I-5, Highway 89, and Highway 299. Several good fishing lakes are found off the roads that junction with W. A. Barr Road (west of Mount Shasta, off the

Central Mount Shasta exit on I-5). A Forest Service map is a necessity.

Contact: Shasta-Trinity National Forest, 530/226-2500, www.fs.fed.us/r5—click on Forest Offices.

Supplies: Sportsmen's Den, Mount Shasta, 530/926-2295, www.mtshastasports.com.

Guide: Jack Trout Guide Service, 530/926-4540, www.jacktrout.com.

17 LAKE SISKIYOU

Rating: 7

near Mount Shasta in
Shasta-Trinity National Forest
Map 2.2, page 120   **BEST (**

Indian legend has it that Mount Shasta was created when the Great Spirit poked a hole in the sky and made a tepee out of the fallen pieces. Some of the fish in nearby Lake Siskiyou are so big that they could have been created in a similarly spectacular fashion.

A true jewel, this lake sits at the base of giant Mount Shasta, which towers above at 14,162 feet, creating one of the prettiest settings for an artificial lake anywhere in the United States. It was created for the sole purpose of recreation—not to store water for farmers—so while reservoirs in the California foothills get drained, Siskiyou remains full. Lake Siskiyou covers 435 acres and is at an elevation of 3,181 feet. In the summer months the lake gets a lot of traffic from RVers, sunbathers, and anglers.

This is known primarily as a trout lake, but the best fishing is for smallmouth bass. They aren't big, typically about 8–13 inches, but they bite great during the evening bite in shaded areas. Use a 1/4-ounce darthead jig with a salt-and-pepper Fat Albert grub. The swimming cove at Wagon Creek is a great spot on early summer evenings, even when kids are jumping into the lake at the rope swing.

The standard fare is trolling for trout. Fish and Game stocks Siskiyou with rainbow trout in the 10- to 12-inch class, brook trout, and brown trout in the six- to eight-inch class.

But there are some surprises along the way. At times, DFG plants as many as 5,000 brood-stock brown trout, along with catchable brook trout, Eagle Lake trout, rainbow trout, and as many as 250,000 fingerlings.

Many techniques work here. Many people do just fine trolling a night crawler behind flashers and are quite content doing that. But you can also have success by fly-fishing, trolling lures, casting deep-water plugs, or drifting with bait. The trout bite is best during the evening, along the Wagon Creek arm or on the north shore.

The biggest trout of the year are caught in late spring and again in October. In the summer, it seems all you get are the DFG planters. On a cold, windy day in early spring, I once hooked a monster brown here and could do nothing with it until finally it wrapped the line around a stump and broke off.

Many fishing techniques have been developed specifically for this lake. One method is to use a lure called a Bingo Bug, which can be slow-trolled at dawn during calm water and an insect hatch. Under those conditions it's a great way to catch fish. When the wind comes up, a quarter-ounce Z-Ray, gold with red spots, or a gold Little Cleo is very good.

In the summer, using leadcore line and a Triple Teaser is quite effective, along with the traditional night crawler/flasher combination. Hey, in the summer, I've seen people catch trout by swimming in the middle of the lake next to their boat and using Power Bait 40 feet deep on an unattended rod.

Fly fishers love Lake Siskiyou in late spring and early summer and again in the fall, fishing from float tubes where the South Fork of the Sacramento River enters the lake. Some of the lake's biggest fish can be taken by float tubers at this time. Best fly patterns in the spring include the black leech, woolly bugger (in a variety of colors), and other small streamers. In the fall, dry fly patterns will work whenever a hatch is occurring. At times in October, the caddis hatch can be sensational; it provides some of the best dry fly-fishing of the year.

Facilities, fees: North shore access is limited to day use only; vault toilets are provided. Full facilities are provided at Lake Siskiyou Marina, including a campground, restrooms, showers, coin laundry, RV cabins, a fish-cleaning station, a marina, a boat ramp, a small tackle shop, and a grocery store. Boat rentals are available. Fishing supplies can be obtained in Mount Shasta at Rite-Aid and Sportsmen's Den. Fishing access is free on the north shore. An entrance fee is charged for day use at Lake Siskiyou Camp Resort and Marina.

Directions: From Redding, take I-5 north to the town of Mount Shasta and the exit for Central Mount Shasta. Take that exit and drive to the stop sign. Turn left and continue a short distance to Old Stage Road. Turn left and drive 0.25 mile to a Y at W. A. Barr Road. Bear right on W. A. Barr Road and drive past Box Canyon, then continue for two miles to the entrance road for Lake Siskiyou Camp Resort and Marina. Bear right and drive a short distance to the entrance station.

Contact: Lake Siskiyou Camp Resort and Marina, 530/926-2617, 530/926-2618, or 888/926-2618, www.lakesis.com; Siskiyou County Visitors Bureau, www.visitsiskiyou.org.

18 UPPER SACRAMENTO RIVER

Rating: 9
near Mount Shasta, upstream of Shasta Lake
Map 2.2, page 120

The river here has experienced the Genesis effect, rebounding from the worst inland toxic spill in California history in 1991 to become a flourishing habitat. I was on the scene and broke the story of how a Southern Pacific freighter derailed and dumped a tanker wheels-up into the river, spilling 19,000 gallons of an all-purpose herbicide. A spill-proof bridge has been built, and the aquatic food chain continues to build, along with the opportunity for a once-great trout stream to reclaim itself.

The river is full of fish. In 2011, the fish were the biggest I'd seen in 25 years—25–200 trout per pool, including at least a pair of 18–20-inchers, and in the lower river, from Sims to Delta, some five-pounders. The key is that the lower levels of the aquatic food chain, from algae to insects, have reestablished themselves, creating a high carrying capacity for the habitat. Just like that, survival rates of newly born trout skyrocketed.

The fishing can be good in many different stretches of river. What makes it work is that the Upper Sacramento River is among the most easily accessed trout streams in the western United States. It flows south from the dam at Lake Siskiyou (near Mount Shasta) for 40 miles to Shasta Lake. With I-5 running alongside, you'll find dozens of side roads that provide excellent fishing access. In addition, the trout season is open year-round.

For most of the summer, the best fly-fishing technique is nymphing in pocket water. Come the cool weather of October, one of the most dramatic caddis hatches in California occurs for about an hour each evening, from about 5:30–6:30 P.M. There are so many caddis that at times you can be reluctant to take a deep breath for fear of choking to death.

The Department of Fish and Game stocks the river from the town of Dunsmuir on downstream about five miles. The stocking boundary is from Scarlett Bridge in north Dunsmuir downstream to Sweetbriar Bridge just downstream of Castle Crags State Park. The plants are extremely popular in the town of Dunsmuir itself, with many access points right in town. There are plenty of signed access points to the river, but there are several other excellent spots.

The most inaccessible portion of the river is from Cantara Loop on downstream to north Dunsmuir. Those who explore this section of river—hiking on the railroad tracks (beware of trains!) and then wading their way for access—will find some of the best fishing here. You can also discover the remains of historic sites, such as the old resort of Shasta Springs.

One beautiful spot is Mossbrae Falls, where an underwater spring flows right out of the cliff, creating a veil effect. It's one of the prettiest places on the entire river, and you might even catch a fish there, too. Access is sometimes cut off to the falls area because you have to walk along railroad tracks to get there.

Upstream of Dunsmuir, from the Cantara Bridge to Box Canyon (accessible off Old Stage Road), a catch-and-release section has been established, where only artificials are permitted. Fly-fishing can be good and is best when using weighted nymphs with a strike indicator; then hope for a binge of surface dry fly-fishing in the evening.

Downstream from Dunsmuir are many other excellent areas. Big fish hunker in the holes around Soda Springs, Gibson, and Lakehead. Some people walk on the adjoining railroad tracks (keep alert for trains!), then scramble down to the river when they see a prime spot. Using spinners, especially small Panther Martins, is usually quite successful around here.

Many special regulations are enforced, making it essential that you scan the DFG rule book first. The one requirement that is likely to stay in effect for some time is the use of single barbless hooks, artificials only, for most of the river.

In winter months, the Upper Sac is open year-round, with catch-and-release with flies and lures with single barbless hooks permitted in what is usually the closed season. Take I-5 to Redding and continue north past Shasta Lake to Lakehead and continue north; river access is available from turnoffs at Vollmers/Delta, La Moine, Pollard Flat, Gibson, Sims and elsewhere. I checked all these spots and there wasn't another car or angler at any of them. I wear Simms waders with wading shoes, a tight-fitted wading belt, a fly-fishing vest with all my fishing gear, polarized sunglasses, and a wide brim hat, and I bring an old ski pole for a wading staff (with a rope tied in a loop to the wrist wrap, so I can throw the rope over my shoulder and fish hands-free). Rod, reel, line: I've tried a lot of rods and combinations and believe the best for this river is a 10-foot, 5-weight Sage fly rod, a fly reel with floating line, with a 4 x 7-foot leader.

For the Upper Sac, I almost always start by tying on a No. 16 olive Prince Nymph, then add 10 inches of 5X fluorocarbon leader and then tie on a No. 16 Copper John. Other flies that have worked for me are the No. 12 golden stone nymph, weighted dark olive wooly bugger, and, if there's a hatch and surface rise, caddis flies in various sizes, touched with a drop of floatant.

The entire Upper Sac from Vollmers/Delta on north to Box Canyon Dam at Mount Shasta can provide excellent fishing at different times of year, but in the early spring, I suggest sticking to the lower river, from Simms Campground on downstream to Delta/Dog Creek, because resident fish are joined here by spring migrants that have swum up from Shasta Lake.

Insider's note: Every year, I try to book with Jack Trout (530/926-4540, www.jacktrout .com) for a rafting/fly-fishing trip. Jack and his small stable of guides are the only fly-fishing guides who are also certified as rafting guides. We usually put in at Simms, then raft down the river, stopping to fish all the spots that you can't reach from shore or by wading. I've caught 12–25 trout on these trips, real easy and effective.

In winter, the best fishing is often right in midday, not at dawn and dusk as in the summer. That's because the water is still cold, so the trout feed more aggressively when the surface water warms up even a degree. The best bet of all is on warm, overcast days roughly 11 A.M.– 2:30 P.M. You get hatches and feeding activity, and when the sky is overcast, the fish are a lot more active and far less shy about striking.

A few fieldscouts who live nearby have reported occasional good dry fly-fishing, but my experience is that most of the feeding is subsurface, so you are better off drift-nymphing along the bottom. I look for pocket water behind boulders, seams along eddies, and the edge of slicks downstream of riffles. Once the spot is identified, I usually cast just 25–40 feet out (sometimes only 10 feet), and then drift the flies right into the spots where trout are likely holding. Short casts are better than long ones because it is easier to see the bite and set the hook. The bite: The trout do not shoot across the river to grab your fly, but rather sit in pocket water or along seams, then move over a few inches and "inhale" the "food." So do not expect an electric shock of a strike. The trick is to watch where your line enters the water or to place a strike indicator on your fly line. All you will see is the line or strike indicator stop or move a bit sideways on the surface—that's the strike. Set the hook and get ready to rock-'n'-roll.

Facilities, fees: Several full-facility campgrounds and RV parks are available along the river and near adjacent towns. Restrooms with flush toilets, vault toilets, and drinking water are provided. A few good ones are Sims Flat in Shasta-Trinity National Forest, Railroad Park (both near Dunsmuir), and Castle Crags State Park (near Castella). Supplies can be obtained in Mount Shasta, Dunsmuir, Castella, Lakehead, and Redding. Fishing access is free.

Directions: Direct access is available off I-5 via nearly every exit between the towns of Lakehead and Mount Shasta.

To CalTrout/Mount Shasta access: Take I-5 to Mount Shasta and then take the exit for Central Mount Shasta. At the stop sign, turn west and drive one mile to W. A. Barr Road. Turn left, drive for a mile to a Y junction with Old Stage Road. Bear left on Old Stage Road and drive to Cantara Road. Turn right and continue down to the river. The put-in is at the CalTrout fishing access above the Cantara Loop Railroad Bridge.

To Sims Road access: Take I-5 to the exit for north Dunsmuir. Take that exit to the stop sign. Turn west and drive a short distance to Dunsmuir Avenue, then continue a short distance to Prospect Avenue. Turn right and drive one mile to the river access (which is well signed in Dunsmuir).

To Prospect Avenue/Dunsmuir access: Take I-5 to the exit for Sims Road (12 miles south of Dunsmuir). Take Sims Road east to Sims Flat Campground and access.

To Dog Creek access: Take I-5 to the exit for Vollmers/Dog Creek. Take that exit and drive west a short distance to the river access.

Contact: Shasta-Trinity National Forest, Mount Shasta Ranger District, 530/926-4511, www.fs.fed.us/r5—click on Forest Offices.

Guides and supplies: Jack Trout Guide Service, 530/926-4540, www.jacktrout.com or www.mtshasta.com; Ted Fay Fly Shop, Dunsmuir, 530/235-2969, www.tedfay.com; J&J Guide Service, 530/222-6253; Wayne Eng Flyfishing, 530/235-4018, www.wayneeng flyfish.wordpress.com; Rick Cox, McCloud Flyfishing Adventures, 530/964-2533, www .mccloudflyfishing.com.

19 TROUT CREEK

Rating: 4
near McCloud in Shasta-Trinity National Forest
Map 2.2, page 120

Just hearing the name Trout Creek can be enough to get the blood pumping. Relax. Cool your jets. Sit down and take a few deep breaths.

Trout in the five- to seven-inch class live in this small stream, the kind of place where the setting is the draw and the fishing just a bonus. It's a quiet spot for camping. The water is pure, and so is the pine-scented air. After a while, it won't matter that the biggest trout in the world aren't in these waters. Trout Unlimited is directing a special habitat-protection project here. Trout Creek is a beautiful place, easy to reach and easy to fish.

Facilities, fees: A small Forest Service campground is provided. There is no drinking water. A vault toilet is available, and garbage must be packed out. Supplies can be obtained in McCloud. Fishing access is free.

Directions: From Redding, take I-5 north for 56 miles to the exit for McCloud/

Reno—Highway 89. Bear right on Highway 89 and drive 10 miles to McCloud, then continue two miles to Pilgrim Creek Road. Turn left on Pilgrim Creek Road and drive 20 miles to a signed road for Trout Creek. Turn left and drive one mile.

Contact: Shasta-Trinity National Forest, McCloud Ranger District, 530/964-2184, www .fs.fed.us/r5—click on Forest Offices. Siskiyou County Visitors Bureau, www.visitsiskiyou .org.

20 McCLOUD RIVER

Rating: 8
near McCloud in Shasta-Trinity National Forest
Map 2.2, page 120

The McCloud River is known throughout the world as the source of the strain of rainbow trout now flourishing in many countries, including New Zealand, Chile, and Argentina. It is known by fly fishers as a blue-ribbon trout stream. And it is now known by many as one of the most beautiful rivers around, especially the downstream section governed by the Nature Conservancy, where emerald-colored water flows over boulders and into pools and gorges.

That's the problem: it's too well known. It is fished hard daily by many skilled fly fishers, including many professional guides who are quick to show strangers the best spots that used to take years for fly fishers to learn. Too many top rods on just a few miles of river knocks the rating down from a 10 to an 8. The saving grace is Shasta Lake. Many fish migrate up into the McCloud from Shasta Lake, so you get the bonus of those newcomers as well as the well-schooled year-round resident trout.

The best results here are gained by adept fly fishers who use weighted nymphs and fish pocket water. The trout rarely attack the fly; most often they simply stop its flow in the current. Know-hows watch their line, realizing that any strange movement will probably be the only sign that they're getting a bite. Short-lining nymphs on the McCloud is nearly an art.

The McCloud can be difficult to wade in and fish successfully. Chest waders with a belt are a must, as is a wading staff. The algae-covered rocks are extremely slippery, and if you don't watch it—kerplunk, you'll go right in the drink. The secret is to stay off the big rocks—they're like launching pads. There is nothing more slippery than a large, flat-topped boulder on the McCloud that looks like a perfect place to stand. Instead, watch where you step, and stick to the gravel and baseball-sized rocks.

The river has become extremely popular with high numbers of anglers coming long distances to fish the prime sections. Despite the rod quota on the Nature Conservancy section (10 rods at a time), the entire river gets fished very hard. It is also professionally guided, so the best spots are shown to people fishing here for the first time.

As a result, the trout here are very smart. They are most likely to be taken nymphing pocket water with strike indicators. As summer arrives, there is a surface bite that can last anywhere from 45 minutes to an hour. It can be a long wait, nymphing pocket water all day for this flash of action at dusk.

The regulations are difficult to understand, with different rules applying to four parts of the river. So let's get it straight:
• Upstream of McCloud Reservoir (the area accessed from Fowler's Camp), there's a five-fish limit and no special restrictions.
• On the Upper McCloud, upstream of Lake Dam, there's a five-fish limit and no special restrictions.
• Downstream of McCloud Reservoir, from the dam to Lady Bug Creek near the Nature Conservancy (near Ah-Di-Na Campground), the limit is two fish, artificials only, single barbless hook (with a move afoot to get this changed to catch-and-release fishing).
• On the 2.5 miles downstream from the Nature Conservancy Cabin, access is limited to 10 rods at a time. All fish must be released.

Fishing is not permitted from the roped-off section on downstream for 2.5 miles.

Confusing? Yes. But that's nothing compared to the confusion you will feel if the trout decide not to bite.

The upstream section near Lakim Dam is much easier to fish. In addition, the nearby side trip to Middle Falls is spectacularly beautiful. A trail from Fowler's Camp traces along the river upstream to Middle Falls, one of the prettiest waterfalls in Northern California. You can stop to fish on the way, zipping short casts to deep, clear pools.

As for catch rates, there's no average to the average. Skunks are common, especially among newcomers. Those who keep returning for more punishment eventually figure out the river well enough to catch three or four trout per visit.

Occasionally, you'll hear of fantastic evening bites during a caddis hatch, or of giant trout on cold, early November days. But folks around here usually talk about the beauty of the McCloud. Pretty soon you'll figure out why: they just got skunked.

Facilities, fees: On the Lower McCloud River, there's the Forest Service–run Ah-Di-Na Campground. On the Upper McCloud, camping is available at Fowler's Camp, Cattle Camp, and Algoma Camp. For the most part, campgrounds have chemical toilets and drinking water. Supplies can be obtained in McCloud. Fishing access is free. Donations are requested for access to the McCloud Conservancy.

Directions: To Lower McCloud: From Redding, take I-5 north for 56 miles to the exit for McCloud/Reno—Highway 89. Bear right on Highway 89 and drive 10 miles to Mc-Cloud and Squaw Valley Road. Turn right on Squaw Valley Road and drive five miles (the road becomes Forest Service Road 11). At the McCloud boat ramp, bear right and drive on Forest Service Road 11 to the end of Battle Creek Cove and Forest Service Road 38N53/Ah-Di-Na Road (a dirt road) on the right. Turn right and drive four miles (past

Ah-Di-Na Campground) to the road's end at Wheelbarrow Creek. The Nature Conservancy boundary is 0.5 mile down the trail.

To Upper McCloud: From Redding, take I-5 north for 56 miles to the exit for McCloud/Reno—Highway 89. Bear right on Highway 89 and drive 10 miles to McCloud, then continue five miles to a signed campground entrance road on the right. Turn right and drive a short distance to a Y, then bear left at the Y to the campground. Access is available along a trail out of the camp.

Contact: Shasta-Trinity National Forest, McCloud Ranger District, 530/964-2184, www.fs.fed.us/r5—click on Forest Offices; Siskiyou County Visitors Bureau, www.visitsiskiyou.org; reservations for sections managed by the Nature Conservancy, 415/777-0487.

Guides: Jack Trout Guide Service, 530/926-4540, www.jacktrout.com or www.mtshasta.com; Ted Fay Fly Shop, Dunsmuir, 530/235-2969, www.tedfay.com; Rick Cox, McCloud Flyfishing Adventures, 530/964-2533, www.mccloudflyfishing.com; Wayne Eng Flyfishing, 530/235-4018, www.wayneengflyfish.wordpress.com; Three Rivers Guide Service, 530/925-7990, www.threeriversguideservice.com.

21 TRINITY ALPS WILDERNESS

Rating: 10

northwest of Redding

Map 2.2, page 120 **BEST (**

From a mountain peak or airplane, the Trinity Alps resemble Switzerland's high mountain backbone. To those who have hiked the southern Sierra, the Trinities look as if they are 13,000–14,000 feet high, with conical peaks poking holes in the sky.

These appearances are deceptive. In the Trinity Alps Wilderness area, the elevation of most lakes and adjoining peaks ranges 6,000–8,000 feet. As a result, the Trinities encompass elements other than granite, ice, and water (the components found in the southern Sierra). These mountains contain more soil, trees, and terrestrial activity, all of which add up to a greater food supply for insects and a longer trout-growing season. The lakes here contain some of California's largest mountain-bred trout. The Trinity Alps offer trout that top out in the 14-inch class (17- to 18-inchers even make an occasional appearance), as opposed to the 7-inchers common to the High Sierra. At Little South Fork Lake, which is reached via an excruciating off-trail grunt, a trout ran 40 feet on me, something I had never experienced with mountain trout.

I have visited most of the wilderness areas in California, and in terms of quality, quantity, and scenic beauty, the backcountry lakes of the Trinity Alps offer the finest wildland fishing I have found.

Difficult-to-reach destinations are the key to this experience. If a particular location is easy to access, the fishing will probably be poor. Camper/anglers tend to throw back small fish and keep the big ones, which results in a lake with a lot of small fish that have been taught valuable lessons by previous anglers.

The lakes with the biggest and best trout are: Little South Fork Lake, Emerald Lake, Sapphire Lake, Canyon Creek Lake, Boulder Lake and Tangle Blue Lake.

These other lakes provide fair to middlin' results: Bear Lakes, Fox Creek Lake, Granite Lake, Grizzly Lake, Holland Lake, Log Lake, Long Gulch Lake, Marshy Lakes, McDonald Lake, Papoose Lake, Smith Lake, Snow Slide Pond, Stoddard Lake, and Summit Lake,.

The pretty Caribou Lakes are a good first-day destination, located on the edge of real wildlands with great fishing amid several lakes. However, the lakes themselves are also popular summer campsites and get fished hard. Soon enough, they will not produce much.

These lakes generally become accessible around mid-June, sometimes earlier. Fishing is usually best in early July, when the water warms up, insects hatch, and the trout begin to feed.

Tremendous day trips are possible in the Trinity Alps, including visits to mountaintops and ridgelines that afford dramatic views. Mount Thompson, which juts out above Sawtooth Ridge, is the most dramatic peak in the range. Life is simple up here, where glaciers once carved out a chunk of the world.

Facilities, fees: No facilities are available. Fishing access is free.

Directions: From Redding, drive west on Highway 299 to Weaverville and Highway 3. Turn north on Highway 3 and drive north to Trinity Lake. Access roads to trailheads for the Trinity Alps Wilderness are available on the west side of Highway 3 at Stuart's Fork, Coffee Creek, and elsewhere. Trailheads are also available on roads north of Highway 299 at Canyon Creek and New River, and also southwest of Callahan. A map is essential.

Contact: Shasta-Trinity National Forest, Weaverville Ranger District, 530/623-2121, www.fs.fed.us/r5—click on Forest Offices.

22 COFFEE CREEK

Rating: 3

in Klamath National Forest

Map 2.2, page 120

Coffee Creek should be renamed Rock Creek in honor of the mountains of rocks lining parts of the bank. Small rocks, big rocks, here a rock, there a rock, everywhere a rock. This abundance of rocks is a symbol of a long-gone era—it is the result of past gold-mining operations.

Floods ripped this river apart in 1964, and it hasn't recovered. The fish aren't long gone, though. The problem is that they just aren't long. Coffee Creek has few areas that provide quality habitat, and most of the trout here are true dinkers. The DFG stocks this river with rainbow trout (in the six- to eight-inch class) and with a mix of smaller fish, depending on water conditions.

Coffee Creek's best fishing spot is fairly close to its entrance into the Upper Trinity, but anglers have experienced problems with landowners in the area. Translation: People get mighty upset if you wander onto their property while walking up the river, so check a current national-forest map to avoid trespassing. Farther upstream, where the river is bordered by national forest, much of Coffee Creek is wide, shallow, and (of course) rocky.

Facilities, fees: Two national-forest campgrounds are provided on Coffee Creek Road—Goldfield and Big Flat. Vault toilets are provided. No drinking water is available, and garbage must be packed out. Supplies can be obtained at Trinity Center and in Weaverville. Fishing access is free.

Directions: From Sacramento, take I-5 north to Redding and Highway 299 West. Take that exit and drive 52 miles west on Highway 299 to Weaverville and Highway 3. Turn north on Highway 3 and continue to Trinity Lake. Continue north (passing through Trinity Center) past the north end of Trinity Lake, and drive nine miles north on Highway 3 to Coffee Creek Road. Turn west on Coffee Creek Road. Fishing access is available along Coffee Creek Road.

Contact: Shasta-Trinity National Forest, Weaverville Ranger District, 530/623-2121, www.fs.fed.us/r5—click on Forest Offices; Trinity Outdoors, 530/623-4999, www .trinityoutdoors.net.

23 SOUTH FORK SACRAMENTO RIVER

Rating: 3

near Mount Shasta, upstream of Lake Siskiyou

Map 2.2, page 120

Most of the year, this river isn't much more than a trickle, but enough water does run down to support a small population of trout. The Department of Fish and Game stocks rainbows in the six- to eight-inch class. The prime riffle-fed deep pools that hold quality trout are practically nonexistent, as are roadside turnouts. Instead you get pocket water,

which requires short, precise casts, and just a few places along the road with enough room to park. The best spot, however, is at the confluence of Wagon Creek, where the DFG occasionally makes stocks.

Facilities, fees: Camping is available at Lake Siskiyou, Gumboot Lake, and in Mount Shasta. Supplies can be obtained in Mount Shasta. Fishing access is free.

Directions: From Redding, take I-5 north to the town of Mount Shasta and the Central Mount Shasta exit. Take that exit to the stop sign. Turn left and drive to Old Stage Road. Turn left and drive 0.25 mile to a Y at W. A. Barr Road. Bear right on W. A. Barr Road and drive past Box Canyon Dam, continuing past the Lake Siskiyou entrance road and the lake. The river parallels the road, and direct access to the lower portion is available in most places. Be careful to park safely off the road.

Contact: Shasta-Trinity National Forest, Mount Shasta Ranger District, 530/926-4511, www.fs.fed.us/r5—click on Forest Offices.

Guides and supplies: Sportsmen's Den, Mount Shasta, 530/926-2295, www.mt shastasports.com.; Jack Trout Guide Service, 530/926-4540, www.jacktrout.com; Ted Fay Fly Shop, Dunsmuir, 530/235-2969, www.ted fay.com; J&J Guide Service, 530/222-6253.

24 CASTLE LAKE

Rating: 5

near Mount Shasta in
Shasta-Trinity National Forest

Map 2.2, page 120

Bring your camera. Not to take pictures of all the big fish, because there are very few of those, but to capture the view from some of California's most scenic lookouts. The view of Mount Shasta on the road just half a mile below the lake is absolutely spectacular. More magazine pictures of the magic mountain are taken from the road to Castle Lake here than from any other lookout. But an even better photo opportunity is available if you hike in from Castle Lake up to Heart Lake, then snap a photo of Shasta with little Heart in the foreground. This is eye-popping stuff. Extremely pure water that is low in nitrogen and phosphates (similar to Lake Tahoe) has resulted in a color that is deeper blue than any lake in the Trinity Divide country, making it the focus of a study by University of California Davis scientists for years.

This is often a good lake to ice fish in winter. However, in summer Fish and Game no longer stocks here. Shoreliners can have a particularly difficult time. Even though the lake is small, the best success by far is had by anglers using some kind of craft, at least a raft or float tube, to cover some of the deeper areas. That's because the shoreline areas are quite shallow in some parts of the lake, and folks on the shore can't reach the fish. If you do stick to the bank, hike around to the far side for the best prospects.

This is one of the best lakes in Northern California for ice-fishing for trout. Castle Lake is easy to reach (there's a paved road all the way), and in the winter it provides one of the few good ice-fishing opportunities in Northern California. Not many out-of-towners take advantage of it, yet it is easy and fun. After cutting your hole in the ice (or using one of the holes cut on a previous day), just dunk a night crawler and stay alert, because the fish here are bigger and more eager in the winter than at any other time of the year.

But that is not the reason this place is so memorable. The views are absolutely unforgettable.

Facilities, fees: A small campground with vault toilets is provided 0.5 mile down from the lake, but there is no drinking water. There are no legal campsites along the lake's shoreline. Fishing supplies can be obtained in Mount Shasta at Sportsmen's Den and Rite-Aid. Fishing access is free.

Directions: From Redding, take I-5 north to the town of Mount Shasta and the Central Mount Shasta exit. Take that exit to the stop sign. Turn left and drive to Old Stage Road.

Turn left and drive 0.25 mile to a Y at W. A. Barr Road. Bear right on W. A. Barr Road and drive past Box Canyon Dam. Turn left at Castle Lake Road and drive 7.5 miles to the end of the road at the foot of Castle Lake.

Contact: Shasta-Trinity National Forest, Mount Shasta Ranger District, 530/926-4511, www.fs.fed.us/r5—click on Forest Offices.

Guides and supplies: Sportsmen's Den, Mount Shasta, 530/926-2295, www.mt shastasports.com; Jack Trout Guide Service, 530/926-4540, www.jacktrout.com.

25 TAMARACK LAKE

Rating: 4

near Castella in Shasta-Trinity National Forest

Map 2.2, page 120

Tamarack is pleasing to the eye and the soul. It is one of the prettiest lakes in the Trinity Divide country, an alpine lake that provides a refuge of peace and beauty. The fishing? Well, that's just fair, since the DFG no longer stocks it. The best and deepest fishing spot is at the south end of the lake, which is good in the fall. The lake is at an elevation of 5,900 feet, covers 21 acres, and is 16 feet deep.

There are actually three lakes in the immediate area: Tamarack, which is the biggest, and nearby Upper and Lower Twin Lakes, to the west. Tamarack also has the biggest fish. Of those two, Upper Twin Lake provides the better fishing.

Tamarack makes a good base camp for people who like to explore. Of course, if you just want to sit back and gaze at it, that's okay, too.

Facilities, fees: There are no on-site facilities. Primitive, do-it-yourself campsites are available 200 yards from the lake. Supplies can be obtained in the town of Castella. Fishing access is free.

Directions: From Redding, drive north on I-5 to the town of Castella (near Castle Crags) and Castle Creek Road. Take that exit, turn west, and drive 11 miles west on Road 25 (Castle

Creek Road) to Twin Lakes Road (Forest Road 38N17). Turn left (south) and drive three miles. Bear left where the road forks and proceed one mile to the lake. (The last four miles of road are very rough, suitable only for high-clearance four-wheel-drive vehicles.)
Contact: Shasta-Trinity National Forest, Mount Shasta Ranger District, 530/926-4511, www.fs.fed.us/r5—click on Forest Offices.

26 TRINITY RIVER

Rating: 9
in Shasta-Trinity National Forest
Map 2.3, page 121

The Trinity River can earn a sure 10 rating from late summer through winter for salmon and steelhead, respectively, and in spring and early summer for brown trout. It's not quite a year-round fishery, but if you time it right, it can be sensational.

The Trinity is the best river in California to fish for steelhead from the shore. Steelhead fishing on the Trinity is a real treat. That is because you can have the sense of fishing a trout stream—and yet the fish can weigh in excess of eight pounds. This stream runs clear and blue, and tumbles around boulders and into deep holes. Framed by a high, tree-lined canyon, it is a beautiful setting for shoreliners chasing steelhead. The river's spring salmon runs have rebounded over the last couple of years and now provide good fishing from May to June.

Increased water releases from Trinity Dam, courtesy of the Bureau of Reclamation, bode well. The Hoopa Indians, who were ready to prove in court that the Trinity was devastated by low flows, threatened to sue the bureau, hence the increase in water. And quite simply, more water equals more fish.

Highway 299 (a yellow-striped two-laner) runs alongside the river, and turnouts are set above many prime fishing spots. The best of these are just below the Lewiston Bridge; in the vicinity of Steel Bridge, midway between Lewiston and Douglas City; at Steiner Flat

(accessible by hiking in), below Douglas City; at the mouth of Canyon Creek, at Junction City; and at the confluence of the North Fork Trinity and Hell Hole, upstream of Big Bar. Don't overlook Burnt Ranch Falls and Gray Falls; although far downstream, they're frequently two of the best spots on the entire river system, especially in spring.

When shoreline fishing, approach the bank like a cat burglar. Most fishing spots are identified as slicks, riffles with a defined edge, or pools above and below rapids. You should quarter your casts; that is, cast at a 45-degree angle above the prime holding area, then walk the bait downstream across the bottom.

The Trinity also provides some of the best steelhead fly-fishing in the state. The river is not wide, which makes it possible for anglers to reach runs and pockets without making difficult casts. The best spots are between Douglas City and Junction City and spots known as "Meat and Potatoes," "Hornet's Nest," and "Flats of Evans Bar." The best spots, by consensus: Steel Bridge (between Lewiston and Douglas City), Steiner Flat (short hike required), mouth of Canyon Creek at Junction City, downstream of Junction City, vicinity of confluence of North Fork Trinity, Hell Hole upstream of Big Bar. My favorite trip in a drift boat is to put in at Douglas City and then work the boat in the canyon along eight miles of river downstream to Junction City.

For fly-fishing for steelhead, use two flies at once. Tie on a No. 8 golden stone, and then from that, add two feet of leader and a weighted nymph (either caddis or mayfly). Sometimes we switch to a red salmon egg pattern to try to entice a salmon. Place a strike indicator (Umpqua Foam Indicator) about five feet above the first fly. The No. 10 Silver Hilton, Brindle Bug, and pink Glo Bug are also good patterns.

The steelhead make their first appearance in fall, and they continue to arrive and move through the river up until spring; this is one of the longest steelhead runs anywhere. If you like to sleep in, this is the place to go.

Midday is the most productive period in winter; the river receives relatively small amounts of sunlight, which (in conjunction with cold temperatures) makes the water frigid and the steelhead reluctant to eat. When the sun comes out and the water warms up a degree or two, the fish can really come to life.

The salmon run is improving on the Trinity because of increased water flows on the river from Trinity and Lewiston lakes. There are two distinct runs. The spring run occurs in May and June and tapers off in midsummer. The other is the fall run, which starts in late summer and continues through October.

Salmon average 10–12 pounds, and occasionally a 20-pounder is taken. The best baits are roe balls or tuna balls, and the best technique is to drift your bait along the bottom of the deeper holes and runs. The fish can also be caught with spinners in the riffles at dawn and dusk.

At times the stretch of river below Lewiston Dam offers great fly-fishing for large rainbow and brown trout. A boat helps a lot in this spot, because access is only fair.

I remember catching a steelhead here once, then just sitting on a rock and looking at my surroundings. The clouds drifted through the trees and gave the area an ethereal feel. I scanned the high mountain ridge, deep canyons, and puffy cumulonimbus clouds sitting on the treetops. It was a scene I'll never forget.

Regulations for steelhead or trout: Limit is one fish, a hatchery-produced steelhead (noted by a missing adipose fin) or one brown trout. All wild steelhead must be released. Regulations for salmon: One adult salmon (over 22 inches) and two jack salmon (under 22 inches) may be caught. Special rules: Barbless hooks are required. No treble hooks with a gap greater than three-quarter inch are allowed. No hook with a shank longer than two inches is allowed. No weight exceeding a half ounce can be located within 18 inches of the hook. Always check DFG regulations for current rules and fish status.

Note: Most of the Trinity River is not stocked. Two small sections (upstream of Trinity Lake and along the Upper Trinity near Highway 3) are planted with rainbow trout and brown trout. Most of these fish migrate into Trinity Lake. In 2011, Scott Bice landed a 15-pound, 2-ounce brown trout while shore fishing.

Facilities, fees: Several campgrounds are along Highway 299 west of Weaverville and off Trinity Dam Boulevard. Burnt Ranch and Hayden Flat are good choices. Two other campgrounds are on Steiner Flat Road, outside of Douglas City. Drinking water and vault toilets are available at most campgrounds. Cabins can be rented at Steelhead Cottages, 530/623-6325. Supplies can be obtained in Weaverville, Lewiston, or Junction City. Fishing access is free.

Directions: To the uppermost part of the river from Redding: Drive west on Highway 299 for 30 miles to the Lewiston turnoff. Turn right and drive through the town of Lewiston, on Trinity Dam Boulevard, until you reach the bridge that crosses the river. Cross the bridge and turn left on Rush Creek Road. Direct river access is available.

To the lower stretches: From Redding, drive west on Highway 299 to Douglas City and then to Steiner Flat Road. Turn left (west) and follow Steiner Flat Road. Direct river access is available off this road.

To the central Trinity: From Redding, drive west on Highway 299 to Weaverville and continue to Junction City. Access is available from several well-signed gravel roads and trails off Highway 299 west of Junction City. The stretch between Burnt Ranch and Hawkins Bar may be restricted; check current fishing regulations.

Contact: Shasta-Trinity National Forest, Big Bar Ranger District, 530/623-6106, www.fs.fed.us/r5—click on Forest Offices; Trinity River Lodge RV Resort, Lewiston, 530/778-3791; Steelhead Cottages, 530/623-6325 or 800/742-3785, www.steelheadcottages.com.

Guides: Paul Catanese, Catman's Trinity

Guide Service, 530/623-2328; Jorgen Moholt, 530/623-2145; Herb Burton, Trinity Fly Shop, 530/623-6757, www.trinityflyshop.com; Jack Trout Guide Service, 530/926-4540, www .jacktrout.com; Liam Gogan, Trinity River Outfitters, 530/623-6376, www.trinityriver outfitters.com; Three Rivers Guide Service, 530/925-7990, www.threeriversguideservice .com.

Supplies: Trinity Fly Shop, 530/623-6757, www.trinityflyshop.com.

27 NEW RIVER

Rating: 5

near Salyer in Shasta-Trinity National Forest
Map 2.3, page 121

The New River is an oft-forgotten tributary of the Trinity River, simply because it feeds into the Trinity on the side opposite Highway 299. Yet here it is, and a small, winding road traces the river up into the Salmon Mountains.

Fishing is no longer permitted on the East Fork; below that point it's catch-and-release, with barbless and artificial lures only. You can access the New River off the road or farther upstream. Upstream, the road feeds into a trailhead that provides hike-in access to rarely fished portions of the river. For a drive-to area so near a highway, this river is actually quite remote. The trout are natives, and special regulations are in effect. A little-known secret is that the New River gets a summer steelhead run. It is challenging, exciting, and all catch-and-release.

Facilities, fees: Denny Campground is available at the end of Denny Road. Picnic tables, fire grills, and vault toilets are provided. No drinking water is available. All garbage must be packed out. Leashed pets are permitted. Supplies can be obtained about one hour away, in Salyers Bar. Fishing access is free.

Directions: From the junction of U.S. 101 and Highway 299 near Arcata, turn east on Highway 299 and drive to Willow Creek. In Willow Creek, continue east on Highway 299 to Salyer

and drive four miles to Denny Road/County Road 402. Turn north on Denny Road and drive about 14 miles on a paved but winding road to the campground for your base of operations. Stream access is available from the road.

Contact: Shasta-Trinity National Forest, Big Bar Ranger Station, 530/623-6106, www .fs.fed.us/r5—click on Forest Offices.

28 CANYON CREEK

Rating: 5

near Junction City in
Shasta-Trinity National Forest
Map 2.3, page 121

Scenic beauty and an opportunity to angle for wild rainbow trout are what this pretty water has to offer.

Check for current regulations. A 14-inch-maximum size limit may be in effect to ensure that when a big one is caught it stays in the river rather than ending up in a frying pan. To protect summer steelies, fishing is restricted below the falls (five miles above the wilderness-area boundary).

Canyon Creek is a tributary to the Trinity River, and it enters the Trinity near Junction City. Gold mining often took place on the stream's upper reaches, and this area is rich in history.

Facilities, fees: Ripstein Campground is available on Canyon Creek Road. Picnic tables, fire grills, and vault toilets are provided, but drinking water is not. Garbage must be packed out. Supplies can be obtained in Junction City, 45 minutes away. Fishing access is free.

Directions: From Redding, head west on Highway 299 and drive past Weaverville to Junction City. At Junction City, turn right on Canyon Creek Road and drive 15 miles to the campground on the left side of the road for your base of operations. Creek access is available off several roads and trails that junction with Canyon Creek Road.

Contact: Shasta-Trinity National Forest, Big

Bar Ranger Station, 530/623-6106; Shasta-Trinity National Forest, Weaverville Ranger Station, 530/623-2121, www.fs.fed.us/r5—click on Forest Offices.

29 EWING GULCH RESERVOIR

Rating: 4

near Hayfork in Shasta-Trinity National Forest

Map 2.3, page 121

Bet you never heard of this one. Am I right? This water is largely unknown, even to anglers who pride themselves on their familiarity with the state's offerings, because the summer fishing is often poor, and few people have any reason to discuss the place. DFG no longer stocks this lake.

During the spring and fall, however, fishing at Ewing Gulch is a whole different ball game. In these parts, winters come cold and summers hot, making both seasons zilch-time. But the trout arrive when the seasons transition. Water temperature is key, so I always carry an aquarium-shop thermometer. The fishing is best here when the water temperature is in the low to mid-50s. Check it out.

Facilities, fees: Picnic tables and restrooms are available for day use. Overnight camping is not permitted; lodging and supplies can be obtained in Hayfork. Fishing access is free.

Directions: From I-5 at Redding, take the Highway 299 West exit. Drive west on Highway 299 to Douglas City and Highway 3. Turn left (southwest) on Highway 3 and drive about 20 miles to the town of Hayfork and Brady Road. Turn right (north) on Brady Road and drive one mile to Reservoir Road. Turn right (east) on Reservoir Road and drive to the lake.

Contact: Shasta-Trinity National Forest, Hayfork Ranger Station, 530/628-5227, www.fs.fed.us/r5—click on Forest Offices.

Information and supplies: Ernie's Department Store, Hayfork, 530/628-5332, www.hayfork.com.

30 RUTH LAKE

Rating: 6

near the town of Mad River in Six Rivers National Forest

Map 2.3, page 121

On California's North Coast, black bass are generally as rare as Bigfoot. Ruth Lake is the exception to this rule. The lake provides a decent bass fishery, trout, and good spring crappie fishing.

If you like to drive fast, getting to Ruth Lake will be difficult. You need patience on winding Highway 36, a route designed for horses and carriages, not cars. Once you arrive, you'll discover a long, narrow lake set at an elevation of 2,700 feet in remote western Trinity County. Shoreline campgrounds are a big plus, especially when the lake is full of water.

In hot weather the bass fishing is good, and in cool weather the trout fishing is good. Although this lake is quite narrow and its two sides seem to resemble one another, better fishing prospects can be found on the west side. There are two reasons. First, coastal winds come from the west most of the year, and the lake's west side is better protected. Second, during the late afternoon, three major west-side coves receive shade earlier than any other part of the lake.

Ruth Lake is stocked with trout. Fish and Game usually plants 10- to 12-inch rainbow trout and Eagle Lake trout. If the bass don't bite, the trout provide an alternative.

The one big problem here is that during the heavy rains in early spring, this lake can get quite muddy, killing prospects for a month or two. But come clear water, the trout bite can be excellent.

Ruth is open to all kinds of boating, and although there's not a lot of traffic, a single water-skier is one too many for a basser trying to sneak up on a quiet cove. I suggest cordoning off half the lake to separate the water-skiers from the anglers, a setup that works at many other lakes. For now, many of the coves are designated as no-wake zones. But you're more likely to be the next person on the moon than see a sheriff boat patrol out here.

Note: All boats must be inspected and certified free of mussels prior to launching at this lake.

Facilities, fees: Two campgrounds, Fir Cove and Bailey Canyon, are provided. Ruth Lake offers boat-in camping. A full-service marina, boat ramps, boat rentals, picnic areas, and a disposal station are also available. Supplies can be obtained in Ruth Lake or Dinsmore. Fishing access is free.

Directions: From Eureka, drive south on U.S. 101 to Alton and the junction with Highway 36. Turn east on Highway 36 and drive about 50 miles to the town of Mad River. Turn right at the sign for Ruth Lake/Lower Mad River Road and drive 12 miles to the lake.

Contact: Six Rivers National Forest, Mad River Ranger District, 707/574-6233, www.fs.fed.us/r5—click on Forest Offices; Ruth Lake Marina, 707/574-6194, www.ruthlake csd.org; Six Rivers Lodge, 707/574-6220; Journey's End, 707/574-6441, www.the journeysend.com.

31 YOLLA BOLLY WILDERNESS

Rating: 4

west of Red Bluff in
Shasta-Trinity National Forest
Map 2.3, page 121

The Yolla Bolly may not rate high on the list of California's 43 significant wilderness areas, but it still appeals to people in the know.

First, how to pronounce the name: Yolla is pronounced "YO-la," not "YAH-la." Bolly is pronounced "BOWL-lee," not "BAH-lee." Have you got it? If so, and if you like primitive, rugged, hot (in the summer), and largely unpopulated country, this wilderness may be your place. You won't see the kind of magnificent mountain peaks as in the Trinity, Marble Mountain, Russian, and Sierra Wildernesses,

nor will you find a lot of lakes. The true appeal is that this is where the headwaters of the Middle Eel River are found, along with other little feeder creeks at the bottoms of steep ravines and canyon draws.

In the northern Yolla Bollies, a handful of hike-to lakes (including Black Rock Lake, Long Lake, Square Lake, and Yolla Bolly Lake) provide decent fishing. They receive aerial stocks of fingerlings in some years.

The primitive feel of this wilderness has its own appeal. The place can evoke gut-level emotions, and after a short time here, layers of civilization will start peeling off as if you were taking a good, long shower.

Facilities, fees: No facilities are available. Fishing access is free.

Directions: From Red Bluff on I-5, turn west on Highway 36. Drive west on Highway 36 (slow and twisty, 90 minutes or more) to Platina. Trailheads are accessible from several unimproved Forest Service roads that junction with Highway 36 near Platina. In winter, four-wheel-drive vehicles can be required.

Contact: Shasta-Trinity National Forest, Yolla Bolla Ranger Station, 530/352-4211, www.fs.fed.us/r5—click on Forest Offices.

32 TRINITY LAKE

Rating: 8

near Weaverville in
Shasta-Trinity National Forest
Map 2.4, page 122

Trinity Lake can be a mountain paradise for fishing, boating, and camping. It is nestled at the eastern foot of the Trinity Alps, at an elevation of 2,300 feet, and covers 17,000 acres with 145 miles of shoreline. The only potential drawback to Trinity is that it can be subject to severe drawdowns because water is diverted and piped over to the Sacramento Valley for farming. In low-water years, less water is around for Trinity Lake, particularly by late summer.

When everything is right, it can support

one of the best smallmouth-bass fisheries in the state and provide good chances of catching largemouth bass and rainbow trout. Trinity receives plants of rainbow and brown trout, and king salmon in the six- to eight-inch class. They can grow big. Kokanee salmon, brown bullhead, and channel catfish are also available.

Smallmouth, however, are the centerpiece. The lake-record smallmouth is 9 pounds, 1 ounce, caught by Tim Brady of Weaverville.

The best fishing for smallmouth takes place as winter transitions to spring, not in summer. The weather is cold then. The spring breeze often has a bite to it (especially if you're in a fast boat), but smallmouth come out of hibernation during this season. For anglers fanning the shoreline with casts, using grubs or spinnerbaits, smallmouth fishing is best on the upper end of the lake, particularly around the dredger tailings.

When spring arrives in May, angler pressure on the Trinity is still quite low, but the largemouth bass come to life. The upper ends of the lake arms are the best spots. Because Trinity Lake has almost zero structure (the bottom is practically barren and steeply sloped), the bass tend to suspend and scatter off points and in the backs of coves. That is why it is critical to cover a lot of water. An electric motor is an absolute necessity.

On Trinity Lake, it can take a newcomer a day or two to find fish, and then another day to figure out exactly how to start hooking them. One way to shortcut this procedure is to use crickets. Use a No. 6 hook and single split shot, then cast the live cricket just off the points and let it sink. Typically between 15 and 30 feet down, you'll find fish. I've used this same method for smallmouth in other lakes, and it seems to be a universal truth that smallmouth like nothing better than a live cricket.

Once the sun is on the water, skilled knowhows using grubs can catch both largemouth and smallmouth bass.

In June, the weather here is often still cool. But if you pick a day when the wind is down, June is prime time for trout trolling. Stuarts Fork and points near the corners of the dam are among the better spots. There are no secrets about it; you'll get more strikes by trailing half a night crawler behind flashers.

Fish and Game has created a new opportunity here with the planting of king salmon. The fish are up to six and seven pounds, but they are not caught consistently. When the salmon start feeding on the undersize kokanee salmon in this lake, a trophy fishery will likely result.

As summer progresses, the weather often heats up, and the fish generally go 25–40 feet below the surface. If you don't go that far down in the thermocline, you'll get skunked. New arrivals who see pictures of fish on the walls of tackle shops and resorts and wonder why they never get a bite can find this particularly frustrating.

Trinity is a big lake with full-service marinas. You can rent houseboats, stay in cabins (at Cedar Stock Resort), head out and set up a boat-in camp (at Captain's Point, on the west shore of the Trinity River arm), and try for a variety of fish. Even when the water level is down, you'll find plenty of lake to explore and fish.

Facilities, fees: Several campgrounds are provided around the lake, including boat-in sites. Full-service marinas, boat ramps, boat rentals, picnic areas, groceries, bait, and tackle are also available. Resorts include: Trinity Center Marina, Pinewood Cove Resort, and Trinity Lake Resort and Marina. There is a parking fee at boat ramps.

Directions: From I-5 at Redding, take Highway 299 west and drive 52 miles to Weaverville and Highway 3. Turn north on Highway 3 and drive 14 miles to the lake. This road will take you directly to a boat ramp; boat ramps are also available farther north, off Highway 3 and Trinity Dam Boulevard.

To Tannery Gulch: From I-5 at Redding,

take Highway 299 west and drive to Weaverville at Highway 3. Turn north on Highway 3 and drive 13.5 miles to County Road 172. Turn right on County Road 172 and drive 1.5 miles to the campground and nearby boat ramp.

To Stuarts Fork Boat Ramp: From I-5 at Redding, take Highway 299 west and drive to Weaverville at Highway 3. Turn north on Highway 3 and drive seven miles to the Stuarts Fork arm of Trinity Lake.

To Bowerman Boat Ramp: From I-5 at Redding, take Highway 299 west and drive to Weaverville at Highway 3. Turn north on Highway 3 and drive to Covington Mill (six miles south of Trinity Center). Turn right (south) on Guy Covington Road and drive two miles to the boat-ramp entrance.

To Pinewood Resort: From I-5 at Redding, take Highway 299 west and drive to Weaverville at Highway 3. Turn north on Highway 3 and drive 14 miles to the resort entrance on the right.

To Trinity Lake KOA: From Redding, take Highway 299 west and drive to Weaverville at Highway 3. Turn north on Highway 3 and drive to Trinity Lake and continue to Trinity Center. At Trinity Center, continue 0.5 mile north on Highway 3 to the resort (on the right).

Contact: Shasta-Trinity National Forest, Weaverville Ranger District, 530/623-2121, www.fs.fed.us/r5—click on Forest Offices; Shasta Cascade Wonderland Association, 530/365-7500, www.shastacascade.com.

Lodging: Trinity Lake Resorts, 530/286-2225 or 800/255-5561, www.trinitylakeresort.com; Trinity Lake KOA, 530/266-3337 or 800/715-3337, www.trinitylakekoa.com; Pinewood Cove Resort, 530/286-2201, www.pinewoodcove.com; Trinity Alps Marina, 530/286-2282, www.trinityalpsmarina.com; Shasta Lake campgrounds, www.shastalakecamping.com; Recreation.gov, 877/444-6777, www.recreation.gov.

33 LEWISTON LAKE

Rating: 8

near Lewiston in
Shasta-Trinity National Forest
Map 2.4, page 122

This is one of California's prettiest lakes, ringed by conifers and always full, and with the Trinity Alps as a backdrop. Long and narrow, Lewiston is at 1,900 feet and spans a length of nine miles and 750 acres, with 15 miles of shoreline.

Enjoy the beauty of the place, because fishing quality does tend to fluctuate wildly. The Trinity Dam powerhouse, at the head of Lewiston Lake, is one key to angling success. When the powerhouse runs, it pours feed down the chute and into the head of the lake, and under these conditions, trout fishing can be outstanding anywhere from Lakeview Terrace on upstream.

If the powerhouse is running, anchor in the current and let a night crawler flutter near the bottom. When the powerhouse is not running, anchor near the point where the current flattens out into the lake and use yellow Power Bait.

Fly-fishing specialists should consider this lake, too. Some tules border the western shoreline near Lakeview Terrace; anglers should wade out here and fish the evening rise. Non–fly fishers might try using a fly behind a bubble (fly-and-bubble technique), which can also attract bites.

If all else fails, you can usually pick up a trout or two by using more traditional trolling methods, such as trailing half a night crawler behind a set of flashers. But typically this is a last resort.

The Department of Fish and Game stocks Lewiston with 10- to 12-inch rainbow trout, 10- to 12-inch brook trout, and 6- to 8-inch brown trout. In addition, several local businesses have teamed up to provide a pen-rearing project at Lewiston, where trout are grown in the pens until they reach three pounds, at which point they are released into the lake.

This is a testimonial of how to do something right, an example for other lakes across the state. Some huge and elusive brown trout also swim in the depths of this lake.

Lewiston Lake provides visitors with an opportunity to enjoy quality camping (with 100 campsites), fishing, boating, and hiking, but it is often overlooked in favor of its nearby big brother, Trinity Lake. There are 15 miles of shoreline. A 10 mph speed limit keeps the water quiet and calm—conditions that are ideal for anglers using canoes and small aluminum boats.

Facilities, fees: Several campgrounds are available; the best is Mary Smith Camp. Lakeview Terrace Resort, 530/778-3803, provides pleasant accommodations for folks who don't want to rough it. A boat ramp is provided. Supplies can be obtained in Lewiston. There is a parking fee at the Pine Cove Boat Ramp.

Directions: From Redding, take Highway 299 west and drive to Buckhorn Summit, continuing for five miles to Trinity Dam Boulevard. Turn right on Trinity Dam Boulevard and drive 10 miles (five miles past Lewiston) to Lakeview Terrace Resort on the left side of the road. To reach Pine Cove Marina, continue 0.5 mile on Trinity Dam Boulevard.

Contact: Shasta-Trinity National Forest, Weaverville Ranger District, 530/623-2121, www.fs.fed.us/r5—click on Forest Offices; Shasta Cascade Wonderland Association, 530/365-7500, www.shastacascade.com; Pine Cove RV Park & Marina, 530/778-3770, www.pine-cove-marina.com; Lakeview Terrace Resort, 530/778-3803, www.lakeviewterraceresort.com; Trinity Fly Shop, 530/623-6757, www.trinityflyshop.com.

34 SHASTA LAKE

Rating: 10
near Redding in Shasta-Trinity National Forest
Map 2.4, page 122   BEST (

Shasta Lake is the outdoor recreation capital of Northern California. It is a massive reservoir with 370 miles of shoreline, 13 campgrounds with 1,200 campsites, 15 boat ramps, 11 marinas, 400 houseboat rentals, and 35 resorts. In addition, getting here is easy (a straight shot on I-5), and it's just north of Redding.

The lake has 22 species of fish, with trout, bass, salmon, crappie, and catfish providing the best results.

"This is simply the best fishery in California," said lure inventor Gary Miralles. "I can live anywhere, and I have chosen to live here, right on Shasta Lake."

Miralles is transfixed at Shasta by a 15-pound brown trout he once hooked—and lost—that he named "Mo." Others are captivated by the chance of catching 15 or 20 trout in a day or 5- to 10-pound salmon—or dunking minnows for crappie, bass, sunfish, and catfish. My top day with Miralles delivered 58 trout, all released.

In addition, every March there comes a 7- to 10-day stretch of clear, warm weather that inspires the start of a three-month cycle where the bass practically shout "Catch me!" In a day, it's typical to catch 25 bass—a mix of spotted, largemouth, and perhaps a Florida. On one trip with my brother, Rambob, we tried to keep track of the number of fish we caught but lost the figure at around 73 when we had a series of doubles; the hookups were just coming too fast to count.

Here is a species-by-species synopsis:

• Trout: Shasta Lake provides one of the most consistent trout fisheries in California. In more than 750 trips, my longtime fishing pal Gary Miralles has been skunked only twice. He is available for guided trips, is the owner of Shasta Tackle, and specializes in trolling Humdingers and Cripplures, as well as Koke-A-Nuts behind Sling Blades.

The trout are big, averaging 14–18 inches, with a sprinkling in the 18- to 22-inch class, mixed in with salmon five pounds and larger. I asked Miralles to show me his logbook for a week of trips, and in four days he took 11 people who caught (and mostly released) a total of 173 trout. This averaged out to nearly

16 per person, with the trout averaging 16 inches; the biggest was 20 inches, caught by my wife, Stephani.

I use downriggers to test depths between 25 and 90 feet all summer, trolling Humdingers. My favorite colors here are purple, blue/silver, red/gold, and black/silver. In the spring, gold Cripplures can work best. Then once schools of shad minnows furnish easy food for the trout, I switch to blue/silver and purple Humdingers. In winter I have had success with the white Z-Ray with red dots, 25-ounce Kastmaster, and silver F-4 Flatfish.

Though the lake is huge, two general spots are the best for trout. For the first, launch near the dam at Clickapudi Ramp and then troll at the corner of the dam, the mouth and inlet of the Dry Creek arm adjacent to Toupee Island, and the inlet to the Big Backbone. It is best on the south-facing shorelines. This is because all summer south winds blow the feed against these shorelines.

The other area that is excellent is up the Mc-Cloud arm, right along the limestone formations that are always so stunningly beautiful. In April and May there seem to be large concentrations of trout farther up the McCloud up from Dekkas Rock, and at the headwaters of the McCloud arm. In the spring, going well up the Pit River arm about five miles past the no-ski marker can provide sensational fishing for the big Pit River strain of rainbow trout. Once you find a school of trout, stay with it, because they don't move out of these areas quickly.

In summer, the lake stratifies into distinct temperature zones, making it easy to locate trout. That is because the trout hold position in the thermocline as if they are locked in jail, and that makes them much easier to find. Average trolling depth in spring and fall is 10–20 feet for best results. By summer, the trout stay put in the thermocline, 45–70 feet deep. In fall, when the lake turns over, bringing shad minnows to the surface, the trout can be caught in the top 10 feet of water. It can be just plain sensational.

• Bass: Shasta Lake is loaded with bass. In the spring and early summer, anglers who know how to fish plastic worms can catch 75–100 bass per boat. Though high fish counts are not unusual at Shasta Lake, catching very many over 13 inches is rare. Getting a limit of bass over 15 inches; well, you might want to declare the day a national holiday. A productive bass area that gets less attention than most other spots is the wooded area of the Squaw Creek arm. A newcomer can tie on a No. 1 hook, clamp on a split shot 17 inches above the hook, then hook a live minnow through the nose (vertically), toss it out, and have a bass on in under a minute. It's the best place for a youngster to learn to fish because you're going to get bit, and the action can be sensational. For anglers experienced with plastics, you can fill your boat (and empty it, of course).

One trick at Shasta is to go out in the late summer, when the water is low, revealing the lake's structure, rocks, timber, and brush. When the lake fills, these are the spots to fish. Do not waste your time casting at bare shorelines.

The spring bass bite, especially for spotted bass, makes Shasta one of the best places to learn how to fish with plastic worms. You can use almost any technique: Dartheads with a Fat Albert grub, Texas-style with a Brush Hog, Wacky-style with a Senko, or drop-shot with a Magic Worm. The best advice is to use a fairly stiff-tipped spinning rod, to cast into the backs of coves in a few feet of water and "dead-stick" the worm. That means you do not move the worm, but keep it "dead" on the bottom. And, get this, you should retrieve enough line to keep it taut. You can then feel and see even the lightest nibble, and so be ready to set the hook.

When I first learned how to do this, I kept reeling in the plastic worms and noticed they appeared all chewed up, yet I was not feeling any bites. Catching nothing was driving me crazy until I switched to a stiff-tipped rod, and just like that I started joining those lucky anglers with the 50-fish days.

Of course, more traditional methods also work: "walking the dog" with a plastic worm (that is, walking a plastic worm along the lake bottom); casting a Zara Spook surface lure and zig-zagging it; and casting white spinnerbaits wherever you find muddy water.

The top spots for bass are along big rock piles, at the backs of coves, near submerged trees, and in the downwind sides of points. Most bassers here fish long hours and cover lots of water; their electric motors keep them on the move as they cast along the shoreline ahead of the boat. Of course, you need to follow the bass through their patterns, from winter mode to pre-spawn, spawn, post-spawn, and summer staging.

• Salmon: Salmon fishing has become popular, especially in the spring, when the water is still cool and the flesh of the salmon is still firm. The most popular way to fish for salmon is to mooch with an anchovy tail 60–80 feet deep right at the dam. Another trick is trolling with a Sling Blade dodger and a Koke-A-Nut, 60–120 feet deep, using a Scotty downrigger to get there.

The average-size salmon runs about three pounds. The most consistent areas for salmon are near the dam and the Dry Creek arm. After a DFG plant, tons of 8- to 10-inch salmon can be caught. Of course, these fish should be released. They represent the lake's future salmon fishery.

Salmon are best caught from March through May. Once the 100°F temperatures of summer arrive, the salmon go very deep, often 90–125 feet down at the dam.

• Crappie: As spotted bass increased in numbers, crappie have gone down. There are still prospects up the Pit River arm; a 5-mph zone is established where a series of submerged trees provide an ideal habitat for crappie as well as big bass. Tie up to one of the trees and vertically jig with white crappie jigs. If you enjoy fishing with live minnows, hook a live minnow vertically through the mouth, attach a small split shot, and send it down there. The bonus at Shasta is that the crappie are often large—12–14 inches long.

• Catfish: Shasta has some giant catfish, as well as good numbers of two- and three-pounders. The best bet is to fish at night for the big ones. If you are staying on a houseboat, keep a line out all night, using chicken livers or dead minnows for bait. Catfish weighing five pounds and up are common on summer nights. Though catfish are caught all over the lake, the best area is also the most difficult to fish: up in the Pit River arm, among the submerged trees.

At Shasta there are several boat-in campgrounds, as well as enough drive-in campgrounds to make sure that the place never fills up. One thing about Shasta to be prepared for is the number of people. Hundreds of houseboaters and hordes of waterskiers converge on this place in the summer. But Shasta is big enough for everybody. If you want to escape the masses, just head into one of the quiet coves.

A final word: There's no other lake like Shasta in the West. Even though you may have been on the lake several times, when Shasta Lake is full, it's like discovering a new body of water.

Facilities, fees: Lodging, cabins, campgrounds, restrooms with showers and flush toilets, drinking water, and convenience stores are available. Many marinas have fishing boats, ski boats, personal watercraft, and accessories for rent. Fees are charged for boat launching, day use, and camping.

• Antlers Resort: A full-service marina, convenience store, and picnic area are available. Houseboats, pontoon boats, aluminum fishing boats, personal watercraft, ski boats, and canoes can be rented. Contact 530/238-2553 or 800/238-3924, www.shastalakevacations.com.

A campground and paved boat ramp are nearby at Antlers RV Park and Campground, 530/238-2322 or 800/642-6849, www.antlersrvpark.com.

• Bridge Bay Resort & Marina: A paved ramp, full-service marina, motel, convenience store, restaurant, and picnic area are available. Houseboats, ski boats, pontoon boats, and aluminum fishing boats are for rent. Contact 530/275-3021 or 800/752-9669, www.seven crown.com/lakes.

• Digger Bay Marina: There is a paved ramp, a full-service marina, gas, and a store. Fishing boats can be rented. Contact 530/275-3072 or 800/752-9669.

• Holiday Harbor: A two-lane paved ramp, full-service marina, RV park, cafe, convenience store, gas, picnic area, and playground are available. Houseboats, ski boats, pontoon boats, personal watercraft, aluminum fishing boats, and canoes can be rented. Contact 530/238-2383 or 800/776-2628, www.lake shasta.com.

• Jones Valley Resort: A boat ramp, full-service marina, and convenience store are available. Houseboats, fishing boats, ski boats, pontoon boats, personal watercraft, canoes, and kayaks can be rented. Contact 530/275-7950 or 877/468-7326.

• Packers Bay: A boat ramp, marina, dock, fuel, and convenience store are available. Houseboats can be rented. Contact 800/331-3137, www.packersbay.com.

• Shasta Marina: A marina, gas, and a convenience store are available. Houseboats can be rented. Contact 530/238-2284 or 800/959-3359, www.shastalake.net.

• Silverthorn Resort: A paved ramp, full-service marina, cabins, mooring, gas, pizza parlor (summer only), and a store are available. Houseboats, pontoon boats, ski boats, aluminum fishing boats, kayaks, and personal watercraft can be rented. Contact 530/275-1571 or 800/332-3044, www.silverthorn resort.com.

Directions: Fishing access points are available all around the shore and can be reached by taking one of several exits off I-5 north of Redding. A popular spot is Fisherman's Point, at Shasta Dam. From Redding, drive four miles north on I-5. Take the Shasta Dam Boulevard exit and drive to Lake Boulevard. Turn right (well signed) and drive to the boat ramp at the dam. Directions to other marinas and access points follow.

• To Antlers: From Redding, drive north on I-5 for 24 miles to the Lakeshore Drive/Antlers Road exit, in Lakehead. Take that exit, turn right at the stop sign, and drive a short distance to Antlers Road. At Antlers Road, turn right and drive one mile south to the campground and nearby boat ramp.

• To Sugarloaf: From Redding, drive north on I-5 for 24 miles to the Lakeshore Drive/Antlers Road exit. Take that exit and turn left on Lakeshore Drive. Drive three miles (look for the "Loaf on Inn" sign) and turn left and drive to the entrance for Sugarloaf. Turn left and drive to the marina and boat ramp.

• To Hirz Bay: From Redding, drive north on I-5 for about 20 miles to the Salt Creek/Gilman exit. Turn right on Gilman Road/County Road 7H009 and drive northeast for 10 miles to the campground/boat launch access road. Turn right and drive 0.5 mile to the boat ramp.

• To Lakeshore Marina: From Redding, drive north on I-5 for 24 miles to Lakehead and the exit for Lakeshore Drive/Antlers Road. Take that exit, turn left at the stop sign, and drive under the freeway to Lakeshore Drive. Turn left and drive three miles to the entrance on the left.

• To Bailey Cove: From Redding, drive north on I-5 over the Pit River Bridge at Shasta Lake to O'Brien Road/Shasta Caverns Road exit. Turn east (right) on Shasta Caverns Road and drive 0.25 mile to a signed turnoff for Bailey Cove. Turn right and drive one mile to Bailey Cove Boat Ramp.

• To Holiday Harbor: From Redding, drive north on I-5 for 18 miles to the O'Brien/Shasta Caverns Road exit. Turn right (east) at Shasta Caverns Road and drive about one mile to the marina entrance on the right.

• To Packers Bay: From Redding, drive north on I-5 for 18 miles to the O'Brien/Shasta Caverns Road exit. Take that exit to the stop sign, turn left, drive a short distance, and then turn left and drive south on I-5 a short distance to the exit for Packers Bay. Take that exit and drive two miles to the marina and boat ramp.

• To Shasta Marina: From Redding, drive north on I-5 for 18 miles to the O'Brien/Shasta Caverns Road exit. Take that exit to the stop sign. Turn west on O'Brien Inlet Road and drive one mile to the entrance to the marina and boat ramp.

• To Jones Valley & Silverthorn: From Redding, turn east on Highway 299 and drive 7.5 miles (just past the town of Bella Vista) to Dry Creek Road. Turn left on Dry Creek Road and drive nine miles to a Y in the road. For Jones Valley Resort and a public ramp, bear right at the Y. For Silverthorn Resort, bear left at the Y.

• To Bridge Bay: From Redding, take I-5 north for eight miles to the Bridge Bay exit. Take that exit and continue one mile to the office. Pay for boat launching, then drive south 100 yards to the boat ramp.

• To Centimudi/Shasta Dam: From I-5 in Redding, drive north for three miles to the exit for the town of Shasta Lake City and Shasta Dam Boulevard. Take that exit, bear west on Shasta Dam Boulevard, and drive three miles to Lake Boulevard. Turn right on Lake Boulevard and drive two miles to a fork. Turn right and drive 0.5 mile to the boat launch.

• To Digger Bay: From I-5 in Redding, drive north for three miles to the exit for the town of Shasta Lake City and Shasta Dam Boulevard. Take that exit and bear west on Shasta Dam Boulevard, then drive about three miles to Shasta Park Drive. Turn right on Shasta Park Drive (which becomes Digger Bay Road) and drive about four miles to the marina and boat ramp.

Contact: Shasta Lake Visitor Information Center, 530/275-1589, www.fs.fed.us/r5—click on Forest Offices/shastatrinity/recreation; Shasta Cascade Wonderland Association, 530/365-7500, www.shastacascade.com.

Lodging: Digger Bay Marina, 530/275-3072 or 800/752-9669; Bridge Bay Resort, 530/275-3021 or 800/752-9669, www.sevencrown .com/lakes; Antlers Resort, 530/238-2553 or 800/238-3924, www.shastalakevacations .com; Antlers RV Park and Campground,

530/238-2322 or 800/642-6849, www.antlers rvpark.com; Holiday Harbor, 530/238-2383 or 800/776-2628, www.lakeshasta.com; Silverthorn Resort, 530/275-1571 or 800/332-3044, www.silverthornresort.com; Shasta Lake, www.shastalake.com; Sugarloaf Cottages, 530/238-2448.

Information: Guide Gary Miralles, Shasta Tackle Company, 530/275-2278; Phil's Propeller & Fishing Tackle, 530/275-4939 or 800/462-3917, www.philsprop.com; Basshole, 530/238-2170, bassholebarandgrill.com.

35 CLEAR CREEK

Rating: 5

west of Redding

Map 2.4, page 122

"Psssst. Want to hear a secret? Just don't tell anybody about it."

That is how a few people talk about Clear Creek. You see, everybody else in this area goes to nearby Whiskeytown Lake. They don't know that Clear Creek, along with its little campground, exists. But it does. Not only that, but the stream also supports a fair population of trout, with many in the 10- to 12-inch class.

Fishable sections lie both upstream and downstream of Whiskeytown Lake. The upstream section receives 800 six- to eight-inch rainbow trout per year. Pretty meager, but at least they're plunking some fish in.

If you visit nearby Whiskeytown Lake during the peak early summer season, tiny Clear Creek just might provide the less-crowded alternative you are looking for.

Facilities, fees: A small primitive campground is north of French Gulch. No drinking water is available. Garbage must be packed out. Other campsites are at Whiskeytown Lake. Supplies can be obtained in Redding. Fishing access is free.

Directions: From Redding, turn west on Highway 299 and drive 17 miles to Trinity Lake Road (just west of Whiskeytown Lake). Turn north on Trinity Lake Road and continue past the town of French Gulch for about 12 miles to the Trinity Mountain Ranger Station. Turn right on County Road 106/East Side Road (gravel) and drive north for about 11 miles to the campground access road (dirt). Turn right on the access road and drive two miles to the campground. Access is available off short roads that junction with Trinity Mountain Road, which parallels the creek.

Contact: Shasta-Trinity National Forest, Weaverville Ranger District, 530/623-2121, www.fs.fed.us/r5—click on Forest Offices.

36 WHISKEYTOWN LAKE

Rating: 7
near Redding in Shasta-Trinity National Forest
Map 2.4, page 122

The improving fishing for kokanee salmon at Whiskeytown Lake is putting it on the map in Northern California. The good-sized lake (elevation 1,200 feet) covers 3,220 acres, with 36 miles of shoreline, and it is just a short drive west of Redding. Thousands of kokanee salmon have been planted by the Department of Fish and Game at Whiskeytown.

One of the great techniques for kokanee salmon at Whiskeytown is to use a Sling Blade dodger trailed by a Koke-a-Nut. But the key at Whiskeytown is depth—typically just 15 feet deep in spring and early summer, but as much as 70 feet deep in later summer.

Another technique is to trail a Luhr Jensen Wedding Spinner behind a small set of flashers, with the hook baited with a piece of corn. The kokanee love it.

If the kokanee aren't biting, just skewer on a night crawler instead of corn, and you're in business for trout. After all, Whiskeytown is stocked with rainbow and brook trout. The best areas for trout are in the vicinity of the Highway 299 bridge and near the powerhouse. In fact, if the powerhouse is running, start and end your trip there. It is the best spot on the lake for trout.

Whiskeytown isn't considered a great bass lake, but bass are in there. Because of the clear water and varying shorelines, bass tend to be very wary. Light lines are a must at Whiskeytown, and most anglers use lines that are too heavy; that is, too visible, and it spooks the fish from biting.

Anglers without boats will find plenty of shoreline to fish, a real bonus. When the lake is full, the Whiskey Creek arm offers several hundred yards of accessible bank on each side. An option is to fish Whiskey Creek above the lake. For access, drive up the road for several miles. It's very brushy, where you work your way through the brush to the stream. Use small lures and light line. In high-water years, it's worth the effort.

Whiskeytown is easy to reach from Redding, has plenty of room to explore (36 miles of shoreline), and offers decent camping accommodations. The biggest problem is the wind in early summer, which can whip up during the spring, making this the favorite lake in the region for windsurfers and sailboaters. The federal ban on personal watercraft at national parks took effect at Whiskeytown in 2003.

Facilities, fees: There are three campgrounds: Brandy Creek, Oak Bottom, and Dry Creek Group Camp. Tents are not permitted at Brandy Creek. A full-service marina, boat rentals, groceries, wood, and an RV dump station are available. Full supplies can be obtained in Redding. There are also three boat ramps:
• Brandy Creek Marina: A paved launch ramp, swimming beach, snack bar, and convenience store are available.
• Oak Bottom Marina: A paved launch ramp, full-service marina, fishing pier, convenience store, and a snack bar are available. Pontoon boats, ski boats, sailboats, fishing boats, canoes, and pedal boats can be rented.
• Whiskey Creek: A paved launch ramp and fishing pier are available. A convenience store is nearby. There is a vehicle-use fee (an annual pass is available).

Directions: To Brandy Creek: From Redding,

drive west on Highway 299 for eight miles to the park's visitors center. Turn left at the visitors center (Kennedy Memorial Drive) and drive five miles to the campground entrance road on the right. Turn right and drive a short distance to the camp.

To Dry Creek: From Redding, drive west on Highway 299 for eight miles to the visitors center. Turn left at the visitors center (Kennedy Memorial Drive) and drive six miles to the campground on the right side of the road.

To Oak Bottom: From Redding, drive west on Highway 299 for 15 miles (past the visitors center) to the campground entrance road on the left. Turn left and drive a short distance to the campground.

Contact: Whiskeytown National Recreation Area, 530/246-1225 or 530/246-1225, www .nps.gov/whis; Shasta Cascade Wonderland Association, 530/365-7500, www.shastacascade .com; Oak Bottom Marina, 530/359-2269.

37 KESWICK LAKE

Rating: 6

near Redding in Shasta-Trinity National Forest
Map 2.4, page 122

Some days, you need a Jaws of Life to get the fish to open their mouths at this narrow, deep, small lake. Few even try this lake, because the trout can be so elusive. Yet the lake is home to some monster-size rainbow trout and brown trout. One of the largest wild rainbow trout ever documented from a California lake (18 pounds, 5 ounces) was caught here.

Because of the year-round cold water, some people claim it takes deep-water trolling techniques, downriggers preferred, to get to them. The Department of Fish and Game stocks rainbow trout and Eagle Lake trout in the six- to eight-inch class here. It might just be feed for the giant trout.

The Redding Fly Shop has figured out how to fish the upper end of the lake to catch some beauties. This is a specialized approach: With fly rod, most will cast with sink-tip lines or a clear intermediate sink line, and use No. 4 or 6 streamers, or brown steel buggers.

Facilities, fees: A boat ramp and a day-use picnic area with vault toilets are provided. There is no drinking water. Camping is available nearby at Whiskeytown Lake. Fishing access is free.

Directions: From I-5 at Redding, take the Highway 299 West exit. Drive four miles west to Iron Mountain Road. Turn right (north) on Iron Mountain Road and drive four miles to the lake. Follow the signs to the boat ramp.

Contact: U.S. Department of Interior, Bureau of Reclamation, Northern California Area, 530/275-1554.

38 SACRAMENTO RIVER: REDDING TO ANDERSON

Rating: 10

near Redding
Map 2.4, page 122   BEST (

From Redding to Anderson, this river can provide some of the best catch rates for trout anywhere in the West. At times (especially from mid-October through November, and also in spring and early summer), it's sensational.

Yet it may be even better known for its stacked holes of salmon (15–25-pounders), which arrive from late July through fall, with the best fishing from mid-August through September. Yet still others rave about the shad fishing in June.

But first note this: when the river is flowing over 9,000 cubic feet per second (CFS), shore fishing is impossible, and you need a boat to fish right.

Many guides from the Fly Shop launch and drift this section with fly fishers aboard, side casting and side drifting. Hank Mautz, a fieldscout and former guide, also has had tremendous success back trolling or side casting with Glo Bugs. Most boaters will put in at the Posse Grounds, then take their drift boats downstream, stopping the boats to work the riffles, cuts, and tails. The best time is in the fall, when two or three anglers often catch and release 50 trout in a day.

In the spring, the preferred setup is to rig with night crawlers for bait, threaded on the hook so that they lie perfectly straight in the water. Crickets can also work well. Another trick with a spinning rod from a drift boat is to cast a No. 2 gold Mepps spinner. Other techniques include anchoring in the side waters, then casting in the riffles.

There are some big trout in this river. Many go 15–20 inches and occasionally to 5 pounds, with documented reports of trout up to 10 pounds. Most catch-and-release all fish in order to keep one of the great fisheries great.

When the river is running below 7,000 CFS, there is opportunity for shoreline prospects right in the town of Redding, wading out and casting. When the river is much higher, you cannot reach the prime spots from shore. One of the better spots from shore is within 40 yards of the Sundial Bridge, on the upstream side.

From a boat you will see how the character of this river changes from mile to mile. One of the prettiest sections is the canyon below the Jones Ferry Bridge. Some call this Iron Canyon Rapids, a Class I drop, where the water rumbles through miniature cliffs and lava outcroppings.

Yet it seems the salmon make even bigger news.

They average 15–25 pounds and are commonly bigger. In fact, the state record—88 pounds—was caught on this river near Red Bluff by Lindy Lindberg. But there's something I didn't learn that day that took many years to discover: fishing for salmon is rarely fast-paced.

You tend to grind out the fish, working the river for long periods, hoping to get a bite every hour or so. The salmon fishing starts to perk up around mid-August, peaks from mid-September–mid-October, and then starts to wane through November. During this time, there are hundreds of boats on the river every day,

back-trolling over the deep river holes, where salmon rest on their upstream journey.

Bumping roe is the best way to go. Another good technique is back-trolling. Rig with a large silver Flatfish or Kwikfish, with a three-inch fillet of sardine tied on the underside of the lure. Place a three-way swivel four feet above the lure, and hang your sinker from the swivel, its weight dependent on the depth of the hole and river current. Four to eight ounces usually does the job. If you don't have a boat, get a guide. One of the few bank-fishing spots for salmon is on the east side of the river, at the mouth of Old Battle Creek.

Note that it's illegal to fish for salmon upstream of the Deschutes Bridge, in Redding.

My first trip here was very special. I fished with north-state legend John Reginato. At first he was skeptical of me, "the Talking Beard," but I quickly hooked a 28-pound salmon and landed it after a fantastic fight that included several jumps. John got a photo of the fish jumping in midair with my profile and bent rod in the foreground (it has since run in more than 50 publications). Then 20 minutes later I got another big one: 32 pounds.

Another option is to fish from Red Bluff on downstream for shad, which arrive in June and remain in force through early July. The experience is just the opposite of salmon fishing. It's fast-paced, the fish are not huge, and you can use light tackle or fly rods. The best spot is the Tehama Riffle, downstream of the Tehama Bridge. Here you can wade out, cast Shad Darts, Teeney Rounders, or T-Killers, and in one evening catch 10 or so shad in the two- to four-pound class.

The Sacramento River is the lifeblood of Northern California, running some 400 river miles from its source at the base of Mount Shasta southward to San Francisco Bay. Water exports to points south have damaged the river, but as long as the water rumbles downstream, the fish will keep coming back.

Facilities, fees: Several full-facility campgrounds and RV parks are available along the Sacramento River and near adjacent towns.

A few good choices include the Marina RV Park and Sacramento River RV Resort. Fishing access is free.

Directions: From Redding, drive south on I-5 and look for exits for Riverside, Balls Ferry, and Jellys Ferry. Access is also available in the city of Redding at Caldwell Park and near the Redding Civic Auditorium.

Contact: U.S. Forest Service, Lake Red Bluff Recreation Area, 530/527-2813; Woodson Bridge State Recreation Area, 530/839-2112, www.parks.ca.gov; Shasta Cascade Wonderland Association, 530/365-7500, www.shasta cascade.com.

Guides: J&J Guide Service, 530/222-6253; Frank Duarte's Guide Service, 530/570-2399, www.worldwidefishing.com; Mike Bogue, 530/246-8457, www.mikebogue.com; Jack Trout Guide Service, 530/926-4540, www .jacktrout.com or www.mtshasta.com; Liam Gogan, Trinity River Outfitters, 530/623-6376, www.trinityriveroutfitters.com; The Fly Shop, 530/222-3555 (stream report) or 800/669-3474 (guide bookings), www.fly shop.com.

39 SACRAMENTO RIVER: RED BLUFF TO COLUSA

Rating: 8

near Redding

Map 2.4, page 122

The old river is an emerald-green fountain, the lifeblood of Northern California, a living, pulsing vein in the very heart of the state.

To put it a little more directly, this section of the river, from Red Bluff downstream to Colusa, is the prettiest part of California's Central Valley. I have canoed the entire length and fished most of it, and it remains a place filled with beauty, power, and big fish. The folks who live on the river don't need a calendar. They just track the migrations of fish, which tell time better than a watch. Trout live in these waters, and shad, salmon, striped bass, and sturgeon—some of which reach state-record sizes—migrate through.

For the most part, to fish it well, you must have a boat and be skilled at operating it, or you must hire a guide who can do the job for you. The reason is that the banks of the Sacramento River throughout most of this section are quite deep, and wading is impossible in many areas. There are exceptions, however.

In late May and June, the river comes to life with the arrival of migrating shad. They move through this entire section of the river, from Colusa on upstream to the Red Bluff diversion dam. Unlike the other fish, shad can be caught by anglers wading at two areas: the Tehama Riffle and around Colusa.

The Tehama Riffle is an outstanding spot. To reach it, take the Tehama/Los Molinos exit off I-5, then drive east. At Tehama, turn right on County Road A8 and drive a few blocks, then cross the Sacramento River. Turn left on a dirt road and park immediately under the Tehama Bridge. The best stretch is just downstream of the bridge.

If you have a boat, you can launch at Woodson Bridge State Recreation Area, Mill Creek Park (at Los Molinos), or the Red Bluff Diversion Dam. The fishing is best in the evening, when one can catch up to 20 shad in the two- to five-pound class by using Shad Darts, T-Killers, or Teeney Rounders, by making quartering casts, and by getting the lure deep.

The shad run continues into July, when the big females arrive, and then starts to wane. By August, however, enough salmon begin moving through to change your entire perspective. These are big spawners, mostly 10- to 20-pounders, and they can jump, strip line, and really raise hell. The salmon run starts in midsummer and peaks in September, continues through October, then wanes in November.

From mid-May through mid-June, the striped bass fishing can be fantastic in the Colusa area. The best way to catch them is using swim baits on a jighead. It can be sensational, where you catch a half dozen 10- to 15-pound bass, with a chance for bigger.

In August, the salmon take over the river. A day of fishing for these big salmon is a long grind, though. You start early and end late, patiently back-trolling with roe, Flatfish, or Kwikfish lures in the deeper holes. You need spirit, tempered with persistence, but it's worth it. The holes in the five miles of river downstream of the Red Bluff Diversion Dam are the top spots. It was here that Lindy Lindberg caught the state-record 88-pounder, a fish so big that Lindberg had to strap it to the side of his boat à la *Old Man and the Sea.*

The cold-water curtain inside of Shasta Dam lowers the river temperature a few degrees on the Sacramento River. That is why salmon now tend to school up several miles downriver from traditional spots, especially early in the season. This stretch of water extends several miles below Woodson Bridge State Park. In turn, this has spread the boats out and made fishing more of a quality experience along the entire river.

Come winter and early spring, the sturgeon and striped bass start moving into this area, and the better holes are in the stretch of water near Colusa. Some huge sturgeon are in the mix, many of them beating the six-foot size limit now in effect. These are strong fish that can put you through a war. Meanwhile, more stripers now spawn in the Sacramento River than in the San Joaquin Delta. Trolling Rebels is the way to catch them, though it can require many hours per hookup. They don't come easy, but they come big. Since the larger individuals are spawning females, I urge anglers to release them. The trade-off is a future of guaranteed improved fishing.

The U.S. Fish and Wildlife Service has a recorded message on the fish counts at Red Bluff Diversion Dam: 530/527-1408.

Facilities, fees: Several campgrounds and RV parks are available along the river. Good choices include the Bend RV Park and Fishing Resort (near Red Bluff), Hidden Harbor RV Park and Marina (near Los Molinos), and Woodson Bridge State Recreation Area (near Corning). Lodging and supplies can be obtained in Red Bluff, Corning, and other towns. Boat ramps and boat rentals are also available. Fishing access is free.

Directions: Access is available off roads that junction with I-5 near Red Bluff, Corning, and Orland. Highway 45 southeast of Orland parallels the river, providing direct access to Colusa.

Contact: Lake Red Bluff Recreation Area, 530/527-2813; Sacramento River Discovery Center, 530/527-1196; Woodson Bridge State Recreation Area, 530/839-2112, www.parks.ca.gov (click on Visit a Park); Shasta Cascade Wonderland Association, 530/365-7500, www.shastacascade.com; Department of Fish and Game, Redding, 530/225-2300.

Information and supplies: Driftwood RV Park, 530/384-2851 or 888/678-1717, www.campdriftwood4fun.com; Hidden Harbor RV and Marina, 530/384-1800, www.hiddenharborrv.com.

Guides: J&J Guide Service, 530/222-6253; Frank Duarte's Guide Service, 530/570-2399, www.worldwidefishing.com; Mike Bogue, 530/246-8457, www.mikebogue.com; Three Rivers Guide Service, 530/925-7990, www.threeriversguideservice.com; Liam Gogan, Trinity River Outfitters, 530/623-6376, www.trinityriveroutfitters.com; The Fly Shop, 530/222-3555 (stream report) or 800/669-3474 (guide bookings), www.flyshop.com.

LASSEN
AND MODOC

Mount Lassen was the last volcano in California

to have a major eruption, blowing its top in 1914. No matter where you go in this region, you can sense the drama of that event and see the area's volcanic past – pumice boulders, volcanic rock, and spring-fed streams from the underground lava tubes.

The fishing is often nearly as explosive. Fishing highlights include the best fly-fishing in Northern California at Hat Creek, Fall River, Pit River, Burney Creek, and Manzanita Lake. Some people buy summer homes here solely because of the fly-fishing for trout.

Others head straight to Eagle Lake. At Eagle Lake, the average trout may be the largest of any lake in California. Lake Almanor is also home to trophy-size brown trout, as well as big rainbow trout, salmon, and smallmouth bass.

In addition, good fishing for smaller trout exists at a series of small, largely hidden lakes in the Caribou Wilderness and in nearby Lassen National Forest. Good prospects for crappie and smallmouth bass are highlights at Lake Britton. When it comes to lakes, the only drawback in this region is at Lassen Volcanic National Park. With the exception of Manzanita Lake, prospects are utterly terrible. There are also small trout streams such as Deer Creek, Yellow Creek, and North Fork Feather, and bass fishing at Round Valley Reservoir.

Lava Beds National Monument is a stark, pretty, and often lonely place, a region sprinkled with small lakes with trout, deer with large racks who migrate in after the first snow (and after the hunting season has closed), and a unique volcanic habitat, featuring huge flows of glass (obsidian) and gray matter (dacite). The highlight is Medicine Lake, formed in the caldera of a volcano and providing good trout fishing, with the bonus of campgrounds near the lakeside.

The northeast corner of California, or "old Modoc country," is among the most remote and least traveled of any area of the state. This is the kind of place where you can literally get away from everybody and poke around and explore. It features Cave and Lily Lakes (two small sister lakes), great little campgrounds, decent fishing, and a series of largely secret spots across the region. Janes Reservoir is the best of the secret fishing spots.

This region is lonely and remote, with many surprises for those willing to explore it. On the high desert plateau where the South Warner Mountains rise up on the edge of the Nevada basin, this region is largely sagebrush country. You'll find a sprinkling of lakes – some with trout, others with bass – and a few small and pristine wilderness streams with short but chunky trout. Herds of antelope and a considerable backcountry for exploration by four-wheel drive are added bonuses.

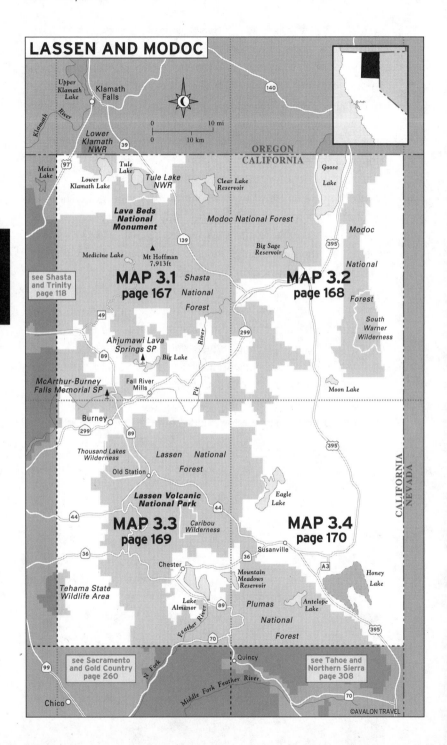

LASSEN AND MODOC

Upper Klamath Lake
Klamath Falls
Klamath River
Lower Klamath NWR
Meiss Lake
Lower Klamath Lake
Tule Lake
Tule Lake NWR
Clear Lake Reservoir
Goose Lake

OREGON
CALIFORNIA

Lava Beds National Monument

Modoc National Forest

Modoc

Big Sage Reservoir

Medicine Lake
Mt Hoffman 7,913ft

see Shasta and Trinity page 118

MAP 3.1 page 167

Shasta National Forest

MAP 3.2 page 168

National Forest

South Warner Wilderness

Ahjumawi Lava Springs SP
Big Lake

Fall River Mills

Pit River

McArthur-Burney Falls Memorial SP

Moon Lake

Burney

Thousand Lakes Wilderness

Lassen National Forest

Old Station

Eagle Lake

Lassen Volcanic National Park

MAP 3.3 page 169

Caribou Wilderness

MAP 3.4 page 170

Chester
Susanville

Tehama State Wildlife Area

Mountain Meadows Reservoir

Honey Lake

CALIFORNIA
NEVADA

Lake Almanor

Plumas National Forest

Antelope Lake

Feather River

see Sacramento and Gold Country page 260

Quincy

N Fork

Middle Fork Feather River

see Tahoe and Northern Sierra page 308

Chico

©AVALON TRAVEL

0   10 mi
0   10 km

Map 3.1

Sites 1-11
Pages 171-177

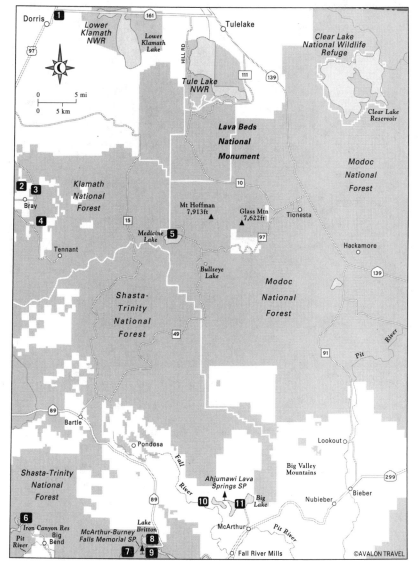

Map 3.2

Sites 12-32
Pages 178-188

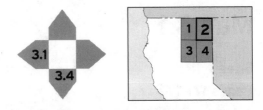

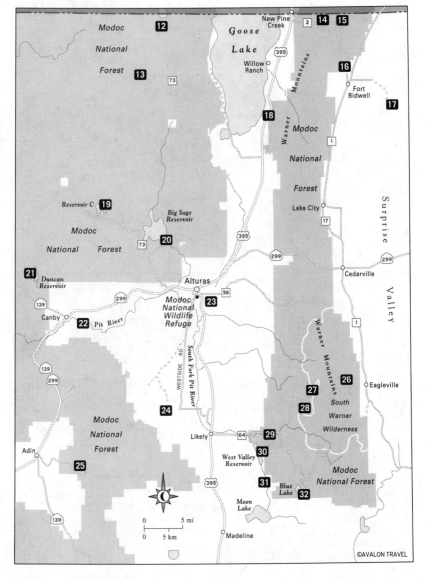

Map 3.3

**Sites 33-58
Pages 189-207**

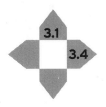

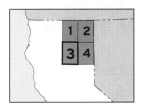

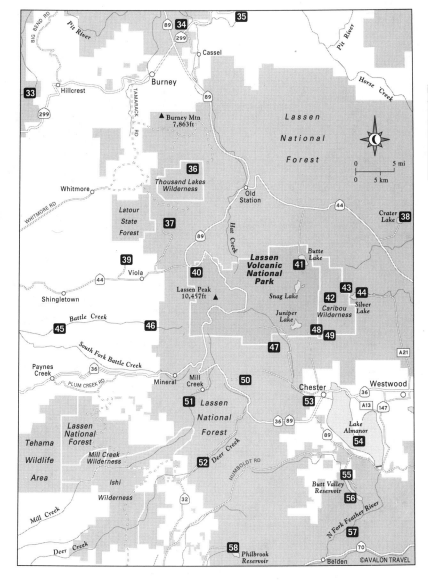

Map 3.4

Sites 59-65
Pages 207-212

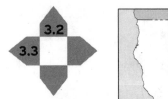

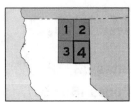

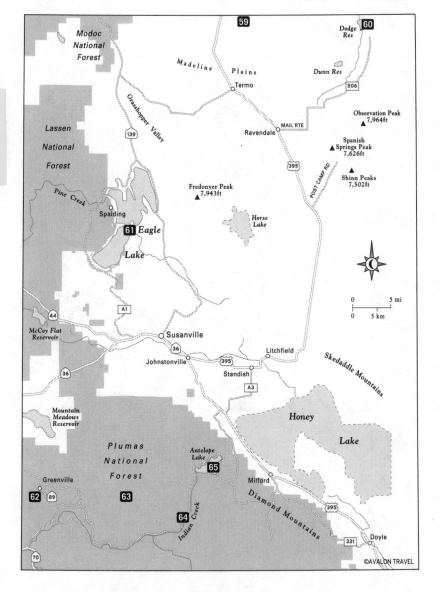

Modoc National Forest

59

Dodge Res

60

Madeline Plains

Dunn Res

Termo

506

Grasshopper Valley

MAIL RTE

Observation Peak
▲ 7,964ft

Lassen National Forest

139

Ravendale

395

Spanish
▲ Springs Peak
7,626ft

POST CAMP RD

Shinn Peaks
▲ 7,502ft

Pine Creek

Fredonyer Peak
▲ 7,943ft

Spalding

Horse Lake

61 Eagle Lake

44

A1

McCoy Flat Reservoir

Susanville

36

Johnstonville

395

Litchfield

Standish

A3

Skedaddle Mountains

36

Mountain Meadows Reservoir

Honey Lake

Plumas National Forest

Antelope Lake

65

Greenville

Milford

62 89

63

64

Diamond Mountains

395

Indian Creek

331

Doyle

70

©AVALON TRAVEL

0   5 mi
0   5 km

■ INDIAN TOM LAKE

Rating: 8

near Dorris

Map 3.1, page 167

For me, this lake's name conjures up images of bark canoes, fall colors, and a quiet, unknown spot comparable to the small lakes in northern Minnesota. Wrong.

Indian Tom Lake is easily accessible and is in flat, fairly stark country, not the pristine setting suggested by its name. Just the same, it offers a unique fishery for Lahontan cutthroat trout. The lake's fishing regulations are also special, so check the Department of Fish and Game's rule book before tossing in a line. The local game warden urges the DFG to stock Indian Tom Lake because the growth rate of fish can be fantastic. DFG biologists can't confirm that the fish always make it through the hot late summer, and that makes it a put-and-take fishery. Because of the lake's high alkalinity, other species of trout cannot live here, only Lahontan cutthroat. So plants have to be cutthroat or nothing.

Most visitors, however, arrive at the lake too late in the year for good fishing. If you come in midsummer and encounter algae growth, you may ask, "What's the big deal about this place?" The lake is not particularly deep, so it is vulnerable to weed growth in warm weather. Go in spring and early summer, when the water is clear and moderate in temperature, and when the fish are hungry and vibrant. Try silver or gold Kastmasters, or anything in hammered silver or hammered gold.

Facilities, fees: No facilities are available. Supplies can be obtained in Dorris. Fishing access is free.

Directions: From Redding, drive north on I-5 to Weed. Take the Central Weed/Highway 97 exit. Turn right at the stop sign and drive one mile through town to Highway 97. Bear right on Highway 97 and drive 52 miles to the town of Dorris. Continue north on U.S. 97 for 1.5 miles to Highway 161. Turn right and drive 0.25 mile to Sheepy Creek Road.

Turn right on Sheepy Creek Road and drive to the lake.

Contact: Department of Fish and Game, Redding, 530/225-2300; Merrill Lumber, Dorris, 530/397-3701; Butte Valley Chamber of Commerce, 530/397-2111, www.buttevalleychamber.com.

■ ORR LAKE

Rating: 5

near Macdoel in Klamath National Forest

Map 3.1, page 167

You can decide whether little Orr Lake is a good or a bad place. First, the negative side: The access road is rough, the larger fish can be elusive, and during the hot summer months, visitors—especially those with kids—should keep a sharp lookout for rattlesnakes. So you should drive a rugged vehicle, bring your angling smarts, and keep your eyes on the ground. If you follow these instructions at Orr Lake, you may be in for a treat.

Orr is one of the few lakes of its size with both brown trout and bass. It also has catfish. The Fish and Game stocks catchable trout. Trout fishing is best during the cool months, of course, and bass angling is optimal during the warm months. Little lily pads provide ideal bass cover, and a nice feeder creek (see listing for *Butte Creek* in this chapter) provides the trout with plenty of food. These conditions encourage the presence of some big browns; because the lake is small, however, these large fish are mighty wary. If you employ a secret technique, Orr Lake is its litmus test. I suggest using a small jointed Rapala, which attracts strikes from bass and browns. The bass are able to spawn naturally. The DFG gives this lake a boost by planting 300 brook trout in the 6- to 8-inch class and 4,700 10- to 12-inch rainbow trout per year.

Facilities, fees: Vault toilets are at the lake. A primitive campground is available. Fishing access is free.

Directions: From Redding, drive north on I-5

to Weed and the exit for Highway 97. Take that exit, turn right at the stop sign, drive through Weed, bear right (north) on Highway 97, and drive 26 miles to Tennant–Bray Road. Turn right (east) and drive five miles to Bray. At Bray, turn left and drive two miles to the lake.

Contact: Klamath National Forest, Goosenest Ranger District, 530/398-4391, www.fs.fed .us/r5—click on Forest Offices.

3 BUTTE CREEK

Rating: 4
near Macdoel in Klamath National Forest
Map 3.1, page 167

You've got your work cut out for you at Butte Creek. Butte is just 6–10 feet wide. It flows freely, but it's a slow-moving "chalk" stream, and it is bordered by meadow with a cut bank. Most trout hide in the shade of that bank. If you saunter right up to the water and start casting, you may not find a single trout.

There are two major problems with this approach: For one thing, you're standing on top of the fish, and for another, you've scared them off. You have to sneak up on the trout at Butte Creek, like a burglar sneaking through an unlocked window. It helps to stand back from the river when you cast; if the fish see the shadow of your rod, detect any casting motion, or—God forbid—see you, you're a goner. This creek is no longer stocked with rainbow trout. Butte Creek can boost your confidence by offering a chance to pass the real test: fooling a native trout.

Facilities, fees: Shafter Campground is adjacent to the creek. Vault toilets, drinking water, and garbage bins are available. Supplies can be obtained in Macdoel. Fishing access is free.

Directions: From Redding, drive north on I-5 to Weed. Take the Central Weed/Highway 97 exit. Turn right at the stop sign and drive one mile through town to Highway 97. Bear right on Highway 97 and drive to Ball Mountain

Road. Turn east on Ball Mountain Road and drive three miles to Old State Highway. Drive south over the railroad tracks and continue six miles to Shafter Campground. Access is available in several spots, but do not trespass where signs are posted.

Contact: Klamath National Forest, Goosenest Ranger District, 530/398-4391, www.fs.fed .us/r5—click on Forest Offices.

4 ANTELOPE CREEK

Rating: 4
near Tennant in Klamath National Forest
Map 3.1, page 167

Don't even think about fishing Antelope Creek unless you have a Forest Service map in hand, so that you can determine what land is public (accessible) and what land is private (inaccessible). Make a mistake and you may get nailed for trespassing. If you are from the Bay Area or Los Angeles, the landowners will particularly enjoy your plight.

Antelope Creek is a classic babbling brook; it runs over rocks and boulders and into pools and pocket water. The DFG once stocked this stream, but no longer. The native trout have exceptional color. They are generally small, but a few 8- to 10-inchers can add a little spice to the day.

Note: Do not trespass on posted private land.

Facilities, fees: No facilities are available. Supplies can be obtained in Weed or MacDoel. Fishing access is free.

Directions: From Redding, drive north on I-5 to Weed. Take the Central Weed/Highway 97 exit. Turn right at the stop sign and drive one mile through town to Highway 97. Bear right on Highway 97 and drive 32 miles to Bray–Tennant Road. Turn right on Bray–Tennant Road and drive about 10 miles to Forest Service Road 43N44/Stephens Pass Road. Turn right on Stephens Pass Road and drive 5.5 miles to Forest Service Road 42N16.

Park at the access point where the road crosses Antelope Creek.

For a free map of Lassen National Forest, contact Lassen National Forest Supervisor's Office, 2550 Riverside Dr., Susanville, CA 96130, 530/257-2151, or download it at www.fs.fed.us/r5—click on Forest Offices.

Contact: Klamath National Forest, Goosenest Ranger District, 530/398-4391, www.fs.fed.us/r5—click on Forest Offices.

5 MEDICINE LAKE

Rating: 7
near McCloud in Modoc National Forest
Map 3.1, page 167

Medicine Lake offers mystery, a challenge, and an answer. What's the mystery? Originally this lake was a caldera, the mouth of a volcano. Naturally, comparisons are drawn between it and Oregon's Crater Lake, but Medicine is neither as deep nor as blue as Crater. Regardless, the lake's volcanic origin gives Medicine a sense of far-reaching history, unique among most lakes in California. It is beautiful, and it offers lakeside campsites and a paved access road. Snow usually clears from the surrounding area by June, if not before. Hit it right and you can get some beautiful limits of big brook trout.

Medicine Lake is not, however, undiscovered. Fishing is the challenge, and the answer is, "You can handle it." Trout fishing is good here, for both brook trout and rainbow trout. In late spring and early summer, brook trout can be voracious. After all, they have a pretty good set of chompers for trout. Trollers get the best results. During the summer, this lake presents a typical morning- and evening-bite scenario. During the spring and fall, when the bite is better throughout the day, beware of surprise storms; they can pour snow on unsuspecting visitors. Some folks, mainly families with youngsters, are content to toss in their bait along the shore near the campgrounds, and seem to catch the odd one. Superior results come from fishing by boat. To improve the boating experience, waterskiing is permitted only between 10 A.M. and 4 P.M. During the morning and evening, anglers can find quiet water for prime-time fishing. I really like this idea—it's a good solution to the never-ending water-skier/angler conflict, and I suggest it be applied to other lakes in the state.

Medicine Lake is stocked by the Department of Fish and Game. Usually the plants consist solely of brook trout, although rainbow trout are sometimes included in the mix. Few know that arctic grayling were stocked in this lake at one point, but they didn't grab much attention. The stocking program ended, natural spawning did not resume, and these fish are never caught anymore.

Notes: If you bring a dog, keep it tied up or take it along in your boat. Dogs are not allowed on the beach, and the rangers here clamp down pretty hard… on a brighter note, there are several exciting side trips in the area, including ice caves, a mountaintop lookout that is available for overnight lodging (for a fee) from the Forest Service, and nearby Bullseye and Blanche Lakes.

Facilities, fees: Four campgrounds (with drinking water and vault toilets) and a boat launch are provided on the lake. Supplies can be obtained in McCloud; limited supplies are available at the Bartle Lodge, which you pass on the drive in. Fishing access is free.

Directions: From Redding, drive north on I-5 past Dunsmuir to Highway 89. Bear right (east) on Highway 89 and drive 28 miles to Forest Road 15/Harris Springs Road (just past Bartle). Turn left on Forest Road 15/Harris Springs Road and drive five miles to a fork with Forest Road 49/Medicine Lake Road. Bear right at the fork at Medicine Lake Road and drive 26 miles to the lake-access road on the left. From Bartle, the route is signed.

Contact: Modoc National Forest, Doublehead Ranger District, 530/667-2246, www.fs.fed.us/r5.

6 IRON CANYON RESERVOIR

Rating: 6

near Big Bend in
Shasta-Trinity National Forest
Map 3.1, page 167

Iron Canyon is a good spot to fish and camp. Some anglers fish from shore, others troll, and fly fishers with float tubes should also consider this a spot to hit. Iron Canyon is at 2,700 feet in elevation and covers 500 acres, with 15 miles of shoreline.

Each year, rainbow trout are stocked, as well as brook trout. In addition to rainbow trout, big brown trout live in these waters. I've caught some beautiful stringers of trout here, and they always seem to come in the spring. In the fall, the lake level often becomes quite low, exposing a long, stump-ridden shore near Deadlun Camp. There can be a good bite in the fall for trout in the 14- to 15-inch class at Iron Canyon. Unfortunately, lake drawdowns are often severe starting in October. By November the lake is often at minimum pool.

Yet even in the spring, this lake doesn't ever seem to fill completely. A PG&E contact told me it is likely that an engineering error when the dam was constructed means the lake never quite fills.

The lake is in a national forest just above the elevation line, where conifers, not deciduous trees, grow. If you feel that you're being watched while you fish, look up. A bald eagle is probably patrolling the lake.

Facilities, fees: Two campgrounds are provided: Hawkins Landing and Deadlun. Neither has drinking water. A boat ramp is also available at Hawkins Landing; small boats are recommended. Supplies can be obtained in Big Bend and Burney. Fishing access is free.

Directions: To Hawkins Landing access/boat ramp: From Redding, take Highway 299 east for 37 miles to Big Bend Road/County Road 7M01. At Big Bend Road, turn left and drive 15.2 miles to the town of Big Bend. Continue for 2.1 miles to Forest Road 38N11. Turn left and drive 3.3 miles to the Iron Canyon

Reservoir Spillway. Turn right and drive 1.1 miles to a dirt road. Turn left and drive 0.3 mile to the campground and boat ramp.

To Deadlun access: From Redding, take Highway 299 east for 37 miles to Big Bend Road/County Road 7M01. At Big Bend Road, turn left and drive 15.2 miles to the town of Big Bend. Continue for five miles to the lake, bearing right at the T intersection, and continue for two miles (past the boat-launch turnoff) to the campground turnoff on the left side of the road. Turn left and drive one mile to the campground. A dirt route is available here to the lake for hand-launched boats.

Contact: Shasta-Trinity National Forest, Big Bend Ranger Station, 530/337-6502, www .fs.fed.us/r5—click on Forest Offices; Shasta Lake Visitor Center, 530/275-1296, www .shastalake.com; PG&E Recreation Desk, 916/386-5164, www.pge.com/recreation.

7 ROCK CREEK

Rating: 6

near Lake Britton in
Shasta-Trinity National Forest
Map 3.1, page 167

Rock Creek provides an option for anglers who have hunkered down at Lake Britton for a few days, fishing smallmouth bass or rainbow trout in the lake. Sound familiar? So you've fished for bass at Lake Britton for a few days, maybe camped at the developed sites at nearby McArthur-Burney Falls Memorial State Park, and would like to try something different.

Maybe you're ready for a primitive camp along a small stream stocked with trout. If so, this is the place. Rock Creek is very close to Lake Britton and the state park, yet rarely will you hear local folks talk about it. In fact, it's usually hikers who stumble upon the good fishing, since the Pacific Crest Trail (PCT) is routed right across the creek. The best stretch of water is just below Lake Britton on downstream a bit, where the DFG stocks rainbow trout in the six- to eight-inch class at various times.

Facilities, fees: A small primitive campground is nearby. More campgrounds and supplies are available at nearby Lake Britton. Fishing access is free. Rock Creek is closed year-round to all fishing from about a mile from Rock Creek Falls downstream to the Pit River.

Directions: From Redding, take Highway 299 east to Burney and continue for five miles to the junction with Highway 89. At Highway 89, turn left (north) and drive five miles to Clark Creek Road. Turn left at Clark Creek Road and drive across Lake Britton Dam to Forest Road 37N02 and continue to Forest Service Road 11. Turn left on Forest Service Road 11. This road parallels Rock Creek, offering direct access.

For a free map of Lassen National Forest, contact Lassen National Forest Supervisor's Office, 2550 Riverside Dr., Susanville, CA 96130, 530/257-2151, or download it at www.fs.fed.us/r5—click on Forest Offices.

Contact: Lassen National Forest, Hat Creek Ranger District, 530/336-5521, www.fs.fed.us/r5—click on Forest Offices; Department of Fish and Game, Redding, 530/225-2300; Vaughn's Sporting Goods & Fly Shop, Burney, 530/335-2381, www.vaughnfly.com.

8 LAKE BRITTON

Rating: 8

near McArthur-Burney Falls Memorial
State Park in Shasta-Trinity National Forest

Map 3.1, page 167

You want the ideal camping/fishing/boating vacation spot in the mountains of Northern California for a family? Lake Britton may be the answer. Campgrounds are available at McArthur-Burney Falls Memorial State Park and also on the north shore. Boat ramps provide easy access, and the lake hosts a wide variety of fish species. Lake Britton is at an elevation of 2,700 feet, covering 1,600 acres with 18 miles of shoreline. Adjacent McArthur-Burney Falls Memorial State Park guarantees heavy use during the summer.

In the spring, Lake Britton is an outstanding destination for fishing for smallmouth bass. The best lures are hard baits, such as the Shad Rap and other Rebel and Rapala shad imitations. Cast exclusively at shoreline areas where you can see rocks, especially rock piles and points. At long exposed stretches of shoreline, or areas devoid of rocks, you will typically find no smallmouth. So keep casting to these rocky shorelines and craggy point areas. Grubs rigged on 1/4-ounce darthead jigs are often effective. Days with 15–20 smallmouth can be in the bargain. Timing is a key, with the best fishing from late April through late May, with the very best in early May.

As summer arrives, most folks here fish for trout or crappie. In summer, your best bet is trolling for trout during the first and last two hours of the day. When I was filming a TV show here, I saw a school of 2,000 or more trout swirling in the cove near the eagle nest. It was like seeing a swarm of big sardines or mackerel in the ocean, just an incredible sight.

A lot of kids try to fish from shore, and sometimes, using two-hook rigs with Power Bait, they even catch a few. This lake provides a lot better prospects by boat than by shore.

A great surprise for many is the outstanding crappie fishing near the railroad trestle located on the upper end of the lake. With crappie you can really have a ball here on a hot summer afternoon and early evening. Fish here with white crappie jigs, dunking with live minnows under a bobber, or fly-fishing with a Marabou. It was here at the railroad trestle that some people were catching crappie by the hundreds and throwing them into garbage buckets to take home. The outrage that followed from this abuse resulted in the present 25-fish limit.

With emerald-green water set in a high-walled granite gorge, the lake headwaters are very pretty. The surrounding landscape is well forested, with many giant ponderosa pines, which are best known for their impressive mosaiclike bark.

This lake also differs from the others by not being hidden. Highway 89 runs right across

Lake Britton, and many people discover it for the first time on vacation, while coming from or going to McArthur-Burney Falls Memorial State Park. Burney Falls is a freshwater fountain, 129 feet high. The park offers outstanding viewing areas and hiking trails near the falls. Seeing the waterfall is a must-do side trip.

Facilities, fees: The state park's small marina has rowboats, boats with motors, canoes, kayaks, and pedal boats for rent. Campgrounds, restrooms with coin showers, flush toilets, vault toilets, and picnic areas are nearby. Boat ramps, boat rentals, groceries, bait, and tackle are available. Fishing access is free.

Directions: To McArthur-Burney Falls Memorial State Park: From Redding, take Highway 299 east to Burney and then continue for five miles to the junction with Highway 89. At Highway 89, turn left (north) and drive six miles to the park entrance on the left side of the road. Turn left, stop at the kiosk, and then continue one mile to the launch ramp and small marina.

To North Shore: From Redding, take Highway 299 east to Burney and then continue for five miles to Highway 89. Turn left (north) and drive 9.7 miles (past the state-park entrance and over the Lake Britton Bridge) to Clark Creek Road. Turn left (west) and drive about a mile to the North Shore access road. Turn left and drive one mile to the North Shore campground and launch ramp.

Contact: McArthur-Burney Falls Memorial State Park, 530/335-2777, www.parks.ca.gov (click on Visit a Park); PG&E Recreation Desk, 916/386-5164, www.pge.com/recreation; Burney Falls General Store, 530/335-5713; Vaughn's Sporting Goods & Fly Shop, Burney, 530/335-2381, www.vaughnfly.com.

⑨ BURNEY CREEK

Rating: 6

near Burney
Map 3.1, page 167

Burney Creek gurgles over rocks polished by centuries of rolling water. Access is good, and the trout fishing often is too. It's a pretty setting, a classic freestone creek. But get this: the most popular area to fish provides the worst results, and the least popular area provides the best results. Sounds crazy, but that's the story here.

The reason is that so many campers stay at McArthur-Burney Falls Memorial State Park and fish the section of Burney Creek that runs over the awesome waterfall, into the deep pool below, and on through the park. That stretch of river gets hammered every day of the season by campers, and the trout have learned a few lessons.

But the stretch of water west of Burney is completely different. It is well stocked, uncrowded, and the catching is often as good as the fishing. If you need fishing tips, advice on access, or a guide, stop in at Vaughn's Sporting Goods & Fly Shop in Burney.

Lower Burney Creek has rainbow trout, brook trout, and a few elusive brown trout. Middle Burney Creek gets six- to eight-inch rainbow trout, and Upper Burney gets six- to eight-inch rainbow and seven- to eight-inch brook trout. That adds up to quite an opportunity, one that you may never have known existed. But if you're camping at Burney Falls, forget fishing the stretch near the waterfall.

Facilities, fees: Camping is available nearby at Cassel Forebay (on Hat Creek) and at McArthur-Burney Falls Memorial State Park, at Lake Britton. An entrance fee is charged at McArthur-Burney Falls Memorial State Park. Other creek access is free.

Directions: One access point is the area around McArthur-Burney Falls Memorial State Park. From Redding, take Highway 299 east to Burney and then continue for five miles to the junction with Highway 89. Turn left at Highway 89 and drive six miles to the park entrance, on the left side of the road.

Fishing access is available above and below the falls. Access is also possible off side roads west of Burney: From Burney, drive south on Tamarack Road (across from the entrance to the Sierra Pacific Mill) and drive 2.5 miles. Access is directly off the roads to the right.

Contact: McArthur-Burney Falls Memorial State Park, 530/335-2777, www.parks.ca.gov; Vaughn's Sporting Goods & Fly Shop, Burney, 530/335-2381, www.vaughnfly.com.

10 FALL RIVER

Rating: 9

near McArthur

Map 3.1, page 167

Fall River does not roll over rocks and boulders. It is a spring-fed stream, deep and slow-moving, slow enough to fish from a float tube. The water is so clear that long leaders (12 feet is the average) and delicate casts are mandatory. This is an artificials-only, single-barbless-hook stream. In all, Fall River is an exclusive, quality water.

This is still one of the prized blue-ribbon trout streams in the western United States. But it is fished nowhere near as heavily as it once was. One reason is the extremely limited access to the river. Another reason is the high skill and talented presentation that are required to inspire the trout to bite.

From the warm days of June through summer and fall, the Fall River is the site of the most amazing insect hatch in California. Hatching insects and rising trout can create so many pools on the calm surface that it looks as if it's raining. This is a unique world-class stream, with water so clear you can spot a dime 30 feet down on the bottom and unconsciously reach in, thinking you can pick it up. The trout are wild, and many are big 16- to 20-inchers, with a sprinkling in the five-pound class.

That right there is enough to inspire people from all over the United States to cast a line here, but it takes more than inspiration to succeed. You'll need fly-fishing skills, knowledge of stream access, and a sense of ethics.

Access can be exclusive. Your best bet is to stay at Spinner Fall Lodge, where you can get onto the prime upper stretch of river. Snow-covered Mount Lassen sits above this trout paradise, watching as it has since its last violent eruption in 1914. If you lose a few big trout, you might just blow your top, too.

Another strategy is to launch a boat from Island Bridge (space for only a few parked cars) and then work the area nearby upstream. Or launch at Rat Farm at Big Lake near MacArthur (see *Big Lake*) and then drive up the Fall River channel to the best spots. My favorite riffle is at the "old farm house" where Ed Rice and I have had 50-fish days. For talented fly fishers, Fall River is one of the top streams in the western United States. The only downers: Bank access is zero, access in general is about the worst of any blue-ribbon trout stream in California, and if you are new to the game, you've got no chance here.

Facilities, fees: Prams can be launched at Spinner Fall Lodge (guests only); only electric motors and paddleboats can be launched at the CalTrout Island Bridge access. Camping is available at Cassel Forebay and at Lake Britton. Fishing access is free.

Directions: The premium upper stretch of the river is bordered by private property, with access limited to guests of Spinner Fall Lodge. Public access is available, however, at the CalTrout access at Island Bridge, off McArthur Road (there's room for just a few cars). You can access the lower part of the river via Glenburn Road, just west of Fall River Mills, off Highway 299.

Contact: Fall River Valley Chamber of Commerce, 530/336-5840, www.fallrivervalleycc .org; Spinner Fall Lodge, 530/336-5300, www .spinnerfalllodge; CalTrout, 530/926-3755, cal trout.org; Vaughn's Sporting Goods & Fly Shop, Burney, 530/335-2381, www.vaughnfly.com.

11 BIG LAKE

Rating: 7

near McArthur

Map 3.1, page 167

One of the most frustrating things in the world is to see a huge fish swim under your boat, and then be unable to get a bite. At Big Lake, this can happen several times a day; giant wild rainbow trout swim right past, and then—no bites! Big Lake supports a low population of large trout, especially wild rainbow trout.

Big Lake is the centerpiece of Ahjumawa Lava Springs State Park. Huge freshwater springs from underground lava tubes make this habitat unique. They produce a tremendous volume of pure water that creates a matrix of clear, slow-moving waterways: Fall River, Lava Creek, Rising River, Tule River, Ja-She-Creek, Eastman Lake, Horr Pond, and Big Lake.

Fly fishers in small boats have their best prospects at Big Lake very early and late in the day. Trollers can do just as well, but a key is using a very long line, typically 125 feet of line out, with light leaders; 3-pound test can be necessary, and fluorocarbon, which is near-invisible, is mandatory. These fish are typically line-shy. The water is very clear and the fish can get spooked easily. The best bet is to anchor near the springs, then cast leeches or marabous with sink-tip lines, fly-fishing, with a strip retrieve. Don't just let it sit there. I've seen two-foot trout swim right up, stop an inch away, study the hook, and then depart to my utter frustration.

One trick is to cast large bass-type lures (such as Rapalas, Rebels, and Shad Raps) from a boat and then fan the shoreline with casts. They don't come easy, but an 18-incher is average, and they range much bigger. One thing is for sure: fish at midday at Big Lake on a typical hot, blue-sky summer afternoon and you have about as much chance of catching one of these bombers as finding Bigfoot.

Facilities, fees: A boat launch is provided. Nine boat-in campsites are available across the lake at Ahjumawa Lava Springs State Park. There's another campground nearby at Cassel Forebay. Supplies can be purchased in Fall River Mills and McArthur. Fishing access is free.

Directions: From Redding, take Highway 299 east for 73 miles to McArthur and Main Street. Turn left on Main Street and drive 3.5 miles (it becomes a dirt road) to the Rat Farm boat launch at Big Lake. Launch your boat. Nine boat-in campsites are along the shore, 1–2.5 miles from the launch site.

Driving note: Those with boats on trailers should be aware that the cattle guards on the entrance road are very old and, in turn, quite narrow. It is possible for a tire of your boat trailer to slip off the side of the cattle guard, and then for the inside of the wheel to catch the cattle guard and rip the axle out of place on the trailer. Guess how I know? Turns out it has happened many times to fishermen towing boats, according to the tow truck driver in MacArthur.

Contact: Ahjumawa Lava Springs State Park, 530/335-2777 or 530/225-2065, www.parks .ca.gov (click on Visit a Park); Burney Chamber of Commerce, 530/335-2111, www .burneychamber.com; Vaughn's Sporting Goods & Fly Shop, Burney, 530/335-2381, www.vaughnfly.com; Fall River Valley Chamber of Commerce, 530/336-5840, www .fallrivervalleycc.org.

12 DIAMOND RESERVOIR

Rating: 4
near Davis Creek in Modoc National Forest
Map 3.2, page 168

This little-known reservoir is way out in lonesome country. Local cowboys, who occasionally run cattle in the area, are among the few people who know about Diamond. The DFG stock consists of rainbow trout. You want obscure? You want cowboy country? You want a chance for a few nice trout? You want a long drive? Diamond Reservoir is the place, with guaranteed quiet.

Facilities, fees: No facilities are available. Supplies can be purchased in Alturas. Fishing access is free.

Directions: From Redding, take Highway 299 east and drive about 144 miles (17 miles past Canby) to Crowder Flat Road. Turn left on Crowder Flat Road and continue approximately 29 miles to the reservoir.

Contact: Modoc National Forest, Devil's Garden Ranger District, 530/233-5811, www.fs.fed.us/r5—click on Forest Offices.

13 JANES RESERVOIR

Rating: 7

near Davis Creek in Modoc National Forest

Map 3.2, page 168

Janes Reservoir gets very little fishing pressure because it's so out of the way. It takes a long time for even the Modoc locals to get there. As a result, the resident fish receive few lessons from know-how anglers, which benefits the people who do make the trek. Little known is that there are some big brown trout and Eagle Lake trout here. So it is ironic that this body of water is not even named on many maps. The best fishing for these big trout is in the cold weather of spring. On a blustery April day, you will likely have the place all to yourself. Set in the high plateau country, it's not the prettiest place in the world. If, however, you have a canoe or car-top boat and are serious about fishing, it's an ideal spot in which to entice those big trout.

Facilities, fees: A boat ramp and campsites for tents and self-contained RVs are available. Picnic tables and fire pits are provided, vault toilets are available, but no drinking water. Supplies can be purchased in Alturas. Fishing access is free.

Directions: From Redding, take Highway 299 east and drive about 144 miles (17 miles past Canby). Turn left on Crowder Flat Road and drive about 30 miles to County Road 73 (signed Janes Reservoir). Turn west and drive 0.25 miles to the dam, campground, and boat ramp.

Contact: Modoc National Forest, Devil's Garden Ranger District, 530/233-5811, www.fs.fed.us/r5—click on Forest Offices.

14 CAVE LAKE

Rating: 5

in Modoc National Forest

Map 3.2, page 168

You'll find two lakes here: Cave Lake on one end and Lily Lake on the other. Both are very quiet and little traveled, and they offer decent fishing for foot-long-class trout. Cave has sparse vegetation, so Lily Lake is the more attractive of the two.

Tiny Cave Lake is at 6,600 feet in elevation and is worth tossing a line into: it is no longer stocked with trout, but still provides okay results relative to the number of anglers who fish the lake. Most of Cave's fish are rainbow trout, but some brook trout are also available. I definitely suggest using a fly-and-bubble here. If you don't have a bobber handy, a piece of bark will float and do the job just fine. A little local knowledge: trout seem to bite best when light breezes cause a slight ripple on the water—especially in the late spring and early summer.

Facilities, fees: A campground with vault toilets and a ramp for small boats are available. All motors are prohibited, even electric. Garbage must be packed out. Supplies are available in New Pine Creek (in Oregon) and Davis Creek. Fishing access is free.

Directions: From Redding, take Highway 299 east and drive 146 miles to Alturas. In Alturas, turn north on U.S. 395 and drive 40 miles to Forest Service Road 2 (if you reach the town of New Pine Creek, on the Oregon/California border, you have driven a mile too far). Turn right on Forest Service Road 2 (a steep dirt road—trailers are not recommended) and drive six miles to the campground entrance on the left side, just beyond Lily Lake picnic area.

Contact: Modoc National Forest, Warner Mountain Ranger District, 530/279-6116, www.fs.fed.us/r5.

15 LILY LAKE

Rating: 6

in Modoc National Forest
Map 3.2, page 168

Although located in no-man's-land, Lily Lake is well worth the trip and is one of the better car-accessible destinations in Northern California. People come for a day or two of camping (at nearby Cave Lake), fishing, and solitude. It's a lot prettier than Cave Lake, primarily because of the conifers sprinkled around its perimeter. The DFG stocks Lily Lake with catchable (1/2-pound) trout. This is a great place for weary visitors to recharge their batteries. Add it up: pretty spot, decent fishing for small trout, and a little-known camp nearby.

Facilities, fees: Picnic tables, a vault toilet, and a gravel boat ramp are available for day-use only. All boat motors are prohibited. Supplies can be purchased in Davis Creek and Fort Bidwell. Fishing access is free.

Directions: From Redding, take Highway 299 east for 146 miles to Alturas and U.S. 395. Turn north on U.S. 395 and drive 40 miles to Forest Road 2 (if you reach the town of New Pine Creek on the Oregon/California border, you have driven a mile too far). Turn right on Forest Road 2 (a steep dirt road, trailers are not recommended) and drive six miles to the Lily Lake picnic area.

Contact: Modoc National Forest, Warner Mountain Ranger District, 530/279-6116, www.fs.fed.us/r5.

16 LAKE ANNIE

Rating: 4

near Fort Bidwell
Map 3.2, page 168

Annie is Fort Bidwell's backyard fishing hole. Fort Bidwell is a unique community seemingly untouched by time; it's a beautiful little spot, with a grocery store, a gas station, and a natural hot spring just west of town. The lake is immediately west of Annie Mountain (hence the name), and it contains good numbers of small rainbow trout. It is stocked with Eagle Lake trout by air, since it's too far away for the Department of Fish and Game to reach by car.

It is also close to the Warner Mountains. The lake is surrounded by fairly sparse country, and nobody gets here by accident. Lake Annie covers 30 acres and is situated at 4,700 feet in elevation, with a rocky shoreline surrounded by sagebrush and grassy hills. That's right: there are no trees. It's also right that the lake is too small for anything but car-top boats.

Since most of the land surrounding the lake is private property, please respect the rights of landowners, and stay clear.

Facilities, fees: No facilities are available. Supplies can be obtained in Fort Bidwell and in nearby Cedarville. Fishing access is free.

Directions: From Redding, take Highway 299 east for 146 miles to Alturas. From Alturas, continue east on Highway 299 to Cedarville and Surprise Valley Road. Turn north on Surprise Valley Road and continue (the road becomes County Road 1) to the town of Fort Bidwell and the junction with County Road 6. At that junction, turn left to continue on County Road 1. Keep bearing left and drive 2.3 miles to the lake.

Contact: Bureau of Land Management, Surprise Field Office, 530/279-6101.

17 FEE RESERVOIR

Rating: 6

near Fort Bidwell
Map 3.2, page 168

Fee Reservoir is one crazy place. The surrounding area is barren, and it doesn't look like a great place to fish. If you haven't caught anything after an hour or so, you might be tempted to forget the whole deal and head elsewhere. Most visitors do just that, which is a major error. There are some big trout here. When the lake is high enough (and we'll get to that), the DFG stocks Fee Reservoir with cutthroat trout, catchable rainbow trout, and Eagle Lake trout.

The high-quality fish of the Eagle Lake strain generally weigh 2.5–3 pounds, but some of these fish are bigger. They can be hard to catch. Persistent individuals with night crawler know-how will fill their stringers. It takes a light touch and experience to know when to set the hook on the light bites. If you fall into this category, you're in business. Skilled fly fishers should put this lake on their radar scopes.

Fee Reservoir's setting is typical of Modoc County's high desert country. You may see a special orange glow at dawn and dusk; in early summer, this normally stark setting comes alive with a variety of blooming wildflowers. It is at 5,329 feet in elevation on the Modoc Plateau. When full, Fee Reservoir covers 337 acres, but because the water is used for irrigation, it is subject to major summer drawdowns and erratic level fluctuations based on water demand.

Facilities, fees: A boat ramp and campground with drinking water and vault toilets are available. Limited supplies can be obtained in Cedarville. Fishing access is free.

Directions: From Redding, take Highway 299 east for 146 miles to Alturas. From Alturas, continue east on Highway 299 for 21 miles to Cedarville and County Road 1. Turn north on County Road 1 and drive 30 miles to Fort Bidwell and Fee Reservoir Road. Turn right on Fee Reservoir Road (a good gravel road) and drive 7.5 miles to the reservoir.

Contact: Bureau of Land Management, Surprise Field Office, 530/279-6101.

18 BRILES RESERVOIR

Rating: 4
near Davis Creek in Modoc National Forest
Map 3.2, page 168

If you feel as if you're in the middle of nowhere when you cruise U.S. 395, it's because you are.

Out-of-towners tend to drive pretty fast on this road, and they miss little spots like Briles Reservoir. A few miles east of the highway, Briles is tucked in a pocket of the Warner Mountains foothills, in Modoc National Forest. The DFG stocks brook trout and Eagle Lake trout with aerial plants. June and July are the best times to fish here, despite the large number of small fish, because this reservoir is also used as a water supply for hay fields. By late summer, the water levels are fairly low.

Facilities, fees: No facilities are available. A campground is available seven miles away. Supplies can be obtained in Davis Creek. Fishing access is free.

Directions: From Redding, take Highway 299 east for 146 miles to Alturas and U.S. 395. Turn north on U.S. 395 and drive to the town of Davis Creek and Westside Road. Turn right on Westside Road (Forest Service Road 11) and continue 2.5 miles east to a fork. At the fork, turn left (north) and drive four miles, bear left again, and drive a short distance to Briles Reservoir.

Contact: Modoc National Forest, Warner Mountain Ranger District, 530/279-6116, www.fs.fed.us/r5.

19 RESERVOIR C

Rating: 5
near Alturas in Modoc National Forest
Map 3.2, page 168

Venturing out to the "alphabet lakes," in the remote Devil's Garden area of Modoc County, is one hell of a trip. Reservoir C and Reservoir F are the best of the lot, but the success can go up and down like a yo-yo depending on water levels. For the most part, the fishing is decent in late spring and early summer; then it goes the way of the dodo bird.

Reservoir C gets a favorable listing because of the small camp that makes it acceptable to overnighters and the hopeful fishing prospects that come in early summer. Year-to-year results depend highly on the weather. If the water level is up, then so is the fishing. It is stocked with brown trout and Eagle Lake trout, each species in the six- to eight-inch class. Reservoir C has decent numbers of largemouth bass as well. The strategy: Fish for trout from late winter to early spring, and then for bass after that. Another option in the alphabet lakes is Reservoir F, which is stocked with catchable trout.

A sidelight here is the number of primitive roads routed through Modoc National Forest—perfect for four-wheel-drive junkies.

Facilities, fees: There are six primitive campsites. Picnic tables and fire pits are provided. A vault toilet is available, but drinking water is not. Garbage must be packed out. Fishing access is free.

Directions: From Alturas, take Highway 299 west for three miles to Crowder Flat Road/County Road 73. Turn right on Crowder Flat Road and drive 3.5 miles to Triangle Ranch Road/Forest Service Road 43N18. Turn left on Triangle Ranch Road and drive six miles to Forest Service Road 44N32. Turn right on Forest Service Road 44N32, drive 0.5 mile, turn right on the access road for the lake and campground, and drive 0.5 mile to the camp at the end of the road.

Contact: Modoc National Forest, Devil's Garden Ranger District, 530/233-5811, www.fs.fed.us/r5—click on Forest Offices; Belligerent Duck, 530/233-4696, www .belligerentduck.bizland.com; Sports Hunt, 530/233-2423.

20 BIG SAGE RESERVOIR

Rating: 6

near Alturas in Modoc National Forest
Map 3.2, page 168

Don't let the dirt access road to Big Sage scare you off—it's smooth enough to trailer a boat over. Follow that road and you will find a good boat ramp, as well as an opportunity to catch largemouth bass.

In fact, this is one of the few bass waters in the entire area. Several islands provide the bass with shoreline habitat, as do some coves along the southwest shoreline. Catfish and crappie also live here.

You're in classic desert plateau country here, at an elevation of 4,400 feet, and the land bordering the lake to the north is particularly sparse. Big Sage is sizable, covering some 5,000 acres, and it is one of the area's most popular lakes. In Modoc County that means you might actually see another person.

Facilities, fees: A campground with picnic tables and fire pits is provided. There are wheelchair-accessible toilets and a ramp, but no piped water. Garbage must be packed out. A boat ramp is also available. Fishing access is free.

Directions: From Alturas, take Highway 299 west for three miles to Crowder Flat Road/County Road 73. Turn right (north) on Crowder Flat Road and drive six miles to County Road 180. Turn right on County Road 180 and drive three miles to a signed access road for the lake. Turn left at the access road for the campground and boat ramp, and drive a short distance to the camp, on the left side of the road.

Contact: Modoc National Forest, Devil's Garden Ranger District, 530/233-5811, www.fs.fed.us/r5—click on Forest Offices; Belligerent Duck, 530/233-4696, www .belligerentduck.bizland.com; Sports Hunt, 530/233-2423.

21 DUNCAN RESERVOIR

Rating: 5

south of the town of Tulelake in
Modoc National Forest
Map 3.2, page 168

Here's a little reservoir that goes unnoticed by most people. It's out in the middle of nowhere, but I'll tell you why you should find it. Once you become familiar with the place, you can catch beautiful trout in the two- to four-pound class. No foolin'. The fish at Duncan

Reservoir don't look like your average rainbow trout, because they aren't. The DFG no longer air-express plants this domesticated strain of Eagle Lake trout.

Facilities, fees: A Forest Service campground, Howard Gulch, is three miles south on Highway 139. Picnic tables, drinking water, and vault toilets are available. Fishing access is free.

Directions: From Redding, take Highway 299 east for approximately 130 miles to the small town of Canby, then continue one mile to the junction with Highway 139. Turn north on Highway 139 and drive 2.5 miles to Forest Service Road 46 (Loveness Road). Turn right on Forest Service Road 46 and drive three miles to Forest Service Road 43N35. Turn right and drive three miles to Duncan Reservoir.

Contact: Modoc National Forest, Doublehead Ranger District, 530/667-2246, www .fs.fed.us/r5.

22 BALLARD RESERVOIR

Rating: 4

near Canby

Map 3.2, page 168

Fish this lake in May or June. Any later than that, and well, in dry years you might as well be fishing in a bucket. That's not because Ballard is small. Ranchers built the lake and then take what they think they deserve, and sometimes more than they deserve. The result is that dropping water levels and hot weather can cause an overgrowth of algae later in the fishing season. Big problem. So big that trout are not stocked here some years. When Ballard is stocked, it receives Eagle Lake trout and catchable rainbows. The lake is shaped kind of like a cucumber, and you can access it on a dirt road along the southwest side. There's no ramp, so anglers with car-top boats and canoes have a big advantage.

Note: Always respect private property rights.

Facilities, fees: A few primitive campsites are available. No drinking water available. Garbage must be packed out. Supplies and fishing tackle can be obtained at the gas station in Canby or in Alturas. Fishing access is free.

Directions: From Alturas, take Highway 299 west for 17 miles to the town of Canby and Centerville Road/County Road 54. Turn left on Centerville Road and drive one mile until the road forks. Continue straight on County Road 175/Forest Service Road 41N04 and drive four miles to Ballard Reservoir (well signed).

Contact: Modoc National Forest, Big Valley Ranger District, 530/299-3215, www.fs.fed .us/r5; Belligerent Duck, 530/233-4696, www .belligerentduck.bizland.com; Sports Hunt, 530/233-2423.

23 DORRIS RESERVOIR

Rating: 6

near Alturas

Map 3.2, page 168

Locals can get a case of lockjaw when asked about this lake. There are some big, big trout in these waters, as well as bass and catfish, and I'm not speaking with a forked tongue. Dorris Reservoir is decent in size and is a short drive out of Alturas in the Modoc National Wildlife Refuge. Bring your camera, because you'll be in a wildlife paradise, with a diverse array of birds (especially large numbers of geese in the fall and winter) and mammals, including coyotes, deer, quail, rabbits, and even antelope. A tour of the adjacent refuge is a must for first-time visitors.

The ol' "Modockers" put a lot of faith in a plain old night crawler, and you might do the same at Dorris. They toss one out with a split shot for weight, perhaps inflating the night crawler so it floats a bit off the lake bottom, then see what they get. In the early summer, when the trout, bass, and catfish are all coming on, the gettin' is good.

A boat is a necessity. That is because most of the lake's shore is privately owned. Always respect private property rights from shore. A boat solves that.

Also note that the reservoir is closed to drive-in access and boating from mid-October through April 1. Walk-in access is permitted after January 15. Shoreline areas, islands, and peninsulas with nesting waterfowl are closed from February through May. Vehicles (on designated roads) and boating are permitted from April through September. As you may have figured, this is a major nesting area for ducks and geese.

Facilities, fees: Two unimproved boat ramps and vault toilets are available, but not drinking water. Two national-forest campgrounds are nearby, and RV parks are in Alturas. Supplies and fishing tackle can be obtained at the gas station in Canby or in Alturas. Fishing access is free.

Directions: From the south end of Alturas, turn east on Parker Creek Road (County Road 56) and drive three miles until the road forks with County Road 57. Bear right on County Road 57 and travel a short distance to the boat ramp, or bear left and continue to the north end of the reservoir.

Contact: Modoc National Wildlife Refuge, 530/233-3572, www.fs.fed.us/r5—click on Forest Offices.

24 BAYLEY RESERVOIR

Rating: 5

south of Alturas
Map 3.2, page 168

The rating for Bayley Reservoir changes in every edition of this book. In 2008, I almost deleted it. In 2012, it gets a 5. Not bad. It used to have some big Eagle Lake trout, and pretty good numbers of them, and the DFG has continued stocking trout here. One problem is water clarity. The lake can still get real muddy.

This lake is way out in the middle of nowhere. What makes it worth seeing? Mainly that it's far from everything. In fact, the first

time I stopped in nearby Likely, which consists of a gas station/store and a cemetery, I asked the old fella at the gas pump why, of all things, they named the town Likely. "Because you are likely not to get there," he answered.

That's the way they are in Modoc. This is cow country, and if you want to have a lake all to yourself, Bayley Reservoir is the one for you. The trees are small, there is plenty of chaparral, and best of all, there are often more fish than people out here. Out here, that could mean there are two fish in the lake and one person fishing for them.

Graven Reservoir (to the north) and Delta Lake (to the south) are in very close proximity to this lake. Delta gets stocked with catchable trout, but Graven does not.

Facilities, fees: A few primitive campsites are available. There are no other facilities and no drinking water. Garbage must be packed out. Supplies can be obtained in Alturas or Likely. Fishing access is free.

Directions: In Alturas, take U.S. 395 to the south end of town and Centerville Road. Turn south on Centerville Road and drive two miles to Westside Road/County Road 60. Turn left and drive 6.5 miles to Bayley Reservoir Road/County Road 62. Turn right on Bayley Reservoir Road/County Road 62 and drive 9.5 miles to the reservoir.

Contact: Bureau of Land Management, Alturas Resource Area, 530/233-4666; Bureau of Land Management, Eagle Lake Field Office, 530/257-0456, www.blm.gov/ca; Belligerent Duck, 530/233-4696, www.belligerentduck.bizland.com; Sports Hunt, 530/233-2423.

25 ASH CREEK

Rating: 4

near Adin in Modoc National Forest
Map 3.2, page 168

Know your water: Ash Creek is visible from Highway 299 north of the town of Adin, and the lower stretch is bordered by private land.

So head east of Highway 299 to Ash Creek Campground, a cozy little spot, and start your fishing adventure. There you will find pocket water with small trout. The pools are small, and the shoreline is brushy, so the best strategy is to wade right down the middle of the creek, kneeling down while you make short, precise casts to these small pockets. Ash Creek gets an allotment of seven- to eight-inch rainbow trout.

Facilities, fees: Picnic tables and fire grills are at Ash Creek Campground. Vault toilets are available, but drinking water is not. Garbage must be packed out. Supplies can be purchased in Adin. Fishing access is free.

Directions: From Redding, take Highway 299 east and drive 100 miles to Adin and Ash Valley Road/County Road 88/527. Turn right on Ash Valley Road and drive eight miles to a signed campground turnoff. Turn left at the signed campground turnoff and drive a mile to the campground, on the right side of the road.

Contact: Modoc National Forest, Big Valley Ranger District, 530/299-3215, www.fs.fed .us/r5.

26 SOUTH WARNER WILDERNESS

Rating: 6

near Likely in Modoc National Forest
Map 3.2, page 168

Many hikers overlook the lonely Warner Mountains, but this area does have a genuine mystique, as well as a remote and extensive trail system. With pine trees, meadows, and streams, the west side of the Warners is something like the Sierra. The east side, however, is high desert country dotted with sagebrush and juniper—quite dry and rugged. One of the best backpacking trips here is the 23-mile Summit Trail Loop, which traverses both sides of the ridgeline, allowing hikers to see the stark contrasts between the east and west slopes.

For anglers, the best lakes in the South

Warner Wilderness are South Emerson Lake and Patterson Lake. The best streams are Cottonwood Creek, Parker Creek, Pine Creek, East Creek, and Mill Creek. Note that North Emerson Lake is shallow and freezes over occasionally, killing many fish. Patterson Lake is always the best of the bunch. Clear Lake, Cottonwood Lake, and Lost Lake no longer receive plants, and all of the creeks have been taken off the DFG plant list to protect small native trout.

Treat this land gently. After fishing here a while, you may even notice that you are talking in soft tones. The Warners can do that to you.

Facilities, fees: There are no developed campgrounds within the wilderness area, but Mill Creek Falls, Soup Springs, and Patterson Campgrounds are at the outskirts. Supplies can be obtained in Likely and Eagleville. Fishing access is free.

Directions: From Alturas, take U.S. 395/ Highway 299 north for about five miles to the junction with Highway 299. Turn right on Highway 299 and drive to Cedarville. From Cedarville, drive 15 miles south on County Road 1, to Eagleville, and continue one mile south on County Road 1 to County Road 40. Turn right on County Road 40 and drive three miles to the campground at the end of the road. The access road is steep and very slick in wet weather. Trailers are not recommended.

Contact: Modoc National Forest, Warner Mountain Ranger District, 530/279-6116, www.fs.fed.us/r5.

27 MILL CREEK

Rating: 7

near Likely in Modoc National Forest
Map 3.2, page 168

Mill Creek flows right out of the South Warner Wilderness, those lonely mountains of the northeast. The best strategy here is to go in from Soup Springs Camp, then hike over the South Warner Wilderness boundary. You will come off a hillside and into a valley floor, at the bottom of which you'll find Mill Creek.

The size of its trout sets this stream apart from others in Modoc County. The one- to three-pound class trout in Mill Creek are not mirages, and if you tangle with them, you'll never forget the experience. Access is good, including a trail along much of the stream as well as a parallel road. Because this is very touchy water, it's best for you to fish while walking upstream. This requires finesse and sneak-fishing techniques. Tie up your rigs behind a tree, don't let 'em see your shadow, and stay low when you cast.

Your reward will be a unique strain of wild trout that are short, dark, and chunky, appearing somewhat compressed. A Mill Creek fishing trip is a lot of fun and a little bit of work, and you won't find fish like this anywhere else. To see Mill Creek Falls, take the trail out of camp and bear left at the Y.

A note of caution: Always refer to a national-forest map when you are fishing a trout stream. This will ensure that you don't tromp on private property. In Modoc County, trespassing is sacrilege.

Facilities, fees: Mill Creek Falls has a campground with picnic tables and fire pits; drinking water and vault toilets are available. Supplies can be purchased in Likely. Fishing access is free.

Directions: From Alturas, take U.S. 395 south for 17 miles to the town of Likely and Jess Valley Road. Turn left on Jess Valley Road/County Road 64 and drive nine miles to the fork. Bear left on West Warner Road/Forest Road 5 and drive 2.5 miles to Forest Road 40N46. Turn right on Forest Road 40N46 and drive two miles to the campground entrance at the end of the road. Access is available off Forest Service roads near the campground, and also along trails that lead into the South Warner Wilderness.

Contact: Modoc National Forest, Warner Mountain Ranger District, 530/279-6116, www.fs.fed.us/r5.

28 CLEAR LAKE

Rating: 6

near Likely in Modoc National Forest

Map 3.2, page 168

Clear Lake is one of the prettiest spots in Modoc County. This is a small, high mountain lake in remote northeastern California. Unlike so many other small, high mountain lakes, this one has some big fish. That goes especially for the brown trout, and there are also a few rainbow trout. Knowing that can add sizzle to the adventure.

The fishing is best in the evening, but don't expect a large haul. There just plain aren't that many fish here. Nearby Blue Lake to the south, for instance, is a better bet. There are, however, some big ones, and the beauty of the surrounding Warner Mountains and Mill Creek Falls makes this spot good for an overnighter.

Clear Lake is in the South Warner Wilderness Area in Modoc National Forest. You enter on a paved road from Likely, then take a short (half-mile) and beautiful hike in from the Forest Service camp near Mill Creek Falls. In recent years the lake has seen increased use, so don't expect solitude.

Facilities, fees: Camping is not permitted at the lake, but a campground is available at Mill Creek Falls. Supplies can be obtained in Likely. Fishing access is free.

Directions: From Alturas, take U.S. 395 south for 17 miles to the town of Likely and Jess Valley Road. Turn left (east) on Jess Valley Road/County Road 64 and drive nine miles, until the road forks with West Warner Road/Forest Service Road 5. Bear left on West Warner Road and drive 2.5 miles to Forest Service Road 40N46. Turn right and drive two miles to Mill Creek Falls. Hike 0.5 mile to the lake.

Contact: Modoc National Forest, Warner Mountain Ranger District, 530/279-6116, www.fs.fed.us/r5.

29 SOUTH FORK PIT RIVER

Rating: 5

near Likely in Modoc National Forest

Map 3.2, page 168

The South Fork Pit, which is fed by Mill Creek, is one of the little surprises in this remote part of California. What's surprising is that the stream runs right along the road, and the adventurous angler will discover some good trout water.

When you turn off at Likely and first see the river, it may be murky, but don't be disheartened. You're looking at water that has been released from West Valley Reservoir. Just keep on driving.

Soon you will reach the South Fork Pit, which runs clear. It is a small stream, home to brown and rainbow trout. Fly fishers who like a small water challenge will be delighted. The DFG no longer stocks the river with rainbow trout in the 10- to 12-inch class, and 7- to 8-inch brown trout.

Facilities, fees: Campgrounds are available at West Valley Reservoir, Mill Creek Falls, and farther north in the town of Alturas. Supplies can be purchased in Likely. Fishing access is free.

Directions: From Alturas, take U.S. 395 south for 17 miles to the town of Likely and Jess Valley Road. Turn left on Jess Valley Road and drive east. Fishing access is available along the road.

Contact: Modoc National Forest, Warner Mountain Ranger District, 530/279-6116, www.fs.fed.us/r5.

30 WEST VALLEY RESERVOIR

Rating: 5

near Likely

Map 3.2, page 168

First the warning: Hazardous high winds can blow here in the spring, and there have been several boating accidents. Some boaters claim that the ghosts of accident victims sometimes hover overhead.

But if you come on a calm day, this place is one of the better choices in the entire region. West Valley Reservoir provides good access and a quality boat ramp, and it usually gets filled during the winter with runoff from the South Fork Pit River.

You don't even need a boat here. Shoreliners and boaters take the same approach: pick a spot, hunker down, and wait for a nibble on the bait. Bait? That's right. Very few people use lures here, and only a sprinkling try trolling. Some anglers fish for Sacramento perch, which tend to be on the small side here.

The lake is at 4,770 feet, covers 970 surface acres, and has seven miles of shoreline. A great bonus is that boat-in camping is permitted anywhere along the shore; it's a do-it-yourself affair, with no resorts, marinas, or facilities of any kind.

In the heat of summer, this is a good lake for swimming. In the cold (and I mean c-o-l-d) winter, it's good for ice fishing. Up here on the Modoc Plateau, temperatures often stay around 0°F for several weeks, starting in mid-December. The DFG stocks 10- to 12-inch and 7- to 8-inch Eagle Lake trout here.

If you are planning a trip here in late summer or fall, it is advisable to call ahead and check the water level. The reservoir is typically drained to very low levels at that time of year to supply water to local ranchers.

Facilities, fees: There are a few unimproved campsites with water and vault toilets. A boat ramp is also available. Supplies can be obtained in Likely or Alturas. Fishing access and camping are free.

Directions: From Alturas, take U.S. 395 south for 17 miles to the town of Likely and Jess Valley Road. Turn left (east) on Jess Valley Road (County Road 64) and drive two miles to the sign for West Valley Reservoir. Turn right and drive four miles to the boat ramp at West Valley Reservoir (the north end of the lake can be accessed via a short road off Jess Valley Road).

Contact: County of Modoc, Public Works, 530/233-6405; Modoc National Forest, Warner Mountain Ranger District, 530/279-6116, www.fs.fed.us/r5. Bureau of Land Management, Alturas Field Office, 530/233-4666, www.blm.gov/ca.

31 PARSNIP CREEK

Rating: 3

near Likely in Modoc National Forest

Map 3.2, page 168

This little creek enters and exits Blue Lake. The best stretch of water is below the lake, as it drops down through forest country.

At first glance you may be unimpressed. Parsnip Creek is quite small, and you can walk a mile and find just a few spots to flick your line. But every once in a while you will find a deep pool where the fish are just sitting, suspended in the current, gorging themselves as they pick up floating morsels. Most of the trout are small, however.

The upper end of the stream above Blue Lake is high plateau country. If you are camping at Blue Lake and want to try something different, you may find it worth a try to hike upstream, rod in hand, as you use extreme stealth to sneak up on every spot.

Facilities, fees: Camping is available at Blue Lake and Patterson Campground. Supplies can be obtained in Likely. Fishing access is free.

Directions: From Alturas, take U.S. 395 south for 17 miles to the town of Likely and Jess Valley Road. Turn left on Jess Valley Road (County Road 64) and drive nine miles until the road forks with Blue Lake Road/Forest Service Road 64. Bear right on Blue Lake Road and drive seven miles to Forest Service Road 39N30 (signed for Blue Lake). Turn right on Forest Service Road 39N30. Access is available along the road.

Contact: Modoc National Forest, Warner Mountain Ranger District, 530/279-6116, www.fs.fed.us/r5.

32 BLUE LAKE

Rating: 7

near Likely in Modoc National Forest

Map 3.2, page 168

Put this one on your must-fish list. As remote as Blue Lake is in a faraway section of Lassen County, the big brown trout that roam this 160-acre lake make it worth a try. Some of these brown trout are in the 10- to 12-pound class, and searching for them among the many rainbow trout in the foot-long class is something of a treasure hunt. The DFG plants foot-long-class rainbows here, as well as Eagle Lake trout of the same size.

One of the legends here is that a former Fish and Game director from Alturas used his power to order a special stock of giant brown trout—30-inchers, about 200 of them—to benefit his brother and friends, who lived in Alturas. The stock did occur, that's a fact, and since browns can live 10–15 years, it is no surprise that some giant fish are occasionally caught here. As is typical with big browns, the best prospects are in late winter and spring on cold, blustery overcast days. There is no shortage of those out here in northeastern California.

For a lake near a wilderness area (South Warner), Blue Lake offers surprisingly good access, with a paved road all the way to the northeast side. The campground has pretty surroundings, a good boat ramp is available nearby, and anglers will discover consistent results trolling from late spring and well into summer.

The egg-shaped lake is rimmed by trees. It borders on the pristine; this is one of the prettiest lakes you can reach on a paved road. Big fish are the bonus.

A 5-mph speed limit assures quiet water for small boats and canoes. A trail circles the lake and takes less than an hour to hike. The elevation is 6,000 feet. A pair of nesting bald eagles live here; over the last several years there have been three fledged chicks. Although their presence negates year-round use of six campsites otherwise available, the trade-off is an unprecedented opportunity to view the national bird.

Facilities, fees: A campground with drinking water and vault toilets is provided. A boat ramp, picnic area, and fishing pier are wheelchair-accessible. Supplies can be obtained in Likely. Fishing access is free.

Directions: From Alturas, take U.S. 395 south for 17 miles to the town of Likely and Jess Valley Road. Turn left on Jess Valley Road/County Road 64 and drive nine miles to the fork with Forest Service Road 64. At the fork, bear right to continue on Forest Service Road 64 and drive six miles to Forest Service Road 38N60. Turn right on Forest Service Road 38N60 and drive two miles to the campground at the lake.

Contact: Modoc National Forest, Warner Mountain Ranger District, 530/279-6116, www.fs.fed.us/r5.

33 PIT RIVER

Rating: 6

northeast of Redding in
Shasta-Trinity National Forest

Map 3.3, page 169

The Pit River is like two sides of a coin—flip it and see if it comes up heads or tails. Heads: When PG&E water releases are ideal for fishing, then the Pit becomes a blue-ribbon trout stream. Tails: When PG&E releases are high, you have no chance.

A good stretch of river for fly-fishing on the Pit is below the dam at Lake Britton. But success is way down here, because access is easy, and also because so many people camp at the nearby McArthur-Burney Falls Memorial State Park.

So it then becomes time to flip that coin again and see if it comes up tails. If so, off you go.

That's because a utility company operates a series of powerhouses along the Pit, and each stretch of the river is unique. For the most part, the stream is brushy, so you have to get out in it and wade. Shoreliners don't have a prayer. Other stretches lie in canyon bottoms,

requiring anglers to be in top physical condition. In addition, the wading is very slippery, and you can wrench a knee slipping on the bowling ball–size boulders.

When stream flows are right, the area between Lake Britton and Big Bend has become a blue-ribbon trout stream. The best portions of the river are below Powerhouse No. 3, Powerhouse No. 5 (difficult access), and near the town of Bend (the easiest access). It is here that the Pit can make a perfect example of a nymph-fishing stream, with challenging wading and pocket-water fishing, and occasional great results. The best fishing is always at dusk, after which hiking out in the dark is always a pain.

The latter is best for people making their first trip to the Pit; you can cast to pools and pockets in this boulder-laden stream. If you so desire, just downstream of town there's a natural hot spring, where you can work out those sore casting muscles. Access is also good near the Big Bend Bridge, which spans a beautiful stream with lots of pocket water.

Not everyone will enjoy this place. Fishing the best sections of the river requires hiking down a canyon, wading skillfully and aggressively, casting precisely during the evening rise, and then hiking back out of the canyon in the dark. Some call it the most challenging fishing experience of their life, wading amid the boulders then hiking out of the canyon at night. Get the picture? If you're still with me, well, maybe I'll see you out there. Hit it right and this can be some of the best fly-fishing for trout in Northern California.

Facilities, fees: Limited, dispersed camping with drinking water and vault toilets is available off Highway 299. Supplies can be obtained in Redding, Big Bend, and Burney. Fishing access is free.

Directions: To the Fender's Ferry section: From Redding, take Highway 299 east and drive 30 miles to Fender's Ferry Road. Turn left on Fender's Ferry Road and drive four miles. Access is available on the left side of the river, below the dam. The river can also be accessed off several roads that intersect Big Bend Road, about 35 miles east of Redding. These roads are unimproved, and high-clearance vehicles are recommended.

To the Big Bend section: From Redding, take Highway 299 east and drive 34 miles to Big Bend Road. Turn left on Big Bend Road and drive to the town of Big Bend and Hagen Flat Road. Turn east on Hagen Flat Road. Access is available directly off this road, near Powerhouse Nos. 3 and 4 and at several spots in between. Access is also possible below the Lake Britton Dam, east of Lake Britton: At the junction of Highways 299 and 89, drive about seven miles north on Highway 299 to Powerhouse No. 1.

Contact: Shasta-Trinity National Forest, Shasta Lake Ranger District, 530/275-1587; Shasta Lake Visitor Center, 530/275-1589; Vaughn's Sporting Goods & Fly Shop, Burney, 530/335-2381, www.vaughnfly.com; Jack Trout Flyfishing, 530/926-4540, www.jacktrout.com; The Fly Shop, 530/222-3555 or 800/669-3474, www.theflyshop.com.

34 BAUM AND CRYSTAL LAKES

Rating: 8

near Burney

Map 3.3, page 169

Brown trout and rainbow trout grow surprisingly large here in big-fish country. The biggest I've seen was a 24-pound brown trout. No foolin'.

Anglers can fish Baum by boat or bank, but no motors are allowed. Most people dunk night crawlers, and a few cast flies behind a bubble. They catch trout in the foot-long class for the most part, until suddenly and unexpectedly hooking something giant. Many big fish are lost, leaving the angler confused about what actually occurred.

Fish and Game takes good care of Baum Lake, stocking it each year with rainbow trout in the 10- to 12-inch class and 6- to 8-inch

browns. It's those browns that grow so large and can be so elusive. It's ironic that on the opening day of trout season, so many fly fishers head to nearby Hat Creek, yet it is Baum Lake that provides the better catches. That's true not only for numbers, but for size of the trout as well.

Good side trips in the immediate area include touring the Crystal Hatchery, which is adjacent to Baum Lake, or hiking on the nearby Pacific Crest Trail.

Facilities, fees: Camping is available nearby at Hat Creek and Lake Britton. No gas motors are permitted on Baum and Crystal Lakes. Electric motors are permitted. Supplies can be purchased in Burney. Fishing access is free.

Directions: From Redding, take Highway 299 east to Burney and continue for five miles to the junction with Highway 89. At the junction, continue straight on Highway 299 for two miles to Cassel Road. At Cassel Road, turn right and drive 3.6 miles to the campground entrance on the left (or turn left on Hat Creek–Powerhouse Road and continue to Baum Lake and the adjoining Crystal Lake).

Contact: PG&E Recreation Desk, 916/386-5164, www.pge.com/recreation; Vaughn's Sporting Goods & Fly Shop, Burney, 530/335-2381, www.vaughnfly.com.

35 HAT CREEK

Rating: 8

near Burney in Lassen National Forest

Map 3.3, page 169

What kind of trip are you in the mood for? Do you want to camp along a stream, have a chance at catching trout up to 12 inches long, and then eat it for dinner? If so, head to Upper Hat Creek. But if you want to fish a classic chalk stream, using a conservation-oriented fishing rod for wild trout and releasing your catch, go to Lower Hat Creek.

Upper Hat provides easy access off Highway 89, streamside campgrounds, and stretches of river that are stocked biweekly through the summer. A good number of rainbow trout and brook trout are stocked in Upper Hat, along with more rainbow trout in Middle Hat.

That adds up to a lot of fish for happy campers in this neighborhood. Anything goes here: Power Bait garnished with a salmon egg is the preferred entreaty, and there's a five-fish limit. In the fall, some huge trout migrate into this stretch of water.

The most reliable section of the river for families who are camping and want to have a little trout fry is this section along Highway 89. The DFG stocks fish in the stream at each of the campgrounds. Even though the upper portion of Hat Creek along the campgrounds is very heavily fished during the summer, when the crowds leave, a chance exists to catch a very big trout from one of the deep lava rock holes.

Each summer, when the crowds are there, there are accounts of kids racing back to their parents with stories of lost fish. Most of these stories are listened to in disbelief, but they may well be true. These trout may run up to six and even seven pounds. The DFG stocks Middle Hat Creek with 10- to 12-inch brook trout, 10- to 12-inch rainbow trout, and 6- to 8-inch brown trout. They grant Upper Hat Creek 10- to 12-inch rainbow trout and 10- to 12-inch brookies.

Such is not the case at Lower Hat. Trout have not been stocked in the section from Powerhouse No. 2 to Lake Britton for some 35 years. It is a fly-fishing stream, where extremely light, long leaders and very small flies are a necessity to even get a rise. Anglers use floating lines, size 5X to 7X tippets, and fly patterns as small as No. 20—though No. 16 can do well during the evening rise. The best patterns for Hat Creek are the Yellow Stone, Humpy, caddis, and duns.

Because all fish are released, some big trout roam these waters, most averaging 10–16 inches. The 18- to 22-inchers seem much more rare in recent years than in the past, but some monsters are still caught. The biggest I have heard tell of on Lower Hat is a 17-pound brown trout, caught in the 1980s.

Lower Hat demands the absolute best of fly fishers. Many say that if you master Lower Hat, you can fish successfully anywhere in the world. The wild trout section of Hat Creek is renowned among many fly fishers. But the truth is that it can be a very difficult stream to catch fish in, especially once summer arrives and angler numbers are very high.

At dusk it can take very sharp eyes. If you are using a surface pattern at dusk, there can be so many insects floating amid your fly that you can lose track of which one is actually yours—and you miss the set when you get a rise.

Facilities, fees: Several campgrounds are on Upper Hat Creek along Highway 89. At Cave Camp and Hat Creek, wheelchair-accessible fishing is available. Supplies can be obtained in Burney, Old Station, and Hat Creek. Fishing access is free.

Directions: To Lower Hat Creek: From Redding, take Highway 299 east for 51 miles to Burney, then continue northeast on Highway 299 for nine miles to where the highway crosses Hat Creek. Access is directly off Highway 299 where the road crosses the stream (at a county picnic area). The stretch from Baum Lake downstream to Lake Britton, excluding the concrete canal, is a designated wild trout stream, and special regulations are in effect. The area from Cassel Forebay to the Powerhouse No. 2 inlet may be fished with no special restrictions.

To reach Upper Hat Creek: From Redding, take Highway 299 east to Burney and continue for five miles to the junction with Highway 89. Turn right (south) on Highway 89 and drive 13 miles to Bridge Campground. Access is available at several campgrounds along the stream for 10 miles along Highway 89.

Contact: Lassen National Forest, Hat Creek Ranger District, 530/336-5521, www.fs.fed.us/r5; Clearwater Lodge, 530/336-5005 or 888/600-5451, www.clearwaterlodge.com; Vaughn's Sporting Goods & Fly Shop, Burney, 530/335-2381, www.vaughnfly.com; Jack Trout Flyfishing, 530/926-4540, www.jacktrout.com.

36 THOUSAND LAKES WILDERNESS

Rating: 7

east of Redding

Map 3.3, page 169

Big news: Tamarack Trailhead has a new location that makes it far preferable to the Cypress Trailhead. Those familiar with the area will remember that you needed a high-clearance four-wheel-drive rig to reach the former Tamarack Trailhead. (That was because the road passed through private property and the owner would not allow the Forest Service to maintain it). The new trailhead is significant, because instead of having to hike/climb more than 1,000 feet to reach Lake Eiler, now it's more like 400 feet. The new location adds only about 0.25-mile more hiking distance to the trip. Get yourself a map of this area, start gazing, and imagine the possibilities. It is hard to go wrong.

From the new Tamarack Trailhead, your first destination is Lake Eiler, a three-mile hike. The trail then routes into the northwestern interior of the Thousand Lakes Wilderness. After two miles, you'll reach a fork in the trail; turn left (south) to reach Barrett Lake in just another mile of hiking.

Note that there is a complex trail network in this area with many junctions, creating a situation in which backpackers can invent their own multiday route. From Barrett Lake, other attractive destinations include Durbin Lake, 0.5 mile to the south, and Everett and Magee Lakes, another (very challenging) 2.7 miles away.

The primary destination is Lake Eiler. It is the largest lake in this region, set just below Eiler Butte. From the south side of Eiler Lake, the trail loops deeper into the wilderness in a clockwise arc. It passes near several other lakes, including Box and Barrett Lakes. Both of these provide good fishing for small trout.

The wilderness area is not large, and most of the lakes are in the northeast sector, south of Freaner Peak, in the Thousand Lakes Valley. If you want to get in some mountain climbing

on your trip, a couple of peaks with great views (Red Cliff and Gray Cliff) are accessible to the southwest out of Everett and Magee Lakes. Note that the Magee Trail is no longer maintained and is more of a route and a trek than a hike.

The reason this wilderness is called the Thousand Lakes Wilderness has nothing to do with a thousand lakes. It's because during snowmelt, or after thunderstorms with intense rain, the standing water gives rise to thousands of small pools in the rocks. That is also why, in the spring and early summer, this is the worst place for mosquitoes in California.

Facilities, fees: No facilities are available in the wilderness area. Several campgrounds are off Highway 89 between the Hat Creek Work Center and the town of Old Station. Fishing access is free.

Directions: From Redding, take Highway 299 east for 50 miles to Burney and continue east five miles to Highway 89. Turn right (south) on Highway 89 and drive about 14 miles to Forest Road 33N25. Turn west on Forest Road 33N25 and drive 7.5 miles to a Y junction. Turn right and drive just about 1.5 miles to the trailhead (this new route is well signed).

Contact: Lassen National Forest, Hat Creek Ranger District, 43225 East Highway 299, P.O. Box 220, Falls River Mills, CA 96028, 530/336-5521, www.fs.fed.us/r5—click on Forest Offices.

37 NORTH BATTLE CREEK RESERVOIR

Rating: 5

near Viola

Map 3.3, page 169

A lot of folks unwittingly bypass this lake while heading east on Highway 44. They're too busy and excited en route to Lassen Volcanic National Park. If they just slowed down, they might see the turnoff for North Battle Creek Reservoir, and in turn, discover a spot that gets far less use.

The fishing, too, is far better here than at the national park. Each year, North Battle Creek Reservoir is stocked with 2,400 seven- to eight-inch brown trout, and they grow a lot bigger than the dink-sized variety found in most of the lakes at Lassen, which hasn't been stocked in a generation.

When the campgrounds are crowded at Lassen, what the heck, just roll on over to North Battle Creek Reservoir. You will probably end up catching more fish anyway.

This is one of several PG&E facilities that is off the mainstream radar.

Facilities, fees: A small campground with both drive-in and walk-in sites and a car-top boat launch are available. Drinking water and vault toilets are provided. Electric motors are permitted on the reservoir, but gas-powered engines are not. Fishing access is free.

Directions: From Redding, take Highway 44 east to Viola. From Viola, continue east for 3.5 miles to Forest Road 32N17. Turn left on Forest Road 32N17 and drive five miles to Forest Road 32N31. Turn left and drive four miles to Forest Road 32N18. Turn right and drive 0.5 mile to the reservoir and the campground, on the right side of the road.

Contact: PG&E Recreation Desk, 916/386-5164, www.pge.com/recreation.

38 CRATER LAKE

Rating: 5
near Susanville in Lassen National Forest
Map 3.3, page 169

Little Crater Lake sits just below the top of Crater Mountain at 6,800 feet, an obscure spot in Lassen National Forest. Anglers will find an intimate setting for trout fishing here. Most of the fish are small rainbow trout, with some brook trout and a sprinkling of larger Eagle Lake trout in the mix. Resident crayfish make for good catching and eating.

This is a small lake, just 27 acres, good for a kayak, canoe, pram, or inflatable (no motors are allowed). A primitive boat ramp and

campground is a nice plus. Not only is Crater Lake remote, but the access road is quite rough. A lot of people don't want to tangle with the drive just for the opportunity to fish for some small rainbow trout planted by the Department of Fish and Game.

The lake receives a variety of stocks, including rainbow trout in the 10- to 12-inch class and fingerling brookies dropped in by the DFG airplane.

For a good side trip, drive up Crater Mountain on the Forest Service road, which loops around near the summit (7,420 feet).

Facilities, fees: A campground is provided, as are drinking water (from a well) and vault toilets. Only nonmotorized boats are permitted on the lake. Supplies can be obtained in Susanville. Fishing access is free.

Directions: From Redding, take Highway 44 east to the junction with Highway 89 (near the entrance to Lassen Volcanic National Park). Turn north on Highway 89 and drive to Highway 44. Turn east on Highway 44 (left) and drive to the Bogard Work Center and adjacent rest stop. Turn left at Forest Service Road 32N08 (signed "Crater Lake") and drive one mile to a T intersection. Bear right and continue on Forest Service Road 32N08 for six miles (including two hairpin left turns) to the campground, on the left side of the road.

Contact: Lassen National Forest, Eagle Lake Ranger District, 530/257-4188, www.fs.fed.us/r5—click on Forest Offices.

39 MACUMBER RESERVOIR

Rating: 5
east of Redding
Map 3.3, page 169

Although little Macumber Reservoir is easy to reach from Redding, it gets missed by a lot of folks. They just drive right by. Whoa there. If you put your foot to the brake, you'll find a lake that's part of the PG&E utility company's hydro system and gets stocked each year with

6,000 foot-long rainbow trout by the Department of Fish and Game.

No gas motors are permitted here. That keeps it quiet and intimate for kayaks, inflatables, and other hand-powered boats.

Macumber was created when a dam was placed across the north fork of Battle Creek, set at 3,500 feet. Remember that. In the warm summer months, most of the fish often hold near the original creek channel, which is on the eastern side of the lake rather than right down the middle. By the way, this lake is spelled wrong as "McCumber" about 90 percent of time. But now you've got it right.

Facilities, fees: A small campground with vault toilets and drinking water is provided. A car-top boat launch is also available; gas motors are not permitted, but electric motors are. Fishing access is free.

Directions: In Redding, take Highway 44 east and drive toward Viola to Lake Macumber Road (if you reach Viola, you've gone four miles too far). Turn left at Lake Macumber Road and drive two miles to the reservoir and campground.

Contact: PG&E Recreation Desk, 916/386-5164, www.pge.com/recreation; Hinkle's Market & Sporting Goods, Redding, 530/243-2214.

40 MANZANITA LAKE

Rating: 8

in Lassen Volcanic National Park
Map 3.3, page 169

Several times early in the season and again late in the season, knowledgeable fly fishers can catch trout averaging 16 inches in Manzanita Lake. Manzanita is small but quite beautiful, and the conversion to a natural trout fishery has been a success. Rules mandate using a lure or fly only with a single barbless hook, and catch-and-release only.

The centerpiece of Lassen Volcanic National Park is, of course, the old Lassen Peak, and the climb up that beauty is one of the best

two-hour (one-way) hikes in California. But on a good day, Manzanita Lake provides the kind of fishing that can make you forget all about hiking.

Manzanita Lake is at 5,890 feet near the park entrance, and its idyllic setting rates high among the park's many attractions. In many ways, the lake makes an ideal vacation destination. The campground adjacent to the lake is Lassen's largest, with 179 sites, so you will almost always find a spot; it's also the easiest to reach, being so close to a major park entrance. In addition, cabins set up near the lake have added to the opportunities.

No powerboats are permitted on the lake, making it perfect for a canoe, raft, or pram. The best technique here is to offer the trout what they feed on: insects. Fly patterns that work best are the No. 14 Callibaetis; No. 16 Haystack; No. 14 or 16 Hare's Ear nymph; or, if a larger hatch is coming off, a No. 6, 8, or 10 leech in brown or olive. Fly fishers come ready with both sinking and floating lines, switching as necessary. Most of the feeding is done subsurface, however. If you want spin fishing here, try a half-ounce gold Kastmaster with a single barbless hook.

Fishing is prohibited at Emerald and Helen Lakes, in the national park, and all stocks ended many years ago at Summit Lakes and other lakes in the park. But considering what Manzanita provides, all is forgiven. Well, almost all.

Facilities, fees: A campground with drinking water and flush toilets is available. A picnic area, a convenience store, a museum, visitors center, an RV dump station, coin showers, and coin laundry are nearby. There is a boat ramp, but only nonmotorized boats are permitted on the lake. A park entrance fee is charged.

Directions: From Redding, take Highway 44 east to the junction with Highway 89. Turn right (south) on Highway 89 and drive one mile to the entrance station to Lassen Volcanic National Park (the state highway becomes Lassen Park Highway/Main Park Road). Continue a short distance on Lassen

Park Highway/Main Park Road to the campground entrance road. Turn right and drive 0.5 mile to the campground.

Contact: Manzanita Lake Camper Store, 530/335-7557; Lassen Volcanic National Park, P.O. Box 100, Mineral, CA 96063, 530/595-4480, www.nps.gov/lavo; Lassen Loomis Museum Association, P.O. Box 220, Mineral, CA 96063, 530/595-3399, www .lassenloomis.info.

41 BUTTE LAKE

Rating: 2

near Old Station in
Lassen Volcanic National Park
Map 3.3, page 169

A handful of old-timers remember when the fishing at Butte Lake was the best they've ever had in a national park. Newcomers wonder what the heck they are talking about.

This lake once received generous stocks of trout in the 10- to 13-inch class. If you happened to be camping here during the week following a fresh stock, well, you were in business. That's no longer the case. Stocks have been discontinued. The fools.

Because access to the lake is via an obscure park entrance, visitors often miss it. Butte Lake borders the Fantastic Lava Beds to the southwest, and nearby hiking destinations include Snag Lake to the south and Prospect Peak to the west. It is large (212 acres), has a high-mountain setting (6,100 feet elevation), and is beautiful. Fishing? There are still a few trout in the lake, but at the rate it's going, this lake probably won't make the cut of most.

Facilities, fees: A campground with drinking water and flush toilets is available. A small boat ramp is available; no motors are permitted. A per-vehicle park entrance fee is charged.

Directions: From Redding, drive east on Highway 44 to the junction with Highway 89. Bear north on Highway 89/44 and drive 13 miles to Old Station. Just past Old Station, turn right (east) on Highway 44 and drive 10

miles to Forest Service Road 32N21. Turn right and drive six miles to the campground at the lake.

Contact: Lassen Volcanic National Park, P.O. Box 100, Mineral, CA 96063, 530/595-4480, www.nps.gov/lavo; Lassen Loomis Museum Association, P.O. Box 220, Mineral, CA 96063, 530/595-3399, www.lassenloomis .info.

42 CARIBOU LAKE

Rating: 7

near Westwood in Lassen National Forest
Map 3.3, page 169

Everyone should fly in an airplane over this area at least once to be able to appreciate it. There are literally dozens of lakes in the region. Most of them are pristine little spots so quiet that you can practically hear the flowers bloom.

Caribou is one of those that is accessible by car, and because it is set on the edge of the wilderness, it provides a jumping-off point to several other small lakes, including Jewel, Eleanor, Black, Turnaround, Twin, and Triangle Lakes, which you hit in that order as you head to the interior of the wilderness.

Caribou Lake is stocked with rainbow trout in the 10- to 12-inch class and 6- to 8-inch brown trout. Fish in the 12-inch class are occasionally caught here. Folks with local knowledge know this and fish the lake year after year.

Facilities, fees: Vault toilets are available, but not drinking water. Garbage must be packed out. Two campgrounds are nearby, at Silver Lake. Only nonmotorized boats are allowed at Caribou Lake. Fishing access is free.

Directions: From Red Bluff, take Highway 36 east to the junction with Highway 89. Continue east on Highway 89/36 past Lake Almanor to Westwood and County Road A21. In Westwood, turn left on County Road A21 and drive 12.5 miles to Silver Lake Road. Turn left on Silver Lake Road/County Road 110 and drive 8.5 miles north to Silver Lake.

Continue past Silver Lake a short distance to Caribou Lake.

Contact: Lassen National Forest, Almanor Ranger District, 900 East Highway 36, P.O. Box 767, Chester, CA 96020, 530/258-2141, www.fs.fed.us/r5—click on Forest Offices.

43 CARIBOU WILDERNESS

Rating: 8

in Lassen National Forest
Map 3.3, page 169

Elevations in the Caribou Wilderness range 5,000–7,000 feet, offering hikes that aren't too rough and a chance to visit many alpine lakes filled with pan-sized trout. Because so many lakes are clustered so close to each other here, the Caribou Wilderness has been called the Walking Lakes Wilderness. Because it isn't hit by high numbers of people, the fishing, camping, and hiking are excellent.

Highlights include exploring volcanic areas, going for one-day hikes on several good loop trails that pass lakes, and taking a multiday expedition into adjoining Lassen Volcanic National Park. Black Lake and Turnaround Lake, both of which are fairly easy for hikers to access, offer some of the better fishing. On a longer trip, you could tie in Snag Lake or Juniper Lake, along with many others. Airplanes stock the following hike-to lakes with trout: Black, Cypress, Eleanor, Emerald, and Evelyn. Lakes no longer stocked with trout are: Gem, Hidden, Long, Jewel, Posey, Rim, Triangle, Twin, and Turnaround Lakes. Other unique points of interest are the Black Cinder Rock, Red Cinder Cone, and Caribou Peaks. Once you set up a base camp in the vicinity of these geologic wonders, you can put a lunch into a day pack and make a great side trip or two. Sound good? It is.

Facilities, fees: There are no facilities available within the wilderness area. Campgrounds are provided nearby at Silver Lake. Supplies can be obtained in Westwood. Fishing access is free.

Directions: From Redding, drive east on

Highway 44 to Old Station. Access roads that lead to trailheads are off Highway 44 to the west. A good scenic trail begins at Silver Lake. The trailhead is accessible off County Road A21 and Silver Lake Road/County Road 110. A map of Lassen National Forest is essential.

Contact: Lassen National Forest, Almanor Ranger District, 900 East Highway 36, P.O. Box 767, Chester, CA 96020, 530/258-2141, www.fs.fed.us/r5—click on Forest Offices.

44 SILVER LAKE

Rating: 5

near Westwood in Lassen National Forest
Map 3.3, page 169

Dozens of lakes dot the adjacent Caribou Wilderness, but Silver Lake, which doesn't require a hike in, often provides the best fishing of the bunch. It is a small and pretty lake, set at 6,400 feet in elevation. That translates to cold water—freezing over in winter, with ice-out usually occurring by June.

While Silver Lake is the largest of the little alpine lakes in the region, it is dwarfed by Lake Almanor, Mountain Meadows Reservoir, and Butte Lake to the south. For that reason, many vacationers never discover it.

Three species of trout live in these waters: brook, Eagle Lake, and brown. They comprise a decent fishery, with a variety of the smaller, easier-to-catch brookies and a few of the larger, more elusive brownies. Eagle Lake trout in the 10- to 12-inch class and brown trout in the 6- to 8-inch class are stocked.

For people making an expedition into the adjoining Caribou Wilderness, Silver Lake is a good first-night camp. It is at an elevation of 6,400 feet. From here you can access routes to Emerald Lake to the northwest and nearby Betty, Trail, and Shotoverin Lakes to the southeast. Fish and Game stocks Emerald and Shotoverin with catchable trout.

If you don't like the company at Silver Lake, nearby Caribou Lake provides an alternative.

Facilities, fees: Two campgrounds are provided: Silver Bowl and Rocky Knoll, with drinking water and vault toilets. An unimproved boat ramp is here; only car-top boats are permitted. Supplies can be purchased in Westwood. Fishing access is free.

Directions: From Red Bluff, take Highway 36 east to the junction with Highway 89. Continue east on Highway 89/36 past Lake Almanor to Westwood. In Westwood, turn left on County Road A21 and drive 12.5 miles to Silver Lake Road. Turn left (west) on Silver Lake Road/County Road 110 and drive 8.5 miles north to Silver Lake.

Contact: Lassen National Forest, Almanor Ranger District, 900 East Highway 36, P.O. Box 767, Chester, CA 96020, 530/258-2141, www.fs.fed.us/r5—click on Forest Offices.

45 GRACE LAKE

Rating: 6

near Shingletown
Map 3.3, page 169

Never heard of this tiny lake? Maybe you should listen up. Despite its size, Grace Lake is stocked with rainbow trout in the six- to eight-inch range. This boils down to a lot of fish for a small lake that doesn't get much fishing pressure. Hit this place early in the season. By mid-June, the sun starts branding everything in sight around these parts. The water temperature gets cranked up, and the trout get cranked down. If you find yourself cruising in this vicinity in April or May and have a hankering for trout, roll on by for some good shoreline bait dunking. Expect to see lots of folks fishing from lawn chairs.

Facilities, fees: A picnic area is available. Campgrounds and RV parks are near Shingletown. Fishing access is free.

Directions: From Redding, take Highway 44 east to Shingletown and Manton Road. Turn right on Manton Road and drive one mile south to a fork. Bear left at the fork on a dirt road and drive 0.8 mile to the lake.

Contact: PG&E Recreation Desk, 916/386-5164, www.pge.com/recreation; Hinkle's Market & Sporting Goods, Redding, 530/243-2214.

46 BATTLE CREEK

Rating: 8

near Red Bluff in Lassen National Forest
Map 3.3, page 169

Fly fishers and trout anglers should put Battle Creek on their target list. It's possible that it could become one of the top 10 trout streams in California. In the coming years, biologists predict that the trout population of Battle Creek could increase to 7,000–8,000 per mile.

Here, at the best trout stream in Lassen National Forest, you get rainbow trout up to a foot long, easy access off Highway 36, and a pretty setting on the edge of Lassen Volcanic National Park at an elevation of 4,800 feet. A lot of anglers drive right on by in both directions, not realizing that there are fish in Battle Creek. But there are. Fish and Game makes sure of that by stocking catchables: rainbows and brookies in the 10- to 12-inch class.

Money to fund hydro dam removal and habitat restoration comes from the Central Valley Improvement Act and cooperation from PG&E. Battle Creek has a relatively high and stable flow of water throughout the year, something unusual in California. That makes it uniquely drought resistant. That also means it is ideal for salmon and steelhead spawning on the lower reaches and trout fishing on the upper reaches. The area near Manton should have the biggest positive impact, but the entire stream will be transformed.

For those who love exploring, some of the upper reaches of Battle Creek (along with Mill Creek) are in some of the most remote canyons in the north state.

Adjacent Paynes Creek, set lower on Highway 36, provides a nearby alternative, though the fish there tend to be smaller, and the seasonal window of opportunity a bit shorter.

Facilities, fees: A campground, drinking water, flush and vault toilets, and a day-use picnic area are available just west of the town of Mineral. Supplies can be obtained in Mineral. Fishing access is free.

Directions: From Red Bluff, turn east on Highway 36 and drive 41 miles to the campground and river access (if you reach Mineral, you have gone two miles too far).

Contact: Lassen National Forest, Almanor Ranger District, 530/258-2141, www.fs.fed .us/r5—click on Forest Offices.

47 WILLOW LAKE

Rating: 5

near Chester in Lassen National Forest

Map 3.3, page 169

Little egg-shaped Willow Lake always comes as a surprise. Though located near some of California's top vacation destinations, this spot is so well off the beaten path that out-of-towners miss it every time.

The lake, which provides an intimate and quiet setting for campers and anglers, is in a national forest just west of Kelly Mountain. Yet it is only three miles from the southeastern border of Lassen Volcanic National Park at Drakesbad, and 10 miles northwest of giant Lake Almanor. The lake is stocked with brown and Eagle Lake trout, primarily 10- and 11-inchers. Shore fishing is easy, and the results are often good. After setting up camp, just walk around the lake, stopping to cast a few times as you go. A fly-and-bubble, Panther Martin, or 1/8-ounce Kastmaster or Z-Ray will usually do the job. If nobody has fished the lake recently, approach the shallows at the Willow Creek inlet and outlets. Trout often hold there unless they get scared off.

Drakesbad at Lassen Volcanic National Park provides a great side trip for hikers, with destinations such as Devils Kitchen and Drakes Lake within an hour's walk.

Facilities, fees: Primitive dispersed campsites are available. Garbage must be packed out. Supplies can be obtained in Chester. Access and camping are free. Supplies can be obtained in Chester. Fishing access is free.

Directions: From Red Bluff, take Highway 36 east and drive to Chester (at Lake Almanor) and Feather River Drive. Turn left on Feather River Drive and drive 0.75 mile to County Road 312. Bear left on County Road 312 and drive five miles to the fork with County Road 311 and 312. Bear left on County Road 311 and drive one mile to Forest Service Road 29N14 (a dirt road). Turn right and drive to Willow Lake.

Contact: Sports Nut, Chester, 530/258-3327; Lassen National Forest, Almanor Ranger District, 900 East Highway 36, P.O. Box 767, Chester, CA 96020, 530/258-2141, www .fs.fed.us/r5—click on Forest Offices.

48 ECHO LAKE

Rating: 4

near Chester in Lassen National Forest

Map 3.3, page 169

Obscure. Hard to reach. Primitive camping. A chance to catch small trout. Not many people around. Most people want these things on a vacation, and that is exactly what Echo Lake provides. The one drawback is its small size, which is only a problem on extended trips.

The Caribou Wilderness lies less than a mile northwest of the lake. With a national forest map in hand to help you navigate, it can be easy to make a quick trip into the nearby wilderness area and hit a string of lakes. Hidden, Long, Posey, and Beauty Lakes are all on the same loop trail.

Facilities, fees: A primitive campground, with drinking water and vault toilets, is provided. Garbage must be packed out. Supplies can be obtained in Chester. Fishing access is free.

Directions: From Red Bluff, take Highway 36 east to Chester. Continue east on Highway 36 for eight miles to Chester Dump Road. Turn left on Chester Dump Road and drive west a short distance on a connector road, then continue north for 9.5 miles to Echo Lake.

Contact: Sports Nut, Chester, 530/258-3327; Lassen National Forest, Almanor Ranger District, 900 East Highway 36, P.O. Box 767, Chester, CA 96020, 530/258-2141, www .fs.fed.us/r5—click on Forest Offices.

49 STAR LAKE

Rating: 4

near Chester in Lassen National Forest
Map 3.3, page 169

Of the three small trout lakes in the area north of Almanor, Star Lake provides the best chance of seeing the fewest people. Unfortunately, the odds are also good that you'll catch the smallest fish.

Some DFG dinkers live in this little mountain lake—you know, those five-inch brook trout. If you catch an eight-incher, you may need to be resuscitated. And the lake is not exactly loaded with these little brookies either. The DFG no longer stocks it, even with dinker fingerlings.

But it is quiet and pretty, and if you have some mountain goat in you, a climb up the adjacent Star Butte to the east can make a good boot-thumping side trip.

Facilities, fees: There are no on-site facilities. A primitive campground is available at nearby Echo Lake, but there is no drinking water. Fishing access is free.

Directions: From Red Bluff, take Highway 36 east to Chester. Continue east on Highway 36 for eight miles to Chester Dump Road. Turn left on Chester Dump Road and drive to Forest Service Road 10. Continue north on Forest Service Road 10 for about nine miles to the trailhead. Park and walk 0.25 mile to the lake.

Contact: Sports Nut, Chester, 530/258-3327; Lassen National Forest, Almanor Ranger District, 900 East Highway 36, P.O. Box 767, Chester, CA 96020, 530/258-2141, www .fs.fed.us/r5—click on Forest Offices.

50 WILSON LAKE

Rating: 3

near Mineral in Lassen National Forest
Map 3.3, page 169

If you want a spot that's pretty enough to visit, even though you wouldn't want to live there, Wilson Lake is worth considering.

You see, the trout fishing just doesn't seem to be up to snuff at ol' Wilson. This round lake is pretty, bordered by meadows on one side and dotted by a few little islands, but it's shallow on the northeast side. At least the salamanders like it.

If you don't catch anything, consider hiking a short distance southeast of the lake to the Ice Cave, the product of ancient glacial activity, or venturing on a more rigorous trek to the top of Ice Cave Mountain.

Facilities, fees: There are no on-site facilities. A primitive campground called Willow Springs is a short distance east of Wilson Lake, but no drinking water is provided. Supplies are available in Mineral. Fishing access is free.

Directions: From Red Bluff, take Highway 36 east for about 45 miles to Mineral. Continue east on Highway 36 for 8.5 miles (2 miles past Childs Meadows parking area) to Wilson Lake Road/Forest Service Road 29N19 (a dirt road). Turn left on Wilson Lake Road and drive 2.5 miles to the lake.

Contact: Lassen National Forest, Almanor Ranger District, 900 East Highway 36, P.O. Box 767, Chester, CA 96020, 530/258-2141, www.fs.fed.us/r5—click on Forest Offices.

51 MILL CREEK

Rating: 5

near Mineral in Lassen National Forest
Map 3.3, page 169

Don't try fishing Mill Creek without a Forest Service map. Much of the land bordering this trout stream is privately owned, and the local ranchers are apt to shoot a load of rock salt into your rear end if they catch you trespassing, so pay close attention to the directions in this listing, and be certain to have a map.

The stretch of stream along the hiking trail is where public access is best. Besides, too much salt isn't good for you.

Facilities, fees: Campgrounds with drinking water and vault toilets are available off the road that leads to the trailhead. Supplies can be obtained in Mineral. Fishing access is free.

Directions: From Red Bluff, take Highway 36 east for 43 miles to the town of Mineral and the junction with Highway 172. Turn right on Highway 172 and drive six miles to the town of Mill Creek and a Forest Service road (at times, this is signed Mill Creek/Hole in the Ground, but the sign is often stolen and missing). Turn right and drive three miles to a parking area and trailhead, or continue five miles to the campground access road. Turn left and drive 0.25 mile to the camp. A hiking trail follows Mill Creek for several miles.

For a free map of Lassen National Forest, contact Lassen National Forest Supervisor's Office, 2550 Riverside Dr., Susanville, CA 96130, 530/257-2151, or download it at www .fs.fed.us/r5—click on Forest Offices.

Contact: Mill Creek Resort, 888/595-4449, www.millcreekresort.net; Lassen National Forest, Almanor Ranger District, 900 East Highway 36, P.O. Box 767, Chester, CA 96020, 530/258-2141, www.fs.fed.us/r5— click on Forest Offices.

52 DEER CREEK

Rating: 8
near Mineral in Lassen National Forest
Map 3.3, page 169

Try to envision the ideal trout stream: A trail leads along the stream, providing you with hiking access. The water is pure and clear, flowing over rocks and into pools. Trout in the foot-long class seem to be in all of the good-looking spots, even though you can't always catch them.

Want more? A small, yellow-striped two-lane highway runs right alongside much of it, allowing anglers to hit several stretches of the river in one day. Yet the road is too curvy for RVs or out-of-towners who aren't willing to pay the price for a chance at quality trout fishing.

You get this at Deer Creek, which has consistently been one of the better stream producers of trout.

When fishing Deer Creek, it is critical to know how the fishing changes as you travel east from Chico. As you drive into the alpine country and cross over a concrete bridge, you'll see a large parking area on the right along Highway 32. This is the prime access point for fly-fishing in a catch-and-release section of water.

An excellent angler's trail here provides access to the river. You cross the highway, catch the trail, and hike downstream along the river with good fly-fishing water about every 35–40 yards. You can hike along, catch these spots, cast to the fish, and spend a day at it, fishing a dozen or so good spots. Note that two miles downstream, there is a no-fishing section within proximity of a fish ladder. It is well signed.

As you drive far upstream, you will find a series of three campgrounds. This is the area that is stocked by the DFG, where you are allowed to keep the fish. In any case, be sure to check the DFG regulations. In this area, the creek is stocked with 10- to 12-inch rainbow and brook trout.

The trail that follows much of the premium upper stretch makes the river special. It allows you to get a good look at the better spots and feel as if you're sneaking up on the fish. Your chances of coming up with a nice stringer are very good.

Facilities, fees: Alder and Potato Patch campgrounds are along the creek on Highway 32. Vault toilets and drinking water are available. Supplies can be obtained in Mineral. Fishing access is free.

Directions: From Chico, take Highway 32 northeast for 40 miles. Just after the small, red, metal bridge (locals call it the "Red Bridge") that crosses Deer Creek, park on the south side of the road, where there's a dirt pullout. The trailhead is just up from the bridge, on the north side of the road. This section is good for fly-fishing for trout. There are also several good swimming holes.

From Red Bluff, take Highway 36 east for 44 miles to the junction with Highway 89. Continue east on Highway 36/89 to the junction with Highway 32. Turn south on Highway 32 and drive eight miles to the campground, on the right side of the road. Trailers are not recommended. Direct access to the creek is available off Highway 32 at pullouts.

Contact: Sports Nut, Chester, 530/258-3327; Lassen National Forest, Almanor Ranger District, 900 East Highway 36, P.O. Box 767, Chester, CA 96020, 530/258-2141, www .fs.fed.us/r5—click on Forest Offices.

53 LITTLE NORTH FORK FEATHER RIVER

Rating: 7

northwest of Lake Almanor in
Lassen National Forest
Map 3.3, page 169

Few either realize the prospects or are willing to find out just what is possible on this trout stream. Depending on where you fish it, the Little North Fork Feather River can provide some very good results. The best spots are out of the way, and anglers must be willing to hike to reach them.

The river's central access points, just off Forest Service roads near Warner Valley, are where the DFG stocks trout. For the most part, stocks consist of rainbow trout in the 9- to 11-inch class. Fishing for them in this intimate setting can be fun.

But if you hike onward, brush-bashing and rock-hopping your way to the difficult-to-reach pools, you will find some surprisingly large brown trout. The theory is that these browns are from Lake Almanor. They are difficult to catch, and there aren't very many of them, so tread lightly. And if you are lucky enough to hook one, maybe it's time to let 'em go and leave some seed for the future.

You need the stealth of a burglar, the nerves of a safecracker, and then you must perform like Derek Jeter in Yankee Stadium with the knowledge that you might be casting for a five-pound brown. Screw up anything along the way and you might as well try eating soup with a fork.

Facilities, fees: High Bridge and Domingo Springs campgrounds are near the river. Picnic tables, fire grills, drinking water, and vault toilets are available. Supplies can be obtained in Chester. Fishing access is free.

Directions: From Red Bluff, take Highway 36 east for 44 miles to the junction with Highway 89. Do not turn left (north) on Highway 89 to Lassen Volcanic National Park entrance, as signed. Continue east on Highway 36/89 to Chester. In Chester turn left (north) on Feather River Drive (Warner Valley Road). Drive 0.75 mile to County Road 312. Bear left and drive six miles to Warner Valley Road. Turn right and drive 11 miles to the campground on the right. *Note:* Access is available directly off Warner Valley Road and off several Forest Service roads and trails that junction with it.

Contact: Lassen National Forest, Almanor Ranger District, 900 East Highway 36, P.O. Box 767, Chester, CA 96020, 530/258-2141, www.fs.fed.us/r5—click on Forest Offices.

54 LAKE ALMANOR

Rating: 10

east of the town of Red Bluff in
Lassen National Forest
Map 3.3, page 169

Lake Almanor grows big trout, tons of small-mouth bass. My brother and I had one three-hour stretch where we caught five over 5 pounds, and then I hooked—and lost—the lake-record 24-pound brown trout. I know it was the lake record because my fieldscout and pal, Hal Jansen, caught, weighed, and released the same fish only a short distance from where it got away from me. The official lake record is a 16-pound brown trout, since Hal released his prize fish. The lake-record rainbow trout is 9 pounds, 14 ounces. That might sound small, but remember these fish fight like steelhead—just fantastic.

It's also a pretty lake, a jewel ringed by conifers. You can stay in a lakeside vacation home or rental cabin and maybe catch a big fish. This is one of the best lakes in the state for large rainbow trout, brown trout, and lake-raised salmon. Smallmouth bass also live in these waters, and they come to life at midsummer, right when the cold-water species go into a short lull.

Methods: 1) Troll using downriggers to reach precise depths on the edge of underwater ledges and channels, near submerged boulder fields, springs or weed beds. 2) Jig, straight up and down at ledges or springs. 3) Flycast with sink-tip lines and leeches, with strip retrieve, on the edges of weed beds. 4) Baitfish with night crawler under slip bobber at springs.

• Leader, swivels: Tie on a black barrel swivel to the fishing line, add 27 inches of 6-pound test fluorocarbon leader, and snap swivel for lure.

• Lures, flies: Use 2 1/4 or 2 1/2-inch Needlefish lure in rainbow, black/silver, red/white/black, or brown trout, with red eye added to head of lure; 2 1/2-inch Z-Ray, yellow with red spots; 2 3/4-inch jointed Rapala (floating), gold/black; marabou trolling flies (no snap swivel); 4 1/2-inch rat lure with double treble hooks.

• Cat-and-mouse: Off downrigger on deep line, run a jointed Rebel or Rapala. On shallow line, run a Needlefish. It will look like a small trout is chasing a pond smelt.

• Rod, reel, line: My favorite for trolling is a 7-foot Loomis PR8400C matched with Abu-5 Ambassadeur level-wind, with 250 yards of fresh 10-pound Maxima Ultra-Green.

If you get the idea it takes some expertise to fool these big trout, you are correct. If there are drawbacks, it's the weather and the fact you have to pay your dues to be successful. In the spring, early summer, and fall, when the trout fishing is best, it is often very cold and windy. In fact, the key is to be out before daybreak, because the wind often comes up by 10 A.M., forcing everybody off the lake. In the fall, it is also quite cold, with absolutely frigid mornings. And in the winter, Almanor gets a lot of snow, often 10 feet, and the place is just about abandoned. That leaves a narrow window of good weather in July and August, when the fishing is the worst.

During those warm months, when most people want to visit, smallmouth bass provide a bridge for anglers. Using crickets for bait and a split shot for weight, cast along the shoreline drop-offs, let the cricket sink to about 30 feet deep, and then twitch it and reel in a few feet—right then is when you will often get a bite. The best area for smallmouth bass is on the west side of the lake, generally near the outlet area, right along the buoy line.

Mount Lassen's mammoth eruptions of 1914 and 1921 are key to the lake's aquatic abundance. Much of the lake bottom is peppered with volcanic boulders the size of bowling balls, and rampant weed growth has covered these boulders. That provides habitat for caddis, mayflies, and other insects emerging from the bottom in larval form. The profuse springs pumping cold water keep the lake cool, fresh, and circulating, and the lake's pond smelt provide additional forage. The final result is a big fish factory like no other in Northern California.

Natural springs keep the water cold and circulating, and, along with the penetrating rays of sunlight, they also help get the aquatic food chain in motion. The minnow population (pond smelt) is thus abundant, providing large amounts of feed for growing sport fish. Finally, Fish and Game stocks yearling and fingerling chinook salmon, Eagle Lake trout, and brown trout. All of these species have the potential to grow big, and with the abundant food supply here, they do. Rather than catching lots of small fish, at Almanor you are apt to catch a few huge ones. That is, if you can handle them.

The best time for trout fishing is in October, when the big brown trout and Eagle Lake trout are on the prowl. It is common to catch browns and Eagle Lakers in the three- to five-pound class during a two- to three-week period when it isn't raining. A technique used religiously by the locals is to spray scents on the lures that they are trailing. The preferred scent always includes anchovy oil.

At the northeast end of the lake, we found a shallow-water weed field that extends for two miles to shore, a perfect area for the big fish to feed and hide. On the edge of that weed field, we found a ledge where the bottom dropped from 3 feet to 25 feet deep on one side, and from 3 feet to 11 feet (in a narrow channel) on the other. We set up to troll the edge of the weed field, 8–15 feet deep, right on the ledge. My brother hit first, with a five-pound brown trout, landed after a 15-minute battle. Rainbow trout that were roughly five and seven pounds, as hot as Dean River steelhead, struck next. We lost three others—two bigger, one smaller—and then landed a rainbow trout and a king salmon. That was just a start to a fall day when the lake was like glass.

Other good spots are the edge of the old river channel at both the north end of the lake and the south end near the dam, as well as the mouth of Bailey Creek and adjacent Bailey Springs (best when it is windy, because it's shallow) along the southeast shore of the lake. Some folks fish by the northern shore of the Almanor Peninsula, trolling, and try almost nowhere else.

If it's windy, blowing up whitecaps, one trick I'll do is run my boat up to the shallows and channel along the southeast shore of the lake north of Bailey Creek. That is when I'll put on my secret weapon, a mouse lure—right, the kind that costs about $35 in the Cabela's catalog—and troll it right along the shore in 4–8 feet of water. I've hooked some monster-size trout with this trick.

Another peak period is from late March through early June, when salmon can provide solid fishing. (It's often good starting in February.) The Big Springs area, on the east side of the lake just north of the Hamilton Branch, is the most consistent spot on the lake. It is only a five-minute boat ride from the former Lassen View Resort. Another well-known spot that attracts big fish is called the A-Frame, named after a nearby A-frame cabin that's used as a navigational landmark. Some anchor in the vicinity of these springs, then use either a small chunk of anchovy or an entire night crawler, letting the bait descend to the lake bottom. When the bait gets picked up, I prefer to point the rod at the water, and when the slack in the line is pulled a few inches—wham!—I slam the hook home. Another technique is to jig straight up and down; crappie jigs and Gitzits work well. While anchored, you simply drop the jig to the lake bottom, jerk it up in two-foot pulls with your rod, then let the jig settle back down. This can get very monotonous but will often entice bites when bait will not, particularly after the main bite is over at 9:30 A.M.

Almanor has tons of salmon, but most of them are small, just 12 or 13 inches. That's a far cry from a few years ago, when they averaged three to five pounds. I once caught a five-salmon limit here that weighed 22 pounds. Because of the fall-off in the size of salmon in Lake Almanor, the DFG is experimenting with planting fewer salmon, and hopefully they will get bigger.

The trout and salmon are often done by midmorning. But don't give up, because the smallmouth bass fishing can be exceptional if you use live crickets for bait. On one trip, every five minutes or so one of us would hook another bass. Between us we caught and released about 25 or 30 smallmouth in a few hours. The biggest landed was a three-pounder that I tussled with for about 10 minutes, but I had a much bigger one (about a four-pounder, with a square body) that broke the line when it dove under the boat. We used long, light spinning rods, like noodle rods, with 4-pound test on spinning reels, then tied on No. 10 hooks and clamped on two tiny split shot each. We hooked on grasshoppers for bait, flipped them out, and let them sink—then kept them barely moving.

This is a big lake, some 13 miles long and covering 28,000 acres. That alone can be frustrating to newcomers who don't know where the heck to start their expedition. It can take a few days of zilches before you figure out where to fish.

PG&E created Almanor to be a reservoir, but it looks more like a natural lake, because it is kept so full most of the year. Meanwhile, water levels always seem to be low at Mountain Meadows Reservoir to the east, which feeds into Almanor, and at Butt Lake to the south, which gets its water from here. Lake Almanor is big and beautiful, filled with sapphire-blue waters and with snowcapped Mount Lassen as a backdrop.

Many people call Lake Almanor a "poor man's Tahoe" because of the lack of lodging and restaurant possibilities. This is the kind of place for a simple fishing weekend, or for families who are content to spend all of their time in campgrounds or in a cabin when not fishing.

Facilities, fees: Several campgrounds are available, as are lodging, boat ramps, a boat dock, groceries, gas, bait, and tackle. Fishing access is free.

Directions: From Red Bluff, take Highway 36 east for 44 miles to the junction with Highway 89. Continue east on Highway 36/89 to Lake Almanor and the next junction with Highway 89 (two miles before reaching Chester). Turn right on Highway 89 and drive eight miles to the southwest end of Lake Almanor. Turn left at your choice of four campground entrances, with a boat ramp nearby.

To North Shore camp and boat ramp: From Red Bluff, take Highway 36 east for 44 miles to the junction with Highway 89. Drive east on Highway 36/89; the camp and boat ramp are two miles past Chester, on the right.

To Almanor North and South camps and nearby ramp: From Red Bluff, take Highway 36 east for 44 miles to the junction with Highway 89. Continue east on Highway 36/89 to Lake Almanor and the next junction with Highway 89 (two miles before reaching Chester). Turn right on Highway 89 and drive six miles to County Road 310. Turn left on County Road 310 and drive one mile to the campground.

Contact: Lassen National Forest, Almanor Ranger District, 900 East Highway 36, P.O. Box 767, Chester, CA 96020, 530/258-2141, www.fs.fed.us/r5—click on Forest Offices; Plumas County Visitors Bureau, 800/326-2247, www.plumascounty.org; Chester-Lake Almanor Chamber of Commerce, 530/258-2426 or 800/350-4838, www.lakealmanor area.com; PG&E Recreation Desk, 916/386-5164, www.pge.com/recreation; Sports Nut, Chester, 530/258-3327; Sportsmen's Den, Quincy, 530/283-2733.

Guides: Big Meadows Guide Service, 530/596-3072; Roger's Guide Service, 530/528-0525; J&J Guide Service, 530/825-3491 or 530/222-6253, jandjguideservice.net; Dick's Guide Service, 530/256-3317; Almanor Fishing Adventures, 530/258-6732, www .almanorfishingadventures.com; Big Daddy's Guide Service, 530/283-4103; Rick's Guide Service, 530/284-6005; Lake Almanor Fly Fishing Company, 530/258-3944, www .almanorflyfishing.com; Tight Lines Guide Service, 530/263-0990 or 530/263-7944, www.fishtightlines.com.

55 YELLOW CREEK

Rating: 7

near Lake Almanor in Lassen National Forest

Map 3.3, page 169

Yellow Creek is a classic spring creek. This meandering stream rolls slowly and gently through a valley. Don't expect raging water rushing over rocks and into pools.

Aside from the fact that it doesn't attract nearly as many people, Yellow Creek is similar to Hat Creek near Burney. Fishing this water is very challenging and difficult; regulations mandate fly-fishing only, and you must use dry flies and match hatches. The evening rise here is a classic scene for skilled fly fishers. That's another way of saying that the trout can be damn hard to catch.

A little-known secret about the stream is that the biggest fish rarely rise to a hatching caddis; instead, they lie under the cut bank, the underwater indentation unique to spring creeks, and wait for morsels to drift by.

A good campground has been provided. So has a fence that keeps the cows out of the creek. You can thank the fine organization California Trout, Inc. for that one.

You should check fishing regulations before heading out on any body of water, but it is critical here, as different rules govern different parts of the river. The middle of the valley is considered something of a temple, however, and the religion practiced there is catch-and-release fly-fishing.

To gain a completely new perspective on Yellow Creek, check out the lower end, those first few miles above the confluence with the Feather River near Belden. The creek flows much more quickly there, tumbling through pools, riffles, and small falls. Spring is the best time to be on this stretch of the creek, because lots of good-sized rainbow trout from the Feather River use it for spawning. In the fall, a few big browns also ascend Yellow Creek.

Facilities, fees: A 10-unit PG&E campground is provided. Drinking water and vault toilets are available. Supplies can be obtained in Chester. Fishing access is free.

Directions: From Red Bluff, take Highway 36 east for 44 miles to the junction with Highway 89. Continue east on Highway 36/89 to Lake Almanor and the junction with Highway 89 (two miles before reaching Chester). Turn right on Highway 89 and drive about five miles to Humbug Road/County Road 308/309. Turn right (west) and drive 0.6 mile to the junction of County Road 308 and 309. Bear left on County Road 309 and drive 1.2 miles to the junction with County Road 307. Bear right on County Road 307 and drive 5.4 miles to a Y. Bear left at the Y and drive 1.2 miles to the campground entrance on the right. Turn right and drive 0.3 mile to the campground at Yellow Creek. Stream access is available in Humbug Valley.

Contact: PG&E Recreation Desk, 916/386-5164, www.pge.com/recreation; Sports Nut, Chester, 530/258-3327; Sportsmen's Den, Quincy, 530/283-2733.

56 BUTT VALLEY RESERVOIR

Rating: 7

near Chester

Map 3.3, page 169

The official name is "Butt Valley Reservoir." But everybody calls this "Butt Lake." That includes me. And most people who show up at Butt Lake look around and wonder what all the fuss is about. With a little luck, you will find out.

After all, the water level is often quite low, exposing lots of stumps on the bare lake bed; the campground is some distance from the water; and camping can be intolerable if your neighbor is some self-obsessed moron with a boom box or a generator. When you discover that the trout can be difficult to catch, you are bound to say, "I should have gone to Almanor." After all, Almanor is right next door.

Maybe so, but when the powerhouse is running, this is the place to be. You see, the powerhouse is on the northern end of this long, narrow reservoir, and when it runs, remarkable numbers of pond smelt come down the tunnel from Almanor and get funneled by the PG&E turbines right into the narrow channel at the head of Butt Lake. In turn, every big trout in the lake congregates in this small area—and you can catch the trout of your life.

Rainbow trout ranging 10–15 pounds have been caught here, compliments of the powerhouse. One month, something like 20 10-

pounders were documented coming from this channel, most of them taken on Countdown Rapalas. The biggest I've heard of was a 17-pound rainbow trout caught by a woman who had cast out a Phoebe, of all things.

So Butt Lake can be either a disaster or a bounty. Rarely is there an in-between.

Note: Closures can be in effect here in the channel at the powerhouse. When that happens, this lake still provides a decent fishery for rainbow trout. Most people catch them trolling. Where? The magic spots are anywhere you can find stumps.

Facilities, fees: Two campgrounds are provided on the eastern shoreline (Ponderosa Flat and Cool Springs). Drinking water, vault toilets, and a boat ramp are available. Supplies can be obtained in Chester, about 10 miles away. Fishing access is free.

Directions: From Red Bluff, take Highway 36 east for 44 miles to the junction with Highway 89. Continue east on Highway 36/89 to Lake Almanor and the next junction with Highway 89 (two miles before reaching Chester). Turn right on Highway 89 and drive about seven miles to Butt Valley Road. Turn right on Butt Valley Road and drive 3.2 miles for Ponderosa Flat Campground or 5.7 miles for Cool Springs Campground and boat ramp, on the right.

Contact: PG&E Recreation Desk, 916/386-5164, www.pge.com/recreation; Sports Nut, Chester, 530/258-3327; Sportsmen's Den, Quincy, 530/283-2733; Big Meadows Guide Service, 530/596-3072; Roger's Guide Service, 530/528-0525.

57 NORTH FORK FEATHER RIVER

Rating: 7

south of Belden Forebay in
Plumas National Forest
Map 3.3, page 169

The North Fork Feather has always been a reliable spot where you could camp and catch planted trout. But the future is in question because increased stream flows by PG&E have helped rafting but can be too high to fish effectively. The jury is still out.

Because the flows of this river are controlled by the releases from Belden Forebay, the water releases determine your fate. For years, this has been one of the most reliable spots during the opening weekend of trout season, when many other rivers have high murky flows from snow melting. The North Fork Feather River has been a top trout producer. The DFG has stocked the river quite heavily, especially from the opening of trout season on the last Saturday of April through early summer. The east branch of the North Fork now receives rainbow trout, as well as at Almanor and at Belden—all in the 10- to 12-inch class.

The aquatic life in these waters is vibrant and productive, making for some very happy campers/anglers. As for the stream, which was pretty to begin with, it has come back quite strong and is a favorite among those who have been following its recovery.

The natural place to start fishing is at the campgrounds. But that is where everybody, and I mean everybody, fishes. Instead, drive up to Belden Forebay and work over the stretch of water in the first 150 yards below the dam. Results can be excellent there. Then continue downstream, making hits along the way, and you'll eventually return to the campgrounds. By then, you will likely have your fish. And just watch. All the hard-pressed campers will ask you where you caught them.

You can just smile and say: "In the water, on a hook, right in the mouth."

Facilities, fees: Three campgrounds are set right along the river, with access off Caribou Road, including Gansner Bar Campground, a good choice. Drinking water and vault toilets are available. A small grocery store is nearby. Fishing access is free.

Directions: From Oroville, take Highway 70 north to Caribou Road (two miles past Belden at Gansner Ranch Ranger Station). Turn left on Caribou Road and drive a short distance to the campground, on the left side of the road.

Contact: Plumas National Forest, Mount Hough Ranger District, 530/283-0555, www.fs.fed.us/r5—click on Forest Offices; Sportsmen's Den, Quincy, 530/283-2733.

Contact: Lassen National Forest, Almanor Ranger District, 900 East Highway 36, P.O. Box 767, Chester, CA 96020, 530/258-2141, www.fs.fed.us/r5—click on Forest Offices; PG&E Recreation Desk, 916/386-5164, www.pge.com/recreation.

58 PHILBROOK RESERVOIR

Rating: 4

near Paradise in Lassen National Forest

Map 3.3, page 169

The first time I visited Philbrook, I figured they got the name wrong. Even though Paradise Lake is so close to the southwest, it looked as if this lake deserved the name more than the original.

Philbrook, set at 5,600 feet, is just hard enough to reach that most folks stay away. And it is larger than you would expect. When I rolled up, insects were hatching and trout were rising, leaving little pools all over the surface. The road is too rough for trailered boats, but I had a canoe strapped to the top of my Ford four-by-four, so it seemed ideal. Shortly thereafter, I realized why this lake was not named Paradise: It's Dinkerville, U.S.A. That's right, it is loaded with little rainbow trout, and it requires a hell of an effort to catch anything else. It's even worse at midsummer, when the weather is very hot and the fishing is poor.

Facilities, fees: A campground with drinking water, vault toilets, and a picnic area is provided. A car-top boat launch is available. Fishing access is free.

Directions: From Orland on I-5, take the Highway 32/Chico exit and drive to Chico and the junction with Highway 99. Turn south on Highway 99 and drive to Skyway Road/Paradise (in south Chico). Turn east on Skyway Road, drive through Paradise, and continue for 27 miles to Humbug Summit Road. Turn right and drive two miles to Philbrook Road. Turn right and drive 3.1 miles to the campground entrance road. Turn right and drive 0.5 mile to the campground.

59 MENDIBOURE RESERVOIR

Rating: 3

near Madeline

Map 3.4, page 170

The trip here is not so much a fishing trip as an adventure. The road in is terrible. You need four-wheel-drive with high clearance, and you must know how to use it, or forget this one. The Bureau of Land Management suggested I take it out of the book because access is so difficult, cell phone reception is zero, and they don't want people to get stuck trying to make it. But for some, a challenge is just what the doctor ordered.

The lake has a few trout in it, but it is not stocked, and the prospects are what I call "limited." Regardless, the ambitious few with a kayak or inflatable can get the lake all to themselves, set up a camp, and perhaps even catch the odd one. The lake does have a light sprinkling of Eagle Lake trout in it. The only prospects are from April through June.

They named this lake after a local rancher. Get the idea? Right, Mendiboure Reservoir was built to provide water to ranchlands, and that means levels are subject to fluctuations, depending on how much water it gets in the winter and how much the ranchers take out in the summer.

Of the lakes you can reach by vehicle in California, this is one of the most remote, challenging, and least-visited.

Facilities, fees: There are no on-site facilities. Supplies are available in Madeline. Fishing access is free.

Directions: From Alturas, take U.S. 395 south for 31.5 miles to the town of Madeline and Clarks Valley Road. Turn east on Clarks

Valley Road and drive two miles to a rough dirt road. Turn south and follow it through the drainage for four miles to the reservoir. A high-clearance four-wheel-drive vehicle is required. Do not attempt to drive this road with a car.

Contact: Bureau of Land Management, Alturas Resource Area, 530/233-4666, www.blm.gov/ca.

60 DODGE RESERVOIR

Rating: 5

near Ravendale

Map 3.4, page 170

Dodge is one of the larger reservoirs in this remote area of the Modoc Plateau, and because of it, Fish and Game has taken a completely different approach here. The DFG plants Eagle Lake trout fingerlings in the hope that the lake will provide enough feed for a high percentage of them to grow to adult size.

The bigger fish here are taken early in the season, but be warned—when the wind blows, it can feel like the coldest place on earth. The colder the weather and the water, the more the fish will be found in shallow waters, as little as a foot deep.

Fly fishers have the advantage here, but spin fishers tossing out a Rapala or Rebel and twitching it through this very shallow water have a very good chance of catching trout in excess of 18 inches.

It's not a major destination, so you'll never feel crowded at this lake. As at all desert lakes, fishing in the middle of summer can be spotty, and very early morning is your best time.

Because of its size and location, over 400 surface acres at an elevation of 5,735 feet, this lake provides more stable fishing conditions than so many of the reservoirs used for water storage. That means better fishing during the summer than at other lakes.

A word of warning: The last mile of road before the turnoff in the Dodge Reservoir can become impassable with just a small amount of rain or snow. The composition of the road just does not hold up well to weather. Snow is your worst enemy, but rain can stop a normal two-wheel-drive vehicle from reaching the lake.

There is also a very good chance that, along the entire length of road from the Madeline Plain into Dodge Reservoir, you'll see some wild horses. There's no sight quite like them. They are considered to be wild, but some will stay close to the road, while others will come no closer than 300 yards.

Facilities, fees: A campground is provided, as are picnic tables and fire pits. A vault toilet is available, but drinking water is not. There is no boat ramp, but hand-launched boats are permitted. Only nonmotorized boats are permitted on the reservoir. Fishing access is free, but a donation box has been provided.

Directions: From Susanville, take U.S. 395 north for 54 miles to Ravendale. Turn right on County Road 502 (Mail Route) and drive 12 miles to County Road 506. Turn right and drive 5.5 miles to a T intersection. Turn left on County Road 506 and continue for six miles to Dodge Reservoir access road. Turn left and drive one mile to the campground, at the end of the road.

Contact: Bureau of Land Management, Eagle Lake Field Office, 530/257-0456, www.blm.gov/ca.

61 EAGLE LAKE

Rating: 9

near Susanville in Lassen National Forest

Map 3.4, page 170

You want big trout? You say you even dream about big trout? You'd do anything for big trout? Anything?

Well, you don't have to do much. Just make a trip to Eagle Lake in the fall, be persistent, and you will indeed get your big trout.

Big? Trout measuring 16–17 inches are average. Four- and five-pounders used to be common, but so many have been caught and kept that they are considered trophies now.

Low water has been a problem in recent years, but all signs look good for 2012.

The lake also has several excellent campgrounds and cabin rentals, but the big trout are what inspire people to visit. The average trout here is often bigger than those at any of the state's 850 other trout-filled lakes and streams.

Not only are these fish impressive, but the techniques used are simple: most people use a night crawler under a slip bobber, and there are good prospects from shore.

Always follow the prescribed procedure for catching the lake's big trout: You rig by placing a tiny plastic bobber stop on your line, adding a red bead and a slip bobber. Then tie on a No. 4 hook, adding a split shot about 12 inches above the hook. Use a night crawler for bait, hooking it with a worm threader so it lies perfectly straight in the water, looking as natural as possible. For those new to the game, the folks at the lake's shops and marinas can demonstrate this rigging.

You then cast along the tules, the bobber floating about. The big trout like the tules, and they will sometimes cruise in and out along the edges looking for food.

There are many good spots at the lake. The tules adjacent to the airport runway, the deep spot adjacent to Eagle's Nest, and Troxel are the top spots by boat. By shore, the best areas are the rock jetty at the Eagle Lake Marina, the shore adjacent to Highway 139 at the northwest end, and in cold weather (including when this lake is iced over in late December), the extreme southern end.

Although the best catches are usually achieved using night crawlers for bait, as the very cold weather arrives and the big trout abandon their deep-water haunts of summer to move into the shallows, some anglers do well by trolling bikini-colored Needlefish lures along the many stretches of tule-lined shore. Bikini is a color pattern developed by Luhr Jensen, the manufacturer of Needlefish.

It is absolutely critical to be on the water at daybreak, when the lake glasses out. Why?

Because the wind can howl at Eagle Lake in the spring and summer, quickly resulting in waves and whitecaps that can make boating unpleasant at the least, and sometimes even very dangerous. If you have a small boat, get off the water at the first sign of wind. Bigger boats can get out of the wind by anchoring on the leeward side of points amid the tules.

Trolling is best at Eagle Lake from its opening clear through October. Best methods are leadcore line at a variety of depths, but the key is trying to regulate your depth so that your lure is within a couple of feet of the bottom. This is known as a Needlefish lake, with a variety of colors working. Frog-pattern Needlefish seem to be the most consistent, but other extremely light patterns will work. In addition, there is one secret lure that seems to be consistent when all others fail: a medium-sized orange Rapala. Never go to Eagle Lake without one. Don't be afraid to test.

Trolling flies is another popular technique developed by Jay Fair, a retired local guide. His methods combine fly line and leadcore and leader to achieve a precise depth with a large trolling fly. You can achieve practically the same by using a small amount of leadcore and a long leader.

Eagle Lake can also get very cold, so cold that even with its immense size—100 miles of shoreline and 27,000 surface acres—the lake usually freezes over solid by Christmas. But the fishing is best when the cold weather arrives, from September on.

In the dead of winter, the best spot is the mouth of Pine Creek. In winter, typically between Christmas and New Year's Day, ice fishing here is just fantastic. Often there can be 30–40 guys in the subfreezing temperatures all hopping from foot to foot to stay warm, and catching two and three big Eagle Lake trout apiece, using a night crawler directly below your little ice hole. It can be quite unnerving to hear the lake surface cracking off in the distance. It is so loud at times it can sound like a jet taking off.

If you've never caught a five-pound trout,

come here and fish until you tangle with one. Then you will know why.

The DFG stocks thousands of wild and domestic Eagle Lake trout in the 10- to 12-inch class here. Basically, a lot of fish. The fishing season here runs from Memorial Day weekend through December 31.

Facilities, fees: Several campgrounds, cabin rentals, and other forms of lodging are available. A full-service marina, boat rentals and ramps, a grocery store, showers, a coin laundry, and an RV dump station are at Eagle Lake Marina. Fishing access is free. Fees apply for launching, docking, and camping.

Directions: To Aspen Grove Campground: From Red Bluff, take Highway 36 toward Susanville to Eagle Lake Road/County Road A1. Just before Susanville, turn left on Eagle Lake Road/County Road A1 and drive 15.5 miles to County Road 231/Forest Road 31N02. Turn right on County Road 231 and drive two miles to the campground on the left side of the road.

To Eagle Lake RV Park and boat ramp: From Red Bluff, take Highway 36 toward Susanville to Eagle Lake Road/County Road A1. Just before Susanville, turn left on County Road A1 and drive (staying left at the junction with County Road 231) to the lake's west shore at Spaulding Tract and County Road 518. Turn right on County Road 518 and drive through a small neighborhood to Strand Way (the lake frontage road). Turn left on Strand Way and drive about three blocks (the boat ramp is on the left) to Palmetto Way. The entrance to the store and the RV park entrance are at 687-125 Palmetto Way. Register at the store.

Contact: Lassen County Chamber of Commerce, 530/257-4323, www.lassencounty chamber.com; Bureau of Land Management, Eagle Lake Field Office, 530/257-0456, www .ca.blm.gov/eaglelake; Eagle Lake Marina, 530/825-3454, www.eaglelakerecreation area.com; Mariners Resort, 530/825-3333, marinersresort.com; Eagle Lake RV Park, 530/825-3133, www.eaglelakeandrv.com;

Eagle Lake General Store, 530/825-2191; Lassen National Forest, Eagle Lake Ranger District, 530/257-4188, www.fs.fed.us/r5— click on Forest Offices.

Guides: J&J Guide Service, 530/825-3491 or 530/222-6253, jandjguideservice.net; Big Meadows Guide Service, 530/596-3072; J&J Guide Service, 530/825-3491 or 530/222-6253, jandjguideservice.net; Roger's Guide Service, 530/528-0525; Tight Lines Guide Service, 530/263-0990 or 530/263-7944, www.fishtightlines.com; Sierra Drifters Guide Service, 760/935-4250, www.sierra drifters.com.

62 ROUND VALLEY LAKE

Rating: 6

near Greenville in Plumas National Forest

Map 3.4, page 170

Even the best bassers can go years without fishing Round Valley. Like so many other people, they forget that a good bass lake can be located in the mountains.

Round Valley is one of the few high-altitude bass lakes in California. It provides the ideal bass habitat, with many stumps and, in the summer, lily pads and some weed cover. That is why the resident bass get big. Before the Florida strain of largemouth bass was introduced to many lakes in California, Round Valley had the state record, a 14-pounder.

Bluegill and catfish also live in this lake, but the bass make it special. The lake becomes productive in early May, and by midsummer it sees a lot of topwater action.

Every June, the businesses and resorts on Round Valley Lake sponsor a bluegill derby for the kids. It's something both kids and adults enjoy. Many big bluegills are caught, which is very rare for a mountain lake.

Facilities, fees: A picnic area is provided for day use. A boat dock is also here. Supplies can be obtained in Greenville. Fishing access is free.

Directions: From Red Bluff, take Highway

36 east and drive 44 miles to the junction with Highway 89. Continue east on Highway 36/89 to Lake Almanor and the next junction with Highway 89 (two miles before reaching Chester). Turn right on Highway 89 and drive about 25 miles to the town of Greenville and Greenville Road. Turn right (south) on Greenville Road and drive three miles to the signed turnoff for Round Valley Lake. Turn left and continue to the lake.

Contact: Plumas National Forest, Mount Hough Ranger District, 530/283-0555, www .fs.fed.us/r5—click on Forest Offices; Sportsmen's Den, Quincy, 530/283-2733.

63 TAYLOR LAKE

Rating: 6

near Taylorsville in Plumas National Forest

Map 3.4, page 170

The water is clear and the fish are shy, but a careful approach in the evening using light line and a 1/16-ounce black Panther Martin spinner can result in an impressive stringer of brookies for a nighttime fish fry. The DFG no longer stocks this quality brook-trout water with fingerlings.

The small, obscure mountain lake is ideal for fishing from a float tube or raft, yet it gets little attention from most anglers and campers. Note that most of the lake is surrounded by private property, so respect the rights of landowners.

Some good drive-to side trips in the area are the lookout point west of Taylor Lake near Kettle Rock and, to the north, the remote area between Rattlesnake and Eisenheimer peaks.

Facilities, fees: A few primitive, dispersed Forest Service campsites are available, but there is no drinking water. Garbage must be packed out. Supplies can be obtained in Taylorsville. Fishing access is free.

Directions: From Oroville, take Highway 70 east to the junction with Highway 89. Turn left on Highway 89 and drive seven miles to

Highway 22. Turn right and drive five miles east to Taylorsville and County Road 214. Turn north on County Road 214 and drive about two miles to Forest Service Road 27N10. Turn right on Forest Service Road 27N10 and drive about 10 miles east (stay to the left). Turn left on Forest Service Road 27N57 and travel one mile to the lake.

Contact: Plumas National Forest, Mount Hough Ranger District, 530/283-0555, www .fs.fed.us/r5—click on Forest Offices; Sportsmen's Den, Quincy, 530/283-2733.

64 INDIAN CREEK

Rating: 4

south of Antelope Lake in Plumas National Forest

Map 3.4, page 170

When Antelope Lake is crowded, Indian Creek provides skilled stream anglers with a good local alternative.

Indian Creek pours from the Antelope Valley Dam, then tumbles well downstream into Genessee Valley and past Taylorsville. Two-lane roads border much of this section of river, and you will find small pullouts along the road, and little trails that lead to the better fishing spots. No trail? Then it's not likely to be a great spot.

One of the best stretches of water is the two miles below the dam. This is where the bigger fish seem to be, including some nice brown trout. In addition, the area where Cold Stream Creek enters Indian Creek holds some small rainbow trout.

Note: This Cold Stream Creek, a small tributary to Indian Creek in Plumas County, should not be confused with the Cold Stream Creek in Sierra County, south of Sierraville near Highway 89.

Facilities, fees: Campgrounds are available at Taylorsville and Antelope Lake. Supplies can be obtained nearby in Taylorsville at Young's Market, 530/284-7024. Fishing access is free.

Directions: From Red Bluff, take Highway 36 east for 44 miles to the junction with Highway 89. Continue east on Highway 36/89 to Lake Almanor and the junction with Highway 89 (two miles before Chester). Turn right on Highway 89 and drive to the Highway 207 turnoff. Turn left and drive five miles east to Taylorsville. From Taylorsville, drive north on Beckwourth and Indian Creek roads. They parallel the creek, and direct access is available.

Contact: Plumas National Forest, Beckwourth Ranger District, 530/836-2575, www.fs.fed .us/r5—click on Forest Offices.

65 ANTELOPE LAKE

Rating: 8
near Taylorsville in Plumas National Forest
Map 3.4, page 170

Wanted: mountain lake circled by conifers with secluded campsites and good fishing.

Some people might want to put an advertisement in the newspaper to find such a place, but that isn't necessary for in-the-know visitors to northern Plumas County. They go to Antelope Lake, which is ringed by a forest, provides campgrounds at each end of the water, and has a boat ramp conveniently located a few miles from each camp.

The lake is at an elevation of 5,000 feet and is just about perfect for a fishing/camping vacation. It is secluded, about 100 miles from Oroville, yet accessible to trailered boats. Although not huge, it is big enough, with 15 miles of shoreline. Little islands, coves, and peninsulas give it an intimate feel.

And then there is the fishing, which is good, particularly in the early summer. Fish and Game stocks rainbow trout, brook trout in the 10- to 12-inch class, and Eagle Lake fingerlings, which join a few large, resident brown trout. Most folks employ standard trolling techniques—that is, use a night crawler trailing a set of flashers—or anchor up along a shoreline point or cove and fish with bait.

While anglers from distant reaches come to Antelope for the early summer trout fishing, locals from Susanville to Reno consider it a bass lake during the summer months. Minnow-type lures like Rapalas and Rebels can be cast in the shallows in early summer, and plastics—such as the Brush Hogs, Senko worm, and most soft four- to six-inch worms—work well throughout the summer.

The best part is that getting here requires quite a drive for most people. If not for that, Antelope Lake would be loaded with vacationers every day of the summer. Indian Creek, just below the Antelope Valley Dam, provides another nearby option.

Facilities, fees: A boat ramp is available, as are several campgrounds with drinking water and vault toilets. An RV dump station and small grocery store are nearby. Supplies can be obtained nearby in Taylorsville at Young's Market, 530/284-7024. Fishing access is free.

Directions: To Long Point Campground: From Red Bluff, drive east on Highway 36 to Susanville and U.S. 395. Go south on U.S. 395 and drive about 10 miles (1 mile past Janesville) to County Road 208. Turn right on County Road 208 (signed Antelope Lake) and drive about 15 miles to a Y (one mile before Antelope Lake). Turn right at the Y and drive one mile to the campground entrance on the left side of the road. The boat ramp is at Lost Cove, a three-mile drive on Indian Creek Road, on the lake's north shore.

Contact: Plumas National Forest, Mount Hough Ranger District, 530/283-0555, www.fs.fed.us/r5—click on Forest Offices; Big Meadows Guide Service, 530/596-3072; Roger's Guide Service, 530/528-0525.

MENDOCINO AND WINE COUNTRY

© TOM STIENSTRA

BEST FISHING SPOTS

⊂ Freshwater Fisheries
Clear Lake, **page 234.**

⊂ Places to Teach Kids to Fish
Clear Lake, **page 234.**
Lake Berryessa, **page 247.**

For many people, this region offers the best possible combination of geography, weather, and outdoor activities around. The Mendocino coast is dramatic and remote, with several stellar state parks for hiking, while Sonoma Valley, in the heart of wine country, produces some of the most popular wines in the world. Add mainstream recreation at Clear Lake, Lake Berryessa, and other lakes, and you have a capsule summary of why the Mendocino coast and the wine country have turned into getaway favorites.

In a perfect world, the Mendocino coast could be one of the best fishing areas imaginable. After all, the salmon fishing can be preeminent out of Fort Bragg in the summer, and the prospects for rockfish and lingcod at nearby inshore reefs are also often beyond compare from summer through fall, and in winter on days when the sea is calm.

But this is not a perfect world. The coast is quite windy in the spring and foggy in the summer, and that makes it all a matter of timing.

The Sonoma coast can be one of the great places on earth to live if you're an angler. Bodega Bay is an outstanding jump-off spot for salmon, rockfish, lingcod, and, in the fall, sometimes even albacore. Meanwhile, Lake Sonoma is excellent for black-bass fishing, and a recovery plan for steelhead is being put in place on the Russian River. Little-tried inshore reefs near Point Arena provide secret spots for rockfish. As at Fort Bragg, only the weather can kill the prospects in this region.

The Sonoma foothills rank just behind the San Diego foothills and just ahead of the Mother Lode and the south delta in providing the best bass fishing in California. Clear Lake, Lake Berryessa, Indian Valley Reservoir, and perhaps Spring Lake provide everything you can ask for — numbers, size, and the opportunity to catch the biggest bass of your life.

Many smaller lakes nestled out of the way also provide hope. Conditions are ideal for bass, catfish, and crappie at lakes throughout this region, and there is the bonus of good trout fishing at Berryessa.

The least-traveled area in this region is the Yolla Bolly Wilderness. It is best known for its sparse population, few small streams, and an absence of lakes. Just outside the wilderness boundary, the surrounding region is highlighted by Lake Pillsbury. In addition, little Hammerhorn and Howard Lakes provide backcountry options.

In the western Sacramento Valley, Stony Gorge and East Park are the biggest of the few reservoirs in this area. Both provide good crappie fishing, with bass always a wild card.

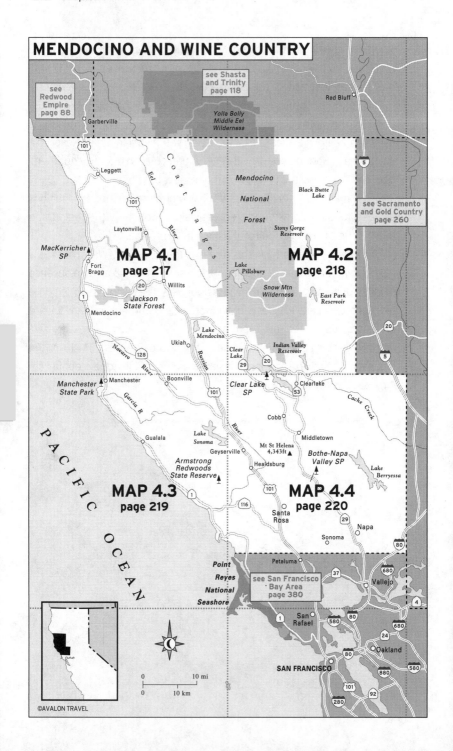

MENDOCINO AND WINE COUNTRY

see Redwood Empire page 88

see Shasta and Trinity page 118

Red Bluff

Garberville

Yolla Bolly Middle Eel Wilderness

Leggett

Mendocino National Forest

Black Butte Lake

see Sacramento and Gold Country page 260

Laytonville

Stony Gorge Reservoir

MacKerricher SP

MAP 4.1 page 217

Lake Pillsbury

MAP 4.2 page 218

Fort Bragg

Willits

Snow Mtn Wilderness

East Park Reservoir

Jackson State Forest

Mendocino

Lake Mendocino

Ukiah

Clear Lake

Indian Valley Reservoir

Manchester State Park

Manchester

Boonville

Clear Lake SP

Clearlake

Cache Creek

Gualala

Lake Sonoma

Cobb

Middletown

Bothe-Napa Valley SP

Lake Berryessa

Geyserville

Mt St Helena 4,343ft

MAP 4.3 page 219

Armstrong Redwoods State Reserve

Healdsburg

MAP 4.4 page 220

PACIFIC OCEAN

Santa Rosa

Napa

Sonoma

Point Reyes National Seashore

Petaluma

see San Francisco Bay Area page 380

Vallejo

San Rafael

SAN FRANCISCO

Oakland

0   10 mi
0   10 km

©AVALON TRAVEL

Map 4.1

Sites 1-13
Pages 221-228

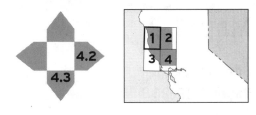

4.2

4.3

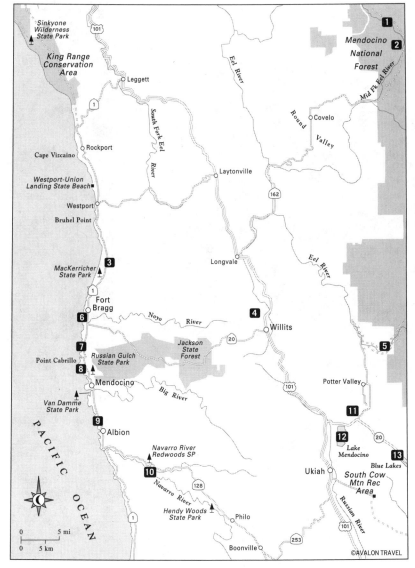

Sinkyone Wilderness State Park

King Range Conservation Area

Leggett

Rockport

Cape Vizcaino

Westport-Union Landing State Beach

Westport

Bruhel Point

1

Mendocino National Forest

2

Eel River

Mid Fk Eel River

Round Valley

Covelo

South Fork Eel River

Laytonville

162

MacKerricher State Park

3

Fort Bragg

6

Noyo River

Longvale

4

Willits

Jackson State Forest

20

Eel River

5

7

Point Cabrillo

Russian Gulch State Park

8

Mendocino

Big River

101

Potter Valley

11

Van Damme State Park

9

Albion

Navarro River Redwoods SP

10

12

Lake Mendocino

13

Blue Lakes

Ukiah

South Cow Mtn Rec Area

Navarro River

128

Hendy Woods State Park

Philo

Russian River

Boonville

253

101

PACIFIC OCEAN

0   5 mi
0   5 km

©AVALON TRAVEL

Map 4.2

Sites 14-22
Pages 229-238

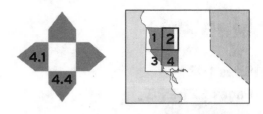

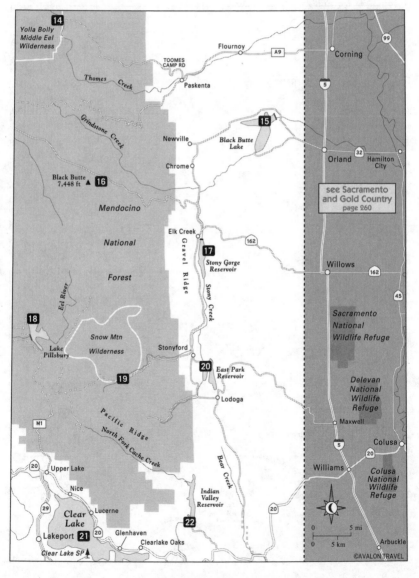

Map 4.3

Sites 23-27
Pages 239-243

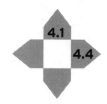

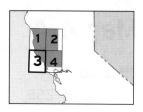

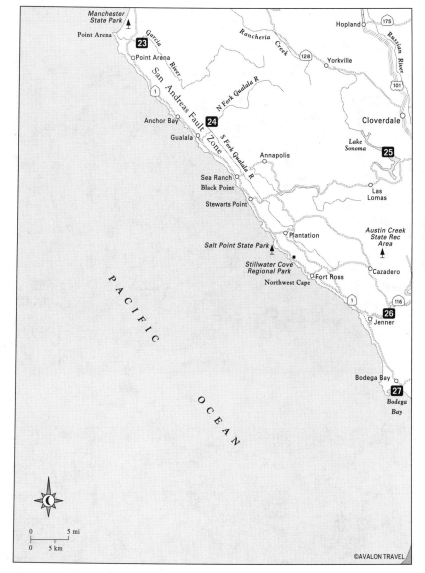

Map 4.4

Sites 28-39
Pages 245-255

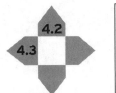

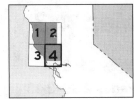

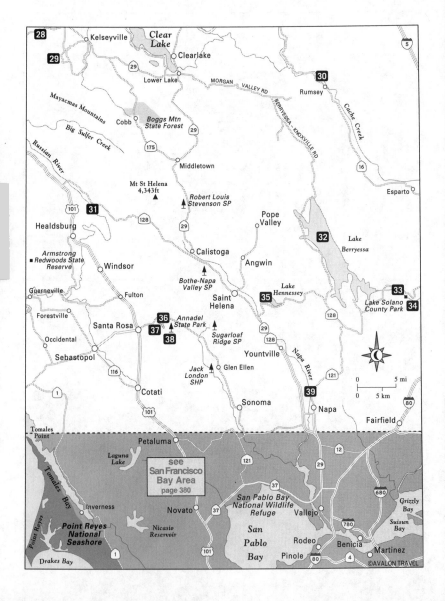

1 HAMMERHORN LAKE

Rating: 5
near Covelo in Mendocino National Forest
Map 4.1, page 217

Hammerhorn Lake is a veritable dot of water, covering just five acres. It is obscure and well hidden, but even so, it is stocked with rainbow trout in the 10- to 12-inch class. The few people who know about this place come here to take advantage of good fishing, camping, and adventuring. A population of golden shiners will drive you nuts by stealing your bait in the late summer, but most anglers can do just fine early in the summer—without needing a boat.

Hammerhorn Lake is at 4,500 feet, near the border of the Yolla Bolly Wilderness, and some hikers will spend the night here before heading off for the Mendocino wildlands; the trailhead is nearby, to the northeast. The irony is that they are more likely to get better fishing at little Hammerhorn than anywhere in the adjacent wilderness.

If you want to explore the surrounding area and have a four-wheel-drive vehicle to help you negotiate the primitive roads, the Hammerhorn Mountain lookout provides a great vista point. Otherwise, bring a backpack and head northeast into the Yolla Bollies.

Facilities, fees: A campground with drinking water (spring and summer only) and vault toilets is available. Garbage must be packed out. Supplies can be obtained in Covelo. The lake has two wheelchair-accessible piers. No motorized boats are allowed. Fishing access is free.

Directions: From Willits, take U.S. 101 north for 13 miles to Longvale and the junction with Highway 162. Turn northeast on Highway 162 and drive to Covelo. Continue east on Highway 162 to the Eel River Bridge. Turn left at the bridge on Forest Road M1 and drive about 17 miles to Forest Road M21. Turn right and drive one mile to the campground entrance and lake.

Contact: Mendocino National Forest, Covelo Ranger District, 78150 Covelo Road, Covelo, CA 95428, 707/983-6118, www.fs.fed.us/r5— click on Forest Offices; Western Auto, Covelo, 707/983-6651.

2 HOWARD LAKE

Rating: 5
near Covelo in Mendocino National Forest
Map 4.1, page 217

Tucked deep in the interior of Mendocino National Forest, between Espee Ridge to the south and Little Doe Ridge to the north, is little Howard Lake, which provides good fishing and primitive camping. For a drive-to lake, it is surprisingly remote.

Howard Lake can be fished well from the shore but is ideal for a small car-top boat, such as a canoe, pram, or raft. Whatever your preference, just plunk it in, paddle around, and fish the areas that are out of reach from land. The trout are often good-sized. It may seem hard to believe, but the Department of Fish and Game (DFG) actually sends a tanker truck way out here instead of stocking the lake by air. The result is rainbow trout in the foot-long class instead of the midgets that take the one-way airplane rides.

Hammerhorn Lake, which is even smaller than Howard Lake, lies six miles to the north, just in case you want to hit two in one trip. Some four-wheel-drive roads also provide opportunities for side trips.

Facilities, fees: There is a dock and a primitive boat ramp for car-top boats (no motorized boats are allowed). Little Doe Campground, just north of the lake, has vault toilets. Garbage must be packed out. Supplies can be obtained in Covelo. Fishing access is free.

Directions: From Willits, take U.S. 101 north for 13 miles to Longvale and the junction with Highway 162. Turn northeast on Highway 162 and drive to Covelo. Continue east on Highway 162 to the Eel River Bridge. Turn left at the bridge on Forest Service Road M1 and drive about 11 miles to the campground, at the north end of the lake.

Contact: Mendocino National Forest, Covelo Ranger District, 78150 Covelo Road, Covelo, CA 95428, 707/983-6118, www.fs.fed.us/r5—click on Forest Offices; Western Auto, Covelo, 707/983-6651.

3 CLEONE LAKE

Rating: 6

near Fort Bragg in MacKerricher State Park

Map 4.1, page 217

Nestled in a pocket between Highway 1 and Laguna Point is Cleone Lake, one of the few lakes in the state actually west of the highway. Along with surrounding MacKerricher State Park, it makes for a weekend vacation destination. This is one of few state parks in California where day-use access is free.

The big question is this: Has the DFG stocked the lake with trout? Yes. Sign up for the trip? No, forget it. Shoreline bait dunkers do very well after a stock, using yellow Power Bait on one hook and half a night crawler on the other. It's great for youngsters, but the rest of the time...

The planted trout join a resident population of largemouth bass, bluegill, and brown bullhead. All three of these warm-water fish species are most active in the summer and fall, but they can be difficult to catch in decent numbers. One reason is that they get nonstop smart lessons from anglers every day of the summer.

Once the tourist season starts, a lot of people plan to camp at MacKerricher State Park, set in an idyllic spot on the Mendocino coast. Many of them are not even aware of Cleone Lake. But once they discover it, out come the fishing rods. What to do? Beat them to the punch by arriving in the spring, when the lake is full, the people are few, and the trout are biting.

Note: A series of warm days can cause algae blooms here, and the DFG will suspend trout stocks until water temperatures cool and the oxygen content improves from cooler weather.

Facilities, fees: A campground is provided at MacKerricher State Park (reservations at 877/444-6777, www.recreation.gov). Picnic tables, fire rings, and food lockers are provided. Drinking water, flush toilets, coin-operated showers, and an RV dump station are available. Supplies can be obtained in Fort Bragg. Nonmotorized boats are permitted on the lake. Fishing access is free.

Directions: From Fort Bragg, take Highway 1 north for three miles to the MacKerricher State Park entrance road, on the left. Turn left and drive 0.5 mile to the lake.

Contact: MacKerricher State Park, 707/964-9112 or 707/937-5804, parks.ca.gov.

4 LAKE EMILY AND LAKE ADA ROSE

Rating: 4

near Willits

Map 4.1, page 217

The locals are going to want to string me up to the yardarm for putting Lake Emily in the book, but my sworn duty to my editor and readers comes first.

It's not that Lake Emily is spectacularly beautiful, because it isn't. And it's not that the fish are giant. They aren't. Well, what is it then? Just this: to the folks around Willits, Lake Emily is like a private backyard fishing hole, and they keep quiet about it.

Alas, access is so easy (just a short jaunt from U.S. 101) that out-of-towners are bound to discover it anyway. What you get at Lake Emily is an easy-to-reach put-and-take fishery that can provide a chance for rainbow trout. It's bait-dunker time, so bring a chair and a bucket after a stock, then wander on over and take a gander. Some years back, DFG removed Emily from the stocking list. Now they are considering stocking again in 2012, but nothing has been decided. Nearby Lake Ada Rose has a few brook trout, but don't hold your breath waiting for a bite.

Note: Swimming, boating, and tubing are

not permitted at Lake Emily or Lake Ada Rose.

Facilities, fees: Flush toilets and drinking water are available. Lodging and supplies are in Willits. Fishing access is free.

Directions: From the San Francisco Bay Area, take U.S. 101 north to Willits and Sherwood Road. Turn left on Sherwood Road and continue north to the Brooktrails Development. Turn left on Primrose Drive and drive 0.5 mile to the lake.

Contact: Brooktrails Township, 707/459-2494; Department of Fish and Game, www.dfg.ca.gov.

5 TROUT CREEK

Rating: 4

near Ukiah
Map 4.1, page 217

Trout Creek is a short feeder stream to the Eel River, a classic babbling brook with enough pocket water to keep a few small wild trout going. Don't expect anything big, and don't expect to catch a lot. But if you want a nearly pristine stream, a campground close by, and some pan-sized trout, you've found the place.

There are very few trout streams in this region, and most people don't have a clue about this one. Those who do visit are often disappointed by the scaled-down size of the water and the fish, but hey, the elevation is just 1,500 feet, so that puts the setting in perspective. It is quiet, peaceful, and pure out here. Sometimes that is reward enough.

Also note that nearby, in Potter Valley (to the south), the DFG stocks the East Fork Russian River (Cold Creek) with catchable rainbow trout and Eagle Lake trout.

Facilities, fees: A PG&E campground is provided. Drinking water and vault toilets are available. Supplies can be obtained in Potter Valley and Ukiah. Fishing access is free.

Directions: From the San Francisco Bay Area, take U.S. 101 north to the junction with Highway 20 (4.5 miles north of Ukiah). Turn east

on Highway 20 and drive five miles to County Road 240/Potter Valley-Lake Pillsbury Road. Turn northwest Potter Valley Road and drive to Eel River Road. Turn right and drive 4.5 miles east to the Eel River Bridge, then continue two more miles to Trout Creek.

Contact: PG&E Recreation Desk, 916/386-5164, www.pge.com/recreation.

6 FORT BRAGG DEEP SEA

Rating: 10

at Fort Bragg
Map 4.1, page 217

Come summer, the offshore waters of Fort Bragg can provide some of the best salmon fishing anywhere in the world. Two runs of salmon can arrive here at the same time, with Klamath River salmon ranging this far south and Sacramento River salmon ranging this far north. This usually occurs between mid-June and mid-July.

In the first part of July, a large number of salmon are caught straight out of Noyo Harbor. Anglers start trolling as soon as they reach open water. Another good spot for salmon and rockfish is Cleone Reef, which sits about three miles north of Fort Bragg in just 60 feet of water. Yet another area that's close to port lies two miles south of town, right offshore from a house on the coast.

Unlike salmon anglers to the south, Fort Bragg boaters don't like to mooch as much. Trolling is the name of the game here, and the most popular setup is a big silver flasher trailed by a white or green hoochie slipped over the head of an anchovy. The rockfishing can also be very good; in addition to Cleone Reef, the reefs off Caspar, Rockport, MacKerricher State Park, and Jughandle State Park are productive with shrimp-fly rigs or Diamond jigs.

A deep-sea trip out of Fort Bragg can be just plain good, but there is a chance for great versatility here. You can make a longer trip and head north of MacKerricher State Park for bigger sacks of rockfish and lingcod—or you can stay in close to shore and have a ball using light tackle.

During September and October the ocean is often calmest. Although the salmon have departed by then, deep-sea fishing is outstanding. Some huge lingcod and a variety of rockfish move into the local fishing grounds, and anglers can leave with limit bags that weigh 100 pounds. Some outfits offer the combination trip of rockfish and Dungeness crab.

In addition, there is always a chance to see whales—gray, humpback, blue, and even killer whales occasionally pass through in the late fall.

Fort Bragg is the classic fishing town, out of the way but worth a trip. Because it is on Highway 1, tourists from all over the country stop by while cruising up and down the coast. One time when I was waiting to be seated at a restaurant, a tourist tapped me on the arm, then asked: "What's the name of that big lake out there?" No kidding.

Note that fishing regulations often change here from year to year, for seasons, depth restrictions, bag limits, size limits, and even annual quotas for the fleet. Always check current regulations with Fish and Game or with a marina or party-boat operator before planning a trip.

Facilities, fees: Several campgrounds and RV parks are nearby, including Woodside and Pomo. Lodging, a full-service marina, a boat ramp, restrooms, groceries, bait, tackle, and party-boat charters are available. Party-boat fees apply.

Directions: To Noyo Harbor: In Fort Bragg, take Highway 1 south through town to North Harbor Drive (right before the Noyo Bridge). Turn left and travel west to Noyo Harbor.

To Noyo Mooring Basin Marina: In Fort Bragg, take Highway 1 to Highway 20. Turn east on Highway 20 and drive a short distance to South Harbor Drive. Turn left on South Harbor Drive and drive two blocks to the harbor.

Contact: Mendocino Coast Chamber of Commerce, 707/961-6300, www.mendocinocoast

.com; Tommy's Marine Service, 707/964-5423, www.tommysmarine.com.

Boating information: Noyo Harbor District and Mooring Basin Marina, 707/964-4719; Dolphin Isle Marina, 866/964-4113 or 707/964-4113, www.dolphinisle.com.

Party-boat information: Noyo Fishing Center, 707/964-3000, www.fortbraggfishing .com; Telstar Charters, 707/964-8770, www .gooceanfishing.com; All Aboard Fishing Adventures, 707/964-1881, www.allaboard adventures.com.

7 CASPAR HEADLANDS STATE BEACH

Rating: 4

near Mendocino

Map 4.1, page 217

A bay protects this beach, access is easy, and the gentle outflow of Caspar Creek gets the marine food chain in gear. Perch are at the top of that food chain.

The irony is that the fishing is best when the fewest number of people visit. From Memorial Day through Labor Day, the perch fishing is only fair, and it can be quite poor in the spring. Yet that is when the tourists show up. From September through early winter, however, the beach is gently sloped, and runoff from fall rains raises the level of Caspar Creek, which begins flowing to the sea. Then the perch start biting, and you'll probably have them all to yourself.

Facilities, fees: A full-facility campground is available across the street from the beach, at Caspar Beach RV Park. Supplies can be obtained in Mendocino. Fishing access is free; a permit is required.

Directions: From Fort Bragg on Highway 1, drive 4.5 miles south to Point Cabrillo exit. Take that exit and drive west to the beach. Fishing access is on the shore and nearby, at Caspar Creek.

Contact: Mendocino Coast Chamber of Commerce, 707/961-6300, www.mendocino coast.com.

Permits: California Parks and Recreation, Mendocino Sector, 707/937-5804, www.parks .ca.gov.

Lodging and supplies: Caspar Beach RV Park, 707/964-3306, casparbeachrvpark.com; Harvest at Mendosa's, Mendocino, 707/937-5879, www.harvestmarket.com.

8 MENDOCINO COAST

Rating: 6

near Mendocino
Map 4.1, page 217

One of the classic spots on the Pacific coast is pretty Mendocino, the kind of place where John Steinbeck would fit right in. The little village shops are loaded with treasures, but the real treasure hunt comes to those who venture to fish the inshore coastal waters.

A boat ramp provides easy access, and once on the water, you can be fishing within a matter of minutes. The rockfishing is good at many nearby reef areas, including just northwest of Goat Island, around the northern point, and along the reefs, southward to Stillwell Point.

Though the Big River flows to the sea through Mendocino Bay, it attracts no salmon. Yet thousands and thousands of salmon swim past this area every summer. That makes this a so-called interception fishery, since the salmon that are here today are on the move and will likely be gone tomorrow. Timing is critical and, as at Fort Bragg, mid-July seems to be the best time for a trip.

Boaters should not venture far out of Mendocino Bay without quality navigation equipment. It is very common for a giant fog bank to sit just off the coast, then quickly move in and blanket everything. If you are boating offshore in clear weather and suddenly find yourself cloaked in the stuff, you'll need that navigation equipment to return safely to harbor.

Autumn is the prettiest time, especially on calm evenings when the lights of Mendocino reflect off the bay.

Note that fishing regulations often change here from year to year, for seasons, depth restrictions, bag limits, size limits, and even annual quotas for the fleet. Always check current regulations with Fish and Game or with a marina or party-boat operator before planning a trip.

Facilities, fees: A boat ramp is provided. Camping, lodging, groceries, gas, bait, tackle, and canoe rentals are nearby. A good camping option is at Russian Gulch State Park, two miles north of Mendocino. Fishing access is free.

Directions: From Mendocino, take Highway 1 south about 300 yards to the exit for North Big River Road. Take the North Big River Road exit and drive east to the end of the flats to the boat ramp with a natural hard-rock base.

Contact: Mendocino Coast Chamber of Commerce, 707/961-6300, www.mendocinocoast .com; Catch a Canoe, 707/937-0273, www .catchacanoe.com; Russian Gulch State Park, 707/937-5804, www.parks.ca.gov; Harvest at Mendosa's, Mendocino, 707/937-5879, www .harvestmarket.com.

9 ALBION COAST

Rating: 6

near Mendocino
Map 4.1, page 217

Getting to the fishing grounds requires a short cruise—either go around Albion Head to the north or make a left turn and head around Salmon Point to the south. There you will find good rockfishing, the occasional salmon passing through in midsummer, and big lingcod in September and October.

The area in the vicinity of Schooner's Landing is well protected—a good launch site for trailered boats. Schooner's Landing has campgrounds on grassy sites and full hookups for RVs, and it can make a good base camp for a multiday fishing trip.

A lot of people with trailered boats bypass this area because they don't know there's a ramp. Well, there is.

Note that fishing regulations often change here from year to year, for seasons, depth restrictions, bag limits, size limits, and even annual quotas for the fleet. Always check current regulations with Fish and Game or with a marina or party-boat operator before planning a trip.

Facilities, fees: Camping, a boat ramp and dock, and a picnic area are on-site. Gas, groceries, bait, and tackle are nearby. Camping also available at Van Damme State Park, 2.5 miles to the north. A fee is charged for boat launching; overnighters get a discount.

Directions: From Mendocino, take Highway 1 south for 5.5 miles to Albion River Road (just before the bridge, on the north side of river). Turn left on Albion River Road and drive 0.25 mile to the bottom of the hill, take another left, and drive to the harbor. A boat ramp is at Schooner's Landing, just north of the Albion Bridge.

Contact: Schooner's Landing, 707/937-5707, www.schoonersrvpark.com; Albion Grocery, 707/937-5784.

10 NAVARRO RIVER

Rating: 4

near Mendocino
Map 4.1, page 217

Highway 128 parallels this river all the way to the ocean, providing prospective anglers with easy access and a good look at conditions. Your safest bet is to park at Paul Dimmick Campground at Navarro River Redwoods State Park, and then hike upstream one or two miles. This is the best stretch of water for steelhead.

Like many coastal streams in this area, the Navarro River depends on one thing for success: timing. If you get the tail end of a storm, then you're doing good, with the best prospects as the water is coming up, then again as the water is dropping. If you fish it after the river has stabilized, most of your day will be spent wondering how these fish disappear.

The fact is this: steelhead here don't waste any time getting up into the upper reaches of the river, where it's illegal to fish.

The river carries a few surprises. At times it can appear very clear and slow moving, and quite wide near the mouth. During peak periods in the steelhead run during the winter, you can sometimes see the fish as you hike on the adjacent trail. You will probably feel awed by the sight of the fish, as well as frustrated by your inability to hook many of them.

Facilities, fees: Campgrounds, restrooms with flush toilets (seasonal; pit toilets are available in off-season), and drinking water (seasonal) are available. Supplies can be obtained in Mendocino, at Harvest at Mendosa's. Fishing access is free.

Directions: From Mendocino, take Highway 1 south for 10 miles to Highway 128. Turn left on Highway 128 and drive east. The highway parallels the lower river. Fishing is permitted from the river mouth to Greenwood Road Bridge. The upper river can be accessed through Hendy Woods State Park, off Highway 128. A path at the south end of the bridge provides excellent access.

To Hendy Woods: From Cloverdale on U.S. 101, turn northwest on Highway 128 and drive about 35 miles to Philo Greenwood Road. Turn left on Philo Greenwood Road and drive 0.5 mile to the park entrance. Check DFG regulations for current status of closed fishing areas.

Contact: Mendocino Coast Chamber of Commerce, 707/961-6300, www.mendocinocoast.com; Navarro River Redwoods State Park, 707/937-5804, www.parks.ca.gov; Hendy Woods State Park, 707/895-3141, www.parks.ca.gov; Harvest at Mendosa's, Mendocino, 707/937-5879, www.harvestmarket.com; Craig Bell, Greenwater Guide Service, 707/884-3012.

11 COLD CREEK

Rating: 6

in Potter Valley
Map 4.1, page 217

Never heard of Cold Creek, eh? Some maps list it as the East Fork Russian River, but the locals call it Cold Creek, and referring to it as such shows a hint of insider knowledge. By any name, however, it provides the best summer trout fishing in a stream anywhere in this region.

The best section by far is the stretch of water in Potter Valley. This is where the Department of Fish and Game stocks rainbow trout and Eagle Lake trout; not dinkers, but decent 11- to 12-inch fish. In an area virtually devoid of trout streams—after all, winter steelhead and summer rainbow trout just don't mix—Cold Creek provides anglers with a unique alternative. Access is easy, and campgrounds are nearby.

Facilities, fees: Campgrounds and supplies are at Lake Mendocino and Blue Lakes. Fishing access is free.

Directions: From Ukiah, take U.S. 101 north to the junction with Highway 20. Turn east (right) on Highway 20 and drive five miles to East Potter Valley Road. Turn northwest on East Potter Valley Road (toward Lake Pillsbury) and drive 5.9 miles to the town of Potter Valley. Continue on East Potter Valley Road. Turnouts that provide fishing access are available along the road (the larger turnouts, where a DFG tanker can get in, are the best spots).

Contact: Department of Fish and Game, Central Coast Region, 707/944-5500; Diamond Jim's Sporting Goods, 707/462-9741.

12 LAKE MENDOCINO

Rating: 6

near Ukiah

Map 4.1, page 217

Lake Mendocino is at 750 feet in elevation, in the foothill country east of Ukiah. It covers 1,750 acres, has 15 miles of shoreline, and is a major destination point for boaters and campers, especially families who appreciate the warm, clear water and the easy driving access (compared to Clear Lake).

Striped bass at Lake Mendocino provide a long shot for the gold ring. A handful of giant striped bass live in this lake. They tend to hang quite deep and feast on the other fish in the lake. At first light, get on the water at Coyote Dam and cast large, deep-diving plugs or troll a diving Rebel down the main river channel. A long shot? Definitely, but sometimes long shots come in.

A pair of binoculars can be a useful tool at Mendocino, especially early in the morning, for scanning the shoreline for signs of striped bass chasing fish in the shallows. If you can get a boat within casting distance without making too much noise and spooking the fish, you've got a chance of catching several stripers before they are put down by the activity.

There are periods when the fishing is very good. The lake level tends to fluctuate quite a bit over the course of a year, which causes problems for largemouth bass and bluegill. That's why the striper fishery has become so important for anglers. In addition, there's been an attempt to improve habitat for catfish. Fish and Game placed several "catfish condominiums" in the lake. Catfish hole up in these little homes.

Traditional baits are in order. Summer evening is the prime time, when those catfish emerge from their condos and go on the prowl for something to eat. The lake is in foothill country, and it gets hot here in the summer.

If you prefer fishing in the morning, get up early, before the water-skiers arrive, and cast small Rapalas in the coves. As long as the water is quiet and shaded, sunfish, bluegill, and bass will hang out in these coves. When the water-skiers start plowing up the water and the sun cranks up the surface temperatures, forget it; it's over.

A marina that once rented all styles of boats used to be in business here, but no more.

Facilities, fees: Several campgrounds are provided around the lake, as well as one boat-in campground (contact Recreation.gov, 877/444-6777, www.recreation.gov). Two boat ramps, picnic areas, and bait are available. Other supplies can be obtained in Ukiah. Fishing access is free. A boat-launching fee is charged. Annual passes may be purchased.

Directions: To Che-Ka-Ka Campground: From Ukiah, take U.S. 101 north to Lake Mendocino Drive. Exit right on Lake Mendocino Drive and continue to the first stoplight at North State Street. Turn left on North State Street and drive to the next stoplight. Turn right (which puts you back on Lake Mendocino Drive) and drive about one mile to the signed entrance for the campground and boat ramp at Coyote Dam.

To Kyen Campground: From Ukiah, take U.S. 101 north for five miles to the Highway 20 turnoff. Bear east on Highway 20 to Marina Drive. Turn right and drive 200 yards to the boat ramp (and campground).

Contact: U.S. Army Corps of Engineers, Lake Mendocino, 707/467-4200, www.spn.wsace.army.mil/mendocino; Diamond Jim's Sporting Goods, 707/462-9741.

13 BLUE LAKES

Rating: 4

near Upper Lake
Map 4.1, page 217

This is one of the few places in California where you can rent a lakeside cabin, go trout fishing, and not have to endure a long, grinding drive to get there.

Lake County is home to these Blue Lakes, which are not to be confused with several other Blue Lakes elsewhere in the state. Many people overlook Blue Lakes because of their proximity to giant Clear Lake, just 10 miles away to the southeast.

The long, narrow lakes are created from the flows of Cold Creek, which eventually runs into the East Fork Russian River and Lake Mendocino. The upper lake is by far the better of the two.

Upper Blue Lake is stocked with rainbow trout and Eagle Lake trout in the 10- to 12-inch class. At times the lake has the most consistent catch rate in the county. That, however, always happens in the cooler months, not in the summer, leaving frustrated visitors who

show up in July wondering, "Where are all the trout I've heard about?"

The answer is that they've either been caught already or they're hiding deep in the thermocline, where the water is cool and oxygenated. When that happens, it is better to switch than to fight. That means fishing instead for bluegill (during the day), largemouth bass (in the morning and evening), or catfish (at night).

With regard to bass, the Blue Lakes have quietly become a secret spot for local anglers. When the Clear Lake bite gets turned off, or when the lake gets too crowded with skiers or tournament anglers, these locals head for Blue Lakes. The size of the bass they will catch is surprising—in some cases the fish are over 10 pounds. Crankbaits, such as the Speed Trap, can be very effective when cast parallel to the shoreline. Another trick here is to work a Brush Hog off any kind of structure. This will give you a chance of catching a large bass. If the bass aren't biting at Clear Lake in the spring or fall, Blue Lakes can provide the ultimate insurance policy.

Note: All boats must be inspected and certified free of mussels prior to launching at this lake.

Facilities, fees: Several resorts are available, providing campsites, lodging, restaurants, boat ramps and rentals, groceries, bait, tackle, and gas. Fishing access is free.

Directions: From Ukiah, drive north on U.S. 101 for five miles to the junction with Highway 20. Turn east on Highway 20 and drive 12 miles. Lake access is available off Highway 20 and Blue Lakes Road.

Contact: Lake County Visitor Information Center, 707/274-5652 or 800/525-3743, www.lakecounty.com; Le Trianon Resort, 707/275-2262, www.letrianon.com; Pine Acres Blue Lakes Resort, 707/275-2811, www.bluelakepineacres.com; Narrows Lodge, 707/275-2718 or 800/476-2776, www.thenarrowsresort.com; The Lodge at Blue Lakes, 707/275-2181, www.thelodgeatbluelakes.com.

14 YOLLA BOLLY WILDERNESS

Rating: 4

west of Red Bluff in
Mendocino National Forest

Map 4.2, page 218

The Yolla Bolly Wilderness is known for its little-traveled trails that lead to an intricate series of small streams, many of which are the source of the first trickles into the Eel River. Lakes? There aren't many, but that's not the appeal here.

As a result, the fishing is often poor. Many of the smaller creeks scarcely even flow in the late summer. Hikers will discover, however, that the wilderness area is sprinkled with cold springs. In this sector of the Yolla Bollies they will also find only a few lakes offering any fishing prospects: Long Lake, Square Lake, and Yolla Bolly Lake.

If you're looking for great fishing, many other wilderness areas rate higher. But if you want a wilderness hiking trip where you'll encounter few people and the climbs aren't killers, then you're talking Yolla Bolly.

Facilities, fees: No facilities are provided. No drinking water is available. Garbage must be packed out. Supplies are in Corning. Fishing access is free.

Directions: From Sacramento, take I-5 to Corning and the exit for Corning Road. Turn west on Corning Road and drive 21 miles (it becomes Paskenta Road) to Paskenta and a fork with Forest Service Road M2. Bear right on Forest Service Road M2 and drive 19 miles (the road is at first paved, then turns to dirt). Continue six miles to Cold Springs Guard Station and Forest Service Road M22. Bear right on Forest Service Road M22 and drive nine miles to Forest Service Road 25N27/Ides Cove. Turn left and drive 3.5 miles to the Ides Cove Trailhead. Park and hike 0.25 mile to Square Lake, or continue one additional mile to Long Lake.

Contact: Mendocino National Forest, 530/934-3316, www.fs.usda.gov/wps.

15 BLACK BUTTE LAKE

Rating: 6

near Orland

Map 4.2, page 218

Hit this lake wrong and you get the vacation from hell. Hit it right and you may wonder why more people aren't taking advantage of "paradise." The reality is that there rarely is an in-between here.

Come in late March, April, and May, and you will find a pretty lake amid fresh green foothills, with about 40 miles of shoreline, lakeside camps, and some of the best crappie fishing in Northern California. But arrive in late July or August, and you'll find low water levels, brown and mostly barren hillsides, camps like sweat pits, and fish with a terminal case of lockjaw. Let there be no doubt as to when you should visit.

This used to be known as "the best" crappie fishing lake in this part of the state. Now it's "occasionally the best" crappie fishing lake in this part of the state. When conditions are perfect, the crappie fishing can still be phenomenal. It's a hit-and-miss affair.

This is the bottom lake in a chain of three lakes: East Park, Stony Gorge, and then Black Butte. For this reason, as well as the spring wind, this lake stays muddy much longer than the other two. That delays fishing at times.

Black bass are often overlooked in this lake. That's a mistake. Though the murky waters may hamper crappie fishing, it can make the bass easier to catch. To solve the murky-water problem, use spinnerbaits with big blades, rattling crankbaits, and even rattles in jigs and worms.

Access to Black Butte is easy; it's just a short jog off I-5, making it a prime attraction to owners of trailered boats. In the spring, not only do the crappie go on the bite, but the lake also becomes a good fishery for large-mouth bass. The lake also has spotted bass, channel catfish, bluegill, and sunfish. Occasionally, even striped bass are caught, often by accident.

The lake is shaped like a giant 7, and when

the water level is up, the better area for fishing is on the north side, just west of the dam and east of Buckhorn Store, where there's a series of protected coves and an island. Avoid open water at this reservoir, and focus on the little coves and protected backwater areas. That is where you will find the fish.

Facilities, fees: The two campgrounds are Orland Buttes and Buckhorn; picnic tables and fire grills are provided. Drinking water, flush toilets, RV dump station, showers, and a playground are available. A boat ramp is available. Fishing access is free.

Directions: To Buckhorn: From I-5 in Orland, take the Black Butte Lake exit. Drive about 12 miles west on Road 200/Newville Road to Buckhorn Road. Turn left and drive a short distance to the campground and boat ramp on the north shore of the lake.

To Eagle Pass: Drive as above to the fork with Buckhorn Road and Road 206. Bear right (signed for the dam) and drive to the turn on the left for the Eagle Pass Picnic Area and boat ramp. Turn left and continue to the paved boat ramp.

To Orland Buttes: From I-5 in Orland, take the Black Butte Lake exit. Drive west on Road 200/Newville Road for six miles to Road 206. Turn left and drive two miles to the camp entrance and boat ramp on the left.

Contact: U.S. Army Corps of Engineers, Sacramento District, Black Butte Lake, 530/865-4781, www.corpslakes.usace.army.mil.

16 PLASKETT LAKES

Rating: 5

northwest of Willows in
Mendocino National Forest
Map 4.2, page 218

This pair of connected dot-sized mountain lakes form the headwaters of little Plaskett Creek. They are difficult to reach, in the middle of nowhere and at an elevation of 6,000 feet, but once here you can fish for rainbow trout in the foot-long class. Newcomers are always surprised about that. Fish and Game plants catchable trout here.

Trout fishing is best at the westernmost of the two lakes. Not only is it bigger, but it just plain seems to have more fish. No motors are permitted in the lakes, and swimming is not recommended. Plaskett Lakes have made something of a comeback since they were drained to kill a weed infestation and then restocked.

There are some good hiking trails in the area to the south. One route heads along Plaskett Creek and then south up to Chimney Rock (which can also be reached from the south via Bushy Mountain Road).

Facilities, fees: Plaskett Meadows Campground is nearby. Drinking water, vault toilets, garbage service, and a picnic area are available. Motorized boats are not permitted on the lake. Supplies are in Elk Creek. Fishing access is free.

Directions: From Sacramento, take I-5 to Willows and the exit for Highway 162. Take the exit for Highway 162 West, and drive west (toward the town of Elk Creek) to County Road 306 (just after crossing the Stony Creek Bridge). Turn north on County Road 306 and drive four miles to Alder Springs Road. Turn left on Alder Springs Road/Forest Highway 7 and drive 31 miles to the lake entrance road (and campground), on the left. Turn left and drive a short distance to the lake.

Contact: Mendocino National Forest, Grindstone Ranger District, 530/934-3316, www.fs.fed.us/r5; Stonyford Work Center, 530/963-3128; Stonyford General Store, 530/963-3235, www.stonycreekhorsemen.org.

17 STONY GORGE RESERVOIR

Rating: 5

near Elk Creek
Map 4.2, page 218

Long, narrow Stony Gorge is in a canyon, and it has an elevation of 800 feet, 1,300 surface acres, and 25 miles of shoreline. A classic foothill reservoir, it experiences hot weather and water drawdowns in the summer but also provides a decent warm-water fishery. This lake keeps anglers away largely because of its barren landscape.

Black-bass fishing is usually best in deeper water. Dark-colored jigs with a bit of red are good in early spring. As summer approaches, orange seems a better color here. You can also occasionally turn up a big bass using a deep, slow Rogue spinnerbait in 15 feet of water.

If you hit this lake in the early summer—that is, before it gets drained too much—you will find catfish, bluegill, crappie, and some largemouth bass. Unlike Indian Valley Reservoir to the south, this is not a great bass lake, but it does provide good boating and a virtual smorgasbord of fishing opportunities.

Facilities, fees: Several campgrounds and a group camp are available. Vault toilets and picnic areas are provided, but drinking water is not. Garbage must be packed out. A paved boat ramp is also on the northeast side of the lake at Skipper's Point. Supplies can be obtained in Elk Creek. Fishing access is free.

Directions: From Sacramento, take I-5 north for 90 miles to Willows and Highway 162. Turn west on Highway 162 and drive 19 miles to County Road 304 (just before the Stony Creek Bridge). Turn left (signed) and drive two miles to the reservoir.

Contact: Bureau of Reclamation, Northern California Area, 530/934-7069; Stony Gorge Reservoir, 530/968-5267.

18 LAKE PILLSBURY

Rating: 7
near Ukiah in Mendocino National Forest
Map 4.2, page 218

It seems that bit by bit, Lake Pillsbury is growing more popular each year. Not so long ago this mountain lake had good weather, plenty of water, few people, and lots of trout. Well, with all those attractions, it isn't surprising that more vacationers than ever before are heading here.

Covering some 2,000 acres, Pillsbury is by far the largest lake in the Mendocino National Forest. At an elevation of 1,800 feet, Pillsbury is big and pretty when full, with 65 miles of shoreline. It is becoming a popular vacation destination with Bay Area folks, who tend to congregate at the north end of the lake, where beaches, Forest Service camps, and two boat ramps are located.

Pillsbury can provide good trolling results (the DFG stocks rainbow trout here). That continues into the summer, when higher temperatures drive the trout deep. The hot summer weather also gets the resident populations of bass, bluegill, and green sunfish active in the top 10 feet of water and makes the lake ideal for swimming, especially right off the Pogie Point Campground.

The better fishing is up the lake arms. Leave the main lake body and explore the Eel River arm, Horseshoe Gulch, or south of Rocky Point, up the Rice Fork.

Although most of the attention is focused on the trout in the early season, a population of Florida-strain bass inhabit the lake. Spring is the time to fish for these bass, some of which exceed 10 pounds. Surface lures can be very effective here in April and May, such as the Rico's, Pop-R, and various models of weedless frogs. Plastics such as the Brush Hog and Senko worm are more consistent with larger fish.

Lake Pillsbury has a high density of squawfish ("Sacramento pike" to the politically correct), which may be one reason the bass grow so big. Bass love to feed on juvenile squawfish. Note that once squawfish reach a foot long, they impact the rest of the fisheries by eating the eggs and fry. There are so many squawfish in Lake Pillsbury, as well as in the headwaters of the Eel River, that at times they have been dynamited successfully in the Eel. The DFG is considering many eradication programs for Pillsbury.

In addition to the surrounding forestland, highlights include lakeside camping and good boat ramps. Groceries and gas are also available.

Note: All boats must be inspected and certified free of mussels prior to launching at this lake.

Facilities, fees: Several campgrounds with drinking water and vault toilets are provided. Lodging, a marina, boat ramps and rentals, groceries, gas, bait, and tackle are also available. Fishing access is free.

Directions: To Lake Pillsbury Resort: From Ukiah, take U.S. 101 north for five miles to the junction with Highway 20. Turn right (east) on Highway 20 and drive five miles to East Potter Valley Road (toward Lake Pillsbury). Turn northwest on East Potter Valley Road and drive 5.9 miles to the town of Potter Valley. Continue on East Potter Valley Road to Eel River Road. Turn right and drive 15 miles to Lake Pillsbury and Forest Road 301F. Turn right at Forest Road 301F and drive two miles to the resort.

To Sunset: From Ukiah, take U.S. 101 north for five miles to the junction with Highway 20. Turn right (east) on Highway 20 and drive five miles to East Potter Valley Road (toward Lake Pillsbury). Turn northwest on East Potter Valley Road toward Lake Pillsbury. Drive 5.9 miles to the town of Potter Valley, and then continue on East Potter Valley Road to Eel River Road. Turn right and drive 15 miles to the Eel River Information Kiosk at Lake Pillsbury. Continue east for 4.1 miles to Lake Pillsbury and the junction with Hall Mountain Road. Turn right and drive three miles to the camp entrance. A boat ramp is available 0.25 mile to the south.

To Fuller Grove: Continue as above to the Eel River Information Kiosk at Lake Pillsbury. Continue for 2.2 miles to the campground access road. Turn right and drive 0.25 mile to the campground.

Contact: Mendocino National Forest, Upper Lake Ranger District, 707/275-2361, www .fs.usda.gov/wps; PG&E Recreation Desk, 916/386-5164, www.pge.com/recreation; Lake Pillsbury Resort, 707/743-9935, wwwlprandm.

com; Lake County Visitor Information Center, 707/274-5652 or 800/525-3743, www .lakecounty.com.

19 LETTS LAKE

Rating: 6
west of Maxwell in Mendocino National Forest
Map 4.2, page 218

It's tough getting to Letts Lake, even with the detailed directions I provide here. Just imagine how difficult it would be to find the place without this book. Result? Advantage, you.

When you eventually get here, you'll find a small lake set at an elevation of 4,500 feet in the Mendocino National Forest, with a few campgrounds on the north shore. Letts has trout ranging to 12 inches and makes a good camping/fishing destination for folks who like to end the day with a trout fry. The lake is just big enough (35 acres) that a small boat comes in handy. Since no motors are allowed on the water and the access road is quite circuitous, car-top rowboats, canoes, and rafts are ideal.

The lake is spring-fed and stocked with trout in early summer, and it also provides an opportunity for largemouth bass and catfish.

The surrounding area is pretty, with excellent views and good hiking. You can turn a hike into a fortune hunt by trying to discover one of several natural springs in the area: Fir Rock Springs, Summit Springs, Cold Springs, Freezeout Springs, Board Camp Springs, Young's Corral Springs, and Sylar Springs.

Facilities, fees: Four campgrounds are on the east side of the lake. Drinking water, vault toilets, and garbage service are available. There is an unimproved boat ramp and a wheelchair-accessible fishing pier. No motorized boats are permitted on the lake. Supplies can be obtained in Stonyford. Fishing access is free.

Directions: From Sacramento, take I-5 north for 67 miles to the exit for Maxwell. Take that exit, turn west on Maxwell–Sites Road, and drive to Sites and Sites–Lodoga Road. Turn left on Sites–Lodoga Road and continue to Lodoga and Lodoga–Stonyford Road. Turn right on Lodoga–Stonyford Road and loop around East Park Reservoir to reach Stonyford and Fouts Spring Road. Turn west on Fouts Springs Road/ Forest Service Road M10 and drive about 17 miles into the national forest (where the road becomes Forest Service Road 17N02) to the campground, on the east side of Letts Lake.

Contact: Mendocino National Forest, Grindstone Ranger District, 530/934-3316; Stonyford Work Center, 530/963-3128, www.fs.fed .us/r5; Stonyford General Store, 530/963-3235, www.stonycreekhorsemen.org.

❷⓿ EAST PARK RESERVOIR

Rating: 6
near Stonyford and Mendocino National Forest
Map 4.2, page 218

East Park Reservoir can produce bass in excess of 10 pounds. This is also one of the best lakes in the Sacramento foothills for crappie.

One of the better areas for bass in spring and early summer is the shallow, weed-infested area at the south end of the lake. Here you can use the weedless plastic worms, Brush Hogs, and some topwater baits. Search and cast into open water pockets. But it is also true that the number of big fish has decreased at the same rate as the number of bass tournaments here has increased.

Once the weed growth becomes thick (in June) and water temperatures rise, then the weedless frog takes over as the top surface lure. Any shallow area with a creek channel can be good fishing in early spring, but the fish soon tend to move out into deeper water, where fishing points and underwater ledges are more productive.

The lake is a local playground for anglers as well as water-skiers, so don't expect to have it to yourself on any weekend during the summer. Weekdays are a different story, and spring offers the best bass and crappie fishing.

It can get hot here. Midsummer temperatures often soar into the 90s and 100s, the water level drops a bit almost daily, and East Park Reservoir turns into a bathtub, complete with the ring.

So the smart angler gets here before the searing heat of summer sets in, before the drawdowns, and before you need to wear ice under your hat to stay cool. Spring arrives early here in the valley foothills, and that can get the bass on a good bite. You should wait for the year's first three- or four-day string of weather in the 80s. That's when the bass come out of their winter slumber and go on the attack.

East Park is shaped like a Y, and when it is full, there is much more habitat for bass than the average reservoir. Many little fingers and coves on the southeast arm of the lake provide ideal haunts for bass. Start searching there during the first warm days of spring, sticking and moving, casting along the shoreline.

The bass fishing remains quite good until the heat gets oppressive; then it is limited to early morning and late-evening sprees when the sun isn't hitting the lake. Anglers should respond by switching gears, fishing instead for bluegill, crappie, or catfish.

One of the great secrets of this lake is that the crappie fishing can be sensational. It is best at night, with live minnows or crappie jigs tossed under a bright light.

Facilities, fees: A picnic area and an unimproved launch ramp are provided. Primitive, dispersed camping and a group site are at the reservoir. Vault and chemical toilets are available. There is no drinking water or electricity. Supplies can be obtained in Stonyford and Lodoga. Fishing access is free.

Directions: From Sacramento, take I-5 north for 67 miles to the exit for Maxwell. Take that exit, turn west on Maxwell–Sites Road, and drive to Sites and Sites–Lodoga Road. Turn left on Sites–Lodoga Road and continue to Lodoga and Lodoga–Stonyford Road. Turn right on Lodoga–Stonyford Road and drive to East Park Reservoir and the boat ramp.

Note: A second entrance can be reached 23 miles from I-5 just past Squaw Creek Inn.

Contact: East Park Reservoir, 530/968-5267 or 530/968-5274, www.usbr.gov/mp; Bureau of Reclamation, Northern California Area, 530/934-7069; Stonyford General Store, 530/963-3235, www.stonycreekhorsemen.org.

21 CLEAR LAKE

Rating: 10

north of Calistoga

Map 4.2, page 218   **BEST (**

A 20-pound Florida-strain largemouth has yet to be caught in Clear Lake, but many people feel that a 20-pounder will be caught here, and perhaps even a new world-record bass.

Maybe Clear Lake should be renamed Fish Lake or Green Lake, because its emerald-green waters are full of fish. It has high levels of nutrients and algae, and you can thank nature for creating such a wonderful problem.

You see, the lake's substantial nutrients (phytoplankton and algae) and huge minnow population support a rich fishery. In simpler terms, a lot of aquatic food equals a lot of fish—including giant bass, catfish, and crappie, along with scads of bluegill. In the 1970s, people said the lake had wall-to-wall crappie. In the '80s, they talked about the wall-to-wall catfish, and in the '90s, wall-to-wall bass. Now, in the 21st century, those same folks are saying that Clear Lake could be the first lake in Northern California to produce a 20-pound bass.

Set amid the foothills of Lake County, Clear Lake is quite pretty, covering 44,000 surface acres. It is the largest natural freshwater lake within California's borders, and with Highway 20 running aside the eastern shore, it often seems topped to the brim. Thanks to dozens of resorts and private campgrounds sprinkled along the 100 miles of shoreline, huge numbers of visitors can be accommodated without feeling crowded. Reservations are advised in the summer, of course. More than 25 fishing tournaments take place every year at Clear Lake. It is the only major lake without boat-launching fees.

The outstanding fish habitat makes for outstanding fishing. And it also produces tons of big crappie and great numbers of catfish, including yellow and channel catfish.

Why is this place so attractive for bass fishing? Because there's ample habitat, there are plenty of bass in the 5- to 10-pound class, and they seem to be in shallow water almost year-round. When the bite is on, it is common to catch 20–30 bass per day.

Much of the western shore, in the vicinity of the state and county parks, has cove after cove lined with tules—ideal haunts for bass and bluegill. In the central part of the lake, the shoreline of a small island and The Narrows also hold a lot of bass. And at the north end of the lake, the bass often hug a series of old pilings and docks.

Tournament anglers use soft plastics such as the Brush Hog, Senko worm, Zoom fluke, and grubs. The No. 1 technique is dropshotting. Jerkbaits and swimbaits are also very effective. In summer, most switch to floating (weedless) frogs. The "frog bite" can be incredible in the summer, with casters getting a lot of action from big bass. Many trophy bass are caught at night during the summer months. Try a 10-inch plastic worm or a Weapon jig. Crankbaits such as the Rattletrap, Shad Rap, Rogue Fat Rap, Rapala, and large spinnerbaits in white or black are also popular.

Casts must be precise as you toss the lure within inches of your desired mark, next to a piling, tule berm, or rock pile. In the spring, if you wear polarized sunglasses, you can often see a bass as you cast to it. Keep doing that, and it becomes difficult to not catch fish.

Early spring through early summer is prime time in Clear Lake. This is when the bass are active in their pre-spawn mood and are easiest to catch. Throughout the year, a variety of techniques are possible. The standard plastic baits, deep-diving crankbaits, and ripping baits all work at appropriate times at Clear Lake. Water temperature and season are the key factors.

Flipping is very popular at Clear Lake in the

tules, especially when the tules border deeper water in early spring or shallow water in early summer.

A favorite method in the middle of spring is to cruise the portions of the lake that have docks set in relatively deep water. Cast a Brush Hog or Senko with no weight, letting it sink slowly to the bottom. That often brings results. Spinnerbaits also work well with this method.

After the spawn in June and into July, as the lake warms up, is when the "frog bite" comes to life. This is when you search out the thickest surface vegetation you can find. You cast a weedless frog on top of the thick mat of vegetation, then hop it along toward small pockets in this vegetation. A bass may bust through a thick mat of vegetation to grab the lure—or wait until the frog hits the small pocket of open water. Heavy line is a must: 25- and even 30-pound test. Use braided line. Some anglers use the new 50-pound test braided lines that have the diameter of a 10-pound line. Clear Lake has some huge bass, and if one grabs that weedless frog in the middle of all those weeds, you don't have a chance to pull that fish out without that heavy line.

When fishing open water, use lighter line, of course; 10- or 12-pound test is the standard.

An overlooked time of year at Clear Lake is the dead of winter, right when it's coldest, sometimes down to freezing. You will see hardly any anglers on the lake. Don't be deceived; even though bass are known as warmwater fish, some of the biggest fish of the year are taken at this time on jumbo minnows. Fish also seem to school up at this time, so much of the shoreline will be barren of fish.

In winter and late spring, many catch the big bass with jumbo minnows. There are two ways to fish with jumbo minnows. You can use a bobber and let the minnow drift into the depth near the shoreline. Or you can fish the minnow with a very small split shot, just enough weight to get the bait down on the edges of rock piles and steep banks. Regardless, you have a chance of catching the biggest

fish in your life when using this method. Many people have done just that.

In the winter months you cast it out, let it sink for several seconds, and then pull it slowly—maybe as little as six inches at a time—always pausing between these slow pulls. Don't be discouraged by the long intervals between fish, because the reward more than makes up for it when you finally find them.

On a calm day, casting a Rattlin' Rogue, either in the clown pattern or with a touch of orange, can inspire bass attacks.

You are apt to catch more than just bass. That is because Clear Lake has a population of huge black crappie, running 15–16 inches and up to three pounds. Anglers often catch these by accident on bass plugs. If you snag one, switch over to a crappie jig in white, yellow, or white with a spinner, or let a live minnow roam down there. Crappie stay tightly schooled, and the angler must present the lure or bait right in front of them. The most difficult part is finding the school, not getting bites.

As a 10-year-old, I had one of my first personal successes at Clear Lake, catching dozens of crappie on a warm summer night. Today you can, too. Private resorts hang bright lights from their dock, attracting gnats, which in turn attract minnows. Eventually, the crappie show up to eat the minnows; you simply toss out a small white jig and start catching fish.

If you have a boat, you can get a kid hooked on fishing by taking a similar approach for bluegill. Just use a red worm or a meal worm under a bobber, toss it out near the tules, and watch that bobber start to dance. For a young kid who thinks fish don't exist, it is quite a thrill. The coves near the state park are excellent for this sport.

For anglers who prefer to relax, catfishing provides the answer. Several deep holes provide excellent fishing. The best two are in Jago Bay and off Rattlesnake Island. Two other good spots are at each end of the lake: at the north end of the lake, a good hole is outside the mouth of Rodman Slough; at the south end of the lake, try just outside the entrance to Cache Creek. I've fished all of these and my favorite is the last spot.

If you think all this sounds too good to be true, you are right. There are a few thorns: One is the traffic, which on summer weekends is horrendous on the two-laners that provide access to the lake. Another is the wind; in the early spring, the north wind sometimes puts the fish off the bite for days on end. Lastly, by late summer, algae blooms can turn the surface waters into a soupy mess. This no longer happens to the extent it once did, but it still is a concern in August.

But that green mess is the stuff of life at Clear Lake. Without it, the lake would likely provide average feed and fish populations. Maybe they should just change the name of the lake.

Lake records: 33.25-pound catfish, 17.52-pound bass; 4-pound, 8-ounce crappie (state record).

Note: All boats must be inspected and certified free of mussels prior to launching at this lake.

Facilities, fees: Camping is possible at Clear Lake State Park (near Kelseyville), as well as at several private campgrounds and resorts around the lake. Full-service marinas, boat rentals, bait, tackle, and supplies are also offered.

Public boat ramps are in the city of Clearlake at Redbud Park; in Kelseyville, at Lakeside County Park; in Lakeport, at 1st Street, 3rd Street, 5th Street, Clear Lake Avenue, and at the junction of Lakeshore Boulevard and Crystal Lake Way; in Lucerne, at Lucerne Harbor County Park; in Clearlake Oaks; and in Nice, at H. V. Keeling County Park, Nice Community County Park, and Hudson Avenue. Most of the ramps are concrete, and a few are unimproved.

Dozens of mom-and-pop operations dot the lakeshore. They vary greatly in quality, but virtually all have their own boat ramps or are situated very close to a public ramp. The most developed operation is at Konocti Harbor Resort & Spa, which has condo-style

units, a restaurant, full marina, and a small concert hall.

Directions: To Clear Lake State Park: From Vallejo, take Highway 29 north to Lower Lake to a lighted junction (still Highway 29). Turn left on Highway 29 and drive seven miles to Soda Bay Road. Turn right on Soda Bay Road and drive 11 miles to the park entrance on the right side of the road.

From Sacramento, take I-5 north to Williams and Highway 20. Turn west on Highway 20 and drive to the junction with Highway 53. Turn left on 53 and drive to Lower Lake and the lighted junction with Highway 29. Turn right on Highway 29 and drive seven miles to Soda Bay Road. Turn right on Soda Bay Road and drive 11 miles to the park entrance on the right side of the road.

From Eureka, take U.S. 101 south to Calpella (17 miles south of Willits), turn east on Highway 20, and continue to Highway 29. Turn right on Highway 29 and drive to Kelseyville and Main Street. Turn left on Main Street and drive a short distance to State Street. Turn right and drive 0.25 mile to Gaddy Lane. Turn right on Gaddy Lane and drive about two miles to Soda Bay Road. Turn right and drive one mile to the park entrance on the left (well signed from Kelseyville).

Several resorts and private boat ramps are in the area:

• Edgewater Resort, at Soda Bay: In Kelseyville on Highway 29, take the Gaddy Lane exit and drive (the road immediately becomes Merritt Road) on Merritt Road for two miles to Soda Bay Road. Turn right on Soda Bay Road and drive three miles to the park entrance and boat ramp on the left. For more information call 707/279-0208.

• Holiday Harbor, near Nice: From north of Ukiah on U.S. 101, drive north to the junction with Highway 20. Turn east on Highway 20 and drive to the town of Nice and Howard Avenue. Turn left on Howard Avenue and drive 200 feet to the park and boat launch at the end of the road. For more information call 707/274-1136.

• Beachcomber Resort & RV, near Lucerne: From north of Ukiah on U.S. 101, or from Williams on I-5, turn on Highway 20 and drive to the town of Lucerne. Continue on Highway 20 to the east side of Lucerne and to the resort at 6345 East Highway 20. For more information call 707/274-6639.

• Glenhaven Beach, at Glenhaven: From north of Ukiah on U.S. 101, or I-5 at Williams, turn on Highway 20 and drive to Clear Lake and the town of Glenhaven (four miles northwest of Clearlake Oaks). In Glenhaven, continue on Highway 20 to the camp and boat ramp at 9625 East Highway 20. For more information call 707/701-6000.

There are also the following free public ramps:

• Clear Lake Avenue: From Main Street in the town of Lakeport, take Clear Lake Avenue east and head to the paved ramp at the lake's edge.

• 5th Street Ramp: From Main Street in the town of Lakeport, turn east on 5th Street and drive to the two-lane paved ramp.

• 1st Street Ramp: From Main Street in the town of Lakeport, turn east on 1st Street and continue to the two-lane paved ramp.

• Hudson Avenue: From Highway 20 in Nice, turn south on Hudson Boulevard and continue to the two-lane paved ramp at the lake's edge. Fishing access is free.

• H. V. Keeling County Park: This park is in the town of Nice at 3000 Lakeshore Boulevard and has a paved ramp.

• Lake County Park: On Highway 29 south of Kelseyville, turn north on Soda Bay Road/Highway 281 and drive to Park Drive. Turn north on Park Drive and drive to the paved ramp at 1985 Park Drive.

• Lakeshore Drive and Crystal Lake Way: From Main Street in the town of Lakeport, turn west on Clear Lake Avenue and continue to High Street. Turn north, drive to Lakeshore Drive, turn right, and continue to the paved ramp at the junction with Crystal Lake Way.

• Lucerne Harbor County Park: A paved ramp

is available in the town of Lucerne at 6225 East Highway 20.

• Redbud City Park: In the town of Clearlake, look for the park entrance at 14655 Lakeshore Drive. A four-lane paved ramp is available.

• 3rd Street Ramp: From Main Street in the town of Lakeport, take 3rd Street east to the two-lane paved ramp.

Contact: Clear Lake State Park, 707/279-2267, www.parks.ca.gov; Lakeport Regional Chamber of Commerce, 866/525-3767 or 707/263-5092, www.lakecochamber.com; Lake County Visitor Information Center, 707/274-5652 or 800/525-3743, www.lakecounty.com; Clearlake Chamber of Commerce, 707/994-3600, www.clearlakechamber.com.

Supplies and lodging: Clearlake Bait & Tackle, 707/994-4399, www.clearlaketackle.net; Clear Lake Cottages & Marina, 707/995-5253, www.clearlakecottagesandmarina.com; Edgewater Resort and RV Park, 800/396-6224; Clearlake Outdoors, 707/262-5852, clearlakeoutdoors.com; Lakeshore Bait and Tackle, 707/994-3474, www.lakeshorebaitandtackle.com; Limit Out Bait & Tackle, 707/998-1006, www.fishinclearlake.com; Pit Stop, 707/262-0931; Tackle It, 707/262-1233, www.tackleit.biz; Ferndale Resort and Marina, 707/279-4866, www.ferndaleresort.com; Shaw's Shady Acres on Cache Creek, 707/994-2236; Holiday Harbor RV Park & Marina (north end of lake), 707/274-1136.

Guides: The King Connection, 707/263-8856; Get-R-Done Fishing Service, 707/272-6640, www.getrdonefishing.com; Bassin' with Bob Myskey, 707/274-0373, www.fishclearlake.com; Team Effort Fishing Guide Service, 707/277-0207, www.TeamEffortFishing.com; Bass Fishin' with Richard, 707/279-4739, www.bassfishinclearlake.com; Big George's, 707/279-9269; Clear Lake Guide Service, 707/349-1427, www.clearlakeguideservioce.com; Taylored Guide Service, 707/349-6797, www.clearlakefishingguide.com; Adam's Whoop Bass Guide Service, 707/391-5685; Jim Munk, 707/479-7961; Bass n Boars Guide

Service, 707/463-1034, www.bassnboars.com; D-R Fishing Guide Service, 707/489-2265, www.drobbersfishing.com; Bob Thein's Fishing Guide Service, 707/994-4886; Larry Hemphill Guide & Instruction, 530/674-0276; Gut Buckets Catfish'n Guide Service, 530/671-1415, www.gutbucketsclearlake catfishn.com.

22 INDIAN VALLEY RESERVOIR

Rating: 8

near Clear Lake

Map 4.2, page 218

After a while, Indian Valley Reservoir becomes more like the ugly dog you love more than anything in the world because inside beats a heart that will never betray you. This is one of the better bass lakes in California, often offering days of fantastic catches every spring. You'll need a boat, but that done, two anglers might just catch 40 or 50 bass on any warm, windless day from mid-March through early June. It happens.

The lake is at 1,475 feet in foothill country, and when full, the lake covers about 3,700 acres and has 39 miles of shoreline. In addition to the bass, it has good fishing for rainbow trout, kokanee salmon, crappie, catfish, and smallmouth bass.

One key is the large number of stickups, or submerged trees, in the lake, which provide a perfect aquatic habitat. Winter inflows from Cache Creek and Wolf Creek provide fresh, cool, oxygenated water and an influx of feed, and the hot weather that follows gets the bass, crappie, and redear sunfish feeling active and ready to eat.

When the Department of Fish and Game made the controversial decision to put kokanee salmon in Indian Valley Reservoir, it didn't take long for it to be a no-brainer. The fish grew, and they grew fast because of the plankton-rich waters; in two years, fish 18 inches long were being caught. Indian Valley is now known as one of the state's best producers of big kokanee salmon.

The fishing rhythm starts in mid-May and lasts well into September. The average kokanee in midsummer run right around 15–16 inches, and the bigger ones run 18 inches, and even slightly bigger than that in August.

Conventional trolling methods for kokanee salmon work here, such as the Sling Blade dodger and Vance's dodger; and then trailing a variety of kokanee bugs, Apex lures, Uncle Larry's spinners, and most small wobblers that are brightly colored, such as Vance's Sockeye Slammer. As always with kokanee, don't forget to tip your hooks with the white corn.

A problem in kokanee fishing here with downriggers is the submerged trees that can snag the downrigger weight. If that happens, you have a very good chance of losing some of your tackle. Make sure you have a pair of wire cutters in your boat to cut the downrigger line; otherwise this could be dangerous. The reason it can be dangerous is that if the ball catches in the top of a tree 50 feet beneath the boat and the wind comes up, the whitecaps could capsize your small boat.

If you divide Indian Valley Reservoir into the north half and the south half, the south half is where you want to concentrate your efforts for kokanee. Early in the season you might get them as shallow as 20 feet deep, trolling trout lures like Needlefish. But as the season progresses, you will need to get down 40, 50, and 60 feet. This is where the snags at Indian Valley become a problem. The best thing to do is to memorize a route, then drive back and forth through that route. You will learn to avoid the worst treetops.

In the late winter and spring, a real surprise at Indian Valley is the quality fishing for trout, which is usually best near the creek inlets and along the dam. Although most of the trout planted in the spring are Eagle Lake trout in the 10- to 12-inch class, a few larger trout are occasionally caught.

Indian Valley is beautiful in its own way. A 10-mph speed limit, clear water, and hot days make for a quiet setting and good swimming in the summer.

Indian Valley is also a very underrated catfish lake, and for years has been known as a bass and crappie lake, but kokanee have now taken center stage. More people travel the 10 miles of dusty washboard roads to fish for kokanee than for any other species.

Facilities, fees: Campgrounds, drinking water, vault toilets, a boat ramp, full-service marina, bait, and tackle are available; supplies are at the Indian Valley Store. A set per-vehicle day-use fee is charged for up to three people, with an additional fee for each additional person. Boat launching is free.

Directions: From Williams on I-5, turn west on Highway 20 and drive 25 miles into the foothills to Walker Ridge Road. Turn north (right) on Walker Ridge Road (a gravel road) and drive north 5.4 miles to a major intersection of two dirt roads. Turn left and drive five miles (you will pass Blue Oak Campground to your right) to the Indian Valley Store and boat ramp, at the south end of the lake near the dam. Note that the access road is dirt and washboarded.

From the north end of Clear Lake, at the town of Nice, drive one mile east on Highway 20, then turn left on Bartlett Springs Road. The twisty road is routed to the north end of the lake, where there's a boat launch. This is a slow, twisty, but scenic route.

Contact: Bureau of Land Management, Ukiah Field Office, 707/468-4000, www.blm.gov/ca (click on Ukiah); Indian Valley Store and Marina, 530/662-0607 (recorded message, infrequently updated). A detailed map is available from the BLM.

23 GARCIA RIVER

Rating: 5

near Point Arena
Map 4.3, page 219

Which of California's coastal rivers clears the fastest after a big storm? The answer is the Garcia River, a short steelhead stream that runs out to sea just north of the town of Point Arena. The prime spot is the tidewater at the Miner Hole, and the prime time is high tide and the first two hours of the outgoing tide in January and February. You can often see the steelhead rolling, a sight that will get your juices flowing. The Miner Hole is a short walk from the parking area on Miner Hole Road. When the fish are in, you'll see other cars parked there.

Waders are a must here as you work downstream, casting along the way. The preferred technique is to cast a Little Cleo or an F7 Flatfish (gold, orange, and silver are the best colors). The critical factor with the Garcia River is timing, of course. You either hit it when the steelhead are in or you get skunked, and out-of-towners commonly experience the latter result. Always phone ahead before planning a trip.

The Garcia has about 10 miles of fishable water, but the best bet is to stick exclusively to the tidewater. This is where fresh-run steelhead hole up for a while, acclimating themselves to the freshwater. They are strong and bright. Hook a big one and you'll never forget it.

Of course, always check the most current DFG regulations whenever fishing anywhere for steelhead.

Facilities, fees: Camping is possible at Point Arena, including at Manchester State Park. Picnic tables and fire grills are provided. Drinking water, vault toilets, and an RV dump station are available. Supplies can be obtained in Point Arena. Fishing access is free.

Directions: From Point Arena, drive west on Miner Hole Road to a parking area that offers access to the Miner Hole, the best spot on the river. An option is to drive east on Eureka Hill Road for five miles. The upper fishing limit is at the bridge there. The river can be accessed by foot downstream of the bridge.

Contact: Manchester State Park, 707/882-2463 or 707/937-5804, www.parks.ca.gov; Gualala Sports & Tackle, 707/884-4247, www.gualalasport.com; Craig Bell, Greenwater Guide Service, 707/884-3012.

24 GUALALA RIVER

Rating: 6

south of Point Arena
Map 4.3, page 219

Among most of California's steelhead streams, the Gualala River is a lance of light in a field of darkness. The steelhead runs are improving, not declining, thanks primarily to regulations designed to protect habitat and a local project that has resulted in the release of 30,000 steelhead smolts per year from rod-and-reel-caught spawners. Some beautiful, big steelhead in the 15-pound class can be caught on the Gualala, but alas, the word is out. When the fishing is on, you can expect crowds. The worst-case scenario is "the gauntlet"; that is, a line of anglers working shoulder-to-shoulder in the same prime piece of water. It may sound crazy, but it happens here fairly often, with surprisingly few feathers getting ruffled.

The key? Get on the water early and be the first to fish several holes. The steelhead can and will spook here once the river gets crowded, so you'll need to be there first.

Want to learn a few secrets? Guide Craig Bell let me in on these: During an evening high tide, fishing the stretch of river just below the Highway 1 bridge at Mill Bend can be outstanding; just cast Little Cleos or peach-colored Puff Balls or Glo Bugs in the direction of rolling steelhead. During the morning, a better bet is to start upstream at Switchvale, cross upstream, and fish the North Fork Hole. From here on down, there are about 10 good spots for steelhead. I've had the best luck on the Gualala when the steelhead enter the river early in the winter and hole up in the tidewater a while. It also provides an opportunity for fly fishers. (Comets and sinking lines are mandatory.) The key is to go deep with your offering and get as natural a drift as possible in the slow-moving water.

If you don't mind the company and the competition, the Gualala provides a rare chance to catch a large steelhead on a small stream. If you arrive when the steelhead are moving through, you will discover some big, strong fish as well. Sure, those are two big "ifs," but few things worth remembering come easy.

And remember: always check current DFG fishing restrictions before heading out.

Facilities, fees: Camping is available at Gualala Point Park and Gualala River Redwood Park. Drinking water, restrooms, flush toilets, coin-operated showers, an RV dump station, convenience store, coin laundry, RV supplies, ice, and firewood are available. Supplies can be obtained in Gualala. Fishing access is free.

Directions: To access the lower river from the town of Gualala, turn east on Old Stage Road (County Road 501) and drive less than one mile to Old State Road (County Road 502). Turn right on Old State Road, where access is available on the road. To reach the upper fishing limit of the river from Gualala, drive south on Highway 1 to Annapolis Road. Turn left (east) on Annapolis Road and travel to the twin bridges. The bridges cross the Gualala.

Contact: Redwood Coast Chamber of Commerce, 707/884-1080 or 800/778-5252, www.redwoodcoastchamber.com; Gualala Sports & Tackle, 707/884-4247, www.gualalasport.com; Craig Bell, Greenwater Guide Service, 707/884-3012; Gualala Point Regional Park, 707/785-2377, www.sonoma-county.org/parks; Gualala River Redwood Park, 707/884-3533, www.gualalapark.com.

25 LAKE SONOMA

Rating: 9

north of Santa Rosa
Map 4.3, page 219

Lake Sonoma has become one of the best recreational areas within the sphere of influence of the Bay Area. It's a great place for fishing for bass, sunfish, and catfish, and has great boat-in camping and a low-speed area of the lake that's ideal for fishing. It provides a good fishery for largemouth bass and sunfish, with excellent habitat well upstream, on the lake arms.

The big lake, 2,700 acres, is set in rich foothill country and has thousands of hidden coves. From the dam, the lake extends nine miles north on the Dry Creek arm and four miles west on Warm Springs Creek. Each of the lake arms has several fingers and miles of quiet and secluded shoreline. The public boat launch is near the junction of the lake arms. In addition, boat rentals are available from the marina.

Lake Sonoma is ideal for people who grew up in the Midwest or in the South, where using live minnows under bobbers is a popular way to fish. Lake Sonoma provides such a place for the same fun.

You can go into a deep cove, dunk minnows, and catch all kinds of bass, bluegill, catfish, and crappie. It's like a potluck trip: you never know what's down there the next time your bobber starts to twitch.

The only thing it doesn't have is trout. And that is to make sure no hatchery trout slip downstream past the dam into the Russian River and potentially cause problems for the steelhead fishery.

Because there are so few lakes of this type and size in the area, it's become the major destination for people from Santa Rosa, as well as for people from the Bay Area. Summer weekends can be chaotic; weekdays are your best bet for quality fishing.

Another thing to remember is that this lake can turn quite muddy in late winter due to runoff from the murky inlet streams. It can take a couple of weeks of rain for it to settle and green up. It's good to track that, because often the best fishing of the year is right after it greens up.

The usual waterskiing/fishing conflict was solved by providing a large area in the main lake body for water-skiers and personal watercrafts. Yet some two miles of the Warm Springs Creek arm and five miles on the Dry Creek arm are off-limits to skiing, and this is where the bass fishing is best. The preferred bait is live minnows, available from the Dry Creek General Store, on the approach road just south of the lake.

One advantage of starting a fishing trip at the Yorty Creek ramp is the big crappie found on the west side of the Yorty Creek arm. During the summer, the sun peeps over the tops of the hills to find belly-boaters already casting toward shore to do battle with scrappy crappie that often outweigh the bass in this neighborhood. Good catfish roam here, too.

On the lake arms, there are lots of stick-ups, or submerged trees. You should cast your lures or let your minnows roam there. Bass and sunfish are abundant, and while there aren't very many large ones, the high numbers of the smaller fellows often make up for the lack of big fish.

Although this lake is not planted with rainbows, it has a self-sustaining, landlocked population of steelhead that makes Sonoma a real "sleeper" for the experienced trout troller. Don't expect easy fishing like that found on some of the fish-factory lakes of California, where heavily planted catchable and trophy trout are common. Although fish up to nine pounds have been taken, most of the fish found here are in the one- to four-pound range. In the spring and summer, anglers troll night crawlers or lures such as Needlefish and Cripplures behind flashers in the main creek channel and the face of the dam. Catch-and-release is advisable here, since these are wild fish.

Lake Sonoma is one place where the government did something right. The construction of Warm Springs Dam created this lake and along with it opportunities for camping (including great boat-in sites), waterskiing (in specific areas), and go-slow zones. And it is now one of the best fishing lakes in Northern California. An adjacent 8,000-acre wildlife area features 40 miles of hiking trails in a woodland setting.

Facilities, fees: A full-service marina, boat ramps, and boat rentals are available. There are 109 primitive boat-in campsites around the lake; two hike-in sites; four group sites (two of which are boat-in); and 95 tent sites and two group sites at Liberty Glen Campground, 2.5 miles from the lake. Picnic tables, fire grills, and vault toilets are provided at the primitive sites, but drinking water is not. At Liberty Glen, picnic tables and fire rings are provided, as are flush toilets, drinking water, lantern holders, solar-heated showers, and an RV dump station. Fishing and other supplies can be obtained at the Dry Creek Store on Dry Creek Road in Healdsburg. Day-use and launch fees apply.

Directions: To primary ramps: From Santa Rosa, drive north on U.S. 101 to Healdsburg. In Healdsburg, take the Dry Creek Road exit, turn left, and drive northwest for 11 miles. After crossing a small bridge, you will see the visitors center on your right. To reach the boat ramp, continue past the visitors center for about three miles. Follow the signs to the public launch ramp across the ridge or to the ramp at Lake Sonoma Marina.

To Yorty Creek access: Car-top boats can be launched at the Yorty Creek access. From Santa Rosa, drive north on U.S. 101 to Cloverdale. Take the first Cloverdale exit and turn left at the stop sign, driving over U.S. 101 to South Cloverdale Boulevard. Turn right and drive to West Brookside Road. Turn left and drive to Foothill Drive. Turn left on Foothill Drive and drive to Hot Springs Road. Turn right on Hot Springs Road and continue on the narrow, winding road several miles to the lake.

Contact: U.S. Army Corps of Engineers, Lake Sonoma, 707/431-4590, www.spn.usace .army.mil/lake sonoma; Lake Sonoma Marina, 707/433-2200 or 707/526-7272, www .lakesonoma.com; Dry Creek General Store, 707/433-4171.

Guides: Jim Munk, 707/479-7961.

26 RUSSIAN RIVER (GUERNEVILLE TO JENNER)

Rating: 5

northwest of Santa Rosa

Map 4.3, page 219

Sometimes just watching the mouth of the Russian River can be an illuminating experience. In late fall, the mouth of the Russian is like a revolving door, with a sandbar that opens and closes according to the strength of river flows. After heavy rains, it busts a hole through the sandbar, opening the mouth, and the river once again flows to the sea. At the same time, that allows anadromous fish such as salmon, steelhead, and, in the spring, shad to enter the river.

That should be all the clues you'll need to help you decide how to fish here. During the summer, when the mouth is closed, the fishing is quite poor. But from winter through spring, when the mouth is open, it can be decent—not great, but decent.

In the winter, after the steelhead start arriving, you can see the anglers standing at the mouth of Dry Creek, casting out. It's the one time there's a crowd. You almost need to bring your own rock to stand on at this one spot, hoping to intercept a migrating steelhead.

The runs of fish on the Russian vary quite a bit from year to year. With increased production of salmon and steelhead upstream from the Dry Creek Hatchery, there is some hope for the future. But without corresponding increased river flows, courtesy of releases from Lakes Sonoma and Mendocino, those runs can be undermined.

Sea lions also seem to be a problem, although, historically, large runs of steelhead and large numbers of sea lions have shared the river. One day in January, I saw something like 75 sea lions (or maybe they were harbor seals) lined up at the mouth of the river, trying to pick off steelhead as they swam through. The balance seemed out of whack.

The key here is water, and when rains are sufficient in fall and early winter, the salmon have a chance to enter the river in September and October, followed by steelhead around Thanksgiving. The bigger steelhead usually show up around mid-January. These fish can be elusive, but every year there are good sprees that provoke excitement and disbelief in those who have never experienced them.

Where to fish? The best spots for steelhead are between the mouth of Dry Creek and Duncans Mills, but access for shore fishing is only fair. One option is to launch a small pram or driftboat from Wohler Bridge to get the best access in this stretch of river. Good launch areas include Steelhead Beach, Vacation Beach, Monte Rio Beach, Casini Ranch Family Campground, and Jenner.

In the spring and summer, fishing activity tapers off on the Russian River. In May, the remainder of a once-great shad run moves through the Russian, with the best spots below the Healdsburg Dam on to Duncans Mills. I caught my first shad on the Russian River in 1966, upstream, near Cloverdale; that run of fish above Healdsburg in the Cloverdale area was depleted over the years because of the dam at Healdsburg. Because of the fish ladder now in place, shad are making a big comeback; with decent water flows, this could be a fishery to watch again in the future.

In the summer, the county places several temporary dams in the river, turning it from a river into a series of greenish sloughs. Some small catfish and smallmouth bass hang out in the Alexander Valley area, but they are rarely fished. The river gets a lot of canoe traffic in the summer.

All salmon fishing is prohibited. From April 1–November 1, only artificials with barbless hooks are allowed. Bait may be used from November through March, although not for salmon (even catch-and-release fishing for salmon is prohibited).

Facilities, fees: Lodging, cabins, campgrounds, restrooms, showers, canoe and kayak rentals, and shuttles are available, as are public beaches with restrooms, picnic facilities, and snack bars. Day use is free in most areas. Casini Ranch Family Campground has a boat ramp and rentals. Unpaved boat ramps are provided at Casini's put-in, Steelhead Beach, and Monte Rio Fishing Access. Summer canoe rentals are in Forestville. Fishing access is free.

Directions: To Burke's put-in: From the Bay Area, drive north on U.S. 101 to the junction with Highway 116 west (just north of Petaluma). Take Highway 116 west and drive 15 miles to Forestville and Mirabel Road (at the gas station). Turn right and drive 1.5 miles until it dead-ends at Burke's and the Russian River.

To Casini's put-in: On U.S. 101 north of Santa Rosa, turn west on River Road and drive 16 miles to Guerneville and Highway 116. Continue west on Highway 116 and drive seven miles to Duncan Mills and Moscow Road. Turn left (southeast) on Moscow Road and drive 0.7 mile to the campground on the left.

To Monte Rio Fishing Access: In the town of Monte Rio, turn south on Church Street and continue down to the ramp.

Contact: King's Sport & Tackle, Guerneville, 707/869-2156, www.guernevillesport.com; Casini Ranch Family Campground, 707/865-2255 or 800/451-8400 (reservations), www.casiniranch.com.

27 BODEGA BAY SALMON AND DEEP SEA

Rating: 10

north of San Francisco
Map 4.3, page 219

A gold mine of fish and good times has turned Bodega Bay into one of the best fishing spots on the coast. The beautiful surroundings make a fun fishing trip all the more enjoyable. Bodega Bay retains a rural feel, even though it is relatively close to the Bay Area. The drive here is pleasant, along a two-lane highway routed through rolling hills and dairy farms.

The most abundant species is the rockfish, and party boats specialize in trips to Point Reyes, and north off Fort Ross, where limits are virtually a daily affair, as are very heavy bags of fish. The rewards are large reds, ling-cod, and a variety of rockfish. In the fall, Captain Rick Powers, of the *New Sea Angler,* offers light-tackle "anything goes" trips to the shallows of Fort Ross, one of the most fun rockfish adventures in California.

The changes in regulations for deep-sea fishing, to a maximum of two hooks per rod, have created this favored technique: Use a 12-ounce Hex Bar or Diamond jig with a single hook, and then tie a shrimp fly or shrimp jig as a cheater; that is, set up on a dropper 18 inches above your Hex Bar. The Hex Bar catches the lings, and the shrimp fly or shrimp jig catches the big rockfish.

Rockfish may provide consistent day-in, day-out results, but salmon provide the sizzle. I have fished here many times when hordes of salmon were waiting just west of Bodega Head at the Whistle Buoy, a short cruise from the excellent boat ramp. Other good spots for salmon lie to the south just off Tomales Point, 10 Mile Beach, and north just outside the mouth of Salmon Creek.

Typically the salmon are in the 8- to 10-pound class early in the season. That is also when it is windiest here, and believe me, the north wind can howl over the top of Bodega Head. Come summertime, the wind lies down and the salmon get bigger. There are periods when there seem to be more 20-pound salmon here than at any other stretch of the coast. This normally sedate spot can turn into a madhouse on July weekends when the salmon are running. By late August, however, only a sprinkling of fish remain, catch rates for salmon are only fair, and most of the boats disappear.

A good spot for salmon is 10 Mile Beach. This is especially good in late summer for big salmon that can average over 15 pounds. The average salmon offshore Bodega Bay seems larger than those caught by the Bay Area fleet to the south. Preferred methods are trolling and mooching, although more trolling is done here with a flasher and an Apex or just a plain Apex off a weight.

When live anchovies for bait are available in Bodega Bay, it can be very productive drifting those anchovies along the beach for halibut.

Another bonus is that albacore often roam just west of Cordell Bank, arriving in mid-September and staying through mid-October. Some extraordinary fish counts are possible. This is also when some of the calmest seas of the year are available, making the long trip a lot easier to handle.

Several adventures on land are also available. In the winter, minus low tides come in cycles, every two weeks, uncovering miles of tidal flats in Bodega Bay, particularly on the western side. Though it is gooey, this is prime clamming territory. During high tides, shore fishing can net you perch, flounder, and, sometimes in the summer, halibut. Bodega Bay is fast becoming a favorite fishing port and weekend vacation site. After a trip here, you will understand why.

One time while returning from a salmon trip here, I saw a deer swimming straight out of the harbor toward the sea. Then the Coast Guard sent out a rescue boat and returned the deer to land. That is as strange as things get here, despite Bodega Bay's legendary status as the place where Alfred Hitchcock filmed his thriller *The Birds.* Instead of attacking birds, you are more likely to see attacking fish. You won't have to beat them off the boat with your oars, but there are some large rockfish and salmon in these waters.

Facilities, fees: Party-boat charters are available, as are a full-service marina, two boat ramps, and several campgrounds. Supplies can be obtained in the town of Bodega Bay. Party-boat fees apply.

Directions: From Petaluma on U.S. 101, take the East Washington exit and turn west (this street becomes Bodega Avenue). Drive west through Petaluma (the road becomes Bodega Highway) and continue for 10 miles to the town of Valley Ford (Bodega Highway will become Highway 1). Stay on Bodega Highway/Highway 1 for seven miles to the town of Bodega Bay. Then continue to your destination as described:

To the charter boat dock at Porto Bodega: In Bodega Bay, continue north to Eastshore Road. Turn left on Eastshore and drive one block to Westside Road. Continue straight and to the charter boat operation parking lot.

To Westside Park launch ramp: In Bodega Bay, continue north to Eastshore Road. Turn left on Eastshore and drive one block to Westside Road. Turn right on Westside and take the road around the bay to the launch ramp at Westside Park.

To Doran Park launch ramp: Turn left on Doran Park Road and continue to the park entrance.

Contact: Spud Point Marina, Bodega Bay, 707/875-3535, www.sonoma-county.org/parks; Bodega Bay Sportfishing, 707/875-3344, www.bodegabaysportfishing.com; Fish On Charters, 707/875-2323, www.bodegabayfishing.com.

Party boats: Bodega Bay Sportfishing Center with *New Sea Angler* and *Sandy Ann,* 707/875-3495 or 875-3344, www.bodegabay sportfishing.com; Fish On Charters with Pay Back and Samantha Irene, 707/875-2323, www.fishoncharters.net; Miss Anita Fishing Charters, 707/875-3474, www.missanitafish ingcharters.com; Reel-lentless, 707/334-4827, www.reellentlesssportfishing.com.

28 HIGHLAND SPRINGS RESERVOIR

Rating: 5

west of Clear Lake

Map 4.4, page 220

People can drive to Clear Lake many times over a lifetime and never discover Highland Springs Reservoir and adjacent Adobe Creek Reservoir, even though they are only about 10 miles west of their giant neighbor. But between them, this overlooked pair of lakes can provide anglers with much-needed alternatives.

Highland Springs Reservoir is in the foothills, just southwest of Big Valley, about a mile west of Adobe Creek Reservoir. Created from a dam on Highland Creek, which is a tributary of Adobe Creek, it covers about 150 acres.

Along with calm water, there's a variety of warm-water fish, including largemouth bass,

sunfish, bluegill, catfish, and bullhead. Fishing is best during the first warm snaps of spring, often in April and early May, especially for bass and bluegill. As the summer sun heats up this reservoir, the fishing for catfish becomes better. And here's a bonus: if your luck is not good at Highland Springs, it's just a quick trip over to Adobe Creek Reservoir.

Because gas motors are prohibited on the lake, Highland Springs offers a perfect alternative for anglers with small, hand-powered boats, such as canoes, rafts, or prams. The rule guarantees quiet water, even on three-day weekends, when nearby Clear Lake gets just about plowed under by all the hot jet boats.

Facilities, fees: Picnic areas, restrooms with flush toilets, and an unimproved boat ramp are provided. Gas-powered motors are not permitted on the lake. Fishing access is free.

Directions: From Vallejo, take Highway 29 north to the town of Lower Lake. Bear left on Highway 29 and drive to Kelseyville, then continue on Highway 29 four miles to Highland Springs Road. Turn left on Highland Springs Road and drive four miles to the reservoir.

Contact: Lake County Visitor Information Center, 707/274-5652 or 800/525-3743, www.lakecounty.com; Lake County Public Works, 707/263-2344, www.co.lake.ca.us; Tackle It, 707/262-1233, www.tackleit.biz; Lakeshore Bait and Tackle, 707/994-3474, www.lake shorebaitandtackle.com.

29 ADOBE CREEK RESERVOIR

Rating: 5

west of Clear Lake

Map 4.4, page 220

The little brother of Highland Springs Reservoir, about a mile to the west, Adobe Creek Reservoir covers 60 acres and provides a quiet retreat in the foothills of the Mayacamas Mountains. Big Valley, to the east, helps separate these two lakes from massive Clear Lake, and as such they are often overlooked.

Adobe Creek Reservoir provides a fair fishery for bass, bluegill, and sunfish, but there's less fish habitat than at adjacent Highland Springs Reservoir due to its squarish shape and fewer coves. Of the two, this one comes in second, but it's a favorite with bird watchers. Still, whenever you can find a lake where no motors are allowed, there's always a chance that you'll have a quality fishing experience. This spot is good for float tubers casting poppers or small floating Rapalas along the shore during the spring bite. Just don't come here expecting large fish.

Facilities, fees: There are no on-site facilities here. No gas motors; only electric motors are permitted on the lake. Fishing access is free.

Directions: From Vallejo, take Highway 29 north to the town of Lower Lake. Bear left on Highway 29 and drive to Kelseyville, then continue on Highway 29 four miles to Highland Springs Road. Turn left on Highland Springs Road and drive 3.5 miles to Bell Hill Road. Turn left on Bell Hill Road and drive 0.5 mile to Adobe Creek Road. Turn right on Adobe Creek Road and drive to the reservoir.

Contact: Lake County Visitor Information Center, 707/274-5652 or 800/525-3743, www .lakecounty.com; Lake County Public Works, 707/263-2344, www.co.lake.ca.us; Tackle It, 707/262-1233, www.tackleit.biz; Clearlake Bait & Tackle, 707/994-4399, www.clear laketackle.net.

30 CACHE CREEK

Rating: 4

southeast of Clear Lake near Vacaville

Map 4.4, page 220

Cache Creek is best known as the closest white-water rafting opportunity to the San Francisco Bay Area. Not as well known is the fact that some huge catfish and a light sprinkling of smallmouth bass roam the slower flows of the river. In past years, the Department of Fish and Game stocked fingerling brown trout, and though that has stopped,

there are a few real beauties in here. The catfish are the main prize.

Don't believe me? Stop in at the little tackle shop in the town of Guinda, because seeing is believing: a 30-pound catfish caught in Cache Creek, then mounted, is on display there.

Much of the upper reaches of Cache Creek (just below Clear Lake) is inaccessible, though you can fish a two-mile stretch of smallmouth bass water on the small road that runs out of Anderson Flat. It is rarely hit. The more accessible area is right along Highway 16, the narrow two-laner that connects tiny towns such as Guinda and Rumsey and then heads north to the rafting put-in spot near the confluence of Bear Creek.

Facilities, fees: You'll find a campground about 10 miles north of Rumsey, in Cache Creek Canyon Regional Park. Drinking water, flush toilets, and an RV dump station are available. Supplies can be obtained in the Clear Lake area and in Guinda. There is a small daily charge per vehicle.

Directions: From Vacaville on I-80, turn north on I-505 and drive 21 miles to Madison and the junction with Highway 16. Turn north on Highway 16 and drive northwest for about 45 miles to the town of Rumsey. From Rumsey, continue west on Highway 16 for five miles to the park entrance. Direct access is available from the town of Rumsey to four miles upstream, at the confluence of Bear Creek. South of Rumsey, the creek runs on private property; be aware of the boundaries.

Contact: Cache Creek Canyon Regional Park, 530/406-4880, www.yolocounty.org.

31 RUSSIAN RIVER (CLOVERDALE TO GUERNEVILLE)

Rating: 7

north of Santa Rosa

Map 4.4, page 220

This section of the river has been greatly enhanced by the operation of the Warm Springs

Hatchery, which is set below Lake Sonoma and the Ukiah Hatchery, on the upper river end. Runs of steelhead have been significantly boosted, and in turn, the stretch of river from Healdsburg on down will provide the closest quality steelhead opportunity for Bay Area anglers.

When the steelhead return to the Russian River in the winter months, they now often stop at the mouth of Dry Creek, then make the turn north there for the trip up to the hatchery. From Thanksgiving on, as long as stream conditions are fishable, you can plan to see at least a few bank anglers casting here. This portion of the Russian River is just a mile downstream from Healdsburg. Dry Creek, a key spawning tributary, is closed to all fishing, of course. Upstream of Healdsburg, the river takes on a different scope. Because of the fish ladder at Healdsburg, shad are making a comeback in the river at points north up to Cloverdale.

I used to fish the Squaw Rock area between Cloverdale and Hopland, and I have enjoyed some success there, but in recent years, the results have been poor at best. Access to the Russian River is not difficult in this area, but catching anything decent certainly is. A much better prospect is fishing the East Fork Russian River (Cold Creek) in Potter Valley, which the Department of Fish and Game stocks with 10- to 12-inch rainbow trout.

For more information about the lower river, see *Russian River (Guerneville to Jenner)*. For more information about the upper river, see *Cold Creek*.

Facilities, fees: Lodging, campgrounds, and supplies are available in several towns along Highway 116 and points upstream. Fishing access is free.

Directions: Many access points are available, including at Wohler Bridge, Steelhead Beach, and Memorial Beach. Access is available with a key obtained from Sonoma County Regional Parks, 707/565-2041, for shore fishing and boat launching.

From the San Francisco Bay Area, take U.S. 101 north to Healdsburg and take either the Dry Creek Road exit or Alexander Valley Road exit to the river. Or continue north on U.S. 101 just past Cloverdale, where there's access to the river under the old U.S. 101 bridge. Another option is to drive farther north, where there are several pullouts on the road and access points between Cloverdale and Hopland. Local tackle shops carry an excellent map of the river, detailing it from Healdsburg to the coast.

Contact: King's Sport & Tackle, Guerneville, 707/869-2156, www.guernevillesport.com; Dry Creek General Store, 707/433-4171; Burke's Canoe Trips, Forestville, 707/887-1222, www.burkescanoetrips.com.

32 LAKE BERRYESSA

Rating: 10

north of Vallejo

Map 4.4, page 220 BEST (

Scads of bass, a trophy-trout fishery, salmon, and several resort areas make Lake Berryessa the Bay Area's most popular vacationland and a great place for families. When full, it is a big lake, covering some 21,000 acres with 165 miles of shoreline, complete with secret coves, islands, and an expanse of untouched shore (on the eastern side) that's off-limits to people.

What you get is quality fishing. If you can visit during the week and thus avoid the partygoers, you will get a chance to enjoy quiet water and good fishing. Come to Berryessa on a Thursday morning, for instance, after seeing the place on a Saturday afternoon, and you'll feel as if you're on a different planet.

As at many large reservoirs, your approach to fishing here is dependent upon time of year, water temperature, and "patterning" the bass (determining what stage they are in). If you want numbers, try the springtime, when the bass move in along shoreline cove areas in the lake arms. The prime areas are the three major lake arms at the south end of the lake, as well as the Putah Creek arm at the north end of the lake. Avoid the main lake body.

The north end of the lake, up the Cache Creek arm above the 5-mph speed limit buoy, can be sensational from first light at dawn to about 9 A.M. Use a 3 1/2-inch Zara Super Spook Junior in light blue/silver (bleeding shad), and dart it so it zig-zags on the surface, with periods of 5–10 seconds where you let it sit until all the ripples have dissipated.

The main lake along the east shore is also good for bass, especially in the spring, using Zoom flukes and Senko worms (often best in root-beer color or motor oil), or with flukes (in white). Rig a Senko in Wacky style (see *Largemouth Bass* in the *Sport Fish* chapter) and dead-stick it along the weeds. A fun trip is to get up before dawn, head up to the Putah Creek arm, and cast spinnerbaits and Spooks. Then once direct sunlight hits the water, head back to the main lake body and work over the eastern shore for largemouth bass. The east shoreline, from the vineyards on into the adjacent cove, is an excellent spot, where bass hold from late March through early June.

Lake Berryessa seems loaded in the spring with bass ranging 11–14 inches. There are some giant bass in this lake. Though Clear Lake is something of a landmark for giant bass, there are giant bass just as big at Berryessa, some in the 15-pound class, though they prove to be extremely elusive. But don't be surprised if you hear of a 20-pound bass at Berryessa, because the lake has the aquatic riches to support large fish.

In the fall and midsummer, bass can become more difficult to catch at Berryessa, especially when you have to compete with heavy water-skier traffic. Sometimes you can catch them with unusual methods that don't work the rest of the year. Believe it or not, a Blue Fox minnow spinner cast along the backs of coves in the fall is a surprising way to take bass in the 14- to 17-inch class. Done it many times.

In the spring, as the surface water temperatures approach the mid-60s, Berryessa can be terrific for surface fishing for bass. This lake has dozens and dozens of flooded islands that bass congregate on during these times, and bass will come from 8 and 10 feet deep to hit the surface lure. Zara Spook, Pop-R, and Rico's can be very successful.

Try two different methods, one keeping the lure moving from the time it hits the water and the other letting it sit and then moving it slowly back towards the boat. Even old-fashioned lures like the Jitterbug can work well here. A secret is to add a small plastic worm on the rear hook, or even a skirt.

It is common to catch 20 or 30 bass in a day, casting a variety of lures—plastics are best—along these protected shoreline coves. During the evening, surface lures such as the Rebel Pop-R can provide some exciting fishing. Most of the bass are small, many in the 10- to 12-inch class, but there are enough bigger ones to keep things interesting. Berryessa boasts nowhere near the numbers of large bass as Clear Lake to the north does, however (although the Putah Creek arm has a good supply of smallmouth).

Trout fishing in the summer is often excellent for people who understand how to troll deep in the thermocline. The lake has a trophy trout fishery. A lot of the trout range 14–17 inches, and what most anglers do is get up before dawn in summer and then troll out at the southern areas of the lake. Portuguese Cove, Skiers Cove, both entrances to the Narrows (especially the Rock Slide, on the east side of the lakeshore), and the mouth of Markley Cove are all good spots. The key in the summer is depth, trolling typically 25–35 feet deep, using lures such as the Rainbow Runners, Triple Teaser (white with a red head), and Humdinger.

Once the hot weather arrives, it's as if the trout are locked in jail, the way they stay about 35–40 feet down in the thermocline. You either go that deep or get skunked. A red Rainbow Runner spoon is the preferred entreaty to catch trout in the 12- to 18-inch class. Using a downrigger is the ideal way to reach the precise depth. If you don't have a downrigger, leadcore trolling line and planer-divers will also help you get deep.

If you don't like trolling deep, wait until the lake "turns over"; that is, when the stratified temperature zones do a flip-flop, bringing cool water and trout to the surface. This usually occurs around the third week of October, and the lake surface becomes dotted with thousands of tiny pools from rising trout—a spectacular scene—best viewed on Hope Creek, Putah Creek, the Markley Cove arm, mouth of Skiers Cove, the Rock Slide at the mouth of the Narrows, and around the Big Island. The lake-record rainbow trout, 38 inches and 14 pounds, was taken during such a period. Using live minnows for bait is very effective at this time.

When the lake turns over is when live minnow fishing can provide a fantastic sport. Use a No. 4 or 6 hook, hook the minnow through the nose vertically, then clamp a very small split shot 18 inches above that; place a bobber four–five feet above the minnow. From a boat, toss it out, then drift along the likely coves and shoreline points, letting the breeze push your boat along. The minnow will swim along with you for the ride. It's best to hook the minnow through the nose, because even if it dies, the action of the drift will make it appear to be swimming. Some people prefer hooking the minnows through the back, but they tend not to last as long, though they may be very active for a few minutes.

One technique is to drift in a cove with live minnows out for bait, and as you push along the shoreline, to simultaneously cast bass lures along the shore. That way you have a chance for bass and trout on a single drift. The two-rod stamp makes this possible.

In the fall, keep your eyes trained to scan the surface for any activity of swirling minnows. Often you can see them swirling or "boiling," and then cast to the fish. Berryessa also attracts a lot of aquatic birds called grebes, and concentrations of grebes usually indicate lots of minnows. Birds never lie. Catfish have become a more popular fish at Lake Berryessa from spring through fall. Anglers using a variety of baits (such as clams, chicken livers,

and night crawlers) catch them from shore, sometimes even in the middle of the day. These fish average two pounds but can easily go over five pounds.

During the winter months, shore anglers can be very productive when fishing for trout in areas like Spanish Flat and Markley Cove. Bait anglers use either a minnow under a bobber, or Power Bait and a night crawler (on separate hooks) off the bottom, and then cast a second rod with lures such as a Kastmaster, Krocodile, or Little Cleo. Be sure to have your California two-rod stamp when doing this.

The Department of Fish and Game now operates a rearing project at Lake Berryessa, where small rainbow trout are grown in pens until they reach a large size and are then released. The DFG has an ambitious plan to turn the lake into a fish and wildlife paradise. If fulfilled, true greatness will be attained. In 2012, the DFG plans to stock Lake Berryessa with 58,000 foot-long rainbow trout and 58,000 foot-long Eagle Lake trout annually. Berryessa is also stocked with king salmon and kokanee salmon fingerlings. The DFG requests that all salmon under 14 inches be released.

Sound good? Well, it is. However, that's the source of the lake's one problem: too many people on weekends. It is particularly frustrating when you cross paths with self-obsessed boaters or jet-skiers ripping up and down the lake during the summer, with little regard for anything but themselves. The campgrounds can get loaded, too. In other words, hardly a pristine experience.

Resorts have been scraped or seized, most have been renamed, trailer cabins razed, and the boat launch fee jacked to a ridiculous $26.25 at Pleasure Cove (while launching is free at most ramps at Clear Lake to the north). When the 40-year contracts with concessionaires expired in 2008–2009, the federal government, through the Bureau of Reclamation, swung the hammer of eminent domain to take control of the lake's seven resort marinas and recreation infrastructure. What's left is

Markley Cove and Pleasure Cove with park model cabins and boat rentals, campsites at four locations, and greatly reduced recreation and lodging facilities, few stores and supplies, and higher prices for everything. News of lawsuits has replaced fishing reports.

On the lake, none of that seems to matter. Once on the water, Berryessa is the kind of place where you can shed your cares. When the water temperature is cool, and you head out on a morning weekday, you can have the lake largely to yourself. I try to fish with guide Jim Munk every spring, and we've had many 60-fish days here using Zara Spooks and Senkos rigged Wacky. One time, I caught an 11-pound catfish by accident on a Senko by the vineyards. With novelist John Lescroart, we caught trout and salmon, one after another; then we caught a stunning five-pound smallmouth for book dealer Tom Hedtke. One summer day, publisher Ed Ow ran over my canoe with a houseboat as he discovered they didn't have brakes. We laughed like hell about it, too. On a trip with Dusty Baker and Elvin Bishop, we floated into Skier's Cove, casting ahead of the boat for bass, trailing live minnows under bobbers for trout. Back in the day, my brother returned from the front lines of Vietnam and off we went, right straight to Berryessa, and how for the first time in my life, it was so great just to be in a boat with him, alive and well, that it didn't matter that we didn't get a single bite that day.

As you venture out, the bright white wake ripples again behind your boat and the water spans for miles. You can watch the deer and turkey browse along the eastern shore, the grebes, geese, and songbirds in the coves, and know you'll always have another fish to cast to. You might remember the old days on the lake with your friends. That can be all the inspiration you need to get out there again.

Facilities, fees: Before launching, self-certify that your boat is mussel-free and get a certificate at www.usbr.gov/mp/ccao/berryessa. Resorts and services can be found at:

• Markley Cove Resort: Park model cabins ($175 per night Mon.–Fri. for four-person cabin, $200 Sat.–Sun.); boat rentals; boat launching $20.

• Pleasure Cove Marina: Park model cabins ($159 per night four-person cabin, $250 per night for eight-person cabin, $550 per night for loaded cabin that sleeps 10, two-night minimum); boat rentals; boat launching $26.25.

Directions: From San Francisco: Take I-80 east over Bay Bridge and continue 50 miles to Exit 51A toward Cherry Glen Road. Take that exit a short distance to Lagoon Valley Road, turn left and go 0.2 mile and continue onto Cherry Glen Road. Drive 0.6 mile (keep right at the fork) and continue a short distance to Pleasants Valley Road. Turn left and drive 12.6 miles to Highway 128. Turn left and drive five miles past the dam and the southern end of the lake at Markley Cove. Continue to west side of lake.

From Napa: Take Highway 121 north three miles through town to a T (with Las Trancos Street on left) with Monticello Road/Highway 121. Turn right on Highway 121 and drive 12.3 miles to Highway 128/Capell Valley Road. Turn left and go 4.8 miles to Berryessa-Knoxville Road. Turn right and drive five miles to west shore of lake, visitor center and day-use areas.

To Pleasure Cove: From Vallejo, take I-80 northeast about 10 miles to the Suisun Valley Road exit. Take Suisun Valley Road and drive north another 10 miles to Highway 121. Turn north right on Highway 121 and drive about eight miles to the end of Highway 121 and the junction with Highway 128. Bear right (southeast) on Highway 128 and proceed four miles to Wragg Canyon Road. Turn left and continue three miles to the end of the road.

To Putah Creek: From Vallejo, take I-80 northeast about 10 miles to the Suisun Valley Road exit. Take Suisun Valley Road and drive north to Highway 121. Turn north on Highway 121 and drive five miles to Highway 128. Turn left on Highway 128, drive five miles to Berryessa–Knoxville Road, and continue 13 miles to 7600 Knoxville Road.

Contact: U.S. Bureau of Reclamation, Lake Berryessa, 707/966-2111, www.usbr.gov/mp/berryessa

Resorts: Markley Cove Resort, 707/966-2134, www.markleycoveresort.com; Pleasure Cove Resort, 707/966-9600, www.goberryessa.com; Lupine Shores, 707/966-9088; Chaparral Cove, 602/977-7358, berryessalake.com.

Guides: Larry Hemphill Guide & Instruction, 530/674-0276; Jim Munk, 707/479-7961.

33 LAKE SOLANO

Rating: 5

near Lake Berryessa in
Lake Solano County Park
Map 4.4, page 220

Sometimes a lake is not a lake at all. Such is the case with Lake Solano, which is actually a section of Putah Creek with a small dam on it.

Whatever you call it, Solano does provide a quiet alternative to nearby Lake Berryessa. That's because motorboats are prohibited from the water here, making this a good bet for folks with canoes, rowboats, and other small, people-powered craft.

The trout-stocking program here was halted in 2008 (this may change once the Environmental Impact Report is finished and reviewed). In the meantime, native trout seem to be steadily repopulating the lake and Putah Creek upstream. Several nice catches have been reported next to the park and the fishing access sites upstream.

A handful of anglers have kept secret for years Lake Solano's occasional trophy trout. These are usually caught by fly fishers float-trolling the upper end of Lake Solano, with the best time from midfall–midspring. Believe it or not, these fish occasionally exceed 20 inches.

The campgrounds are popular on summer weekends, but they rarely fill during the week.

When Berryessa is teeming with people and fast boats, you might want to spend a few quiet hours here.

Facilities, fees: A campground, restrooms with flush toilets, showers, drinking water, an RV dump station, and picnic areas are provided. Pedal boats and canoes can be rented on weekends. Supplies can be obtained nearby. No motorized boats are permitted on the lake. There is a day-use parking fee; an annual pass is available.

Directions: From Sacramento, take I-80 west to Davis and the exit for Highway 113. Take that exit and drive north on Highway 113 to Russell Boulevard. Turn west on Russell Boulevard and drive to Winters (the road becomes Highway 128), then continue up Putah Creek four miles to Pleasant Valley Road. Turn left on Pleasant Valley Road and continue to the signed entrance to the park.

From the Bay Area, take I-80 east to Vacaville and I-505. Bear north on I-505 and drive to Winters and Highway 128. Turn west on Highway 128 and continue up Putah Creek to the signed entrance to the park.

Contact: Lake Solano County Park, 530/795-2990, www.solanocounty.com.

34 PUTAH CREEK

Rating: 5

downstream of Lake Berryessa
Map 4.4, page 220

During the open period of the general trout season, this is generally a put-and-take stream. After November 15 and the closing of the general trout season, however, the rules mandate fly-fishing only, barbless hooks, and catch-and-release. When the masses of people have departed, the larger native trout in this system start appearing. As in adjacent Solano, there are occasional fish that measure up to 20 inches.

These big rainbows and occasional browns will surprise the angler expecting no more than a 10-inch trout. When there is a rare hatch in the winter months, fish will come to a dry fly. But that is rare. Most fish are caught by fishing upstream with nymphs. You need to get the fly right on the bottom, in a natural drift.

A trick here is to wade the sections of stream that are very difficult to access by most anglers. There are about a half a dozen of these difficult-to-reach sections between the dam and Lake Solano, and they all hold big fish.

Since trout plants were stopped in 2008, native trout seem to be steadily repopulating Putah Creek. These fish can be smart. The fishable section is actually quite short, set just below the little dam at Lake Solano, right downstream from the releases from Lake Berryessa. Some Bay Area fly fishers use Putah Creek to hone their craft before heading off for more serious stuff in the mountains. Sometimes they even catch trout.

Facilities, fees: The nearest campground and facilities are at Lake Solano County Park, just upstream of Putah Creek. Supplies are available in Winters. Fishing access is free.

Directions: In Vacaville, take I-505 north and drive 11 miles to the junction of Highway 128. Turn west on Highway 128 and drive about five miles (past Winters). Putah Creek runs along the road, and the best fishing is found in the two miles just below the dam at Lake Solano.

Contact: Department of Fish and Game, Yountville, 707/944-5500.

Guides: Greg Bonovich, Putah Creek Fly Fishing, 800/480-5285, www.putahcreekfly fishing.com.

35 LAKE HENNESSEY/ CONN DAM

Rating: 6

north of Napa in Lake Hennessey City Recreation Area
Map 4.4, page 220

One great thing about Hennessey is that the road goes right by the lake. So it can be fun for locals to just go out on a late afternoon drive to see if anyone is fishing. Quite often nobody is. But if you do see action, there is a reason for it. In the summer, fishing for bass, bluegill, and sunfish is a lot of fun for families, often while enjoying evening picnics.

So over time, what Hennessey has become is Napa's backyard fishing hole. All the locals call it "Conn Dam." The one catch: No motors over 10 horsepower are permitted.

As with so many places, timing is everything. Fish and Game stocks Hennessey with 10- to 12-inch Eagle Lake trout and rainbow trout, and fingerling rainbow trout. The best stocks are in cool-weather months, best in late winter through late spring. They provide hope for shoreline bait dunkers and a handful of trollers.

Spring arrives with warmer days, as well as resident bass, bluegill, and sunfish. This is a good bass lake and there is a good number of decent bass in the 14- to 18-inch class. Because the bass boats with the big engines do not fish here, those in small boats with electric motors or in canoes (all must be registered with DMV with a vessel number and current stickers to be legal here) can work in quiet water and get some nice fish.

I've found that whatever is working at nearby Berryessa at the time for bass works at Hennessey. So if guide Jim Munk is deadsticking Senkos and getting 50-fish days at Berryessa, you might try that here, without enduring the traffic. Rarely will a basser like Munk launch his boat here; if he does, the prop of the big engine never touches the water. Instead, he uses the electric trolling motor on the front of his boat. It's rare to see this, maybe just a few times a year. Bassers do it because the fishing is good. Considering all the trouble it is to load a pro-style bass boat without using the motor, seeing one in the lake is the best indicator of all that the lake is on fire.

At least you can fish here. Some other lakes in this area are off-limits to the public.

Facilities, fees: A boat launch is provided at the lake; boats with engines over 10 horsepower are not permitted on the water, and nonregistered boats such as canoes, prams, and rafts are also prohibited. A picnic area, drinking water, and vault toilets are provided. Supplies can be obtained in the town of Napa. There is a per-day boat-launching fee. Annual passes are available. A fishing permit is required for those over 16 and is available at the boat ramp.

Directions: In Napa, take Highway 128/29 to Trancas Street. Turn east (right if coming from the south) on Trancas and drive to the Silverado Trail. Turn north on Silverado Trail and drive about 15 miles to Highway 128 East (also known as Conn Creek Road). Turn right and drive three miles to the boat launch and recreation area. The road runs along the lake.

Contact: Lake Hennessey, City of Napa Public Works, 707/257-9521; Department of Fish and Game, Yountville, 707/944-5500.

36 SPRING LAKE

Rating: 5

in Santa Rosa at Spring Lake County Park

Map 4.4, page 220

Spring Lake was the site of the biggest hoax pulled off in the fishing world in many years. A fellow claimed to have caught a 24-pound largemouth bass, which would have shattered the world record—what the people would call the "Million Dollar Bass." As the story goes, the angler had his wife bring a bathroom scale to the lake, where they photographed and weighed the 24-pound bass, then released the fish back in the lake.

Despite claims that a world-record fish was caught, and even stories in national magazines about the fish, many remained extremely skeptical. A nuclear engineer pal of mine, Ray Rychnovsky, conducted a careful analysis of the photograph, spending days determining the actual length and girth of the fish based on other elements in the photograph, such as the length between the thumb and forefinger of the gent holding the fish. Rychnovsky

concluded the bass might possibly weigh 14–17 pounds, but was still well short of the world record of 22 pounds, 4 ounces.

Yet anglers will bite on anything. *Outdoor Life* even ran a cover story on this fish, a story in which I was castigated for not believing such a tale. Years later, the consensus is that a lot of people were duped by a ridiculous tale that never passed the first rule of journalism: independent verification by two individuals who don't have a stake in the outcome.

This lake does have a few bass in it, but not enough to be considered a serious bass fishery. There are reports of maybe three or four 10-pound fish a year being caught by some local Santa Rosa anglers. I have done some TV shows at this lake, and so when it came out that the hoax was attempted here, no one laughed harder than I did.

Now, let me tell you more about Spring Lake. A precious handful of lakes near the San Francisco Bay Area have campgrounds, and this is one of them.

Spring Lake is stocked with rainbow trout, usually twice a month in late winter and early spring. Most are 10–12 inches. Did you ever think you could go on a fishing/camping trip right in Santa Rosa, of all places? It may sound crazy until you see this lake, which is fairly good sized (75 acres) and surrounded by parkland.

The fishery here is very similar to that of nearby Lake Ralphine, with trout in the cool months and some small bass and bluegill in the summer. In fact, Spring Lake and Ralphine Lake are stocked on the same days when the DFG tanker truck is on the route. The difference here is you can turn it into an overnighter.

Facilities, fees: A campground, drinking water, flush toilets, RV dump station, swimming lagoon, and picnic areas are available. A boat ramp (boats with gas motors are not permitted on the water), summer boat rentals, and bait are also available. A day-use fee is charged.

Directions: In the North Bay, take U.S. 101

to Santa Rosa and the junction with Highway 12. Turn east on Highway 12 to the first traffic light (at this light, Highway 12 turns left; do not turn). At the light, continue straight on Hoen Avenue and drive 0.5 mile (crossing Summerfield Road) to Newanga Avenue. Turn left and drive 0.25 mile to the park and boat ramp at the end of the road.

Contact: Spring Lake County Park, 707/539-8092 or 707/565-2267 (camping reservations); Sonoma County Parks, 707/565-2041, www .sonoma-county.org/parks; Santa Rosa Convention and Visitor's Bureau, 707/577-8674, www.visitsantarosa.com; Outdoor Pro Shop, 707/588-8033.

37 LAKE RALPHINE

Rating: 5

in Santa Rosa at Howarth Park

Map 4.4, page 220

Along with Spring Lake, this is one of two backyard fishing holes in Santa Rosa. Twenty-six acre Ralphine Lake is the smaller of the two (it's one-third the size of Spring Lake). Bait dunkers on the shore and in small rowboats are the primary users. You can go far here with a jar of Power Bait, a tub of night crawlers, and two No. 6 hooks.

Ralphine is stocked solely by the Department of Fish and Game, and that means no large bonus trout; in fact, anything over 12 inches is a fluke. But the stocks of 10- to 12-inch rainbow trout and Eagle Lake trout are consistent when the water temperatures are cool enough to allow it, usually October through March. In the summer, small bass and bluegill provide kids with an opportunity to give it a try.

Facilities, fees: Picnic facilities are provided in the park. A boat ramp and boat rentals are available. No motors are permitted on the lake. A campground is nearby, at Spring Lake. Supplies are in Santa Rosa. Fishing access is free.

Directions: In the North Bay, take U.S. 101 to Santa Rosa and the junction with Highway 12. Turn east on Highway 12 to the first traffic light (at this light, Highway 12 turns left; do not turn). At the light, continue straight on Hoen Avenue and drive a short distance to Summerfield Road. Turn left and continue to Howarth Park.

Contact: Howarth Park, 707/543-3424; Santa Rosa Recreation and Parks, 707/543-3282; Santa Rosa Convention and Visitor's Bureau, 707/577-8674, www.visitsantarosa.com.

38 LAKE ILSANJO

Rating: 6

in Santa Rosa in Annadel State Park

Map 4.4, page 220

"You've got to walk there" may be the most frightening thing you can say to an angler. It certainly is enough to discourage most folks from visiting Lake Ilsanjo.

The centerpiece of Annadel State Park, which has 5,000 acres of rolling hills, meadows, and oak woodlands, with a few seasonal creeks, Ilsanjo is a classic bass pond, something many anglers never get a chance to fish. Alas, here you have the chance, but you must walk five miles round-trip for the privilege. It takes a little over an hour in both directions, and you should bring a full canteen to make the trip a bit easier. You're better off riding a mountain bike, with an ultralight float tube and tackle in a daypack. Annadel is a great park for biking, and fishing Ilsanjo is how you take it the extra mile.

That done, this is the perfect place to bring a light spinning rod and small bass lures for the spring bite. One great lure to use here is a one-inch Countdown Rapala, black over gold. Most of the bass are right along the shore, so it's wise not to rush right up to the shoreline and cast as far out as possible. Instead, creep up and cast along the bank, moving deeper with each cast.

As the water warms, forget the "hard baits," like Rapalas, and switch over 1/4-ounce Dartheads with grubs or plastic worms. Sneak-fish the entrances to the coves.

While the majority of the bass are small, they are fun to catch, and it's exciting knowing there are a few big fellows swimming around in there. The lake record is an eight-pounder.

Facilities, fees: A campground is nearby, at Spring Lake Regional Park. Supplies can be obtained in Santa Rosa. Fishing access is free.

Directions: From U.S. 101 in Santa Rosa, drive east on Highway 12 to Montgomery Drive. Bear right at Montgomery Drive and drive 3.5 miles to Channel Drive. Turn right on Channel Drive and drive a short distance to the park. Park and hike 2.5 miles to the lake.

Contact: Annadel State Park, 707/539-3911, www.parks.ca.gov; Outdoor Pro Shop, 707/588-8033.

39 NAPA RIVER

Rating: 4

near Napa

Map 4.4, page 220

The Napa River has started a comeback. Yes, there's a long way to go, but when people, habitat, and fish are pointed in the same direction, they often have a way of getting there.

Of course, the best section of the Napa River is the lower section, the last mile or two before it pours into the bay. In the fall, large striped bass often congregate here, followed by sturgeon all winter and into early summer. The largest fish ever taken from a Bay Area pier was landed here—a 194-pound sturgeon caught by George Gano at the Vallejo Pier, near Wilson Avenue. Because the Vallejo Pier has been long-closed due to structural problems, fishing prospects are best along the nearby wall, with access still possible off Wilson Avenue.

A sprinkling of steelhead return to the river every winter, marching upstream to spawn. Even with severe catch restrictions in place on most steelhead streams, my suggestion is to give the steelhead a rest and leave them alone so they can complete their spawning mission. Perhaps one day there will be a significant steelhead run in the Napa River again, enough to provide a viable fishery.

Lower portions of the Napa River can be good for decent-sized striped bass, but the fishing never seems to be sustained. It's there for a week or two and then gone. Local information is important here. Call ahead.

Starting in December and January, after the Napa River has had a chance to muddy up from big rains a few times, sturgeon tend to gather in the lower sections of this river. When the bigger waters outside the harbor are too rough to fish, this is an area in which you'll be relatively protected from wind and have an excellent chance of catching sturgeon.

Most of the time, reality overshadows dreams, and at the Napa River—especially upstream in and above the town of Napa—you primarily get good numbers of small striped bass. I have fished behind homes right in Napa and caught and released scads of these little six- and seven-inch bass. With an ultralight spinning rod, it's a real kick. I call them "Napa River trout," though of course, there is no such thing. They stay in the river all the way into July, and once the flows start warming, the little bass head downstream and into their summer nursery area in San Pablo Bay.

For many years the Napa River looked like a green slough, not a real river, and it is no mystery why the steelhead fishery in the winter and the striped bass fishery in spring and early summer went right down the tubes. Now the river is on its way back.

A coalition of the Friends of the Napa River, U.S. Army Corps of Engineers, and the Department of Fish and Game is hoping their work on the Napa River will be a testimonial to stream restoration. It starts by exercising flood control without a dam; that is, where the river is allowed (for the most part) to take its natural course. Although this floods out some riparian zones in the short term, it creates wetlands and in turn improves habitat for the entire aquatic food chain here.

This is no short-term deal either. The residents of Napa passed a voter initiative to slightly increase sales tax in order to pay for the work. Every dime of restoration money that the City of Napa raises with this small tax is matched with grant money from federal agencies, so funding is in place.

Facilities, fees: A public boat ramp is provided at Moore's Landing. Bait and tackle can be obtained nearby. Lodging is in Napa. Fishing access is free.

Directions: From Napa, drive southwest on Highway 121/Highway 12 to Cuttings Wharf Road. Turn left on Cuttings Wharf Road and continue to the end of the road to reach the boat ramp.

Contact: Napa Valley Marina, Napa, 707/252-8011, www.napavalleymarina.com; Sweeney's Sports, 707/255-5544, sweeneyssports.com.

SACRAMENTO AND GOLD COUNTRY

BEST FISHING SPOTS

❰ Freshwater Fisheries
San Joaquin Delta, **page 292.**

This landscape is filled with Northern California's most significant rivers – the Sacramento, Feather, Yuba, American, and Mokelumne. All of these provide opportunities for fishing and water sports in both lakes and rivers, in addition to serving as the lifeblood for a series of wildlife refuges.

These rivers attract runs of salmon, shad, and striped bass for what is called an "interception fishery." This is where the fish are migrating through, and your mission is to try to "intercept" them along the way. That is why timing is everything here.

Several reservoirs are sprinkled across the Mother Lode country like little jewels. Many of them provide excellent fishing. The best are Camanche Lake (for bass), Lake Pardee (for trout and kokanee salmon), Lake Amador (for trout and a few big bass), and New Hogan Reservoir (for bass and striped bass).

But the region also includes a few other surprises: Bucks Lake and its giant Mackinaw trout and excellent rainbow fishery; the small and largely hidden trout streams of Middle Fork Feather and Spanish Creek; and kokanee salmon at Bullards Bar Reservoir.

I rank three of this chapter's lakes among the top 10 lakes for fishing in the state – Lake Oroville and Camanche Lake make the list for bass (25-fish days for bass are common at Lake Oroville from late March through mid-May), and Lake Amador makes it for bluegill and catfish. That is no small feat, considering they were rated against more than 300 other lakes.

Add it up and put it in your cash register – this is a great area to have a boat in which you can roam from lake to lake finding your own secret spots.

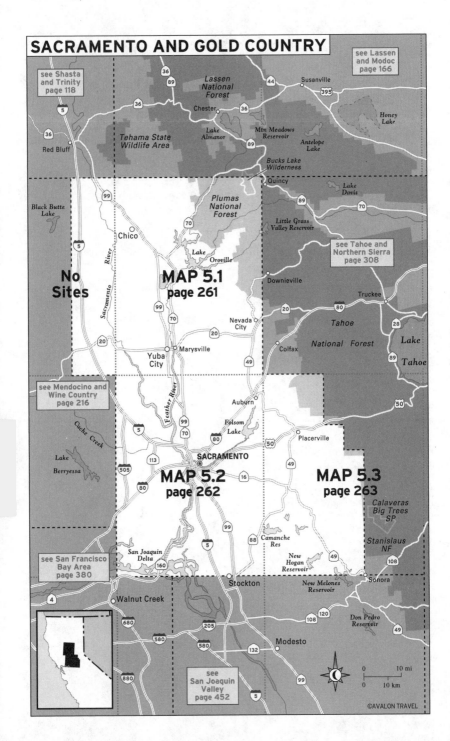

SACRAMENTO AND GOLD COUNTRY

see Shasta
and Trinity
page 118

see Lassen
and Modoc
page 166

Lassen
National
Forest

Susanville

Chester

Honey
Lake

Lake
Almanor

Mtn Meadows
Reservoir

Tehama State
Wildlife Area

Antelope
Lake

Red Bluff

Bucks Lake
Wilderness

Black Butte
Lake

Quincy

Lake
Davis

Plumas
National
Forest

No
Sites

Chico

Little Grass
Valley Reservoir

see Tahoe and
Northern Sierra
page 308

Lake
Oroville

MAP 5.1
page 261

Downieville

Truckee

Sacramento River

Feather River

Nevada
City

Tahoe

National   Forest

Lake
Tahoe

Colfax

Marysville

Yuba
City

see Mendocino and
Wine Country
page 216

Cache Creek

Auburn

Folsom
Lake

Placerville

Lake
Berryessa

SACRAMENTO

MAP 5.2
page 262

MAP 5.3
page 263

Calaveras
Big Trees
SP

Stanislaus
NF

see San Francisco
Bay Area
page 380

San Joaquin
Delta

Camanche
Res

New
Hogan
Reservoir

Sonora

Stockton

New Melones
Reservoir

Walnut Creek

Don Pedro
Reservoir

Modesto

see
San Joaquin
Valley
page 452

0   10 mi

0   10 km

©AVALON TRAVEL

Map 5.1

Sites 1-21
Pages 264-280

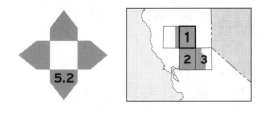

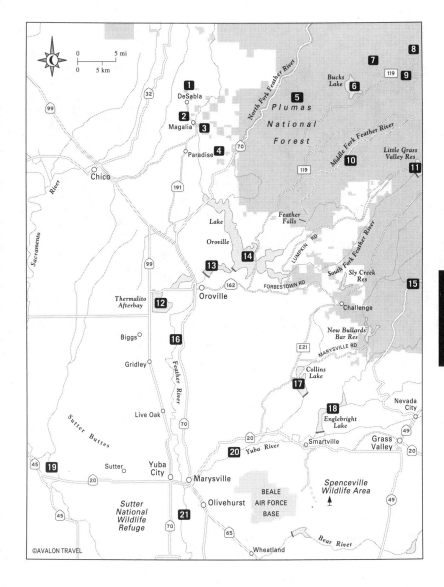

Map 5.2

Sites 22-34
Pages 281-294

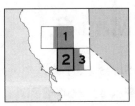

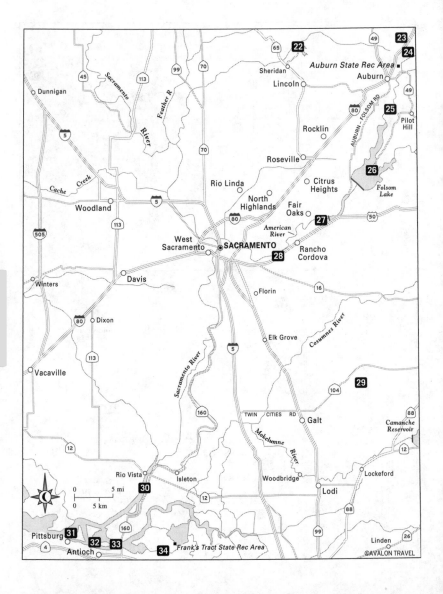

Map 5.3

Sites 35-43
Pages 296-303

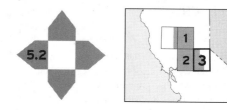

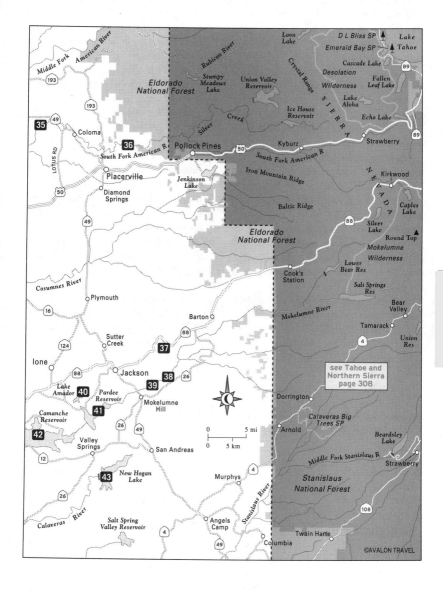

❶ BUTTE CREEK

Rating: 5

near Paradise in Lassen National Forest
Map 5.1, page 261

For the angler who has grown tired of the reservoirs in the area, especially on a hot day when a cold stream sounds even better than a cold beer, Butte Creek may be the answer. A trail follows the canyon, which makes access perfect for the angler who loves to hike and fish, stick-and-move. The shoe fits.

It is stocked with 10- to 12-inch trout, and not just little slim-jims. Virtually all out-of-towners miss this place because it's just far enough out of the way. As you drive to the stream you can have fun exploring the vicinity of Doe Mill Ridge and the surrounding Lassen National Forest.

Note that Butte Creek is subject to closures and catch-and-release sections, and that all anglers should carefully study the Department of Fish and Game (DFG) regulations before fishing.

Facilities, fees: There are no on-site facilities. A campground is available north of Butte Creek at Philbrook Reservoir, and in Paradise. Supplies can be obtained in Paradise. Fishing access is free.

Directions: From Chico, drive south on Highway 99 to Skyway Road. Turn east on Skyway Road and drive 10 miles to Paradise. Continue on Skyway Road for five miles to Doe Mill Road. Turn left on Doe Mill Road. Access is at the bridge nearby and farther north along the road.

Contact: Paradise Sporting Goods, 530/877-5114; The Tackle Box, Chico, 530/898-9761; Bureau of Land Management, Redding Field Office, 530/224-2100, www.blm.gov/ca.

❷ DE SABLA FOREBAY

Rating: 7

near Paradise
Map 5.1, page 261

Ever wanted to fish somebody's personal fishing reserve? If so, De Sabla Forebay, set at 2,800 feet in the Paradise foothills, provides that opportunity.

This little lake is a favorite of PG&E employees. Public access is permitted on the south and east sides of the lake, with access off Skyway Road. It's shoreline bait-dunking time, with no boats allowed.

The lake is stocked with rainbow trout. It also has some surprise brown trout. Here's an insider's note: if you can get hold of the vacation schedules of the PG&E hotshots who fish here, you will always know the best times to fish—that's when the best stocks are. Even though De Sabla is quite small, the water level always seems to be high, another perk for PG&E folks who enjoy the place.

Note: The group picnic area is booked nearly every summer weekend; if you plan on reserving it, do so far in advance.

Facilities, fees: No camping is permitted, but a recreational group picnic area is available by reservation on the east side. Boats are not permitted, but prams and float tubes are okay. Fishing access is free.

Directions: From Chico, take Highway 99 south to Skyway Road. Turn east on Skyway Road and drive 10 miles to Paradise. Drive through town and continue 10 more miles north to De Sabla Forebay.

Contact: The Tackle Box, Chico, 530/898-9761; Paradise Sporting Goods, 530/877-5114; Chico Fly Shop, 530/345-9983, www.chicoflyshopinc.com; PG&E Recreation Desk, 916/386-5164, www.pge.com/recreation.

❸ PARADISE LAKE

Rating: 5

near Paradise
Map 5.1, page 261

Anglers with any kind of imagination can conjure up all kinds of fantastic notions about a lake named Paradise. But keep your lid on before you overheat, because while it's nice, it's not quite that nice.

The best thing about Paradise Lake is that

it provides a more intimate setting to fish for trout in the spring and bass in the summer than Lake Oroville to the south. Because motors are not allowed, you don't have to worry about getting plowed under by water skiers and wakeboarders as you do at Oroville. Instead you get quiet water, ideal for small paddle-powered boats.

In the early summer, this can be a perfect place to bring a canoe, with the stern man paddling and the bow man casting along the shore for bass. Occasionally you might even pick up a large brown trout while casting for bass. Paradise Lake is stocked with rainbow trout ranging 10- to 12-inches, with a sprinkling of others in the two- to five-pound class.

In addition to largemouth bass, Paradise Lake has a resident population of catfish. The bass and catfish provide prospects in the summer months when the water is warmest. Lake records include: brown trout at 15 pounds; largemouth bass at 15 pounds; and catfish at 26 pounds.

The area experiences huge swings in temperature from season to season. It is at an elevation of 3,000 feet, where it gets heat from the valley in the summer and cold from Lassen National Forest in the winter.

Boating season runs from the last Saturday in April–November 15. No gas motors. Electric motors are okay. But fishing from shore is permitted year-round in designated areas.

Facilities, fees: A day-use picnic area is provided. No gas motors are permitted on the lake. No dogs are allowed. Camping is possible near Paradise. Supplies are in Paradise. The lake is closed on Wednesday. Boat-launching and day-use fees apply (either per day or by an annual pass).

Directions: From Chico, take Highway 99 south to Skyway Road. Turn east on Skyway Road and drive 10 miles to Paradise and Coutolenc Road. Turn right on Coutolenc Road and drive 3.5 miles to the lake entrance.

Contact: Paradise Lake, Paradise Irrigation District, 530/877-4971, www.paradise irrigation.com; Paradise Sporting Goods,

530/877-5114; The Tackle Box, Chico, 530/898-9761.

4 CONCOW RESERVOIR

Rating: 2

near Paradise

Map 5.1, page 261

The key to understanding Concow Reservoir lies in what the lake doesn't have, rather than what it does. No boats are allowed on this lake, there are no on-site facilities, and fishing is only in designated areas.

The fishing? That's not so great either. There are virtually no fish stocks of any kind. There are some resident rainbow trout, a few big brown trout that hide out and are difficult to find, and scarcely anything else. Other than that, it's a great place (heh, heh, heh). The easiest area to fish is the southern end, where a road drops down to the water.

Facilities, fees: Concow Campground has lake access, drinking water, and vault toilets. Supplies can be obtained in Oroville. Fishing access is free.

Directions: From Oroville, take Highway 70 north for 12 miles to Concow Road. Turn left and drive three miles to the reservoir.

Contact: Paradise Sporting Goods, 530/877-5114; The Tackle Box, Chico, 530/898-9761.

5 PLUMAS NATIONAL FOREST

Rating: 7

south of Lake Almanor

Map 5.1, page 261

Many of the lakes in this forest have been detailed elsewhere in this chapter. Three that have not been discussed are Smith Lake (just north of Snake Lake), Big Bear Lake, and Long Lake, in the Gold Lakes Basin.

All support populations of fish, but of the three, Long Lake is the premier attraction.

This lake is particularly beautiful—very clean, very deep—and requires only a half-mile hike to reach. The evening trout fishing can be good there. In addition to Long Lake, little Big Bear Lake, to the immediate south, adds an extra hike-in dimension to the Gold Lakes Basin, a premier destination.

Facilities, fees: Several campgrounds are provided on the Gold Lake Highway. Supplies are available in neighboring towns. Fishing access is free.

Directions: Access to the forest is off roads that junction with Highway 70, and also off the Gold Lake Highway from Graeagle to Gold Lake.

Contact: Plumas National Forest Headquarters, 530/283-2050, www.fs.fed.us/r5—click on Forest Offices.

6 BUCKS LAKE

Rating: 9

near Quincy in Plumas National Forest

Map 5.1, page 261

You want fish? Instead of searching all over creation, try Bucks Lake, where the fish come to you.

Bucks Lake is one of the most consistent trout producers in the western United States. It makes a good family destination, with clean, quality campsites, and is also perfect for know-hows who want to try for something special. Mackinaw trout nearing the 20-pound class are hooked every spring and the lake-record brown trout weighed 16 pounds. The lake is also home to rafts of rainbow trout and a sprinkling of kokanee salmon.

Rainbow trout supply the best fishing here. The top spot for that is by Rocky Point, close to where Bucks Creek enters the lake. The old river channel near where Mill Creek pours in is also quite good and has a sprinkling of the big Mackinaws.

Bucks Lake is at an elevation of 5,150 feet, so it gets snow—and plenty of it. As soon as the ice melts and the access road is plowed clear, the fishing tends to be the best of the year. That usually happens in the first week of May, but it all depends on the amount of late snow. Sometimes the lake is open on the last Saturday of April, the annual trout opener for mountain trout streams. Other times, it isn't open until Memorial Day weekend, or later, because the snow is so high. The stocks early in the season are large and consistent, with rainbow trout and brook trout in the 10- to 12-inch class and Eagle Lake fingerlings.

Most people fishing Bucks Lake are campers with trailered boats who launch in the late afternoon and then troll to catch the DFG planters. Most are very happy with this. Every once in a while, though, somebody catches one of those big ones, and it provides a glimpse of what is really possible here.

Many people like this lake because of the high catch rate for rainbow trout. When it comes to the Mackinaw, however, there is no rate to the catch. You can go a whole day without a nibble and the next morning get two in a half hour. It's like the fishing lottery of the northern Sierra.

Anglers catch good numbers of trout both trolling and fishing from shore. Since there are several good campgrounds and lodges at the lake, it makes an ideal destination for either hard-core anglers or families wanting to try trout fishing for the first time.

Know-hows fishing here eventually turn to the big ones, the Mackinaw trout. Mackinaw at Bucks Lake range to 20 pounds, with a number in the 10- to 18-pound class; most all are released to fight again another day. Whereas Mackinaws in Lake Tahoe have been caught as deep as 400 feet, at Bucks Lake you don't have to go much deeper than 70 feet and as little as 40 feet deep early in the year. The best methods are to troll a J plug or a silver M2 Flatfish or Kwikfish. Others prefer vertical jigging, using a Gibbs Minnow, Horizon minnow jig, or a Buzz Bomb.

Bucks Lake is one of the few lakes in this part of the mountains that produce a hexagenia hatch in early summer. This is when fly fishers in float tubes cast along the shallow muddy shorelines and often get into some of the lake's big trophy rainbow trout.

When I was a kid, I latched onto a friend's family, and they brought me with them on a fishing trip to Bucks Lake, where I limited on trout on back-to-back days. The next morning, just before leaving for home, I decided to brag about it in the little store there and found a game warden with willing ears.

After listening patiently to the 12-year-old who needed a straitjacket to stand still, the warden informed me that I had been fishing in a closed area—where all the fish were planted—and that I must go to jail.

I started crying, figuring it was the end of my life.

Then the warden put his arm around me and said, "Well, son, maybe I don't have to take you to jail after all. But from now on, make sure you check the fishing regulations every time before you start fishing."

I vowed I would, and it's a promise I've never broken.

Facilities, fees: Several campgrounds are provided on or near the lake. Drinking water, vault toilets, and garbage service are provided. A full-service marina, boat ramps, boat rentals, groceries, bait, and tackle are available. Fishing access is free.

Directions: From Oroville, take Highway 70 north to the junction with Highway 89. Turn south on Highway 89/70 and drive 11 miles to Quincy and Bucks Lake Road. In Quincy, turn right at Bucks Lake Road and drive 16.5 miles to Bucks Lake and the junction with Bucks Lake Dam Road/ Forest Service Road 33.

Contact: Sportsmen's Den, Quincy, 530/283-2733; Bucks Lake Lodge, 530/283-2262 or 800/481-2825, www.buckslakelodge.com; Bucks Lake Marina, 530/2i3-4243, www .BucksLakeMarina.com; Plumas National Forest, Mount Hough Ranger District, 530/283-0555, www.fs.fed.us/r5—click on Forest Offices; Plumas County Visitors Bureau, 800/326-2247, www.plumascounty.org.

▐ SILVER LAKE

Rating: 5

near Quincy in Plumas National Forest

Map 5.1, page 261

If you want a pan-sized fish to fry, Silver Lake can provide just that. These waters contain a lot of brook trout that are perfectly suited for the frying pan, though about one of every five trout caught here seems to be a rainbow. The DFG stocks rainbow and brook trout fingerlings annually. Silver Lake often seems to have so many brookies they need to be thinned out so that a few have a chance to grow bigger.

The surrounding area is quite attractive. The Pacific Crest Trail (PCT) is routed just above (west of) the lake, and little Gold Lake is a short distance south of here.

Facilities, fees: A campground is available. Vault toilets are provided, but drinking water is not, and garbage must be packed out. Supplies can be obtained in Quincy. Fishing access is free.

Directions: From Oroville, take Highway 70 north to the junction with Highway 89. Turn south on Highway 89/70 and drive 11 miles to Quincy. In Quincy, turn right at Bucks Lake Road and drive west for nine miles to Silver Lake Road. Turn right and drive seven miles to the campground, at the north end of the lake.

Contact: Sportsmen's Den, Quincy, 530/283-2733; Plumas National Forest, Mount Hough Ranger District, 530/283-0555, www.fs.fed .us/r5—click on Forest Offices.

▐ SNAKE LAKE

Rating: 3

near Quincy in Plumas National Forest

Map 5.1, page 261

A hard winter can cause Snake Lake to freeze nearly all the way to the bottom, killing about 70 percent of the fish. It does happen. Another more recent problem is the growing thatch of pond lilies. Worst of all, the Department of

Fish and Game (DFG) stopped planting the lake with rainbow trout fingerlings.

Snake Lake is quite shallow, so shallow in fact that the summer sun can heat up the lake enough to provide habitat for warm-water fisheries despite its mountain setting. Because of this, Snake Lake is home to bass, catfish, and bluegill, which are certainly a surprise. That's what keeps it in the book. It can be a shock for newcomers who think lakes in Plumas National Forest grow only trout.

Facilities, fees: A campground is provided. Vault toilets are available, but drinking water is not. Garbage must be packed out. There is a car-top boat launch (motors are not permitted on the lake). Supplies can be obtained in Quincy. Fishing access is free.

Directions: From Oroville, take Highway 70 north to the junction with Highway 89. Turn south on Highway 89/70 and drive 11 miles to Quincy. In Quincy, turn right at Bucks Lake Road and drive five miles to County Road 422. Turn right and drive two miles to the Snake Lake access road. Turn right and drive one mile to the campground on the right.

Contact: Plumas National Forest, Mount Hough Ranger District, 530/283-0555, www .fs.fed.us/r5—click on Forest Offices.

9 SPANISH CREEK

Rating: 6
near Quincy in Plumas National Forest
Map 5.1, page 261

The name of this creek doesn't mean much to most anglers, but it should. According to the Department of Fish and Game, each year some one million people try to go fishing on the opening day of trout season in California. If you want to avoid most of 'em, Spanish Creek is a good bet.

A multitude of various types of insects hatch on this water, which offers anglers good access, a mix of rainbow trout and brown trout, and a light sprinkling of quality brown trout. In addition, a habitat-enhancement program that

has been under way on Greenhorn Creek, a tributary to Spanish Creek, is helping restore the river to the way it was in the good old days. Insiders know that these waters are home to some huge but elusive brown trout.

Facilities, fees: Picnic tables, drinking water and vault toilets are available. Supplies can be obtained in Quincy. Fishing access is free.

Directions: In Quincy, take Bucks Lake Road west. Or take Quincy Junction north. Excellent access to the creek is available from either of these roads.

Contact: Sportsmen's Den, Quincy, 530/283-2733; Plumas National Forest, Mount Hough Ranger District, 530/283-0555, www.fs.fed .us/r5—click on Forest Offices.

10 MIDDLE FORK FEATHER RIVER

Rating: 9
northeast of Oroville in
Plumas National Forest
Map 5.1, page 261   BEST (

The Middle Fork Feather River is one of the top 10 trout streams in California—that is, providing you know which piece of the river to fish. The stretch above Quincy, while not unique, is decent: Fish and Game stocks it with 10- to 12-inch rainbow trout, access is quite easy, and if you want a quick evening hit, it can answer the request.

The stretch of river below the confluence of Nelson Creek, however, is a different chunk of territory. The river is unbridled, and so are the trout. This hike-in wilderness is for those with a pioneering spirit, which is another way of saying it takes one hell of a trek to get in and out of the canyon. As you make your way down to the river, you'll need a Forest Service map, a keen eye for spotting rattlesnakes, and a willingness for brush-bashing. Once there, you will find an untouched stream filled with wild trout that have never seen a Purina Trout Chow pellet.

Six-piece backpack rods are ideal, the kind

that can be converted instantly to a spinning rod or fly rod. During most of the day, when hatches are few and the trout are feeding subsurface, use the rod as a spinning rod and cast small lures into the heads of pools. At dawn or dusk, when the trout are rising to hatching insects, convert it to a fly rod and cast dry flies.

Obviously, this is not for everybody. But that is just one more reason this river is so special.

Facilities, fees: There are dispersed hike-in campsites along the river. Supplies can be obtained in Oroville, Quincy, and Blairsden. Fishing access is free.

Directions: In Oroville, drive to the junction of Highway 70 and 162. Turn north on Highway 162 (Olive Highway) and drive 26 miles to the town of Brush Creek and Bald Rock Road. Turn right (south) on Bald Rock Road and drive 0.5 mile to Forest Service Road 22N62 (Milsap Bar Road). Turn left and drive (steep, rough, and narrow) to Middle Fork Feather. Access is available directly off the road. Other sections of the Middle Fork Feather are accessible by hiking or driving to other trailheads and access points.

From Blairsden, take Highway 70/89 north. Access is available off the highway between the towns of Blairsden and Sloat, and off trails that junction with it.

Contact: Sportsmen's Den, Quincy, 530/283-2733; Plumas National Forest, Feather River Ranger District, 530/534-6500, www.fs.fed.us/r5—click on Forest Offices.

11 LITTLE GRASS VALLEY RESERVOIR

Rating: 7
near La Porte in Plumas National Forest
Map 5.1, page 261

This is your standard trolling/hardware lake. The way most fish it is to get a boat, rig with flashers trailing a night crawler, and troll slowly for rainbow trout in the foot-long class.

Little Grass Valley Reservoir, set at 5,000 feet in Plumas National Forest, provides popular lakeside camping and decent catch rates. Stocks are quite good, consisting of foot-long rainbow trout and fingerling kokanee salmon. By summer, when the fish descend to the thermocline, a number of boaters use leadcore lines to get 35–40 feet deep.

Kokanee seem to be off the radar here. By midsummer in a good water year, kokanee can reach 16 inches in length. A number of good-sized rainbows and browns are taken each year, many approaching five pounds. The biggest rainbow trout documented approached 19 pounds.

Add it up: a mountain lake with a decent amount of water, lakeside camps, boat ramps, and good trout stocks. Now put it in your cash register, and don't plan on being out here alone. This lake gets plenty of visitors.

Facilities, fees: Eight campgrounds, with flush toilets, drinking water, and an RV dump station, are available. There are three boat ramps and a fish-cleaning station. Fishing access is free.

Directions: To Wyandotte: From Oroville, take Highway 162 east for about eight miles to the junction signed Challenge/LaPorte. Bear right (to LaPorte) and drive east past Challenge and Strawberry Valley to LaPorte. Continue two miles past LaPorte to the junction with County Road 514/Little Grass Valley Road. Turn left and drive one mile to a junction. Turn left and drive one mile to the campground entrance road, on the right.

To Black Rock: Drive as above to LaPorte. Continue two miles past LaPorte to the junction with County Road 514/Little Grass Valley Road. Turn left and drive about five miles to the campground access road on the west side of the lake. Turn right on the access road and drive 0.25 mile to the campground and nearby boat ramp.

To Peninsula Tent: Drive as above to County Road 512 (which becomes County Road 514/Little Grass Valley Road) for three miles to Forest Road 22N57. Continue on Forest

Road 514 for one mile to the campground entrance on the right. Turn right and drive 0.25 mile to the campground.

Contact: Plumas National Forest, Feather River Ranger District, 530/534-6500, ww.fs.fed.us/r5—click on Forest Offices.

12 THERMALITO AFTERBAY

Rating: 5

near Oroville
Map 5.1, page 261

After spending a day at crowded Lake Oroville, people who own canoes, rowboats, and rafts might be ready to throw their boats over Feather Falls. But nearby Thermalito Afterbay provides a much saner option, with some good bass fishing as a bonus.

Anglers who poke and probe in small boats during the early morning and late evening hours will get good bass fishing results in the spring and early summer. When the water temperature is 65–70°F, the bass in the southeastern part of the lake can provide quite a surface bite.

The problem for small-boat owners at neighboring Oroville is that they can just about get plowed under by a speeding ski boat rounding a point on one of the upper lake arms. That doesn't seem to happen here.

In addition, Thermalito Afterbay doesn't look like the typical lake. The southwest portion is squarish, while the water to the east is shallow. The shallow areas provide good habitat for waterfowl in the winter. The reservoir regulates water levels downstream, and boaters should note any warning signs regarding changing water levels.

Facilities, fees: Two paved boat launches are provided, and all boats are permitted. Campgrounds are nearby at Lake Oroville. Supplies can be obtained in Oroville. Fishing access is free.

Directions: From Oroville, take Highway 162 (Oroville Dam Boulevard) west to the afterbay. Just before reaching the bridge on the afterbay, turn left on a paved road and drive a short distance to the launching area at Monument Hill.

To the ramp at Wilbur Road: From Oroville, take Highway 162 (Oroville Dam Boulevard) west to Wilbur Road. Turn right and continue (well-signed) to the boat launch.

Contact: Lake Oroville State Recreation Area, Lake Oroville Visitors Center (open weekends), 530/538-2219, www.parks.ca.gov; Huntington's Sportsman's Store, Oroville, 530/534-8000, www.huntingtonsports.com; Pro Bass Guide Service, 530/533-1510.

13 THERMALITO FOREBAY

Rating: 5

near Oroville in Lake Oroville
State Recreation Area
Map 5.1, page 261

With so many boaters, campers, and anglers heading over to nearby Lake Oroville, Thermalito Forebay is an option to those who prefer a quiet water with no motorized boats.

It may seem small compared to giant Lake Oroville, but the forebay is no pint-size cup of water. It provides some good fishing as well, and is best for trout in the spring, then bass in the early summer. Fish and Game stocks rainbow trout and brook trout, both in the 10- to 12-inch class. Shoreline prospects are decent, especially for anglers who keep on the move, exploring new spots rather than sitting like a statue all day.

The quality of camping is seasonally dependent. Set at an elevation lower than 1,000 feet, this area gets blasted with blowtorch heat day after day beginning midsummer—you might as well camp in the caldera of a volcano.

Facilities, fees: A day-use picnic area and a boat ramp are at the North Forebay. Restrooms with drinking water and flush toilets are available. No motorized boats are permitted, except for on the South Forebay, which also has a boat ramp. Camping is nearby at

Lake Oroville. Supplies can be obtained in Oroville. Day-use fees apply, and an annual day-use permit can be purchased.

Directions: To the North Forebay: Take Highway 70 to Oroville and continue two miles to Garden Drive. Turn left on Garden Drive and drive 0.5 mile to the picnic area.

To the South Forebay: Take Grand Avenue west and drive three miles to the parking area.

Contact: North Thermalito Forebay, 530/538-2221; Lake Oroville State Recreation Area, Lake Oroville Visitors Center (open weekends), 530/538-2219, www.parks.ca.gov; Huntington's Sportsman's Store, Oroville, 530/534-8000, www.huntingtonsports.com; Oroville Chamber of Commerce, 530/538-2542 or 800/655-4653, www.orovillechamber.net.

14 LAKE OROVILLE

Rating: 10

near Oroville

Map 5.1, page 261

At first glance, Oroville seems to have it all: campgrounds, enough water for all kinds of boating, and a fish for every angler. I've had some great days on Oroville. One time on my TV show, we filmed a bass trip here, and as you might figure, the jinx of a TV camera has a way of bringing out rain and causing the fish not to bite. Sure enough, it poured rain. The batteries on my boat had to be replaced. But by the time we got on the lake, it was midday. In three hours we caught about 20 bass, including several 14- to 17-inchers, the cameras rolling like crazy. Anywhere else I would have been in panic. Not at Oroville. In the spring, this is one of the best lakes to catch bass in the state.

Covering more than 15,000 acres, Lake Oroville is a huge reservoir with extensive lake arms and a large central body of water. Fish? It's got 'em—a wide variety, including rainbow trout, brown trout, largemouth bass, catfish, bluegill, crappie, and a significant salmon population. The DFG plants fingerling brown trout and fingerling and yearling chinook salmon.

The bass fishery has undergone a dramatic change from a decade ago. Spotted bass are now the main bass species taken. Largemouths are still caught by anglers fishing in the coves, brush, and wood throughout the lake; smallmouths are relatively rare in the catches, but spotted bass are abundant.

The introduction of the spotted bass has created a great winter bass fishery that didn't exist before, since the "spots" continue to be active after the water temperatures dip below 50°F, unlike their largemouth and smallmouth cousins, according to DFG fishery biologist Dennis Lee. In fact, some of the prime fishing is from December through March, when everything from spooning with Kastmasters and Hopkins spoons in deep water to tossing spinnerbaits into the mouths of rain-gorged creeks yields results at times. Dropshotting can be sensational, sometimes where you can get directly over the bass, fish vertically, jigging lightly.

The "slot" limit, where only fish under 12 inches or over 15 inches may be kept, is largely credited with making Oroville one of the better bass lakes in the state. That is why there are more big spotted bass at Oroville than at any other lake in Northern California. Also, it has the Northern California record: 14 pounds, 11 ounces.

The bass fishing can be fantastic in the spring, the one time of year when greatness is possible. In late spring, bass anglers can experience spurts of fantastic days when everything comes together: no wind, the bass hanging out in the top five feet of water up the lake arms, and a catch of 15 or 30 fish. It is best to try for bass at high water in the spring, casting to the backs of caves. The fish often hide below floating debris and wood.

If you're unfamiliar with the lake, one of the best areas to try for bass is the Middle Fork, especially from the mouth of the canyon up to the Bidwell Bar Bridge. Fish here from late winter into early summer, working the north shoreline along the steep rocks. How good is it? This can produce 30-fish days, with most of the bass running 12–14 inches and about one out of five running bigger. One of the best lures is a salt-and-pepper worm with a chartreuse tail, either four or six inches long and rigged on a darthead.

Some big trout also live in this lake, and they provide good trolling results during the seasonal transitions from winter to spring and from fall to winter. The fishing is best well up the lake arms, particularly if you troll for big browns with a jointed Rapala during the cool fall months, or for small rainbow trout using the traditional flasher/night crawler combination. Most of the year, however, the surface waters get so warm that the trout stay very deep—60–80 feet down, sometimes even deeper—and few anglers like to fish that deep in a lake. A Scotty downrigger can solve that.

For trollers, the most common catch at Lake Oroville is chinook salmon.

Salmon can be found all over the lake, but two spots are best. The first is by the dam, where water is pumped back into the depths of the lake to infuse oxygen into the cool depths. Trolling 125 feet is common near the dam. The second is about halfway up the North Fork arm; 60 feet down is usually about right here.

You have to use your fish locator to find the schools of fish, but when you find them, rest assured they will be there for weeks at a time—and you have your very own secret spot. Try trolling Speedy Shiners, Rapalas, or Sparklefish.

There is a chance of catching brown trout ranging over five pounds by trolling the points between the Bidwell Bar Bridge and Canyon Creek either very early in the morning or very late in the evening. Use large Rebels and Rapalas trolled on a long line anywhere from 15–35 feet deep.

The Lake Oroville Fishery Enhancement Committee (LOFEC) is demanding improved management of fishery habitat, water levels, and recreation sites. Significant black-bass habitat projects have been completed.

At an elevation of 900 feet in foothill country, the lake gets some very hot temperatures in the summer, and anybody who isn't prepared will shrivel like a raisin.

The Department of Water Resources has funded recreation opportunities at this lake, and it provides some unique opportunities for camping. They include a floating barge of a campground. It's like a houseboat without a motor and is one of the best group campground deals anywhere in California. There are also floating restrooms, as well as floating platforms for tents.

Lake records: 15.48-pound largemouth bass (released); 19-pound, 11-ounce king salmon; 9-pound silver salmon; 15-pound brown trout; 15-pound rainbow trout; 2-pound, 10-ounce black crappie; 3-pound, 4-ounce white crappie; 6-pound smallmouth bass; 25-pound channel catfish; 27-pound white catfish; 97-pound sturgeon.

Facilities, fees: Several campgrounds, including Bidwell Canyon, Limesaddle, and Loafer Creek, are available in addition to floating platforms for camping and boat-in camping. There are restrooms with flush toilets, coin showers, and RV dump stations. Two full-service marinas, boat ramps, boat rentals, groceries, gas, bait, and tackle are nearby. Day-use fees apply, or an annual day-use permit can be purchased.

Directions: From Oroville, take Highway 162 east for seven miles east to Canyon Drive. Turn left and drive two miles to Oroville Dam. Turn left and drive over the dam to the spillway parking lot at the end of the road. Register at the entrance station. Boats can be launched from this area.

To the state recreation area: From the Sacramento area, take I-5 north to the junction with Highway 99/70. Turn north on Highway 99/70 and continue on Highway 70 into Oroville to Highway 162. Turn east and drive two miles to the Olive Highway. Turn right on Olive Highway (still Highway 162) and drive six miles to Kelly Ridge Road. Turn left (north) on Kelly Ridge Road and drive 1.5 miles to Arroyo Drive. Turn right on Arroyo Drive and drive one mile to the state park entrance.

Contact: Lake Oroville State Recreation Area, Lake Oroville Visitors Center (open weekends), 530/538-2219, www.parks.ca.gov; Oroville Chamber of Commerce, 530/538-2542 or 800/655-4653, www.orovillechamber.net; Bidwell Canyon Marina, 530/589-9175, bidwellcanyonmarina.com; Lime Saddle Marina, 530/877-2414.

Supplies: Huntington's Sportsman's Store, Oroville, 530/534-8000, www.huntingtonsports.com.

Guides: Cash Colby, 530/533-1510; Larry Hemphill, 530/674-0276, www.imhooked.com; G&J Outdoor Enterprises, 530/885-1492, www.gandjoutdoors.com.

15 BULLARDS BAR RESERVOIR

Rating: 10

near Camptonville in Tahoe National Forest

Map 5.1, page 261

Compared to other reservoirs in the Central Valley foothills, Bullards Bar stands out like a silver dollar in a field of pennies. Many believe it is the No. 1 lake in California for spotted bass. The lake appears remote, but by midday Sunday, I guarantee that skilled bassers have cast to every good spot on the lake Friday through Sunday. If you can go on Tuesday, Wednesday, or Thursday, prospects for being the first to cast to a fish that day are much better. The results can be spectacular; five-fish, 15-pound limits aren't unusual at all, and many do better.

So many of the 155 major reservoirs in California are simply water-storage facilities, drawn down at the whim of water brokers, regardless of the effects on recreation and fisheries. The folks who control the plumbing at Bullards Bar somehow manage to keep it nearly full through July, even in low-rain years, when other reservoirs are turned into dust bowls. The reservoir, which is at an elevation of 2,300 feet, has 55 miles of shoreline and covers a lot of territory. So you get good lakeside camping and boating, and the kind of beauty that goes with high water levels.

Bullards Bar has a growing population of smallmouth bass and largemouth bass. Anglers who toss split-shotted four-inch plastic worms off the points in the Yuba and Willow Creek arms of the lake seem to do the best, but all the familiar tricks for bass in reservoirs can work. The best fishing takes place from late winter through early summer. Other options include catfish, crappie, sunfish, and kokanee salmon.

From late May through the month of November, limits of kokanee are quite common. Most years, the fish are much smaller than in other kokanee lakes. An 11- to 12-inch kokanee is about par. The DFG stocks fingerling kokanee salmon here in the thousands every year.

The trolling depth varies with water temperatures, with trolling depths down to 80 feet common by late August. The best combination is the Sling Blade dodger or any other dodger with a kokanee bug, Koke-a-Nut, Uncle Larry's spinner, Wedding Ring spinner, or any small, brightly colored wobbler—all of which should be tipped with a piece of white corn.

When fishing the lake for the first time and looking for kokanee, start near the dam and work your way up the lake. Sooner or later you'll find small concentrations of boats, and you can bet there are kokanee in those areas.

Fish and Game stocks Bullards Bar with rainbow trout fingerlings, and trolling results are excellent. In the spring, don't be surprised if you hook a big resident brown trout. One of the best techniques is to start with a set of Cousin Carl's Half-Fast Flashers, then hook on a No. 0 Luhr Jensen Wedding Spinner, which comes with a tied leader. With a worm threader, add half a night crawler on the hook, then slow troll until you find fish.

The main feeder stream to this reservoir is the North Fork Yuba River. That's a good place to start fishing. If the lake is full, two boat-in camps are available, as well as dispersed boat-in camping around the lake. Boat-in campers are required to have a portable chemical toilet.

Facilities, fees: A full-service marina is at Emerald Cove, which offers fishing-boat, ski-boat, pontoon-boat, and houseboat rentals. A snack bar and convenience store are also available. Boat-in camping includes two developed boat-in campgrounds with vault toilets, as well as many primitive boat-in sites with no drinking water, where boaters are required to bring portable chemical toilets (they are also available for rent). Garbage must be packed out. Full supplies can be obtained in Marysville, Camptonville, Dobbins, Grass Valley, and Nevada City. Fishing access is free.

Directions: To Emerald Cove Marina: From Marysville, take Highway 20 northeast to Marysville Road/County Road E21. Turn north at Marysville Road (signed Bullards Bar Reservoir) and drive 12 miles to Old Marysville Road. Turn right and drive 14 miles to reach the entrance road for Cottage Creek Launch Ramp and the marina (turn left just before the dam).

To reach the Dark Day boat ramp: Continue over the dam and drive four miles. Turn left on Dark Day Road and continue to the ramp.

Contact: For boat-in camping, reservations, and a shoreline camping permit contact Emerald Cove Resort and Marina, 530/692-3200, www.bullardsbar.com; Tahoe National Forest, Yuba River Ranger District, 530/288-3231, www.fs.fed.us/r5—click on Forest Offices; Yuba County Water Agency, 530/741-6278.

Guide: Tight Lines Guide Service, Grass Valley, 530/263-0990 or 530/263-7944, www.fishtightlines.com.

16 FEATHER RIVER (OROVILLE TO YUBA CITY/MARYSVILLE)

Rating: 8

upstream of Yuba City/Marysville

Map 5.1, page 261

The Feather has become one of the brightest spots in California for salmon, striped bass and shad. Good natural spawning in the river's low-flow section, combined with a state-of-the-art hatchery facility in Oroville, have made the Feather a salmon factory. The main interception point is the Thermalito Afterbay outlet hole, where shore anglers casting spinners or bead/yarn combinations, as well as boaters back-bumping roe or Kwikfish lures or jigging Gibbs Minnows, catch thousands of fish per season. Do not snag salmon. Got it?

Salmon can be caught in the Feather River as early as March to May, but the runs peak in September. Fishing starts at the mouth of the Feather River at Verona. The technique is to anchor a boat, then let a Flatfish or Spinner wobble in the current downstream of the boat.

There are several boat ramps. One is on the Yuba City side of the river. The other is on the Marysville side of the river, near the mouth of the Yuba. Above Yuba City there are about 10 miles of river you can fish if you have a jet boat, but there is no public access from shore anywhere in this section. There's also river access adjacent to the towns of Live Oak and Gridley.

Unlike the Sacramento River, the Lower Feather River has no salmon closures and can offer the finest salmon fishing in the valley.

The best opportunity for bank anglers to catch salmon is at the Thermalito Outlet Hole and downstream, in the several miles of riffles and pools. This section of river is a Fish and Game Wildlife Area. Bank fishing is also accessible at Shanghai Bend and various places just below Yuba City. When boating through this area, be extremely careful at low flows because there can be many shallow spots. Another good spot is below the Highway 99 bridge. This is a big hole known as Beer Can Beach.

The upper river above Yuba City is confined to jet boats and drift boats because of the many shallow riffles.

The salmon run peaks in September here. The season closes September 30 above Honcut Creek. In late fall, steelhead start entering the river. Check DFG regulations for rolling closures.

Note that the upstream low-flow area can provide prime steelhead fishing, but that both bank and jet-boat access are severely limited. Unless you take the time to learn the bank access points, most success is with a drift boat.

Steelhead can be caught throughout the winter, providing storms don't muddy up the upper sections. That happens rarely, since flows are controlled at Oroville Dam. Pink or champagne-colored Glo Bugs are the top steelhead patterns.

Striped bass fishing usually peaks in late May. In the spring, striped bass can provide very good fishing, especially in the lower sections. The area downstream of Boyd's Pump (which is below the town of Yuba City) can provide outstanding striped bass fishing. A bonus is that the river is usually high at this time of year, so boats can use propellers without severe risk of prop strikes. Check river levels for safe operation.

Many people simply anchor and fish with bait, and others troll. But the technique that can result in tremendous numbers of fish is to drift the major holes and runs with jumbo live minnows. Most of the stripers you catch will be about 4–10 pounds.

Shanghai Bend is one of the best spots in the state for shad, which move into the river in good numbers in May. It is downriver from the mouth of the Yuba River, a prime, wadable piece of water that can provide tremendous fishing when flows are below 3,500 cubic feet per second (CFS). In the first and second weeks of May, anglers

sometimes catch 20–25 shad in an evening. The best years are when stream flows are up, not down. There can be long periods, of course, when catches are sparse, but if you get in on one of these runs, you'll never forget it.

The odds are better, however, if you have a boat. The shad arrive at the river's confluence with the Sacramento River, at Verona. Boaters anchor there and cast right at the point where the two rivers blend, one of the top spots for shad anywhere.

With a boat, it is also much easier to chase migrating salmon and striped bass.

Facilities, fees: Campgrounds and supplies are in the Oroville area. Fishing access is free. A shuttle service for drift boats is available from McGrath's (530/533-8564).

Directions: From Sacramento, take I-5 north to the exit for Highway 99/70. Turn north on Highway 99/70 and drive to Marysville and continue north on Highway 70 (the river is about one mile to the west, bridged by East Gridley Road). The area north of the Table Mountain bicycle bridge is closed to all fishing. Areas south of the bridge are open seasonally; check current DFG regulations.

To boat ramps: Riverbend Park has a boat ramp with good adjacent parking. To reach it, from Oroville take Highway 70 north to Montgomery Street. Take that exit, turn left on Montgomery Street, and drive 0.25 mile to Riverbend Park.

Palm Avenue launch ramp is an unimproved ramp at the bottom of the Oroville Wildlife Area. The Vance Avenue ramp and Thermolito Afterbay Outlet launch are off Larkin Road. River Reflections RV Park (530/534-1995) has a launch ramp and campsites, restrooms, and showers. A ramp is available in Gridley off of East Gridley Road; get a pass and key at 685 Kentucky Street in Gridley.

Contact: Huntington's Sportsman's Store, Oroville, 530/534-8000, www.huntington sports.com; G&J Outdoor Enterprises, 530/885-1492, www.gandjoutdoors.com.

17 COLLINS LAKE

Rating: 9

north of Marysville in
Collins Lake Recreation Area

Map 5.1, page 261

Every reservoir goes through a unique evolution, and Collins Lake seems to be peaking in productivity. This is one of the few lakes where both bass and trout thrive. Trout fishing is excellent in the spring, when the cool, pure flows of Dry Creek and Willow Glen Creek fill the lake. Then in early summer, when the surface temperatures warm significantly, the largemouth bass come to life. More than 50,000 trout are planted here every spring; thousands of these are 3–8 pounds.

Set at 1,200 feet in the foothill country of Yuba County, this is a pretty spot that's ideal for the angler who wants to camp and has a boat. I prefer fishing here in April or early May, and then again from mid-September through October, when the lake is quiet, the surface temperatures are cool, and the fishing is best. During the hot summer months in between, the trout are deep (though good results are possible using deep-water trolling techniques), bass fishing is a dawn/dusk affair, and you can run into water-skier traffic.

Before the water warms in summer, Collins provides outstanding prospects for trout. From shore, Power Bait and night crawlers are the preferred entreaties.

There are about 12 miles of shoreline, and you can explore most of it in a weekend while trolling for trout. That is how most of the trout here are caught, by people using standard trolling techniques. Depth is always the key factor. The trout are found in shallow water during the cool months, then they go deeper and deeper month after month into summer. By late July it is common to fish for trout 40–45 feet deep.

The reward is rainbow trout that average 14–16 inches, plus a few similar-sized brown trout and, once in a while, a huge brown that will make you think you've hooked Moby Trout. As part of the largest private stocking program north of Sacramento, trout 1–10 pounds are planted here.

Collins is also an outstanding bass lake, with smallmouth, largemouth, and spotted bass. The lake record for spotted bass is over 8 pounds, while large bass of over 10 pounds are occasionally caught. Smallmouth bass exceeding three pounds are also taken.

The brushy shoreline and river arm are ideal bass habitat, and other areas of rocky shoreline are perfect for smallmouth. If you're careful in the willows and weeds, you can cast crankbaits for some of the bigger fish. Since snags seem inevitable, most prefer plastics.

A 10-inch Power Worm fished at night here has enticed some huge bass. In the late winter and early spring, the small, soft, hand-poured worms in both four- and six-inch sizes (in translucent colors) can work well with all three bass species.

Waterskiing is permitted in only the lower half of the lake in the summer, saving the upper half of the lake for anglers and those seeking solitude. In the fall, winter, and spring months, no waterskiing is allowed at all.

This is a good fishing lake. If you are one of those poor anglers who believe they are afflicted with a terrible jinx, show up here during late April or early May and get the cure.

Lake records: 15-pound, 4-ounce largemouth bass; 8-pound, 9-ounce spotted bass; 13-pound, 4-ounce rainbow trout; 9-pound brown trout; 21-pound, 2-ounce catfish; 2-pound, 13-ounce crappie.

Facilities, fees: Campgrounds, a full-service marina, a boat ramp and rentals, and supplies are at the lake. Restrooms, drinking water, flush toilets, an RV dump station, coin-operated showers, sandy swimming beach, volleyball, grocery store, coin laundry, wood, ice, and propane gas are also available. A per vehicle day-use fee is charged, as well as a daily boat-launch fee.

Directions: From Marysville, drive east on Highway 20 about 12 miles to Marysville Road. Turn north and drive approximately

eight miles to the recreation area entrance road, on the right. Turn right, drive a mile to the entrance station, and then continue to the campground, on the left side of the road.
Contact: Collins Lake Recreation Area, 800/286-0576, www.collinslake.com; Tight Lines Guide Service, 530/263-0990 or 530/263-7944, www.fishtightlines.com.

18 ENGLEBRIGHT LAKE

Rating: 7

northeast of Marysville
Map 5.1, page 261

Remember this place—providing, that is, you have a boat. Englebright always seems to have plenty of water, waterskiing is prohibited on the upper end, and in the spring it's as if the lake is waging a trout war with Collins Lake to the north to determine which can provide the best fishing. Best of all, it has some of the nicest boat-in campsites anywhere. One little problem: There's almost zero access for shore fishing.

The reservoir is in the foothills of Yuba and Nevada Counties at an elevation of about 500 feet. It has an unusual shape. With 24 miles of shoreline, it looks something like a water snake winding its way through the Yuba River Canyon, called "The Narrows" by locals.

Anglers are better off visiting in the spring, when the water is cool, the skiers few, and the trout near the surface. That is also when the water starts getting stocked. Plants continue at frequent intervals for a total of 18,000 rainbow trout. Although most of the rainbows planted in Englebright range in size 10–12 inches, they seem to add inches to their bodies in a relatively short time. During the spring, trollers dragging flasher/night crawler rigs nab 16- and 17-inchers pretty regularly. Every once in a while somebody will hang a big brown.

If you can get away during a weekday in March, you may be surprised by bass up to 2.5 pounds. My best suggestion here is to work the drop-offs along the shore with a four- or six-inch plastic worm (with a chartreuse tail). By summer, the catch rates fall off.

The weather gets hot here in the summer, and water-skiers really like this place, because narrow channels provide calmer water for waterskiing than a wide-open lake.

If you visit during the peak summer months, you can escape all of the water-skiers by heading upstream. Waterskiing is not permitted upstream of a line of demarcation called Upper Boston. The trolling is often quite good near the point where the South Fork Yuba enters the lake, especially in the fall.

Facilities, fees: There are 100 boat-in sites. Vault toilets are provided, as are two paved ramps—one just east of the dam, adjacent to the picnic area, and one at the marina, at Skipper's Cove. There are signs for each on the entrance road. Drinking water is at each boat launch and at the marina. Boat rentals (including houseboats), mooring, fuel dock, and groceries are available. There is a boat-launching fee and day-use fee, however, fishing access is free.

Directions: From Auburn, take Highway 49 north to Grass Valley and the junction with Highway 20. Turn west on Highway 20 and drive to Mooney Flat Road (if you reach Smartville, you have gone a mile too far). Turn right on Mooney Flat and drive 2.5 miles to the park entrance on the left. Turn left at the fork and drive a mile to park headquarters and the boat ramp, just east of the dam.

Contact: Skipper's Cove, 530/432-6302, www .englebrightlake.com; U.S. Army Corps of Engineers, Sacramento District, Englebright Lake, 530/432-6427, www.corpslakes.usace .army.mil.

19 SACRAMENTO RIVER

Rating: 7

from Colusa to Sacramento
Map 5.1, page 261

From Colusa to Sacramento, this stretch of river represents the best and worst of the

Central Valley. The upside includes good prospects for big salmon, striped bass, and sturgeon (and many shad, too) during their respective migrations upriver. The downside is what the U.S. Army Corps of Engineers has done to much of the area here.

During the months of March, April, and May, the Sacramento River within the city limits of Sacramento and through Freeport offers excellent striped bass fishing. The preferred method here is to anchor in a boat and fish with sardines. Of course other baits will work, such as shad and anchovies, but sardines rule the roost. Little trolling is done here for striped bass, especially compared to downstream, in the vicinity of Walnut Grove and Isleton.

In the fall, salmon fishing takes hold of the entire Sacramento River. In Sacramento proper they start catching them as early as late August, but the fishing isn't strong until mid-September, and October is the peak.

Both spinners and Flatfish and Kwikfish are used in the Sacramento area. As you move up into the Knights Landing area, it's almost all Flatfish and Kwikfish. However, in the vicinity of Grimes and Colusa, it's almost all spinners. This may be because most resort owners in this area manufacture their own spinners. Regardless, they do catch fish. Then when you get above Colusa, everybody is again using Flatfish and Kwikfish.

The Colusa portion of the river is the most attractive. In the spring this is where striped bass spawn in large numbers. Some 75 percent of the striper spawning originally took place in the San Joaquin Delta until the giant state and federal water pumps at Clifton Court virtually destroyed the stripers there; now they head up to Colusa on the Sacramento River to do their thing.

If you have a boat, a graph, and a good supply of lures, you can do your thing, too. The river cannot be fished effectively from shore, and the graph helps locate the major holes and bottom drop-offs where the fish hold. These spots are where you troll the large

Rebel minnows for striped bass (March into early June). Or anchor and cast leadheads with plastic grubs into the holes; 20-fish days can be common when the bite is on in April. For salmon, use T-55 or M-2 Flatfish (mid-August through mid-October); and anchor and use mud shrimp or ghost shrimp for sturgeon (December through March).

The section of the Sacramento River from Discovery Park to Freeport produces top-notch bank fishing for both stripers and king salmon at times. Bank anglers trying for stripers in the spring from March–May will often do better than boaters, particularly while fishing during high runoff conditions, when it's difficult for boaters to get out on the river. There are usually two or three weeks every May, usually late May, when this can be some of the best fishing in California.

The stretch of river below the Freeport Bridge is a local hot spot for bank anglers to toss out Blue Fox Vibrax and Mepps No. 5 spinners for salmon from July–November. Bank anglers seem to do better than boaters in August and September, while the boaters seem to prevail in October. This may be because the salmon tend to hold close to the bank earlier in the season, so the bank anglers have a better shot than boaters. Many boaters seem to be convinced that the top place to fish is right in the middle of the river, regardless of whether the chinooks are holding there or not.

In the Sacramento area, many natural areas hold fish in the course of their respective migrations. The most famous are the Minnow Hole, just south of Sacramento; the mouth of the American River, at Discovery Park; and the mouth of the Feather River, at Verona. This is no secret, and you can expect plenty of company on the water when the fish are moving through.

Other good spots include the I-880 bridge; Government Dock, north of Discovery Park; Miller Park, Sacramento; Brickyards, south of Minnow Hole; Garcia Bend; the "Line," just below the Freeport Bridge; and Clarksburg Flat, in Clarksburg.

The Sacramento River in and around the metropolitan Sacramento area can also be good for summer potluck fishing. Use a depth finder to locate 12- to 17-foot-deep holes on the outsides of bends and then anchor close to shore. Catfish and small schoolie-sized stripers, 16–20 inches, tend to hang in these areas, and you can catch them on chunks of anchovy or sardine.

A newcomer to the area may be puzzled about where to begin, but it's quite simple. The fish are either moving through or they're not. When they are, get on the river, pick one of the recommended spots, and wait in line with the rest of the boats.

When I canoed the entire Sacramento River, this particular section left the most lasting memories. The Colusa area is beautiful. But downstream of Grimes, many long segments have been converted into a canal by the U.S. Army Corps of Engineers, which turned the riverbanks into riprapped levees, complete with beveled edges and 90° turns. These parts of the river are treeless and virtually birdless, and the fish simply use it as a highway, migrating straight upriver without pausing. They have little reason to.

But around Colusa and Sacramento, it's a different story. Near Colusa, the river is quite beautiful as it winds its way southward. The banks are lined with trees, and there are some deep holes, gravel bars, and good fishing in season. And while the river is leveed off near Sacramento, there are also some good holes where fish will hold up on their upriver journey. In between, there are precious few spots, the best being in the vicinity of Grimes and Knight's Landing.

Facilities, fees: Campgrounds, lodging, boat rentals, and supplies are available in the Sacramento area. Fishing access is free.

Directions: Access is off roads that intersect I-5. You'll find boat ramps at the following locations: Colusa–Sacramento River State Recreation Area, in Colusa; Ward's Boat Landing, on Butte Slough Road, south of Colusa; Verona Marina, on Garden Highway, in Verona; Elkhorn Boat Launch, northwest of Sacramento, on Bayou Way; Alamar Marina, on Garden Highway, in Sacramento; Discovery Park, in Sacramento, at the confluence of the Sacramento and American Rivers; Miller Park, below the Capitol City Freeway; and Garcia Bend, off I-5, in South Sacramento.

Contact: Sacramento Department of Parks & Recreation, 916/808-5200, www.sacramento river.org (click on Access).

Marinas: Freeport Marina, 916/665-1555; Sherwood Harbor Marina, 916/371-3471; Clarksburg Marina, 916/744-1505; Stan's Yolo Marina, 916/371-7040.

Supplies: Broadway Bait, Rod & Gun, Sacramento, 916/448-6338; Freeport Bait, Sacramento, 916/665-1935; Johnson's Bait & Tackle, Yuba City, 530/674-1912, www .johnsonsbait.com.

20 YUBA RIVER

Rating: 7

east of Marysville from
Brown's Valley to Marysville
Map 5.1, page 261

The Yuba, unique among the major Central Valley rivers, is having a wild, self-sustaining run of steelhead; the fisheries of the Feather, American, and Sacramento Rivers are for the most part hatchery-supported. The clear, deep pools and cool water found in the stretch from Englebright Dam to Highway 20 sustain steelhead throughout the summer months. The Yuba is a popular river for catch-and-release fly-fishing enthusiasts using a variety of steelhead flies. Over the years, the biggest problem has been that the Yuba has poor public access, but that has been largely solved (and we'll get to that).

There are 30 miles of river along Highway 20, from Englebright Dam to Yuba City. Yet no other river in the state has less public access, and even what is provided can change each year. The upper section of the Yuba above the Parks Bar Bridge can hold good populations of native rainbow trout. However, it's virtually all private, and access is at the whim of the owner.

The lower part of the Yuba has the ability to attract steelhead in the winter and shad in the spring. But the key with anadromous fish is freshwater. That's what attracts them. When the flows are low, there is little else that can compel them onward. But when the river is flowing sufficiently, the Yuba provides know-how anglers with a unique opportunity. The shad arrive in May and the steelhead in January and February, and though access is limited, some fine catches can be made. When everything is right, this can be an exceptional water. But it's rare when everything is right.

The river also attracts wild runs of spring and fall chinook salmon. The runs vary widely from year to year, depending upon water conditions. Like so many rivers in the Central Valley, the Yuba is a prisoner of water releases from reservoirs upstream.

Since this is a wild fishery, it is subject to barbless hooks and artificial-lure-only restrictions; check your "Fish and Game Sportfishing Regulations Summary and Supplements" for the latest restrictions.

And what of increased access? A special drawing is held that provides access to the Lower Yuba River in Brown's Valley. Each year, fishing dates are announced in April, May, June, July, and August, usually two days per month. To apply, contact: DFG, River Fishing Access, 1701 Nimbus Road, Suite A, Rancho Cordova, CA 95670. The access is limited to 15 anglers per day to the site location 1.5 miles upstream from the Highway 20 Bridge. Access allows anglers to fish both banks between posted boundaries. In addition, anglers can launch car-top boats, canoes, kayaks, rafts, and float tubes. But any boat, such as a large inflatable, that requires the use of a trailer is not allowed. For more information, call 916/358-2926.

Facilities, fees: Camping is available at Live Oak Campground (north of Yuba City) and at Sycamore Ranch in Brown's Valley. Boat ramps are at both campgrounds. Lodging and supplies are in Yuba City. Fishing access is free.

Directions: At the junction of I-5 and Highway 20, just north of Williams, take Highway 20 east for 30 miles to Marysville. Access is at the Simpson Lane Bridge in Marysville, and at the E Street Bridge on Highway 20.

Contact: Sycamore Ranch RV Park, 530/741-1190 (group camping reservations) or 800/834-1190; Johnson's Bait & Tackle, Yuba City, 530/674-1912, www.johnsonsbait.com; Star Bait & Tackle, Marysville, 530/742-5431.

Guides: Three Rivers Guide Service, 530/925-7990, www.threeriversguideservice.com; G&J Outdoor Enterprises, 530/885-1492, www.gandjoutdoors.com.

21 FEATHER RIVER (YUBA CITY/MARYSVILLE TO VERONA)

Rating: 8

downstream of Yuba City/Marysville

Map 5.1, page 261

If you want fish, and I mean lots of fish, show up at Shanghai Bend during the second week of May, and you won't be disappointed.

The Feather River is on the road to becoming the No. 1 shad river in the Central Valley. How? With low flows most years on the American River to the south, many shad seem to be bypassing the American and heading farther up the Sacramento River, then turning right at the Feather.

You hear the tales: 35, 40, 50 shad in a single evening, sometimes even more. It actually happens here in May, when the shad arrive en masse and head upstream. If the shad army moves through while you're in a boat at the mouth of the Feather River at Verona, or while you're wading at Shanghai Bend, greatness is possible. The more likely scenario is catching 5–10 fish, enjoying the first warm days of the year, and maybe getting a sunburn. Every year the best fishing falls somewhere in a 15-day span starting in early May. Johnson's Bait & Tackle provides the most reliable information on the timing and the strength of the run.

You'll have a different tale to tell the rest of the year. The river gets doses of striped bass (fall and spring), salmon (fall), and steelhead (winter), but they are sprinkled in holes from Marysville on upstream to the Thermalito Bay outlet hole. Below Marysville, the river is home to a sizable population of smallmouth. On summer evenings they'll hit grubs or top-water lures.

A boat is a virtual necessity if you want to do it right here. Two good fishing spots north of Yuba City are the Car Body Hole and Long Hole; south of Yuba City there's Boyd's Pump (a boat ramp is available near this spot) and Star Bend. The folks at Johnson's Bait & Tackle can provide detailed directions.

Facilities, fees: Camping is at Live Oak Campground (north of Yuba City). Picnic areas, drinking water, and flush toilets are available. Boat ramps are near Yuba City and at Verona Marina. Fishing supplies can be obtained in Yuba City and Marysville. Fishing access is free.

Directions: To Shanghai Bend: Take I-5 to Williams and the junction with Highway 20. Turn east on Highway 20 and drive 30 miles to Yuba City and the Garden Highway. Turn south on Garden Highway and drive four miles to Shanghai Bend Road. Turn left and continue on a dirt road to the parking area.

To the Verona Marina: At the junction of I-5 and Highway 99 (north of Sacramento), take Highway 99 north and drive eight miles to Sankey Road. Turn left and drive two miles west to the Verona Marina.

To Riverfront Park: From Yuba City, take Highway 20 east into Marysville (cross the bridge) and continue to the second stoplight. Turn left and continue to a stop sign. Continue straight to a second stop sign. Turn left (continuing over a levee) and follow the signs to Riverfront Park.

Contact: Verona Marina, 916/927-8387; Johnson's Bait & Tackle, Yuba City, 530/674-1912,

www.johnsonsbait.com; Star Bait & Tackle, Marysville, 530/742-5431; G&J Outdoor Enterprises, 530/885-1492, www.gandjoutdoors.com; Three Rivers Guide Service, 530/925-7990, www.threeriversguideservice.com.

22 CAMP FAR WEST RESERVOIR

Rating: 7

southeast of Marysville

Map 5.2, page 262

Set eyes on this lake and you'll instantly say "bass." With 29 miles of shoreline, cove after cove, and perfect weather for bass, Camp Far West Reservoir has become one of the better bets for bass fishers in the foothills of the Sacramento Valley.

Spring comes early here in the foothill country (elevation 320 feet), followed by hot summers. Give this lake four straight days of warm weather in the spring, and it will give you bass on the bite in return.

Be sure to avoid the main lake body, both in front of the two launch ramps and near the dam. Not only is there a lot less bass habitat there, it's also where most of the waterskiing action takes place. You'll find what you're looking for at many other spots on the lake.

A key is that before the lake was created, portions of the Bear River arm were left uncut. That provides excellent aquatic habitat and bass structure. As the water warms and bass go into their pre-spawn mode, the deep shoreline of the Bear River arm is an excellent spot. The same holds true for the Rock Creek arm.

Wherever there is a bush in the water, there is a chance for a good-sized bass to be there. Flipping can be very productive with large worms or 3/8-ounce jigs in darker colors.

The lake draws down quite dramatically in early fall, and all but a few hardy anglers visit the lake. Yet the fishing turns on in the fall again for largemouth bass.

Among the top areas for smallmouth bass are the rocky islands and ledges along the north end of the lake. Small jigs and spinners, small baits, and minnow-type plugs work well here from early March through April.

For some tasty crappie fillets, fish around the submerged trees at the upper end of the Rock Creek arm on summer evenings. Brown trout are occasionally caught in the same area, but they are few and elusive.

A sprinkling of striped bass can also provide a surprise at this lake. The lake record is reportedly 44 pounds. At one time they were quite abundant. No more.

One word of caution: Summer weekends can be a real zoo—too many people.

For the most part, users split the lake into two areas. Most powerboaters and waterskiers head to the lake's southern side. It can get outrageous on the weekends, when a few impromptu boater parties get under way with lots of liquids and suntan lotion flowing almost as fast as the jet boats. In fact, jet-boat races are held here during the summer.

Facilities, fees: Campgrounds, flush toilets, drinking water, and picnic areas are available. On the north shore, there is a boat dock with fishing-boat, personal watercraft, and pedal-boat rentals. A convenience store with bait and tackle is nearby. On the south shore, there is gas, a boat dock, and limited facilities. There are two paved boat ramps, one on the north side and one on the south side. Clearly marked signs for both boat ramps are posted on the entrance road. Day-use and boat-launch fees apply.

Directions: From Sacramento, take I-80 east toward Roseville to Highway 65. Turn north on Highway 65 and drive to the town of Sheridan and Rio Oso Road. Turn right on Rio Oso Road and drive about five miles to McCourtney Road. Turn left on McCourtney Road and drive to the lake. The road circles the lake and provides access to campgrounds and launching ramps at the north and south shores.

Contact: Camp Far West Lake, www.camp farwestlake.net; North Shore, 530/633-0803; South Shore, 916/408-5037; Wet 'n Wild boat rentals, 530/315-2560; Johnson's Bait & Tackle, Yuba City, 530/674-1912, www .johnsonsbait.com.

23 HALSEY FOREBAY

Rating: 5

north of Auburn

Map 5.2, page 262

The Bear River Canal feeds into this small lake that's known only by locals who track the latest trout stocks. Set at 1,800 feet in the foothill country north of Auburn, Halsey Forebay is one of those lakes that only produces well in the few days following a plant.

Similar small lakes, such as Rock Creek Lake, Lake Arthur, Lake Theodore, and Siphon Lake, are within five miles of here, but Halsey is the only one the DFG stocks with trout, providing some good-sized ones at that (10- to 12-inchers). And get 'em Haley does, just as spring turns into summer.

If you hit it just after the "trout mobile" has made its rounds, you're in good shape, but your chances diminish with each passing day. For some reason, there is not much of a holdover bite here between the plants. The best spots to try are along the rail near the inlet and on the shore directly across the lake from there. Nearby Rock Creek Lake and Lake Theodore are terrible for fishing (both get drained almost completely from time to time), but Lake Arthur is okay for pan-sized cats and green-eared sunfish.

Facilities, fees: PG&E provides a picnic area at the lake. A campground, lodging, and supplies are in Auburn. Fishing access is free.

Directions: From Sacramento, take I-80 east through Auburn and continue two miles past Auburn to the Dry Creek Road exit. Take that exit to Christian Valley Road. Turn right on Christian Valley Road and drive one mile to Bancroft Road. Turn left on Bancroft Road and drive a short distance.

Contact: Auburn Chamber of Commerce, 530/885-5616, www.auburnchamber.net; G&J Outdoor Enterprises, 530/885-1492, www

.gandjoutdoors.com; PG&E Recreation Desk, 916/386-5164, www.pge.com/recreation.

24 CLEMENTINE LAKE

Rating: 4

northeast of Auburn on the American River

Map 5.2, page 262

Some lakes must be fished by boat. When you visit Clementine Lake, you'll quickly discover this is one of those places. The shoreline is very brushy, making it near impossible to walk along the bank. Ah, but the angler with a boat has it made. Facing the shore, boaters can zip casts along the brush, right where the bass often hang out.

Although the lake harbors a small population of trout, it is best known for its spring and summer smallmouth-bass fishery. The fish aren't big—ranging 8–15 inches—but you can sometimes catch good numbers of them, providing you have that boat. Fish with live crawdads, crickets, or night crawlers for the best action, but crawdad crankbaits and plastic worms also work. Make sure you get here early in the late spring or throughout the summer—the lake tends to crowd up with water-skiers and drunken watercrafters during a hot summer day.

The long, narrow reservoir is a dammed-up gorge on the North Fork American River, part of the Auburn State Recreation Area, and is at an elevation of 1,200 feet. In the summer this stretch of river is the temperature of bathwater. In the spring you will find cooler water as you move well upstream, where the lake's modest population of trout tend to congregate. Get your boat as far upstream as possible, anchor, and toss out a night crawler, letting it flutter a bit in the current.

Some anglers never bother fishing Clementine Lake—the launch area has parking for only 25 boat trailers (spaces are usually taken by skiers in the summer), and there are very few fish. The lake is not stocked by the DFG. With a little experimentation, however, you can catch some nice natives. The wise few can limit on June mornings by trolling from the dam buoys up to Robber's Roost. Try going 20–28 feet down with a silver dodger trailed by a small silver shad Needlefish. When you first get out on the lake and look at your depth finder, you may think you're in trout heaven—but, alas, most of those marks you'll see are bubbles rising from the bottom vegetation. About 10 miles of river upstream of the lake has been snorkeled and is home to just a few smallmouth bass, suckers, squawfish, and the occasional trout. Regardless, the lake is an awesome spot for a canoe trip in the fall or winter; you'll feel as if you're the only person on the planet.

Facilities, fees: Boat-in campgrounds, floating chemical toilets, picnic areas, and gas are available, but drinking water is not. Garbage must be packed out. Supplies can be obtained in Auburn. Fishing access is free.

Directions: From Sacramento, take I-80 east for 31 miles to Auburn and continue to the exit for Foresthill. Take that exit to Foresthill Road. Turn northeast on Foresthill Road and drive three miles to Lake Clementine Road. Turn left and drive 2.5 miles to the boat launch. (A sharp, hairpin turn makes it impossible for pickups and trailers to make the boat ramp; bring a kayak instead.)

Contact: Auburn State Recreation Area, 530/885-4527, www.parks.ca.gov; Auburn Chamber of Commerce, 530/885-5616, www.auburnchamber.net.

25 NORTH FORK AMERICAN RIVER

Rating: 4

near Auburn

Map 5.2, page 262

Access to this section of river is extremely limited. The one decent access point is at the Highway 49 bridge, just below the confluence of the North and Middle Forks.

Make it down to the river, though, and you'll find a good spot to fish for smallmouth bass, either fly-fishing with dark woolly worms or plugging with crankbaits. Don't expect large fish; there aren't many of those. But there are enough in the 9- to 12-inch class to feed a smallmouth fan's addiction. For trout, a better bet is up the cooler Middle Fork.

Facilities, fees: A boat ramp is off Highway 49 north of Folsom Lake, on Rattlesnake Bar Road. Campgrounds are nearby, including boat-in sites at Auburn State Recreation Area. Supplies can be obtained in Auburn, Colfax, and in the Emigrant Gap area. There's no drinking water on-site. Fishing access is free.

Directions: From Sacramento, take I-80 east for 31 miles to Auburn and Highway 49. Take Highway 49 north and drive to the river. Access the river where the bridge crosses (a trail leads along the river here). Limited access is also available off roads that intersect I-80 near Colfax. Access to the North Fork of the North Fork American is farther north, off I-80 via the Emigrant Gap exit.

Contact: Auburn State Recreation Area, 530/885-4527, www.parks.ca.gov; Bureau of Land Management, Mother Lode Field Office, 916/941-3101, www.blm.gov/ca.

26 FOLSOM LAKE

Rating: 6

northeast of Sacramento in
Folsom Lake State Recreation Area

Map 5.2, page 262

Thousands and thousands of people come to Folsom Lake, Sacramento's backyard playland, to fish, water-ski, camp, or just lie around in the sun.

When full, Folsom Lake covers some 18,000 acres. But because it has such shallow arms, the water level can fluctuate from winter to spring as much as at any other California lake. I've seen it look almost empty before the onset of December rains, and then seen it fill to the brim seemingly overnight. In addition, catch rates suffer because of high boater traffic. Weekends can be so crowded that many anglers throw their hands up in frustration and leave with plenty of time still left in their day to get a bite.

Still, there's hope, but you have to treat Folsom like an urban lake. Fishing for bass and trout is often quite good in spring and early summer, and a fast-growing population of kokanee salmon is adding some sparkle. Stocks of kokanee and king salmon provide hopes for the future. For being so close to a large population center, it provides a decent fishery.

The character of the place can change from month to month. In late winter and spring, the lake is excellent for trout fishing. The water is cool and fresh, and as long as it remains that way, rainbow trout in the 10- to 12-inch class are stocked on a regular basis. The water around Dike 8, between the dam and Folsom Marina, has consistently produced more trout for trollers than any other area. Then, in early May, hot weather starts hammering away at the Central Valley. Suddenly, hundreds of mermaids come out to get suntans. And just as fast, the lake becomes better suited to bass fishers. If you want trout, you'd best get on the water at daybreak and be done by 9 A.M. After that, water-skiers take over, and the sun sends the trout down into the abyss.

There are two different trout seasons on Folsom Lake, not by law, but by the way you fish. One is midspring through midfall; the other takes up the rest of the year in the cool winter months. The summer season is for boaters and trollers; the winter season is for bank anglers. Believe it or not, bank anglers catch far more trout during this period than the trollers do.

The shallow flats between Granite Bay and Beal's Point are one of the best areas of the lake. A good strategy is to use a boat to access the shoreline here, and then fish from the bank for the cruising trout off the gradual sloping shoreline.

With a two-rod stamp, many people fish with Power Bait or night crawlers and then also cast lures, hoping to intercept cruising fish. Some of these trout go up to 20 inches.

For planted trout, try using Power Bait near the boat ramp at Granite Bay. For larger holdovers, shore anglers can toss live minnows under a bobber near Elephant's Foot at Rattlesnake Bar (on the North Fork arm) or near the Salmon Falls Bridge (on the South Fork arm), while trollers can pull silver Kastmasters in the top 10 feet of water along the shoreline just north of the Peninsula boat ramp.

Largemouth bass respond quickly to warmer temperatures. Miles of decent bass water can be found up both lake arms, the North Fork American and the South Fork American, where skilled bassers can do very well. Skill? Yes, that is required. Over the course of a few months, these bass will see damn near every lure ever invented. You'll have to present your offering in a way that fools the fish into thinking the thing is actually alive.

Fingerling king salmon are also planted. In the spring, when water surface temperatures are still cool, salmon in the two- to five-pound range are available to anglers bank fishing minnows and night crawlers off the dam and Beal's Point. For some reason, none of the local trollers have figured out how to catch the kings consistently in the summer, when the fish move into deep water.

Crappie fishing has greatly improved at Folsom in recent years due to the efforts of private clubs creating cover, including planting willow trees at low water. When the lake fills, these trees will provide aquatic habitat. This is also helping jump-start an already good bass fishery.

The best fishing for crappie usually takes place during the spring and summer months in years that have had good rainfall. A promising place to start looking for crappie is around the submerged trees and brush in New York Creek Cove. If you can locate it with your depth finder, try the sunken bridge near the mouth of Sweetwater Creek Cove, which also holds fish.

Those who want something big to sink a hook into should try catfishing at night in July and August. Folsom is loaded with cats that range up to 24 pounds and are fairly easy to catch. Using chicken liver, fish the shallow coves near Granite Bay, Five Percent, and Beal's Point. If you can get down to the lake a day after the first substantial rain of the season, your reward will be the best catfishing of the year. Look for spots where small feeder streams enter the lake; this is where cats gather to intercept the tasty morsels that wash in with the current. Another insider's tip: Fish the old Salmon Falls Bridge for lunker-sized catfish.

Plan on sharing the water with a lot of young drunken sailors. If you stick around long enough, you'll see just about every stunt imaginable that comes with hot sun, cold suds, and lots of people.

Facilities, fees: Campgrounds, picnic areas, restrooms with flush toilets, drinking water, mooring, ice, bait and tackle, and a snack bar (summer only) are available. Folsom Lake Marina has full boating services. Folsom Lake Rentals rents out fishing boats in summer. Rentals of pontoon boats, ski boats, fishing boats, and personal watercraft are possible near the Granite Bay boat launch. Supplies can be obtained in Folsom. Day-use and boat-launching fees are charged.

Directions: To Beal's Point: From Sacramento, take U.S. 50 east to the Folsom Boulevard exit. Take that exit, turn left, and drive seven miles (the road changes name to Folsom–Auburn Road) to Beal's Point. Turn right and continue to the entrance.

To other paved boat ramps:

• Folsom Point: From Sacramento, take U.S. 50 east to the exit for Folsom. Take that exit to Folsom Boulevard and drive to Blue Ravine Road. Turn right on Blue Ravine Road and drive four miles to East Natoma Road. Turn right and drive to the boat ramp adjacent to a picnic area. A multilane paved ramp is here.

• Folsom Lake Marina: From Sacramento, take U.S. 50 east to the exit for Eldorado Hills Boulevard. Take that exit and drive 4.5 miles to Green Valley Road. Turn left on Green Valley Road and drive one mile (to the bottom of the hill) to the entrance to the marina. Turn right and continue to the ramp.

• Granite Bay: From Sacramento, take I-80 east to the exit for Douglas Boulevard. Take that exit to Douglas Boulevard East and drive to where it dead-ends, at Granite Bay. A multilane paved ramp is here.

• Rattlesnake Bar: From Sacramento, take I-80 east to the exit for Elm Street. Take that exit and drive east 0.5 mile to High Street. Turn left on High Street (which becomes Highway 49) and continue on Highway 49 into Pilot Hill and Rattlesnake Bar Road. Turn right and drive 2.5 miles to the entrance. A paved ramp is here.

• Rattlesnake Bar: From Placerville, take Highway 49 north (toward the town of Coloma) for 8.3 miles into the town of Pilot Hill and Rattlesnake Bar Road. Turn left on Rattlesnake Bar Road and drive nine miles to the end of the road and the park entrance.

Contact: Folsom Lake State Recreation Area, 916/988-0205, www.parks.ca.gov; Folsom Lake Marina, 916/933-1300, www.folsom .lakemarina.com; Folsom Lake Rentals, 916/223-8129; Folsom Chamber of Commerce, 916/985-2698, www.folsomchamber .com.

27 LAKE NATOMA

Rating: 7

east of Sacramento at Nimbus Dam

Map 5.2, page 262

It seems that the many big rainbow trout caught at Lake Natoma each year are taken right after a trout plant of dinkers by Fish and Game. The theory is these big fish are eating the dinkers. Somehow these big fish know that when the DFG tanker trunk shows up, the dinner bell is ringing. It's no accident that so many big trout are here. Below every major reservoir there's a small lake called an afterbay, and Lake Natoma is just that for big Folsom Lake, to the east. For the size of some of the trout in this lake, and the high number

of people who live in the area, it is surprising more people do not fish here.

Natoma is known, just like Butt Lake below Lake Almanor, as a regular producer of some of the largest rainbow trout in the state. What do they have in common? Pond smelt and other forage that are chopped up and sent into the lake (river) below when the hydroelectric turbines are running. In Natoma, there are periods when hundreds of rainbows in the 4- to 8-pound class and dozens in the 8- to 12-pound range have been caught out of this afterbay. It is the best prospect for a football-sized rainbow over eight pounds in the Sacramento area.

This narrow lake covers 500 acres, and because it gets water from the bottom of Folsom Dam, Natoma tends to be colder than its big brother, Folsom. That's what makes this a good trout lake, with foot-long rainbows stocked by the Department of Fish and Game, plus a few large resident fish that hang near the upper end and gobble up the passing morsels in the flows from Folsom Dam. Natoma also has good smallmouth fishing in the summer; just hit it with a float tube and some crayfish imitations.

Waterskiing is prohibited, and boaters must obey the 5-mph speed limit. That's welcome news for anglers who don't like to compete with personal watercraft and speedboats. Instead you get quiet trolling water.

The California lake record rainbow trout was caught here on January 17, 2000: a fish weighing 23 pounds, caught by Jeremy Brucklacher.

Note: No motors are permitted in the lower half of the lake. There are also many good spots to bait-fish from the bank. There are a few resident bass and sunfish in Lake Natoma, but nearby Folsom Lake is a much better spot for bass fishing.

Facilities, fees: Ramps for launching small boats are at the east and west ends of the lake, at Negro Bar and Willow Creek. Restrooms with flush toilets and drinking water are available. A day-use fee is charged.

Directions: From Sacramento, take I-80 north to the exit for Douglas Boulevard. Take that exit east and drive five miles to Auburn–Folsom Road. Turn right on Auburn–Folsom Road and drive south six miles until the road dead-ends into Greenback Lane. Turn right on Greenback Lane and merge immediately into the left lane. The park entrance is approximately 0.2 mile down, on the left.

Contact: Folsom Lake State Recreation Area, 916/988-0205, www.parks.ca.gov.

28 AMERICAN RIVER

Rating: 5

from Fair Oaks to Sacramento

Map 5.2, page 262

Don't like the action? Just stick around. On the American River, it always seems as if another run of fish is on the way.

Steelhead arrive from December through mid-March; shad from late April through early July; striped bass in April, May, and June; and salmon from September through November. By December the cycle starts anew. No fish? What, me worry?

This section of the American flows from the outlet at Nimbus Basin on downstream past Fair Oaks and Rancho Cordova before entering the Sacramento River at Discovery Park. In that span, several spots offer excellent access by boat or by bank (although chest waders are a necessity at some).

The upper river (see DFG regulations) is closed from October 16 through December 31 to all fishing. When it reopens on January 1, the river is full of steelhead and steelhead anglers. Many fish are caught the first few days, then it tapers off to more typical results for steelhead.

Bank fishers use Glo-Bugs, night crawlers, and spinners such as the Blue Fox and Mepps to get their fish. Anglers in drift boats pull plugs such as Hot Shots and Wee Warts, and occasionally use roe for their fish.

The peak of the salmon run in the American

River occurs during late September and October. The lower river has three major areas where trollers catch tons of fish: the two dredger holes on the lower river, one below the 16th Street Bridge, and one above it. Another good spot is the run behind Sacramento State University, accessed by either boat ramp on the south side of the Howe Avenue Bridge.

Above that, riffles and runs are fished by bank fishers or by the occasional drift-boat angler. On the upper river, there are unimproved boat ramps near the Sunrise Bridge and also from an access road a mile upstream. Small boats are put in and anchored here, letting Kwikfish or Flatfish wobble in the river current. This is best during the end of the open season, which ends October 15. Limits are the rule. The sardine wrap on the Kwikfish and Flatfish lures makes a big difference here; be sure to use it.

Some bank anglers still use the traditional methods of casting spinners and wobblers like Mepps and Krocodiles to catch their salmon. One of my favorite spots in May is River Bend Park, where I walk downstream a bit, then wade in and start casting for shad. There's a footbridge overhead, and from it kids can often see the shad and tell me where to cast. Cheating? Maybe, but I release all the fish anyway. Another favorite spot is Sunrise Avenue; many more shad are caught in that area than at River Bend Park, but it's usually loaded with anglers.

The shad need decent water flows to be attracted upstream, and when that happens, the American is one of the best shad rivers anywhere. The same is true for the other anadromous species that migrate here: salmon, steelhead, and striped bass. However, the converse is also true. If the flows are very low, as can be the case, the river turns into a skunkhole. Little water equals few fish.

In the best years, the late-summer striped bass fishing is best in the section of river just upstream from its confluence with the Sacramento River. You need a boat to have much of a chance. Salmon and steelhead, on the other hand, are sprinkled throughout the river all the way to Nimbus Basin during fall and winter, and they can be caught from shore as well as from a boat.

Facilities, fees: Boat ramps are provided at Discovery Park and near Watt Avenue. Lodging and supplies are in the Sacramento area. Restrooms with flush toilets, drinking water, picnic areas, and barbecues are at many river-access points. Fishing access is free.

Directions: Easy access is off the roads in Rancho Cordova and Fair Oaks that cut off from U.S. 50. Excellent shore-fishing access is at the following locations: Nimbus Basin, Ancil Hoffman Park, River Bend Park, the Sunrise Avenue access areas, the Watt Avenue Bridge area, Paradise Beach, the area behind Cal Expo, and Dredger Hole. By boat, the best and most easily accessible spot is at the confluence of the Sacramento and American Rivers in Discovery Park, in Sacramento.

• To Ancil Hoffman Park: In Sacramento, take I-80 to the exit for Arden Way. Take that exit east and drive 4.5 miles to Fair Oaks Boulevard. Turn left on Fair Oaks Boulevard and drive 1.5 miles to Oak Avenue. Turn right and drive to Van Alstine Avenue. Turn right on Van Alstine and drive to California Avenue. Turn left on California Avenue and drive to Tarshes Drive. Turn right and drive a short distance to the entrance to Ancil Hoffman Park. There is no boat ramp. Hand-launching is difficult, and the former put-in area is washed out.

• To Discovery Park: In Sacramento, take I-5 to the exit for the Garden Highway. Take that exit, turn left, and drive to Natomas Park Drive. Turn right and drive to the signed park entrance. A paved ramp is available.

• To River Bend Park: In Sacramento, take U.S. 50 east to the exit for Bradshaw Road. Take that exit, turn north, and drive to Folsom Boulevard. Turn right on Folsom Boulevard and drive about one mile to Rod Beaudry Drive. Turn left on Rod Beaudry Drive and continue to River Bend Park. This place has no boat ramp; there is hand-launching only.

• To Harrington Way: In Sacramento, take I-80 to the Arden Way exit. Turn west on Arden Way and drive 4.5 miles to Kingsford Drive. Turn right on Kingsford Drive (which turns into Harrington Way) and continue to the access. This place has no boat ramp; there is hand-launching only.

• To Howe Avenue: From Sacramento, take U.S. 50 east to the exit for Howe Avenue. Take that exit, turn north, and drive to La Riviera Drive. Turn right on La Riviera Drive and drive to the sign for the river access.

• To Gristmill (also known as Mira Del Rio): From Sacramento, take U.S. 50 east to the exit for Bradshaw Road. Take that exit, turn north, and drive to Folsom Boulevard. Turn left and drive a short distance west to Butterfield Way. Turn right and drive to Stoughton Way. Turn right and drive to Mira Del Rio Drive. Turn left on Mira Del Rio, and then immediately turn right for river access. No boat ramp is available. Some boats are launched from the gravel bar, but this will be difficult for two-wheel-drive vehicles or four-wheel-drive vehicles without significant tires.

• To Rossmoor Drive: From Sacramento, take U.S. 50 east to the exit for Sunrise Boulevard. Take that exit, turn north, and drive 0.5 mile to Coloma Road. Turn left turn on Coloma Road and drive 1.5 miles west to Rossmoor Drive. Turn right on Rossmoor Drive and continue into the park to the car-top boat ramp at the end of the road.

• To Sailor Bar: From Sacramento, take U.S. 50 east to the exit for Hazel Avenue. Take that exit, turn north, and drive 1.5 miles to Winding Way. Turn left and drive about 0.5 mile to Illinois Avenue. Turn left on Illinois Avenue and continue to the end of the road. There is a paved boat ramp.

• To Upper Sunrise: From Sacramento, take U.S. 50 east to the exit for Sunrise Boulevard. Take that exit, turn north, and drive 1.5 miles to South Bridge Street. Turn right and drive to the car-top boat ramp. A paved launch for hand-launched boats was installed in 2003.

• To Watt Avenue South: From Sacramento, take U.S. 50 east to the exit for Watt Avenue.

Take that exit and drive about 0.5 mile to the sign for the launching area. A paved ramp is available for launching small boats.

Contact: G&J Outdoor Enterprises, 530/885-1492, www.gandjoutdoors.com; Fly-fishing Specialties, Citrus Heights, 916/722-1055, www.flyfishingspecialties.com; Sacramento County Parks, 916/875-6961 (park rangers), www.msa2.saccounty.net.

29 RANCHO SECO LAKE

Rating: 6

southeast of Sacramento in
Rancho Seco Recreation Area
Map 5.2, page 262

Here's a spot that's ideal for a family picnic, especially if Dad and Mom like to get away after dinner for some evening fishing, with a chance for big bass and a sprinkling of bluegill, redear sunfish, crappie, and catfish. Trout are stocked from November through March. The lake, part of the 400-acre Rancho Seco Recreation Area, has a boat ramp (no gas motors are permitted), a picnic area, and several docks for shore fishing.

The lake covers 160 acres and provides a variety of prospects, all of them weather dependent. In the spring and fall, the bass fishing can be good, but it is best in April, May, and October. The lake's bass record is 16 pounds, 15 ounces.

The key to catching largemouth bass here can be to use diving crawdad lures in the late spring, as well as shad-patterned lures.

Rancho Seco has some huge Florida-strain largemouth bass, with many exceeding the 15-pound mark. A night crawler retrieved very slowly along the bottom has enticed many big fish, along with traditional plastic-worm methods.

When the water is cold, the lake is stocked with some rainbow trout in the 10- to 12-inch class, joining others in the two- to four-pound class. These are sought after primarily by shoreline bait dunkers. In the summer, it

really heats up, and the majority of anglers are either kids trying for sunfish or persistent old-timers waiting for catfish. Some big catfish inhabit the lake and will bite lines baited with chicken liver. Remember, you can't use live minnows at Rancho Seco.

The park is open for day use only. Since no gas motors are permitted on the lake (electric motors only), you get quiet water and fair fishing, along with good access and picnic sites. Bring the family.

The area also has wetland habitat that provides homes for ducks, geese, hawks, bald eagles, blue herons, and other migratory birds.

Facilities, fees: A campground, RV dump station, coin showers, flush toilets, and a picnic area are provided. A boat ramp, fishing piers and docks, rentals of kayaks and pedal boats, and a fish-cleaning station are available. No gas motors or live bait are permitted on the lake. Lodging and supplies are in Sacramento. Day-use and boat-launching fees are charged.

Directions: From Sacramento, take Highway 99 south for 12 miles to the Highway 104 exit. Take Highway 104/Twin Cities Road east (look for the twin towers) and drive 12 miles to the signed entrance for Rancho Seco Recreation Area. Turn right and continue to the lake.

Contact: Rancho Seco Recreation Area, 209/748-2318 or 916/732-4913 (camping reservations).

30 SACRAMENTO RIVER DELTA

Rating: 8

near Rio Vista
Map 5.2, page 262

The delta is an extraordinary place, with some 1,000 miles of navigable waterways—a mosaic of rivers, sloughs, and lakes. When I fly over it, I always think that it looks like intricate masonry work. When I fish it, it looks more like paradise.

Right off, though, you must check the water temperature. If it is 57°F or warmer, trolling is often better than bait fishing. If it's colder than 57°F, the opposite is true. At 50°F or colder, trolling can become very difficult.

The striped bass start arriving in decent numbers to the Sacramento River in mid-September, and through mid-April different schools will arrive at different times. For instance, the biggest delta stripers of the year often are caught the week before Christmas, when it's very cold and foggy. Then in early April, there is usually a short-lived but wide-open trolling bite, which then turns off completely—a total zilch so sudden you'd swear the fish disappeared. During the summer months, a few resident stripers hang around the area, but for the most part, water-skiers take over the delta.

Some of the best spots for striped bass are in the vicinity of the boat ramp at Rio Vista. Good prospects include the Rio Vista Bridge, Isleton Bridge, Steamboat Slough (upstream of Rio Vista), the southern tip of Decker Island (downstream of Rio Vista), the Towers (which are actually power lines downstream of Decker Island), and the deep holes in Montezuma Slough.

By early November, good numbers of striped bass have spread throughout the lower Sacramento River near Rio Vista and have infiltrated sloughs such as Steamboat Slough, Sutter Slough, and Miner Slough. Farther to the northeast, the least-fished sections of the delta are Prospect Slough, Shag Slough, and Lindsey Slough. These can all offer very good fall and winter striped bass fishing. Bait fishing with shad is the preferred technique. Trolling usually stays good until early November.

The sign that fishing is over in this area is when the first big rains come, muddying up the waters. That pushes the fish toward Rio Vista. But even during periods of muddy water, the area off upper Cache Slough in the vicinity of Shag Slough is one of the best sturgeon spots in the entire region.

Because this area is not a spawning route for striped bass, fishing is very poor here in the spring.

Options here are sturgeon and salmon, and sometimes they're more than options—they can be the fish of choice. Some huge sturgeon have been caught on the Sacramento River Delta in this area, including several in the 250- to 300-pound class. One November day, Bill Stratton was on his first trip on a new boat with a new rod, fishing for striped bass, when he hooked a monster sturgeon here by accident. He had to hop aboard another boat to fight the fish, and after several hours, he landed a 390-pound sturgeon that stands as the world record for 30-pound line. The better sturgeon spots are downstream, especially in the vicinity of the southern tip of Decker Island, holes in Montezuma Slough, and in the center of the channel adjacent to the Pittsburg PG&E Plant. The number of sturgeon attracted to these areas is linked directly to rainfall. In high-rain years, a lot of sturgeon move in. In low-rain years, you won't find very many.

Salmon have also become a viable alternative to striped bass, especially from late August through September, when the salmon pass through this area en route to their upstream spawning areas. The better results have come trolling in the area adjacent to the Rio Vista boat ramp.

If you like to anchor and fish with bait, the best way to avoid bait robbers is to fish the stronger tides or the sloughs, cuts, and inlets. Montezuma Slough and Little Honker Bay are among the best spots of all. If you have crab problems, move your boat immediately. Once they find you, you're dead meat. Some years the mitten crabs are no problem at all. Others years, they can be a pain. In recent times, they haven't been much of a concern.

If you are new to the game, then book a trip with Barry Canevaro and learn the ropes. He can be as much a teacher as a guide. In one four-hour spree with Barry, I caught and released 12 striped bass of up to 23 pounds—a reminder of what is possible when everything is right.

Facilities, fees: Campgrounds are at Brannan Island State Recreation Area. Lodging, full-service marinas, bait, tackle, and supplies can be found near the boat ramps. Fees are charged for day-use at private resorts, boat launching, boat rentals, and camping.

Directions: To Brannan Island State Recreation Area: From I-80 in Fairfield, take the Highway 12 exit, drive southeast 14 miles to Rio Vista, and continue to Highway 160 (at the signal before the bridge). Turn right on Highway 160 and drive three miles to the park entrance, on the left. From Antioch, take Highway 4 to Antioch and continue over the Antioch Bridge (where the road becomes Highway 160) to the park, on the right.

• To B&W Resort, Isleton: Take I-5 to Highway 12 (south of Sacramento, near Lodi). Turn west on Highway 12 and drive 11 miles to Brannan Island Road (after the second bridge). Turn right and drive a very short distance. The resort is on your immediate left.

• To Korth's Pirates' Lair Marina, Isleton: Take I-5 to Highway 12 (south of Sacramento, near Lodi). Turn west on Highway 12 and drive 11 miles to Brannan Island Road (after the second bridge). Turn right and drive three miles to the marina.

• To Vieira's Resort, Isleton: Take I-5 to Highway 12 (south of Sacramento, near Lodi). Turn west on Highway 12 and drive 17 miles to the four-way stop at Highway 160 (just before the Rio Vista Bridge). Turn right (northeast) on Highway 160 and drive three miles to the sign for Vieira's on the left. Turn left and drive a short distance into the resort.

• To Sandy Beach County Park, Rio Vista: Take I-80 to Fairfield and the exit for Highway 12. Take that exit southeast and drive 16 miles to Rio Vista and the intersection with Main Street. Turn right on Main Street and drive a short distance to 2nd Street. Turn right and drive 0.5 mile to Beach Drive. Turn left (west) on Beach Drive and go 0.5 mile to the park.

• To Delta Marina RV Resort, Rio Vista: Take I-80 to Fairfield and the exit for Highway 12. Take that exit and drive 16 miles to Rio Vista

and the intersection with Main Street. Turn right on Main Street and drive a short distance to 2nd Street. Turn right on 2nd Street and drive to Marina Drive. Turn left on Marina Drive and continue another short distance to the harbor.

• To Snug Harbor Resort: Take I-80 to Fairfield and Highway 12. Turn east on Highway 12 and drive 16 miles to Rio Vista and Front Street. Turn left on Front Street and drive under the bridge to River Road. Turn right on River Road and drive two miles to the Real McCoy Ferry (signed "Ryer Island"). Take the ferry (free) across the Sacramento River to Ryer Island and Levee Road. Turn right and drive 3.5 miles on Levee Road to Snug Harbor on the right.

Contact: California Delta Chamber & Visitor Bureau, 916/777-4041, www.californiadelta .org; Sandy Beach County Park, Solano County Parks, 707/374-2097, www.solanocounty .com; Brannan Island State Recreation Area, 916/777-6671, www.parks.ca.gov; Riverside Bait Shop, 916/777-6661.

Marinas and lodging: Holland Riverside Marina, 925/634-2345 or 925/634-8080, www.hollandriverside.com; Korth's Pirates' Lair Marina, Isleton, 916/777-6464 or 888/776-6464, www.korthsmarina.com; Snug Harbor Marina and RV Camp/Park, 916/775-1455, www.snugharbor.net; Duck Island RV Park, 916/777-6663 or 800/825-3898, www.duckislandrv.com; B&W Resort, Isleton, 916/777-6161, www.bandwresort .com; Vieira's Resort, Isleton, 855/843-4727 or 916/777-6661, www.vieirasresort.net; Delta Marina RV Resort, Rio Vista, 866/774-2315, www.deltamarina.com.

Boat rentals and charters: Herman & Helen's, 209/951-4634, www.hermanand helensmarina.com; KOA Boat Rentals, 209/369-1041, www.towerparkboatrentals.com.

Guides: Fish Hookers Sportfishing, 916/777-6498, www.fishhookers.com.

Hal Schell's *Delta Map and Guide* can be bought online at www.californiadelta.org/ ordermap.html.

31 PITTSBURG PIER

Rating: 6

in Pittsburg

Map 5.2, page 262

The warm water from the nearby PG&E outfall attracts fish to this spot. The pier can be one of the best in the Bay Area for striped bass (in the fall), sturgeon (winter through spring), and even steelhead (late fall).

Facilities, fees: The newer pier has restrooms, parking, picnic tables, and drinking water. Fishing access is free.

Directions: Take I-680 to Martinez and the exit for Highway 4. Take the Highway 4 exit eastbound and drive to the Railroad Avenue exit. Take that exit and turn left on Railroad Avenue. Drive on this road to the end at 3rd Street. Turn left on 3rd Street and drive to Marina Boulevard. Turn right and follow the road to where it ends at the harbor. To get to another pier, proceed as directed above, but turn left on Marina Boulevard and keep to the right until you come to Bayside. Turn right and continue to the road's end. You will see signs indicating the access road to the pier.

Contact: Pittsburg Marina, 925/439-4958.

Fishing charter: Fish Hookers, 916/777-6498, www.fishhookers.com.

32 ANTIOCH PIER

Rating: 5

in Antioch

Map 5.2, page 262

Besides having a good view of the waterway, this pier offers some of the better prospects for striped bass in the area. It's best from late September into early December and then again in the spring, typically April and May. The pier is open for fishing 24 hours per day.

Facilities, fees: Restrooms, parking, a fish-cleaning station, and picnic tables are available. Swimming is not permitted. Fishing access is free.

Directions: Take Highway 4 to Antioch and the exit for Wilbur Avenue. Take the Wilbur Avenue exit and turn right on Wilbur Avenue. Make an immediate left on Bridgehead Road; the parking area is at the end of the road.

Contact: For a park brochure, call or go online to East Bay Regional Park District, 888/327-2757, ext. 5, www.ebparks.org, then follow the directions and leave your name, address, and the park brochure requested.

33 SAN JOAQUIN DELTA

Rating: 7

near Antioch

Map 5.2, page 262   BEST (

The old green San Joaquin provides a viable fishery for striped bass, largemouth, and catfish. Striped bass arrive in late September, although in modest numbers. Come winter, so do the sturgeon. They provide a fair chance for skilled anglers with boats, but it takes time and persistence to get a bite—and when you do, you had better not blow the set.

One of the advantages to fishing the San Joaquin rather than the Sacramento River side of the delta is the wide variety and the number of good spots. Some of the better places are just west of the Antioch Bridge (with good trolling from Mayberry Slough to the Antioch PG&E power plant), Big Break, Blind Point (at the mouth of Dutch Slough, upriver from Buoy 17), the mouth of False River (near Buoy 25), and Santa Clara and San Andreas shoals (with good trolling in fall and spring).

This is a great playground for a boat owner, with calm water and hundreds of options. I love to scan a map and dream of where to visit next. You could fish every weekend of the year and not see the entire delta in your lifetime. There is just too much of it.

That factor causes it to be inundated with boats in the summer, particularly waterskiers in unbelievable numbers. The place gets wild, with very heavy drinking and wet T-shirt contests at marinas, and occasional arrests for under-age drinking. In low-rain years, the sheriffs can be more entertaining than the fishing.

The amount of striped bass, sturgeon, and salmon that swim up the San Joaquin is nearly equivalent to the amount of freshwater flowing through the San Joaquin. When rain and snowmelt runoff is low, the pumps continue to gorge themselves 24 hours a day, and the fish have very little reason to choose to swim here.

Maybe there will come a day when the pumps get shut down for the spring spawn, once again allowing the rivers to take their natural courses westward through the delta, bays, and out to sea. The day that happens is the day the fisheries will start their recovery.

Facilities, fees: Lodging, cabins, and campgrounds are provided; full-service marinas and supplies are available at or near many of the boat ramps listed under *Directions*. Fees are charged for day use at private resorts, boat launching, boat rentals, and camping.

Directions: Take Highway 4 to Antioch and continue to Oakley and Cypress Road. Turn left on Cypress Road, drive over the Bethel Island Bridge, and continue 0.5 mile to Gateway Road. Turn right and drive on Gateway Road. This route provides access to the interior San Joaquin Delta.

• To Emerald Pointe Marina, Bethel Island: Take Highway 4 to Antioch and continue east to Oakley and Cypress Road. Turn left on Cypress Road and drive three miles (drive over the Bethel Island Bridge; the road name changes to Bethel Island Road) to Stone Road. Turn right on Stone Road and continue 1.5 miles to the sign on the right for the marina entrance.

• To Bethel Harbor, Bethel Island: Take Highway 4 to Antioch and continue east to Oakley and Cypress Road. Turn left on Cypress Road and drive three miles (drive over the Bethel Island Bridge; the road name changes to Bethel Island Road) to Harbor Road (on the island's northern side). Turn right and drive to the end of the road.

• To Lundborg Landing, Bethel Island: Take

Highway 4 to Antioch and continue east to Oakley and Cypress Road. Turn left on Cypress Road and drive three miles (drive over the Bethel Island Bridge; the road name changes to Bethel Island Road) to Gateway Road. Turn right on Gateway Road and drive two miles to the park entrance on the left (look for the large sign and tugboat).

• To Sugar Barge Marina, Bethel Island: Take Highway 4 to Antioch and continue east to Oakley and Cypress Road. Turn left on Cypress Road and drive three miles (drive over the Bethel Island Bridge; the road name changes to Bethel Island Road) to Gateway Road. Turn right on Gateway Road and drive 0.25 mile to Piper Road. Turn left and drive two miles to Willow Road. Turn right and drive a short distance to the marina.

• To Eddo's Harbor & RV Park, Sherman Island: Take Highway 4 to Antioch and continue over the Antioch Bridge (where the road becomes Highway 160). Continue to Sherman Island East Levee Road. Turn right and drive to 19530 East Levee Road.

• To Lauritzen Yacht Harbor, Antioch: Take Highway 4 to Antioch and the exit for Wilbur Avenue. Take that exit, turn right, and drive to Bridgehead Road. Turn left on Bridgehead Road and drive 0.25 mile to the signed entrance for the yacht club on the right.

Contact: California Delta Chamber & Visitor Bureau, 916/777-4041, www.californiadelta .org.

Marinas and lodging: Anchor Marina, 925/684-9148, www.anchormarinainc .com; Beacon Harbor, 925/684-2174, www .beacon-harbor.com; Bethel Harbor, Bethel Island, 925/684-2141, www.bethelharbor .com; D'Anna's Bethel Island Marina Resort, 925/684-3720; Eddo's Harbor & RV Park, 925/757-5314, www.eddosresort.com; Emerald Pointe Marina, Bethel Island, 925/684-2388, www.emeraldpoint-marina.com; Frank's Marina, 925/684-2101; Hennis Marina, 925/684-3333; Lauritzen Yacht Harbor, Oakley, 925/757-1916, www.lauritzens.com; Lundborg Landing, 925/684-9351; Russo's Marina,

925/684-2024, www.russosmarina.com; Rusty Porthole Marina, 925/684-3607, www.rusty porthole.com; Seahorse Marina, 925/684-3606; Sugar Barge Marina, Bethel Island, 925/684-9075 or 800/799-4100, www.sugarbarge.com; Sunset Harbor, 925/684-3522.

Boat rentals and charters: Lundborg Landing, 925/684-9351; Paradise Point Marina, 800/752-9669, www.sevencrown.com/lakes.

Guides: Fish Hookers, 916/777-6498, www.fishhookers.com.

Hal Schell's *Delta Map and Guide* can be bought online at www.californiadelta.org/ordermap.html.

34 SOUTH DELTA

Rating: 10

near Stockton

Map 5.2, page 262

In many ways, the delta provides the pinnacle of California water sports: the best waterskiing, wakeboarding, the best bass fishing, and the fastest relief valve from the Bay Area pressure cooker. Out on the delta, everybody suddenly acts nice to each other, even though just a few miles away on the highways, it is exactly the opposite.

The fishing for largemouth bass is considered among the best in America, especially in the vicinity of Victoria Slough, Old River, and the Grant Line. Some of the most consistently good fishing for black bass in the delta occurs in 14-Mile Slough and White Slough. Many professional tournaments are won in these waters for bass. If there is a problem, it's that by the time you make your cast at a good-looking spot, it's likely a pro or two has already hit the area. You have to be like my friend "Hoover," who can vacuum up after everybody else has gone through.

I like to power up the San Joaquin River and head to the edge of Frank's Tract, along tule-lined False River. Along the way, there are dozens of good fishing spots: extended walls of tule berms, coves overgrown by weed mats, tule-lined points, and submerged fence lines from former fields flooded by levee breaks. My favorite strategy here is to use Senko worms rigged with No. 4/0 Gamakatsu hooks (no weight), white spinnerbaits, and Rattletraps. What work best are the Senko plastic worms, usually dark green and maroon sparkle. Cast toward shore, often along the rock-bedded levees in just a foot of water, let the worm sink, and then work it slowly along the bottom toward the weed mats. The bass hang in the weeds and under the mats. The bass mainly eat crawdads and threadfin shad in the delta, which try to hide from the bass in the submerged cover.

In a typical day, fish 15–25 spots and catch 20–30 bass. The delta is not always like a lake, because you have to master the tides. It can all be about timing. The best bites are at the turn of the tides: during high tides, the bass often move deep into the tule berms; on low tides, they get flushed out of the tules by low water and often can be found under the adjoining weed mats. Got it? The high tide is when the fish move back into the cover. The low tide is when they move out of the structure in the shallows.

The bass fishing in particular is quite good in spring, summer, and fall. The water gets very cold in the winter, sometimes in the low 40s, and that freezes the bite.

The crowds on weekends during the summer in the delta can be phenomenal—just as phenomenal as the lack of crowds during the week. This is when black-bass anglers have their time, even in the middle of summer during the hottest days. They search out the thickest weed beds and use weedless frogs and weedless rats. Skipping the lures across the top of this very thick vegetation seems to drive some of the biggest bass wild. They'll bust through to take the lure.

Working on the edges of the weed mats is not quite as productive; you have to force yourself to cast into the thickest cover. This requires heavy line, no less than 20-pound test, or even heavier with braided Fire Line.

Flipping is very popular in the delta because of the cover that can be accessed by this technique. The best two lures used are the 3/8-ounce jig with a crawdad trailer, or any 8- to 10-inch Power Worm.

In the winter, bass tend to migrate to the back of sloughs, out of the way of any current. In spring, they move toward the mouths of these sloughs. This is true off the South Fork of the Mokelumne River, with nearby Hog, Sycamore, or Beaver Slough.

Catfish can be caught virtually anywhere in this section of the delta. In the delta, remember that catfish are on the edges of the current, so don't be afraid to fish in 12–15 feet of water during incoming or outgoing tides. The turn of the tide and two hours after the turn are the prime times for catfish.

One of the best places for catfish in the entire delta is Fishermen's Cut. Almost all the side channels off the Stockton deep-water channel produce good catfishing. Rows of old pilings also can hold catfish; just make sure to fish in at least 12 feet of water.

In the summer, because of the high numbers of water-skiers and personal watercraft careening around, the superior bass waters are naturally the quiet, out-of-the-way spots with navigation hazards.

As you get deeper into the back delta, the better fishing is for catfish. West of Stockton, the area around King Island is one of the finer spots, particularly in Disappointment Slough and White Slough. Farther north, the Mokelumne River also holds a lot of catfish, with the best places just inside Sycamore Slough, Hog Slough, and Beaver Slough, which you run into in a row while cruising north on the Mokelumne River, north of Terminous.

The areas farther south used to provide excellent fishing for catfish, as well as striped bass, but no more. I remember fishing here, anchored and using anchovies for bait for striped bass or catfish, and needing just a one-ounce sinker to hold my bait on the bottom during an incoming tide. Now, with the pumps running, the tide direction is reversed, and even with a five-ounce sinker, it won't hold bottom. The pull is too strong. The pumps have the biggest negative impact on fishing at the area in the vicinity of Clifton Court, at Old River, and the Grant Line Canal.

There's some irony to this. Water flows have become minimal, because reduced amounts of water are allowed to run through the delta, yet pumping to points south has been increased, so the back delta now has the qualities of a lake, not a river. Instead of striped bass and salmon, there are largemouth bass and catfish.

Facilities, fees: Campgrounds, lodging, boat rentals, bait, tackle, and supplies are in the Stockton area. Fees are charged for day-use at private resorts, boat launching, and camping. Boat-launching facilities are at Discovery Bay Yacht Harbor (which charges a launching fee for nonresidents), Holland Riverside Marina, Lazy M Marina, and Orwood Resort.

Directions: To Discovery Bay Yacht Harbor, Byron: From Martinez, take Highway 4 east to Antioch/Oakley. Turn east on Highway 4 and drive (past Brentwood) to Discovery Bay Boulevard. Turn left and drive about one mile to Willow Lake Road. Turn right and drive 0.5 mile to Marina Road. Turn right and drive 0.25 mile to the marina (it's well signed).

• Holland Riverside Marina, Brentwood: From Martinez, take Highway 4 east to Antioch/Oakley. Turn east on Highway 4 and drive (near Brentwood) to the Byron Highway. Turn left on the Byron Highway and drive six miles to Delta Road. Turn right on Delta Road and drive two miles to the marina at the end of the road.

• Lazy M Marina, Byron: From the East Bay, take I-580 east to the split with Highway 205. Take Highway 205 to the exit for Grant Line Road (near Tracy). Take that exit, turn northwest, and drive to the Byron Highway. Turn right on the Byron Highway and drive eight miles to Clifton Court Road. Turn right and drive 0.5 mile to the marina.

• Orwood Resort, Brentwood: From Martinez, take Highway 4 east to Antioch/Oakley. Turn east on Highway 4 and drive (near Brentwood) to Bixler Road. Turn left and drive four miles to road's end, at Orwood Road. Turn right and drive 0.25 mile to the resort, on the right.

Contact: California Delta Chamber & Visitor Bureau, 916/777-4041, www.californiadelta .org.

Marinas and lodging: Ladd's Marina, Stockton, 209/477-9521; River's End Marina, near Clifton Court Forebay, 209/835-8365, www.riversendmarina.com; Discovery Bay Yacht Harbor, Byron, 925/634-5928, www .discoverybayyachtharbor.com; Holland Riverside Marina, 925/634-2345 or 925/634-8080, www.hollandriverside.com; Lazy M Marina, Byron, 925/634-4555; Orwood Resort, Brentwood, 925/634-7181, www.orwoodresort .com; Paradise Point Marina, 800/752-9669, www.sevencrown.com/lakes; Cruiser Haven Marina, 925/634-3822, www.cruiserhaven .com; Tracy Oasis Marina, 209/835-3182, tracy oasismarina.com; Whiskey Slough Harbor, 925/698-8100, www.whiskeyslough.com.

Supplies: Thornton Road Bait & Tackle, Stockton, 209/473-2239.

Boat rentals: Walnut Grove Marina, 916/776-1181, www.walnutgrovemarina.com.

Hal Schell's *Delta Map and Guide* can be bought online at www.californiadelta.org/ordermap.html.

35 SOUTH FORK AMERICAN RIVER

Rating: 5
near Placerville in Eldorado National Forest
Map 5.3, page 263

The upper South Fork American River offers one excellent fishing spot near U.S. 50, while two good stretches are available on the lower South Fork, just north of Placerville. Take your pick.

The best stretch of water in the entire canyon lies near Riverton along U.S. 50. Why is it so good? During the prime fishing season, there are simply more trout here than anywhere else on the river, because many are stocked here weekly from opening day, on the last Saturday in April, through July. This stretch is also very pretty. Anyone who makes the trip up U.S. 50 to Tahoe should keep a rod rigged and ready

so that they can park at a turnout and make a few casts to regain their sanity.

The lower stretch of the American, from Chili Bar on downstream, is very popular with rafters, whom you'll see in various stages of dress. On weekends, so many rafts can clog the water that they disrupt the fishing. The trout here are also smaller and warier, necessitating sneak-fishing techniques.

The solution is to head farther east toward the Coloma area, where rainbow trout in the 10- to 12-inch class are stocked, adding to a fair population of native fish.

Facilities, fees: Campgrounds are off U.S. 50. Supplies can be obtained in Placerville. Fishing access is free.

Directions: Excellent access to the upper South Fork American is off U.S. 50 east of Placerville; there are several turnouts where you can park and hike down to the river. The best area is near Riverton. Two good spots are also available on the lower South Fork American. From Placerville, drive north on Highway 193 to Chili Bar. Direct access is provided there, and there are trails for hiking downstream. Another option is near Coloma. From Placerville, drive north on Highway 49/193, then northwest on Highway 49, which crosses the river just north of town.

Contact: Eldorado National Forest, Placerville Ranger District, 530/644-2324, www.fs.fed .us/r5; Bureau of Land Management, Mother Lode Field Office, 916/941-3101, www.blm .gov/ca.

Guides: G&J Outdoor Enterprises, 530/885-1492, www.gandjoutdoors.com.

36 JENKINSON LAKE

Rating: 7
east of Placerville in Sly Park Recreation Area
Map 5.3, page 263

In many ways this is the ideal fishing destination. In fact, about the only thing wrong with Jenkinson Lake (also known as Sly Park Lake) is that it's hardly a secret.

The trout fishing is excellent in the spring, the bass fishing comes on strong in the summer, the upper end of the lake has a 5-mph speed limit (which keeps all the water-skiers out of your hair), and five lakeside camps are set along the north shore, on the upper end.

Sound good? It is. But this popular spot also attracts boaters with its easy accessibility and three-lane paved boat ramp, so you can expect plenty of company. Once on the water, though, just head well up the main lake arm, away from the water-skiers, and you will hardly notice the others.

With a surface area of 640 acres and set at 3,500 feet in the lower reaches of Eldorado National Forest, Jenkinson Lake has the perfect climate for fishing. Winters are cold and snowy, and spring and early summer bring cool water temperatures, creating ideal conditions for trout. In response, a lot of trout are stocked: rainbows in the 10- to 12-inch class, along with Eagle Lake fingerlings and a whopping number of brown-trout fingerlings. Just plain forget about fishing the main lake body. Instead head straight up the lake, trolling from the narrows on upstream, then exploring both lake arms.

Some big browns weighing over 10 pounds are in here, as are a few scattered Mackinaw. The Macks, however, don't get that big, usually running a couple of pounds at best. Some of the top trolling spots include the second dam and in front of both boat launches.

Smallmouth bass predominate here because of the excellent smallmouth habitat (flats, rocky points, and underwater ledges) throughout the lake. But when the hot weather arrives, get out your bass gear, because a surprisingly strong largemouth population has been established here. As with the trout, the bass fishing is better well up the lake arms. Watch out, though: you can pepper shoreline haunts with casts, hoping a big bass gets riled up enough to strike, and a large brown trout will strike your lure. It happens.

During winter and early spring, Jenkinson Reservoir is drawn way down, and the successful anglers fish from shore. It's one of the few lakes that I know of where you can catch a Mackinaw fishing from shore. These are usually caught by accident by anglers using night crawlers, hoping to entice a plant of rainbow or brown trout. Other tips: No personal watercraft are allowed on the lake and there is a horse trail that circles the lake.

Note: All boats must be inspected and certified free of mussels prior to launching at this lake.

Facilities, fees: There is a small marina with docks, campgrounds, vault toilets, drinking water, picnic areas, an RV dump station, and bait and tackle, and a convenience store with a bar and grill is across the street. Supplies can be obtained in Placerville or Pollock Pines. Two paved boat ramps, Stonebraker and West Shore, are available. Day-use and boat-launch fees apply.

Directions: From Sacramento, take U.S. 50 east to Pollock Pines and take the exit for Sly Park Road. Take that exit south and drive five miles to Jenkinson Lake and the campground access road. Turn left and drive one mile to the campground, on the left.

To the Stonebraker boat ramp: On the entrance road, continue straight past Pine Cone Campground to the Stonebraker Campground and launch ramp.

To the West Shore boat ramp: Once inside the lake entrance, drive 50 feet past the kiosk to the boat-ramp access road, on the right. Turn right and drive 0.25 mile to the ramp.

Contact: Sly Park Recreation Area, El Dorado Irrigation District, 530/295-6824 (information) or 530/295-6810 (reservations), www .eid.org; Sly Park Resort, 530/409-1328, www .slyparkresort.com.

❸❼ TIGER CREEK AFTERBAY

Rating: 5

northeast of Jackson
Map 5.3, page 263

Little Tiger Creek Afterbay is one of the most overlooked fishing spots along the Highway

88 corridor. Most people probably figure that since the elevation is 2,400 feet, the weather will be too hot and the lake too small to provide much of anything.

Wrong. It's not at all hot here during the spring. And in the cooler months, the water is stocked with 10- to 12-inch rainbow trout, providing good prospects for those with good timing. Most of the trout range in the 10- to 11-inch class. No float tubes or swimming are allowed.

Facilities, fees: A PG&E picnic area is provided. Supplies are in Pioneer. Fishing access is free.

Directions: From Jackson, take Highway 88 east for 18 miles to Tiger Creek Powerhouse Road (at Buckhorn Lodge). Turn right on Tiger Creek Powerhouse Road and drive one mile to a junction. Bear right at the junction and drive 1.4 miles to the reservoir.

Contact: PG&E Recreation Desk, 916/386-5164, www.pge.com/recreation.

38 LAKE TABEAUD

Rating: 5

near Jackson

Map 5.3, page 263

Set at 2,000 feet, an hour's drive east of Stockton, the lake is just high enough to keep the water cool into early summer. Tabeaud (how do you pronounce it?) provides quiet water and a chance to catch trout in a small lake that is often overlooked by the masses. The lake is stocked with rainbow trout in the 10- to 12-inch class, offering decent prospects, especially in the spring.

It's always funny to hear people try to pronounce the name of this lake on their first visit. My pal Foonsky, who commonly mangles names, called it Lake "Tay-Be-A-Ud."

It's pronounced "tah-BOW." Nice and simple. So is the fishing.

Facilities, fees: A picnic area is available. Supplies can be obtained in Jackson. No motors are permitted on the lake. Access is free.

Directions: From Stockton, drive east on Highway 88 to Highway 49. Turn south on Highway 49 and drive to Jackson. From Jackson, continue south on Highway 49 for 0.5 mile to Clinton Road. Turn left on Clinton Road and drive east for 5.1 miles to Tabeaud Road. Bear right on Tabeaud Road and continue two miles to the lake.

Contact: PG&E Recreation Desk, 916/386-5164, www.pge.com/recreation.

39 MOKELUMNE RIVER

Rating: 5

northeast of Stockton

Map 5.3, page 263

From the powerhouse on downstream, the Mokelumne has many riffles, drop-offs, and pools that hold trout. On summer evenings, it gives skilled fly fishers or spin fishers an opportunity to make quiet approaches and precise casts. This section of water is also good for kayaking. Flows used to fluctuate up and down at the crazy whim of the water master, but that problem no longer occurs. This is a huge plus.

Only the north fork of the river gets stocked. The Department of Fish and Game plants rainbow trout in the 10- to 12-inch class here. For anglers who specialize in using bait in rivers for trout, the first two months of the season, May and June, are the time to hit the river.

Facilities, fees: A picnic area is available on Electra Road, 2.7 miles east of Highway 49. Access is free.

Directions: From Stockton, take Highway 88 east for 24 miles past the town of Clements, and then continue on Highway 88 past Camanche Lake and Lake Pardee to Martel and Highway 49. Turn south on Highway 49, drive through Jackson, and continue 4.5 miles to Electra Road. Go east on Electra Road. The river is accessible off this road for four miles upstream, to the powerhouse at Electra.

Contact: Bureau of Land Management,

Mother Lode Field Office, 916/941-3101, www.blm.gov/ca; PG&E Recreation Desk, 916/386-5164, www.pge.com/recreation.

⁴⁰ LAKE AMADOR

Rating: 9

northeast of Stockton

Map 5.3, page 263

Imagine a fish factory that turned out giant bass and trout in numbers as if they were being made on an assembly line. At times, Lake Amador is like that fictional fish factory.

Amador is in the foothill country east of Stockton at an elevation of 485 feet, covering 425 acres and with 13.5 miles of shoreline. The lake is perfect for fishing, with several extended coves—the Carson arm, Cat Cove, Big Bay, the Jackson Creek arm, Rock Creek Cove, and Mountain Springs—and a law that prohibits waterskiing and personal watercraft. The top spots are the Carson arm and the Jackson Creek arm.

Lake Amador is famous for producing giant largemouth bass. In late March, it seems more bass weighing 5–12 pounds are caught here than at any lake in Northern California. In summer, some of the largest bass are caught at night. Bass-fishing instructor Larry Hemphill hooks lots of big bass here on summer nights using Weapon or Rod-Strainer jigs, or 10-inch plastic worms.

So that means everybody is fishing for the big bass, right? Wrong. The catch rates for rainbow trout have become so good from late winter through early summer that now the trout attract most of the fishing pressure. Lake Amador runs its own hatchery, which stocks thousands of pounds of trout; planting usually begins about the middle of October. These fast-growing trout are bred from wild rainbows in Summit Lake, Washington, and can reach up to 10 pounds in 16 months. The Department of Fish and Game also supplements the lake with rainbow trout in the 10- to 12-inch class. The best fishing is in the launch ramp cove (where the trout are planted), using Power Bait or small Kastmasters. Trollers can do okay in late spring out on the main lake and near the mouth of Jackson Creek.

One of the problems with Lake Amador in winter and early spring is that the lake muddies up easily with rain. That is why bait anglers off the bank can do better than the boat anglers trolling lures.

A trick here is trolling a Flatfish or Apex with at least 100 feet of line out, and then making S turns. Don't hurry to put any weight in front of these lures. You want them to go as shallow as possible. The trout are right up near the surface. Bright colors are best.

In the spring, the best bet for landing one of the big bass is using live crawdads for bait on the Jackson Creek, Mountain Springs, or Carson Creek arm of the lake. If you can't get crawdads, casting plastic worms right along the shoreline may also work. The skill and light touch required for both of these techniques can take a lot of time to develop, however. That is why the trout fishing has become so popular at Amador. With weekly stocks, it takes no time at all to figure out how to do it.

The lake is open year-round, and the trout fishing provides the best hopes. As the weather warms, there are days when everyone on the lake limits. The Jackson Creek area is my favorite spot for trout.

The only time this lake frustrates is in late summer, when week after week of warm temperatures puts the trout deep and makes the bass wary. That is when people switch to catfish in Big Bay and Cat Cove. Giant catfish over 40 pounds are also a very real possibility here in the spring and summer. The Mountain Springs and Carson Creek arms, as well as the dam, are the most productive spots for cat hunters using mackerel, sardines, or liver—though trout anglers soaking Power Bait near the launch ramp also get surprised by a big cat now and again. Crappie and bluegill fishing is another good prospect at Amador; fish the brushy coves with small jigs, minnows, or red worms.

There's one little problem at Lake Amador, as well as at nearby Pardee and Camanche. Listen close and you'll hear it. It's the sound of ka-ching. Fees are charged for your vehicle, another for each person over two, another for boat launching, and that's before you buy any tackle, bait, drinks, or food. Hear it? Ka-ching, ka-ching, ka-ching.

Facilities, fees: A small marina rents fishing boats. Campgrounds, a picnic area, drinking water, restrooms, showers, an RV dump station, fishing supplies (including bait and tackle), a snack bar, restaurant, a convenience store, gas, propane gas, a seasonal swimming pond, a boat ramp, and a playground are available. There is an entrance fee per vehicle for two people, plus more for each additional person. A fishing fee is charged per person per day, and a launch fee is charged.

Directions: From Stockton, take Highway 88 east for 24 miles to Clements. Just east of Clements, bear left on Highway 88 and drive 11 miles to Jackson Valley Road. Turn right (well signed) and drive four miles to Buena Vista Drive. Continue straight one mile to Lake Amador Drive. Turn right and drive over the dam to the campground office.

Contact: Lake Amador Resort, 209/274-4739, www.lakeamador.com; Dale's Foothill Fishing (guide), 530/295-0488, www.dalesfoothill fishing.com.

41 PARDEE LAKE

Rating: 9

northeast of Stockton
Map 5.3, page 263

Pardee is the prettiest of the lakes in the Mother Lode country, covering more than 2,000 acres with 37 miles of shoreline. It is most beautiful in early spring, when the lake is full, the hills are green, and the wildflowers are blooming. And one other thing, the rainbow trout are biting, too. Then, during the summer, attention turns to bass (both smallmouth and largemouth), as well as kokanee salmon and catfish.

The lake is set up exclusively for anglers, with no waterskiing or personal watercraft permitted. Most anglers use boats, get on the water early, and troll from the boat launch right down the north arm. Start in the center of the lake, then work along the east side, turning east down the long channel arm of the lake.

The Department of Fish and Game stocks 6- to 8-inch rainbow trout and tons of fingerling kokanee salmon. In addition, the lake manager stocks 70,000-plus pounds of rainbow trout that weigh 2–8 pounds. There's plenty of feed for kokanee, so they grow quickly and survive over winter. In the best years, some kokanee approach 17 inches long. This lake is one of the best lakes in California for kokanee salmon.

When the lake opens in February, it's a big event that draws thousands of people. The night before the opener, cars with and without boat trailers form a line just outside the gate, and by dawn, the end of the line is usually several miles down the road. Opening day is not for the faint of heart—the crowds can be overwhelming. On the plus side, there are bazillions of trout planted here before the opener (and usually all season long for that matter). Since the truck trout get dumped in at the boat ramp, that's where the best fishing takes place early in the season. Shore anglers in the marina cove—using Power Bait, night crawlers, or assorted spoons and spinners—cash in on the planters.

In addition to the boat ramp vicinity, two other favorite spots receive far less pressure. One is the extreme southern portion of the lake, specifically just as the cove narrows. Beach your boat on the left and bank fish, using Power Bait for trout. It can be a real hot spot. In addition, trollers often find kokanee and trout in the same area here because of a light prevailing north wind that pushes food into the area.

The other spot is at the uppermost outhouse on the Mokelumne River. An outhouse? Yes, an outhouse! It is one of several floating outhouses on Pardee.

This is where the cold water of the Mokelumne enters the warm water of the lake. Look for any kind of light debris line—that will indicate the change. The upstream side will be very cold; the transition to the lower side is obvious. Most fish are just below the change. It is worth trolling or bait fishing from a boat here.

When you see trout rising, one strategy is to allow your boat to drift and to cast lures such as a Kastmaster, a Krocodile, or a brown Roostertail spinner; all can produce some nice fish.

Until the water near the launch area warms up, later in the spring, shore anglers do the most damage, but trollers take over as summer approaches and the fish begin to disperse. Boaters usually drop their gear just outside the marina and troll through the Narrows until they clear the 5-mph buoys. If they pick up a fish or two, they'll turn around and make another pass. If not, they usually try around the dam, near Woodpile Gulch, or off the mouth of the Mokelumne arm.

Pardee also has a nice population of smallmouth bass, but not many people try for them. Hmm, maybe that's why there's a good number of them. In the spring, when the lake is full and all the shoreline grass is flooded, a tip for bass anglers is to cast a dark ripple-tailed grub (rigged with a weedless hook) toward the backs of coves, then retrieve very slowly. Always watch closely for your line to move sideways—often that is all you see when you get a pickup—and set the hook immediately.

As summer arrives, anglers must be on the water very early or must fish quite deep. Some anglers get their trout limit and are done by 9 A.M. One of the easiest ways is just to troll a Needlefish lure 5–15 feet deep, although many rely on the traditional flashers, followed by a night crawler. Shoreliners don't try anything fancy either, using Power Bait and a night crawler on separate hooks.

Another possibility is trolling for kokanee salmon, using flashers followed by a No. 10 Wedding Spinner, made by Luhr Jensen. The kokanee also seem to be a morning bite.

Because of Pardee's proximity to the other Mother Lode lakes, one option is to connect on the trout at Pardee in the morning, then skip over to Amador in the evening for the bass. It's a great combination and an offer too good to refuse.

The state record for smallmouth bass was caught here in July of 2007. The fish weighed 9.83 pounds and broke a 40-year-old record. The lucky angler was Harold Hardin of Stockton, who said he lost a fish larger than the state-record fish and has seen others that are much larger. Hardin said he used a swim bait off Leveque Point at the mouth of the Mokelumne River.

Lake records: 9.83-pound smallmouth bass; 13-pound, 4-ounce largemouth bass. Both were caught in 2007.

Facilities, fees: A full-service marina has fishing boats and pontoon boats for rent, boat moorings, a boat ramp, and boat storage. A campground, drinking water, restrooms, showers (in the RV section of the campground), an RV dump station, a fish-cleaning station, coin laundry, a convenience store, propane gas, full-service restaurant, RV storage, a wading pool, and a seasonal swimming pool are available. There is an entrance fee per vehicle, a fishing fee per person per day, and a boat and float-tube launch fee per day.

Directions: From Stockton, take Highway 88 east for 24 miles to the town of Clements. Just east of Clements, bear left on Highway 88 and drive 11 miles to Jackson Valley Road. Turn right and drive to a four-way stop sign at Buena Vista. Turn right and drive for three miles to Stony Creek Road, on the left. Turn left and drive a mile to the campground, on the right.

Contact: Pardee Recreation Area, 209/772-1472, www.pardeelakerecreation.com; Pardee Marina, 209/772-8108; Dale's Foothill Fishing (guide), 530/295-0488, www.dalesfoothillfishing.com.

42 CAMANCHE LAKE

Rating: 9

northeast of Stockton

Map 5.3, page 263

Come the first warm days of spring, some of the best lake fishing in California can be had here. Like most foothill reservoirs, Camanche can produce small fish, but if you hit it right in late winter or early spring, bass average two pounds or better. There is a wide variety of fish—bass, trout, crappie, bluegill, catfish—and on a spring or early summer weekend it is possible to catch all of them. During this time, Camanche provides an outstanding fishery—a take-your-pick deal. This is the homewater for Bob Simms, the Sacramento radio angler legend, and he's shown me all his tricks here on many trips.

Camanche is a large, multifaceted facility set in the foothills east of Lodi at an elevation of 325 feet, covering 7,700 acres and with 53 miles of shoreline. Camanche is known among anglers as one of the best lakes in the West with regards to structure. This is because of all the mine tailings—that is, piles of rocks and ditches left over by 19th-century miners.

This is a great lake to fish using light tackle, anywhere from 6- to 10- pound test line, and split-shotting four- to six-inch plastic worms. A key is to use the smallest split shot possible to get your worm down.

The bass tend not to be huge at Camanche, but they can often be found in abundance by boaters working the shoreline, casting lures as they go. Most of the bass are in the 12- to 14-inch class, with a sprinkling of 15- and 16-inchers, and just occasionally a monster. They provide excellent sport. Bass in Camanche are very color-conscious and very particular about the time of day, so don't be afraid to experiment.

Because of the abundance of threadfin shad in Camanche, small deep-diving crankbaits and spinner baits in shad patterns can be very good year-round. Some of the most exciting bass action can be had with topwater baits, such as Pop-Rs, on summer evenings. With plenty of structure, the entire upper lake can be excellent for bass fishing.

Camanche can be one of the better crappie lakes in the Sierra foothills, and there are times in the spring when the crappie fishing at Camanche can be the best thing going in the state. One trick is to fish at night, bringing one of those bright minnow lights. The light sits in the water and attracts both gnats and minnows, and in turn, crappie show up to eat both. If you toss a live minnow or white crappie jig their way, you can have periods of a fish per cast.

Camanche gets decent trout stocks from the Department of Fish and Game, which plunks in 10- to 12-inch rainbow trout and kokanee salmon fingerlings. It is also stocked by Urban Park Concessionaires with 80,000 pounds of trout, as well as an annual stock of largemouth bass.

Trout anglers have many options at Camanche. The lake is big enough so that the planters can take on the characteristics of wild fish and grow to 10 pounds. Trollers catch as many fish as anybody, and the best time to try it is in the late winter or early spring. Trolling right along the surface with a silver-blue Kastmaster works as well as just about any other method. Try near the dam and off the north-shore and south-shore boat ramps. If the trout aren't biting in the big lake, there's always the South Shore Trout Pond, which is well stocked with trout ranging from pan-sized to several pounds. The rock wall, just off the mouth of China Cove, can be an excellent area to troll for trout, too. So can the bridge area farther up the lake.

Another popular area to troll is between Big Hat Island and Little Hat Island. A great trick is to use a Rainbow Runner lure, rigged with a single hook. Add half a night crawler on the hook, then troll it, varying depths. The slow, rolling, back-and-forth action of the lure with the scent of the night crawler can prove irresistible.

Because Pardee Dam is just a few miles

above Camanche, this lake doesn't muddy up like others do after a heavy storm. That is why trolling for trout here can be good in the winter months, when so many other lakes are still muddy. After big rains, when the water is a little cloudy, a favorite lure is a fire tiger Rapala or Rebel trolled on a long line, paralleling the shoreline.

A good tip here is to never be afraid to troll near any stickups or islands. In winter, many trout hang close to shore or near cover.

Alas, there is always a snag. Here it's called summertime, when the place is inundated by water-skiers and personal watercraft riders, and if those goofs hit the coves, the best spots get spooked. If the traffic is heavy, head to the area above the Narrows—it's quiet here, courtesy of a 20-mph speed limit and the banning of waterskiing and personal watercraft riding.

Camanche is probably the most misspelled lake name in California, "Comanche" being a frequent foul-up. But by any name, this lake fishes great. As at Pardee and Amador, multiple fees are charged for access for anglers with boats.

Lake records: 19.42-pound rainbow trout, 14.33-pound largemouth bass, 2.49-pound crappie.

Note: All boats must be inspected and certified free of mussels prior to launching at this lake.

Facilities, fees: Full-service marinas offer fishing-boat and pontoon-boat rentals, mooring, and boat storage. Lodging, campgrounds, restrooms, showers, an RV dump station, a trout pond, boat ramps, coin laundry, a snack bar, and a convenience store are available. Restaurants are nearby. Fees are charged for day use, boat launching, mussel inspection, and fishing.

Directions: To the north shore: From Stockton, drive east on Highway 88 for 24 miles to Clements. Just east of Clements, bear left on Highway 88 and drive six miles to Camanche Parkway. Turn right and drive seven miles to the Camanche North Shore entrance gate.

To the south shore: From Stockton, drive east on Highway 88 for 24 miles to Clements. Just east of Clements, continue east on Highway 12 and drive six miles to South Camanche Parkway. Turn left and drive six miles to the entrance gate.

Contact: Lake Camanche North Shore, 209/763-5121, www.camancherecreation.com; North Shore Marina, 209/763-5166; Lake Camanche South Shore, 209/763-5178; South Shore Marina, 209/763-5915; Dale's Foothill Fishing (guide), 530/295-0488, www.dalesfoothillfishing.com.

43 NEW HOGAN RESERVOIR

Rating: 8

northeast of Stockton

Map 5.3, page 263

New Hogan has reclaimed its stock as a great fishing lake, for bass in the spring and early summer, and then for striped bass in late summer and fall. Plus, unlike nearby Amador, Pardee and Camanche, you don't get charged over and over—for vehicle access, for fishing, for boat launching.

The unique quality of New Hogan is striped bass. And with good reason: The fishery is booming. The lake is loaded with stripers that run 2–20 pounds, and they can be caught in a variety of ways. A 31-pounder was caught in 2006.

The period from July through September provides some of the most entertaining fishing to be had anywhere. That's when big schools of stripers herd balls of shad to the surface. When the shad run out of water, the stripers hammer them from below and create wild boils that can be seen from several hundred yards away. Anglers employ a blast-and-cast method to fish the boils. They sit out in the middle of the lake until they see stripers thrashing on the surface, then crank up their outboards and dash madly toward the activity. They then cut the motor and drift up to the edge of the school and cast topwater baits to the boils.

It's not as easy as it sounds, however. First of

all, you usually only get one to three casts per boil (when the shad get dispersed, the stripers drop back down and try to round 'em up again). Next, you have to "match the hatch" at times. The stripers can get locked into one particular size of bait and won't hit anything that isn't that exact size. I've seen guys fish boils all day without a touch because they were using five-inch-long Zara Spooks that were much larger than the shad that the bass were feeding on. Most of the shad you're going to see here are about one-half to three-quarters of an inch long, so things like Teeny Torpedoes and Zara Pooches work great. The best lure I've ever used here for boiling stripers, though, is a 1/12-ounce silver Kastmaster. It is so light that you need to go with 2-pound test to get any casting distance, but it sure is fun when you hook up! When the fish are not boiling, trolling Rapalas on downriggers or jigging with Hopkins spoons works well.

At New Hogan, you can enjoy chasing stripers or spend a little time catching bluegill, or even enjoy some pretty good crappie fishing at times. The lake-record crappie is 3 pounds, 8 ounces—right, a monster. But to many, this is still a bass-fishing lake. As you work the shoreline, casting with a variety of plastics or crankbaits, keep a wary eye on the depth finder. Track every drop-off or rock pile. These structures always hold bass.

Although New Hogan is not believed to be in the same league for largemouth bass fishing as Camanche, it can be excellent from mid-March through late May. Almost everything here is grubs, Brush Hogs and Senkos, and a lot of finesse fishing drop-shotting with Senkos rigged Wacky style (see *Largemouth Bass* in the *Sport Fish* chapter).

During the summer, you have to fight the waterskiing traffic, but there are excellent spots with quiet water up the lake arms. The best areas are at the far north end of the lake up the Calaveras River arm, and at the far south end of the lake up the Bear Creek and Whisky Creek arms.

New Hogan covers 4,000 acres and has 50 miles of shoreline. It is at an elevation of 680 feet and offers many boat-in camping spots along the eastern shore near Deer Flat, a tremendous vacation spot for boaters, campers, and anglers.

One problem is that since 2000, no marina operator or boat rentals have been available at New Hogan. The U.S. Army Corps of Engineers has been hoping for a replacement. But hoping, whether in fishing or in government, never is the best strategy to get something done.

Facilities, fees: Two drive-in campgrounds, drinking water, restrooms with flush toilets, showers, a fish-cleaning station, two boat ramps, and an RV dump station are available. Boat-in campsites, a picnic area, and a golf course are nearby. A day-use fee is charged. A boat-launching fee is charged daily or annually. Supplies are available in Valley Springs.

Directions: From Stockton, drive east on Highway 26 for about 35 miles to Valley Springs and Hogan Dam Road. Turn right and drive 1.5 miles to Hogan Parkway. Turn left and drive one mile to South Petersburg Road. Turn left and drive 0.25 mile to the campground at the lake, on the right.

Contact: U.S. Army Corps of Engineers, Sacramento District, 209/772-1343, www.corpslakes.usace.army.mil.

TAHOE AND NORTHERN SIERRA

© RAMBOB STIENSTRA

BEST FISHING SPOTS

❰ Freshwater Fisheries
Lake Tahoe, **page 341.**

❰ Most Unusual Fisheries
Independence Lake, **page 322.**
Martis Creek Reservoir, **page 336.**
Hell Hole Reservoir, **page 340.**
Kirman Lake, **page 371.**

This is one of California's most beautiful and

diverse landscapes. From the foothills to the Sierra crest, there is a vast spectrum of opportunity for people who love to fish, camp, and explore.

Tahoe and the northern Sierra feature hundreds of lakes, including dozens you can drive to. The best for scenic beauty are Echo, Donner, Fallen Leaf, Sardine, Caples, Loon, Union Valley... well, I could go on and on. It is one of the most beautiful regions anywhere on earth.

The northern end of the Sierra starts near Bucks Lake and extends to Bear River Canyon (and Caples Lake, Silver Lake, and Bear River Reservoir). In between are the Lakes Basin Recreation Area (containing Gold, Sardine, Packer, and other lakes), in southern Plumas County; the Bowman Lakes Recreation Area (dozens of small lakes); the Crystal Basin (featuring Union Valley Reservoir and Loon Lake, among others), in the Sierra foothills west of Tahoe; Lake Davis (with the highest catch rates for trout), near Portola; and the Carson River Canyon and Hope Valley, south of Tahoe.

With so many fish and so little time, Plumas National Forest offers the ultimate paradox for anglers, especially those on vacation. Plumas has it all: great natural beauty, dozens of lakes, streams, and campgrounds, a chance at big fish, and tremendous variety.

Of course, Lake Tahoe itself can provide a special opportunity for Mackinaw trout. When it's good, it's great, with 5- to 10-pound trout in a stellar setting. On a clear, quiet dawn, the beauty is electrifying. There are beautiful lakes elsewhere in the region that provide good fishing for trout, such as Beardsley, Spicer Meadows, and Alpine.

Another big plus is increasing quality of kokanee salmon at several lakes near Tahoe, including Stampede, Boca, and Donner (along I-80), as well as Caples (along Highway 88). There are also several small streams, such as the South Fork American, the East Fork Carson and West Fork Carson, and of course the well-known Truckee River.

You could spend weeks exploring any of these places, having the time of your life, and still not get to Tahoe's magic. But it is Tahoe where the adventure starts for many, especially in the surrounding Tahoe National Forest and Desolation Wilderness.

So many fish, so little time.

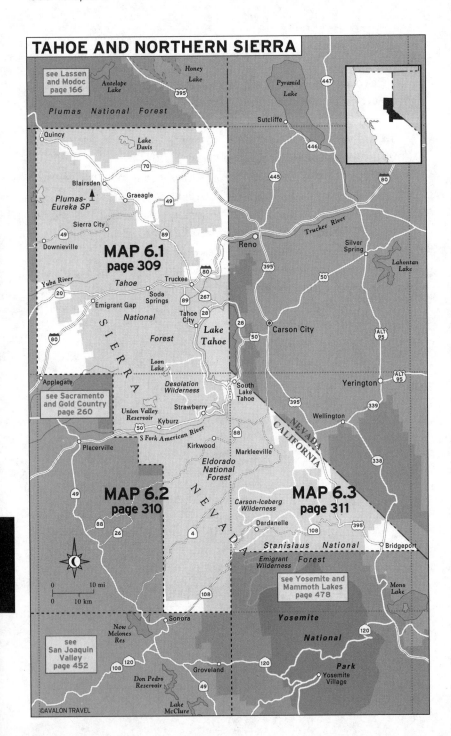

TAHOE AND NORTHERN SIERRA

see Lassen
and Modoc
page 166

Honey
Lake

Pyramid
Lake

Antelope
Lake

447

395

Plumas National Forest

Sutcliffe

446

Quincy

445

Lake
Davis

70

80

Blairsden

Graeagle

49

Reno

Truckee River

Silver
Spring

Plumas-
Eureka SP

Sierra City

89

Lahontan
Lake

49

Downieville

MAP 6.1
page 309

Truckee

80

395

50

20

Tahoe

Soda
Springs

89

267

28

ALT
95

Emigrant Gap

National

Tahoe
City

28

Carson City

80

Forest

Lake
Tahoe

50

Loon
Lake

ALT
95

Applegate

Desolation
Wilderness

South
Lake
Tahoe

Yerington

see Sacramento
and Gold Country
page 260

Union Valley
Reservoir

Strawberry

395

339

50

Kyburz

Wellington

Placerville

S Fork American River

88

338

Kirkwood

Markleeville

49

MAP 6.2
page 310

Eldorado
National
Forest

MAP 6.3
page 311

88

Carson-Iceberg
Wilderness

26

4

Dardanelle

108

395

Bridgeport

Stanislaus National

0   10 mi

Emigrant
Wilderness

Forest

0   10 km

see Yosemite and
Mammoth Lakes
page 478

Mono
Lake

Sonora

New
Melones
Res

Yosemite

120

see
San Joaquin
Valley
page 452

National

108

120

Groveland

120

Park

Yosemite
Village

49

Don Pedro
Reservoir

Lake
McClure

©AVALON TRAVEL

NEVADA

CALIFORNIA

SIERRA

NEVADA

Map 6.1

Sites 1-43
Pages 312-341

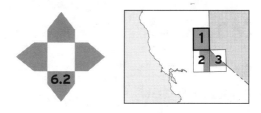

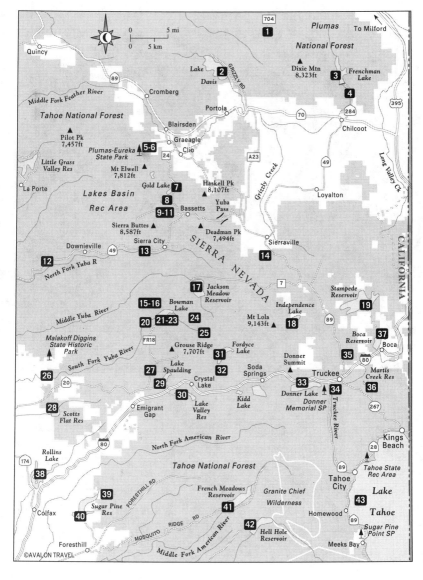

Map 6.2

Sites 44-67
Pages 345-361

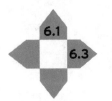

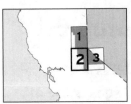

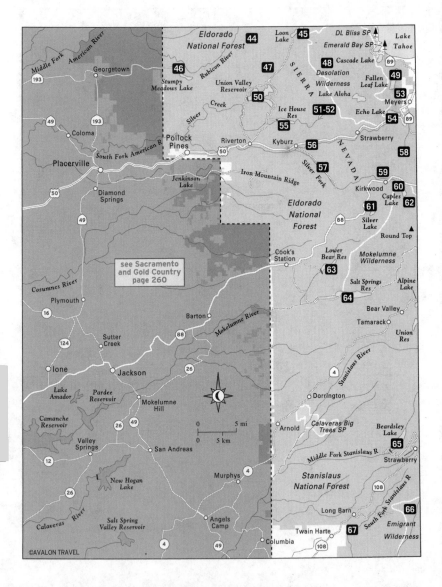

Map 6.3

Sites 68-85
Pages 361-373

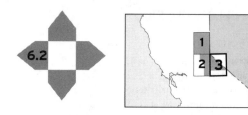

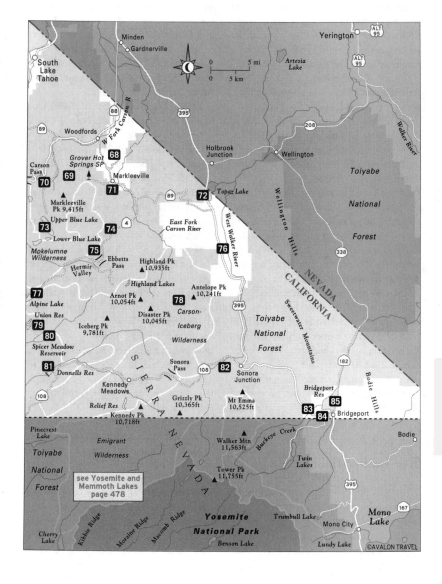

1 WILLOW CREEK

Rating: 4
near Milford in Plumas National Forest
Map 6.1, page 309

If you want a quiet, small stream with good access, you want to know about Willow Creek.

This obscure little stream flows through the Diamond Mountains southwest of Honey Lake (shallow, alkaline, few fish). The trout are on the small side, but they are wild, not planters. The area is quiet and gets little traffic. There are a number of four-wheel-drive roads in the area.

A camp (Conklin Park) is situated along little Willow Creek, on the northeastern border of the Dixie Mountain State Game Refuge. The area has greened up, although there remains some evidence of a big wildfire. The campground is little known, primitive, rarely used, and is not likely to change anytime soon. The elevation is 5,900 feet.

Facilities, fees: Conklin Park campground is on Willow Creek. Vault toilets are available, but drinking water is not. Garbage must be packed out. Supplies can be obtained in Milford at Doyle Pay-Less, (530/827-2880), Beckwourth, or Chilcoot. Fishing access is free.

Directions: From Susanville, take U.S. 395 south for 24 miles to Milford. In Milford turn right (east) on County Road 336 and drive about four miles to a Y. Bear left on Forest Service Road 70/26N70 and drive three miles. Turn right at the bridge at Willow Creek, turn left on Forest Service Road 70 (now paved), and drive three miles to the camp entrance road, on the left.

Contact: Plumas National Forest, Beckwourth Ranger District, 530/836-2575, ww.fs.fed.us/r5—click on Forest Offices.

2 LAKE DAVIS

Rating: 10
near Portola in Plumas National Forest
Map 6.1, page 309

What is occurring at Lake Davis is the resurgence of California's preeminent trout fishery at a mountain lake. The Department of Fish and Game is trying to create a fishery where the trout say, "Catch me!"

In late 2007, the DFG tried again to rid Lake Davis of pike by drawing the lake down to a puddle and then poisoning it. Ever since, the DFG shows up with a fleet of tankers full of trout like you've never seen to bring the lake back. DFG biologists have projected that many of the trout introduced to the lake will spawn in the future, and their progeny will take on the characteristics of the previous wild-born trout that made Davis one of the special travel destinations for anglers throughout the western United States.

The DFG's first attempt to poison Lake Davis was botched in the fall of 1997. I was at the lake the day the first pike was caught here, and I couldn't believe someone could be so stupid as to plant pike in a great trout lake. The DFG feared the pike would get downstream and eventually into the delta, where they would threaten to wipe out salmon, steelhead, and several endangered species, such as the delta smelt.

Historically, Davis has always been one of the best mountain trout fisheries in America because of its rich aquatic food chain. This differs from most mountain lakes, where the stark, pristine waters provide little food and the fish stay very small. The trout at Davis are often in the 14- to 20-inch class, sometimes bigger, and always beautiful and healthy, with the brightest black spots imaginable. It's a great lake for people camping or staying in the cabins, fishing from shore, trolling, fly-fishing, and float tubing.

The peak times to fish for trout are from the late spring ice-out through June and then in the fall. They span all sizes, from dinkers to 24-inch trophies.

Lake Davis is in the southern reaches of Plumas National Forest, just 50 miles from Reno, a bonus if you want to end your trip with a little gambling binge. It's good-sized, with 30 miles of shoreline. Even so, it can freeze over. That's because it's high in the northern Sierra, at an elevation of 5,775 feet, so it freezes over and gets plenty of snow in the winter.

Many people just show up, pick a spot along the shore at Camp 5, and then throw out Power Bait with a very light weight, floating the bait just off the bottom. They average two or three fish and are very content with that.

Others with boats troll just off the island or from Camp 5 up to the mouth of Freeman Creek, trolling woolly buggers or Cripplures. The bite is excellent from April through early June, then slows down during warm days of summer. The fishing picks up again from about the first week of September, is better yet in October, and continues until snow and bad weather shut the lake down in November. Skilled trollers can take 20–30 fish per trip when things are going great guns. There's a real nice spot just to the far side of the island, a slot that can be extremely productive.

If that doesn't score, head up toward the mouth of the creeks. Needlefish work well here, and so does the fire-tiger-colored Countdown Rapala. In fact, when the water is cool, as in the late spring and again in the fall, trolling a Rapala on a long line where the lake shallows up can result in some really big fish.

This lake is ideal for fly-fishing from a float tube, particularly on the northwest end, near the outlets of Freeman Creek (the best spot) and Grizzly Creek (second best). In fact, the whole northwestern end seems to hold more of the larger resident trout, while the southern end has more of the smaller planters. Davis has become a favorite among float tubers. They'll spend the day fly casting with woolly worms and woolly buggers, using a strip retrieve and doing well. Ten per rod is doing well, and again, there is a good chance for 16- and 17-inchers, sometimes bigger.

All boating is permitted here, and trolling is quite popular. But if you arrive in the spring, beware of afternoon winds, which can howl out of the north. So dress warmly, get out early, and enjoy the quiet time. As summer arrives, the evening trout rise can be quite a sight.

Facilities, fees: Several campgrounds are available. The largest is Grasshopper Flat. Drinking water and vault toilets are provided. A boat ramp, grocery store, and an RV dump station are nearby. Supplies are at the Grizzly Store (at Lake Davis) and at Dollard's (in Portola). Fishing access is free.

Directions: From Truckee, turn north on Highway 89 and drive to Sattley and County Road A23. Turn right on County Road A23 and drive 13 miles to Highway 70. Turn left on Highway 70 and drive one mile to Grizzly Road. Turn right on Grizzly Road and drive about six miles to Lake Davis.

To Lightning Tree Campground: From Truckee, turn north on Highway 89 and drive to Sattley and County Road A23. Turn right on County Road A23 and drive 13 miles to Highway 70. Turn left on Highway 70 and drive one mile to Grizzly Road. Turn right on Grizzly Road and drive about six miles to Lake Davis. Continue north on Lake Davis Road along the lake's east shore, and drive about five miles to the campground entrance, on the left.

Contact: Plumas National Forest, Beckwourth Ranger District, 530/836-2575, www.fs.fed.us/r5—click on Forest Offices; Plumas County Visitors Bureau, 800/326-2247, www.plumascounty.org; Lake Davis Cabins, 530/832-1060; Grizzly Store, Lake Davis, 530/832-0270, grizzlystore.portola-ca.com; Dollard's, Portola, 530/832-5251; Sportsmen's Den, Quincy, 530/283-2733; Dillard Guided Fishing, 530/832-6394, www.dillardguidedfishing.com.

❸ FRENCHMAN LAKE

Rating: 7

near Chilcoot in Plumas National Forest

Map 6.1, page 309

Frenchman Lake provides a solid put-and-take trout fishery. The DFG stocks Eagle Lake trout here, both catchables and fingerlings.

By boat, most anglers slow-troll with night crawlers until getting a strike, then rework the area. A lot of folks make the mistake of quickly getting away from the boat ramp area. It is my experience that this is one of the better spots to fish, along with the narrows, and upstream near the creek inlet.

This is a good lake for shore fishing, particularly from the inlet on the west side, which is directly accessible from the road. Because it is well protected from winds, that same area is ideal for fishing from a float tube or a small raft, on either side of the road.

The lake gets a solid 7 rating. It would be higher except for the size of the fish; they just don't quite have the big ones you might expect when you fish the place. You'd think that fish in excess of three pounds would be quite common at this lake, but they're not.

This lake also has fluctuations of success according to the time of year. You can come here in midsummer, when the campgrounds are full with happy families eagerly heading to the lake, and then the fishing just doesn't quite match up to the fantasies. But after Labor Day, those fish go on the bite, just like in the spring.

A bonus before Memorial Day and after Labor Day is that you can have the lake to yourself when the fishing is best, though the nights are cold. That is when catch rates are often outstanding at Frenchman Lake, a great spot that is easy to hit for anyone visiting Reno, only 35 miles away.

Water demands often cause the lake level to drop substantially in late summer and fall. During this time of the year, it is wise to phone the U.S. Forest Service before planning a trip with a boat to make sure the water level isn't below the ramp.

This is fairly high country, at an elevation of 5,500 feet, so the lake gets cold and windy in the spring and fall.

Facilities, fees: A boat ramp is provided, and several campgrounds are nearby. Drinking water and vault toilets are available, as are groceries. Supplies are seven miles away in Chilcoot. Fishing access is free.

Directions: From Reno, take U.S. 395 north to the junction with Highway 70. Turn west on Highway 70 and drive to Chilcoot and the junction with Frenchman Lake Road. Turn right on Frenchman Lake Road and drive nine miles to the lake and to a Y. At the Y, turn right and drive 1.5 miles to the campground, on the left side of the road. The boat ramp is nearby.

Contact: Wiggin's Trading Post, Chilcoot, 530/993-4721; Plumas National Forest, Beckwourth Ranger District, 530/836-2575, www.fs.fed.us/r5—click on Forest Offices; Plumas County Visitors Bureau, 800/326-2247, www.plumascounty.org.

4 LITTLE LAST CHANCE CREEK

Rating: 4

near Chilcoot in Plumas National Forest

Map 6.1, page 309

Little Last Chance Creek is a beautiful stream full of riffles, bends, and pools. It once provided excellent fishing, but now it is largely overgrown with brush, making access very difficult. Trying to work your way through the brush to reach the stream and then trying to cast is like standing in a spider web. It will drive you crazy. When you move to another spot, you then repeat the frustration all over again. So even though there are miles of river, what you find is everybody fishing the same 50 yards below the dam, over and over again, catching the planters.

Over the years I have caught some beautiful trout in this stream. The best section is the first 200 yards below the outlet at Frenchman Lake Dam. Little Last Chance Creek is stocked here.

Even though Little Last Chance Creek is only a 45-minute drive from Reno, the place has a remote feeling to it.

I remember when this was a real quality trout fishery, with some big native fish. I once released a 16-inch while a local bait dunker was standing by. He practically gagged. Just couldn't believe it.

"Why fish if you're going to throw 'em back?" he said. "Because I'd like to catch 'em again next year," I answered. He looked at me as if I had antlers growing out of my head.

Facilities, fees: The Chilcoot Campground is on Frenchman Lake Road near the stream. Drinking water and flush toilets are available. Supplies are in Chilcoot, at Wiggin's Trading Post. Fishing access is free.

Directions: From Reno, take U.S. 395 north to the junction with Highway 70. Turn west on Highway 70 and drive to Chilcoot and the junction with Frenchman Lake Road. Turn right on Frenchman Lake Road and drive 5–7 miles. The stream is alongside the road. The best access is directly below the outlet for Frenchman Lake Dam.

Contact: Wiggin's Trading Post, Chilcoot, 530/993-4721; Plumas National Forest, Beckwourth Ranger District, 530/836-2575, www .fs.fed.us/r5—click on Forest Offices; Plumas County Visitors Bureau, 800/326-2247, www .plumascounty.org.

5 EUREKA LAKE

Rating: 5

near the town of Graeagle in
Plumas-Eureka State Park
Map 6.1, page 309

The trout fishing at this beautiful little lake is best during the first part of the season, usually from late May through June and into early July. If you are camping at Plumas-Eureka State Park, it is well worth the short walk to the lake to make a few casts. There are primarily brook trout.

Some fly fishers work this lake with a float tube. There is often an evening hatch. But the more predictable bite is on black leech patterns, sink-tip lines, strip retrieve.

Note: This park is on the closure list developed by the California Department of Parks, pending final state budget decisions or the possible transfer of park management to other park agencies or volunteer groups.

Facilities, fees: A campground is provided in Plumas-Eureka State Park. Motorized boats are not permitted on the lake. Drinking water and flush toilets are available. An RV dump station is nearby. A grocery store, coin laundry, and propane gas are within five miles. Supplies are at the Blairsden Mercantile and in Graeagle. Fishing access is free.

Directions: From Truckee, take Highway 89 north to Graeagle. Just after passing Graeagle (one mile from the junction of Highway 70), turn left on County Road A14/Graeagle–Johnsville Road and drive west for about five miles to the park entrance.

Contact: Plumas-Eureka State Park, 530/836-2380, www.parks.ca.gov.

6 JAMISON CREEK

Rating: 5

near the town of Graeagle in
Plumas-Eureka State Park
Map 6.1, page 309

Most streams are not good for family fishing trips. Extensive hiking, special fishing techniques, and lack of elbow room make most streams better suited to folks who don't mind splitting up. Jamison Creek is the exception. Year after year it is stocked with trout (catchable 10- to 12-inch rainbows). The stream also holds a few brown trout. A campground is nearby, as are many squirrels to help keep the kids interested. In addition, access is quite easy; no grueling hike is required.

Note: This park is on the closure list developed by the California Department of Parks, pending final state budget decisions or the possible transfer of park management to other park agencies or volunteer groups.

Facilities, fees: A campground is in Plumas-Eureka State Park. Drinking water, flush toilets, and coin showers are available. An RV dump station is nearby. A grocery store, coin laundry, and propane gas are within five miles. Supplies can be obtained at the Blairsden Mercantile and in Graeagle. Fishing access is free.

Directions: From Truckee, take Highway 89 north to Graeagle. Just after passing Graeagle (one mile from the junction of Highway 70), turn left on County Road A14/Graeagle–Johnsville Road and drive west for about five miles to the park entrance. Creek access is off the road near the campground.

Contact: Plumas-Eureka State Park, 530/836-2380, www.parks.ca.gov.

⁊ GOLD LAKE

Rating: 7

near Sierraville in Plumas National Forest

Map 6.1, page 309

All anglers hate the wind, right? Wind is the one thing that can kill the fishing, right? Nobody catches anything when it's windy out, right?

When it comes to Gold Lake, the answers are wrong, wrong, and wrong. Because the water at Gold Lake is extremely clear, the trout are easily spooked when it is calm. That presents a tremendous challenge. But when the wind kicks up, the trout get a lot braver. The big brown trout, rainbow trout, and Mackinaws emerge from the depths and cruise the shallows to feed.

That is when you can catch the trout of your life. The DFG stocks rainbow in the 10- to 12-inch class here. A 10-pound brown and a 14-pound Mackinaw have been documented in recent years out of this lake, and there will be more catches in that class. Why? Because of the minnows, their favorite forage (in addition to juvenile trout). The lake is loaded with them.

Gold Lake, which is at an elevation of 6,400 feet in Plumas National Forest, is bigger than most people expect. Since it is a natural body of water, it is always full and makes for a beautiful sight.

Almost all the fish caught at Gold Lake are taken by anglers with boats, by trolling. It's difficult to catch fish from shore. And by midmorning, when the wind often comes up, a lot of boaters get driven off the lake and try to cast into it from shore. It's one of those frustrating encounters in life. If you can hit it just right in the spring, when at least half the lake is free of ice, trolling a big woolly bugger on the surface on a long line will catch some big browns and rainbows.

If you hit one of those stretches where catching a fish is like finding Bigfoot, there are many hike-to options in the surrounding Gold Lakes Basin. Good destinations include Summit, Bear, Round, Long, Silver, and Squaw Lakes. Of these, Squaw Lake provides the steadiest fishing, although you'll only end up with some tiny brook trout.

Facilities, fees: Lodging and campgrounds with vault toilets are nearby. No drinking water is available. Garbage must be packed out (Lakes Basin Campground has drinking water and garbage service). A boat ramp is provided. Limited supplies are at nearby resorts; additional supplies can be obtained in Graeagle and Bassetts. Fishing access is free.

Directions: From Truckee, take Highway 89 north and drive 20 miles to Sierraville and Highway 49. At Sierraville, turn left on Highway 49 and drive about 10 miles to the Bassetts Store. Turn right on Gold Lake Highway and drive to the lake access road (well signed), on the left.

Contact: Gold Lake Lodge, 530/836-2350; Gold Lake Beach Resort, 530/836-2491; Sportsmen's Den, Quincy, 530/283-2733; U.S. Forest Service, www.fs.fed.us/r5.

⒏ SNAG LAKE

Rating: 4

near Sierra City in Tahoe National Forest

Map 6.1, page 309

Snag Lake is stocked with rainbow trout in the 10- to 12-inch class and brook trout fingerlings. The larger resident fish that have avoided getting caught for a year or two are very smart. You might see them cruising the lake, but darn if they'll bite something with a hook in it.

There are better lakes in this area, and there are worse. So as far as the competition goes,

Snag Lake rates in the so-so range. But when you consider how beautiful this section of Tahoe National Forest is, on a larger scale you could do a lot worse. It is at an elevation of 6,600 feet.

Snag Lake is a neat little spot and doesn't get much fishing pressure. That is the best thing going for it.

Facilities, fees: A primitive campground is nearby. Picnic tables and fire grills are provided. Vault toilets are available, but drinking water is not. Garbage must be packed out. Only hand launching is allowed. Supplies can be obtained in Sierra City and Bassetts. Fishing access is free.

Directions: From Truckee, take Highway 89 north and drive 20 miles to Sierraville and Highway 49. At Sierraville, turn left on Highway 89/49 and drive about six miles to Highway 49. Turn left at Highway 49 and drive about 10 miles to the Bassetts Store. Turn right on Gold Lake Highway and drive five miles to the Snag Lake Campground on the left.

Contact: Tahoe Flyfishing Outfitters, 530/541-8208, www.tahoeflyfishing.com; Tahoe National Forest, Yuba River Ranger District, 530/288-3231, www.fs.fed.us/r5—click on Forest Offices.

9 SALMON LAKE

Rating: 6
near Sierra City in Tahoe National Forest
Map 6.1, page 309

Salmon Lake is a beautiful spot for a family to make a day of it and catch some trout while they're at it. It's bait-dunker time, with most of the trout caught from the shoreline by folks using night crawlers, Power Bait, or crickets under a float. Upper Salmon receives catchable brook trout in the 10- to 12-inch class. The Lower Salmon also receives catchable trout.

Salmon Lake used to be known for some very big brown trout. Not many. But they were caught every year, some up to seven and eight pounds. Right or wrong, the reason for the decline here is largely blamed on a handful of snowmobilers who have targeted the lake for ice fishing.

If you are more ambitious and don't mind a steep hike, some quite spectacular sights are available to you in the surrounding area. Lower Salmon, Horse, and Deer Lakes are all nearby. Deer Lake is absolutely pristine and beautiful, filled with crystal-clear water and golden trout. You can access it via a trail out of Packer Lake.

Facilities, fees: Lodging is at Salmon Lake Lodge. Campgrounds are nearby. No boat ramp is provided, but boats can be launched at the shore. Supplies are in Sierra City and Bassetts. Fishing access is free.

Directions: From Truckee, take Highway 89 north and drive 20 miles to Sierraville and Highway 49. At Sierraville, turn left on Highway 89/49 and drive about six miles to Highway 49. Turn left at Highway 49 and drive about 10 miles to the Bassetts Store. Turn right on Gold Lake Highway and drive about three miles north to a signed road for Salmon Lake. Turn left at the sign for Salmon Lake and drive one mile to the lake.

Contact: Sportsmen's Den, Quincy, 530/283-2733; Salmon Lake Lodge, 530/852-0874; Tahoe National Forest, Yuba River Ranger District, 530/288-3231, www.fs.fed.us/r5—click on Forest Offices.

10 LOWER SARDINE LAKE

Rating: 8
near Sierra City in Tahoe National Forest
Map 6.1, page 309

Sometimes there is just no substitute for spectacular natural beauty, which is why you must visit the Sardine Lakes when you're in the Sierra Buttes area.

Set in a rock bowl beneath the Sierra Buttes, Lower Sardine Lake is among the prettiest drive-to lakes in California. It's always full of water from melted snow. This is a small, intimate setting for low-speed boats only. That is reason enough to visit, but the lakes do receive an extra boost.

The fishery here is outstanding for pan-size rainbow trout, with high catch rates common. Troll along the far shore, where there's a small creek inlet. If you land here and follow that creek, you can hike upstream and see a hidden waterfall.

Lower Sardine Lake is stocked with brook trout, all at least 10 or 11 inches, and with holdover fish, it provides a consistent summer fishery. Most anglers here troll or bait-fish from the shore using standard techniques. The lodge, boat rentals, and the chance to get fishing reports make this place really special.

Because this area has lakeside cabins with a backdrop of the Sierra Buttes, the whole place is drop-dead gorgeous. The waiting list for the cabins here is 10 years plus, and that includes folks waiting for someone to cancel. That's why the resort employees go crazy when people call repeatedly, saying, "Hey, I'd like to stay the coming weekend."

Some anglers fish the upper lake but discover only very small fish. You see, Upper Sardine Lake just doesn't compare with the lower lake as a fishery. It is stocked with fingerling rainbow trout rather than catchable brookies.

Facilities, fees: Limited supplies, a restaurant, and boat rentals are at Sardine Lake Lodge. Note that Sardine Lake cabins have a long waiting list and are available only when there are cancellations. A campground is at Lower Sardine Lake. Picnic tables, fire grills, drinking water, and vault toilets are provided. There is a small, primitive, dirt boat ramp. Fishing access is free.

Directions: From Truckee, take Highway 89 north and drive 20 miles to Sierraville and Highway 49. At Sierraville, turn left on Highway 89/49 and drive about six miles to Highway 49. Turn left at Highway 49 and drive about 10 miles to the Bassetts Store. Turn right on Gold Lake Highway and drive one mile to Sardine Lake Road. Turn left and drive a short distance to a fork. Bear left at the fork (signed Sardine Lake) and drive one mile to the lake.

Contact: Sardine Lake Resort, 530/862-1196; Sportsmen's Den, Quincy, 530/283-2733; Tahoe National Forest, Yuba River Ranger District, 530/288-3231, www.fs.fed.us/r5—click on Forest Offices.

11 PACKER LAKE

Rating: 5

near Sierra City in Tahoe National Forest

Map 6.1, page 309

Packer Lake occasionally provides a good evening bite for rainbow trout in the top 5–10 feet of water for about two hours. Because boat rentals are at the lodge, this has become a lake where you can have a lot of fun, even if the fish tend not to be very big. The lake is stocked with catchable rainbow trout.

Packer Lake is at an elevation of 6,218 feet, near the trailhead for the hike up the west side of the dramatic Sierra Buttes. The lodge has lakefront log cabins and low-speed boats. The nearby hike to Sierra Buttes is a world-class romp.

Facilities, fees: A lodge with cabin rentals and boat rentals is available. Packsaddle Campground is 0.5 mile from the lake. Vault toilets are provided, as is (hand-pumped) drinking water. Pack and saddle animals are permitted, and corrals and hitching rails are available. Supplies can be obtained in Sierra City and Bassetts. Fishing access is free.

Directions: From Truckee, take Highway 89 north and drive 20 miles to Sierraville and Highway 49. At Sierraville, turn left on Highway 89/49 and drive about six miles to Highway 49. Turn left at Highway 49 and drive about 10 miles to the Bassetts Store. Turn right on Gold Lake Highway and drive one mile to Sardine Lake Road. Turn left and drive one mile to a fork. Bear right and drive three miles to the lake on the right.

Contact: Packer Lake Lodge, 530/862-1221; Tahoe National Forest, Yuba River Ranger District, 530/288-3231, www.fs.fed.us/r5—click on Forest Offices.

12 TAHOE NATIONAL FOREST (YUBA RIVER HEADWATERS)

Rating: 4

north of Nevada City

Map 6.1, page 309

This chunk of national forest is known for its four-wheel-drive roads, mountain biking routes, tiny hike-to lakes, and small trout.

The best lakes in this sector are Horse, Deer, Lower Salmon, Tamarack, Hawley, and Spencer Lakes. With a large number of roads, this place is perfect for anglers into four-wheel drive or ATVs. A Forest Service map details all the back roads, trails, and hidden lakes.

These lakes do attract some hiking anglers, most of whom end up disappointed not only with the small size of the fish but also with the numbers. A lot of snow falls in this country, making it inaccessible to hikers until sometime around early June—later if there is a particularly large snowpack.

Facilities, fees: Several campgrounds are on or near Highway 49. Supplies are along the highway. Fishing access is free.

Directions: From Auburn, take Highway 49 north to Nevada City and continue (the road jogs left, then narrows) to Camptonville. Drive 9.5 miles to the campground entrance and North Yuba River trailhead, on the right.

Contact: Tahoe National Forest, Yuba River Ranger District, 530/288-3231, www.fs.fed .us/r5—click on Forest Offices.

13 NORTH FORK YUBA RIVER

Rating: 7

near Sierra City in Tahoe National Forest

Map 6.1, page 309

The Yuba has become a favorite challenge for skilled fly fishers hoping for an evening rise. There is a lot of beautiful water here. This is a pool-and-drop river, with slicks leading to short drops over boulders and riffles that resemble miniature rapids. Fish hold on the edges of these little rapids and riffles.

Many of the trout on the North Fork Yuba have definitely taken smart pills. It takes skill, persistence, and timing to pull off a great weekend.

Highway 49 provides good access to the river, and as you travel along, you will see good turnouts and easy access to many good pools and riffles. This river gets fished pretty hard on weekends, and as a result, the fish are wary. They also tend to be small, because most of the big ones are kept, and the small ones are thrown back.

As you can learn at the Stanislaus and so many other rivers, show me a river where the big fish are kept, and I'll show you a river with few big fish.

However, there is an exception to this on the Yuba. Although the large rainbows seem to be extremely rare, there are some big elusive browns that eat the small rainbows. These big browns mostly reside in the upper reaches of the river near Sierra City (check for special regulations) and are very rarely caught.

If you have ever driven along Highway 49 in this region, you have probably seen the North Fork Yuba and said to yourself, "That's pretty. I wonder if there are any trout in it?" So many vacationers stop to find out for themselves that this stretch of the river gets a lot of activity. But Fish and Game takes that into consideration and stocks some 10- to 12-inch rainbow trout every year.

The best fishing for DFG planters is near the campgrounds. The best fly-fishing for wild fish is upstream, from just below Shangri-La Resort on upstream several miles.

Facilities, fees: Numerous campgrounds are off Highway 49. Two good ones are Union Flat and Chapman Creek. Supplies are in Bassetts Station, Sierra City, Downieville, and Camptonville. Fishing access is free.

Directions: From Auburn, take Highway 49 north to Nevada City and continue (the road jogs left, then narrows) to Camptonville. Drive 9.5 miles to the campground entrance, on the right. This is a good starting spot. Access is at pullouts along Highway 49 up past Sierra City.

Contact: Tahoe National Forest Headquarters, 530/265-4531, www.fs.fed.us/r5—click on Forest Offices; Nevada City Anglers, 530/478-9301, www.nccn.net.

14 COLD CREEK

Rating: 5

north of Truckee in Tahoe National Forest
Map 6.1, page 309

If you want to learn how to fish a small trout stream and have a very good chance of catching rainbow trout in the 9- to 11-inch class, head over to Cold Creek.

This little stream provides mountain-style fishing but offers easy access and planted trout. The easy access is off Old Truckee Road, which runs right alongside the river, and the planters are rainbow trout, of which some 1,900 10- to 12-inchers are stocked. The surroundings are quite pretty, and you'll often see deer in the vicinity, especially during the evening. If you take Highway 89 or Highway 49 to get here, be sure to slow down, because deer can jump out of the woods and into the road at any time.

Side note: The rangers at the Forest Service call it Cold Creek. The DFG prefers Cold Stream. In honor of the campground, we're going with Cold Creek.

Facilities, fees: Cold Creek Campground is on Highway 89, 20 miles north of Truckee. Drinking water and vault toilets are available. Supplies can be obtained in Truckee and Sierraville. Fishing access is free.

Directions: From Truckee, take Highway 89 north and drive to Little Truckee Summit (access to one stretch of the stream is available directly off the road, north of the Bear Valley Road turnoff). Continue to Old Truckee Road (about one mile south of Sierraville) and turn left (north); the road parallels the stream, offering direct access.

Contact: Tahoe National Forest, Sierraville Ranger District, 530/994-3401,www.fs.fed .us/r5—click on Forest Offices.

15 WEAVER LAKE

Rating: 6

north of Emigrant Gap in
Tahoe National Forest
Map 6.1, page 309

Tucked away in the granite slopes of Sierra Nevada country, Weaver Lake is one of dozens of lakes in a 10-mile radius. On the way in, you will pass several of them, including little McMurray Lake and large Bowman Lake, within a mile to the south.

Weaver has a good mix of trout, primarily rainbow trout, plus some browns and a few elusive Mackinaws. The DFG makes regular stocks, beginning when snow is cleared from the access road in late spring and continuing into midsummer. Catchable rainbow trout ranging 10–12 inches are usually stocked during this period, along with 10,000 Eagle Lake fingerlings. This is just the place for family campers with car-top boats.

For the mom and dad who want to get away from it all, but whose family is not ready for the wilderness experience, Weaver Lake provides a rare drive-to alternative.

Facilities, fees: Vault toilets are available. A primitive campground is at Jackson Creek just east of Bowman Lake. No drinking water is provided. Garbage must be packed out. Fishing access is free.

Directions: From Auburn, take I-80 east for 45 miles to the exit for Highway 20. Take that exit, turn west, and drive four miles to Bowman Lakes Road (Forest Road 18). Turn right and drive 19 miles to Graniteville Road. Turn left and drive one mile to Forest Road 41. Turn right and drive two miles to Weaver Lake. Continue past the private lodge for one mile to the lake access road. Bear right and drive 1.5 miles to the lake.

The road is rough, and although four-wheel-drive vehicles are not required, they are recommended.

Contact: Tahoe National Forest, Yuba River South Ranger District, 530/265-4531, www .fs.fed.us/r5—click on Forest Offices; SPD Market, Nevada City, 530/265-4596; Nevada City Anglers, 530/478-9301, www.nccn.net.

16 McMURRAY LAKE

Rating: 5

north of Bowman Lake in
Tahoe National Forest
Map 6.1, page 309

Little McMurray Lake, nestled in the Sierra at 5,832 feet, is often lost in the shadow of its nearby big brothers: Weaver Lake, half a mile to the north, and Bowman Lake, half a mile to the south. Aside from size, one reason may be that McMurray doesn't have a campground. Another is that much of the shoreline is on private property.

But it does have trout. And folks who don't connect at Weaver or Bowman should saunter on over here and make a few casts. The lake is stocked with catchable rainbow trout in the 10- to 11-inch class and rainbow-trout fingerlings. Although usually not in great numbers, it is plenty for this small body of water. If you hit it after a plant, it will be plenty for you, too.

Fishing from a float tube, kayak, or pram can be ideal here, giving anglers the mobility to cover much of the lake in an evening.

Facilities, fees: There are no on-site facilities. Primitive campgrounds are available at Bowman Lake. Fishing access is free.

Directions: From Auburn, take I-80 east for 45 miles to Highway 20. Take the Highway 20 exit and head west, driving four miles to Bowman Lake Road (Forest Service Road 18). Turn right and drive 19 miles until you reach Meadow Lake Road. Turn right (east) on Meadow Lake Road and drive one mile to McMurray Lake Road. Turn north on McMurray Lake Road and drive one mile to the lake. The road is rough; four-wheel-drive

vehicles are recommended, and trailered boats are not advised.

Contact: SPD Market, Nevada City, 530/265-4596; Nevada City Anglers, 530/478-9301, www.nccn.net; Tahoe National Forest, Yuba River South Ranger District, 530/265-4531, www.fs.fed.us/r5—click on Forest Offices.

17 JACKSON MEADOW RESERVOIR

Rating: 7

northwest of Truckee in Tahoe National Forest
Map 6.1, page 309

Jackson Meadow Reservoir receives a good number of 10- to 12-inch rainbow trout. In addition, rainbow- and brown-trout fingerlings are also trucked in. Plants are usually made in early summer, after ice-out has occurred and snowplows have cleared the access road. Standard trolling techniques and shoreline bait dunking are popular, with okay results.

The best fishing occurs in late June, when limits are common for trollers. Fishing slows gradually after that, with the early-morning anglers having the best chance of getting a few fish for the frying pan.

This isn't the wilderness, and it isn't A-1 fishing, but it does score high in all categories. You will find a pretty mountain lake where you can camp and boat and maybe catch a trout now and then.

Campers use Jackson Meadow Reservoir as headquarters for multiday trips into this many-faceted mountain region. The lake is at 6,200 feet in a pretty area featuring forests, meadows, and the trademark granite of the Sierra Nevada. For side trips, there are many other lakes in the vicinity, and the trailhead for the Pacific Crest Trail is just to the east, along the access road.

Because levels are often kept higher here than at other mountain reservoirs, the lake itself is quite beautiful. Lakeside camping, a decent boat ramp, and fair fishing add up to a pleasant trip for most visitors.

Facilities, fees: Several campgrounds (including a boat-in campground), two picnic areas, drinking water, flush and vault toilets, and an RV dump station are available, as are two paved boat ramps. Supplies can be obtained in Truckee and Sierraville. Fishing access is free.

Directions: To Woodcamp Campground: From Truckee, take Highway 89 north for 17.5 miles to Forest Road 7. Turn left on Forest Road 7 and drive 16 miles to Jackson Meadow Reservoir. At the lake, continue across the dam around the west shoreline and then turn left at the campground access road. The campground entrance is on the right, just before the Woodcamp boat ramp.

To Pass Creek Campground: From Truckee, take Highway 89 north for 17.5 miles to Forest Road 7. Turn left on Forest Road 7 and drive 16 miles to Jackson Meadow Reservoir; the campground and boat launch are on the left, at the north end of the lake.

Contact: Nevada City Anglers, 530/478-9301, www.nccn.net; Tahoe National Forest, Yuba River South Ranger District, 530/265-4531, www.fs.fed.us/r5—click on Forest Offices; Truckee–Donner Chamber of Commerce, 530/587-2757; SPD Market, Nevada City, 530/265-4596.

18 INDEPENDENCE LAKE

Rating: 10
north of Truckee in Tahoe National Forest
Map 6.1, page 309   BEST (

Independence Lake is undergoing a transformation from the Sierra's gated, off-limits fantasyland to a recreation gem with a new walk-in campground, boat rentals, and public access. The Nature Conservancy, the new owners of the lake and its surrounding 2,200 acres, announced a new recreation plan in 2011. This cobalt-blue gem nestled at 6,949 feet in a deep, forested canyon north of Truckee in the central Sierra is home for huge but elusive cutthroat and brown trout, as well as kokanee salmon and brook trout—and according to

past caretakers, a ghost that watches over the place.

Independence was originally two smaller lakes named Loon Lakes. After a forest fire in 1945, the surrounding slopes were logged and a new dam was built. As the water rose, the land bridge (now about 15 feet underwater) between the two lakes was submerged and a single, two-mile-long lake was created. Some of the original logging equipment is still underwater.

Sierra Pacific, a power company based in Reno, bought Independence Lake, two houses, and the surrounding forest in 1947 and then used the lake as its own playground and party site. The power company often locked a pipe gate across the road near the caretaker's house to block public access to a small boat ramp. When a Peninsula billionaire tried to buy the lake and surrounding forest for $22 million, the Nature Conservancy stepped in and managed enough donations to buy it for $15 million. The Nature Conservancy's challenge was to protect the lake's pristine, clear waters and unique strain of Lahontan cutthroat trout while improving public access.

To guarantee no invasive mussels or plants infect the lake, the new plan bans private boats, which are blamed in Southern California for spreading the invasive quagga mussel. Boats with 4-cycle motor engines will be available for rent. That will provide safety against the occasional howling winds that blow through the canyon, as well as the ability to fish for the lake's elusive but huge trout.

Anglers will discover huge trout and crystal-clear water that require using light, near-invisible line. I verified a 14-pound cutthroat trout and heard of a 25-pound brown trout netted and released in a DFG survey. Yet these huge fish are hypersensitive to light in the clear water; in addition, when hooked, they can break you off by wrapping around the submerged logging booms. They can seem impossible to catch from shore, and the new ability to rent a boat, kayak, or float tube will provide a window of chance.

The prize fish here are the 10- to 15-pound cutthroat trout and brown trout in the 20- to 25-pound class. All cutthroat trout must be released. Although there are good numbers of kokanee salmon ranging 8–14 inches and a fair sprinkling of brown trout, there are also some monster-size browns, including one I've named "Son of Mo."

To catch the big ones, the best strategy is to head up to the far end of the lake with a boat. With a depthfinder, you will see how the lake bottom suddenly comes up, then drops back down. That is because the lake used to be two small lakes, and then a dam was built, creating one big lake with this shallow spot. You'll find the big fish on the ledges of these drop-offs, always drifting toward the ledge with the wind.

There are old cranes under water, left from the logging days, and the big fish will grab your lure and then wrap it around these cranes and break off. If you go to heavy lines, you won't get a bite, because the water is too clear, and the fish will see your line. The only answer is going to fluorocarbon leaders, which are both strong and invisible.

From a downrigger, stack two lines. Troll a big jointed Rebel on the bottom and a large Needlefish on the upper line. Another option is to stop your boat near the ledge and cast Torpedoes or Jake's for the big cutthroat.

For kokanee salmon, some people troll a Sling Blade dodger with a Koke-A-Nut or Wedding Rings tipped with corn. You must generally troll deep to have a chance, and it's best just off those deep-water ledges on the far end of the lake.

The best strategy when the wind is blowing is to let it move your boat along at a perfect speed for slow trolling, allowing you to turn your engine off and enjoy the quiet (there is a 10-mph speed limit). No bait is permitted at this lake, and no rainbow trout are stocked by the DFG.

When the cutthroat trout head up from the lake into the entrance stream to spawn, black bears arrive in significant numbers to catch them. Many bald eagles then show up for easy pickings from the leftovers.

Viewed from the air, Independence Lake is one of the prettiest lakes in the Sierra, with azure water contrasted against the rising walls of the rich, forested canyon. For 60 years, that was pretty much all most could do, look from a distance, that is, not touch. A new day is at hand.

There are other sights you won't see anywhere else in California. On my visit, the friendly caretakers told me that several visitors had seen a ghost that wears a plaid shirt, who looks out the window at a 150-year-old, boarded-up structure (once a historic resort) located near the boat ramp. Some have even said the ghost is the specter of a photographer who drowned in the 1940s when his boat capsized in the wind, or maybe the pilot who crashed into a towering slope above the lake in a snowstorm in 1950. Neither body was found and put to rest.

Facilities, fees: There are seven primitive walk-in campsites ($10 per night, first-come first-served, six people per site max.) with bear-proof food storage box, picnic tables, and a fire ring; there is no developed, piped water or garbage service (pack it in, pack it out). Boat rentals are available: three 14-foot aluminum boats with 10-horsepower 4-cycle outboard ($50 full day, $25 half day); eight kayaks, including two tandems, and four pontoon float tubes ($20 full day, $10 half day). Supplies can be obtained in Truckee. Boat-launching fees apply.

No live bait is allowed; use of artificials is required. All cutthroat trout must be released; limit of five kokanee salmon or brook trout. Leashed dogs are permitted on trails and campsites. No private watercraft permitted; no hunting; and no campfires outside of designated rings. There is no smoking, firewood cutting, felt-soled waders, or live bait.

Directions: From Truckee, take Highway 89 north for 15 miles to turnoff signed for Independence Lake, Webber Lake, Jackson Meadow Reservoir. Turn left and go 1.5

miles (on paved road) to a junction signed "Independence Lake–5 miles." Turn left and drive 2 miles (road becomes dirt, rough for some vehicles) to a fork signed "Independence Lake–3 miles." Take right fork and drive 0.5 mile to another fork. Bear left and drive across a stream. (If you do not drive across a stream just after taking this fork, you have taken the wrong fork.) Continue to the signed entrance road for "Independence Lake Preserve." High-clearance vehicles are required.

Contact: Nature Conservancy, www.nature .org (type Independence Lake in search box).

19 STAMPEDE RESERVOIR

Rating: 8

north of Truckee in Tahoe National Forest
Map 6.1, page 309

The fishing for kokanee salmon at Stampede can be some of the best in California.

Kokanee salmon is king at Stampede Reservoir. Each year thousands of anglers plan vacations at this lake because of the fishing. The DFG is hoping to manage this lake so that there are not only good numbers of kokanee, but also good size, with fish measuring 15–18 inches. Kokanee approaching the state record of four pounds have been taken here. They may be the finest-tasting freshwater fish around and can make for an excellent fishery.

The best fishing starts in June and is centered at the confluence of the Little Truckee River arm and the Sage Hen Creek arm. Kokanee school in here for about a month before moving to other areas in the lower lake. These fish are as shallow as 20 feet deep in early summer, when it is still cold. As the summer temperatures take over, fish will be caught 45–60 feet deep.

A good area is just across from the main boat ramp near the islands. Fish school in front of these islands throughout the entire season. The biggest fish will be caught in August; then the trolling slows down as the fish get closer to spawning.

That is when jigging for them becomes the most productive. The method here is to locate a school with your depth finder, hold the boat over the school, and then jig a Horizon minnow or Buzz Bomb. This method of fishing does get tiring, but at this time of year, it works.

Always focus on the early season, picking days when the wind is down; this will give you good results catching kokanee salmon and foot-long rainbow trout along the southern shoreline and near the inlet of the Little Truckee River. As a bonus, anglers have an honest chance at catching a monster brown trout or Mackinaw trout. The best way to entice 'em is to be out on the water at dawn or dusk, then troll a Rapala directly across from the boat launch along the northern shoreline. Trollers usually concentrate their efforts on the dam, the Sage Hen arm, and the Little Truckee arm.

Stampede provides a viable alternative to Lake Tahoe, and the DFG knows it. That is why it stocks rainbow trout in the 10- to 12-inch class, along with huge numbers of kokanee fingerlings, typically about 100,000 per year.

The classic Sierra Nevada experience can be had at Stampede Reservoir—an easy-to-reach, drive-to lake that is hard to beat. At 3,400 acres, the lake is a big one, the second largest in the area after Lake Tahoe. It is at 6,000 feet in the Sierra Nevada and usually becomes accessible by mid-May. It has just about everything you could want: an extended launch ramp, several campgrounds, and good fishing. The speed limit on the lake is 45 mph, so in midsummer, hot-rod recreational boating can be popular (though it's not as bad as at nearby Boca).

There's just one problem. Note the "extended" launch ramp. Why would a ramp need to be extended? Because the level falls quite low in late summer and fall, when water is poured out of the dam via the Little Truckee River and Boca Reservoir to keep the fish going in the Truckee River along I-80.

In late summer and fall, the kokanee fishing

falls off as the fish prepare to spawn. They stop biting around the end of September.

Facilities, fees: Several campgrounds and a boat ramp are on the south side of the lake. Drinking water, vault toilets, and an RV dump station are available. Supplies can be obtained in Truckee. Fishing access is free.

Directions: From Truckee, take I-80 east for seven miles to the Boca–Hirschdale/County Road 270 exit. Take that exit and drive north on County Road 270 for about seven miles (past Boca Reservoir) to the junction with County Road S261 on the left. Turn left and drive 1.5 miles to the campground, on the right.

Contact: Tahoe Flyfishing Outfitters, 530/541-8208, www.tahoeflyfishing.com; Tahoe National Forest, Truckee Ranger District, 530/587-3558, www.fs.fed.us/r5—click on Forest Offices; Mountain Hardware, Truckee, 530/587-4844.

20 TAHOE NATIONAL FOREST

Rating: 7

northwest of Lake Tahoe

Map 6.1, page 309

Granite peaks, beautiful lakes set in rock bowls, and a mixed conifer forest filled with trees that seem to have been sprinkled from heaven above are the hallmarks of this chunk of national forest.

The area has a special look, one that becomes apparent to visitors immediately. It is neither as heavily wooded as the national forests of Northern California, nor as sparse as the high southern Sierra near Mount Whitney. Instead, with its perfect granite backdrop, it provides a unique setting for a fishing trip. In addition, on a summer afternoon you might be witness to a fantastic thunderstorm in which thunder rolls down the canyon and lightning harpoons the ridge tops, and it's all over in just an hour.

The following hike-to lakes have been stocked by air in the past and provide the best chance in the area, though most of the trout

are on the small side: Lake of the Woods and Rock, Feely, Island, Long, Round, Milk, Sanford, Downey, Lower Beyers, Blue, Warren, Upper and Lower Lola Montez, Upper and Lower Loch Leven, Fisher, and Hysink Lakes. Nearby drive-to lakes in the region are also stocked and are detailed in separate listings.

Although this area does not provide the isolation found at some of the lesser-traveled wildlands of the state, it does have great natural beauty and spectacular mountain scenery. And, of course, don't forget the quiet camps along jeweled lakes, where rising trout leave little pools on the surface in the evening.

The nearby Desolation Wilderness, southwest of Lake Tahoe, draws so many people that quotas on trailheads are almost always filled, and there seems to be a camper at every lake, no matter how difficult it is to reach. But this stretch of forestland provides a good alternative to the wilderness area, with similar terrain and lesser-known destinations. The hiking and mountain biking are outstanding.

Facilities, fees: Several campgrounds are available off I-80 and near adjacent towns. Supplies can be purchased in Nevada City, Truckee, and at locations off I-80. Fishing access is free.

Directions: To Lindsey Lake Trailhead: From Auburn, take I-80 east for 45 miles to Highway 20. Take the Highway 20 exit and head west, driving four miles to Bowman Lake Road (Forest Service Road 18). Turn right and drive 8.5 miles north until you see a sign that says "Lindsey Lake, Feely Lake, Carr Lake." Turn right and follow the signs to the parking area for Lindsey Lake. The road can be rough for the last half mile; high-clearance vehicles are advised.

To Grouse Ridge Trailhead: From Sacramento, take I-80 east past Emigrant Gap to Highway 20. Turn west on Highway 20 and drive to Bowman Road/Forest Service Road 18. Turn north on Bowman Road and drive five miles to Grouse Ridge Road. Turn right on Grouse Ridge Road and drive six miles on rough gravel to the trailhead.

Contact: SPD Market, Nevada City, 530/265-4596; Nevada City Anglers, 530/478-9301, www.nccn.net; Tahoe National Forest, Yuba River South Ranger District, 530/265-4531, www.fs.fed.us/r5—click on Forest Offices.

21 BOWMAN LAKE

Rating: 9

north of Emigrant Gap in
Tahoe National Forest
Map 6.1, page 309

Bowman is so pretty, a sapphire jewel set in granite at an elevation of 5,558 feet, that it is difficult to pass by without making camp for the night. It is the centerpiece of the Bowman Lakes Recreation Area. Stay here and you might discover Bowman's secret: brown trout. This is the best lake in the immediate region for them. These brownies will strike hard and fight hard, but after you take them out of the frying pan, they'll go down easy.

While the browns are a target for some anglers in Bowman, big rainbows exist as well. These can be very difficult to catch after the water warms up. As soon as you can get in (once the snow has cleared) is the best time for these rainbows and browns. Once summer arrives, they often only feed during the first half hour to 45 minutes of daylight.

In early summer, the better fishing is found on the upper end of the lake, near where Canyon Creek and Jackson Creek feed in. This is also a good area in the fall, when some big browns prowl around. But once the flows of those feeder creeks are reduced to a trickle, the fish seem to scatter, and your search is best rewarded by trolling about 30 yards offshore, covering most of the lake. That way you can cover the maximum amount of water in the minimum amount of time.

The Department of Fish and Game plants kokanee salmon in this lake as well. It can be one of the best lakes in California for kokanee salmon. Also, Bowman is stocked with fingerling Eagle Lake trout. You need a boat in order to troll to catch kokanee, yet the road to Bowman is not suitable for most trailered boats. It is a long, rough ride in to the lake and the last few miles in can cause damage to a trailer. That makes this a potential goldmine fishery for someone with a car-top boat, such as a kayak or canoe that is rigged with a downrigger. The speed limit is 10 mph.

Though a boat helps things tremendously, alas, there is no launch ramp, just an unimproved gravel bar that some anglers make do with, with small aluminum boats that they launch by hand. Nearby Weaver Lake to the north and Jackson Meadow Reservoir, six miles to the northeast, provide options.

Facilities, fees: A free primitive campground with vault toilets is at the lake. There is no drinking water. Garbage must be packed out. Supplies can be obtained in Truckee. Fishing access is free.

Directions: From Sacramento, take I-80 east past Emigrant Gap to Highway 20. Head west on Highway 20 and drive 4.6 miles to Bowman Lake Road/Forest Service Road 18. Turn right and drive about 16 miles to Bowman Lake and the campground on the right side of the road, at the head of the lake. The road starts out paved, but gets rough; four-wheel-drive vehicles are recommended.

Contact: Nevada City Anglers, 530/478-9301, www.nccn.net; SPD Market, Nevada City, 530/265-4596; PG&E Recreation Desk, 800/743-5000, www.pge.com/recreation; Tahoe National Forest, Yuba River South Ranger District, 530/265-4531, www.fs.fed.us/r5—click on Forest Offices.

22 SAWMILL LAKE

Rating: 3

north of Emigrant Gap
Map 6.1, page 309

No campground and no large trout. Several nearby lakes provide both, so why come here? Because Sawmill Lake is beautiful, and sometimes that is enough.

Set at about 6,000 feet amid Sierra granite and pines, the lake attracts the curious, mainly people fishing for small trout. Car-top boats (canoes, kayaks) are okay, but you must carry your boat in from wherever you park.

The lake is home to the ubiquitous DFG dinker, those puny five-inchers that go into a swoon when hooked. The DFG stocks fingerling rainbow trout from time to time. The fish make a pretty sight rising atop the still waters at dusk on a windless day, but if you want to camp and fish, then move it on down the line.

Facilities, fees: Limited walk-in tent sites are near the north shore. There are no facilities and no drinking water. Garbage must be packed out. Access to the lake is free. More camping is at nearby Jackson Creek.

Directions: From Auburn, take I-80 east for 45 miles to the Highway 20 exit. Take that exit and head west on Highway 20 four miles to Bowman Lake Road (Forest Service Road 18). Turn right on Bowman Lake Road and drive 16 miles to Bowman Lake. Turn right and drive along Bowman Lake to Faucherie Lake Road. Turn right on Faucherie Lake Road and drive 0.5 mile to the north end of Sawmill Lake. The last part of the drive is rough, and four-wheel-drive vehicles are recommended.

Contact: Tahoe National Forest, Yuba River South Ranger District, 530/265-4531, www .fs.fed.us/r5—click on Forest Offices.

23 FAUCHERIE LAKE

Rating: 7

north of Emigrant Gap in
Tahoe National Forest
Map 6.1, page 309

It's hard to believe that you can drive to Faucherie Lake. But you get out of your vehicle, and there it is: a classic alpine lake in the Sierra Nevada, set at 6,100 feet, created by clear pure water from melting snow, filling a glacier-carved granite bowl.

This is the kind of place that I have backpacked many miles to reach. It is quiet and pristine and offers fair fishing for rainbow trout. The DFG stocks fingerlings of rainbow, Eagle Lake, and brown trout.

Imagine arriving at Faucherie Lake on a summer afternoon, plopping in a canoe, then paddling around and enjoying the natural beauty. While you're at it, you can trail a lure behind the boat, your fishing rod propped against your shoulder while you paddle. There's a decent chance that a trout or two will come along for the ride, and that you'll end a perfect day with an evening fish fry over a campfire.

If you would like to camp on the lake, load all your camping gear into your boat or canoe and find a spot on the opposite side. The setting is spectacular.

Radio star, pal, and fieldscout Bob Simms explained that the lake was named after the engineer (Faucherie) who directed construction of this lake and nearby French Lake. Both were designed to transport water to a hydraulic mine outside of Nevada City. In the mid-19th century, that link was also the site for the world's first long-distance telephone lines.

Note that that the road in is long and rough; a four-wheel-drive, high-clearance vehicle is required.

Facilities, fees: A group campground (reservations required) and vault toilets are available. There is no drinking water. Garbage must be packed out. A campground is one mile away. There is a concrete boat ramp along with limited parking. Fishing access is free.

Directions: From Sacramento, take I-80 east past Emigrant Gap to Highway 20. Head west on Highway 20 and drive four miles to Bowman Road/Forest Service Road 18. Turn right and drive about 16 miles (much of the road is quite rough) to Bowman Lake; continue four miles to a Y. Bear right at the Y and drive about three miles (four-wheel-drive, high-clearance vehicle required) to the campground, at the end of the road.

Contact: Tahoe National Forest, Yuba River South Ranger District, 530/265-4531, www .fs.fed.us/r5—click on Forest Offices.

24 JACKSON LAKE

Rating: 4

north of Emigrant Gap in
Tahoe National Forest
Map 6.1, page 309

Like neighboring Catfish Lake (surrounded by private land with no public access), Jackson Lake just doesn't cut it. The few trout here are midget-sized brook trout, and with so many other waters to pick from in the area, this is not the place to wind up. Oh, and there's no campground, either.

But if you just want a spot to sit and enjoy the scenery, Jackson does provide a classic mountain view. It is set below a high back wall in a granite cirque, a kind of mountain temple.

Facilities, fees: There are no on-site facilities. Campgrounds are nearby at Jackson Meadow Reservoir. Supplies are in Truckee. Fishing access is free.

Directions: From Auburn, drive east on I-80 for 45 miles to Highway 20. Take the Highway 20 exit and head west, driving four miles to Bowman Lake Road (Forest Service Road 18). Turn right and drive 19 miles until you reach Meadow Lake Road. Turn right on Meadow Lake Road and drive four miles to Jackson Lake Road. Turn right and drive one mile to Jackson Lake. Four-wheel-drive vehicles are required.

Contact: Tahoe National Forest, Yuba River South Ranger District, 530/265-4531, www .fs.fed.us/r5—click on Forest Offices.

25 FRENCH LAKE

Rating: 4

north of Emigrant Gap in
Tahoe National Forest
Map 6.1, page 309

For a remote mountain lake, French Lake surprises many with its size and grandeur. Surrounded by rugged terrain at an elevation of 6,000 feet, it covers close to 350 acres and reaches a maximum depth of 150 feet.

This lake surprises many that venture into it. The surprise, however, is not the kind of surprise you want. Although French Lake looks as if it could be a great fishing lake, it just has never lived up to that billing. It does harbor some Mackinaw, so the chance for a big fish is always there.

The DFG stocks French Lake with fingerling rainbow trout. But alas, the fishing is largely hit-and-miss: a lot of misses interspersed with hits of primarily small trout. Catch anything larger than 10 inches and you might as well head to Reno, because you've got luck on your side. Since it is difficult to reach and the rewards are poor-to-fair fishing, French Lake gets little attention from visitors to Tahoe National Forest.

Facilities, fees: No facilities are available. Fishing access is free.

Directions: From Auburn, drive east on I-80 for 45 miles to Highway 20. Take the Highway 20 exit and head west, driving four miles to Bowman Lake Road (Forest Service Road 18). Turn right and drive 19 miles until you reach Meadow Lake Road. Turn right on Meadow Lake Road and drive seven miles to French Lake Road. Turn right and drive two miles to French Lake. Four-wheel-drive vehicles are required.

Contact: Tahoe National Forest, Yuba River South Ranger District, 530/265-4531, www .fs.fed.us/r5—click on Forest Offices.

26 SOUTH FORK YUBA RIVER

Rating: 5

east of Nevada City in Tahoe National Forest
Map 6.1, page 309

With clear blue water flowing over boulders that have been polished smooth through the centuries, the South Fork Yuba provides a beautiful setting for trout fishing.

The best stretch of water on the South Fork Yuba is no longer in the high Sierra near Eagle Lakes. You are better off working the Sierra foothills east of Nevada City (see *Directions*).

The stretch of water near Eagle Lakes is no longer stocked, and that area is fished relatively hard because of nearby campsites. In addition, if you fish the area near I-80, carry a Forest Service map detailing which lands are public and which are private to keep you from straying onto someone's property. The area gets enough traffic that any trespasser is viewed as intolerable.

I first fished the South Fork Yuba many years ago, and I am still fascinated with its beauty. The river is bordered by a stark granite landscape, and its flows are such a deep shade of blue that it looks like a picture postcard.

Facilities, fees: Campgrounds are off Washington Road and near I-80. Supplies can be obtained in Grass Valley, Nevada City, and off I-80. Fishing access is free.

Directions: From Nevada City, take Highway 49 east to Grizzly Hill Road. Turn right (south) on Grizzly Hills Road and drive about three miles to the campground and river access there. Alternatively, from Nevada City, take North Bloomfield east to Edward's Crossing for river access.

Optional access: From Sacramento, drive east on I-80 to Cisco Grove and continue one mile to the Big Bend exit. Take that exit, turn left on Hampshire Rock Road, and drive east 1.5 miles. Direct access is possible from I-80 near Donner Summit via the Eagle Lakes or Big Bend/Rainbow Road exits.

From Nevada City, take Highway 20 for 12 miles to Washington Road. Turn left (north) on Washington Road and drive about eight miles to Maybert Road. Turn right (east) on Maybert Road. River access is near the campgrounds and picnic areas.

Contact: Tahoe National Forest, Yuba River South Ranger District, 530/265-4531, www .fs.fed.us/r5—click on Forest Offices; Bureau of Land Management, Mother Lode Field Office, 916/941-3101; SPD Market, Nevada City, 530/265-4596; Nevada City Anglers, 530/478-9301, www.nevadacityanglers.com.

27 FULLER LAKE

Rating: 7

east of Nevada City in Tahoe National Forest
Map 6.1, page 309

As you pass Fuller Lake while heading north on Bowman Road, you might be tempted to keep driving. Knowing that dozens of other lakes are set farther back in the mountains makes it hard to stop, but stopping might be a good idea.

Not only is Fuller Lake much easier to reach than the other, more remote lakes in this region, it often provides much better fishing. That's because it's just as easy for the Department of Fish and Game to get here as it is for campers, and they plant the heck out of the water, stocking rainbow and brown trout in the 10- to 12-inch class yearly, not to mention the occasional brook trout. This is a good lake to fish from a float tube, using olive woolly buggers. For bait dunkers, the dam area is a pretty decent spot. A bonus is that this is one of the few lakes in the entire backcountry region that provide any sort of boat ramp.

Fuller Lake is at 5,400 feet, and the road in is usually free of snow by mid-May. Late snowstorms are common in this area, however, so always phone the Forest Service first to check on road conditions.

There are more than a fair number of brown trout in excess of two pounds in Fuller Lake. As the summer goes on, these become harder to catch.

Fly fishers in spring and fall do quite well. So do trollers who can put their lures a foot off the bottom. Rebel and Rapala lures work well here. So do large spoons, such as the Speedy Shiner and Sparklefish.

This lake also receives supplemental fish from the canal that runs from Bowman Lake and empties into Fuller Lake.

Facilities, fees: No camping or drinking water is on-site. A paved boat ramp and paved parking area are at the northern end of the lake. Supplies can be obtained in Nevada City. Fishing access is free.

Directions: From Sacramento, take I-80 east past Emigrant Gap to Highway 20. Head west on Highway 20 and drive to Bowman Road/Forest Service Road 18. Turn right (north) and drive four miles to the lake on the right.

Contact: Tahoe National Forest, Yuba River South Ranger District, 530/265-4531, www .fs.fed.us/r5—click on Forest Offices; PG&E Recreation Desk, 800/743-5000, www.pge .com/recreation.

28 SCOTTS FLAT RESERVOIR

Rating: 7

east of Nevada City in
Scotts Flat Recreation Area
Map 6.1, page 309

First: No personal watercraft. Hallelujah!

Second: When Scotts Flat Reservoir is full to the brim, it is one of the prettier lakes in the Sierra Nevada foothills. The reservoir is shaped like a teardrop, with 7.5 miles of shoreline circled by forest at an elevation of 3,100 feet. With two campgrounds near the water's edge, decent trout stocks, and two nearby boat launches, it makes an ideal family camping destination.

And third: Trout stocks usually start in April and continue well into summer. Lower Scotts Flat receives 10- to 12-inch rainbow trout; Upper Scotts Flat gets 10- to 12-inch rainbows and 10- to 12-inch brown trout. Most of the fish are caught by boaters using standard techniques, slow-trolling with flashers trailed by a night crawler and zigzagging about 30 yards adjacent to the shore. But shoreline bait dunkers can also catch some fish—especially on green Power Bait—from the camp on the north side of the reservoir. Only a quarter mile from where the fish are planted, this camp has a 200-foot-long, barrier-free fishing pier. The pier automatically adjusts to changing lake levels. Another 100-foot pier is equally accessible and offers even more opportunity.

Planted rainbows make up the bulk of the catch for trouters here, but these waters do hold some huge brown trout that can top 10

pounds. The best bet is to troll large rainbow-trout pattern plugs, such as Rapalas, along the shoreline during early spring or late fall storms; the worse the weather is, the more active the big brownies become.

This lake is also one of the best in California for kokanee salmon. Kokanee fingerlings are planted by the thousands every year by the DFG. It is loaded with smallmouth bass, which can provide great topwater action on summer mornings and evenings. When the fish are not taking surface baits, try split-shotting four-inch finesse worms or small black or brown grubs.

While this lake has many species of fish, they don't usually all bite at the same time. You must pattern your approach according to time of year, water temperature, and the depth of the fish according to those factors, of course.

Let's cheer one more time: personal watercraft are not permitted at this lake!

Facilities, fees: Two campgrounds, restrooms, coin showers, coin laundry, and an RV dump station are available, as are a general store, a bait and tackle shop, boat rentals, moorings, gas, a fish-cleaning station, a picnic area, boat and trailer storage, and a playground. A restaurant is four miles away. There are two boat ramps, Cascade Shores and Scotts Flat Marina. A day-use fee is charged.

Directions: To the reservoir and Scotts Flat Marina: From Auburn, take Highway 49 north to Nevada City and the junction with Highway 20. Turn right (east) and drive five miles to Scotts Flat Road. Turn right (south) and drive four miles to the camp entrance road, on the right (on the north side of the lake).

To Cascade Shores: On Highway 49 in Nevada City, drive to Red Dog Road. Turn south on Red Dog Road and drive three miles to Quaker Hill Road. Turn left on Quaker Hill Road and drive east to the sign for the Cascade Shores Day-Use Area.

Contact: Scotts Flat Marina, 530/265-0413, www.scottsflatlake.net.

29 LAKE SPAULDING

Rating: 8

near Emigrant Gap in Tahoe National Forest
Map 6.1, page 309

Spectacular beauty. Easy to reach. Good boat ramp. Campground. Decent fishing. Good side trip options. What else could an angler want?

Lake Spaulding is one of the few lakes that can provide all of these things. About the only thing it doesn't have is water that's warm enough to swim in. I froze my buns off once after taking a dunk on a dare.

The lake is at 5,000 feet in the Sierra Nevada. This is classic granite country, and the setting features huge boulders and a sprinkling of conifers around a gray, slablike shoreline. The entire area looks as if it has been cut and chiseled. The drive here is nearly a straight shot up I-80, and the boat ramp is fine for small aluminum boats. If there's a problem, it's the amount of company you'll have at the campground.

With morning and evening bites, the trout fishing is good. The fish are scattered about, however, since this lake is really just a big rock canyon filled with water and lacking natural holding areas. That mandates trolling, which gives boaters a huge advantage over shoreliners. Also, a few giant brown trout live in this lake, but they are rarely caught.

To increase your chances with the very wary brown trout in this lake, try using the minnow-type lures with a luminescent finish. They are more expensive, but their three-dimensional effect works on the browns.

The lake has many unimproved campsites around the lake built by campers and anglers. Explore and you'll find one suited to your needs.

Many people will be watching Lake Spaulding with great interest in the near future: the DFG started planting chinook salmon here, and some of those fish should be pretty good-sized. Anglers aren't the only ones who are benefiting from the salmon plants; the big brown trout have been enjoying them as well.

If you're trolling and start catching lots of small salmon, put on a big silver plug and fish for browns, because they're probably nearby.

In addition to salmon, rainbow- and brown-trout fingerlings are stocked. For good rainbow fishing in the spring, troll near the surface with night crawlers and flashers around any floating driftwood that's been washed into the lake by spring floods. When the Rim Powerhouse (on the northwest shore) is running, trout fishing can be good in that area also.

Nearby lakes, including Bowman, Weaver, and Faucherie, can make excellent side-trip destinations. Visitors should set aside half a day to explore the area.

Facilities, fees: PG&E provides a campground and a paved boat ramp. Drinking water, vault toilets, and a picnic area are available. Supplies are in Nevada City. Fishing access is free.

Directions: From Sacramento, take I-80 east past Emigrant Gap to the exit for Highway 20. Take that exit and drive west on Highway 20 for 2.3 miles to Lake Spaulding Road. Turn right and drive 0.5 mile to the lake.

Contact: SPD Market, Nevada City, 530/265-4596; Nevada City Anglers, 530/478-9301, www.nevadacityanglers.com; Tahoe National Forest, 530/265-4531; PG&E Recreation Desk, 800/743-5000, www.pge.com/recreation; G&J Outdoor Enterprises, Auburn, 530/885-1492.

30 LAKE VALLEY RESERVOIR

Rating: 4

near Yuba Gap
Map 6.1, page 309

Lake Valley Reservoir is gorgeous when full, its shoreline sprinkled with conifers and boulders. The setting is similar to nearby Lake Spaulding, just north of I-80, although the fishing is not as good and the lake not quite as large. One plus is that waterskiing is prohibited here. The speed limit is 15 mph.

The reservoir, which has a surface area of

300 acres, is at 5,786 feet and offers a decent campground with a nearby boat ramp. At times in the past, rainbow trout in the 10- to 12-inch class, rainbow fingerlings, and brown trout have been stocked here. In some years, DFG has not stocked this lake.

The best long shot hope is for trolling, not shoreline bait dunkers. You'll need a boat to best cover this elliptical-shaped lake. On a windy spring day, you can turn off your engine and let the wind push you, often at the perfect speed for presenting a night crawler trailing behind flashers.

Facilities, fees: PG&E provides a campground. Drinking water and vault toilets are available. A picnic area is nearby. The lake has a boat ramp. Supplies can be obtained off I-80. Fishing access is free.

Directions: From Sacramento, take I-80 east to the exit for Yuba Gap. Take the Yuba Gap exit and drive south 0.4 mile to Lake Valley Road. Turn right on Lake Valley Road and drive 1.2 miles until the road forks. Bear right and continue 1.5 miles to the campground entrance road, to the right.

Contact: PG&E Recreation Desk, 800/743-5000, www.pge.com/recreation; G&J Outdoor Enterprises, Auburn, 530/885-1492; SPD Market, Nevada City, 530/265-4596; Nevada City Anglers, 530/478-9301, www.nccn.net.

31 FORDYCE LAKE

Rating: 8
east of Nevada City in Tahoe National Forest
Map 6.1, page 309

Dams in Sierra gorges can create lakes with strange shapes, and Fordyce is one of them. This long, curving lake has a very deep southern end near the dam, several coves, and six feeder streams.

This place is ideal for four-wheel-drive junkies with car-top boats, who can make their way to the west side of the very narrow part of the lake, then hand-launch their craft. It takes some muscle and spirit, but if you get the job done, the fishing can be decent for rainbow trout and brown trout. A good number of fingerling rainbow trout are stocked here.

There are some downright huge browns in the lake and a 15-incher is considered small. You'll need persistence and spirit to hook up with one, and your chances are best by trolling Rapalas near the inlets, especially in the fall and spring.

Beware that Fordyce draws way down in the late summer. Although it still may offer good fishing, it is not the beautiful, full lake that graces the scenery here in spring. The area has some good hiking trails, which are detailed on the Forest Service map.

Facilities, fees: There are no on-site facilities. Garbage must be packed out. Primitive campgrounds are at nearby Lake Sterling (a well-marked trail connects the two lakes) and three miles away at Rattlesnake Creek. Supplies can be obtained off I-80. Fishing access is free.

Directions: From Sacramento, take I-80 east to Yuba Gap and continue about four miles to the Cisco Grove exit north. Take that exit, turn left on the frontage road, and drive a short distance onto Rattlesnake Road (just prior to reaching Thousand Trails). Turn right, continue on Rattlesnake Road (which is gravel, steep, and curvy; trailers are not recommended), and drive three miles (look for the campground on the right). When the road forks, bear left and drive three miles to the lake. Four-wheel-drive vehicles are recommended.

Contact: Tahoe National Forest, Yuba River South Ranger District, 530/265-4531, www.fs.fed.us/r5—click on Forest Offices; PG&E Recreation Desk, 800/743-5000, www.pge.com/recreation.

32 LAKE STERLING

Rating: 4
east of Nevada City in Tahoe National Forest
Map 6.1, page 309

Perched in a granite pocket at 7,000 feet, this small, pretty lake offers sparse results for anglers. Before you come, though, call ahead and ask the key question: "How high's the water?" Lake Sterling has always been subject to severe fluctuations.

The few resident trout consist primarily of rainbows (fingerlings are stocked). There may not be a lot of them, but they're pretty good-sized for a small mountain lake, averaging 12–13 inches. They can be taken early in the morning, in the shallows near shore, by fishing tiny nymph or scud patterns on an extremely light tippet. Get into stealth mode if you want to be successful, because these fish are quite wary.

Most visitors are not serious anglers but campers, who are drawn by the beauty of the area, fish a bit, then take off on a hike. (A good trail leads north from here to Fordyce Lake.) As you drive to Lake Sterling, plan on spending 35–45 minutes on the last 6.5 miles. The final 0.75 mile is the worst, and vehicles with low axle clearance are not recommended.

The lake is a nice place once you get here, but don't be surprised to hear lots of noise (guns, vehicles, bugle calls, campfire chants, etc.) coming from the nearby Glacial Trails Scout Camp. Most of the land surrounding Lake Sterling is private property, so stay clear where this is signed.

Facilities, fees: A small, primitive campground is available. Garbage must be packed out. Fishing access is free.

Directions: From Sacramento, take I-80 east to Yuba Gap and continue about four miles to the Cisco Grove exit north. Take that exit, turn left on the frontage road, and drive a short distance onto Rattlesnake Road. Turn right, continue on Rattlesnake Road (which is gravel, steep, and curvy; trailers are not recommended), and drive four miles to Lake Sterling Road. Turn left and drive 2.5 miles (the road is steep and curvy) to the lake. Four-wheel-drive vehicles are recommended.

Contact: Tahoe National Forest, Yuba River South Ranger District, 530/265-4531, www.fs.fed.us/r5—click on Forest Offices; PG&E Recreation Desk, 800/743-5000, www.pge.com/recreation.

33 DONNER LAKE

Rating: 8

west of Truckee in
Donner Memorial State Park
Map 6.1, page 309

Even though Donner Lake is visited by millions of vacationers cruising past on I-80, the first glimpse is always a stirring one. The remarkable beauty of this place evokes a heartfelt response.

The large, oblong lake (three miles long and three-quarters of a mile wide) is filled with gemlike blue water and set near the Sierra crest at 5,900 feet. Easy to reach, it makes a good family camping destination. The area is well developed, with cabins and maintained access roads. Those exact reasons, however, are often cited as why some people never stay at Donner. They want more seclusion.

Trout fishing is often good near the boat ramp at the west end. Because the lake is so big, it is best fished by boat, but shoreliners who toss Kastmasters do stand a chance. If you go by boat, heed this warning: afternoon winds can run you off the lake during the spring, just as afternoon thunderstorms can in late summer. In summer, clear water can make it a very difficult proposition for anybody but the earliest risers on the water at first light.

For rainbows and kokanee, troll the south shore from China Cove on west. Stay very close to shore, but be respectful of the folks fishing off the docks; they can congregate on weekends. Although much smaller than nearby Lake Tahoe, Donner gives up more big Mackinaw to anglers each season. Macks ranging to well over 20 pounds are taken each spring by trollers dragging pearl T-55 Flatfish or big silver-and-black Rapalas, or by jiggers yo-yoing Hopkins, Crippled Herring, or Bomber spoons. The most productive Mack holes include the Guard Rail on the north shore and China Cove to the south (boaters need to be careful of the big submerged boulders just east of China Cove.)

The best fishing for the big Mackinaw trout

is usually on cold, windy spring days when nobody else is on the lake. You need a boat that can handle the whitecaps to keep it safe.

Donner Lake is stocked with 10- to 12-inch rainbow trout, along with fingerling kokanee salmon. The lake gets fished hard by trollers, with the trout and kokanee being the primary fare.

Still, the odds of catching a real beauty, a rainbow, brown, or Mackinaw in the 10-pound class, are just good enough that a few wise anglers know the next nibble may be the very trout they have been waiting for all their lives.

Because the lake is such a favorite, reservations are an absolute must if you want to camp at the state park, the only campground at the lake. Also note that boats rented at the state park can be hand-launched only.

Facilities, fees: Campgrounds, vault toilets, drinking water, and picnic areas are available, as is lodging. Powerboats, fishing boats, personal watercraft, kayaks, canoes, and pontoon boats can be rented at Donner Lake Village Resort, and pedal-boat, canoe, kayak, fishing-boat, and personal-watercraft rentals are at the state park marina. A paved public boat ramp is on the lake's northwest corner, about half a mile from the resort on Old Highway 40. Supplies are in Truckee. Fishing access is free. Boat-launching fees apply.

Directions: From Auburn, take I-80 east just past Donner Lake to the Donner State Park exit. Turn south on Donner Pass Road and drive 0.5 mile to the park entrance and the southeast end of the lake.

Contact: Donner Memorial State Park, 530/582-7892 or 530/582-7894; Truckee–Donner Chamber of Commerce, 530/587-2757, www.truckee.com; Mountain Hardware, Truckee, 530/587-4844; Tahoe Flyfishing Outfitters, 530/541-8208, www.tahoeflyfishing.com; boat-launching information, 530/582-7720.

Lodging: Donner Lake Village Resort, 530/587-6081 or 855/621-6664, www.donnerlakevillage.com.

34 TRUCKEE RIVER

Rating: 7
near Truckee in Tahoe National Forest
Map 6.1, page 309

The Truckee River stands apart as one of the few trout streams that provide both easy access and quality trout fishing. The river has a mix of wild trout and planters, providing good prospects for fly fishers and family bait dunkers alike.

If you are new to the area, be aware that the regulations here are under intense debate and in constant flux. Artificials, barbless hooks, and catch-and-release fishing could be required along much of this river. Check with the DFG before casting a line.

Historically, the Highway 89 section, where the road runs alongside the river from Truckee to Tahoe City, was stocked with lots of rainbow trout every summer.

While the section of Truckee River from the town of Truckee up to the entrance of Alpine Meadows is lined with campgrounds and filled with planted trout, there is a respectable number of native trout as well. A skilled fly fisher with dry flies or weighted nymphs can do well at dawn and dusk. The best spots for this along Highway 89 are between the campgrounds, not adjacent to the campgrounds. When releases are right from the dam at Tahoe City, the rafters make the river unfishable—there are too many of them in the low-flow section. By about 11 A.M. on any warm Saturday, the river will be so clogged with rafters that you'll begin to wonder how the water gets through. Get on the water very early to avoid the onslaught.

The area from Truckee to the Nevada state line is considered the trophy section of Truckee River, and there are special regulations in place. Trout in the five-pound class are available here for skilled anglers.

Spinners such as Mepps and Vibrex work in some of the slower pools early and late in the day, and Rapalas and Rebels can be effective at the tail end of riffles.

Regardless, if you're driving through the area, keep your rod ready. If you see a spot that looks good (and there are lots of them), pull off the road, hoof it down to the stream, and make a few casts. It is always worth the effort. Farther downstream, east of Truckee along Glenshire Drive, there are fewer fish and far fewer anglers. Access to this stretch is still quite easy, though, and the trout hold in pockets and pools. In the evening, fly fishers who take a careful approach and make short, gentle casts can be successful.

The Truckee River has become famous just because so many people drive right by it. Only those who have fished it, however, know its best qualities.

Need inspiration? No problem. Just stop by Fanny Bridge, in Tahoe City, and check out the big (and protected) trout that live beneath the span; they'll get any angler's blood pumping. The river is closed here, from the dam downstream 1,000 feet.

Facilities, fees: Several campgrounds are on Highway 89 and around the Truckee area. Lodging, bait, tackle, and groceries can be obtained in Truckee. Fishing access is free.

Directions: From Truckee, take Highway 89 south. The road parallels the river for 14 miles to Tahoe City, and excellent roadside access is available.

To reach the section of river east of Truckee, take Highway 267 east for 0.5 mile to Glenshire Drive. Turn right on Glenshire Drive, which parallels the river for several miles, offering direct access. Access is also possible off I-80 east of Truckee.

Contact: Mountain Hardware, Truckee, 530/587-4844; Nevada City Anglers, 530/478-9301, www.nccn.net; Tahoe Flyfishing Outfitters, 530/541-8208, www.tahoeflyfishing.com; Tahoe National Forest, Truckee Ranger District, 530/587-3558, www.fs.fed.us/r5—click on Forest Offices.

35 PROSSER CREEK RESERVOIR

Rating: 5

north of Truckee in Tahoe National Forest

Map 6.1, page 309

If you hit Prosser Creek Reservoir wrong and hope to eat trout for dinner, you'd best plan on having dinner in Truckee. Hit it right and this lake is a universe apart from the other place. Fish and Game stocks catchable-size rainbow trout here and along with holdovers from previous years, Prosser Creek Reservoir can provide a decent fishery.

While Prosser maintains its status as a put-and-take fishery for most people, locals target this lake in early summer for rainbows that may go up to 18 inches. Both shore anglers and trollers have success. By July, it's back to the planters.

It's a pretty spot set at 5,741 feet, and the 10-mph speed limit keeps the fast boats from interfering. A lakeside campground provides good camping. The lake draws way down in early fall, but a secret is that fishing improves after a drawdown, unlike at most lakes.

Facilities, fees: Campgrounds, drinking water, vault toilets, and a picnic area are provided. Supplies can be obtained in Truckee. Fishing access is free.

Directions: From Truckee, take Highway 89 north for three miles to the campground entrance road, on the right. Turn right and drive less than a mile to the campground.

Contact: Tahoe National Forest, Truckee Ranger District, 530/587-3558, www.fs.fed.us/r5—click on Forest Offices; Mountain Hardware, Truckee, 530/587-4844; Tahoe Flyfishing Outfitters, 530/541-8208, www.tahoeflyfishing.com.

36 MARTIS CREEK RESERVOIR

Rating: 6

near Truckee

Map 6.1, page 309   **BEST (**

Martis is a landmark victory for fly fishers. Martis Lake, set at 5,800 feet, is one of the few lakes in California set aside exclusively for wild trout.

If you want wild trout, catch-and-release fishing is required. A lake or stream can be fished out when there is no tanker truck showing up every other week to replenish what has been taken. Unless that is, you let 'em go. That is why catch-and-release is the law here, and it's working. To jump-start things, the DFG occasionally stocks fingerling Eagle Lake trout and, in a nice touch, cutthroat trout fingerlings as well.

Successful fishers do two things at this reservoir: 1) They are both patient and persistent enough to know that the bites here occur in one-hour periods during a hatch and that the rest of the time can be a zilch. 2) They use very long leaders on their fly lines and very small flies, even size 22 dry flies and size 18 nymphs.

It can be frustrating fishing because the trout are very smart here, schooled by some of California's most talented fly rods, caught and released. But when you hook an 18- or 19-inch trout, it all becomes worthwhile.

When no fish are killed in a water, the average size of the fish becomes much larger than many anglers are accustomed to. That's because at lakes where catch-and-release isn't mandated, most folks like to throw back the little guys and keep the big ones. That is the worst scenario for any body of water, because soon all you get is lots of little fish. But at Martis, where all fish are returned, not only do the little ones have a chance to grow big, the big ones can get even bigger. That means Lahontan cutthroat trout that range to 25 inches. There is a sprinkling of equally huge brown trout.

But these fish are difficult to catch, and with all the special regulations regarding tackle and catch-and-release, this is not the best place

for people who want to camp and fish with their children. Another rule bars motors from the water, so most fly fishers arrive with float tubes or prams and use sinking lines, leech or woolly-worm patterns, and a strip retrieve.

One rarely hears stories about the number of trout caught at Martis Lake. You will, however, hear about the size of the trout and the challenge of catching one. Whatever you do, don't show up with one of those big black frying pans.

Facilities, fees: A developed campground is at the lake. Drinking water, vault toilets, tent pads, and pay phones are available. No reservations are taken, except for wheelchair-accessible sites. The grounds are open May through mid-November. Motorized boats are not permitted on the water, and fishing is limited to catch-and-release, with single, barbless hooks and artificials. Bait is not permitted. Fishing access is free.

Directions: From Truckee, take Highway 267 south for about three miles (past the Tahoe-Truckee airport) to the entrance road to the lake on the left. Turn left and drive another 2.5 miles to the campground, at the end of the road.

Contact: Mountain Hardware, Truckee, 530/587-4844; Nevada City Anglers, 530/478-9301, www.nevadacityanglers.com; Tahoe Flyfishing Outfitters, 530/541-8208, www.tahoeflyfishing.com.

37 BOCA RESERVOIR

Rating: 7

northeast of Truckee in Tahoe National Forest

Map 6.1, page 309

Boca is often one of the Sierra Nevada's solid producers of kokanee salmon. In some years, Boca can produce kokanee that even rival those at Stampede for size, at 15–16 inches.

In spring and early summer, during snowmelt, fishing near the inlet can be very productive for rainbows. The same stream can be productive for kokanee as they make their fall migration in late September.

A good sprinkling of stocked rainbow trout join the kokanee and a few giant brown trout to make Boca a decent lake for campers who want a chance to catch a fish or two. Access is very easy (just a quick hop off I-80). Yet a lot of folks miss this place because the dam faces the road (so you can't see the lake driving by), unlike at nearby Donner Lake, which is right along the highway and which everybody gawks at.

Stocks are intermittent at Boca. At times, it has received stocks of 10- to 12-inch rainbow trout, and it sometimes a bonus stock of rainbow trout in the five- to eight-pound class, along with kokanee salmon fingerlings. There are other times when it seems the DFG makes no stocks at all.

The best prospects are on the west side of the lake, where a series of coves line the shore from the dam all the way up to the north side, where the Little Truckee River enters the lake.

Boca is at 5,700 feet and covers 980 acres. Once on the water, you may find it hard to believe that I-80 is only two miles away. It can feel many miles away.

But all is not perfect at Boca. If you dislike personal watercraft, plan on fishing Boca before Memorial Day or after Labor Day. In between, Boca can sometimes seem like the personal watercraft capital of the Sierra Nevada.

In drought years Boca can be drained so low that the boat ramp is rendered totally unusable. It's a long drive to the boat ramp, so if you are unsure about conditions, call ahead before starting out. In high snow years the lake is usually full by June and is a beautiful and inviting sight.

Finally, sometimes the DFG doesn't stock the lake, and then you are left with fair to middling prospects for smartened-up holdovers.

Facilities, fees: Two campgrounds with vault toilets are on the lake and another is nearby, at Boca Springs. A boat ramp is available. Drinking water is at Boca Rest campground. Supplies can be obtained in Truckee. Fishing access is free.

Directions: From Truckee, take I-80 east for seven miles to the Boca–Hirschdale exit. Take that exit and drive north on County Road 270 about 2.5 miles to the campground on the right side of the road. The boat ramp is on the southwest end of the lake.

Contact: Tahoe National Forest, Truckee Ranger District, 530/587-3558, www.fs.fed .us/r5—click on Forest Offices; Mountain Hardware, Truckee, 530/587-4844; Tahoe Flyfishing Outfitters, 530/541-8208, www .tahoeflyfishing.com.

38 ROLLINS LAKE

Rating: 6

southeast of Grass Valley

Map 6.1, page 309

The search for decent-sized trout ends at Rollins Lake, where a great number of 10- to 12-inch rainbow trout are stocked. Add in the growing kokanee salmon population, the holdovers from trout stocks from previous years, and you have an opportunity to come up with an impressive limit.

Rollins Lake extends far up two lake arms, covering 900 acres, with 26 miles of shoreline. It lies at an elevation of 2,100 feet, right where foothill country and forest meet. In late winter, the snow line is usually around here, too. The result is a lake that crosses the spectrum, supporting both trout and bass, along with channel cat, bluegill, and crappie. The lake is stocked with rainbow trout March through April, and the trout fishing is best in the springtime and at the lower end of the lake, near the dam. When summer weather sets in, anglers make the switch to bass; the best bass-fishing spots are in coves midway up the lake arms. The DFG also stocks fingerling kokanee salmon.

It can get quite hot here in the summer, and this place is very popular for swimming and waterskiing. Boat ramps are available near all four campgrounds; the most remote one is on the peninsula, accessible via Highway 174 and You Bet Road.

Facilities, fees: There is a full-service marina with floating gas dock, boat rentals, and four boat ramps. Lodging, cabins, campgrounds, restrooms with showers, convenience stores, an RV dump station, a restaurant, and a swimming beach with water slide are available. Supplies can be obtained in Colfax. Day-use and boat-launch fees apply.

Directions: To Long Ravine: From Auburn, take I-80 east for about 20 miles to Colfax/Highway 174. Turn north on Highway 174 (a winding, two-lane road) and drive about two miles to Rollins Lake Road. Turn right on Rollins Lake Road and drive to the campground and boat ramp, at 26909 Rollins Lake Road.

To Orchard Springs/Rollins Lakeside Inn: From Auburn, take I-80 east for about 20 miles to Colfax and Highway 174. Turn north on Highway 174 (a winding, two-lane road) and drive 3.7 miles (bear left at Giovanni's Restaurant) to Orchard Springs Road. Turn right on Orchard Springs Road and drive 0.5 mile to the road's end. Turn right at the gatehouse and continue to the campground and boat ramp.

To Peninsula Campground: From Auburn, take I-80 east for about 20 miles to Colfax and Highway 174. Turn north on Highway 174 and drive about eight miles (a winding, two-lane road) to You Bet Road. Turn right and drive 4.3 miles (turning right again to stay on You Bet Road), and continue another 3.1 miles to the campground entrance and boat ramp, at the end of the road.

To Greenhorn: From Auburn, drive northeast on I-80 for about 20 miles to Colfax and Highway 174. Turn north on Highway 174 and drive (a winding, two-lane road) to Greenhorn Road. Turn right and drive to the boat ramp.

Contact: Rollins Lake Resort/Long Ravine Campground, 530/346-6166, www.longravine campground.com; Orchard Springs, 530/346-2212 (winter at 530/265-5302), www.osresort .net; Peninsula Campground, 530/477-9413 or 866/4MY-CAMP (866/469-2267), www

.penresort.com; Greenhorn Campground, 530/272-6100.

39 MORNING STAR LAKE (BIG RESERVOIR)

Rating: 5

northeast of Auburn in Tahoe National Forest

Map 6.1, page 309

This 70-acre pocket of freshwater surrounded by forest is very pretty and is usually quiet. It's ideal for small boats and for either trolling for trout or casting along the shore for bass. A picnic area is at the water's edge. The lake is stocked with trout. As for bass, there are a few of those, providing a rare opportunity to fish for bass at a mountain lake (elevation 4,000 feet). There are catfish as well, another surprise for newcomers. If you are spending a weekend up here, you might visit Morning Star one day, then head to nearby Sugar Pine Reservoir the next.

Facilities, fees: Morning Star Lake is privately owned, and a fishing permit must be purchased from the campground office. A California fishing license is not required. Boats can be rented. A campground has drinking water, vault toilets, showers, and a store; picnic areas are nearby. A primitive boat ramp is also available. Supplies are in Foresthill. Day-use and fishing fees apply, with a discount if camping.

Directions: From Sacramento, take I-80 east to the north end of Auburn and the Foresthill Road exit. Take that exit and drive east 20 miles to Foresthill. Drive through Foresthill (road changes to Foresthill Divide Road) and continue eight miles to Sugar Pine Road. Turn left and drive about 3.5 miles to Forest Service Road 24 (signed Big Reservoir). Bear right on Forest Service Road 24 and drive 2.5 miles to the campground entrance road, on the right.

Contact: Morning Star Lake Campground, 530/367-2129, www.morningstar.icyspicy .com.

40 SUGAR PINE RESERVOIR

Rating: 7

northeast of Auburn in Tahoe National Forest
Map 6.1, page 309

In the 150-square-mile area surrounding Sugar Pine Reservoir, there is only one other lake, Morning Star, and the two happen to be within a mile of each other. But don't make the mistake of thinking they are similar. They aren't.

Sugar Pine has the fish, and Morning Star has the better-known campground. Given the choice, head to Sugar Pine, which is relatively new and has better facilities. The fishing is better, too, because the reservoir is stocked with rainbow catchables and fingerlings. Sugar Pine is at a 3,500-foot elevation, so it gets stocked earlier than mountain lakes do; plants usually start in late April and continue into early summer.

A great time to visit Sugar Pine is in the fall, after the lake has "turned over" (the stratified thermal layers do a flip-flop) and after the summer crowds have disappeared. On just about any given autumn afternoon, you'll see trout rising everywhere and few, if any, people. In the summer, the trout drop down in the water column, but smallmouth bass fishing can still be very good in the shallows. Try chartreuse grubs or four-inch purple plastic worms with green tails.

Besides smallmouth bass, the lake has a surprising population of Florida-strain largemouth. A couple of 10-pound largemouths and a 14-pounder have been reported in recent years. Electrofishing surveys conducted by the DFG have turned up a 50/50 mixture of smallmouth and largemouth bass.

Facilities, fees: A paved boat ramp is on the south shore. There is a campground with drinking water, vault toilets, a picnic area, and a camp host. An RV dump station is near the boat ramp. Supplies are in Foresthill. A day-use fee is charged.

Directions: From Sacramento, take I-80 east to the north end of Auburn and the Foresthill Road exit. Take that exit and drive east 20 miles to Foresthill. Drive through Foresthill (the road changes to Foresthill Divide Road) and continue eight miles to Sugar Pine Road. Turn left and drive five miles to the lake and campground.

Contact: Tahoe National Forest, American River Ranger District, 530/367-2224, www.fs.fed.us/r5—click on Forest Offices.

41 FRENCH MEADOWS RESERVOIR

Rating: 9

northeast of Auburn in Tahoe National Forest
Map 6.1, page 309

The road to this lake is long and winding, and if you get stuck behind an RVer who refuses to pull over, you may feel like adding a gun turret to the front of your rig. What's the big rush? The trout, that's what. They're waiting for you.

French Meadows Reservoir, set at 5,300 feet on a dammed-up section of the Middle Fork American River, has turned into one of the top trout lakes in the Sierra Nevada. It is stocked with rainbow trout in the foot-long class and fingerling rainbows, which join a resident population of brown trout (supplemented by the DFG with 10- to 12-inchers) and holdovers from stocks of rainbow trout in previous years. Trollers in search of these trout work the dam area and up near the inlet with Needlefish and flashers.

The big lake covers nearly 2,000 acres when full in the spring, covering a lake bottom that is full of stumps and boulders. That is why the trout like this place so much: lots of habitat. The big browns in particular will hang out around the submerged logs, much like bass do in a warm-water lake.

It seems everybody who trolls French Meadows Reservoir uses flashers and night crawlers. Although that can be very productive, the trout can shy away from that method. Try instead threading a night crawler, with the hook on a four-foot leader behind a ball-bearing snap swivel, then trailing 100 feet of line and trolling very slowly. Even stop the boat to let the worm settle gently. This can work wonders when the trout are tired of seeing all that hardware, over and over again.

There are several excellent campgrounds, including one boat-in site.

Facilities, fees: Several campgrounds and two lakeside picnic areas are provided. Drinking water, some flush toilets, and several vault toilets are available. There are two paved boat ramps, one at the picnic area two miles east of the dam, and one on the opposite side of the lake, next to McGuire Picnic Area. Both are directly off the lake's access road and are well signed. Supplies are in Foresthill. Fishing access is free.

Directions: From Sacramento, take I-80 east to the north end of Auburn and the Foresthill Road exit. Take that exit and drive east to Foresthill and Mosquito Ridge Road (Forest Service Road 96). Turn right (east) and drive 40 miles (the road is curvy) to Anderson Dam and to a junction. Turn left (still Mosquito Ridge Road), then continue along the southern shoreline of French Meadows Reservoir for four miles to the campground.

Contact: Tahoe National Forest, American River Ranger District, 530/367-2224, www .fs.fed.us/r5—click on Forest Offices.

42 HELL HOLE RESERVOIR

Rating: 8

in Eldorado National Forest
northeast of Auburn

Map 6.1, page 309   **BEST (**

To some, Hell Hole Reservoir, at 4,700 feet, has the appearance of a mountain temple. Its crystal-pure water, fed by the most remote stretches of the pristine Rubicon River, is the color of sapphires. The mountain country to the east, the Granite Chief Wilderness, rises high for miles, crowned by Twin Peaks on the crest above Tahoe.

Once on the lake, the surprises keep coming. If you aren't ready for them, you'll get zilched.

Kokanee salmon, brown trout, and Mackinaw trout are the primary fish in these waters. The DFG stocks rainbow trout. The fish often usually stay very deep in the summer. I use downriggers to get there, usually 60–80 feet deep. If you do not have downriggers, use leadcore line and go down 10 colors; leadcore line is color coded, of course, so that you can determine how deep you are fishing.

If you fish shallow or use techniques for rainbow trout, again, you can be headed for trouble.

Fish and Game stocks brown trout that range 10 inches–4 pounds, fingerling and catchable rainbow trout, and fingerling kokanee salmon here. The latter provide a bonus for most anglers who visit mountain lakes.

Browns and Mackinaws can grow quite large, and they do just that at Hell Hole. Fish in the 10-pound class are in here, and though they might be your goal, there are enough brownies in the foot-long class to keep things interesting while you pursue the big fellows.

Don't try to make a fast hit. This is not the kind of place where you show up, catch your fish in an hour or two, and then leave. Big brown trout and lake trout play by their own rules and on their timetable, not yours. Besides, this place is so beautiful you'll want to spend some slow, lazy days getting to know it.

You may need to use special deep-water techniques during the day and take a very quiet, careful approach in the evening, because the water is often very clear and you'll be trying for brown and Mackinaw trout. Fishing from the shore is usually not very productive, as the walls of the lake are too steep. Watch out for wind in the afternoon.

Troll the sides of this steep lake. Note that the boulders and underwater rocks are home to the brown trout during the daylight hours, and they can only be enticed out if the lures get within a few feet. You may snag up occasionally, but that comes with the territory.

In the last half hour of daylight, troll a Rebel or Rapala 125 feet behind the boat, then make big S turns.

In the spring and early summer, it is not necessary to get your line down deep, particularly as dusk approaches. The browns will be watching the surface as it gets dark. Later in summer you'll have to go deeper.

There are some good-sized Mackinaw trout in Hell Hole, but they are tough to catch. One problem is the uneven bottom terrain in the lake. That makes it difficult to troll deep, at 60–80 feet, where the Mackinaw cruise. One option is to use a downrigger to troll a J-Plug (rainbow trout–colored) fairly fast in 60–80 feet of water around the lake structure. You may get a nice Mackinaw or a big brown.

One of the best fishing spots in the lake is just to the east of the boat ramp. That is where water is pumped into the lake, creating a river effect. It's a natural place for fish to wait for food. That includes the planted rainbows, as well as the big browns and Mackinaw trout that feed on the planters. Kokanee can be attracted here as well.

Kokanee in this lake can run quite deep in midsummer. Because they school in open water, snags are not a problem as with deep-water trolling for Mackinaw.

There are very few rainbow trout in the lake, but in the spring they can be eager if you know where to find them. Then, where there are dozens of small waterfalls entering this lake, approach these spots cautiously by boat and cast an unweighted night crawler where the water comes in. Let it drift in the current for 15 seconds. If you don't get a fish, move on to the next waterfall. Because there are so few big rainbows in this lake, it would be nice to practice catch-and-release if you don't need food for the frying pan.

One insider's note: In summer, the boat-in, hike-in campground at the head of the lake often has rattlesnakes in the vicinity.

Finally, Hell Hole can be subject to lake drawdowns by early fall.

Facilities, fees: A paved boat ramp is available.

There are four Forest Service campgrounds: Hell Hole, Big Meadows, Upper Hell Hole, and Middle Meadows Group Campground. Boat-in campsites, vault toilets, drinking water, and picnic areas are provided. Supplies can be obtained in Foresthill or Georgetown. Fishing access is free.

Directions: From Sacramento, take I-80 east to the north end of Auburn. Take the Elm Avenue exit and turn left at the first stoplight onto Elm Avenue. Drive 0.1 mile, turn left on High Street, and continue through the signal where High Street merges with Highway 49. Travel on Highway 49 for about 3.5 miles, turn right over the bridge, and drive about 2.5 miles into the town of Cool. Turn left on Georgetown Road/Highway 193 and drive about 14 miles into Georgetown. At the four-way stop turn left on Main Street (which becomes Wentworth Springs/Forest Road 1) and drive about 25 miles. Turn left on Forest Road 2 and drive 22 miles to the campground on the left. Continue one mile to the dam, boat ramp, and parking.

Note: There is another route to the lake, but it takes far longer to get here.

Contact: Eldorado National Forest, Georgetown Ranger District, 530/333-4312, www .fs.fed.us/r5.

43 LAKE TAHOE

Rating: 8

east of Sacramento in the Lake Tahoe Basin

Map 6.1, page 309   **BEST (**

So few places evoke an emotional response at first glance. Lake Tahoe, along with Crater Lake in Oregon and the Yosemite Valley, is one of those rare natural wonders that make you feel something special just by looking at them.

Of course, Tahoe is huge: 22 miles long, 12 miles wide, and 1,645 feet deep at its deepest point. It is filled with 39 trillion gallons of water, enough to cover California to a depth of 14 inches (hypothetically), and enough so that it would take 300 years of severe drought for it to drain significantly. It also has unmatched purity. This water is 99.9 percent pure, similar to distilled water. It is so clear that on a calm day, you can see a dinner plate 75 feet or more below the surface.

That purity, however, is what prevents the lake from becoming a world-class fishery, undermining its ability to support large amounts of aquatic life. Nevertheless, it remains a quality fishery. The Mackinaw trout are the resident trophy fishery, the rainbow trout provide fair prospects, and the kokanee salmon offer sprees most years during late summer.

What I learned first about Tahoe is that the fish hold in relatively small pockets, and that 95 percent of the water has no fish at all. Newcomers arriving green are unlikely to catch anything. But once you start to figure out this lake, great things become possible. Without a boat, you have virtually no chance.

The Mackinaw can provide the best battle. They average 5 pounds but commonly reach 8, and are occasionally much bigger, with 10- to 25-pounders a possibility. Some say that 50- and 60-pounders swim the depths of the lake, but nobody has ever landed one. The biggest one documented is 38 pounds, the state record.

When Mackinaws weigh more than 10 pounds, they are usually called "lakers," as in lake trout. Well, most of the lakers are taken in a few key spots: in the northwest section of the lake along the steep underwater ledge, 160–220 feet deep; in the southern part of the lake in the vicinity of Emerald Bay; and near underwater knobs and domes, such as the one that rises to 160 feet below the surface, about a mile offshore of Casino Row at South Shore. The water is so clear that light penetration causes the Mackinaws to live quite deep, commonly 150 feet down. They will go much deeper on bright, sunny days and when there's a full moon. That is why know-how anglers at Tahoe get on the water at first light, prefer overcast days, always troll deep for the lakers, and are usually done fishing by 9 or 10 A.M.

It's a different deal, however, for rainbow trout and kokanee salmon. In good kokanee years, trollers from Tahoe City to Homewood (on the west shore) begin to catch some fish in the early summer. The fish seem to use the west side of the lake as a migration route as they head for their spawning stream (Taylor Creek) at the south end of the lake. By August, the kokes will be camped out off the mouth of Taylor Creek and around Camp Richardson. They begin moving up the creek to spawn in early October.

The size and numbers of kokanee vary dramatically from year to year at Lake Tahoe, usually due to the amount of plankton produced. The best fishing occurs at the south end of the lake in midsummer, from mid-July through the month of August. Fishing for kokanee is an early-morning affair, even though you can reach them in midday. Tahoe is one lake where they don't seem to bite so much after 8 A.M.

The kokanee bite can be a wild affair, a one-after-another proposition. When does that happen? Like a long-shot romance, sometimes never. When it does, it is usually in late summer or early fall; by September, enough kokanee have either been caught or not caught to determine whether the year is a winner or a loser. The DFG plants kokanee salmon at several points around the lake on a fairly regular basis.

The lake-record kokanee salmon weighed 4 pounds, 15 ounces.

Trolling for rainbow trout is okay sport at Tahoe, and it is aided by the stocking of 10- to 12-inch-class rainbow trout, a fairly sparse number though, considering the huge amount of water available. These fish avoid areas with sandy bottoms and instead congregate where rocky terrain supports more aquatic life and provides better feeding. Such spots are found along the northwestern shore near Kings Beach and along the southeastern shore just inside the Nevada line. Every once in a while, somebody catches a monster brown trout by accident while trolling for rainbows in these areas. The browns like to eat the small trout, you see.

The flats outside Tahoe City can be a wonder for rainbow trout. These flats cover several hundred acres with an average depth of 25–35 feet. Then as you head south, it drops off dramatically into several hundred feet of water.

Tahoe can be a very windy lake, and therefore very dangerous for those with small boats. When the wind blows from the south at Lake Tahoe, the waves become 1.5–2 feet high.

Big rainbows move up out of the depths and onto the flats to feed. Troll a speedy shiner, sparkle fish, or a Rebel or Rapala at at least 4 mph with leadcore line, letting out at least 150 feet of line. If you hook three, you'll be lucky to land one; they're terrific fighters. The average size can run close to four pounds.

Always remember that Tahoe is a special place. You may never see water so clear in the outdoors. Thus it requires a special approach, and you must be out on the water early or late in the day. What to do in between? After you've had your fill of the casinos, maybe you can sit on the ridge above Emerald Bay or take the chairlift to the top of Heavenly Valley and just look at the lake. The sight will conjure some of the greatest feelings possible.

There is no place on earth like Lake Tahoe. The Lake Tahoe Visitors Authority provided the following facts about the lake:

• It is North America's largest alpine lake.

• The elevation is 6,226 feet, making it the highest lake of its size in the United States.

• With a depth of 1,645 feet (near Crystal Bay), it is the third-deepest lake in North America and the 10th-deepest in the world (Lake Baikal, in Russia, is the deepest, at over 4,600 feet). The average depth is 989 feet.

• About 95 percent of the lake's fish live in only 5 percent of the water.

• If drained, the lake would take 700 years to refill.

• Sixty-three streams flow into Lake Tahoe, but only one, the Truckee River, flows out, running past Reno and into Pyramid Lake.

• The sun shines at Lake Tahoe an average of 274 days per year, but snowfall has been recorded every month and averages 420 inches per year.

• The water is so deep, cold (39°F below 700 feet), and devoid of light and oxygen on the bottom that, according to legend, 1930s mobsters wearing "cement shoes" have been perfectly preserved on the lake bottom, complete with vintage clothing.

Note: All boats must be inspected and certified free of mussels prior to launching at this lake.

Facilities, fees: Campgrounds, lodging, marinas, boat rentals, groceries, bait, and tackle are at several locations around the lake. Boat ramps are at the following locations.

North Lake Tahoe:

• Kings Beach Recreation Area: There is a paved ramp suitable for small boats. Picnic areas and restrooms are available. Ski boats, sailboats, and personal watercraft can be rented. It's off Highway 28, in Kings Beach. For more information, call 530/546-7248.

• North Tahoe Marina: The paved ramp here can only be used by special arrangement; it's closed to the public. A full-service marina, with accessories and moorings, is available. Powerboats are for rent. It's on Highway 28 in Tahoe Vista. For more information, call 530/546-8248.

• Sierra Boat Company: A full-service marina, hoist, and boat storage are available. It's at 5146 North Lake Boulevard, in Carnelian Bay. For more information, call 530/546-2551.

• Lake Forest Boat Ramp: A paved ramp is available. It's on North Lake Forest Road, off Highway 28 in Lake Forest. For more information, call 530/583-3796, ext. 29. A fee is charged for parking.

• Tahoe City Marina: There is a boat lift, a full-service marina, moorings, slip rentals, and boat storage. Powerboats, fishing boats, and sailboats are for rent. Parasailing, sailing charters, and fishing charters are available. It's on Highway 28 in Tahoe City. Contact 530/583-1039 or www.tahoecitymarina.com.

• Sunnyside Marina: A marina, hoist, boat

rentals, and boat storage are available at 1850 West Lake Boulevard (Highway 28, 530/583-7201), two miles south of Tahoe City; to contact the High Sierra water-ski school across from the marina, call 530/583-7417.

• Homewood High and Dry Marina: A hoist, a full-service marina, moorings, and boat storage are available. Powerboats, ski boats, sailboats, canoes, and kayaks are for rent. It's on Highway 89 (West Lake Boulevard) in Homewood. Contact at 530/525-5966.

• Obexers Boat Company: A paved ramp, travel lift, boat storage, and limited marina services are available. It's at 5355 West Lake Boulevard, in Homewood. Contact at 530/525-7962 or www.obexersboat.com.

• Meeks Bay Marina: A paved ramp and full-service marina are provided. Powerboats, canoes, kayaks, and pedal boats are for rent. A chartered speedboat is available. It's on Highway 89, 10 miles south of Tahoe City, marina information, call 530/525-5588, www.action-watersports.com. For Meeks Bay Lodge reservations, call 877/326-3357 or visit www.meeksbayresort.com.

• Sand Harbor Ramp: A paved ramp and limited marina facilities are available. It's on Highway 28, two miles south of Incline Village. For more information, call 775/831-0494.

South Lake Tahoe:

• Camp Richardson Resort and Marina: A paved ramp and a full-service marina with moorings are available. Powerboats, personal watercraft, kayaks, and pedal boats are for rent. Fishing charters, parasailing, and water-ski schools are available. It's on Highway 89, 2.5 miles north of South Lake Tahoe. For boat rentals, call the marina at 530/542-6570 or 800/544-1801, www.camprichardson.com.

• Lakeside Marina: A paved ramp and a full-service marina with moorings are available. Ski boats, sport boats, and pontoon boats are for rent. It's at the junction of Lakeshore Boulevard and Park Avenue, off Highway 50 in South Lake Tahoe. Contact at 530/541-6626 or 530/541-9800, www.action-watersports.com.

• Ski Run Marina: Powerboats, personal watercraft, fishing boats, and pontoon boats are for rent. It's at 900 Ski Run Boulevard, in South Lake Tahoe, 1.5 miles south of Stateline. Contact at 530/541-5448 or 800/696-7797, or www.tahoesportfishing.com.

• South Lake Tahoe Recreation Area/El Dorado Boat Ramp: A paved ramp and kayak rentals are available. It's on Lakeview Avenue, off Highway 50, in South Lake Tahoe. Contact at 530/542-6056.

• Tahoe Keys Marina: A paved ramp, full-service marina, and fishing and sailing charters are available. Ski boats, personal watercraft, sailboats, kayaks, and canoes are for rent. It's on Tahoe Keys Boulevard, off Highway 50. For boat rentals, call 530/544-8888 or visit www.tahoesports.com; for the marina, call 530/541-2155.

• Timber Cove Marina: An unimproved boat ramp and limited marina services and moorings are available. Ski boats, personal watercraft, pontoon boats, sailboats, kayaks, pedal boats, and water bikes are for rent. It's at 3411 Lake Tahoe Boulevard, in South Lake Tahoe. Contact at 530/544-2942, www.action-watersports.com.

• Zephyr Cove Marina: A full-service marina is available. It's on Highway 50 in Zephyr Cove. Ski boats, personal watercraft, canoes, kayaks, and pedal boats are for rent. Contact at 775/586-9338 or 800/696-7797, www.tahoe sportfishing.com.

• Cave Rock Ramp: A paved ramp is available. It's on Highway 50, three miles north of Zephyr Cove. In summer months, call 775/588-7975; in winter months, call 775/831-0494. Fishing access is free. Fees are charged for parking, boat launching, mooring, and camping.

Directions: To North Shore/Kings Beach: From Sacramento, take I-80 east to Truckee, then continue east three miles to Highway 267. Turn south on Highway 267 and drive to North Shore/Kings Beach and Highway 28. Turn left (east) to access Kings Beach, Crystal Bay, and Incline. Turn right (south) to access Tahoe Vista, Agate Bay, and Carnelian Bay.

To North Shore/Tahoe City: From

Sacramento, take I-80 east to Truckee and Highway 89. Turn south on Highway 89 and drive to Tahoe City and the junction with Highway 89/28. Turn left on Highway 28 to access the North Shore (Tahoe City, Carnelian Bay). Turn right on Highway 89 to access the west shore (Tahoma, Homewood, Meeks Bay).

To South Shore: From Sacramento, take U.S. 50 east over Echo Summit to Meyers and the junction with Highway 89. Continue straight on U.S. 50/Highway 89 to Four Corners at South Lake Tahoe. Continue straight (north) on Highway 89 to access the southwest shore (Camp Richardson, Emerald Bay, Fallen Leaf Lake). Turn east on U.S. 50 to access the south shore and Nevada (South Lake Tahoe, casino row, Kingsbury Grade).

Contact: Lake Tahoe Basin Management Unit, Visitor Center, 530/543-2674; North Lake Tahoe Resort Association, 530/581-6900; Lake Tahoe Visitors Authority, 800/AT-TAHOE (800/288-2463); South Lake Tahoe Chamber of Commerce, 775/588-1728.

General information: www.gotahoenorth.com, www.tahoesouth.com, www.tahoeinfo.com, www.puretahoe.com.

Fishing information in North Lake Tahoe: Captain Bob Reynolds, 530/318-6272; Captain Chris, 530/583-4857, tahoefishingcharters.com; Swigards Hardware, 530/583-3738.

Fishing information in South Lake Tahoe: Captain Gene St. Denis, 530/544-6552, www.blueribbonfishing.com; The Sportsman, 530/542-3474; Tahoe Keys Marina, 530/541-2155; Tahoe Flyfishing Outfitters, 530/541-8208, www.tahoeflyfishing.com.

Guides: Blue Ribbon Fishing Charters, 530/544-6552, www.blueribbonfishing.com; Kingfish Guide Service, Homewood, 530/525-5360; Mickey's Big Mack Charters, 800/877-1462; Lake Tahoe Fishing, 530/541-5566 or 877/270-0742, www.tahoefishingguides.com; Tahoe Flyfishing Outfitters, 530/541-8208, www.tahoeflyfishing.com; Captain Bob Reynolds, 530/318-6272; Captain Chris, 530/583-4857, www.tahoefishingcharters.com.

44 ELDORADO NATIONAL FOREST

Rating: 4

southwest of Lake Tahoe

Map 6.2, page 310

Eldorado National Forest provides an option to the heavily traveled and adjacent Desolation Wilderness. This forest has many wilderness qualities, but it gets far less hiker traffic. Most of the trails to the better fishing lakes here are not as long as the one you must hike when entering Desolation.

Start by getting a Forest Service map and scanning it for the following lakes. Richardson, McKinstry, Winifred, Spider, Emigrant, and Cody Lakes have been stocked in the past. The DFG may stop aerial plants at these lakes. Many of these make day-hike destinations from trailheads at some of the drive-to lakes featured in this chapter.

Facilities, fees: Campgrounds and supplies are off U.S. 50 and Highway 88. Fishing access is free.

Directions: Access to roads and trailheads is off U.S. 50 from Placerville and off Highway 88 from Jackson to the north and south. See a Forest Service map for details.

Contact: Eldorado National Forest, Pacific Ranger District, 530/647-5415, www.fs.fed.us/r5.

45 LOON LAKE

Rating: 7

south of Lake Tahoe in Eldorado National Forest

Map 6.2, page 310

Loon Lake is a crown jewel in the Crystal Basin: gorgeous, good fishing, great camping, and a jump-off point for hiking. This weekend camping destination is best if you have a small boat. Set near the Sierra crest at 6,400 feet, this lake covers 600 acres and reaches a depth of 130 feet at its deepest point. It is surrounded by Eldorado National Forest, and a forest trail leads to Winifred, Spider, and Buck Island Lakes, all to the east. If you don't like roughing it, consider Ice House Resort, on the access road about 20 miles from Loon Lake.

You want trout? This lake has 'em. It is stocked with 10- to 12-inch rainbow trout, and because the lake tends to open late due to heavy snow, it typically gets stocked just about every week once it's accessible. That's a good thing, since this place is popular and can get quite a bit of fishing pressure when the weather turns good for keeps in the summer.

Because of the water clarity, the best fishing occurs in the morning and late hours at Loon Lake. Fishing in the middle of the day in summer is a pure waste of time.

When fishing with a downrigger, you'll have to be careful, because, like other Sierra Nevada Lakes, this granite-filled basin loves to eat downrigger weights. Always carry a pair of wire cutters with you when using a downrigger in a lake like this, in case you get snagged up.

Each year brown trout in the two- to four-pound class, occasionally larger, are caught at Loon Lake, mostly early in the season.

In the early summer, afternoon winds can drive anglers off the lake and delight windsurfers (no boating restrictions are in effect). When that happens, nearby Union Valley Reservoir provides an option.

It also can make for a jump-off point for a weeklong backpacking trip (wilderness permits are required through the Forest Service and are not available at the lake).

Facilities, fees: There is one drive-to campground with drinking water, vault toilets, and picnic areas. A primitive campground can be accessed by boat or trail. A boat ramp is available. Fishing access is free.

Directions: From Sacramento, take U.S. 50 east to Placerville and continue 23 miles to Riverton and the junction with Ice House Road/Forest Road 3 on the left. Turn left and drive 34 miles to a fork at the foot of Loon Lake. Turn right and drive three miles to a picnic area and boat ramp.

Contact: Eldorado National Forest, Pacific Ranger District, 530/647-5415, www.fs.fed.us/ r5; Ice House Resort Campground, 530/293-3321; Ice House Lake and all other campgrounds, 877/444-6777 or www.recreation .gov; Dale's Foothill Fishing (guide), 530/295-0488, www.dalesfoothillfishing.com.

46 STUMPY MEADOWS RESERVOIR

Rating: 8

northeast of Placerville in
Eldorado National Forest

Map 6.2, page 310

Stumpy Meadows has a good supply of brown trout in excess of four pounds, but people do not usually try special tricks for them. My suggestion is to occasionally try exclusively for the big brown trout by using larger lures, such as a No. 11 Rapala or a Sparklefish, and to troll faster than typical for rainbow trout. You may get a big one.

If you've never been to Stumpy Meadows, don't let the name fool you into thinking this is a stodgy, algae-filled reservoir. Quite the opposite. The water is cold, clear, and surrounded by national forest, and this is the ideal spot to camp, fish, and boat. Best of all, a 5-mph speed limit for boaters keeps the water calm, creating the perfect conditions for fishing.

Stumpy Meadows, which covers 320 acres, is in snow country at 4,400 feet in Eldorado National Forest. Snow shuts down the access road every winter, but as soon as the road is plowed (usually in April), the fishing is often excellent. That's because the lake is stocked with trout nearly every week once the road has been cleared, for a yearly total of 9,300 10- to 12-inch rainbows, 1,500 10- to 12-inch browns, and 10,000 fingerling browns. Most of the trout are caught using standard trolling techniques; just adjust for depth according to the time of year. In the early spring and late fall, some big brown trout move up into the head of the lake near the entrance point for Pilot Creek.

Even at 4,400 feet, the lake has some surprise catfish.

Facilities, fees: Campgrounds, picnic areas, and a boat ramp are provided. Drinking water and vault toilets are available. Supplies can be obtained in Placerville and Georgetown. Fishing access is free.

Directions: From Sacramento, take I-80 east to the north end of Auburn. Turn left on Elm Avenue and drive about 0.1 mile. Turn left on High Street and drive through the signal that marks the continuation of High Street as Highway 49. Drive 3.5 miles on Highway 49, turn right over the bridge, and drive 2.5 miles into the town of Cool. Turn left on Georgetown Road/Highway 193 and drive 14 miles into Georgetown. At the four-way stop, turn left on Main Street, which becomes Georgetown–Wentworth Springs Road/Forest Service Road 1. Drive about 18 miles to Stumpy Meadows Lake. Continue about a mile and turn right into Stumpy Meadows Campground.

Contact: Eldorado National Forest, Georgetown Ranger District, 530/333-4312, www.fs.fed.us/r5.

47 GERLE CREEK RESERVOIR

Rating: 5

west of Lake Tahoe in
Eldorado National Forest

Map 6.2, page 310

This small reservoir at 5,231 feet in Eldorado National Forest is pretty and offers limited fishing opportunities.

Small? It doesn't have a boat ramp, making it perfect for those with car-top boats, kayaks, canoes, or inflatables that are easily launched by hand. Quiet? Yep; no motors are permitted on the lake. Pretty? Definitely; it's nestled in the canyon of Gerle Creek, which feeds into the South Fork Rubicon. And limited? That, too, is affirmative.

Trout are not stocked here, but the lake supports a natural, self-sustaining population of brown trout. Some big browns do live in these waters, but they can be elusive.

The surrounding scenery is beautiful, and the campground is quite nice, making Gerle Creek Reservoir decent for a layover. However, nearby Loon Lake, Union Valley Reservoir, and Ice House Reservoir all provide much better fishing. The campground was renovated for the 2012 season.

Facilities, fees: No motors are permitted on the lake. A campground, vault toilets, drinking water, a picnic area, and a wheelchair-accessible fishing pier are provided. Supplies are available in Placerville. Fishing access is free.

Directions: From Sacramento, drive east on U.S. 50 to Placerville and continue 23 miles to Riverton and the junction with Ice House Road/Forest Road 3. Turn left (north) and drive 27 miles (past Union Valley Reservoir) to a fork with Forest Service Road 30. Turn left, drive two miles, bear left on the campground entrance road, and drive a mile to the campground.

Contact: Eldorado National Forest, Pacific Ranger District, 530/647-5415, www.fs.fed.us/r5.

48 DESOLATION WILDERNESS

Rating: 7

in Eldorado National Forest

Map 6.2, page 310

A "frog vs. trout" war has been fought here. (The environmentalists hate the trout: "Not natural. They eat pollywogs, etc."). The DFG stopped stocking trout by airplane in Desolation Wilderness in 2001 because of lawsuits by environmentalists to protect some pollywogs. The good news is that several lakes are not going to be touched. There are plenty of trout in Velma, Gilmore, and many others of the best lakes in Desolation for camping, hiking, and fishing.

Trout can live 14 years in mountain lakes

after being stocked. In rare cases, the trout may have found a way to spawn in some lakes. Before the stocking ban, the following hike-to lakes were planted by air: Avalanche, Cagwin, Cathedral, Clyde, Cup, Doris, Eagle, Floating Island, Forni, Gertrude, Gilmore, Granite, Grass, Grouse, Hemlock, Hidden, Highland, Horseshoe, Kalmia, Lake of the Woods, Lawrence, LeConte, Lost, Maud, No. 3, No. 5, Pyramid, Lower Q, Middle Q, Ralston, Rockbound, Ropi, Rubicon, Shadow, Snow, Stony Ridge, Sylvia, Tallac, Toem, Triangle, Twin, Tyler, Middle Velma.

This wilderness area is one of the most stunning in the country, with viewpoints across Lake Tahoe and the wilderness interior of granite, ice, ridges and peaks, more than 120 pristine lakes, and a diverse trail system that ranges from elevations of 6,330 feet to 9,900 feet. The Pacific Crest Trail (PCT) is routed through here, and those who have hiked the entire PCT from the Mexican border to Canada say the Desolation portion is among the prettiest stretches.

The drawback is that once the snow melts enough to provide access to backpackers, there seems to be lots of campers at every lake. The area has grown so popular that entry is now granted on a strict permit system for half of the approximately 700 overnight slots available. The rest are on a first-come, first-served basis. Getting a permit in advance is always advised.

That done, you can spend hours gazing over a map of the wilderness and dreaming of visiting a different spot every night. The fishing is decent at many of the lakes here, though the trout are universally few at all lakes.

The trailhead out of Echo Lakes provides access to some of the best views and prettiest lakes in Desolation Valley, set just below the Crystal Range. A hiker's shuttle boat operates out of Echo Lake Marina and will ferry you to the PCT trailhead at the head of the lake for a fee. You have your choice of a series of lakes from spur trails en route to Aloha Lake.

Of course, it also happens to be one of the busiest sections of the wilderness area. If you plan your trip for sometime in September or early October, when the nights are cold and most of the vacation traffic has passed by, you may find a setting similar to the one that John Muir found so compelling a century ago.

Facilities, fees: No facilities are available. Fishing access is free.

Directions: There are many trailheads in the area; the most popular is at Echo Lakes.

From South Lake Tahoe, take Highway 89 to the junction with U.S. 50. Turn west on U.S. 50 and drive 5.5 miles to the signed turnoff for Echo Lakes (Johnson Pass Road) on the right (one mile west of Echo Summit.) Turn right and drive 0.5 mile on Johnson Pass Road to Echo Lakes Road. Turn left on Echo Lakes Road and drive one mile to a series of parking lots 0.25 mile before the road ends at Echo Lakes Resort. Park and hike to the boat dock. Take the hiker's shuttle boat across Echo Lakes to the trailhead for the Pacific Crest Trail (visitors not staying at the resort must park in one of the upper lots or alongside the road, not in the lower lot by the resort).

Contact: Eldorado National Forest, Pacific Ranger District, 530/647-5415, www.fs.fed .us/r5.

49 FALLEN LEAF LAKE

Rating: 5

near South Lake Tahoe in
the Lake Tahoe Basin
Map 6.2, page 310

Here's a gorgeous lake with some huge but elusive Mackinaw trout. Fallen Leaf Lake is at an elevation of 6,377 feet, only three miles from the town of South Lake Tahoe. The lake is big, three miles long and three-quarters of a mile wide, and as much as 430 feet deep in places. Forest land encircles the lake, and some of the shore is on private property, so you'll need a boat to do it right.

The only boat ramp on Fallen Leaf Lake is operated by a resort at the far end. They sometimes keep a chain across the boat ramp until 8 A.M. Occasionally you might be able to make an arrangement to get in early. If not, one option is to bring a car-top boat that you can carry around the chain, and hand-launch in order to get on this lake as early as possible. The crack of dawn is not too early. Mackinaw to 20 pounds are in this lake, but they tend to bite at first light, then clamp down tight after that. The big Macks get very little pressure because of the late opening of the boat ramp. (The late opening protects the lake from introduced weed infestations, and boats must be washed off before launching.)

One of the best methods is to troll along the shoreline next to the road coming in. You'll notice a long point extending out into the lake. From that point to the campground is the best area. An M-2 or a T-50 Flatfish trolled in 100–120 feet of water will get a few snags and a few Mackinaw averaging five pounds.

Most anglers troll slowly near the shoreline for rainbow trout, or toss out bait from spots near the campground at the north end of the lake. Others try for kokanee salmon, which are stocked each year. Catch rates are only fair though, and there are many days when the lake is better for looking at than for fishing. Shore fishing is usually poor.

Millions of people drive within a mile of this large, beautiful lake and don't even know it exists. But if you make the effort to get here, you'll discover water that's almost as deep and blue as Lake Tahoe, its giant neighbor to the east. It's always a glorious sight at Fallen Leaf Lake to look up at Mount Tallac and see the snow in the shape of a cross near the peak.

Note: All boats must be inspected and certified free of mussels prior to launching at this lake.

Facilities, fees: Camping, drinking water, flush and vault toilets, a small marina, a convenience store, and bait and tackle are available. Fishing boats, kayaks, and canoes can be rented. Fishing access is free. A boat-launching fee is charged.

Directions: From South Lake Tahoe, at the junction of U.S. 50 and Highway 89, turn north on Highway 89 and drive two miles to the Fallen Leaf Lake turnoff on the left. Turn left on Fallen Leaf Lake and drive to the head of the lake and the signed turn to the marina and boat ramp on the right. *Note:* The road is very narrow and subject to idiotic, fast oncoming drivers. Use extreme caution and show courtesy. When towing a boat, drive very slowly and expect oncoming traffic. RVs are not permitted on this road. There are no turnarounds for trailers.

Contact: Lake Tahoe Basin Management Unit, Taylor Creek Visitor Center, 530/543-2674; Fallen Leaf campground, 530/544-0426, www.fallenleaflakecabins.com; Fallen Leaf Lake Marina, 530/544-0787; Tahoe Flyfishing Outfitters, 530/544-8208, www.tahoefly fishing.com.

50 UNION VALLEY RESERVOIR

Rating: 8

west of Lake Tahoe in
Eldorado National Forest

Map 6.2, page 310

The fishing for rainbow trout always seems reliable here. While you're at it, you might pick up a nice brown trout or brook trout. That's what draws anglers to Union Valley Reservoir. It's a big lake, 3,000 acres, set in a beautiful area. But there's more to it than that.

Some very large Mackinaw trout live here, ranging to 20 pounds and up. The best way to catch them is to troll near underwater structures with big Rapalas or to jig the bottom with Hopkins Spoons. Like Donner Lake, Union Valley produces some of the largest Mackinaws in the state, including fish in the 15- to 25-pound range, but it doesn't give up its secrets easily. Mackinaws in the 12- to 20-inch class are much more common; try trolling night crawlers or Flatfish behind flashers at 60–120 feet deep in the spring, summer, and fall.

Union Valley is at an elevation of 4,900 feet, near Ice House Reservoir to the south and

Loon Lake farther to the north. It is stocked with 13,400 10- to 12-inch rainbow trout, providing shoreline prospects for campers, and 25,000 kokanee salmon fingerlings. This provides good results for those who troll in the evening. The lake is shaped kind of like a horseshoe, with several feeder streams located up each of the arms. The fishing is typically better in these two areas.

Union Valley gets planted with rainbows, and there's a surprising number of holdover rainbows in the 15-inch class that provide bonus fishing. From June and into late August, kokanee salmon take off.

Kokanee salmon run in cycles at Union Valley. Some years the kokanee are located in schools near the front of the boat ramp or down by the dam, and they can be caught regularly by just about everyone who trolls for them. Other years they just seem to disappear. It is still a mystery where they go. One theory is that during high-water years, they get washed through the dam and downstream, out of the lake. The other theory is that the increasing numbers of Mackinaw in the lake are using them for a delightful dinner.

Whenever you can locate a school of kokanee in Union Valley Reservoir, if you switch to Mackinaw methods and then troll beneath the kokanee, you will get a chance for a whopper lake trout.

The secret fish of Union Valley Reservoir is smallmouth bass, present in good numbers. Very few big ones are caught; this crystal-clear mountain water makes them line-shy. It may be necessary to go down to 4-pound test line and a small, hand-poured four-inch worm to entice them.

The reservoir is in the Crystal Basin Recreation Area, among the most popular backcountry destinations for campers from the Sacramento area. A prominent granite Sierra ridge that looks like crystal when covered with frozen snow is the source of its name.

Facilities, fees: Campgrounds, vault toilets, drinking water, coin showers, and an RV dump station are available. Supplies can be obtained in Placerville or at the store at Ice House Resort. Fishing access is free.

Directions: From Sacramento, take U.S. 50 east to Placerville and continue 23 miles to Riverton and the junction with Ice House Road/Forest Road 3. Turn left (north) and drive 15 miles to the campground entrance road (a mile past the turnoff for Jones Fork Campground). Turn left and drive 1.5 miles to the campground at the end of the road (a nearby boat ramp is on the left on the way in).

There are two other boat ramps:

• West Point: From Sacramento, take U.S. 50 east to Placerville and continue 23 miles to Riverton and the junction with Ice House Road/Forest Road 3. Turn left (north) and drive four miles to Peavine Ridge Road. Turn left and drive three miles to Bryant Springs Road. Turn right and drive five miles north to the paved ramp, adjacent to the dam.

• Yellowjacket: From Sacramento, take U.S. 50 east to Placerville and continue 23 miles to Riverton and the junction with Ice House Road/Forest Road 3. Turn left (north) and drive 21 miles to Union Valley Road (at the head of Union Valley Reservoir). Turn left and drive a mile to the campground entrance road. Turn left and drive a mile to the campground. A paved ramp is available.

Contact: Eldorado National Forest, Pacific Ranger District, 530/647-5415, www.fs.fed.us/r5; Dale's Foothill Fishing (guide), 530/295-0488, www.dalesfoothillfishing.com.

51 WRIGHTS LAKE

Rating: 6

southwest of Lake Tahoe in
Eldorado National Forest
Map 6.2, page 310

Wrights Lake is an ideal jump-off point for backpackers, day hikers, and anglers with cartop boats. No motors are permitted.

This classic alpine lake, which is fairly small at just 65 acres, is high in the Sierra Nevada at 7,000 feet. Anglers with hand-launched boats (no boat ramp) can poke around, trolling for rainbow trout and brown trout, with 10- to 12-inch class stocks of each here. Year-to-year holdover rates are decent, and these fish include a sprinkling of big brown trout.

The beauty of this little lake lies in the number of side-trip possibilities. You can drive less than a mile to little Dark Lake and from there hike farther north to the Beauty Lakes or Pearl Lake. For multiday trips, another option is to take a backpack trip to the east in the Crystal Range and the Desolation Wilderness (permit required).

The campground and nearby trailhead make this a very popular spot, and it gets a good share of visitor traffic in the summer.

Facilities, fees: A campground is provided. Drinking water, vault toilets, and a picnic area are available. Supplies can be obtained in Placerville or Pollack Pines. Fishing access is free.

Directions: From Sacramento, take U.S. 50 east to Placerville and continue 23 miles to Ice House Road/Forest Road 3. Turn left on Ice House Road and drive north 11.5 miles to Ice House Reservoir. Turn right (east) on Road 32 and drive 10 miles to Wrights Lake Road. Turn left on Wrights Lake Road and drive two miles to the campground.

Contact: Eldorado National Forest, Pacific Ranger District, 530/647-5415, www.fs.fed .us/r5.

52 DARK LAKE

Rating: 5

southwest of Lake Tahoe in
Eldorado National Forest

Map 6.2, page 310

Most people first visit Dark Lake simply out of curiosity. Wrights Lake, a more popular destination, lies just a mile to the east, and they figure that as long as they are heading to Wrights, they might as well drop by and see what's happening here.

What these adventurous anglers discover is a little lake (about a quarter of the size of

Wrights Lake) tucked in the high Sierra, with decent numbers of trout. Rainbow and brown trout are stocked here, all ranging 10–12 inches in length. Prospects for shoreliners are pretty decent.

A trailhead at the north end of Dark Lake is routed north to the two Beauty Lakes and then Pearl Lake, three alpine lakes that are even smaller than Dark Lake.

Facilities, fees: No facilities are provided. A campground is nearby at Wrights Lake. Fishing access is free.

Directions: From Sacramento, take U.S. 50 east to Placerville and continue 23 miles to Ice House Road/Forest Road 3. Turn left on Ice House Road and drive north 11.5 miles to Ice House Reservoir. Turn right (east) on Road 32 and drive 10 miles to Wrights Lake Road. Turn left on Wrights Lake Road and drive two miles to the campground and lake access road. Bear left and drive one mile to Dark Lake.

Contact: Eldorado National Forest, Pacific Ranger District, 530/647-5415, www.fs.fed .us/r5.

53 ANGORA LAKES

Rating: 4

south of Lake Tahoe in the Lake Tahoe Basin

Map 6.2, page 310

For some visitors to Lake Tahoe, the Angora Lakes provide the perfect side trip. Getting here requires a quick drive from South Lake Tahoe, followed by a short walk, but that alone keeps most people from wanting to give this place a try.

Upper Angora Lake is gorgeous, with clear, blue water, backed by a granite wall that leads to Angora and Echo peaks. It has been occasionally stocked with fingerling brook trout. The fishing is typically poor. It is more popular for rowing around with your sweetheart for an hour, or for children, jumping off boulders into the lake. The upper lake has the best fishing for small trout caught trolling or casting lures. Because the water is so clear, they often only bite when the lake is shaded at dawn and dusk, and they go into lockjaw mode when sunlight is on the water.

The lower lake isn't much more than a large pond, surrounded by forest, a pretty setting for a series of rustic cabins.

En route to the lake, the views of Fallen Leaf Lake and Lake Tahoe are sensational from the ridge-top road on the way up to Angora Lakes.

Facilities, fees: Rowboat rentals, drinking water, restrooms, and a small café noted for its lemonade are available. Supplies can be obtained in South Lake Tahoe. Cabin rentals are on the lake, but it can take 10 years or more on a waiting list; there is the possibility of cancellations, so it may be worthwhile to sign up. Fishing access is free.

Directions: From South Lake Tahoe, at the junction of U.S. 50 and Highway 89, turn north on Highway 89 and drive two miles to the Fallen Leaf Lake turnoff on the left. Turn left on Fallen Leaf Lake and drive about two miles to a fork. Turn left at the fork and drive 0.25 mile to Forest Service Road 12N14. Bear right and drive 2.3 miles (past the Angora Fire Lookout) to the end of the road and a parking lot. A 0.5-mile shuttle ride to the cabins is available for guests and their gear; otherwise you must make the short hike uphill.

Contact: Lake Tahoe Basin Management Unit, Taylor Creek Visitor Center, 530/543-2674; Angora Lakes Cabin Rentals, 530/541-2092 (summer), www.angoralakesresort.com.

54 ECHO LAKE

Rating: 8

south of Lake Tahoe in the Lake Tahoe Basin

Map 6.2, page 310

Afternoon sunlight and a light breeze will cover the surface of Echo Lake with slivers of silver. By evening, the lake, now calm, takes on a completely different appearance: deep and beautiful, almost foreboding. Being here

for the transformation is like watching the changing expressions of a loved one.

Echo Lake is carved out of granite near the Sierra ridge at 7,500 feet, the gateway to the southern portion of Desolation Wilderness. The big blue body of water covers 300 acres and reaches depths of 200 feet. It was once actually two lakes connected by a stream in a canyon, but a small dam on Lower Echo Lake raised the water level and created a narrow connecting stream that you can navigate with a boat to Upper Echo Lake.

This lake can provide excellent trolling for trout and also has some big cutthroat. The best lures for cutthroat trout are the Jake's Spin-o-lure and the Torpedo.

Because of the elevation, the fishing season is relatively short here. The lake freezes over in winter and ice-out usually occurs in May. In some years, the lake opens by Memorial Day weekend, but the place doesn't really get going until well into June. Shortly after Labor Day weekend, cold nights and mornings drive a lot of people away.

Lower Echo gets most of the traffic, and it receives a variety of stocks: rainbow trout in the foot-long class and fingerling Lahontan cutthroat trout. These fish join a fair population of kokanee salmon and brown trout, though the latter can be difficult to locate.

Waterskiing is not permitted on Upper Echo Lake. But you can also end up with a quiet rod, because the fishing is not as good. The DFG stocks cutthroat fingerlings at Upper Echo Lake.

On the north side of the lake, the Pacific Crest Trail is routed up to Upper Echo Lake and then beyond, into Desolation Wilderness. To hike into the wilderness area, you'll need to obtain the required overnight permit from the Forest Service; because of the area's popularity, trailhead quotas are enforced. A lot of outstanding destinations can be reached via the PCT, including Aloha Lake, Tamarack Lake, and many other nearby lakes. A hiker's shuttle boat operates out of Echo Lake Marina; it will ferry you to the PCT trailhead at the head of the lake. There is a fee per person each way.

Facilities, fees: Drinking water and vault toilets are provided. A marina offers docks; a boat launch; fishing boat, canoe, and kayak rentals; and a hiker's shuttle-boat taxi. Lodging, a convenience store, and a snack bar are nearby. Campgrounds are nearby, at Lake Tahoe. There is a fee for boat launching. Other access is free.

Directions: From Placerville, take U.S. 50 east toward South Lake Tahoe; near the summit, look for Sierra-At-Tahoe Ski Resort on the right. At the ski resort, continue east on U.S. 50 for 1.8 miles to a road on the left signed "Berkeley Camp/Echo Lakes." Turn left and drive 0.5 mile on Johnson Pass Road to Echo Lakes Road (signed). Turn left and drive one mile to a series of parking lots. Continue 0.25 mile down the hill to the Echo Lake Chalet and marina. For day use, you must park in the upper lot.

From South Lake Tahoe, take Highway 89 south for five miles to U.S. 50. Turn west on U.S. 50 and drive 5.5 miles to the signed turnoff for Echo Lakes on the right (one mile west of Echo Summit). Turn right and drive 0.5 mile on Johnson Pass Road to Echo Lakes Road (signed). Turn left and drive one mile to a series of parking lots. Continue 0.25 mile down the hill to the Echo Lake Chalet and marina. For day use, you must park in the upper lot.

Contact: Echo Lake Chalet, 530/659-7207, www.echochalet.com; Lake Tahoe Basin Management Unit, Taylor Creek Visitor Center, 530/543-2674, www.fs.fed.us/r5.

55 ICE HOUSE RESERVOIR

Rating: 9

west of Lake Tahoe in
Eldorado National Forest
Map 6.2, page 310

This is one of my favorite lakes in the Sierra for the elusive big brown trout. Three major lakes lie within the beautiful Crystal Basin: Ice House Reservoir, Union Valley Reservoir, and Loon Lake. Ice House, the first one you reach as you drive north, attracts most of the anglers who come to the area during the summer, while Union Valley gets many more campers. Ice House is stocked, and not just with a bunch of dinkers. It receives rainbow and brown trout, all in the 10- to 12-inch class, which join a decent resident holdover population that includes some big brown trout. It also receives 10,000 brown trout fingerlings. The result is a very good trout fishery.

A lot of limits are taken here, mostly by trollers. The fish don't congregate at any particular area in the reservoir, so trolling is the best way to explore the lake, picking up a fish every now and then. The dam is always a good bet for the occasional big fish.

Ice House was created when a dam was placed on the South Fork Silver Creek. It sits at an elevation of 5,500 feet and covers about 650 acres when full. The deepest spot I could find was 130 feet, which explains why the lake seems to have a good holdover population through the ice-cold winters.

Facilities, fees: There is one well-developed campground at the lake, Ice House, which has drinking water, wheelchair-accessible sites, a picnic area, an RV dump station, a swimming beach, and an adjacent boat ramp. Vault toilets, picnic area, and an RV dump station are available at Northwind and Strawberry Point campgrounds. Supplies can be obtained at the Ice House Resort, a few miles south of the reservoir on Ice House Road. Fishing access is free.

Directions: From Sacramento, take U.S. 50 east to Placerville and continue 23 miles to Riverton and the junction with Ice House Road/Forest Road 3. Turn left (north) and drive about 11 miles to Ice House Road. Turn right on Ice House Road and drive two miles east to the boat ramp.

Contact: Ice House Resort Campground, 530/293-3321; Ice House Lake and all other campgrounds, 877/444-6777 or www.rec reation.gov; Dale's Foothill Fishing (guide),

530/295-0488, www.dalesfoothillfishing.com; Eldorado National Forest, Pacific Ranger District, 530/647-5415, www.fs.fed.us/r5.

56 SOUTH FORK AMERICAN RIVER

Rating: 4

east of Placerville in Eldorado National Forest
Map 6.2, page 310

Access is easy and the river does look fishy, but after spending a little time here, reality sets in: catch rates are very poor. The DFG stocks trout weekly, or so they say, but I don't believe it. One-third of all money from fishing licenses is supposed to go to trout plants and this river is a perfect example of a waterway that should be full of fish—with easy access and a large population nearby. But you just don't see it here.

For most folks, the stream is one of the bigger disappointments in an otherwise very pretty and much-visited area. The South Fork American runs through granite chutes, over boulders, and around bends, then drops into tempting pools. Millions of drivers admire this water every year as they cruise U.S. 50 to and from Tahoe. Some even stop to cast a line. After all, with all the pullouts along U.S. 50, access is so easy. The only time it's a problem is when the traffic is heavy and you must wait a while to merge back onto the highway into the procession of cars.

But then you get down to the river and make a few casts, and voilà!—you catch nothing. This happens time and time again. The stream just doesn't seem to produce very often.

Facilities, fees: Several campgrounds with drinking water and vault toilets are available off U.S. 50. Supplies can be obtained in towns along U.S. 50. Fishing access is free.
Directions: From Sacramento, drive 45 miles east on U.S. 50 to Placerville. From Placerville, continue east on U.S. 50. Direct access is available off the road between Pollock Pines and Echo Summit.

Contact: Tahoe Flyfishing Outfitters, 530/541-8208, www.tahoeflyfishing.com; Eldorado National Forest, Placerville Ranger District, 530/644-2324, www.fs.fed.us/r5.

57 SILVER FORK AMERICAN RIVER

Rating: 4

in Eldorado National Forest east of Placerville
Map 6.2, page 310

Kyburz isn't a big town. It's really just a dot on the map. But to anglers it's a key location on U.S. 50 and the adjacent American River. One reason is that the snow line often starts right at Kyburz, which in the early season can make the difference between easy and terrible access. The second reason is that on the South Fork American along U.S. 50, fish populations are very low upstream of Kyburz. Wise anglers ignore this stretch of the American River and instead turn off at Kyburz to fish the Silver Fork.

That is because there are campgrounds along the Silver Fork American, which used to be stocked with rainbow trout. No more. This area can get pretty crowded in the summer with campers, RVs, and jeeps, and without stocks, the river will get fished out.

The native rainbows and browns in this stretch are rare unless you are a fly fisher and concentrate your efforts during the last half hour of daylight. One hope for the future: Improved water flow has the chance to improve the quality of habitat and trout populations.

Facilities, fees: Two campgrounds (China Flat and Silver Fork) are on Silver Fork Road. Supplies are in Placerville. Fishing access is free.
Directions: From Sacramento, take U.S. 50 east to Kyburz and Silver Fork Road. Turn right and drive eight miles. The best fishing is from Silver Fork Camp on downstream.
Contact: Eldorado National Forest, Placerville Ranger District, 530/644-2324, www.fs.fed.us/r5.

58 WEST FORK CARSON RIVER

Rating: 6

near Markleeville in
Humboldt-Toiyabe National Forest

Map 6.2, page 310

Imagine setting up camp just 100 feet away from casting into a beautiful trout stream, or staying in a log cabin that's within a five-minute walk of several good trout-fishing holes. Or finding a mountain stream where the odds of catching a cutthroat trout are in your favor.

The impossible dream? The West Fork Carson River provides all those elements.

Although larger than a babbling brook, this is a fairly small stream. The better spots are often found below the bridges that span it. If you search for trout-filled pools there, you'll be trying for fish that have trouble resisting a well-presented 1/16-ounce Panther Martin, black body, yellow spots.

The best section of the river runs through Hope Valley. This is where most of the 10- to 12-inch rainbow trout that are planted in these waters are plunked in. It is also where a series of small Forest Service campgrounds are set along the stream, and where you can rent a genuine log cabin from Sorensen's Resort. An option is to fish the West Carson at the point where Highways 88 and 89 intersect.

This is definitely a put-and-take river, with the exception of a few wily rainbow and brown trout that manage to hide underneath the undercut banks of this stream. They can only be taken very early and very late in the day by a properly presented fly or by the smallest of lures on 2- or 3-pound test line.

The section between Sorensen's Resort and Woodfords is all pocket water and is very heavily fished, with easy access points. But by taking the time and trouble to creep and crawl and sneak around the bushes and trees and hit some of the out-of-the-way pockets, you have a chance to catch the biggest fish in this section of the river.

The early-season weather in this area can spring a few surprises on visitors. I once got ambushed by quite a snowstorm the night before one trout opener on the West Carson. It turns out that snow is common in late April and early May, and the fishing doesn't really get started here until late May and early June.

Facilities, fees: Campgrounds are off Highway 88 near Woodfords, and also in Hope Valley. Cabins are at Sorensen's Resort, in Hope Valley. Fishing access is free.

Directions: From South Lake Tahoe, take U.S. 50/Highway 89 west to Meyers and Highway 89 on the left. Turn left (south) on Highway 89 and drive over Luther Pass to the T junction with Highway 88. Turn left and drive east through Hope Valley. Roadside access is available at several Forest Service campgrounds.

From Stockton, drive east on Highway 88 to Hope Valley.

Contact: Humboldt-Toiyabe National Forest, Carson District, 775/882-2766; Sorensen's Resort, 530/694-2203 or 800/423-9949, sorensens resort.com; Tahoe Flyfishing Outfitters, 530/541-8208, www.tahoeflyfishing.com.

59 KIRKWOOD LAKE

Rating: 4

south of Lake Tahoe in
Eldorado National Forest

Map 6.2, page 310

The Carson Pass area has become a great alternative to crowded Tahoe to the north (the casinos are only an hour's drive away). At the center of the area is Kirkwood Mountain Resort, which offers year-round accommodations and makes a deluxe base of operations for a fishing or hiking trip.

Little Kirkwood Lake, set at a 7,600 feet elevation, is near the resort. It's a good place to get young novice anglers started, with good shoreline access, quiet water, some small rainbow trout, and not much else. It is stocked with a few (1,500 to be exact) 10- to 12-inch rainbow trout each year. For those in search of larger trout, there are many options in the area, all worth fishing.

Facilities, fees: A campground with drinking water and vault toilets is available. Lodging, a restaurant, restrooms with flush toilets, a convenience store, a gas station, and horseback riding rentals are nearby. Motorized boats are not permitted on the lake. Fishing access is free.

Directions: From Jackson, take Highway 88 east for 60 miles (4 miles past Silver Lake) to the campground entrance road on the left (if you reach the sign for Kirkwood Mountain Resort, you have gone 0.5 mile too far). Turn left and drive 0.25 mile (road not suitable for trailers or RVs) to the campground, on the left.

Contact: Eldorado National Forest, Amador Ranger District, 209/295-4251, www.fs.fed.us/r5; Kirkwood Mountain Resort, 209/258-6000.

60 CAPLES LAKE

Rating: 9

south of Lake Tahoe

Map 6.2, page 310

This is a high mountain lake, set at an elevation of 7,950 feet and covering 600 acres. As long as the wind doesn't blow too hard, this is one of the best mountain lakes for fishing in the Sierra. The trout are abundant and can come big. The three-week period after ice-out can provide some of the best fishing of the year at Caples. The only problem is that cold, early summer wind, which can just about turn you into petrified wood.

It is always great to fish a lake that has brooks, browns, and rainbows in it. But Caples has Mackinaws as well, some up to 18 pounds. The best time to fish for them is as soon as the ice is off the lake, usually in late May or early June. In addition, when the lake is only partially cleared from ice, some of the biggest brown trout here, in excess of four pounds, are taken each year by bank anglers casting Rapalas from shore, right near the shoulder of the road.

Besides offering dramatic surroundings and

easy access off Highway 88, it has a 10-mph boating speed limit, which keeps things calm. Good hiking trails are available in the adjacent national forest. The best is a route that starts just off the highway near the dam at the westernmost portion of the lake and is routed into the Mokelumne Wilderness.

The lake gets a lot of anglers at midsummer, but not nearly as many in early summer and fall. The stocks are quite large: rainbow trout, brook trout, and brown trout, all in the 10- to 12-inch range. For the best fishing results, troll the northern shoreline near the surface during early summer. Just pray the wind is down.

Facilities, fees: There is a campground across the road. A boat ramp, boat rentals, groceries, and bait are nearby. Drinking water and vault toilets are available. Fishing access is free. A boat-launching fee is charged.

Directions: From Jackson, take Highway 88 east for 63 miles (one mile past the entrance to the Kirkwood Ski Resort) to the lake entrance road, on the right.

Contact: Eldorado National Forest, Amador Ranger District, 209/295-4251; Caples Lake Resort, 209/258-8888, www.capleslakeresort.com; Eldorado Irrigation District, 530/295-6810, www.eid.org; Dale's Foothill Fishing Guide Service, 530/295-0488, www.dalesfoothillfishing.com; Tahoe Flyfishing Outfitters, 530/541-8208, www.tahoeflyfishing.com.

61 SILVER LAKE

Rating: 7

in Eldorado National Forest

Map 6.2, page 310

The Highway 88 corridor provides access to several excellent lakes, including three that lie right in a row from west to east: Lower Bear River, Silver, and Caples. Of the three, Silver Lake is most often overlooked.

Why? Because both Lower Bear River Reservoir and Caples Lake have developed resorts nearby that promote fishing and trout stocks.

Silver Lake does not, yet it provides quality trolling and a chance at catching a big brown or Mackinaw trout.

The lake is at a 7,200-foot elevation, in a classic granite cirque just below the Sierra ridgeline. You are provided a solid opportunity for trout fishing by boat or from the shore. DFG stocks the lake with rainbow and brown trout, all in the 10- to 12-inch class. The top spots are the northwest corner near the boat ramp, especially at dawn and dusk, and in the narrows along Treasure Island on toward the inlet stream, the headwaters of the Silver Fork American River.

The lake is usually free of ice by late May or early June, and by summer it gets quite a lot of use. Most visitors congregate on the lake's north side, where the campgrounds, picnic areas, and marina are located.

Facilities, fees: Kit Carson Lodge rents fishing boats, rowboats, canoes, and kayaks. A small marina at Kay's Silver Lake Resort rents fishing boats. There are two campgrounds, vault toilets, drinking water, picnic areas, a convenience store, restaurants, a bar, gas, and a coin laundry. Cabins and motels are available, as is a boat ramp. Fishing access is free. A boat-launching fee is charged.

Directions: From Jackson, take Highway 88 east for 52 miles to the lake entrance road.

Contact: Eldorado National Forest, Amador Ranger District, 209/295-4251, www.fs.fed .us/r5; Kit Carson Lodge, 209/258-8500 (summer) or 530/676-1370 (winter), www .kitcarsonlodge.com; Plasse's Resort, 209/258-8814, www.plassesresort.com; Dale's Foothill Fishing Guide Service, 530/295-0488, www .dalesfoothillfishing.com.

62 WOODS LAKE

Rating: 5

in Eldorado National Forest
Map 6.2, page 310

Even though Woods Lake is only two miles from Highway 88, it can make visitors feel as if they are visiting some far-off land.

This small lake in the high Sierra, set at an elevation of 8,200 feet, always seems to be full and looks very pretty against its granite backdrop. There's a campground and an area for launching car-top boats. In addition, it is stocked with rainbow trout in the 10- to 12-inch class, providing fair hopes for shoreliners. The best area to fish is a radius of 50 yards near the outlet of Woods Creek, which pours downstream into Caples Lake.

This is one of several lakes in the area that offer some of the best shoreline fishing access at mountain lakes in California.

Facilities, fees: A campground and picnic area are provided. Motorized boats are not permitted on the lake. Drinking water (hand-pumped) and vault toilets are available. Supplies are nearby. Fishing access is free.

Directions: From Jackson, take Highway 88 east to Caples Lake and continue for a mile to the Woods Lake turnoff on the right (two miles west of Carson Pass). Turn right (south) and drive a mile to the campground on the right (trailers and RVs are not recommended).

Contact: Eldorado National Forest, Amador Ranger District, 209/295-4251, www.fs.fed .us/r5.

63 BEAR RIVER RESERVOIR

Rating: 7

southwest of Lake Tahoe in
Eldorado National Forest
Map 6.2, page 310

As you rise out of the San Joaquin Valley on Highway 88 and venture east into the mountains, Bear River Reservoir is the first of three quality mountain lakes you come to. Silver Lake and Caples Lake are the other two, up the hill.

With a lower elevation (at 5,800 feet), Bear River Reservoir has one advantage over the others. The ice here melts off sooner than at Silver and Caples Lakes. Correspondingly, the spring stocks and fishing get going earlier, too.

Another edge is that the Department of Fish and Game and the private resort here (Bear River Resort) each stock the lake. The DFG stocks the lower reservoir with rainbows, browns, and brookies, all in the 10- to 12-inch class. On top of that, the resort dumps in thousands more trout, including some in the trophy-size range. These plants join a small resident population of large brown trout.

You get the picture: lots of fish. Almost every week someone catches a trout in the 5- to 10-pound class. The people at the resort do a good job of providing detailed fish reports.

This is a deep, decent-sized lake, at 725 acres. During the summer, most trollers use leadcore trolling line to get the desired depth—and catch the majority of the fish. People shore-fishing at the campgrounds on either side of the boat ramp on the western end of the lake do only fair.

The upper lake has primarily small rainbow trout (dinkers galore), but it does provide a decent short hike.

On summer weekends, campground reservations are essential.

Facilities, fees: A boat ramp, a small marina with fishing boat, kayak, and canoe rentals, lodging, a grocery store, a restaurant, coin laundry, a lounge, campgrounds, restrooms with flush toilets and showers, a playground, volleyball, a beach area, and a game room are nearby. Fishing access is free.

Directions: From Stockton, take Highway 88 east for 80 miles (through foothill country and into the mountains) to the Bear River Road/resort area entrance on the right. Turn right and drive about two miles to a junction with the resort entrance road (if you drive over the dam, you have gone 0.25 mile too far). Turn left on the resort entrance road and drive 0.5 mile to the entrance on the right.

Contact: Bear River Lake Resort, 209/295-4868, www.bearrivercampground.com; Dale's Foothill Fishing, 530/295-0488, www.dales foothillfishing.com; Eldorado National Forest, Amador Ranger District, 209/295-4251, www.fs.fed.us/r5.

64 SALT SPRINGS RESERVOIR

Rating: 6

east of Jackson in Eldorado National Forest

Map 6.2, page 310

Most brown trout at Salt Springs Reservoir run 11–13 inches. But if you get your technique down and fish the prime bite during dusk on cold nights, you can get bigger ones. There are 10-pounders in the lake, and some say far bigger. There's also a catch here, and we'll get to that.

Salt Springs Reservoir could be called the twin of Hell Hole Reservoir. It is at about the same elevation, is in a steep canyon, and is fed by a similar river. You can also fish Salt Springs the same way you do Hell Hole for brown trout. That is, use leadcore line and a depth finder, then troll the edges of the rocky shoreline. Because of submerged boulders, you may lose some lures. But getting the Rapala, Rebel, or frog-colored Needlefish close to the rocks in 20–30 feet of water is the key to catching fish. Downriggers don't work as well here because you can get the downrigger weighs stuck in the rocks. If you do use a downrigger, bring wire cutters or you can get your boat stuck.

Another trick is to get on the lake in late winter on foul, windy days. That is when the big browns, the 10-pounders, choose to feed. I use a Cabela's swimming rat, large jointed Rebels and Rapalas, and then test different depths, starting right on the surface at dawn.

Salt Springs is not stocked. Remember that you are fishing for wild brown trout. This takes a special approach or you will get zilched.

Skilled anglers who boat upstream can find trout congregating at the Mokelumne River inlet in the early summer. Below the dam, though, the Mokelumne River itself seems to provide higher catch rates.

Everyone should visit Salt Springs Reservoir at least once, for it has just about everything. The long, narrow lake is in the Mokelumne

River Gorge, a dramatic canyon with spectacular surroundings for boaters. Hikers will be satisfied, too: a trail leading into the Mokelumne Wilderness starts just north of the dam. Set at an elevation of 4,000 feet, the lake covers 950 acres. Even though the location is fairly obscure, this place is so beautiful that it attracts vacationers who return year after year.

From a boat in the middle of Salt Springs Reservoir, looking to the south of the dam, you'd swear you're in a portion of Yosemite National Park. There's a huge granite face that rises several thousand feet from the canyon bottom: striking beauty.

Now for the catch: Only car-top boats that can be carried to the lake and hand-launched are permitted. Access is a real pain. And small boats, like canoes, can be dangerous in the spring when fishing is best, because winds can howl through here. The Mokelumne Wilderness boundary extends 350 feet to the west from where the river enters the reservoir at the east end. Under the Wilderness Act, mechanized and motorized equipment, including motorboats, are not permitted in designated wilderness areas in order to provide opportunities for solitude and primitive recreation experiences. The Forest Service will install buoys in 2012 to mark the boundary.

Facilities, fees: A picnic area and vault toilet are available. There is no camping at the lake, and no drinking water. Garbage must be packed out. Primitive campgrounds are nearby, on the Mokelumne River. Supplies can be obtained in Pioneer and Ham's Station. Fishing access is free.

Directions: From Jackson, take Highway 88 east to Pioneer and then continue for 18 miles to Ellis Road/Forest Road 92 (78 miles from Jackson), at a signed turnoff for Lumberyard Picnic Area. Turn right on Ellis Road and drive 12 miles to Salt Springs Road (Forest Road 9). Turn left, cross the Bear River, and continue two miles to the dam. The road is steep, narrow, and curvy in spots. RVs and large trailers are not advised.

Contact: Eldorado National Forest, Amador Ranger District, 209/295-4251, www.fs.fed.us/r5; PG&E Recreation Desk, 800/743-5000, www.pge.com/recreation.

65 BEARDSLEY RESERVOIR

Rating: 8

near Strawberry in Stanislaus National Forest

Map 6.2, page 310

Beardsley Reservoir is set deep in the Stanislaus River canyon and is reached by an eight-mile access road off Highway 108 that drops about 2,000 feet.

In the spring, during a short period in April, this lake can produce both big rainbow trout and big brown trout. Occasionally, you see a rare brook trout. In the late afternoon, the wind blows out of the west, and you turn off your engine and let the wind push you along. It is the perfect speed to drift with a set of flashers trailed by half a night crawler for limits of trout (both foot-long rainbow and brown trout, with the chance of a big brown).

On a trip here with Ed "The Dunk" Dunckel, we kept getting our night crawlers bit off right behind the hook. So we added a trailer hook, a "stinger," that is, and that got 'em. We limited in about two hours, a hell of a trip, even though I lost about a 19-inch brown at the boat, right before The Dunk could get him in the net.

A depthfinder can work wonders. Even when fishing in my canoe, we make sure the depthfinder is bouncing sonar off the bottom. That is because this lake has underwater ledges. The wind will push the feed against these ledges and, in turn, attract the fish. We've seen big schools of trout stacked up against these sloping ledges, and then caught one or two every pass by either letting the wind push us over the top of the ledge or slowly trolling with the motor to accomplish the same thing. One trout opener, my brother Rambob and I had one of the most beautiful 10-fish limits you've ever seen in California, and this was in wind so bad it kicked up whitecaps and kept most people on shore. Yeah, that was us out there.

Because the access road is steep, the people at TriDam Project often close it down in the winter months. The reason for this closure is that if the road gets iced up, it is easy to get stuck down at the lake; a two-wheel-drive vehicle towing a boat would not be able to make the steep climb up the icy road. So the key is to pay attention when the gate is open, then flat jump on it. This is when the biggest fish of the year are caught. With The Dunk, we've been the first rods on the lake in many years by keeping tabs when the gate is opened.

Once May arrives, the DFG stocks catchable (10- to 12-inch) rainbow trout here. Once the lake is planted, the summer pattern evolves with good results—not great, not bad, but good—for the planters. In the summer months, there is a good fishery for pan-sized rainbow trout during a short evening snap. This is the lake you learn to hate. It requires very slow trolling, or heading east to the powerhouse and then anchoring, or tying up along the shoreline and using night crawlers, Power Bait, or salmon eggs.

Beardsley can be subject to severe drawdowns, particularly in drought years, making it look something like the Grand Canyon. When the lake is low, you have to drive down on the dry lake bed to hand-launch your boat. Believe it or not, that is often preferable to the situation during high water, when the walk up the boat ramp to the parking area is so long that some old-timers call it "Cardiac Hill."

Facilities, fees: A boat launch is provided. A campground, picnic area, and flush toilets are available, but drinking water is not. Garbage must be packed out. Supplies are in Strawberry and Pinecrest. Access is free.

Directions: From Sonora, take Highway 108 east for approximately 25 miles to Strawberry and the turnoff for Beardsley Reservoir/Forest Road 52. Turn left and drive seven miles to Beardsley Dam.

Contact: Stanislaus National Forest, Summit Ranger District, 209/965-3434, fax

209/965-3372, www.fs.fed.us/r5—click on Forest Offices; Rich & Sal's Sporting Goods, Pinecrest, 209/965-3637; TriDam Project (for road information), 209/965-3996, www.tridamproject.com.

66 EMIGRANT WILDERNESS

Rating: 8

north of Yosemite National Park in Stanislaus National Forest

Map 6.2, page 310

What if you flipped a coin and it landed on its side?

That is what trying to pick a fishing destination in the Emigrant Wilderness can be like. There are more than 100 lakes to choose from, with elevations ranging from 4,500 feet (the trailhead at Cherry Lake) to peaks topping out at over 9,000 feet. The most popular trailheads are the Crabtree Trailhead and at Kennedy Meadows, along Highway 108. From Kennedy Meadows, you can hike south past Relief Reservoir and on to the Emigrant Lake area. At the latter you will discover dozens and dozens of lakes situated fairly close together.

Of all the options, however, note that golden trout are available only in a few lakes: Black Hawk, Blue Canyon, Iceland, Red Bug, Ridge, Sardella, and Wilson Meadow. Many of these are off-trail, accessible for those willing first to hike the Pacific Crest Trail and then head off on their own route to these lesser-known lakes. The Huckleberry Trail also provides this option.

Many other lakes provide decent fishing for small rainbow and brook trout. The following are the lakes in Emigrant Wilderness that have been stocked by airplane by the Department of Fish and Game: Bear, Big, Bigelow, Black Bear, Buck, Camp, Upper Chain, Chewing Gum, Coyote, Dutch, High Emigrant, Estella, Fisher, Fraser, Frog, Gem, Granite, Grizzly Peak, Grouse, Hyatt, Jewelry, Karls, Kole, Leighton, Leopold, Lertora, Lewis, Long, Maxine Lakes, Mercer, Mosquito, Olive, Pingree, Pinto, Powell, Pruitt, Red Can, Relief,

Rosasco, Shallow, Snow, Starr Jordan, Yellow-hammer, Toejam, Waterhouse, Wire Lakes, and "W."

The wilderness area also is home to sizable populations of wildlife. Hikers who explore the high country near the Sierra ridgeline will discover good numbers of deer, including some bucks sporting very impressive racks.

Facilities, fees: Campgrounds and supplies can be found in and near the towns of Pinecrest and Dardanelle. Access is free.

Directions: Forest Service roads that lead to trailheads are available off Highway 108.

Contact: Stanislaus National Forest, Summit Ranger District, 209/965-3434, www.fs.fed .us/r5—click on Forest Offices.

67 SOUTH FORK STANISLAUS RIVER

Rating: 7

near Strawberry in Stanislaus National Forest

Map 6.2, page 310

The mountain symphony is the sound of rushing water pouring over rocks and into pools. That is the music you hear on the South Fork Stanislaus River.

This is a beautiful river, one that is often underestimated only because it rarely produces large trout. Like many of the streams on the western flank of the Sierra Nevada, this river doesn't seem to grow big trout. But once the mosquitoes and caddis start hatching during the evening, it doesn't much seem to matter. The rush of the water, the sneak up to the hole, a short cast, and bingo, you've got one.

There are two good stretches. My favorite is the section upstream of Lyons Reservoir, which requires a fairly bumpy ride in, and then an evening of stalking each spot and zipping short casts with your fly rod. I've had a lot of wonderful evenings here. Most of these are not big fish, but they take a No. 16 mosquito pattern tossed lightly at the head of a pool. You need to have shade on the water to get the evening rise. Otherwise, traditional

nymphing techniques, or skilled bait techniques, are needed. The fish are spooking until the witching hour at dusk.

The reaches accessible by car are stocked with rainbow trout in the 10- to 12-inch class. But again, if you hike onward up the stream, you will get into areas inhabited only by natives.

Facilities, fees: Camping is available at Fraser Flat. Drinking water and vault toilets are provided. Supplies can be obtained in Strawberry or Sierra Village. Fishing access is free.

Directions: To Fraser Flat from Sonora, take Highway 108 east to Long Barn. Continue east for six miles to Spring Gap Road/Forest Road 4N01. Turn left and drive three miles to the campground, on the left side of the road. Access is available at the campground for those who pay the day-use fee along the trail that parallels the river west of Fraser Flat. Another dirt access road, Forest Service Road 4N13, is available out of Strawberry, about five miles farther north on Highway 108.

Contact: Rich & Sal's Sporting Goods, Pinecrest, 209/965-3637, www.pinecrestsport shop.com; Stanislaus National Forest, Mi-Wok Ranger District, 209/586-3234, www.fs.fed .us/r5—click on Forest Offices.

68 INDIAN CREEK RESERVOIR

Rating: 6

near Markleeville in

the Indian Creek Recreation Area

Map 6.3, page 311

In the space of just a few miles, the terrain completely changes in this country. When you cross over the ridge from the western Sierra into the eastern Sierra, the land becomes sparsely forested, with not nearly as many classic granite features. That is why Indian Creek Reservoir gets missed by so many anglers. It's on the eastern side, at an elevation of 5,600 feet, and most vacationers are off yonder.

The lake covers 160 acres, and a 10-mph

speed limit keeps anglers happy. Access is quite easy (there's even a small county airport within a mile of the lake), and the trout trolling is fair. Not great, fair. The DFG plunks in catchable-size Eagle Lake trout here.

If you have time for a side trip, hike one mile to little Summit Lake, just west of the reservoir. The trailhead is just southwest of the campground area.

Facilities, fees: Campgrounds, restrooms with drinking water, flush toilets and showers, and picnic areas are available, as are two primitive boat ramps. Supplies are nearby in Markleeville. Fishing access is free.

Directions: From Sacramento, take U.S. 50 east to Meyers and Highway 89. Turn south (right) on Highway 89 and drive over Luther Pass to Highway 88. Turn left (east) on Highway 88/89 and drive six miles to Woodfords and Highway 89. Turn right (south) on Highway 89 and drive about four miles to Airport Road. Turn left on Airport Road and drive four miles to Indian Creek Reservoir. At the fork, bear left and drive to the campground, on the west side of the lake.

From Markleeville, take Highway 89 north for about four miles to Airport Road. Turn right on Airport Road and drive about three miles to Indian Creek Reservoir. At the fork, bear left and drive to the campground, on the west side of the lake.

Contact: Bureau of Land Management, Carson City Field Office, 775/885-6000, www.blm.gov/nv.

69 BURNSIDE LAKE

Rating: 5

southeast of Lake Tahoe
Map 6.3, page 311

The first time I fished little Burnside Lake, I didn't bring my canoe. Instead I walked along the shoreline near the outlet, casting a variety of small lures. By 11 A.M., I had caught only a five-inch rainbow trout. My buddies Ed "the Owl" Ow and Buster "Rob" Brown had also

caught just one each. By noon, we were in South Tahoe, sitting at a blackjack table. I had much better luck there.

The odd thing was that in the middle of the lake, there were these two women in a small boat, just rowing along, trailing their lines behind them and trolling. They caught a rainbow trout about every 10 minutes, and though they, too, caught a few small ones, they ended up filling their stringer with two limits and returning to shore right as we were leaving. The lesson: Bring your boat and your night crawlers and start trolling. Note that vehicles are not permitted on the lake shoreline.

The DFG provides modest stocks and plants 10- to 12-inch rainbow trout.

Facilities, fees: There are no facilities. Cabins can be rented at Sorensen's Resort (in Hope Valley), and campgrounds are east of Sorensen's Resort. Fishing access is free.

Directions: From Sacramento, take U.S. 50 east to Meyers and Highway 89. Turn south (right) on Highway 89 and drive over Luther Pass to Highway 88. Turn right (west) on Highway 88 and drive six miles to Burnside Lake Road. Turn left (south) and drive 6.5 miles to the lake.

Contact: Humboldt-Toiyabe National Forest, Carson Ranger District, 775/882-2766; Sorensen's Resort, 530/694-2203 or 800/423-9949, www.sorensensresort.com.

70 RED LAKE

Rating: 5

south of Lake Tahoe in
Humboldt-Toiyabe National Forest
Map 6.3, page 311

Red Lake is the brook-trout capital of Humboldt-Toiyabe National Forest. That's kind of like being the best second baseman in Iceland. But what the heck, an award is an award.

Here a brook trout, there a brook trout, every once in a while a brook trout. And not just dinkers, though you can be guaranteed there are plenty of those around. A fair mix of seven- to nine-inchers help flesh out the frying pan.

Red Lake is in high mountain country, set at 8,200 feet, just southeast of Carson Pass. It is fair-sized, about four times larger than nearby Woods Lake, and shaped like a lima bean. The DFG stocks catchable-size brook trout and fingerling cutthroat trout here.

The lake was once the subject of an intense dispute between the public and some local landowners, who wanted to deny them access. The state resolved the problem by purchasing much of the adjoining land and the water rights. Now you are free to bring a kayak, canoe, inflatable, or other hand-launched boat and do your own thing. No motors are permitted.

Facilities, fees: On-site facilities are not available, though there are a few primitive campsites on the lake's east side. A campground is nearby at Woods Lake. Fishing access is free.

Directions: From Sacramento, take U.S. 50 east to Meyers and Highway 89. Turn south (right) on Highway 89 and drive over Luther Pass to Highway 88. Turn right (west) and drive about six miles southwest to the turnoff for Red Lake. Turn left and continue to the lake.

An optional route from the Sacramento Valley: From Jackson, take Highway 88 east over Carson Pass to the turnoff for Red Lake. Turn right and drive to the lake.

Contact: Humboldt-Toiyabe National Forest, Carson Ranger District, 775/882-2766; Tahoe Flyfishing Outfitters, 530/541-8208, www .tahoeflyfishing.com.

71 EAST FORK CARSON RIVER

Rating: 8

near Markleeville in
Humboldt-Toiyabe National Forest

Map 6.3, page 311

The East Fork Carson provides a more stark, remote setting than the West Fork, but just as many fish are stocked: 13,500 rainbow trout in the 10- to 12-inch class. Roadside access is excellent. That is why this stream is a favorite for those who know of it.

My favorite section is just upstream from Highway 4 along Wolf Road. You can find a lot of pocket water and several pools here, and the water is clear, cold, and pure. The fishing is better here during the evening hatch. In the spring, you might need mosquito repellent.

Another good section is just downstream from where Monitor Creek enters the East Fork, at the junction of Highways 89 and 4. There just always seem to be good numbers of fish in this area.

You can spend a great day on the East Fork Carson, exploring up and down the river, fishing a half dozen spots or so. Compared to most trout streams, catches are better on the East Fork Carson than dozens of other trout waters. Here you talk about what you caught, not how pretty the water looks.

Facilities, fees: A campground is near Markleeville. Supplies can be obtained in Markleeville. Fishing access is free.

Directions: From Sacramento, take U.S. 50 east to Meyers and Highway 89. Turn south (right) on Highway 89 and drive over Luther Pass to Highway 88. Turn left and drive to Woodfords and Highway 89. Turn right on Highway 89 and drive to Markleeville, then continue six miles. Direct access along the highway is in this area between Markleeville and Highway 4.

From Stockton, take Highway 4 east over Ebbetts Pass (which is long, slow, narrow, and curvy) and continue on 88/89 to Woodfords and the junction with Highway 89. Turn right. Direct access is available along Highway 89 between Markleeville and Highway 4.

Contact: Humboldt-Toiyabe National Forest, Carson Ranger District, 775/882-2766; Tahoe Flyfishing Outfitters, 530/541-8208, www .tahoeflyfishing.com.

72 TOPAZ LAKE

Rating: 8

on the California/Nevada border in
Humboldt-Toiyabe National Forest
Map 6.3, page 311

The wind can howl at Topaz, but so can your fishing reel when the big trout go on the bite. The lake is at an elevation of 5,000 feet, at the foot of the eastern Sierra, right on the California/Oregon border.

It has big trout, often averaging 14–18 inches, with a sprinkling of bigger and smaller ones. When the wind kicks up, it can get downright ugly. If you fish from a small aluminum boat, always remember: safety first.

That done, come prepared for some extensive trolling and the very real possibility of catching a trophy-sized trout. And please, please, please remember to bring a net that's suitable for landing a big fish. Every week someone pulls a five- to eight-pounder up to his or her boat and then loses it because the net is too small.

There are plenty of trout in the foot-long class, since the lake is stocked by both Nevada and California. (The California DFG stocks 10- to 12-inch rainbow trout.) Did I say a lot of fish? Yes, so many that on one trip, Ed "The Dunk" Dunckel looked at his fishfinder and just about croaked. "There are so many black spots that it looks like an attack of gnats," he said.

They weren't gnats, of course, but trout, some 40,000 fresh, from a recent plant near the Topaz Marina ramp. Ironically, none of the fish would bite. After some intense effort, I left for better prospects, and by day's end, The Dunk had one of the most beautiful stringers of trout I've ever seen.

The contrast between the high desert of Nevada and the timbered slopes of California is accented here. The state line goes through the middle of Topaz Lake, with the border seemingly dividing the habitat as well as the states. The lake traditionally opens on January 1.

Facilities, fees: Several boat ramps are available. A 40-boat marina with a launch and boat-trailer storage is lakeside. Four RV parks are nearby. Tent camping is at Douglas County Park, on the northeast side of the lake. Boat launching is free to overnight campers at the Topaz Lake RV Park. For noncampers, a boat-launching fee is charged. A small casino is available on the Nevada side.

Directions: From Carson City, Nevada, take U.S. 395 south for 33 miles to Topaz Lake and the campground/marina, on the left side of the road.

From Bridgeport, California, take U.S. 395 north for 45 miles to the campground/marina, on the right side of the road.

Contact: Topaz Lake RV Park, 530/495-2357, www.topazlakervpark.com.

73 BLUE LAKES

Rating: 7

south of Lake Tahoe in
Humboldt-Toiyabe National Forest
Map 6.3, page 311

The water is cold and the fishing can be hot at this spot in the high country, elevation 8,200 feet. Both Upper and Lower Blue Lakes, which are linked by Middle Blue Creek, are among the most consistent producers of rainbow trout in the region.

The access road to both of these lakes runs on only one side. Bank anglers always fish near the access road. With a boat, always fish the far side, and if you don't have a boat, be willing to hike to it.

Upper Blue seems to be the better choice for shoreline fishing, particularly the area stretching west from the boat ramp for about 200 yards. Lower Blue is decent from the shore, but trolling from a boat can be deadly dull. The north end of that lake, just past the drop-off, provides the best results. Both are well stocked. Upper Blue gets 10- to 12-inch rainbow trout and bonus cutthroat fingerlings. Lower Blue receives 10- to 12-inch rainbow trout and fingerling brook trout.

The first time I fished the Blue Lakes was on

a trip to nearby Hope Valley, where the mission was to fish the Carson River, then head over to the Rubicon. But the Carson was a zilch that day, and a freak snowfall blocked access to the Rubicon. So it was off to the Blue Lakes, which had just become ice-free and had a clear access road. This turned out to be the best insurance policy for a fishing trip that I could've wanted.

Now when I visit this area, I come here first and keep the Carson and Rubicon in mind as possible side trips.

Since the DFG is supposed to spend 33 percent of fishing license fees on hatcheries, you've got to wonder why fewer plants, not more, have been made here.

Facilities, fees: A campground, vault toilets, and drinking water are nearby. There is a boat ramp. Fishing access is free. A boat-launching fee is charged.

Directions: From Sacramento, take U.S. 50 east to the junction with Highway 89. Turn south on Highway 89 and drive over Luther Pass to the junction with Highway 88. Turn right and drive 2.5 miles to Blue Lakes Road. Turn left and drive 11 miles (the road becomes dirt) to a junction at the south end of Lower Blue Lake. Turn right and drive three miles to Upper Blue Lake on the left side of the road.

From Jackson, take Highway 88 east over Carson Pass and continue east for five miles to Blue Lakes Road. Turn right (south) and drive 11 miles (the road becomes dirt) to a junction at the south end of Lower Blue Lake. Turn right and drive three miles to Upper Blue Lake, on the left side of the road.

Contact: PG&E Recreation Desk, 800/743-5000, www.pge.com/recreation.

74 SILVER CREEK

Rating: 6

near Markleeville in
Humboldt-Toiyabe National Forest
Map 6.3, page 311

For a small, pristine stream that is out of the way, Silver Creek is easy to reach. Try it. The creek

sends its pure water, from snowmelt, tumbling over small boulders for about six miles until pouring into the East Fork Carson River.

Large granite slabs border most of the stream, and you walk along them as you move from spot to spot. The little two-lane highway crosses the river in several places, and it is just downstream from these points where the largest numbers of trout hold in pools.

The stream is stocked with rainbow trout in the 10- to 12-inch class, decent numbers for such a short stretch of river.

Facilities, fees: A campground is nearby, on Silver Creek. Supplies are in Markleeville. Fishing access is free.

Directions: From Markleeville (southeast of Lake Tahoe), take Highway 89 south for six miles to Highway 4 and the confluence of the Carson River and Silver Creek. Turn southwest on Highway 4; direct access is available.

Contact: Humboldt-Toiyabe National Forest, Carson Ranger District, 775/882-2766.

75 KINNEY LAKES

Rating: 5

south of Markleeville in
Humboldt-Toiyabe National Forest
Map 6.3, page 311

The three Kinney Lakes are perched high in granite country, just east of Ebbetts Pass along the Pacific Crest Trail. Each has its own niche for anglers.

The biggest, Kinney Reservoir, is near Highway 4 and provides shoreline fishing prospects for rainbow trout in the 9- to 11-inch class and small brook trout. The Department of Fish and Game stocks the reservoir with 10- to 12-inch rainbow trout. In addition, the lake is small enough and often calm enough to fish from a raft or float tube.

The other lakes, Upper and Lower Kinney, can be reached by hiking short distances from the reservoir. The first you will come to is Lower Kinney, which is the prettiest of the three and nearly as big as the reservoir. For the most part it has only small brook trout, however. Upper Kinney lies just a short jaunt upstream and feeds into Lower Kinney through a creek. After close inspection, you'll probably get the feeling that Upper Kinney has nothin'. But there must be something, because the DFG gives Upper Kinney fingerling cutthroat trout (Lower Kinney gets some as well).

One of the lesser-traveled sections of the Pacific Crest Trail runs just west of Upper Kinney, and it's a good spot to start a backpacking adventure. Head north over Reynolds Peak, circle around Raymond Peak, and you will be routed into a basin that has eight small lakes. When I camped at Raymond Lake, I was unimpressed with the fish—just a few dinker-size brook trout.

Facilities, fees: There are no on-site facilities. A campground is available nearby on Silver Creek. Supplies can be obtained in Markleeville. Fishing access is free.

Directions: From Woodfords, take Highway 89 south to Highway 4. Turn right (south) on Highway 4 and drive about 10 miles to Kinney Reservoir on the right. A short walk is required.

Contact: Humboldt-Toiyabe National Forest, Carson Ranger District, 775/882-2766.

76 WEST WALKER RIVER

Rating: 7

northwest of Bridgeport in
Humboldt-Toiyabe National Forest
Map 6.3, page 311

The West Walker River is for the angler who is not the specialist, or for the camper who wants an easy-to-reach stream where chances are good that he or she will catch a trout or two for dinner. It is a good place to bring a kid for a first stream-fishing experience. The West Walker River receives plants of rainbow trout in the 10- to 12-inch class. This river also receives a supplemental plant of Alpers rainbow trout that range 2–10 pounds.

After high flows from the spring snowmelt,

regular plants and improved fishing go from late June on through summer. Once summer days arrive, the stream runs quite clear, making midday prospects terrible. By evening, however, the insects start hatching, shade is on the water, and the bite is on.

After the water flows stabilize in early summer, one of the best places to fish is in Pickle Meadows, adjacent to Highway 108, just up from U.S. 395. When the fish get finicky here, try using 3-pound test and the smallest clear plastic bubble available, and use a nymph about four feet below the bubble. Best patterns for this are a Pheasant Tail or a Prince nymph in size 12 or 14.

Cast directly upstream, then retrieve at the same speed as the current. Watch for any hesitation in the bubble; that means a trout is stopping the drift of the nymph. Strike! You can be surprised by the number of trout that can be caught with this method. But note: Avoid casting into the fastest current; choose secondary currents that will give you a consistent drift.

Several campgrounds are positioned along the West Walker right off U.S. 395, providing fishing for brook trout and camping access. Rainbow trout are stocked near the campgrounds, as well as at accessible locations from the bridge (downstream is a good spot).

Facilities, fees: Several campgrounds with drinking water and vault toilets are off U.S. 395 and Highway 108. Supplies are in Walker or Bridgeport. Fishing access is free.

Directions: From Bridgeport, take U.S. 395 north to Highway 108. The West Walker runs along Highway 108 downslope to near 395, with access off 108, and also from 395 north to Walker and beyond for several miles.

From Carson City, take U.S. 395 south to Coleville and then continue south for 13 miles to the campground on the west side of the highway (six miles north of the junction of U.S. 395 and Highway 108).

Contact: Ken's Sporting Goods, Bridgeport, 760/932-7707, www.kenssport.com; The Trout Fly, 760/934-2517, www.thetroutfly

.com; Tahoe Flyfishing Outfitters, 530/541-8208, www.tahoeflyfishing.com; Humboldt-Toiyabe National Forest, Bridgeport Ranger District, 760/932-7070, www.fs.fed.us/r5—click on Forest Offices.

77 LAKE ALPINE

Rating: 8

northeast of Arnold in
Stanislaus National Forest
Map 6.3, page 311

Quite a few people have discovered Lake Alpine, its camp, and the easy access off Highway 4. Many now return to vacation here every year. You no longer get the solitude and the absolute Sierra quiet like in the old days, but you still get good camping and decent fishing in a beautiful setting. In 2011, the county helped the DFG and added bonus trout plants. As a result, the lake had one of its best years ever. More of the same is expected in 2012 and beyond.

Lake Alpine is at 7,320 feet in the Sierra Nevada, just above where the snowplows stop in winter. It usually becomes accessible sometime in April. Because of the good access and increased number of vacationers, Fish and Game stocks 10- to 12-inch rainbow trout in here. It's a good idea to get here in May, prior to the summer rush.

Once school is out for summer, the campgrounds are loaded with families.

This lake is so pretty. I first saw it back in the day, when I was taking the long way home over the Sierra Nevada via Ebbetts Pass on Highway 4 during a cross-country motorcycle/camping/fishing trip. I arrived at little Lake Alpine at about 7 P.M., when there wasn't a hint of breeze on the surface, just little pools from hatching bugs and rising trout. I parked my bike, turned the key, and let the giant engine rumble to silence. I had my six-piece pack rod together and rigged in minutes.

On my first cast I got a strike, missed the set, but knew I was on to something special. The next cast got him, a frisky 11-incher that shortly thereafter ended up in my small frying pan at a beautiful little camp set near the lake.

Facilities, fees: There are cabins, a restaurant, a convenience store, bait and tackle, coin showers, a boat ramp, and rentals for fishing boats, rowboats, canoes, and kayaks at Lake Alpine. Campgrounds, flush and vault toilets, drinking water, and picnic areas are available. Fishing access is free.

Directions: From Angels Camp, take Highway 4 east to Arnold and continue for 29 miles to Lake Alpine. Alpine Resort is on the left. Campgrounds and the boat ramp are off an access road to the right.

Contact: Lake Alpine Lodge, 209/753-6350, www.lakealpinelodge.com; Ebbetts Pass Sporting Goods, Arnold, 209/795-1686, www.ebbettspasssportinggoods.com; Stanislaus National Forest, Calaveras Ranger District, 209/795-1381, www.fs.fed.us/r5—click on Forest Offices.

78 CARSON-ICEBERG WILDERNESS

Rating: 4

north of Yosemite National Park in
Stanislaus National Forest
Map 6.3, page 311

Hikers always cast a knowing, smiling nod when people start talking about the Carson-Iceberg Wilderness. Despite being in the heart of the Sierra Nevada, this is one of the more overlooked wilderness areas, especially when compared to Desolation Wilderness to the northwest of Tahoe and Emigrant Wilderness to the south, just north of the Yosemite border.

The Carson-Iceberg Wilderness is a place where hiking and mountaineering come first and fishing comes second (or third). The Pacific Crest Trail passes through this high Sierra country, providing access to numerous small streams, including the headwaters of the Carson River. I've hiked most all of the PCT and the section through here is one of the easiest, fastest, and prettiest. The whole area is stark and pristine, and hikers should be cautious whenever crossing rivers. During an early summer day, a river that is low and easily crossed in the morning can become high in the afternoon due to increases in snowmelt.

Compared to other wilderness areas, few lakes here provide decent fishing. Then once you find them, you discover that most of the fish are dinkers. The following lakes have been stocked in the past by the Department of Fish and Game: Rock (rainbow trout), Bull Run (brook trout), Lost (rainbow trout), and Sword (brook trout). Bull Run Lake has been the best, with some big brook trout, but with stocks suspended, the future is a guess.

Regardless, the Carson-Iceberg Wilderness is a place with a special sense of history, beauty, and quiet. For a backpacker on vacation, that is what really counts, not the size of fish and number of lakes.

A side note: I work with all 200 Forest Service districts in California, Washington, and Oregon, and it's my experience that the Summit Ranger District is one of the best at providing accurate, up-to-date reports on trail conditions, fire danger, and other information that can affect a trip.

Facilities, fees: No facilities are available. Campgrounds and supplies can be found in and near adjacent towns. Trailheads are off Highway 4 east of Lake Alpine, and off Highway 108 in the Dardanelle area. Access is free.

Directions: From Sonora, take Highway 108 east past Strawberry, to Dardanelle and the campground, on the left side of the road. A trailhead for the PCT is near Sonora Pass, and a parking lot is available.

Contact: Stanislaus National Forest, Summit Ranger District, 209/965-3434, www.fs.fed .us/r5—click on Forest Offices.

79 UNION RESERVOIR

Rating: 8

northeast of Arnold in
Stanislaus National Forest
Map 6.3, page 311

For some, just getting here is far enough "out there." But you can get a lot farther "out there" if you want.

Union Reservoir and the adjoining Utica Reservoir are set in Sierra granite at 6,850 feet. Union provides the better fishing, since it is stocked with 10- to 12-inch rainbow trout and Eagle Lake trout each summer, while Utica gets none. It also receives kokanee salmon fingerlings. The best of it comes to visitors with car-top boats, who can carry them down to the water and then hand-launch them. The 5-mph speed limit keeps everything quiet. The north end of the lake has a few shallow spots, with some small islands poking through, but the south end is quite deep.

Keep an eye on this one. Union is one of the up-and-coming lakes for kokanee salmon.

Then there's another option. A trailhead with an adjacent parking area at Union Reservoir has a trail routed deep into the Carson-Iceberg Wilderness. Several lakes are within little more than a mile's hike, including Summit Lake and Mud Lake. Farther east, the trail runs alongside Highland Creek and near Iceberg Peak.

Facilities, fees: A boat ramp is available. Walk-in campsites are off Forest Service Road 7N75 at the reservoir. A vault toilet is provided, but drinking water is not. Garbage must be packed out. Supplies are off Highway 4 in Tamarack. Fishing access is free.

Directions: From Angels Camp, take Highway 4 east for 32 miles to Spicer Reservoir Road. Turn right and travel east about seven miles to Forest Service Road 7N75. Turn left and drive three miles to Union Reservoir.

Contact: Ebbetts Pass Sporting Goods, Arnold, 209/795-1686, www.ebbettspasssport inggoods.com; Stanislaus National Forest,

Calaveras Ranger District, 209/795-1381, www.fs.fed.us/r5—click on Forest Offices.

80 SPICER MEADOW RESERVOIR

Rating: 9

in Stanislaus National Forest
northeast of Arnold
Map 6.3, page 311

Hit it right and you'll swear Spicer is the best trout lake on the planet. There have been evenings when a group of us had 20, 30 trout, all caught on gold Cripplures, surface to 10 feet deep. This is always early in summer, when the lake has sparked to life after a long winter, yet before the vacation season and warm weather has taken hold.

It isn't a giant lake by reservoir standards, covering 2,000 acres, but it is large and quite pretty from a boat, surrounded by canyon walls and set at 6,418 feet. Apex lures can be sensational here, but we'll try all our favorites, including the aforementioned gold Cripplures.

The lake has a lot of big trout in it, many 14- to 18-inchers, and the fishing has improved in recent years. At one time, long ago, there were many giant brown trout in this lake. Every once in a while, someone still catches one. A few nice browns are in the mix of rainbows, and the DFG started to truck in large numbers of rainbow trout fingerlings. All stocks stopped here, but this is one of the few lakes where fishing got better after the plants stopped, not worse.

This is one of the older reservoirs in the high-central Sierra Nevada. Spicer Meadow was established in 1929, when a dam was built in the canyon on Highland Creek, creating a short, narrow lake.

Note that a section of lake is within Alpine County and no motors are allowed here.

Facilities, fees: A small boat ramp, campground, drinking water, and vault toilets are available. Fishing access is free.

Directions: From Angels Camp, take Highway 4 east about 32 miles to Spicer Reservoir Road/Forest Service Road 7N01. Turn right, drive seven miles, bear right at a fork with a sharp right turn (Forest Road 7N75), and drive a mile to the campground, at the west end of the lake.

Contact: Stanislaus National Forest, Calaveras Ranger District, 209/795-1381, www.fs.fed .us/r5—click on Forest Offices.

81 DONNELL RESERVOIR

Rating: 9

near Strawberry in Stanislaus National Forest
Map 6.3, page 311

Only the deranged need apply. But like my old pal, the late Waylon Jennings, said, sometimes being a little crazy can keep you from going insane.

Donnell Reservoir is in a deep canyon with high granite walls and clear, cobalt-blue water. It is beautiful, like a miniature Yosemite, complete in the spring with a waterfall, two-tiered, 500-foot Niagara Falls, and a massive granite massif that looks like cross between a miniature Half Dome and El Capitan. Set at 4,921 feet, this lake is one of the toughest lakes to reach and fish in California. But if you drag in a kayak, the insanity ends. This lake has big, beautiful trout, but it'll practically kill you to get here and try to catch them.

The reason anglers, myself included, will go through a little hell to get a boat on the lake here is that you have a chance at fishing heaven. There are some monster-sized rainbows. At the head of the lake, you can drift a night crawler under a bobber in the current flow, and then watch a giant trout come up and swallow the bobber. Then, when you try to fight the fish, the bobber pops out of the mouth of the fish and is gone. Have that happen to you even once and your brain cells will be zapped like you've never felt.

For first-timers, start the trip by driving to

Donnell Vista, at an elevation of 6,100 feet. From here, you can see the dramatic gorge and sweeping beauty of the place. It also gives you a picture of how difficult it is to get a boat in.

There are two options. You make a drive on an unsigned network of forest roads through Hell's Half Acre and then reach a high fence and gate. From here, you hoist your boat over the top of the high fence and then portage it about 0.5 mile to the dam. At the dam, you then rope it down to the lake, and then take the ladder on the dam down to the water. You have to be a mix of Cro-Magnon and lunatic. Very few people are willing to do this. It gets worse; when it's time to leave, it can be near impossible to rope your boat back up to the top of the dam. Try this only in June, when the lake is at its highest level. Earlier in the year, the lake is often kept very low and it really is impossible to get a boat in and out of the water by roping it down from the dam.

At low water, one trick we've pulled off is to climb down the ladder to a large boulder field. Then you scramble over the boulders down to lake's edge on the right. Often there are cheap, dented-up aluminum boats here that were dragged over the boulders and then left here, because there's no logical way to get the boat out. At one point there were quite a few boats, but the water authority can confiscate them and pull them out, so this is far from a sure thing.

The other option is preferable if you don't mind dragging a kayak and your gear through forest and down the canyon to the lake. It's just as difficult, but in a different way. You drive up to Clark Fork with a Forest Service map and turn left, looking for an unsigned spur road on the left. Sometimes there'll be a few ribbons tied on trees to mark the best spot. Turn on the spur road and drive in a short distance. From here, you trek cross-country down to the lake on deer trails. The best route is down into the canyon near the head of the lake; when near water level, lateral west to the boulder field near the head of the lake. To make it worse, you need to drag a kayak with you in order to fish the lake right.

If you make it to water's edge, your troubles are not over. If you don't have a boat, the lake is terribly hard to fish because so much of the lake is edged by high walls and big boulders. And if you do have a boat, like a kayak, you have to be extremely competent because wind typically howls through this canyon every day. It often starts at midmorning and picks up through the afternoon, with whitecaps common by midafternoon.

So don't go jumping off on this trip without a good look in the mirror and a long talk with yourself. If you go anyway, I have one thing to say: Don't blame me. I warned you.

At this point, because it is so difficult to get to the lake, I have barely touched on fishing techniques. Well, if you go, it is best to camp and be on the lake at dawn.

The consensus is you need night crawlers for bait. For anglers who never use bait, well, your fly-fishing buddy isn't watching over your shoulder, and you should know: night crawlers work best at Donnell. You must use a worm threader so the worm lies perfectly straight along the shank of the hook. Most use a bobber, others just a single split shot. Then, in your boat, drift in the current at the head of the lake, with the night crawler trailing behind the boat, and then let the breeze push you along the old river channel.

The handful of anglers who bring reels with leadcore line, or those fewer still who have portable downriggers mounted on hand-carried boats (like my Old Town canoe and Scotty Junior), should slow-troll a jointed gold/black Rapala about 30, 40 feet deep on one side, and a rainbow-colored Needlefish with a red eye added 20–30 feet deep on the other. It will look like a small fish chasing a smaller fish. Try different depths, but in early summer, this is usually where they stay once the sun is up. The water is clear and deep, and once sun is on the water, the fish can go deep. That is why you need a way to fish deeper, from about 8 A.M. on.

When the wind comes up, if you are not confident in your boat and skills to stay safe, then get off the lake. Otherwise, the wind can push you to the end of the lake and it is difficult to return. Yet we've caught some of our biggest trout when the wind is pushing us at a pretty good clip. I don't use a lot of hardware, but when the wind is up, there is an exception: Cousin Carl Half-Flat Flashers, just two blades, hammered chrome/bronze, 18 inches of fluorocarbon leader, and then a night crawler rigged so it lies perfectly flat in the water, so the end of it undulates in the current. The trout often can't resist that just as shade takes over the lake in the evening.

The whole affair is kind of crazy. The things we do to chase a big fish, eh?

Facilities, fees: No facilities are provided. Garbage must be packed out. Access is free.

Directions: To Donnell Dam: From Sonora, take Highway 108 east for 31 miles (just past the Dodge Ridge turnoff) to the town of Strawberry. Continue on Highway 108 for four miles to Beardsley Road. Turn left and drive one mile to Forest Road 5N95 (Hells Half Acre Road). Turn right and drive 2.1 miles to a fork with Forest Road 5NO9X (the "4700 Road"). Bear right at the fork and drive 8.1 miles to the gate. Park and walk 0.5 mile (passing two gates) to the dam. High-clearance vehicles are recommended; it takes roughly 75 minutes to get there from Highway 108.

To Donnell Trailhead: From Sonora, take Highway 108 east for 31 miles (just past the Dodge Ridge turnoff) to the town of Strawberry. Continue on Highway 108 for 19 miles (three miles past Donnell Overlook) to Clark Fork Road on the left. Turn left and drive one mile to a fork. Bear left at the fork on Forest Road 6N06 and drive about 2.5 miles to an unsigned spur road on the left. Bear left on that spur road, drive a short distance, and park. Look for the blue marker ribbons (usually present) at the trailhead and hike 2.5

miles on a faint route to the inlet of Donnell Reservoir. Detailed topographical and Forest Service maps and off-trail mountaineering experience are required.

Note: There is no direct vehicle access to the lake.

Contact: Stanislaus National Forest, Summit Ranger District, 209/965-3434, fax 209/965-3372, www.fs.fed.us/r5—click on Forest Offices; Rich & Sal's Sporting Goods, Pinecrest, 209/965-3637.

For a regular map of the area, contact the U.S. Forest Service. For a topographic map, ask for Donnell Lake, California, from the U.S. Geological Survey (888/275-8747). Major credit cards are accepted.

82 KIRMAN LAKE

Rating: 7

near Bridgeport

Map 6.3, page 311   BEST (

Once all but unknown, little Kirman Lake has become renowned as a unique, quality fishery. It has been the best brook-trout lake in the state, but it declined during the years that DFG failed to stock it. It started making a comeback in 2007. Brookies weighing three pounds are starting to get more common again. The biggest fish are caught when the cold weather arrives near the end of the season in October. Cutthroat trout of over five pounds also inhabit the lake.

The DFG stocks fingerling cutthroat and brook trout. The fish grow very fast and have a relatively short life expectancy, so stocks are a must.

The hike in to Kirman used to keep most people out, but now fly fishers have discovered it en masse, and you can see them daily, hiking in with float tubes.

You get an intimate setting, specialized angling, and large cutthroat trout at little Kirman Lake. Some people feel this is a fly fisher's paradise.

The trail in is 2.75 miles, including an easy hop over a fence, and that stops some anglers from bringing much gear. But this is where a light float tube or a small raft is essential for the best access and for being able to reach the key areas outside the shallows. The best area is on the left side of the lake near the beaver dams. By shore, it is very difficult to have much success.

The rules mandate special restrictions (always check the Department of Fish and Game rule book before fishing anywhere), including mandatory use of lures or flies with a barbless hook.

The best fly patterns are shrimp patterns, based on the food supply in the lake. But many fly fishers catch the big trout on leeches, Zug Bugs, Scuds, and Matukas.

The best lure is the 1/16-ounce Panther Martin, black body with yellow spots, of course, rigged with a single, barbless hook. Another pattern that works great is a 1/16-ounce Daredevil that has one side painted flat black, then has five small red dots on it. This was developed by Ed Dunckel, and we appropriately call it "The Mr. Dunckel Special." But remember that from shore, this is an extremely difficult lake to reach the fish. Other good lures are the Roostertail White Coach Dog and Trout Teasers.

An average day here is to catch one of these cutthroats, maybe a brook trout, too. But among those fish is the chance for a 20-incher. Or bigger.

Facilities, fees: No facilities are on-site. Campgrounds are nearby. Supplies can be obtained in Bridgeport. Access is free.

Directions: From Bridgeport, take U.S. 395 north for 17 miles to Highway 108. Turn west on Highway 108 and drive about 0.5 mile. Parking is past the cattle guard on the road. From the parking area, walk the 2.75-mile trail to the lake (there's one hill).

Contact: Ken's Sporting Goods, Bridgeport, 760/932-7707, www.kenssport.com; The Trout Fly, 760/934-2517, www.thetroutfly.com; Rich & Sal's Sporting Goods, Pinecrest, 209/965-3637, www.pinecrestsportshop.com; Tahoe Flyfishing Outfitters, 530/541-8208, www.tahoeflyfishing.com.

83 BUCKEYE CREEK

Rating: 6

east of Bridgeport in
Humboldt-Toiyabe National Forest
Map 6.3, page 311

Buckeye Creek is known for its brush-free, grassy banks (no tangled casts), with occasional deep pools and cut banks. It takes a cautious wader to fish this right. This is where Chief Lone Wolf became famous by catching big trout with his bare hands, lying on his side along the shoreline and then scooping them right out from under the bank.

If you want something easier, brook trout are planted at the Buckeye Camp where Buckeye Creek Road crosses the creek. Try from there on upstream a bit. Lots of brookies; lots.

If you want more of a challenge and a chance for some big fish, hike to the upper stretches of Buckeye Creek, where you will discover some brush-filled beaver dams. They create some deep holes, where a mix of brown trout and rainbow trout hang out. Toss out a night crawler (no weight, not even a split shot), keep your reel on free spool, and you can catch some beauties in this area.

Buckeye Creek also receives small plants of catchable-size rainbow trout.

A star attraction at Buckeye Creek is some little hot springs, and most vacationers don't even realize they exist (they are two miles from the campground).

Like neighboring Robinson Creek, Buckeye Creek once provided fabulous fishing for brown trout migrating up the streams from Bridgeport Reservoir in the fall. Not so much anymore. Locals claim that out-of-town anglers fished out the big browns, keeping all the big ones and not leaving enough fish for the future.

Facilities, fees: A campground, flush toilets, and drinking water are near the creek, off Buckeye Creek Road. Primitive campgrounds are on the creek itself. Supplies can be obtained in Twin Lakes and Bridgeport. Fishing access is free.

Directions: From the town of Bridgeport on U.S. 395, drive seven miles southwest on Twin Lakes Road to Twin Lakes Resort and Buckeye Creek Road. Turn right (north) on Buckeye Creek Road (dirt, often impassable when wet) and continue 3.5 miles to the creek.

Contact: Ken's Sporting Goods, Bridgeport, 760/932-7707, www.kenssport.com; The Trout Fly, 760/934-2517, www.thetroutfly .com; Doc & Al's Resort, 760/932-7051; Inyo National Forest, Mono Lake Ranger District, 760/647-3044, www.fs.fed.us/r5—click on Forest Offices.

84 ROBINSON CREEK

Rating: 5

near Bridgeport
Map 6.3, page 311

Robinson Creek has a mix of wild brown trout, including a rare lunker, along with brook trout and planted 10- to 12-inch rainbow trout. The best bet for newcomers is to start fishing at the bridge adjacent to Twin Lakes Resort, on downstream a bit, and also near campgrounds set along Twin Lakes Road. Why? Because this is where the Department of Fish and Game plunks in their hatchery trout. Along with those planters are an awful lot of people.

Only rarely are the big brown trout caught out of Robinson Creek. Consider that there are several camps here, with anglers working the water near all of them. By early summer, those big browns have been well-schooled, getting fishing lessons every day.

But even those browns have to eat now and then, and the best bet is to try for them early

in the season, before the summer vacationers arrive. Offer a night crawler in front of a big brown in mid-May or late October, drifting it past with no weight, and it will likely be an offer it can't refuse.

Facilities, fees: Campgrounds are available. Supplies can be obtained in Bridgeport. Limited supplies are available at Annett's Mono Village and Twin Lakes Resort. Fishing access is free.

Directions: Take U.S. 395 to Bridgeport and Twin Lakes Road. Turn southwest (toward the Sierra) on Twin Lakes Road and drive about seven miles. Direct access is available from the road and at the campgrounds.

Contact: Ken's Sporting Goods, Bridgeport, 760/932-7707, www.kenssport.com; The Trout Fly, 760/934-2517, www.thetroutfly .com; Twin Lakes Resort, 760/932-7751; Humboldt-Toiyabe National Forest, Bridgeport Ranger District, 760/932-7070.

85 BRIDGEPORT RESERVOIR

Rating: 10

near Bridgeport
Map 6.3, page 311

Some waters just seem to grow large fish, others small ones. Bridgeport Lake is one of the lakes that grow big fish. Giant. Gargantuan. They are in there.

The biggest fish of the year in Mono County are often caught at the end of the season in late October (as well as the first week of the season after the last Saturday of April). When weather turns cold, that is when the big rainbow trout often gorge before the winter doldrums take over. Occasionally, huge browns are also caught, fish occasionally even ranging over 10 pounds. The irony is that relatively few anglers are out in the late season, fighting the cold, occasional snow flurries, and the chance for a giant trout.

As you read this, it is likely that there are a few 20-pound brown trout roaming around this lake, along with a sprinkling over 10 pounds and a fair number ranging above 5 pounds. Catching them is no easy deal. But it's the kind of thing that can put an angler on attention for months at a time.

Even though the lake has 13 miles of shoreline and has been emptied several times, it seems to respond at a few spots: at Rainbow Point (the one obvious point on the western shore), as well as near the outlets of Buckeye, Robinson, and Swauger Creeks, at the southern end of the lake.

When full, Bridgeport covers 4,400 surface acres and is quite pretty, the bright blue water contrasting with the stark surrounding countryside of the eastern Sierra. It is in a valley at an elevation of 6,500 feet. The lake is stocked with rainbow trout in the 10- to 12-inch class, 1,300 brood-stock rainbow trout weighing two pounds and up, and mostly catchable browns that provide seed for the future.

From shore, research editor Kathie Morgan and her husband, David, fish the very accessible southeast shore. They use Thomas Buoyants and have caught rainbow and brown trout to 20 inches.

Yet a boat, or at least a float tube, provides a tremendous advantage. Many people arrive for the trout opener in late spring. Waters are clear, trollers have good lanes to fish, and a lot of big fish are caught. Early in the season, trollers try for big trout by using orange or fire-tiger Rapalas and Rebels. These lures seem to have a magic effect on the bigger fish, though it can take long hours to finally hook a big brown. Conventional trolling techniques using Needlefish or a variety of lures, including flashers and night crawlers, can also work here.

With the two-rod stamp and a friend, you can keep two or three rods out trolling for rainbow trout to keep the action going, and make every hour a chance for fun. At the same time, always keep one rod out with a special lure for a big brown trout, like a Castaic Trout,

Bomber, or large Rapala or Rebel, or even a Thunderstick. These big browns eat trout for breakfast and dinner, so you need a giant lure to properly simulate their food.

As the summer warms, however, weed growth can choke off the trolling, except for a small area of water near the dam. This is when bait fishers take over, using Power Bait and night crawlers in pockets between the weeds, or anchored in a boat next to weeds.

The same weeds that foul trollers create a wonderful opportunity for fly fishers. Float tubing in the weeds is a technique to hook some of the lake's biggest fish, both rainbow trout and brown trout in the 19-pound class. Landing them, however, is another story.

Fly fishers use streamers here, with the woolly bugger and Zonker the most popular.

The northern end of the lake is shallow, so it warms up and receives abundant nutrients from the feeder streams, resulting in a tremendous aquatic food chain. Because of these factors, there can be an algae-bloom problem late in the summer during years that are quite warm.

You can try all summer and not get a 5-pounder. You can try for years and not get a 10-pounder. But now and then, just when you forget about them, one is caught, and its King Kong size will get you back out there fishing for the fish of your dreams.

Facilities, fees: Bridgeport Reservoir RV Park and Marina has a full-service marina, boat slips, fishing-boat rentals, convenience store, and campsites. Paradise Shores RV Park (no tents) has two rental trailers, restrooms with flush toilets, and coin laundry. The public day-use area has drinking water and restrooms. Picnic areas are provided along the eastern shore. Many campgrounds are in the area. Supplies can be obtained in Bridgeport. Fishing access is free.

Directions: From Southern California, take U.S. 395 north to Bishop and continue to

Bridgeport and Highway 182. Turn east on Highway 182 and continue for one mile to the lake. The boat ramps are directly off the highway.

From Sacramento, take U.S. 50 east to Echo Summit (near South Lake Tahoe). Turn south on Highway 89 and drive to its junction with U.S. 395. Turn south on U.S. 395 and drive through Bridgeport to Highway 182. Turn east on Highway 182 and continue one mile to the lake.

To the three boat ramps:
• Bridgeport Reservoir RV Park and Marina: From Bridgeport, take Highway 182 east for three miles to the marina entrance. A paved ramp and docks are available.
• Paradise Shores RV Park: From Bridgeport, take Highway 182 east to the signed turnoff (just past Bridgeport Marina). A dirt launching area is available.
• Bridgeport Public Ramp: From Bridgeport, take Highway 182 east for 3.5 miles to the sign for public access. A paved ramp is available.

Contact: Bridgeport Marina, 760/932-7001, www.bridgeportreservoir.com; Paradise Shores RV Park, 760/932-7735, www.calparadise.com; Ken's Sporting Goods, Bridgeport, 760/932-7707, www.kenssport.com; The Trout Fly, 760/934-2517, www.thetroutfly.com; Stay Bent Fishing Guide Service, 775/450-5516, www.staybentfishing.com; Sierra Drifters Guide Service, 760/935-4250, www.sierradrifters.com (fish report available by email).

SAN FRANCISCO BAY AREA

© TOM STIENSTRA

BEST FISHING SPOTS

【 Hike-In Fisheries
Henry W. Coe State Park, **page 434.**

【 Places to Teach Kids to Fish
San Pablo Reservoir, **page 399.**
Lake Chabot, **page 403.**
Del Valle Reservoir, **page 410.**

A huge undersea mountain range along the Bay
Area coast gives rise to a fishery that is among the richest in the world.
This fishery extends roughly along a reef from the Farallon Islands on
north to Soap Bank and Cordell Bank. It is a year-round home to salmon
(fishing only in season, of course) and to more than a dozen species of
rockfish and lingcod.

Believe it or not, the Bay Area has 58 lakes. I've counted them. Of these,
29 lakes are stocked with trout in season, and of those, 11 provide bonus
trophy-size rainbow trout. Another 20 have no stocks. Public access for
fishing is prohibited at 18 lakes – most notably, every lake on the peninsula
between Lake Merced (in San Francisco) and Stevens Creek Reservoir
(near Monta Vista).

The feature programs are in Alameda and Contra Costa Counties, where
bonus trophy-size rainbow trout are available at San Pablo Reservoir,
Lake Chabot, Lafayette Reservoir, Shadow Cliffs Lake, and Quarry Lakes.
The Del Valle Reservoir has developed one of the best urban fishing programs for trout in America, while the the Los Vaqueros Reservoir gives
the region a long-needed chance at an excellent warm-water fishery.
Trophy-size fish are also occasionally planted at Contra Loma Reservoir,
Lake Temescal, Don Castro Reservoir, and Parkway Lake. These are but
a small sprinkling compared to the typical dinkers that are plunked in by
the hatchery trucks.

While most of the Bay Area's streams have been lined with concrete and
channeled for flood control, there is still limited opportunity for steelhead
at San Gregorio Creek and Pescadero Creek.

The Bay Area has many piers and significant shore-access points for
fishing. The highlights are salmon at Pacifica Pier; halibut and perch at

Berkeley Pier; sturgeon at Dumbarton Pier, Candlestick Point, McNear's Pier, and Point Pinole Pier; and striped bass at Crockett Pier, Pittsburg Pier, and Antioch Pier.

Other pluses are the perch and jacksmelt at Fort Point Pier and the jacksmelt and giant bat rays at Oyster Point Pier. The key is timing, of course. You either intercept the fish during their seasonal migrations, scheduling each day's trip for the tides, or you might as well get hired to simulate a statue.

The Bay Area has 150 significant parks (including 12 with redwoods), 7,500 miles of hiking and biking trails, 45 lakes, 25 waterfalls, 100 miles of coast, mountains with incredible lookouts, bays with islands, and 1.2 million acres of greenbelt — and hundreds of acres are being added each year as land is bought with money earmarked from property taxes.

In the foothills that separate the San Joaquin Valley from the Santa Clara Valley — with miniature mountains that rise to 3,000 feet bordered by deep canyons — you will find Henry W. Coe State Park. This wilderness park provides a great destination in the spring into the back country for pond-style bass fishing.

It may stun some anglers who live in the Bay Area that catch rates for salmon are often the highest on the Pacific Coast, better even than Alaska. That can stun people from the Bay Area who go to Alaska expecting to catch one giant king salmon after another, only to find out the hours-per-fish ratio is often better right out of San Francisco.

The only downers are that you must board a boat to make it work — either your own private boat or a party boat — and that the traffic is often jammed, making the return trip home a pain in the butt. But the beauty of the Bay Area and its coast, especially when viewed from a boat, is nonpareil.

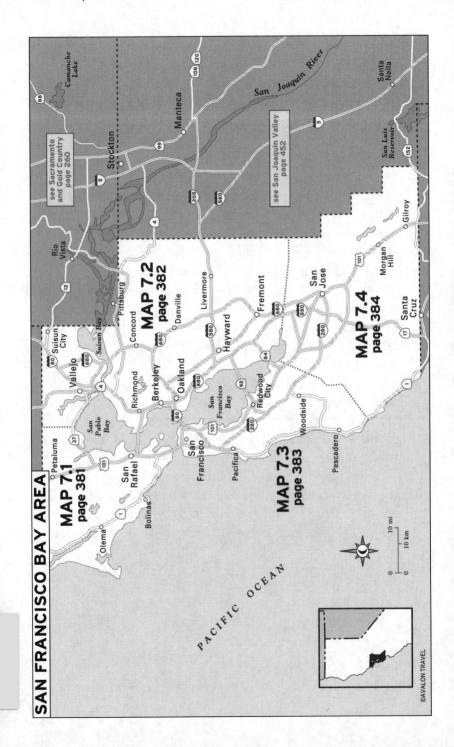

SAN FRANCISCO BAY AREA

MAP 7.1 page 381

MAP 7.2 page 382

MAP 7.3 page 383

MAP 7.4 page 384

see Sacramento and Gold Country page 260

see San Joaquin Valley page 452

PACIFIC OCEAN

©AVALON TRAVEL

Map 7.1

NORTH BAY

Sites 1-13

Pages 385-393

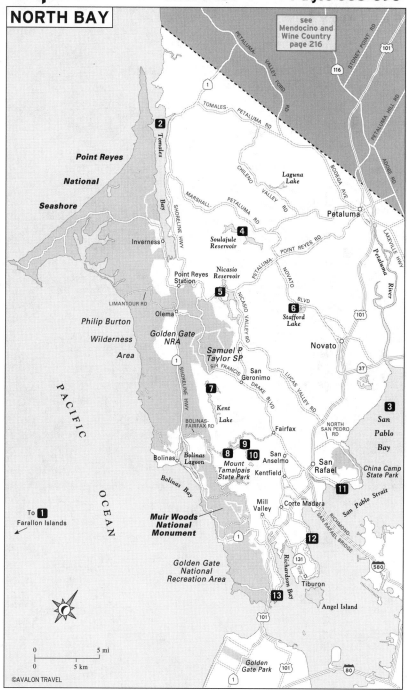

see Mendocino and Wine Country page 216

Point Reyes

National

Seashore

PETALUMA VALLEY FORD RD

STONEY POINT RD

101

116

TOMALES PETALUMA RD

1

2

Tomales Bay

ADOBE RD

PETALUMA HILL RD

CHILENO VALLEY RD

Laguna Lake

BODEGA AVE

Petaluma

LAKEVILLE HWY

MARSHALL-PETALUMA RD

4

Soulajule Reservoir

POINT REYES RD

Petaluma River

SHORELINE HWY

Inverness

Nicasio Reservoir

Point Reyes Station

5

NICASIO VALLEY RD

PETALUMA

NOVATO

BLVD

6

Stafford Lake

101

LIMANTOUR RD

Philip Burton

Olema

Golden Gate NRA

Wilderness

Area

Samuel P Taylor SP

SIR FRANCIS

San Geronimo

DRAKE BLVD

LUCAS VALLEY RD

Novato

37

1

7

Kent Lake

BOLINAS-FAIRFAX RD

Fairfax

NORTH SAN PEDRO RD

3

San

Pablo

Bay

PACIFIC

Bolinas

Bolinas Lagoon

8

9

10

San Anselmo

Kentfield

Mount Tamalpais State Park

San Rafael

China Camp State Park

11

RICHMOND-SAN RAFAEL BRIDGE

San Pablo Strait

Bolinas Bay

Corte Madera

OCEAN

To **1**
Farallon Islands

Mill Valley

1

Muir Woods National Monument

12

131

Richardson Bay

Golden Gate National Recreation Area

580

Tiburon

13

Angel Island

101

0   5 mi

0   5 km

Golden Gate Park

101

80

1

©AVALON TRAVEL

Map 7.2

Sites 14-41

Pages 394-411

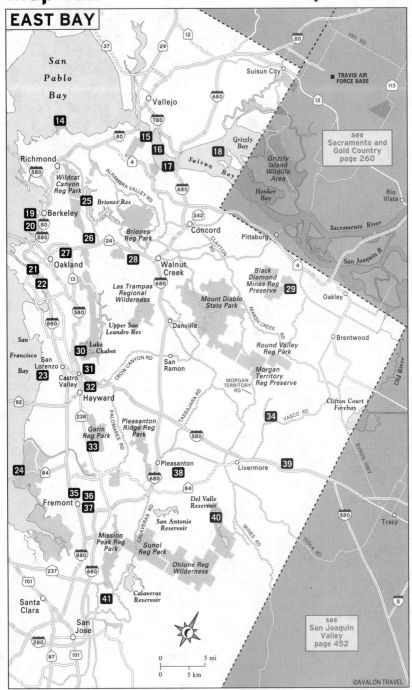

EAST BAY

©AVALON TRAVEL

Map 7.3

Sites 42-62   **Pages 411-426**

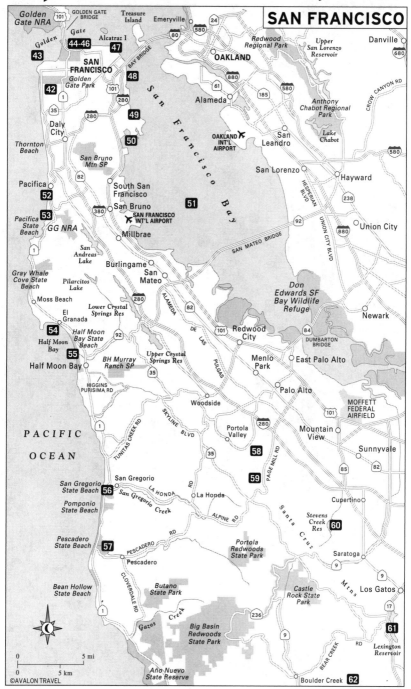

SAN FRANCISCO

Golden Gate NRA · 101 · GOLDEN GATE BRIDGE · Treasure Island · Emeryville · 24 · 580 · 80 · Redwood Regional Park · Upper San Lorenzo Reservoir · Danville · 680

Golden · Gate · Alcatraz I · **44-46** · **47** · BAY BRIDGE · **OAKLAND** · 680

43 · SAN FRANCISCO · **48** · 880 · 61

42 · Golden Gate Park · 1 · 101 · 280 · 280 · San · Alameda · 185 · 580 · Anthony Chabot Regional Park · CROW CANYON RD

35 · **49** · Francisco · OAKLAND INT'L AIRPORT · San Leandro · Lake Chabot

Daly City · **50** · Bay · 580

Thornton Beach · San Bruno Mtn SP · San Lorenzo · Hayward · 238

Pacifica · 82 · South San Francisco · SAN FRANCISCO INT'L AIRPORT · **51** · HESPERIAN BLVD

52 · San Bruno · 380 · SAN MATEO BRIDGE · 92 · UNION CITY BLVD · Union City · 880

Pacifica State Beach · **53** · GG NRA · Millbrae · Don Edwards SF Bay Wildlife Refuge

Gray Whale Cove State Beach · San Andreas Lake · Burlingame · San Mateo · 280 · 82 · 101 · Redwood City · Newark

Moss Beach · Pilarcitos Lake · Lower Crystal Springs Res · DE LAS · Menlo Park · 84 · East Palo Alto · DUMBARTON BRIDGE

El Granada · **54** · 92 · Half Moon Bay State Beach · Upper Crystal Springs Res · PULGAS · Palo Alto · MOFFETT FEDERAL AIRFIELD

Half Moon Bay · **55** · 35 · BH Murray Ranch SP · Woodside · 101

Half Moon Bay · HIGGINS PURISIMA RD · SKYLINE BLVD · Portola Valley · 280 · Mountain View · Sunnyvale

PACIFIC · 1 · TUNITAS CREEK RD · **58** · Page Mill RD · 85 · 82

OCEAN · 35 · **59**

San Gregorio · LA HONDA · Cupertino

San Gregorio State Beach · **56** · San Gregorio Creek · La Honda · ALPINE RD · Santa · Stevens Creek Res · **60**

Pomponio State Beach · RD · Cruz · Saratoga · 9 · 9

Pescadero State Beach · **57** · PESCADERO · RD · Portola Redwoods State Park · Mts · Los Gatos

Pescadero · CLOVERDALE RD · Castle Rock State Park · 17

Bean Hollow State Beach · 1 · Butano State Park · 236 · **61**

Gazos · Creek · Big Basin Redwoods State Park · 9 · BEAR CREEK · RD · Lexington Reservoir

0 — 5 mi · 0 — 5 km · ©AVALON TRAVEL · Año Nuevo State Reserve · Boulder Creek · **62**

Map 7.4

Sites 63-74

Pages 428-434

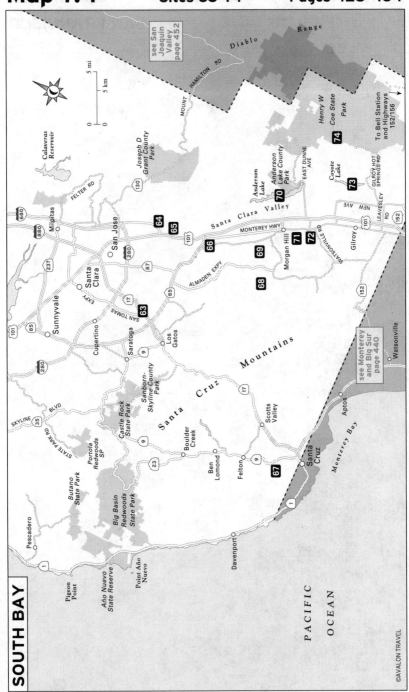

SOUTH BAY

©AVALON TRAVEL

1 FARALLON ISLANDS

Rating: 10

off the San Francisco coast
Map 7.1, page 381

A huge undersea mountain range gives rise to a fishery that is among the richest in the world. The fishery extends roughly along a reef from the Farallon Islands on north to Soap Bank and Cordell Bank. It is a year-round home to salmon (fishing only in season, of course) and to more than a dozen species of rockfish and lingcod. When conditions are right, this area can attract albacore, several species of whales (featuring grays, humpbacks, and blues), and a wide variety and number of seabirds.

This extraordinary habitat extends from the Bay Area coast out about 30 miles to the continental shelf. Marine upwelling occurs here in late winter and spring, when strong winds out of the northwest push surface currents to the side, bringing deep, cold, nutrient-rich waters to the surface. Sunlight penetration of this water starts a plankton boom, and in turn, the marine food chain flourishes.

Note that in order to protect seabirds and marine mammals from being disturbed, boats are not allowed to fish right up against the island. Fishing depths are limited to no deeper than 180 feet in order to protect deepwater species. Water less than 60 feet deep around the Farallon Islands and Noonday Rock is closed to fishing at all times for rockfish and lingcod.

Charter boats depart early, usually by 5:30 A.M.; traveling at 12 knots, they usually hit the Farallones by 8:45 A.M. With Abe and Angelo Cuanang in their matched pair of Boston Whalers, I have reached the Farallones in 56 minutes from the Golden Gate on a flat, calm sea.

Much of the area is loaded with rockfish, but the vicinity of South Farallon Island seems most abundant.

Skippers turn their engines off and drift, allowing the boats to float above tremendous schools of yellows and blues that are 50–100 feet below the surface, and large numbers of lingcod on the bottom, as deep as 180 feet deep. This allows for light tackle fishing for shallow school fish, as well as traditional bottom-style fishing for lings and the wide variety of rockfish that live near the ocean floor.

Again, note that fishing regulations often change here from year to year, for seasons, depth restrictions, bag limits, size limits, and even annual quotas for the fleet. Always check current regulations with Fish and Game or with a marina or party-boat operator before planning a trip. The limits seem to have stabilized at 10 rockfish.

The Farallon Islands are actually the emerging tops of an underwater mountain range that provides a perfect habitat for the aquatic food chain. To the north is the Pimple, and beyond that, the North Farallon Islands. All three areas provide rich marine regions where rockfish thrive. The South Island is the largest, has a few structures, and is used as a research lab by the Scripps Institute. The Pimple is just a single rock, and the North Farallon Islands are sharp-tipped rocks resembling the mountain peaks in the jagged southern Sierra near Mount Whitney.

In the winter and spring, huge schools of krill can actually tint the surface water red and, in the process, attract large schools of salmon. There have been fantastic schools of sardines in spring and summer. During the first week of the salmon season, the vicinity of the South Farallones is particularly attractive if the weather is calm enough to allow people to make the long trip. All through spring, balls of shrimp, squid, and a significant number of juvenile rockfish lure salmon to the area. As for rockfish, they tend to stay deep during this time of the year.

As summer arrives, the salmon move inshore with the arrival of large schools of anchovies. In addition, rockfish start moving to shallower and easier-to-fish areas, with midwater school fish becoming abundant by mid-June. By fall, the salmon move out, and rockfish take over (they're found in both shallow and deep waters), with a bonus of large numbers of lingcod.

Of the latter, most are in the 5- to 10-pound class, with about 10 percent in the 15- to 20-pound range and a few larger ones.

On quiet fall mornings I have seen yellows swirling on the surface, ready to take a large silver streamer delivered by a fly rod or a Hair Raiser cast from a spinning rod.

All this diverse and abundant marine life adds up to one of the best fisheries in California.

Facilities, fees: Bait and tackle can be rented on each boat. Party-boat fees are charged per person.

Directions: The Farallon Islands are 27 miles west of the Golden Gate Bridge and can be reached by charter boat from the following locations:

• To Fisherman's Wharf from the Golden Gate Bridge: Take U.S. 101 to the southern end of the Golden Gate Bridge in San Francisco and look for the marina exit. Take that exit and drive southeast toward Fisherman's Wharf. The boats are at the foot of Jones and Jefferson, along the front row of Fisherman's Wharf, between Castagnola's and Tarantino's restaurants. A parking garage is nearby, at Beach and Jones.

To Fisherman's Wharf from the Bay Bridge: Take I-80 west to the exit for Embarcadero/Harrison Street. Take that exit (on the left-hand side of the road) and drive to Harrison Street. Turn right on Harrison Street and drive five blocks to the Embarcadero. Turn left on the Embarcadero and drive past the piers on the right to Bay Street. Continue on the Embarcadero to Fisherman's Wharf and the parking garages.

• To the Berkeley Marina: Take I-80 to Berkeley and exit at University Avenue West/Berkeley Marina. Drive west to a T intersection. Turn left for the pier and bait shop. Turn right for the boat ramp.

• To the Emeryville Marina: Take I-80 to Emeryville. Take the Powell Street exit west to Powell Street. Drive west on Powell Street for 0.75 mile to the parking area, marina, and bait shop, at the end of the road.

• To Clipper Yacht Harbor, Sausalito: Take U.S. 101 to Sausalito and the exit for Sausalito–Marin City. Take the Sausalito–Marin City exit and bear left, heading under the freeway. Turn right on Bridgeway and proceed a few blocks to Harbor. Turn left and continue to the marina.

Contact: Hi's Tackle, South San Francisco, 650/588-1375, www.histackleboxshop.com; Gus' Discount Tackle, San Francisco, 415/752-6197, www.gusdiscounttackle.com.

Party boats: Berkeley Marina Sports Center, 510/849-2727, www.berkeleymarina sport-fishing.com; Emeryville Sportfishing, 510/654-6040 or 800/575-9944, www .emeryvillesportfishing.com; Huck Finn Sportfishing, 650/726-7133, www.huck finnsportfishing.com; Riptide Sportfishing, 650/728-8433, www.riptide.net; Half Moon Bay Sportfishing, 650/728-3377, www.hmb fishing.com.

❷ TOMALES BAY

Rating: 5

north of San Francisco

Map 7.1, page 381

This is among the most unusual places in California: a long, narrow bay cut by the San Andreas Fault, one of the earth's most feared earthquake fault lines. Because Point Reyes shields the bay from north winds, these quiet waters are ideal for paddling a kayak or motoring around in a small boat (a hoist is available in Inverness; look for the sign on the east side of the road). In the summer, the adventuresome angler can discover huge halibut on the northwestern side. Schools of perch also await, though they can require a lot of searching out. For nonboaters, clamming is quite good in season during minus tides at Tomales Bay State Park.

On calm days, however, small boats can reach prime salmon-fishing areas just outside the bar. One popular salmon mooching spot is Bird Rock, which is close enough to the bay's protected waters that small boats can get back to safety if the weather suddenly turns ugly. Other favored salmon spots just south of the mouth of Tomales Bay include Elephant Rock, the Key Holes, and Ten-Mile Beach.

Inside the bay near Hog Island you'll find a good halibut fishery. Another great opportunity is out of Dillon Beach: in clam season, visitors can rent small boats for the short ride to the prime clam beds. Leopard sharks and bat rays are common in summer months in the channel.

Tomales Bay is largely undeveloped, bordered by the Point Reyes National Seashore to the west and by Highway 1 and small towns to the east. A few warnings are necessary, however: Every year, dozens of clammers get nailed at Tomales Bay State Park for not possessing a state fishing license. A license is required for clamming, and the rangers will check.

If you have a small boat, it is unwise to try to "shoot the jaws" (to head through the mouth of Tomales Bay and out into the ocean). The water is very shallow near the buoy here and can get quite choppy and dangerous. In addition, this is a breeding area for great white sharks. In fact, one great white actually bit the propeller off a boat in these parts.

Note: Tomales Bay State Park is on the closure list developed by the California Department of Parks, pending final state budget decisions or the possible transfer of park management to other park agencies or volunteer groups.

Facilities, fees: Campsites are reachable by boat or bike, or on foot, at Tomales Bay State Park. A day-use fee is charged.

Directions: To Lawson's Landing: From Marin, take U.S. 101 north to Petaluma and the exit for Washington Boulevard. Take the Washington Boulevard exit and drive west for 10 miles (it turns into Bodega Avenue) to Tomales Road. Turn left at Tomales Road and drive six miles to the town of Tomales at Highway 1. At the stop sign, turn right on Highway 1 and drive 0.25 mile to Dillon Beach Road. Turn left on Dillon Beach Road and drive four miles to Lawson's Resort.

To Tomales Bay State Park: Take U.S. 101 to Marin and the exit for Sir Francis Drake Blvd. Take that exit and drive west for 20 miles to the town of Olema. Turn right on Highway 1, drive about four miles, turn left at Sir Francis Drake Boulevard, and drive north for seven miles to Pierce Point Road. Turn right and drive 1.2 miles to the access road for Tomales Bay State Park. Turn right and drive 1.5 miles to the park entrance.

Contact: Tomales Bay State Park, 415/669-1140, www.parks.ca.gov; Lawson's Landing, Dillon Beach, 707/878-2443, www.lawsonslanding.com.

🮊 SAN PABLO BAY

Rating: 10

from the Richmond Bridge to the Carquinez Bridge

Map 7.1, page 381

If you could create the perfect place to position yourself to intercept migrating sturgeon and striped bass, San Pablo Bay would be it.

Set between the freshwater delta and the saltwater San Francisco Bay, this bay lies in the center of the migration path for thousands of fish that come and go every year. Sturgeon and striped bass provide the best fishing. During years of heavy rainfall, the magic point where saltwater mixes with freshwater shifts down into western San Pablo Bay. Some 90 percent of the marine food production in the bay/delta takes place in this mixing zone, and with enough rain, it will position itself in an area I named the "Sturgeon Triangle." The triangle is bordered by the Pumphouse (it looks like an outhouse on stilts, three miles east of Hamilton Field); China Camp, to the southwest; and Buoy 5, to the southeast. The Pumphouse and China Camp attract sturgeon during outgoing tides, while Buoy 5 is a good spot at incoming tides.

You have several other excellent spots to choose from. These include the Richmond Bridge area, both above and below the bridge during outgoing tides, particularly in the fall; and just off the Point Pinole Pier, especially in March. On the east side of San Pablo Bay, prospects are good just south of the Mare Island Rock Wall, along with offshore Rodeo on the edge of the channel, but usually only after periods of significant rain runoff.

During years of high rainfall, large numbers of sturgeon abandon the ocean and enter the bay/delta system to spawn. Sturgeon, which are capable of living 70 and 80 years, live primarily in the ocean and spawn only once every seven or eight years. They'll often wait for ideal conditions before heading upstream, hence the apparent dramatic fluctuations in population levels from year to year. These fish need a reason to leave the ocean, and high stream flows moving through the bay system provide the incentive.

Striped bass are more predictable in their annual cycles. They arrive in the spring months at San Pablo Bay and again (often in better numbers) from September through December. If the water isn't too muddy from storm runoff, these fish provide good opportunities for trollers. The best times are during the top of high tides and during the first two hours of a moderate outgoing tide. You'll find the best spots along the Marin shoreline from San Quentin prison on north, including along the Marin Islands, the Brickyard, the Pumphouse, and on the southeast side of San Pablo Bay, at Point Pinole and the Rodeo Flats.

Water clarity is key when it comes to striper trolling. If it's muddy, you might as well be searching for a polar bear in the desert. If it's clear and you time things right, you'll have decent prospects for four- to eight-pound fish using white one-ounce Worm-Tail jigs.

In the early summer, when larger striped bass move down from the delta, another option is available. The reefs adjacent to the Brothers Islands (on the east side) and the Sisters Islands (on the west side) provide a habitat where the stripers can pin baitfish against the rocks. Anglers who allow their boats to drift and dangle live shiner perch, mud suckers, or bullheads near the bottom can get some

beauties. These spots are real tackle grabbers, however, so come prepared.

Shoreline fishing can be quite good, too. McNear's Pier (in San Rafael) and Point Pinole Pier provide the rare chance to fish for sturgeon in the winter and striped bass in the spring. During the spring, the Loch Lomond Jetty is a fair spot to try for big bat rays, some weighing as much as 60 pounds; the spring and the fall are good for stripers.

At times the fishing in San Pablo Bay is among the best in the country. One March day after very heavy rains, 14 sturgeon in the 100-pound class were caught in a two-hour span at the Richmond Bridge. It was the best short period of sturgeon fishing ever documented in Bay waters. In the fall, San Pablo Bay also provides an opportunity to fish for perch and shark.

Facilities, fees: Marinas and boat ramps are at Loch Lomond, Benicia, Crockett, and Glen Cove Marinas. Several piers and shoreline jetties are available. Party-boat fees are charged per day.

Directions: To Loch Lomond Marina: Take U.S. 101 to San Rafael and exit for central San Rafael. Take that exit to 2nd Street. Turn east, pass Montecito Shopping Center (the road becomes South San Pedro Road), and continue two miles to Loch Lomond Drive (signed Marina). Turn right and drive a short distance to the marina parking area. Walk to Dock A (next to the boat ramp).

Contact: Point Pinole Regional Park, 510/237-6896.

Supplies: Loch Lomond Live Bait, San Rafael, 415/456-0321; Western Boat, San Rafael, 415/454-4177, www.westernboatshop.com; Martinez Marina Bait, 925/229-9420; M&M Market & Bait, Vallejo, 707/642-3524; Leonard's Bait & Tackle, Petaluma, 707/762-7818, www.leonardsbaitandtackle.com.

Party boats: Touch of Gray, San Rafael, 415/456-0321; Executive Fishing Charters, 415/460-9773, www.executivefishingcharters.com; Bass-Tub, 415/456-9055, www.basstub.net; Fish Hooker Charters, 916/777-6498, www.fishhookers.com; Happy Hooker

Sportfishing, 510/223-5388 or 510/222-5279; *Morning Star,* Crockett, 707/745-1431 or 800/464-1431, www.morningstarfishing.info; in Pittsburg: Fin Addict, 209/367-4665, www .finaddictsportfishing.com; Fury Sportfishing, 916/920-8487, www.furysportfishing .com; Jim Cox Sportfishing, 650/369-3807, www.jimcoxsportfishing.com; Sole Man Sportfishing, 510/703-4148, www.soleman fishing.com.

Marinas: Loch Lomond Marina, San Rafael, 415/454-7228, www.lochlomondmarina .com; Benicia Marina, 707/745-2628, www .beniciamarina.net; Glen Cove Marina, Vallejo, 707/552-3236, www.glencovemarina.net.

4 SOULAJULE LAKE

Rating: 6

near Novato

Map 7.1, page 381

This little-known hike-in lake is tucked away in northern Marin County. You can drive to the left of the dam, then make the short hike to the water's edge. The quiet and crafty angler will discover many small largemouth bass (a few of the elusive big fellas) and the best crappie fishery in the county.

Walk the many shoreline points. Use 1/2-ounce spinnerbaits, Carolina-rigged lizards or diving crawdad-style crankbaits. The best fishing for big bass is February to April. Sure, they've gotta eat the rest of the year, but they sure seem reluctant to eat something with a hook in it.

So timing is always a key, and the first warm weather of the year marks the prime time for crappie. Tie on a crappie jig, either white, chartreuse, or yellow, then make a cast, walk on, and make another cast. If you hit crappie, stick to that spot; they're a school fish. The evening bass fishing, using small crankbaits, can also be decent, though most of the fish are small.

Start by trying not to butcher the name of this lake. It is pronounced soo-la-HOO-ley, not

SOLE-lay-jewl. It may not sound right to you, but once you start catching bass here, saying the name will become easier. Now, one more time: How do you pronounce Soulajule?

Facilities, fees: There are no on-site facilities. Lodging and supplies are in Novato and Petaluma. There is a per vehicle day-use fee.

Directions: Take U.S. 101 to Novato and the San Marin exit. Take the San Marin exit and continue west to Novato Boulevard. Turn right and drive nine miles to Petaluma–Point Reyes Road. Turn right on Petaluma–Point Reyes Road and drive 0.25 mile to Hicks Valley Road. Turn left on Hicks Valley Road and drive three miles to Marshall–Petaluma Road. Turn left on Marshall–Petaluma Road and drive three miles to the signed turnoff on the left. Turn left and drive 0.5 mile to the parking area.

Contact: Marin Municipal Water District, 415/945-1180; Fishing Information Hotline, 415/945-1194; Sky Oaks Ranger Station, 415/945-1181; Western Sport, San Rafael, 415/456-5454, www.westernsportshop.com; Western Boat, San Rafael, 415/454-4177, www.westernboatshop.com.

5 NICASIO LAKE

Rating: 5

near Novato

Map 7.1, page 381

The biggest lake in the North Bay Area is Nicasio Lake, which covers 825 acres. On spring evenings during the week, it can seem abandoned and you may wonder whether it is even worth a look. Turns out Nicasio is one of the surprises of Marin's hidden lakes, and lots of small bass and a chance at a big catfish make this a good destination for a parent-child team looking for action.

In the spring, the bass and crappie fishing is good during the evening. In the early evening through darkness, catfishing can also be good. Explore the lake's backside for the best results.

As the first warm weather arrives and spring gives way to summer, shoreliners can cast surface plugs (such as small Jitterbugs) and then, with a hesitating retrieve, entice strikes from smallmouth bass in the 8- to 13-inch class. The fish may not be big, but they provide surface action and a lot of fun. Crappie fishing is often excellent in the early summer. Just walk and cast with a crappie jig until you hit a school; it can be great if you hit it right. Some big bass are also in here, but they seem to have wised up to our tricks.

Nicasio does provide good bank fishing for catfish, as well as the best catfish prospects in this region of California. A few Marin and Sonoma County residents are aware that Nicasio is home to a sprinkling of giant catfish. It seems they never bite in the daytime, just on those warm summer nights when they come out to prowl for food. There is an exception, however. You can catch catfish on sunny days by using the "Mr. Catfish" method described in the *Catfish* section of the *Sport Fish* chapter. But remember, this method has to be followed exactly or you will likely get zilch.

What typically happens is an angler will be fishing here for catfish and will hook one of these monsters completely by surprise and get his or her tackle all torn up. Hence a believer is born. After that experience an angler might return three or four nights in a row to the same spot, hoping to hook up the same fish. It can take a whole summer, but you just might do it.

The drawbacks: Trout are not stocked, there are no picnic tables, and since the lake is set amid rolling hills that aren't very wooded, the hiking is only fair.

Facilities, fees: No facilities are available. Boats and water-body contact are not permitted. The lake is open from sunrise to sunset. Fishing access is free.

Directions: Take U.S. 101 to Marin and the exit for Sir Francis Drake Boulevard. Take that exit west and drive seven miles to Nicasio Valley Road. Turn right on Nicasio Valley Road and drive five miles to the lake.

An alternate route: Take U.S. 101 in Marin to the Lucas Valley Boulevard exit and drive west for seven miles to Nicasio Valley Road. Turn right on Nicasio Valley Road and drive about one mile to the lake.

Contact: Marin Municipal Water District, 415/945-1180; Fishing Information Hotline, 415/945-1194; Sky Oaks Ranger Station, 415/945-1181; Western Boat, San Rafael, 415/454-4177, www.westernboatshop.com.

6 STAFFORD LAKE

Rating: 6

near Novato

Map 7.1, page 381

Imagine sitting along this lake, fishing and enjoying the scenery with your rod propped up on a stick. Then whoosh! The rod gets whipped into the lake and disappears forever.

That is exactly what was happening at Stafford Lake. Rumors started circulating about some giant, rod-stealing fish, "the Monster of Stafford Lake." Now and then, someone would hook the fish and lose all his or her line, and the legend would grow. Nobody could handle it.

Then the water district drained the lake to work on the dam, and what happened? As the water level decreased, a five-foot sturgeon was spotted: the Monster.

Volunteers completed a major habitat-improvement project here for bass, redear sunfish, and bluegill. It is one of the better little lakes for bass fishing in the Bay Area. At 245 acres, it is big enough to provide a quality fishery. April through July, and then again from September to October, it's the best topwater lake in the county.

The one regret is that boats and even float tubes are not allowed on the water. That is one rule that needs changing. Caution: Be sure to stay out of the areas signed No Trespassing.

In the meantime, Stafford Lake has become the kind of place where people go to throw Frisbees, have picnics, and enjoy the sights of the lake. Meanwhile, anglers, persistent as ever, still go out on weekends hoping for that elusive monster.

Facilities, fees: A picnic area is on the west side of the lake. Lodging and supplies are in Novato. A day-use parking fee is charged, or an annual pass is available.

Directions: Take U.S. 101 to Novato and the San Marin exit. Take that exit and drive west to Novato Boulevard. Turn right and drive three miles to the lake. Continue past the first entrance to the main gate.

Contact: Stafford Lake Park, 415/897-0618.

7 KENT LAKE

Rating: 3

near Lagunitas

Map 7.1, page 381

The only way to get to Kent Lake, set in a canyon on Lagunitas Creek, is to hike. When you first arrive you will be surprised at how big it is—460 acres, set in a long, deep canyon edged by redwoods. The fishing is not easy, as stocks are never made. Specialists, however, can still manage to catch trout and bass. One trick is to bring a minnow trap, catch your own minnows, and then use them as live bait. The best area to fish is to the left of the dam, along the back side.

Parking access is lousy, and once you've found a spot, you face a half-hour walk to the lake.

Facilities, fees: No facilities are available. Boats and water-body contact are not permitted. The lake is open from sunrise to sunset. Fishing access is free.

Directions: Take U.S. 101 to Marin and the exit for Sir Francis Drake Boulevard. Take that exit west and drive about 12 miles (just past Shafter Bridge, which spans Paper Mill/Lagunitas Creek). Park here and look for the locked gate at the entrance to the trailhead on the left.

Contact: Marin Municipal Water District, Fishing Information Hotline, 415/945-1194; Sky Oaks Ranger Station, 415/945-1181, www.marinwater.org; Western Boat, San Rafael, 415/454-4177, www.westernboatshop.com.

8 ALPINE LAKE

Rating: 3

near Fairfax

Map 7.1, page 381

Most first-time visitors find Alpine Lake to be much larger and prettier than they had expected. By Bay Area standards it is a good-sized reservoir (224 acres), as well as one of the prettiest around, set in a tree-bordered canyon on the slopes of Mount Tamalpais. Trailheads that begin at the dam and lead to excellent hikes are just a bonus for anglers.

Very few rainbow trout are in these waters, though a small percentage of them are large; there's also a sprinkling of largemouth bass. The lake is not stocked, and the resident fish have apparently gone to Smart School. Your best bet is to walk around the back side of the lake and cast plugs such as the Husky Jerk at dawn and dusk, or Senkos or Brush Hogs when direct sun hits the water.

Facilities, fees: No facilities are available. Boats and water-body contact are not permitted. The lake is open from sunrise to sunset. Fishing access is free.

Directions: Take U.S. 101 in Marin to the exit for Sir Francis Drake Boulevard. Take that exit west and drive six miles west to the town of Fairfax. Look for the Fairfax sign (in the center median) and turn left (the road is unsigned; do not continue to the lighted intersection, where no left turn is possible); then turn right immediately on Broadway Avenue (a frontage road). Drive one block to Bolinas Road. Turn left and drive west for eight miles (continuing along Alpine Lake) to the Alpine Dam.

Additional access is available 0.5 mile west, at the Cataract Trailhead, on the left.

Contact: Marin Municipal Water District, Fishing Information Hotline, 415/945-1194; Sky Oaks Ranger Station, 415/945-1181, www .marinwater.org.

9 BON TEMPE LAKE

Rating: 6

near Fairfax

Map 7.1, page 381

Of the lakes in Marin County, pretty Bon Tempe has the highest catch rates for trout. When stocks were stopped at Marin County's other lakes, they were doubled at Bon Tempe by the DFG, primarily 10- to 12-inch rainbows. After a plant, the result is many smiling, happy anglers who often get five-fish limits in the 9- to 11-inch class.

Shoreline bait dunking is the way to go. Timing is critical, as there are zero stocks from May through October. From November through April, though, plants are made nearly every other week, immediately boosting catch rates.

Bon Tempe covers 140 acres and is on the slopes of Mount Tamalpais, just below Lagunitas Lake and above Alpine Lake. It seems to get more sun than the others, picnic areas are available, and you can access a network of outstanding hiking trails near here. No wonder this is the most popular of Marin's eight lakes.

Facilities, fees: A parking area is provided. Vault toilets are available. Boats and water-body contact are not permitted. The lake is open from sunrise to sunset. A day-use fee is charged per vehicle.

Directions: Take U.S. 101 in Marin to the exit for Sir Francis Drake Boulevard. Take that exit west and drive six miles west to the town of Fairfax. Look for the Fairfax sign (in the center median, just after a gas station) and turn left (the road is unsigned; do not continue to the lighted intersection, where no left turn

is possible); then turn right immediately on Broadway Avenue (a frontage road). Drive one block to Bolinas Road. Turn left and drive west for 1.5 miles to Sky Oaks Road, on the left. Bear left and drive 0.5 mile to the Sky Oaks entrance station.

Contact: Marin Municipal Water District, Fishing Information Hotline, 415/945-1194; Sky Oaks Ranger Station, 415/945-1181, www .marinwater.org.

10 LAGUNITAS LAKE

Rating: 6

near Fairfax

Map 7.1, page 381

Though Lagunitas covers only 22 acres, by some standards a large pond, this lake has gained national attention as a testing ground for a natural wild-trout fishery in an urban area. The plan is to make very few stocks, permit primarily catch-and-release fishing, and allow the trout to spawn on the lake's feeder streams. The results have proven to be good in March and April. Cormorants have really pounded this lake, undermining the program. Stocks subsidize the lake to keep it a viable fishery.

The prime angling spot is at the steep side opposite the dam, and the most successful technique is to use flies behind a Cast-A-Bubble or a Kastmaster (with the hook removed). Another trick is casting a No. 16 olive nymph or a 1/8-ounce Roostertail spinner. Success fluctuates tremendously according to season, with a very slow bite in the summer and winter.

Regulations are sometimes adjusted in response to changing spawning success, so always, always, always check the current rules before heading out.

Facilities, fees: A parking area is provided. Pit toilets are available. Boats and water-body contact are not permitted. The lake is open from sunrise to sunset. A day-use fee is charged per vehicle.

Directions: Take U.S. 101 in Marin to the

exit for Sir Francis Drake Boulevard. Take that exit west and drive six miles west to the town of Fairfax (get in the left lane). Look for the Fairfax sign (in the center median, just past a gas station) and turn left (the road is unsigned; do not continue to the lighted intersection, where no left turn is possible); then turn right immediately on Broadway Avenue (a frontage road). Drive one block to Bolinas Road. Turn left and drive west for 1.5 miles to Sky Oaks Road on the left. Bear left and drive 0.5 mile to the Sky Oaks entrance station.

Contact: Marin Municipal Water District, Fishing Information Hotline, 415/945-1194; Sky Oaks Ranger Station, 415/945-1181, www.marinwater.org; Western Boat, San Rafael, 415/454-4177, www.westernboatshop.com.

11 McNEAR'S PIER

Rating: 6

in San Rafael at McNear's Beach

Map 7.1, page 381

Of all the piers in the Bay Area, this one, located adjacent to one of the five best sturgeon areas in San Pablo Bay, provides anglers with the best chances of landing a sturgeon. Fishing can also be good for striped bass in the fall months, using pile worms for bait.

Facilities, fees: Restrooms, parking, drinking water, fish-cleaning stations, a swimming pool, tennis courts, a beach, and a concession stand are available at the pier. An entrance fee is charged.

Directions: Take U.S. 101 to San Rafael and take the exit for central San Rafael to 2nd Street. Turn east, pass Montecito Shopping Center (the road becomes South San Pedro Road), and continue four miles (the road becomes Point San Pedro Road) to Cantera Way. Turn right and drive to the park and fishing pier.

Contact: McNear's Beach Park, 415/499-6388, www.maringov.org; Loch Lomond Live Bait, San Rafael, 415/456-0321.

12 PARADISE PIER

Rating: 6

in Tiburon in Paradise Beach County Park

Map 7.1, page 381

This place is not only pretty, but it is situated where anglers can intercept passing fish. Part of a well-landscaped 11-acre county park, Paradise Pier offers chances for sturgeon in the winter. During the summer months, prospects are best for striped bass, halibut, and sharks.

Facilities, fees: Benches, tap water, and fish-cleaning sinks are provided. Restrooms and picnic tables are nearby. An entrance fee is charged.

Directions: From San Francisco, drive north on U.S. 101. Take the Tiburon exit and proceed on Paradise Drive to the pier.

Contact: Paradise Beach Park, www.maringov.org; Loch Lomond Live Bait, San Rafael, 415/456-0321.

13 EAST FORT BAKER PIER

Rating: 4

west of Sausalito

Map 7.1, page 381

In late summer and fall, migrating salmon pass within casting range of this beautiful spot just inside the entrance to the bay, near the Golden Gate Bridge. East Fort Baker provides anglers with a wild-card long shot. This is on the Marin County side of the Golden Gate Bridge.

Facilities, fees: Portable restrooms are provided. Fishing access is free.

Directions: From San Francisco, drive north on U.S. 101 over the Golden Gate Bridge, get in the right lane to the exit for Alexander Avenue. Take that exit and drive 500 yards to the Marin Headlands sign. Turn left and drive to the tunnel. Turn right and continue to the Coast Guard Station, and look for the entrance to the pier adjacent to the station.

From Marin, drive south on U.S. 101 to the last Sausalito exit (just before the Golden

Gate Bridge). Follow the signs for Sausalito/ East Fort Baker. To get to the pier, turn right at the baseball field.

Contact: Golden Gate National Recreation Area, Marin Headlands Visitor Center, 415/331-1540; Bay Discovery Museum, 415/339-3900, www.baykidsmuseum.org.

14 POINT PINOLE PIER

Rating: 5

near Pinole

Map 7.2, page 382

The pier is situated perfectly for anglers to have a chance to intercept migrating striped bass, sturgeon, the rare salmon, king, and resident flounder, perch, and sharks.

On rare occasions, sturgeon can arrive to the area in large numbers, particularly during significant outgoing tides in the winter and spring. I've seen days where there were so many anglers here that the pier looked like a porcupine from all the rods sticking out. A ride on a park shuttle out to the pier makes the trip unique and fun, and the shoreline views of San Pablo Bay add texture to the day. No fishing license is necessary at the pier. If you fish from shore, however, a license is required.

Facilities, fees: A shuttle bus is available from the parking area to the pier. Restrooms, drinking fountains, benches with windscreens, and shaded picnic sites are on-site. Bicycle trails and a beach path are available. A parking fee is charged on weekends and holidays.

Directions: Take I-80 to San Pablo and the exit for Hilltop Drive. Take that exit and drive west on Hilltop Drive to the intersection with San Pablo Avenue. Turn right on San Pablo Avenue and drive north for a short distance to Richmond Parkway. Turn left on Richmond Parkway and drive a few miles to Giant Highway. Turn right and drive a short distance to the park entrance (it's well signed), on the left. Take the shuttle bus to the bay.

Contact: Park Headquarters, 510/237-6896; for a park brochure, call or go online to East

Bay Regional Park District, 888/327-2757, option 3, ext. 4551, then follow the directions and leave your name, address, and the park brochure requested, or download it from www.ebparks.org.

15 CARQUINEZ STRAIT

Rating: 5

from the Carquinez Bridge to the Mothball Fleet

Map 7.2, page 382

Joey Pallotta hooked a sturgeon here one day off Benicia, and when the fish rolled near the surface, it looked as big as a whale. Turns out it nearly was. It weighed 468 pounds and measured nine feet, six inches, a world record.

Now get this. Bigger fish have been seen in these parts. Some PG&E divers who were laying cable on the bottom say they came across a sturgeon that they paced off at something like 12 feet long. Another time, a big ship's propeller cut a sturgeon in two, and according to witnesses, both pieces added up to 11 feet.

You'd think this is where everyone would fish for sturgeon, right? Well, it doesn't work that way. That's because the best area is in deep water, 70–90 feet down, off Benicia. Strong tides and, in the spring, heavy freshwater outflows make the use of heavy sinkers a necessity just to get the bait near the bottom, where the sturgeon are prowling around. You also need a huge length of anchor line to get your boat to stay put, especially in the spring, when freshwater flows double the strength of outgoing tides. This remains a sport and spot for specialists.

Striped bass, however, provide short periods of excellent fishing. They migrate through the Carquinez Strait in the spring, and trollers can get excellent results in the evening. For stripers, water clarity is all-important. The water tends to clear at the top of the tide here. In some years the Department of Fish and Game plants juvenile salmon in Benicia, and when that happens, the striped bass go into a feeding frenzy. If you are on the spot, you can catch quick limits of stripers here, casting Rebels, Pencil Poppers, or Hair Raisers, or using threadfin shad for bait.

Facilities, fees: See *Contact* for phone numbers and websites for boat ramps and party-boat operators. Party-boat fees are charged per day.

Directions: Take Highway 4 to Martinez. Exit at Alhambra Avenue and drive north for two miles to Escobar Street. Turn right on Escobar Street and drive three blocks to Ferry Street. Turn left and drive across the railroad tracks, to Joe DiMaggio Drive. Bear right onto Joe DiMaggio Drive and drive to North Coast Street. Turn left on North Coast Street and drive to the parking area next to the fishing pier. The route is well signed.

Contact: Boat ramps: Martinez Marina, 925/313-0942, www.martinez-marina.com; Glen Cove Marina, Vallejo, 707/552-3236, www.glencovemarina.net; Benicia Marina, 707/745-2628, www.beniciamarina.net; Pittsburg Marina, 925/439-4958, www.pittsburg marina.com.

Party boats: The website www.sfsport fishing.com offers booking information for boats operating from San Francisco (Fisherman's Wharf), Emeryville Marina, Berkeley Marina, Half Moon Bay (Pillar Point Harbor), and Point San Pablo; Happy Hooker Sportfishing, 510/223-5388; *Morning Star*, Crockett, 707/745-1431 or 800/464-1431, www.morningstarfishing.info.

Supplies: Martinez Marina Bait, 925/229-9420; M&M Market & Bait, Vallejo, 707/642-3524; Benicia Bait & Tackle Shop, Benicia, 707/745-4921.

16 BENICIA PIERS

Rating: 4

in Benicia

Map 7.2, page 382

Striped bass are hard to catch here in the fall months, but there are plenty of bullheads. Your best bet is to catch a few bullheads, then use them for bait for striped bass.

Facilities, fees: Ninth Street Park has restrooms, a picnic area, and a launch site. The Benicia Marina has restrooms, a store, benches, and parking. Access is free.

Directions: From Concord, take I-680 to I-780 and the East 5th Street exit. Take that exit, turn left on 5th Street, and drive 0.6 mile to the road's end at East E Street. Turn right on East E and drive 0.3 mile to East 2nd Street. Turn left on East 2nd and drive a short distance to East B Street. Turn left on East B and drive a short distance to the marina.

Contact: Benicia Marina, 707/745-2628, www.beniciamarina.net.

17 MARTINEZ PIER

Rating: 6

in Martinez

Map 7.2, page 382

Visitors to Martinez Pier get fine views of the bay and marina, and a fair chance at catching passing fish in season, including striped bass in the spring and fall, sturgeon in the winter, and (get this) steelhead in late fall.

Facilities, fees: Benches, fish-cleaning sinks, restrooms (at marina headquarters), and a bait shop are provided. Fishing access is free.

Directions: Take Highway 4 to Martinez and the exit for Alhambra Avenue. Take that exit and drive north on Alhambra Avenue for two miles to Escobar Street. Turn right on Escobar Street and drive three blocks to Ferry Street. Turn left and drive across the railroad tracks, to Joe DiMaggio Drive. Bear right onto Joe DiMaggio Drive and drive to North Coast Street. Turn left on North Coast Street and drive to the parking area next to the fishing pier. The route is well signed.

Contact: Park headquarters, 925/228-0112; Martinez Marina, 925/313-0942, www.mar tinez-marina.com; for a park brochure, call or go online to East Bay Regional Park District, 888/327-2757, option 3, ext. 4551, then follow the directions and leave your name, address, and the park brochure requested, or download it from www.ebparks.org.

Supplies: Martinez Marina Bait, 925/229-9420; M&M Market & Bait, Vallejo, 707/642-3524; Benicia Bait & Tackle Shop, Benicia, 707/745-4921.

18 SUISUN BAY

Rating: 8
from the Mothball Fleet to Pittsburg
Map 7.2, page 382

The rod tip dipped, then straightened. Fish on? Fish off? With the reel on free spool, I thumbed the line, poised like a safecracker to detect any minute sign. Suddenly, I felt pressure. Under my thumb I sensed the line starting to peel off the fishing reel.

"One, two, three," I counted aloud while some 15 feet of line was stripped; then I locked the spool and set the hook home. Fish on! A nice striped bass. My brother Rambob and I caught something like 15 in one three-hour tide swing with Barry Canevaro.

This is the method anglers use to fish the fall and winter runs of striped bass in Suisun Bay and adjacent Honker Bay. You should fish from an anchored boat, using bullheads for bait. The whole process is very exciting because you keep your reel on free spool and must have the nerve to wait to set the hook until you are certain the striped bass has taken it into its mouth.

While you are anchored and waiting for a big striped bass, a giant sturgeon just might wander by and gobble your bait. Some of the biggest sturgeon ever caught have been taken by complete accident this way.

The preferred spots to anchor and "bullhead for stripers" are immediately east of the Mothball Fleet (in the shallows of Honker Bay along the Firing Line, across from Pittsburg) and in holes and ledges in Montezuma Slough. When the stripers are in during the fall and winter, some of the most productive fishing in the entire bay/delta takes place here.

Sturgeon, on the other hand, provide a steadier fishery, although in this area you may need to spend long hours on the water to catch one. The best spots are between the Martinez/Benicia Bridge and the Mothball Fleet, the third row of ships at the Mothball Fleet, just off the sandbar at the Mothball Fleet, immediately east of the Mothball Fleet, and in the center of the channel adjacent to the Pittsburg PG&E plant.

A good rule of thumb is to locate the area where freshwater from the delta mixes with saltwater from the bay, then anchor in the best spot. Most of the aquatic food for the bay system is produced in this mixing zone, which is a natural holding area for sturgeon. Depending on rainfall and reservoir releases, this zone can shift throughout the year, necessitating some detective work on your part.

Here's good news for those who like to anchor and fish: compared to San Pablo and San Francisco Bays, Suisun Bay has far fewer bait robbers. Not only does this help keep the bait bill down, but you can rest assured that when you get a bite, it is probably a big striped bass or sturgeon—not a pesky crab or bullhead.

Facilities, fees: Several piers are available. Party-boat fees are charged per day.

Directions: Take Highway 4 to Martinez and the exit for Railroad Avenue. Take that exit, turn left on Railroad Avenue, and drive to the end, where it meets 3rd Street. Turn left on 3rd Street and drive to Marina Boulevard. Turn right and continue to where the road ends at the harbor.

Contact: Boat ramps: Martinez Marina, 925/313-0942, www.martinez-marina.com; Glen Cove Marina, Vallejo, 707/552-3236, www.glencovemarina.net; Benicia Marina, 707/745-2628, www.beniciamarina.net; Pittsburg Marina, 925/439-4958, www.pittsburg marina.com.

Party boats: Barry & Diane Canevaro, Fish Hooker Charters, 916/777-6498, www.fish hookers.com; Happy Hooker Sportfishing, 510/223-5388 or 510/222-5279; *Morning Star,* Crockett, 707/745-1431 or 800/464-1431, www.morningstarfishing.info.

Supplies: Martinez Marina Bait, 925/229-

9420; M&M Market & Bait, Vallejo, 707/642-3524; Benicia Bait & Tackle Shop, Benicia, 707/745-4921.

19 BERKELEY PIER

Rating: 6

in Berkeley

Map 7.2, page 382

One of the most popular piers in the Bay Area, Berkeley Pier is license-free. It extends some 3,000 feet into the waters of the bay. Perch fishing can be very good along the pilings in the winter months, and in the early summer, anglers have a chance at halibut. You can catch shiner perch and then use them as live bait for halibut. In late spring and early summer, striped bass occasionally show up and surprise anglers, but this is unpredictable and extremely sporadic, year to year. Starry flounder, sharks, and jacksmelt move in and out along the pilings in winter and early spring.

Facilities, fees: Restrooms, fish-cleaning racks, overhead lighting, and benches are provided. Fishing access is free.

Directions: Take I-80 to Berkeley and the exit for University Avenue/Berkeley Marina. Take the University Avenue exit west, drive over the overpass, and follow the signs to the Berkeley Marina. The pier is at the foot of University Avenue, just past the bait shop and marina.

Contact: Berkeley Marina Sports Center, 510/849-2727, www.berkeleymarinasportfishing.com.

20 EMERYVILLE PIER

Rating: 5

in Emeryville

Map 7.2, page 382

This pier, just west of Trader Vic's on Anchor Drive, extends about 750 feet and was rebuilt in 2007. Fish at high tides only; it is just a mudflat at low tide. But during high tides, the potential here is great. A handful of insiders show up on high tides and cast 3/4-ounce Kastmasters and catch striped bass. Others toss out bait, usually anchovy, and wait for a bite. But when the fish move in, you're better off chasing them down with lures.

Note: Do not confuse the Emeryville Pier with the Emeryville Boardwalk, where fishing is not permitted.

Facilities, fees: Seats, lighting, water taps, and fish-cleaning racks are provided on the pier. Also in the marina are restrooms, a picnic area, a fish market with bait and tackle sales, and several restaurants. Fishing access is free.

Directions: Take I-80 to Emeryville and take the Powell Street exit at Emeryville. Drive west on Powell Street to the road's end in the Emeryville Marina. The pier is at the foot of Powell Street.

Contact: Emeryville Sportfishing, 510/654-6040 or 800/575-9944, www.emeryville sportsfishing.com; Emeryville Marina, 510/654-3716, emeryvillemarina.com.

21 PORT VIEW PARK/ MIDDLE HARBOR SHORELINE PARK

Rating: 5

in Oakland

Map 7.2, page 382

Prospects for striped bass are good at Port View Park, especially on early summer nights, when this area gets heavy use.

Facilities, fees: Benches and lighting are provided on the pier. Restrooms, a bait shop, snack bar, a drinking fountain, and an observation tower are at the park area. Fishing access is free.

Directions: Take I-880 to Oakland/Alameda and take the Broadway off-ramp. At the bottom of the road, continue straight on 6th Street, then drive six blocks to Castro Street. Turn right on Castro Street and drive one block to 7th Street. Turn left on 7th Street, continue two miles to the shipping terminal area, and look for the sign for Port View Park.

Contact: Port of Oakland, 510/627-1100, www.portofoakland.com; Central Bait, Alameda, 510/522-6731.

22 ESTUARY PARK PIER

Rating: 5

in Oakland

Map 7.2, page 382

Fine views of the Oakland–Alameda Estuary and all the activity there—including ship-repair work—can be had from this pier, which is one in a series of piers in the estuary. You'll have a chance for perch in the winter months, and even an outside shot at landing a striped bass in the summer.

Facilities, fees: Restrooms, benches, a drinking fountain, a launch ramp, and tables are provided. A bait shop and several restaurants are eight blocks away, at Jack London Square. Fishing access is free.

Directions: Take I-880 to Oakland and take the Jackson Street exit. Drive south on Jackson Street to Embarcadero. Turn left on Embarcadero and continue four blocks to the park.

Contact: Oakland Parks and Recreation Department, 510/238-3187; Central Bait, Alameda, 510/522-6731.

23 SAN LEANDRO PIER

Rating: 4

in San Leandro

Map 7.2, page 382

This is the southernmost San Francisco Bay pier along the East Bay shoreline. On high tides in late spring and early summer, striped bass occasionally show up in the area. When they do, toss a 3/4-ounce Kastmaster.

Facilities, fees: Restrooms, drinking water, and picnic tables are provided. Fishing access is free.

Directions: Take I-880 to San Leandro and the exit for Marina Boulevard. Take that exit and drive west on Marina Boulevard to Monarch

Bay Drive. Turn left on Monarch Bay and drive to Pescador Point Drive. Turn right (south) and continue to the marina.

Contact: San Leandro Marina, 510/577-3488, www.sanleandro.org; Central Bait, Alameda, 510/522-6731.

24 DUMBARTON PIER

Rating: 6

in Newark

Map 7.2, page 382

This pier extends from the Newark shoreline to the channel of the South Bay. It is the former roadbed of the old Dumbarton Bridge, and the designers were smart enough to make sure you could reach the main channel with your casts from the end of the pier. In the winter, during periods of heavy rain, many sturgeon congregate in this area. Use grass shrimp for bait. In the summer, small sharks and rays also make an appearance in significant numbers. Occasionally in February and March, anglers using hunks of squid for bait hook with bat rays in the 50- to 70-pound class. Plaques installed along the pier let you know about the different species of fish here.

Note that Marshlands Road is closed to cars and motorcycles from April 1 to August 31. A free shuttle service is offered on weekends.

Facilities, fees: Running water for drinking and cleaning fish is provided. Restrooms and windbreaks are also available. Fishing access is free.

Directions: From San Francisco: Take U.S. 101 south to the exit for Willow Road–Dumbarton Bridge. Take that exit and drive east across the Dumbarton Bridge and to the first exit after the toll plaza, Thornton Avenue. Take that exit (Thornton Avenue). Turn right and drive to Marshlands Road. Turn right again and drive to the signed entrance for the Don Edwards San Francisco Bay National Wildlife Refuge entrance and visitors center.

To reach Dumbarton Pier, continue past the entrance for the visitors center for about three miles, following the signs to Dumbarton Pier (and the entrance to a leg of the Bay bicycle trail).

Contact: Don Edwards San Francisco Bay National Wildlife Refuge, P.O. Box 524, Newark, CA 94560, 510/792-0222, www.fws.gov/desfbay.

25 SAN PABLO RESERVOIR

Rating: 9

near Orinda

Map 7.2, page 382   **BEST (**

Daybreak at San Pablo Reservoir highlights one of the most beautiful scenes in the Bay Area, distinguished by blues and greens, placid water, and boats heading out with eager fishers aboard. Anglers are scattered about, many of them eager to catch rainbow trout. San Pablo provides a unique combination of beauty, boating, and good fishing.

San Pablo has 866 surface acres and 14 miles of shoreline, and is in a canyon near El Sobrante. The best opportunities here are for fishing, both from shore and boat, but low-speed boating is also very good. It's big enough to accommodate good-sized powerboats, yet small enough to provide an intimate setting for small rowboats, even kayaks. The rules prohibit body contact with the water, so waterskiing, personal watercraft, wading, swimming, and inner tubing are not allowed. In addition, a 5-mph rule in the Waterfowl Management Area and along the shoreline keeps it quiet for fishing.

Another big plus is that there is an excellent marina and a small store with a tackle shop, and boat rentals and a ramp are available. There are also more trout stocked here than at any other lake in the Bay Area, an average of about 200,000 per year from the DFG and lake manager.

If there's a catch, it's the linkage of small fees that can really add up to a significant total for a fishing trip. But the fish plants at San Pablo are among the highest of any lake in the western United States, courtesy of a system where anglers pay an entry fee per vehicle and also purchase a daily fishing permit, which funds trout plants.

The trout average a foot long, with an ample dose of 3- to 5-pounders and a few every year in the 10-pound class.

The key for trout at San Pablo is depth: the magic level in summer, whether bait fishing or trolling, is 25–30 feet deep. If you use bait, try two hooks with yellow Power Bait and half a night crawler, or one hook loaded with mushy salmon eggs. Trollers do best with flashers trailed by a Needlefish lure or half a night crawler. Shore fishing is good right in front of the tackle shop, and results are often excellent along the far shore just inside leeward points.

A bonus is good bass fishing, but usually only right at first and last light. The waterfowl area at the south end of the lake holds some nice bass. There are some big catfish here as well.

San Pablo Reservoir is large and beautiful and has a good boat ramp. It is open most of the year, from mid-February to early November. The only problem is that it's very popular on three-day weekends, when catch rates always drop significantly. Most of the time, however, the lake offers one of the most consistent fisheries in the state.

This is a great destination for boating, big enough to accommodate sizable boats, yet small enough to provide an intimate setting for tiny aluminum boats and even canoes.

The lake is big for one in a metropolitan area, and it's the No. 1 recreation lake out of 45 with public access in the Bay Area. Two major lake arms are featured. The main arm extends south, into a waterfowl management area with a 5-mph speed limit, while the Scow Canyon arm, across the reservoir from the San Pablo Recreation Area, extends east, into the remote foothills of Contra Costa County.

An excellent marina supplies a variety of boat rentals. One drawback is that the boat ramp is some distance from the marina. A

5-mph speed limit is enforced along the shoreline and in the coves; there is a 25-mph limit on the main lake body. Work to restore the dam was completed in 2011 and seismic issues no longer restrict lake levels.

Lake records: 21-pound, 12.8-ounce rainbow trout, by Steve Dwy of San Pablo; 18-pound, 11-ounce largemouth bass, by Victor Barfield of Daly City; 31-pound, 4.8-ounce catfish, by Dave Edwards of Vallejo; 105-pound sturgeon, by Nai Saephan of San Pablo; 3-pound, 6.4-ounce redear sunfish, by Bob Laughlin of San Pablo; 3-pound, 3.2-ounce crappie, by Calvin Warren of Hayward.

Note: All boats must be inspected and certified free of mussels prior to launching at this lake.

Facilities, fees: Picnic areas, a playground, a small marina, a multilane paved launch ramp, docks, and a snack bar/fishing shop are available. Fishing boats and rowboats can be rented. Fees are charged for fishing permits, parking, and boat launching. Annual passes can be purchased.

The lake supplies drinking water to the Bay Area, so body contact with the water is forbidden; hence, swimming, wading, waterskiing, personal watercraft, and inner tubing are strictly prohibited. All boaters must wear Coast Guard–approved life jackets. No two-cycle engines are permitted.

Directions: From the north: Take I-80 and exit on San Pablo Dam Road. Turn south (toward Orinda) on San Pablo Dam Road and drive six miles to the main lake entrance, on the left. If you have a boat to launch, continue to the second entrance on the left.

From the south (San Jose): Take I-680 to Highway 24. Bear west on Highway 24 and drive to Orinda and the exit for Camino Pablo Road. Take Camino Pablo Road north and drive to the lake on the right. The first entrance leads to the boat ramp; the second is the main entrance.

Contact: San Pablo Recreation Area, San Pablo Reservoir, 510/223-1661, www.rockymountainrec.com/lakes.

26 LAKE ANZA

Rating: 2

in Berkeley in Tilden Regional Park
Map 7.2, page 382

Don't expect this lake to set your heart a-pumping. It is small, just 11 acres, and the main attraction is the surrounding parkland. The fishing isn't all that great either. There are a few bluegill and some small bass, but the fishing is generally poor.

It has a sandy beach that has maximum sun exposure yet is largely sheltered from the summer's prevailing winds. Early in the summer, it can make for a good swimming hole. Your odds of seeing a mermaid are often better than catching a fish.

Facilities, fees: Picnic areas and restrooms are provided. The facilities are wheelchair-accessible. Fishing access is free.

Directions: Take Highway 24 to Fish Ranch Road (near the Caldecott Tunnel). Take that exit and drive to Grizzly Park Boulevard. Turn right on Grizzly Peak Boulevard and continue to South Park Drive. Turn right and drive one mile to Wildcat Canyon Road. Turn left on Wildcat Canyon Road and drive to Central Park Drive. Turn right on Central Park Drive and drive to the Lake Anza entrance (near the merry-go-round), on the right.

Contact: For a park brochure, call or go online to East Bay Regional Park District, 888/327-2757, option 3, ext. 4551, then follow the directions and leave your name, address, and the park brochure requested, or download it from www.ebparks.org; for fishing information, call 888/327-2757.

27 LAKE TEMESCAL

Rating: 6

in the Oakland hills
Map 7.2, page 382

Little Temescal, one of the original three parks that started the East Bay Regional Park District in 1936, covers just 15 acres. Because of its size, it responds instantly to trout plants. The cormorants often respond just as quickly. After a plant, birds and anglers engage in a fish-catching contest. The trout are caught, and quick. Attempts to improve the summer prospects, by stocking small catfish when the water is warm, have been successful.

As a lake in East Bay Parks, it gets bonus stocks and fishery management. Lake records include a 17-pound largemouth bass and a 16-pound, 6-ounce rainbow trout—but these are anomalies.

Prospects are often good in the spring for shoreline bait dunkers at Temescal, where you often spot children fishing from shore with a parent. The DFG stocks 3,500 10- to 12-inch rainbow trout, and the park district adds 3,700 more, including trophy-sized trout and 1,250 pounds of channel catfish. Other fish in residence include largemouth bass, redear sunfish, bluegill, and catfish.

Lake Temescal is a stunning surprise for many. It provides a refuge of peace for swimming, fishing, and sunbathing.

The whole place was barbecued in the terrible Oakland Hills firestorm in the fall of 1991. The East Bay Regional Park District rehabilitation program has been a success, with a special silt collector to maintain water quality, and little Temescal is healthy and full of life.

The swimming area is open spring through fall, with lifeguards on duty during posted periods.

Facilities, fees: Boats are not permitted on the lake. A snack stand is nearby, and many facilities are wheelchair-accessible. There are picnic areas at both ends of the lake adjacent to eight acres of lawn. A parking fee is charged when the kiosk is attended; at all other times, it's free.

Directions: Take Highway 24 in Oakland to the exit for Broadway. Take that exit and bear left through the intersection, continuing on Broadway (toward Highway 13 southbound). Within 0.5 mile, look for the signed entrance to the Temescal Regional Recreation Area, on the right. Turn right and drive to the park.

Contact: Park headquarters, 510/652-1155; for a park brochure, call or go online to East Bay Regional Park District, 888/327-2757, option 3, ext. 4551, then follow the directions and leave your name, address, and the park brochure requested, or download it from www.ebparks.org; for fishing information, call 888/327-2757.

28 LAFAYETTE RESERVOIR

Rating: 8

near Walnut Creek

Map 7.2, page 382

Lafayette Reservoir provides excellent results for folks who fish here from winter through early summer. Trout are stocked regularly by the DFG and the concessionaire, and some large but elusive bass are roaming about.

The East Cove is the most consistent trout producer. Whether fishing from a boat or the shoreline, most anglers catch trout here by bait fishing. Some beautiful limits of one- to three-pound trout are caught in the spring.

If you limit on trout, you might test the shoreline and docks for bass. The lake has some big ones, including 10-pounders, but few people try for them. The lake also has bluegill, black crappie, and several kinds of catfish.

Canoe and rowboat rentals are available (no dogs are allowed in the boats). A primitive launching area (hand launching only) is provided.

The lake was completed in 1933 and provides a backup water supply for East Bay Municipal Utility District customers. It was opened to public recreation in 1966.

Lafayette Reservoir is a 126-acre lake that is very pretty, a little paradise in the East Bay hills. The surrounding oak-covered hills create a pleasant, quiet setting for picnics. The reservoir is used only for fishing, canoeing, and sailing. With access restricted to boats that can be hand-launched, you are assured peace and lots of space on the water. Gas motors are not permitted, but electric motors are okay, which keeps things quiet.

Talk about the ideal spot for easy flat-water kayaking; this can be it.

Privately owned rowboats, canoes, kayaks, and sailboats are allowed at the reservoir. There is a fee for boat registration. In addition, there are rowboats and pedal boats for rent at the activity center on an hourly, half-day, or all-day basis.

Peak use is in late winter and spring, when the weather begins to warm yet the water temperature is still cool, making for good trout fishing.

Facilities, fees: A small boathouse, dock, bait shop, and launch ramp are available. Picnic areas, restrooms, and hiking and bicycle trails are provided. No gas motors are permitted on the lake. Rowboats and pedalboats can be rented. A fishing permit and parking fee are required. An annual parking pass can be purchased.

Directions: Take Highway 24 to Walnut Creek and the exit for Acalanes. Take that exit, which feeds you onto Mount Diablo Boulevard. Drive about a mile on Mount Diablo Boulevard to the signed park entrance, on the right.

Contact: Lafayette Reservoir, 925/284-9669, www.ebmud.com/recreation.

29 CONTRA LOMA RESERVOIR

Rating: 6

near Antioch

Map 7.2, page 382

This little lake is on the map for surprise giant striped bass, decent trout fishing from late winter through spring, and a chance for catfish in summer. The lake also has catfish, largemouth bass, bluegill, and redeared sunfish.

The striped bass are here only because they get sucked in. You see, this reservoir gets its water via the fish-stealing California Aqueduct. Most of the stripers seem to be on the small side. But get this: 20-pounders are taken every year. The best fishing is usually the southern shoreline.

A trout-planting program that takes place from fall through spring is a success. Both the park district and the Department of Fish and Game now make regular trout stocks, often on a weekly basis during cooler weather. Some small catfish are stocked in the summer. Still, relatively few anglers are taking advantage of the situation, even though the fishing has been good during the spring. In the summer, with trout on the wane, success ranges from poor to fair.

Contra Loma Reservoir is the first stop for water being shipped out of the delta and bound for points south. It covers 70 acres, is easily accessible to residents of Antioch and nearby towns, and provides a good place for fishing, swimming, and boating. No gas motors are permitted; electric motors only. The surrounding parkland is crisscrossed with hiking and horseback-riding trails.

Antioch is one of the Bay Area's fastest growing cities—thank heaven that the East Bay Regional Park District protected this beautiful landscape first by making it a park well prior to the growth spurt.

Contra Loma Reservoir is the centerpiece, an 80-acre lake with a swim lagoon and fishing prospects. The park covers 776 acres in the foothills near Antioch, with trail connections into adjacent Black Diamond Mines Regional Preserve. It is also an excellent spot for windsurfing from April through early July.

One thing to remember is that it gets hot here in the summer, and afternoon winds are common. This makes it ideal for windsurfing and sailing. Both sports are popular here, and the conditions are particularly attractive to beginning windsurfers. Swimming is permitted at a beautiful little lagoon with a sandy beach, but not in the main lake. Boating rules ensure that the reservoir remains quiet and peaceful.

Note: All boats must be inspected and

certified free of mussels prior to launching at this lake.

To make certain the water quality at this lake is not compromised, the Contra Costa Water District enforces several rules:

• Boats no longer than 17 feet with electric motors are permitted. Gas motors are prohibited (they can be mounted on boats, but must not touch the water).

• Anglers using float tubes must wear waders or other wetsuit material to eliminate the chance of body contact with the water.

• All windsurfers must shower a minimum of two minutes prior to entering the reservoir and must wear at least a short wetsuit; showers are outside the restrooms and next to the beach used by windsurfers.

• Kayakers with self-bailing kayaks must shower prior to entering the reservoir and must wear at least a short wet suit. Dry-type kayaks are permissible, but no rollovers or other activities that cause body contact with the water are permitted.

Lake records: 12-pound, 1-ounce largemouth bass; 17-pound, 9-ounce rainbow trout; 26-pound, 6-ounce channel catfish; 40-pound striped bass; 4-pound black crappie.

Facilities, fees: A boat launch, fishing pier, picnic areas, and a snack bar are available. The facilities are wheelchair-accessible. Fees are charged for parking, boat launching, and daily fishing permits.

Directions: Take Highway 4 to Antioch and the exit for Lone Tree Way. Take that exit and drive south to Golf Course Road. Turn right and drive to Frederickson Lane. Turn right at Frederickson Lane and drive about one mile to the entrance kiosk.

Contact: Park headquarters, 925/757-9606; for a park brochure, call or go online to East Bay Regional Park District, 888/327-2757, option 3, ext. 4551, then follow the directions and leave your name, address, and the park brochure requested, or download it from www.ebparks.org; for fishing information, call 888/327-2757.

30 LAKE CHABOT

Rating: 9

near Castro Valley
Map 7.2, page 382   BEST

Here's a lake that just plain looks fishy. And it is, with abundant stocks of trout in the winter and spring: 10- to 12-inch rainbow trout from the DFG, and trout measuring a foot or longer from the park district. In the summer, catfish are stocked in good numbers. They join a resident population of the biggest largemouth bass in the Bay Area. Schools of crappie and bluegill hold in several coves. The best spots for trout are Coot Landing, Honker Bay, and Bass Cove; avoid the open lake body.

The giant bass are very difficult to catch. I've seen them swim right under my canoe. Your best chance is in the spring, using grubs or tube baits. There is an unofficial 10-pounders club here who release all the bass, and I suggest you do the same to keep this fishery strong. The trout are easier to come by. Most anglers shoreline bait-dunk near the marina. Others troll. Bait dunkers seem to outcatch the trollers.

The lake covers 315 acres and is the centerpiece of a 5,000-acre regional park that has 31 miles of hiking trails, horseback-riding rentals, and a campground. It's too bad that privately owned boats (apart from canoes and kayaks) aren't permitted to launch here; otherwise the fishing program would be nearly as strong as that at San Pablo Reservoir. But rentals are available, and shore fishing for trout is often quite good.

Lake records: 17-pound, 10-ounce largemouth bass; 21-pound, 4-ounce rainbow trout; 35-pound catfish; 13-pound, 8-ounce sturgeon.

Note: All boats must be inspected and certified free of mussels prior to launching at this lake.

Facilities, fees: Restrooms, parking, boat rentals, horseback-riding, camping spots, bicycle trails, picnic areas, and drinking water are available. Privately owned boats, apart from canoes and kayaks, are not allowed. A small marina office sells bait and tackle. Day-use fees are charged.

Directions: From San Francisco: Take I-80 east across the Bay Bridge for 6.4 miles to the MacArthur split and bear right on I-580. Drive 14.2 miles south to San Leandro. Take the exit for 150th Avenue toward Fairmont Drive for 0.2 mile and merge with Freedom Avenue. Drive 0.1 mile to Fairmont Drive. Turn left at Fairmont and go 1.9 miles (it becomes Lake Chabot Road) to the park entrance on the left.

From San Jose: Take I-880 north for 27 miles to San Lorenzo and the Hesperian Boulevard exit. Take that exit, drive 0.2 mile to Hesperian, and turn right. Drive 1.1 miles to Fairmont. Turn right at Fairmont and drive 2.6 miles to the park entrance on the left.

Contact: For a park brochure, call or go online to East Bay Regional Park District, 888/327-2757, option 3, ext. 4551, then follow the directions and leave your name, address, and the park brochure requested, or download it from www.ebparks.org; Urban Park Concessionaires, www.norcalfishing.com (click on Lake Chabot); Chabot Queen boat tours, 510/247-2526.

their gear and hike around the surrounding parkland instead.

Facilities, fees: Restrooms, parking, drinking water, hiking trails, picnic areas, a swimming lagoon, and a food concession are available. There are no boating facilities, and boating is not allowed. Fishing-permit and swimming fees are charged.

Directions: From I-580 eastbound: In Castro Valley, drive to the exit for Center Street. Take that exit and drive north to Heyer Avenue. Turn right on Heyer and drive to Cull Canyon Road. Turn left and drive to the park entrance.

From I-580 westbound: In Castro Valley, drive to the exit for Castro Valley. Take that exit to Castro Valley Boulevard. Turn left onto Castro Valley Boulevard and drive to Crow Canyon Road. Turn right and drive 0.5 mile to Cull Canyon Road. Turn left on Cull Canyon Road and drive to the park entrance.

Contact: Cull Canyon Regional Recreation Area, 510/537-2240; for fishing information, call 888/327-2757; for a park brochure, call or go online to East Bay Regional Park District, 888/327-2757, option 3, ext. 4551, then follow the directions and leave your name, address, and the park brochure requested, or download it from www.ebparks.org.

31 CULL CANYON RESERVOIR

Rating: 3

in Castro Valley

Map 7.2, page 382

With the East Bay heat hammering away at it all summer long, this tiny reservoir, just 18 acres, supports only small populations of warm-water species, including catfish, bass, and sunfish.

The results won't exactly make you want to cancel that trip you had planned for Alaska. Your best bet is to come in the summer and try for small catfish, which are stocked once or twice per month. Otherwise, the fishing is quite poor, and visitors are apt to pack up

32 DON CASTRO RESERVOIR

Rating: 2

in the Hayward hills

Map 7.2, page 382

Little Don Castro, at just 23 acres (at last count), is going down the drain. The lake is rapidly silting up and may disappear. Don Castro is the focal point of a small regional park that doesn't get much attention. And why should it? No boats are allowed, and there are very few trout, plus just a sprinkling of catfish. That doesn't add up to a heck of a lot. The only time this spot is worth a look is in the spring and early summer, when small bass and bluegill can provide some sport for shoreliners. Dunk a worm under a bobber and see what happens. Don Castro gets 2,000 10- to 12-inch rainbow trout from the DFG, plus a few bonus fish from the park district.

Lake records: 10-pound largemouth bass; 17-pound, 4-ounce rainbow trout; 22-pound channel catfish. But don't get any big ideas. Your chance of hooking a fish like one of these is like winning the lottery.

Facilities, fees: Parking, restrooms, a swimming lagoon, a lakeside hiking trail, picnic areas, several fishing piers, and a seasonal food concession are available. There are no boating facilities, and boating is not allowed. An entrance fee is charged. A daily fishing permit is required.

Directions: From I-580 east in Castro Valley, take the Center Street exit. Turn right and drive to Kelly Street. Turn left and drive a short distance to Woodroe. Turn left onto Woodroe and drive to the park entrance.

From I-580 west, take the Castro Valley exit and drive west on East Castro Valley Boulevard to Grove Way. Turn left and drive to Center Street. Drive a short distance, turn left, and drive to Kelly Street. Turn left at Kelly Street and drive to Woodroe. Turn left once again and drive to the park entrance.

Contact: For a park brochure, call or go online to East Bay Regional Park District, 888/327-2757, option 3, ext. 4551, then follow the directions and leave your name, address, and the park brochure requested, or download it from www.ebparks.org; for fishing information, call 888/327-2757.

33 JORDAN POND

Rating: 3

in Garin Regional Park, Hayward
Map 7.2, page 382

Jordan Pond is a five-acre pond with a self-sustaining population of largemouth bass, bluegill, and redear sunfish. These fish are augmented in the summer by monthly plants of 250 pounds of channel catfish.

Jordan Pond has a fishing pier, and in the summer, organized groups occasionally take over the place for a youth fishing program. The park district prohibits boats and float tubes.

Facilities, fees: A fishing pier, restrooms, drinking water, picnic tables, and a visitor center are available. The park is open 5 A.M.–10 P.M. A parking fee is charged.

Directions: Take I-680 to Fremont and the exit for Mission Boulevard. Take that exit and go north on Mission Boulevard to Garin Avenue. Turn right (east) on Garin and drive to the park entrance.

Contact: Garin Regional Park, 510/582-2206; for a park brochure, call or go online to East Bay Regional Park District, 888/327-2757, option 3, ext. 4551, then follow the directions and leave your name, address, and the park brochure requested, or download it from www.ebparks.org.

34 LOS VAQUEROS RESERVOIR

Rating: 9

near Livermore
Map 7.2, page 382

The Bay Area's newest lake has emerged as one of the best of the region's 150 significant parklands. If you haven't seen it yet, Los Vaqueros Reservoir, with its surrounding watershed parkland, is a sight that will pop your eyes out. When you clear the rise and Los Vaqueros first comes into view, you'll be stunned at the lake's size and beauty. It is surrounded by 18,500 acres of watershed wildlands, in addition to two regional parks (Morgan Territory and Round Valley), creating roughly 225 square miles of greenbelt.

Los Vaqueros provides year-round fisheries, for trout in the cool months and for bass in the summer and fall. Its location and warm weather virtually assure a quality warm-water fishery (that is, for bass, bluegill, crappie, and catfish), a much-needed opportunity in a region where most lakes are prisoners of trout plants.

The best fishing in summer is often for

striped bass. Fly-fishers toss Hair Raiser-style or Worm-Tail jigs, or bucktail jigs or Kastmasters. The fact that striped bass have become such a star at this lake shows how many fish get sucked down the Delta pumps.

The best fishing in late winter and spring is for trout. That is the result of very solid stocks by East Bay MUD, which runs the lake. In addition, the lake has a high population of minnows and plankton, 10 times the forage in San Pablo Reservoir, according to water district scientists. Because of that, many are predicting that the lake will eventually provide the best fishery in the Bay Area for bass and catfish. In addition, since there are underwater drop-offs close to shore, fishing from the bank or the piers provides much better opportunities than at most lakes.

The lake is stocked with rainbow trout, including some of the biggest one-time stocks, 10,000 pounds in one shot, in the Bay Area. The lake also receives largemouth bass, bullhead and channel catfish, bluegill, and green sunfish. Kokanee salmon were planted in 2004, 2005, and 2007, and should have reached catchable sizes by 2008. Yet they haven't really been heard from—my guess is that the stripers have mowed them down.

A big focus at the reservoir is the marina at the south end, where there are electric-powered boats for rent and two fishing piers.

The South Gate (off Vasco Road out of Livermore) is set up for anglers and hikers, with access to both the marina and Los Vaqueros Trail, which extends about halfway around the lake and offers sweeping views of the watershed.

Two big problems: wind, and no access for private boats. The lake is in rolling foothills in the little-known terrain of remote Contra Costa County, well southeast of Mount Diablo, roughly between Livermore to the south and Brentwood to the north, not far from Altamont Pass and its windmill farms. The wind can howl through here, and it often does, especially from late April through early July. That's right when trout and bass fishing should peak, but the wind keeps a lot of people off the water.

It's a downer that no private boats and no gas engines, not even the clean-burning four-cycle outboards, are permitted on the lake. That's an issue, because not having a large-enough boat powered by an engine could compromise your safety if you get caught in a wind out here. (Seems ridiculous—the lake is filled with water that has already been boated on in the Delta.)

With Sunol Regional Wilderness to the south, this region has the greatest concentration of golden eagles in the western hemisphere. There are 19 varieties of raptors (mostly hawks and owls), along with blacktail deer, wild boar, coyote, and fox. It is possible that a mated pair of bald eagles at nearby Del Valle Reservoir, south of Livermore, could produce offspring that would take up residence at Los Vaqueros. A major planting of oaks, which provide food for wildlife, will support fauna further; for many years, cattle had eaten all the oak seedlings.

Side note: Research editor Kathie Morgan unearthed that the first bass tournament held at Los Vaqueros was won by Howard Bass. The winning fish, also named Bass (no relation), weighed 7.11 pounds.

Lake records: 45.2-pound striped bass; 12-pound largemouth bass; 6-pound salmon; 13.14-pound rainbow trout; 6.97-pound brown trout; 29.09-pound catfish; 2.34-pound crappie.

Access note: The South Gate (off Vasco Road out of Livermore) is best for hikers and anglers, with access to both the marina and the Los Vaqueros Trail. No bikes are permitted at South Gate. The North Gate (on Walnut Avenue, out of Brentwood) is best for bikers. Due to the steep terrain that surrounds some of the reservoir, there are no vehicle roads connecting the north and south watershed, so bikers and hikers are separated.

Special regulations: No pets are permitted. On the lake, no privately owned boats or gas motors are permitted. No swimming or other body contact with the water is permitted. On trails, youth 12–17 must not hike alone, and children under 12 must hike with an adult.

Facilities, fees: Restrooms; boat rentals; a small marina with bait, tackle, snacks, and ice; picnic areas; and an interpretive center are available. Fees are charged for parking.

Directions: To South Gate: Take I-580 to Livermore and the exit for Vasco Road. Turn north on Vasco Road and drive five miles to Los Vaqueros Road. Turn left (north) and drive to the south entry station of the watershed.

Contact: Los Vaqueros Marina, 925/371-2628; Urban Park Concessionaires, 925/426-3060, www.norcalfishing.com; fishing information hotline, 925/248-2474; Contra Costa Water District, 925/688-8175, www.ccwater.com (click on Los Vaqueros).

35 QUARRY LAKES

Rating: 6

in Fremont at Quarry Lakes
Regional Recreation Area
Map 7.2, page 382

What started as a good idea in the '70s has come to fruition. The Bay Area's newest park and public lake, Quarry Lakes Recreation Area provides good fishing. This recreation area has also unveiled new opportunities for biking, hiking, fishing, low-speed boating, wildlife watching, picnics, and swimming.

The centerpiece at Quarry Lakes Recreation Area is Horseshoe Lake. The lake is stocked with trout. Park district staff are also trying to create a self-sustaining fishery for largemouth and smallmouth bass. The lake seems to respond very quickly to trout plants, and fishing from shore is often as good as it is from boats.

There is a small boat launch, a picnic area with a lawn, a swimming area with changing rooms, a snack bar, and a beach with wheelchair access. Boats up to 17 feet (including canoes, kayaks, and prams) are permitted at Horseshoe Lake only. No gas motors are permitted, but electric motors are.

This park started as an uncertain concept in 1975, when the East Bay Regional Park District and the Alameda County Water District started purchasing an old gravel quarry with three water holes, about 450 acres in all. The park district has since spent $5.8 million in grants and bond money to transform the property into a park.

Visitors will find a water-based park with three small lakes—Horseshoe Lake, Rainbow Lake, and Lago Los Osos, all separated by levees. Lago Los Osos and Rainbow Lake will be managed in different ways. Lago Los Osos, which means "Lake of the Bears," is managed solely as a wildlife preserve, attracting both waterfowl and shorebirds from the nearby wildlife refuge along South San Francisco Bay, and no fishing is allowed. Rainbow Lake will provide limited fishing for bass and carp, but the park district may create a one-of-kind trophy-trout fishery here, with an additional fishing fee to support it.

The one factor that screws this place up is the wind. It can really howl here. I've seen the little lakes practically awash in whitecaps. In the summer, from late May through July, mornings can be very foggy. By noon, the fog burns off, but then the wind comes on, some days howling through the place and making it so nobody can fish. The best months of the year here include the first break of warm weather in February, and then again in March.

Note: All boats must be inspected and certified free of mussels prior to launching at this lake.

Facilities, fees: Facilities include a boat ramp, picnic areas, and a bike trail. Fees are charged for day use and boat launching, and a daily fishing permit must be purchased.

Directions: From I-880 in Fremont: Drive to the Decoto Road East exit. Take that exit and drive east for 1.2 miles to Paseo Padre Parkway. Turn right and drive 0.8 mile to Isherwood. Turn left and drive 0.7 mile to the park entrance, on the right.

From I-680 in Fremont: Drive to the exit for Mission Boulevard. (Highway 238). Take that exit, turn north (keeping the hills on your right), and drive 4.7 miles to Nursery

Avenue. Turn left and drive 100 yards (across the tracks) to Niles Boulevard. Turn right and drive 1.3 miles (crossing a bridge) to Osprey Drive. Turn left and drive 100 yards to Quarry Lakes Drive. Turn left and drive 0.3 mile to the park entrance, on the left.

From the peninsula: Take U.S. 101 to the exit for Highway 84/Dumbarton Bridge. Take that exit and drive east to Fremont (Highway 84 becomes Decoto Road) and continue to Paseo Padre Parkway. Turn right and drive 0.8 mile to Isherwood. Turn left and drive 0.7 mile to the park entrance, on the right.

Contact: For a park brochure, call or go online to East Bay Regional Park District, 888/327-2757, option 3, ext. 4551, then follow the directions and leave your name, address, and the park brochure requested, or download it from www.ebparks.org.

36 SHINN POND

Rating: 3

in Fremont
Map 7.2, page 382

An old gravel pit here was filled with water, then stocked with bass and bluegill. The result is a 23-acre pond that doesn't provide much of anything. In the summer, the East Bay Regional Park District stocks 250 pounds of catfish each month. You may see some folks sit there with their lines in the water for hours. After a while, you'll wonder if they are statues.

Facilities, fees: Restrooms and drinking water are at the pond. You can leave your car at the park. Fishing access is free.

Directions: Take I-680 to Fremont and the exit for Mission Boulevard/Highway 238. Take that exit and turn south on Nursery Avenue and drive to Niles Boulevard. Turn right and drive to Osprey Drive. Turn left on Osprey Drive and drive to Quarry Lakes Drive. Turn left and drive to the park entrance on the left.

Contact: For a park brochure, call or go online to East Bay Regional Park District, 888/327-

2757, option 3, ext. 4551, then follow the directions and leave your name, address, and the park brochure requested, or download it from www.ebparks.org.

37 LAKE ELIZABETH

Rating: 4

in Fremont
Map 7.2, page 382

During the hot summer months, Lake Elizabeth and the surrounding parkland provide a relatively cool spot in the East Bay flats. Unfortunately, the fishing is also quite cool at the 83-acre lake, no matter what the temperature is. A few small bass, bluegill, crappie, and catfish provide long-shot hopes. The DFG stocks trout in the winter months and a few catfish in the summer. So with all these fish—five species—what's the problem? Answer: There's just not enough of them.

Facilities, fees: A boat ramp, boat rentals, and restrooms are available. Fishing access is free.

Directions: Take I-880 to Fremont and the exit for Stevenson Boulevard. Take that exit and drive east for two miles to Paseo Padre Parkway. Turn right on Paseo Padre Parkway and drive about one block to Sailway Drive. Turn left on Sailway Drive and drive a short distance to Central Park.

Contact: City of Fremont, Recreation Services at Lake Elizabeth Boathouse, 510/790-5541, www.fremont.gov.

38 SHADOW CLIFFS LAKE

Rating: 7

in Pleasanton
Map 7.2, page 382

Shadow Cliffs shows what is possible when you put no limits on your vision. This place started off as nothing but an old gravel quarry with a squarish water hole. When it was donated to the East Bay Regional Park District, its value was assessed at only $250,000. As a park, it is near priceless.

A key is that the water is high quality and clear, even during the winter. It is not affected by storm runoff, like most of the lakes with public access in the Bay Area, so it doesn't get muddy.

An outstanding water-sports and boating program has been established. The fishing program is also excellent, with the prospects best in fall, winter, and spring. The Department of Fish and Game stocks the lake with trout about twice per month, and it receives more plants from the park district. Among these are trophy-size rainbow trout, stocked in the winter and spring, and catfish, stocked in the summer. So fishing is often excellent, and fishing derbies are popular.

Besides the main lake, Shadow Cliffs has an arroyo with a chain of smaller lakes and ponds. No swimming or boating is allowed at these ponds, but their shorelines are well shaded and provide several hideaways. But here's a plus: float tubes and hand-carried boats are allowed.

A squarish shape and steep banks give Shadow Cliffs an odd, submerged appearance, but you won't mind, because the lake offers a good fishery in the cool months. The park district plants 21,500 rainbow trout and 5,000 channel catfish. DFG supplements this with 11,000 rainbow trout. This is the only lake in the Bay Area stocked with Thunder Trout, the genetic wonders that outfight all the other planters. Included in the mix are trout in the five-pound class. Even rainbow trout weighing 10–15 pounds are occasionally caught. The better fishing is always along Stanley Boulevard or in the vicinity of the third dock, and at times, the top spot is right in the middle of the lake. Don't ask why, but things just work out that way.

This bears repeating: in high-rain years, when all the lakes get so muddy in the Bay Area, Shadow Cliffs is one of the few that stay clear. It doesn't get roiled by mucky runoff like virtually all the other lakes. So even in the biggest rain years, remember this lake.

The weather gets very hot out this way in the summer, and instead of planting trout, the park district stocks one- and two-pound catfish. There are also resident bluegill and largemouth bass. Bait, tackle, and snacks are available. Boat rentals include rowboats, canoes, and paddleboats.

Lake records: 39-pound channel catfish; 18-pound, 8-ounce rainbow trout; 18-pound, 1-ounce largemouth bass; 2-pound black crappie.

Facilities, fees: A boat launch, boat rentals, picnic areas, and a snack bar are available. Boats with electric motors are permitted on the lake (they must be no longer than 17 feet), but gas-powered engines are not. Some facilities are wheelchair-accessible. Fees are charged for parking and for daily fishing permits.

Directions: Take I-580 to Pleasanton and the exit for Santa Rita Road South. Take that exit and drive south for two miles to Valley Avenue. Turn left on Valley Avenue and drive to Stanley Boulevard. Turn left and drive to the park entrance.

Contact: For a park brochure, call or go online to East Bay Regional Park District, 888/327-2757, option 3, ext. 4551, then follow the directions and leave your name, address, and the park brochure requested, or download it from www.ebparks.org.

ⓕ BETHANY RESERVOIR

Rating: 4

near Livermore in Bethany Reservoir
State Recreation Area

Map 7.2, page 382

A smorgasbord of fish is available at Bethany Reservoir, but it definitely isn't "all you can eat." Bethany has rainbow trout, largemouth bass, striped bass, catfish, bluegill, and crappie living in it. Catching them is another matter.

This 162-acre reservoir is similar to Contra Loma Reservoir, to the north, in that it gets its water via the California Aqueduct. That is why striped bass are in the lake; they're sucked out of the delta and pumped here. The better fishing is on the southwest side of the lake, across from the boat ramp, where you'll find a series of coves.

Though all boats are allowed on the lake, a 5-mph speed limit keeps the water quiet. The exception to this rule of quiet is in the spring, when the winds can howl through this area. A bonus is that a good bike trail traverses the park.

Facilities, fees: Picnic areas, portable toilets, and a boat ramp are available. There are fees for day use and boat launching.

Directions: From I-580 at Livermore, travel east and take the Altamont Pass exit. Turn right on Altamont Pass Road and travel to Kelso–Christianson Road. Turn right and continue to the park entrance.

Contact: Bethany Reservoir State Recreation Area, California Parks and Recreation Department, 209/532-0150, www.parks.ca.gov.

⁴⁰ DEL VALLE RESERVOIR

Rating: 10

southeast of Livermore in
Lake Del Valle State Recreation Area

Map 7.2, page 382   BEST (

Del Valle is one of the Bay Area's top adventure lands for fishing, camping, boating, and hiking.

The lake sits in a long, narrow canyon in Alameda County's foothill country, covering 750 acres with 16 miles of shoreline. It provides a setting for the newcomer or the expert, with very good trout stocks during winter and spring, and an excellent population of bass. They are joined by more elusive smallmouth bass, catfish, bluegill, and a few rare but big striped bass. It's one of the few lakes in the Bay Area that also provide camping, rental boats, and a good ramp for powerboats. The trailhead for the Ohlone Wilderness Trail is also nearby.

As long as water clarity is decent in the winter months, trout fishing is usually excellent.

My favorite two spots are: 1) The river channel at the head of the lake, about 50 yards from the inlet, anchored, fishing with bait. 2) East corners of the dam, trolling 20–35 feet deep with the cat-and-mouse trick (see *Trout* in the *Sport Fish* chapter). On a TV show, I demonstrated these techniques, and on Day 1 with kids who had never fished before, we had 10 trout that weighed 25 pounds. On Day 2, we had two six-pounders, one on bait, one trolling, along with another half dozen trout.

Other good spots are Swallow Bay, the Narrows, and from shore near the boat launch. Most of the trout are in the one- to two-pound class but range to eight pounds and up. The bigger ones are usually caught by accident by folks bait fishing with Power Bait and night crawlers on separate hooks.

The rigging for trout, bait fishing, is simple: Place a small bullet sinker on the line and then tie on a small snap swivel. From the snap swivel, use 6-pound leader and about 18 inches of line to a No. 8 hook, and about 12 inches of line to another hook. Then place three Power Bait nuggets (chartreuse is best) on each hook. When you cast out, the bullet sinker will drop to the bottom, and the Power Bait will float up a bit, right where the big ones roam.

The largemouth bass population has exploded. To catch them, drop-shot grubs at dawn at points outside Swallow Bay. For striped bass, at dawn, cast Worm-Tail jigs or Castaic Trout at corners of the dam.

The DFG planted 10,000 king salmon in the early 21st century, along with 10,000 kokanee salmon back in 2005. They seemed to have disappeared without even a croak.

In the summer months, the trout fishing slows at Del Valle Reservoir, with bass, catfish, and bluegill offering the best of it until October. Trolling in the thermocline for salmon could bridge this gap. Then in the fall, as the water cools, the park district trout plants resume, including trophy-size fish, and more fish are supplemented by the DFG.

Lake records: 18-pound, 2-ounce largemouth bass; 22.6-pound rainbow trout;

30-pound channel catfish; 40-pound striped bass; 25-pound sturgeon; 2-pound, 2-ounce bluegill; 5-pound, 12-ounce smallmouth bass; 2-pound, 2-ounce crappie; 9-pound king salmon; 1-pound, 14-ounce redear sunfish.

Note: All boats must be inspected and certified free of mussels prior to launching at this lake.

Facilities, fees: A campground is available. Picnic areas, a full-service marina, a boat launch, boat rentals, a concession stand, and paved walking and bike trails are provided. The facilities are wheelchair-accessible. Fees are charged for access, boat launching, and a required daily fishing permit.

Directions: Take I-580 to Livermore and the exit for North Livermore Avenue. Take that exit and turn south (right if coming from Bay Area) and drive eight miles (the road becomes Tesla Road) to Mines Road. Turn right on Mines Road and drive 3.5 miles to Del Valle Road. Continue straight on Del Valle Road (note that Mines Road turns left; do not turn left) and drive four miles to the Del Valle Regional Park entrance. After passing through the entrance, bear right at the fork and continue to the marina, boat launch, and parking area.

Contact: Del Valle Marina, 925/449-5201; for a park brochure, call or go online to East Bay Regional Park District, 888/327-2757, option 3, ext. 4551, then follow the directions and leave your name, address, and the park brochure requested, or download it from www.ebparks.org; for recorded fishing information, call 925/248-3474.

41 SANDY WOOL LAKE

Rating: 2

near Milpitas in Ed R. Levin County Park
Map 7.2, page 382

The lake may be small, just 14 acres, but it is surrounded by parkland crisscrossed by 16 miles of hiking trails. Like many lakes and reservoirs in Santa Clara County, Sandy Wool is closed indefinitely to boating.

The fishing varies from fair to downright terrible. The best hopes are in the winter, when the Department of Fish and Game stocks Sandy Wool twice a month with trout (14,000 10- to 12-inch rainbow trout). During that time you'll have a decent chance of catching fish here. In the summer, when the water heats up, you might as well dunk a line in a bucket.

Facilities, fees: Restrooms, parking, a golf course, horseback-riding rentals, and picnic areas are available. A day-use fee is charged.

Directions: Take I-680 to Milpitas and the exit for Calaveras Road East. Take that exit and drive east for 3.5 miles to Downing Road. Turn left (north) on Downing Road and drive 0.5 mile to the park entrance (straight ahead). Proceed to the parking area, which is near Sandy Wool Lake.

Contact: Santa Clara County Parks and Recreation, 408/355-2255, www.parkhere.org; Ed R. Levin County Park, 408/262-6980, www.sccgov.org.

42 LAKE MERCED

Rating: 2

in San Francisco
Map 7.3, page 383

If you sit in a boat along Lake Merced's tule-lined shore, San Francisco and its 700,000 residents will seem like a whole different world. From that perspective, it is a resource of tremendous public value. It is also a place of peace and potential. Unfortunately, the fishing does not live up to that potential.

In many ways, the fishing operation is a shipwreck, and the money spent so far by the City of San Francisco at the lake has not addressed many of the defining issues, such as establishing a trout-planting program that provides a chance for anybody to catch a fish; contracting a concessionaire to operate a bait and tackle shop and rent boats; clearing rampant tule growth that blocks so much of the shore access; and maintenance of bathrooms, piers, hoists, and docks.

An agreement was reached to restore the lake levels at Lake Merced. A water-treatment plant provides irrigation water for the golf courses nearby, which has limited pumping from the lake's aquifer. The groundwater basin beneath the lake is recharging. That allows the lake to rise and levels to stabilize.

Lake Merced has a long, colorful history. In 1893, 90,000 muskies were planted but were never heard from again. In the mid-1980s, it was the most successful urban trout fishery in America; *Field & Stream* hired me to write a cover feature about it. No more. The glory days may be over for good, despite catchable trout plants made by the Department of Fish and Game. So what you have now is the occasional small plant by the DFG in the North Lake, a few days of fair prospects by shoreline bait dunkers, then back to zilch.

Because it's right on the coast, Merced can be buried in heavy fog and mist in the summer, keeping water temperatures cool, while the San Joaquin Valley is baking in the 100s day after day. Unlike at most other Bay Area lakes, the trout fishing here has the chance to remain good in the summer, because the daily doses of morning and evening fog keep the water temperatures cool, allowing for continued stocks.

There are three lakes here: Lake Merced North (105 acres), Lake Merced South (203 acres), and the Merced Impoundment (17 acres, but typically too low on water for public use). The north and south lakes are linked by an underground pipe. Despite ongoing problems with water levels and other screwups, there are still recreational benefits.

The south lake is the largest of the trio, larger than most expect. When it is full, it is quite pretty. It has been damaged greatly by low water levels and unchecked tule growth, with most of the shoreline access now choked off. Only clearing tules in several areas and raising lake levels will solve this. The south lake, while more of a recreation lake for rowers and sailboaters, can also provide a chance for trout in the 10- to 11-inch class. Because

tules have choked off access, the best spot is near the dam. Some large catfish and bass live along the tules, but few people have figured out how to catch them.

The impoundment is smaller than many expect. In low-rain years, it is reduced to a puddle, and no trout are stocked.

Catch rates are best at the north lake. The best spots in the north lake are the cove offshore from the 18th hole of the adjacent golf course and the northwest corner of the lake. The DFG occasionally stocks the lake with trout, but not enough to provide a viable fishery with a real chance to show up and catch a fish. CalTrout sponsors a big youth day, one big shot a year, and it would be great if they could step in and take a year-round role and bring back this lake.

An option is bass fishing on the far side of the little bridge. I've heard stories of 10-pound bass, and I believe them. It's possible the south lake has some huge bass along the tules on the east side of the lake.

Back in the day, as we say, the lake's record trout was caught, a 17-pound, 8-ounce rainbow landed by Jesse Rappenecker of San Bruno. That was just one of two 17-pound trout taken at Lake Merced. The other, weighing in at 17 pounds, 6.5 ounces, was landed by Will Rose of Daly City. But the days of those fish were when Urban Parks ran the lake, and since that organization departed, in frustration with the city government, the once-great days here seem like a mirage. The City of San Francisco has shown a rare example of humankind's ability to screw up a good thing.

Facilities, fees: Facilities include restrooms, a boat launch, dock, and fishing pier. Fishing access is free.

Directions: From the peninsula: Take I-280 to Highway 1 in San Bruno. Turn west and drive one mile to Highway 35/Skyline Boulevard. Turn right (north) on Highway 35 and drive five miles to the lake. Turn right at the lake entrance.

From San Francisco: Take Geary Boulevard west until it dead-ends at the ocean and the Cliff House Restaurant. Turn left on the Great Highway and drive four miles to the lake, on the left.

From Daly City: Take I-280 to the exit for John Daly Boulevard West. Take that exit and drive west to Skyline Boulevard. Turn right at Skyline Boulevard and drive to the lake entrance, on the right.

Contact: San Francisco Recreation & Parks Department, 415/831-2700; sfrecpark.org/LakeMerced.

43 GOLDEN GATE SALMON

Rating: 8

along the Bay Area coast

Map 7.3, page 383

The richest marine region on the Pacific coast from Mexico to Alaska lies along San Francisco. Salmon are king of these waters. The key is that an underwater shelf extends 30 miles out to sea before dropping off to never-never land. The relatively shallow area is perfect for an ocean upwelling in the spring, which brings cold, mineral-rich waters to the surface. Sunlight penetrates that water, causing tiny aquatic organisms to be born in great numbers. Shrimp, squid, anchovies, and herring are attracted to the plankton-filled water and in turn draw hordes of hungry salmon, which roam the Bay Area coast searching for baitfish. This is the only portion of the Pacific coast where salmon can be found year-round.

Regulations here change often, so it's wise to check before each trip. The season usually starts in April and runs through October. During that time, anglers get some widely varied, quality fishing. In spring, the primary feed for salmon is sardines, shrimp, and squid (which are often found in tight balls near the Farallon Islands), as well as a sprinkling of juvenile rockfish and small schools of anchovies off Pedro Point near southern Pacifica, the Deep Reef southwest of Half Moon Bay, and Duxbury Reef offshore near Marin. The fishing is usually best around the shrimp balls just off the Farallon Islands, in 55- to 90-foot-deep water.

Early in the season you'll get top results by trolling, not mooching, often well offshore. In their search for fish, the big charter boats fan out like the spokes of a bicycle wheel. A skipper who finds fish often alerts the rest of the fleet. If you are on the water in a private boat, you can listen in by tuning your marine radio to Channel 67 and, occasionally, Channel 59.

By mid-June to early July huge numbers of anchovies and small sardines migrate into the inshore waters off Half Moon Bay, Pacifica, and Marin. This causes the salmon to swarm in large schools, then move inshore to corral the baitfish. The result can be the best fishing of the year, with calm seas and packs of salmon on the bite within close range.

Drift-mooching, in which the engine is turned off and the boat is allowed to drift with the current, is a popular technique at this time. Trolling tends to provide higher catch rates, while mooching nets larger fish, since anglers can use lighter tackle and sense every bite (it can also be much more fun).

By fall, many of the salmon school in the vicinity of the Channel Buoys, 10 miles west of the Golden Gate, or what I call "The Salmon Highway" (from Duxbury to Rocky Point and then down to Stinson Beach) as they prepare to journey through the bay and upriver to their spawning grounds. This is when the largest salmon of the year are caught, with a sprinkling of 25- to 40-pound fish in the area from mid-August through early October.

If you are new to the game, learning how to play is as easy as tumbling out of bed in time to board the boat. Bring a lunch, drinks, warm clothing, and, if vulnerable to Neptune, seasickness pills. Before heading out, the skippers will provide brief instructions on the techniques planned for the day. If you need help at any time, a professional deckhand will be there for you.

The salmon fishery remains one of the best in the state, despite dramatic fluctuations in population due to perpetually troubled water conditions in spawning areas.

I have opened and closed more than 20 seasons. On the last day of one particular season, I took my buddy Dave "Hank" Zimmer out on the *Wacky Jacky* for his first salmon trip. About midway through the day, I hooked a salmon I figured for a 10-pounder, then passed the rod to ol' Hank.

"Here ya go, Hank," I said. "Enjoy it."

Well, 40 minutes later, he brought a 32-pounder alongside. It was one of the greatest fights with a salmon I have ever witnessed, the fish streaking off on long runs the first three times it saw the boat. Afterward, Hank just sat down kind of stunned, and looked at the giant fish.

Then he calmly said: "Hey, this fishing is fun."

I still can't believe I passed a 30-pounder.

Facilities, fees: Party boats depart at 6 A.M. daily from San Francisco, Sausalito, Emeryville, Berkeley, and Bodega Bay. Skippers ask that those who will be fishing arrive at 5:30 A.M. for an orientation. Bait is provided, and tackle and rod rentals are available on each boat. Party-boat fees are charged per day.

See *Contact* for information on specific boats and on launch ramps for private boats.

Directions: To Fisherman's Wharf from the Golden Gate Bridge: Take U.S. 101 to the southern end of the Golden Gate Bridge in San Francisco and look for the exit for Marina. Take that exit and drive southeast toward Fisherman's Wharf. The boats are at the foot of Jones and Jefferson, along the front row of Fisherman's Wharf between Castagnola's and Tarantino's restaurants. A parking garage is nearby at Beach and Jones.

To Fisherman's Wharf from the Bay Bridge: Take I-80 west to San Francisco and the exit for Embarcadero/Harrison Street. Take that exit (on the left-hand side of the road) and drive to Harrison Street. Turn right on Harrison Street and drive five blocks to Embarcadero Street. Turn left on Embarcadero and drive past the piers on the right to Bay Street. Continue on Embarcadero Street to Fisherman's Wharf and the parking garages.

• To the Berkeley Marina: Take I-80 to Berkeley and the exit for University Avenue West/Berkeley Marina. Take that exit and drive west to a T intersection. Turn left for the pier and bait shop. Turn right for the boat ramp.

• To the Emeryville Marina: Take I-80 to Emeryville and the exit for Powell Street. Take that exit west to Powell Street. Drive west on Powell Street for 0.75 mile to the parking area, marina, and bait shop, at the end of the road.

• To Clipper Yacht Harbor, Sausalito: Take U.S. 101 to Sausalito and take the Sausalito–Marin City exit and bear left, heading under the freeway. Turn right on Bridgeway and proceed a few blocks to Harbor. Turn left and continue to the marina.

Contact: For general information, go to the Fisherman's Wharf Merchants Association, www.fishermanswharf.org. Following is contact information for specific boats.

• San Francisco: *Bass-Tub,* 415/456-9055, www.basstub.net; *Chucky's Pride,* 415/564-5515; Captain Joey, 415/892-2353; *Lovely Martha,* 650/871-1691, www.lovelymartha .com; Riptide Sportfishing, 650/728-8433, www.riptide.net; *Wacky Jacky,* 415/586-9800, www.wackyjackysportfishing.com; SoleMan Sportfishing, 510/703-4148, www.soleman fishing.com.

• Sausalito: *Blue Runner,* 415/458-8700, www.bluerunnercharters.com; *Flying Fish,* 415/898-6610, www.flyingfishsportfishing .homestead.com; *Hog Heaven,* 415/382-7891; *New Rayann,* 415/924-6851, www.newrayann .com; *Outer Limits,* 415/454-3191; *Salty Lady,* 415/674-3474, www.saltylady.com; Sea Turtle Charters, 415/332-4200, www.seaturtle fishingcharters.com.

• Berkeley Charter Boats, 510/849-3333, www .berkeleycharterboats.com; *Golden Eye 2000,* 510/610-0888; Happy Hooker Sportfishing, 510/223-5388 or 510/222-5279.

• Emeryville Sportfishing, 510/654-6040

or 800/575-9944, www.emeryvillesportfish ing.com.

• Half Moon Bay Sportfishing, 650/728-3377, hmbfishing.com; Huck Finn Sportfishing, 650/726-7133, www.huckfinnsportfishing .com; Riptide Sportfishing, 650/728-8433, www.riptide.net.

Launch ramps for private boats: Berkeley Marina, 510/981-6740, www.ci.berkeley .ca.us; Clipper Marina, Sausalito, 415/332-3500, www.clipperyacht.com; Loch Lomond Marina, San Rafael, 415/454-7228, www .lochlomondmarina.com; Richmond Marina, 510/236-1013, www.marinabayyachtharbor .com; Oyster Point Marina, South San Francisco, 650/871-7344, www.smharbor.com/ oysterpoint; Emeryville Marina, 510/654-3716, www.emeryvillemarina.com; Pillar Point Marina, Princeton, 650/726-5727, www .smharbor.com/pillarpoint.

Supplies: Hi's Tackle, South San Francisco, 650/588-1375, www.histackleboxshop .com; Gus' Discount Tackle, San Francisco, 415/752-6197, www.gusdiscounttackle.com; Liberal Fishing Tackle, 415/391-1947; Berkeley Marina Sports Center, 510/849-2727, www .berkeleymarinasport-fishing.com or www .fishingthebayarea.com; Emeryville Sportfishing, 510/654-6040 or 800/575-9944, www.emeryvillesportfishing.com; Huck Finn Sportfishing, 650/726-7133, www .huckfinnsportfishing.com; Berkeley Bait & Tackle, 510/849-0432; Central Avenue Bait & Tackle, Alameda, 510/522-6731; Grand Street Bait, Alameda, 510/521-2460; Mike's Bait, Oakland, 510/532-8505; Outdoor Pro Shop, Oakland, 510/532-2824, www.out doorproshop.com.

44 FORT POINT

Rating: 5

in San Francisco

Map 7.3, page 383

This pre–Civil War fortification, just under the Golden Gate Bridge on San Francisco Bay, once guarded the entrance to the bay. Today it is an attractive spot where anglers can fish along a seawall or on a nearby pier. Striped bass are sometimes caught at the wall in the evenings in late June. Smelt fishing is often excellent in June as well. In the winter, perch fishing is often good here. Rangers host a program that teaches children to fish crabs.

Facilities, fees: Restrooms are available near the entrance to the fort. Fishing access is free.

Directions: Take U.S. 101 to San Francisco and the southern end of the Golden Gate Bridge in San Francisco to the Marina Boulevard exit. Take the Marina Boulevard exit and drive southeast toward Fisherman's Wharf. Turn left at Marina Green and drive west to the parking area near Fort Point Pier or Fort Point.

Contact: Fort Point Visitors Center, 415/556-1693; Presidio Visitor Center, 415/561-4323; Hi's Tackle, South San Francisco, 650/588-1375, www.histackleboxshop.com.

45 MUNI PIER

Rating: 5

in San Francisco

Map 7.3, page 383

Try for jacksmelt, shiner perch, and flounder at this pier just west of Aquatic Park. While you fish you'll be surrounded by views of San Francisco Bay and Fisherman's Wharf.

Facilities, fees: Restrooms, a snack shop, and a drinking fountain are near the pier. Benches, bleachers, and a grassy area are available for picnicking. Fishing access is free.

Directions: In San Francisco, drive north on Van Ness Avenue to where the road ends.

Contact: Golden Gate National Recreation Area, Fort Mason Visitor Center, 415/345-7500, www.fortmason.org; Hi's Tackle, South San Francisco, 650/588-1375, www.histackle boxshop.com.

46 GOLDEN GATE

Rating: 8

in San Francisco Bay and along the coast

Map 7.3, page 383

Your trip starts with a cruise past national treasures such as Alcatraz and the Golden Gate Bridge, surrounded by Bay Area skylines. It ends with a treasure chest of striped bass, halibut, and rockfish. In between, you get the excitement of dangling a live anchovy or shiner perch while trying to catch a variety of fish. This is called potluck fishing, and it kicks off in June, when the striped bass begin arriving at San Francisco Bay after wintering upstream in the delta. First come the scout fish, the 5- to 10-pound stripers. By the third or fourth week of June, the best fishing of the year in the Bay Area is under way. That is when the striped bass often show up en masse from the delta, halibut show up in large numbers from the ocean, and rockfish can be found at the reefs just west of the Golden Gate Bridge.

One little problem. Some years, the stripers don't show in big-time numbers. You practically need an Ouija Board to predict what will happen every June, July, and August. It's something that can add to the excitement and help stamp fishing as the world's second-greatest mystery.

With moderate outgoing tides during the evenings in late June and mid-July, anchovies become trapped along the South Tower of the Golden Gate Bridge, luring big schools of striped bass that move right in along the pillar to attack the baitfish. Because of National Homeland Security, the feds don't like boats getting too close to the South Tower. So another nearby good spot on outgoing tides is Yellow Bluff. Earlier in the day, during incoming tides, stripers congregate along the rocky reefs west of Alcatraz: the rock pile, Harding Rock, Shag Rock, Arch Rock, and Mel's Reef.

Also consider upbay at the reefs at the Brothers Islands (see the *San Pablo Bay* listing) near the Richmond Bridge.

This is some of the fastest fishing of the year, and greatness is possible. On one trip, I caught and released 13 striped bass ranging 8–22 pounds in two hours. There is often a fantastic limit streak in late June and early July, and then again in late September through October. If you own your own boat, keep your marine radio tuned to Channel 88, where the latest news is usually exchanged.

All saltwater species are tidal-dependent, and that is especially the case with halibut and striped bass. During slow-moving tides, halibut provide the best fishing; during stronger tides, striped bass come to the front. Since tide cycles phase in and out from fast to slow, skippers have quality stripers or halibut to shoot for on most summer days. The only tides to be wary of are minus low tides, which muddy the water and put a damper on all fishing in the bay.

Those minus low tides cause outgoing water to move swiftly, apparently pushing a big school of stripers out the Golden Gate and along the inshore coasts by early July. That is when surf fishing gets good at Thornton Beach and Pacifica, and when the *Happy Hooker, Huck Finn,* and other boats specializing in beach fishing have tremendous results along Pacifica.

By August things slow down, because most of the fish have migrated to the Pacific Ocean. They start returning in September, however, and another good spree for striped bass takes place from mid-September to mid-October. During this time, the fish typically show up during outgoing tides at the reef off Yellow Bluff, upstream of the Golden Gate Bridge on the Marin shore, and during incoming tides at the rock piles west of Alcatraz.

Striped bass are as strong as bulldogs, and when hooked, they give a mercurial sensation at the rod.

Another fish to try for is the shark. Leopard sharks in the 40- to 45-inch class are most common in these waters. The best spots are near the Bay Bridge, west of Angel Island, and just north of Belvedere Point on the east side. Fish on the bottom with midshipmen for bait.

Facilities, fees: Many piers are in the area. See *Contact* for phone numbers for marinas and specific boats. Party boats depart at 7 A.M. daily from San Francisco, Emeryville, Berkeley, San Rafael, Point San Pablo, and Crockett. Skippers ask that those who will be fishing arrive at 6:30 A.M. for an orientation. Bait is provided, and tackle and rod rentals are available on each boat. Party-boat fees are charged per day.

Directions: To Fisherman's Wharf from the Golden Gate Bridge: Take U.S. 101 to the southern end of the Golden Gate Bridge in San Francisco and look for the Marina exit. Take that exit and drive southeast toward Fisherman's Wharf. The boats are at the foot of Jones and Jefferson, along the front row of Fisherman's Wharf, between Castagnola's and Tarantino's restaurants. A parking garage is nearby, at Beach and Jones.

To Fisherman's Wharf from the Bay Bridge: Take I-80 to San Francisco to the exit for Embarcadero/Harrison Street. Take that exit (on the left-hand side of the road) and drive to Harrison Street. Turn right on Harrison Street and drive five blocks to the Embarcadero. Turn left on the Embarcadero and drive past the piers on the right to Bay Street. Continue on the Embarcadero to Fisherman's Wharf and the parking garages.

To the Berkeley Marina: Take I-80 to Berkeley and the exit for University Avenue West/Berkeley Marina. Take that exit and drive west to a T intersection. Turn left for the pier and bait shop. Turn right for the boat ramp.

To the Emeryville Marina: Take I-80 to Emeryville and the exit for Powell Street. Take that exit west to Powell Street. Drive west on Powell Street for 0.75 mile to the parking area, marina, and bait shop, at the end of the road.

Contact: For specific boats:
• San Francisco: *Bass-Tub,* 415/456-9055, www.basstub.net; *Chucky's Pride,* 415/564-5515.
• Berkeley: Berkeley Charter Boats, 510/849-

3333, www.berkeleycharterboats.com; *Golden Eye 2000,* 510/610-0888; *Happy Hooker,* 510/223-5388.
• Emeryville: Emeryville Sportfishing, 510/654-6040 or 800/575-9944, www.emeryvillesportsfishing.com.
• Pittsburg: *Fin Addict,* 209/367-4665, www.finaddictsportfishing.com.
• Point San Pablo: Fury Sportfishing, 916/920-8487, www.furysportfishing.com.
• San Rafael: Loch Lomond Live Bait, San Rafael, 415/456-0321; Executive Fishing Charters, 415/460-9773, www.executivefishingcharters.com.

Marinas: Berkeley Marina Sports Center, 510/849-2727, www.berkeleymarinasportfishing.com; Marina Bay Yacht Harbor, Richmond, 510/236-1013; Emeryville Marina, 510/654-3716, www.emeryvillemarina.com; Caruso's, Sausalito, 415/332-1015; Loch Lomond Marina, San Rafael, 415/454-7228; Oyster Point Marina, South San Francisco, 650/871-7344.

Supplies: Hi's Tackle, South San Francisco, 650/588-1375, www.histackleboxshop.com; Emeryville Sportfishing, 510/654-6040 or 800/575-9944, www.emeryvillesportfishing.com; Berkeley Marina Sports Center, 510/849-2727, www.berkeleymarinasport-fishing.com; Loch Lomond Live Bait, San Rafael, 415/456-0321.

47 PIER SEVEN

Rating: 3

in San Francisco

Map 7.3, page 383

At the far end, anglers will find benches and a fishing area. It's a long shot for striped bass in summer.

Facilities, fees: No facilities are available. Fishing access is free.

Directions: In San Francisco, take Broadway east to where it ends at the pier.

Contact: Port of San Francisco, Public Affairs, 415/274-0400.

48 AGUA VISTA PIER

Rating: 4

in San Francisco
Map 7.3, page 383

The most commonly caught fish at this spot are jacksmelt (in the spring) and shiner perch (in the summer). It is often a great spot to catch live bait.

Facilities, fees: Picnic tables are at this 1,000-square-foot pier. The adjoining Mission Rock Resort has restrooms, a public phone, a bait shop, and a restaurant. Fishing access is free.

Directions: In San Francisco, drive north on 3rd Street to the intersection with Terry Francois Boulevard (formerly China Basin Street).

Contact: Port of San Francisco, Public Affairs, 415/274-0400; Hi's Tackle, South San Francisco, 650/588-1375, www.histacklebox shop.com.

49 WARM WATER COVE PIER

Rating: 6

in San Francisco
Map 7.3, page 383

With its industrial setting adjacent to a power-plant outfall, Warm Water Cove sure doesn't look like much. However, the warm water from the outfall attracts a wide variety of fish throughout the year, making this place popular with local anglers. The perch fishing can be outstanding in the winter from late November through January. This can be a good spot for schoolie-size striped bass on pile worms for bait.

Facilities, fees: A small T-shaped pier, benches, and a chemical toilet are provided. Fishing access is free.

Directions: In San Francisco, drive north on 3rd Street, turn right (east) on 24th Street, and proceed two blocks to the pier.

Contact: Port of San Francisco, Public Affairs, 415/274-0400; Hi's Tackle, South San Francisco, 650/588-1375, www.histacklebox shop.com.

50 CANDLESTICK POINT

Rating: 6

in San Francisco
Map 7.3, page 383

Fish only high and outgoing tides here, when striped bass and halibut make appearances on the flats. Leopard shark and flounder are common in the winter. And the lucky rod might hook a sturgeon, best usually just after the top of the tide. That is when ol' diamond-back roams the shallows looking for food. I've heard of perch in the winter and jacksmelt in the spring being caught.

During low tides, mud flats are often exposed. Afternoons can be very windy, especially in June and July.

Facilities, fees: Benches are available on two piers. Restrooms and picnic facilities shielded by windbreaks are available nearby. Fishing access is free. There's no fee if parking outside the state recreation area. A parking fee is charged at a kiosk when entering the parking area for the SRA.

Directions: From San Francisco: Take U.S. 101 south to the 3rd Street exit. Drive to the stop sign, turn left, drive to the Monster Park frontage road, and continue two miles to the state park entrance, on the right. Turn right and drive a short distance to the Candlestick Point Recreation Area.

Note: The main day-use parking lot and Last Port parking area are closed on Thursday and Friday. Event parking fees are charged on San Francisco 49ers home game days.

From the peninsula: Take U.S. 101 north to the Monster Park exit (historically known as the Candlestick Point exit). Bear right and drive three miles to the state park entrance, on the right. Turn right and drive a short distance to the Candlestick Point Recreation Area (on the State Parks closure list).

Contact: Candlestick Point State Recreation Area, Ranger Station, 415/671-0145, www .parks.ca.gov; Oyster Point Bait, 650/589-3474.

51 SOUTH SAN FRANCISCO BAY

Rating: 7

from the Bay Bridge to Alviso

Map 7.3, page 383

The South Bay is not really a bay at all, but an estuary that experiences huge changes in water temperature and salinity levels throughout the year. Key factors are rain and the resulting storm runoff that enters the bay. It can provide just the right freshwater/saltwater mix during the spring, and the result is huge bumper crops of grass shrimp, the favorite food of most fish in the South Bay, especially perch and sturgeon.

When heavy rains hit the South Bay, the first thing to look for is an upturn in the number of perch and sturgeon. Perch are common during good-moving tides along rocky areas (such as the cement-block breakwater at Coyote Point), near pilings (at the Dumbarton and San Mateo Bridges and adjacent to San Francisco and Oakland international airports), and in sloughs that experience a good tidal flush (such as Burlingame's Showboat Slough and the Alameda Estuary). What to use for bait? Live grass shrimp, of course.

The same bait works well for sturgeon, although it also attracts pesky bullheads and small sharks. After decent rains, the areas in the main channel just south of the San Mateo Bridge and in the vicinity of the Dumbarton Train Bridge are often excellent fishing spots. After very heavy rains, big sturgeon can be found farther south along the PG&E towers. Another option is to wait for herring spawns in late December and January, then anchor off Candlestick Point or Alameda and use herring eggs (during a spawn) or whole herring for bait. Some of the best sturgeon scores have been recorded in these areas.

School-sized striped bass sometimes arrive in mid-March and early April in the vicinity of Coyote Point, where they can be taken by trolling white, one-ounce Hair Raisers during high tides. They can also show near the flats off Candlestick Point and at the nearby Brisbane Tubes, and also off the Alameda Rock Wall in June during high and incoming tides and, even more rarely, again in September. The higher the rainfall during the previous winter, the better the chance of getting a bite.

The same formula holds for excellent runs of jacksmelt in the spring, primarily from mid-February through early April. After decent winter rains, head to the western side of the South Bay near Burlingame's Fisherman's Park for the best fishing, using a chunk of pile worm under a big float. Timing is important: be there at the top of the tide, then focus on the first two hours of the outgoing tide, when it will take your float out to deeper points.

Although you'll need a boat, timing, technique, persistence, and the willingness to keep a constant vigil, the South Bay can still provide the stuff of magic. This is one place where you'll have to tailor your schedule to the demands of the fish. Otherwise, you might as well buy a ticket for a slow boat to China.

Directions: To Oyster Point Marina: Take U.S. 101 to South San Francisco and the exit for Oyster Point Boulevard. Take that exit and drive east on Oyster Point Boulevard to Marine Boulevard. Turn right and drive to a sign indicating the public boat ramp.

To the Port of Redwood City: Take U.S. 101 to Redwood City and exit for Seaport Boulevard–Woodside Road. Take that exit and drive east on Seaport Boulevard (toward the bay) to Chesapeake Street. Turn left and drive to the launching area sign, on your right.

Facilities, fees: No party boats are available from South Bay harbors, but boats from Berkeley, Emeryville, and San Francisco occasionally fish the South Bay when sturgeon fishing is best in the winter, and for halibut along the Alameda Rock Wall in May and June.

Piers include Oyster Point, Coyote Point, San Mateo Pier, Dumbarton Piers (from Newark), and Alameda Estuary. Access to piers is free.

Contact: Fish and Wildlife Service, San Francisco Bay Wildlife Refuge, 510/792-0222.

Marinas: Oyster Point Marina, South San Francisco, 650/871-7344, www.smharbor.com/oysterpoint; Coyote Point Marina, 650/573-2594; Port of Redwood City Marina, 650/306-4150; San Leandro Marina, 510/577-3488, www.sanleandro.org.

Supplies: Oyster Point Bait, 650/589-3474; Central Bait, Alameda, 510/522-6731.

52 PACIFICA PIER

Rating: 6

in Pacifica
Map 7.3, page 383

At times, Pacifica Pier can seem like the best fishing pier on the Pacific Coast. It's a good spot for crabbing in the winter. And in some summer months, Pacifica Pier provides a rare chance to catch salmon using an anchovy under a pier bobber. This is the only Bay Area pier that allows direct access to ocean fishing. The shoreline gets brief flurries of striped bass when they corral schools of anchovies. From the beaches (Linda Mar, Rockaway, Manor, Center Hole), cast chromed jigs (such as Krocodile, Hopkins, or Miki); from the rocks (Mori Point, Mussel Rock, Pedro Point), cast the large floating plugs known as Pencil Poppers. Fishing for striped bass is always best here at the turn of the tide, especially during the first two hours of an incoming tide.

A few smarts are required, but nothing that can't be learned quickly. The standard rigging is the trolley rig, named after a fishing system unique to Pacifica Pier. You start with a four- to eight-ounce pier sinker (it looks like a four-legged spider), tie it to your line, then make a short underhand cast; the sinker will grab the bottom and hold tight, despite the ocean surge. Attach a pier bobber, which is about the size of an apple, to the line with a snap swivel along with six feet of leader and a size 5/0 hook. Hook a whole anchovy, then let the bobber and bait "trolley" down the line to the water. That giant bobber will float on the surface with the anchovy below it while you wait for the thing

to get tugged under, perhaps by a giant salmon. When the pier is full of anglers doing this, the fishing actually improves, because all those anchovies in the water are like a chum line, drawing the fish right in.

Everything seems perfect for such a scene to unfold from mid-June through August, when water temperatures are ideal for salmon and the first migrating anchovies arrive. The water is often tinted green like a champagne bottle, a color my Pacifica fieldscout and pal Jim Klinger claims can herald the best prospects, especially compared to the murky browns of winter. A vibrant essence of life seems to fill the water, with all the birds, the baitfish, and the first salmon of the year.

Most people at the pier help their neighbors. But just like in the big city, there are exceptions, as illustrated by a story told by Klinger:

"One day, this guy was just plain making life miserable for everyone around him. He was bumping into people, hitting people with his rod, then when things finally settled down and we got back to fishing, his bobber goes bye-bye. We knew he had a huge fish on. Sure enough, he started to fight it, reeling, his rod doubled over, but then he got all screwed up, and before long, his line started getting tangled with several others. He looks over at us and asks, 'What do I do now?' And the guy next to him says, almost automatically, 'Cut your line.' So the guy pulls out his knife, cuts his line, and proceeds to lose one of the biggest salmon you could dream of."

Facilities, fees: Drinking fountains, restrooms, benches, lighting, and fish-cleaning facilities are provided. There's also a snack shop. Fishing access is free.

Directions: From San Francisco, take Highway 280 south to Daly City and Highway 1. Bear right on Highway 1 and continue to Pacifica and the Paloma Avenue exit. Take the Paloma Avenue exit and drive west to Beach Boulevard. Turn left (south) on Beach Boulevard and drive to the pier at Sharp Park.

Contact: Pacifica Pier, www.pacificapier

.com; Chit Chat Coffee Shop, 650/359-7025; The New Coastside No. 2 Bait & Tackle, 650/359-9790; The Rusty Hook, 650/355-8303; Pacifica Parks, Beaches, and Recreation, 650/738-7381, www.cityofpacifica.org.

53 PACIFICA

Rating: 7
from Devils Slide to Mussel Rock
Map 7.3, page 383

During a magical five-week period from the last week of June through July, and into the first week of August, some of the best fishing in the United States can often be had in the inshore waters off Pacifica. The rocky coast is made up of a series of small bays where striped bass can corral schools of anchovies, pinning them against the back of the surf line. Salmon often move in as well, rounding up the anchovies just a mile offshore. Want more? Halibut are commonly found off the sandy flats here, especially in the Devils Slide area.

The only problem is that sometimes there are just too many fish, namely kingfish. Also known as white croaker, kingfish can be so abundant that they disrupt drift-moochers who are trying to catch salmon.

Wind and the resulting ocean surge determine how productive these waters will be. When the wind is up and the waves are high, the motion disturbs the ocean bottom, causing the anchovies to move offshore. When that happens, the inshore striper and salmon fishery goes belly up. But if the wind is down and there is no ocean surge, the anchovies will move right in, bringing large marauding schools of striped bass and salmon with them.

Salmon fishing can be outstanding too, but some years it just doesn't happen. According to my logbook, salmon often show up just off Pedro Point in mid-March, then disappear until July, when they return about a mile offshore from the Pacifica Pier. When this happens, there can be so many boats on the water that together they resemble a flotilla.

When the striped bass show up, and some years they don't, the live-bait boats head out from Berkeley and Emeryville and chum the stripers into a frenzy. Onboard anglers using live anchovies for bait will catch one striper after another until reaching their limits. These big boats back into the surf line near Mussel Rock or in Linda Mar Bay, then owners of small boats will head into the same general area and either use live bait (available at Fisherman's Wharf in San Francisco, Berkeley, and Emeryville) or cast Hair Raisers. Small boats should stay clear of the surf zone, where it is very easy to capsize and drown. Meanwhile, surf casters on the beach send casts out to the fish, using chrome Hopkins, Krocodile, or Miki jigs. There are also runs of striped bass independent of those started by the chumming, usually in late June at Center Hole (north of Mussel Rock), then in July off the Manor Apartments (at the north end of town) and Rockaway Beach. In August, the fishing is better from the rocks at Mori Point; use large Pencil Poppers. The best fishing always occurs at high tide.

Since most of the fishing here takes place from the end of June through early August, what should you do the rest of the year? Maybe crab a little at Pacifica Pier in the winter, try for a perch at Linda Mar Bay in the spring, or go rockfishing off Pedro Point in the fall—always dreaming of those few magical weeks in the summer.

Facilities, fees: There is no boat ramp in Pacifica. Some hardy souls hand-launch small boats through the surf at the southern end of Linda Mar Bay. The nearest boat ramp is at Pillar Point Harbor at Princeton, in Half Moon Bay. Beach and pier access is free. Partyboat fees are charged per day.

Directions: To Pacifica Pier: Take Highway 1 to Pacifica and the exit for Paloma Avenue. Take the Paloma Avenue exit and drive west to Beach Boulevard. Turn left (south) on Beach Boulevard and drive to the pier at Sharp Park.

Contact: Pacifica Pier, www.pacificapier.com;

Chit Chat Coffee Shop, 650/359-7025; The New Coastside No. 2 Bait & Tackle, 650/359-9790; The Rusty Hook, 650/355-8303.

The following is contact information for specific boats.

Berkeley: Berkeley Charter Boats, 510/849-3333, www.berkeleycharterboats.com; Golden Eye 2000, 510/610-0888; Happy Hooker Sportfishing, 510/223-5388 or 510/222-5279.

Emeryville: Emeryville Sportfishing, 510/654-6040 or 800/575-9944, www.emery villesportsfishing.com.

Point San Pablo: Fury Sportfishing, 916/920-8487, www.furysportfishing.com.

Half Moon Bay: Half Moon Bay Sportfishing, 650/738-3377, www.hmbfishing.com; Huck Finn Sportfishing, 650/726-7133, www .huckfinnsportfishing.com.

54 HALF MOON BAY

Rating: 8

from Devils Slide to Pigeon Point

Map 7.3, page 383

Half Moon Bay is often a quality act. So is the fishing.

The most consistent results are gained from rockfishing at the Deep Reef (12 miles southwest of the harbor), and off Pescadero and Pigeon Point (to the south) and Devils Slide and Pedro Point (to the north).

Rockfish are coming back in decent numbers and have increased in size as well. With protections ordered against commercial fishing, in time this fishery could come all the way back. Deep-sea fishing for rockfish is also good off Montara, San Gregorio, and Bean Hollow. In the fall, shallow-water rockfishing can be exceptional, often just 30–50 feet deep. I like casting three-ounce Point Wilson Darts, then retrieving over the top of the reefs. There can be sensational shallow-water fishing at the shallow reefs between San Gregorio and Pigeon Point. Occasionally, some big halibut are caught by accident when fishing the sandy transition zone edging up to the reef.

Not as predictable are the salmon. Because there's no salmon stream near Half Moon Bay, boaters must try to intercept passing fish. There are, however, usually three periods during which success can be great. The first is in April, when salmon often school in the vicinity of the Deep Reef. The next is in late June and early July, when salmon are often found at the Southeast Reef (which is marked by three buoys, adjacent to the Miramar Restaurant), Martin's Beach (to the south), or Pedro Point (to the nearby north). After a lull, another large batch of small salmon, 20- to 24-inchers, show up in early August off the far buoy northwest of Pillar Point. At other times, ranging from March through September, there is usually a sprinkling of salmon in the area.

The biggest problem with early-season salmon is the wind. When I lived here, I remember one May when there were small-craft warnings posted 28 of 31 days, and those three days that were fishable in my boat, I was booked on a trip.

For the owner of a small boat, it can be ideal when the fish are schooling. During the week, when it's not nearly as crowded, you can launch at 5:30 P.M., cruise over to the fishing grounds, limit out between 6 and 8 P.M., and be back at the ramp by nightfall.

Perch fishing along the beach just south of the Princeton Jetty is excellent during the first two hours of an incoming tide, just after a good low tide has bottomed out. People here employ a system using plastic grubs with a sliding-sinker rigging. Shoreliners can try the Princeton Jetty, where they'll get lots of snags but a decent number of fish. For the best results, fish the incoming tide with bait just after low water. Another possibility is a beach run of striped bass during the summer. Although now rare, this event does occur, usually during the second week of June, then on and off in July—and most commonly at Venice Beach.

Note that fishing regulations often change here from year to year, for seasons, depth restrictions, bag limits, size limits, and even annual quotas for the fleet. Always check current regulations with Fish and Game or with a marina or party-boat operator before planning a trip. The Marine Protection Act is the ultimate trump card in shutting us out from traditional fishing spots.

Directions: From San Francisco: Take I-280 south to Daly City and the junction with Highway 1. Bear right (south) on Highway 1, drive through Pacifica, over Devil's Slide, and continue five miles to Princeton. Turn right, drive 0.25 mile, and then turn left into Pillar Point Harbor.

From the East Bay or peninsula: Drive west on Highway 92 into Half Moon Bay and the junction with Highway 1. Turn north and drive five miles to Princeton. Turn left, drive 0.25 mile, and turn left into Pillar Point Harbor.

Facilities, fees: A boat ramp is at Pillar Point Harbor at Princeton. A fee is charged for launching. The Pillar Point Pier offers very limited success.

Party boats can be arranged through Huck Finn Sportfishing and Riptide. Party-boat fees are charged per day.

Contact: Pillar Point Harbor, 650/726-5727, www.smharbor.com/pillarpoint/; Half Moon Bay Sportfishing, 650/728-3377, www.hmbfishing.com; Huck Finn Sportfishing, 650/726-7133, www.huckfinnsportfishing.com; Riptide Sportfishing, 650/728-8433, www.riptide.net; Hilltop Bait, Tackle & Deli, 650/560-9544.

55 PILLAR POINT JETTY

Rating: 3
in Princeton
Map 7.3, page 383

The outer jetty rims Pillar Point Harbor. It provides prospects for a variety of rockfish, sea trout, and some perch. Snags are a problem. At low tides, some try to poke-pole the rocks at the outer end of the jetty. Others fish for halibut right at the end of the jetty at the jaws of the harbor entrance. Timing is a key: the halibut show up here only during the first two

hours of the outgoing tide after a significant high tide, usually in May, June, and early July. In July, anchovies often move right inside the harbor. Striped bass can follow them right in, creating a wild scene. You have to be lucky to see this, then pounce. It usually lasts for 20 or 30 minutes, no more.

Facilities, fees: Restrooms, a drinking fountain, a restaurant, a snack bar, and a bait shop where tackle is sold are available. The pier is open 24 hours daily. Fishing access is free.

Directions: From Pacifica, take Highway 1 south until you reach the second light at Princeton and Capistrano Road (signed "Harbor"). Turn right (west) and drive a short distance to the marina access road, on the left, to buy bait.

Contact: Huck Finn Sportfishing, 650/726-7133, www.huckfinnsportfishing.com; Half Moon Bay Sportfishing, 650/738-3377, www.hmbfishing.com.

56 SAN GREGORIO CREEK

Rating: 2
south of Half Moon Bay
Map 7.3, page 383

A meager steelhead run still returns to little San Gregorio Creek, but the fish are hard-pressed to make it upstream. Anglers have an even more difficult task trying to intercept them.

Runs can vary in size from year to year, but the conditions that attract them do not change. The season starts with heavy rains in December and early January; then during high tides from around January 10 to mid-February, pods of steelhead shoot out of the river, head under the Highway 1 Bridge, and move eastward toward their spawning grounds. Fishing is allowed only on Wednesdays and weekends, so timing becomes tricky. Most steelhead are caught in the 150 yards upstream of the Highway 1 bridge by anglers using night crawlers or roe for bait. Occasionally, small trout are caught as well. Be sure to check regulations prior to fishing.

If nothing is doing, Pescadero Creek, nearby

to the south, provides an alternative and has larger runs of fish.

Note: Always check DFG regulations before fishing anywhere for steelhead. This fishery is subject to closures. A published account that this stream has been selected for reintroduction of coho salmon by the DFG is incorrect.

Facilities, fees: No facilities are available. Fishing is allowed east of the bridge. Fishing access is free.

Directions: From Half Moon Bay, take Highway 1 south for 14 miles to San Gregorio Bridge. Creek access is just to the east of San Gregorio Beach. You can park on the east side of the highway.

Contact: Pescadero State Beach, 650/879-2170, www.parks.ca.gov; Hilltop Grocery Bait, Tackle & Deli, Half Moon Bay, 650/560-9544.

57 PESCADERO CREEK

Rating: 4

south of Half Moon Bay

Map 7.3, page 383

Most of the steelhead caught here are tricked just upstream of the Highway 1 bridge in the lagoon. It happens right at sunrise and at dusk, when a high tide and good river flows out to sea allow pods of steelhead to enter the stream.

Those circumstances are rarely aligned, and since fishing is permitted only on Wednesdays and weekends, timing becomes the most difficult aspect of the trip. But it can happen. This stream still attracts steelhead in the 15-pound class, though 4- to 8-pounders are average, along with a fair number of juvenile steelhead that locals call rainbow trout.

The steelhead are difficult to catch. They're usually taken by anglers wading in the lagoon and bait fishing with roe or night crawlers in the nearly still flows. It can take remarkable persistence, staring at your line where it enters the water, waiting for any movement—a sign that a fish is moving off with the bait.

Once hooked, the steelhead are outstanding fighters, both jumping and streaking off on runs. Although catching one has become a rare event, they remain the fightingest fish in the Bay Area. Be sure to check regulations prior to fishing.

I've watched this river for years, and right under the DFG's nose, the lagoon near the bridge is being filled in with mud. I was told that is because when the new Highway 1 bridge was built, they didn't completely remove an old base for the temporary dam, so it blocks the downstream flow of silt to the ocean. In addition, farmers put in diversions and temporary dams upstream that reduce stream flows and can raise havoc with steelhead reaching upstream spawning grounds.

If you decide to wait for a tremendous strike, call the Pescadero Store. I hear they are looking for a cigar-store Indian.

Note: Always check DFG regulations before fishing anywhere for steelhead. In addition, this fishery is subject to closures.

Facilities, fees: No facilities are available. Fishing is allowed east of the bridge. Fishing access is free.

Directions: Take Highway 92 west to Half Moon Bay and the junction with Highway 1. Turn south on Highway 1 and drive 17 miles to Pescadero Road. Turn left and drive about 200 yards to an unsigned dirt road on the left. Turn left and drive a short distance to a dirt parking lot and trailhead. Walk a short distance to the creek and lagoon.

Contact: Pescadero State Beach, 650/879-2170, www.parks.ca.gov; Hilltop Grocery Bait, Tackle & Deli, Half Moon Bay, 650/560-9544.

58 ARASTRADERO LAKE

Rating: 3

near Palo Alto in the peninsula foothills

Map 7.3, page 383

A 20-minute hike through pretty foothill country gets you to this classic bass pond, part of a 600-acre preserve. Several good trails weave their way through the area, and hikers share them with squirrels, chipmunks, and hawks.

The pond is circled by tules, and there are few openings along the shoreline where anglers can cast. (You'll see fishing line snarled on branches.) Some decent-sized bass live in these waters, but they are hard to catch.

One royal pain in the rear end is the rule laid down by the Palo Alto Recreation Department banning all rafts and float tubes from the water. This is a perfect setting to fish from a float tube, which would allow fly fishers with poppers to send casts along the tule-lined shore. But no, that is forbidden.

Facilities, fees: A few marked hiking trails lead through the area. Fishing access is free.

Directions: Take I-280 to Palo Alto and the exit for Page Mill Road. Take that exit and drive west on Page Mill Road for about one mile to Arastradero Road. Turn right on Arastradero Road and drive 1.5 miles to the signed parking lot on the right. Park and hike 20 minutes to the lake.

Contact: Parks, Recreation, & Open Spaces Division, 650/496-6962, www.cityofpaloalto.org; Foothills Park, 650/329-2423.

59 BORONDA LAKE

Rating: 2

near Palo Alto in Foothills Park
Map 7.3, page 383

After seeing how a park district got things right at Shadow Cliffs Lake, turn to Boronda Lake, where the government botched a good idea. Boronda Lake was originally set in a deep canyon, and after being dammed, it could have provided fantastic habitat for bass, bluegill, sunfish, and catfish.

Instead, the bureaucrats decided to fill in the canyon with dirt and cap it, making the lake very shallow. Sunlight can penetrate to the bottom, raising water temperatures, fostering intense weed and algae growth, and

ruining all chances for a decent fishery. To top it off, only Palo Alto residents and their guests are allowed to visit.

A few meager fish plants have been attempted. What you get are a few dinker-sized bass and a scattering of sunfish. That and a lot of weeds. This is hard evidence for the argument that fishery-habitat decisions should be taken out of the hands of local bureaucrats and given over to fishery biologists, who could still turn this place around. If that doesn't happen, it's hopeless.

Facilities, fees: A parking area, drinking water, picnic tables, and restrooms are available at the park, which is open to Palo Alto residents only. A small boat dock is also provided; only nonmotorized boats are allowed. Swimming and wading are prohibited. An entrance fee is charged.

Directions: Take I-280 to Palo Alto and the exit for Page Mill Road. Drive west on Page Mill Road (very curvy) for 2.7 miles to the park entrance, on the right. Proof of Palo Alto residency is required.

Contact: Parks, Recreation, & Open Spaces Division, 650/496-6962, www.cityofpaloalto.org; Foothills Park, 650/329-2423.

60 STEVENS CREEK RESERVOIR

Rating: 5

near Cupertino
Map 7.3, page 383

When full, Stevens Creek is quite pretty, covering 95 acres. A series of heavy rains can fill the reservoir quickly, and when that happens, Fish and Game stocks it with rainbow trout in the foot-long class. Stocks are rarely scheduled in advance, but when they happen, Stevens Creek can become a respectable prospect. Keep tabs on this place in late winter and early spring. The stocks usually occur in late February or March.

In late summer, the place can just about go dry. It is capable of holding bass, sunfish, and catfish, but fluctuating water levels have reduced the spawning success and the population to just about zilch.

Note: All boats must be inspected and certified free of mussels prior to launching at this lake.

Facilities, fees: This reservoir is in a county park, so there are full facilities available, such as parking, restrooms, picnic areas, hiking trails, and a launch ramp. Fees are charged for parking and access.

Directions: Take I-280 to the exit for Foothill Boulevard. Take that exit and drive south for four miles on Foothill Boulevard (which becomes Stevens Canyon Road) to the reservoir.

Contact: Stevens Creek County Park, 408/867-3654; Santa Clara County Parks and Recreation, 408/355-2255, www.parkhere.org.

61 LEXINGTON RESERVOIR

Rating: 8
near Los Gatos in the Santa Cruz foothills
Map 7.3, page 383

When Lexington fills, it creates a beautiful lake that covers over 450 acres, a place with much potential. A few insiders who know of it take advantage of the outstanding bass fishing in the spring. From late February through April, you can get an excellent bite on spinnerbaits and shad-type lures along the submerged trees and brush.

When it is full, the survival rate of planted rainbow trout is very high, making for good trolling (often near the dam) and shoreline fishing (in the coves). The DFG stocks 12,000 10- to 12-inch rainbow trout, usually twice a month from March through Memorial Day.

A reasonably skilled bass angler with a boat and electric motor, heading out on a spring morning, can have some excellent days at Lexington. That's pretty startling when you consider the millions of people within close range of the reservoir.

Note: All boats must be inspected and certified free of mussels prior to launching at this lake.

Facilities, fees: Parking, picnic areas, vault toilets, and a boat ramp are available. Fees are charged for day-use and boat launching. No powerboats are allowed, but electric motors are permitted.

Directions: From San Jose: Take Highway 17 to the exit for Bear Creek Road. Take that exit, bear right, cross over the freeway, and re-enter Highway 17 and drive a short distance to the exit for Alma Bridge Road. Take that exit and drive east for 1.5 miles (across the Lexington Dam). The boat ramp is near the dam. Parking is available just east of the dam, in Lexington Reservoir County Park.

From Santa Cruz: Take Highway 17 to the exit for Alma Bridge Road. Take that exit and drive east for 1.5 miles (across the Lexington Dam). The boat ramp is near the dam. Parking is available just east of the dam, in Lexington Reservoir County Park.

Contact: Lexington Reservoir, 408/356-2729; Santa Clara County Parks and Recreation, 408/355-2255, www.parkhere.org.

62 LOCH LOMOND RESERVOIR

Rating: 7
near Ben Lomond in the Santa Cruz Mountains
Map 7.3, page 383

Getting into heaven is supposed to be a little more difficult than this.

Loch Lomond is a gorgeous recreation area set in a forested canyon in the Santa Cruz Mountains. It provides outstanding hiking, low-speed boating (with rentals available), and good fishing for bass, bluegill, and trout.

It is just far enough away for most that every trip here is something special. The access route to the lake entrance, though well signed, can still confuse some newcomers. And when you first arrive at the entrance kiosk, the lake is out of sight, and you might even say, "So, what's the big deal?" In minutes, however, you will find out. The access road drops down to the canyon floor, and suddenly, the lake comes into view.

Redwoods frame the lake. This is a second-growth forest that has not only taken hold, but dominates the surrounding landscape. Huckleberry forms thick stands in the coves along the shoreline.

The lake, created when a dam was placed on Newell Creek, sits in a long, narrow canyon surrounded by forest in the Santa Cruz Mountains. Boating and trout fishing can be exceptionally good, and this is one of the top day-trip destinations for Bay Area anglers.

Loch Lomond is one of the best bass lakes in the Bay Area's nine counties, with good numbers of two- and three-pound bass, which are best caught during an early-morning bite in spring for those using white spinnerbaits and Senkos. There are also some monsters in this lake. Nobody gets one by accident. Use swimbaits, like a Huddleston or a Castaic Trout, and be out early, late, when the wind is up, or in rain—never at midday on pretty, blue-sky days.

The future of trout fishing here is now a question mark. This was one of the lakes that got the kibosh from the DFG in the infamous lawsuit brought by the Citizens of Biological Diversity. Chief Ranger Scot Lang said he hopes Loch Lomond will be restored to the DFG's planting list—and soon.

Many years, the trout fishing is good, even from holdovers in the 14- to 18-inch class from past year's plants. In addition, the lake often has great bluegill fishing on summer evenings, especially fly-fishing with woolly worms or bait-dunking a worm under a bobber in sheltered, warm coves.

Some people just like fishing for trout from shore and with bait; they'll catch a few and enjoy the scenery. That's how the biggest fish ever caught in the lake was hooked, by accident—a 32-pound catfish.

The one thing this place lacks is trophy-sized trout, but that is made up for somewhat by a good bass bite in the very early morning

hours and right at dusk. Not many people know about the bass at Loch Lomond, and fewer ever dream of throwing a bass plug out for a wild-card try. If you hit it right on summer evenings, you may also find tons of bluegill that are often eager to hit a woolly-worm fly.

Those contraptions that look like lunar landing vehicles are actually solar-powered aerators and water circulation devices that keep the lake oxygenated and weed-free.

Trolling for trout is often quite good here. Just keep your boat about 30 yards offshore, paralleling the shoreline. One day my friend Dave "Gus" Zimmer and his dad, Ed, caught a few trout at Loch Lomond, landed the boat at the island, and barbecued them right then and there. "Magic stuff," Hank reminisces.

Boating rules here have changed dramatically. Boats are subject to a 14-day quarantine before they are allowed to launch. Unless you keep a boat at the lake, you are better off renting a boat from the marina.

Facilities, fees: Restrooms, parking, picnic tables, a tackle shop, boat rentals, and a boat launch are available. No gas motors are allowed; powerboats and sailboats are not permitted. Unfortunately, swimming, wading, windsurfing, and other water-contact sports are not allowed.

Loch Lomond opens for the year on March 1, sunrise to sunset, seven days a week; from Labor Day to mid-October, the lake is open on weekends only, and closes in winter. A day-use fee is charged. There is a fee for boat launching.

Directions: From San Jose: Take Highway 17 south to Scotts Valley and the Mount Hermon Road exit. Take that exit and drive west for 3.5 miles to Graham Hill Road. Turn left and head south for 0.5 mile to East Zayante Road. Turn left and drive 1.5 miles to West Drive. Turn left and drive 0.75 mile to Sequoia Drive. Turn right at Sequoia Drive and continue to the park entrance. This route is very well signed.

From Santa Cruz: Take Highway 1 to Highway 9. Turn north on Highway 9 and drive to Felton and Graham Hill Road. Turn right and drive (across the railroad tracks) to East Zayante Road. Turn right and drive 2.5 miles to Lompico Road. Turn left and drive 1.5 miles to West Drive. Turn left and drive 0.75 mile to Sequoia Drive. Turn right and continue to the park entrance. Route is well-signed.

Contact: Loch Lomond Reservoir, 831/420-5320, www.cityofsantacruz.com (click on Water, then Recreation); Santa Cruz Mountains Interactive Online Guide, www.hwy9 .com/site/info/center.html.

63 CAMPBELL PERCOLATION PONDS

Rating: 5

in Los Gatos Creek County Park
Map 7.4, page 384

Just five acres in all, this dot of water can provide some surprisingly good trout fishing during the winter and spring. The fish aren't big, but stocks from the DFG are decent (16,000 rainbow trout in the 10- to 12-inch class annually) and provide good opportunities for shoreliners. The percolation ponds are closed indefinitely to all boating.

It becomes critical to track the DFG's stocking schedule for the Campbell Percolation Ponds. Because the lake is so small, it reacts quickly and strongly to stocks.

Facilities, fees: Restrooms, water, parking, and a grassy picnic area are available. A day-use fee is charged from Memorial Day to Labor Day.

Directions: Take Highway 17 to Campbell and the Camden Avenue/San Tomas exit. Take that exit and drive west on San Tomas Expressway to the exit for Winchester Boulevard. Take Winchester South exit and drive to Hacienda. Turn left on Hacienda and drive to Dell Avenue. Turn left and drive a short distance to the park entrance.

Contact: Los Gatos Creek County Park, ranger station, 408/356-2729; Santa Clara County Parks and Recreation, 408/355-2255, www.parkhere.org.

64 LAKE CUNNINGHAM

Rating: 4

in San Jose
Map 7.4, page 384

Trout fishing in an urban setting? It doesn't get much more urban than this.

Lake Cunningham, covering 50 acres, is adjacent to the Raging Waters water-slide park. If you bring the kids along and the fish don't bite, you can always salvage the day by using the water slide as an insurance policy. And that might be necessary, because the fishing can go down the tubes. However, prospects are decent after DFG trout plants from late winter through spring. Typically, the lake is stocked every other week with 10- to 12-inch rainbow trout. Channel catfish are stocked in summer months.

Boats to 16 feet in length (no gas engines) are allowed here, but float tubes are not.

Facilities, fees: This is a regional park and has full facilities, including restrooms, water, and parking. A daily parking fee is charged in summer and during the weekends in the off-season.

Directions: From San Jose, drive south on U.S. 101 to the Tully Road East exit. Take that exit and drive east on Tully Road. After the intersection with Capitol Expressway, look for the park entrance on the left, and follow the signs to the lake.

Contact: Lake Cunningham Park Headquarters, 408/794-7577.

65 COTTONWOOD LAKE

Rating: 2

in San Jose
Map 7.4, page 384

The definition of the word "lake" has been stretched a bit here. The lake is more like a pond, eight acres in all, but it is pretty. However, Cottonwood Lake is closed indefinitely to all boating. The DFG stopped stocking Cottonwood, and if they don't start again, there is no reason to fish here, or for this lake to make it in the next edition of this book.

Access to the city park where the lake is located is quite easy, a short hop off U.S. 101. There are pleasant picnic sites and six miles of bike trails.

Facilities, fees: This lake is in a county park and has full facilities, including restrooms, water, parking, and picnic areas. A day-use fee is charged.

Directions: From San Jose, take U.S. 101 south to the Hellyer exit. Take that exit west and drive a short distance to the entrance for Hellyer County Park.

Contact: Santa Clara County Parks and Recreation, 408/355-2255, www.parkhere.org; Hellyer County Park, 408/225-0225.

66 PARKWAY LAKE

Rating: 7

in Coyote

Map 7.4, page 384

Your search for trout has ended. Instead of driving across the state in search of fish, you have the fish brought to you at 40-acre Parkway Lake. And they come big. There are records of several trout weighing over 20 pounds.

The scenery isn't the greatest, and at times on weekends your fellow anglers aren't exactly polite, but the rainbow trout are large and abundant, with catch rates often averaging three fish per rod or better. No trout measures under a foot long, one out of three is longer than 16 inches, and many bonus fish are in the 5- to 12-pound class, sometimes even bigger. From fall through spring, the most consistent stocks of large trout anywhere in California are made here. About 45,000 rainbow trout and 35,000 catfish are planted annually, along with bonus sturgeon.

In the summer the lake is converted to sturgeon and catfish. Catfishing at night can be a good bet, but in general, catch rates for catfish and sturgeon are inconsistent. Not so for trout. The expensive access fee goes toward purchasing big fish, and plenty of them. A typical allotment is about 8,000–10,000 trout per month, about what Bon Tempe Lake, a decent place in Marin, gets in an entire year. In June and July, the lake stays open until midnight to provide the best catfishing.

The best technique is to use a woolly worm, half a night crawler, or Power Bait, casting it behind an Adjust-A-Bubble with a hesitating retrieve. Spinners such as the Mepps Lightning, Panther Martin, and gold Kastmaster can go through binges as well.

If you want to get a kid hooked on angling, try coming here on a Thursday, when the crowds are down. You'll be able to demonstrate that fishing often results in catching, maybe even a lot of catching.

Lake records: 22-pound, 4-ounce rainbow trout; 52-pound sturgeon; 40-pound catfish; 10-pound largemouth bass.

Facilities, fees: A small tackle shop, refreshments and snacks, restrooms, and boat rentals are available. No private boats or gas engines are permitted. An access fee is charged. A fishing license is not required.

Directions: From San Jose, take U.S. 101 south to Coyote and the Bernal Avenue exit. Take Bernal west and drive to Highway 82 (Old Monterey Road). Turn left and drive two miles to Metcalf Avenue. Turn left and cross the bridge. You will see the lake on your left.

Contact: Parkway Lake, 408/629-9111, www.parkwaylake.com; Coyote Discount Bait & Tackle, 408/463-0711, www.coyotebait.com.

67 SAN LORENZO RIVER

Rating: 4

in Santa Cruz

Map 7.4, page 384

This is a cool wild card for local steelhead anglers who don't want to make the long drive north to more promising waters.

As with all small steelhead streams, a key to success is having a good phone contact to learn exactly when the fish are moving through. Steelhead leave the ocean to enter the river in the winter months, when high stream flows correspond with high tides. The best fishing is right after one of these periods. Bank fish in the lagoon just upstream from the mouth of the river or hitting upriver spots along Highway 9 up to Felton. In any case, it's something of a pipe-dream that is cause for celebration when you hit the bull's-eye and get steelhead.

Fishing is permitted here only on Wednesday and weekends from December through February, on legal holidays, and on the first and last days of the fishing season. This is the case for most small coastal streams. Current regulations require barbless hooks and catch-and-release practices; always check the Department of Fish and Game regulations.

If you want a special treat in the spring, you can actually see large steelhead spawn. Just explore the headwaters of the San Lorenzo in the Santa Cruz Mountains, farther east along Highway 9 near San Lorenzo Park. You can also get a good view of most of the river by taking a ride on the old train that runs here, operated by Santa Cruz Big Trees and Pacific Railway. Named the Roaring Camp Big Trees Railroad, it's a slow-moving steam engine that runs from Felton to Santa Cruz.

A local anglers/conservation group is doing wonders to try to bring this steelhead run back.

Facilities, fees: Henry Cowell Redwoods State Park provides a campground and fishing access. Drinking water, flush toilets, picnic areas, and coin-operated showers are available. Fishing access is free, but there is an entrance fee at Henry Cowell Redwoods State Park.

Directions: To Henry Cowell Redwoods: In Scotts Valley on Highway 17, take the Mount Hermon Road exit and drive west toward Felton to Graham Hill Road. Turn left and drive 2.5 miles to the Henry Cowell campground, on the right. *Note:* Access to the river is available at many pullouts off Highway 9 at Santa Cruz.

Contact: Henry Cowell Redwoods State Park, 831/335-4598 or 831/438-2396, www.parks.ca.gov; Roaring Camp Big Trees Railroad, 831/335-4484, www.roaringcamp.com; for updates on the San Lorenzo River and fishing regulations, call the Department of Fish and Game, Monterey, 831/649-2870.

68 ALMADEN RESERVOIR

Rating: 5

in Almaden Quicksilver County Park

Map 7.4, page 384

A handful of shoreliners fish for bass here, catch-and-release, on late spring and summer evenings. I've seen some decent surface bites at dusk, where fly fishers casting small poppers were having a ball. The best spots are in the sheltered tule-lined coves at the head of the lake.

Despite so many people in the nearby Santa Clara Valley, a lot of folks bypass the place. Like nearby Calero Reservoir, it is set near some abandoned mines, where mercury runoff has made all fish too contaminated to eat.

Some shoreline bait dunkers practice catch-and-release with the few small resident bass and pan fish.

Facilities, fees: Picnic tables are available and drinking water is available at two entrances. No boats are permitted. Fishing access is free.

Directions: Take Highway 85 to the exit for Almaden Expressway. Take that exit and drive south on Almaden Expressway to Almaden Road. Turn right on Almaden Road and drive through New Almaden to the Hacienda park entrance, on the right. To reach Almaden Reservoir, continue one mile south to the lake entrance.

Contact: Almaden Quicksilver County Park office, 408/268-3883; Santa Clara County Parks and Recreation, 408/355-2255, www.parkhere.org; Coyote Discount Bait & Tackle, 408/463-0711, www.coyotebait.com.

69 CALERO RESERVOIR

Rating: 8

near Coyote

Map 7.4, page 384

The value of catch-and-release fishing can be seen at Calero Reservoir, where populations of bass and crappie are strong and fishing success is quite good. Nobody keeps anything, because the fish are contaminated with mercury and are dangerous to eat.

Calero has provided excellent fishing for bass and crappie, often rating with Coyote Reservoir as the best in Santa Clara County. Just keep throwing them back, and it will stay that way. At times, this is one of the best bass lakes in the Bay Area, and amid the 12-inchers, there are some true monsters, scaling 10 pounds and up.

Calero is the one lake in the Santa Clara County foothills that is often full to the brim. As such, the place is very popular for boating, fishing, and all forms of lakeside recreation. On weekends, water-skiers can be a pain in an angler's rear end.

The lake covers 333 acres. Operations at the lake close a half hour before sunset: I know! You miss the dusk rise.

Note: All boats must be inspected and certified free of mussels prior to launching at this lake.

Facilities, fees: Portable restrooms, picnic tables, parking, and a boat ramp are available. No drinking water. A day-use fee is charged. There is a boat-launching fee. Reservations for the boat launch are recommended and can be required on popular weekends and holidays from April through October.

Directions: From San Jose, drive south on U.S. 101 for five miles to Bailey Avenue. Turn right on Bailey and drive until the road ends at McKean Road. Turn right on McKean Road and drive 0.5 mile to the park/reservoir entrance.

Contact: Ranger kiosk, 408/268-5240; Santa Clara County Parks and Recreation, 408/355-2255 or 408/355-2201 (boat-launching reservations), www.parkhere.org; Calero Reservoir County Park, 408/268-3883; Coyote Discount Bait & Tackle, 408/463-0711, www.coyotebait.com.

70 LAKE ANDERSON

Rating: 6

near Morgan Hill

Map 7.4, page 384

The lake covers more than 1,000 acres in the oak woodlands and foothills of the Gavilan Mountains and is the boating capital of Santa Clara County. Don't worry, though, because a 5-mph speed limit on the southern half keeps the water quiet and calm for fishing.

A lot of water is needed to fill this lake, and when levels are high, boating and fishing conditions are great. The area near the dam can be especially good for crappie and bass, particularly in the morning. When the lake is full, the best prospects are at the extreme south end of the lake, from the Dunne Bridge on south. This area can be very good for bass, bluegill, and crappie in the early spring, before too many anglers have hit it and smartened up the fish.

The area near the dam is often best for crappie. As spring turns to summer, you can find bass suspended off points 10–25 feet deep, often all around the lake. At times, Anderson can provide sensational fishing, even the best bass prospects in the Bay Area. But don't get too excited. At other times, there seems no chance to catch a fish.

Once Memorial Day arrives, the water warms up, boat-launching reservations are required, the fast boats show up, and most anglers bail on the place. On warm weekends when the lake level is up, the fast boats will ruin it on the north end of the lake.

When I was a mere lad of 12, my dad and I were fishing along the shore at the head of the lake above the Dunne Avenue Bridge, catching bass, bluegill, and crappie. A boat pulled up on the opposite side, and two young women proceeded to lay down towels and sunbathe naked "as jaybirds," as my dad called it. While our attention was diverted, a turtle snuck up and ate all the fish off our stringer.

Note: All boats must be inspected and certified free of mussels prior to launching at this lake.

Facilities, fees: Picnic areas, parking, restrooms, and launch ramps are available. A day-use fee is charged. There is a boat-launching fee. Boat-launching reservations are required on weekends and holidays from Memorial Day through Labor Day.

Directions: To reach the head of the lake: From San Jose, take U.S. 101 south for seven miles to the exit for Dunne Avenue. Take that exit and turn east on Dunne Avenue and drive through Morgan Hill. Continue to the Dunne Avenue Bridge (for shore fishing) or to the marina access road, on the left. Turn left and drive to the boat ramp.

To reach the primary reservoir entrance: From San Jose, take U.S. 101 south for five miles to Cochran Road exit. Take that exit and turn east on Cochran and drive two miles to the reservoir entrance on the left near the dam.

Contact: Anderson Lake County Park, 408/779-3634; Coyote Discount Bait & Tackle, 408/463-0711, www.coyotebait.com; Santa Clara County Parks and Recreation, 408/355-2255, www.parkhere.org; boat-launching reservations, 408/355-2201.

71 CHESBRO RESERVOIR

Rating: 5

near Morgan Hill
Map 7.4, page 384

The official name is Chesbro Reservoir, but locals refer to this place as Chesbro Dam. Whatever you call it, during the spring, it is certainly worth a look for a chance at the bass.

While there are lots of small bass in this lake, there are also some absolute giants that are quite elusive. So you might see a monster swimming around and end up catching midgets, but you will be hooked on the place, just the same. Anglers often leave here in wonderment over a fish they glimpsed.

When full, the reservoir covers 300 acres, and some years provide prospects for good-sized crappie during the spring.

The bass follow the classic patterning of other lakes in the area, especially Calero and Coyote. From winter trend through pre-spawn, post-spawn, and summer staging, you must pattern the fish first before you can start getting the kind of action this lake is known for among know-hows.

Facilities, fees: Chesbro is closed to all boating. No facilities are provided.

Directions: From San Jose, drive south on U.S. 101 to the exit for Tennant Avenue. Take that exit west and drive one mile (Tennant becomes Edmondson Avenue) and continue on Edmondson 1.8 miles to Oak Glen Avenue. Turn right on Oak Glen and drive 1.6 miles to Llagas Avenue. Turn left to continue on Oak Glen Avenue and drive 0.6 mile to the launch ramp.

Contact: Santa Clara County Parks and Recreation, 408/355-2255, www.parkhere.org; Chesbro Reservoir, 408/779-9232; Coyote Discount Bait & Tackle, 408/463-0711, www.coyotebait.com.

72 UVAS RESERVOIR

Rating: 6

near Morgan Hill
Map 7.4, page 384

At times Uvas Reservoir can be the best bass lake in Santa Clara County. When it's full to the brim with water, largemouth bass can be located in the coves in the spring. They can be caught with a purple plastic worm, small Countdown Rapala, white crappie jig, or all the favorites: Brush Hogs, Senko, and Zoom worms.

Uvas Reservoir is closed to boating. Fishing the shoreline can be good, and when I first discovered this, I remember how excited I was sneaking up on the coves on a cool spring morning.

Uvas used to be stocked with trout in late winter by the DFG, but no more.

Facilities, fees: No facilities are provided. Shore-fishing access to the reservoir is free.

Directions: From San Jose, drive south on U.S. 101 for five miles to Coyote and Bernal Road. Take the Bernal Road exit west and drive 0.2 mile to the Monterey Highway exit. Turn left on Monterey and drive a short way to Bailey Road. Turn right and drive 2.8 miles to McKean Road. Turn left on McKean Road and drive 10 miles (passing Calero and Chesbro; the road becomes Uvas Road) to the park and reservoir.

Contact: Uvas Reservoir, 408/779-9232; Santa Clara County Parks and Recreation, 408/355-2255, www.parkhere.org; Coyote Discount Bait & Tackle, 408/463-0711, www.coyote bait.com.

73 COYOTE RESERVOIR

Rating: 8

near Gilroy

Map 7.4, page 384

Coyote Lake is a jewel among Bay Area parks and recreation lands. In the early spring, it is often the No. 1 bass lake in the Bay Area. It has an outstanding campground with bluff-top sites overlooking the south end of the lake, within walking distance of casting for fish, and it provides access for powerboating, canoeing, kayaking, and windsurfing.

Coyote Lake is a pretty surprise to newcomers: a long, narrow lake set in a canyon just over the ridge east of U.S. 101, about five miles upstream (south) of Lake Anderson. The lake covers 635 acres and is surrounded by an additional 796 acres of parkland. All boating is permitted, bass fishing is good during the summer, trout fishing is good in the spring, hiking trails are available along the shoreline, and the entire setting provides a pretty respite from the chaos of crowded San Jose to the north.

If you get the opportunity to fish Coyote on a weekday morning in spring or summer, do not pass up the chance. My preference is the structure along the south and southwest end of the lake. Most who learn this lake will fish it with Senkos, Zoom flukes, pig-and-jig, and drop-shotting. Some of the catches can boggle

the mind. Not only are there often more bass caught at this lake than at any other Bay Area lake, but more big bass, the 8- to 12-pounders that have a way of getting inside your mind and realigning your senses.

There is an informal agreement here to release these fish to fight another day. That is one reason the fishery has stayed so strong, despite many big fish being caught. Instead of ending up dead, they are returned to propagate and fill the lake with their progeny. And in the laws of genetics, big fish have a way of creating more big fish with their offspring.

In the winter and early spring (usually from March through early June), when the lake is cool, the Department of Fish and Game stocks Coyote with rainbow trout. After the warm weather moves in, bass take over.

All you need for this lake to click is lots of water and quiet mornings. At one time Coyote Reservoir was considered simply an alternative to Lake Anderson, its big brother just to the north. Those days are over. The appeal of this lake has made it equally popular, and a visit here will quickly demonstrate why.

The campground, bass fishing, and boating access make this a special place. There are also two hiking trails available along the lakeshore.

One slightly frustrating element here is that the lake is never quite allowed to fill. A problem with the dam means that at the highest level, the lake looks about 80 percent full. So by midsummer, it is often down to 50 percent full. The boat ramp is often closed in the fall due to low water. A 35-mph speed limit is strictly enforced.

There is also a great side trip. From the park's entrance road, if you turn left on Gilroy Hot Springs Road and drive east about four miles, you will reach two trailheads for Henry W. Coe State Park, Hunting Hollow, and Coyote Gate. Wildlife is abundant here, including deer, wild turkey, and bobcats. Sometimes when I'm at Coyote, I'll make this quick driving tour just to see what wildlife I might come across. The wild turkeys in particular seem to have a rapidly growing population along the stream here. The hot springs have been closed down for years (there's always talk about reopening the place).

Note: All boats must be inspected and certified free of mussels prior to launching at this lake.

Facilities, fees: Camping, parking, picnic areas, restrooms, and a boat launch are available. A day-use fee is charged. There is a boat-launching fee.

Directions: From San Jose, take U.S. 101 south to Gilroy and the exit for Leavesley Road. Take that exit and drive east on Leavesley Road for two miles to New Avenue. Turn left (north) on New Avenue and drive 0.5 mile to Roop Road. Turn right on Roop Road and drive 3.5 miles (it becomes Gilroy Hot Springs Road) to Coyote Lake Road. Turn left on Coyote Lake Road and drive to the park entrance.

Contact: Coyote Lake-Harvey Bear Ranch County Park, 408/842-7800; Coyote Discount Bait & Tackle, 408/463-0711, www.coyotebait.com; Santa Clara County Parks and Recreation, 408/355-2255, 408/355-2201 (camping reservations), or 408/355-2201 (boat-launching reservations), www.parkhere.org.

74 HENRY W. COE STATE PARK

Rating: 10

southeast of San Jose

Map 7.4, page 384   BEST (

This is the Bay Area's backyard wilderness, with 100,000 acres of wildlands, all of it is networked by 100 miles of ranch roads and 300 miles of hiking trails—providing access to 140 ponds and small lakes, hidden streams, and a habitat that is paradise for fish, wildlife, and wild flora. There are drive-in campsites, at park headquarters, that are set on a hilltop and are ideal for stargazing and watching meteor showers. However, it is at the wilderness hike-in and bike-in sites where you will get the full flavor of the park—the matrixes of valleys, creeks, and foothill grasslands for wildflowers and wildlife.

There's a catch, of course. The only way to the backcountry is by hiking, biking, or on horseback—no cars are permitted on the ranch roads—and the trails feature long, heart-pounding climbs to reach the park's interior. Even though Coe may appear to be 120 square miles of oak foothills, the terrain is often steep, and making ridges often involves climbs of 1,500 feet. Always consult with the rangers before setting out here; the ambitious plans of many hikers cause them to suffer from dehydration and heatstroke. Expect hot weather in the summer; spring and early summer are the prime times. And bring a water purifier for hikes, because there is no drinking water.

From headquarters, it takes a hellacious 56-mile round-trip with about a 15,000-foot aggregate vertical climb to reach Jackrabbit Lake and the best pond-style bass fishing in California. The trip can easily hit 75–90 miles if you include Rooster Comb and Jackrabbit Lake, Mustang Pond, and Kingbird Pond—the best small lakes for fishing. It's so grueling that almost nobody tries it.

For the best fishing, the real key is the park entrance at the Dowdy Ranch Visitors Center, near Bell Station on Highway 156. In 2011, that entrance was closed to the public as part of state park cutbacks. Since volunteers are likely to take over operations at Henry W. Coe, it's possible that the Dowdy Ranch entrance could reopen. When open, it provides landmark access to the previously impossible-to-reach sectors of the park. From the entrance, it is only two miles to a fantastic swimming hole on Pacheco Creek, eight miles to Kingbird Pond, 11 miles to Mustang Pond, 14 miles to Jackrabbit Lake, and a round-trip of about 28 miles to all these spots, including Rooster Comb. Add in a Saturday-night campout and this could be the perfect weekend mountain-bike trip; or maybe the best outdoor adventure in California, with biking, camping, fishing, swimming, wildflowers, and wildlife. For hikers, it is all backpack-style in the oak woodlands landscape. You can set up camp (primitive sites) pretty much anywhere you choose.

Most of the bass are in the 10- to 13-inch class at the ponds, but most of the little lakes have a pond king in the five-pound range. The Brush Hog, Senko, lizard, and frog lures are all good here.

To reach the best fishing ponds in the remote Orestimba region of the park takes a difficult multiday expedition, yet it is even possible to embark on a 70-mile loop trip here, the longest contiguous hiking route in the Bay Area. You go up one canyon, then down the next, over and over. Some people get so worn down, hot, and exhausted that they are practically reduced to nothing more than a little pile of hair lying in the dirt. From the trailhead at Dowdy Ranch/Bell Station, here are the best trips:

• Hole in the Rock, 1.9 miles: Your destination is a fantastic swimming hole on Pacheco Creek. To get there, from the new trailhead, take the main Kaiser–Etna Road (two miles) or the North Fork Trail (2.7 miles). When you reach the creek, walk upstream a few hundred yards to find Hole in the Rock. Another decent swimming hole is downstream.

• Kingbird Pond, 7.9 miles: Little Kingbird Pond provides bass fishing and is the first fishing spot out of Bell Station. To reach it, take Kaiser–Etna Road five miles to a four-way junction. Go straight (north) on Orestimba Creek Road for 2.4 miles to the Kingbird Pond Trail. Turn right and go 0.5 mile to the pond. *Note:* Once you get to Orestimba Corral, about six miles in, the route is pretty flat, with just gentle hills.

• Mustang Pond, 11.1 miles: This little lake is only 3.2 miles from Kingbird Pond, but there are several creek crossings on this route. At high water you might get a little wet, but it's a lot of fun on a mountain bike. From Kingbird Pond, head 0.5 mile back to the Orestimba Creek Road. Turn right (so you're going north again) and head 2.2 miles to the Mustang Pond Trail on the right. It's 0.5 mile to this pond.

• Jackrabbit Lake, 13.9 miles: This lake is about twice the size of Kingbird and Mustang, and it provides what is probably the best bass fishing in the park. It is only 2.8 miles from Mustang Pond. To get there, from Mustang Pond continue on the Mustang Pond Trail (it horseshoes) northwest to Orestimba Creek Road. Turn right, heading north again, and go 0.75 mile to a spur junction with Long Ridge Road. Turn right and go 1.2 miles, a bit of a climb, to an unsigned spur junction on the left that I call Jackrabbit Lake Road. Turn left and push out a short climb and drop of 0.4 mile to the lake.

• Base of Rooster Comb, 16.5 miles: The Rooster Comb is a large, rocky exposed ridge formation that rises up 500 feet from the valley floor to an elevation of 1,836 feet. For the creative eye, it looks something like a, well, you guessed it! Below, Orestimba Creek Flat is a good area to camp. To get here from Jackrabbit Lake, it's 2.6 miles: Backtrack on Jackrabbit Lake Trail to Long Ridge Road. Turn right and return to Orestimba Creek Road. Turn north (right) and go one mile to the base of the Rooster Comb.

• Return to park entrance: From the Rooster Comb, it's 11 miles back to the park entrance. This makes for a fantastic 27.5-mile loop, with three lakes and the opportunity to camp wherever your spirit takes you.

Any place easy to reach from headquarters sees a fall-off in catch rates. That's most true of Frog Lake and Bass Pond.

Another good jump-off point is Coyote Creek Trailhead, upstream of Coyote Reservoir, near Gilroy. From here you can head to Kelly Lake and, a mile later, to Coit Lake. Coit has a backcountry campground and a chance for swimming and bass fishing. Do not take this trip out of the trailhead from headquarters. That forces a much tougher route, including a hellacious, hot, dry climb out of China Hole on the way back. Instead, start this trip on the Coyote Creek Gate, past Coyote Reservoir.

From the Coyote Creek Gate, the trip starts with a steady climb on a former ranch road, climbing past Coit Camp. From here, detour east on single-track up to Mahoney Ridge.

Then turn right, and the trail drops quickly down to Kelly Cabin Lake, a beautiful spot, though it is fished hard and often yields little. From Kelly Cabin Lake it is a nine-mile hike to Coit Lake—seven miles to Kelly Lake (typically more off-color than the pretty Coit Lake), then another two miles from the earth dam to Coit, a well-signed, mostly uphill tromp.

Over this entire route, stay alert for wildlife. It is common to see wild turkeys, coyotes, deer, wild pigs, and hawks. In the spring, wildflowers are also sensational all through here, with yarrow (clusters of white blooms), columbine (like bells), poppies, and large spreads of blue-eyed grass being the most common.

Unfortunately, visitors often leave from headquarters disappointed. The increased popularity of the park has caused much greater fishing pressure and oftentimes less success. What happens with most folks is that they get up on Saturday morning, make the drive (longer and more twisty than they expect), and finally start hiking off at noon, when the heat is worst. They come to little Frog Lake (the first pond on the route out), stop and make a cast, don't catch anything, and declare the trip a bust. Or, an uneducated, unsuccessful effort is made to reach the more inaccessible lakes, and the rangers have to haul them out. Either way, with more information and better planning, Coe can be a great experience.

Mississippi Lake once had a rare population of large, native rainbow trout, but low water prevented spawning through 1991, devastating the population. Then in 1992 and 1993, an unknown party planted bass in the lake, and they are thriving. If any trout survived the drought, their young are likely to have been eaten by the voracious bass. Mississippi Lake now offers excellent bass fishing.

Henry W. Coe State Park is one of my favorite places in California. It's a place for someone who wants solitude and quality fishing in the same package, and isn't averse to rugged hiking to find it. I've made about 15 extensive trips in here and have seen just about all of it. I never get tired of it, just tired.

Facilities, fees: Drive-in campsites and primitive hike-in sites are available. Drinking water, pit toilets, fire rings, and picnic tables are provided in the drive-in sites. Hike-in sites don't have potable water. Dogs and fires are not allowed in the backcountry. Camp stoves with bottled gas are permitted in backcountry camping areas. Supplies can be obtained in Morgan Hill. A day-use fee is charged for parking. All campers and backpackers must pay camping fees and register in advance.

A map/brochure is available at park headquarters. For a detailed topographic map, send a check for $7 ($10.25 for a plastic map) to Pine Ridge Association, Map Request, P.O. Box 846, Morgan Hill, CA 95037.

Directions: To headquarters: From San Jose, take U.S. 101 south to Morgan Hill and the exit for Dunne Avenue. Take that exit and turn east on Dunne Avenue exit and drive over Morgan Hill and Anderson Lake for 13 miles (a twisty road) to the park headquarters and visitors center.

To Hunting Hollow/Coyote Gate: From San Jose, take U.S. 101 south to Gilroy and the exit for Leavesley. Take that exit, turn east on Leavesley, and drive two miles to New Avenue. Turn left and drive 0.25 mile to Roop Road. Turn right and drive about six miles (many small turns; after three miles, it becomes Gilroy Hot Springs Road) to the Hunting Hollow parking lot, on the right. Park or continue one mile to the Coyote Gate, which has limited parking along the shoulder of the road.

To Bell Station: From San Jose, drive south on U.S. 101 to Gilroy and Highway 152. Turn east on Highway 152 and drive to Highway 156/Pacheco Pass Highway. Turn east on Highway 156 and drive about five-plus miles to Bell Station (look for a restaurant and a dirt road on left). Turn left on the dirt road (graded) and go 6.6 miles to the new visitors center, parking, and trailhead.

Contact: Henry W. Coe State Park, 408/779-2728; Pine Ridge Association, 408/779-2728, www.coepark.org.

MONTEREY
AND BIG SUR

The scenic charm seems to extend to infinity

from the seaside towns of Santa Cruz, Monterey, and Big Sur. The primary treasure is the coast, which is rock-strewn and sprinkled with inshore kelp beds, where occasionally you can find sea otters playing "Pop Goes the Weasel." The sea here is a color like no other, often more of a tourmaline than a straight green or blue.

There are so many days when the beauty of Monterey Bay can take your breath away. With a recent upswing in the salmon fishing in late spring and early summer, there are times when the fishing matches the scenic charm. In addition, the surge in white sea bass out of Monterey has made this one of the top attractions on the California coast.

Rockfish are abundant at kelp forests near Capitola, Santa Cruz, and Point Lobos; in the legendary, deep Monterey Underwater Canyon; and in a light sprinkling of reefs. Perch fishing is just okay for folks throwing baits out from the beach, with the best results during the first two hours of the incoming tides. The big bonus for those without boats is that skiff rentals are available in Santa Cruz and Capitola.

From Monterey, most head south to Big Sur to take in a few brush strokes of nature's canvas, easily realizing why this area is beloved around the world. At first glance, however, it's impossible not to want the whole painting. That is where the campgrounds come in. They provide both the ideal getaway and a launching point for adventure. The inland strip along Highway 1 provides access to state parks, redwoods, coastal streams, Los Padres National Forest, and the Ventana Wilderness.

One note of caution: The state park campgrounds on Highway 1 are among the most popular in North America. Reservations far in advance are required all summer, even for weekdays. They are always the first to fill on the state's reservation system. So get the game wired to get your site.

During the summer, only the fog on the coast and the intense heat just 10 miles inland keep this region from attaining perfection.

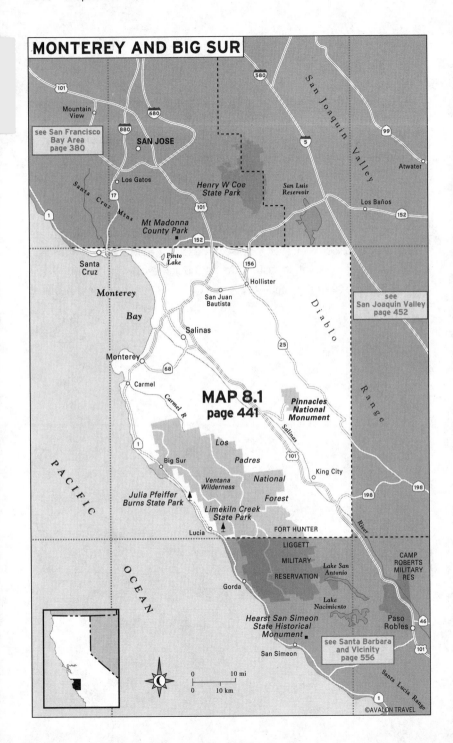

MONTEREY AND BIG SUR

Map 8.1

Sites 1-10
Pages 442-447

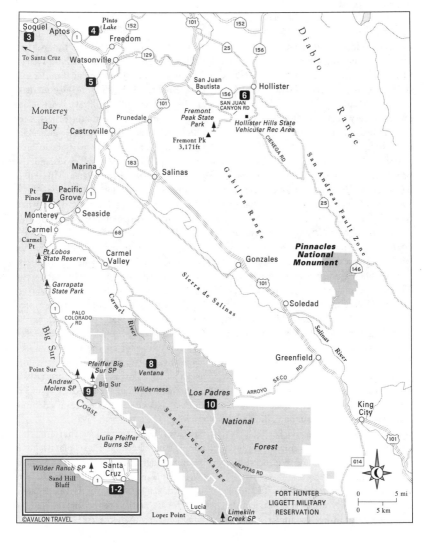

©AVALON TRAVEL

❶ SANTA CRUZ DEEP SEA

Rating: 10
south of San Francisco at Santa Cruz Wharf
Map 8.1, page 441

It would be nice to have a crystal ball to help predict where the best places to fish will be in the next 10 years. But when it comes to Santa Cruz, no crystal ball is needed. This is one place that shouldn't be missed. The fishing here can be sensational.

Good marine habitat, abundant levels of baitfish, plenty of young fish being recruited into the adult population, and (most important) no gillnetting all ensure a promising future. The Department of Fish and Game (DFG) says closed areas from the Marine Life Protection Act (MLPA) will allow spawning and a nursery area and, in turn, keep the placed filled with fish. We'll see. I hope they are right for once.

Fishing access is also good, with charters, boat launches, and boat rentals all available. The opportunity to rent a boat and motor is what gives this spot a slight edge over Monterey. Santa Cruz is a beautiful area, set on the northwestern tip of Monterey Bay. A rejuvenated boardwalk, a pretty beach, and nearby redwood forests are among the highlights.

The salmon season generally opens in April. The best spots in the early season are usually adjacent to the Cement Ship or farther south, off Moss Landing, when mooching very deep. According to my logbook, by April 5–10, a big school of salmon always schools up just a mile offshore in an area known as "Three Trees." This area, which is named for three large cypress trees that sit in a group on an otherwise stark coastal bluff, is just north of Santa Cruz and provides the best salmon fishing of the year. The logbook rarely lies.

Rockfish are the most consistent producer, with chilipepper, black, and blue rockfish the most abundant species.

Note that fishing regulations often change here from year to year, for seasons, depth restrictions, bag limits, size limits, and even annual quotas for the fleet. Always check current regulations with Fish and Game or with a marina or party-boat operator before planning a trip. Note that the MLPA prohibits rockfishing in some areas.

Special trips for large lingcod are offered from late August through October, and in the spring and early summer, migrating salmon march through the area in a procession of schools. There are a few halibut and white seabass, and there are always huge numbers of kingfish (white croaker) in the area.

At the inshore reefs, which provide an easy shot on the small rental skiffs, the rockfish tend to be small. Most of the rockfish average 3–5 pounds, sometimes even smaller. Because the big red rockfish, the 6- to 12-pounders, are 20–25 years old, it will take years before they are recruited back into the fishery, a reminder of the devastation of the commercial fish killers. For bigger fish, party boats offer special trips north to Año Nuevo Island, the best lingcod habitat in the area. This trip is most popular in the fall, when the big lings move inshore at Año Nuevo and also when the north winds are lightest, making the ride "uphill" an easy one.

Halibut in the spring and white seabass in summer and fall can provide big surprises. In late August, trips run out of Santa Cruz for albacore. Wind is always a key when fishing the ocean, but the Santa Cruz area often gets lighter winds than farther north on the California coast.

When you add it up, the Santa Cruz area makes a very attractive fishing picture. It is one of the few places on the Pacific coast where boat rentals are available (nearby Capitola is another) and where fisheries are on a definite upswing.

Facilities, fees: Party-boat charters, boat ramps, a boat hoist, and boat rentals are in the area. Lodging, campgrounds, and supplies can be found in Santa Cruz. Rod rentals, bait, and tackle can be obtained at the wharf. Party-boat fees are charged per person.

Directions: From San Jose, take Highway 17 to

Santa Cruz and the junction with Highway 1. Turn south on Highway 1 to Santa Cruz and the exit for Soquel Avenue/Santa Cruz Harbor. Take that exit and drive west for one mile to Capitola Road. Turn left on Capitola Road and drive 0.3 mile to 7th Avenue. Turn right and drive a short distance to the harbor. Boat launches are at Santa Cruz Harbor and farther south on Highway 1, at Moss Landing.

Contact: Santa Cruz Harbor, 831/475-6161.

Party boats: Leo's Sport Fishing, 831/476-2648; Stagnaro's Charters, 831/427-2334, www.stagnaros.com; Captain Jimmy Charters, 831/662-3020, www.captainjimmycharters.com; Kahuna Sportfishing, 831/633-2564, www.kahunasportfishing.com; Ultimate Fish Charters, 831/566-9407, www.ultimatefishcharters.com.

Supplies: Bayside Marine, Santa Cruz, 831/475-2173, www.baysidemarinesc.com.

2 SANTA CRUZ MUNICIPAL WHARF

Rating: 5
in Santa Cruz
Map 8.1, page 441

At most piers, folks are content to catch a fish, any fish. At Santa Cruz you can do better than that from late summer through fall. Mackerel are particularly abundant, and large jacksmelt sometimes arrive in good numbers; between them you can fill your bucket. The rest of the year, you'll have kingfish to keep you company.

If you are among the lucky, you might hook a halibut in the summer, even a striped bass in the fall. And in some years, there are tons of mackerel from midsummer through mid-October.

Facilities, fees: Restrooms, benches, and fish-cleaning tables are provided. Rod rentals, bait, tackle, a boat launch, and boat rentals are available. Several shops and restaurants are on the wharf. A parking fee is charged.

Directions: From San Jose, take Highway 17 west to Santa Cruz. Continue straight on Highway 17 (past the Highway 1 turnoff) where the highway feeds into Ocean Street. Continue on Ocean Street to its end at Riverside. Turn right on Riverside and drive two blocks to Laurel Street. Turn left, drive over a bridge, and immediately turn left on Front Street. Drive approximately 0.3 mile to Washington Street. Turn left and drive a short distance to the wharf.

Contact: Santa Cruz Municipal Wharf, 831/420-6025, www.cityofsantacruz.com; Stagnaro Fishing Trips, 831/427-2334; Santa Cruz Boat Rentals, 831/423-1739, www.capitolaboatandbait.com.

3 CAPITOLA PIER

Rating: 6
south of Santa Cruz at Capitola Fishing Wharf
Map 8.1, page 441

Spots such as Adams Reef, Surfers Reef, Soquel Reef, Capitola Reef, and South Rock hold good populations of small rockfish. You can rent a boat here. If a sea lion shows up around a kelp bed, the fish stop biting; if you find yourself over a sand bottom, you get kingfish, with a chance at a halibut; and in the fall, large blue sharks can still be enticed with a hunk of smelly, bloody bait. Every once in a while, somebody ties up with big white sea bass.

Deep-water rockfishing, once popular here, was prohibited.

Note that fishing regulations often change here from year to year, for seasons, depth restrictions, bag limits, size limits, and even annual quotas for the fleet. Always check current regulations with Fish and Game or with a marina or party-boat operator before planning a trip.

The Capitola Pier itself provides a decent fishery in the fall months, when jacksmelt and mackerel can move in hordes into the area, and the inevitable kingfish will always nibble at your bait.

When I look at Capitola Pier, it's as if many years have flashed by in a day or two. It was back in the 1960s when my dad, Bob Stienstra Sr., first took me and my brother, Rambobby, to Capitola. While fishing, we'd listen to the baseball game on the radio, and while Willie Mays made basket catches, we'd catch small rockfish like crazy on the inshore reefs and edges of the kelp beds.

I remember a big white seabass that snapped my grandfather's old Calcutta rod in half, a rod that he said couldn't be broken (heh, heh, heh).

Facilities, fees: Restrooms, fish-cleaning tables, benches, lights, and picnic tables are provided. Rod rentals, bait, tackle, a boat hoist, and boat rentals are available. Several shops and restaurants are nearby. A parking fee is charged.

Directions: From San Jose, take Highway 17 west to Santa Cruz and Highway 1. Turn south on Highway 1 and drive to the 41st Avenue exit. Turn right and drive to Capitola Road. Turn left on Capitola Road and drive 0.75 mile to the wharf. Parking lots are nearby.

Contact: City of Capitola, Public Works, 831/475-7300; Capitola Boat & Bait, 831/462-2208, www.capitolaboatandbait.com.

4 PINTO LAKE

Rating: 6

near Watsonville

Map 8.1, page 441

The first time I saw Pinto Lake I was making an approach in an airplane at Watsonville Airport. I looked down and saw this horseshoe-shaped lake bordered by a parklike setting and said to myself, "There's got to be fish in there." Well, after landing the plane, I decided to find out for myself. There were.

Trout are stocked on a fairly regular basis here. Then when the water heats up, fair populations of crappie, bluegill, and catfish take over. Rainbow trout are the mainstay, however, except from August through October. That is when the focus shifts to warm-water species. The crappie fishing was once fantastic here, but crappie populations always seem to cycle up and down, with little regard to anything. It won't exactly get you panting.

The lake is one of the few in the area that offer camping, and when all the nearby state-beach campgrounds are jam-packed with RVs, Pinto provides an excellent option for over-nighters. The trout fishing isn't too shabby either, and occasionally the bass fishing can be excellent, too. Swimming and tent camping are not permitted, and a 5-mph speed limit on the lake is enforced.

Facilities, fees: A campground for RVs only, restrooms with flush toilets, drinking water, picnic areas, a paved boat ramp, and a snack bar (in summer season) are provided. Row-boats and pedal boats are for rent. A day-use fee is charged on weekends. A boat-launching fee is charged.

Directions: From Monterey, drive north on Highway 1 to the exit for Green Valley Road. Take that exit, turn right on Green Valley Road and drive 2.7 miles (0.5 mile past the Holohan intersection) to the lake.

Contact: Pinto Lake Park, 831/728-6194, www.pintolake.com.

5 MONTEREY BAY SHORELINE

Rating: 5

along Monterey Bay

Map 8.1, page 441

The best thing about surf fishing the beach in Monterey Bay is the view. On a calm, blue-sky day, the water just kind of laps at the shore. It looks almost like Hawaii. Bring a sand spike for your rod and some eats and drinks, and enjoy yourself.

The best thing going is perch. One of the best tricks is to use a string of motor oil–colored plastic grubs. Use either three grubs on a surf leader or, even better, set up with a sliding sinker rig. You need to cast in the underwater sand hollow between breaker lines. Perch fishing is best just after a low tide has bottomed out and the incoming tide starts.

Nature provides long stretches of beach with

only a gentle curve to them. That is why you get a sprinkling of surf perch.

Facilities, fees: Some state beach campgrounds are available. Lodging and supplies can be found in Santa Cruz, Capitola, Moss Landing, and Monterey. A day-use fee is charged at some of the state beaches.

Directions: From Santa Cruz, drive south on Highway 1 and continue south along the coast. Fishing access can be found at Grey Hound Rock County Beach, and several state beaches off Highway 1, including Moss Landing State Beach, Natural Bridges State Beach, Sunset State Beach, New Brighton State Beach, Salinas River State Beach, Seacliff State Beach, Zmudowski State Beach, Monterey State Beach South, Carmel River State Beach, and Marina State Beach.

Contact: Santa Cruz County Conference & Visitors Council, 831/425-1234, www.scparks .com; Monterey County Convention & Visitors Bureau, 877/666-8373, www.seemon terey.com; Carmel Visitors Center, 831/624-2522; California State Parks, Santa Cruz District, 831/335-6318; California State Parks, Monterey District, 831/649-2836.

Information and supplies: Capitola Boat & Bait, 831/462-2208, www.capitolaboatand bait.com; Compass, Boat and Fishing Supply, Monterey, 831/647-9222; Quarterdeck Marine Supply, Monterey, 831/375-6754.

6 SAN JUSTO RESERVOIR

Rating: 1
near Hollister
Map 8.1, page 441

The shock of what the zebra mussel can do to a lake is a sad reality at San Justo Reservoir. Officials have blocked all access in the fear that someone could transfer the invasive mussel to other waters, just as has been done to many lakes in Southern California. I kept it in the book in the hope of shocking every boater to take care when traveling and exploring across California, lake to lake.

It's also important to remember how it got to this point. San Justo had developed into a good local fishery for stocked rainbow trout in late winter and early spring. There were also prospects for bass and catfish in spring and summer, respectively. All that is gone. Because somebody launched a boat here and brought in the zebra mussels.

San Justo Reservoir covers 200 surface acres. The surrounding landscape is sparse, with no facilities other than covered picnic areas. There are no trees, no grass, and no beach, just dirt and rocks. In late summer and early fall, water levels can fall significantly. A rule prohibiting gas motors (electric is okay) means that there are no speedboats or personal watercraft rocketing around, which was another plus for enthusiasts of nonpowered water sports.

Lake records: 18-pound, 3-ounce largemouth bass; 6-pound, 10-ounce rainbow trout.

Facilities, fees: Portable toilets, a picnic area, bait and tackle, a snack bar and small store, and fishing-boat rentals are available. A paved launch ramp is on the lake's northeast side. No camping is allowed. Full facilities are in Hollister. Fees are charged for day use and boat launching.

Directions: Take U.S. 101 to Highway 156 (north of Salinas). Turn east on Highway 156 and drive seven miles (through San Juan Bautista) to Union Road. Turn right (south) and continue a short distance to the reservoir (up the hill).

Contact: San Justo Reservoir, 831/638-3300; San Benito County Parks Public Works, 831/636-4170.

7 MONTEREY DEEP SEA

Rating: 10
south of San Francisco at Monterey Wharf
Map 8.1, page 441

Monterey stands apart from the rest of California. It has the best of both worlds: Southern

California's weather and Northern California's beauty. To get a picture of the fishing here, all you have to do is stroll through the Monterey Bay Aquarium, where the tanks are like giant houses, allowing an inside view of the multiple levels of marine life in Monterey Bay.

The key for marine life in Monterey Bay is the 5,000-foot-deep canyon that generates nutrient-rich water, which in turn sets off one of the West Coast's most diverse marine systems.

The salmon season usually starts in April. Most of the salmon caught in Monterey Bay are taken between Moss Landing and Fort Ord. There is a larger percentage of big fish in Monterey's spring run than anywhere else on the coast, with occasional trips where a 15-pound salmon is average; a number of 20- to 25-pounders are caught as well.

Salmon fishing is often excellent just a few miles out of Moss Landing and at the drop-off/entrance to the Monterey Underwater Canyon. Occasionally, salmon show up offshore of Point Sur, but this is far less predictable than the other spots mentioned.

As summer arrives, most of the salmon head north, and the focus at Monterey turns to rockfish, which have been rejuvenated in recent years due to the ban on gillnetting. The better spots are the edge of Monterey Canyon and also "around the corner," off Cypress Point, Point Lobos, Carmel Bay, and Big Sur. Note that the MLPA has closed some of the deep-water spots; check with the DFG's Monterey office for current restrictions.

Longer trips south to the Big Sur area can be fantastic, especially in the shallow reef areas, using light tackle and casting three-ounce split-tail Scampi jigs, Point Wilson Darts, and other swim baits. The salmon season continues through summer. Albacore fishing usually is best from August through November.

If you have your own boat, Monterey Bay is an excellent destination. Because the wind is much calmer here than at points north, especially in the late summer and early fall, the big bay can get so flat that it looks like a big frog pond.

Catches of white seabass can be sensational on the edge of kelp. Keep in mind that Monterey is a world-class destination, and other people want to visit, too, so it gets crowded. But that aside, Monterey is a beautiful area with a returning abundance of all marine life. It will always be a favorite.

Facilities, fees: Party-boat charters, boat ramps, boat hoist, full-service marina, lodging, and supplies are in the vicinity. Rod rentals, bait, and tackle can be obtained at Fisherman's Wharf. Party-boat fees are charged per person. Parking fees are charged.

Directions: Take Highway 1 to Monterey and the exit for Pacific Grove/Del Monte Avenue exit. Take that exit and drive one mile to Figueroa Street. Turn right and drive west to Wharf No. 1. Boat ramps are at the wharf area and at the Coast Guard Pier, 0.5 mile away.

Contact: Monterey County Convention & Visitors Bureau, 877/666-8373, www .seemonterey.com; Monterey Harbor, 831/646-3950; Fisherman's Wharf, www.monterey wharf.com.

Supplies: Compass, Boat and Fishing Supply, Monterey, 831/647-9222; Quarterdeck Marine Supply, 831/375-6754.

Party boats: Randy's Fishing Trips, 831/372-7440 or 800/251-7440, www.randysfishing trips.com; Chris' Fishing Trips, 831/375-5951, www.chrisfishingtrips.com.

8 VENTANA WILDERNESS

Rating: 3

southeast of Monterey in
Los Padres National Forest
Map 8.1, page 441

The Ventana Wilderness is a rugged coastal environment with spans of time every summer and fall where it is little traveled. It can be hot and dry, with severe fire danger in the summer and fall, when just finding drinking water can be difficult. But spring arrives here early, often in March, and by the time the trout season opens (on the last Saturday in

April), the wilderness provides a quiet, beautiful setting, as well as a few secret spots for hikers who fish.

Salmon Creek provides more than 10 miles of fishable stream. Other prospects are on the headwaters of the Carmel, Big Sur, and Little Sur Rivers. Upper Carmel River is the best, with trout as large as 10 or 11 inches. No trout are stocked in the Ventana Wilderness; all waters contain only native trout, mostly rainbows, with a few scarce brown trout mixed in.

Regulations change often here; expect more closures in the future. Check regulations for current status.

The rivers still provide viable fisheries, but they are only a shadow of the former glory that was here before the Marble Cone Fire. After that fire, heavy rains caused erosion damage, and silt was washed into the streams, covering some spawning gravels. That in turn lowered spawning success, which explains the sustained low population levels since the fires. It is something that only time will heal, but as the soils stabilize and as spring rains scour the river, this fishery will again rebound. That, of course, could take a generation or more.

Facilities, fees: No facilities are available. A parking fee is charged at the Big Sur/Pine Ridge Trailhead, but other access points are free.

Directions: Access to trailheads is available off several roads that junction with Highway 1 near Big Sur. See a U.S. Forest Service map for details (www.fs.fed.us/r5).

Contact: Los Padres National Forest, Monterey Ranger District, 831/385-5434, fax 831/385-0628; Department of Fish and Game, Monterey, 831/649-2870.

9 BIG SUR RIVER

Rating: 3

near Big Sur in Los Padres National Forest
Map 8.1, page 441

This stream is set amid a stand of coastal redwoods, a pretty spot known primarily as a summer vacation site, not as a winter destination for steelhead anglers. Regardless, from January through early March, the river attracts anglers from the Monterey area. It takes the combination of rain and high tides for the steelhead to feel compelled to leave the ocean and swim upstream. When that combination occurs, anglers should be out on the stream and ready to go.

Catch rates are quite low. There are long periods when nothing happens, interspersed with short sprees when the steelhead move through the area. If you are like most people, you'll show up and come to the conclusion that there are no fish here. Wrong. There are. But finding them requires perfect timing. Ken Oda, a biologist for the Department of Fish and Game, says that this river is different from other rivers because the steelhead here like to hide in logjams.

Always check ahead for low-flow closures and current DFG regulations.

Facilities, fees: Campgrounds, lodging, picnic areas, and supplies are at Pfeiffer-Big Sur State Park and along Highway 1. A day-use fee is charged for vehicles at Pfeiffer-Big Sur State Park and Andrew Molera State Park; walk-in access is free at both.

Directions: From Monterey, take Highway 1 south for 26 miles to Pfeiffer-Big Sur State Park. Other limited access is available off the highway.

Contact: Pfeiffer-Big Sur and Andrew Molera State Parks, 831/667-2315, fax 831/667-2886; California State Parks, Monterey District, 831/649-2836; Department of Fish and Game, Monterey, 831/649-2870.

10 ABBOTT LAKES

Rating: 3

near Greenfield in Los Padres National Forest
Map 8.1, page 441

This spot is known to the locals simply as "the lakes," and you might expect a lot more than what you get here. You might also get more than you expect (and we'll get to that).

Abbott Lakes are just two little reservoirs in the Los Padres foothills, more like small ponds. Canoeing and fishing are permitted at the ponds, but no swimming is allowed. During the evening, maybe you toss out a line to see if there are any fish in the lakes. Alas, it is not the kind of fishing that will get you champing at the bit—just some pint-sized bluegill, with poor catch rates at that, and nothing else.

The lakes are just inside the border for Los Padres National Forest. A river runs through steep canyons, and the area is covered with oaks, chaparral, with a fair amount of poison oak in most areas.

There are days every year here when the temperatures hit 100-plus degrees, and the surrounding canyon traps heat, often making it 10°F hotter than down in the valley. You might feel as if you're sitting in a pizza oven, not a boat. If you hit it wrong, you can end up feeling something like a pepperoni pizza.

Now, what about getting "more than you expect?" Research editor Kathie Morgan unearthed a detailed report filed with the Forest Service in which an employee claims the following (seriously): "I then heard a noise off to my left on the hillside… I notice what appeared to be a man walking up the hill about 20 feet in front of me. I then realized this was too tall and too wide to be a person. It was about 8 feet tall. It stopped, turned its head and stared back at me for about 30 seconds. It turned and walked back up the hill. I ran back to the station knowing what I had seen was not human."

Now for the rest of the story: "Late that day I was with my supervisor alone, and I asked him if he had ever seen anything weird near the lakes or the bone yard (trash area). He looked at me and said, 'Oh, you seen it too?' He went to tell me that other members of the Forest Service had seen it."

Facilities, fees: A campground, a restroom with flush toilets and coin showers, drinking water, and a picnic area are available. There is no boat ramp; car-top boats may be hand-launched. A day-use fee or pass is required.

Directions: From Salinas, take U.S. 101 south for 25 miles to the town of Greenfield and Greenfield–Arroyo Seco Road. Turn west on Greenfield–Arroyo Seco Road/County Roads G16 and 3050 and drive 19 miles to the lakes, which are within the Arroyo Seco Campground. The road runs right alongside the northernmost of the two lakes. A walk is required to reach the smaller lake to the south (the smaller lake may be closed in dry years).

Contact: Los Padres National Forest, Monterey Ranger District, 831/385-5434, fax 831/385-0628; Arroyo Seco Campground, 831/674-5726. For a map of the area, contact the U.S. Forest Service, www.fs.fed.us/r5.

SAN JOAQUIN VALLEY

The lakes in the foothills of the San Joaquin Valley are like Gardens of Eden for boating and water-sports enthusiasts. The heart is the San Joaquin Delta and its 1,000 miles of mosaic-like waterways, accessible only by boat.

In the San Joaquin arm of the lower delta, outstanding opportunities for striped bass are available. Note that some of the biggest striped bass in the world are at O'Neill Forebay and in San Luis Reservoir. Every year or so, another 50- or 60-pounder is caught. There are also tons of smaller bass, and for both shoreliners (who drive around the lake looking for action) and boaters, this place can be a real thrill. The recent trout programs in the spring at nearby Los Banos Creek Reservoir are a blessing.

The lakes in the San Joaquin Valley are the primary recreation attraction; all summer long, the refreshing, clean water is revered as a tonic against the valley's heat. During the hot summer nights, the Mendota (Fresno) Slough has catfish on the prowl.

When viewed from the air, the short distance between these lakes and the Sierra Nevada mountain range is surprising to many. This proximity results in cool, high-quality water – the product of snowmelt sent down river canyons on the western slope. Examples of this can be found at Don Pedro Reservoir, east of Modesto, and Lake McClure, near Merced. Some even rate Don Pedro as the best all-around fishing lake in the state.

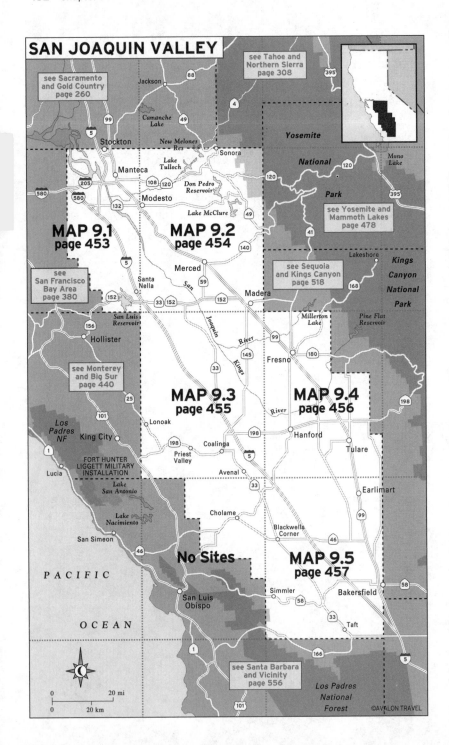

SAN JOAQUIN VALLEY

see Sacramento
and Gold Country
page 260

see Tahoe and
Northern Sierra
page 308

Jackson

88

Camanche
Lake

49

99

Stockton

New Melones
Res

Sonora

Yosemite

National

120

Mono
Lake

395

Manteca

Lake
Tulloch

205

108 120

Don Pedro
Reservoir

120

Park

580

580

132

Modesto

Lake McClure

49

140

MAP 9.1
page 453

MAP 9.2
page 454

see Yosemite and
Mammoth Lakes
page 478

41

395

see
San Francisco
Bay Area
page 380

5

Merced

59

San

Madera

Santa
Nella

152

33 152

152

see Sequoia
and Kings Canyon
page 518

Lakeshore

168

Kings

Canyon

National

Park

156

Hollister

San Luis
Reservoir

Joaquin

Kings

River

145

Millerton
Lake

99

Fresno

180

Pine Flat
Reservoir

see Monterey
and Big Sur
page 440

25

101

33

MAP 9.3
page 455

MAP 9.4
page 456

198

Los
Padres
NF

King City

Lonoak

River

198

Hanford

1

198

Coalinga

5

Tulare

Lucia

FORT HUNTER
LIGGETT MILITARY
INSTALLATION

Priest
Valley

Avenal

Earlimart

Lake
San Antonio

33

99

Lake
Nacimiento

Cholame

San Simeon

46

Blackwells
Corner

46

No Sites

MAP 9.5
page 457

58

PACIFIC

Simmler

58

Bakersfield

San Luis
Obispo

33

Taft

OCEAN

0   20 mi

0   20 km

1

see Santa Barbara
and Vicinity
page 556

166

5

Los Padres

National

101

Forest

©AVALON TRAVEL

Map 9.1

Sites 1-4
Pages 458-460

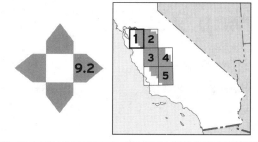

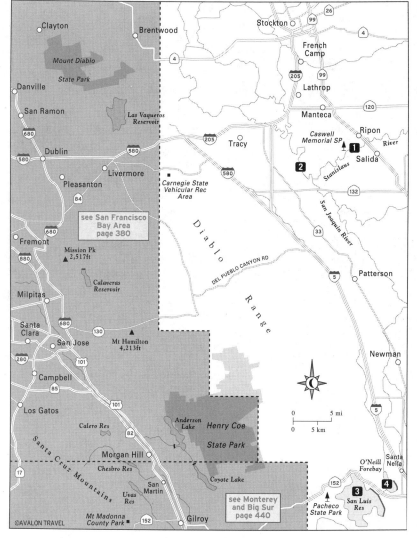

©AVALON TRAVEL

Map 9.2

Sites 5-14
Pages 461-469

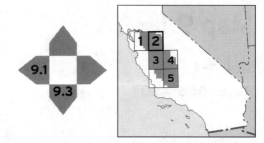

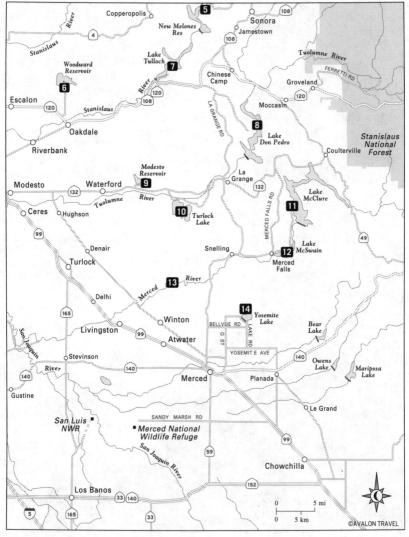

Map 9.3

Sites 15-20
Pages 469-472

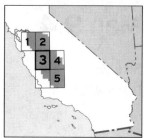

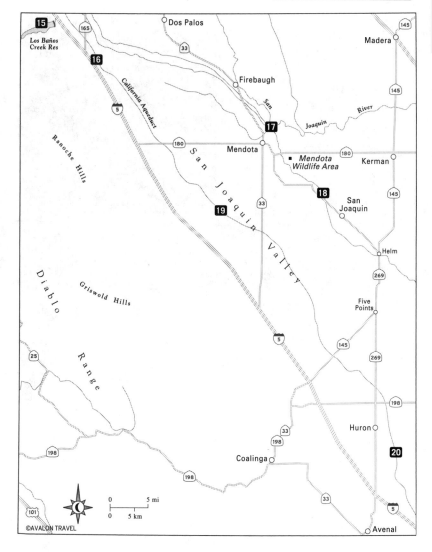

Map 9.4

Site 21
Page 473

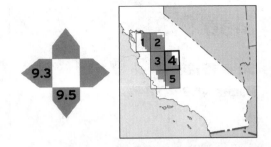

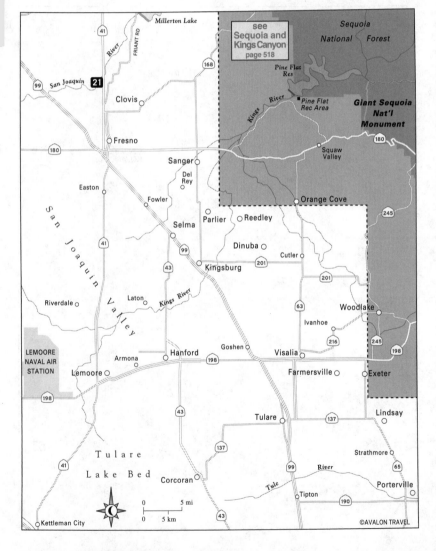

Map 9.5

Sites 22-23
Pages 473-474

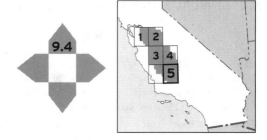

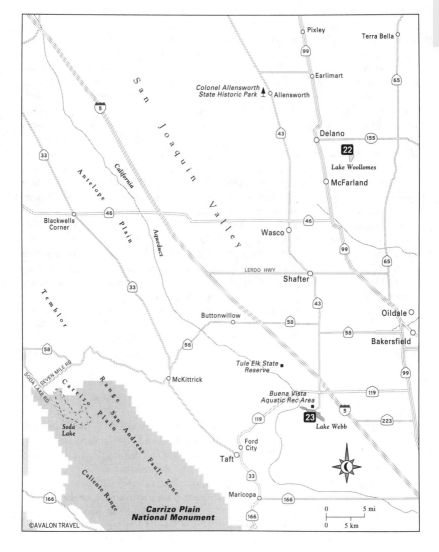

1 STANISLAUS RIVER

Rating: 4

near Stockton

Map 9.1, page 453

Caswell Park provides an access point to the Stanislaus River. It also offers surrounding parkland covering 250 acres, a visitors center, and a nature trail.

This section of the Stanislaus is a green, slow-flowing waterway, much of it bordered by various hardwoods. Even in the worst years, it provides a suitable habitat for catfish. Most folks show up at the park on a summer evening, toss their line out with a chicken liver or cut a chunk of sardine or anchovy for bait, and wait for a catfish to come along.

In its best years, when good water flows are running from the mountains to the delta, this river can still attract salmon and striped bass as far upriver as Caswell Park and beyond.

Facilities, fees: A campground and picnic areas are at the park. Drinking water, flush toilets, showers, wood, a swimming beach, a nature trail, and exhibits are on-site. Supplies are in Stockton and Manteca. There is a day-use fee at Caswell Memorial State Park.

Directions: From Manteca, take Highway 99 south for 1.5 miles to the Austin Road exit. Turn south and drive four miles to the park entrance.

Contact: Caswell Memorial State Park, 209/599-3810, www.parks.ca.gov; California State Parks, Four Rivers District, 209/826-1196.

2 SAN JOAQUIN RIVER (PATTERSON TO STOCKTON)

Rating: 6

near Stockton

Map 9.1, page 453

Striped bass still make the push up the San Joaquin River, and if they get by the pumping plant at Clifton Court, they will swim up past Stockton, then south past Mossdale, and perhaps even make it all the way to the mouth of the Stanislaus River.

In the process, they provide short periods of good fishing and long periods of bad fishing. The best of it comes when a pod of fish arrives in the Stockton Turning Basin, right at the Port of Stockton—but again, this can last for just a short period. If you have a boat; if you hear about the run; if you are on the spot; if you get a bite. As I say, that's a lot of ifs.

As you move south (upstream), the San Joaquin becomes less of a river and more of a slough, providing better habitat for catfish and a sprinkling of largemouth bass than for anadromous fish such as striped bass, salmon, and sturgeon. This is certainly the case at George J. Hatfield State Recreation Area and Fisherman's Bend, which provide opportunity for catfish. Access can be tough on any river, particularly one such as this section of the San Joaquin, which flows through so much private, diked-off farmland. Fisherman's Bend provides a fair opportunity to catch catfish, best on hot summer nights.

Note: George J. Hatfield State Recreation Area is on the closure list developed by the California Department of Parks, pending final state budget decisions or the possible transfer of park management to other park agencies or volunteer groups.

Facilities, fees: Camping is possible at the state recreation area and Fisherman's Bend. Supplies can be found in adjacent towns. There are day-use fees at George J. Hatfield State Recreation Area.

Directions: To George J. Hatfield State Recreation Area: South of the junction of I-5 and I-580, take I-5 south to the Newman/Stuhr Road exit. Turn east on County Road J18/Stuhr Road and drive to Newman and the junction with Highway 33. Turn right and drive a short distance to Hills Ferry Road. Turn left and drive five miles (it becomes Kelly Road) to the park entrance, on the right.

To Fisherman's Bend: South of the junction of I-5 and I-580, take I-5 south to the

Newman/Stuhr Road exit. Turn left (east) on County Road J18/Stuhr Road and drive 6.5 miles to Hills Ferry Road. Turn left and drive a mile to River Road. Turn left on River Road and drive to 26836 River Road.

Contact: George J. Hatfield State Recreation Area, 209/826-1197, www.parks.ca.gov; California State Parks, Four Rivers District, 209/826-1196; Fisherman's Bend River Camp, 209/862-3731.

❸ SAN LUIS RESERVOIR

Rating: 7

near Los Banos in San Luis Reservoir
State Recreation Area
Map 9.1, page 453

The best spot for fishing is the San Luis Creek area, accessible after launching from the nearby San Luis Creek boat ramp.

Most of the striped bass here are in the 10- to 15-inch class; after all, most of the fish are pumped in via the Delta when they are quite small. But there is also a sprinkling of 25- to 40-pounders, some even bigger. The lake also has black bass, channel catfish, and crappie. Though San Luis is well known, neighboring O'Neill Forebay usually produces more stripers, bigger stripers, and has better protection from the wind.

San Luis Reservoir is a huge, squarish, man-made lake set in otherwise desolate country, covering nearly 13,800 acres with 65 miles of shoreline. Whenever I fly through the area, heading to or from Monterey Bay, I use the giant lake as a checkpoint and maybe do a circle to scan for boats. The reservoir was built on the edge of the San Joaquin Valley for the sole purpose of storing water on line with the California Aqueduct. By fall, the water gets drawn way down, and its vast, barren appearance can seem quite stark. Tule fog is common in winter. The elevation is 575 feet.

Come fall, this reservoir, as ugly as it is with the annual drawdowns to send water south, suddenly comes to life with all manner of birds, bait, and bass. You don't even need a boat, though it can help plenty. This reservoir is absolutely huge and subject to drastic drawdowns. That is one reason why most boaters prefer the O'Neill Forebay. Many of the record stripers have been caught at the forebay as well.

Remember this: birds never lie. When you see birds cruising, you know they are on the move, looking for food. When they circle, hover, or dive, you know they have found it. At San Luis Reservoir, schools of striped bass will corral large schools of shad, which send the baitfish near the surface and, in turn, cause the birds to feed in dive-bomb raids. The angler, seeing this, then cruises to the scene, stops short of a surface boil, and casts to the fish.

It can be done by boat or bank. By boat is simplest, of course, although there can be a tremendous amount of water to cover. Trolling a broken-back Rebel is effective when there are no birds to chase it. By bank, you scan shoreline waters for diving birds, and when you find them, drive around the lake to the spot, jump out, and make long casts—just like you're surf fishing for stripers off Pacifica or bait fishing with mud suckers or jumbo minnows.

In the spring and early summer, the wind can howl through here, particularly in the afternoon, and warning lights and horns have been installed to alert boaters to get off the lake during periods of dangerous wind. It is also in the spring and early summer when the striped bass are most difficult to catch, tending to head deep, scatter, and roam the wide-open expanses of the lake in search of baitfish. Few are caught by deep-water trolling techniques using large diving plugs.

With every striped bass caught at San Luis Reservoir and the adjacent O'Neill Forebay comes a degree of irony, for every striped bass in this lake has been sucked right out of the delta by the California Aqueduct pumps and then delivered via the canal. In addition, the Department of Fish and Game stocked three million striped bass here, the biggest striper stock at any lake in California history.

After pumping fish and water since 1967, the lake often seems to be full of both of them.

Facilities, fees: Campgrounds, picnic areas, drinking water, coin showers, an RV dump station, flush toilets, and boat ramps are available. A store, coin laundry, a gas station, a restaurant, and propane gas are 1.5 miles away. Supplies can be obtained in Gilroy and Los Banos. A day-use fee is charged. Fees are charged for day use and boat-launching. An annual pass can be purchased.

Directions: To San Luis Creek boat ramp: From Los Banos, drive west on Highway 152 for 14 miles to the park entrance (marked San Luis Creek State Recreation Area/O'Neill Forebay). Turn right and drive 1.5 miles to the boat ramp.

To Basalt boat ramp: From Los Banos, drive west on Highway 152 for 12 miles to Gonzaga Road (the park entrance road). Turn left and drive four miles to the boat ramp.

To Dinosaur Point: Take Highway 152 to the west side of San Luis Reservoir and Dinosaur Point Road. Turn east on Dinosaur Point Road and continue to the boat ramp, at the road's end.

Contact: San Luis Reservoir State Recreation Area, 209/826-1197, Four Rivers District, 209/826-1196, www.parks.ca.gov.

❹ O'NEILL FOREBAY

Rating: 9
near Gilroy in San Luis Reservoir
State Recreation Area
Map 9.1, page 453

Six different fly-fishing line-class world records for striped bass have been set at San Luis Reservoir and neighboring O'Neill Forebay. These are highlighted by a 54-pound, 8-ounce striped bass caught on 16-pound tippet by Al Whitehurst, who owns four of the records.

This is proof that sometimes bigger is not better. O'Neill Forebay is the little brother of the adjacent and giant San Luis Reservoir. But even though it's by far the smaller of the pair, the opportunities for boating and water sports are far more attractive here.

O'Neill Forebay covers 2,000 surface acres with 14 miles of shoreline, providing the recreation for the recreation area. The Forebay is far prettier than the main lake, and provides a chance at great fishing. If you time it right, you can catch striped bass, large in both in size and numbers. The lake also has largemouth bass and crappie.

There are many excellent ways to catch those striped bass. Many anglers use live minnows, anchovies, Hair Raiser–style jigs, or Kastmasters. Guides Dan Blanton and Dave Sellers have developed outstanding fly-fishing methods here, casting streamers that simulate small baitfish. This lake is often best in the fall, starting usually in late October, when the first cool weather of the year brings the fish to the surface. This is often when the biggest fish of the year are caught.

For swimmers, there is a large developed beach, complete with outdoor showers for rinsing off. Boaters can dock at the beach to have lunch, go for a swim, and then head back out on the water to ski.

O'Neill Forebay is a very attractive recreation lake, but sometimes it can be too attractive. On weekends and holidays from May through October, it can get so congested that some folks simply surrender and head over to the bigger San Luis Reservoir to avoid the crowds.

Note that the Medeiros boat ramp has been closed since the September 11 attacks. It will not reopen. In addition to security concerns, there were problems with launching in low water here.

Facilities, fees: Two campgrounds, chemical toilets, drinking water, and showers are available. Fees are charged for day use and boat launching. A paved launch ramp is available. Waterskiing, wakeboarding, and personal watercraft are permitted. All boaters must wear life jackets. Sailboarding and swimming are allowed; a large, sandy beach is on the west side of the forebay.

Directions: Take Highway 152 to San Luis Reservoir (12 miles west of Los Banos) to the signed forebay entrance road. Turn north and drive to the forebay and beach area.

To San Luis Creek boat launch: Drive on Highway 152 to San Luis Reservoir (12 miles west of Los Banos) and the signed campground entrance road (15 miles west of Los Banos). Continue straight and drive two miles to the campground, on the left, and continue to the boat ramp.

Contact: San Luis Reservoir State Recreation Area, 209/826-1197, Four Rivers District, 209/826-1196, www.parks.ca.gov.

5 NEW MELONES RESERVOIR

Rating: 9

near Sonora

Map 9.2, page 454

For know-hows with boats, New Melones can be a fish factory. Rainbow trout in the two- to three-pound class are very common, and fish up to five or six pounds are definitely not out of the question. Because stocked rainbow trout become naturalized quickly at this lake, five-pounders look and fight like wild fish. The lake also has excellent fishing for largemouth bass from late winter through early summer. The biggest bonus is the kokanee salmon. At times this is the best lake in California for kokanee salmon.

The best time to hit the lake for trout is in the winter and on into spring. That's when the trout feed near the surface and can be caught without the aid of downriggers or leadcore line. Parrots Ferry to Horseshoe Bend is a hot spot to troll silver spoons such as Needlefish with or without flashers. As the weather warms, downriggers become necessary to get down to the trout. In the summer, try fishing near the spillway.

The big brown trout of New Melones are becoming more popular. Most of the big browns are caught in winter months, well up the river arm. Two techniques stand out here

for the browns: One is trolling a whole thread-thin shad, allowing it to spin in the water. The other is trolling the minnow-type lures such as Rebela or Rapalaa. Many anglers will tell you they caught their browns on these lures, but the truth is it goes a step further. The Rebel mystic lure, for instance, which comes in minnow and diving models, has a reflective finish that emits hues and colors like no other finish. The big predator browns seem to be fooled by it.

New Melones is a huge reservoir in the Sierra foothills that covers 12,500 acres and offers 100 miles of shoreline and good fishing. At Tuttletown, there is a mammoth camping area that encompasses three campgrounds (Acorn, Manzanita, and Chamise) and two group camping areas (Oak Knoll and Fiddleneck). Aquatic habitat is excellent, with groves of submerged trees. The lake provides a quality fishery for trout, bass, and kokanee salmon. The Department of Fish and Game stocks 10- to 12-inch rainbow trout and kokanee salmon here.

Planted rainbows seem to do quite well in the lake. They feed primarily on shad and quickly lose their dull planter colors and grow back their fins.

The Department of Fish and Game was surprised to find out how fast kokanee grew in New Melones. In just two years, these fish reach lengths of 18 inches and are as fat as can be. This lake is now one of the best lakes in California for kokanee salmon. That indicates there is a good supply of plankton in the lake.

As with most kokanee fisheries, the dam area is a good spot to start. But other areas can be extremely productive. One is the far south end of the lake, especially after a couple of days of a light prevailing north wind, which will blow food to the south. Other good spots are toward the Glory Hole boat ramp area, around the islands, and 100 yards off of Glory Hole Point.

During early summer, you can troll 40–60 feet down and catch kokanee. But starting in late July, you may have to go as deep as 120 feet to find these fish. A trick when fishing deeper than 80 feet is to add glow-in-the-dark tape on your dodger and lure.

Kokanee anglers prefer trailing a dodger, such as a Sling Blade or Vance, followed closely by a Sockeye Slammer, hoochie, Apex, Uncle Larry's spinners, Koke-a-Nut, or a variety of bugs. And as in most kokanee waters, adding scents by ProCure to the lure makes a difference.

One of the most popular fisheries that New Melones has to offer is its spring crappie action. Head up the Mormon or Angels arm of the lake and look for submerged trees on your depth finder. The fish usually hang 20–40 feet deep and bite best at night. To increase your success, drop a "crappie" light over the side—shad will flock to the light, and crappie won't be far behind.

New Melones is a big lake, almost giant when full, but my advice is to avoid the main lake body, to the south, and instead focus on the northern arms. This upper section is the new part of the lake, the area created by rising water from the higher dam, and it is here where you will find the best aquatic habitat for bass, bluegill, and trout.

The bass bite can be good in the spring, if you probe the protected coves and cast around the submerged trees. If you approach the area quietly, then make precise, soft-landing casts, you can catch bass up to 15 or 16 inches. My preference is for Shad Raps, Rattletraps, and similar crankbaits, working the early-morning and late-evening bites. If you find yourself wading through the dinks, then it's time to move to another spot.

On a trip with Ed "The Dunk" Dunckel, I had a real beauty on that managed to get around a submerged tree and break my line. When we moved the boat closer, though, we discovered the bass was still hooked and fighting away, and the line was still wrapped around the tree limb. "The Dunk" managed to grab the bass, unhook it, and let it go. The fish deserved it.

An option here is to head your boat well up the lake arms, as far as is possible and right into the current, then anchor and let a night crawler drift downstream of the boat. It's a system that can take some beautiful native rainbow trout. A bonus at New Melones is fishing up the canyon. Even if you don't catch any fish, the scenery is spectacular.

But most folks just troll the main lake body, content to pick up a fish now and then. In the summer, trollers in the main lake must go quite deep.

Lake records: 13-pound, 1-ounce brown trout; 18.11-pound largemouth bass; 7.97-pound spotted bass; 36-pound catfish.

Facilities, fees: A full-service marina; rentals for fishing boats, pontoon boats, ski boats, personal watercraft, and houseboats; moorings; bait and tackle; and slip rentals are at New Melones Lake Marina. Five campgrounds, restrooms with flush toilets, drinking water, showers, boat ramps, an RV dump station, and picnic areas are nearby. Supplies can be obtained in Sonora and Angels Camp. Fishing access is free.

Directions: To Tuttletown: From Sonora, take Highway 49 north to Reynolds Ferry Road. Turn left and drive about two miles to the entrance road for Tuttletown Recreation Area.

To Glory Hole: From Manteca, take Highway 120 east (it becomes Highway 108) to Jamestown and Rawhide Road. Turn left and drive five miles to Highway 49. Turn left and drive 10 miles to Whittle Road (signed "New Melones," with Glory Hole Sports on the left). Turn left on Whittle and drive five miles to the marina and boat launch.

Contact: Bureau of Reclamation, New Melones Administrative Office, 209/536-9094, www.usbr.gov/mp/ccao/newmelones; New Melones Visitors Center, 209/536-9543; New Melones Lake Marina, 209/785-3300; Whistle Stop, Jamestown, 209/984-5554; Glory Hole Sports, Angels Camp, 209/736-4333, www.gloryholesports.com.

Sierra Sportfishing, Ripon, 209/599-2023, www.sierrasportfishing.com; Fish'n Dan's Guide Service, Twain Harte, 209/586-2383, www.fishndans.com; Dale's Foothill Fishing, 530/295-0488, www.dalesfoothillfishing.com; Bassin' 1A Guide Service, 209/586-0948, www.bassin1a.com; Gold Country Sport-fishing, 209/848-2746, www.goldcountry fishingguide.wordpress.com; Randy Pringle, The Fishing Instructor, 209/543-6260, www .thefishinginstructor.com; Tight Lines Guide Service, 530/263-0990 or 530/263-7944, www.fishtightlines.com.

6 WOODWARD RESERVOIR

Rating: 5

near Oakdale in
Woodward Reservoir County Park
Map 9.2, page 454

Woodward is a large reservoir covering 2,900 acres with 23 miles of shoreline, set in the rolling foothills just north of Oakdale at an elevation of 210 feet. The lake was completely drained in 2004. In 2005, as the lake started to fill again, bass, catfish, and sunfish were stocked, and in October, rainbow trout were added as well. It filled in 2006, and the fish started to take hold. Lakes are often most productive in their fifth to eighth years of existence, so Woodward Reservoir could be headed to a new golden age.

The Department of Fish and Game stocks rainbow trout in the 10- to 12-inch class. The fishing is fair for bass and catfish, with bass best during the early summer and catfish best during summer evenings. There are plenty of little coves along the shoreline for you to stick casts for bass. Most of the bass aren't big, and they aren't necessarily easy to come by, either. But the future is a wild-card mystery, and this could change.

Part of the lake's rebirth is a $1.87 million renovation at Heron Point, on the south shore of the lake, that includes a new boat ramp, parking, fish-cleaning station, and other facilities. This will greatly help congestion that has been a pain in the butt at the old one-lane ramp here.

Note: All boats must be inspected and certified free of mussels prior to launching at this lake.

Facilities, fees: Drinking water, flush toilets, showers, a campground, three boat ramps, a marina, mooring, a boat ramp, dry boat storage, and some equestrian facilities are available. An entrance fee is charged per vehicle per day; a boat-launching fee is also charged.

Directions: From Manteca, take Highway 120 east (it becomes Highway 108) for 20 miles to Oakdale and the junction with County Road J14/26 Mile Road. Turn left and drive four miles to Woodward Reservoir.

Contact: Woodward Reservoir County Park, 209/847-3304 or 209/525-6750, www.stan county.com/er/parks; Bob's Marine, 209/551-2165, www.bobsmarine-ca.com.

7 LAKE TULLOCH

Rating: 7

near Jamestown
Map 9.2, page 454

The first time I flew an airplane over Tulloch Lake, I couldn't believe how different it looked by air than from a boat. It resembled a giant X more than a lake. After landing at the strip in Columbia and making the trip to the lake, I understood why.

The reservoir is in two canyons that crisscross each other, and by boat you never even see the other canyon. The lake is actually the afterbay for New Melones Reservoir, with the water to fill Tulloch coming from the New Melones Dam, on the northeastern end of the X. With such extended lake arms, there are 55 miles of shoreline. A five-lane boat ramp makes launching and loading your boat easy. The elevation is 500 feet.

Fishing? It can be like a yo-yo, and sometimes like a yo-yo without the string. The best thing going is the chance for smallmouth bass. This is one of the better spots in the Central Valley for smallmouth, but not quite in the class of Trinity Lake.

Smallmouth are different from their large-mouth counterparts in that they start feeding earlier in the season. It can still be very cold in early March when the smallmouth go on the bite. The smallmouth like to hang out around submerged rock piles and shoreline points, often suspended about 15–20 feet deep. Diving plugs, grubs, and Gitzits all work the best, and it is much more difficult to get them to strike a surface lure or plastic worm.

Tulloch also has a fair trout fishery, but that, too, goes up and down. The Department of Fish and Game stocks catchable-sized rainbow trout here. Vacationing anglers catch most of the trout in summer, when they troll with leadcore line and flashers/minnows, going deep during the warmer months. In October and November, a trick to take big trout is to troll fast and deep, using lures such as the Sparklefish and Rapala, 20–30 feet down.

From about February through May, some fabulous holdover rainbow trout fishing can be had. Chunky rainbows weighing in at 1–6 pounds are common for trollers dragging Kastmasters, night crawlers, Needlefish, and Z-Rays near the surface this time of year. Guide Jay Chojnacki, of California Fishing Adventures, says that his best success with Tulloch's cold-weather trout comes on days that the lake is socked in with fog. It's kind of like steelhead fishing—the colder and wetter, the better.

Tulloch also boots out pretty impressive crappie during the spring spawn. And don't forget the crawdads; there are lots of them.

Facilities, fees: Marinas with boat launches, rentals, and docks are at both the north shore and south shore. Lodging, a campground, picnic areas, drinking water, restrooms with showers, coin laundry, an RV dump station, convenience stores, a restaurant, and a bar are available. Fees are charged for camping. Day-use and boat-launch fees are charged.

Directions: From Manteca, drive east on Highway 120 (it becomes Highway 108/120) to Oakdale. Continue east for 13 miles to the South Shore/Tulloch Road on the left. Turn left and drive 4.6 miles to the campground entrance and gatehouse, at the south shore of Lake Tulloch. For the north shore, continue for 10 more miles on Highway 108/120 to O'Byrnes Ferry Road. Turn left and drive to the north shore.

Contact: Lake Tulloch Resort, 209/785-2286, www.laketullochresort.org; Lake Tulloch Campground and Marina, 209/881-0107 or 800/894-2267, www.laketullochcampground .com; Fish'n Dan's Guide Service, Twain Harte, 209/586-2383, www.fishndans.com; Bassin' 1A Guide Service, 209/586-0948, bassin1a.com; Gold Country Sportfishing, 209/848-2746, www.goldcountryfishing guide.wordpress.com.

8 DON PEDRO RESERVOIR

Rating: 10
northeast of Modesto

Map 9.2, page 454

This is one of the best lakes for fishing in California. It seems that each year, one species takes over as a star. Some years it is bass. Others it is salmon. You never know which. But what you do know is that this is one of the fishiest lakes around.

Don Pedro is a giant lake with many extended lake arms, providing 160 miles of shoreline and nearly 13,000 surface acres when full. It's in the foothill country at an elevation of 800 feet, and many travelers see the lake when they take the Highway 49 route to Yosemite National Park.

The rainbow trout in Don Pedro can go from stocker size to five pounds, and the best trolling takes place from Rodgers Creek to Jenkins Hill and on to Middle Bay and the Highway 49 bridge. The lake also has a great supply of kokanee. They include some of the state's biggest and Don Pedro rivals New Melones and Indian Valley for that honor. The Department of Fish and Game also stocks catchable-sized rainbow trout here.

Bass fishing can be good at Don Pedro, and some big bass can surprise you. One suggestion is to fish well up the lake arms, where there is plenty of cover available, and then gently cast a night crawler or live minnow out under the cover. In the process, you can get not only bass, but also some nice bluegill.

Don Pedro's natural production of largemouth bass is given a big bonus plant of fingerling largemouth bass. Because of the large amount of aquatic food in the lake, survival rates are high, and the fish grow quite quickly.

An option can be salmon. Salmon ranging 4–6 pounds can occasionally be caught by trolling frozen anchovies or shad on Rotary Salmon Killer rigs.

Don Pedro can also produce large kokanee, at times averaging 1.5–2.5 pounds by mid-August. Anglers troll for kokanee here with a variety of enticers, including Needlefish, Humdingers, Sockeye Slammers, and kokanee "bugs" behind dodgers; make sure you put white corn on the hook. The top areas include Middle Bay and Jenkins Hill. Trolling depths range 30–80 feet, depending on the time of year. The fishing generally picks up by mid-May and lasts into early September.

Boat-in campers should always bring a shovel and a light tarp with some poles. The shovel is to dig out flat spots in the shoreline for sleeping areas, and the tarp and poles are to create a sunblock. Because the water can recede quickly here, the spot you fished three weeks ago could be high and dry for the coming weekend.

Regardless, this lake offers outstanding opportunity for boaters, campers, and anglers. You might even catch a salmon.

Facilities, fees: Don Pedro Marina (south shore) and Moccasin Point Marina (north shore) have rentals of fishing boats, houseboats, and pontoon boats; mooring; boat storage; motor repairs; and bait and tackle. Campgrounds, boat-in campsites, restrooms with flush toilets and showers, three RV dump stations, three boat ramps, picnic areas, snack bars, two cafés, a convenience store, coin laundry, and gas are available. Day-use and boat-launch fees are charged. No pets are allowed in campsites.

Directions: The following are directions to the reservoir's campgrounds and boat ramps.

To Moccasin Point: From Manteca, drive east on Highway 120 (it becomes Highway 108/120) for 30 miles to the Highway 120/Yosemite exit. Bear right on Highway 120 and drive 11 miles to Jacksonville Road. Turn left on Jacksonville Road and drive a short distance to the campground and lake, on the right.

To Blue Oaks: From Manteca, take Highway 120 east to Oakdale (the road becomes Highway 120/108). Continue east on Highway 108 for 20 miles to La Grange Road/J59 (signed "Don Pedro Reservoir"). Turn right on La Grange Road and drive 10 miles to Bonds Flat Road. Turn left on Bonds Flat Road and drive 0.5 mile to the campground and boat ramp, on the left.

To Fleming Meadows: From Manteca, take Highway 120 east to Oakdale (the road becomes Highway 120/108). Continue east on Highway 108 for 20 miles to La Grange Road/J59 (signed "Don Pedro West Shore"). Turn right on La Grange Road and drive 10 miles to Bonds Flat Road. Turn left on Bonds Flat Road and drive 2.5 miles to the campground and boat ramp, on the left.

Contact: Don Pedro Lake Recreation Agency, 209/852-2396, www.donpedrolake.com; Don Pedro Marina, 209/852-2369 or 800/255-5561, www.lakedonpedromarina.com; Moccasin Point, 209/989-2206.

Guides: Sierra Sportfishing, Ripon, 209/599-2023, www.sierrasportfishing.com; Fish'n Dan's Guide Service, Twain Harte, 209/586-2383, www.fishndans.com; Bassin' 1A Guide Service, 209/586-0948, www.bassin1a.com; Gold Country Sportfishing, 209/848-2746, www.goldcountry fishingguide.wordpress.com; The Fishing Instructor, 209/543-6260, www.thefishing instructor.com.

9 MODESTO RESERVOIR

Rating: 5

near Modesto

Map 9.2, page 454

Here lies one of California's highest-quality bass lakes, yet it's relatively undiscovered. The southern shoreline of the lake is loaded with submerged trees, coves, and inlets, and it is protected with a 5-mph speed limit to keep the water quiet. All this adds up to good prospects for bass fishing, although many of the fish are small—a fact that keeps this place from being counted among the great bass lakes of California. Modesto Reservoir is a big lake, covering 2,800 acres and with 31 miles of shoreline. It's set in the hot-weather foothill country, just east of guess where?

Get on the lake early for the largemouth bass, casting Rattletraps along the stickups. Eventually the lure will land practically right on top of a bass, and it will seem as if the lure is whacked almost as soon as it hits the water. Fishing for bass is good, though the fish are often small. The overwhelming majority of fish range 9–13 inches, including the rainbow trout that the Department of Fish and Game stocks here. Maybe in future years, they will get bigger.

The best trout fishing is usually had by shore casters using Power Goo near the inlet.

Waterskiing is excellent in the main lake body. Anglers head to the southern shore of the lake, which is loaded with submerged trees and coves and is also protected by a 5-mph speed limit.

One of the great things here is the opportunity for boat-in camping in many coves at the southern end of the lake. It's a good idea to bring a shovel to dig out a flat spot to sleep, something that is often necessary when boat-in camping at a reservoir.

Note: All boats must be inspected and certified free of mussels prior to launching at this lake.

Facilities, fees: Campgrounds, picnic areas, drinking water, restrooms with flush toilets, showers, an RV dump station, a marina, a store, and propane gas are available. Day-use and boat-launch fees are charged.

Directions: From Modesto, take Highway 132 east for 16 miles (past Waterford) to Reservoir Road. Turn left (north) on Reservoir Road and continue to the reservoir.

Contact: Stanislaus County, Parks and Recreation, 209/525-6750, www.stancounty.com/er/parks; Modesto Reservoir Regional Park, 209/874-9540.

10 TURLOCK LAKE

Rating: 6

east of Modesto in Turlock Lake
State Recreation Area

Map 9.2, page 454

Turlock Lake is fed with cold, fresh water from the bottom of New Melones Reservoir. Despite its low elevation (250 feet) in the Modesto foothills, that cool water in combination with trout stocks from the Department of Fish and Game (10- to 12-inch rainbow trout) creates one of the few year-round trout fisheries in the Central Valley. The lake is simply cooler than many Central Valley reservoirs, only 65–74°F in the summer, when other lakes in the region are 75–82°F.

You'll find the best prospects trolling on the western end of the lake, across from the boat launch and near a series of small islands.

When full, Turlock Lake covers 3,500 acres and has 26 miles of shoreline.

For bass, try casting around the islands (on the eastern section of the lake as well as the western), which provide a decent morning/evening bite, or toss out bait at night for the catfish.

Note: Turlock Lake State Recreation Area is on the closure list developed by the California Department of Parks, pending final state budget decisions or the possible transfer of park management to other park agencies or volunteer groups.

Facilities, fees: A campground, a full-service

marina, boat rentals, a boat ramp, bait, tackle, gas, and groceries are at the lake. Drinking water, flush toilets, coin showers, and a swimming beach are in the state recreation area. A day-use fee is charged.

Directions: From Modesto, go east on Highway 132 for 14 miles to Waterford. Continue eight miles on Highway 132 to Roberts Ferry Road. Turn right and drive one mile to Lake Road. Turn left and drive two miles to the campground, on the left.

Contact: Turlock Lake State Recreation Area, 209/874-2008 or 209/874-2056, www.parks .ca.gov.

11 LAKE McCLURE

Rating: 7

east of Modesto

Map 9.2, page 454

Every lake usually has a few spots that seem to produce year after year. So it is at McClure.

The best areas for bass are the two major coves in the southeastern end (the left half of the H) of the lake, where both Cotton Creek and Temperance Creek enter the lake. Since they are directly across from the dam, they are not affected by water drawdowns as much as the northern arm of the lake, up Piney Creek.

In late winter, the upriver half of McClure (the right half of the H) is best for trout. There is a boat launch just east of where Highway 49 crosses the lake, providing access to the upper Merced River arm. Here, you can get a mix of wild trout and recently stocked rainbows. Like Lake Oroville, McClure is known as a place where a boater can catch-and-release multitudes of spotted bass, including many in the 12- to 15-inch slot-limit size.

McClure is shaped like a giant H, with 82 miles of shoreline, warm water, and lots of water activity, including waterskiing and houseboating. Its primary fisheries are warm-water species, including bass, crappie, bluegill, and catfish. In the cool months of late winter,

however, it receives a few bonus stocks of rainbow trout from Fish and Game. The DFG stocks catchable-sized rainbow trout here. Fingerling kokanee salmon are also stocked and are a coming fishery. The elevation is 900 feet.

Some people think that Lake McClure and adjoining Lake McSwain are the same lake. That will teach them to think. Although they are connected by the Merced River, they are two separate lakes with separate identities.

Facilities, fees: Full-service marinas with mooring are at McClure Point and Barrett Cove. Barrett Cove Marina rents fishing boats, ski boats, personal watercraft, houseboats, and pontoon boats. McClure Point rents fishing boats. Campgrounds, fish-cleaning stations, picnic areas, restrooms with flush toilets and showers, convenience stores, snack bars, coin laundry, RV dump stations, and gas are available at all major access points. Five boat ramps are around the lake. Day-use, boat-launching, and pet fees apply.

Directions: To McClure Point Recreation Area: From Turlock, take County Road J16 east for 19 miles to the junction with Highway 59. Continue east on Highway 59/County Road J16 for 4.5 miles to Snelling, and bear right at Lake McClure Road. Drive seven miles to Lake McSwain Dam and continue for seven miles to the end of the road, to the campground and boat launch.

To Horseshoe Bend Recreation Area: From Modesto, take Highway 132 east for 31 miles to La Grange and then continue for about 17 miles (toward Coulterville) to the north end of Lake McClure and the campground entrance road on the right side of the road. Turn right and drive 0.5 mile to the campground and boat launch.

To Barrett Cove: From Modesto, take Highway 132 east for 31 miles to La Grange and then continue about 11 miles (toward Coulterville) to Merced Falls Road. Turn right and drive three miles to the campground entrance on the left. Turn left and drive a mile to the campground, on the left side of the road.

To Bagby Recreation Area: From Modesto, take Highway 132 east for 31 miles to La Grange and then continue for 20 miles to Coulterville and the junction with Highway 49. Turn south on Highway 49, drive about 12 miles, cross the bridge, and look for the campground entrance, on the left side of the road. Turn left and drive 0.25 mile to the campground.

Contact: Lake McClure Recreation Area, 800/468-8889 (reservations) or 209/378-2521, www.lakemcclure.com; Horseshoe Bend Recreation Area, 209/878-3452.

Guides: Sierra Sportfishing, Ripon, 209/599-2023, www.sierrasportfishing.com; Fish'n Dan's Guide Service, Twain Harte, 209/586-2383, www.fishndans.com; Gold Country Sportfishing, 209/848-2746, www.goldcountryfishingguide.wordpress.com; The Fishing Instructor, 209/543-6260, www.thefishinginstructor.com.

12 LAKE McSWAIN

Rating: 6

east of Modesto
Map 9.2, page 454

If you find Lake McClure to be just too big and with too many big boats, then Lake McSwain provides a perfect nearby option: it's small, and waterskiing is prohibited. The water is much colder here than at McClure to the east, and the trout fishing is better.

McSwain is like a pond compared to its big brother McClure, but the water level is usually near full. That gives it a more attractive appearance, especially in low-water years, when McClure can look almost barren by late fall. Since McSwain is small, the Department of Fish and Game gets a lot more mileage out of the catchable-sized trout it stocks each year.

The top lure here for trollers is the No. 7 rainbow trout Rapala. There are a few bass in the lake, but they're pretty small, and due to the cold water here, they don't bite all that well.

Lake McSwain is actually the afterbay for adjacent Lake McClure, and this camp is near the McSwain Dam on the Merced River. If you have a canoe or car-top boat, this lake is preferable to Lake McClure, because waterskiing is not allowed.

Facilities, fees: A full-service marina is available and has rentals for fishing boats and pedal boats. A campground, boat ramp, drinking water, restrooms with showers, an RV dump station, coin laundry, a playground, a snack bar, and a convenience store are nearby. A day-use fee is charged.

Directions: From Turlock, drive east on County Road J17 for 19 miles to the junction with Highway 59. Continue east on Highway 59/County Road J17 for 4.5 miles to Snelling and Lake McClure Road. Bear right at Lake McClure Road and drive seven miles to the Lake McSwain Recreation Area turnoff, on the right.

Contact: Lake McSwain Recreation Area, 209/378-2521 for information or 800/468-8889 for reservations, www.lakemcclure.com; Lake McSwain Marina, 209/378-2534.

13 MERCED RIVER

Rating: 7

near Newman in
George J. Hatfield State Recreation Area
Map 9.2, page 454

Catfish and trout are the best thing going in this stretch of the Merced River, especially in the areas that are the most accessible, such as Hatfield Park.

The DFG stocks 22,000 rainbow trout ranging to 10 pounds in March and April. Once the area heats up, catfish take over. That's when folks show up in the evenings, toss out their bait, maybe sip a refreshment and nibble some fried chicken, and hope a catfish gets interested in their bait.

Salmon are always a wild card. When high rain and snowmelt result in high flows for the Merced River, something like 15,000 salmon make the journey up the Merced, and for the entire San Joaquin River system, the count can be as high as 70,000. But in drought years, with little water being allowed to flow from reservoirs to the sea, less than a hundred salmon return to the Merced, and only 600 return to the San Joaquin system.

The connection has become clear: High river flows equal high fish counts. It's about that simple.

Note: This park is on the closure list developed by the California Department of Parks, pending final state budget decisions or the possible transfer of park management to other park agencies or volunteer groups.

Facilities, fees: A campground and picnic areas are provided. Supplies are in Newman. A day-use fee is charged.

Directions: To George J. Hatfield State Recreation Area: South of the junction of I-5 and I-580, take I-5 south to the Newman/Stuhr Road exit. Turn east on County Road J18/Stuhr Road and drive to Newman and the junction with Highway 33. Turn right and drive a short distance to Hills Ferry Road. Turn left and drive five miles to the park entrance, on the right.

Contact: California Parks and Recreation, Four Rivers District Office, 209/826-1197, www.parks.ca.gov; George J. Hatfield State Recreation Area, 209/632-1852; McConnell State Recreation Area, 209/394-7755; Tim Bermingham's Drift Boat Guide Service, 209/984-4007.

14 LAKE YOSEMITE

Rating: 5

north of Merced in Lake Yosemite Park
Map 9.2, page 454

Lake Yosemite has a sprinkling of resident bass, bluegill, and catfish, most of which refuse to bite during the daytime. There is a late-afternoon chance for bluegill and a short binge for bass at dusk—and then only at night do the catfish go on the prowl here.

Lake Yosemite Lake is on the outskirts of east Merced. It is a 25-acre lake that provides backyard opportunity for local residents. It's stocked with 10- to 12-inch rainbow trout, usually during early spring, but then the hot temperatures take over, and it is good-bye trout. You see, it gets hot here, with temperatures of 95–105°F being common all summer. But unlike many lakes in the San Joaquin Valley, the water is cool, not warm.

One problem is that on hot summer nights, there are occasional groups of young drinkers that can create havoc here. The county sheriff has tried to round them up with varying success.

Note: Lake Yosemite, of course, is not in Yosemite National Park and it has nothing to do with Yosemite National Park.

Facilities, fees: Picnic areas, drinking water, and restrooms are provided. A boat ramp is available just past the park entrance. Group picnic areas and buildings can be reserved. A concessionaire with boat rentals may be in business; check current status. Lodging and supplies are in Merced. Day-use and boat-launch fees are charged by day or year.

Directions: From Modesto (or north of Merced), take Highway 99 south to Highway 59 near Merced. Take Highway 59 north and drive four miles to Bellevue Road. Turn right on Bellevue Road and drive five miles east to Lake Road. Turn left on Lake Road and drive to the lake.

From Fresno (or south of Merced), drive north on Highway 99 to Merced and the 16th Street exit. Take that exit and drive a short distance to G Street. Turn right on G Street and drive five miles to Bellevue Road. Turn right and drive 2.5 miles to Lake Road. Turn left on Lake Road and drive to the lake.

Contact: Merced County Parks and Recreation, 209/385-7426, www.co.merced.ca.us.

15 LOS BANOS CREEK RESERVOIR

Rating: 4

near Los Banos
Map 9.3, page 455

This is catfish country, the kind of place where some of the locals will stay up through the night during the summer, sitting on a lawn chair along the bank, waiting for a catfish to nibble their baits. The big catfish roaming these waters can be worth the wait.

In the spring there is usually a good bass fishery, and some large bass have been caught here. The better spots are along the Los Banos Creek arm and in Salt Springs Cove. The reservoir was once stocked with rainbow trout when the water is cool enough to support them, but no more.

During typical summer days, it can get really hot at Los Banos Reservoir. It is in a long, narrow valley, with the surrounding hills often baked brown by late May. The lake is at 330 feet, covers 410 acres, has 12 miles of shoreline, and has a 5-mph speed limit.

As at nearby San Luis Reservoir, the wind can howl through this country in the early summer. That is why the top activities here have become windsurfing (where the speed limit is often exceeded) and sailing. This is not exactly paradise, but for anybody making the long cruise up or down nearby I-5, Los Banos Reservoir is an excellent spot to camp overnight or take a quick fishing hit as a respite from the grinding drive.

Facilities, fees: A paved launch ramp is available on the reservoir's northeast side. A campground, picnic areas, drinking water, and chemical toilets are available. Supplies can be obtained in Los Banos. Day-use and boat-launch fees are charged.

Directions: Take Highway 152 to Volta Road (five miles west of Los Banos). Turn south on Volta Road and drive about a mile to Pioneer Road. Turn left on Pioneer Road and drive a mile to Canyon Road. Turn south (right) onto Canyon Road and drive about five miles to the park.

Contact: San Luis Reservoir State Recreation Area, 209/826-1197; Four Rivers District, 209/826-1196, www.parks.ca.gov.

16 CALIFORNIA AQUEDUCT (MERCED COUNTY)

Rating: 2

east of Fresno

Map 9.3, page 455

The Department of Water Resources likes to call the California Aqueduct the "World's Longest Fishing Hole." What it really is, however, is the "damnedest fish trap in the world," as Charles Fullerton, former Fish and Game director, called it.

All the fish in the aqueduct have been sucked out of the delta by the giant pumping station at Clifton Court Forebay, then sent south with the water. Striped bass and catfish are the primary victims and have the highest survival rates in the aqueduct, feeding on the latest crop of baby fish pulled out of the delta. The stripers and catfish are of all sizes, from the tiny juveniles recently arriving from the delta to stripers in the 40-pound class and catfish to 20 pounds. The chance of hooking one of the latter is what gets people out here.

There are several fishing access points, where folks can sit along the cement-lined canal, toss in their bait, and hope a striped bass or catfish isn't too full from eating all the newly arrived baby fish to consider taking a nibble. There is no "structure" or habitat in the aqueduct. It is just a canal—steeply lined at that, so don't fall in. There is neither great strategy nor any particularly good spots. You just toss out your bait and wait, and spend your time watching all that water go by.

Facilities, fees: Parking areas, trash cans, and vault toilets are provided. No camping is provided along the aqueduct. Fishing access is free.

Directions: To the Mervel Avenue site from I-5 (south of Los Banos): Take I-5 to Highway 33 (near Los Banos). Turn east on Highway 33 and drive eight miles to Los Banos, then continue 12 miles to the junction with Highway 152. Continue straight (Highway 33 turns right) to the Mercy Springs Road exit. Turn north and drive five miles to Mervel Avenue.

Turn right and drive three miles to the access site.

To the Fairfax site from I-5 (about 60 miles north of Kettleman City): Take the Panoche Road exit. Turn east and drive about three miles to Fairfax Road. Turn left and drive three miles north to the access site.

To the Cottonwood site: Take I-5 to the Santa Nella/Highway 33 exit. Take that exit and drive north on Highway 33 for five miles to Cottonwood Road. Turn left and drive to the access site.

To the Canyon Road site: Take I-5 to the Los Banos/Mercy Springs exit. Take that exit and drive west on Highway 152 for two miles to Volta Road. Turn right and drive one mile to Pioneer Road. Turn left and drive one mile to Canyon Road. Turn right and drive three miles to the access site.

Contact: Department of Water Resources, Gustine, 209/827-5100.

🔟🟦 MENDOTA POOL

Rating: 3
near Mendota
Map 9.3, page 455

Mendota Pool is just the northern access point to Fresno Slough, which is the centerpiece for surrounding county parkland.

Boaters can reach the prime spots (where the slough has a deep bend on both sides), as well as a small island on the eastern side. You can also fish from shore for catfish, the main attraction. A few striped bass are also here. For a second option, bring a small spinning rod, a hook, a bobber, and a tub of worms, and you may catch some pan fish, which hold in the same areas as the catfish. This is a popular waterskiing area.

Facilities, fees: A paved launch ramp is available. Restrooms, picnic areas, drinking water, a softball field, and barbecue pits are at Mendota Pool Park. Supplies are available in Mendota. Fishing access is free.

Directions: From Fresno, take Highway 180 west (Whites Bridge Road) for 11 miles, through the town of Kerman, and continue 19 miles to the Mendota Wildlife Area entrance. Cross the bridge at the slough and drive five miles to Mendota and Bass Avenue. Turn right on Bass Avenue and drive 3.5 miles to a gravel road (past Mendota Pool Park). Turn right and drive 0.25 mile.

Contact: Mendota Pool Park, City of Mendota, 559/655-4298, www.mendota.il.us/parks; Department of Fish and Game, Mendota Wildlife Area, 559/655-4645.

🔟🟦 MENDOTA (FRESNO) SLOUGH

Rating: 5
west of Fresno in the Mendota Wildlife Area
Map 9.3, page 455

If you visit Mendota Slough, try to arrive before dawn so you can see the surrounding marsh wake up with the rising sun. It is one of the highlights of the San Joaquin Valley. You get to watch all manner of waterfowl waking up, lifting off, and flying past in huge flocks while the morning sun casts an orange hue on everything.

The Mendota Slough is the water source for the surrounding Mendota Wildlife Area and offers a quiet spot to fish for catfish amid a wetland vibrant with life. Striped bass, crappie, and perch are also in these waters but are caught only occasionally.

Most anglers launch off the Highway 180 access point, then cruise south for three miles to the first major cove on the east side. This is the best catfish area in the slough. It is also adjacent to prime wetland habitat, where lots of waterfowl take up residence. Hunting is allowed in the fall.

Another bonus to fishing the southern part of Mendota Slough, as opposed to the Mendota Pool, is that no waterskiing is permitted south of the Highway 180 overpass, to avoid disturbing the ducks. The obvious side benefit is that anglers are not disturbed either.

Facilities, fees: A boat launch, restrooms, and dispersed camping are at Mendota Wildlife Area. A boat launch, campground, restrooms with flush toilets and drinking water, a restaurant, and bait and tackle are at Jack's Resort. Boat launching and fishing access at the wildlife area is free. Fees apply for day use and boat launching at Jack's Resort.

Directions: From Fresno, take Highway 180 west (Whites Bridge Road) for 11 miles, through the town of Kerman, and continue 19 miles to the wildlife area entrance (just before the bridge at the slough).

Take I-5 (driving north) to the Highway 33/Mendota exit to Derrick Avenue. Turn north on Derrick Avenue and drive to Mendota and Belmont Avenue. Turn right (south) on Belmont Avenue and drive one mile to Highway 180. Turn right and drive four miles to the wildlife area entrance. The entrance for Jack's Resort is directly across from the entrance to Mendota Wildlife Area.

Contact: Department of Fish and Game, Mendota Wildlife Area, 559/655-4645; Jack's Resort, 559/655-2335.

19 CALIFORNIA AQUEDUCT (FRESNO COUNTY)

Rating: 3

southeast of Fresno

Map 9.3, page 455

For people cruising the endless monotony of I-5, the California Aqueduct provides a rare respite. Along with the water pumped out of the Sacramento–San Joaquin Delta come striped bass and catfish, and they provide poor to fair fishing at special access sites. It is nothing complicated, with two options. You might try what I do when I make the long drive in the San Joaquin Valley. I'll bring along a spinning rod for the trip, with a Rattletrap lure tied on, and then when I need a break from the driving, I stop at these aqueduct access spots. I hardly wait to reach the water and then make 5–10 casts. Sometimes a striped

bass will be wandering by right where I am casting. The other option is to take it more seriously, sitting on your fanny, tossing out your bait, and then waiting for a striper or catfish to come cruising down the aqueduct. The best hope is in the early evening and into the night, with anchovies being the preferred entreaty.

Facilities, fees: Parking areas and toilets are provided. No other facilities are available. Fishing access is free.

Directions: From I-5 take the Highway 33/Mendota exit. Turn north on Highway 33/Derrick Avenue and drive five miles to Three Rocks and Clarkson Avenue. Turn right on Clarkson Avenue and drive east to the fishing access sign.

Contact: Department of Water Resources, Gustine, 209/827-5100.

20 CALIFORNIA AQUEDUCT (FRESNO AND KINGS COUNTIES)

Rating: 2

from Huron to Kettleman City

Map 9.3, page 455

This may be the ugliest fishing spot on earth. The California Aqueduct is an engineer's dream, endless and straight, with beveled edges made of concrete. The surrounding area is hot, flat, and desolate, a paragon of nothingness. But for people cruising I-5, it provides a rare respite. Along with the water pumped out of the delta come striped bass and catfish, and they provide poor to fair fishing at the California Aqueduct fishing access sites. It's nothing complicated. You sit on your fanny and toss out your bait, with anchovies the preferred entreaty, and wait for a striper or catfish to come cruising down the aqueduct. The best fishing is in the early evening on into the night. For highway cruisers who want to break the monotony of I-5, a long shot is making a quick hit at these access points, casting out Rattletrap lures. Who knows? Maybe a striped bass will be wandering by. On the other hand, maybe not.

Facilities, fees: Toilets are provided at all California Aqueduct access sites. Camping, lodging, and supplies are available in Kettleman City. Fishing access is free.

Directions: To reach the Huron site from Kettleman City, take I-5 north for 24 miles to the Highway 198 exit. Turn east on Highway 198/Dorris Avenue and drive six miles to the fishing site.

To reach the Avenal Cutoff site from Kettleman City, take I-5 north for 10 miles to the Highway 269 exit. Loop around over the freeway to Avenal Cutoff Road. Turn left (northeast) on Avenal Cutoff Road and drive four miles until the road crosses the California Aqueduct.

To reach the Kettleman City site from the north end of Kettleman City, turn west on Milham Avenue and drive one mile to the access site at the aqueduct crossing.

Contact: California Department of Water Resources, Coalinga, 209/827-5451.

21 SAN JOAQUIN RIVER (PINEDALE TO PATTERSON)

Rating: 6

near Fresno
Map 9.4, page 456

From its headwaters in the Sierra Nevada to its outlet into the delta, the San Joaquin River takes on more characteristics and changes its appearance more often than a chameleon.

In this stretch of water, the river is a gentle stream that rolls its way slowly through the San Joaquin Valley, skirting just north of Fresno. The best areas to fish are at Lost Lake Park and Broken Bridges, where access is good, and where significant numbers of rainbow trout are planted, usually in the spring and early summer months. Another good access point is at the Highway 99 crossing, where catfish provide hope. This relatively short stretch of

river is very heavily planted, getting 10- to 12-inch rainbow trout. The stocks are made virtually weekly and for as long as the river is cool enough to support them.

Public access is extremely limited. There is no free public shoreline access from Fresno (at the Highway 99 crossing) all the way up to Lost Lake Park. In this span, the only access is through a private riverside property that is named Fort Washington Beach Park.

Facilities, fees: Lost Lake Park has a campground, drinking water, a picnic area, and chemical toilets. Supplies are in Fresno. A day-use fee is charged per vehicle per day. No boat launching is allowed.

Fort Washington Beach Park has a boat ramp and a campground. There is a day-use fee. There is no fee for boat launching.

Directions: To Lost Lake Park: From Highway 41 (at the north end of Fresno), take the Friant Road exit and drive north on Friant Road for 9.5 miles to Lost Lake Park. Access is available at Lost Lake Park and at the Broken Bridges, about a mile past the park, in Friant.

To Fort Washington Beach Park: From Highway 41 (at the north end of Fresno), take the Friant Road exit and drive north on Friant Road for one mile to Rice Road. Turn left and continue until the road forks. Bear left at the fork and continue to the park. The river can also be accessed northwest of Fresno, where Highway 99 crosses the river.

Contact: Lost Lake Park, Fresno County, Parks and Grounds, 559/600-3004; Fort Washington Beach Park, 559/434-9600.

22 LAKE WOOLLOMES

Rating: 4

near Delano
Map 9.5, page 457

Little Lake Woollomes (pronounced WOOL-ums) provides a respite, set as it is in a small park—the kind with lawns and a few picnic spots. An angler's paradise it is not, with some bluegill, catfish, and occasionally a bass. It gets catchable 10- to 12-inch rainbow trout from the Department of Fish and Game. Some folks spend evenings here having a picnic along the shore, tossing out their bait, and waiting for a nibble. Woollomes does cover about 300 acres, and in the barren south valley, any lake, even this one, is considered something special.

Facilities, fees: An unimproved boat ramp for car-top boats is next to the picnic areas. Picnic areas, restrooms, drinking water, and boat docks are provided. Supplies are nearby. An annual permit is required for all boats, including canoes and kayaks. Permits can be purchased at the park. Boats are limited to sailboats, rowboats, and canoes; no powerboats, motorboats (not even trolling motors), or motorized personal watercraft are allowed. No permit is required for shoreline fishing. A day-use fee is charged on weekends from Easter to September 15.

Directions: From Bakersfield, take Highway 99 north for 25 miles to Delano and Highway 155. Turn east on Highway 155 and drive one mile to Mast Avenue. Turn right (south) on Mast Avenue and drive one mile to Woollomes Avenue. Turn left (east) on Woollomes Avenue and continue a short distance to the lake.

Contact: Kern County Parks and Recreation Department, 661/868-7000, www.co.kern .ca.us/parks; Bob's Bait Bucket, Bakersfield, 661/833-8657, www.bobsbaitbucket.com.

23 BUENA VISTA AQUATIC RECREATION AREA

Rating: 4

near Bakersfield

Map 9.5, page 457

It may not resemble your idea of paradise, but in the desolate western San Joaquin Valley, any body of water is something of a haven. Buena Vista is at an elevation of 330 feet and is actually two connected lakes fed by the West Side Canal—little Lake Evans to the west and larger Lake Webb to the east. It is critical that you know the difference between the two.

Lake Webb, covering 875 surface acres, is open to all boating, including personal watercraft. With a 45-mph speed limit, jet boats towing skiers are a common sight all summer long. No trout stocks are made; it's primarily a catfish lake.

Lake Evans, on the other hand, is small (85 acres) and quiet, with no boats allowed. It is stocked with trout when water temperatures are cool, in the winter months. It also provides fair fisheries for bass, bluegill, catfish, and crappie. The bass and crappie are best in the spring, before the west valley gets fried by the blowtorch heat of summer. By then, the fishing is decent only at dusk (for bass) and into the night (for catfish).

A maximum of 300 boats and 125 personal watercraft are allowed per day.

Facilities, fees: A paved boat ramp is available on the north side of Lake Webb. A marina and fishing supplies are available. A campground with restrooms, drinking water, flush toilets, showers, a playground, store, and an RV dump station is nearby. Two swimming lagoons, a snack bar, and groceries are also nearby. A PGA-rated golf course is two miles west. Day-use, boat-launching, and fishing fees are charged; the fishing fee is only charged when trout are stocked.

Directions: From Bakersfield, take I-5 south a short distance to Highway 119. Turn west on Highway 119 and drive two miles to Highway 43. Turn left (south) on Highway 43 and drive two miles to the campground, at the road's end.

Contact: Buena Vista Aquatic Recreation Area, 661/763-1526; Kern County Parks and Recreation Department, 661/868-7000, www.co.kern.ca.us/parks; Bob's Bait Bucket, Bakersfield, 661/833-8657, www.bobsbait bucket.com.

YOSEMITE AND MAMMOTH LAKES

© TOM GRUNDY/123RF.COM

BEST FISHING SPOTS

◖ Hike-In Fisheries
Ansel Adams Wilderness, **page 494.**

◖ Places to Teach Kids to Fish
Pinecrest Lake, **page 481.**
Convict Lake, **page 508.**

Some of nature's most perfect artwork was created on the east side of the Sierra crest, where you'll also find many of California's best lakes for trophy-sized trout. More big brown trout are caught here than anywhere else, and they add a special sizzle to the excellent Alpers trout programs that are provided at many lakes.

There are beautiful lakes elsewhere in the region that provide good fishing for trout, such as Twin Lakes, Convict Lake, and Crowley Lake. Twin Lakes probably produces more 10-pound brown trout than any other lake in California. This region also includes Saddlebag Lake, the highest drive-to lake, at 10,087 feet. In addition, almost every lake's outlet stream provides prospects. This region has it all: beauty, variety, and a chance at the fish of a lifetime. There is also access to the Ansel Adams Wilderness, which features Banner and Ritter peaks and lakes filled with small fish.

Fly fishers have the chance to float tube in lakes for giant trout or to hike, then sneak and stalk trout in small mountain streams. Of the latter, the headwaters of the San Joaquin River, with access on the River Trail, provide the best chance in California of catching the grand slam of trout – rainbow, golden, brown, and brook, as well as some hybrid versions that can't be categorized.

Of course, most visits to this region start with a tour of Yosemite Valley – framed by El Capitan, the Goliath of Yosemite, on one side, and the three-spired Cathedral Rocks on the other. As you enter the valley,

Bridalveil Fall comes into view, a perfect freefall of water over the south canyon rim, then across a meadow. To your left you'll see the two-tiered Yosemite Falls, and finally, Half Dome, the single most awesome piece of rock in the world. Yosemite Valley is the world's greatest showpiece, and yet no place has as much unfulfilled potential for fishing as Yosemite National Park. Of 318 lakes, only 127 have ever had fish, and of those, only a handful provide a viable opportunity. Why? Because trout are not stocked here, the spawning habitat becomes very limited, and the lakes get fished out.

The irony is that although 24,000 people jam into five square miles of Yosemite Valley each summer day, the park is actually 90 percent wilderness. What most see of Yosemite represents but a fraction of the fantastic land of wonder, adventure, and unparalleled natural beauty.

For those who hike, another world will open up: the Grand Canyon of the Tuolumne River, Matterhorn Peak, Benson Lake (with the largest white-sand beach in the Sierra), and dozens of spectacular waterfalls.

If you explore beyond the park boundaries, the adventures just keep getting better. Over Tioga Pass, outside the park and just off Highway 120, are Tioga and Ellery Lakes, which often provide much better fishing than any other lakes in the park.

This region has it all: beauty, variety, and a chance at the hike or fish of a lifetime. Nothing compares to it.

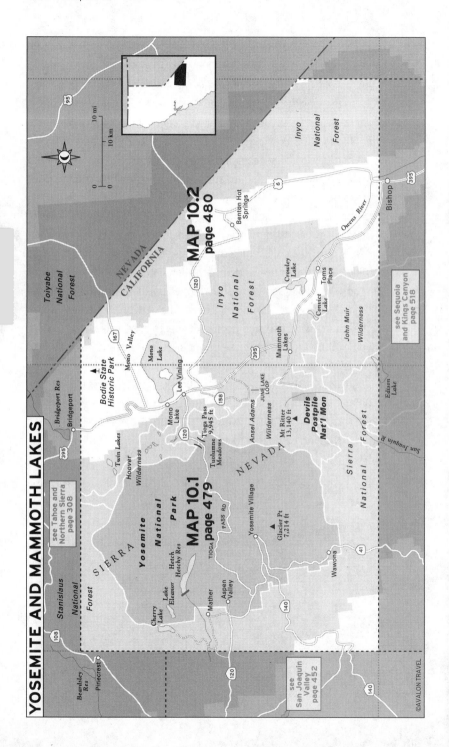

Map 10.1

Sites 1-31
Pages 481-502

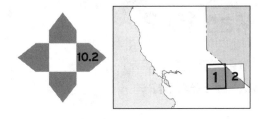

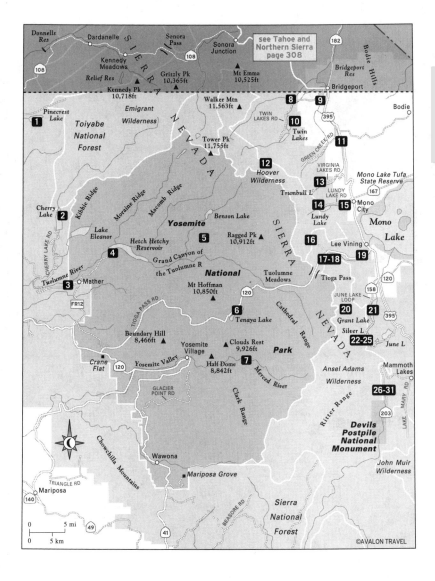

Map 10.2

Sites 32-42
Pages 504-512

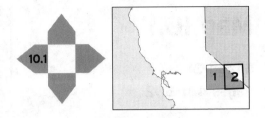

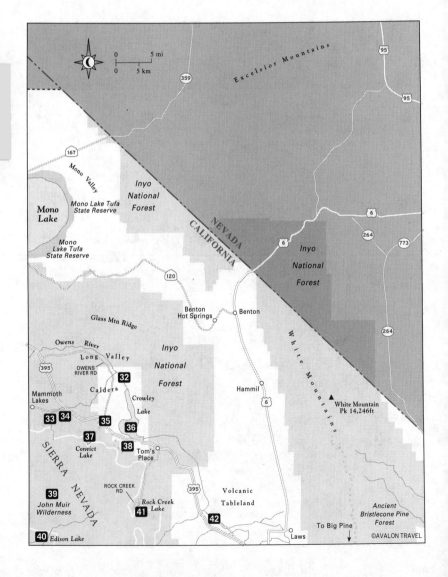

©AVALON TRAVEL

1 PINECREST LAKE

Rating: 5

near Strawberry in Stanislaus National Forest

Map 10.1, page 479 **BEST (**

No secrets here. The word is out about Pinecrest Lake, a family-oriented vacation center that provides the most consistent catch rates for pan-sized rainbow trout in the region. It is near the Dodge Ridge Ski Resort, and the lake provides in summer what Dodge Ridge provides in winter: a fun spot with full amenities. It is pretty and has decent fishing, but quiet wilderness it is not. The campground usually has plenty of takers.

Pinecrest Lake is at 5,621 feet, covers 300 acres, and gets regular stocks of rainbow trout to join a resident population of brown trout. Every now and then someone catches a big brown that causes quite a stir, but it is usually by accident and not design. Most of the fishing is done by trolling the flasher/night crawler combination, or by bait dunking. Note that a 20-mph speed limit is in effect and waterskiing is prohibited.

Stanislaus National Forest, Summit Ranger District, and Pacific Gas and Electric Company are working together to update and rehabilitate Pinecrest's day use areas and campgrounds. Most of the work will be complete by 2015, but will continue through 2019.

Facilities, fees: A boat ramp and boat rentals are available at Pinecrest Lake Resort. There is a marina, lodging, campgrounds, drinking water, and wheelchair-accessible fishing pier. There are four restrooms with flush toilets and sinks, including two restrooms that are winterized. A grocery store, coin laundry, gas, restaurant, and pay showers (in summer only) are also available. Fishing access is free.

Directions: From Manteca, take Highway 120 east to Oakdale and Highway 108/120. Turn east on Highway 108/120 and drive to Sonora. Continue northeast on Highway 108 for 30 miles toward Sonora Pass to the Pinecrest Lake turnoff. Turn right and drive a short distance to the lake.

Contact: Stanislaus National Forest, Summit Ranger District, 209/965-3434, www.fs.fed .us/r5—click on Forest Offices; Pinecrest Lake Marina, 209/965-3333; Pinecrest Lake Resort, 209/965-3411, www.pinecrestlake resort.com; Rich & Sal's Sporting Goods, Pinecrest, 209/965-3637, www.pinecrest sportshop.com.

2 CHERRY LAKE

Rating: 7

northwest of Yosemite National Park in Stanislaus National Forest

Map 10.1, page 479

Cherry Lake is a jewel of a mountain lake surrounded by national forest. It is just outside the western boundary of Yosemite National Park, set at 4,700 feet. It is much larger than most people anticipate, about three miles long, and is stocked regularly with rainbow trout in the 10- to 12-inch class, joining larger holdovers and providing much better trout fishing than anything in Yosemite.

The camp is on the southwest shore of the lake, a very pretty spot that is about a mile ride to the boat launch on the west side of Cherry Valley Dam. The lake is bordered to the east by Kibbie Ridge; just on the other side is Lake Eleanor in Yosemite National Park.

Fishing is best in May and early June, although the weather can be quite nasty during late spring. Pick one of the nice days, troll adjacent to the shoreline, and you should pick up fish. If you show up instead at midsummer and try fishing from shore, you may be out of luck.

Fishing is just one of the reasons people love to visit Cherry Lake, which provides a base of operations for many activities. The dam at Cherry Lake marks the start of a trail that is routed north into the Emigrant Wilderness, or to the east to Lake Eleanor and farther into Yosemite National Park. Between the two wilderness areas are literally dozens of backcountry lakes.

Here's an insider's tip: During periods of

campfire restrictions, which are often most of the summer in this national forest, the campground here is the only one in the area where campfires are permitted. That makes the idea of camping here extremely compelling. A fire permit is required from the Forest Service.

Water levels can fluctuate, often dropping precipitously from mid-July through September. The gate across Cherry Lake Dam is closed the weekend following Labor Day and usually reopens Memorial Day weekend, weather permitting.

Facilities, fees: A paved boat ramp is available, depending on water levels. Boat-in camping is permitted on the lake's east side. A campground, vault toilets, and drinking water are 0.5 mile from the lake. Supplies can be obtained in Groveland. Fishing access is free.

Directions: From Groveland, take Highway 120 east for about 15 miles, to Forest Service Road 1N07/Cherry Lake Road, on the left side of the road. Turn left and drive 18 miles to the south end of Cherry Lake and the campground access road, on the right. Turn right and drive one mile to the campground.

Contact: Stanislaus National Forest, Groveland Ranger District, 209/962-7825, www.fs.fed.us/r5—click on Forest Offices.

🖪 TUOLUMNE RIVER

Rating: 5

west of Yosemite National Park in
Stanislaus National Forest
Map 10.1, page 479

The Tuolumne is not the greatest stream you've ever seen, but it isn't the worst either.

For starters, you must have a Forest Service map in hand before trying to figure out the best access points, then follow the directions in this listing. That will get you to the more promising spots, where rainbow trout are stocked by the Department of Fish and Game (DFG). A breakdown of stocks is as follows: Middle Fork, South Fork, and North Fork all get 10- to 12-inch rainbow trout.

For finishers, if you are more ambitious and want to chase wild trout, you must scan the Forest Service map to make sure you are not trespassing on private property. This country is "checkerboarded"; that is, parcels are owned by private individuals and the Forest Service in a checkerboard pattern. If a sign says "No Trespassing," you'd best believe it.

The hard-to-reach sections of the Tuolumne River don't offer large fish, which is frustrating considering the effort required to reach them. I think my biggest catch here was an 11-incher, and most have been in the 5- to 7-inch class.

Regardless, it is a small, pretty stream.

Facilities, fees: Several campgrounds with vault toilets can be found near the river, but they offer no drinking water. Fishing access is free.

Directions: From Groveland, take Highway 120 east for about 18 miles (4 miles past the Groveland District Office). Campgrounds along the highway provide access to the planted sections of the Tuolumne. There are also access points in more remote sections on Forest Service roads.

Contact: Stanislaus National Forest, Groveland Ranger District, 209/962-7825, www.fs.fed.us/r5—click on Forest Offices; Bureau of Land Management, Mother Lode Field Office, 916/941-3101, www.blm.gov/ca; Fish'n Dan's Guide Service, Twain Harte, 209/586-2383, www.fishndans.com; Rich & Sal's Sporting Goods, Pinecrest, 209/965-3637, www.pinecrestsportshop.com.

🖪 HETCH HETCHY RESERVOIR

Rating: 2

in Yosemite National Park
Map 10.1, page 479

Hetch Hetchy is a beautiful granite-edged canyon filled with an azure-blue lake, a second Yosemite Valley, complete with waterfalls. But no boats are permitted, no trout stocks are made, and the fishing is regularly horrible and can seem impossible from shore. The lake is huge (covering 2,000 acres) and is at 4,000 feet in the northwest corner of Yosemite National Park. It has brook trout, rainbow trout, and a few large brown trout, but they are almost never caught.

One suggestion is to hike across the dam, then hike up on the far side of the lake toward the Tuolumne River Canyon, then drop down and fish the headwaters, where the Tuolumne enters the head of the lake. This is ambitious, but it's really your only chance.

For purely entertainment purposes, let me tell you a story of the secret adventures of an outlaw friend, but be forewarned: This is totally illegal. If you try it, you're likely to end up in jail. This outlaw friend of mine, whom I call Josey Wales, used a trap to catch live mice. Then under a waning moon, he'd plunk his scull boat in Hetch Hetchy at about 1 A.M., and he'd scull over near Wapama Falls just as the moon was coming up. At about 2 A.M., he'd arrive, take out his cage of mice, and hook one through the skin of the neck. Then, with the wiggling mouse dangling from his fishing line, he'd plop the little guy on a square piece of floating wood. The outlaw Josey Wales would have his bail open on his spinning reel and would oar off quietly in the night. About 60 yards off, he'd stop. He'd flip his bail over, turn toward that little mouse jumping around on the piece of floating wood, and give his rod a twitch. That mouse would get tugged into the water, and it would swim like crazy, illuminated by the bright moon rising in the night sky. That's how this outlaw caught 10-pound brown trout at Hetch Hetchy. Can you tell me how many violations he committed? Probably would end up in San Quentin but he never got caught doing it. (He did end up in county for something else, but that's another story.)

I think it's equally criminal that no boats are allowed on this lake, not even human powered. The only exception is when honchos from the San Francisco Water Department and politicians have been seen on gas-powered motorboats (!). What's the bigger outrage?

Facilities, fees: A walk-in campground (wilderness permit required), a picnic area, and parking are available. No private boats are permitted on the lake. A park entrance fee is charged.

Directions: From Manteca, take Highway 120 east and drive to Oakdale and Highway 108/120. Turn left on Highway 108/120 and drive east for 25 miles to the turnoff for Chinese Camp and Highway 49/120. Turn right on Highway 49/120, drive about 5 miles to Groveland, and continue 28 miles (6 miles past Harden Flat) to Evergreen Road. Turn left (north) and drive to the reservoir. Call the number under *Contact* for road/gate information.

Contact: Yosemite National Park, 209/372-0200, www.nps.gov/yose.

5 YOSEMITE NATIONAL PARK

Rating: 4

east of Stockton

Map 10.1, page 479

Many people don't realize that just 150 years ago there were no fish at all in 95 percent of the thousands of lakes in the Sierra Nevada range. That includes the high country of Yosemite National Park, where the lakes are barren rock bowls, filled with pure water and with few nutrients to provide for aquatic life.

The only lakes that had any fish were the few that had inlets to large streams, where the trout were able to live in the lake in summer, and then swim upstream in the rivers to spawn in the winter and spring.

But as time passed, trout were stocked in the high Sierra lakes, with golden trout, rainbow trout, brook trout, and sometimes brown trout and even cutthroats planted. Well, while aerial plantings have continued at lakes in national forests, they were stopped long ago at Yosemite National Park. There are no plants, and those high mountain lakes are again returning to their natural state as barren rock bowls.

Of the 318 lakes in Yosemite National Park, only 127 have ever had fish. Of those 127, only a handful now provide viable prospects. And despite the 3.5–4 million visitors to Yosemite each year, the Park Service is only now forming a fisheries management plan, which largely consists of ways to get rid of fish, not to provide a fishing program.

Many hike-to streams provide good fishing for tons of small brook trout. The best are Matterhorn Creek and Lyell Fork, and the Tuolumne River (near Glen Aulin) is another. These are your best bets because the trout have a chance to spawn in the rivers.

Lakes? The following provide the better fishing: Benson, Bernice, Dog, Lower Edna, Edyth, Harriet, Ireland, Matthes, Mattie, Minnow, Rodgers, Shepherd, Skelton, Smedberg, Tallulah, Tilden, Twin, Virginia, Washburn, Wilma, and Young.

Cathedral Lake is a good example of what can happen without stocks, and also without natural production and no rules that require catch-and-release fishing. Because of its unique rock spire, its natural beauty, and its small, pristine, lakeside camps, Cathedral has always been a favored destination. It is also a perfect layover spot for hikers on the John Muir Trail. In the 1970s, Cathedral Lake provided very good fishing despite getting hit every day by anglers. Well, with no more stocks, no natural spawning, and no catch-and-release fishing, Cathedral Lake is now fished out. This same scenario has played itself out at many lakes in Yosemite National Park.

Regardless, Yosemite is God's country, one of the most beautiful places on earth, and I have hiked most of it. You get the classic glacial-sculpted domes, cirques, moraines, and canyons, with some of the best vista points anywhere.

Facilities, fees: Campgrounds, lodging, and supplies are in the park. Horse, bike, and raft rentals can also be obtained. A park entrance fee is charged.

Directions: Trailheads leading into the park can be reached via Forest Service roads that

junction with Highways 99, 140, 41, and 120, and with U.S. 395. The following routes lead to major park entrances:

From Stockton, take Highway 99 south to Highway 120. Turn east on Highway 120 and drive 75 miles to the park entrance.

From Merced, take Highway 140 east for 55 miles to the park entrance. Check the status of this route due to repairs, closures, delays, and rerouting because of damage from Ferguson Rock Slide.

From Fresno, take Highway 41 north for 65 miles to the park entrance.

Take U.S. 395 to the town of Lee Vining and Highway 120. Turn west on Highway 120, then continue for about 10 miles to the park entrance.

Contact: Yosemite National Park, 209/372-0200, www.nps.gov/yose.

6 TENAYA LAKE

Rating: 2
west of Lee Vining in Yosemite National Park
Map 10.1, page 479

Tenaya Lake is in a natural rock basin in the pristine, high granite country of Yosemite, and like Lake Tahoe or Crater Lake in Oregon, it is one of the few places that provide a sense of "feeling" just by looking at it. It is at 8,141 feet and covers 150 acres. John Muir called it a mountain temple. The lake was named after Chief Tenaya of the Ahwahneechee Indian tribe, who was Yosemite's last Indian chief and caretaker before the entire tribe was deported to a reservation by an army troop.

Perhaps that is why the fishing is so terrible. I call it "Chief Tenaya's Revenge." There are no stocks, natural reproduction is very poor, and only a sprinkling of small brook trout and rainbow trout have managed to survive. You might as well fish in an empty bucket.

No matter. Just being able to spend a day sitting and looking at this place can be plenty.

Facilities, fees: A picnic area is at the lake. Campsites are nearby, at Tuolumne Meadows.

Nature trails are provided. No motorized boats are permitted on the water. There is no boat ramp, but car-top boats can be hand-launched. Supplies can be obtained in Lee Vining and in the park. A park entrance fee is charged.

Directions: From Merced, drive east on Highway 140 to the Arch Rock entrance station. Continue east to the Big Oak Flat Road junction (0.5 mile before entering Yosemite Valley). Turn left and drive 14 miles to Tioga Road. Turn right and drive about 31 miles (past Tuolumne Meadows) and through the Tioga Pass entrance station. Continue two miles to the lake on the right side of the road (15 miles west from Tioga entrance station).

From Lee Vining, take U.S. 395 south to the junction with Tioga Pass Road/Highway 120. Turn west on Tioga Pass Road/Highway 120 and drive about 11 miles to the Tioga Pass/Yosemite National Park entrance. Continue another 15 miles to the lake.

Contact: Yosemite National Park, 209/372-0200, www.nps.gov/yose; Inyo National Forest, Mono Lake Visitors Center, 760/647-3044, www.monolake.org; Bells Sporting Goods, 760/647-6406; Tioga Pass Resort, www.tiogapassresort.com.

⑦ MERCED RIVER

Rating: 7

west of Yosemite National Park in
Sierra National Forest
Map 10.1, page 479

Here is the stream that so many vacationers drive right by in their scramble to get to Yosemite National Park. The irony is that as they pass the Merced River, they are passing better fishing water than can be found anywhere in the park. There are also several campgrounds along the Merced that have fewer people in them compared to the camps in Yosemite. Of course, the surroundings are nowhere as dramatic; it is a pretty river set in a canyon and the fishing is often good.

In summer, all the spots near the campgrounds are stocked with catchable (10- to 12-inch) rainbow trout by the Department of Fish and Game. The fishing is best from June through July, then it starts to wane a bit in August, as temperatures climb and water flows drop.

Though this river is better known for its rafting, it does provide good fly-fishing for those who learn the river. It is best in the evening, when the canyon is shaded and there can be a surface hatch and bite. During midday, it is very difficult to catch anything. At dusk, it is like a different river. There are pullouts along the highway that provide access. But watch out for fast-moving vehicles. They can really howl up and down the canyon here.

In the summer, this is an ideal river to jump into during the day, with many deep holes and rocks situated perfectly for jumping platforms (always check the depth of the hole before jumping in, and never dive headfirst into a river, of course). Then, as the day cools off and shade falls on the river, it becomes better for fishing, not swimming, with a good evening bite for rainbow trout in the 9- to 12-inch class (some smaller, very few bigger).

Facilities, fees: Campgrounds are along the river west of the park entrance near El Portal. Supplies are in El Portal. Fishing access is free.

Directions: To Merced River above the Bureau of Land Management's Briceburg Visitors Center: From Merced, take Highway 140 east for 45 miles to the Briceburg Visitors Center. Continue north; the road parallels the river, and direct access is available.

To Merced River near BLM's Briceburg Visitors Center: From Merced, take Highway 140 east for 45 miles to a Briceburg Visitors Center. Near the Briceburg Visitors Center, turn left at a road that is signed BLM Camping Areas (the road remains paved for about 150 yards). Drive over the suspension bridge and turn left, traveling downstream (up to five miles), parallel to the river.

To South Fork Merced: From Mariposa, take Highway 140 east for about 5 miles to

Triangle Road (if you reach Midpines, you have gone 1.5 miles too far). Turn right on Triangle Road and drive about six miles to Darrah and Jerseydale Road. Turn left and drive three miles to the campground, on the left side of the road (adjacent to the Jerseydale Ranger Station).

Contact: Bureau of Land Management, Mother Lode Field Office, 916/941-3101, www.blm.gov/ca; Briceberg Visitor Center, 209/379-9414; Sierra National Forest, Bass Lake Ranger District, 559/877-2218, www.fs.fed.us/r5—click on Forest Offices.

8 GREEN CREEK

Rating: 5

near Bridgeport in
Humboldt-Toiyabe National Forest
Map 10.1, page 479

Most people don't come to Green Creek to fish. They come here to hike. This is a small meadow creek, pretzeling its way along, with deep-cut banks, all very pretty.

The access road leads to a nice little camp at streamside, with an adjacent trailhead for backpackers. The trail is routed past Green Lake and then into the magnificent Hoover Wilderness. Visitors often arrive in the afternoon after a long drive, then overnight it and plan to start their backpacking trip the next morning, rested and ready.

In the meantime, they should get out their fishing rods. Green Creek is stocked with rainbow trout at the campground, as well as at several obvious access points along Green Creek Road. Some browns up to 12 inches join the planters. Most people don't know that.

Facilities, fees: A campground, drinking water, and vault toilets are available. Supplies are in Bridgeport. Fishing access is free.

Directions: From the town of Bridgeport, take U.S. 395 south for four miles to Green Lakes Road (dirt). Turn right and drive eight miles to Forest Road 142. Turn right and go four miles to the Green Creek Campground. Access

is available at the campground and at several access points on the road in.

Contact: Humboldt-Toiyabe National Forest, Bridgeport Ranger District, 760/932-7070, www.fs.fed.us/r5—click on Forest Offices; Ken's Sporting Goods, Bridgeport, 760/932-7707, www.kenssport.com; The Troutfitter, 760/934-2517, www.thetroutfly.com; Bridgeport Chamber of Commerce, 760/932-7500, www.bridgeportcalifornia.com.

9 EAST WALKER RIVER

Rating: 9

north of Bridgeport
Map 10.1, page 479

The East Walker River always sets off passions from trout anglers. It's one of the top brown trout streams in the western United States, although some may debate that suggestion.

The number of big brown trout (three- to five-pounders and occasionally even bigger) can make every visit to this river an exciting but eclectic adventure. You know the fish are there. You know that a lot of fly fishers try to coax them to take a streamer, day after day, all season. You know they are smart and elusive. But you also know that at some point in their lives, these fish have to eat, right?

That is your chance. This is a very difficult stream to fish for newcomers to fly-fishing. You need remarkable stealth in your approach, then casting skill, so that you can make your presentation with an extremely light touch, just kind of floating your fly or streamer out on the water. There are also a lot of cut banks here that the trout hide under. It can be very difficult to get the big fish to emerge, and it can be almost impossible when there is direct sunlight on the water. A little wind (a pain when fly casting) is actually a good thing here, as it ruffles the water a bit, helping to disguise your approach.

What helps is using sink-tip lines and large streamers, especially in the cold weather, early in the season, when the wind is typically a frustrating element for casting. Ken's Sporting Goods, the headquarters around these parts, advises using Marabous, Matukas, and Sculpins, as well as strong fluorocarbon leaders. Standard trout leaders will break if you hook a big brown. That's the kind of thing that can make strong men cry and weak men drink.

Far more big fish break off in this river than get landed. I urge you to release every fish you catch here to help this fishery continue to rebuild to its former preeminent status. An intriguing aspect of the East Walker is that you can entertain yourself by catching fish in the 10- to 14-inch class (a lot of fun with a fly rod) and then get stunned and rung up when a five-pounder (or bigger) grabs your fly and says good-bye. The favored patterns include Pheasant Tail nymphs, Prince nymphs, Hare's Ear nymphs, and a variety of streamers, such as the woolly bugger, Zonker, and sculpin patterns.

When water flows are about 200 cubic feet per second, that is often when fishing is best. The first mile of river below the dam is typically sprinkled with fly fishers.

Most everybody fishes below the dam on down about a mile, so these fish get a very keen eye for what might pass their way. But this is where the big fish are. Blow the presentation and you have no chance. In the fall, I've seen anglers lined up below the dam, taking turns, and I just say forget it, I want to be by myself.

You have to travel farther downstream to get by yourself, but as you depart the dam area, you leave the big fish behind, too. The river has more riffles and a fair number of 12-inch trout, a more standard-type trout stream. There is an occasional surface caddis hatch here, but again, those giant browns are nowhere to be found.

The Department of Fish and Game and CalTrout have done an outstanding job of protecting the riparian habitat and future access with a land deal, and of monitoring the recovery of the river since it was damaged by a silt flow in 1989. The projections are for the river's premium numbers of big brown trout to continue their return in the coming years.

What is called "microhabitat" is developing, and this is the key to the entire aquatic food chain. Since the silt flush, spawning success is way up, approximately 80 percent now, compared to the less than 5 percent–20 percent spawning success that was the case immediately before that. The Department of Fish and Game is planting fingerling brown trout to help reestablish the fishery.

Another bonus is that all the carp that had detracted from the experience seem to have taken up residence far downstream, well out of range of the prime fishing area downstream of Bridgeport Reservoir.

It is an absolute necessity that you make a close check of all state regulations prior to beginning your fishing trip here. As the fishery continues to recover, the rules will be adjusted and fine-tuned.

My best suggestion is to do as I do: stop in at Ken's, in nearby Bridgeport, to get the lowdown.

One thing you can count on is that the river will be jammed with anglers in October, when the big browns swim upstream to spawn below the dam. There is a famous spot called "The Big Hole," and it seems people will come for miles to make a cast into it.

For newcomers, the East Walker River generally flows through ranch land, the flat, high country for which the region east of the Sierra is well known. It is quite pretty, running blue and hip-deep as it flows toward Nevada.

And it deserves all the desire you will feel as you fly-cast a big streamer, hoping that maybe this will be the time when you meet the giant brown trout of your life.

Note: Always check with the DFG for current fishing regulations pertaining to the East Walker River.

Facilities, fees: Campgrounds and supplies are in the Bridgeport area. Fishing access is free.
Directions: From Bridgeport on U.S. 395, take Highway 182 and drive north along

Bridgeport Reservoir, then continue past the dam. The road runs right along the river, providing direct access.

Contact: Ken's Sporting Goods, Bridgeport, 760/932-7707, www.kenssport.com; Sierra Trout Magnet, 760/873-0100, www.sierratroutmagnet.com; The Troutfitter, 760/934-2517, www.thetroutfly.com; Sierra Drifters Guide Service, 760/935-4250, www.sierradrifters.com; Performance Anglers, 818/288-0583, www.performanceanglers.com; Bridgeport Chamber of Commerce, 760/932-7500, www.bridgeportcalifornia.com.

🔟 TWIN LAKES

Rating: 10

near Bridgeport in
Humboldt-Toiyabe National Forest

Map 10.1, page 479

More big brown trout are caught at Twin Lakes than at any other water in California, but it is hardly assembly production. The two biggest brown trout recorded in California were caught here. The state record brown trout, 26 pounds, 5 ounces, was caught here in 1985. One of the wildest catches I've ever heard of occurred in 1991, when 11-year-old Micah Beirle of Bakersfield caught a trout that weighed in at 20 pounds, 8 ounces. In addition, browns in the 5- to 10-pound class are caught here nearly every week.

However, what most people catch are not the giant browns, but the planted rainbow trout in the 9- to 11-inch class, and if they're lucky, maybe a three-pounder or enough kokanee salmon to fill a frying pan.

The Twin Lakes are actually two lakes, of course, connected by a short stream (no fishing here) and located high in the eastern Sierra, at an elevation of 7,000 feet. Twin Lakes Resort is near Lower Twin, and Annett's Mono Village Resort is on Upper Twin. Waterskiing is permitted at Upper Twin (35-mph speed limit) from 10 A.M.–3 P.M. If there are too many people around for you, a nearby trailhead leads into the Hoover Wilderness, where there are many small but quality trout waters.

Anybody can see the big brown trout, but most of the big browns are not caught by accident; the lake gets too much fishing pressure for that to happen. Instead, they are taken by specialists trolling Rapalas. The No. 18 Rapala is probably the best lure ever designed for these big browns. But it takes a lot of time on the water, and some anglers work at it all summer and never get one of the big ones.

The best of the two lakes is Lower Twin, by a mile. At Lower Twin, the speed limit is 35 mph, and the better spots include the shallows near Marti's Marina, where trolled woolly worms are productive early and late in the day for rainbow trout. The best fishing is just off a stepped shelf that drops very steeply, on the south side of Lower Twin. Another good spot is in the northeast bay in Lower Twin.

Lower Twin gets 10- to 12-inch rainbow trout, courtesy of the DFG. Upper Twin usually gets a few more than Lower Twin, in the same class. At Upper Twin, the kokanee salmon usually go on their best bite of the year when the weather cools off in September.

If you want to try for the big boys, the 10-pounders and up, remember this: the preponderance of big brown trout are caught when the weather is cold, often windy, often early in the season after ice-out. That is because in warm, calm weather, they are more easily spooked and more apt to hide under deep ledges until nightfall. So if you want a real try at a big brown, show up during the miserable weather of early May and troll until you're so cold that you feel like petrified wood. If you can plan your trip to Twin Lakes after a plant of Alpers rainbow trout, you'll limit out by adding a three- or four-pounder on top of a stringer of 12-inchers.

Facilities, fees: Full-service marinas, mooring, and fishing- and pontoon-boat rentals are at Twin Lakes Resort and Annett's Mono Village Resort. Both resorts have paved boat ramps. Lodging, restaurants, and groceries are at the lake. Campgrounds, vault toilets, and drinking water are on Twin Lakes Road. Fishing access is free. A boat-launching fee is charged, except at the Forest Service unimproved ramp at South Twin Lakes road.

Directions: Take U.S. 395 to Bridgeport and the junction with Twin Lakes Road. Turn west and drive 12 miles to the lakes. Boat ramps are at the far east end of the lower lake and the far west end of the upper lake.

Contact: Humboldt-Toiyabe National Forest, Bridgeport Ranger District, 760/932-7070, www.fs.fed.us/r5—click on Forest Offices; Twin Lakes Resort (Lower Twin Lake), 760/932-7751 or 877/932-7751, www.lower twinlakesresort.com; Annett's Mono Village Resort (Upper Twin Lake), 760/932-7071, www.monovillage.com; Ken's Sporting Goods, Bridgeport, 760/932-7707, www.kenssport .com; The Troutfitter, 760/934-2517, www .thetroutfly.com.

11 VIRGINIA CREEK

Rating: 6

south of Bridgeport
Map 10.1, page 479

This is a snaggy creek, made even more confounding by the large but elusive brown trout that live here. Because of the limbs and brush in the creek, it can be difficult to land a big brown trout.

Of course, there is an easier way to fish it. From Virginia Creek Settlement Resort on upstream for two miles, Virginia Creek is stocked with 10- to 12-inch rainbow trout by the Department of Fish and Game. Several spots along this stretch of water are easy to fish.

The chance for big brown trout shadows the prospects with every cast. The best habitat for these brown trout is around the pools created by beaver dams. The prime areas are found south of Bridgeport to the top of Conway Summit, which entails a rough ride followed by a hike. But thanks to the hike, you won't have to contend with competition from all the U.S. 395 bait dunkers.

Facilities, fees: Campgrounds are off U.S. 395. Vault toilets and dispersed campsites are available. Supplies can be found in Bridgeport. Fishing access is free.

Directions: From Bridgeport, take U.S. 395 south. The highway parallels the creek, and direct access is available. Some access points require a short hike to reach.

Contact: Ken's Sporting Goods, Bridgeport, 760/932-7707, www.kenssport.com; The Troutfitter, 760/934-2517, www.thetroutfly .com.

12 HOOVER WILDERNESS

Rating: 9

east of Stockton in Humboldt-Toiyabe
and Inyo National Forests
Map 10.1, page 479

Nine trailheads offer access to the remote interior of the Hoover Wilderness, which has many lakes within range of one-day hikes. Among the best trailheads to reach lakes quickly are those out of Virginia Lakes, Lundy Lake, and Saddlebag Lake. The latter, at 10,087 feet, is the highest drive-to lake in California.

The best areas of the wilderness are Sawtooth Ridge and Matterhorn Peak, which look like the Swiss Alps and make for fantastic lookouts and off-trail clambering. Robinson Creek is a good choice as well. Most of the backcountry provides good fishing in early summer, with Green Lake, East Lake, Barney Lake, Crown Lake, and Peeler Lakes the best of the lot.

In addition to those mentioned above, the following lakes have been stocked from the air by Fish and Game: Anna, Barney, Bergona, Cascade, Cooney, Crown, East, Frog, Gilman, Glacier, Green, Hoover, Oneida, Odell, Shamrock, Steelhead, Summit, and West.

This is a special area, and with such easy one-day access, it has become quite popular for hikers. Those who go beyond the one-day range and explore the interior and high wilderness ridge, however, will discover a place that is difficult to improve upon: there's good fishing, beautiful scenery, and very few people.

Facilities, fees: No facilities are available. Campgrounds and supplies can be found off U.S. 395 in the Bridgeport area and off Highway 108. Fishing access is free.

Directions: Trailheads that lead into the wilderness are off the Forest Service roads that junction with U.S. 395 and Highway 108.

Contact: Humboldt-Toiyabe National Forest, Bridgeport Ranger District, 760/932-7070, www.fs.fed.us/r5—click on Forest Offices; Inyo National Forest, Mono Lake Visitors Center, 760/647-3044, www.monolake.org.

13 VIRGINIA LAKES

Rating: 6

near Lee Vining

Map 10.1, page 479

Virginia Lakes are the gateway to a beautiful high-mountain basin that has eight small alpine lakes within a two-mile circle. The lakes are set at 9,600 feet between mountain peaks that reach 12,000 feet. The best fishing is at the larger of the Virginia Lakes and at little Trumbull Lake (the first lake on the north side on Virginia Lakes Road). Big Virginia gets the heaviest fishing traffic.

Both Virginia and Trumbull offer decent fishing for small trout and excellent shoreline access. Occasionally, Virginia is planted with brood fish. The upper Virginia Lakes are stocked by the Department of Fish and Game with catchable 10- to 12-inch rainbow trout. The lower Virginia Lakes also get rainbow trout in the 10- to 12-inch range. (Mono County adds a monthly plant of two- to eight-pound rainbows in the Virginia Lakes.) Most lakes have brook trout and a few golden trout.

The area is a great value for anglers who like to test different waters. The Virginia Lakes are the gateway to many lakes, including Red Lake, Blue Lake, Moat Lake, and Frog Lake. The latter three almost form a triangle.

In addition, a trail passes just north of Blue Lake, inside the boundary of the Hoover Wilderness, leading west to Frog Lake, Summit Lake, and beyond into a remote area of Yosemite National Park. The entire area has great natural beauty that's best seen on foot, exploring the different lakes as you go.

At Big Virginia Lake, no gas motors are permitted.

Facilities, fees: An unimproved boat ramp is available at Big Virginia Lake. Boat rentals, lodging, a café, and a convenience store are available at Virginia Lakes Resort. Gas motors and water-body contact are prohibited. Rentals for horsepack trips are available as well. Supplies can be obtained in Bridgeport or Lee Vining. Access is free.

Directions: From Bridgeport, take U.S. 395 south to Virginia Lakes Road. Turn west (right) on Virginia Lakes Road and drive six miles to Big Virginia Lake.

Contact: Humboldt-Toiyabe National Forest, Bridgeport Ranger District, 760/932-7070, www.fs.fed.us/r5—click on Forest Offices; Virginia Lakes Resort, 760/647-6484, www.virginialakesresort.com; Virginia Lakes Pack Outfit, 760/937-0326, www.virginialakes.com; Ken's Sporting Goods, Bridgeport, 760/932-7707, www.kenssport.com.

14 LUNDY LAKE

Rating: 7

near Lee Vining

Map 10.1, page 479

Lundy Lake is in a high mountain valley in the stark eastern Sierra, a short drive from U.S. 395. Yet even though the lake provides good fishing and a campground and makes an ideal jump-off point for hikes, compared to the other lakes in the area, it gets less traffic.

Lundy always seems to please and surprise, with good trout fishing and a sprinkling of big fish. Rainbow trout and mostly catchable brown trout have been planted here. Some of the latter grow old and huge. You need a boat to do it right, with most fish caught by trolling.

Both nature and history accent a visit to Lundy Lake. The lake is long and narrow and set at 7,800 feet. Nature decided to block Mill Creek with several thousand tons of rock, creating a natural dam. In addition, if you explore Lundy Canyon, you can discover the remains of some of the highest-elevation gold mines during the gold rush. A hike up Mill Creek to the beaver dams, either to catch fish or take pictures, is always an option.

There are also several options for non-boaters. Mill Creek is just below the outlet at the dam and is a good spot, with several primitive camps available. In addition, a trail starting near the west end of the lake leads along upper Mill Creek and into the Hoover Wilderness. With two cars to shuttle, a great short trip is possible by hiking from Lundy Lake, up over Lundy Pass, and over to Saddlebag Lake.

Most people become fascinated with giant Mono Lake, just east of the highway. The area is something of a moonscape, with a giant saline lake as its centerpiece. It is also the nesting site for nearly all the species of gulls found in California. If you have ever seen seagulls in the mountains and wondered what they were doing there, Mono Lake is the answer. As vacationers stare at the lake, though, they usually don't even see the adjacent turnoff marking Lundy Lake Road.

Facilities, fees: Cabins, hot showers, a small campground, and fishing-boat rentals are at Lundy Lake Resort (which has no phones). A boat ramp is near the resort. A picnic area and primitive campsites are near the lake's east side, on Mill Creek. Campgrounds are also at Saddlebag Lake to the south and Virginia Creek to the north. Limited groceries and supplies can be obtained at the lake. Full supplies can be obtained in Lee Vining. Fishing access is free.

Directions: From Lee Vining, take U.S. 395 north for seven miles to Lundy Lake Road. Turn left (west) on Lundy Lake Road and drive five miles to the lake at the end of the road.

Contact: Inyo National Forest, Mono Lake Visitors Center, 760/647-3044, www.mono lake.org; Lundy Lake Resort, P.O. Box 550, Lee Vining, CA 93541, reservations 626/309-0415 (winter only); Ken's Sporting Goods, Bridgeport, 760/932-7707, www.kenssport .com; Mono County Public Works, 760/932-5440.

15 MILL CREEK

Rating: 4

north of Lee Vining near Lundy Lake

Map 10.1, page 479

Hit-and-run isn't against the law when it comes to fishing. In fact, when it comes to fishing a stream like Mill Creek, it is exactly the approach you need.

That is because Mill Creek is bordered by Lundy Lake Road, the stream pouring from the dam at Lundy Lake on downstream (eastward) until it eventually runs into the west end of Mono Lake. The strategy should be to hit a good spot on Mill Creek along the road, parking and making the quick stick, then returning to your vehicle and heading to the next spot. Hit-and-run. The sections of river below Lundy Lake are stocked with rainbow trout in the 10- to 12-inch class. For smaller, wild trout, an option is hiking the river above Lundy Lake.

Facilities, fees: A campground is on Lundy Lake Road. Supplies can be found in Lee Vining. Fishing access is free.

Directions: From Lee Vining, take U.S. 395 north for seven miles to Lundy Lake Road. Turn west (left) on Lundy Lake Road. The road parallels the creek, and direct access is available.

Contact: Inyo National Forest, Mono Lake Visitors Center, 760/647-3044, www.mono lake.org; Mono County Public Works, 760/932-5440; Ernie's Tackle, June Lake, 760/648-7756.

16 SADDLEBAG LAKE

Rating: 7

west of Lee Vining in Inyo National Forest

Map 10.1, page 479

If you want to feel as if you are standing on top of the world, just try this trip. Your vehicle will lug as it makes the climb, gasping for breath, but when you finally make it, you will be at the highest car-accessible lake in California—Saddlebag Lake, at 10,087 feet.

It is an outstanding destination, either to camp, boat, and fish for a while, or to use as a jump-off point for a wilderness backpacking trip.

Saddlebag is one of the bigger lakes in the region, set off by stark, pristine granite well above the tree line. The fishing is especially good on summer evenings. The water is clear and pure, and the fishing is best by boat during the evening bite. Like at all high mountain lakes, the trout get a case of lockjaw during still, blue-sky afternoons. Saddlebag Lake receives plants of rainbow trout in the 10- to 12-inch class from the Department of Fish and Game.

When other lakes get too warm, the DFG plants large brood stock here (and at Virginia Lake) because of the cold water. The fish hang out where the snowmelt enters the lake.

A bonus is the trail that loops around the eastern side of the lake, then heads north and splits into two wilderness routes. It's a take-your-pick deal. At the fork, head right to go up Lundy Pass and reach Odell Lake and Shamrock Lake, or head left to Greenstone, Wasco, and Steelhead Lakes. These are all close enough to reach on an afternoon hike—a fantastic way to spend a day. There is a hiker's shuttle boat. Note that with the elevation and the high mountain pass, it can be windy and cold here, and some people find it difficult to catch their breath on simple hikes.

The camp is about a quarter mile from the lake and is within walking range of the little store and the boat rentals. The boat ramp is a one-minute drive away. The scenery is stark; everything is granite, ice, or water, with only a few lodgepole pines managing precarious toeholds. RV users should note that level sites are extremely hard to come by.

Facilities, fees: Boat rentals, a hiker's shuttle boat, and an unimproved boat ramp are available. A campground, drinking water, vault toilets, and a small store are nearby. Fishing access is free. There is a fee for boat launching.

Directions: From the eastern Sierra, take U.S. 395 to the junction with Highway 120/Tioga Pass Road (just south of Lee Vining). Turn west on Tioga Pass Road/120 and drive about 11 miles to Saddlebag Lake Road. Turn right and drive three miles to the lake.

From Merced, take Highway 140 east to the Arch Rock entrance station. Continue east to the Big Oak Flat Road junction (0.5 mile before entering Yosemite Valley). Turn left and drive 14 miles to Tioga Road. Turn right and drive about 65 miles (past Tuolumne Meadows) and through the Tioga Pass entrance station. Continue two miles to Saddlebag Lake Road. Turn left and drive three miles to the lake. *Note:* Check the status of the Highway 140 route to see about repairs, closures, delays, and rerouting because of damage from Ferguson Rock Slide. Other routes are available from the San Joaquin Valley.

From Fresno, take Highway 41 north for 65 miles to the park entrance.

Contact: Inyo National Forest, Mono Lake Visitors Center, 760/647-3044, www.mono lake.org; Saddlebag Lake Resort, P.O. Box 303, Lee Vining, CA 93541, www.saddle baglakeresort.com; Tioga Pass Resort, www .tiogapassresort.com; Bells Sporting Goods, 760/647-6406.

17 ELLERY LAKE

Rating: 6

west of Lee Vining in Inyo National Forest

Map 10.1, page 479

Congress blew the deal when they set the borders for Yosemite National Park. They didn't include Tioga and Ellery Lakes within park boundaries. Both are just two miles outside the Highway 120 entrance on the eastern side of the park and are Yosemite-like in all ways but one: the fishing. It's actually often good, unlike at so many places at the national park.

The lakes offer spectacular deep-blue waters set in rock and at the 9,500-foot range. It looks like Yosemite, feels like Yosemite, but is not Yosemite. Whereas all plants have been suspended at the national park, turning the lakes into barren water bowls, Ellery gets stocked with rainbow trout in the 10- to 12-inch class. They join a fair population of rainbow and brook trout.

There is often a very good evening rise, best fished from a float tube, raft, or car-top boat. There is no boat ramp, but small boats can be hand-launched.

While shoreline prospects are decent during the evening bite, anglers with car-top boats do best on the far southwest side. Options? Nearby Saddlebag Lake provides them.

Facilities, fees: A campground is on the west side of the lake. Pit and portable toilets are available. Drinking water is provided from a wellhead at the entrance to the camp. Nearby Tioga Pass Resort offers cabins, a café, and a convenience store. Supplies can be obtained in Lee Vining. Fishing access is free.

Directions: From Lee Vining, take U.S. 395 south to the junction with Tioga Pass Road/Highway 120. Turn west on Tioga Pass Road/Highway 120 and drive about 10 miles to the campground and lake entrance, on the left.

From Merced, take Highway 140 east to the Arch Rock entrance station. Continue east to the Big Oak Flat Road junction (0.5 mile before entering Yosemite Valley). Turn left and drive 14 miles to Tioga Road. Turn right and drive about 65 miles (past Tuolumne Meadows) and through the Tioga Pass entrance station. Continue two miles to the campground and lake entrance, on the right.

Contact: Inyo National Forest, Mono Lake Visitors Center, 760/647-3044, www.mono lake.org; Bells Sporting Goods, 760/647-6406; Tioga Pass Resort, www.tiogapass resort.com.

18 TIOGA LAKE

Rating: 6

west of Lee Vining in Inyo National Forest

Map 10.1, page 479

Some rare golden trout can be found in Tioga Lake, one of the very few drive-to lakes where you have any chance at all at a golden. Just don't plan on it. The few golden trout join more abundant numbers of rainbows; the latter are planted occasionally by the Department of Fish and Game. Tioga Lake, like nearby Ellery Lake, is a gorgeous spot. It is located just outside the borders of Yosemite National Park at 9,700 feet. If the park boundaries had been drawn to include Tioga, it would get no stocks and provide about the same results as the nearly fishless Tenaya Lake.

The four major lakes in this region—Tioga, Ellery, Tenaya, and Saddleback—are usually locked up by snow and ice until late May. The 15 hike-to lakes in the vicinity seldom become accessible until mid-June, with the high-mountain spring arriving in July.

Facilities, fees: A campground, vault toilets, an unimproved boat ramp, and drinking water are available. Nearby Tioga Pass Resort offers cabins, a café, and a convenience store. Supplies can be obtained in Lee Vining. Fishing access is free. Fees are charged for boat launching and camping. If you're arriving through Yosemite, a fee is charged for park entrance.

Directions: From Lee Vining, take U.S. 395 south to the junction with Tioga Pass Road/Highway 120. Turn west on Tioga Pass Road/Highway 120 and drive about 11 miles to the campground and lake entrance, on the left.

From Merced, drive east on Highway 140 to the Arch Rock entrance station. Continue east to the Big Oak Flat Road junction (0.5 mile before entering Yosemite Valley). Turn left and drive 14 miles to Tioga Road. Turn right and drive about 65 miles (past Tuolumne Meadows) and through the Tioga Pass entrance station. Continue two miles to the campground and lake entrance, on the right.

Contact: Inyo National Forest, Mono

Lake Visitors Center, 760/647-3044, www
.monolake.org; Bells Sporting Goods,
760/647-6406; Tioga Pass Resort, www
.tiogapassresort.com.

19 LEE VINING CREEK

Rating: 6

east of Lee Vining in Inyo National Forest
Map 10.1, page 479

When worse comes to worst at Yosemite, you
can always bail on the park, head to Lee Vining Creek, and throw a line in. Lee Vining
Creek pretzels through a meadow near the
base of Tioga Pass. It's real pretty, with lots of
stocked trout near the campgrounds.

The jinx got ya? Been kiboshed all week?
Want to turn your rod into firewood kin-
dling? Then try an evening here. This section
of stream is often overlooked, but hatchery-
planted rainbow trout are along Poole Power
Plant Road, from the bridge to where the road
crosses the creek. Look for the obvious access
points. That is where the fish are. The creek's
south fork also gets 10- to 12-inch rainbow
trout, and lower Lee Vining gets brown-trout
fingerlings.

The trout aren't big. The trout aren't wild.
But if you haven't caught anything for a while,
a trout is still a trout. Night crawlers or fly-
fishing works best here.

Facilities, fees: Four campgrounds are nearby.
Pit and portable toilets are available, but drinking water is not. Fishing access is free.

Directions: From Lee Vining, take U.S. 395
south to the junction with Tioga Pass Road/
Highway 120. Turn west on Tioga Pass Road/
Highway 120 and drive about 3.5 miles to
Poole Power Plant Road. Turn left into the
campground entrance. An access road parallels the creek.

Contact: Inyo National Forest, Mono Lake
Visitors Center, 760/647-3044, www.mono
lake.org; Mono County Building and Parks
Department, 760/932-5440; Bells Sporting
Goods, 760/647-6406.

20 ANSEL ADAMS WILDERNESS

Rating: 8

east of Yosemite National Park in
Inyo National Forest
Map 10.1, page 479   BEST (

This is one of the prettiest backpacking areas in
the world. John Muir and Ansel Adams coun-
seled with heaven here, with Banner and Ritter
peaks and the Minarets providing the backdrop
for some of nature's finest architecture. Dozens and dozens of small lakes speckle this high
mountain country, all of them created by glacial
action and then filled by the melting drops of
snow. The John Muir Trail (JMT) is routed
right through this wilderness, and only hikers
who get deep into its interior will discover its
greatest rewards. The best approach is connecting to the JMT, then taking side trips (off-trail
if necessary) to reach remote, pristine lakes.

That approach also makes for better fishing.
Any lake within a day's hike of a trailhead often
provides poor to fair fishing. Get in deeper, two
or three days from pavement, however, and you
will have the opportunity to cast a line in crystal
pure waters where fish have seen few lures.

The lakes have been stocked by airplane
with fingerlings, and while the trout are not
big, they do provide good sport and evening
campground fish fries. The deeper lakes have
high survival rates from year to year, however,
with last year's holdovers (a bit larger) joining
this year's recruits.

Here is the complete list of lakes in the Ansel
Adams Wilderness that have been stocked by
airplane: Alger, Altha, Anne, Beck, Blackie,
Cecile, Cora, Dana, Davis, Ediza, Emerald,
Fernandez, Flat, Frying Pan, Gale, Garnet,
Gem, Gibbs, Holcomb, Iceberg, Joe Crane,
Kidney, Lady, Lillian, Lost, Marie, McClure,
McGee, Minaret, Monument, Nydiver, Parker,
Porphury, Post, Rainbow, Rockbound, Rod-
gers, Rosalie, Ruby, Ruth, Rutherford, Sadler,
Sardine, Shadow, Shirley, Slab, Staniford,
Thousand Island, Trinity, Twin Island, Lower
Twin Lake, Vandenburg, Ward, and Waugh.

The trail system in the wilderness is very extensive, with more than 250 miles in the Minarets alone, and it connects to even more trails on the Inyo side of the wilderness. Elevations range from trailheads at 7,200 feet to the peak at Mount Ritter at 13,157 feet. For views alone, the vista of Banner and Ritter from Thousand Island Lakes is the kind of scene where you could sit and stare for hours, letting it all sink in.

One of the better fishing/hiking routes for newcomers is the Lillian Lake Loop. The trout are small but abundant at Staniford, Vandenburg, and Lillian Lakes, and the trip provides a glimpse into one of the rare, special places on this planet.

Facilities, fees: No facilities are available. Numerous campgrounds are near trailheads. Supplies can be obtained in Lee Vining and at June Lake and Mammoth Lakes. Fishing access is free.

Directions: Trailheads, and roads that lead to them, are off the following highways: Highway 120, U.S. 395 between Lee Vining and Mammoth Lakes, Highway 158 (June Lake Loop), and Highway 203 (Mammoth Lakes Road). Some roads are closed in winter.

Contact: Inyo National Forest, Mono Lake Visitors Center, 760/647-3044, www.mono lake.org; Frontier Pack Train, 888/437-6853, www.frontierpacktrain.com.

21 GRANT LAKE

Rating: 5

near June Lake in Inyo National Forest

Map 10.1, page 479

Dramatic panorama sunsets and good fly-and-bubble fishing make Grant Lake a special place. This is the largest of the waters among the June Loop lakes. The hourglass-shaped lake is at an elevation of 7,600 feet and covers 1,100 surface acres. The lake is sometimes referred to as the "Home of the German brown trout."

The June Lake Loop features a series of quality waters that are accessible by car in a loop road off U.S. 395. They are Grant Lake, Silver Lake, Gull Lake, and June Lake, as well as a fishable section of Rush Creek between Silver and Grant Lakes. There are several hike-to lakes nearby, including Agnew Lake, Waugh Lake, and Gem Lake, all on the Rush Creek drainage.

Grant Lake provides good trolling in the morning and good fly-and-bubble prospects in the evening. The better spots for shore fishing are at the lake narrows (when the lake is full), at the peninsula, and also where Park Creek enters the lake near the dam. It is stocked regularly with 10- to 12-inch rainbow trout and has been stocked in the past with brown trout.

But Grant Lake does not come problem-free. It is the only lake in the June Lake Loop that allows waterskiing, and that drives a lot of anglers to more quiet waters. (A 10-mph speed limit is in effect daily until 10 A.M.) The lake is also subject to drawdowns, courtesy of the Los Angeles Department of Water and Power, those lovely folks for whom fish just get in the way of their raid on the mountains' water. The lake is often low, it seems. It also sits in a fairly barren landscape, and the wind can whistle across the lake. In addition, there is the history of Rush Creek, which was wiped out by Grant Lake.

Note: One of the state's newest fisheries is here, at Rush Creek on downstream to Mono Lake: wild browns. They're small, but they're here.

Facilities, fees: A campground, an RV park, a boat ramp, flush toilets, drinking water, a picnic area, a store, and a small marina are provided. Fishing-boat and dock rentals are also available. Supplies can be obtained in Lee Vining and June Lake. Fishing access is free.

Directions: From Lee Vining, take U.S. 395 south for six miles to the first Highway 158 north/June Lake Loop turnoff. Turn west (right) and drive five miles on Highway 158 to the Grant Lake access road.

Contact: Inyo National Forest, Mono Lake Visitors Center, 760/647-3044, www.mono lake.org; June Lake Chamber of Commerce, www.junelakeloop.org; Grant Lake Marina, 760/648-7964; Ernie's Tackle, June Lake, 760/648-7756; The Troutfitter, 760/934-2517, www.thetroutfly.com; Bells Sporting Goods, 760/647-6406.

22 SILVER LAKE

Rating: 7

near June Lake in Inyo National Forest

Map 10.1, page 479

Silver Lake is a small, intimate lake, covering just 80 acres and set at 7,200 feet. Yet all services are provided, and it is near an outstanding trailhead that is routed up the beautiful Rush Creek drainage.

The lake is stocked regularly with rainbow trout, providing good evening fishing for both trollers and shore casters tossing the fly-and-bubble combination. Occasional plants of trophy-sized rainbow trout are also made, joining a small population of quality browns. The lake receives plants of 10- to 12-inch rainbow trout, along with cutthroat fingerlings.

Unlike Grant Lake, Silver Lake doesn't seem to have the problems of lake drawdowns. It is filled with snowmelt in spring and glacial water in summer, creating a pure setting that is easily accessible. A good spot is near the dam and boat ramp. There always seem to be trout there.

Wilderness it is not, but that is not far away, either. The trail routed west from Silver Lake along the Rush Creek drainage runs past Agnew Lake, Gem Lake, and Waugh Lake into the Ansel Adams Wilderness. To experience one of the great hikes in California, take this trail all the way up to the ridge, where it connects to the Pacific Crest Trail, then head north over Donohue Pass into Yosemite, and out down Lyell Fork to Tuolumne Meadows. You'll need two cars to complete this trip, using the shuttle system, parking one at Silver Lake and the other at Tuolumne Meadows.

Facilities, fees: Two boat ramps are available at the lake's south end near Silver Lake Resort.

A small marina with fishing boats for rent, an RV park, cabins, a store, coin laundry, RV supplies, gas, and a café are at Silver Lake Resort. A campground, restrooms with flush toilets, and drinking water are nearby. A 5-mph speed limit is enforced on the lake. Fishing access is free. Launching is free next to the Forest Service campground.

Directions: From Bishop, take U.S. 395 north for 54 miles to the Highway 158/June Lake Loop turnoff. Turn left on Highway 158, drive past June Lake and Gull Lake, and continue for another three miles to Silver Lake. The boat ramp is at the south end of the lake.

From Lee Vining, take U.S. 395 south for six miles to the first Highway 158 north/June Lake Loop turnoff. Turn west (right) and drive nine miles (past Grant Lake) to Silver Lake. Just as you arrive at Silver Lake (a small store is on the right), turn left at the entrance for the boat launch and campground.

Contact: Inyo National Forest, Mono Lake Visitors Center, 760/647-3044, www.monolake .org; June Lake Chamber of Commerce, www .junelakeloop.org; Silver Lake Resort, 760/648-7525, www.silverlakeresort.net; Ernie's Tackle, June Lake, 760/648-7756; The Troutfitter, 760/934-2517, www.thetroutfly.com.

23 REVERSE CREEK

Rating: 4

near Lee Vining in Inyo National Forest

Map 10.1, page 479

It is no secret how Reverse Creek got its name. This is the only stream in the region that flows toward the mountains, not away. Reverse Creek is a small, tree-lined stream that provides a quiet alternative to the nearby lakes in the June Lake Loop.

The creek starts quite small but builds to a respectable size by the time it reaches past Fern Creek Lodge. Small lures, such as the 1/16-ounce Panther Martin, and small baits do the job just fine during the evening bite. Wading is advised, and hip waders work well.

Results are spotty. Occasionally a big lunker trout gets caught here, always a happy shock, with smiles all around.

The land bordering the stream is owned by the Forest Service, and the adjoining private property owners legally can't prevent you from walking down the stream. Expect a lot of Power Baiters here.

Facilities, fees: Campgrounds, lodging, dining, and supplies are nearby. Fishing access is free.

Directions: From Lee Vining, take U.S. 395 south (past the first Highway 158/June Lake Loop turnoff) to June Lake Junction (a gas station/store is on the west side of the road) and Highway 158 south. Turn right on Highway 158 south and drive three miles to the campground, on the left side of the road (across from Gull Lake).

From Bishop, take U.S. 395 north for 54 miles to the Highway 158/June Lake Loop turnoff. Turn left (southwest) on Highway 158 and drive past June Lake and Gull Lake to Reverse Creek campground, or where the creek crosses the road. Access is available here and from access roads near the creek.

Contact: Inyo National Forest, Mono Lake Visitors Center, 760/647-3044, www.monolake.org; June Lake Chamber of Commerce, www.junelakeloop.org; Reverse Creek Lodge, 760/648-7535 or 800/762-6440 (reservations), www.reversecreeklodge.com; Ernie's Tackle, June Lake, 760/648-7756; The Troutfitter, 760/934-2517, www.thetroutfly.com.

24 GULL LAKE

Rating: 8
near June Lake in Inyo National Forest
Map 10.1, page 479

Little Gull Lake is the smallest of the June Loop lakes, covering just 64 acres. Set in a rock bowl at 7,600 feet, below the peaks of the eastern Sierra, it is intimate and dramatic, and small but beautiful.

Don't sell it short just because it is the smallest of the lakes in the immediate area. The lake is stocked with rainbow trout that are 10- to 12-inchers, courtesy of the Department of Fish and Game, and it also gets cutthroat fingerlings yearly. They provide opportunities for shoreline bait dunkers, trollers, and evening fly fishers with float tubes. Bonus Alpers trout can knock your eyes out.

The people who run the marina are among the nicest you'll find anywhere.

Facilities, fees: A boat ramp is on the lake's southwest corner. A campground, boat rentals, and a full-service marina are available. Drinking water, fire grills, picnic tables, and flush toilets are provided. A grocery store and a coin laundry are nearby. A 10-mph speed limit is in effect. Fishing access and boat launching are free.

Directions: From Lee Vining, take U.S. 395 south (past the first Highway 158/June Lake Loop turnoff) to June Lake Junction (a gas station/store is on the west side of the road) and Highway 158. Turn right on Highway 158 and drive three miles to the campground entrance, on the right side of the road.

From Bishop, take U.S. 395 north for 54 miles to the Highway 158/June Lake Loop turnoff. Turn left on Highway 158, then drive past June Lake and continue another mile to Gull Lake.

Contact: Inyo National Forest, Mono Lake Visitors Center, 760/647-3044, www.monolake.org; June Lake Chamber of Commerce, www.junelakeloop.org; Gull Lake Marina, 760/648-7539, www.gulllakemarina.com; The Troutfitter, 760/934-2517, www.thetroutfly.com.

25 JUNE LAKE

Rating: 8
in Inyo National Forest
Map 10.1, page 479

This lake gets as much intense fishing pressure as any in California. And it deserves it. The lake has a lot of trout, including Alpers trout, which are not only big, but take on the characteristics of wild fish after living in the lake a while.

June Lake is a fully developed resort area, with everything going for it except solitude. Beauty? It's a 160-acre mountain lake set at 7,600 feet below snowcapped peaks. Good fishing? Weekly stocks make sure of it. Accommodations? If you need something, you can get it here.

A great spot from shore is next to the swimming beach. Another good one is on the far side along the steep wall. The lake is clear and deep, and the trout are sensitive to light and temperatures.

You will have a chance for trout in the five- to eight-pound class, along with the more typical-sized rainbows that range 10–12 inches. The lake receives plants of rainbow trout each year, along with cutthroat fingerlings. You can outfish a lot of people by using fluorocarbon leaders, which are virtually invisible to the fish. People who show up with 8- or 10-pound test are the ones that get skunked. The fish can see the line.

Facilities, fees: There are two paved boat ramps, one at June Lake Marina and one at Big Rock Resort. A full-service marina; docks; and fishing-boat, pontoon-boat, and canoe rentals are at June Lake Marina. Cabins, a small marina, and fishing-boat and kayak rentals are at Big Rock Resort. Campgrounds, restrooms with flush toilets, and drinking water are available. A store, propane gas, lodging, and cabins are nearby. There is a 10-mph speed limit on the lake. Fishing access is free. There is a fee for boat launching.

Directions: From Lee Vining, take U.S. 395 south for 20 miles (six miles past Highway 158 north) to June Lake Junction (a sign is posted for "June Lake Village") and Highway 158 south. Turn west (right) on Highway 158 south and drive two miles to June Lake. Turn right (signed) and drive a short distance to the campground.

From Bishop, take U.S. 395 north for 54 miles to the Highway 158/June Lake Loop turnoff. Turn left on Highway 158 and drive two miles to June Lake. Turn right (signed).

Contact: Inyo National Forest, Mono Lake Visitors Center, 760/647-3044, www.mono lake.org; June Lake Chamber of Commerce, www.junelakeloop.org; June Lake Marina, 760/648-7726, www.junelakemarina.net; Big Rock Resort, 760/648-7717, www.bigrock resort.net; Pinecliff Resort, 760/648-7558; Ernie's Tackle, June Lake, 760/648-7756; The Troutfitter, 760/934-2517, www.thetrout fly.com; Fern Creek Lodge, 760/648-7722, www.ferncreeklodge.com.

26 HORSESHOE LAKE

Rating: 5

near Mammoth Lakes in Inyo National Forest

Map 10.1, page 479

The Mammoth Lakes Basin is often compared to the June Lake Loop to the nearby north, but it isn't nearly as traveled or as developed.

Horseshoe Lake is a good example. It is at 8,900 feet and equals the natural beauty of any lake in the eastern Sierra. There is no resort here, no boat rentals, and no boat ramp, and as for trout stocks, the Department of Fish and Game plants very few brook-trout fingerlings per year. A few brook trout and rainbow trout are available, however. For fishing alone, the other lakes near Mammoth are better prospects.

But what makes this lake special is the trailhead at the northern side of the lake. The trail heads west up to Mammoth Pass and then connects shortly with the Pacific Crest Trail. I have hiked all of this, and the best bet is to head south into the John Muir Wilderness and take cutoff trails along Deer Creek to Deer Lake, or to continue another five miles south on the PCT and head to Duck Lake or Purple Lake.

Warning: The campground at Horseshoe Lake was closed because of dangerous carbon dioxide releases, although the lake is still safe.

Rangers warn they may close the parking area at any time, which would make lake access more difficult.

Facilities, fees: Vault toilets are available. Supplies can be obtained in Mammoth Lakes and at Lake Mary. Fishing access is free.

Directions: From Lee Vining, take U.S. 395 south for 25 miles to Mammoth Junction and Highway 203. Turn right (west) on Highway 203 and drive through the town of Mammoth Lakes to the junction of Minaret Road/Highway 203 and Lake Mary Road. Continue straight through the intersection and drive 3.6 miles to Lake Mary Loop Drive. Turn right and drive past Lake Mary and Lake Mamie to Horseshoe Lake, at the end of the road.

From Bishop, take U.S. 395 north for 40 miles to Mammoth Junction and Highway 203. Turn left (west) on Highway 203 and drive through the town of Mammoth Lakes to the junction of Minaret Road/Highway 203 and Lake Mary Road. Continue straight through the intersection and drive 3.6 miles to Lake Mary Loop Drive. Turn right and drive past Lake Mary and Lake Mamie to Horseshoe Lake, at the end of the road.

Contact: Inyo National Forest, Mammoth Lakes Visitors Center, 760/924-5500, www.fs.fed.us/r5—click on Forest Offices; Mammoth Lakes Visitors Bureau, 888/466-2666, www.visitmammoth.com; Rick's Sport Center, 760/934-3416; Kittredge Sports, Mammoth Lakes, 760/934-7566, www.kittredge.net; The Troutfitter, 760/934-2517, www.thetroutfly.com; Lake Mary Marina, 760/934-5353.

27 TWIN LAKES

Rating: 7

near Mammoth Lakes in Inyo National Forest
Map 10.1, page 479

These Twin Lakes, west of Mammoth, are a pair of small lakes on little Mammoth Creek, high in Inyo National Forest and at an elevation of 8,700 feet. The DFG stocks them with rainbow trout in the 9- to 11-inch class. The lakes are absolutely beautiful, set amid the Sierra granite country and ringed by old stands of pines. The view of the waterfall here always makes a picture-postcard photograph.

The waterfall area of the north lake holds the trout—try a night crawler here. Otherwise, this is the kind of place where an angler with a float tube arrives for an evening of fly-fishing. It's not the place to get ambitious. After all, you're on vacation. Leave your ambitions behind. There are pockets between weeds where it becomes an art to present tiny dry flies.

Don't get this Twin Lakes confused with the Twin Lakes farther north, just west of Bridgeport. They are two different animals.

Facilities, fees: A campground, drinking water, and flush toilets are available. Twin Lakes Store rents rowboats and canoes. Lodging and a restaurant are at Tamarack Lodge. A grocery store, coin laundry, coin showers, and propane gas are nearby. No motors are allowed. There is no boat launch; car-top boats may be hand-launched. Fishing access is free.

Directions: Take U.S. 395 to Mammoth Junction and Highway 203. Turn west on Highway 203 and drive through the town of Mammoth Lakes to the junction of Minaret Road/Highway 203 and Lake Mary Road. Continue straight through the intersection to Lake Mary Road and drive 2.3 miles to Twin Lakes Loop Road. Turn right and drive 0.5 mile to the campground at Lake Mary.

Contact: Inyo National Forest, Mammoth Lakes Visitors Center, 760/924-5500, www.fs.fed.us/r5—click on Forest Offices; Mammoth Lakes Visitors Bureau, 888/466-2666, www.visitmammoth.com; Tamarack Lodge and Resort, 760/934-2442 (information) or 800/626-6684 (reservations), www.tamaracklodge.com; Twin Lakes Store, 760/934-7295; Rick's Sport Center, 760/934-3416; Kittredge Sports, Mammoth Lakes, 760/934-7566, www.kittredge.net; Pat Jaeger, 760/872-7770, www.jaeger-flyfishing.com; The Troutfitter, 760/934-2517, www.thetroutfly.com.

28 LAKE MAMIE

Rating: 5

near Mammoth Lakes in Inyo National Forest
Map 10.1, page 479

Lake Mamie is one of the marquee waters in the Mammoth Lakes Basin that is stocked by the Department of Fish and Game. The others are Twin Lakes, Lake Mary, and Lake George.

It is little Mamie, however, that often provides the best fishing. The lake is small and narrow and is easily fished by boat, bank, or float tube. A variety of methods work. Shoreline bait dunking, trolling, and the fly-and-bubble technique, which is traditional during the evening at all lakes in the eastern Sierra, can all catch fish. In addition, the DFG stocks Lake Mamie with brood-stock rainbow trout ranging in size 10–12 inches.

One trick at Lake Mamie is using light line. The water is quite clear, and line heavier than 6-pound test can be detected and avoided by the larger fish. My suggestion is to use 3-pound Fenwick line and fluorocarbon leaders. Some people really love this lake. For others, it scarcely inspires a pulse.

Facilities, fees: A boat ramp, picnic area, rental cabins, bike and boat rentals, bait and tackle, and groceries are at Wildyrie Lodge. Campgrounds are at nearby lakes. No motors are permitted on the lake. No swimming is allowed. Fishing access is free.

Directions: Take U.S. 395 to Mammoth Junction and the junction of U.S. 395 and Highway 203. Turn west on Highway 203 and drive through the town of Mammoth Lakes to the junction of Minaret Road/Highway 203 and Lake Mary Road. Continue straight through the intersection to Lake Mary Road and drive 2.3 miles to Twin Lakes Loop Road. Turn right and drive past Twin Lakes and Lake Mary to Lake Mamie and the boat ramp on the left.

Contact: Inyo National Forest, Mammoth Lakes Visitors Center, 760/924-5500, www.fs.fed.us/r5—click on Forest Offices; Mammoth Lakes Visitors Bureau, 888/466-2666, www.visitmammoth.com; Wildyrie Lodge, 760/934-2444; Lake Mary Marina, 760/934-5353; Rick's Sport Center, 760/934-3416; The Troutfitter, 760/934-2517, www.thetroutfly.com; Pat Jaeger, 760/872-7770, www.jaeger-flyfishing.com; Kittredge Sports, Mammoth Lakes, 760/934-7566, www.kittredge.net.

29 LAKE MARY

Rating: 7

near Mammoth Lakes in Inyo National Forest
Map 10.1, page 479

This is headquarters for the Mammoth Lakes area. Lake Mary is the largest and most developed of the 11 lakes in the immediate vicinity. It provides a resort, a launch, and boat rentals, and it is the most heavily stocked of the lot. The plants include trout in the 10- to 12-inch class and a sprinkling of lunkers.

It only takes one look to see why this lake is so popular: The natural beauty is astounding. Lake Mary is high in the mountains, at 8,900 feet, and stands out among some of nature's most perfect artwork.

Standard fishing techniques work just fine here, either trolling (best), casting a bubble and fly (okay), fly-fishing from a float tube with a sink-tip line, black leech and strip retrieve, or fishing from shore with bait (fair). A trip to Lake Mary isn't exactly roughing it, but you get decent fishing and great natural beauty anyway.

If there are too many people for you, an excellent trailhead for backpackers is on the east side of the lake. The trail is routed south along Mammoth Creek to Arrowhead Lake, Skeleton Lake, Barney Lake, and then finally big Duck Lake. The latter is larger than Lake Mary and is just a mile from the junction with the Pacific Crest Trail. They are all gorgeous.

The Forest Service campsites here are available on a first-come, first-served basis. In the summer, visitors should arrive as early as possible to secure a spot. Reservations are necessary to stay at one of the lodges.

Facilities, fees: Cabins and fishing-boat

rentals are at Crystal Crag Lodge. A campground, store, and docks are at Pokonobe Resort, along with rentals for pontoon boats, fishing boats, canoes, and pedal boats. Lake Mary Marina has docks and a boat ramp, and rents out fishing boats, pontoon boats, canoes, and pedal boats. Another paved boat ramp is available at Pokonobe Resort. Campgrounds for tents and RVs are nearby. Drinking water and restrooms with flush toilets are available. A 10-mph speed limit is enforced and swimming is prohibited. Fishing access is free. There is a fee for boat launching.

Directions: Take U.S. 395 to Mammoth Junction and the junction of U.S. 395 and Highway 203. Turn west on Highway 203 and drive through the town of Mammoth Lakes to the junction of Minaret Road/Highway 203 and Lake Mary Road. Continue straight on Lake Mary Road and drive 2.3 miles to Twin Lakes Loop Road. Turn right and drive past Twin Lakes to Lake Mary. The road is well signed and circles Lake Mary.

Contact: Inyo National Forest, Mammoth Lakes Visitors Center, 760/924-5500, www.fs.fed.us/r5—click on Forest Offices; Mammoth Lakes Visitors Bureau, 888/466-2666, www.visitmammoth.com; Lake Mary Marina, 760/934-5353; Crystal Crag Lodge, 760/934-2436, www.crystalcrag.com; Pokonobe Resort Marina, 760/934-2437, www.pokonobe resort.com; Lake Mary Store and Marina, 760/934-5353; Rick's Sport Center, 760/934-3416; The Troutfitter, 760/934-2517, www.thetroutfly.com; Pat Jaeger, 760/872-7770, www.jaeger-flyfishing.com; Kittredge Sports, Mammoth Lakes, 760/934-7566, www.kittredge.net.

30 LAKE GEORGE

Rating: 6

near Mammoth Lakes in Inyo National Forest

Map 10.1, page 479

You get a two-for-one offer at Lake George. You can camp and fish here, with decent prospects for rainbow trout and brook trout to 12 inches, or you can strap on a backpack and hoof it down the trail. Either way, it is tough to go wrong.

Set at the 9,000-foot range, Lake George is a small, round lake fed by creeks coming from Crystal Lake and TJ Lake, both just a mile away. The entire lake is designated as a wake-free zone. It is just west of Lake Mary, yet doesn't get nearly the number of people. That makes it attractive, along with decent fishing for trout up to a foot long, sometimes larger. A sprinkling of rainbow trout in the 10- to 12-inch class and rainbow-trout fingerlings are planted here. In the spring, it is often last of the major lakes in the Mammoth Lakes area to melt off ice.

Another option is to lace up your hiking boots and go for broke. The trail that starts at the northwest end of the lake travels past Crystal Lake (a beautiful little lake below giant Crystal Crag) and then up, up, up to the Mammoth Crest, and on south a few miles to the little Deer Lakes. The latter provide quiet, seclusion, and great natural beauty.

Facilities, fees: Cabins, dock, fishing boats, a primitive boat ramp, and rowboats are at Woods Lodge. A campground, restrooms with flush toilets, and drinking water are available. A convenience store, coin laundry, coin showers, and propane gas are nearby. Neither swimming nor motors larger than six horsepower are permitted. Fishing access is free. There is a fee for boat launching.

Directions: Take U.S. 395 to Mammoth Junction and the junction of U.S. 395 and Highway 203. Turn west on Highway 203 and drive through the town of Mammoth Lakes to the junction of Minaret Road/Highway 203 and Lake Mary Road. Continue straight through the intersection and drive 0.3 mile to Lake George Road. Turn right and drive a short distance to the lodge at the end of the road.

Contact: Inyo National Forest, Mammoth Lakes Visitors Center, 760/924-5500, www.fs.fed.us/r5—click on Forest Offices; Mammoth Lakes Visitors Bureau, 888/466-2666, www.visitmammoth.com; Crystal Crag Lodge, 760/934-2436, www.crystalcrag.com; Woods Lodge, 760/934-2261; Rick's Sport Center, 760/934-3416; The Troutfitter, 760/934-2517, www.thetroutfly.com; Pat Jaeger, 760/872-7770, www.jaeger-flyfishing.com; Kittredge Sports, Mammoth Lakes, 760/934-7566, www.kittredge.net.

31 MIDDLE FORK SAN JOAQUIN RIVER

Rating: 8

near Devils Postpile National Monument in Inyo National Forest

Map 10.1, page 479

If you've never felt it or seen it, you may not understand. It's that moment when a trout grabs your dry fly. It starts when you see the trout rise before you feel the grab. A millisecond later, the trout jolts you, and it's almost an electric sensation, as if you are wired direct to the fish. For a lot of people who fly-fish, it's the single most exciting moment in all sport. This is better than watching any sport because here you are the participant, not the observer.

And the way you take this to the highest level is by casting a dry fly to wild fish in a pristine wilderness stream.

That is what has always led me back to the Middle Fork San Joaquin River, high in the Sierra in the Ansel Adams Wilderness, the best place in the West to try to catch the grand slam of wild trout in a single day: rainbow trout, brook trout, golden trout, and brown trout. Sometimes I add in a strange-looking hybridized mix I call the "golden-brook."

Even though the trout are not large here, you have a chance to get 20–50 grabs in a day. Whether you convert is up to you. To get here, you have to range far, first to the eastern Sierra; from U.S. 395, head west on 203 to the Mammoth Mountain Ski Area. If you arrive after 7 A.M.—or aren't camping—you have to take a shuttle bus over Minaret Summit and then down into the canyon to the

San Joaquin River and the trailheads (or on to Red's Meadow and Devils Postpile National Monument).

The best launch point for this trip is at the Agnew Meadows Campground (some prefer Upper Soda Springs Campground). But first-timers must be wary and bring a map of Inyo National Forest. That is because you can accidentally take the Pacific Crest High Trail, which is routed uphill to the ridge. Instead, take the well-worn (unsigned) "fisherman's trail" downhill to the river, where you turn right and hook up with the River Trail. Another caution: If you take the shuttle bus, do not miss the correct stop and do not expect the bus driver to provide much help. If you end up at Devils Postpile, you can end up hiking instead on the John Muir Trail, which is routed for several miles to Gladys, Rosalie, and Shadow Lakes before dropping down and linking up with the River Trail/PCT (once you get it right, you'll always get it right).

Gear is pretty standard. I wear waders and a small internal-frame backpack loaded with my tackle, lunch, and canteen. For gear I used a light, fast rod, an 8-foot, 5-weight (a standard 8 1/2-foot, 6-weight is okay), with the reel set up with floating line and a 7 1/2 or 9-foot 3X or 4X leaders. My favorite flies here are the No. 16 Royal Coachman, caddis (all different styles), and a local favorite, Brite Dot. Always add floatant to dry flies.

When you arrive at the river, be ready to approach the river like a burglar sneaking through an unlocked window. You start by hiking upstream on the River Trail, looking for the likely spots. The trout hide where riffles tumble into little pools, in pockets behind boulders, and along current seams. These are all spots where a trout can sit near-motionless, pointed upstream, out of the primary current, and wait for a hatched insect to come floating by overhead. That's when you step up to the plate and take your swings. Creep upstream, stay low to keep the trout from detecting the shadow of your casting motion, and then zip a short cast upstream of the spot. The fly must land softly and then drift downstream as if no line were attached. This is best accomplished with precise short casts, often just 15–30 feet, and not a lot of back-and-forth and long-distance sail jobs like you see at the sports shows. If the line slaps the water, lands with a large slack loop, or the fly skids, it will be a swing and a miss. But there are hundreds of spots here for trying again. Stay on the move and enjoy the magic of a wilderness stream.

The water is clean and cold, and the surroundings are pristine, with pockets of thin forest amid dramatic granite landscape. The trailhead is at 8,300 feet, and the route in gradually climbs and extends 11 miles to Thousand Island Lake at 9,800 feet for sensational views of the Minarets, crowned by Banner and Ritter peaks.

I've hiked and fished all of this several times and have had some of my highest catch days with a fly rod here, 40–50 trout, catch-and-release. The fish tend not to be very big, almost nothing over 11 inches, but they're often willing to a take a dry at almost any time. According to a Fish and Game survey, the average angler catches nearly three fish per hour here, one the highest catch rates of wild fish in California.

If your idea of paradise is a pristine high-mountain stream where small trout hide in pocket water, then you'll be in ecstasy here.

The stream is high in the Sierra, running through a canyon at 7,700 feet in elevation, tumbling over boulders and into pockets and holes, sometimes even slicing deep runs in the granite. It is very beautiful, especially in early summer, when snow melting from the surrounding mountains fills the river with fresh, oxygenated water.

In early summer, to do it right, you need at least hip waders (but be careful) to gain access to the best spots. Later in the year, as the snowmelt subsides and the river drops, you can rock-hop your way along and do just fine. However, the fishing is nowhere as good late in the year (when flows are low) as it is earlier in the year.

How early? Well, consider that in big snow years, the road in is not even open until the Fourth of July. So in a typical year, mid-June and early July are usually ideal for the trip. In poor snow years, the river can be a trickle by late August.

But know this: You must hike. If you are not willing to hike several miles, forget it.

Facilities, fees: A campground, drinking water, and chemical toilets are available. Limited supplies can be obtained at Red's Meadows. Lodging and restaurants are in Mammoth Lakes. Fishing access is free. If you take the shuttle bus, there is a charge.

Directions: Take U.S. 395 to Mammoth Junction and the junction of U.S. 395 and Highway 203. Turn west on Highway 203 and drive through the town of Mammoth Lakes to the junction of Minaret Road/Highway 203 and Lake Mary Road. Turn right and drive five miles to Minaret Station (past the Mammoth Mountain Ski Area). Continue for 2.6 miles to the campground entrance road, on the right. Turn right and drive just under a mile to the Agnew Meadows Campground. This is the best of several access points.

Access note: A shuttle bus is required for noncampers arriving between 7 A.M. and 7:30 P.M. ($7 per person, no discounts) from the Mammoth Mountain Ski Area to this area. If you take the shuttle bus, get off at the Agnew Meadows Campground (some prefer Upper Soda Springs Campground).

Contact: Inyo National Forest, Mammoth Lakes Visitors Center, 760/924-5500, www.fs.fed.us/r5—click on Forest Offices; Mammoth Lakes Visitors Bureau, 888/466-2666, www.visitmammoth.com; Devil's Postpile National Monument, 760/934-2289; Rick's Sport Center, 760/934-3416; The Troutfitter, 760/934-2517, www.thetroutfly.com; Kittredge Sports, Mammoth Lakes, 760/934-7566, www.kittredge.net; Red's Meadow Resort and Pack Station, 800/292-7758, www.redsmeadow.com; Mammoth Lakes Pack Outfit, 888/475-8747, www.mammothpack.com.

32 OWENS RIVER

Rating: 5

east of Mammoth Lakes

Map 10.2, page 480

Comparing the Owens River to most other trout streams in California is like comparing the North Pole and South Pole. Owens River is a world apart.

The Owens is a spring creek, a meandering stream whose quiet flows pretzel their way through meadows for 30 miles before entering Crowley Lake. The water is very clear, sometimes deep, full of a huge assortment of aquatic life, and loaded with large, fast-growing trout that you can often see cruising along. Loaded with them? Loaded. It is an amazing phenomenon. The Department of Fish and Game stocks 10- to 12-inch rainbow trout here. Occasionally some big trout are stocked here as well. They can stun anglers used to the 10-inchers.

But before you throw the gear in your car and make a dash for the Owens River Valley, put on the brakes and read on. Why? Because it is my opinion that while the Owens River can conjure up visions of greatness in the mind of most any angler, the reality is that it produces very few trout on the end of a fishing line. There are two reasons. One is that so much of the river is bordered by private property that access is largely a pain in the butt. For all the 30 miles of river, the one decent publicly accessible spot is at Big Springs. This stretch of water, as well as that bordering the private resorts, gets fished so hard that it takes absolutely preeminent skills to get bit.

The fish spook very easily. I watched my brother Rambob sneak up on his hands and knees, yet the fish still spooked downriver. That kills it right there for most anglers. Strike one. The presentation has to be perfect, very soft—and the fly can't skid across the water, but must drift downstream as if no line were attached. Strike two. The water is so clear and so slow-flowing that the trout have all day to inspect the fly, and then decide not to bite. I've seen five-pound browns swim right up

to my Hare's Ear, just to slough it off. Strike three, and you're out.

There are few resident fish in the Owens River. The big guys tend to live in Crowley Lake and then enter the river to spawn; the big browns do so in the fall, the rainbows in the spring. Fall and spring—the windows of opportunity, during which monster-sized fish can be found—are the best times to fish. In the summer, the river gets hit hard every day, catch rates are low, and only very rarely is a true trophy-sized rainbow or brown trout actually caught.

The Owens River demands the best out of the best fly fishers in America—and it is always a challenge that the best find most compelling. If this flips your pancake, be sure to try dinging your dong at Hot Creek (see the *Hot Creek* listing).

Note: Always check DFG regulations for laws governing the river. They vary according to section.

Facilities, fees: Campgrounds are available. Supplies can be obtained in Lee Vining, Mammoth Lakes, and Tom's Place. Fishing access is free.

Directions: From Bishop, take U.S. 395 north for 46 miles to Owens River Road. Turn right and drive two miles east to Big Springs Road. Turn north on Big Springs Road and drive 0.25 mile to the campground, where the river's headwaters are located.

Access notes: Public access is available from the campground downstream about a mile. Beware of crossing onto private property. Do not try to access the river through Alper's. Access is available through Alper's Owens River Ranch for guests only.

Other public access is available via Benton Crossing Road, approximately 13 miles south of the Owens River Road turnoff from U.S. 395. Turn east and continue to the bridge. The area between the Arcularius Ranch and Crowley Lake is accessible to the public. But note that Arcularius Ranch is a private, members-only facility and isn't open to the public.

Contact: Inyo National Forest, Mono Lake

Visitors Center, 760/647-3044, www.mono lake.org; Rick's Sport Center, 760/934-3416; The Troutfitter, 760/934-2517, www.the troutfly.com; Kittredge Sports, Mammoth Lakes, 760/934-7566, www.kittredge.net; Sierra Trout Magnet, 760/873-0100, www .sierratroutmagnet.com; Performance Anglers, 818/288-0583, www.performanceanglers .com.

33 MAMMOTH CREEK

Rating: 4

near Mammoth Lakes in Inyo National Forest
Map 10.2, page 480

Little Mammoth Creek flows downstream (east) from Twin Lakes and provides an option amid the Mammoth area known mostly for a series of small, productive lakes.

Always start your day here at the bridge on Old Mammoth Road. From there, you will find access points to the creek along the road to U.S. 395. That's it. This stretch of water is stocked with rainbow trout in the 10- to 12-inch class and provides decent public access.

As the river flows east past U.S. 395, it runs into the Hot Creek geyser and forms Hot Creek, where less than a mile of the stream is open to the public.

Facilities, fees: Campgrounds are at nearby lakes. Supplies can be obtained in Mammoth Lakes. Fishing access is free.

Directions: From Bishop, take U.S. 395 north for 39 miles to Mammoth Junction. Turn west on Highway 203 and drive to the town of Mammoth Lakes. Turn left on Old Mammoth Road and continue to Mammoth Creek Road, just before the bridge. Turn left and continue west.

Contact: Inyo National Forest, Mammoth Lakes Visitors Center, 760/924-5500, www .fs.fed.us/r5—click on Forest Offices; Rick's Sport Center, 760/934-3416; The Troutfitter, 760/934-2517, www.thetroutfly.com; Kittredge Sports, Mammoth Lakes, 760/934-7566, www.kittredge.net.

34 CONVICT CREEK

Rating: 5

north of Bishop in Inyo National Forest
Map 10.2, page 480

Little Convict Creek can provide a stunner. It doesn't look like much, but this little trout stream has some huge brown trout, five-pounders, and also receives decent plants of catchable-size rainbow trout.

Catchable trout are planted from the dam on the east end of the lake on downstream toward U.S. 395, with access right along Convict Lake Road. Your best bet is below the campground, which is also the section that is best stocked with rainbow trout. The best spot for the big brown trout is at the outlet of Convict Lake. It can occasionally stun people just how big these brown trout can be.

If you get zilched from shore at Convict Lake, this small stream provides a viable option.

Convict Lake is one of the prettiest places anywhere, and it also offers a multitude of recreational choices. Of them all, fishing below the dam on Convict Creek is the most overlooked. The campground is in a stark setting.

Facilities, fees: A campground, drinking water, and flush toilets are available. An RV dump station, a boat ramp, a store, a restaurant, and horseback-riding facilities are nearby. Cabins can be rented through the Convict Lake Store. Fishing access is free.

Directions: Take U.S. 395 to Convict Lake Road (five miles south of Mammoth Junction, adjacent to Mammoth Lakes Airport). Turn west on Convict Lake Road and drive two miles to Convict Lake. Cross the dam and drive a short distance to the campground entrance road, on the left. Turn left and drive 0.25 mile to the campground. Creek access is best there and below the dam.

Contact: Inyo National Forest, Mammoth Lakes Visitors Center, 760/924-5500, www .fs.fed.us/r5—click on Forest Offices; Convict Lake Resort & Cabins, 760/934-3800 or 800/992-2260, www.convictlake.com.

35 HOT CREEK

Rating: 8

near Mammoth Lakes
Map 10.2, page 480

So many trout are caught and released at Hot Creek that through the process of natural selection, they soon might start being born with grommets in the sides of their mouths. This is the most popular catch-and-release fishery in California, with each trout caught an average of five or six times a month. Crazy? Not so crazy. What will drive you crazy is when you spot several 22-inch, four-pound rainbow trout and then try to catch them. The biggest brown trout documented was hooked, landed, and released: a 27-incher.

Hot Creek is a classic meandering spring creek, wandering through a meadow in the eastern Sierra. Only two small pieces of it, totaling just three miles, are accessible. Below the Hot Creek hatchery, there are two miles of stream bordered by private land, where access is allowed only to fly fishers who have booked one of the nine cabins at Hot Creek Ranch. Downstream of that section is another piece of water just under a mile long that is accessible to the public. The best time to fish is from the season opener (on the last Saturday in April) through early July. After that, weed growth becomes a problem.

The Hot Creek Ranch section of river is something of a legend, where the big trout have names and where some of the most expert fly fishers in the world come to practice their art. All wear polarized sunglasses so that they can see the trout in the river. Almost never will the trout actually smack the fly, but more often simply stop it. The know-hows, seeing this through their special glasses, then set the hook. Newcomers to the game, without polarized glasses, just keep waiting for the bite that never comes. All fish are released on this stretch of river. The best fly patterns are the standards for spring creeks. They include caddis, duns, and parachutes. Don't expect fireworks. Most of the river is off-limits to the public, making it very confusing for newcomers trying to figure out where to fish. In addition, catch rates are much lower than advertised. You can often see the fish but not catch them.

The free-to-the-public stretch of water is one of the most intensely fished streams in California. Gear type is restricted to flies and lures with single barbless hooks. There are a lot of big fish here.

The stream is called Hot Creek because just below the public-accessible stretch of water, hot springs boil into the stream, way too hot to support trout. The Forest Service prohibits swimming here because of high levels of arsenic and rapid fluctuations in water temperature.

So there you have it, a tiny piece of water, just three miles long, from the hatchery to the hot spring, where there are not only a lot of big, native rainbow trout, but where you can actually see them. It comprises a one-of-a-kind fishery that every fly fisher should sample at some time.

Facilities, fees: A picnic area with restrooms is provided near the fish hatchery. Campgrounds, lodging, and supplies can be found in the Mammoth Lakes area. Fishing access is free.

Directions: Take U.S. 395 to Hot Creek Hatchery Road (three miles south of Mammoth Junction; 36 miles north of Bishop). Turn east on Hot Creek Hatchery Road and look for the sign for Hot Creek Geologic Area. Continue for about three miles to the dirt parking areas and hike down to the creek.

Contact: Inyo National Forest, Mammoth Lakes Visitors Center, 760/924-5500, www.fs.fed.us/r5—click on Forest Offices; Mammoth Lakes Visitors Bureau, 888/466-2666, www.visitmammoth.com; Rick's Sport Center, 760/934-3416; The Troutfitter, 760/934-2517, www.thetroutfly.com; Kittredge Sports, Mammoth Lakes, 760/934-7566, www.kittredge.net; Culver's Sporting Goods, Bishop, 760/872-8361; Sierra Trout Magnet, 760/873-0100, www.sierratroutmagnet.com; Pat Jaeger, 760/872-7770, www.jaeger-flyfishing.com; Sierra Drifters Guide Service, 760/935-4250, www.sierradrifters.com.

36 CROWLEY LAKE

Rating: 10

north of Bishop
Map 10.2, page 480

At some point, every angler should experience a trout opener at Crowley Lake. It is a wild scenario. In the big years, thousands of anglers arrive on the Friday evening prior to the annual opener (the last Saturday in April) and convert the little nearby town of Tom's Place into an all-night cowboy rocker. The idea of "trout, trout, trout," mixed with favorite elixirs, whips the place into a frenzy. Before dawn, there can be so many anglers on the northwestern and southern shores of Crowley Lake that the Department of Fish and Game sometimes even puts up a rope barricade to keep people from fishing too early. When the legal opening time arrives, the DFG fires off a flare into the morning sky to signify the start of trout season.

Then comes the reward. By 9 A.M. there are usually many limits, including good numbers of large rainbow trout in the three- and four-pound class (sometimes even bigger) and maybe a few monster brown trout. Then by early afternoon, everybody has either passed out or gone to sleep from exhaustion.

We're not talking the good ol' days. Crowley is a happening place. Crowley, at 6,720 feet, is bordered by high desert country (sparse and dry looking) and has 45 miles of shoreline. The White Mountains are off in the distance to the east, and the Sierra is to the west. The west winds can occasionally be nasty, particularly on early summer afternoons.

The lake is boosted by giant plants of fingerling rainbow, cutthroat, and brown trout; subcatchable Eagle Lake and rainbow trout; and 10- to 12-inch rainbows. A newly developed strain of brown trout hopes to bring the glory days of giant browns back to Crowley, and fingerlings are planted by the thousands. The big Alpers rainbow trout always provide a happy shock to the lucky few.

The lake is fed from the north by the Owens River and by Convict Creek to the west, and between those two inlets is the best shore fishing on the lake. By boat, many fish are caught trolling, but another technique is straight-line jigging with small purple or white crappie jigs with a small worm trailer. You might catch more than trout with that method.

You can catch Sacramento perch, which have a large population in the lake. Or you might get a big brown trout, maybe in the 15-pound class or bigger. For several years, the state-record brown was one taken from Crowley, a fish that weighed 25 pounds, 11 ounces. It has been beaten twice by browns landed at Twin Lakes near Bridgeport. Because of the high amount of aquatic life in the lake, trout can grow as fast as an inch per month during the summer months.

A trick for big browns at Crowley is to troll a Rapala or drift a whole night crawler well up the Owens River arm of the lake. In the fall, most of the lake's population of browns will head up in this area to spawn, the one time the big ones are vulnerable. All it takes is to hook one, and you will be back. After all, only those who see the invisible can do the impossible. Alligator Point and the mouth of the Owens are good spots.

When the wind is down, the northwest corner is good for float tubers. In peak season, they always seem to be bobbing around here. On the opener, it can look like a flotilla of tubers.

Facilities, fees: Crowley Lake Fish Camp offers a full-service marina, docks, a boat ramp, fishing- and pontoon-boat rentals, tackle, and a convenience store. Floating chemical toilets are on the lake. Several campgrounds are nearby. Swimming is not permitted. Boats must be registered at the lake entrance. Day-use and boat-launching fees are charged.

Directions: From Bishop, take U.S. 395 north for 21 miles to the Crowley Lake Road exit. Turn left on Crowley Lake Road and drive northwest for 5.5 miles (past Tom's Place) to the campground entrance on the left (well signed) or continue to the Crowley Lake Fish Camp.

Contact: Bureau of Land Management, Bishop

Field Office, 760/872-5000, www.blm.gov/ca; Interagency Visitor Center, 760/876-6222; Crowley Lake Fish Camp, 760/935-4301, www.crowleylakefishcamp.com; Tom's Place Resort, 760/935-4239, www.tomsplaceresort.com; Rick's Sport Center, 760/934-3416; The Troutfitter, 760/934-2517, www.thetroutfly.com; Kittredge Sports, Mammoth Lakes, 760/934-7566, www.kittredge.net; Culver's Sporting Goods, Bishop, 760/872-8361; Sierra Drifters Guide Service, 760/935-4250, www.sierradrifters.com; Historic Highway 395, www.395.com; Pat Jaeger, 760/872-7770, www.jaeger-flyfishing.com; Sierra Trout Magnet, 760/873-0100, www.sierratroutmagnet.com; Performance Anglers, 818/288-0583, www.performanceanglers.com.

37 CONVICT LAKE

Rating: 10

north of Bishop in Inyo National Forest

Map 10.2, page 480   BEST (

Convict Lake is a mountain shrine. This is a place where people who love untouched, natural beauty, lots of trout, and a chance for a trophy can practice their religion. The lake is framed by a back wall of wilderness mountain peaks and is fronted by a conifer-lined shore. All this is at 7,583 feet, bordered by the John Muir Wilderness to the west. Yet access is very easy off U.S. 395 to the east.

At times the fishing is outstanding, with lots of fish and a sprinkling of giants. Time your trip when the moon is dark and the lake surface has become ice-free, and you will get excellent trolling results. Most of the summer catches are rainbow trout and brook trout, but in the early summer and early fall, when the weather is cold and the fishing pressure is low, some huge brown trout are always caught. Catch rates fluctuate greatly, and there are lots of shoreline bait dunkers on the southern shoreline.

The best fishing of the year here is usually during the annual late-summer, early-fall trout derby. The lake is stocked with both DFG catchable 10- to 12-inch rainbow trout and big Alpers trout. But even the DFG occasionally plunks in some big ones here. I caught a 23-inch rainbow trout that had a DFG tag on it, and that is proof enough.

Some of my best catches here have been while trolling two lures simultaneously (with two rods), so that it appears as if a trout is chasing a minnow. Start by tying a snap swivel on your line. Then tie a 25- to 28-inch leader (fluorocarbon) to the snap swivel and a large Countdown Rapala (rainbow-trout pattern or gold/black). Then, on another rod, tie another 12- to 14-inch leader to the snap swivel with a floated jointed Rebel (gold/black). When you troll, the Countdown Rapala appears to be chasing the smaller jointed Rebel. With another person in the boat, on another rod, add a silver/black Needlefish or purple Humdinger, and put that out in front of the Rebel and Rapala. It will look like a fish chain on a feeding-attack mission. I almost won the Convict Lake fish tournament one year with this trick, landing a big rainbow trout that actually broke one of the hooks on the treble hook of the jointed Rebel.

The best strategy is to troll just off the underwater ledge/dropoffs, best at the head of the lake near the creek inlet at dusk. I hooked a monster brown here once, but it got away from me without warning. Another strategy is to rip troll at dusk with big Rapalas. This works best on windy spring evenings. You won't get a lot of fish, but after all, you're going for the big one. I've seen 10-pounders here, even if I haven't landed one yet.

There are many bonuses: the trail on the north side of the lake goes west along the lake and then up through a canyon alongside Convict Creek. In the space of a challenging five-mile climb, the trail leads into the John Muir Wilderness and a series of nine lakes, including Bighorn Lake, which is bigger than Convict Lake. Another option is fishing for the planters stocked in Convict Creek just downstream of the dam along Convict Lake Road. In September, the aspens coating the mountain slopes turn yellow and then golden.

You could be a world-class artist and not paint a prettier picture.

When you put it all together, this is a great place to spend a week—beauty, quality fish, and hiking options.

Facilities, fees: Boat docks, a boat ramp, a small marina, boat rentals, a fish-cleaning station, bait and tackle, an RV dump station, a convenience store, cabin rentals, and a restaurant are at Convict Lake Resort. A campground, restrooms with flush toilets, and drinking water are nearby. The speed limit is 10 mph on the lake. Fishing access is free. There is a fee for boat launching.

Directions: From Bishop, take U.S. 395 north for 35 miles to Convict Lake Road (adjacent to Mammoth Lakes Airport). Turn left and drive three miles to the boat ramp.

From Lee Vining, take U.S. 395 south for 31 miles (5 miles past Mammoth Junction) to Convict Lake Road (adjacent to Mammoth Lakes Airport). Turn west (right) on Convict Lake Road and drive two miles to the boat launch.

Contact: Convict Lake Resort & Cabins, 760/934-3800 or 800/992-2260, www.convictlake.com; Tom's Place Resort, 760/935-4239, www.tomsplaceresort.com; Inyo National Forest, Mammoth Lakes Visitors Center, 760/924-5500, www.fs.fed.us/r5—click on Forest Offices; Mammoth Lakes Visitors Bureau, 888/466-2666, www.visitmammoth.com.

38 McGEE CREEK

Rating: 4
north of Bishop in Inyo National Forest
Map 10.2, page 480

When the wind is blowing a gale at Crowley Lake, an occasional event, little McGee Creek provides the answer to an angler's prayer. The wind can really howl at Crowley, particularly during the afternoon in the early summer. It drives everybody off the lake, looking for cover. Only a few folks who know little spots like McGee Creek keep looking for trout.

McGee Creek is just southwest of Crowley Lake. It flows eastward until it joins up with Lower Convict Creek and enters the big lake. The section between Old Highway 395 and the Upper Campground is stocked with some 10- to 12-inch rainbow trout. When a hurricane is blowing at Crowley, any trout is a good trout.

Another option at McGee Creek is using the end of the road as a trailhead for a wilderness adventure. The trail is routed west into the John Muir Wilderness, passing Horsetail Falls and then heading to the high country, where you discover dozens of lakes. One of the better destinations is the source of McGee Creek: Big McGee and Little McGee lakes, set amid the stunning, high granite country of the Silver Divide.

Facilities, fees: A campground with restrooms, showers, drinking water, and RV hookups is on the creek. Supplies are in Bishop. Fishing access is free.

Directions: From Mammoth Junction (the junction of U.S. 395 and Highway 203), take U.S. 395 south for 10 miles to McGee Creek Road. Turn right (southwest) and look for the park entrance on the left.

Contact: Inyo National Forest, White Mountain Ranger District, 760/873-2500, www.fs.fed.us/r5—click on Forest Offices; McGee Creek RV Park, 760/935-4233, www.mcgeecreekrv-campground.com; The Troutfitter, 760/934-2517, www.thetroutfly.com; Sierra Drifters Guide Service, 760/935-4250, www.sierradrifters.com; Mammoth Lakes Pack Outfit, 888/475-8747, www.mammothpack.com.

39 JOHN MUIR WILDERNESS

Rating: 10
east of Fresno in Sierra National Forest
Map 10.2, page 480

Trails reaching as high as 12,000 feet, mountaintops poking holes into the heavens, and hundreds of pristine lakes set in granite bowls make for paradise in the John Muir Wilderness. It is the kind of place where a hiker can get religion without making a single donation in an offering plate. I'll tell you the kind of impact it had on me. Visiting it is such a transcendent experience that it has made me stay in good physical condition, with the idea in the back of my mind that I could return at any time, any day.

There are many trailheads and access points into the John Muir Wilderness. The best are at Edison Lake, Florence Lake, and at the end of Highway 180, in Kings Canyon National Park. I suggest that you scan the fishing notes for other waters within this chapter to find jump-off points and suggested routes.

Usually if you plan on eating trout for dinner when backpacking, it guarantees you will get skunked. An exception is in the John Muir Wilderness, where my brother Rambob and I have never failed to limit on trout every evening (bring plenty of jerky just to be safe). The trout are not large (very seldom over eight inches long), but they include the rare golden trout, California's state fish. Most of the lakes here harbor lots of small brook trout and some rainbow trout, the kind that practically jump into the frying pan come the evening rise.

The following hike-in lakes have been stocked in recent years with golden trout by the Department of Fish and Game's flying tanker: Apollo, Aweetasal, Bearpaw, Beartrap, Big Bear, Bighorn, Black Bear, Brown Bear, Chapel, Claw, Coronet, Den, Hooper, Island, Neil, Upper Nelson, Orchid, Pemmican, Rose, Rosebud, Silver Pass, Spearpoint, Teddy Bear, Three Island, Toe, Tooth, Ursa, Vee, Virginia, and White Bear.

Meanwhile, the following lakes have been on the DFG's list for stocking with rainbow trout and brook trout in recent years: Anne, Chimney, Cirque, Coyote, Crown, Davis, Geraldine, Maxon, Minnie, Pearl, Rainbow, Scepter, and Vermilion.

This list is constantly changing; check with the DFG for current status.

Note that all trout plants in Kings Canyon National Park have been stopped! That should be taken into consideration before planning your backcountry route.

Many visitors to the John Muir Wilderness hike primarily on the John Muir Trail, partially in reverence for the master. In the process, however, they miss many of the more hidden and lesser-visited lakes. Remember, when Muir hiked from Mount Whitney to Yosemite Valley, there was no trail, but rather a general route. Much of it was cross-country, and on the way, he was apt to explore any lake and any mountain. That is the best approach to take. Once in the high country, head off the trail, clambering your way to lakes that are like mountain temples, where humankind is only a temporary visitor, and where Muir's ghost may still linger.

Facilities, fees: No facilities are in the wilderness area. Campgrounds are at many trailheads. Fishing access is free.

Directions: Access to trailheads can be found off roads that intersect U.S. 395 to the east and Highway 168 to the west.

Contact: Sierra National Forest Headquarters, 559/297-0706; for a map of the area, contact the U.S. Forest Service, www.fs.fed.us/r5—click on Forest Offices; Mammoth Lakes Pack Outfit, 888/475-8747, www.mammothpack.com.

40 LAKE EDISON

Rating: 7

northeast of Fresno in
the Sierra National Forest
Map 10.2, page 480

Here is one of the most remote camping and fishing destinations in California. Lake Edison offers good fishing, tent cabins, campgrounds, a rustic mountain lodge and restaurant, a boat launch, boat rentals, horse rentals, and a nearby trailhead to the John Muir Trail. A 15-mph speed limit keeps the lake ideal for anglers, and a ferry service runs across the lake twice a day for hikers on the John Muir Trail.

Edison Lake is at an elevation of 7,650 feet and is fed by Mono Creek, a cold, pure, and pristine trout stream. It is one of the most remote lakes you can drive to in California. Edison is stocked with fingerlings as well as catchable trout. There are some giant brown trout in this lake, but they are difficult to inspire. These big browns are best caught at ice-out (during the first two weeks of the season). This may sound crazy, but you go in by snowmobile and cast in breaks between the ice; that is your best chance of getting one of the monsters. Do not try to walk on the ice. This can result in death.

After ice-out, when the road opens up, most boaters use standard trolling techniques and do well enough on rainbow trout, with occasional brook trout and big brown trout. Shoreliners who are willing to hike fare no worse. You should take the hiker's shuttle boat, or hike the trail on the north side of the lake and hike up toward the inlet of the lake, about a three-mile tromp. The fishing in Mono Creek can be excellent, especially during the evening bite.

If you like hiking, Edison Lake provides one of the better jump-off points. The trail along the north side of the lake is routed along Mono Creek and then connects to the John Muir Trail. This provides excellent stream-fishing access along Mono Creek. From there, if you don't mind a steep climb, head south up Bear Mountain. It takes about a 40-minute hike to reach an absolutely wondrous aspen grove that is pretty any time of the year.

Because many people start their backpacking trips here, lake use is high in summer. Hang out here for long enough, and you are bound to see JMT hikers taking a break, eating everything in sight at the small restaurant. Nearby Mono Hot Springs offers mineral baths and access to hot springs.

Note that the drive to Edison Lake is on an extremely twisty and narrow road. If you want a near-death experience, try driving it on a Friday or Sunday afternoon, when there's a good chance of a head-on collision with idiots trying to race to and from Mono Hot Springs. If you are towing a boat, it is extremely precarious. My pal, fieldscout Gary Miralles, who contributed to this book, towed a 21-foot Alumaweld here and said he narrowly avoided several near-death head-on collisions and that he'd never go back, no matter how good the fish might be. What to do? Drive slowly, take your time, and enjoy the Sierra views. My personal preference is to make the trip at night, when you can more easily spot oncoming vehicles because of the headlight beams boring holes in the darkness, making for no surprises on the blind turns on the narrow road.

Facilities, fees: A paved boat ramp is on the west shore; Kaiser Pass Road leads directly to it. Lodging, tent cabins, restrooms, showers, a convenience store, flush toilets, a primitive boat ramp, fishing-boat and canoe rentals, bait and tackle, and a hiker's water taxi are at Vermillion Valley Resort. A campground with drinking water and vault toilets is nearby. Fishing access is free.

Directions: From the town of Shaver Lake, take Highway 168 north for 21 miles to Kaiser Pass Road/Forest Road 80. Turn right and drive 16 (narrow and twisting) miles to a fork in the road. Bear left onto Edison Lake Road (right goes to Florence Lake) and drive approximately six miles to the resort, at the end of the road. For a map of the area, contact the U.S. Forest Service (www.fs.fed.us/r5—click on Forest Offices).

Note: You pass Mono Hot Springs on the access road. On Friday and Sunday afternoons and evenings, some drivers from L.A. will shred this curvy two-laner as if it's a racecourse and forget it's actually a two-way road. Avoid driving to this lake during these time periods.

Contact: Vermilion Valley Resort, 559/259-4000, www.edisonlake.com; Sierra National Forest Headquarters, 559/297-0706.

41 ROCK CREEK LAKE

Rating: 8

northwest of Bishop in Inyo National Forest

Map 10.2, page 480

Most natural lakes are often prettier and smaller than reservoirs, and Rock Creek Lake, at just 63 surface acres, is a perfect example. The lake has great natural beauty, at 9,682 feet in the high Sierra, near the Little Lakes Valley, just north of the boundary to the John Muir Wilderness.

A 5-mph speed limit for boats guarantees quiet water. Although there is no similar guarantee of fishing, it is decent enough. Plants of rainbow trout start as soon as the ice melts and the access road is plowed (usually sometime in May); most stocks range 9–11 inches. The resort here adds additional fish. Those rainbows join a light sprinkling of brown trout along with fair numbers of brook trout. Brown trout in the 10-pound class are occasionally hooked, sometimes landed. The lake-record brown trout weighed 15 pounds, 8 ounces. A bonus is the plants of big Alpers rainbow trout, the locally raised trophy hybrid. Shoreline bait dunkers will find the best prospects by far near the outlet of the lake. Many of the higher-elevation lakes nearby have golden trout.

You mainly see fishing boats on the lake. Note that at times, especially in the afternoon in the late spring, wind out of the west can be cold and frustrating. The lake is in a slot in a high mountain canyon, and the wind can whip right in through. Traffic is heavy in the summer months, with a lot of people using this as a base camp and jump-off point for trips into the John Muir Wilderness.

There are some 35 other lakes nearby, many within range for a one-day round-trip. The hike out west to Mono Pass gets quite steep, but you can stop on the way at Ruby Lake, named for its gemlike qualities.

There is an excellent trailhead here for wilderness trips into the Little Lakes Valley. It is an easy day hike, featuring excellent fishing for brook trout. Horseback rentals are available at the Rock Creek Pack Station.

Facilities, fees: Lodging, a campground, an unimproved boat ramp, restrooms with flush toilets, drinking water, a picnic area, a café, and a convenience store with bait and tackle are available. Fishing boats and rowboats can be rented at Rock Creek Lakes Resort. Fishing access is free.

Directions: From Mammoth Junction (the junction of U.S. 395 and Highway 203), take U.S. 395 south for 15 miles to Tom's Place and Rock Creek Road. Turn right (south) on Rock Creek Road and drive eight miles to the lake.

From Bishop, take U.S. 395 north for 30 miles to the town of Tom's Place and Rock Creek Road. Turn left on Rock Creek Road and drive eight miles to Rock Creek Lake.

Contact: Rock Creek Lakes Resort, 760/935-4311, www.rockcreeklake.com; Rock Creek Lodge, 760/935-4170, www.rockcreeklodge.com; Tom's Place Resort, 760/935-4239, www.tomsplaceresort.com; Inyo National Forest, White Mountain Ranger District, 760/873-2500, www.fs.fed.us/r5—click on Forest Offices; Rock Creek Pack Station, 760/935-4493 (summer only), www.rockcreekpackstation.com.

42 PLEASANT VALLEY RESERVOIR

Rating: 7

near Bishop

Map 10.2, page 480

Pleasant Valley Reservoir is a long, narrow reservoir, created from a small dam on the Owens River. It is at 4,200 feet and borders the volcanic tableland to the immediate east. You have to hike or bike about 15 minutes from the campground at Pleasant Valley Park to reach the lake, meaning only the hardy few who are willing to portage a kayak on their shoulders or hoist in a float tube will have the advantage of fishing from a boat. This lake was restricted to shore fishing for decades, but no more, and that provides a great plus for float tubers. No trailered-in boats or motors are permitted.

This lake has also improved because of locally produced bonus stocks made by the Bishop Chamber of Commerce, along with big Alpers rainbow trout weighing up to eight pounds, courtesy of the Adopt-a-Creek Foundation. The Department of Fish and Game adds reasons to cast a line: rainbow trout in the 10- to 12-inch class, which join a fair population of native brown trout, some of them huge and almost impossible to catch.

Timing is critical. The trout fishing can be decent from late winter through early June, and then again in the fall, from mid-September through October. During this period, there is a chance for some big browns in the uppermost stretches of the lake. In the summer? Chances are fair, with evenings being decent.

The lake also has bass, but they are kept largely a secret by the locals. At Culver's, the owner showed me some photos of some beauties. Another option here is fishing the Owens River Gorge, above the reservoir. This nine-mile stretch is being restored and has increased water flows. The brown trout population is now estimated at more than 3,000 fish per mile (compared to 800 fish per mile in 1996). The average length of the fish has increased in the same period from 7 inches to 12 inches. It can be difficult to access, but there can be lots of action.

Facilities, fees: No facilities are available on-site. Campgrounds and supplies are in Bishop. Fishing access is free.

Directions: From Bishop, take U.S. 395 north for seven miles to Pleasant Valley Road and the signed turnoff for the reservoir. Turn north on Pleasant Valley Road and drive for 1.5 miles to the barrier across the road. Park and walk to the dam. A trail travels along the eastern side of the lake.

Contact: Inyo County Parks Department, 760/875-5577, www.inyocounty.us; Bishop Area Chamber of Commerce and Visitors Bureau, 760/873-8405 or 888/395-3952, www.bishopvisitor.com; Culver's Sporting Goods, Bishop, 760/872-8361; Mac's Sporting Goods, Bishop, 760/872-9201; The Troutfitter, 760/934-2517, www.thetroutfly.com; Sierra Drifters Guide Service, 760/935-4250, www.sierradrifters.com.

SEQUOIA AND KINGS CANYON

© MARIUSZ JURGIELEWICZ/123RF.COM

BEST FISHING SPOTS

❰ Hike-In Fisheries
Golden Trout Wilderness, **page 549.**

❰ Places to Teach Kids to Fish
Pine Flat Lake, **page 540.**

There is no place on earth like the high Sierra,

from Mount Whitney north through Sequoia and Kings Canyon National Parks. This is a paradise filled with deep canyons, high peaks, and fantastic natural beauty. The largest living things in the history of the earth – giant sequoias – can be found in pockets of spectacular groves on the western slopes.

Near Whitney, the alpine wilderness is filled with small lakes, streams, and trout, including more golden trout in the John Muir Wilderness than anywhere else. On the western slopes of the Sierra, the best trout fishing is at Edison, Florence, and Hume Lakes, all of which include opportunities for some large browns and stocked rainbows.

The eastern slopes hold a series of small streams that offer good vehicle access, Lake Sabrina and South Lake, and great wilderness trailheads at the end of almost every road. The additional private stocking programs of big rainbow trout in the Bishop area are a great bonus.

The western slope of the Sierra Nevada here is known for its charm, small trout, and a number of hidden spots, such as in the Dinkey Creek Wilderness. Other highlights include good trout fishing on the Kings River, bass at Pine Flat Lake, and excellent camping, boating, fishing, and recreation at Huntington, Shaver, and Bass Lakes, as well as at Wishon and Courtright Reservoirs. The hidden spots in Sierra National Forest provide continual fortune hunts, especially up the Dinkey Creek drainage above Courtright Reservoir.

When full, Lake Kaweah is a great destination for a chance at trophy-sized bass, and Lake Success and Bravo Lake are improving to trophy status. Winter trout plants are also exceptional in this area.

The remote Golden Trout Wilderness is one of the most pristine areas of California, and its small streams, called stringers here, provide an outstanding destination for backpackers who carry fishing rods.

Giant Isabella Lake has big bass and lots of trout (stocked in winter), and is the highlight among the fishing spots at the foot of the southern Sierra. Other fishing areas nearby feature several small drive-to streams; of these, the Middle Fork Tule River is the best of the lot.

The Sierra rivers that feed these lakes (and others) also offer the opportunity to go fly-fishing for trout. In particular, the Kaweah and Kings Rivers boast many miles of ideal pocket water for fly fishers. Although the trout on these streams are only occasionally large, the catch rates are often high, and the rock-strewn beauty of the river canyons is exceptional.

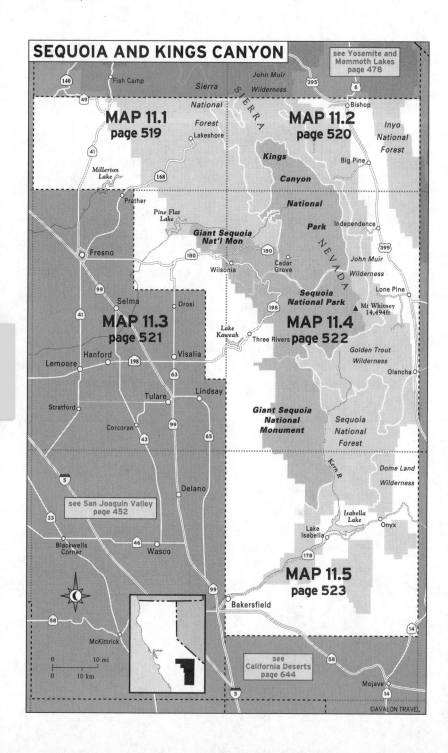

SEQUOIA AND KINGS CANYON

see Yosemite and Mammoth Lakes page 478

MAP 11.1 page 519

MAP 11.2 page 520

MAP 11.3 page 521

MAP 11.4 page 522

MAP 11.5 page 523

see San Joaquin Valley page 452

see California Deserts page 644

©AVALON TRAVEL

Map 11.1

Sites 1-12
Pages 524-531

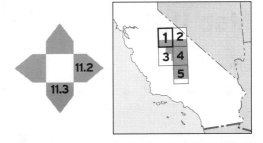

11.2

11.3

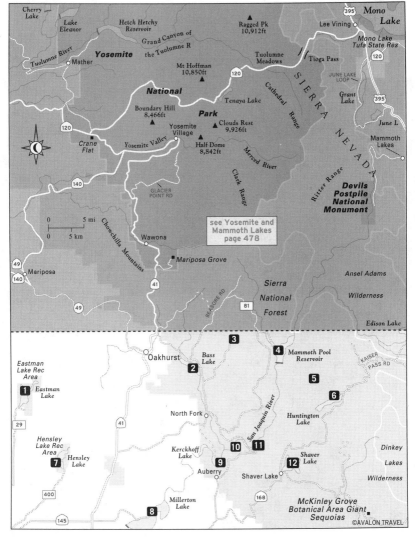

©AVALON TRAVEL

Map 11.2

Sites 13-24
Pages 531-540

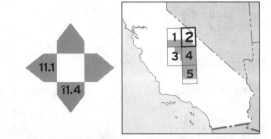

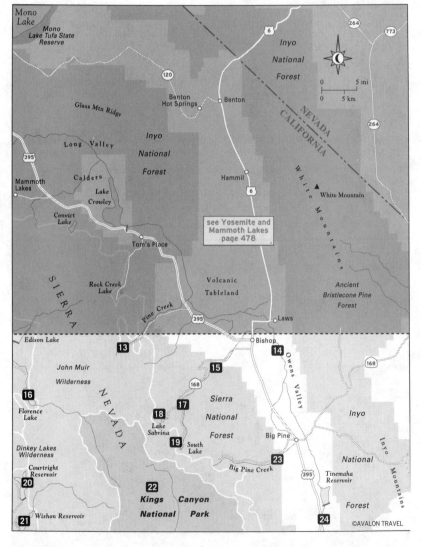

©AVALON TRAVEL

Map 11.3

Sites 25-27
Pages 540-542

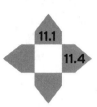

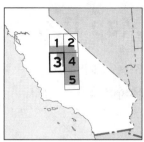

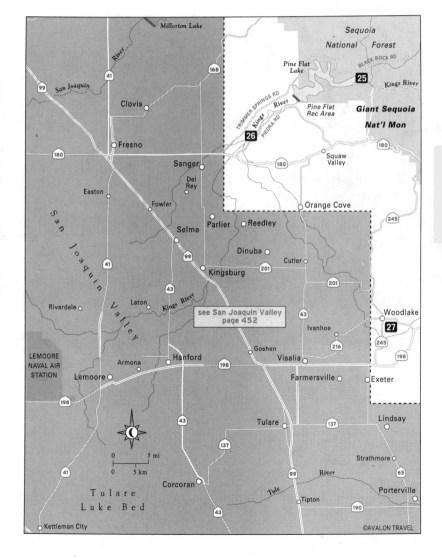

see San Joaquin Valley
page 452

©AVALON TRAVEL

Map 11.4

Sites 28-42
Pages 542-550

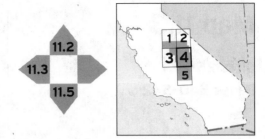

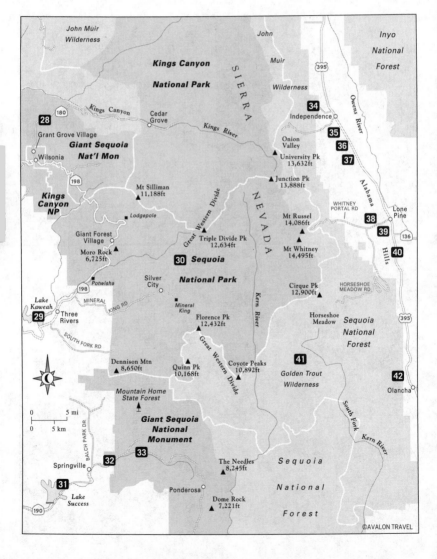

Map 11.5

Sites 43-45
Pages 550-552

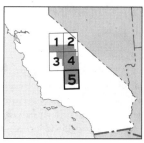

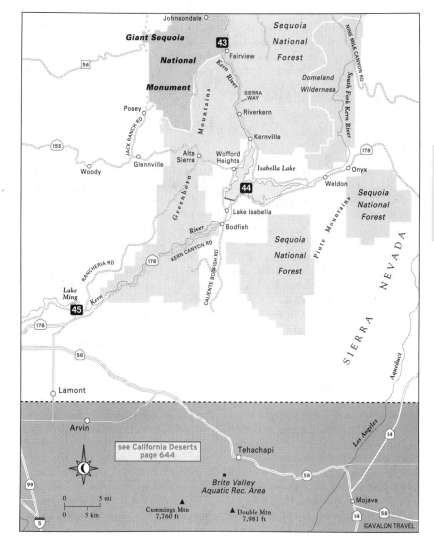

❶ EASTMAN LAKE

Rating: 7

southeast of Merced

Map 11.1, page 519

One of the most fascinating experiments in California is taking place at Eastman. In the attempt to create a trophy bass fishery—that is, lots of big bass 15–22 inches—the limit is only one bass, and that one bass must measure at least 22 inches.

Before the lake was opened to the public in 1978, many brush piles were anchored along the lake bottom to provide aquatic habitat in what would otherwise be a barren water hole. Well, it worked.

Another thing that has worked is a weed-control program. At one time, Eastman was plagued by rampant weed growth. That has largely been solved. Good work! Another bonus is a trophy-bass program. Fishing can be good for not only bass and catfish, but for rainbow trout, bluegill, crappie, and redear sunfish. The Department of Fish and Game stocks Eastman with half-pound catchable trout.

Eastman Lake is tucked in the foothills of the San Joaquin Valley at an elevation of 650 feet. It covers 1,800 surface acres. The reservoir was created when the federal government built a dam on the Chowchilla River. Eastman Lake has become the kind of place where you can make an evening hit for the bass after getting off work. The northern arm of the lake usually provides the best prospects.

In summer, decent catfishing is often available near the campgrounds on the southeastern shore of the lake.

Note that a small area at the upper end of the lake is closed to boating to protect a bald-eagle nesting site. The area is marked by a buoy "keep out" line. Bring your binoculars, look for the big nest, and check it out. This lake is designated as a "Watchable Wildlife" site, and it has 163 species of birds.

Facilities, fees: Two boat ramps are available, one on the lake's east side and one on the west side. Campgrounds and picnic areas are at the lake. Drinking water, flush toilets, showers, and an RV dump station are provided. An equestrian staging area is available for overnight use, and there are seven miles of hiking, biking, and equestrian trails. Supplies can be obtained in Chowchilla or Madera. A day-use fee is charged per vehicle. Boat launching is free.

Directions: Take Highway 99 to Chowchilla and exit at Avenue 26. Take that exit and drive 11 miles to County Road 29. Turn left (north) on County Road 29 and drive eight miles to the lake.

Contact: U.S. Army Corps of Engineers, Sacramento District, Eastman Lake, 559/689-3255, www.corpslakes.usace.army.mil.

❷ BASS LAKE

Rating: 8

northeast of Fresno in Sierra National Forest

Map 11.1, page 519

There are two worlds at Bass Lake. Come to this lake in late winter through late spring and you can have a great time fishing for bass and rainbow trout. After that, the kokanee salmon come on strong.

But arrive after the Fourth of July and weekends can resemble the racetrack at the Indianapolis 500.

Bass Lake is popular with a huge diversity of people. It is a long, beautiful lake, set in a valley at 3,400 feet and surrounded by national forest. The lake covers nearly 1,200 acres when full and has five campgrounds, four resorts, and two boat launches.

The lake also has a variety of fish, making it a take-your-pick deal. In the winter and spring, Fish and Game stocks it with rainbow trout in the 10- to 12-inch class, which provide a good troll fishery through May. This lake is one of the best lakes in California for kokanee salmon; the Department of Fish and Game (DFG) plants kokanee fingerlings here. By June, though, the weather heats up, and nature converts the lake to a warm-water special, with bass (not quite as good as the lake's name implies), bluegill, crappie, and catfish all coming to life.

My fly-fishing pal Rick Martin reports he's had some great times here, with small poppers for bass. The best surface bite is at dawn, mid-May to early June. To do it right, you just have to have a boat. Note that during the summer season, all boats must be registered at the Bass Lake Sheriff's Tower. And you thought you lived in a free country? Ha.

The best spots are along the southeastern shore, from the area south of Pines Village on to the dam. There you will find one deep cove and a series of smaller ones, where warm-water species hold during the summer months.

A bonus at Bass Lake is that there are designated areas for personal-watercraft riding, waterskiing, and fishing. That has kept the peace.

Facilities, fees: Two boat ramps are available: one on the lake's northeast side, off Road 274 at the Pines Resort, and one on the southwest side, off County Road 222 near Miller's Landing. Lodging, gas, snack bars, full-service marinas, picnic areas, coin laundry, and small stores are available. There are campgrounds with flush toilets or vault toilets. Ski boats, personal watercraft, pontoon boats, fishing boats, kayaks, and canoes are for rent at Miller's Landing Resort and the Pines Marina. The Forks Resort rents fishing boats, pontoon boats, rowboats, and canoes. Day use is free; county boat-launch fees are charged based on engine horsepower.

Directions: From Fresno, take Highway 41 north to Oakhurst and continue 2.5 miles to Yosemite Forks and Bass Lake Road/County Road 222. Turn right at Bass Lake Road and drive six miles (staying right at two forks) to the lake's southern shore and access points.

Contact: Bass Lake Chamber of Commerce, 559/642-3676, www.basslakechamber.com; Miller's Landing Resort, 559/642-3633, www.millerslanding.com; The Forks Resort, 559/642-3737, www.theforksresort.com; Bass Lake Watersports and Marina, 559/642-

3200, www.basslakeboatrentals.com; Sierra National Forest, Bass Lake Ranger District, 559/877-2218, www.fs.fed.us/r5—click on Forest Offices.

Boat permits: Sheriff's Tower, 559/642-3606 (summer only).

❸ SIERRA NATIONAL FOREST

Rating: 8

northeast of Fresno

Map 11.1, page 519

You could spend many years exploring Sierra National Forest and never tire of it. This is a vast, beautiful area that includes several wilderness areas and provides backpackers with an opportunity to spend many days in paradise.

Let's get one thing straight, however: the trout are not big. But that's okay. Just bring a very small (lightweight) frying pan, and they'll look big at dinnertime. They do bite readily and can often provide an antidote to those suffering from a serious fishing jinx. Get a Forest Service map, scan the following lakes, and then route your trip, planning at least three or four days in the backcountry.

The following hike-to lakes are stocked by airplane with fingerling brook trout and/or rainbow trout: Deer, Dinkey, Doris, Ershim, Hidden, Jackass, Mirror, Mystery, Red, South, Swamp, Swede, and Tocher. You won't find any golden trout in these lakes. A wilderness permit is required for overnight use.

One of the best destinations is along Dinkey Creek, northwest of Courtright Reservoir and southwest of Florence Lake. The trail is routed to First Dinkey Lake, the centerpiece of the area, but Mystery Lake, South Lake, Rock Lake, and Cliff Lake are all within a few miles.

Facilities, fees: Facilities and supplies can be found in adjacent towns. Fishing access is free. Day-use fees may be charged where there are facilities.

Directions: Access to roads and trailheads is

off Highways 168, 41, 49, and 140, east of Fresno.

Contact: Sierra National Forest Headquarters, 559/297-0706, www.fs.fed.us/r5—click on Forest Offices; the Forest Service office on Highway 168 in Prather may be the most convenient for anglers arriving from the San Joaquin Valley.

4 MAMMOTH POOL RESERVOIR

Rating: 6

northeast of Fresno in Sierra National Forest

Map 11.1, page 519

This lake was created by a dam in the San Joaquin River gorge, a steep canyon that drops nearly 3,000 feet, creating a long, narrow lake with steep, high walls. Because of the surrounding high ridges, Mammoth Pool always seems to be much higher in elevation than its listed 3,330 feet.

The lake opens each year when the snow clears, sometime between May 1 and mid-June. Just before the lake opens to the public, the Department of Fish and Game provides rainbow trout stocks. The best fishing is then and is usually located from just east of the boat launch (where you can troll adjacent to the shoreline) on up to the narrows. Trolling directly in front of the dam also provides good chances.

In years with significant snowmelt, the better fishing is well up the San Joaquin arm, at the mouth of the river and the mouths of the creeks. A boat-in camp is at China Bar, in a cove on the northwest side of this arm, and provides a perfect location for a boating/fishing vacation.

One word of caution: If you'll be visiting from late August through November, always call ahead and ask about lake levels. Because the water is used to generate hydroelectric power at the dam, water levels can drop significantly late in the season. The lake covers 1,270 surface acres when full, early in the

season, but usually drops about 90 feet by the close of summer. This often renders the paved launch ramp useless.

Note: Boats and water sports may be restricted from May 1 through June 15 because of deer migration—that's right, deer migration through the lake.

Facilities, fees: A paved boat ramp is on the reservoir's north side, next to Mammoth Pool Campground. A gravel launch is available on the south side, next to the picnic areas. Campgrounds, drinking water, vault toilets, picnic areas, bait and tackle, a snack bar, and a grocery store are provided. A boat-in camp is on the lake's upper reaches. The speed limit is 35 mph up to China Bar; it is 20 mph above China Bar. Fishing access is free.

Directions: From Fresno, take Highway 41 north for about 25 miles to North Fork Road/County Road 200. Turn right and drive northeast for 17.5 miles to Auberry Road/County Road 222. Turn left (north) and drive one mile to the town of North Fork and Mammoth Pool Road. Turn right and drive 1.5 miles to County Road 225 (still Mammoth Pool Road). Turn right and drive about 37 miles (the road becomes Minarets Road/Forest Road 81) to a junction. Bear right (still Mammoth Pool Road) and drive three miles to Mammoth Pool Reservoir and the campground. The drive from North Fork takes 1.5–2 hours and is narrow and twisty.

Contact: Sierra National Forest, Bass Lake Ranger District, 559/877-2218, www.fs.fed.us/r5—click on Forest Offices.

5 KAISER WILDERNESS

Rating: 6

northeast of Fresno in Sierra National Forest

Map 11.1, page 519

Many of the wilderness areas in the southern Sierra Nevada include huge portions that are above the tree line, comprising stark granite country and lakes set in rock bowls. The Kaiser Wilderness, however, is an exception.

The area is mostly wooded, though Kaiser Peak is bare and provides a great lookout. The best jump-off spot is at Huntington Lake, where there are two trailheads. One popular loop hike starts near Lakeshore and heads north to Kaiser Peak, then loops back around to Nellie Lake and south along Home Camp Creek to the west end of Huntington Lake. The other starts from the trailhead at Lakeshore, continues about a mile, turns right at the fork, and then leads to Lower Twin and Upper Twin Lakes, both stocked with trout.

The following hike-to lakes have been stocked by airplane in the Kaiser Wilderness: Campfire, Nellie, Upper Twin, and Walling. They have received fingerling rainbow trout, but no brook or golden trout. This stocking program is subject to change; check for current status.

Facilities, fees: No facilities are in the wilderness area. Campgrounds are at Huntington Lake and at some trailheads. Fishing is free.

Directions: Access to trailheads is off Highway 168 east of Fresno, and off Forest Service roads that junction with Highway 168 near Huntington Lake.

Contact: Sierra National Forest, High Sierra Ranger District, 559/855-5355, www.fs.fed.us/r5—click on Forest Offices.

6 HUNTINGTON LAKE

Rating: 8

northeast of Fresno in Sierra National Forest

Map 11.1, page 519

Huntington Lake is planted with rainbow trout, usually as soon as snowplows start rolling and the access road is cleared. The stocks also usually continue regularly through summer, providing good catch rates for trollers and a good evening bite. We're talking big-time plants, with 10- to 12-inch rainbow trout, as well as thousands of fingerling kokanee salmon. There are also some big but elusive brown trout in this lake.

Huntington Lake is at 7,000 feet in the Sierra Nevada and surrounded by national forest. This is a big lake, at 4 miles long and half a mile wide, with 14 miles of shoreline. It also has many campgrounds and resorts, and is a jump-off point for backpacking trips into the nearby Kaiser Wilderness.

It is pretty, popular, and often provides very good fishing for know-hows. Many summer visitors get zilch because they fish only once a year. You need a boat, that's for starters.

The best camps for anglers are the Deer Creek and College Camps (on the northeast shore) and the Lower Billy Creek Camp (on the northwest shore). Boat launches are near both of them.

Lake use is heavy from May through September and diminishes greatly after Labor Day weekend. By mid-October, when the cold weather moves in for good, most operations shut down for winter. The Rancheria Falls National Recreation Trail is near the eastern end of the lake. It provides access to beautiful Rancheria Falls.

Facilities, fees: A paved boat ramp is on the northeast shore, near Lakeshore Resort. Campgrounds, restrooms, drinking water, lodging, picnic areas, a marina, boat slips, bait and tackle, propane gas, restaurants, and groceries are available. Fishing boats, pontoon boats, canoes, kayaks, personal watercraft, and sailboats can be rented at Huntington Lake Marina, on the west shore. Horseback riding is possible nearby. Parking fees are charged in some areas.

Directions: From Fresno, take Highway 168 east to Shaver Lake, then continue 21 miles to Huntington Lake and Huntington Lake Road. Turn left on Huntington Lake Road and drive one mile. Continue on Huntington Lake Road to a series of several campgrounds and access points, on the left.

Contact: Rancheria Marina, 559/893-3234, www.rancheriaenterprises.com; Lakeshore Resort, 559/893-3193, www.lakeshoreresort.com; Sierra National Forest, High Sierra Ranger District, 559/855-5355, www.fs.fed.us/r5—click on Forest Offices.

◢ HENSLEY LAKE

Rating: 7

north of Fresno

Map 11.1, page 519

What makes a reservoir good for largemouth bass? This is what: plenty of shoreline coves, lots of points, and sheltered bays. Most reservoirs don't have all these assets, but Hensley is an exception, making it one of the best fishing bets in the immediate region.

Set at 540 feet in the Central Valley foothills, northeast of Fresno, Hensley is a good-sized lake covering 1,500 acres, with 24 miles of shoreline when full. Spring comes early here, and so does the bass fishing, often starting up in early March and continuing at a good clip until late May. At that time the better bass fishing becomes a dawn or dusk proposition. Catfish, sunfish, and bluegill also live in the lake.

The northern shore is best for bass and also offers some protection from the spring winds. If it is windy, another good spot is the cove east of the dam, which is protected by a stubby peninsula. The lake is ideal for bass boats with foot-controlled electric motors, allowing you to glide adjacent to the shoreline, fanning the shallows with casts.

Hensley is also stocked with rainbow trout by the Department of Fish and Game. It gets 10- to 12-inch rainbow trout, usually spaced out over the cool months. Once the water warms up in late spring, water-skiers take over during the day, and they just love hitting the coves. The resulting wakes slap against the shore and spook the bass. If the skiers would just remain in the vicinity of the dam, they wouldn't hurt the fishing, but they don't.

The solution is to take advantage of the Central Valley's warm weather in early spring, which is not only before the water-skiers arrive but also when the bass start waking up at Hensley (far earlier in the year than at lakes farther north).

Facilities, fees: Two paved launch ramps are available: one on the lake's east side, off County Road 400, and one on the west side, next to Hidden View Campground. Campgrounds, restrooms with flush toilets and showers, an RV dump station, and picnic areas are available. Supplies can be obtained in Madera. A day-use fee is charged that includes boat launching.

Directions: From Madera, take Highway 145 northeast for about six miles to County Road 400. Bear left on County Road 400 and drive to County Road 603 (below the dam). Turn left and drive about two miles to County Road 407. Turn right on County Road 407 and drive 0.5 mile to the Hidden View Campground and boat launch.

Contact: U.S. Army Corps of Engineers, Sacramento District, Hensley Lake, 559/673-5151, www.corpslakes.usace.army.mil.

◢ MILLERTON LAKE

Rating: 7

north of Fresno in Millerton Lake
State Recreation Area

Map 11.1, page 519

Millerton Lake may seem like the perfect setting for a bass bonanza. Sometimes it actually is. A slot limit where only bass under 12 inches or above 15 inches may be taken has resulted in a lot of beautiful (and protected) fish in the 12- to 15-inch class.

At an elevation of 578 feet and in the foothills of the San Joaquin Valley, Millerton gets good bass weather, providing for a nine-month growing season, although it's very hot during midsummer. The lake also has a lot of shoreline bass habitat, with 43 miles of shoreline in all, including many little coves on the San Joaquin arm.

This is becoming a very good bass lake; it's on a definite upswing. A bass-stocking program looks to keep it that way.

Regardless, Millerton gets a lot of traffic because of its proximity to Fresno and Madera.

The shape of the lake, a large body and a long narrow inlet, seems to naturally separate water-skiers from anglers. Rules guarantee it: no waterskiing is allowed on the upriver portion of the lake. But beware: at the main lake, personal watercraft plow water like an armada of water jets.

One major problem here is that this lake seems to be a perennial victim of low water levels, with summer and fall drawdowns a visual impact.

No trout have been stocked at Millerton for years. Catfishing can be good in summer. A bonus is that the lake provides a wintering habitat for bald eagles, and eagle boat tours can be arranged.

Facilities, fees: Boat ramps are on the south shore by the day-use areas and at the end of the campground entrance road. Campgrounds, three boat-in campsites, picnic areas, restrooms with flush toilets and coin showers, drinking water, an RV dump station, a full-service marina, and a snack bar are provided. Fishing boats, ski boats, personal watercraft, pontoon boats, canoes, and kayaks are available for rent at the marina. Supplies can be obtained in Friant. A day-use fee is charged; an annual pass may be purchased. A fee is charged for boat launching.

Directions: From Madera, take Highway 99 and exit onto Highway 145 East. Drive 22 miles (six miles past the intersection with Highway 41) to the park entrance on the right.

Contact: Millerton Lake State Recreation Area, 559/822-2332, www.parks.ca.gov.

9 SAN JOAQUIN RIVER

Rating: 4

northeast of Fresno in Sierra National Forest
Map 11.1, page 519

The San Joaquin is the chameleon of California rivers, changing its appearance from one stretch to the next. In this area, the only stretch planted significantly with trout by the Department of Fish and Game is below Millerton Lake, downstream of Friant (the best stretch of river upstream of Millerton Lake is near Devils Postpile National Monument). So what you get here are a few accessible spots near the campgrounds; that is, spots that get picked over year after year. The fish tend to be small for the most part and are not particularly amenable to donating themselves to your frying pan. The DFG stocks the South Fork and Middle Fork San Joaquin with rainbow trout in the 10- to 12-inch class.

The river also has dramatic changes in water flows, even during the summer, due to unpredictable releases from dams at Redinger Lake and Kerckhoff and Mammoth Pool Reservoirs. It doesn't take long to figure out what's happening here. Maybe sample it for an hour, then head on up the mountain.

A secret is that in remote sections of the San Joaquin, rainbow and brown trout in the 24- to 28-inch class have been spotted. It requires a one- to two-day backpacking trip to reach them.

The local water district is supposed to provide increased river flows to improve fish health and numbers.

Facilities, fees: Campgrounds are along the river and at Millerton Lake. Supplies are in Friant and Auberry. Fishing access is free.

Directions: From Fresno, take Highway 41 north for to the exit for Highway 168. Take the exit for Highway 168 east. Drive east on Highway 168 for 22 miles to Auberry Road. Turn left and drive two miles to Smalley Road (signed "Smalley Road and San Joaquin River Gorge Management Area"). Turn left and drive four miles to the campground, on the right. River access is limited to campgrounds on the river.

Contact: Sierra National Forest, Bass Lake Ranger District, 559/877-2218, www.fs.fed .us/r5—click on Forest Offices; Bureau of Land Management, Bakersfield Field Office, 661/391-6000; The Troutfitter, 760/934-2517, www.thetroutfly.com.

10 KERCKHOFF RESERVOIR

Rating: 4

northeast of Fresno in Sierra National Forest
Map 11.1, page 519

Well, you can't win 'em all, and when it comes to Kerckhoff, it can be difficult to win ever. The lake is something of a dud, with no trout and virtually no largemouth bass, but it does present a chance for striped bass.

It is not an easy chance, however. The fishery goes up and down faster than the lake levels; hit it wrong and you'll swear there isn't a single fish in the entire lake. Hit it right and you'll think that you have discovered a secret spot that everybody else ignores. The stripers tend to be deep most of the year, requiring specialized trolling with diving deep-water plugs, but there are short spurts in the fall when the show moves up on the surface. It takes a boat to chase them, but only those with car-top boats need apply, since there are only primitive boat-launching facilities. Nearby Redinger Lake, five miles to the east, provides an alternative and has a boat launch.

Kerckhoff is in the foothill country east of Fresno at 1,000 feet, and it can seem hotter than the interior of Mount Vesuvius. If you camp here, be sure to bring a plastic tarp and some poles so you can rig a makeshift roof to provide a shade shelter from the sun.

Because the reservoir is remote and small, and the use of boat motors more than five horsepower is prohibited, it gets fairly light use, even in summer. Most of the visitors are anglers and folks out paddling kayaks, canoes, and other small boats.

Facilities, fees: An unimproved boat ramp is on the north shore. A picnic area and small campground with drinking water and vault toilets are provided by PG&E. Supplies are available in Auberry or North Fork. Fishing access is free. No motors over five horsepower are allowed.

Directions: From Fresno, take Highway 41 north to the exit for Highway 168. Take the exit for Highway 168 east and drive east on Highway 168 for about 22 miles to Auberry Road. Turn left and drive 2.8 miles to Powerhouse Road. Turn left and drive 8.4 miles to the lake.

Contact: Sierra National Forest, Bass Lake Ranger District, 559/877-2218, www.fs.fed .us/r5—click on Forest Offices; PG&E Recreation Desk, 916/386-5164, www.pge.com/ recreation.

11 REDINGER LAKE

Rating: 3

northeast of Fresno in Sierra National Forest
Map 11.1, page 519

Redinger Lake is on the Department of Fish and Game's thumbs-down list: the list of waters that get nothing, as in no stocked trout, no bass, no catfish, no fishery management of any kind, and no pressure for water-level management. No nothin'.

They might as well just turn it over to the water-skiers. There can be plenty of the latter, since the lake, which is at 1,400 feet in the hot Sierra foothills, is only about an hour's drive from Fresno. Redinger is three miles long and a quarter mile wide and has a 35-mph speed limit.

The best option for anglers/boaters is to head well up the San Joaquin arm, where there are primitive boat-in camps along the north shore. In the spring, there can be fair trout fishing at the headwaters of the lake, almost always on night crawlers for bait.

Redinger gets far lighter boating traffic than nearby Shaver and Huntington Lakes. This area has high fire danger in summer and fall. No open fires are allowed at any time of year. Campfire permits are required for charcoal barbecues and camping stoves.

Facilities, fees: A paved boat ramp is on the lake's south end. A primitive campground has pit toilets, and a picnic area is provided. No drinking water is available, and garbage must be packed out. Supplies can be obtained in Auberry. Access is free.

Directions: From Fresno, take Highway 41 north for about 25 miles to North Fork Road/County Road 200. Turn right and drive northeast for 17.5 miles to Auberry Road/County Road 222. Turn left (north) and drive one mile to the town of North Fork and Mammoth Pool Road. Turn right and drive 1.5 miles to County Road 225 (still Mammoth Pool Road). Turn right and drive about four miles to Italian Bar Road. Turn right and drive seven miles to the lake.

Contact: Sierra National Forest, Bass Lake Ranger District, 559/877-2218, www.fs.fed .us/r5—click on Forest Offices.

12 SHAVER LAKE

Rating: 8

northeast of Fresno in Sierra National Forest
Map 11.1, page 519

Shaver Lake can be an excellent lake for early-summer trout fishing and is becoming exceptional for kokanee salmon. By summer, waterskiing takes over, making it time for anglers to head to higher country. Though Shaver is not as high in elevation as nearby Huntington (Shaver is at 5,370 feet, while Huntington is at 7,000 feet), it is very pretty and popular.

The Department of Fish and Game stocks Shaver with catchable trout from late spring through midsummer. They provide good fishing for trollers and bait dunkers alike. It gets 10- to 12-inch rainbow trout, along with kokanee-salmon fingerlings. Fishing is good here all over this lake. You might find some big browns here, too, even caught by accident by people fishing for the lake's smallmouth bass.

The fishing is best when the surface of the lake starts to warm up in spring and into midsummer. The last two hours of daylight provide the best summer action.

Facilities, fees: Paved boat ramps are at Camp Edison (two miles from the town of Shaver Lake on the west shore) and Sierra Marina (seven miles north of the town of Shaver Lake) on Highway 168. Campgrounds, lodging, restrooms, flush toilets, picnic areas, restaurant, bar, bait and tackle, and a convenience store are available. Sierra Marina has full services and rents out fishing boats and pontoon boats. Fishing boats, pontoon boats, canoes, and kayaks can be rented at Shaver Lake Lodge. Day-use and boat-launching fees are charged at private boat ramps; boat launching at the public boat ramp is free.

Directions: From Fresno, take Highway 168 east for 50 miles to the town of Shaver Lake. Continue 2–7 miles to access points on the west shore of the lake.

Contact: Sierra Marina, 559/841-3324, www .sierramarina.com; Shaver Lake Lodge/Lakeside Rentals, 559/841-3326, www.lakeside atthepoint.com; Camp Edison, 559/841-3134, www.sce.com/campedison; Sierra National Forest, High Sierra Ranger District, 559/855-5355, www.fs.fed.us/r5—click on Forest Offices.

13 PINE CREEK

Rating: 4

north of Bishop in Inyo National Forest
Map 11.2, page 520

The relatively few people who have even seen this little stream usually just keep on going. Most visitors taking the Pine Creek Road exit are heading for the wilderness, using the trailhead at the end of the road to hike off to Honeymoon Lake, Pine Lake, Upper Pine Lake, and beyond into the high country of the John Muir Wilderness.

The problem is that this creek is very brushy and steep, making it difficult to fish. In the early season, in spring and early summer, it is often nearly unfishable.

The irony is that there are often bigger trout in the stream right along the access road. It is stocked with trout from where Pine Creek Road first crosses the stream on upstream to where the road crosses the stream again, near the mining operation. The plants are usually made right from both bridges, with the Department of Fish and Game plunking in rainbow trout in the 10- to 12-inch class.

Put that in your cash register and add it up. It is worth the quick hit, but no more.

It's not just the fishing that always makes me hit this spot. During the spring-to-summer transition, you can almost always see Sierra bighorn sheep on the northern wall. Drive up to the fishing access at the bridge near the mining operation and then scan the mountain slope in 20-degree sections. At first, the bighorns seem invisible. But they are almost always there in spring. Bring binoculars or a spotting scope for a close-up look. If you walk toward them, you will scare them off.

Facilities, fees: No facilities are on-site. Campgrounds and supplies can be found in Bishop. Fishing access is free.

Directions: From Bishop, take U.S. 395 north for about 10 miles to Pine Creek Road, on the left. Turn and drive west to where the road crosses the creek. A parking area is on the left. This is the best access point.

Contact: Culver's Sporting Goods, Bishop, 760/872-8361; Mac's Sporting Goods, Bishop, 760/872-9201; Brock's Flyfishing, 760/872-3581 or 888/619-3581, www.brocksflyfish.com; Bishop Area Chamber of Commerce, 760/873-8405 or 888/395-3952, www.bishopvisitor.com; Inyo National Forest, White Mountain Ranger District, 760/873-2500, www.fs.fed.us/r5—click on Forest Offices.

14 OWENS RIVER

Rating: 9

from Bishop to Big Pine
Map 11.2, page 520

You want trout? The Department of Fish and Game, the Bishop Chamber, and Inyo County answer your request. They stock large numbers of rainbow trout in the Owens River on a regular basis, often year-round.

The best spots: The river is stocked in the Bishop area from Laws Bridge on U.S. 6 on downstream to Collins Road, with the plants usually made at those two major access points. South near the town of Big Pine, the stream is stocked at Westgard Pass Road and Steward Lane. The DFG and Adopt-a-Creek Foundation also plant on East Line Street. The Upper Owens from Benton Crossing Bridge to the Fishing Monument is also stocked. These spots also receive Alpers trout, courtesy of Adopt-a-Creek Foundation, a sensational program. There are also reports of bass that can provide a surprise in spring.

Water flows are projected to be maintained to increase the health of the river and the quality of the fishery. It has the potential to turn this into a little trout factory in the otherwise desolate Owens River Valley. The saving grace is the trout plants.

The Owens River has been dammed, diverted, pumped, tunneled, and sometimes run till it's just about dry. The piece of water between Bishop and Big Pine provides a glimpse of what once was.

Facilities, fees: Campgrounds and supplies are in the Bishop and Big Pine areas. Fishing access is free.

Directions: Take U.S. 395 to north Bishop and the junction with U.S. 6/East Line Street. Turn east on U.S. 6/East Line Street. Drive to Warm Springs Road or Collins Road. Access is available where these roads cross the river and off roads that junction with them.

Another option: Take U.S. 395 to Big Pine and Steward Lane or Westgard Pass Road. Turn east on Steward Lane or Westgard Pass Road, from where direct access is available.

Contact: Bishop Area Chamber of Commerce, 760/873-8405 or 888/395-3952, www.bishopvisitor.com; Interagency Visitor Center, 760/876-6222; Inyo County Parks Department, 760/873-5577, www.inyocountycamping.com; Culver's Sporting Goods, Bishop, 760/872-8361; Mac's Sporting Goods, Bishop, 760/872-9201; Los Angeles Department of Water & Power, 760/872-1104.

Guide service: Sierra Drifters Guide Service,

760/935-4250, www.sierradrifters.com (fishing reports by email available by request); Brock's Flyfishing, 760/872-3581 or 888/619-3581, www.brocksflyfish.com; Sierra Trout Magnet, 760/873-0100, www.sierratroutmagnet.com; The Troutfitter, 760/934-2517, www.thetroutfly.com; Sierra Guide Group, 760/872-9836, www.sierraguidegroup.com; Pat Jaeger, 760/872-7770, www.jaeger-flyfishing.com.

15 BISHOP CREEK

Rating: 8

near Bishop in Inyo National Forest
Map 11.2, page 520

The Bishop Creek drainage is one of the most diverse and productive fishing streams in the eastern Sierra. Access is easy, with turnouts right along Bishop Creek Road, but most folks just sail on by on their way up to gorgeous Lake Sabrina or nearby North Lake and South Lake. But if you stop, you will discover good evening trout fishing. The DFG stocks Bishop Creek with large numbers of stocks. It can provide very good fishing if you know where to hit. In addition, it receives bonus Alpers trout, the big ones.

So pay close attention to the following information. The stream is stocked with rainbow trout in four main areas: upstream from Bullpit Park to Powerline Road; from Intake II to Cardinal Lodge; downstream of Lake Sabrina to the North Lake turnoff; and on the South Fork from South Lake to the Forest Service campgrounds; and from Parcher's Resort to Weir Lake. Got it?

There are two forks where most of the best spots are located: the South Fork and Middle Fork. These spots also receive Alpers trout, courtesy of Adopt-a-Creek Foundation. There are some big native brown trout. The biggest documented in the past few years was an 11-pounder, caught on the Middle Fork. The general feeling is that this giant brown somehow found its way through the spillway from Lake Sabrina during a preseason water release.

Facilities, fees: Several campgrounds are available on the road in. Supplies can be found in Bishop. Fishing access is free.

Directions: Take U.S. 395 to Bishop and Highway 168. Turn west on Highway 168 and follow the road to access points off Bishop Creek Road.

Contact: Inyo National Forest, White Mountain Ranger District, 760/873-2500, www.fs.fed.us/r5—click on Forest Offices; Bishop Area Chamber of Commerce, 760/873-8405 or 888/395-3952, www.bishopvisitor.com; Interagency Visitor Center, 760/876-6222; Inyo County Parks Department, 760/873-5577, www.inyocountycamping.com; Culver's Sporting Goods, Bishop, 760/872-8361; Mac's Sporting Goods, Bishop, 760/872-9201; Brock's Flyfishing, 760/872-3581 or 888/619-3581, www.brocksflyfish.com; Sierra Trout Magnet, 760/873-0100, www.sierratroutmagnet.com.

16 FLORENCE LAKE

Rating: 5

northeast of Fresno in
the Sierra National Forest
Map 11.2, page 520

The drive to Florence is hellacious, a long, twisty, narrow route that will test your nerves, courage, and sanity. Most people coming here are hikers en route for the wilderness John Muir Lodge or the JMT trailhead, or heading to the Mono Hot Springs.

Florence is smaller and less developed than its northerly neighbor, Edison Lake. It doesn't have large numbers of trout, but it does have just about everything else, including mountain beauty; excellent hiking, kayaking, canoeing, rafting, and float-tubing options; and fair enough trout fishing.

The lake is at 7,327 feet, with the awesome Glacier Divide country providing a backdrop to the east. A 15-mph speed limit maintains the sanity of the place. A hiker's water taxi makes trips across the lake and back for a fee.

The lake usually becomes ice-free around

Memorial Day weekend, although it can be later in big snow years, and it remains open through late September, sometimes later. Florence is not stocked with rainbow trout. Brown trout is the primary species in this lake. Boaters should start trolling immediately upon launching, and then head along the western shore on up to the inlet, where the South Fork of the San Joaquin River enters the lake. Shoreliners will discover a trail along the western side of the lake, with the better prospects being both near the dam and near the inlet, and only fair in between. Water levels can fluctuate, and the lake is often quite low in the summer and fall.

If you like hiking, then strap on a backpack and just keep on going. From the inlet, the trail winds up the South Fork to the Pacific Crest Trail (PCT) about five miles in. From there you can continue southeast along the San Joaquin, turning into Evolution Valley, one of the prettiest meadows/woodlands in the entire high Sierra. Backpackers are required to obtain a wilderness permit for overnight use.

This lake is very remote and on the edge of wilderness. See *Directions* for driving tips.

Facilities, fees: A paved boat ramp, campground, picnic area, vault toilets, drinking water, a water taxi, bait and tackle, and a small store are available. Fishing-boat rentals and water taxis are at Florence Lake Resort. There is a wheelchair-accessible pier. Fishing access is free. There is a fee for the water taxi.

Directions: From the town of Shaver Lake, take Highway 168 north for 21 miles to Kaiser Pass Road/Forest Road 80. Turn right and drive 16 miles (narrow and twisting) to a fork in the road. Bear right at the fork to Florence Lake Road (left goes to Edison Lake) and drive five miles to the lake.

Driving tip: On Friday and Sunday afternoons and evenings, some drivers from L.A. en route to and departing from Mono Hot Springs, respectively, shred this narrow, curvy two-laner as if it's a race course and forget it's actually a two-way road. Avoid driving to this lake during these two time periods. It is safer at night because you can see oncoming headlights around the blind curves.

Contact: Florence Lake, www.florence-lake .com; Sierra National Forest, High Sierra Ranger District, 559/855-5355, www.fs.fed .us/r5—click on Forest Offices.

17 NORTH LAKE

Rating: 6

southwest of the town of Bishop in
Inyo National Forest

Map 11.2, page 520

North Lake is a beautiful setting in the high country, well known for its awesome aspen groves and towering granite cliffs. It provides decent shoreline prospects for a mix of brook trout and rainbow trout.

It is at an elevation of 9,500 feet and has a surface area of 13 acres. It is very pretty. Some anglers bring float tubes or kayaks for improved access. The best fishing is with a fly-and-bubble combination or fly fishers casting leeches with sink-tip lines, strip retrieve. Plants of rainbow trout in the 10- to 12-inch class usually reach a fair number here. The Adopt-a-Creek Foundation stocks the big Alpers trout. Brook trout and brown trout can also be found.

Fishing pressure is moderate compared to nearby lakes. A variety of flies and lures can work here.

North Lake makes a good layover before heading off on a backpacking expedition. Just west of the lake is a trailhead for a route that follows the North Fork of Bishop Creek up to a remarkable granite basin that is loaded with similar small mountain lakes. Loch Leven (10,740 feet) and Piute Lake (11,420 feet) are 3 and 4.5 miles away, respectively, and if you head over the pass into Humphreys Basin, you can venture cross-country to your choice of 25 lakes, many holding golden trout.

If you don't want to hike, nearby Lake Sabrina and South Lake provide good prospects.

This is a beautiful spot for trout fishing.

It is surrounded by aspens and is gorgeous year-round, especially in early fall, when each side of the canyon comes alive in golds and yellows.

Facilities, fees: There is no boat ramp, but car-top boats can be hand-launched. A campground, drinking water, and vault toilets are available. No motors allowed. Supplies can be obtained in Bishop. Fishing access is free.

Directions: Take U.S. 395 to Bishop and Highway 168. Turn southwest (toward the Sierra) on Highway 168 and drive 17 miles to Forest Road 8S02 (signed North Lake). Turn right (north) on Forest Road 8S02 and drive for two miles to the campground.

Contact: Culver's Sporting Goods, Bishop, 760/872-8361; Mac's Sporting Goods, Bishop, 760/872-9201; Inyo National Forest, White Mountain Ranger District, 760/873-2500, www.fs.fed.us/r5—click on Forest Offices; Interagency Visitor Center, 760/876-6222.

18 LAKE SABRINA

Rating: 9

southwest of the town of Bishop in Inyo National Forest

Map 11.2, page 520

Lake Sabrina is one of the prettiest lakes in America that you can reach by car. It is nestled in a high mountain canyon, framed by wilderness slopes and backed by snowcapped peaks.

This is the largest of the three lakes in the immediate vicinity of the Bishop Creek drainage. It is also the most popular of them. Lake Sabrina is at 9,130 feet and covers nearly 200 acres, yet it is only a 20-mile drive out of Bishop.

Sound good? It is. It's small, intimate, and provides consistent fishing, a boat ramp, rentals, and has a 10-mph speed limit to guarantee quiet water. It also has good hiking options (and there are two other lakes within 2.5 miles).

The best shore fishing is usually at the south end, near the inlets, and on rocks near the boat ramp. But it seems everybody who shows up makes a cast here. By boat, you can fish the northwest shore, either trolling or casting a fly-and-bubble. When the wind is down, the evening bite is often a good one during the summer months. Sabrina is stocked regularly with 10- to 12-inch rainbow trout by the Department of Fish and Game, and with Alpers trout by the concessionaire. There are also some big browns. Because of the lake's depth, holdover survival is good.

Shoreline fishing is good with bait, with a genuine chance for a lunker Alpers or brown trout. Big fish are common at this lake. Since the lake is deep, the big ones can be anywhere, and yet they pull surprises. The best bet is to fish at the inlets toward the back end of the lake.

This lake is almost always frozen over for opening day.

If you want to go off by yourself, the trail on the southeast side of the lake provides an opportunity. Shortly after leaving the lake's shore, it forks; head to the left to hike to Lake George; head to the right to hit Blue, Donkey, and Baboon Lakes. All are excellent day-hike destinations.

Note: It's pronounced "sa-BRY-na," not "sa-BREE-na" (like my editor's name).

Facilities, fees: A boat ramp is available on the lake's north end. A campground with drinking water and vault toilets is nearby. Fishing boats, canoes, and pontoon boats are rented out at Sabrina Lake Boat Landing. Supplies can be obtained in Bishop. Fishing access is free.

Directions: Take U.S. 395 to Bishop and Highway 168. Turn southwest (toward the Sierra) on Highway 168 and drive 17 miles to a signed fork (signed "Lake Sabrina"). Take that fork and drive 0.5 mile to the lake.

Contact: Sabrina Lake Boat Landing, 760/873-7425; Culver's Sporting Goods, Bishop, 760/872-8361; Mac's Sporting Goods, 760/872-9201; Inyo National Forest, White Mountain Ranger District, 760/873-2500, www.fs.fed.us/r5—click on Forest Offices; Bishop Area

Chamber of Commerce, 760/873-8405 or 888/395-3952, www.bishopvisitor.com; Interagency Visitor Center, 760/876-6222.

19 SOUTH LAKE

Rating: 8

southwest of the town of Bishop in
Inyo National Forest

Map 11.2, page 520

This is the high country, where visitors get a unique mix of glacial-carved granite, lakes the color of gems, and good evening fishing for rainbow trout or sometimes a big brown. This is a beautiful setting, in a deep Sierra canyon filled with aspen and peppered with conifers.

Set at 9,755 feet and covering 166 acres, South Lake was created by a small dam on the South Fork of Bishop Creek. A good boat ramp is available, making for good access for owners of trailered aluminum boats, who can launch easily and then troll along the lake's shore. South Lake is the most developed of the three lakes in the area (the others are North Lake and Lake Sabrina).

The Department of Fish and Game stocks South Lake with rainbow trout in the 10- to 12-inch class, usually starting at ice-out (in early summer, when the access road gets plowed) and continuing regularly through the summer. The concessionaire regularly stocks Alpers trout as well.

It used to be that most of the big browns, Alpers, and rainbows were caught in the deepest part of the lake, near the dam. Now it's unpredictable as to where you'll hook up with these big fish. Yet for the best chance of a limit, head to the shore, where streams pour runoff into the lake. These small inlets attract feeding trout.

While boaters do quite well here, so can shoreliners. The outlet area with Power Bait can be dynamite early in the season. The lake level is often dropped in late winter to encourage the ice to melt—and to get that water to Los Angeles. Look for breaks near the inlet, where some shoreliners will risk a slip and a fall to cast a Rapala for giant and unsuspecting brown trout. I've seen many big brown trout taken here.

A bonus is below the lake, where anglers can fish the South Fork Bishop Creek as it traverses along the road, between Bishop Creek Lodge and the lake.

In addition, there are good hike-to lakes within a two-hour hike. A trail routed along the southeast part of the lake forks off, providing trails to two different series of lakes. If you head to the right, you will reach the Treasury Lakes after about a 2.8-mile hike—a good day trip. If you head to the left, you will be on the trail up to Bishop Pass, in the process passing Bull Lake, Long Lake, Saddlerock Lake, and Bishop Lake. Ruwau Lake has some beautifully colored brook trout in the foot-long class. Cast a small Panther Martin spinner, black with yellow spots, and get it deep enough so it swims just over the top of the big boulders on the bottom of the lake at the far end.

Lake record: 10 trout (two 5-fish limits) weighing 50 pounds, caught in 2006 by Marlon Meade and Dave Finkelstein.

Facilities, fees: Several campgrounds are on South Lake Road. Picnic areas are at the lake. A convenience store, bait and tackle, an unimproved boat ramp, moorings, a café, and fishing-boat rentals are at South Lake Boat Landing. A 5-mph speed limit is in effect. Fishing access is free.

Directions: Take U.S. 395 to Bishop and Highway 168. Turn southwest (toward the Sierra) on Highway 168 and drive 15 miles to South Lake Road. Turn left and drive seven miles south to the lake.

Contact: South Lake Boat Landing, 760/873-4177; Inyo National Forest, White Mountain Ranger District, 760/873-2500, www.fs.fed.us/r5—click on Forest Offices; Bishop Area Chamber of Commerce, 760/873-8405 or 888/395-3952, www.bishopvisitor.com; Interagency Visitor Center, 760/876-6222; Inyo

County Parks Department, 760/873-5577, www.inyocountycamping.com.

Lodging: Parcher's Resort 760/873-4177, www.parchersresort.net.

Supplies: Culver's Sporting Goods, Bishop, 760/872-8361; Mac's Sporting Goods, Bishop, 760/872-9201.

20 COURTRIGHT RESERVOIR

Rating: 7
northeast of Fresno in Sierra National Forest
Map 11.2, page 520

Courtright Reservoir provides good trout fishing and camping, as well as a wilderness trail. You can camp, boat, and fish—or you can park at the trailhead at Voyager Rock Campground (northeast side of the lake) and head off into the John Muir Wilderness. Most of the traffic here is not from boaters but from wilderness campers. They use the lake's campground as home base before exploring the John Muir Wilderness.

Courtright is in the high Sierra at 8,200 feet, and if you plan to stick around, it is best visited in the early summer, when the lake level is the highest by far (it can drop quickly from mid-August on through to the fall). Stocks of rainbow trout are made regularly, and cool but warming water temperatures keep the trout biting. The Department of Fish and Game stocks Courtright with 10- to 12-inch rainbow trout, and the fishing can be good here. A 15-mph speed limit guarantees zero waterskiing and, in turn, calm water. The boat launch is just west of the dam.

The surrounding scenery is very pretty, and this is a good place for a picnic site, as it is typically very peaceful and quiet.

Backpackers have several options. The best is to head east from the trailhead at Voyager Rock Campground and into the high granite country of the LeConte Divide to poke around the Red Mountain Basin. There are six lakes in the basin: Arctic Lake, Blackrock Lake, Disappointment Lake, Devils Punchbowl, Hell For

Sure Lake, and Horseshoe Lake. Backpackers are required to obtain a wilderness permit for overnight use.

Facilities, fees: Campgrounds, drinking water, vault toilets, picnic areas, and a paved boat ramp are available. Supplies can be obtained in Fresno and the town of Shaver Lake. Fishing access is free.

Directions: From Fresno, take Highway 168 east to Dinkey Creek Road (on the right just as you're entering the town of Shaver Lake). Turn right and drive 13 miles to McKinley Grove Road (Forest Road 40). Turn right and drive 14 miles to Courtright Road. Turn left (north) and drive 12 miles to the campground entrance road, on the right. *Note:* This route is slow and twisty and is closed in the winter.

Contact: Sierra National Forest, High Sierra Ranger District, 559/855-5355, www.fs.fed .us/r5—click on Forest Offices; PG&E Recreation Desk, 916/386-5164, www.pge.com/ recreation.

21 WISHON RESERVOIR

Rating: 6
northeast of Fresno in Sierra National Forest
Map 11.2, page 520

Wishon is a pretty lake when full, set at 6,500 feet, surrounded by national forest, and filled with snowmelt poured from the North Fork Kings River. It's just that the lake doesn't ever seem to be full, and the interminable fluctuations in water levels can hurt the trout trolling. When the level is stable, the fishing is good, courtesy of stocks of 10- to 12-inch rainbow trout from the Department of Fish and Game, plus a few lunker browns that rarely show. A 15-mph speed limit keeps the lake quiet.

Conditions here are much the same as at nearby Courtright Reservoir; however, Wishon is easier to reach than Courtright.

A five-mile hike starts at the trailhead at Woodchuck Creek and heads east into Woodchuck Country and the John Muir Wilderness. Woodchuck Country has three lakes—Chimney Lake, Marsh Lake, and Woodchuck Lake—that provide good spots for a quick overnight backpack. If you have more time, you can extend the trip to Half Moon Lake, over Scepter Pass, and beyond into the Blackcap Basin, where there are more than a dozen high mountain lakes in pristine granite country.

Facilities, fees: Campgrounds, restrooms with coin showers, a picnic area, coin laundry, a bar, bait and tackle, gas, a paved boat ramp, and a convenience store are available. Fishing boats can be rented at Wishon Village. Fishing access is free.

Directions: From Fresno, take Highway 168 east to Dinkey Creek Road (on the right just as you're entering the town of Shaver Lake). Turn right and drive 13 miles to McKinley Grove Road (Forest Road 40). Turn right and drive to the Wishon Dam. To reach the boat ramp, continue for about three miles to the boat ramp on the southeast shore. *Note:* This route is slow and twisty and is closed in winter.

Contact: Sierra National Forest, High Sierra Ranger District, 559/855-5355, www.fs.fed.us/r5—click on Forest Offices; PG&E Recreation Desk, 916/386-5164, www.pge.com/recreation; Wishon Village RV Resort, 559/865-5361, www.wishonvillage.com.

22 KINGS CANYON NATIONAL PARK

Rating: 8

east of Fresno in
Sequoia-Kings Canyon National Park
Map 11.2, page 520

For anglers, the centerpiece of Kings Canyon National Park is the South Fork Kings River. It often provides outstanding catch rates for small trout by fly fishers, despite the number of visitors to the park and the easy access along Highway 180. The river sits at the bottom of a dramatic canyon, with an 8,350-foot drop from the top of Spanish Mountain down to the river.

It can be common for fly fishers to catch 20 or 25 trout (catch-and-release) from late afternoon to dusk on the South Fork Kings, with the good fishing starting at Boyden Cave on upstream. It is here that you have the best chance in the park of catching a large native rainbow trout. The big ones come only rarely, but they do come. Many people instead fish in the vicinity of Cedar Grove (which is close to the campgrounds), where if you catch one or two, you're doing good. Check fishing regulations for the take limit of trout.

The park has remarkable beauty and variety, with 1,100 miles of streams, 864 lakes (depending on your definition of a lake), and 353 miles of trails in the backcountry. Even the drive-to areas are spectacular in natural beauty. From lookouts along the highway, you can see the Sierra crest and the Monarch Divide, with a long series of peaks over 11,000 feet high and higher, as well as the awesome Kings Canyon and the river below. One of the biggest downers imaginable for anglers was the park's decision to stop aerial stocks of trout.

Those who get such a glimpse of the backcountry wilderness may want to take a week or more to explore it. One of the best loop hikes in the country is available starting at the trailhead where Highway 180 dead-ends. The trail from here routes up into the high country along Bubbs Creek, circles the awesome Sixty Lakes Basin, then returns via Woods Creek. Included in this hike are the climb over Glen Pass, at 11,978 feet, and a one-night camp at Rae Lakes, in the John Muir Wilderness. It takes a minimum of five days to a week to cover the 43 miles and do this trip right.

A wilderness permit under a quota system is required here. The trailhead quota fills quickly, and reservations are advisable.

Rangers at Kings Canyon require that backpackers carry their food in bear-proof canisters. Food canisters for rent, wilderness permits, and trailhead reservations and sign-in are at the Road's End wilderness permit station.

Rae Lakes is the spot where my brother Rambob and I caught limits of brook trout on a bare hook, catching nearly a fish per cast, right in the middle of the day. We would have caught a trout on every cast except they kept hitting the split-shot sinker we had for weight rather than the bare hook. When we finally put a lure on and pinched down the barbs, we each caught and released 70 or 80 trout before finally turning our backs on them. With no more stocks ("they aren't natural"), that kind of success will never happen again. Rae Lakes is near a fragile meadow area, and camping is limited to one-night stays; backcountry rangers make sure you abide by the rules.

There are many other spectacular areas. One of the most breathtaking is the Kearsarge Lakes, set just below the Kearsarge Pinnacles. They are pristine, sapphire blue, bordered by granite, and overlooked by mountain peaks. This hike takes you past Bullfrog Lake, which has good fishing but lots of food-raiding bears (hence the requirement for food canisters) and no campsites.

Since aerial stocks are no longer made in Kings Canyon National Park, fishing success can vary greatly, especially in the smaller lakes.

I still hike back here a lot because of the gorgeous high country and good stream fishing. Another great pleasure is watching short, intense thunderstorms during hot summer afternoons, especially in the vicinity of Rae Lakes and below in the canyon. On hot, clear days, the sky can suddenly cloud up with giant cumulonimbus over the peaks, then cut loose by hurling lightning bolts on the mountain rims and giant thunderclaps down the canyons. The rain is intense; then suddenly, as fast as it started, it ends. The sky clears, and the trout start their evening bite.

Facilities, fees: Campgrounds, lodging, and supplies are in the park. A vehicle entrance fee is charged.

Directions: From Fresno, take Highway 180 east for 55 miles (to the former Big Stump entrance station). Continue 1.5 miles to a junction (left for Grant Grove/Kings Canyon, right for Sequoia National Park). Turn left

(north) on Highway 180 and drive east (curvy at times) into the canyon and past Boyden Cave. The best fishing is found along South Fork Kings River between Boyden Cave and Cedar Grove. For backcountry access, continue on Highway 180 along the South Fork Kings until it dead-ends (28 miles from the park entrance) at the Road's End wilderness permit station. The best fishing in the wilderness is in Bubbs Creek and other streams.

Contact: Sequoia-Kings Canyon National Park, 559/565-3341, www.nps.gov/seki.

23 BIG PINE CREEK

Rating: 6

south of Bishop in Inyo National Forest

Map 11.2, page 520

Big Pine Creek is frequently bypassed in the excitement to get somewhere else, just like so many streams that border two-lane access roads to wilderness areas. The road along Big Pine Creek travels westward to one of the best trailheads for the John Muir Wilderness. If you hike up the trail along the north fork of Big Pine Creek, it takes only four miles of walking to hit a short loop trail that passes seven different lakes.

That is why folks just keep on driving. But here is the surprise: this little stream is stocked with 10- to 12-inch rainbow trout from the Sage Flat Campground to Glacier Lodge. Just upstream from the campground is a good area, particularly in the vicinity of where a little feeder stream enters on the north side of the creek. It should blow your mind.

Facilities, fees: Campgrounds are on the creek. Supplies can be obtained in Big Pine. Fishing access is free.

Directions: Take U.S. 395 to Big Pine (16 miles south of Bishop) and Crockett Street. Turn west (toward the Sierra) on Crockett Street and drive west (the road turns into Glacier Lodge Road) to the creek, from Sage Flat Campground to Glacier Lodge. Direct access is available.

Contact: Glacier Lodge, 760/938-2837; Culver's Sporting Goods, Bishop, 760/872-8361; Mac's Sporting Goods, Bishop, 760/872-9201; Inyo National Forest, White Mountain Ranger District, 760/873-2500, www.fs.fed.us/r5—click on Forest Offices; Bishop Area Chamber of Commerce, 760/873-8405 or 888/395-3952, www.bishopvisitor.com.

24 TABOOSE CREEK

Rating: 4

south of Big Pine

Map 11.2, page 520

Not many people know about Taboose Creek and the adjacent campground. It is at an elevation of 3,900 feet in the Owens Valley.

Yet access is easy, the landscape is sparse chaparral, and the fishing can be good. Here's the trick: stick to the stretch of water from Old Highway 395 on upstream for one mile. That is where the rainbow-trout stocks are concentrated.

By the way, the trail from the end of the road up to the Sierra crest at Taboose Pass is one of the worst butt-kicking, endless climbs in California. I'll never do it again! (Famous last words.)

Facilities, fees: A campground is on the creek. Drinking water (hand-pumped from a well) and vault toilets are available. Supplies can be obtained in Big Pine or Independence. Fishing access is free.

Directions: From Big Pine (16 miles south of Bishop), take U.S. 395 south for 11 miles to Taboose Creek Road. Turn west (right, toward the Sierra) and fish the area from 395 on upstream one mile.

From Independence, take U.S. 395 north for 14 miles to Taboose Creek Road. Turn west (left) and fish the area from 395 on upstream for one mile.

Contact: Lone Pine Sporting Goods, 760/876-5365; Gardner's Hardware, 760/876-4208; High Sierra Outfitters, 760/876-9994; Inyo County Parks Department, 760/873-5577,

www.inyocountycamping.com; Lone Pine Chamber of Commerce, 760/876-4444, www.lonepinechamber.org; Independence Chamber of Commerce, 760/878-0084, www.independence-ca.com; Interagency Visitor Center, 760/876-6222.

25 PINE FLAT LAKE

Rating: 8

east of Fresno

Map 11.3, page 521   BEST (

Spotted bass provide good catch rates for anglers throughout most of the year at Pine Flat Lake, despite the fluctuating water level. Although spotted bass are the mainstay of the lake (the last two world records have been caught here), these waters also support largemouth and smallmouth bass, bluegill, white catfish, black crappie, and a lot of planted trout. The biggest spotted bass verified weighed 10 pounds, 4 ounces, and was caught here.

When Pine Flat is full, courtesy of snowmelt in the Sierra, the lake becomes quite pretty. It is in the foothills east of Fresno, 970 feet above sea level, and the lake sprawls 20 miles in length, has 67 miles of shoreline, and covers 5,790 surface acres.

When water levels are high enough and water temperatures are cold enough, usually in the spring, the Department of Fish and Game plunks in rainbow trout in the 10- to 12-inch class. Until the hot weather arrives, the trout fishing is quite good using standard trolling techniques, as well as by bait fishing from the shore near the boat ramp.

The best bet, however, is always fishing for the spotted bass up the main lake arm, where there are two major coves where the fish hold. As spring gives way to summer, Pine Flat comes alive. That is when Pine Flat becomes one of the most popular lakes in the entire region. This is a highly developed commercial destination that includes a resort and numerous private campgrounds and RV parks that offer full facilities. Reservations are advised for camping.

One crazy element about Pine Flat is that the conditions are actually best in the fall, when the weather is cooler and much more bearable. Yet by fall, the lake can be empty. That is because the lake has a terrible reputation for being extremely low. How low? Would you believe about 80 percent empty? Happens way too many years. This lake could rate a 9 or 10 if this didn't happen. So there you have it, a 10 in the spring and a 3 in the fall.

Facilities, fees: Lodging, campgrounds, restrooms with coin showers, an RV dump station, a fish-cleaning station, four boat ramps, full-service marinas, and a convenience store are available. Fishing boats, pontoon boats, and houseboats can be rented at Pine Flat Lake Marina. Boat-launch fees are charged.

Directions: From Fresno, take Highway 180 east for 17.5 miles to Trimmer Springs Road. Turn left and drive eight miles to the town of Piedra. Continue on Trimmer Springs Road for one mile to Pine Flat Road. Turn right and drive 0.25 mile to the park entrance (signed Island Park).

Contact: Pine Flat Lake Marina, 559/787-2506, www.pineflatlakemarina.com; Benson's Lakeside Resort, 559/787-2207 (information), 888/328-9588 (reservations), www.bensonslakesideresort.com; Lakeridge Resort, 559/787-2260; Lakeridge Campground, 877/787-2260, www.lakeridgecampground.com; U.S. Army Corps of Engineers, Sacramento District, Pine Flat Field Office, 559/787-2589, www.spk.usace.army.mil.

26 KINGS RIVER

Rating: 7

northeast of Fresno

Map 11.3, page 521

There are two stretches of river here, both below and above Pine Flat Reservoir. They are like two different rivers, and each produces a surprise.

In the Pine Flat Lake area, the Kings River just below the dam is stocked with foot-long rainbow trout, which isn't too shabby. The river gets stocked with brood-stock brook trout now and then, along with trophy rainbow trout to 10 pounds. Hook one of them and you'll rate this a 10, not a 7.

Upstream of the lake, DFG in the past has stocked token plants of 10- to 12-inch rainbow trout. Because those fish have mixed with wild trout, it is likely that plants will end. As a wild trout stream, the best bet for this stretch of river is to drive all the way to Garnet Dike Camp, surveying the river as you go, and then to fish your way back downstream to Pine Flat Lake, driving, parking, and making several quick hits.

This upper section of the Kings is better known for providing some of the best rafting and kayaking water in California. Because rafting is so popular in the early summer, it is better to fish here during the evening rather than from morning to midday.

Facilities, fees: No boat ramp is available. Several campgrounds are on the river. Supplies can be obtained in Piedra. Fishing access is free.

Directions: To the Kings River south of Pine Flat Lake: From Fresno, take Highway 180 east and drive 17.5 miles to Trimmer Springs Road. Turn left (north) on Trimmer Springs Road (which parallels the west side of the river). Or continue a few miles east to Minkler and Piedra Road. Turn left (north) on Piedra Road (which borders the river's east side). Access is available from here, all the way upstream to the bridge at Piedra and downstream off numerous county roads.

To the Kings River north of Pine Flat Lake: From Fresno, take Highway 180 east for 17.5 miles to Trimmer Springs Road. Turn left (north) on Trimmer Springs Road and drive 26 miles (past Pine Flat Lake). Continue east on Trimmer Springs Road for seven miles. Access is available off the road and off unimproved roads that parallel both sides of the river.

Contact: Sequoia National Forest, Hume Lake Ranger District 559/338-2251, www.fs.fed.us/r5; Pierce's Park, 559/787-3450.

Supplies (near Piedra): Doyal's, 559/787-2387; I Forgot Store, 559/787-3689.

27 BRAVO LAKE

Rating: 6

in Woodlake

Map 11.3, page 521

Bravo Lake has been on a continued upswing. The highlights are the bass, with surprising improving numbers in the five- to seven-pound class, as well as the catfish. The minimum size for bass here is 12 inches.

The lake has a lot of catfish and they provide good fishing in the summer. A 27-pounder is believed to be the lake record. Offer a night crawler on a warm summer evening. That's the preferred entreaty. Crappie provide an option. Additional fish at Bravo Lake have trickled down from Lake Kaweah (more catfish than anything).

The Department of Fish and Game plants catchable (half pound) trout here. The lake is also used by locals, who jog on the paths around it.

No night fishing (or access) is permitted, a downer considering the hot summer nights. Another is that no boats are permitted. Another is that permits are required and are available only at City Hall (see *Contact*).

Facilities, fees: There are trails around the lake, but no other facilities. No boating is permitted. A fishing access fee is charged. Permits are available only at City Hall.

Directions: From Visalia, take Highway 198 east for eight miles to Highway 245/Spruce Avenue. Turn left (north) and drive 10 miles to the town of Woodlake and Highway 216. Turn right (east) on Highway 216 and drive 0.25 mile to the lake entrance.

Contact: Woodlake City Hall, 350 N. Valencia Blvd., 559/564-8055, www.cityofwoodlake.com.

28 HUME LAKE

Rating: 7

east of Fresno in
Giant Sequoia National Monument

Map 11.4, page 522

When you first see Hume Lake, you may figure that it has a lot of dinkers but very few large trout. After all, a highly developed camp center is just a mile away, and you may deduce that the lake gets hammered by vacationers day after day, all summer long.

Yet the shore fishing is often very good. The trout that are stocked here are not the little slim-jims but good-sized rainbow trout, often 12–14 inches long, even though the lake is small. They become naturalized to the lake quickly, feeding, growing, and taking on the characteristics of wild fish.

Hume is a good lake for shore fishing, with the best spot on the southern corner of the dam, using the inevitable Power Bait. Winter provides some decent ice fishing. The lake is within Sequoia National Forest at an elevation of 5,200 feet and covers 85 acres. This is a gorgeous lake with emerald-green water. Hume Lake makes a good stop and fishing break amid an excellent tour of the area, with nearby Sequoia and Kings Canyon National Parks.

Note: Hume Lake Christian Camp is on the lake's south side, and they are friendly folks who are more than happy to rent you a boat. They also rent bicycles. In the summer, there are often youth camps here, tons of happy kids enjoying this beautiful spot to the max. To reach the best fishing spot, you must pass through the camp.

Facilities, fees: A campground, restrooms with flush toilets, drinking water, and a picnic area are provided. A convenience store, a primitive boat ramp, bait and tackle, gas, and a café are also available. Boats can be rented at Hume Lake Christian Camp. Gas-powered motors are not permitted, and a 15-mph speed limit is enforced. A park entrance fee is charged.

Directions: From Fresno, take Highway 180

east for 55 miles (to what used to be the Big Stump Entrance Station at Sequoia-Kings Canyon National Park). Continue 1.5 miles to a junction (signed left for Grant Grove, right for Sequoia National Park). Turn left and drive six miles to the Hume Lake Road junction. Turn right and drive three miles to Hume Lake and the campground entrance road. Turn right and drive 0.25 mile to the campground, on the left.

Contact: Sequoia National Forest, Hume Lake Ranger District 559/338-2251, www.fs.fed.us/r5; Hume Lake Christian Camp, 559/305-7770, www.humelake.org.

29 LAKE KAWEAH

Rating: 8

east of Visalia

Map 11.4, page 522

If you visit Kaweah in late March, April, or early May, you will discover a big reservoir set in foothill country, where the prospects for trout (late winter) and bass (spring) are good. When the lake is full, it covers nearly 2,000 acres, has 22 miles of shoreline, and is amazingly pretty. The elevation is 694 feet.

This lake has come full circle and is turning into one of the better bass lakes around. Fishing is often excellent, both for quality as well as quantity for skilled bassers. The minimum size is 15 inches, with a two-fish limit, and these regulations have resulted in a lot more big fish.

Kaweah was poisoned in the fall of 1987 (to kill off white bass) and then was restocked with Florida bass and spotted bass. Habitat-improvement work was also conducted during this period. Well, you always get paid back. Those Floridas are getting giant-sized, and the habitat is providing plenty of needed homes for them. The lake record is an 18-pounder.

A bonus is the trout fishing. In late winter, the action starts when the Department of Fish and Game stocks rainbow trout. Kaweah receives 10- to 12-inch rainbow trout, enough to provide decent fishing when the water is cool. This is followed by rising water levels in spring, and then by good bass fishing as the water warms up. Because the lake is drawn down, a lot of vegetation grows on the lake bottom every year—vegetation that provides good cover for bass when the lake starts filling. The Horse Creek area is one of the best for this reason.

The lake also has good populations of crappie, bluegill, and channel catfish.

In late summer and fall, when Kaweah starts to get low, unmarked rocks just beneath the surface can create boating hazards; boaters should be sure to stay in deep water. It's a no-brainer, of course. I've seen Kaweah get down to about 10 percent full.

Visalia is my favorite town in the San Joaquin Valley, but the folks think nothing of draining Kaweah down to near nothing to irrigate the citrus orchards in the foothills east of town. They make this vast assumption that it will refill every winter. That plays havoc with the lake, of course. In many years, the lake is very low by the start of winter, and then in dry years, it stays low all through the next year. That simply lowers the carrying capacity of the habitat; that is, the lake can support far fewer fish in extended low-water periods created by diversions.

Facilities, fees: Boat ramps are on the lake's west end at Kaweah Recreation Area and Lemon Hill Recreation Area. There is also a boat ramp at Slick Rock. A marina, boat rentals, and bait are available. A campground with restrooms, drinking water, flush toilets, and showers is nearby. A grocery store, coin laundry, ice, a snack bar, a restaurant, a gas station, and propane gas are also nearby. A day-use fee is charged. An annual pass may be purchased (accepted at any U.S. Army Corps of Engineers lake nationwide).

Directions: From Visalia, take Highway 198 east for 20 miles to Lake Kaweah's south shore and the boat ramps.

Contact: Kaweah Marina, 559/597-2526, www.kaweahmarina.com; U.S. Army Corps of

Engineers, Lake Kaweah, 559/597-2301, www
.corpslakes.usace.army.mil; Visalia Visitors
Bureau, 559/334-0141, www.visitvisalia.org.

30 SEQUOIA NATIONAL PARK

Rating: 4

east of Visalia

`Map 11.4, page 522`

Sequoiadendron giganteum, the massive mountain redwood, is the world's largest tree, with
a diameter so awesome that it can take 30
people joining hands to ring one. The General
Sherman Tree, a sequoia for which the park is
named, is the largest living tree in the world;
it is 102.6 feet in circumference, 2,200 years
old (give or take a few centuries), and the most
famous of its species.

Sequoia National Park is connected to
Kings Canyon National Park, to the north.
Together they comprise 865,000 acres and 65
consecutive miles of national parkland. Kings
Canyon often provides the better fishing of the
two parks, but after admiring the groves of
giant redwoods, you can explore many excellent waters in Sequoia, including the native
habitat of golden trout. Note that pamphlets
showing fishing regulations for the park are
free at the visitors centers.

The best of the fishing is at the headwaters
of the Kern River, in the high country of Kern
Canyon (see the *Golden Trout Wilderness* listing). The Kaweah River is more accessible, set
along the southern access road (Highway 198),
and it provides poor-to-fair fishing.

As at so many national parks, anglers who
are willing to backpack will experience the
best fishing. Stocks are not made in national
parks, and heavy angler pressure results in
small fish populations at lakes. Some can get
fished out.

Those visitors who explore the interior of
Sequoia National Park will find a far different
world. Instead of big trees, there are scarcely
any trees at all. Much of the high country of
the Great Western Divide is above tree line,
with bare, glacial-cut granite ridges, canyons,
and bowls. The canyons have the streams, and
the bowls have the small lakes. Among the
better destinations is the Nine Lakes Basin
(just below Kaweah Peaks Ridge), where the
lakes are untouched and beautiful, and include
a series of stream-connected lakes that can be
reached by off-trail hiking.

At Forester Lake, located near Franklin Pass
in the Great Western Divide, so many trout
were jumping during the evening rise that it
sounded like popguns going off.

Facilities, fees: Campgrounds, lodging, and
picnic areas are available. There are limited
supplies in the park. A park entrance fee is
charged.

Directions: From Visalia, take Highway 198
east for 36 miles to the Ash Mountain entrance station of Sequoia National Park. Access to the upper Kaweah River is below the
road; some scrambling and hiking is required
to reach the stream.

Contact: Sequoia-Kings Canyon National
Park, 559/565-3341, www.nps.gov/seki.

31 LAKE SUCCESS

Rating: 9

near Porterville

`Map 11.4, page 522`

Lake Success is rising in quality faster than
any other bass lake in California. There are
very high catch rates in late winter and spring.
Some people even call it a fish factory. Like
Lake Kaweah, it too has benefited from regulations mandating a 15-inch minimum size,
with a two-fish limit for bass. The lake record
bass is 18 pounds, and many think this lake
will eventually produce a 20-pounder.

Success is a big lake with a series of major
lake arms, set in bare foothill country at an elevation of 650 feet. When full, it covers nearly
2,500 acres and has 30 miles of shoreline, yet it
is much shallower than most reservoirs. Water
levels can fluctuate from week to week, with
major drawdowns during the summer.

Catch rates are often excellent for bass in the 10- to 15-inch class. There are days where you can catch 14- and 15-inchers all day long. Aquatic food levels are high, and with them come the chance for some monster-sized bass. The south fork is a favorite area for bassers, with submerged trees and vegetation that provide cover for fish.

Bluegill, crappie, and catfish are options in the summer months. In the cool months, the lake is stocked with 10- to 12-inch rainbow trout.

This lake is on the map as something special.

Facilities, fees: Boat ramps are on the east and west shores of the lake. A campground, restrooms with flush toilets, a full-service marina, picnic areas, an RV dump station, and a convenience store with bait and tackle are available. You can rent fishing boats, pontoon boats, personal watercraft, and houseboats at Success Marina. Gas and a restaurant are nearby. A day-use fee is charged that includes boat launching.

Directions: From the junction of Highways 65 and 190 in Porterville, turn east on Highway 190 and drive eight miles to Lake Success.

Contact: U.S. Army Corps of Engineers, Lake Success, 559/784-0215, www.corpslakes.usace. army.mil.

32 TULE RIVER

Rating: 4

northeast of Bakersfield
Map 11.4, page 522

The Tule River runs out of Sequoia National Forest, winding its way down the western slopes of the southern Sierra. The best stretch of river covered in this chapter is well upstream of Lake Success, along Highway 190 from Springville on upriver. The Department of Fish and Game stocks it with 9- to 11-inch rainbow trout every year, with most of the stocking taking place during the early summer. Other species include brown trout, smallmouth bass, and green

sunfish. You can cruise the highway, making quick stops at the turnouts, and hit many spots while heading east into the mountains.

Facilities, fees: Campgrounds are at Lake Success. Supplies can be obtained in Porterville. A day-use fee is charged.

Directions: From Porterville, take Highway 190 east for eight miles past Lake Success. Access is available off the highway at day-use areas at Upper and Lower Coffee Camps, both set on the Tule River.

Contact: Sequoia National Forest, Western Divide Ranger District, 559/539-2607, www .fs.fed.us/r5—click on Forest Offices.

33 MIDDLE FORK TULE RIVER

Rating: 5

northeast of Bakersfield in
Giant Sequoia National Monument
Map 11.4, page 522

The Tule River is created from the many tiny drops of snowmelt that join in rock fissures in the high Sierra. Gravity takes them downhill to the west, where they eventually meld in a canyon and form this stream. It runs through Sequoia National Forest/Giant Sequoia National Monument on down to Lake Success. In the process, it is stocked at several access points along Highway 190. One good spot is in the vicinity of the Wishon Drive turnoff. Another option is to take the Wishon Drive turnoff and then the road (paved, but narrow and curvy) that borders the upper reaches of the river. The river gets rainbow trout, most ranging 9–11 inches.

Note that the day-use areas here get crowded during the summers. The best advice is to forget it during midday and afternoon, and instead fish early morning or early evening.

Facilities, fees: Belknap Campground is along the river. Pit toilets, picnic tables, and drinking water are available. Supplies can be obtained in Porterville or Camp Nelson. A fee is charged at the campground or in day-use parking areas.

Directions: From Porterville, take Highway 190 east and continue past Lake Success. Access is available off the highway up to Camp Nelson.

Contact: Giant Sequoia National Monument, Tule River/Hot Springs Ranger District, 559/539-2607, www.fs.fed.us/r5—click on Forest Offices.

34 INDEPENDENCE CREEK

Rating: 6

near the town of Independence in
Inyo National Forest
Map 11.4, page 522

The lower stretches of Independence Creek are fairly desolate, where you see patches of chaparral in high desert.

The creek is stocked with rainbow trout at the little Independence Campground, 0.5 mile west of Independence, on upstream for 7 miles to where the road crosses the stream above Seven Pines Village. It gets 10- to 12-inch rainbow trout. Nearby Symmes Creek provides another fishing option. The elevation at the campground is 3,900 feet.

Most visitors head past Independence Creek on westward to the Onion Valley Trailhead, which leads to the Pacific Crest Trail and the John Muir Trail. The trailhead also leads to several lakes (Bullfrog and Kearsarge are the most notable) after a day's hiking. This is the area where a large bear ripped open my brother Rambob's backpack and scored the Tang. Bears are food-conditioned here: food canisters are now required; hanging food is not permitted.

Facilities, fees: Campgrounds are on the creek. Supplies can be obtained in Independence. Fishing access is free.

Directions: Take U.S. 395 to Independence and Market Street. Turn west (toward the Sierra) on Market Street and drive 0.5 mile to the county campground and Creek Road. Turn west on Creek Road and drive approximately 2.5 miles to the first of the campgrounds along the creek.

Contact: Inyo County Parks Department, 760/873-5577, www.inyocountycamping .com; Independence Chamber of Commerce, 760/878-0084, www.independence-ca.com; Inyo National Forest, Mount Whitney Ranger Station, 760/876-6200, www.fs.fed.us/r5— click on Forest Offices.

35 SYMMES CREEK

Rating: 4

near Independence
Map 11.4, page 522

Little Symmes Creek is not going to make anybody's list of California's great trout waters. But it might show up on the list of places you can reach by car that are very quiet and visited by few people, and where you might catch a trout. When nearby Independence Creek to the north is stocked, the Department of Fish and Game driver usually makes a quick hit at Symmes Creek at the same time, dropping a small load right at the campground. If the water is too low, it is bypassed. The access road, by the way, heads up to a little-used trailhead that routes backpackers up over Shepherd Pass just north of Mount Tyndall—a genuine butt-kicker climb, one of the worst in California.

Facilities, fees: A primitive campground is available. Supplies can be obtained in the town of Independence. Fishing access is free.

Directions: Take U.S. 395 to Independence and Market Street. Turn west (toward the Sierra) on Market Street and drive for about five miles (along Independence Creek) to Foothill Road. Turn left and continue south until you cross the creek. There is direct access from the roadside.

Contact: Inyo National Forest, Mount Whitney Ranger Station, 760/876-6200, www .fs.fed.us/r5—click on Forest Offices; Bureau of Land Management, Bishop Field Office, 760/872-5000,www.blm.gov/ca.

36 SHEPHERD CREEK

Rating: 5

near Independence

Map 11.4, page 522

For a place such a short distance off a major highway, it is hard to believe how remote little Shepherd Creek feels. It is basically out in the middle of the nowhere land of the Owens River Valley, yet it is easy enough to reach to get stocked with rainbow trout. Where? Right near the sand trap, where the road meets the creek.

The DFG stocks Shepherd Creek with about 1,000 pounds of 10- to 12-inch trout each year.

Beautiful? No. Big fish? No. A chance to catch something? Yes. Well, just about everything has at least one redeeming quality.

Facilities, fees: No facilities are on-site. A campground and supplies can be found in Independence. Fishing access is free.

Directions: From Independence, take U.S. 395 south for five miles and look on the east side for the road with a cattle guard. Turn east on that road and continue until it ends at the Los Angeles Aqueduct. Turn right and continue to the creek.

Contact: Department of Fish and Game, Bishop Field Office, 760/872-1171.

37 GEORGE CREEK

Rating: 5

south of Independence

Map 11.4, page 522

This creek is just a little trickle of water that provides limited opportunity in the spring and early summer. George Creek is stocked with trout at the sand trap, the main access point for the Department of Fish and Game tanker truck. How many? Typically about 1,300 pounds of 10- to 12-inch trout each. That's decent for a stream this small. This provides a quick-hit option that is overlooked

by most, many who might yearn for such a spot.

By the end of the season, the creek is literally a trickle, and you might as well cast on the desert sand.

Facilities, fees: No facilities are on-site. A campground and supplies can be found in Independence. Fishing access is free.

Directions: From Independence, take U.S. 395 south for seven miles to a road 0.25 mile northwest of the Los Angeles Aqueduct crossing. Turn south; direct access to the creek is available here.

Contact: Department of Fish and Game, Bishop Field Office, 760/872-1171.

38 LONE PINE CREEK

Rating: 6

near Lone Pine

Map 11.4, page 522

Whitney Portal is the world-class trailhead that hikers take to climb Mount Whitney and start the John Muir Trail. The road climbs from 3,700 feet–8,361 feet in just 13 miles.

In the process of making this trip, visitors discover that Lone Pine Creek is adjacent to the road for most of the ride up to the Whitney Portal Camp. It is stocked with rainbow trout in the lower stretches just west of Lone Pine, between the Los Angeles Aqueduct and Lone Pine Campground, and at the other camps along the creek (as well as at the little pond near the Whitney Portal Store). On the road, you may not think the stream has much promise. Guess again. The Department of Fish and Game plants rainbow trout in the 10- to 12-inch class, and the people who take the time to try the stream out rarely have an empty frying pan come dinnertime. This river can really surprise you.

The best fishing is right at the campgrounds, where you have to share the stream, naturally, with all the other campers. Unfortunately, if you try to break off and hike the stream to discover your own secret spots, you will discover the stream quite brushy, with poor access. Sure enough, you'll be back at the campground with everybody else. There are also some accessible spots along the road.

This spot is best known, of course, as the jump-off for climbing Mount Whitney; at 14,497 feet (says so on my T-shirt), it's the highest point in the lower 48 states. From the trailhead at Whitney Portal, the trail climbs more than 6,000 feet to the Whitney Summit, including 100 switchbacks to get above Wotan's Throne. That journey can completely overshadow the fishing at Independence Creek. Regardless, check it out.

Facilities, fees: Campgrounds can be found on Whitney Portal Road. Supplies can be obtained in Lone Pine. Fishing access is free. A permit is needed to hike the Whitney Trail; contact the Mount Whitney Ranger Station.

Directions: Take U.S. 395 to Lone Pine and Whitney Portal Road (at a traffic light in the center of town). Turn west at Whitney Portal Road and drive up the foothills of Mount Whitney to Lone Pine Creek. Direct access is available.

Contact: Lone Pine Sporting Goods, 760/876-5365; Gardner's Hardware, 760/876-4208; High Sierra Outfitters, 760/876-9994; Inyo National Forest, Mount Whitney Ranger Station, 760/876-6200, www.fs.fed.us/r5—click on Forest Offices; Lone Pine Chamber of Commerce, 760/876-4444, www.lonepine chamber.org.

39 TUTTLE CREEK

Rating: 4

near Lone Pine
Map 11.4, page 522

The trout in Tuttle Creek can provide some evening entertainment for campers. The campground here, at an elevation of 5,120 feet, is used as an overflow area if the camps farther up Whitney Portal Road are full.

Also close by is Lone Pine Creek, which provides an option for both camping and fishing. Tuttle Creek is stocked with rainbow trout adjacent to the campground, with plants of rainbow trout in the 10- to 12-inch class. You could roll in on an early summer afternoon, set up camp, fish for a few hours during the evening, and then have a trout fry for dinner. There may be no better way to fortify yourself before climbing Mount Whitney.

Note: Just upstream is a fishery for wild brown trout. This hike-to section of stream is not planted, but it often provides a good stream fishing opportunity.

Facilities, fees: A campground, picnic area, and pit toilets are available. There is no drinking water. Supplies are in Lone Pine. Fishing access is free.

Directions: Take U.S. 395 to Lone Pine and Whitney Portal Road (at a traffic light in the center of town). Turn west at Whitney Portal Road and drive for 3.5 miles to Horseshoe Meadow Road. Turn south on Horseshoe Meadow Road and drive 1.5 miles to Tuttle Creek Road. Turn west on Tuttle Creek Road (a winding dirt road) and drive directly into the campground. Access is possible both at and near the campground.

Contact: Lone Pine Sporting Goods, 760/876-5365; Gardner's Hardware, 760/876-4208; High Sierra Outfitters, 760/876-9994; Bureau of Land Management, Bishop Field Office, 760/872-5000, www.blm.gov/ca/. Lone Pine Chamber of Commerce, 760/876-4444, www .lonepinechamber.org.

40 DIAZ LAKE

Rating: 5

south of Lone Pine
Map 11.4, page 522

Diaz Lake covers 85 surface acres and is at an elevation of 3,650 feet in the Owens Valley. It is often overshadowed by nearby Mount Whitney and the Sierra range to the west.

The lake has three camping areas along the western shore, making this a decent spot for campers/boaters. In the summer months, waterskiing and running personal watercraft are popular activities, and fishing for a few resident bass, bluegill, and catfish becomes just a sideline.

From late winter through April, the lake is stocked with 10- to 12-inch rainbow trout, and a 15-mph speed limit for boaters goes into effect (from November through April). Alpers trout are also stocked here intermittently, and occasionally some big brood stock rainbow trout. After stocks, results can be good, both for shore fishing with bait near the campgrounds and for trollers who explore in the vicinity of the boat launch.

One sidelight here is hang gliding, which is very popular on the leeward side of Mount Whitney from May through July. On a rare day you might even see hang gliders along the Whitney face as high as 14,000 feet, an extraordinary sight.

Note: All boats must be inspected and certified free of mussels prior to launching at this lake.

Facilities, fees: A paved boat ramp, campgrounds, restrooms with flush toilets, a picnic area, a boat dock, and playground are available. A nine-hole golf course is nearby. Supplies can be obtained in Lone Pine. Boats over 20 feet long are prohibited. The speed limit is 35 mph from May through October and 15 mph from November through May 14. Boat-launching fees are charged.

Directions: From Lone Pine, take U.S. 395 south for two miles to the entrance, on the right (west) side of the road.

Contact: Lone Pine Sporting Goods, 760/876-5365; Gardner's Hardware, 760/876-4208; High Sierra Outfitters, 760/876-9994; Inyo County Parks Department, 760/873-5577, www.inyocountycamping.com; Interagency Visitor Center, 760/876-6222; Diaz Lake Campground, 760/876-4700; Lone Pine Chamber of Commerce, 760/876-4444, www.lonepinechamber.org.

41 GOLDEN TROUT WILDERNESS

Rating: 6

east of Cartago in Inyo National Forest

Map 11.4, page 522 **BEST (**

Those who start fantasizing about trips into the Golden Trout Wilderness usually dream about one lake after another loaded with giant golden trout. Well, the reality just doesn't work out that way. What you get at Big Whitney Meadow are small streams (actually called "stringers") that pretzel their way through meadows and that are loaded with small golden trout.

For the ambitious few, the headwaters of the Kern River, below the Great Western Divide in the Kern Canyon, is a fantastic trout stream. It is 19 miles to just reach the canyon, no matter which of the three routes you choose. The trout are the biggest in the Sierra, averaging about 10–14 inches, and the river is loaded.

There are actually very few lakes available, especially when compared to the backcountry of the John Muir Wilderness and Kings Canyon National Park, to the immediate north.

The difference, however, is that the waters here have native golden trout and that the headwaters of the Kern River are a rare native habitat for goldens and wild rainbow trout. Another hike-to water that also has native golden trout is Golden Trout Creek. These waters are not planted by air with hatchery fish. They are wild fish: native born and bred, descendants of original lake inhabitants.

Note that Chicken Spring Lake, Johnson Lake, Rocky Basin Lakes, and in general the Cottonwood Creek Basin are being reestablished as native golden-trout fisheries. The fish in these waters were killed off, and in the coming years, a native strain of golden trout will be introduced and managed as a native wild-trout fishery. It is an ongoing project. Another plus is that the cows are out; a herd of 900 cows was once permitted to graze Big Whitney Meadows.

One option for access is taking the Pacific Crest Trail from the Horseshoe Meadow Trailhead. Hike up to Cottonwood Pass and then down the other side to Big Whitney Meadow. There's a nice campsite here and tons of small golden trout in a cut-bank stream in a meadow. In the days that follow you might roam up to the Rocky Lakes Basin (no fish) and then north over the Boreal Plateau to Funston Lake. It is remote, little visited, off-trail, and set just south of the Siberian Outpost.

Another option is hiking straight up the Kern River Canyon. This is an awesome canyon, deep and pristine. It can take a long, difficult trek for this trip. You need to be willing to carry your backpack well up the canyon to the headwaters. That is where you will find the genetically pure strain of goldens. I completed a Sierra crossing, from Horseshoe Meadow on the flank of Whitney, up the PCT to Wallace Creek, then down the Kern Canyon, up Rattlesnake Creek, and over the Great Western Divide and out to Mineral King in Sequoia National Park. This was nearly as good as hiking the JMT, and the fishing in the Kern Canyon was some of the best wilderness fishing I've had—up there with Little South Fork Lake in the Trinity Alps, headwaters of Rush Creek (in wet years), Mono Creek above Lake Edison, and Rae Lakes in Kings Canyon National Park.

The area is home to some of the quietest country you will ever find, with most hikers exploring the John Muir Wilderness and its hundreds of lakes. Is it quiet? It's so peaceful you can practically hear the tiny wildflowers bloom.

Facilities, fees: No facilities are in the wilderness area. Fishing access is free. A permit is required for camping in the Golden Trout Wilderness.

Directions: Access to trailheads is available in the east Sierra out of Lone Pine at Horseshoe Meadow, and in the west Sierra from Mineral King in Sequoia National Park.

Contact: Cottonwood Pack Station, 760/878-2015; Inyo National Forest, Mount Whitney Ranger Station, 760/876-6200, www.fs.fed.us/r5—click on Forest Offices.

42 COTTONWOOD CREEK

Rating: 3

north of Olancha in Inyo National Forest
Map 11.4, page 522

If it is an angler's paradise you want, this is not the place. But if you don't mind the desolate surroundings and fairly limited fishing opportunity, Cottonwood Creek is the spot for a quick hit. The stream is stocked with rainbow trout from the campground (near the powerhouse intake) to the road's end. The Department of Fish and Game plunks in 10- to 12-inch rainbow trout during the summer in this stretch. Stick and move, hit and run, and a few trout will come along for the ride. There is no campground along the stream.

Facilities, fees: Dispersed camping sites are along Lower Cottonwood Creek. Supplies can be found in Lone Pine, about 10 miles north of the turnoff. Campfire permits are required. Fishing access is free.

Directions: From the junction of Highway 190 and U.S. 395 at Olancha, drive 11.5 miles north on U.S. 395 to the Cottonwood Powerhouse turnoff. Turn left and continue west, keeping to the left as you cross the Owens Canal. Direct access is available off the road.

Contact: Lone Pine Sporting Goods, 760/876-5365; Gardner's Hardware, 760/876-4208; High Sierra Outfitters, 760/876-9994; Inyo National Forest, Mount Whitney Ranger Station, 760/876-6200, www.fs.fed.us/r5—click on Forest Offices; Lone Pine Chamber of Commerce, 760/876-4444, www.lonepinechamber.org.

43 KERN RIVER

Rating: 8

northeast of Bakersfield in
Sequoia National Forest
Map 11.5, page 523

This stretch of the Kern River is stocked from the mouth up past Fairview to Johnsondale Bridge with 10- to 12-inch rainbow trout and a sprinkling of trophy-size trout up to six pounds. The best fishing for trout is 5–7 miles upstream of the town of Lake Isabella. This is a very popular fishery and gets hit hard, but it can provide good results during shaded evenings in the early summer.

A great bonus is a chance for smallmouth bass at the lower end of the river, just above the headwaters of Lake Isabella.

You will find that afternoon swimming and evening fishing make for a good camping vacation. Downstream of Johnsondale Bridge is also the best place to fish, not up near South Creek Falls.

Facilities, fees: Campgrounds are on Highway 178 and Mountain 99, as well as at Isabella Lake. Supplies can be obtained in Bakersfield, Kernville, or Lake Isabella. Day-use fees are charged at some parking areas.

Directions: From Bakersfield, drive east on Highway 178 for about 40 miles to the town of Lake Isabella. Access to the lower river is available directly off the highway, 10 miles east of Bakersfield (to Lake Isabella).

To the upper river: From the town of Lake Isabella, take Highway 155/Burlando Road north for 10 miles to Kernville and the Mountain 99/Sierra Way. Turn left (north); direct access is available off the road.

Contact: Sequoia National Forest, Kern River Ranger District, Kernville Office, 760/376-3781, www.fs.fed.us/r5—click on Forest Offices.

44 ISABELLA LAKE

Rating: 8

east of Bakersfield

Map 11.5, page 523

This is the largest freshwater lake in Southern California, covering almost 38,400 acres and offering 38 miles of shoreline when full. It provides good fisheries for largemouth bass (including some monsters), rainbow trout, and fair numbers of bluegill, crappie, and channel catfish. Bass fishing is the best thing going here. The French Gulch area commonly produces largemouth bass weighing up to 5 pounds, and occasionally up

to 10 pounds. The North Fork area has a lot of submerged trees where the bass hang out during the summer. Some locals say a 20-pounder will surely be caught here some day.

A trout derby is held each May at this lake; in the past, the top tagged fish has been worth $10,000, crowning $60,000 in total prizes.

The lake is heavily stocked with rainbow trout by the Department of Fish and Game, which funnels in 10- to 12-inch rainbow trout from two hatcheries. This provides good opportunity for trollers, with the best fishing (and also plenty of food for the giant bass) near the dam. Standard trolling techniques are used, varying the depth according to water temperature, with the best of it coming on flashers trailed by a Needlefish lure or half of a night crawler. Most of the trout are in the 1.5- to 2-pound class, with a sprinkling of 18-inchers and bigger.

Chinook salmon have been stocked, and if they take hold and grow, perhaps this lake could be as special for fishing as it is as a water storage facility.

It gets windy here in the spring, so like at a lot of big reservoirs, the water gets muddy around shoreline points. Boater and camper traffic is heavy here into the fall. After that, when the weather cools, anglers arrive in significant numbers. The water is usually very calm in September and October, but low lake levels are a continual problem from water drained from the lake all summer.

The lake is at 2,600 feet in the foothills east of Bakersfield and is the centerpiece for a wide variety of activities, including waterskiing, bird-watching, and camping. In addition, the nearby Kern River, which feeds the lake, has a good stretch of white water for rafters.

Lake records: 18-pound, 13-ounce largemouth bass; 36-pound, 4-ounce catfish; 3.85-pound crappie; 2-pound, 9-ounce bluegill.

Facilities, fees: Several campgrounds are available. There are full-service marinas, an RV dump station, restaurants, gas, lodging, and convenience stores. Fishing boats, pontoon boats, ski boats, and personal watercraft can be rented at North Fork Marina and at French Gulch Marina.

All boaters must purchase a three-day or an annual permit to boat on the lake; you can obtain one at any of the marinas or local businesses. The permit includes launching privileges. A day-use fee is charged at some spots around the lake.

Directions: From Bakersfield, take Highway 178 east and drive 40 miles to the town of Lake Isabella. Continue two miles to the lake.

To various boat ramps from the town of Lake Isabella:

• Take Highway 178 east for a short distance to Ponderosa Drive. Turn left and drive a short distance to the boat ramp (between the auxiliary dam and the main dam).

• Take Highway 178 east for six miles to Paradise Cove Campground and the boat ramp. This ramp is closed during low lake levels.

• Take Highway 178 east for nine miles to Kissack Bay and the boat ramp. This ramp is closed during low lake levels.

• From Highway 155/Burlando Road, turn right (south) and drive six miles to Camp 9.

• From Highway 155/Burlando Road, turn left (north) and drive three miles to French Gulch Campground.

• Turn west on Highway 155 and drive approximately four miles around the lake's west side. The ramp is between North Fork Marina and Tillie Creek Campground. *Note:* This ramp may be unusable when water levels are low.

• Drive east on Highway 178 for approximately two miles to Old Isabella Road. Turn left and continue to the ramp.

• Continue east on Highway 178 for approximately four miles to the sign for South Fork Recreation Area. Turn left and continue to the ramp, between Paradise Cove and Kern Valley Marina.

Contact: North Fork Marina, 760/376-1812, www.northforkmarina.com; French Gulch Marina, 760/379-8774, www.frenchgulch marina.com; Sequoia National Forest, Kern River Ranger District, 760/376-3781, www .fs.fed.us/r5/sequoia; Kern River Valley Chamber of Commerce, 760/379-5236 or 866/578-4386, www.kernrivervalley.com.

45 LAKE MING

Rating: 4

near Bakersfield in Kern River County Park

Map 11.5, page 523

This lake has a natural calendar. From November to March, the lake is cool enough for trout fishing. The Department of Fish and Game stocks the lake with 10- to 12-inch rainbow trout, usually in the winter months. They join a sprinkling of bluegill, catfish, crappie, and bass, which provide hope during the spring and summer months.

Lake Ming is near the Kern River. It has an elevation of 450 feet and covers only 104 acres. The little lake is a popular spot for water sports in the hot summer months. About 20 days a year the lake is closed to the public and reserved for special organized boating activities. Also note that on one weekend per month in spring and fall, private boat races and waterskiing events are scheduled, and the lake is closed to the public. No boats are allowed on Tuesday and Thursday afternoons. Inflatables are not allowed at all. Always call ahead if you are planning a day trip.

Facilities, fees: A paved boat ramp is on the lake's east side. A campground is approximately 0.25 mile west of the lake. A picnic area, restrooms with flush toilets and coin showers, drinking water, an RV dump station, and a concession stand are available. An annual permit is required for all boats, including canoes and kayaks. No permit is required for shoreline fishing. Permits can be purchased at the park.

Directions: Take Highway 99 to Bakersfield and the exit for Highway 178. Turn east on Highway 178 and drive 11 miles to Alfred Harrell Highway. Turn north and drive four miles to Lake Ming Road. Turn right and drive 0.25 mile to the lake.

Contact: Kern County Parks and Recreation Department, 661/868-7000, www.co.kern .ca.us/parks; Bob's Bait Bucket, Bakersfield, 661/833-8657, www.bobsbaitbucket.com.

SANTA BARBARA AND VICINITY

© EUGENE TOCHILIN/123RF.COM

BEST FISHING SPOTS

◖ Saltwater Fisheries
Ventura Deep Sea/Channel Islands, **page 573.**

For many, this region of California coast is like a dream, the best place in the world to live. It's a unique mix of surprise inland coastal forests and sunswept sand beaches that stretch 200 miles. The natural charm extends to a largely untouched coast, as well as to some of the top bass lakes in California: San Antonio, Nacimiento, Cachuma, and Casitas.

Some of the best inshore rockfishing in California can be found along the inshore coast of San Simeon, and there are excellent sportfishing operations out of Morro Bay and Avila Beach. The Santa Barbara area is one of the promised lands of California. The saltwater fishing is excellent, with a huge variety of species, habitats, and opportunities. The coast is very beautiful, with some of the prettiest state-park beaches anywhere. But that's not all.

The central coast features many little-known areas. Since both U.S. 101 and Highway 1 shift inland north of El Capitan State Beach, access to the coast is limited to a handful of small roads. One long-term problem – for years on end – has been the limited access by the marginal boat hoist at Gaviota State Park.

Of course, nothing is perfect. The Marine Life Protection Act (MLPA) has put coastal areas off limits to fishing. For anglers who make their trips on commercial sportfishing boats, it is up to the boat captain to make sure your line isn't set down in a closed area. For owners of private boats, it's advisable to follow the party boats around until you get it down, or get the

GPS coordinates of the closures as they develop and input them into your GPS or mapping units. Don't hesitate to call the DFG office and request an exact detail of the boundaries. You'll also have to deal with summer fog on the coast and the intense summer heat – just 10-15 miles inland.

My favorite adventure in this area is bass fishing. Lake San Antonio has developed into a stellar bass fishery, and Lake Nacimiento can provide 50-fish days on white bass (plus, the fishery has benefited from the recent introduction of spotted bass).

At Cachuma Lake and Lake Casitas, you get the full spectrum of bass fishing: The former is now one of the best bass lakes around, and the latter has a sprinkling of some of the biggest bass in America. Los Padres National Forest provides a vast region to roam and explore.

The fishing in the Channel Islands is exciting and unpredictable, with fish such as albacore tuna, bonito, marlin, and – my favorite – yellowtail all found in this region. Those who have been out here know that San Miguel Island is an awesome kind of place, where you feel as though you have the entire world to yourself. Of course, it's a terribly long boat ride, but the reward in the summer can be the best of Southern California fisheries. Every year is a roll of the dice, however, but the sure things are the resident rockfish, lingcod, and kelp bass. But always remember the MLPA closures.

This region is dramatic in every sense. The ocean seems to stretch to forever. Maybe it does. For many, forever is how long they wish to stay here.

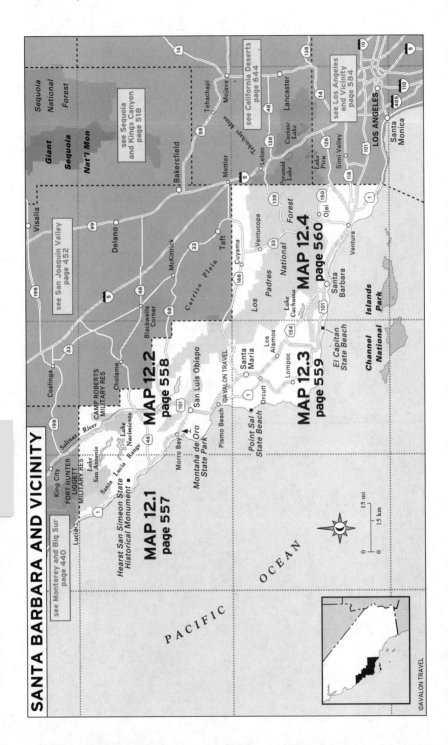

SANTA BARBARA AND VICINITY

see Monterey and Big Sur
page 440

see San Joaquin Valley
page 452

see Sequoia and Kings Canyon
page 518

see California Deserts
page 644

see Los Angeles and Vicinity
page 584

Sequoia National Forest

Giant Sequoia Nat'l Mon

MAP 12.1
page 557

MAP 12.2
page 558

MAP 12.3
page 559

MAP 12.4
page 560

Los Padres National Forest

Channel Islands National Park

Hearst San Simeon State Historical Monument

Montaña de Oro State Park

Point Sal State Beach

El Capitan State Beach

PACIFIC OCEAN

CAMP ROBERTS MILITARY RES

FORT HUNTER LIGGETT MILITARY RES

Lake Nacimiento

Lake San Antonio

Santa Lucia Range

Salinas River

Carrizo Plain

Lake Cachuma

Pyramid Lake

Castaic Lake

Lake Piru

King City
Lucia
Coalinga
Visalia
Bakersfield
Delano
McKittrick
Blackwells Corner
Cholame
Coalinga
San Luis Obispo
Morro Bay
Pismo Beach
Santa Maria
Orcutt
Los Alamos
Lompoc
Santa Barbara
Ventura
Ojai
Simi Valley
Santa Monica
LOS ANGELES
Lancaster
Mojave
Tehachapi
Mettler
Lebec
Cuyama
Ventucopa
Taft

LOS ANGELES

Tehachapi Mtns

0   15 mi
0   15 km

©AVALON TRAVEL

Map 12.1

Site 1
Page 561

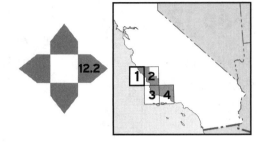

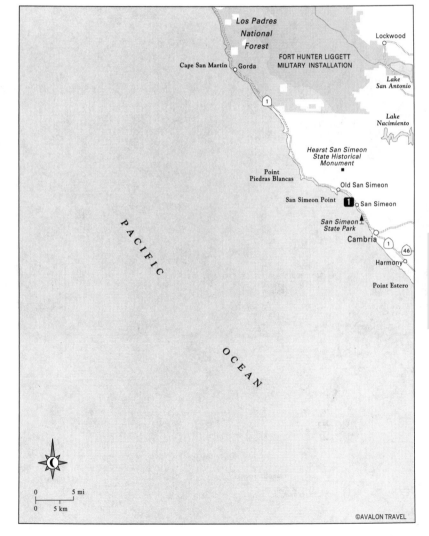

Map 12.2

Sites 2-13
Pages 561-569

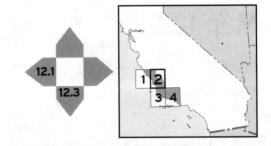

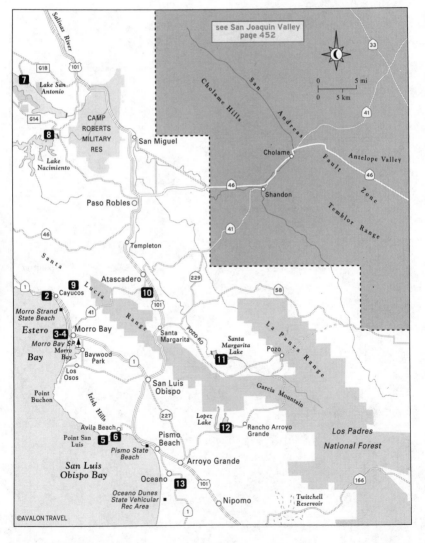

Map 12.3

Sites 14-15
Page 570

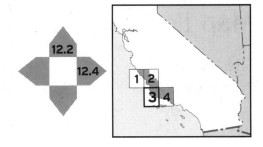

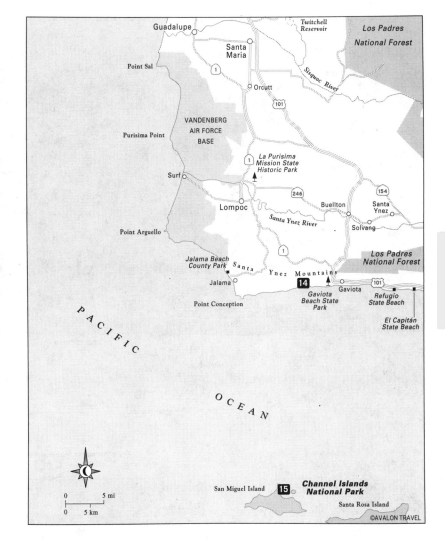

Map 12.4

Sites 16-25
Pages 571-578

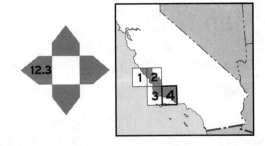

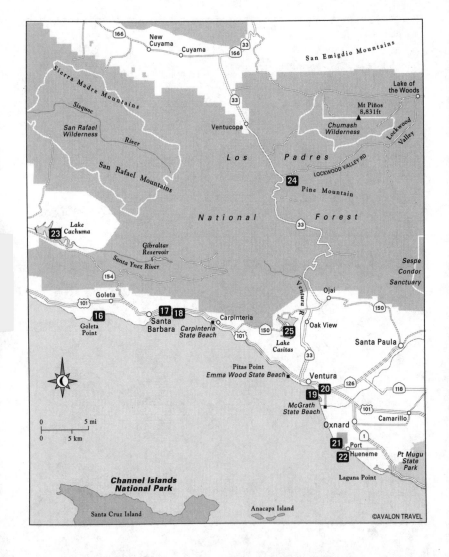

1 SAN SIMEON

Rating: 5

north of San Luis Obispo at San Simeon Bay

Map 12.1, page 557

This area has the potential to be great for anglers with a sea kayak. Be careful, of course, to fish only on days with calm seas, and to stay outside of areas closed by the MLPA.

This used to be called "San Simeon Landing." Now it is called just "San Simeon" because about nobody but the marine birds "lands" anything. There are no party boat operations anymore, and a lot of areas have been closed to fishing.

It is one of the most beautiful areas in the world, with giant cliffs, sheer drop-offs, and shallows strewn with rocks and kelp beds. It is also a sanctuary for otters. Commercial netting is outlawed between Point Sur Rock and San Simeon to protect the otters. The San Simeon Shoal provides excellent habitat for rockfish.

From the pier, you can fish for surfperch, rockfish, and halibut. Surf fishing is allowed from the beach.

A key to the marine abundance is the undersea habitat. Just two miles offshore, the bottom of the ocean drops off to 1,500–2,000 feet. Because of this, the ocean has a dramatic upwelling here, kicking up nutrient-rich water—and with it, all matter of baitfish to the shoal area, about 120–190 feet deep.

Note that fishing regulations often change here from year to year, for seasons, depth restrictions, bag limits, size limits, and even annual quotas for the fleet. Always check current regulations with Fish and Game. It's too bad no sportfishing operators work out of Simeon Landing. No boats can launch from this area.

State records from this area: 11-pound, 4-ounce starry flounder; 2-pound, 9-ounce kelp greenling.

Facilities, fees: A pier, restrooms, a sink for cleaning fish, benches, kayak rentals, and picnic tables are at San Simeon State Park. Two campgrounds are nearby. Access is free.

Directions: From San Luis Obispo, take Highway 1 north for 41 miles to the beach entrance across from the entrance to Hearst Castle.

Contact: Hearst San Simeon State Park, 805/927-2020, www.parks.ca.gov; San Simeon Chamber of Commerce, 800/342-5613, www.sansimeonchamber.org; Virg's Landing, Morro Bay, 800/ROCK-COD (800/762-5263) or 805/772-1222 (party boats), www.morrobaysportfishing.com (note that no sportfishing boats operate from San Simeon Landing).

2 CAYUCOS BEACH PIER

Rating: 6

north of San Luis Obispo

Map 12.2, page 558

Cayucos is often one of the more productive piers on the California coast. The centrally located pier juts well out into the ocean, providing a chance for a variety of species. The best bets are in the summer for mackerel and in the fall for smelt. You might get a rare bonus: perch, the rare halibut, and even salmon are sometimes caught here. The pier is lighted for night fishing. Check Department of Fish and Game (DFG) regulations before the trip.

Facilities, fees: A pier, restrooms, benches, fish-cleaning tables, showers, and picnic areas are provided. Fishing access is free.

Directions: From San Luis Obispo, take Highway 1 north for 14 miles to Cayucos Drive. Turn west on Cayucos and drive several blocks to the end of the road. Park at the Veterans Hall or on Ocean Front Lane.

Contact: Cayucos Chamber of Commerce, 805/995-1200, www.cayucoschamber.com; Cayucos State Beach, 805/781-5930, www.slostateparks.com or www.parks.ca.gov.

3 MORRO BAY CITY NORTH AND SOUTH T-PIERS

Rating: 5

north of San Luis Obispo

Map 12.2, page 558

The best fishing here is for perch. An average number of fish are caught at these piers, making it a spot for Mom and Dad to take the kids fishing. The best of it is in the late summer and fall. In the fall, the jacksmelt arrive in good numbers, along with fair numbers of perch. For a wild card in the spring and summer, try using a live anchovy for bait (available at Virg's), and keep it right on the bottom for halibut.

Facilities, fees: Restrooms are available only at the North T-Pier. A bait shop is nearby. Fishing access is free.

Directions: To the South T-Pier: From San Luis Obispo, take Highway 1 north for 12 miles to Morro Bay and the Morro Bay Boulevard exit. Take that exit and continue straight at the stop sign. Drive several blocks to Main Street. Turn right and drive two blocks to Beach Street. Turn left and drive a short distance to the Embarcadero. Turn right and continue to the pier.

To the North T-Pier: From the South T-Pier, continue for 0.25 mile to the North T-Pier.

Contact: San Simeon Chamber of Commerce, 800/342-5613, www.sansimeonchamber.org; Morro Bay Harbor Master's Office, 805/772-6254, www.morro-bay.ca.us; Virg's Landing, Morro Bay, 800/ROCK-COD (800/762-5263) or 805/772-1222 (party boats), www.morrobaysportfishing.com; Morro Bay Chamber of Commerce, 805/772-4467 or 800/231-0592, www.morrobay.org.

4 MORRO BAY DEEP SEA

Rating: 10

at Morro Bay

Map 12.2, page 558

The drive here along Highway 1 can be worth the trip in itself, coming from either the south or the north. Cruising the great coastal highway can be an ideal way to shake the cobwebs free, regardless of what time of year you plan your visit. The party boats offer a wide range of trips, including excursions for salmon in March and April, for albacore July through November, and for rockfish and lingcod year-round. Virg's bait boat (see *Contact*) brings in live anchovies and sardines from May through November, and Virg's runs regular two-day trips to Cape San Martin and the Point Sur area, making it the only open party boat to do so below Sur. Virg's Landing also offers overnight long-range trips. The top destination is usually between San Simeon Point and Piedras Blancas.

It is the rockfishing that provides day-in, day-out meat on the table. Limits are common, along with good numbers of lingcod, which spawn in the fall months. The party boats focus on three areas for rockfish: south off Point Buchon, and north off Point Estero and at Radar Dome. The boats leave early, and the anglers aboard start catching fish almost as soon as they are over the reefs. It is about the closest thing there is to a guarantee in the world of fishing. Another good spot is Purisima.

An option for private boat owners is to use the hoist at Port San Luis to launch, especially in the spring for salmon and in the summer or fall for shallow-water rockfish. Another opportunity is fishing Morro Bay itself for sand bass and halibut. In the spring, trolling hoochies, spoons, or anchovies for salmon is popular. Try live-bait drifting with anchovies for halibut in the summer and jig fishing the shallows for rockfish in the summer and fall.

Another spot to watch is the Cambria area to the north, just below San Simeon. This has become a great place for white seabass. In fact, the whole Morro Bay/San Simeon area has been good for seabass. Note that in late winter and spring, the ocean can really howl here.

The salmon and albacore fluctuate year to year, but albacore can add some sizzle when schools move into the area.

These fish are far less predictable. Some years, well, it's like they are on a mission from hell. Albacore like clear, blue water that is 62–66°F, and they will roam anywhere from 25–150 miles off the coast to find it. On most trips, you practically troll your little petunia off searching for them, moving along at six or seven knots, with feather jigs trailing behind the boat. When there is a strike, the boat stops, deckhands chum, and anglers rush to the rail, using live anchovies for bait.

Cape Martin's inaccessibility to all but the most adventurous rockfishers (via two-day charter) may be the reason the bottom fishing here is legendary. Huge lingcod dwell here, and they are fish that have spent their lives fantasizing about Tady lures, Diamond jigs, and the like. Cannibalistic lingcod also dwell here, and tall tales have been told about anglers peeling off layer after layer of lingcod before finally reaching the original fish that swallowed the bait, some three fish down.

Note that fishing regulations often change here from year to year, for seasons, depth restrictions, bag limits, size limits, and even annual quotas for the fleet. Always check current regulations with Fish and Game or with a marina or party-boat operator before planning a trip.

Morro Bay is an excellent vacation site, a good fishing town that has a decent charter operation. The area is pretty and less populated than many good coastal areas. When you put it all together, it makes a great headquarters for a saltwater angler.

Private boaters should head north and fish southward if they are concerned about weather conditions.

Facilities, fees: Party-boat charters, restrooms with showers, drinking water, boat ramps, bait, tackle, and supplies are at the bay. Lodging, restaurants, and shops are in the town of Morro Bay. Party-boat fees are charged per person.

Directions: From San Luis Obispo, drive 12 miles north on Highway 1 to Morro Bay and the Morro Bay Boulevard exit. Take that exit and continue straight at the stop sign. Drive several blocks to Main Street. Turn right and drive two blocks to Beach Street. Turn left and drive a short distance to the Embarcadero. Turn right and continue to the pier.

Contact: Virg's Landing, Morro Bay, 800/ROCK-COD (800/762-5263) or 805/772-1222 (party boats), www.morrobaysportfishing.com; Morro Bay Chamber of Commerce, 805/772-4467 or 800/231-0592, www.morrobay.org; San Simeon Chamber of Commerce, 800/342-5613, www.sansimeonchamber.org.

5 SAN LUIS OBISPO BAY DEEP SEA

Rating: 8

south of San Luis Obispo at Port San Luis
Map 12.2, page 558

The day starts early at Avila Beach, and it isn't difficult to wake up in the middle of the night if it means going fishing out of Port San Luis. Calm water equals good fishing, and since the sea breezes are often light here, the prospects usually justify setting your alarm clock.

The best and most predictable fishing here is for rockfish, sand bass, and calico bass. The better spots for rockfish include a reef just offshore of Point Sal to the south and also Diablo Canyon, Santa Rosa Reef, and Pecho Rock.

Note that fishing regulations often change here from year to year, for seasons, depth restrictions, bag limits, size limits, and even annual quotas for the fleet. Always check current regulations with Fish and Game or with a marina or party-boat operator before planning a trip.

In the late winter and spring, from April through July, salmon provide a long shot. But long shots can come in, especially when salmon are involved. They often show up anywhere from Avila Beach to Pismo Beach, and right on down to the mouth of the Santa Maria River. In good years, salmon often school outside the Santa Maria River in early April.

When the salmon move in here, it is often within very close range. One of the best areas is often the vicinity of the "The Abalone Farm."

When the salmon move in this close, you can catch them trolling as shallow as 15 or 20 feet deep at daybreak, and as deep as 80 feet down at midday. Salmon charters often head south of Point Buchon, where salmon may congregate in the spring. As the season progresses, salmon go very deep here, sometimes as deep as 300 feet down, requiring trollers to use a downrigger. As a migratory fish, salmon will travel to where the conditions best suit them: 52–58°F water, heavy plankton (green water with low clarity), and high numbers of baitfish.

Come July, the albacore are apt to be anywhere from 25–150 miles offshore in that warm, crystal-blue water. Albacore can provide the best fishing of the year when the water is warm and the schools of fish move within range of small boats 20–30 miles out, but that seems to happen only two or three years per decade. In the fall, there is a friendly competition for albacore with charter operations in Morro Bay to the nearby north.

Facilities, fees: Party-boat charters, a pier, restrooms, kayak rentals, picnic areas, bait, tackle, and supplies are at the harbor. Party-boat fees are charged per person.

Directions: From San Luis Obispo, take U.S. 101 south to the San Luis Drive exit. Take that exit west and drive to Avila Drive. Turn right and continue west to the parking area, at the end of the street. Party boats operate from the third pier.

Contact: Patriot Sportfishing, 805/595-7200 or 800/714-3474, www.patriotsportfishing.com; Port San Luis Harbor, 805/595-5400, www.portsanluis.com; Port San Luis Boatyard, 805/595-7214, www.portsanluis boatyard.com.

6 SAN LUIS PIERS

Rating: 6
south of San Luis Obispo at Avila Beach
Map 12.2, page 558

There may be no better pier in California from which to try for halibut than right here, and statistics gathered by the Department of Fish and Game prove it: halibut like this harbor. There are three piers here, and they are set in prime habitat. Fishing is permitted at the first and third piers. A halibut tournament is held each July.

Just get your bait, a live anchovy, on the bottom. It takes persistence with spirit, and even then you can still blow it on the set. Regardless, halibut in the 10- to 15-pound class, sometimes bigger, are worth the effort.

For less of a wait, the fall months bring good jacksmelt numbers. Other options in the summer are perch (fair), sardines, and sometimes mackerel, sharks, and rays.

The pier is open 24/7. Two boat hoists are at the third pier. One hoist is large (a 60-ton mobile hoist) and is on the left side as you enter the pier, while another, a coin-operated hoist for smaller boats (1,000-pound limit), is on the pier itself.

Facilities, fees: A bait shop, concession stand, restrooms, a fish-cleaning area, restaurants, and a bar are at the piers. Fishing access is free.

Directions: From San Luis Obispo, drive south on U.S. 101 to the Avila Beach Drive exit. Take that exit west and drive four miles (past the town of Avila Beach) until the road ends at the piers. Fishing is permitted off the first and third piers.

Contact: Port San Luis Harbor, 805/595-5400, www.portsanluis.com; Port San Luis Boatyard, 805/595-7214, www.portsanluis boatyard.com; Patriot Sportfishing, 805/595-7200 or 800/714-3474, www.patriotsport fishing.com.

7 LAKE SAN ANTONIO

Rating: 10
north of San Luis Obispo
Map 12.2, page 558

Can you imagine catching 25 bass in a day? More? At San Antonio, this vision has been no mirage. The lake has become one of the best in California for high catches of largemouth bass, with 25-fish days possible for know-hows on the water. In late spring, just after the spawn, the best bet has been for anglers in boats casting topwater crankbaits, poking along the shoreline on the lake's arms.

Fishing is always best from March through early May. The lake has two arms on the southwest part of the lake and another on the northwest side. These are the superior spots during the spring bass bite. As at all reservoirs, you must pattern the bass as they go through winter mode, early spring, pre-spawn, spawn, post-spawn, and summer mode. Even though San Antonio ranks a 10, that does not mean you simply show up, hold out a bag, and then have the fish start jumping in.

Lake records include: 9-pound, 4-ounce largemouth bass; 3-pound, 14-ounce small-mouth bass; 36-pound, 4-ounce striped bass; 3-pound, 8-ounce crappie; 25-pound channel catfish; 1-pound, 12-ounce bluegill.

A 36-pound striped bass? Yep, there are some huge ones in here. If you want striped bass, however, the timing of your trip is critical. You'd do best to show up in the fall, from late September through mid-October, when the striped bass emerge from the depths and roam near the surface, corralling schools of baitfish. Stripers can also be caught in the early summer by trolling or casting diving plugs. They can be difficult to catch the rest of the year.

There are also good numbers of catfish, crappie, sunfish, and bluegill. No trout are stocked here.

By summer, the water-skiers take over (this is the most popular waterskiing lake in the region). In the winter, eagle tours (on the south shore) are the main attraction, and there is an excellent chance of seeing both bald and golden eagles by boat. Lake San Antonio has the largest population of bald eagles in central California. Winter is the best time to spot them.

San Antonio is a big lake (16 miles long and covering 5,500 surface acres), but it is long and narrow, with about 60 miles of shoreline, four boat ramps, and several campgrounds. It is at 780 feet in the dry, hilly grassland country. The average temperature in the summer is in the 70s, courtesy of the lake's location (20 miles from the coastline).

If you make the trip, keep an eye out to the skies. You never know when a bald eagle might be watching.

Facilities, fees: Campgrounds, restrooms with showers, mobile home rentals, picnic areas, a full-service marina, four paved boat ramps, mooring and slips, a snack bar, a restaurant, a gas station, coin laundry, an RV dump station, and a convenience store are available. Fishing boats, pontoon boats, ski boats, canoes, and kayaks can be rented at Lake San Antonio Marina. Day-use and boat-launch fees are charged.

Directions: To the north shore: Take U.S. 101 to Jolon Road/G-14 exit (just north of King City). Take that exit, turn south on Jolon Road, and drive 27 miles to Pleyto Road (a curvy road). Turn right and drive three miles to the north-shore entrance of the lake. *Note:* When arriving from the south or east on U.S. 101 near Paso Robles, it is faster to take the G-18/Jolon Road exit.

To the south shore from the south: Take U.S. 101 to Paso Robles and the 24th Street exit (G-14 west). Take that exit and drive 14 miles to Lake Nacimiento Drive. Turn right and drive across Lake Nacimiento Dam to Interlake Road. Turn left and drive seven miles to Lake San Antonio Road. Turn right and drive three miles to the south shore entrance.

To the south shore from the north: Take U.S. 101 to the Jolon Road/G-14 exit (just north of King City). Turn south on Jolon Road and drive 20 miles to Lockwood and Interlake Road (G-14). Turn right and drive 18 miles to San Antonio Lake Road. Turn left and drive three miles to the south-shore entrance of the lake.

Contact: Lake San Antonio, 805/472-2311, www.co.monterey.ca.us/parks; Lake San Antonio Resort, 800/310-2313, www.lakesanantonioresort.com; Lake San Antonio Marina boat rentals, 805/472-2313.

8 LAKE NACIMIENTO

Rating: 10

north of San Luis Obispo
Map 12.2, page 558

Just add water and Nacimiento most likely provides the highest bass-per-cast rate in California. For starters, there are white bass, so many there is not even a limit on them. For finishers, the spotted bass and smallmouth can measure up to the fishing anywhere else in the state. A fair number of largemouth bass provide the kicker.

Nacimiento is a big lake set in the coastal foothill country, covering more than 5,000 acres (with 165 miles of shoreline when full of water) and with remarkable numbers of lake arms and coves. By the way, no fish stocks are made here of any species, regardless of water conditions.

Fishing for spotted bass is often great from late winter through early summer. The spotted bass, similar to largemouth, just a bit smaller, have provided such a good fishery that many locals ignore the white bass completely. Dropshot a grub or Senko in late winter, then follow the bass through their spring to summer cycles.

The key here is to think numbers, not size. Most of the white bass are like big crappie, but if you use ultra-light tackle and 2-pound line, you'll still have all the tussle you could want. All you have to do is tie on a Horizon jig, get over the fish, and then vertical jig, straight up and down. You can catch one after another. The best spots are the narrows of the Nacimiento River, Las Tablas Creek, and Town Creek.

The white bass go on wild feeds just after they move into one of the several tributaries of the lake to spawn. It typically happens the first time the water temperature hits 58°F, usually after the first week of good warm weather in the spring.

The best lures for white bass are a Rooster Tail, silver-blue Horizon jig, a small Luhr Jensen Crippled Herring, or a Pt. Wilson Dart.

The white bass average 10–12 inches long and a pound in weight, with several a bit bigger, in the 1.5-pound class—feisty little fellows, certainly strong enough to put some sizzle in your pan. Only rarely do they get bigger, to two and three pounds. They look like a cross between a crappie and a striped bass, with the body of a large crappie and the eyes and fins of a striper.

You need a boat (rentals are available), and then you need to search for shad minnows, which are often spotted swirling on the lake surface. Since shad feed on algae, always search along the shoreline that faces the breeze, where algae will concentrate—and with it, so will the minnows. In turn, that's where the white bass will be.

Another trick is to tie a dropper loop in your line 18 inches above your jig, then put a crappie jig on the dropper. This is called rigging a "cheater." Do this and you can catch two white bass at once, and it's a happy shock how strong and wild two on at the same time can be.

If you're not getting bites, then move, because these fish roam in huge packs, not small pods, so keep searching until you find them. The hunt is usually short and easy, especially with a fish finder.

Fishing for largemouth and spotted bass has become so good that the lake hosts 25 fishing tournaments a year. The 70°F water in summer is not only good for water sports, it is also ideal for bluegill and catfish.

Want more? Try not to laugh: the carp record here is 52 pounds.

Facilities, fees: A paved boat ramp is on the southeast shore, next to Lake Nacimiento Resort. Another boat ramp is available intermittently during the summer season on the north shore. Campgrounds, a picnic area, lodging, restrooms with showers, a restaurant, gas, a full-service marina, boat docks, coin laundry, an RV dump station, and a grocery store are available. Fishing boats, pontoon boats, ski boats, personal watercraft, canoes, and kayaks can be rented at the Lake Nacimiento Marina. There are swimming beaches and a swimming pool. Day-use and boat-launch fees are charged.

Directions: Take U.S. 101 to Paso Robles and the 24th Street/Lake Nacimiento exit. Take that exit, turn west on 24th Street (it becomes Lake Nacimiento Road/G-14), and drive for nine miles. Bear right on Lake Nacimiento Road and continue for seven miles to the resort entrance on the left. *Note:* If you cross the Lake Nacimiento dam, you've gone too far.

Contact: Lake Nacimiento Marina, 805/238-1056 or 805/238-0786; Lake Nacimiento Resort, 800/323-3839 or 800/323-3839, www.nacimientoresort.com.

9 WHALE ROCK RESERVOIR

Rating: 2

near Cayucos

Map 12.2, page 558

Whale Rock Reservoir is a unique place that provides a unique fishery. At one time the water from here flowed to the sea. The lake now covers nearly 600 acres and is just a mile from the Pacific Ocean. When the dam was built here, apparently some steelhead were trapped in the lake, and the descendants of these fish still spawn in the feeder streams when flows are sufficient in winter. That makes this lake one of the few in California with landlocked steelhead. Steelhead are also stocked here sporadically and the lake also has catfish and bluegill.

The lake is open from late April–mid-November, Wednesday through Sunday, and all federal holidays.

The fishing does not come easy, nor does access. In addition to the no-boating law, most of the lake's shoreline is off-limits because it's private property. Fishing pressure is light, and so are the catches. Boaters need not apply, and the same holds true for any angler who wants to have an easy go at it.

Facilities, fees: Pit toilets and picnic tables are available, but drinking water is not. A campground is at Morro Bay. Supplies can be obtained in Morro Bay or Cayucos. No boating or water-body contact is permitted at the reservoir. A day-use fee is charged.

Directions: From San Luis Obispo, take Highway 1 north to Morro Bay and continue north for about five miles (just south of the town of Cayucos) to Old Creek Mountain Road. Turn right (east) and drive two miles to the access gate. Park and walk 100 feet to the reservoir.

Contact: Whale Rock Reservoir, 805/995-3701; City of San Luis Obispo, Parks and Recreation, 805/781-7300, www.slocity.org/parksandrecreation.

10 ATASCADERO LAKE

Rating: 4

north of San Luis Obispo in Atascadero Memorial Park

Map 12.2, page 558

This 30-acre lake is the centerpiece of a nice city park that provides a variety of activities. Most folks do just fine bait dunking from the shoreline. In summer months, the lake has some small bass and bluegill, catfish and carp. There is no boat launch, and there are no gas motors, so get your ambitions in focus: this is a pleasant little park, not an angler's paradise. A 5-mph speed limit is strictly enforced. The DFG once stocked trout here. No more—adios.

Facilities, fees: Restrooms, a café, and pedal-boat and kayak rentals are available. A zoo is nearby. Gas motors and swimming are not permitted. Fishing access is free.

Directions: From San Luis Obispo, take U.S. 101 north to Atascadero and the Morro Road/Highway 41 exit. Take that exit onto El Camino Real. Drive a short distance to the stoplight at Morro Road. Turn left on Morro Road and drive 1.5 miles to the park entrance, on the left.

Contact: City of Atascadero, Parks and Recreation Department, 805/461-5000.

11 SANTA MARGARITA LAKE

Rating: 7

east of San Luis Obispo
Map 12.2, page 558

When anglers go to fishing heaven, it is assumed there will be no water-skiers there. Well, Santa Margarita Lake brings a little bit of heaven to earth by not allowing waterskiing or any other sports that involve body/water contact.

Santa Margarita Lake should have a sign at its entrance that proclaims, "Fishing Only!" The excellent prospects for bass fishing, along with the prohibitive rules, make this lake a favorite among anglers.

The lake has a fair fishery for a variety of species. As the lake warms up in spring, the fishing is converted over for largemouth bass, bluegill, catfish, and crappie. A very few striped bass are also in these waters; every once in a while, someone hooks a big one and loses all their line. Whoo-ya! In a non-whoo-ya moment, the DFG has stopped all trout stocks. Fishing for largemouth has improved enough for know-hows to put this lake on their must-do list.

The lake covers nearly 800 acres, most of it long and narrow. It is in a dammed-up valley in the foothill country at an elevation of 1,300 feet, just below the Santa Lucia Mountains, and is five miles southeast of the town of Santa Margarita. It is fed by the Salinas River.

Boaters with craft under 10 feet long or with inflatables must get approval prior to launching. Float tubes are allowed, providing the user wears waders. In April, a kids' fishing jamboree is held.

Note: All boats must be inspected and certified free of mussels prior to launching at this lake.

Facilities, fees: A paved boat ramp is on the southwest shore and another ramp is on the south shore. Several campgrounds are in the park. Picnic areas, a full-service marina, and a convenience store are available. Fishing boats, kayaks, canoes, and pontoon boats can be rented. No water-body contact is permitted. The speed limit is 30 mph. Day-use and boat-launch fees are charged.

Directions: From San Luis Obispo, take U.S. 101 north for eight miles to the Highway 58/Santa Margarita exit. Take that exit and drive through the town of Santa Margarita to Entrada. Turn right on Entrada and drive seven miles (Entrada becomes Pozo Road) to Santa Margarita Lake Road. Turn left and drive to the lake.

Contact: Santa Margarita Lake Recreation Area, 805/788-2397, www.slocountyparks.org; Santa Margarita Lake Marina, 805/438-1522.

12 LOPEZ LAKE

Rating: 8

east of San Luis Obispo
Map 12.2, page 558

Lopez provides one of the more consistent fisheries in central California. The lake has three major arms: the Arroyo Grande Creek arm, the Wittenberg Creek arm, and the Lopez arm. All are worth exploring for crappie and especially bass. The best areas are up the two main creek arms, where shad and crawdads get the bass feeding. Summer evenings are quite good, often with surface bites in the coves along the lake arms.

At 940 acres and 22 miles of shoreline when full, Lopez is a decent-sized lake, and there are plenty of times when the wind is down and the fishing is up. The lake is set amid oak woodlands and is shaped somewhat like a horseshoe. In the spring, this isn't the lake for any boat that can't handle wind. Why? You guessed it: spring is very windy here, especially in the afternoon in the main channel and Wittenberg arm, making it great for windsurfers and sailboaters but lousy for fishing. You can avoid the wind in the Arroyo Grande or Lopez arm.

Another bonus is Lopez Lake's proximity to the coast, which keeps the lake colder than reservoirs farther inland, making it hospitable to cool water–loving smallmouth bass as well. The crappie can also provide good fishing in late winter. Even though you pay for them, the DFG has stopped all the trout stocks.

As winter merges into early spring, bass come on strong, best for dropshotters. It stays good for bass through May. When summer arrives, this lake gets hot, and that is when the bluegill and catfish get active.

Lopez Lake has become an example of how to do something right. Special marked areas are set aside exclusively for waterskiing, personal-watercraft riding, and windsurfing, and the rest of the lake is designated for fishing and low-speed boating. There are also reserved areas for swimming. That makes it perfect for just about everyone, and, with good bass fishing, the lake has become very popular, especially on spring weekends when the bite is on.

A 25-mile trail system provides opportunities for biking, hiking, and horseback riding. There are also full facilities for swimming, with a big swimming beach, two giant water slides, and a children's wading pool. A nice picnic area is also provided. Scenic boat tours, available on Saturday, are a bonus.

Note: All boats must be inspected and certified free of mussels prior to launching at this lake.

Facilities, fees: A campground, restroom with showers, a full-service marina, mooring, a paved boat ramp, gas, coin laundry, a snack bar, and a convenience store are available. Fishing boats, ski boats, kayaks, and pontoon boats can be rented at Lopez Lake Marina. The speed limit is 40 mph. Day-use and boat-launch fees are charged.

Directions: Take U.S. 101 to Arroyo Grande and the exit for Grand Avenue. Take that exit, turn east, and drive through Arroyo Grande to Lopez Drive. Turn northeast on Lopez Drive and drive 10 miles to the park.

Contact: Lopez Lake Recreation Area, 805/788-2381, www.slocountyparks.org; Lopez Lake Marina, 805/489-1006.

13 OSO FLACO LAKE AND LITTLE OSO FLACO LAKE

Rating: 4

in the Oceano Dunes State
Vehicular Recreation Area
Map 12.2, page 558

If you have this book in your hands because you want to find easy-to-reach lakes for small bass that almost nobody knows about, then Oso Flaco and Little Oso Flaco qualify to be on your list. These two lakes are set in the middle of sand dunes at Oceano Dunes. Even though they're just a few miles from U.S. 101, literally millions of tourists pass right on by with nary a notion of their existence. Only the locals seem to fish here, catching bass from the shore during the warmer months.

The lakes cover 110 acres, and because they are within a mile of the ocean, they remain fairly cool year-round. This is the kind of place where you fish from the shore, hiking around the lakes (a three-mile trip). The fishing is fair, mostly for small bass, but remember, every pond has a king. It's all catch-and-release.

A boardwalk goes across the lake, and fishing is allowed from all points off the boardwalk. If the fish don't bite, you can try clamming on the ocean side of the dunes. An option: Nearby Pismo State Beach offers surf fishing and wheelchair-accessible lagoon fishing without the vehicle noise.

Facilities, fees: No boat-launch or other facilities are on-site. A campground with vault toilets is at Oceano Dunes SVRA, and supplies can be obtained in Arroyo Grande. A day-use fee is charged.

Directions: From Arroyo Grande (about 16 miles south of San Luis Obispo), take Highway 1 south and drive 9.5 miles to Oso Flaco Lake Road. Turn west and drive three miles to the parking area. A short hike is required to reach the lakes.

Contact: Oceano Dunes State Vehicular Recreation Area, 805/773-7170, www.slostateparks .com or www.parks.ca.gov; Oceano Campground, Pismo State Beach, 805/489-1869, or ranger station, 805/473-7220; The Outdoorsman, Grover City, 805/473-2484; The Guadalupe-Nipomo Dunes Center, 805/343-2455, www.dunescenter.org.

🔢 GAVIOTA BEACH

Rating: 7

north of Santa Barbara
Map 12.3, page 559

Whether you're fishing from the beach or by boat, this is an outstanding stretch of coast. A wide array of species is available, and various methods can be used. From Gaviota Beach on east to El Capitan State Beach, 10 miles of coast provide good surf fishing.

The biggest fish are halibut, which arrive within range in the spring, and the most abundant are surf perch and barred perch, which are best in the fall and winter. The rocky areas have kelp bass, sand bass, and some rockfish. The stretch of coast from El Capitan State Beach and Tajiguas in the south to the Hollister Ranch and Cojo Point (Point Conception) in the north is usually solid for calico bass and can be excellent at times for white seabass and halibut.

If you have a boat, you have access to some prime territory. Kelp beds along the inshore coast attract a number of species of bass (and less frequently, halibut and sometimes even white seabass). If your boat is fast and stable, you can roam way out to San Miguel Island, Santa Cruz Island, north to Point Conception, or even around the corner to Point Arguello. In the area, there are also some seamounts that are identified on ocean charts (always carry a chart); lingcod and rockfish numbers are quite good at these places.

The one problem if you have a boat is using the hoist. It comes with a hook, but that's it, which means you must supply your own strap or ANSI-approved sling. In addition, no driving is permitted on the pier, so boats have to be "walked" to the hoist. That means boats in the 17- to 22-foot class need a transport dolly,

and smaller, lighter boats on trailers must be pulled along by hand. All these conditions keep most boaters away, but if you are willing to put up with the difficulty, you get access to a prime piece of coast.

The hoist is open only to boaters with key cards and certification. It is rated at two tons; it can be used from 7 A.M. to one hour before sunset.

Note that fishing regulations often change here from year to year, for seasons, depth restrictions, bag limits, size limits, and even annual quotas for the fleet. Always check current regulations with Fish and Game or with a marina or party-boat operator before planning a trip.

Facilities, fees: A pier, a campground, and a boat hoist are available. Restrooms, drinking water, flush toilets, and coin showers are at the campground. A convenience store (open summer only) is nearby. The weight limit for boats is two tons, and the length limit is 22 feet. Driving on the pier is not permitted, so boat owners must have their own transport dolly if they can't tow their craft by hand. A day-use fee is charged. There is an additional fee for boat hoisting, and you must provide your own sling.

Directions: From Santa Barbara, drive 33 miles north on U.S. 101 to the Gaviota State Beach exit. Take that exit, turn west, and drive a short distance to the park entrance.

Contact: Gaviota State Park, Channel Coast District, 805/968-1033, www.parks.ca.gov; Goleta Valley Chamber of Commerce, 805/967-2500 or 800/646-5382, www.goleta valley.com.

🔢 SANTA BARBARA OFFSHORE/SAN MIGUEL

Rating: 10

Channel Islands, north of Ventura
Map 12.3, page 559

The wide-open sea is the savior for Southern California residents, and in many ways the

Channel Islands are the savior for anglers. Four islands lie in a row here. From west to east, they are San Miguel, Santa Rosa, Santa Cruz, and Anacapa. Each offers a distinctive habitat and fishery, and each receives a different level of fishing pressure. Together they give the area its unique identity, along with the unusual west-to-east geographical alignment of this stretch of coast. The islands are far enough offshore to provide total separation from the noise of the city, and they provide the marine habitat to support a fishery with its own brand of excitement.

San Miguel Island is the westernmost of the four, stretching seven miles long and three miles wide; it's a long grind of a trip by boat to reach it. The trip is worth the ride, however, for the best shallow-water reds you can imagine as well as prospects of halibut ranging to 40 pounds, sometimes even bigger.

San Miguel gets far less fishing pressure than the other islands. The setting is primarily rocky, with major shoals on the west and north sides. The most productive fishing is for a variety of rockfish and lingcod (best at the reefs on the southern and northwestern side).

Just east of Harris Point at Cuyler Harbor, kelp bass and sometimes halibut and rockfish can be located. White seabass, yellowtail, and sheepshead can also be stars of this show. Bennett Reef and Wescott Shoal are two other good bets. Be sure you are inside a line between 34° 03.5' north latitude 120° 21.3' west longitude and 34° 02.9' north latitude 120° 20.2' west longitude; these are the edges of the Harris Point State Marine Reserve, which is a no-take area. If this is your first visit, make a side trip to the beach on the west end of the island near Point Bennett; there is a huge population of sea lions—so many that it can look as if the beach is paved black.

Facilities, fees: Party-boat charters, campgrounds, lodging, and supplies are in the Santa Barbara area. Live bait is usually for sale next to the sportfishing operation.

Directions: From the south: From Ventura, take U.S. 101 north for 28 miles to Santa Barbara and the Cabrillo Boulevard exit. Take that exit and turn left at the bottom of the off-ramp. Drive west for approximately two miles to Harbor Drive. Turn left onto Harbor Way and drive to the sportfishing operations, on the left.

From the north: Take U.S. 101 south to Santa Barbara and the Castillo Street exit. Take that exit, turn right on Castillo Street, and drive to Cabrillo Boulevard. Turn right and drive to Harbor Drive. Turn left onto Harbor Way and drive to the sportfishing operations, on the left.

Contact: Sea Landing, 805/963-3564, www.sealanding.net; WaveWalker Fishing Charters, 805/964-2046, www.wavewalker.com; Stearn's Wharf Bait and Tackle, 805/965-1333, www.stearnswharfbaitandtackle.com; Hook Line & Sinker, 805/687-5689; Santa Barbara Harbor Master, 805/564-5531, www.santabarbaraca.gov; Santa Barbara Conference and Visitors Bureau, 805/966-9222.

16 GOLETA PIER

Rating: 7

north of Santa Barbara

Map 12.4, page 560

This pier and the adjacent beach area are symbolic of much of the quality fishing that nonboaters can take advantage of in Southern California. This particular stretch of water attracts good numbers of perch, both barred and walleye, and they can be caught in decent numbers from the Goleta Pier. In the spring, though halibut are rarely caught at the pier, the chance of hooking one will always be in the back of your mind.

Boaters who use the hoist at the pier can make short trips to inshore kelp beds, then fish on the edges of them. The hoist is available for public use on weekends and most holidays 7 A.M.–4 P.M.

Summers are good here, with mackerel, the rare barracuda, and sometimes even a white seabass swimming through and joining the infrequent rockfish and sheepshead. A lot of people take the small rockfish at the kelp beds for granted. Don't. They add a tremendous dimension to the quality of local sportfishing. This is real plus for kayak fishing.

The halibut fishing in this area is often very good for boaters. Occasionally, one is even caught from the pier. Prospects are nebulous in these waters for calico bass. Some people even fish from float tubes, a rare saltwater opportunity, though most use small boats. This is also a good spot for kayak fishing.

Within reach are the Elwood and Naples reefs, two of the best bass spots, where anglers fish with surface irons or plastic lures. A bonus is that Naples always has lots of barracuda in the summer months.

Facilities, fees: A pier, picnic areas, restrooms, a boat hoist, and a restaurant are available. Frozen bait is for sale at the snack bar at the pier. Supplies are in Goleta. Beach access is free; a fee is charged for use of the boat hoist, and you must provide your own sling.

Directions: From Santa Barbara, take U.S. 101 north to Goleta and Highway 217. Turn west on Highway 217 and head toward the University of California to the Goleta Beach exit. Take that exit, turn left on Sandspit Road, and drive a short distance to the park entrance, on the right.

Contact: Goleta Beach County Park, 805/967-1300, www.sbparks.org.

17 STEARNS WHARF

Rating: 5

in Santa Barbara
Map 12.4, page 560

You watch and you learn. Over the course of time, it's amazing how many different species of fish are caught at Stearns Wharf. Perch? Halibut? Rockfish? Mackerel? They all move through here on a seasonal basis.

The best and most consistent fishing is for perch in the winter and early spring. Many species of perch are caught during this period,

and when the sea is calm and storms infrequent, the perch seem to move in along the pier pilings in large numbers. In the summer, mackerel can be even more abundant. There is no middle ground: they arrive in hordes or they don't show at all.

When they do show, anybody with a bait on a hook has a good chance of getting a bucketful. When that occurs, they are so common that the entire affair is just taken for granted. Not so with halibut, which provide a long shot in late spring and early summer. They are always treated as the king of the piers. A sprinkling of small rockfish, jacksmelt, and croakers are also caught during the summer. There are also rare visits of salmon in the early spring.

Facilities, fees: A pier, restrooms, fish-cleaning tables, benches, and bait are available. A boat launch is nearby. A passenger loading ramp on the wharf can be arranged for use by calling the Santa Barbara Harbor Patrol (see *Contact*). There is a parking fee.

Directions: From Ventura, take U.S. 101 north to Santa Barbara the exit for Cabrillo Boulevard. Exit left on Cabrillo Boulevard. Drive west on Cabrillo for two miles to the wharf.

Contact: Stearn's Wharf Bait and Tackle, 805/965-1333, www.stearnswharfbaitandtackle.com; Santa Barbara Harbor Master, 805/564-5531, www.santabarbaraca.gov; Santa Barbara Conference and Visitors Bureau, 805/966-9222.

18 SANTA BARBARA INSHORE

Rating: 9

offshore Santa Barbara
Map 12.4, page 560

The unique stretch of coast along Santa Barbara is characterized by dense kelp forests, oil platform drilling rigs, and the offshore Channel Islands.

The half-day boats out of Santa Barbara usually work One Mile Reef, Camby's Kelp, and spots off Carpinteria for bass, halibut, bonito, barracuda, rockfish, and white seabass. Boats that stay out longer head all the way up to Point Conception and usually have the area to themselves, fishing for bass at Elwood, Devereaux, and Naples.

A key to the Carpinteria area is that fishing for white seabass has been improving since cutbacks on commercial fishing. All the kelp and reef areas favored for bass are also getting good numbers of croaker and barracuda in the 10- to 12-pound class.

The kelp beds provide outstanding marine habitat for a variety of species. The best area is just west of Santa Barbara. It is here where many species can be caught, with rockfish, kelp bass, and cabezon being the most common. Although these fish tend not to be large, they are often abundant. This is why the kelp forests provide an excellent destination, especially for parents who want to introduce their children to marine fishing. My first ocean-fishing trips were as a 10-year-old out to the kelp beds, and these trips produced some of the first feelings of real success I can remember. Another advantage to fishing around kelp is that light tackle can be employed to get a lot of sizzle out of even rockfish. It is becoming popular to use gear designed for freshwater fishing, casting jigs as if you were fishing for largemouth bass in lakes but instead catching ocean-tough rockfish. I've burned up a couple of reels designed for largemouth bass in lakes doing this.

There are other options. The sandy-bottomed areas attract good numbers of halibut along the coast from El Capitan State Beach on westward to the vicinity of Gaviota State Park. In summer, bonito and yellowtail also arrive in the vicinity. These migratory fish are nomads whose location year to year can't be predicted with any degree of precision. The oil platforms are often good spots for calico bass, barracuda, and sometimes yellowtail.

Don't drive a boat in the dark here if you aren't up to speed on offshore construction. Cables used to secure structures are often not lit. If you own your own boat or are new to the area, it is advisable to have a global positioning system (GPS) to assist in navigation. In fog without a GPS or radar, you can easily head off course. For the most part, boaters do not get lost, and the Santa Barbara area provides an outstanding fishery.

Note: It is often foggy out here in the summer months.

Facilities, fees: Party-boat charters, campgrounds, lodging, and supplies are in the Santa Barbara area. Sea Landing has slip rentals, live bait, tackle store, and boat fuel.

Directions: From the south: From Ventura, take U.S. 101 north for 28 miles to Santa Barbara and the Cabrillo Boulevard exit. Take that exit and turn left at the bottom of the off-ramp. Drive west for approximately two miles to Harbor Drive. Turn left onto Harbor Way and drive to the sportfishing operations, on the left.

From the north: Take U.S. 101 south to Santa Barbara and the Castillo Street exit. Take that exit, turn right on Castillo Street, and drive to Cabrillo Boulevard. Turn right and drive to Harbor Drive. Turn left onto Harbor Way and drive to the sportfishing operations, on the left.

Contact: Sea Landing, 805/963-3564, www .sealanding.net; WaveWalker Fishing Charters, 805/964-2046, www.wavewalker.com; Stearn's Wharf Bait and Tackle, 805/965-1333, www.stearnswharfbaitandtackle.com; Hook Line & Sinker, 805/687-5689; Santa Barbara Harbor Master, 805/564-5531, www .santabarbaraca.gov; Santa Barbara Conference and Visitors Bureau, 805/966-9222.

19 VENTURA DEEP SEA/ CHANNEL ISLANDS

Rating: 8

at Ventura Harbor north of Los Angeles

Map 12.4, page 560   BEST (

From land, the sea looks just like a broad, flat expanse of nothingness, something nice for the sun to set into each evening. The Channel Islands in general have been outstanding for barracuda, especially during warm-water years. They may not be quite as consistently productive as the Coronados Islands farther south, but they are hands down the finest fish habitat this side of the border.

Santa Rosa Island is not only big, but getting there requires a long trip. This combination means that anglers must have a clear plan of attack. What do you want? Halibut? Rockfish? Maybe a chance at landing a big bluefin tuna in the late summer? Each significant fishing area offers something a little different. The northwest end between Sandy Point and Brockway Point is a good example; the shoreline and sea bottom are quite rocky and hold large numbers of rockfish, lingcod, sheepshead, and occasionally white seabass. The southwest end in the vicinity of Bee Rock is similar, harboring significant numbers of rockfish and some kelp bass. If you want halibut, there are several excellent spots to try, including the southeast side of Bechers Bay. These are among the better places for halibut anywhere in the Channel Islands. Another good halibut area is on the southeastern side of the island, just west of East Point. When varieties of tuna start roaming throughout the area, they often use the Santa Cruz Channel around the southeastern side of the island as a gateway. The Gap, the fertile area between the two islands, is a great spot for rockfish. Or try Talcott Shoal, and don't overlook Ford Point.

Santa Cruz Island is the biggest of the four Channel Islands, and its proximity to the coast makes it a much more popular destination than the other islands here. When the wind is down, there is good rock fishing nearly all along the northern shore, best in the vicinity of Double Point and Arch Rock and near the reefs between those island points. When the wind is up, boaters instead duck to the southeast side to get protection from the north wind and also to get decent rock fishing.

Other decent spots at Santa Cruz are Chinese Harbor, Prisoners Harbor, Willows, Yellow Banks, Alberts, and Platts. The bonus appeal here is for bonito, yellowtail, and occasionally larger tuna, which sometimes roam in schools on the southeast side of the island, as well as in the Santa Cruz Channel (near Santa Rosa Island to the west). Some years the tuna show, some years they don't. Keep tuned in, and when they show, don't miss out.

The days are gone when skipper Gordy Starr, a legend among the old-timers, could run his charter boat out to Santa Cruz Island and catch a dozen or more black seabass. The Fish and Game Department now prohibits anglers from taking these giants, but you might get lucky and experience the thrill of seeing one come up and roll on the surface to try for the hooked fish you are winding in. Look for blacks at Blue Banks or Bowen, at the Aquarium at Anacapa Island, or at Santa Barbara Island. In addition, there has been some great action for white seabass, both in early summer and fall, using live squid around the west end of Santa Cruz Island and the east end of Santa Rosa Island.

The Ventura Flats are a spawning ground for sand bass, and they have developed into an excellent fishery. The Flats are known for attracting halibut in the summer and sometimes salmon in the spring. The sea bottom here is a sand-and-mud mix, perfect for halibut. One problem has been commercial netting, which tends to crop the larger halibut out of the picture. As inshore net bans are implemented, this is one area that stands to make prominent gains. It is not fished as heavily as many other areas of the Southern California coast, primarily because locating large concentrations of halibut over such an expansive area can be difficult. But those who keep tuned in to the week-to-week movements of halibut can do well here. Some years bonito even move through the Ventura Flats in the summer; barracuda and white seabass are seen less frequently.

To the north, Rincon Reef provides an outstanding destination for rockfish. Another option is the oil rigs, which attract baitfish and in turn are like a magnet for salmon in the spring and barracuda in the summer.

Vast kelp forests in a few inshore areas north of Ventura provide good fishing, holding a variety of small rockfish and kelp bass. They are just south of Point Pitas to Point Dume.

Whenever you fish the ocean, remember to look at the sea as if you were a fish, not a person. You don't need to sprout a set of gills, but you will certainly have better prospects.

Facilities, fees: Charter boats, boat rentals, bait, tackle, a full-service marina, launch ramp, campgrounds, lodging, and supplies are in and near Ventura.

Directions: Take U.S. 101 to Ventura and the Seaward exit. Take the Seaward exit, turn west, and drive to Harbor Boulevard. Turn left (south) and drive 1.5 miles to Spinnaker Street. Turn right and continue to Entrance No. 2. The sportfishing office is adjacent the parking lot.

Contact: Ventura Sportfishing, 805/676-3474, www.venturasportfishing.com; Ventura Boat Rentals, 805/642-7753, www.venturaboatrentals.com; Eric's Tackle Shop, 805/648-5665, www.ericstackle.blogspot.com; Fisherman's Supply, 805/642-2522; West Marine, 806/654-8233, www.westmarine.com; Ventura Harbor, 805/642-8538 or 877/894-2726, venturaharbor.com; Ventura Visitors and Convention Bureau, 805/648-2075 or 800/483-6214, www.ventura-usa.com.

20 VENTURA PIER

Rating: 5

in Ventura near San Buenaventura State Beach

Map 12.4, page 560

The pier at this state beach is on the edge of some good halibut grounds, the Ventura Flats. Halibut often move inshore within range of the pier anglers here during high tides, with the bite best at the top of the tide, then the first few hours of the outgoing tide. This occurs in the spring and early summer. The pier also provides a decent fishery for perch, best in the

winter and early spring. In fact, the shore from Pier Point Bay on south to Emma K. Wood State Beach can provide good surf fishing for perch and corbina.

Facilities, fees: Restrooms and fish-cleaning sinks are provided. A campground, a restaurant, and picnic areas are nearby. A parking fee is charged. The pier is open 24/7.

Directions: Take U.S. 101 to Ventura and the exit for California Street. Take the California Street exit. Turn left and continue one block to Harbor Boulevard. Turn left on Harbor Boulevard and drive past the pier to the park entrance station and parking area.

Contact: City of Ventura, Parks Division, 805/652-4550; San Buenaventura State Beach, 805/968-1033, www.parks.ca.gov; Emma Wood State Beach, 805/968-1033; Eric's Tackle Shop, 805/648-5665, www.ericstackle.blogspot.com; West Marine, 806/654-8233, www.westmarine.com.

21 PORT HUENEME PIER

Rating: 4

near Oxnard inside Port Hueneme Beach Park

Map 12.4, page 560

Most of the fish come and go with the seasons. Perch are best in the winter, halibut in the late winter and spring, and bonito, barracuda, and shark in the fall and early winter. The summer season is only fair, with some resident kelp bass in the area. Results can be decent for periods of two to three weeks at a time, then suddenly it's a complete dud. Then the telephone becomes your most important piece of fishing equipment. That and the correct pronunciation of "Hueneme."

It's "wy-NEE-mee," of course.

Facilities, fees: Restrooms, lights, benches, fish-cleaning stations, bait and tackle, and a snack bar are available. A parking fee is charged.

Directions: From Ventura drive south on Highway 1 to the city of Oxnard and Hueneme Road. Turn right on Hueneme Road and drive west to Ventura Road. Turn left and drive to Surfside Drive. Turn left and drive to Port Hueneme Beach Park.

Contact: Port Hueneme Beach Park, 805/986-6542, www.ci.port-hueneme.ca.us.

22 OXNARD-PORT HUENEME DEEP SEA/ ANACAPA ISLAND

Rating: 9

offshore of Oxnard-Port Hueneme
Map 12.4, page 560

Directly offshore of Port Hueneme is the Hueneme Canyon, a massive underwater gorge that drops quickly to never-never land. North of the canyon, just offshore of Ventura, are the Ventura Flats, and just 15 miles west are the tops of an undersea mountain range, the Anacapa Islands. Of the four Channel Islands in a row here, Santa Cruz and Anacapa are fished the most extensively because of their proximity to ports, and also because of the more severe weather conditions that affect San Miguel and Santa Rosa Islands. Of course, the MLPA has closed large areas to fishing. For yellowtail, Anacapa has been the most consistent producer in the fall.

Anacapa Island once really got hammered by anglers, as you might expect, but no more because of all the closures. After all, it's a relatively short cruise out here during a calm sea, and there are decent numbers of a large variety of fish. The best fishing tends to be at either end of the island on the southern, leeward side. The southwest end requires a longer trip out but has better fishing, with kelp bass, sheepshead, rockfish, barracuda (less frequently, in the summer months), and, if the gods are smiling, yellowtail. Don't count on the latter, though. If you pull up at Arch Rock, the first land you come to on the eastern side, small rockfish hold on the bottom, which isn't enough to put on the brakes. What is enough, however, is that barracuda and yellowtail roam through this area. It can happen. Cat Rock, Fish Camp, and the Aquarium are excellent places to start

an adventure that could lead you to kelp bass, halibut, white seabass, and yellowtail.

Other options when fishing from Oxnard-Port Hueneme are the sunken cruise ship *La Jenelle,* Harrison's Banks, and the Deep Hole down the coast, famous for its kelp and sand-bass fishing spiced by frequent appearances by yellowtail and white seabass.

White seabass are on a big-time upswing, and a red-hot white bite can get the adrenaline pumping and make an old man feel young. These big croakers have neither the speed of a tuna nor the power of a yellowtail, but they have a pure cussedness when it comes to trying to bring them to the boat. Might as well try to drag up one of those reef-building auto bodies if you hook it. Worse, they are so delicious, their meat so firm and white, that losing one is like losing the winning lottery ticket. In some ways, white seabass are like your cat. Today they love you, can't get enough of your attention, and whatever you put in front of them they will eat. Tomorrow, not. They like a white lure that flutters. An angler willing to yo-yo a lure will probably outfish his or her buddies. To yo-yo, drop the lure to the bottom, take all the slack out of the line, then raise and lower the rod just as you would raise and lower your hand when working a yo-yo. Be alert for the wily white that hits the lure on the sink.

When schools of barracuda show up, anglers can hone their lure-casting skills. Barries will snap at lures, be they white feathers on lead heads or metal lures in a variety of colors. In bright sunshine, the best color combination is yellow and chrome, suggesting that barracuda are quite as cannibalistic as they look. Whatever the color of your fingers, care should be taken when working near the toothy mouth of a barracuda.

Facilities, fees: Party-boat charters, bait, bait receivers (with live anchovies, sardines, or squid), and tackle are at both harbors. A boat ramp, a boat hoist, and boat rentals can be found at Channel Islands Harbor. Full facilities are in Ventura and Oxnard. Party-boat fees are charged per person. A boat ramp, a boat hoist, and boat rentals can be found at

Channel Islands Harbor. Full facilities are in Ventura and Oxnard.

Directions: To Channel Islands Harbor and CISCO Sportfishing: From Santa Barbara, take U.S. 101 south to the Victoria Avenue exit. Take that exit and continue to Victoria Avenue at the end of the off-ramp. Turn right (south) on Victoria Avenue and drive 5.5 miles to Channel Islands Boulevard. Stay on Victoria Avenue for another 0.8 mile to the harbor and the sportfishing operations. Party boats that run excursions to the islands are available here.

To Channel Islands Harbor and Captain Hook's Sportfishing: From Santa Barbara, take U.S. 101 south to the Victoria Avenue exit. Take that exit and continue to Victoria Avenue at the end of the off-ramp. Turn right (south) on Victoria Avenue and drive 5.5 miles to Channel Islands Boulevard. Turn right on Channel Islands Boulevard and drive to Harbor Way. Turn left on Harbor Way and drive a short distance to Captain Hook's Sportfishing on the left.

To Port Hueneme Harbor: From Ventura, take Highway 1 south to Oxnard and Hueneme Road. Turn right on Hueneme Road and drive west to Ventura Road. Turn left and follow the signs to the beach.

Contact: Hook's Landing, 805/382-6233, www.corolomasportfishing.com; CISCO Sportfishing, 805/382-1612, www.channelislandssportfishing.com; Channel Islands National Park Visitors Center, 805/658-5730, www.nps.gov/chis.

23 CACHUMA LAKE

Rating: 10

north of Santa Barbara
Map 12.4, page 560

Cachuma has become one of the hottest bass lakes going in California, for both largemouth and smallmouth bass. Though the lake has never been officially planted with Florida bass, they show up, too. These secret plants have resulted in some giant catches.

When Cachuma Lake is full, you are apt to think you have come upon an angler's paradise, and maybe you have. Several lake arms with protected coves hold bass, trout plants are abundant, and, best of all, waterskiing and personal watercraft riding are not permitted. Cachuma is at an elevation of 750 feet, in the foothills east of Santa Ynez. When full it covers 3,200 acres of what appears to be an abundance of bass habitat. All manner of aquatic vegetation, stickups, shaded coves, rocky points, and drop-offs should make for large numbers of big bass. The lake-record largemouth bass is 16 pounds, 7 ounces, which shows what is possible.

Very little water recreation is permitted, because this is a reservoir used to store drinking water. So no waterskiing, personal-watercraft riding, swimming, or sailboarding is allowed. Canoes and kayaks are prohibited from the lake, as are boats under 10 feet long. That leaves it all to the fishing boats, and with a speed limit of 5 mph in the coves, 10 mph elsewhere, and 40 mph in the center of the lake, it's the perfect setup for high-speed bass boats.

Since a lot of good-looking spots don't have bass, you need to cover a lot of water to be successful. Anglers using bass boats with electric motors have a tremendous advantage. The best spots to start are around Arrowhead Island, Cachuma Bay, Jackrabbit Flat, and the Narrows, where catch rates are highest. Few of the truly big bass can be found at such spots, however. They prefer to stay down, 15–20 feet deep, often suspended next to drop-offs. In March, pulling these bass out requires substantial effort on the part of anglers. Most folks catch a few of the smaller bass, figure they'll do better next time, and only very rarely get one over five pounds. The lake also has smallmouth bass, and they are growing in numbers and opportunity. The ends of the dam are the best bets.

This lake gets hit pretty hard by quality anglers, so count on needing your best game. It's likely you are casting to a bass that has already snubbed another angler's offering.

Cachuma could be a consistent producer of giant bass. For one thing, the food supply is excellent. The lake is stocked with catchable-size trout by the Department of Fish and Game and the county. It is one of the most heavily stocked lakes in California relative to its size. The trout are like growing pills for the big bass. But those trout also provide a good fishery. Stocks are made from October through April. Shore fishing for trout is decent enough from the campground area near the boat ramp when the water is cool, and standard trolling techniques do fine, especially in late spring.

Note: All boats must be inspected and certified free of mussels prior to launching at this lake.

Facilities, fees: Three boat ramps are on the south shore. A campground, yurts, cabins, boat fuel, boat rentals, coin laundry, picnic areas, bait, tackle, restrooms with flush toilets, and showers are available. Lake tours are given year-round. A playground, a general store, propane gas, a swimming pool, bicycle rentals, ice, and a snack bar are nearby. Watercraft under 10 feet are prohibited, and inflatables must be at least 12 feet long. The speed limit is 40 mph in the middle of the lake, 10 mph elsewhere, and 5 mph in the coves. No waterbody contact is allowed. Day-use and boat-launch fees are charged.

Directions: From Santa Barbara, drive north on Highway 154 for 20 miles to the lake.

Contact: Cachuma Lake Recreation Area, Santa Barbara County, 805/686-5054, www .cachuma.com; Cachuma Marina and Boat Rentals, 805/688-4040; Cachuma Boat Tours, 805/686-5050; Hook Line & Sinker, 805/687-5689.

24 REYES CREEK

Rating: 4

north of Ventura in Los Padres National Forest
Map 12.4, page 560

Small Reyes Creek is in the remote Pine Mountain area of Los Padres National Forest.

It is stocked with small rainbow trout in the 10- to 12-inch class from the campground on downstream, but these stocks could be at risk of stopping. This is the kind of trout stream that gets ignored by all but the few people who know the area, yet it can provide a good weekend adventure. The stream could be reduced to a trickle in the summer and fall, so if you come to fish, plan your trip for spring or early summer. Several trails in the area offer options for side trips. Sespe Creek and the North Fork Ventura River to the south, along Highway 33, are nearby alternatives for anglers, but they get far more attention.

DFG requires artificials with barbless hooks. There is a two-fish limit for landlocked steelhead.

Facilities, fees: A campground with pit toilets and a horse corral is available, but drinking water is not. Garbage must be packed out. A small seasonal store, bar, and café are nearby. Supplies can be obtained in Ojai. A daily fee per parked vehicle is required. An annual pass may be purchased.

Directions: From Ojai, take Highway 33 north for 36 miles to Lockwood Valley Road. Turn right on Lockwood Valley Road (Ozena Road) and drive about 3.5 miles to Forest Road 7N11. Turn right and drive about 1.5 miles to the village of Camp Scheideck.

Contact: Los Padres National Forest, Mount Pinos Ranger District, 661/245-3731, www .fs.usda.gov.

25 LAKE CASITAS

Rating: 9

north of Ventura
Map 12.4, page 560

Lake Casitas is known as one of Southern California's world-class fish factories, with more 10-pound bass produced here than anywhere else. The ideal climate in the foothill country gives the fish a nine-month growing season, in addition to providing excellent weather for camping. Casitas (elevation 285 feet) is north of Ventura, in the foothills bordering Los Padres National Forest. Covering 2,700 acres, the lake has 32 miles of shoreline and a huge number of sheltered coves.

Casitas is managed primarily for anglers. Waterskiing, personal watercraft riding, and swimming are not permitted, and only boats between 11 and 25 feet are allowed on the lake, except by special permit. The speed limit is 35 mph except in designated areas, where it is 15 mph. Coves have a speed limit of 5 mph, and near the marina the limit is 3 mph. These restrictions are very similar to those at Cachuma Lake.

It was at Lake Casitas where Ray Easley caught the lake-record 21-pound, 3-ounce largemouth bass that first attracted world attention to Southern California bass lakes. It was also at Casitas where a crawdad I planned to use to catch an even bigger bass clamped onto one of my fingers. I had one response to that: "Yeeeeeeeeow!"

Most of the shockwaves here are caused by fish, however, not finger-grabbing crawdads. Casitas has always been loaded with crawdads, perfect for growing big bass, and perfect as well for bait. But take note that fishing techniques continue to be revolutionized here in the pursuit of giant bass. The big wood plugs (such as Huddleston, Castaic Trout, Stocker Trout, Osprey, and the AC Plug) have become as popular as using crawdads. With the two-rod rule, the best bet is to have a crawdad out for bait while casting with a trout swim bait or other lure.

A lot of people figured Casitas would dominate the world's line-class bass records, but it hasn't worked out that way; Castaic Lake has that honor. Regardless, lots of big bass are caught at Casitas, so many that it takes a 10-pounder to raise any eyebrows. Casitas also has big redear sunfish, crappie, and catfish. It was a former state record–holder for the largest catfish and bass ever caught, and it still holds the record for redear sunfish (3 pounds, 7 ounces). The shad population is huge here, and shad are often used for bait.

With all the bass habitat, you can get confused as to where to start your search. Simplify your mission by starting along the eastern shore, the lake's most productive stretch of water. If you want big bass, crawdads are a must, and so is a lot of time on the water, with plenty of dud days. If you want a higher catch rate but smaller fish, wait until the water has warmed up to 63–64°F, when shad move into the shallows. Then fan the shoreline with casts with shad-patterned plugs. The clear water and the fishing pressure make low-visibility 6-pound line a must. Anything heavier can spook the bass. As at all lakes, the bass here change their temperament, depth, and feed patterns according to time of year and water temperature. You must follow accordingly.

At Casitas, as at many lakes in Southern California, the large stocks of rainbow trout are a big bonus. They provide not only an alternative fishery, but also food to help the bass grow to giant sizes. Casitas is stocked with trout averaging 10–12 inches, usually in large numbers. Shoreline bait dunking for trout is good right near the campgrounds, especially in the early summer, before the water has heated up too much.

Because of the trout, rumors surface here that anglers are using them illegally as bait for the big bass. One bizarre story from the good ol' days is that a guy believed two anglers in a boat were doing just that to catch a huge stringer of bass. He pulled up in his boat, produced a gun, and demanded to see what bait the two fellows were using. Shocked and frightened, they managed to reel in their lines, whereupon he saw their bait: crawdads. "Sorry about that," he mumbled. One of the problems is that the large swim baits often look like trout.

Note: All boats must be inspected and certified free of mussels prior to launching at this lake.

Facilities, fees: Campgrounds, trailer rentals, two paved boat ramps, a full-service marina, fishing docks, floating restrooms, bait and tackle, slip rentals, a water park, picnic areas, showers, a snack bar, and a convenience store are available. Fishing boats, pedal boats, rowboats, and pontoon boats can be rented at the marina. Craft under 11 feet or over 25 feet are prohibited, except by permit. Fees are charged for day use and camping. Night fishing is permitted on select weekends.

Directions: From Los Angeles, take U.S. 101 north to Ventura and the junction with Highway 33 (at the north end of Ventura). Turn north on Highway 33 and drive 10.5 miles to Highway 150/Baldwin Road. Turn left (west) and drive three miles to Santa Ana Road. Turn left and drive 100 yards to the lake entrance on the right.

From Santa Barbara, drive south on U.S. 101 for 11 miles to Highway 150/Baldwin Road. Turn left (east) and drive three miles to Santa Ana Road. Turn left and drive 100 yards to the lake entrance on the right.

Contact: Lake Casitas Recreation Area, 805/649-2233 or 805/649-1122 (camping reservations), www.casitaswater.org; Lake Casitas Marina, 805/649-2043; Eric's Tackle Shop, 805/648-5665.

LOS ANGELES AND VICINITY

© ERIC BRODER VAN DYKE/123RF.COM

BEST FISHING SPOTS

◖ Saltwater Fisheries
Catalina Island, **page 588.**
Santa Monica/Redondo Deep Sea, **page 589.**

◖ Places to Teach Kids to Fish
Santa Ana River Lakes, **page 606.**
Lake Perris, **page 607.**
Irvine Lake, **page 608.**

The best chance at freedom here is on a boat

in the open water, heading across the sea or a lake, hoping for a fish.

The best fishing is near the many islands along the Southern California coast. It takes just a few minutes on a boat heading out to sea to understand why anglers consider this experience the ultimate freedom. Of course, it's not quite free: Not only can it be expensive, but the Marine Life Protection Act (MLPA) has closed many areas to anglers. The numerous regulations and closures may make you feel like consulting a lawyer in order to fish the ocean, but try the DFG instead before you go, or rely on a professional boat captain from a sportfishing operation.

Catalina Island is simply one of the most spectacular places on the entire Pacific coast. The best fishing for tuna, albacore, yellowtail, and marlin tends to be at Catalina or at nearby offshore locations farther out, so starting out on the island rather than the mainland will save you a long boat ride. Because of the distance and the size of boat required to make it out to the island, Catalina is available to those with time and a pretty good pile of money.

On the mainland, bonito fishing at Redondo can be surprisingly exciting, despite the fact that the fishery is so close to so many people. There is also a series of municipal piers that are more promising than any other public piers along the coast.

As you venture south, you can escape the wall-to-wall people and get at the best thing going – the ocean fishing from San Pedro, Long Beach, Newport, and Dana Point, with prospects at kelp beds, bays, sandy bottoms, reefs, and underwater canyons. These areas collectively hold an amazing array of species, with sheepshead, barracuda, halibut, yellowtail, and all matter of rockfish. In the spring, even salmon is a possible find in the deep canyons, and albacore and tuna can be found in the late summer and fall.

There are also some small lakes that are stocked with large trout during cool weather. Because people are willing to pay a daily fishing permit, lake managers are able to stock 20-pound rainbow trout and 30-pound catfish. You could pay thousands of dollars for trips to Alaska, New Zealand, and elsewhere and not catch trout even remotely close to this size. The biggest fish are at Irvine Lake and Santa Ana River Lakes.

In the national forests and mountains surrounding the Los Angeles Basin, the centerpiece is Big Bear Lake, which is always beautiful. And although it is often crowded on the best weekends, weekdays can be very sane, with little pressure and very good trout fishing.

The adjacent San Bernardino National Forest provides relief for folks in Riverside and San Bernardino, with a beautiful drive (the Rim of the World), great hiking (the Pacific Crest Trail), and a sprinkling of lakes that provide seasonal fishing for bass, trout, and catfish. This region quickly gives way to desert in the east, making the beauty of Big Bear Lake something of a phenomenon in comparison.

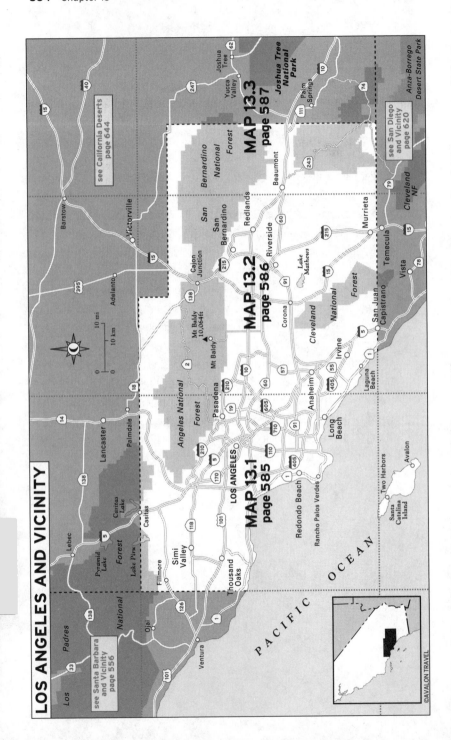

Map 13.1

Sites 1-13
Pages 588-598

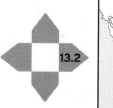

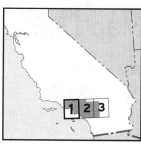

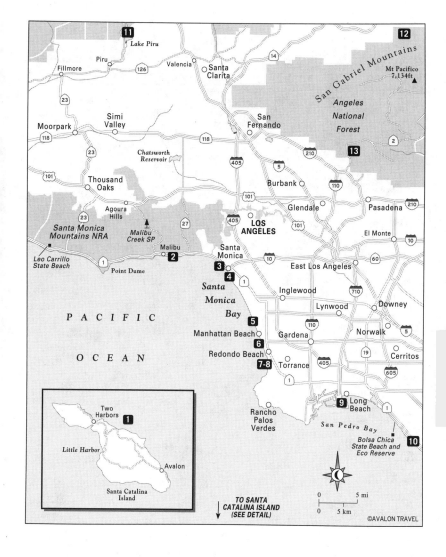

Lake Piru **11**

12

Fillmore
Piru
Valencia
Santa Clarita

126

14

San Gabriel Mountains

Mt Pacifico
7,134ft

23

Moorpark

Simi Valley

118

San Fernando

Angeles National Forest

2

23

Chatsworth Reservoir

118

210

13

101

Thousand Oaks

405

5

Burbank

110

23

Agoura Hills

101

Glendale

Pasadena

210

Santa Monica Mountains NRA

Malibu Creek SP

27

405

LOS ANGELES

101

El Monte

10

Leo Carrillo State Beach

1

Point Dume

Malibu

2

Santa Monica

3

10

East Los Angeles

60

4

1

Inglewood

710

Santa Monica Bay

Lynwood

Downey

5

110

Norwalk

5

Manhattan Beach

Gardena

6

Redondo Beach

19

Cerritos

7-8

Torrance

405

1

605

PACIFIC

OCEAN

9

Long Beach

1

Rancho Palos Verdes

San Pedro Bay

Bolsa Chica State Beach and Eco Reserve

10

Two Harbors

1

Little Harbor

Avalon

Santa Catalina Island

TO SANTA CATALINA ISLAND (SEE DETAIL)

0   5 mi

0   5 km

©AVALON TRAVEL

Map 13.2

Sites 14-38
Pages 598-611

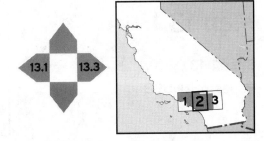

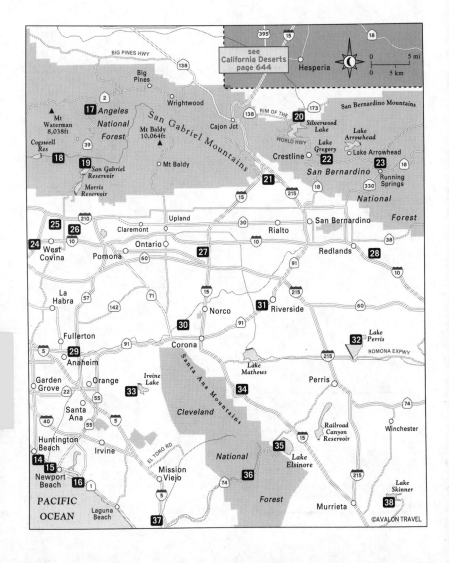

Map 13.3

Sites 39-44
Pages 612-616

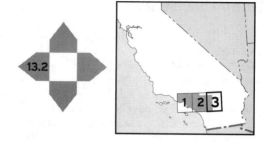

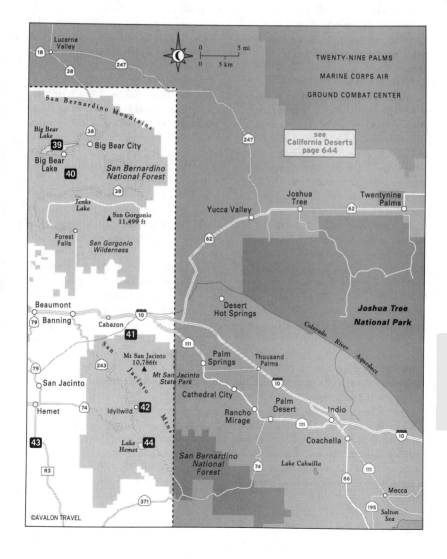

Lucerne Valley

18

38

247

0 5 mi
0 5 km

TWENTY-NINE PALMS

MARINE CORPS AIR

GROUND COMBAT CENTER

San Bernardino Mountains

Big Bear Lake

38

39 Big Bear City

Big Bear Lake **40**

San Bernardino National Forest

38

Jenks Lake

▲ San Gorgonio 11,499 ft

Forest Falls

San Gorgonio Wilderness

247

see California Deserts page 644

Joshua Tree

Yucca Valley

62

Twentynine Palms

62

Beaumont

79 Banning

Cabazon

10

41

79

243

San Jacinto

▲ Mt San Jacinto 10,786ft

Mt San Jacinto State Park

San Jacinto

Hemet

74

Idyllwild **42**

Jacinto Mtns

43

Lake Hemet **44**

R3

371

Desert Hot Springs

111

Palm Springs

Thousand Palms

10

Cathedral City

Palm Desert

Rancho Mirage

111

Coachella

Joshua Tree National Park

Colorado River Aqueduct

Indio

10

74

San Bernardino National Forest

Lake Cahuilla

86

111

195 *Salton Sea*

Mecca

©AVALON TRAVEL

1 CATALINA ISLAND

Rating: 10

west of Long Beach

Map 13.1, page 585 **BEST (**

The first time you see Avalon, moving your eyes across the water to its secluded cove, you may feel as though you've discovered a miniature Monte Carlo. As you approach by ferry, moving past the small boats sheltered in the bay, you will see villas built on terraces shaped like half moons, framed by a small line of mountains in the background, and a white-sand beach and miles of ocean in the foreground. Avalon is like nothing else in California, and after just a day or two here, you will discover that it is one of the most unusual and stellar destinations for outdoor travel adventure anywhere on the Pacific coast.

I'd heard about the remarkable fishing at Catalina, and when I ventured along the southwest shore of the island, I immediately started catching jacksmelt on small jigs. I then put those smelt on hooks, let them down, and started catching yellowtail.

Now get this: After my compadre Jim Klinger caught a beautiful yellowtail, the fish was filleted out right on the spot and the meat cut into three-inch chunks. We dipped the chunks into a bowl of soy sauce and wasabi, then ate the fish raw. At sushi restaurants, yellowtail is called *hamachi* and is among the sweetest-tasting of all sashimi. But it costs a fortune at the restaurants, and here we were off Catalina, eating all the freshly caught yellowtail we could hold. At one point, Klinger took a bite, absorbed the succulent taste like a king, and said with a laugh, "I wonder what the rest of the world is doing right now?"

Can you imagine that all of this, and a ton more, is just 25 miles from Los Angeles and millions of people? It's true. Catalina is not just an island, it's another world, running in a completely different orbit from everybody else.

Catalina Island can be reached by ferry out of Long Beach, San Pedro, and Marina del Rey, as well as by charter plane out of Dana Point, Long Beach, Newport Beach, and San Pedro, landing at the 3,200-foot airstrip called "Airport in the Sky." The ferry ride takes anywhere from 1–2 hours, and the big boats are often escorted by porpoises, bounding and jumping alongside like greyhounds. The ferry boats dock in Avalon, where most visitors stay at rooms and cottages. The first thing you notice is the lack of cars; residents have to sign up on a multiyear waiting list to get one. Instead, the locals get around on electric golf carts, and visitors either walk, rent bikes, take a golf-cart taxi, or sign up for one of the tours.

Extraordinary things can happen on Catalina Island. Scott Costa, a fishing companion, was in his 14-foot skiff, just 30 yards offshore, catching white sea bass on nearly every cast, when he drifted around a point and spotted a bison walking down a secluded beach as if it were a tourist in Hawaii, waves occasionally lapping at its ankles. Where else could you see something like that?

Nowhere else. And nowhere else are you going to have stellar fishing within minutes of the harbor for yellowtail, white sea bass, halibut, and calico bass, and even dorado and marlin, within just an hour's cruise. That makes it one of the top marine fisheries in the world, so good for so long that legendary folks such as Zane Grey, Winston Churchill, and General George Patton have ventured here in the past. What seems most captivating to those with expensive boats are the tuna and marlin, particularly the big yellowfins.

So much phenomenal marine adventure is possible at Catalina Island that many people begin their visits by taking a seat at one of the shoreline restaurants in Avalon and sitting there for hours, soaking up the surroundings. It doesn't take long before they start dreaming of the possibilities.

Note that the Department of Fish and Game (DFG) can set closures and change regulations as part of the Marine Life Protection Act (MLPA). Always check for the current laws.

Facilities, fees: There are five campgrounds on the island; three are hike-in (Parson's Landing, Black Jack, and Little Harbor). The other two (Two Harbors and Hermit Gulch) have tent cabins, chemical and flush toilets, showers, picnic tables, and barbecues. Lodging, a nine-hole golf course, a casino, restaurants, a marine preserve, and an underwater dive park are in Avalon. An adult round-trip ferry ride is available for a fee.

Directions: Avalon, the gateway to Catalina Island, can be reached by a one- to two-hour ferry out of Long Beach, San Pedro, Dana Point, or Newport Beach. Reservations can be made through one of the recommended companies listed in *Contact.*

Contact: Catalina Island Chamber of Commerce, 310/510-1520, www.catalinachamber .com.

Ferries: Catalina Express, 800/481-3470, www.catalinaexpress.com; Catalina Flyer, 800/830-7744, www.catalinainfo.com; Catalina-Marina Del Ray Flyer, 310/305-7250 or 888/663-3779, www.catalinaferries.com; Catalina Explorer, 888/317-3576, www.catalinatours.net; Catalina Classic Cruises, 562/495-3565, www.catalinaclassiccruises.com.

Fishing charters: Fish Catalina, 310/510-2440, www.fishcatalina.com.

Helicopter transport: Island Express, 800/2AVALON (800/228-2566), www .islandexpress.com.

Shuttle from Avalon to Airport in the Sky: 310/510-0143, www.catalina.com/airport.

Camping reservations: Catalina Island, 310/510-8368, www.catalina.com.

2 MALIBU PIER

Rating: 5

west of Los Angeles in Malibu
Map 13.1, page 585

Over the course of a year, the Malibu Pier gets a huge variety of fish in all sizes. The biggest are shark (many species) and halibut, and although rare, they provide a chance at a top prize. More abundant are perch, bass, corbina, and sargo. In the summer, schools of mackerel can move in, and anyone with a line in the water can hook up. One of the best ways to catch them off the pier is to jig a Cripplure. On the fall, this lure has a lot of action, and the macks will smack it with a vengeance. A few large rays are also caught off the end of the pier. The best prospects are in late spring and early summer, when the ocean has calmed down and baitfish are roaming the area, which in turn starts attracting the larger species in the vicinity of the pier.

This area is known more for its beach-house residents, who make up a definitive list of the rich and famous. For many visitors, that tends to overshadow the Malibu Pier, but for anglers without boats, it is the fishing that is attractive, not the chance of seeing a celebrity jogging down the beach.

Facilities, fees: Benches and rod holders are available. The state parks plan to contract a concessionaire to run a tackle shop and concession stand. A daily parking fee is charged.

Directions: From Los Angeles, drive west on the Santa Monica Freeway (I-10) until it turns into Highway 1. Continue west to Malibu and look for the pier directly off the highway (just before Surfrider Beach).

Contact: Malibu Pier Sportfishing, 888/310-7437, www.malibupiersportfishing.com; Malibu Lagoon State Beach, 310/456-8031 or 818/880-0363.

3 SANTA MONICA/ REDONDO DEEP SEA

Rating: 7

from Malibu to Redondo Beach
Map 13.1, page 585   **BEST** (

This stretch of coast is among the most popular in California for saltwater anglers. It sits adjacent to the most densely populated area in California, yet for the most part, the fisheries have been able to keep up with the demand. The most consistent fishery is for rockfish, but there are seasonal options, with halibut in the spring and often bonito and yellowtail in the summer.

Santa Monica Bay is fairly shallow, but it's cut by the Redondo and Santa Monica canyons, and the rockfishing is best in the rocky edges of those canyons. Always check fishing regulations before planning a trip. Most of the local sportfishing boats work along the southern edge of Redondo Canyon. Here you will find a wide variety of rockfish species, including vermilion, gopher, chilipepper, and canary rockfish. In the spring and early summer, halibut often move into the flats of Santa Monica Bay.

My longtime friend and mentor, Bill Beebe, a columnist with *Western Outdoor News,* won the halibut derby here one year and donated his entire $1,000 cash prize to the United Anglers of California. It paid off big, because the UAC has been instrumental in helping to restrict commercial fishing to enhance many fish species and fighting the ridiculous MLPA.

Another good area for rockfish and kelp bass is the kelp beds offshore of Zuma Beach, north of Malibu and El Pescador Beach. The fish tend to be smaller but can offer light-tackle saltwater action, not to mention a lot of fun. The area provides an excellent opportunity for anglers who want to try freshwater techniques but catch saltwater-strength fish. Sea kayaks can even be used for this type of fishing.

Several other options exist. Bonito often move into Redondo Harbor and can be caught from small boats by anglers using light tackle and live anchovies. One trick is to use spinning tackle, 4-pound line, and small gold hooks; you'll hook bonito like crazy. The key is the light line. The fish get so much angling pressure that anything heavier is too visible and will spook them. Bonito in the three- to four-pound range are the norm these days.

Calico bass, sand bass, barracuda, and yellowtail can be caught near the rocky shore from Redondo Harbor south to Rocky Point. Live anchovies are the key.

Yellowtail are always the wild-card option here.

Facilities, fees: Party-boat charters, bait, and tackle are at the sportfishing operations. Lodging, restaurants, and shops can be found in towns along the coast. A paved boat ramp and a hand-launching area are at the Marina del Rey small-craft harbor. Party-boat fees are charged per person.

Directions: To King Harbor in Redondo Beach: From Los Angeles, take I-110 south to I-405. Turn north on I-405 and drive to the Western Avenue exit. Take that exit, turn left, and drive under the freeway to 190th Street. Turn right and drive on 190th Street until it ends, at the beach on Harbor Drive. Turn left on Harbor Drive and continue for 0.7 mile to the pier.

To the Marina del Rey boat launch: From Los Angeles, take I-405 south to Highway 90 West/Marina del Rey Freeway. Turn west on Highway 90 West and drive until it dead-ends at Lincoln Boulevard. Turn left and drive 0.5 mile to Fiji Way. Turn right and drive to 0.25 mile to Harbor Village and the boat ramp. Marina del Rey Sportfishing is on your right at Dock 52.

Contact: Redondo Sportfishing, 310/372-2111 (fish count 310/376-1622), www.redondo sportfishing.com; Marina del Rey Sportfishing, 310/822-3625 or 800/822-3625, www.marinadelreysportfishing.com; Santa Monica Chamber of Commerce, 310/393-9825; Santa Monica Pier, 310/458-8901, www.santamonicapier.org; Redondo Beach Chamber of Commerce and Visitors Bureau, 310/376-6911, www.visitredondo.com.

◢ SANTA MONICA PIER

Rating: 4

in Santa Monica

Map 13.1, page 585

The marine habitat in any coastal area determines the variety of fish available. It's primarily a sand bottom off Santa Monica, and that in turn dictates what fish you might catch. For the most part, anglers at this pier catch opaleye, surfperch, calico bass, shallow-water rockfish, sargo, white sea bass, calico bass, and sand bass. Sardines and herring are also caught; they are then used as baitfish for halibut. It's not great, but it's not bad either. It's a fair year-round fishery that produces a few fish, as long as the ocean surge is not too great.

In some years, this area gets a good run of halibut, most going 20 pounds or better. The most favorable period for halibut is March through May.

The beach area just to the south of the pier can be quite productive in the summer for California corbina, assorted surfperch, yellowfin croaker, and the occasional sand shark.

If you hit it right, the corbina fishing is a blast. The magical combination of factors that sparks the best bite happens at high tide right at sunset. If you get a full moon thrown in, that's even better, because the corbina bite well after dark also.

Rig up with an ultralight spinning outfit and 8- or 12-pound test. Use a small 1/8-ounce egg sinker sliding setup with eight-inch leader. Finish up with a small live bait or bait-holder hook and dig up sand crabs at the beach for bait. The best crabs are the soft-shell variety. Corbina eat them like candy. Casts need not be long; fling your offering out in front of the first set of breakers and hang on. The corbina here will run 12 inches to three pounds and fight 10 times harder than any trout of the same size.

When surf fishing here, you'll get some strange looks from sunbathers on the beach and will often have to field a bunch of questions ranging from "Are there really fish here?" to "Which way to the old *Baywatch* lifeguard tower?"

Facilities, fees: Restrooms, benches, lights, and fish-cleaning sinks are provided. Bait and tackle are for sale on the pier. Numerous shops and restaurants are nearby. A fee is charged for parking.

Directions: From Los Angeles, take I-10 (Santa Monica Freeway) west to the 4th Street exit. Take that exit and drive north to Colorado Avenue. Turn left on Colorado and continue to the pier.

Contact: Santa Monica Chamber of Commerce, 310/393-9825; Santa Monica Pier, 310/458-8901, www.santamonicapier.org; Santa Monica Pier Bait and Tackle, 310/576-2014.

5 MANHATTAN BEACH MUNICIPAL PIER

Rating: 4

southwest of Los Angeles

Map 13.1, page 585

Anglers are discovering that year-round seasonal fisheries are at this pier. In the spring and early summer, halibut roam this area, providing a rare hope. Corbina fishing can be good in the surf. In the summer, there are larger numbers of mackerel and shark in the area, providing the best prospects of the year. In the winter, perch are rare, but large bat rays offer the best prospects. Because the fisheries are in a perpetual cycle here, fishing success fluctuates greatly.

The pier is open 6 A.M.–midnight. This pier has been in operation since 1992, and when fishing is good, you'll wonder why they didn't build this pier much longer ago. When it's bad, you'll wonder why they ever built it at all.

A bonus here is the aquarium.

Facilities, fees: Lights, restrooms, benches, fish-cleaning sinks, a snack bar, and an aquarium are provided. Parking fees vary. Admission to the aquarium is free, but donations are accepted.

Directions: Take I-405 to the exit for Inglewood Avenue South (near Manhattan Beach). Take that exit and turn south on Inglewood Avenue and drive to Manhattan Beach Boulevard. Turn west (right) on Manhattan Beach Boulevard and continue to the pier, at the end of the street.

Contact: City of Manhattan Beach, Parks and Recreation, 310/802-5410; Manhattan Beach Chamber of Commerce, 310/545-5313; Roundhouse Marine Studies Laboratory and Aquarium, 310/379-8117, www.roundhouse aquarium.org.

⑥ HERMOSA BEACH MUNICIPAL PIER

Rating: 5

north of Redondo Beach

Map 13.1, page 585

At the Hermosa Beach Pier, you get a chance for something big and a chance for something small. Big? Sharks, bat rays, halibut, and even the occasional white sea bass, yellowtail, and sand bass roam this area. Small? Surfperch, mackerel, and bonito can arrive in large numbers. Occasionally, corbina, smelt, and sardines are also caught here. Most people come with modest expectations, hoping to catch a few perch, but they are always ready for something better. A good catch is most likely to happen in the summer, when bonito and sharks are most abundant. Wild cards? Bat rays and halibut in the winter and spring, respectively; keep the chance of hooking one in the back of your mind.

The pier is open 6 A.M.–10 P.M.

Facilities, fees: Lights, restrooms, benches, and fish-cleaning tables are provided. Parking fees vary.

Directions: Take I-405 to the exit for Artesia Boulevard West (south of Los Angeles). Take that exit west to Artesia Boulevard and drive west to Highway 1. Turn south on Highway 1 and drive a short distance to Pier Avenue. Turn right and drive west for 0.25 mile to the pier. Parking is available on Hermosa Avenue.

Contact: City of Hermosa Beach, 310/318-0239, www.hermosabch.org; Hermosa Chamber of Commerce, 310/365-6942, www.hbchamber.net.

⑦ REDONDO BEACH PIER

Rating: 5

southwest of Los Angeles

Map 13.1, page 585

In the spring and early summer, halibut provide a quality fishery, though it can take time, persistence, and skill to get a keeper.

Wild cards at Redondo are the sharks and rays. Don't overlook them. The bat rays in particular can get quite large; they have tremendous strength in their initial runs, and provide a good long shot during the winter months. Redondo Pier is a quarter mile away and provides another viable option.

Facilities, fees: Restrooms, benches, fish-cleaning tables, a tackle shop, and restaurants are available. A per-day parking fee is charged.

Directions: From Los Angeles, take I-110 south to the exit for Torrance Boulevard. Turn right on Torrance Boulevard and drive west to the pier.

Contact: Turner's Outdoorsman, 310/214-8724, www.turners.com; Redondo Beach Chamber of Commerce and Visitors Bureau, 310/376-6911, www.visitredondo.com; City of Redondo Beach, 310/318-0631, www.redondo.org.

⑧ REDONDO SPORTFISHING PIER/KING HARBOR

Rating: 6

southwest of Los Angeles

Map 13.1, page 585

Redondo Pier is only a quarter mile away from the much larger Horseshoe Pier in Redondo Beach, but they are worlds apart.

The little Redondo Pier is much smaller and less commercialized, but the fishing is just as good as at its larger neighbor. When the bonito are in, Redondo provides one of the great inshore fisheries on the Pacific coast. Schools of them roam the harbor, searching for anchovies, and the angler who has the opportunity to offer them one can have some exciting hookups. They are most abundant in summer months. Bat rays are another option during the winter.

Facilities, fees: Restrooms, a restaurant, and bait and tackle are available. Fishing access and parking are free.

Directions: From Los Angeles, drive south on

I-110 to I-405. Turn north on I-405 and take the Western Avenue exit. Turn left and drive under the freeway to 190th Street. Turn right and drive on 190th Street until it ends at the beach, at Harbor Drive. Turn left on Harbor Drive and continue for 0.7 mile to the pier.

Contact: Turner's Outdoorsman, 310/214-8724; Redondo Beach Chamber of Commerce and Visitors Bureau, 310/376-6911, www .visitredondo.com; City of Redondo Beach, 310/318-0631, www.redondo.org; Redondo Beach Sportfishing, 310/372-2111, www .redondosportfishing.com.

🟨 LOS ANGELES COAST/ DEEP SEA

Rating: 8
from San Pedro to San Clemente
Map 13.1, page 585

The closest thing to freedom in Southern California is on the open ocean, cruising across the smooth briny green to a favorite fishing spot. No traffic jams, no stoplights, no concrete, no angry people, and no problems. Just the open sea, the friendly hum of the boat engine, and a clean wake as you leave your troubles behind on the mainland.

This stretch of coast offers not only the opportunity for peace of mind, but also a varied and sometimes excellent fishery. The variety is tremendous: anglers can try their luck at inshore kelp beds, mud or sand bottoms, bays, shallow reefs, underwater canyons, and along the mainland at several piers set in the path of passing fish. Four major sportfishing centers are located at San Pedro, Long Beach, Newport Beach, and Dana Point. Between them, dozens of sportfishing charters are available, offering trips covering the spectrum of Southern California saltwater angling.

Note that rules and closures of the coast have taken some areas out of play. The deepwater reefs and seamounts are now off-limits.

When schools of Spanish (jack) mackerel roam the waters offshore from Southern California, many anglers sniff "mackerel!" and thus miss out on exciting action on light tackle. The Spanish mackerel is a member of the jack family, a first cousin to the prized yellowtail, and can be located in fishable numbers by trolling a small bonito feather. When hooked on light tackle, especially on artificial lures, they can put up quite a tussle. Another plus is their mild flavor, unlike that of the Pacific mackerel, a true mackerel.

The primary attraction here has been yellowtail, which can at times be excellent at Rocky Point and Horseshoe Kelp. In the summer, sand bass migrate to the Huntington Flats, often furnishing easy pickings, with a large number of barracuda in the same area. Overnight boats, on the other hand, rely on trips primarily to Catalina Island.

Albacore are the biggest wild card. A good albacore bite is like nothing else, especially when the fish are chummed to the surface in a frenzy. Occasionally large tuna may be in the mix. (Albacore alone are something else, but when a big tuna grabs your bait, you can look down at your reel and say, "Good-bye fishing line." They are line burners.) But with albacore, there is a high level of unpredictability that can make strong men practically cry. When will they show? How far out? Can they be chummed to the surface? The answers change every year. Usually they start arriving sometime in August, anywhere from 30–120 miles offshore.

Marine habitat determines the species of fish available. In turn, the diversity of habitat means that a huge variety of fish call this area home, making it a take-your-pick kind of deal. Here is a capsule listing:
• Inshore kelp beds: Taking a boat out and fishing around kelp beds can provide good action for a large number of species. Kelp beds can change dramatically in size as a result of sea temperatures and inshore surges during big storms. The areas where kelp beds are located include just off Point Vicente, just off Royal Palms State Beach, south of Newport, and northwest of Laguna Beach. Another kelp

bed is just south of Los Angeles Harbor, yet it's virtually submerged, making it more difficult to locate. Several more kelp beds are along the inshore coast south of Dana Point, between San Clemente and Dana Harbor, and also between San Clemente and San Mateo Point.

Although most of the fish are not large, they are usually abundant and can be caught on light tackle and jigs. In the summer months there is always the chance of a bonus—catching one of the larger species. The most common species are kelp bass, sand bass, and many kinds of rockfish, including olive, grass, and vermilion. Sheepshead are also resident fish of these areas. In the summer, barracuda are caught. If you have the luck of hooking one of the latter while fishing for the former, believe me, you will have your hands full.

• Mud and sand bottom: Halibut arrive in large numbers every spring and can provide good fishing through the summer where the sea bottom is flat and made of mud or sand. Whereas halibut were hammered in shallow areas by netters in the 1980s, there is a real opportunity for population increases, as the netters were moved out to deeper water in the 1990s. Some of the better spots for halibut are just offshore of Huntington Beach, Santa Monica Bay, just off Point Fermin, and also in San Pedro Bay.

• Inshore bays: Anglers who own their own boats have the opportunity to fish a number of bays that attract primarily shark, rays, some perch, and, sometimes in the summer, mackerel and bonito. In the best of years during the spring and early summer, in places such as San Pedro Bay, halibut fishing is the top prize, and the bonus of a variety of saltwater bass make Newport Bay attractive. Other good areas are at Alamitos and Seal Beach.

• Underwater canyons: These canyons provide occasional migratory routes for a variety of somewhat rare, alluring species. The most famous such canyon is the Newport Submarine Canyon, directly southwest of the pier at Newport Beach. To the north is the Santa Monica Canyon, in the center of Santa Monica Bay. Redondo Canyon is directly west of Redondo Beach Pier, and Hueneme Canyon lies directly west of Port Hueneme, off Oxnard. During years when the ocean temperatures are cool, schools of salmon roam up through these canyons in March and early April. During years when the ocean temperatures are warm, the prized striped marlin and even schools of tuna cruise through in late summer. If either occurs, don't miss out; it's a rare opportunity.

• Beaches: Surf fishing can be excellent at Huntington Beach and Laguna Beach. Sandy stretches yield up corbina, yellowfin croaker, and the occasional spotfin croaker, halibut, barred and other perches, and sand sharks. Sand crabs (especially soft-shelled) are the bait of choice, and fresh mussels are right behind them. In the winter, anglers cast small trout lures into the surf for surf perch on light tackle, and the fun is enhanced by fighting the surf as well as the fish.

Rockfishing in Laguna Beach's many coves can be excellent. In the north part of town, at Crescent Bay, I have seen 12 different species caught on 12 casts: scorpionfish, corbina, black perch, opaleye, halfmoon, calico bass, barred perch, white perch, cabezon, yellowfin croaker, sand bass, and sargo. All were caught on mussels grown right there on the rocks. Shallow-water rockfish, greenlings, halibut, and sheepshead are less common, but they do exist here. You will also find one of the world's most beautiful species here—the brilliant garibaldi. If you catch one of these fat, bright orange, perch-shaped lovelies, put it back. They are protected by the laws of California.

When the tide allows access to the rocks on the cove's south side, it's possible to catch barracuda and bonito on small chrome lures or white feathers there.

Crescent Bay's small beach is just as productive for grunion as the longer beaches of Huntington and Laguna's Main Beach. You don't need expensive gear for grunion—your oldest blanket, a flashlight with good batteries, and a bucket or bag to put your catch in are all you need. The only legal way to catch these tasty wigglers is by hand, and it's easy. That is, like most fishing, the hardest part is connecting with the fish, putting yourself where the fish are when they are there. In the case of grunion, they're most likely to be at Crescent Bay's beach from late February to early September on the three or four nights after each full moon or new moon.

Here's how to fish grunion: When the tide is at its highest, spread the blanket on the sand and get comfortable. In one or two hours, the surf should start tossing grunion up onto the beach, at which point you brush the sand off your legs, grab the fish, and tuck them into your bucket or bag. There is no limit. (Always check DFG regulations for current restrictions.)

In case the fish don't show, which happens more often than not, full-moon nights are very romantic, but new moons offer more privacy.

Facilities, fees: Lodging, campgrounds, piers, restaurants, shops, bait, tackle, and groceries are available all along the coast.

Boat ramps are at the following locations: in San Pedro at Cabrillo Beach; in Long Beach at Golden Shores (known as the 2nd Street Offramp), Marine Stadium, and Davies Launch Ramp; in Seal Beach at Sunset Aquatic Marina; in Newport Beach at the Newport Dunes Marina; and in Dana Point at Embarcadero Marina.

Embarcadero Marina offers a sling hoist (25-foot maximum boat length) and boat rentals, and Davey's Locker, in Newport Beach, offers motorboat rentals.

Party-boat fees are charged per person. Parking and/or boat-launching fees are charged at most marinas and launch ramps.

Directions: To San Pedro Harbor: From Los Angeles, take I-110/Harbor Freeway south to San Pedro and Gaffey Street. Turn south (left) on Gaffey Street and drive 1.5 miles to 22nd Street. Turn left and drive for 0.75 mile to the 22nd Street Landing, on the right.

• To L.A. Harbor Sportfishing: From Los Angeles, take I-110/Harbor Freeway south and merge with onto Highway 47 North. Drive a short distance to the Harbor Boulevard exit. Take that exit to Harbor Boulevard. Turn right and drive to West 6th Street. Turn left and drive to Sampson Way. Turn right and drive to Nagoya Way. Turn left and drive to L.A. Harbor Sportfishing.

• To Long Beach Sportfishing: From Los Angeles, take the Long Beach Freeway/I-710 south to the sign for Queen Mary/Port of Long Beach. Bear right and take the Pico Avenue exit. Turn right on Pico Avenue and continue to Long Beach Sportfishing, on the right, at 555 Pico Avenue.

• To Pierpoint Landing: From Los Angeles, take the Long Beach Freeway/I-710 south to the sign for Queen Mary/Port of Long Beach. Bear left and follow signs to the Aquarium of the Pacific. Drive past the aquarium to Aquarium Way. Turn right and follow the road along the back side (bearing left) of the aquarium and Pierpoint Landing, at 200 Aquarium Way.

• To Newport Harbor: From Los Angeles, take I-405 south to Highway 55. Take Highway 55 south and drive to Newport Beach (where the highway becomes Newport Boulevard) and continue past Highway 1 (about 0.25 mile past the Pacific Coast Bridge; Newport Boulevard becomes Balboa Boulevard) and drive 1.6 miles on Balboa to Adams Street. Turn left and continue to Newport Landing Sportfishing, at 309 Palm Street, at the end of the road. Parking is available behind the Newport Landing Restaurant.

• To Davey's Locker: From Los Angeles, take I-405 south to Highway 55. Take Highway 55 south and drive to Newport Beach (where the highway becomes Newport Boulevard) and continue past Highway 1 (about 0.25 mile past the Pacific Coast Bridge; Newport Boulevard becomes Balboa Boulevard) and drive on Balboa for 1.5 miles to Main Street. Turn west (left) and continue to 400 Main Street.

• To Dana Point Harbor: From Los Angeles,

take I-5 south through Mission Viejo and San Juan Capistrano to the exit for the Pacific Coast Highway/Dana Point Harbor off-ramp. Take that exit and continue to Dana Point Harbor Drive. Turn left on Dana Point Harbor Drive and drive through two more signals to Golden Lantern Street. Turn left on Golden Lantern Street and to Dana Wharf Sportfishing and the harbor.

Contact: City of San Pedro, 310/831-6245, www.sanpedro.com; Paul's Fishing Bait and Tackle, 310/833-3279; The Rusty Hook, 310/832-2429; Long Beach Area Convention and Visitors Bureau, 562/436-3645 or 800/452-7829, www.visitlongbeach.com; Newport Beach Conference and Visitors Bureau, 949/719-6100, visitnewportbeach.com; Dana Point Chamber of Commerce and Visitors Center, 949/496-1555, danapointchamber.com; Jig Stop, 949/496-3555, www.jigstop.com; Turner's Outdoorsman, 562/424-8628, www.turners.com.

Boat ramps: Cabrillo Marina, San Pedro, 310/732-2252, www.cymcabrillo.com; Sunset Aquatic Marina, Huntington Beach, 562/592-2833, www.sunsetaquaticmarina.com; Newport Dunes Marina, Newport Beach, 949/729-1100, www.newportdunesmarina.com; Embarcadero Marina, Dana Point, 949/496-6177, danapointchamber.com.

Party boats:

• San Pedro: 22nd Street Landing, 310/832-8304 (fish count 310/521-0222); LA Harbor Sportfishing, 310/547-9916 (fish count 310/547-1318), www.laharborsportfishing.com.

• Long Beach and Seal Beach: Long Beach Sportfishing, 562/432-8993, longbeachsportfishing.com; Pierpoint Landing, 562/983-9300 (fish count 310/435-7123), www.pierpoint.net.

• Newport Beach: Newport Landing Sportfishing, 949/675-0551, www.newportlanding.com; Davey's Locker, 949/673-1434, www.daveyslocker.com.

• Dana Point: Dana Wharf Sportfishing, 949/496-5794, www.danawharf.com.

🔟 SEAL BEACH PIER

Rating: 5

at Seal Beach

Map 13.1, page 585

This is one of the longest remaining wooden piers in the United States. Anglers have a long-shot chance for a halibut at this pier; the near-shore area is one of the better places for halibut along the coast. Perch, kingfish, jacksmelt, corbina, croaker, and shark are more common.

Facilities, fees: Restrooms, a restaurant, benches, and fish-cleaning areas are available. Bait can be obtained nearby. A per-day parking fee is charged.

Directions: From Huntington Beach, take Highway 1 north to Seal Beach and Main Street. Turn left on Main Street and drive about two blocks to the pier at the end of the street.

Contact: Seal Beach Chamber of Commerce, 562/799-0179, www.welcometosealbeach.com; Big Fish Bait & Tackle, Seal Beach, 562/431-0723.

🔟 LAKE PIRU

Rating: 8

northwest of Los Angeles

Map 13.1, page 585

Here is a wild-card lake. It may be just the place to shuffle your cards and deal them face up. Piru often is overlooked because of its proximity to Lake Casitas to the west and Castaic Lake to the east (lakes where many believe a world-record bass will be caught). Piru may not produce immense bass, but the catch rates are much higher. Trout fishing is also good.

The lake covers 1,200 acres when full and is at 1,055 feet in Los Padres National Forest. Afternoon winds are predictable on most days. It is a popular waterskiing lake, and to the credit of the lake managers, they have largely solved the conflict between anglers and water-skiers. Waterskiing is restricted to a designated area, roughly in the middle of the lake, with a 35-mph speed limit. Personal watercraft are prohibited. This is a fantastic improvement here: it is no longer the war on the water that it once was.

As at so many lakes with bass and trout, the prime time is in March, April, and May. Bass fishing can be excellent during this time (before the water-skiers take over, in the summer). The catch rates are excellent, especially during very strong morning and evening bites. The three principal cove areas, one on the west side of the lake and two on the east side, are natural spots for the bass at Piru. In the spring, it is common to catch five or more in a few hours, most in the 11- to 13-inch class but sometimes measuring to 15 or 16 inches. To get anything bigger, it helps plenty to use crawdads for bait. The lake has lots of crawdads and a sprinkling of rainbow trout, and the big bass here often take a pass on anything smaller.

Piru once had plenty of trout. No more. Holdovers provide a long shot. The best areas to troll for trout are the cove just north of the boat ramp, up the main lake arm, and then late in the summer in the deep water along the dam. Shoreliners do best just north of the boat ramp and along the cove, around the corner from the ramp. There are also designated areas for shoreliners and float tubers.

Note: All boats must be inspected and certified free of mussels prior to launching at this lake.

Facilities, fees: A paved boat ramp is on the lake's western side. A marina, temporary mooring, motorboat rentals, tackle, bait, and ice are available. A campground with RV sites, restrooms, drinking water, flush toilets, showers, an RV dump station, fish-cleaning stations, boat storage, and a snack bar is nearby. Boats less than 12 feet long or over 26 feet long are prohibited. Canoes and kayaks over eight feet long are permitted in the special-use area. Day-use and boat-launching fees are charged.

Directions: From Ventura, take Highway 126 east for about 30 miles to the exit for Main Street. Drive northeast on Main Street for about six miles (the road becomes Piru Canyon Road) to the campground, at the end of the road.

Contact: Lake Piru Recreation Area, 805/521-1500, www.camplakepiru.com.

12 LITTLEROCK RESERVOIR

Rating: 3

near Palmdale in Angeles National Forest

Map 13.1, page 585

Times can be tough at Littlerock Reservoir, where the DFG sliced off the trout plants. It was never good here, but without plants, there are some days that when it comes to fishing, you might as well go for a walk on the moon. Fair shoreline access is available on the west side.

The lake is at an elevation of 3,258 feet in Angeles National Forest but covers just 150 acres. When it is drained down the Palmdale Ditch and into the California Aqueduct to the north, it can go from being a pretty mountain lake to a muddy mess in just a few months. When that happens, you might as well see when the next spaceship is departing for the moon. At that time, the lake is used for off-highway-vehicle use, and the campgrounds pretty much get taken over by the off-road enthusiasts.

The 5-mph speed limit keeps things quiet, eliminating most powerboating, personal-watercraft riding, and sailboarding. Gas motors up to 10 horsepower are permitted, a good thing because there are times when the wind really whips through here in the late afternoon.

Facilities, fees: A primitive launching area is on the lake's northwest shore. Picnic areas and a wheelchair-accessible boat ramp are available. Boat rentals, bait, tackle, and a snack shop are expected to be available in 2012; call ahead to confirm. A day-use fee is charged per vehicle. An annual pass may be purchased.

Directions: From Los Angeles, take I-5 north to the Highway 14/Lancaster/Palmdale exit. Turn east and continue to Palmdale and Highway 138/Pearblossom Highway. Turn east on Highway 138/Pearblossom Highway and drive about five miles (through the stoplight at the four-way intersection) to Cheseboro Road. Turn right on Cheseboro Road and continue for four miles to the reservoir.

Contact: The Dam Store, 661/533-1923, www.littlerockdam.org; Angeles National Forest, Santa Clara/Mojave Rivers Ranger District, 661/296-9710, www.fs.fed.us/r5—click on Forest Offices.

13 ARROYO SECO CREEK

Rating: 4

north of Pasadena in Angeles National Forest
Map 13.1, page 585

I discovered this little stream by accident. After giving a seminar in Pasadena, I just headed straight toward the mountains. It wasn't long before the traffic was left behind and this little stream flowed alongside the road. I parked at the camp near the Forest Service station, just to watch the water roll by and get my bearings.

Suddenly I saw a trout roll. I couldn't believe it. I quickly retrieved my rod, then caught a few of them, which provided a nice boost after a frustrating day. Later I found out that Arroyo Seco Creek is stocked with trout averaging 7–8 inches, with the plants made right at the Gould Mesa Campground. Note that after an extended rain, the Department of Fish and Game postpones stocks. The best time is always winter to spring.

Facilities, fees: Walk-in campgrounds are available. Supplies can be obtained in surrounding towns. A Forest Service Adventure Pass is required.

Directions: Take I-210 north of Pasadena to the Highway 2/Angeles Crest Highway exit. Turn north and drive 10 miles to the Switzers

Picnic Area. Creek access is available at the picnic area. This access point is designed for the athletic, since it features steep, treacherous banks.

For gentler access: Take I-210 north of Pasadena to the exit for Arroyo Boulevard. Take the Arroyo Boulevard exit and go north on Arroyo Boulevard (road becomes Windsor Avenue) to Ventura Street. Turn right at Ventura Street. You can park in the paved lot on the left, walk through the yellow gate, and hike about one mile to the creek. Gould Mesa Walk-In Camp is two miles north of the Jet Propulsion Labs, which are at the mouth of Arroyo Seco Canyon. Oakwild, a primitive walk-in campground, is two miles north of Gould Mesa Walk-In Camp.

Contact: Angeles National Forest, Los Angeles River Ranger District, 818/899-1900, www.fs.fed.us/r5—click on Forest Offices.

14 HUNTINGTON BEACH PIER

Rating: 5

at Huntington Beach
Map 13.2, page 586

The rebuilt Huntington Beach Pier opened in the summer of 1992. It is in an area that has both good numbers of halibut in the spring and resident populations of croaker and sand bass. Also caught here are corbina, mackerel, perch, and a few sharks.

Facilities, fees: A bait shop, restrooms, benches, lights, and fish-cleaning areas are available. Parking fees vary.

Directions: From Los Angeles, take I-10 east and drive to I-405. To merge onto I-405, take the 3B exit (heading toward Long Beach) and go 35 miles to the exit for Bola Avenue West. Take the Bolsa Avenue West exit and drive a short distance to Westminster Mall, and then make an immediate right turn onto Goldenwest Street. Drive five miles to the Pacific Coast Highway. Turn left (south) on the Pacific Coast Highway and drive about a mile to the pier on the right side of the highway.

Contact: Let's Go Fishing, Huntington Beach, 714/960-1392; City of Huntington Beach, Beach Headquarters, 714/536-5281, www.ci.huntington-beach.ca.us.

15 NEWPORT PIER

Rating: 5

at Newport Beach

Map 13.2, page 586

This spot is just on the edge of the Newport Canyon, providing a chance for a wider variety of fish to roam within casting range than at many piers. It is very popular with anglers, as the pier fishing can be excellent. In addition to the typical parade of kingfish, perch, jacksmelt, and shark, there is also a chance for opaleye and a variety of rockfish. The pier also produces mackerel and sculpin. This pier is open 5 A.M.–midnight.

Facilities, fees: Restrooms, fish-cleaning sinks, lights, benches, and a restaurant are available. Supplies can be obtained in Newport Beach. Parking fees vary.

Directions: Take Highway 1 to Newport Beach and Newport Boulevard. Turn west on Newport Boulevard and continue to the pier.

Contact: Newport Pier, 949/644-3000; City of Newport Beach, 949/644-3151; Visit Newport Beach, 800/942-6278, www.visit newportbeach.com.

16 BALBOA PIER

Rating: 4

at Newport Beach

Map 13.2, page 586

Balboa Pier gets less fishing pressure and is less promising than nearby Newport Pier to the north. The primary species available are kingfish, other croakers, and perch, with some binges of jacksmelt in the spring and occasionally a large bat ray or shark. This pier is open 5 A.M.–midnight.

Facilities, fees: Restrooms, a fish-cleaning area, lights, benches, a restaurant, and picnic areas are available. Supplies can be obtained in Newport Beach. Parking fees vary.

Directions: Drive on Highway 1 to Newport Beach and Newport Boulevard. Turn west on Newport Boulevard and drive to 26th Street. Turn right on 26th Street and then make an immediate left onto Balboa Boulevard and continue to the pier (about two miles south of Newport Pier).

Contact: City of Newport Beach, 949/644-3151; Visit Newport Beach, 800/942-6278, www.visitnewportbeach.com.

17 CRYSTAL LAKE

Rating: 4

northeast of Los Angeles in
Angeles National Forest

Map 13.2, page 586

Crystal Lake is more of a pond than a lake, a little dot of water set deep in the San Gabriel Mountains. But it provides a chance at trout fishing during the cool months. When the lake fills from rain in late winter, the Department of Fish and Game responds by stocking it with rainbow trout ranging from seven inches to over a foot. As long as water conditions are suitable, the DFG continues the plants. This is not the place to bring a boat—it's way too small for that. But rather it's a spot to fish from shore using standard bait-dunking techniques. Most folks come here for recreation and camping, and if there's been a plant, maybe fish a little.

Facilities, fees: Picnic areas, a campground, drinking water, vault toilets, and a visitors center are available. No motors are permitted on the lake. A Forest Service Adventure Pass is required.

Directions: Take I-210 to Azusa and the exit for Azusa Canyon. Take the exit for Azusa Canyon and San Gabriel Canyon Road/

Highway 39. Drive north on San Gabriel Canyon Road/Highway 39 for 25 miles to the Crystal Lake Recreation Area and the signed turnoff for Crystal Lake.

Contact: Angeles National Forest, San Gabriel River Ranger District, 626/335-1251, www .fs.fed.us/r5—click on Forest Offices.

18 WEST FORK SAN GABRIEL RIVER

Rating: 5

northeast of Los Angeles in
Angeles National Forest
Map 13.2, page 586

Of the three forks of the San Gabriel River, this is the place to come if you like to hike and have the option of catch-and-release fishing for wild trout. The best strategy is to park and hike upstream.

The first piece of water, from the mouth of the West Fork on upstream to the first bridge, was once stocked with rainbow trout. No more. There is a very sparse number of fish here. Once you pass the second bridge, however, on up 4.5 miles to Cogswell Reservoir, this is a designated wild trout stream with catch-and-release fishing. The DFG requires artificials with barbless hooks. Considering it's in the Angeles National Forest, it's a rare opportunity.

Facilities, fees: Pit toilets are available. No drinking water. A hike-in campground is six miles from the highway. Supplies and lodging can be found in Azusa and surrounding towns. A Forest Service Adventure Pass is required.

Directions: Take I-210 to Azusa and the exit for Azusa Avenue and San Gabriel Canyon Road/Highway 39. Take that exit north to San Gabriel Canyon Road and drive 39.25 miles. Look for the entrance gate on the left. You can park at the mouth of the West Fork and fish upstream.

Contact: Angeles National Forest, San Gabriel River Ranger District, 626/335-1251, www .fs.fed.us/r5—click on Forest Offices.

19 NORTH FORK SAN GABRIEL RIVER

Rating: 4

north of Azusa in Angeles National Forest
Map 13.2, page 586

The San Gabriel River is the most famous trout stream in Angeles National Forest, but the North Fork is the least-known and least-fished section of it. The East Fork gets most of the fishing pressure. The best section of water here is three miles upstream from its confluence with the West Fork San Gabriel. This spot is stocked with trout in the seven- to eight-inch class when river flows are decent in the spring. The San Gabriel Reservoir area is no longer stocked in order to protect the mountain yellow-legged frog.

Facilities, fees: Coldbrook Campground is 18 miles north of Azusa. Supplies can be obtained in Azusa. A Forest Service Adventure Pass is required.

Directions: Take I-210 to Azusa and the exit for Azusa Avenue and San Gabriel Canyon Road/Highway 39. Take that exit north on San Gabriel Canyon Road and drive 18 miles to the campground on the left. Direct access is available off the highway.

Contact: Angeles National Forest, San Gabriel River Ranger District, 626/335-1251, www .fs.fed.us/r5—click on Forest Offices.

20 SILVERWOOD LAKE

Rating: 7

north of San Bernardino at
Silverwood Lake State Recreation Area
Map 13.2, page 586

Silverwood not only has good trout fishing, it also has a decent population of largemouth bass and a sprinkling of bluegill, crappie, and catfish. Crappie fishing can be so good, in fact, that the dock is sometimes closed when it gets too crowded in the off-season.

Fishing for striped bass can be good: Stripers in the 30- to 40-pound range have been caught here, occasionally some even larger. The lake record is a 45-pounder.

Most of the largemouth bass feed on shad minnows, and know-hows often look for diving birds in the area before picking their spots. From winter through summer, water temperatures swing widely, which has a great effect on the bass. The best fishing is usually in late March, when the water temperature can climb from 56°F–63°F, which causes the bass to start moving into the shallow areas (often in the backs of coves).

Silverwood is at an elevation of 3,350 feet, and when full to the brim, it covers 1,000 acres and has 13 miles of shoreline. It is bordered by San Bernardino National Forest to the south and the high desert to the north, and its proximity to San Bernardino makes it very popular for boaters, especially during hot summers. One problem for anglers is that afternoon winds are usually strong in the spring and early summer.

Someone must have taken some smart pills when they made the boating rules at Silverwood Lake. All of the significant coves that provide good fishing have 5-mph speed limits, and that keeps the water-skiers and anglers separated and happy.

That means you should be on the water early, when the best fishing is: in the cooler months, when water-skiers are few and trout are plentiful. In the summer, that quotient is reversed, though the boating regulations do help (read on). This lake does receive large numbers of trout stocks, courtesy of the Department of Fish and Game—rainbow trout averaging 10–12 inches in length. Survival and growth rates are high because the water is imported from the delta via the California Aqueduct and is rich in aquatic food. From February through early June, the high catch rates keep anglers busy and content. If it's a significant snow year, that schedule can be delayed by a month, making March through July the prime time for fishing.

In addition to the 5-mph speed limits enforced in all of the major coves, several other boating rules help keep the place relatively sane. There are designated areas for boating, waterskiing, fishing, and sailboarding. The main lake area south of the dam is where waterskiing takes place, and there is a 35-mph speed limit. The entire lake is closed to boating 7 P.M.–7 A.M.; in other words, boats must be off the water by sundown. A maximum of 175 boats per day are allowed. Boat-launch reservations are recommended and are required on summer weekends and holidays

Note: All boats must be inspected and certified free of mussels prior to launching at this lake.

Facilities, fees: A paved boat ramp is on the lake's south shore. Campgrounds, restrooms with flush toilets and showers, a full-service marina, picnic areas, an RV dump station, and a convenience store are at the lake. Fishing boats and pontoon boats can be rented at the marina. Supplies can be obtained in Cajon Junction or Crestline. Day-use and boat-launching fees are charged.

Directions: From San Bernardino, take I-15 north to Palmdale/Cajon Junction and exit onto Highway 138 east. Drive 13 miles to the park entrance on the right.

Contact: Silverwood Lake State Recreation Area, 760/389-2303 or 760/389-2281, www .parks.ca.gov; Silverwood Lake Marina, 760/389-2299.

21 GLEN HELEN PARK LAKES

Rating: 6

northwest of San Bernardino at
Glen Helen Regional Park

Map 13.2, page 586

These two little lakes are a bait dunker's haven. They are so small that they get overlooked by most out-of-towners, yet they receive decent plants during the cool months. Just over a mile from the intersection of I-15 and I-215, the lakes are veritable dots of water and offer easy access. They are stocked regularly with trout and catfish, and bass are occasionally caught.

No boating is permitted, but that's not really a problem, because the lakes are too small for that anyway. Instead, you show up with your bait and your bucket, take a seat, and wait for that telltale nibble. The nibbles are forthcoming after stocks of trout, which are made by both the local park district and the Department of Fish and Game. The state adds trout averaging 8 inches and some averaging 11 inches.

Facilities, fees: A swimming lagoon, water slides, pedal-boat rentals, picnic areas, a snack bar (weekends only), and a bait and tackle shop are provided. Supplies can be obtained nearby. No boating is permitted. Day-use and fishing fees are charged. An annual pass may be purchased.

Directions: From San Bernardino, take I-215 north for nine miles to the exit for Devore Road. Take the Devore Road exit. Turn left (west) on Devore Road and drive 0.5 mile across the railroad tracks. Continue for 0.5 mile to the park.

Contact: Glen Helen Regional Park, 909/887-7540, cms.sbcounty.gov/parks.

22 LAKE GREGORY

Rating: 7

north of San Bernardino at
Lake Gregory Regional Park
Map 13.2, page 586

Little Lake Gregory, all of 86 acres, is like the personal backyard fishing hole for the lucky few who own vacation homes near it. The lake is at 4,700 feet on the edge of San Bernardino National Forest, and it is just a short drive north of San Bernardino. Silverwood Lake, to the northwest, is a nearby alternative.

Despite its relatively small size, Lake Gregory provides a viable trout fishery, one of the better in the region. The best fishing can be had by trolling in the late winter and early spring. Once the hot weather shows up, the fish become very difficult to catch. To make up for that lapse, the Department of Fish and Game comes to the rescue with consistent trout plants of catchable rainbow trout; they stock rainbow trout averaging 7–8 inches, with some 10- to 12-inchers. A sprinkling of bass and catfish are also available.

This is a popular lake, one of the relatively few in California where you can buy property near a lake. You get here via Highway 18, taking the slow but pretty Rim of the World Drive.

Note: Brown trout have not been stocked here since 1993.

Facilities, fees: A bait shop is nearby. A campground, restrooms with flush toilets, drinking water, a picnic area, and a snack bar are available. Rowboats, pedal boats, sailboards, sailboats, and water bikes can be rented at the boathouse in summer. A water slide is available. Cabins are nearby, at Camp Switzerland. No private boats may be launched; boating is restricted to rentals only. Electric motors are allowed (you may bring your own), but not gas motors. Supplies are nearby. A day-use fee is charged.

Directions: From San Bernardino, take Highway 18/Rim of the World Highway north for 14 miles to Crestline/Highway 138. Turn north (left) on Highway 138 and drive two miles to Lake Drive. Turn right on Lake Drive and drive three miles to the lake.

Contact: Lake Gregory Regional Park, San Bernardino County, 909/338-2233, cms. sbcounty.gov/parks; Camp Switzerland, 909/338-2731, www.campswitzerland.net.

23 GREEN VALLEY LAKE

Rating: 6

north of San Bernardino
Map 13.2, page 586

This is a small and pretty family-oriented lake. The regulars just keep coming back. It's set at 6,854 feet in San Bernardino National Forest, and because of its proximity to nearby Lake Arrowhead to the west and Big Bear Lake to the east, many folks just don't get around to making the trip.

Green Valley Lake is quiet and intimate, good for kayaks, canoes, and rowboats, as well as for shoreline bait dunkers. The lake receives enough plants of trout to provide good fishing for much of the year. The Department of Fish and Game adds trout in the 7- to 8-inch class and some averaging 10 or 12 inches, and private hatcheries add even more. The lake-record trout is 13 pounds, 3 ounces. The lake also has some bass, crappie, and catfish, which are sometimes caught by accident during the summer by trout anglers using night crawlers for bait.

Facilities, fees: A campground is nearby. Picnic areas; rowboat, kayak, and paddleboat rentals; a snack bar (summer only); convenience store; and bait are at the lake. All motorized craft and privately owned boats are prohibited. Day-use and daily fishing fees are charged.

Directions: From San Bernardino, take Highway 30 east to the junction with Highway 330 (near Highland). Take Highway 330 north (signed Mountain Resorts) and drive to Running Springs and the junction with Highway 18. Turn east on Highway 18 and drive to Green Valley Road. Turn left and drive 3.5 miles to the lake.

Contact: San Bernardino National Forest, Mountaintop Ranger District, 909/382-2790, www.fs.fed.us/r5—click on Forest Offices.

24 PECK ROAD PARK LAKE

Rating: 5
east of Los Angeles in Arcadia
Map 13.2, page 586

This lake is a good example of how large stocks of rainbow trout can turn an urban water hole into a viable fishery. And stocks it gets. As soon as the weather turns cool enough in the fall, the plants start. The lake receives rainbow trout in the 10- to 12-inch class and some in the over-12-inch class (fair numbers for a small lake). When the weather heats up the water in the spring, the trout plants stop at Peck Lake, and catfish stocking begins.

Santa Fe Reservoir (see listing in this chapter) to the east, provides a nearby option and is a more popular destination because it allows hand-powered boats such as kayaks and canoes.

Facilities, fees: A parking lot, restrooms, and picnic areas are provided. Boating is not permitted on the lake. Entrance to the park is free.

Directions: From Los Angeles, take I-10 east to the Peck Road exit. Turn north on Peck Road and drive 2.5 miles to Peck Road Park on the left. Watch for the signed turnoff.

Contact: Santa Fe Dam Recreation Area, 626/334-1065, www.parks.lacounty.gov/parkinfo.

25 SANTA FE RESERVOIR

Rating: 6
east of Los Angeles in Irwindale
Map 13.2, page 586

This lake was built as a flood-control area for the San Gabriel River. Given a fair shot of rainfall in the San Gabriel Mountains, when decent water releases from San Gabriel and Morris Reservoirs, the Santa Fe Dam will have enough water to provide a viable urban trout fishery. It is stocked with rainbow trout in the 7- to 8-inch class, as well as some in the 10- to 11-inch range and even some over 12 inches. Catfish are stocked here in the summer. The lake is also home to bass and bluegill.

Since the lake has a boat ramp, it is more desirable to many than nearby Peck Road Park Lake to the west. No gas motors are permitted.

Facilities, fees: A paved boat ramp is on the south side of the lake. A picnic area, rowboat rentals, a concession stand, and bait are available. No gas motors are permitted. Boats under 8 feet or over 18 feet long are prohibited. Open year-round, sunrise to sunset. Entrance and boat-launching fees are charged.

Directions: From Los Angeles, drive east on I-10 to I-605. Turn north and drive to the

Live Oak exit. Turn right on Live Oak Avenue and drive east for about 1.5 miles to the park entrance, on the left.

Contact: Santa Fe Dam Recreation Area, 626/334-1065, www.parks.lacounty.gov/parkinfo.

26 PUDDINGSTONE LAKE

Rating: 7

in San Dimas at Frank G. Bonelli Regional Park
Map 13.2, page 586

The "old mud puddle," as Puddingstone Lake is called, provides a good chance to catch bass and trout during the morning and evening and is a place to go waterskiing during the day. That's not too shabby, considering the lake is in such close proximity to so many people. It is just south of Raging Waters in San Dimas, bordered on its southern side by Bonnelli Regional Park.

When full, the lake covers 250 acres, and during the winter and spring months, it is an excellent destination. As soon as the weather turns cold, the general public abandons the place (water-skiers included). Yet that is when the trout plants start up, and they are generous: the lake gets large numbers of rainbow trout from fall through spring. They provide good catch rates for shoreliners and trollers alike. In addition, there are some big catfish (the lake record is 45 pounds). Other species include largemouth bass, bluegill, and crappie.

As the warm weather begins to arrive, usually in late February here, the bass fishing gets quite good. The water is still too cool for water-skiers, but it's not too cool for the bass to bite. The best areas are around the docks, as well as at the underwater drop-offs, which are 40–50 feet deep in the winter, 15–20 feet deep in the early spring, and then quite shallow from mid-March through early April.

By May this lake begins to turn into a hell hole for anglers because of the fast boats. From May through early September, folks suddenly remember how much fun it is to go boating,

and Puddingstone provides an easy-to-reach outlet for it. Even though the lake is small, waterskiing is allowed, and the skiers dominate the place.

The nickname of the lake, as mentioned, is the "old mud puddle." Why? Because after particularly intense rains, runoff from the southern slopes of the San Gabriel Mountains muddies up the lake significantly. When that occurs, the fishing turns off. But how often does it rain enough around here for runoff to be a factor? Not very often. The ideal situation is a moderate rain, which freshens the lake and clears the air, allowing anglers an excellent view of the mountains to the north. During the summer it gets so smoggy in this area that the mountains are often not even visible. When that happens, no problem—just leave the lake to the water-skiers. After all, fall through spring is the prime time for anglers anyway.

The speed limit at Puddingstone is 35 mph. The minimum length for powerboats is 12 feet and the maximum length is 26 feet. Fishing, sailing, and sailboarding are allowed daily. Canoes, kayaks, and inflatables are permitted. Shoreline fishing is allowed daily sunrise–9 p.m. Fishing from a boat is permitted sunrise–sunset. The lake is open from sunrise–9 p.m. March through October, and sunrise–7 p.m. November through February.

Note: All boats must be inspected and certified free of mussels prior to launching at this lake.

Facilities, fees: A campground, picnic areas, and boat ramp are available. Supplies are available nearby. The RV park has restrooms with showers, a recreation room, a swimming pool, modem hookups, cable TV, a grocery store, propane-gas delivery, and coin laundry. Day-use and boat-launching fees are charged.

Directions: From Pomona, take I-10 west for five miles to the Fairplex exit. Take the Fairplex exit north to the first traffic light and Via Verde. Turn left on Via Verde and drive to the first stop sign. Drive straight to enter the park, or turn right at Campers View and drive to the RV park.

Contact: Frank G. Bonnelli Regional Park, Los Angeles County, 909/599-8411, www .bonellipark.org/fishing; East Shore RV Park, 909/599-8355 or 800/809-3778, www.east shorervpark.com.

27 CUCAMONGA-GUASTI REGIONAL PARK

Rating: 4

northeast of Ontario

Map 13.2, page 586

This is a 150-acre day-use park that is especially popular with local residents because of its swimming lagoon and water slide.

Shore fishing is possible year-round at the largest lake, just 10 acres, and fishing is allowed at the smaller lake in the winter months. The lakes are stocked with trout and catfish in the 10-acre lake only. Other species include bass and bluegill.

Although no water-body contact is permitted in the two small lakes, visitors can still cool off on hot summer days in the lagoon. No private boats are allowed, but pedal boats and water bikes can be rented at the smaller lake during the summer months.

In winter, no fishing is permitted on Thursdays.

Facilities, fees: Pedal-boat and water-bike rentals are available, as are a water slide, a swimming lagoon, picnic areas, and a snack bar. Fees are charged for day use, fishing, swimming, and the water slide, which is wheelchair-accessible. No private boats are allowed, including inflatables. No water-body contact is allowed in the lakes. The park is open daily from Memorial Day weekend through Labor Day weekend, 7:30 A.M.–7 P.M., and daily the rest of the year 7:30 A.M.–5 P.M. In winter, no fishing is permitted on Thursdays.

Directions: From Ontario, take I-10 east for 3.5 miles to the exit for Archibald Avenue. Take that exit and drive north on Archibald Avenue for about 0.25 mile to the park entrance, on the right.

Contact: Cucamonga-Guasti Regional Park, 909/481-4205, ww.cms.sbcounty.gov/parks.

28 YUCAIPA REGIONAL PARK

Rating: 4

near Redlands

Map 13.2, page 586

This is a family-oriented county park, complete with water slides and pedal boats for the kids and fishing access and hiking trails for adults.

A one-acre swimming lagoon and two 350-foot water slides make this a favorite for youngsters. Three lakes are stocked weekly with catfish in the summer and trout in the winter—the closest thing around to an insurance policy for anglers.

Spectacular scenic views of the Yucaipa Valley, the San Bernardino Mountains, and Mount San Gorgonio are highlights from the park. The park covers 885 acres and is in the foothills of the San Bernardino Mountains. The Yucaipa Adobe and Mousley Museum of Natural History are nearby.

Facilities, fees: A swimming lagoon, fishing ponds, water slides, and pedal-boat and water-bike rentals are available. A campground, restrooms, drinking water, flush toilets, showers, a pay phone, a snack bar (summer only), picnic shelter, a playground with volleyball and horseshoes, and an RV dump station are nearby. The water slide is open Memorial Day weekend through Labor Day weekend. Fees are charged for day use, for use of the water slide, and for swimming and fishing. There is a rental-boat dock. No private boats, canoes, kayaks, or inflatables are permitted. Water-body contact is not permitted at the main lake.

Directions: Take I-10 to Redlands and the exit for Oak Glen Road. Take that exit, turn left, and drive 4.5 miles to the park, on the left.

Contact: Yucaipa Regional Park, 909/790-3127, www.cms.sbcounty.gov/parks.

29 SANTA ANA RIVER LAKES

Rating: 9

in Anaheim

Map 13.2, page 586   **BEST (**

Want to know what spot gets the most anglers in Southern California? Well, the Santa Ana River Lakes in Anaheim attract 2,000–5,000 anglers per week.

So how does it work? You pay a hefty access/fishing fee, which in turn goes to purchase the giant trout and catfish, and then you fish away, hoping to catch a big one. The odds are good.

Two state records have been set here: 27-pound, 8-ounce rainbow trout (California lake record) and 52-pound, 10-ounce channel catfish. There are also bass, crappie, sturgeon, wiper (a hybridized striped bass), and bluegill.

There are three lakes: a main fishing lake, a catfish lake, and a children's fishing pond. The fish factory is open daily 6 A.M.–11 P.M. year-round, and it is occasionally kept open during full moons for all-night fishing.

No water-body contact is permitted, although float tubes are allowed, and the anglers using them must wear waders.

Facilities, fees: A boat launch is on the northeast side of Big Lake. A rowboat dock is on the west side of Catfish Lake. Rowboat and powerboat rentals, rod rentals, tackle, a picnic area, a campground, and a convenience store are available. Other supplies can be obtained nearby. Fees are charged for day use/fishing, float tubes, and boat launching. No fishing license is required. Powerboats, rowboats, and inflatables are permitted. Only four-cycle motors are allowed. Personal watercraft, sailboarding, swimming, and other forms of water-body contact are not permitted. Signed speed limits are enforced.

Directions: Take Highway 91 to Anaheim and the exit for Tustin Avenue. Take that exit and drive north on Tustin Avenue for 0.25 mile to La Palma Avenue. Turn right and drive 0.5 mile to the lake entrance, on the right.

Contact: Santa Ana River Lakes, 714/632-7830 (recorded info), www.fishinglakes.com.

30 PRADO PARK LAKE

Rating: 5

near Corona in Prado Regional Park

Map 13.2, page 586

Prado Park Lake is the centerpiece of a 2,280-acre recreation-oriented park that features an equestrian center, athletic fields, a shooting range, and a golf course. This lake is a backyard fishing hole for folks in Corona and Norco. Catfish are stocked from April–September, and folks fish for catfish and bass.

In the early winter, it undergoes a complete transformation. A little rain and cold temperatures, and the water becomes oxygenated and cool. The Department of Fish and Game steps in and starts planting rainbow trout, and keeps at it until hot weather closes the door in April. By boat or bank, most folks here have the best luck by bait fishing.

Facilities, fees: A campground, restrooms with showers, coin laundry, a snack bar, a picnic area, a boat ramp, and a water playground are available. No gas motors, swimming, water-body contact, or inflatables are permitted. Open year-round, 7:30 A.M.–sunset. Fees are charged for day use, fishing, and boat launching.

Directions: From Riverside, take Highway 91 west to Highway 71. Turn north on Highway 71 and proceed four miles to Highway 83/Euclid Avenue. Turn right on Euclid Avenue and drive a mile to the park entrance, on the right.

Contact: Prado Regional Park, 909/597-4260, www.cms.sbcounty.gov/parks.

31 LAKE EVANS

Rating: 5

in Fairmount Park in Riverside

Map 13.2, page 586

The catfish program here has turned into a huge success. It is not only stocked now with thousands of pounds of channel catfish to help jump-start the fishery, but there are several catfish derbies to celebrate the good fishing. It has bluegill, trout, bass, and carp; trout are stocked in the winter, bass in the spring.

Evans is a good spot to bring a kayak, small rowboat, or canoe, then anchor and go bait fishing for trout in the winter or spring, or catfish in the summer. Shoreliners do well enough during the cool months. If there is a catch, it's that you must monitor water temperature. That decides what you are fishing for.

Lake Evans, a tiny lake on the northern flank of Riverside, would be barren without the plants. It receives trout averaging 8 inches and some in the 10- to 12-inch class.

This area gets smoking hot for weeks in the summer and fall.

The lake is open 10 A.M.–7 P.M. Thursday–Tuesday from Memorial Day weekend through Labor Day weekend. Otherwise, it's open 10 A.M.–sunset. Motorized boats and inflatables are not permitted. Boats under 8 feet or over 15 feet long are prohibited, with the exception of canoes and kayaks.

Facilities, fees: Boat rentals are available. A campground is at Jurupa Regional Park. Restrooms and picnic areas are provided. Supplies can be obtained in Riverside. Access is free. A boating permit must be obtained at the park.

Directions: From Riverside, take Highway 60 north and take the Market Street exit. Turn left (south) on Market Street and continue to the park entrance on the right.

Contact: Riverside County Department of Parks and Recreation, 951/826-2000, www.riversideca.gov.

32 LAKE PERRIS

Rating: 10

southeast of Riverside at
Lake Perris State Recreation Area
Map 13.2, page 586   **BEST (**

Legends can throw newcomers off the track, and the legend of Lake Perris as one of the best lakes for spotted bass sends many anglers on their first adventure here on a wild goose chase.

Perris dominates the line-class world records kept by the International Game Fish Association for spotted bass like no other water in the world does for any species. But the big spotties are not as easy to catch as you might think, and in the attempt to track down a monster, many anglers overlook outstanding surface fishing for largemouth bass and solid trout fishing. In addition, there are some truly awesome, monster-sized bluegill at the lake, courtesy of the fast-growing Florida strain. They bite best in the spring.

The lake annually produces dozens of double digit–weight bass, and the current lake-record largemouth bass is 17 pounds, 6 ounces. To catch the big ones here, try using big swim baits; the Huddleston is probably the best. Old favorites, such as the AC Plug and Castaic Trout, are some tried and true ones. One crazy option is to use saltwater swim bait with built-in scent, like the Berkley Gulp series of baits. Big fish have seen just about everything. Showing them something different can be the trick to get them to take.

World records aside, the largemouth bass fishing here is often much better than that for spotted bass. It's an ideal place to learn how to fish the surface, either casting a floating Rapala, Zara Spook, Jitterbug, or Chugger, or even fly-fishing with a popper or mouse. As long as the water isn't too cold, the popping and plugging can produce excellent catch rates. In the warm months, get on the water early or late, and leave it to the water-skiers between 10:30 A.M. and 5 P.M.

I remember one early summer morning when I first gave up on the spotted bass here and instead tried for largemouth. I caught and released nearly a dozen and figured I'd really done something special. But back at the launch ramp at 11 A.M., I learned that nearly everyone was catching 10–15 fish apiece, even more for some anglers. It completely changed my focus.

The irony is that there are still a few huge

spotted bass at Perris. But the truth is that the largemouth bass are taking over. The better fishing for spotted bass is not with surface lures, but with grubs, fishing them 20–25 feet deep. The top spots for spotties are in breaks between a submerged structure that is bottomed out by rocks. It can take a lot of searching.

What do not take a lot of searching are the trout. The Department of Fish and Game stocks large numbers of rainbow trout, in the 7- to 8-inch and 10- to 12-inch classes. In the cooler months, when the bass are sluggish, the rainbow trout provide good catch rates for both trollers and bait dunkers. The lake also has catfish, crappie, bluegill, and redear and green sunfish.

The lake (elevation 1,500 feet) is in Moreno Valley just southwest of the Badlands foothills. It's a roundish lake that covers 2,200 acres, with an island that makes a good boat-in picnic site. And, unfortunately, it can have a ton of water-skiers during the summer. The weather out here can be like a fire pit in the summer and fall, and that makes waterskiing very popular.

Note: All boats must be inspected and certified free of mussels prior to launching at this lake.

Facilities, fees: A large, multilane paved launching area is on the lake's north shore, just east of the marina. Campgrounds, restrooms with flush toilets, showers, an RV dump station, picnic areas, a full-service marina, moorings, two swimming beaches, and a convenience store are available. Fishing boats and pontoon boats are for rent. The speed limit is 35 mph, except in a few areas where it is reduced to 5 mph. A day-use fee and boating fee are charged. Lake hours are 6 A.M.–6:30 P.M. in winter, and 6 A.M.–8:30 P.M. in summer. All vessels must be on their trailers by the designated close time.

Directions: From Riverside, take I-215/Highway 60 east for about five miles to the I-215/60 split. Bear south on I-215 at the split and drive six miles to Ramona Expressway. Turn left

(east) and drive 3.5 miles to Lake Perris Drive. Turn left and drive 0.75 mile to the park entrance. Boat ramps are located on the north shore of the lake.

Contact: Lake Perris State Recreation Area, 909/940-5603, www.parks.ca.gov.

33 IRVINE LAKE

Rating: 9

southeast of Los Angeles

Map 13.2, page 586　　　　　BEST (

Instead of searching across miles and miles of country to catch a fish, at 750-acre Irvine Lake you get the opposite approach: they bring the fish to you. A hefty access fee is charged, which is turned around and used in part to purchase stocks of huge trout in the winter and huge catfish in the summer. How big? Well, it is kind of mind-boggling: rainbow trout in the 10-pound class and occasionally even at 20 pounds can be found here, and a lake-record catfish of 89.6 pounds was caught in October of 1999.

Irvine Lake is the best place around these parts. The species that are selected are dependent on water temperature; trout plants usually occur from mid-November through March, when the water is cool, and the big catfish are planted for the rest of the year, when the water is warm. Almost never is a trout under a foot stocked in the lake; they leave the dinkers to the Department of Fish and Game. Most of the fish are caught on bait. The top spots are Sierra Cove and the buoy line.

For bass, fishing is strictly catch-and-release. A five-acre fishing pond for children is available.

The fish are often so big that it can be a real mind-bender. On a trip to Alaska's famed Kulik River, I ran into world-class fly fisher Ed Rice, and it wasn't long before we started discussing the size of Alaska's rainbow trout. Then he smiled and said, "You want to know where the biggest trout in the world are? They aren't in Alaska. They're at that Irvine Lake and Santa Ana Lake in Los Angeles." We both laughed. After all, he was right.

Powerboats, canoes, kayaks, and inflatables are allowed. A 5-mph speed limit is enforced from sunrise to 4 P.M. Waterskiing is permitted after 4 P.M. All boats, including inflatables, must be at least eight feet long. The rental-boat fleet numbers 100 boats here. They are very popular among anglers.

Other lake records: 22.6-pound rainbow trout; 12.5-pound brown trout; 17.0 pound steelhead; 50-pound channel catfish; 14-pound, 7-ounce largemouth bass; 49.6-pound sturgeon; 35-pound carp; 4-pound, 2-ounce crappie.

Facilities, fees: A paved boat ramp is on the south side of the lake. Powerboats, rowboats, pontoon boats, and fishing rods are for rent. A children's fishing pond, a picnic area, a campground, restrooms, a café, bait and tackle, and RV and boat storage are available. Access, fishing, and boat-launching fees are charged. No fishing license is required.

Directions: From I-5 (east of Los Angeles), drive to the Highway 91 exit east and drive about nine miles to Highway 55. Turn south on Highway 55 and drive four miles to Chapman Avenue. Turn east and drive nine miles (Chapman Avenue will become Santiago Canyon Road) and look for the lake entrance, on the left side of the road.

Contact: Irvine Lake, 714/649-9111 or 714/649-9113, www.irvinelake.net.

for rainbow trout is 23.5 pounds. Other species include hybridized striped bass, sturgeon, largemouth bass, crappie, and bluegill.

Corona Lake is in the foothills of Corona and is surrounded by oak canyons and meadows. No water-body contact is permitted, but float tubing is allowed, providing anglers wear waders. Powerboats are allowed, but a 5-mph speed limit is strictly enforced. No fishing license is required.

Facilities, fees: A primitive boat ramp is on the west side of the lake. Powerboats, rowboats, and fishing rods are for rent. A picnic area, restrooms, campground, a convenience store, and tackle are available. Supplies can be obtained nearby. The lake is open 6 A.M.–11 P.M. Fees are charged for day use/fishing, float tubes, and boat launching. Powerboats, rowboats, and inflatables, including float tubes, are permitted. A 5-mph speed limit is strictly enforced. Personal watercraft, sailboarding, swimming, and other forms of water-body contact are not allowed.

Directions: From Corona, take I-15 south for about nine miles to the exit for Indian Truck Trail. Take that exit and drive (under the freeway) to Temescal Canyon Road. Turn right and drive 0.25 mile to the lake entrance, on the left.

Contact: Corona Lakes, 951/277-4489 (recorded information), www.fishinglakes .com.

34 CORONA LAKE

Rating: 9

southeast of Corona

Map 13.2, page 586

If you're looking for fishing action, this is the place. This is one of the Southern California lakes where the concept of pay-to-fish has turned the lake into a winner. Corona Lake is heavily stocked at least twice per week with trout and catfish, and it receives heavy fishing pressure. Corona has held state records for catfish, with a lake-record 61-pounder, while the lake record

35 LAKE ELSINORE

Rating: 6

south of Riverside at

Lake Elsinore Recreation Area

Map 13.2, page 586

This is the home of the legendary Whiskers, a very special catfish. It is a hybrid channel catfish that was stocked in the lake. It is a genetic cross between a blue and channel catfish, meaning that Whiskers could grow to more than 100 pounds. So far, as far as I know, Whiskers is still out there...

The city also stocks hybrid striped bass and largemouth bass, which helps give the lake a nice boost. They join resident populations of bullhead, channel catfish, crappie, bluegill, and largemouth bass.

The lake is at 1,239 feet in a region where water is like gold, especially for recreation. As the largest natural freshwater lake in Southern California, there is a lot of gold. It covers 3,300 acres and has 15 miles of shoreline. A fishery program has greatly improved prospects at this lake.

The squarish Elsinore is popular for waterskiing, and on summer afternoons, the place is loaded with skiers. The speed limit is 35 mph, except in designated high-speed areas. Fishing hours are sunrise–10 P.M. There are several fully developed RV parks nearby.

One word of caution: In low-rain years, Elsinore's water level can be subject to fluctuations and drawdowns. It is advisable to call ahead or check the website for lake conditions before planning a trip. In high-rain years, the problem isn't nearly as extreme, of course.

Facilities, fees: Campgrounds, lodging, picnic areas, an RV dump station, a snack bar, bait and tackle, and small stores are available. Day-use and boat-launching fees are charged.

Directions: To the west shore boat ramp: Take I-15 to the Bundy Canyon Road exit. Take that exit, turn west (driving under the freeway), and drive to where the road dead-ends, at Mission Trail. Turn right and drive 0.75 mile to Corydon Road. Turn left and drive one mile to its end, at Grand Avenue. Turn right and drive four miles to the Playland RV Park and boat launch, on the right. Or continue on Grand Avenue to Weekend Paradise and Crane Lakeside Park & Resort—if you reach the Ortega Highway (Highway 74), you have gone too far.

To the east shore boat ramp: Take I-15 to the exit for Main Street. Turn west on Main Street and drive one mile to Graham Street. Turn right on Graham Street and drive to Lindsay Street. Turn left on Lindsay Street and drive to Lakeshore Drive. Turn left on Lakeshore Drive and drive a short distance to Lake Elsinore City Public Launch Ramp, on the left (this ramp is not usable when lake levels are low).

To the north shore boat ramp: Take I-15 to the exit for Central Avenue/Highway 74. Turn west on Highway 74 and drive for three miles to the entrance for the ramp, on the left. Or continue a short distance on Highway 74 to reach boat ramps at The Outhouse, Roadrunner RV Park, and Elsinore West Marina. The ramp at The Outhouse is suitable for personal watercraft and small boats only. The ramp at Roadrunner is not usable when the lake level is low.

Contact: Lake Elsinore Marina, 800/328-6844, www.lakeelsinoremarina.com; The City of Lake Elsinore, 951/674-3124, ext. 265; Lake Elsinore City Public Launch Ramp, 951/245-9308; Elsinore Valley Municipal Water District, www.evmwd.com (water levels).

Lodging: Lake Elsinore City Campground, 951/471-1212; Playland RV Park, 909/678-4663, www.playlandrvpark.net; Crane Lakeside Park & Resort, 951/678-2112, www.cranelakeside.com; Roadrunner RV Park, 951/674-4900.

36 TRABUCO CREEK

Rating: 4

east of Mission Viejo

Map 13.2, page 586

A lot of folks overlook little Trabuco Creek. Access is not easy, and a high-clearance vehicle is recommended. In addition, many anglers from the L.A. area think the only nearby stream fishing is in the Angeles or San Bernardino National Forests. Not so, not with Trabuco Creek flowing down the slopes of lesser-used Cleveland National Forest.

The stream is decent only in the spring months, when flows can support planted trout. The Department of Fish and Game responds by stocking trout in the seven- to eight-inch class, and this is where they go: 4–5 miles above O'Neill Regional Park, with

Trabuco Creek Road providing easy access. Most DFG stocks have been stopped at small streams in Southern California, and I have removed them from this book. This one could be an exception—but for how long? Before planning your trip, check with DFG.

About 70 percent of the campsites in the area are set under a canopy of sycamore and oak. Several roads near this park lead to trailheads into Cleveland National Forest, which is generally at about 1,000 feet in elevation in this area. Occasionally, rangers post mountain lion warnings.

Facilities, fees: A campground and firewood are available at O'Neill Regional Park. A National Forest Adventure Pass is required.

Directions: Take I-5 to Laguna Hills and the County Road S18/El Toro Road exit. Take that exit east and drive past El Toro for 7.5 miles to Live Oak Canyon Road. Turn right at Live Oak Canyon Road/County Road S19 and drive about four miles to Trabuco Canyon Road. After crossing the bridge over Trabuco Creek, turn left for stream access. Access is available upstream of the O'Neill Regional Park.

Contact: Cleveland National Forest, Trabuco Ranger District, 951/736-1811, www.fs.fed .us/r5—click on Forest Offices; O'Neill Regional Park, 949/923-2260, www.ocparks .com/oneillpark.

37 LAGUNA NIGUEL LAKE

Rating: 9

in South Laguna
Map 13.2, page 586

Maybe little Laguna Niguel will shock the world. Some say the lake has become a world-class bass fishery. It has become the site of catch-and-release bass events, and the chance of giant bass appears inevitable. Trout, bass, black crappie, bluegill, and catfish are stocked, and the lake also has carp. The stocks include Alpers trout that average 2–5 pounds.

The lake record for blue catfish is 68 pounds. All bass fishing on Laguna Niguel Lake is

catch-and-release only. No private boats are permitted, but float tubes are allowed, and it's become quite a spectacle to get out in a float tube and cast for these big bass.

Laguna Niguel is a very pretty 44-acre lake set in a canyon in the coastal foothills south of the L.A. Basin. It is the centerpiece for a regional park, a nice spot for picnics and walks, and a great place for folks who might want to toss out a fishing line and see what bites.

Facilities, fees: Picnic areas, bait and tackle, a fish-cleaning station, and a concession stand are available. No private boats are permitted, but boats and rods can be rented; there is a rental dock on the west side of the lake. Supplies can be obtained nearby. An entrance fee is charged, and there is a charge per day for boat launching, fishing, and float tubes.

Directions: Take I-5 to the La Paz exit (near Mission Viejo). Turn south on La Paz Road and drive four miles to the park, on the right.

Contact: Laguna Niguel Regional Park, 949/923-2240 or 949/362-9227, www .lagunaniguellake.com; Sports Chalet, Laguna Niguel, 949/362-0342.

38 LAKE SKINNER

Rating: 7

near Temecula at
Lake Skinner Recreation Area
Map 13.2, page 586

Don't like water-skiers? Don't like personal watercraft? Don't like fast boats of any kind? Then this is the right place.

While Lake Elsinore to the nearby west can be dominated by water sports, Skinner is dominated by anglers and a 10-mph speed limit. And anglers can be rewarded with tremendous numbers of trout plants (considering the size of the lake) and catfish plants as well.

Skinner is set within a county park at 1,470 feet in sparse foothill country, and it covers 1,200 surface acres when full. It usually receives trout planted by the county.

They provide good prospects for trollers, with

the northeast cove and northern shore the best stretches of water. Shoreline anglers have their best hopes in the southeast arm of the lake, within walking distance of the parking area and campgrounds. The lake also has striped bass, largemouth bass, bluegill, and channel catfish.

The big question mark is how striped bass will affect this lake in the future. As Skinner evolves, it has become one of the better striper lakes in Southern California.

No water-body contact is permitted at the lake, and you know what that means. Right: no water-skiers. Kayaks must be the sit-inside-enclosed type, not the sit-on-top style, and all boats must be inspected before launching.

Lake records: 39-pound, 8-ounce striped bass; 33-pound catfish; 14-pound, 8-ounce largemouth bass.

Facilities, fees: Paved launch ramps are available on the lake's northeast and southeast arms. A marina, moorings, boat rentals, and bait are available. A campground with restrooms, drinking water, flush toilets, showers, a convenience store, a snack bar (weekends only), an RV dump station, and a swimming pool (in the summer) is nearby. Boats under 10 feet long and all inflatables are prohibited. A 10-mph speed limit is enforced at all times. Day-use, fishing, and boat-launching fees are charged.

Directions: Take I-15 to Temecula and the exit for Rancho California. Take that exit northeast and drive 9.5 miles to the entrance for Lake Skinner Recreation Area on the right.

Contact: Lake Skinner Recreation Area, Riverside County, 909/926-1541, www.rivcoparks .org; Lake Skinner Marina, 951/926-8515.

39 BIG BEAR LAKE

Rating: 9

northeast of San Bernardino in
San Bernardino National Forest
Map 13.3, page 587

Big Bear is at 6,743 feet, and its beauty is unmatched by the other waters in the region. In the spring, the surrounding snowcapped ridge makes a striking contrast. The lake covers some 3,000 acres and has 22 miles of shoreline. It is a favorite vacation destination for faithful locals and even those from farther afield, making this something like the Lake Tahoe of Southern California.

Trout fishing is often very good. Big Bear gets huge numbers of rainbow trout, typically more than 150,000, courtesy of the Department of Fish and Game. They join a good population of holdover fish from previous years' stocks, as survival rates are quite good. More trout and catfish are stocked in the fall.

You'll get the best results by slow-trolling adjacent to the shoreline. The best spots are from Eagle Point west to the dam.

In the summer months, the fishery here can become primarily an early-morning/late-evening affair, as the water becomes the domain of water-skiers during the midday hours. There are a few largemouth and smallmouth bass, bluegill, crappie, sunfish, catfish, and carp. A great fishing tournament is held every May, right when fishing is the best. Another tournament is in October, and a bowfishing carp tournament takes place in June.

For wild-trout fly fishers, nearby Bear Creek, below Big Bear Lake, provides an option. Getting there involves a short but rugged hike, about a quarter mile. For hikers, the Pacific Crest Trail passes just a few miles north of the lake. Easy trailhead access is available, so if you want to break away from the crowds and take a hike, you can.

Big Bear has everything. It is big and beautiful. It has good trout fishing, quality boating opportunities, many campgrounds, and a few resorts. Access is easy. And it is near the highest regions of San Bernardino National Forest. Fish, boat, camp, and hike—you can do it all at this prime Southern California destination. Just don't expect to have the place to yourself. At times it can also have a lot of people. As I said, it has everything.

Lake records: 14.69-pound rainbow trout; 7-pound, 4-ounce largemouth bass.

Note: All boats must be inspected and

certified free of mussels prior to launching at this lake.

Facilities, fees: There are campgrounds, cabins, lodging, picnic areas, full-service marinas, boat ramps, boat rentals, bait, tackle, and groceries. Boats more than 26 feet long are prohibited. At most campgrounds, drinking water and flush toilets are provided. A boating permit, available by day or by annual pass, is required and can be purchased at all marinas. A day-use fee is charged.

Directions: From San Bernardino, take Highway 18 north and drive 15 miles to the Arrowhead Ranger Station. Continue east for about 15 more miles to Big Bear Lake.

The following are directions to the lake's marinas, as well as information on their facilities:

• To Big Bear Marina: Take Highway 18 (on the lake's south shore) toward Big Bear Lake Village to Paine Road/Highway 18 (look for the big wooden arch that goes across the road). Turn left on Paine Road and continue about two blocks to the marina. Fishing boats, pontoon boats, personal watercraft, pedal boats, canoes, and kayaks are for rent. Storage docks, moorings, a boat ramp, tackle, and guide service are available.

• To Holloway's Marina & RV Park: Take Highway 18 (on the lake's south shore) toward Big Bear Lake Village. Continue over the dam and drive three miles to Edgemore Street (look for the Log Cabin Restaurant). Turn left on Edgemore Street and drive about 0.5 mile to the marina. Fishing boats, pontoon boats, sailboats, pedal boats, and personal watercraft are for rent. Docks, moorings, a boat ramp, gas, bait and tackle, and groceries are available.

• To Municipal Water District East Launch: Take Highway 18 (on the lake's south shore) toward Big Bear Lake Village. Continue to the dam and the junction with Highway 38. Turn east on Highway 38 and drive nine miles to the public launch (it's well signed) on the northeast shore.

• To Municipal Water District West Launch: Take Highway 18 (on the lake's south shore)

toward Big Bear Lake Village. Continue to the dam and the junction with Highway 38. Turn east on Highway 38 and drive 2.5 miles to the public launch (well signed) on the northwest shore.

• To Pine Knot Landing: Take Highway 18 (on the lake's south shore) toward Big Bear Lake Village to Pine Knot Road (the first stop sign after the wooden arch that goes across the road). Turn left on Pine Knot Avenue and drive to the marina, at the road's end. Fishing boats, pontoon boats, speedboats, personal watercraft, sailboats, kayaks, and canoes are for rent. Docks, mooring, slips, storage, bait and tackle, a small store, gas, boat tours, and parasailing are available, as are waterskiing, wakeboarding, and kneeboarding lessons.

• To Pleasure Point Marina: Take Highway 18 (on the lake's south shore) toward Big Bear Lake Village. Continue over the dam and drive two miles to Cienega Way. Turn left on Cienega Way and drive 0.5 mile to Landlock Landing Road. Turn right and drive into the marina. Docks, moorings, boat storage, bait and tackle, a snack bar, and rentals for fishing boats, pontoon boats, pedal boats, and canoes are available.

• To North Shore Landing: Take Highway 18 (on the lake's south shore) toward Big Bear Lake Village. Continue to the dam and the junction with Highway 38. Turn east on Highway 38 and drive two miles to the marina. Fishing boats, sailboats, personal watercraft, speedboats, pontoon boats, canoes, and kayaks are available. Guides, pirate-ship cruises (summer only), and lessons for sailing, waterskiing, wakeboarding, and kneeboarding are available, as are docks, moorings, bait and tackle, and a snack bar.

• To Big Bear Shores & RV Resort: Take Highway 18 (on the lake's south shore) toward Big Bear Lake Village. Continue to the dam and the junction with Highway 38. Turn east on Highway 38 and drive 6.5 miles to the resort. Fishing boats and pontoon boats are for rent. Docks and moorings are available.

Contact: San Bernardino National Forest,

Mountaintop Ranger District and Big Bear Discovery Center, 909/866-3437 or 909/382-2790, www.fs.fed.us/r5—click on Forest Offices; Big Bear Municipal Water District, 909/866-5796, www.bbmwd.org; Big Bear Lake Resort Association, 800/424-4232, bigbearinfo.com.

Marinas: Big Bear Marina, 909/866-3218, www.bigbearmarina.com; Holloway's Marina & RV Park, 909/866-5706 or 800/448-5335, www.bigbearboating.com; Municipal Water District East Launch, 909/866-5200; Municipal Water District West Launch, 909/866-2917; Captain John's Marina, 909/866-6478; Pine Knot Landing, 909/866-7766, www.pineknotmarina.com; Pleasure Point Marina, 909/866-2455, www.pleasurepointbbl.com; North Shore Landing, 909/878-4386, www.bigbearboating.com; Big Bear Shores RV Resort and Yacht Club, 909/866-4151, www.bigbearshores.com.

Guides: Big Bear Charter Fishing, 800/475-3166, www.bigbearfishing.com; Cantrell Guide Service, 909/585-4017 or 909/239-7867, www.bigbearfishing.net; Fish Big Bear, 909/635-7501, www.fishbigbear.net; Lucky Bear Fishing Charters, 909/866-7303, www.luckybearfishing.com.

Supplies: Big Bear Sporting Goods, 909/866-3222, www.bigbearlakesporting goods.com.

40 SANTA ANA RIVER

Rating: 6

east of Redlands in
San Bernardino National Forest
Map 13.3, page 587

This gem is no secret. The Santa Ana River provides a trout stream alternative to the heavily used Big Bear Lake to the nearby north, and a lot of people take advantage of it. Access is easy, trout stocks are quite high, and catch rates are decent enough.

Where are the trout stocked? From Seven Oaks on upstream about seven miles to the

South Fork Bridge on Highway 38. Several turnouts provide direct access to the better spots. The south fork gets an additional number of the seven- to eight-inchers. There are also some brown trout well upstream, but it requires a dangerous scramble across slippery, smooth granite. One slip and you can fall into the river.

Facilities, fees: Campgrounds are off Highway 38. Supplies can be obtained in Redlands or Angeles Oaks. A Forest Service Adventure Pass is required.

Directions: Take I-10 to Redlands and the exit for Highway 38. Take the Highway 38 exit and turn east. Drive past Angeles Oaks to Seven Oaks Road and turn left; access is available off the road.

Contact: San Bernardino National Forest, Mill Creek Ranger District, 909/382-2882, www.fs.fed.us/r5—click on Forest Offices.

41 FULMOR LAKE

Rating: 5

near Banning in
San Bernardino National Forest
Map 13.3, page 587

Wanted: a lake that not everyone knows about. Found: Fulmor Lake.

Little Fulmor Lake is a tiny sliver set at 5,300 feet on the western slopes of the San Jacinto Mountains, near the Black Mountain National Scenic Area. It's small, obscure, and often discovered accidentally by folks heading to nearby Mount San Jacinto State Park or by hikers heading into the adjacent wilderness area to the east.

The lake can be a decent spot for shoreline fishing. Just pick a spot, cast out, and wait for a trout to wander by. The best prospects are in the spring, of course, when water conditions are ideal. The Department of Fish and Game stocks Fulmor with some trout averaging 7 or 8 inches, as well as with some in the 10- to 12-inch class.

A side-trip option is to continue on the road

past the lake, which leads to a trailhead. The trail runs east up to the ridgeline, intersects with the Pacific Crest Trail, and provides a route to Fuller Ridge, Castle Rocks, or south to San Jacinto Peak.

Facilities, fees: Campgrounds are north and south of the lake, off Highway 243. A picnic area with drinking water and pit toilets is at the lake. Supplies can be obtained in Banning. A wheelchair-accessible fishing pier is available. A National Forest Adventure Pass is required.

Directions: From Idyllwild, take Highway 243 north for 12 miles to the entrance on the right.

Contact: San Bernardino National Forest, Idyllwild Ranger Station, 909/382-2922, www.fs.fed.us/r5—click on Forest Offices.

42 STRAWBERRY CREEK

Rating: 4

in Idyllwild

Map 13.3, page 587

In this particular area, it's Lake Hemet to the south that gets most of the attention and Fulmor Lake to the north that gets the hikers. But in between is Strawberry Creek, which flows right through the center of Strawberry Valley and provides a backyard fishing hole for folks who live in the Idyllwild area. Out-of-towners miss it every time.

It's stocked with rainbow trout, mostly seven- and eight-inchers, right where Highway 243 crosses the stream. Park your car, hike a little, cast a little, and maybe you'll catch a few, and add another little fishing spot to your list of successes.

Note that there is a lot of private land along the creek here. Be sure to respect property rights. Also note that fishing fluctuates greatly each year according to stream flows. Also note that DFG could choose to stop stocking this stream, as they have done most all creeks in Southern California.

Facilities, fees: Campgrounds are north of

Idyllwild at Idyllwild County Park or Mount San Jacinto State Park. Supplies can be obtained in Idyllwild. A day-use fee is charged. An annual pass may be purchased.

Directions: From Idyllwild, take Highway 243 south to where the creek crosses the road (just south of the town of Idyllwild); direct access is available. This is usually where the stream is stocked in late winter.

Contact: San Bernardino National Forest, Idyllwild Ranger Station, 909/382-2922, www.fs.fed.us/r5—click on Forest Offices.

43 DIAMOND VALLEY LAKE

Rating: 8

near Hemet

Map 13.3, page 587

Diamond Valley Lake is the region's crown jewel for recreation and boating, and it might become an angler's paradise. The lake spans 4.5 miles long and two miles wide, the largest body of fresh water in Southern California.

In the winter months, outstanding trout stocks jump-start good fishing, with rainbow trout as large as 5–10 pounds, occasionally even bigger. The vicinity of the marina is often a good spot. In the spring and fall, bass fishing takes center stage, often best fairly deep near the dam, with fish ranging over 10 pounds.

The lake-record largemouth bass weighed 16.43 pounds.

Channel and blue catfish are also available, yet may be difficult to target for many anglers because no night fishing is permitted. Bluegill and redear sunfish also are part of the fishery mix.

Note: All boats must be inspected and certified free of mussels prior to launching at this lake.

Facilities, fees: Portable toilets are available on shore, and floating toilets are available for boaters. A small marina with boat rentals, bait and tackle, and a snack shop is available. No water-body contact is permitted. No alcohol is permitted anywhere at the lake.

Open sunrise–sunset. There is a wheelchair-accessible dock. Fees are charged for entrance, boat launching, daily fishing permits, and reservations.

Directions: From Los Angeles County, take I-60 southeast to I-215. Turn south on I-215 to the exit for State Route 74. Take State Route 74 east (toward Hemet; the road changes names to Florida Avenue) to Sanderson Avenue. Turn right on Sanderson and drive to Domenigoni Parkway. Turn left on Domenigoni and drive to Searl Parkway. Turn right and drive to the east marina.

From San Diego County: Take I-15 north to the exit for State Route 79 North/Winchester Road. Turn right on Winchester Road and drive 12 miles to Domenigoni Parkway. Turn right and drive to Searl Parkway. Turn right and drive to the east marina.

Contact: Diamond Valley Lake Marina, 800/590-5253, www.dvlake.com.

44 LAKE HEMET

Rating: 7

near Hemet

Map 13.3, page 587

Every now and then, Hemet can really turn on, and when that happens, don't wait. You have to be here right away to get in on it. At other times, things can be very tough.

Best of all, Lake Hemet receives rainbow trout from the Department of Fish and Game, usually a large allotment for a lake of this size. Most are in the 7- to 8-inch class, and some are in the 10- to 12-inch class. If catch rates weren't good, there are times when it seems that the fish would have to be planted vertically in order to fit.

The lake also has largemouth bass, bluegill, and catfish, which provide other options during the summer months. But it's the spring-through-summer transition period, and then again in early winter, when Hemet really shines. The weather is cooler, the trout plants abundant, and the catches good for both bass and trout.

Lake Hemet, at an elevation of 4,340 feet, is just west of Garner Valley, in Riverside County near San Bernardino National Forest. It has a campground, a boat ramp, and a 10-mph speed limit that keeps the place quiet and fairly intimate.

With just 420 surface acres, Lake Hemet is not about to be mistaken for the well-known bigger lakes in Southern California. At the same time, however, that can be one of the best things about little Hemet. Because of its small size, some folks just pass on by, never really allowing the lake to enter into their consciousness. But it is a good camping/fishing destination, especially when the water is cool and the lake receives large stocks of trout. The lake is under the jurisdiction of the Lake Hemet Municipal Water District.

Kayaks are acceptable if the owner is certified. Boats under 10 feet long are not allowed, nor are canoes, sailboats, and inflatables of any length. Swimming and wading are prohibited.

Note: All boats must be inspected and certified free of mussels prior to launching at this lake.

The lake is open April through September 6 A.M.–10 P.M. and October through March 7 A.M.–8 P.M., Fridays to 10 P.M.

Facilities, fees: A paved boat ramp is on the east shore of the lake. Boat rentals and bait are available. A campground with restrooms, drinking water, flush toilets, coin showers, an RV dump station, a playground, a convenience store, coin laundry, and propane gas is nearby. Additional supplies can be obtained in Hemet. Day-use and boat-launching fees are charged.

Directions: From Palm Desert, take Highway 74 southwest for 32 miles to the lake entrance, on the left.

Contact: Lake Hemet, 909/659-2680, www.lakehemet.org.

SAN DIEGO AND VICINITY

© KLOTZ/123RF.COM

BEST FISHING SPOTS

◖ Saltwater Fisheries
San Diego Deep Sea, **page 626.**

◖ Most Unusual Fisheries
Dixon Lake, **page 628.**

The San Diego area is rated the No. 1 region in

California for fishing – it doesn't get any better than this.

The deep-sea operations are the best anywhere. There are opportunities for local trips for yellowtail, white sea bass, albacore tuna, and marlin, and there are also long-range trips for world-class-sized fish, such as tuna weighing over 300 pounds. All of these fish are line-burners, and when there are multiple hookups aboard, it is absolutely the most exciting fishing imaginable.

This area is a gem, and the coastline from San Diego on up to San Onofre provides the crown jewels of Mission Bay and Oceanside – great for a variety of stellar ocean-fishing trips. The variety of habitat makes it captivating and exciting, with vast kelp forests and warm-water outfall (at San Onofre) in the shallows, and deep underwater shelves and blue-water fishing offshore. The area has a lot of baitfish, squid, mackerel, sardines, and anchovies, providing the basis for a rich fishery.

For many, the weather is near perfect. It is a warm coastal environment, with an azure-tinted sea that borders foothills and mountains. In other words, in a relatively small geographic spread, you get it all.

Yet some anglers do not even venture to the salt. That is because they have the fever for largemouth bass and instead fish a series of fantastic lakes in the area, such as Barrett Lake (by reservation only), Lower Otay, El Capitan, San Vicente, Hodges, Cuyamaca, Henshaw, and Morena. Some of the biggest lake-record bass ever caught in the world have been caught here. These lakes also offer opportunities for giant catfish and bluegill. If there is one problem, it's that a high number of people fish a relatively small number of lakes, so the fish are smart. Catch-and-release is advised to keep the bass fishery strong, so bass have been caught a number of times. At the same time, they have to eat, and right there is your chance.

In an unofficial vote at a national conference for the Outdoor Writers Association of America, San Diego was picked as one of the best regions to live in America.

It is easy to understand why: the weather, the ocean and beaches, the lakes and the fishing, Cleveland National Forest, the state parks, the Palomar Mountains, and the hiking, biking, and water sports. What more could you ask for? For many, the answer is you don't ask for more, because it does not get any better than this.

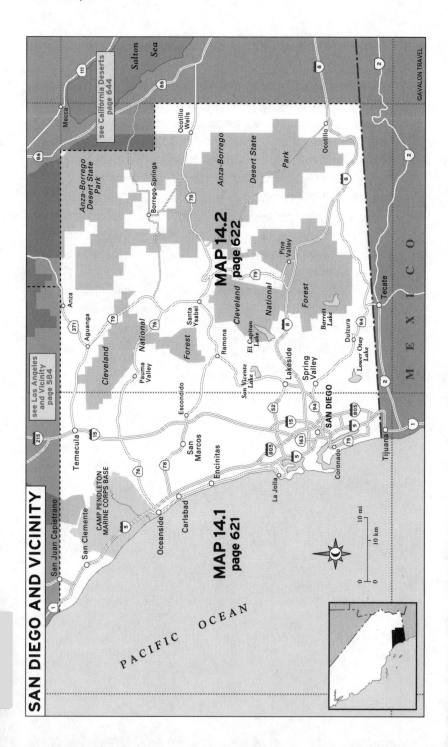

SAN DIEGO AND VICINITY

MAP 14.1
page 621

MAP 14.2
page 622

see Los Angeles
and Vicinity
page 584

see California Deserts
page 644

©AVALON TRAVEL

PACIFIC OCEAN

MEXICO

Map 14.1

Sites 1-13
Pages 623-631

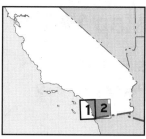

14.2

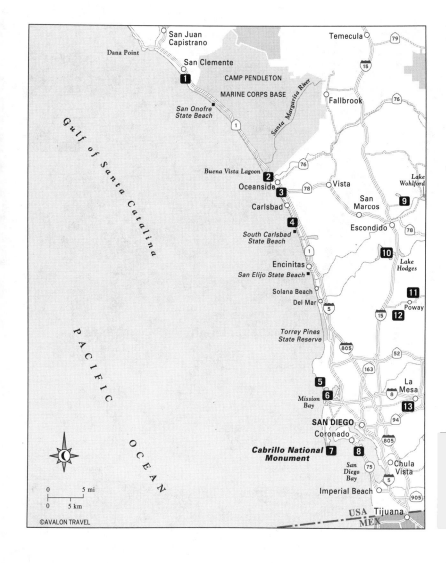

Map 14.2

Sites 14-23
Pages 632-639

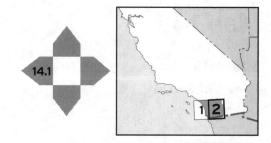

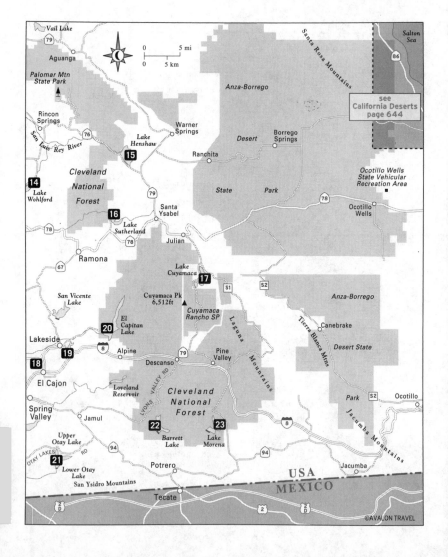

1 SAN CLEMENTE PIER

Rating: 4

south of San Juan Capistrano

Map 14.1, page 621

The stretch of shore surrounding San Clemente Pier is the classic sandy beach. As long as the inshore surge of the surf is light, a large variety of perch hold in the area. They are joined by the inevitable kingfish, croakers, some sharks and rays, and every so often the best prize of them all: halibut. In the summer months, corvina are also caught here.

Facilities, fees: Restrooms, a bait and tackle shop, a restaurant, and fish-cleaning sinks are available. A parking fee is charged.

Directions: Take I-5 to San Clemente and take the Avenida Palazada exit. Turn west (right) and drive two blocks to El Camino Real. Turn left and drive to Avenida del Mar. Turn right and drive to the parking lot at the beach. Walk across to the pier.

Contact: City of San Clemente, Marine Safety, 949/361-8210; San Clemente Chamber of Commerce, 949/492-1131.

2 OCEANSIDE DEEP SEA

Rating: 9

north of San Diego

Map 14.1, page 621

Oceanside is headquarters for anglers who own their own boats, as well as for those who board the big sportfishing vessels. Access to several good fishing areas requires just a 20- to 40-minute run, rarely longer. The engine gets a fair run at it, you have a chance to feel the sea breeze in your face, and the final reward is an array of different fisheries.

You can book an overnight trip during which boats might fish either Catalina or San Clemente. White seabass and yellowtail provide the excitement, but the angling is unpredictable and can go up and down. Remember this: when the squid arrive—go, and go immediately!

The marine habitat provides two attractive settings: inshore kelp beds and deep-water shelves. Take your pick. The kelp forests are widespread and abundant north of Oceanside, both off Camp Pendleton and farther north, off the San Onofre power-plant outfall. Another good stretch of water is along the inshore coast from Carlsbad on south. This habitat is ideal for kelp bass, all manner of rockfish, and sometimes sheepshead, barracuda, and yellowtail (you can always pray). The lush undersea forests give anglers a chance to use light saltwater tackle, casting jigs along the kelp almost as if they are in a lake, casting jigs for largemouth bass.

For larger fish, however, you need to go deeper. The deep undersea shelves are made for a wide variety of bottom-dwelling rockfish, the most common being chilipepper and canary rockfish, with some large, ugly bocaccio. I mean, hey, they don't make fish any uglier, right? These fish hang along the ledges between 280 and 600 feet deep, both northwest and southwest of the harbor. The bonus here is that the bottom of the ocean drops off to never-never land quite quickly—just two or three miles offshore. Instead of a long, boat-thumping grind to reach the fishing grounds, it is a short trip.

Note that fishing regulations often change here from year to year, for seasons, depth restrictions, bag limits, size limits, and even annual quotas for the fleet. Always check current regulations with Fish and Game or with a marina or party-boat operator before planning a trip.

The charter-boat operation out of Oceanside offers all kinds of trips, with both local and offshore focuses. In the best of years, when warm water and abundant baitfish populations move in along the coast, trips for all types of blue-water fish can be arranged. They can even include striped marlin and tuna, although the spotlight always starts with albacore. Then as summer progresses into fall, the "whatever happens" approach follows. This is one place where "whatever happens" is often worth getting in on. When live squid, mackerel, sardines, or anchovies are in use, do exactly as the deckhand tells you.

Restrictions are in place for lingcod, cowcod, bocaccio, and other rockfish. Check current Department of Fish and Game (DFG) regulations before keeping any of these species.

Note: San Clemente is a Naval Gunnery Range. Monitor channel 16 on your marine radio. When they announce a closure, get out of the area.

Facilities, fees: Party-boat charters, a boat ramp, restrooms, a picnic area, and bait and tackle are at the harbor. Lodging, campgrounds, and supplies can be found in Oceanside. Party-boat fees are charged per person.

Directions: From I-5 at Oceanside, take the Oceanside/Harbor Drive exit. Turn west on Harbor Drive and continue (bearing to the left) to the harbor.

Contact: Helgren's Sportfishing, 760/722-2133, www.helgrensportfishing.com; Oceanside Bait Company, 760/434-1183; Pacific Coast Bait and Tackle, Oceanside, 760/439-3474, www.pacificcoast-baitandtackle.com; Oceanside Harbor, 760/435-4000, www.ci.oceanside.ca.us; Oceanside Chamber of Commerce, 760/722-1534.

❸ OCEANSIDE PIER

Rating: 4

in Oceanside

Map 14.1, page 621

Habitat always determines what species are available. At Oceanside Pier, the sandy bottom means you get a chance at halibut in the spring and early summer, along with steady numbers of croaker, kingfish, perch, and sand bass. There are occasional runs of jacksmelt, and at best, bonito and even barracuda can roam within casting range in the summer.

Facilities, fees: Restrooms, fish-cleaning tables, a bait shop, a restaurant, and benches are available. Fishing access is free. Parking fees vary.

Directions: From I-5 in Oceanside, take the Mission Boulevard exit and turn west. Go as far as you can on Mission Boulevard, to Pacific Street. Turn right and continue one block to the pier on the left. Parking is available on Mission Boulevard and Meyers Street.

Contact: Oceanside Pier Bait & Tackle, 760/966-1405; Oceanside Harbor, 760/435-4000, www.ci.oceanside.ca.us; Pacific Coast Bait and Tackle, Oceanside, 760/439-3474, www.pacificcoast-baitandtackle.com; Oceanside Bait Company, 760/434-1183.

❹ AGUA HEDIONDA LAGOON

Rating: 4

near Carlsbad

Map 14.1, page 621

Want to fish from your kayak? Then pay attention. An outlet to the ocean allows halibut, seabass, and even the occasional perch to sneak in to the lagoon. But what makes this place so popular is a stellar boating opportunity.

Kayak fishing, for instance, is popular here. So is powerboating, with a 45-mph speed limit from sunrise to sunset, and with it, waterskiing on the calm days, when there is no chop on the water. There are a few windsurfers, who are restricted to specified areas of the lake. For many people, fishing is an afterthought.

At some times, fishing is allowed only in the designated nonmotorized-use area, in the lower east end of the lagoon, due to an invasive algae. Always check for current fishing status. Anchoring is prohibited in the entire lagoon.

Facilities, fees: A boat ramp, a marina, restrooms, boat rentals, and a picnic area are available. There are separate areas for powerboats, personal watercraft, and nonmotorized boats. Permits are required for boats over 20 feet, 6 inches. Permits can be obtained at the marina. Day-use and boat-launching fees are charged. Passes can be purchased at the marina or from Carlsbad city offices; discounts are given to Carlsbad residents.

Directions: From Oceanside, drive south on I-5 to Tamarack Street. Take that exit and turn left (east) and drive one block to Adams Street. Turn right (south) and drive 0.5 mile to Chiquapin. Turn right and drive two blocks to Harrison Street. Turn left and drive on Harrison Street to the lagoon.

Contact: City of Carlsbad, 760/602-4685; Lagoon Patrol, Carlsbad Police Department, 760/931-2203; California Watersports, 760/434-3089, www.carlsbadlagoon.com.

5 CRYSTAL PIER

Rating: 5

north of San Diego in Pacific Beach

Map 14.1, page 621

In addition to kingfish, perch, jacksmelt, and sharks, the rocky shoreline just south of the pier provides an opportunity for opaleye, kelp bass, and the rare cabezon. Get this: there are rental cottages right on the pier. *Note:* The pier is open only during daylight hours (sunrise to sunset). Crystal Pier is privately owned as part of the adjacent hotel, which is made up of cottages situated on the pier.

Facilities, fees: Cottage rentals and fish-cleaning areas are available. Camping is nearby. Bait, tackle, and fishing-equipment rentals can be found in the hotel lobby. Fishing access is free.

Directions: From San Diego, take I-5 north to the Grand/Garnet exit. Take that exit and turn onto Garnet Avenue. Continue west for several miles to the end of Garnet; you will see the pier as you cross Mission Boulevard.

Contact: Crystal Pier Hotel, 800/748-5894, www.crystalpier.com.

6 MISSION BAY COAST

Rating: 10

northwest of San Diego

Map 14.1, page 621

California's southern coast is a fantastic place with excellent fishing opportunities. A reason for that is Mission Bay and its nearby coast.

The coastal fishing grounds provide outstanding fisheries for just about any warm-water ocean species. Yet if you don't want to venture out to sea, you can catch a variety of smaller species right in the sheltered confines of the bay itself. Just match the habitat.

• Kelp forests: A series of huge, easy-to-reach kelp forests harbor a large variety of species. One large expanse of kelp is between Point La Jolla on south past Bird Rock, and another is to the south, spanning the area from off Ocean Beach to Point Loma. The bottom ranges 60–140 feet deep here, with most catches being kelp bass, rockfish, and sheepshead. In the summer, yellowtail, barracuda, white seabass, and even bonito roam these waters.

• Deep-water shelves: A deep underwater drop-off is directly west of Point Loma, where the bottom of the ocean drops off from 280 feet to 600 feet deep in a matter of a few miles. This is an excellent spot for big cowcod, lingcod, and rockfish. It's about a seven-mile ride out of Mission Bay. Note that restrictions are in place for lingcod, cowcod, bocaccio, and other rockfish. Check current DFG regulations before keeping any of these species.

• Bluewater: Come summer, and the best of the best often arrive—marlin, tuna, albacore, bonito, and yellowtail. Often you don't have to venture far for yellowtail and bonito, which move through just off Point La Jolla, along the southern edge of La Jolla Canyon. Marlin, tuna, and albacore are another matter. From year to year, you never know how close to shore they will come. In the lucky years, when they move in close during September and October, they can be about 10 miles offshore, almost never any closer.

• Flat sea bottom: A bonus at Mission Bay is that between La Jolla kelp beds and Point Loma kelp beds is a flat-bottomed area directly west of Mission Bay, within quick reach of owners of small boats. In the spring, halibut move right in along this area, a once-a-year chance that offers a welcome change of pace.

• Mission Bay: If the sea is rough or if you desire a quiet water option, Mission Bay itself has a variety of fisheries. The most abundant are kingfish, smelt, and perch, but sometimes even sand bass, halibut, bonito, and barracuda will enter the bay. Mission Bay is used more often as a private parkland, like a big lake. It has 27 miles of shoreline, and waterskiing and sailboarding are popular. Note, however, that strict boat-noise limits are in effect; a 5-mph speed limit is also in effect 11 A.M.–5 P.M. on the northwest bay, and from sunset to sunrise on the entire bay.

Facilities, fees: Party-boat charters, a campground, boat ramps, boat hoists, boat rentals, bait, tackle, groceries, and restaurants are at the bay. Party-boat fees are charged per person. A Mexican fishing license is required for some deep-sea sportfishing trips; they can be obtained at the sportfishing operations.

Boat ramps: Dana Landing Ramp, De Anza Cove Ramp, Santa Clara Cove Ramp, Ski Beach Ramp, and South Shores Ramp are all managed by the City of San Diego. A ramp, a marina, boat storage, and boat rentals are all available at Campland on the Bay. A sling hoist (travel lift) is at Driscoll Mission Bay.

Directions: Take I-5 north of San Diego to exit for Sea World Drive. Take the Sea World Drive exit. Turn west and drive past the Sea World entrance to West Mission Bay Drive. Continue (staying to the right) to the first stoplight. Turn left onto the access road. Drive a short distance to Quivira Drive. Turn left and drive a short distance to the bay and Seaforth Sportfishing, on the right. Boat ramps are located throughout the bay.

Contact: San Diego Convention & Visitors Bureau, 619/232-6101, www.sandiego.org.

Boat rentals: Action Beach and Bay Rentals, 619/275-8945, www.actionsportrentals .com; Seaforth Boat Rental, 888/834-BOAT (888/834-2628), www.seaforthboatrental .com; Driscoll Mission Bay Boatyard & Marina, 619/221-8456, www.driscoll-boats. com; Dana Landing, 619/226-2929, www .danalanding.com.

Party boats: Seaforth Sportfishing, 619/224-3383, www.seaforthlanding.com.

7 SHELTER ISLAND PIER

Rating: 6

south of San Diego
Map 14.1, page 621

This is the major shoreline-access point in San Diego Bay and is near the entrance to the bay in the migration path of a Heinz 57 variety of fish. The most consistent results are for perch—many species of them—along with smelt, sand bass, sharks, and rays. The lucky few even intercept halibut (in the spring) or bonito (in the summer) when they sneak through the mouth of the bay. This pier was rebuilt and is quite comfortable.

Facilities, fees: Restrooms, fish-cleaning tables, benches, and a bait and tackle shop are available. Lodging and camping are nearby. Fishing access is free.

Directions: Take I-5 to the west end of San Diego and the exit for Rosecrans exit. Turn west on Rosecrans and drive approximately five miles to Shelter Island Drive. Turn left and drive 0.5 mile to the pier, on the left.

Contact: San Diego Unified Port District, 619/686-6200; Best Western Island Palms Hotel and Marina, 619/222-0561.

8 SAN DIEGO DEEP SEA

Rating: 10

at San Diego Bay
Map 14.1, page 621   BEST (

The term "hot rail" was invented to describe the boats out of San Diego. That is what happens when there are multiple hookups on a boat. The anglers must chase along the railing, following the fish, often in different directions. You duck under poles and jump over the top of other lines, and when there are enough simultaneous hookups, it's absolute bedlam. This can be some of the most exciting fishing anywhere in the world. The term "no angles, no tangles" is well understood by anybody who has had to chase a fish down the rail.

The San Diego sportfishing fleet offers a wide variety of trips, but the best local trips are often for albacore, yellowtail, or white seabass at the Coronado Islands. Longer trips, of course, have become legendary here, ranging from a week to even more than three weeks, all the way south of Cabo San Lucas to Clarion Island and other regional hot spots. Hot rail? It can get so hot you can't touch the thing.

The top spot for yellowtail is at the Coronados, as well as the kelp beds. Albacore are always a question mark, with anglers wondering when and where they'll arrive and how close they will get to land. When they do show in force, it's almost always on the inner and outer banks.

When the sea is warm, courtesy of El Niño, higher temperatures in the ocean bring with them bluefin tuna, yellowfin tuna, and dorado, and the trips fishing for them can take over much of the one- and two-day trips offered out of this port.

Also note that boats out of San Diego rarely fish San Clemente Island, only when results are poor everywhere else. Since that is seldom the case, San Clemente doesn't get nearly the attention of the other spots. The fishing fleet from Long Beach is far more likely to fish San Clemente Island.

More locally oriented trips are also available. One of the favorites and most consistent is the short trip "around the corner" north of Point Loma to the vast kelp forest there. The Point Loma kelp forest is home to many resident species, including kelp bass, rockfish, and sheepshead, and it also attracts yellowtail and barracuda. Sometimes bonito even roam the area during the summer. Another option is right along the world-famous Coronado Beach, where halibut arrive during the spring and early summer.

There are also several deep-water rockfish and lingcod areas. The current depth limit for fishing for rockfish is 180 feet. This rule is subject to change.

Note that fishing regulations often change here from year to year, for seasons, depth restrictions, bag limits, size limits, and even annual quotas for the fleet. Always check current regulations with Fish and Game or with a marina or party-boat operator before planning a trip.

There's more. Marlin and tuna are always a wild card here. Warm ocean temperatures and large amounts of baitfish can compel marlin to migrate north from their typical waters off Baja, and they sometimes can show during the fall just 10–15 miles offshore. People catch giant tuna, wahoo, yellowtail, dorado, marlin, grouper, pargo, skipjack—it's possible to catch a thousand pounds of fish, and believe me, you'll know it.

San Diego is the home port of several world-known skippers, including Frank LoPreste, Tom Rothery, John Grabowski, and Steve Loomis (and the late Bill Poole), all pioneers for long-range trips. These are the fellows who are the top public fish catchers anywhere, who guide their customers across miles of ocean in search of the best saltwater angling on the Pacific coast. Very often they find it.

Facilities, fees: Party-boat charters, boat ramps, fishing piers, full-service marinas, restaurants, lodging, bait, tackle, and supplies are at the bay. Boat ramps can be found at the bay in Chula Vista and National City. Boat rentals are in San Diego. Party-boat fees are charged per person.

Directions: From I-5 in San Diego (heading north), take the Hawthorne Street/Airport exit. Turn west on Harbor Drive and continue to the sportfishing operations.

Contact: San Diego Convention & Visitors Bureau, 619/232-6101, www.sandiego.org.

Boat hoists: Shelter Island Boat Yard, 619/222-0481; Marine Group Boat Works, Chula Vista, 619/427-6767.

Party boats: Fisherman's Landing, 619/221-8500, www.fishermanslanding.com; H & M Landing, 619/222-1144, www.hmlanding.com; Royal Polaris Sportfishing, 619/226-8030, www.royalpolaris.com; Point Loma Sportfishing, 619/223-1627, www

.pointlomasportfishing.com; Excel Sportfishing, 619/223-7493, www.excelsportfishing.com; Red Rooster III, 619/224-3857, www.redrooster3.com.

9 DIXON LAKE

Rating: 8

near Escondido at Dixon Lake Recreation Area

Map 14.1, page 621   BEST (

The world-record bass lives at Dixon Lake. It has been caught twice and is identified not only by its King Kong size, but by a black spot near its head. It was snagged by accident in the fin, landed, weighed, and released in 2006. At that time, it weighed 25 pounds, 1 ounce, which makes it bigger than the most legendary world record of all, 22 pounds, 4 ounces. The same fish, identified by the black spot, was also caught in 2003, when it weighed 21 pounds, 11 ounces.

This is the Million Dollar Bass; that is, the angler who catches it is said to become an instant millionaire from endorsements. Maybe. Maybe not. But by any imagination, the lucky angler will become an instant legend, no matter who it might be.

Most people who fish for this world record do it by sightfishing. That is, they cruise the shallows with the rental boats and electric motors, and with high-quality polarized sunglasses, they search the shallows during the pre-spawn hoping to see the fish. This is no easy trick, because the fish is likely to see you at the same time. If it spots you, this makes the task almost impossible. If you get this far, and actually see the fish, as many have, you then anchor away from it, then cast tube baits right on it. If you irritate the giant bass, it may pick up the bait to move it. At that moment, you must strike, not a moment too soon, not a moment too late. This is how the fish was snagged. The set happened when the fish did not have the hook in its mouth, and in turn, it was snagged by the fin.

As you might figure, Dixon Lake is very popular. Anglers have come from near and far to try to catch this bass.

Dixon is the centerpiece of a regional park in the San Diego foothills at an elevation of 1,405 feet. The fishing is often excellent, with big largemouth bass, besides Mr. World Record, and channel catfish. Stocks of trout add to hopes during the cool winter months. For trout, the best spot is on the east side. You'll see the drop-offs.

No private boats are permitted on Dixon Lake (a downer), but a 5-mph speed limit for the rentals (electric motors only) keeps the small lake quiet. The water is clear and fishable most of the year.

Rainbow trout and catfish are stocked here, as well as a sprinkling of brown trout and now some steelhead. Shoreline fishing can be good here.

A bonus in the summer is that the lake is open to night fishing for catfish Wednesday–Saturday, until 11:45 P.M. Otherwise the lake is open 6 A.M.–sunset daily. Fishing derbies are held in April and November.

Facilities, fees: Powerboats, pedal boats, and rowboats can be rented. A campground with restrooms, drinking water, flush toilets, and showers is nearby. Three fishing piers (one is wheelchair-accessible), bait and tackle, ice, a snack bar, and a picnic area are available. Supplies can be obtained in Escondido. No float tubes are permitted. No private boats are permitted; boating is restricted to rentals. No glass containers or alcoholic beverages are permitted. No pets are allowed. A fishing fee is charged. On weekends, a vehicle entry fee is charged.

Directions: In Escondido, take El Norte Parkway northeast for four miles to La Honda Drive. Turn left and drive to Dixon Lake, at 1700 North La Honda Drive.

Contact: Dixon Lake Recreation Area, 760/839-4680, www.escondido.org/dixon-lake.aspx; City of Escondido, 760/741-3328 (camping reservations); Turner's Outdoorsman, San Marcos, 760/741-1570; Outlaw Bait & Tackle, 760/747-2503.

10 LAKE HODGES

Rating: 9

south of Escondido

Map 14.1, page 621

How you feel about Hodges all depends upon your perspective. You might feel that it's the best lake you have ever fished, where you have a better chance of catching a 10-pound bass than any other place in the United States. Or you might feel that it's the aquatic version of the San Diego Zoo: too many people, ridiculous lines at the boat ramp at dawn, and no such thing as a secret spot.

Hodges encompasses both of those outlooks. It's a fantastic producer of big bass, and, in fact, it is one of the few lakes ever to produce a 20-pounder. But the place is very heavily fished and has a lot of negatives because of it. Yet since the lake is closed four days per week, the fish get a regular, needed rest.

Lake Hodges is at an elevation of 314 feet in the coastal foothills just west of I-15. It's a long, narrow, snakelike reservoir shaped like an inverted V. It is on the San Dieguito River, spans 1,234 surface acres when full, and has 27 miles of shoreline and a maximum water depth of 115 feet. It is home to Florida-strain largemouth bass, crappie, bluegill, channel catfish, bullhead, and carp. The minimum size limit for bass is 15 inches.

The bass come big at Hodges, and in the spring they are also abundant during the first few hours after an opener. There are no secret spots at Hodges; at one time or another, everybody fishes the same areas: both corners of the dam, the Bernardo arm (early in the year), the Narrows (just west of Felicita Bay), and anyplace where you see stickups. The big bass, the 10-pounders and up, tend to be 15–20 feet deep. The crappie fishing is excellent at times.

Because of the amount of fishing pressure and the fact that catch-and-release is growing in popularity, the bass in Hodges are quite smart. Newcomers with little experience can have problems getting anything, particularly if they show up after 10 A.M.; by then, every good spot in the lake has already been hit. On the other hand, know-hows who get on the lake early and then fish plastic worms, spinnerbaits, and crankbaits with a delicate-enough touch to discern the most subtle bites may come up with a fish approaching the world record.

This lake is notorious for low water levels, which can close it to boating or limit the activities: in fall 2003, the lake was 13 percent full, then 100 percent full in 2006, and then down a bit in 2007, then full again in 2011. You get the idea. Hodges has been open for years on Wednesdays and weekends, as well as on holidays, from March through October (water levels permitting), but access days have been up for debate. The lake could be closed Wednesdays, yet open on Fridays. Check for status of water levels and access days.

Lake records: 20-pound, 4-ounce largemouth bass; 2-pound, 8-ounce bluegill; 35-pound channel catfish; 3-pound, 3-ounce crappie.

Note: All boats must be inspected and certified free of mussels prior to launching at this lake.

Facilities, fees: At the time of publication, the concessionaire had closed temporarily because of low water levels, and no boat rentals were available. There is a paved boat ramp, picnic area, snack bar, bait and tackle, and a wheelchair-accessible fishing float. Full facilities can be found in Escondido to the north or San Diego to the south. The speed limit is 35 mph. Fishing and boat-launching fees are charged.

Directions: Take I-15 to Escondido and turn west on Via Rancho Parkway and drive to Lake Drive. Turn left on Lake Drive and continue to the lake entrance. From the entrance, continue one mile to the boat ramp.

Contact: San Diego City Lakes, 619/465-3474 (recorded message) or 619/668-2050, www .sandiego.gov/water/recreation; boat rentals, 760/432-2023.

11 LAKE POWAY

Rating: 7

south of Escondido
Map 14.1, page 621

This lake has gained a reputation for trophy trout-fishing. The biggest yet weighed 17 pounds, 14 ounces, and there are also many fish over 10 pounds. And with all the fishing records in this county, that isn't bad. The lake is stocked with rainbow trout during the winter and catfish during the summer. In some years, steelhead and brown trout have been added.

The bass fishing here is no longer a secret either. Summer catfishing and night fishing are popular, and anglers can add bluegill, bass, sunfish, and pan fish to the list of possibilities here.

In the coastal foothills, about 20 miles northeast of San Diego, the lakeshore setting includes groves of eucalyptus and chaparral. A walk-in (one mile) campground is at the base of the dam. The lake is surrounded by 400-acre Clyde E. Rexrode Wilderness Area. This features several trails, including a three-mile loop around Lake Poway.

The lake covers just 60 acres and provides rental boats, but privately owned boats, even canoes, are not permitted.

Note: Boating and fishing are allowed Wednesday through Sunday year-round. Shoreline fishing is permitted daily. Night fishing is allowed from May through early September on Fridays and Saturdays.

Facilities, fees: Powerboats, rowboats, pedal boats, sailboats, and canoes are for rent at a marina. A hike-in campground, picnic area, bait and tackle, and snack bar are available. Private boats are not allowed, but float tubes are permitted. A day-use fee is charged (excluding Poway residents), and fishing fees are charged.

Directions: From Escondido, take I-15 south to Rancho Bernardo Road. Turn east and drive four miles to Lake Poway Road. Turn left and drive a short distance to the park entrance.

Contact: Lake Poway Recreation Area, 858/668-4772 (ranger), 858/668-4595 (reservations), 858/486-1234 (concession), www.poway.org.

12 LAKE MIRAMAR

Rating: 8

north of San Diego
Map 14.1, page 621

The stories just don't get any more outlandish than at Lake Miramar. This is where a 21-pound, 10-ounce bass was caught and was later found to have a lead diving weight in its stomach. It's also where a 20-pound, 15-ouncer is said to have been floating, dead of old age, then was allegedly scooped up and presented as a record catch. The actual lake-record bass weighed in at 20 pounds, 15 ounces.

Miramar is something of a miniaturized factory when it comes to making big bass. It is a small lake, covering just 160 acres. Stocked trout are like growing pills for bass, and good numbers of threadfin shad are available as prime forage as well. Anglers casting shad-patterned crankbaits can have a lot of success during the early summer. Another technique that can work at Miramar is split-shotting worms just above the grassy, weedy, muck-covered bottom. Miramar also has sunfish.

Because Miramar is so small, really more like a large pond, the entire shoreline gets picked over again and again, often many times in one day. The lake has little structure and the water is quite clear, adding to the difficulty. Sometimes anglers with kids will give up on the bass after midmorning and try for bluegill along the tules. You can't blame them. The trout opener is usually excellent every November. The top spot is Moe's Hole, where the water pumps into the lake.

The lake has just four miles of shoreline, and you can walk completely around the lake, but it is very difficult to fish from shore, since most of the shore is choked off by rampant tule growth. The lake has a maximum depth of 114 feet. The minimum size for bass is 12 inches.

Rainbow trout are stocked here and provide a good winter fishery (in addition to acting as growing pills for the big bass). After a while, you even feel like putting a few lead weights in a fish. Just don't claim the fish as a new state record.

The lake is open seven days a week, but boats are rented on Saturdays and Sundays only. Access days have been up for debate. Check for status of water levels and access days. Even when other San Diego area lakes are drawn down, this lake normally stays full.

Other lake records: 31.4-pound channel catfish; 22.4-pound blue catfish; 2.05-pound redear sunfish; 2-pound, 2-ounce bluegill; 15-pound, 8-ounce rainbow trout.

Facilities, fees: There is a paved boat ramp. Fishing boats, rowboats, and canoes are for rent at a small marina. A picnic area, a snack bar, and bait and tackle are available. The nearest campground is 25 miles away, at Lake Dixon. Other supplies can be obtained in Mira Mesa. Full facilities are in San Diego. Float tubes are allowed, but no water-body contact is permitted. The speed limit is 5 mph. Fishing and boat-launching fees are charged.

Directions: From San Diego, take I-15 north and drive about 10 miles to Mira Mesa. Take Mira Mesa Boulevard east and continue to Scripps Ranch Boulevard. Turn right (south) and drive to Scripps Lake Drive. Turn east (left) and drive to the lake entrance.

Contact: San Diego City Lakes, 619/465-3474 (recorded message) or 619/668-2050, www.sandiego.gov/water/recreation; boat rentals, 858/527-1722.

13 LAKE MURRAY

Rating: 7

northeast of San Diego
Map 14.1, page 621

Lake Murray covers 171 surface acres and has 3.2 miles of shoreline and a maximum water depth of 95 feet. The lake has a two-lane boat ramp, docks, restrooms, a parking lot, and landscaping.

This is primarily a lake for fishing. That is because no activities involving water-body contact are allowed. Since water levels can fluctuate greatly, check the status before making a trip.

Lake Murray has Florida-strain largemouth bass, bluegill, channel catfish, black crappie, and trout (stocked November to May). The minimum size limit for bass is 12 inches. Fish limits are 5 trout, 5 bass, 5 catfish, and 25 crappie, with no limit on other species.

Lake record: 18 pound, 55 ounce largemouth bass, a 2 pound, 15 ounce bluegill, a 3 pound black crappie, a 33 pound, 9 ounce channel catfish, a 12 pound rainbow trout, and a 20 pound, 4 ounce carp.

Murray usually opens in December with excellent trout plants. Fishing is often good through winter for trout, with some giant bass occasionally taken as well. Bass fishing peaks here in late winter and early spring.

In addition to fishing from boats, patrons can use a float tube or fish from shore. Use of float tubes is restricted to within 150 feet from shore. Float tubers must wear chest waders and have a Coast Guard–approved personal-flotation device readily available at all times; it is also required that float tubers have 144 square inches of international orange visible at least 12 inches above the water line. In addition, float tubers must possess a horn or whistle to warn approaching craft. Any float tube that uses oars or has a motor must purchase a private-boat use permit for $5.

This reservoir is part of Mission Trails Regional Park, a few miles east of San Diego. The park is popular for bicycling, jogging, walking, in-line skating, and picnicking. There is a 6.4-mile round-trip walk to the dam gate and back.

Lake Murray is open sunrise–sunset seven days a week, but boats are available for rent only Thursday through Sunday.

Facilities, fees: A paved boat ramp is on the south shore of the lake. Fishing boats, rowboats, and canoes are for rent at a small marina. A boat dock, a picnic area, and restrooms are available. The nearest campground is at Kumeyaay Lake, two miles north. Supplies can be obtained in La Mesa. Powerboats, canoes, kayaks, sailing, and float tubes are permitted. A 5-mph speed limit is enforced. Boaters can bring their own small outboard motors for use on rental boats. No waterskiing, wakeboarding, personal watercraft riding, swimming, sailboarding, or water-body contact is allowed. No alcohol is permitted. Access is free. Fees are charged for boat launching and fishing.

Directions: From San Diego, take I-8 east and drive to La Mesa and Lake Murray Boulevard. Turn north and drive about 0.75 mile to Kiowa Drive. Turn left and continue to the lake.

Contact: San Diego City Lakes, 619/465-3474 (recorded message) or 619/668-2050, www .sandiego.gov/water/recreation; boat rentals, 619/466-4847; Kumeyaay Lake and Campground, 619/668-2748, www.mtrp.org.

14 LAKE WOHLFORD

Rating: 7

east of Escondido
Map 14.2, page 622

San Diego County has several of California's top bass lakes, but Lake Wohlford isn't quite in the top tier of world-class opportunities. Believe it or not, that can be a plus, since the lake gets a lot less pressure than the more famous waters. And regardless of its status, some huge fish are in here just the same.

Wohlford does provide decent trout fishing prospects from winter through early summer, and a 5-mph speed limit keeps the water quiet. The lake is stocked with rainbow trout, brown trout, steelhead, channel catfish, and blue catfish. A bald eagle winters here. The best place to spot it is at Lusardi Point, its favorite perching area.

In the summer, the lake transforms. We're talking bass, bluegill, and catfish, with some crappie on the side. The results are decent enough, but there is a key period here when the water warms up from 58–63°F, about a two- to three-week window of opportunity. When that happens, the bass move up to just 5–10 feet deep and provide a good bite for anglers casting toward the shore from boats.

Lake Wohlford covers 190 surface acres and has two miles of shoreline. It is at 1,500 feet in elevation, and that's right, it gets scorching hot out here in the summer. That is why the prime time to visit is in spring and fall, when the campground gets a fair amount of use.

The lake is open daily from mid-December to the weekend after Labor Day from 6 A.M.– dusk; it's open weekends only from early September–mid-December.

Lake records: 19-pound, 3-ounce largemouth bass; 27-pound blue catfish; 16-pound, 4-ounce rainbow trout; 3-pound, 8-ounce black crappie; 1-pound, 4-ounce bluegill.

Facilities, fees: A paved boat ramp, cabins, an RV park, picnic areas, bait, a snack bar, a restaurant, and limited supplies are available. Fishing boats, rowboats, and pedal boats are for rent at a small marina. All private watercraft are banned due to quagga mussel infestations. No alcoholic beverages, glass containers, or pets are permitted. Fishing, day-use, and boat-launching fees are charged.

Directions: Take I-15 to Escondido and the exit for Via Rancho Parkway. Take the Via Rancho Parkway exit. Turn east on Valley Parkway/County Road S6 and drive four miles to Lake Wohlford Road. Turn right and go 2.8 miles to the lake. The boat ramp is on the north shore.

Contact: City of Escondido, Lake Wohlford, 760/839-4346, www.wohlfordlake.com; Lake Wohlford Resort, 760/749-2755, www .lakewohlfordresort.com; Oakvale RV Park, 760/749-2895; Woods Valley Kampground, 760/749-2905, www.woodsvalley.com.

15 LAKE HENSHAW

Rating: 6

east of Escondido
Map 14.2, page 622

The best things going here are catfish and crappie, and prospects are often good starting in early summer. This lake, like so many, has responded to high water levels. Many of the cabins even smell like fish, a testimonial to recent good times.

There are some big fish in here, and they brighten up the uneven results over the course of the year. The lake-record channel catfish weighed 39 pounds, 5 ounces, and the lake-record crappie was 3 pounds. It also produced a lake-record bass that weighed 14 pounds, 4 ounces. Stocks of largemouth bass were planted at one time, and remnants of them (and their progeny) remain. There is also a nice population of bullhead. However, no stocks of rainbow trout, bluegill, and channel catfish are made anymore.

Henshaw is at 2,727 feet near Cleveland National Forest. It is the biggest lake in San Diego County, covering 1,100 acres and offering 25 miles of shoreline. Swimming is not permitted, and a 10-mph speed limit is in effect. Like many reservoirs, Lake Henshaw is sometimes plagued by low water levels. In big rain years, however, it's never a problem.

Facilities, fees: Fishing boats are for rent. Cabins, a paved boat ramp, a campground, picnic areas, flush toilets, showers, a swimming pool, a whirlpool, a clubhouse, a convenience store, a café, coin laundry, a playground, and an RV dump station are available. No canoes, inflatables, or craft under 10 feet long are permitted. No water-body contact is allowed. A 10-mph speed limit is enforced. Day-use and boat-launching fees are charged.

Directions: From Santa Ysabel, drive seven miles north on Highway 79 to Highway 76. Turn east on Highway 76 and drive four miles to the lake and campground on the left.

Contact: Lake Henshaw Resort, 760/782-3501 or 760/782-3487, www.lakehenshaw resort.com.

16 LAKE SUTHERLAND

Rating: 7

near Ramona
Map 14.2, page 622

The intense number of anglers who hammer away at Dixon, Hodges, El Capitan, San Vicente, and Otay just don't seem to make it out here. The lake is just distant enough from the San Diego metropolitan area and just small enough (only 557 acres) that many of the go-getters do their go-getting somewhere else. The lake has five miles of shoreline and a maximum depth of 145 feet.

In addition, the bass have four days off each week to relax, then five months off each year to think about it. All that adds up to good news for the anglers who visit Lake Sutherland.

The lake, at an elevation of 2,059 feet, was created from the dammed flows of Santa Ysabel Creek and Bloomdale Creek, in the foothills near Cleveland National Forest. In a five-year period at Sutherland, the bass population went from an estimated 10,000–40,000. There are also some big channel catfish in the lake, along with redear sunfish, blue catfish, bullhead, and crappie. The minimum size limit for bass is 12 inches. Strict rules prohibit most water sports.

The lake is small enough that in a day or two you can fish nearly all of it. After a while, particularly with the use of electronics, you can get to know the lake as well as your own home with the lights off. The trends here are pretty typical. After early-rising anglers get in on the dawn bite, the know-hows then settle in and fish the ledges 12–15 feet down, with bait, for a chance at the big ones.

The lake is open to boating sunrise–sunset Saturday and Sunday, plus select holidays, from mid-March through early October. Shore fishing and float-tubing are allowed on Monday. Access days have been up for debate; check for the status of water levels and access days before planning a trip here.

A few notes: The west shore and Santa Ysabel arm of the lake are accessible on foot, just under two miles of shore. From November through January, waterfowl hunting is permitted, usually only on Thursdays and Sundays. Turkey hunting is offered late March–early April. There is no camping at the lake; the nearest campground is 12 miles away, at Dos Picos County Park.

Lake records: 16 pound, 55 ounce largemouth bass; 3 pound, 25 ounce black crappie; 2 pound, 7 ounce bluegill.

Note: All boats must be inspected and certified free of mussels prior to launching at this lake.

Facilities, fees: No concession services are available at the lake. Supplies can be obtained in Ramona. Water-body contact and boats less than 10 feet long are prohibited. The speed limit is 20 mph. Fishing and boat-launching fees are charged.

Directions: Take I-15 to Escondido and the junction with Highway 78. Turn east on Highway 78 and drive about 30 miles to Sutherland Dam Road (about eight miles past Ramona). Turn left and drive north to the lake. Continue 0.7 mile to the boat ramp on the west shore.

Contact: San Diego City Lakes, 619/465-3474 (recorded message) or 619/668-2050, www .sandiego.gov/water/recreation.

17 LAKE CUYAMACA

Rating: 9

northeast of San Diego near
Cuyamaca Rancho State Park
Map 14.2, page 622

Lake Cuyamaca often has outstanding bass fishing, as well as excellent trout fishing in the winter. Cuyamaca has plenty of large bass, as well as high numbers in the two- and three-pound class. The lake also has smallmouth bass, channel catfish, crappie, blue catfish, bluegill, and sturgeon (more about that later). By early summer, the bass and crappie take over. Most of the attention in this chapter is on bass, not trout, but Cuyamaca is an exception, with the best trout fishing by far in the area.

This is the only lake in San Diego County where trout are stocked year-round.

Lake Cuyamaca is at 4,620 feet on the eastern slopes of the Cuyamaca Mountains. This makes it just far enough away from the San Diego area to make a trip here something special, and anglers are usually rewarded appropriately. The lake provides solid prospects for a number of species, with good trout fishing in the cool months, good bass and crappie fishing in the spring and summer, and also prospects for catfish (which are stocked) and bluegill in summer and fall. It is one of the best-improved bass lakes in California. The fishing is best during the last three hours of daylight, depending on the phase of the moon.

Because it is at a much higher elevation than the other area lakes, the water stays cooler longer. In turn, the Department of Fish and Game rewards it with consistent stocks, all joining larger holdovers from previous years; additional trout from a private hatchery are planted as well. The best spots for trout in this shallow lake are at the pumphouse and at Fletcher Island (straight across from the boat ramp; walk across the dike to get there). The lake is stocked with rainbow, brown, and California golden trout, as well as with steelhead and sturgeon.

Cuyamaca is often a great choice for the boater/camper/angler. A bonus is a free fishing class that takes place at 10 A.M. every Saturday.

Now about those sturgeon?... Sturgeon were stocked in the late 1990s and they now weigh 30–50 pounds. Occasionally an angler hooks one. In any case, if you are trout fishing with a light spinning rod, eating a sandwich, and then see your rod get ripped into the lake, well, you know that Mr. Sturgie just came by for a lunch of his own.

The lake is open seven days a week 6 A.M.–sunset. A bonus here is a 10-mph speed limit, which makes the lake ideal for boaters sneaking up on quiet coves to cast surface lures along the shoreline. Water temperatures are always key here.

Lake records: 14-pound, 3-ounce largemouth bass; 14-pound, 1-ounce rainbow trout; 28-

pound, 5-ounce channel catfish; 2-pound, 8-ounce crappie; 1-pound, 6-ounce bluegill; 33-pound, 4-ounce sturgeon.

Facilities, fees: A boat ramp is on the west shore. Fishing boats, canoes, and pedal boats are for rent (arrive by 8 A.M. on Saturday and Sunday for fishing boats). Cabins, a campground, restrooms, drinking water, flush toilets, coin-operated showers, and an RV dump station are at the state recreation area. Free fishing classes are offered at 10 A.M. on Saturday. A convenience store and café are nearby. Supplies are available in Julian. Boats, inflatables, and rafts under 10 feet long are prohibited. Canoes, paddleboats, and Zodiac-type rafts are allowed. A youth fishing program is offered, and a fishing derby is held in September. A 10-mph speed limit is enforced. No water-body contact is allowed. Day-use, fishing, and boat-launching fees are charged.

Directions: From El Cajon, drive east on I-8 to Highway 79 (near Descanso Junction). Turn north (left) and drive nine miles to the park entrance on the left.

Contact: Cuyamaca Rancho State Park, 760/765-3020; Lake Cuyamaca, 760/765-0515 or 877/581-9904, www.lakecuyamaca.org.

18 SANTEE LAKES

Rating: 5

near Santee

Map 14.2, page 622

This is a 190-acre park built around a complex of seven lakes. So how many lakes can you boat on? Answer: Only one, Lake 5. Float tubing is allowed on Lakes 1, 2, and 5, if you're fishing. And campers can fish from their own boats on 6 and 7, subject to approval.

Most campsites are lakefront, and the park is best known for its fishing. The lakes are stocked with 44,000 pounds of trout and catfish annually, with fantastic lake records including a 39-pound catfish, a 16-pound rainbow trout, a 12-pound largemouth bass, and a 2.5-pound bluegill. A catch-and-release policy for largemouth bass is enforced.

Quiet, low-key boating is the name of the game here. Rowboats, pedal boats, and canoes are for rent. This small regional park is 20 miles east of San Diego. It receives more than 100,000 visitors per year. The camp is at 400 feet.

Facilities, fees: Rowboats, canoes, kayaks, and pedal boats are for rent at Lake 5 (9 A.M.–5 P.M.). A campground, restrooms, drinking water, flush toilets, showers, an RV dump station, a playground, two swimming pools, Jacuzzi, picnic areas, a convenience store, a snack bar, a recreation center, a pay phone, propane, and coin laundry are available. Fees are charged for access, fishing, and camping.

Float tubes permitted on Lakes 1, 2 and 5, but only if used for fishing. No sailing, sailboarding, swimming, or water-body contact is allowed. No state fishing license is required. The lakes are open sunrise–sunset.

Directions: Take I-8 to El Cajon and Highway 125. Turn north on 125 and drive four miles to Mast Boulevard. Turn east on Mast and drive two miles to Fanita Parkway. Turn right on Panita and drive 0.25 mile to the entrance on the right.

Contact: Santee Lakes Regional Park, 619/596-3141, www.santeelakes.com.

19 LAKE JENNINGS

Rating: 6

northeast of El Cajon at
Lake Jennings County Park

Map 14.2, page 622

Lake Jennings is a nice little backyard fishing hole and recreation area just outside of Johnstown and at an elevation of 700 feet. It covers 108 surface acres and has a maximum depth of 160 feet. The surrounding landscape is chaparral-covered hills. It's your basic catfish hole, thanks to the channel catfish that are stocked here. Thanks to stocks, trout fishing in the winter is good, too. Night fishing is permitted in the summer.

This is the kind of place where you would come for an evening weekend picnic to enjoy yourself and maybe toss out a fishing line. Bluegill and sunfish can be caught from shore. More serious anglers can try to track down the lake's largemouth bass, but for the most part, this lake doesn't try to compete with the nearby "bass factories," San Vicente and El Capitan.

But surprises happen here. You could be enjoying a summer evening fishing for catfish and have one of the giant blue catfish decide to grab your bait. Some huge fish are in here.

The lake is open for boating Friday–Sunday and on holidays. However, campers can fish here daily. The lake is open for night fishing Fridays and Saturdays, June through August.

Lake records: 17 pound, 4 ounce largemouth bass, 68-pound blue catfish.

Facilities, fees: Rowboats and boats with 5-horsepower motors are for rent. A campground, boat ramp, restrooms, showers, snack bar, picnic areas, an RV dump station, bait and tackle, a fishing float, a fish-cleaning station, and a convenience store are at the lake. Canoes are permitted. Kayaks, inflatables, and sailboats are prohibited. Fishing and boat-launching fees are charged.

Directions: From San Diego, take I-8 east for 21 miles to Lake Jennings Park Road. Turn left (north) on Lake Jennings Park Road and continue one mile to the lake.

Contact: Lake Jennings Fishing Information, 619/443-2510; San Diego County Parks, 858/694-3049; Helix Irrigation District, camping reservations, 619/390-1623, www.lakejennings.org.

20 EL CAPITAN LAKE

Rating: 10

northeast of San Diego
Map 14.2, page 622

The bassers call this place "El Cap," and nearly always with a hint of reverence. Although you may hear stories about the bass at other lakes, El Cap is the one that produces them more often.

Covering 1,562 acres when full, it is the biggest of the lakes managed by the City of San Diego, and it produces the most consistent results for bass anglers. The lake is in a long canyon, at an elevation of 750 feet, and is fed by the San Diego River. It has a maximum depth of 197 feet, with 22 miles of shoreline. It is within easy reach for many anglers.

The minimum size for bass is 15 inches, and 10 inches for crappie. Four off-days per week keep the fish from being stressed.

I have always had my best luck here using large spinnerbaits, Shad Raps, or Rattletraps. To do it right, you need a boat with an electric motor; then you need to pepper the shoreline with casts, trying different depths. The magic number is 58, as in 58 degrees. When the lake is warmer than 58°F, the bass emerge from the depths and cruise 5–10 feet deep, looking for shad minnows. When it is colder, they are deeper—15–20 or sometimes 30–35 feet deep. Fluctuating water levels can be a real problem.

The water clarity is usually only fair at El Capitan, especially in early spring, so the fish are less spooky than at most lakes. That makes this a good lake to break in newcomers to bass fishing. If wind bothers you, get on the lake early and get it done early, because the wind shoots right down the canyon that this lake sits in, especially during the prime spring months. A little wind is good, though, because it keeps water clarity down, allowing the bass to come up to the top 10 feet of water. Crappie are an option, at times a quite outstanding one. The lake also has sunfish, bluegill, and carp.

The best area is the Conejos Creek arm, but this is no secret, and if you don't have an early spot in the line at the boat ramp, someone else will fish it first. No problem; just keep on the move, casting spinnerbaits in the spring and crankbaits in the early summer. You'll get 'em. The lake has too many bass, and conditions that are too good to miss.

As you might have guessed, this place is special and gets a lot of use in the summer months. It attracts a moderate-sized crowd the rest of the time. The lake is open for fishing Monday and

Thursday through Saturday. Access days have been up for debate; check for status of water levels and access days before planning a trip here.

The lake has been subject to major water drawdowns in recent years. Check for current status.

Lake records: 15-pound, 5-ounce largemouth bass; 1-pound, 9-ounce bluegill; 20-pound, 6-ounce channel catfish; 45-pound, 5-ounce blue catfish.

Facilities, fees: A boat ramp and picnic areas are available. The nearest camping is at Lake Jennings. Full facilities and supplies can be found in the San Diego area. The speed limit is 35 mph. Day-use fees are charged in the summer. Fishing and boat-launching fees are charged.

Directions: From San Diego, take I-8 east and drive 16 miles to Lake Jennings Park Road. Turn north and drive about two miles to the town of Lakeside and El Monte Road. Turn right on El Monte Road and drive about eight miles to the entrance for El Capitan Lake. The boat ramp is on the south shore, 2.5 miles from the entrance.

Contact: San Diego City Lakes, 619/465-3474 (recorded message) or 619/668-2050, www.sandiego.gov/water/recreation; boat rentals, 619/443-4110.

21 LOWER OTAY LAKE

Rating: 8

southeast of San Diego
Map 14.2, page 622

This lake has produced some giant fish that can make your brain gears squeak: a 92 pound, 1 ounce blue catfish; a 33 pound, 7 ounce channel catfish; an 18 pound,75 ounce largemouth bass; and a five-bass limit that weighed 53 pounds, 14 ounces. The state record for bluegill (3 pounds, 5 ounces) was held here from 1991–2002.

That record limit was caught by Jack Neu at Otay. I fished with Jack on that legendary March day. There were 35 bass that weighed eight pounds or better over a two-hour span at the marina.

From hearing this, you may think all you have to do is show up and you'll catch a 10-pounder. Unfortunately, it rarely works that way. Otay has long periods of very slow results despite intense fishing, then short periods of unbelievable snaps with giant fish.

Otay, in the foothills near Chula Vista, just north of the California/Mexico border, is at a 490-foot elevation. The lake's surface spans 1,100 acres, there are 25 shoreline miles, and it has a maximum depth of 137.5 feet. The lake has a variety of habitat, including submerged trees, tules, and underwater holes and ledges. Shad, crawdads, and primary levels of aquatic life are abundant, so the bass have plenty of food and grow quite fast. The minimum size is 12 inches. The catfish get big. Crappie fishing has taken a big upswing, too. The DFG stocks Otay with rainbow trout about twice monthly in the cooler months.

The key is the shad. When the bass start rounding up the shad, the entire lake seems to come alive. Most anglers use golden shiners or crawdads, or cast large Countdown Rapalas, Shad Raps, or Rattletraps. By the way, Jack Neu caught his limit with crawdads.

After launching, the best bet is to head up one of the two major lake arms, not to go down toward the dam area. One of the phenomena at Otay is that early in the year, the Otay arm always has warmer water compared to the Harvey arm. That can make a big difference in February and early March, when the bass can be in the top 10–15 feet of water in the Otay arm but still 25–35 feet deep in the Harvey arm.

A few other notes about Otay are worth mentioning. In summer, an aeration system creates a wider vertical habitat zone, raising carrying capacity and survival rates for fish. That should make for higher bass populations. Also, in the fall, catch rates can be very good for know-hows casting plastic worms around the tules, though newcomers can feel like ramming their heads against a wall.

Finally, between those short periods with wide-open bites, the best fortune comes to anglers who use precision graphs to find groups of fish, toss out a buoy to mark the spot, then cast shiners or crawdads toward the buoy. That is how Jack Neu did it, and you can't argue with the only 50-pound limit in history.

Otay is the home of the U.S. Olympic Training Center for rowing sports.

The lake is open Wednesday, Saturday, and Sunday, from sunrise–sunset. Access days have been up for debate; check for status of water levels and access days before planning a trip here. Waterfowl hunting is allowed November through January.

Note: Nearby Upper Otay Lake allows only catch-and-release fishing and only from shore or float tubes.

Facilities, fees: Fishing boats and rowboats are for rent. Picnic areas, a snack bar, a paved boat ramp, and bait and tackle are available. Water-body contact is prohibited. A 35-mph speed limit is enforced. Fishing and boat-launching fees are charged.

Directions: From San Diego, drive south on I-805 to Chula Vista and Telegraph Canyon Road. Turn east on Telegraph Canyon Road and drive five miles to Wueste Road. Turn right and drive to the lake access road, on the left.

Contact: San Diego City Lakes, 619/465-3474 (recorded message) or 619/668-2050, www.sandiego.gov/water/recreation; boat rentals, 619/397-5212.

22 BARRETT LAKE

Rating: 10

near Tecate, east of San Diego
Map 14.2, page 622

When you arrive at Barrett Lake, you will discover a beautiful, 811-acre lake set in a remote valley. Except for one gated road, which crosses private property, there is no public access. Access will be permitted as long as there is no abuse of private property, such as littering, trespassing, or petty damage. If you witness any wrongdoing, immediately try to correct the situation, or the rare chance to fish Barrett Lake will again be taken away.

Along with Upper Otay Lake, this is one of only two reservoirs in the region operating under highly restrictive rules. One of the reasons for this is to protect the last significant local population of northern-strain largemouth black bass. The Florida-strain bass has replaced these fish in nearly all of Southern California.

Other species include bullhead and black and white crappie. Threadfin shad and silverside minnows have been planted for forage. They are reproducing successfully, resulting in healthier and bigger bass.

The lake is in chaparral-covered hills. It offers good fishing structure, including rock piles, sunken timber and brush, and drop-offs—and the result is that you can catch bass regardless of your preferred style. For instance, submerged rock piles are available for those who like trying for monster-sized bass using pig-and-jig or plastic worms. There are plenty of sunken brush piles for those who like casting spinnerbaits. And there are also plenty of coves with midwater fish for anglers who prefer throwing crankbaits. Got it? You can do just about anything you want?…

Just about. Fishing is catch-and-release, with barbless hooks on lures or flies. All parties must be escorted to and from the lake.

All the lake needs is years of high water and it fills with bass, bullhead, bluegill, and black and white crappie. Set in a remote valley near the California/Mexico border, Barrett Lake was closed to the public starting in 1969; it then reopened in the summer of 1994 with a genius-level fishing program. Talented anglers on good days have caught more than 100 bass. Even in slow periods, the average catch is 10 bass per day.

You can go to the best reservoirs in Mexico, like El Salto, and not have a better experience. Under the reservation system, Barrett continues to have the highest bass catch rates, and because the number of anglers is controlled, it is a far more enjoyable experience than at crowded areas, and the high quality of the fishery is maintained.

Access is controlled through a reservation system (see *Contact*) and special fishing rules. The only problem has been the lake level. It really suffers in the dry years, and the fishing with it.

Barrett Lake is open Wednesday, Saturday, and Sunday. Access days have been up for debate. Check for status of water levels and access days. You cannot see the lake from the road.

Facilities, fees: Rental boats with 4-horsepower motors are provided. Visitors are allowed to bring their own outboard motors (up to 25 horsepower). Vault toilets are available, but drinking water is not. Garbage must be packed out. No glass containers or pets are permitted. No more than two vehicles per group and no more than 100 persons per day are let in, and RVs are not permitted. Access is by reservation only through Ticketmaster. A fishing package fee (boat rental included) is charged. Arrangements for lake escort are made after reservations are complete.

Directions: From San Diego, take I-8 east about 30 miles to Japatul Road. Turn south (right) on Japutal Road and drive 5.6 miles to Lyons Valley Road. Bear left on Lyons Valley Road and drive six miles (just past milepost 12) to Barrett Lake Road and an unsigned entrance gate. A ranger will be waiting to check your entrance pass. The lake is approximately 2.5 miles beyond the gate.

Contact: San Diego City Lakes, 619/465-3474 (recorded message) or 619/668-2050, www .sandiego.gov/water/recreation.

Fishing reservations: Ticketmaster, 800/745-3000, www.ticketmaster.com.

23 LAKE MORENA

Rating: 10

east of San Diego at Lake Morena County Park
Map 14.2, page 622

You want fish? You got fish. The lake is remote, but it's worth the trip. If you like bass, make the effort.

The key here is the elevation. The lake is at 3,200 feet and is just south of Cleveland National Forest, only seven or eight miles from the California/Mexico border. Because of the altitude, everything gets going a little later in the season than at lakes at lower elevations and closer to San Diego. Some folks show up in early March, find the bass deep and sluggish, and wonder, "What's all the fuss about Morena?" Show up a month later, however, and you'll find out.

From April through July, Morena consistently produces bass—small ones, big ones, and medium ones. It's just plain a fish-catching place. The lake has a lot of brush-lined shore and plenty of rocks, and the bass hang amid these areas. Since Morena covers 1,500 surface acres when full and has 26 miles of shoreline, a boat with an electric motor will help you cover all the good spots in a single weekend. The back side of Goat Island used to be a prime spot on the lake, but due to low water levels, the back side has been dry, and there has been no Goat Island since the early 2000s.

Before the fish move into the shallows, the fishing is best on plastic worms, salt-and-pepper-colored reapers, and eight-inch cinnamon-colored Blue Veins. Then, just like that, when the fish move into the top 5–10 feet of water, it's a great lake for casting surface lures. It's exciting fishing, with the strikes coming right on top. Try the Rebel Pop-R, Jitterbug, Zara Spook, floating Rapala, or Chugger. If you have a fly rod, bring it along and lay small poppers along the surface. Bass? There are plenty.

The lake is also stocked with trout, and they provide a fair alternative. The Department of Fish and Game plunks in rainbow trout in the 7- to 8-inch class and some up to 12 inches. They are more like growing pills for bass, however, and the lake record proves it. Morena also has catfish, bluegill, crappie, and redear sunfish. The lake experiences something of a drawdown over the course of a year, and by fall, it isn't unusual for it to be about two-thirds full. Lake levels are always a key here. The higher, the better.

Lake records: 19-pound, 3-ounce largemouth bass; 9-pound, 6-ounce rainbow trout.

Facilities, fees: There is a paved boat launch. Campgrounds, cabins, restrooms with flush toilets, showers, and picnic areas are available. Developed facilities are at Morena Village to the east. Boats under 9 feet or over 18 feet long are prohibited. No swimming is allowed. The speed limit is 10 mph. Day-use, fishing, and boat-launching fees are charged.

Directions: From El Cajon, take I-8 east to Pine Valley, then continue east for four miles to Buckman Springs Road/County Road S1. Take the Buckman Springs off ramp, turn right (south) on Buckman Springs Road and drive 5.5 miles to Oak Drive. Turn right on Oak Drive and drive 1.5 miles to Lake Morena Drive. Turn right on Lake Morena Drive and drive to the lake (there's an RV park on the right).

Contact: Lake Morena, San Diego County Parks, 619/579-4101, www.co.san-diego.ca.us/parks; San Diego County Parks, 858/694-3049.

CALIFORNIA DESERTS

© LARRY CRUIKSHANK/123RF.COM

BEST FISHING SPOTS

《 Most Unusual Fisheries
Salton Sea, **page 659.**

There is no region so vast in California — yet with fewer people — than the broad expanse of Anza-Borrego State Desert, Joshua Tree National Park, Mojave National Preserve, Salton Sea, and endless land handled by the Bureau of Land Management (BLM). And yet the area is best loved not for the desert, but for the boating, fishing, and other water sports of the Colorado River.

Each of these respective areas along the Colorado River corridor has distinct qualities that are separate and special, yet they are also joined at the edges.

A favorite is Lake Havasu and its striped bass fishing, which is most opportune in the spring, but the lake also has some giant catfish, and in the winter, there is decent crappie fishing. The Colorado River holds some promise for bass, bluegill, and catfish; fishing for these is best in the upper stretch of Parker Valley. One certainty is that you must have a boat in this area (with the lone exception of Davis Dam) to do it right.

Another highlight of the Colorado River is the striped bass fishing downstream of Laughlin/Bullhead City in late spring, and the trout fishing just below Needles from winter to spring.

Other stretches of the Colorado River are more remote, but they are even more captivating to some. From near Blythe on downstream, there exists a sprinkling of big striped bass, catfish, and other warm-water fisheries.

Just upstream of Martinez Lake, the area becomes very isolated but intriguing. It has marshy regions that can be explored by canoe, giant catfish, and schools of bluegill. Martinez Lake also has some monster-sized catfish.

There are also some surprises hidden about the desert. For instance, only the folks living around Palmdale know about the few fishing spots. Many others think there's no fishing at all. But hey, at least Little Rock Reservoir gets a few decent Department of Fish and Game (DFG) trout plants of small fish in the spring; plus, the California Aqueduct has four access points, and Little Rock Creek has a few small trout plants as long as the snowmelt keeps the river high and cool enough to support them.

Of course, there is also the Salton Sea. Ugly? An iguana looks cute compared to this region. Love? Oh yeah, when the corvina go on the bite, this lake is capable of producing excellent results during the cooler months, in winter and spring. The long-term health of this lake will be an ongoing battle due to water-quality concerns.

Just south of Calipatria, there are two small hideaways: little Ramer Lake, and its bass, catfish, and carp; and Wiest Lake, with its viable trout fishery in the winter months. Almost nobody knows about these two spots.

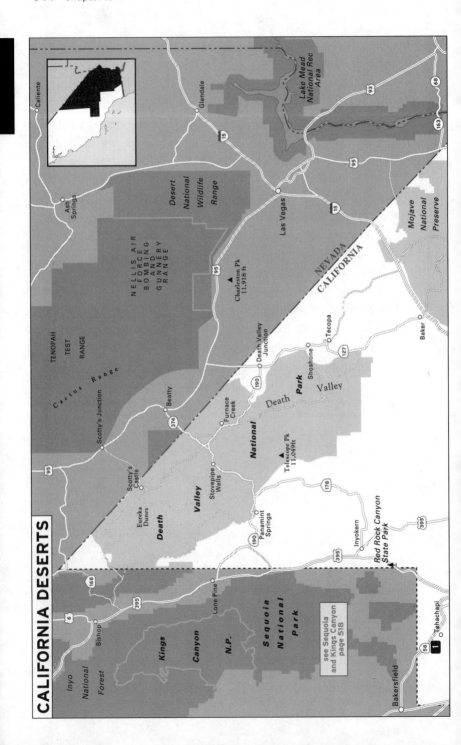

CALIFORNIA DESERTS

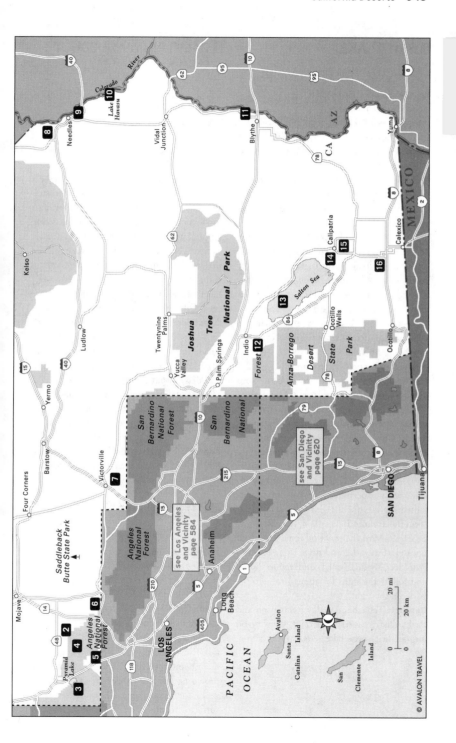

1 BRITE LAKE

Rating: 6

near Tehachapi at Brite Valley
Aquatic Recreation Area
Map pages 644-645

Here's a hidden spot that is often overlooked by the out-of-towners. Brite Valley Lake is a 90-acre lake in the northern flanks of the Tehachapi Mountains. Set at an elevation of 4,000 feet, it is stocked with 10- to 12-inch rainbow trout, which provide good shoreline prospects for bait dunkers.

In the hot summer months, fishing for resident warm-water species is only fair, and evening fishing for catfish is the best thing going. Although gas engines are prohibited, it is a good lake for hand-powered craft such as canoes and rafts. You get a little-known spot, quiet water, and, in the cool months, decent trout fishing. No swimming is permitted.

The lake is open year-round.

Facilities, fees: An unimproved boat ramp and a fish-cleaning station are available. There is a campground with restrooms, drinking water, flush toilets, showers, an RV dump station, picnic areas, a playground, and three pavilions with electricity and tables. Supplies can be obtained about eight miles away in Tehachapi. Gas motors and swimming are not permitted. Day-use and boat-launching fees are charged.

Directions: From Bakersfield, take Highway 58 east toward the town of Tehachapi. Exit onto Highway 202 and drive three miles to Banducci Road. Turn left on Banducci Road and follow the signs for about a mile to the park, on the right.

Contact: Tehachapi Valley Recreation and Parks District, 661/822-3228, www.tvrpd .org/facilities/brite-lake.

2 CALIFORNIA AQUEDUCT (KERN COUNTY)

Rating: 2

west of Lancaster
Map pages 644-645

At least it provides a place to toss a line, and in the south valley, that's saying something.

This access point on the California Aqueduct is just a mile from Quartz Hill and a short hop west from both Palmdale and Lancaster. You bring your bait and your bucket, bait up, toss out your line, and hope a wandering striped bass or catfish roams past and decides to take a bite. You might bring some reading material for a quick read between bites, something short and snappy, like *War and Peace*.

Facilities, fees: A parking area and toilets are provided. Fishing access is free.

Directions: From Los Angeles, take I-5 north for about 40 miles to Castaic and Lake Hughes Road. Turn north on Lake Hughes Road and drive to Elizabeth Lake Road. Turn right and drive about three miles east (past Lake Hughes and Munz Lake) to Elizabeth Lake and Munz Ranch Road. Turn left (north) on Munz Ranch Road and continue to the fishing site, at the aqueduct crossing.

Contact: Department of Water Resources, 800/272-8869, www.water.ca.gov/recreation.

3 PYRAMID LAKE

Rating: 7

north of Los Angeles in
Angeles National Forest
Map pages 644-645

This is one of the cornerstones of California's Central Valley Project: Pyramid Lake is a major storage facility for water being moved from north to south. Since the pumps in the delta take fish as well as water, Pyramid Lake is frequently pumped full to the brim with both, providing a decent fishery for striped bass as well as for rainbow trout. The lake covers 1,300 surface acres and has 22 miles of shoreline.

Striped bass provide a bonus; fish in the 20-pound class are occasionally caught, and stripers to 35 pounds have been taken here. The stripers can be difficult to catch most of the year, although there are a few periods when they are vulnerable, such as in the spring (if trout plants are made at the head of the lake). The stripers often feed on the trout, and if you are on the spot during such activity, you can cast a Rattletrap, Hawg Raiser jig, or AC Plug in a rainbow-trout pattern and have a chance at a quick hookup. Finally, in the fall, the stripers occasionally emerge from the depths and chase their feed near the surface.

Catchable rainbow trout are planted at Pyramid Lake, despite the high predation from striped bass. Plants are made every two weeks, which have improved the prospects, especially for trolling. After launching your boat, start trolling immediately along the western shore. Many boaters rush through this area to reach the main lake and bypass some good water. Trout fishing is decent until summer, when the fish go deep (most anglers troll right over the top of them). In addition to striped bass and trout, the lake provides fishing for largemouth bass, catfish, crappie, and bluegill.

Pyramid Lake is at an elevation of 2,600 feet, and although the lake is surrounded by Angeles National Forest, I-5 is routed right past several lake arms. Yet the lake is difficult to fish without a boat. In fact, most of the shoreline is accessible only by boat.

The lake is also a favorite destination for powerboaters, especially water-skiers (a 35-mph speed limit is enforced) and personal watercraft users. In an attempt to get a handle on the high-speed boating activity, only 50 personal watercraft are allowed on the lake at any one time.

Pyramid is one of the more heavily used recreation lakes in California. Always keep that in mind and your expectations will have a better chance of being fulfilled.

Facilities, fees: Picnic areas, restrooms with flush toilets, and a paved boat ramp are provided. A campground is two miles away, and several boat-in picnic sites are available. Day-use and boat-launching fees are charged. Fishing before sunrise is prohibited.

Directions: From Los Angeles, take I-5 north for about 60 miles to the exit for Smokey Bear Road (about eight miles south of Gorman). Take that exit west and drive 1.7 miles to the lake.

Contact: Pyramid Lake Marina, 661/295-7155; Department of Water Resources, Gorman, Vista del Lago Visitors Center, 661/294-0219, www.water.ca.gov/recreation.

🖪 ELIZABETH LAKE

Rating: 5
west of Lancaster in Angeles National Forest
Map pages 644-645

Elizabeth is at 3,300 feet in the northern outskirts of Angeles National Forest below Portal Ridge. It's a small, pretty lake that provides fair trout fishing in the cool months and bass fishing in the spring and summer. When the water is cool enough and high enough to support trout, it is stocked with rainbow trout in the 8-inch class and in the 10- to 12-inch class. Standard trolling and shoreline bait-fishing techniques do fine here, and in late spring, the water is warm enough to swim in during the day, yet cool enough to catch trout in the evening.

The shoreline of the eastern half of Elizabeth Lake is private and off-limits to the public.

An exceptional side trip is to the Antelope Valley California Poppy State Reserve, a few miles to the north. In the spring, it's usually wall-to-wall blooming poppies, about nine square miles of the bright flowers—a fantastic sight some years, a complete dud in others.

Facilities, fees: Picnic areas, vault toilets, and an unimproved launch ramp are available. There's no drinking water. Motors are restricted to a maximum of 10 horsepower. A daily parking fee is charged. An annual pass may be purchased.

Directions: From Los Angeles, take I-5 north for about 40 miles to Castaic and Lake Hughes Road. Turn north on Lake Hughes Road and then drive to Elizabeth Lake Road. Turn right and drive about three miles east (past Lake Hughes and Munz Lake) to Elizabeth Lake.

Contact: Angeles National Forest, Santa Clara/Mojave Rivers Ranger District, 661/296-9710, www.fs.fed.us/r5—click on Forest Offices.

5 CASTAIC LAKE

Rating: 9

north of Los Angeles

Map pages 644-645

For many years, it seemed almost certain that a world-record largemouth bass was swimming around at Castaic Lake. This is the place where Bob Crupi caught a 22-pound, 1-ounce fish in 1991, just a few ounces shy of the most legendary of all world records (22 pounds, 4 ounces). Crupi did the admirable thing and released that fish. Yet no one ever caught one bigger. We hope that world-class bass passed on its big-fish genes to many equally huge offspring.

Because of that vision, anglers from all over the world head to Castaic (as well as Dixon near San Diego, where another world record–size bass was documented). They want to be the one who lands it. In the meantime, however, a series of giant bass have been caught, world records for several different line classes. Crupi is responsible for several of them.

Castaic is easy to reach, just a short hop from the junction of I-5 and Highway 126. Set at 1,535 feet in the foothills adjoining Angeles National Forest to the north, it is shaped like a giant V and covers nearly 2,400 acres when full. Castaic is a big lake that gets fantastic stocks of rainbow trout and intense fishing pressure by experienced bass anglers. The lake also has striped bass, catfish, bluegill, and crappie.

Because of all the people out to catch giant fish, the bass have smartened up here. Line weight has become critical; too heavy a test will spook the fish, and you'll rarely get a nibble. Because of that, most bassers use 6- to 12-pound line, never heavier, and then they pray that if they hook the world record, the fish won't break them off. Unlike in a lot of lakes, the bass here are deep almost all year (except when spawning), and it takes a lot of persistence and skill to work jigs slowly over structures 25–40 feet deep. The best bet is to carefully graph areas, then fish the deep-water structures. Always start at the upper lake areas. A big change in technique has come with the introduction of huge plastic worms and wood plugs. Use a Huddleston, Worm King, AC Plug (the standard), Megabait, or Stocker Trout, the latter being lures that imitate trout (the favorite food of big largemouth bass).

Some pretty good-sized bass have been caught here from shore, too. Bass in the 10- to 15-pound class are caught fairly regularly—a testimonial to this lake's ability to grow big bass.

If you get the idea that catch rates are not high, you are right. But at Castaic, there is another option: trout. Standard trolling techniques result in good catches, providing that anglers adjust for depth according to water temperatures.

Many newcomers to Castaic arrive with tremendous excitement over the chance at a world record. Then the lack of action makes them feel that the jinx has them by the throat. "All these giant bass are here and I can't even get a bite," they start thinking. Finally they either switch over to trout, slink quietly away to more familiar territory, or grit their teeth and renew the effort, realizing it takes remarkable persistence and skill to entice a trophy.

Waterskiing is also popular at Castaic (there's a 35-mph speed limit), and the bassers do their share of jetting around as well. The lake rules are designed so that the main body of the lake is for waterskiing, and the outer edges and coves are for fishing. The area closest to the dam is for personal watercraft.

Another option is the adjacent Castaic Lagoon, less than a mile to the south. Except for small trolling motors, no motors are permitted on the lagoon, and the trout fishing is often excellent for anglers with canoes and rowboats, as is fishing with bait from shore. Float tubing at the lagoon is good, too. Rainbow trout are stocked, and there are also catfish, bluegill and crappie.

Locals call Castaic "the upper lake," and the afterbay is referred to as "the lower lake" or "the lagoon." A bonus is that fishing is allowed 24 hours a day at the lagoon on the east side. The west side closes at sundown.

Swimming is prohibited at Castaic but is permitted at Castaic Lagoon from mid-June through September. Use is quite heavy into fall.

Facilities, fees: Paved boat ramps are on the main lake's east and west arms (near the dam) and on the lagoon's south shore. A primitive campground is 0.5 mile east of the lagoon. Picnic areas are at the lake and at the lagoon; drinking water and flush toilets are available. Castaic Boat Rentals (on the main lake) rents out fishing boats. Bait and tackle are at the marina. Day-use and boat-launching fees are charged.

Directions: From Los Angeles, take I-5 north for 40 miles to Castaic and Lake Hughes Road. Turn north on Lake Hughes Road and drive 0.5 mile to Ridge Route Road. Turn left and drive 0.75 mile to Castaic Lake Drive. Turn right and drive a short distance to the west lake entrance. Continue two miles to the main lake entrance.

Contact: Castaic Lake, Los Angeles County, 661/257-4050, www.castaiclake.com; Castaic Boat Marina and Rentals, 661/775-6232.

6 CALIFORNIA AQUEDUCT (LOS ANGELES COUNTY)

Rating: 2

from Quartz Hill to Pearblossom
Map pages 644-645

What's the longest fishing hole in the world? The California Aqueduct qualifies, stretching from the delta on south for hundreds of miles. In this region are four different access points that look remarkably similar: concrete beveled edges, a high water level, an adjacent parking area, and a little outhouse. This area of the California Aqueduct has fewer striped bass than the access points farther north; after all, in order to make it here, the fish must survive being pumped several hundred miles through a series of lakes and over the Tehachapi Mountains. However, catfish and the occasional trout and bass are pumped out of Pyramid Lake.

The benefit of the fishing access points is for people who want to make a quick hit or those ready for an all-night stand. The quick hit comes for people cruising through the area who need a break from the driving; they park and cast lures for 5 or 10 minutes, then drive on. The all-nighters bring a lawn chair, cast out their bait, and wait for a fish to wander by.

Facilities, fees: Parking areas are provided at all sites; most offer toilets as well. Supplies can be obtained in Palmdale. Fishing access is free.

Directions: To the 70th Street West site: From Los Angeles, drive north on I-5 to the Highway 14/Palmdale exit. Turn east and continue past Palmdale to the Avenue N exit. Take the exit and turn west. Continue on Avenue N (which becomes 70th Street West). Keep bearing left and travel a short distance south to the fishing site.

To the Avenue S site: From Los Angeles, drive north on I-5 to the Highway 14/Lancaster/Palmdale exit. Turn east and continue to the Avenue S exit (about two miles south of Palmdale). Turn west and continue to the fishing site, just past Tierra Subida Avenue.

To the 77th Street East site: From Los Angeles, drive north on I-5 to the Highway 14/Lancaster/Palmdale exit. Turn east and continue to the Pearblossom/Highway 138 exit. Turn east on Highway 138 and drive southeast to Littlerock. Turn right (south) at 77th Street East, drive south to Avenue V, turn right, and continue to the fishing site.

To the Longview Road site: From Los

Angeles, drive north on I-5 to the Highway 14/Lancaster/Palmdale exit. Turn east and continue to the Pearblossom/Highway 138 exit. Turn east on Highway 138 and drive southeast to Pearblossom and Longview Road. Turn right on Longview Road and drive south to the fishing site.

Contact: Department of Water Resources, Gorman, Vista del Lago Visitors Center, 661/294-0219, www.water.ca.gov/recreation.

7 MOJAVE NARROWS REGIONAL PARK

Rating: 4

on the Mojave River near Victorville

Map pages 644-645

Almost no one (except the locals) knows about this little county park. It is like an oasis in the Mojave Desert.

There are actually two small lakes here: the larger Horseshoe Lake and Pelican Lake. Rowboats and pedal boats are for rent on weekends. Private boats are not allowed.

The park is at 2,000 feet and provides a few recreation options, including a pond stocked in season with trout and catfish, and horseback-riding facilities and trails.

The Mojave River fluctuates in water level here, almost disappearing in some years in summer and early fall. One of the big events of the year here is on Fathers Day in June: the Huck Finn Jubilee. Note that the gate is closed each evening.

Facilities, fees: A campground, restrooms, drinking water, flush toilets, showers, an RV dump station, a picnic area, a snack bar, pay phone, playground, archery range, bait, boat rentals, horse rentals, and horseback-riding facilities are available. A store, propane gas, and coin laundry are three miles from the campground. Fees are charged for day use, fishing, and camping.

A boat rental dock is on the east side of Horseshoe Lake. Rental rowboats and pedal boats are permitted on weekends. No private boats are permitted, including canoes, kayaks and inflatables. Swimming and other water-body contact sports are not allowed. The park is open daily 7:30 A.M.–5 P.M. from mid-October–mid-April; from mid-April–mid-October, it's open 7:30 A.M.–6 P.M. Sunday–Thursday, and 7:30 A.M.–7 P.M. on Friday and Saturday.

Directions: Take I-15 to Victorville and the exit for Bear Valley Road. Take that exit and drive east on Bear Valley Road for six miles to Ridgecrest. Turn left on Ridgecrest, drive three miles, and make a left into the park.

Contact: Mojave Narrows Regional Park, 760/245-2226, cms.sbccounty.gov/parks.

8 COLORADO RIVER (STATELINE TO LAKE HAVASU)

Rating: 7

north of Needles on
the California/Nevada border

Map pages 644-645

Bring your suntan lotion and a big towel. This section of the Colorado River is a big tourist spot, where the body oil and beer can flow faster than the river. There are a lot of hot bodies and hot boats, and waterskiing is the dominant activity in the summer. That doesn't mean there is no fishing. Just the opposite is true—there is great fishing nearly year-round.

Because the river is big and deep, and because it flows 4–8 miles per hour, you really need a boat to do it right. A great trick here is to inspect the river at low water, driving on the dirt road that runs along the east side. That's how you find the secret spots. The best spot for stripers is often below the dam at the buoy line. The striper population here seems to cycle with that of a primary forage, perch.

The fishing lasts from late winter through spring, when the Department of Fish and Game stocks rainbow trout in the stretch of river between Topock Bridge upstream to

Needles. Most of the trout are not large; they are seven–eight inches, with a sprinkling of bigger fellows.

As summer approaches, the trout bite wanes, and striped bass, largemouth bass, and catfish start taking over. In May, there is usually a striped bass derby, and it can be quite a big deal, with prizes and intense competition. Following that weekend, however, the most serious competition has more to do with suntans and fast boats.

About 30 miles of the Colorado River, from Needles to Lake Havasu City (Arizona), is part of the Havasu National Wildlife Refuge. One of the last remaining natural stretches of the lower Colorado River flows through the Topock Gorge.

Note: The last takeout before Lake Havasu is at the town of Topock, Arizona, where I-40 intersects with the river. If you miss it, you have to float approximately 17 more miles to the next takeout at Lake Havasu.

Facilities, fees: Lodging, cabins, campgrounds, full-service marinas, picnic areas, gas, restaurants, tackle, and groceries are in the Needles area. Day-use and boat-launching fees are charged.

Directions: From Southern California, take I-15 north to I-40 at Barstow. Drive east on I-40 for approximately 150 miles to Needles.

From Northern California, drive south on U.S. 395 to Highway 58 at Kramer Junction. Turn east on Highway 58, then cross over on I-15 to I-40. Turn east on I-40 and drive approximately 150 miles to Needles.

Paved boat launches are at the following locations:

To Needles Marina Park and Jack Smith Memorial Park: Drive on I-40 to Needles and the exit for J Street. Take that exit and drive to Broadway. Turn left on Broadway and drive 0.75 mile to Needles Highway. Turn right on Needles Highway and drive 0.5 mile to Needles Marina Park, on the left. Continue 0.5 mile to Jack Smith Memorial Park.

Moabi Regional Park: From Needles, drive east on I-40 for 11 miles to Park Moabi Road. Turn left on Park Moabi Road and continue 0.5 mile to the Moabi Regional Park entrance, at the end of the road.

Rainbo Beach Resort: Drive on I-40 to Needles and River Road. Turn north on River Road and drive 1.5 miles to Rainbo Beach Resort, on the right.

Contact: Needles Chamber of Commerce, 760/326-2050, www.needleschamber.com; Needles Marina Park, 760/326-2197, www.needlesmarinapark.com; Topock Marina (Topock, Arizona), 928/768-2325, www.topock66.com; Rainbo Beach Resort, 760/326-3101, www.rainbobeach.com.

Boat rentals: Moabi Regional Park, 760/326-3831, www.cms.sbccounty.gov/parks; Paradise Boat Rentals, 928/854-4214 or 877/736-6131, www.paradiseboatrentals.com.

9 COLORADO RIVER (PARKER DAM TO PALO VERDE DAM)

Rating: 7

south of Needles on
the California/Arizona border

Map pages 644–645

For fishing, the best section of water in this area is in the upper stretch of Parker Valley. Because an access permit is required by the tribal office, water-skiers tend to bypass it. This piece of water provides good fishing for smallmouth bass, bluegill, catfish, and sometimes crappie, and it's a good duck-hunting area during the early winter.

Below Parker Dam is a spot for a lot of flathead catfish and channel catfish, including some occasional giants. Note that if you catch a razorback sucker, it must be released, as it is an endangered species. They have been caught as far north as Davis Dam near Bullhead City.

Look at all the powerboats racing around! On hot summer days, the Colorado River is about the only thing liquid around these parts that isn't in a can or bottle. One way or another, the natural response is to get in the water—by boat, water skis, personal watercraft, inner tube, or just your swimsuit. If this sounds like a primary place for water recreation, that's because it is.

Note: The Parker Valley portion of the river is part of the Colorado River Indian Reservation, and the tribe requires all anglers to obtain a permit. Permits are available at the tribe's Fish and Game Department in Parker, Arizona. Fishing permits can also be obtained from retail outlets and marinas in Ehrenberg, Arizona, and Poston, Arizona, and at two resorts near Blythe, California: Aha Quin Resort and Lost Lake Resort.

Facilities, fees: Campgrounds, resorts, marinas, boat ramps, boat rentals, bait, tackle, and supplies are off U.S. 95 near Parker, Palo Verde, and Blythe. A free boat ramp, Rockhouse, is operated by the Bureau of Land Management and is several miles north of Parker on the California side of the river. Day-use and boat-launching fees are charged. A permit fee is charged in the upper section of Parker Valley.

See *Directions* for information on the facilities that can be found at specific access points.

Directions: From Southern California, take I-10 east to Blythe and turn north on U.S. 95. Or take Highway 62 east to Vidal Junction at the intersection of U.S. 95 and Highway 62 and turn south on U.S. 95. There are numerous access points off U.S. 95 between Blythe and Vidal Junction in the Parker Valley area. To reach the Parker Dam section of the river, drive about 20 miles east of Vidal Junction on Highway 62 (crossing the Colorado River) to the town of Parker. From Parker, Arizona, turn north on either U.S. 95 or Parker Dam Road (in California, before crossing the California side of the river). Numerous access points are available off these roads.

From Northern California, drive south on U.S. 395 to I-15. Turn south on I-15 and drive to I-10. Turn east on I-10 and drive to Blythe. Turn north on U.S. 95 or turn north off I-10 on Highway 62 near Palm Springs and continue northeast to Vidal Junction, at the intersection of U.S. 95 and Highway 62. Turn south on U.S. 95. There are numerous access points off U.S. 95 between Blythe and Vidal Junction in the Parker Valley area. To reach the Parker Dam section of the river, drive about 20 miles east of Vidal Junction on Highway 62 to the town of Parker, Arizona. From Parker, turn north on either U.S. 95 or Parker Dam Road (in California). Numerous access points are available off these roads.

Directions to other boat launches and access points:

• Rockhouse, Arizona: From Vidal Junction turn east on Highway 62 and drive to Earp. Continue straight on Parker Dam Road for nine miles to the BLM ramp. Contact Bureau of Land Management, Lake Havasu Field Office, 928/505-1200, www.blm.gov/az.

• Buckskin Mountain State Park, Arizona: From Vidal Junction turn east on Highway 62 and drive to Parker and Arizona Highway 95. Turn north on Arizona Highway 95 and drive approximately 12 miles to the state park entrance. A campground, restrooms with showers, a restaurant, convenience store, gas, and a swimming beach are available. Contact Arizona State Parks at 602/542-4174, www.azstateparks.gov.

• River Island State Park, Arizona: From Vidal Junction turn east on Highway 62 and drive to Parker and Arizona Highway 95. Turn north on Arizona Highway 95 and drive approximately 13.5 miles to the state park entrance. A tent campground and swimming beach are provided. Contact Arizona State Parks at 602/542-4174, www.azstateparks.gov.

• La Paz County Park, Arizona: From Vidal Junction turn east on Highway 62 and drive to Parker and Arizona Highway 95. Turn north on Arizona Highway 95 and drive approximately seven miles to Golf Course Drive. Turn left on Golf Course Drive and drive 0.25 mile to Riverside Drive. Turn right and drive 0.5 mile to the park entrance on the left. A campground is available. Contact La Paz County Park, 928/667-2069.

• Cienega Springs Public Ramp, Arizona: From Vidal Junction, take Highway 62 east to Parker, Arizona, and Business 95. Turn north on Business 95 and drive approximately five miles to Cienega Springs and the boat ramp, Contact La Paz County Park, 928/667-2069.

• Patria Flats County Park, Arizona: From Vidal Junction, take Highway 62 east to Parker, Arizona, and Business 95. Turn north on Business 95 and drive approximately seven miles to Golf Road. Turn left and drive 0.25 mile to Riverside Drive. Turn left and drive 0.5 mile to the park on the right. Contact La Paz County Park, 928/667-2069.

• River Land Resort, California: From Vidal Junction, take Highway 62 east to Earp. Continue straight on Parker Dam Road and continue five miles to the resort. A campground, cabins, gas, and convenience store are available. Contact 760/663-3733, www .riverlandresort.net.

Contact: Bureau of Land Management, Lake Havasu Field Office, 928/505-1200, www .blm.gov/az; Bureau of Land Management, Yuma Field Office, 928/317-3200, www.blm .gov/az; La Paz County, Arizona, 928/667-2069; Parker Area Chamber of Commerce, 928/669-2174, www.parkerareachamberof commerce.com.

Fishing permits: Colorado River Indian Tribes, 928/669-9285.

Boat ramps and marinas: Aha Quin Resort, California, 760/922-3604; Bluewater Resort, Arizona, 888/243-3360, www.bluewater fun.com; Lost Lake Resort, California, 760/664-4413.

Lodging: Bluewater Resort, Arizona, 888/243-3360, www.bluewaterfun.com; Big River RV Park, California, 760/665-9359, www.bigriverrvpark.com; Oxbow Campground, California, 938/317-3200, www .blm.gov/az.

Note that a good fishing map of the Colorado River is available for sale at retail outlets and at the BLM Lake Havasu Field Office, 520/505-1200.

10 LAKE HAVASU

Rating: 8

from Topock to Parker Dam
on the Colorado River

Map pages 644-645

Giant Lake Havasu is like a lone sapphire in a vast field of coal. Created with the construction of the Parker Dam across the Colorado River, Havasu is 45 miles long and is one of the most popular boating areas in the southwestern United States.

You need a boat to do it right at Havasu (with one exception, so read on). It's virtually impossible to fish, get a secluded camping spot, or enjoy the area to the maximum without one. With a boat, you can cover the largest amount of water in the search for fish, pick a do-it-yourself boat-in campsite along the Arizona side of the lake, and see the varied shoreline habitat and scenic beauty.

The most sought-after fishing here is for striped bass, with largemouth coming in second, but the results come with tremendous swings in catch rates, areas fished, and techniques. Large catfish are also available, as are some bluegill and redear sunfish. But the star of the show is the striped bass, and because the striper is a migratory fish, you have to track them according to time of year. Your telephone is the most important piece of fishing equipment you could ask for at Havasu; make a phone call to learn up-to-the-minute conditions just prior to your trip—it could prevent a busted weekend.

The best striper fishing is in the spring (March, April, and May), and a big striper derby is held to celebrate it. In the winter, before the first warm weather starts arriving, most of the stripers are down near Parker Dam. Nearby Havasu Springs Resort is a good headquarters for anglers early in the year. But believe me, the stripers are not easy to catch during this period. They tend to be deep, and if the water is very cold, they don't much like hitting lures and are quite subtle on the bite when presented with bait. This all begins to change quickly as March arrives, bringing with it the first warm weather of the year. Chumming for stripers while at anchor is another popular method here.

From late March through April and into May, the striped bass are on the move and on the prowl, providing the best fishing of the year. Most people fish for them as if they were fishing for largemouth bass, using large jigs that simulate baitfish. Some of the best patterns are the Hair Raiser, Striper Razor, and Worm-Tail jig.

One of the best areas is at Site Six near Lake Havasu City, in the middle of the lake in Cottonwood Cove at Cattail Cove State Park in Arizona. Another good spot is at the southern portion of the lake, near Havasu Springs Resort.

The fish start migrating upstream, past Lake Havasu City and beyond. The best spots in Lake Havasu for striped bass during this migratory period are just north of Lake Havasu City, including Grass Island and Skier's Island. Eventually the bass keep going all the way up to Davis Dam (Lake Mojave), adjacent to Bullhead City. In this area, Havasu isn't so much a lake as a semblance of the once-mighty Colorado River. This is also the one time when you don't necessarily need a boat to catch stripers. From the shore at the Davis Dam area, you can use gear styled for surf casting and reach the migrating fish with long casts. This can be a lot of work, and if you aren't in shape, you will be after one weekend. Fishing deep-running Rapalas is best by boat here; Hair Raisers are best by shore.

Once summer arrives, the stripers scatter all over creation, and for the folks willing to work at it, they provide fair trolling results. The best luck comes for those out at daybreak, with the best bite at dawn just after a night with a dark moon. After that, the stripers tend to stay deep, and you can troll your little petunia off looking for one. The exception is late in the summer and early fall, when stripers can corral schools of baitfish near the surface, complete with diving gulls, just like in the ocean. If you are lucky enough to see such an affair, circle it with your boat and cast Hair Raisers in the direction of the birds. While waiting for a surface boil, a good idea is to drift, use anchovies for bait 30 feet down, and hope to pick up a stray or two.

Hundreds of acres of artificial reef have been installed to create more aquatic habitat, and dividends are paying off. It has helped bass, catfish, bluegill, and redear sunfish. Havasu also has some big channel catfish. The best fishing for these fish is usually in the backs of coves, where there can be lots of aquatic vegetation.

The best spot for crappie is on the Bill Williams arm of Lake Havasu, on the south end of the lake. Spring is best. The fishing for black crappie is not like it once was. Their numbers have declined in recent years. In addition, some monster-sized flathead catfish have been caught in the same area, including some ranging to 45 pounds.

By summer, there are a lot of sideshows. There are dozens of personal watercraft, many hot and oiled-down bodies, and beer flowing faster than the river. Some anglers just bait up for catfish, toss out their fishing line, and watch all the passing action. A few giant catfish roam this area, by the way, and every once in a while, someone catches an absolute monster with a head the size of a salad bowl.

One option at Havasu is often overlooked. In the winter months, when the place is virtually abandoned, the trout fishing is pretty decent, and the crappie fishing is fair. The trout are way upstream near Bullhead City, in the stretch of water below Davis Dam. The crappie fishing can be good in Topock Bay, which is just upstream of the I-40 bridge. Another good area is just downstream of the bridge. Fishing for largemouth bass is popular, and tournaments are held consistently from fall through spring. Due to increased catch-and-release rates, the bass population has remained healthy.

With Lake Havasu, you have a tremendous amount of water to pick from and a series of fisheries that provide wildly varied results, depending on the time of year. What to do? Enjoy yourself. Get a boat, pick out a spot along the shore for a boat-in camp, and enjoy the water—a jewel in the desert.

In an effort to better promote fishing, there is a joint effort between various public agencies to provide fishing sites for those without boats. There are numerous such sites, primarily platforms and docks, around the lake, and they are wheelchair-accessible. You can find them at Take Off Point, Havasu Springs Resort, Mesquite Bay, and Site Six. Access is free.

Facilities, fees: Campgrounds, resorts, marinas, boat ramps, boat rentals, bait, tackle, and supplies are along Arizona Highway 95 in the vicinity of Lake Havasu City as well as along Highway 95 on the California side. There are approximately 40 shoreline miles of boat-access camping on the Arizona side of the lake between the dam and Lake Havasu City. There are free shoreline-fishing access sites with platforms and docks. A fee for day use and/or boat launching is charged at most resorts and marinas.

For a comprehensive listing of all boat rentals, charters, and tours, contact Lake Havasu Tourism Bureau or the Lake Havasu Area Chamber of Commerce. Scuba diving is also possible; see *Contact*.

A fishing map of Lake Havasu and the Colorado River is available for sale at retail outlets and the BLM Lake Havasu Field Office.

Note: When driving here, do not turn at the first Highway 95 exit, as that is U.S. 95, which will add hours of travel time and frustration. Take Exit 9 for State Route 95.

Directions: From Southern California: Take I-10 east to Blythe and turn north on U.S. 95. Continue to Vidal Junction, at the intersection of U.S. 95 and Highway 62 (or take Highway 62 directly east to Vidal Junction). To access the west side of the lake, turn north on U.S. 95 and drive about 28 miles to Havasu Lake Road; turn right (east) and continue to the lake.

To reach the east side of the lake, drive east on I-40 and take Exit 9 to Arizona Highway 95. Turn north on Arizona Highway 95 (the Arizona side) or Parker Dam Road (the California side) and drive to Parker Dam. Continue north on State Highway 95 to Lake Havasu City, on the east side of the lake.

From Northern California: Take U.S. 395 south to Highway 58. Turn east and drive to Barstow and I-40. Turn east on I-40 and drive to Exit 9 for Arizona Highway 95. Turn right (south) on Highway 95 and continue 20 miles to Lake Havasu City, on the east side of the lake. To access the west side of the lake, after going east on I-40, turn south on California U.S. 95 (south of Needles) and drive about 17 miles (instead of 20) to Havasu Lake Road. Turn left (east) and continue to the lake.

Paved ramps are available at the following locations:

• Lake Havasu State Park, Arizona: From Parker Dam, drive north on Arizona Highway 95 for 40 miles (2 miles north of London Bridge) to the park entrance. There are three multilane ramps; one is for personal watercraft only. Facilities include a campground, restrooms with showers, and a swimming beach.

• Site Six Ramp, Arizona: Take Arizona Highway 95 north to Lake Havasu City and to Swanson Boulevard. Turn left on Swanson Boulevard and drive a short distance to Lake Havasu Boulevard. Turn left and drive one block to McCulloch Boulevard. Turn left, cross the London Bridge, and continue for two miles to the far end of the island and the ramp, on the left. A fish-cleaning station and a wheelchair-accessible fishing pier are available.

• Cattail Cove State Park, Arizona: Drive north on Arizona Highway 95 to milepost 168 (15 miles north of Parker Dam) and the park entrance road.

• Crazy Horse Campground, Arizona: Take Arizona Highway 95 north to Lake Havasu City and to Swanson Boulevard. Turn right on Swanson Boulevard and drive a short distance to Lake Havasu Boulevard. Turn left and drive one block to McCulloch Boulevard. Turn left, cross the London Bridge, and continue 0.25 mile to the entrance, on the right.

• Havasu Landing Resort & Casino, California: From Vidal Junction, drive north on U.S. 95 toward Needles to 17 Mile Road (about halfway between Vidal Junction and Needles). Turn right and drive 13 miles to the resort. A launch ramp, marina, bait and tackle, fuel dock, campground, a restaurant, a convenience store, and a deli are available.

• Lake Havasu Marina, Arizona: Take Arizona Highway 95 north to Lake Havasu City and to Swanson Boulevard. Turn right on Swanson Boulevard and drive a short distance to Lake Havasu Boulevard. Turn left and drive one block to McCulloch Boulevard. Turn left, cross the London Bridge, and continue to the marina, on the left, at 1100 McCulloch Boulevard.

• Sandpoint Marina & RV Park, Arizona: Take Arizona Highway 95 north and drive 15 miles north to Milepost 168 and the exit for Cattail Cove/Sandpoint Marina. Turn left and drive to the park entrance. Fishing boats, pontoon boats, personal watercraft, and houseboats are for rent. Full service marina and boat repair are available. Bait and tackle are available.

Contact: Lake Havasu Tourism Bureau, 928/453-3444 or 800/2-HAVASU (800/242-8278), www.golakehavasu.com; Lake Havasu Area Chamber of Commerce, 928/855-4115, www.havasuchamber.com; Bureau of Land Management, Lake Havasu Field Office, 928/505-1200, www.blm.gov/az.

Boat ramps and marinas: Lake Havasu State Park, Arizona, 928/855-2784, azstateparks. com; Site Six Ramp, Arizona, 928/453-8686; Cattail Cove State Park, Arizona, 928/855-1223, azstateparks.com/parks; Crazy Horse Campground, Arizona, 928/855-4033, www .crazyhorsecampgrounds.com; Havasu Landing Resort & Casino, California, 760/858-4593 or 800/307-3610, www.havasulanding .com; Lake Havasu Marina, Arizona, 928/855-2159; Sandpoint Marina & RV Park, Arizona, 928/855-0549, www.sandpointresort.com.

Boat rentals: Arizona Watersports, 928/667-7368 or 888/393-7368, www.arizona watersports.com; Paradise Boat Rentals, 928/854-4214 or 877/736-6131, www.para diseboatrentals.com; Nautical Sports Center, 928/855-7000, www.boatrentalshavasu.com.

Houseboat rentals: Havasu Springs Resort, 928/667-3361, www.havasusprings .com; Sandpoint Marina & RV Park, Arizona, 928/855-0549, www.sandpointresort.com; Nautical Sports Center, 800/843-9218, www .boatrentalshavasu.com.

Scuba diving: Aquastrophics Dive & Travel, 928/680-3483, www.aquastrophics.com.

Lodging: Black Meadow Landing, near Parker Dam, 800/742-8278 (camping), www.blackmeadowlanding.com; Crazy Horse Campground, Arizona, 928/855-4033, www .crazyhorsecampgrounds.com; Havasu Landing Resort & Casino, California, 760/858-4593 or 800/307-3610, www.havasulanding .com; Sandpoint Marina & RV Park, Arizona, 928/855-0549, www.sandpointresort.com.

Supplies: Bass Tackle Master, 928/854-2277; Havasu Bait and Tackle, 928/764-2248.

Guides: Captain Doyle's, Topock, Arizona, 866/284-3262, www.funfishing.net.

🔟 COLORADO RIVER (PALO VERDE DAM TO YUMA)

Rating: 8

north of Blythe on
the California/Arizona border

Map pages 644-645

When most people think of the Colorado River, they picture parties and speedboats. Yep, that's the way it is, here as well as upstream, especially on summer weekends and holidays. For fishing in the spring and summer and for duck hunting in the fall, well, you came to the right place as well. Actually, this section has two major stretches of water, the Palo Verde area and the Yuma area. One of the best spots in this region is the backwater-lake area of Martinez Lake, where Martinez Lake Resort has a full-service marina.

Martinez Lake, created by the construction of the Imperial Dam, is the best spot for catfish. The area features lots of stickups. Upstream, there are tunnel-like openings along the bank, often overgrown with cattails. By canoe, you can gain access to several small hidden lakes here, great spots for bluegill and catfish. All of these backwater lakes are good for largemouth bass and catfish. The record in this area is a 70-pound catfish.

The span of water in the Blythe–Palo Verde area is flanked by agricultural areas, although several developed recreation areas and county parks are on the California side of the river, near Palo Verde. Most visitor accommodations are found in the Blythe area. The fishing is fair, with striped bass, largemouth bass, bluegill, crappie, and catfish roaming the area. It's not great, but it's not terrible. It's fair.

The stretch of river in the Yuma–Winterhaven area is farther south, of course, and is less developed than the Palo Verde area. That is another way of saying there's damn near nothing out here, other than some recreation opportunities near Imperial Dam. Some areas are marshy, and they provide an opportunity for duck hunting in the fall. For anglers, there are some big catfish roaming these waters, along with small largemouth bass and a sprinkling of bluegill.

Note: Waterskiing is prohibited below Imperial Dam and in the Imperial National Wildlife Area, with the exception near the Picacho State Recreation Area.

Facilities, fees: Campgrounds, lodging, picnic areas, full-service marinas, boat ramps, bait, tackle, and groceries are in California at Blythe, Palo Verde, Picacho State Recreation Area, and Senator Wash Recreation Area and in Arizona in Yuma and Winterhaven. Most resorts and marinas charge a low day-use and/or boat-launching fee.

Directions: To the Blythe–Palo Verde area: From the Los Angeles area, take I-10 east and travel to Blythe, about three miles west of the California–Arizona border. Numerous resorts, marinas, and access points are available in Blythe, as well as in Palo Verde, farther south. The Palo Verde area may be reached by driving south on Highway 78 to the town of Palo Verde.

To the Yuma–Winterhaven area from San Diego: Take I-8 east and drive to Winterhaven on the California–Arizona border. In Winterhaven, take the Winterhaven/4th Avenue exit. Turn left on 4th Avenue and then turn right on County Road S24. Turn left on Picacho Road and drive under the railroad tracks. Continue on Picacho Road. When you cross the American Canal, the road becomes dirt. Continue north for 18 miles on the winding dirt road (not suitable for large RVs) to the Picacho State Recreation Area. This takes about an hour. Note that there are signed access spots on both County Road S24 and Picacho Road.

Boat ramps are available at the following locations:

• Oxbow Campground, California: Drive on I-10 to Highway 78 (two miles west of Blythe). Take Highway 78 south and drive to Palo Verde. Continue three miles south to a gravel road signed "Colorado River." Turn east (left) and drive 0.75 mile to the campground and boat launch. A boat launch, boat-trailer parking, a campground, and vault toilets are available. A bridge here crosses the river. There is an off-channel boat ramp with access to the Colorado River.

• Palo Verde County Park, California: Drive on I-10 to Highway 78 (two miles west of Blythe). Take Highway 78 south and drive about 20 miles (past Palo Verde) to the park entrance road. A boat ramp, restrooms with flush toilets, and a campground are available, but drinking water is not.

• Picacho State Recreation Area, California: From El Centro, take I-8 east to Winterhaven and the exit for Winterhaven/4th Avenue. Take that exit to 4th Avenue. Turn left and drive 0.5 mile to County Road S24/Picacho Road. Turn right and drive 18 miles (crossing rail tracks, a railroad bridge, and the American Canal; the road becomes dirt) to the campground. The road is not suitable for large RVs. The drive takes one hour from Winterhaven. In summer, thunderstorms can cause flash flooding, making short sections of the road impassable. Two boat ramps, a campground, three boat-in campsites, drinking water, pit toilets, solar showers, an RV dump station, and a camp store are available.

• Imperial National Wildlife Refuge, Arizona: From Yuma, Arizona, take Highway 95 north for 25 miles to Martinez Lake Road. Turn west (left) and drive 13 miles to the lake and visitors center. The boat launch is on the north side of the lake at Meers Point. Direct access to the Colorado River is available. There is a boat launch, a day-use area, and toilets.

• Senator Wash Recreation Area, California: Drive on I-8 to Yuma, Arizona, and the exit for 4th Avenue. Take that exit and drive to Imperial Highway/County Road S24. Turn north and drive 22 miles to Senator Wash Road. Turn left and drive four miles to the day-use boat launch area. The day-use area provides restrooms with flush toilets, outdoor showers, drinking water, a buoyed swimming area, and boat-in access to campgrounds at the north and south shores. There is no direct boat access to the Colorado River.

• Squaw Lake, California: Drive on I-8 to Yuma, Arizona, and the exit for 4th Avenue. Take that exit and drive to Imperial Highway/County Road S24. Turn north and drive 22 miles to Senator Wash Road. Turn left and drive about four miles to the lake (it's well signed). Two boat ramps, boat-trailer parking, two buoyed swimming areas, campgrounds, restrooms with flush toilets, outdoor showers, drinking water, an RV dump station, and a hiking trail are available. Direct access to the Colorado River is possible. There is a 5-mph speed limit.

Contact: Picacho State Recreation Area c/o Salton Sea State Recreation Area, 760/393-3059 or 760/996-2963, www.parks.ca.gov; Bureau of Land Management, Yuma Field Office, 928/317-3200, www.blm.gov/az; California State Parks, Colorado Desert District, 760/767-4037; Imperial National Wildlife Refuge, Arizona, 928/783-3371, www.fws.gov/refuges; McIntyre Park, Blythe, 760/922-8205; Palo Verde County Park, 760/482-4236, www.desertusa.com; Martinez Lake Resort, 800/876-7004, www.martinezlake.com.

12 LAKE CAHUILLA

Rating: 5
near Indio at Lake Cahuilla County Park
Map pages 644-645

What a place. If it weren't for this little patch of water, there would be times when it would be appropriate to put up a sign on I-10 that says, "You are now entering Hell."

Lake Cahuilla covers just 135 acres (with 3.5 miles of shoreline), but they are the most important acres in the entire region. Temperatures are commonly in the range of 100°F, and the desert winds can blow a gale.

The best time to fish this lake is during the cool months, all three of them, when trout are stocked at a good clip by the Department of Fish and Game. The lake receives trout in the 7- to 8-inch class and some ranging to 12 inches. Those are added to by special plants by the county. Together they provide a viable fishery.

The lake also has bluegill, largemouth bass, and carp, and in the summer months, the county also stocks catfish to join some bigger resident holdovers. A resident bass population somehow manages to sustain itself.

No gas motors are permitted on the lake, and no swimming is permitted. A 15-mph speed limit is strictly enforced. The lake is open year-round but is closed Tuesday, Wednesday, and Thursday in summer.

This lake provides the one beacon of hope in a large region of fishing bleakness. If you find yourself out this way during the winter, a good side trip is to Joshua Tree National Park, to the northeast. God help you if you are here any other time of the year.

Facilities, fees: There is an unpaved, beach boat launch. A campground with restrooms, showers, an RV dump station, a playground, a seasonal swimming pool, and picnic areas are available. Supplies can be obtained in Indio. No gas-powered motors are permitted on the lake. Day-use fees are charged.

Directions: From I-10 in Indio, take the Monroe Street exit and follow Monroe Street south for 10 miles to Avenue 58. Turn right and continue three miles to the lake at the end of the road.

Contact: Lake Cahuilla County Park, 760/564-4712 or 800/234-7275 (camping reservations), www.rivcoparks.org/parks.

13 SALTON SEA

Rating: 3

east of San Diego

Map pages 644-645　　　　**BEST (**

The Salton Sea is on the edge of extinction as a viable fishery. Once a fantastic fishery, corvina have virtually disappeared. Since it was once great, it can be great again if habitat, salinity, and water conditions are protected. The lake has tilapia, sargo, and croaker.

The lake has a unique history. The Salton Sea was created in 1905 when a dike broke and the basin was flooded with saltwater. This is one of the world's true inland seas. It is about a three-hour drive from the Los Angeles Basin. The lake is 35 miles long but has an average depth of just 15 feet. This vast body of water covers 360 square miles, and it is surrounded by nothingness for miles in every direction. The Salton Sea is 228 feet below sea level.

The lake record for orangemouth corvina is 39 pounds (a real monster), but that was in the good old days.

When the wind blows, there's nothing to slow it down, so it can howl across the water, whipping up large waves that are dangerous to boaters. To help alert newcomers that hazardous winds are in the offing, local authorities have posted a flashing red light on the northeast shore; get off the lake if you see the light flashing.

In the spring, the fishing here is exciting, as you cast lures in shallow water. Tilapia, a perchlike fish that can range up to four pounds, can be caught by the hundreds. For tilapia and croaker, use worms. At that time, this lake can provide some of the best catch rates in California. Fishing is best from March–July and again in October and November. All you need is a boat and a little luck with the weather; then you can start exploring.

In the summer, fish the lake surface; in the winter, fish deeper. In the winter and early spring, the first area of the lake that comes to life is the southeastern end, but any backwater bay where the water temperature is warm enough to get the fish active is worth exploring. But enjoy the cooler temperatures while you can, because when it gets hot here, you might think you are in hell, and you would be right.

Timing is critical. When the water conditions are ideal, the top spot is often on the southern end of the lake, from the buoy toward Red Hill. This lake can provide one of the state's unique and great fisheries. It's a good thing, too, because the place is ugly, maybe the ugliest fishing spot on planet Earth. For sheer ugliness, the Salton Sea is right up there with the California Aqueduct west of Bakersfield.

Since the water is, for the most part, quite shallow, boaters who aren't used to the place should be aware of unmarked underwater obstacles that are at the lake's far north and south ends and can pose navigational hazards. Most of the boaters here are fishermen casting about for corvina, and they rarely have any unusual problems.

Use is moderate at Salton Sea year-round but is lowest in the summer and highest in the winter, when quite a few retirees make the trip to take advantage of the temperate off-season climate. Other activities in the area include golfing, bird-watching, and hiking.

Facilities, fees: Campgrounds, boat ramps, marinas, picnic areas, lodging, bait and tackle, restaurants, and groceries are available. There are no boat rentals. A nominal fee is charged at most marinas and resorts for day use and/or boat launching.

Directions: From the Los Angeles area, take I-10 east to Indio and exit onto the Highway 86 Expressway. Drive south for 12 miles to 66th Avenue. Turn left and drive less than one mile to Mecca and Highway 11. Turn right (south) and drive 12 miles to Salton Sea.

Boat ramps are available at the following locations:

• To Desert Shores Trailer Park (west shore): From Indio, take Highway 86 Expressway south and drive 30 miles to Desert Shores.

• To Red Hill County Park Marina (east shore): From Mecca, take Highway 111 south to Niland, and continue to Sinclair Road. Turn right and drive 3.5 miles to Garst Road. Turn right and drive 1.5 miles to the end of Garst Road, at Red Hill Road. Turn left on Red Hill Road and drive to the park, at the end of the road.

• To Salton Sea Beach Marina (west shore): From Indio, take Highway 86 Expressway south and drive to Salton Sea Beach and Brawley Avenue. Turn right and drive to Santa Rosa Street. Turn left and drive two blocks to Coachella. Turn right and drive one block to the marina.

• To Salton Sea State Recreation Area (east shore): From Mecca, take Highway 111 south for about 12 miles to the Headquarters Campground. A boat ramp is available.

• To West Shores RV Park (west shore): From Indio, take Highway 86 Expressway south and drive to Salton City and North Marina Drive. Turn left and drive two miles to Sea Garden and the sign for Johnson's Landing. Turn left and drive 0.3 mile to the resort, at the end of the road.

• To Bombay Beach Marina (east shore): From Mecca, take Highway 111 south for about 25 miles to the exit for Bombay Beach Campground (in Salton Sea State Recreation Area) and the Bombay Beach Marina (next to the recreation area). Turn right and drive a short distance to the boat launch.

Contact: Salton Sea State Recreation Area, 760/393-3052 or 760/393-3059, www.parks.ca.gov; Salton Sea West Shores Chamber of Commerce, 760/332-8102; Imperial County, 760/482-4236; Salton Sea Beach Marina, 760/395-1066, www.ssbmarina.com; West Shores RV Park, 760/394-4755; Desert Shores Trailer Park, 760/395-5280.

14 RAMER LAKE

Rating: 4

in Imperial Wildlife Area near Calipatria

Map pages 644-645

Almost nobody knows about little Ramer Lake, except for a few bird hunters hoping for ducks, doves, or quail. It is in the Imperial Wildlife Area, which provides waterfowl habitat and duck-hunting grounds during the winter. The rest of the year it is largely ignored, except for a handful of folks who fish the lake for bass, catfish, and that world favorite, carp.

The lake is in the Imperial Valley, surrounded by farmland and overshadowed by the massive Salton Sea, to the north. You must register at the entrance station to the wildlife area, then leave a written record of anything you've caught. That way they can keep track of the carp.

Facilities, fees: Chemical toilets are provided. No drinking water is provided. A campground is to the south, at Wiest Lake. A paved boat ramp is available. Supplies can be obtained in Calipatria or Brawley. Motorized boats and water-body contact are not allowed. Fishing access is free.

Directions: From Brawley, take Highway 111 north toward Calipatria. At the signed turn on the right for "Imperial Wildlife Area" (five miles before reaching Calipatria), turn right and continue to the lake.

Contact: Department of Fish and Game, Imperial Wildlife Area, 760/359-0577.

15 WIEST LAKE

Rating: 5

in Wiest Lake County Park south of Calipatria

Map pages 644-645

This place can seem almost like an oasis. The water comes from a canal and is emptied into the Alamo River, where this lake is formed. It covers just 50 acres, is at 110 feet below sea level, and provides fishing for trout and catfish.

The Department of Fish and Game plunks in trout here, and they aren't dinkers. They average in the 11-inch class, with a few bigger and smaller. The trout fishing is in the winter, of course, when temperatures are habitable. In the spring and summer, this place really heats up, and the trout fishing goes kaput. That is when catfish are stocked. There are also fair prospects for bass, with a sprinkling of bluegill. The Imperial Valley is something of a wasteland, but little Wiest Lake provides a welcome respite that only locals know about. The Salton Sea is about a 20-minute drive to the northwest. Alcoholic beverages are not permitted.

Facilities, fees: A campground, a restroom with flush toilets and showers, picnic areas, and an RV dump station are available. No drinking water. A store, coin laundry, and propane gas are nearby. Supplies can be obtained in Calipatria or El Centro. A day-use fee is charged.

Directions: From El Centro, take Highway 111 north to Brawley and Highway 78/Main Street. Turn west (left) on Highway 78/Main Street and drive a short distance to Highway 111. Turn right (north) on Highway 111 and drive four miles to Rutherford Road (well signed). Turn right (east) and drive two miles to the park entrance, on the right.

Contact: Wiest Lake County Park, 760/344-3712; Imperial County, 760/482-4236.

16 SUNBEAM LAKE/LAGOON

Rating: 6

near El Centro

Map pages 644-645

Sunbeam Lake is an oasis in desertlike country. It is even surrounded by palm trees. This popular little lake has three miles of shoreline and a lagoon that is about half the size of the lake. The lake is below sea level and is operated by Imperial County.

The lagoon is primarily for fishing, while recreational boaters and swimmers use Sunbeam Lake. All water sports are allowed at the lake, including swimming (when lifeguards are present).

The lagoon is stocked with rainbow trout in the winter months and catfish during the summer. Other species occasionally caught are largemouth bass, bluegill, crappie, and carp.

Temperatures are pleasant in the fall, winter, and spring. But in the summer, the average temperature is over 100°F—and everybody heads to Sunbeam to take a dunk and try to cool off. The lake is open year-round from sunrise to 10 P.M.; the lagoon is open from sunrise to sunset.

Facilities, fees: Paved boat ramps are available on the south side of the lake at the Imperial County Park and at the northwest end of the lagoon (adjacent to Sunbeam Lake). Picnic areas, restrooms with flush toilets, drinking water, and a swimming beach are available at Imperial County Park. An RV resort is nearby. Supplies are available in El Centro. No gas motors are permitted at the lagoon. No alcoholic beverages are allowed. Fees are charged for day use and boat launching.

Directions: From El Centro, take I-8 west for seven miles to the exit for Drew Road. Take that exit and drive north on Drew Road for 0.5 mile to the county park entrance on the left.

Contact: Imperial County, 760/482-4236; Sunbeam Lake RV Resort, 760/352-7154 or 800/900-7154, www.sunbeamlake.com.

RESOURCES

NATIONAL FORESTS

The Forest Service provides access to many hikes—from the remote wilderness to public recreation lakes—and allows camping unless specifically prohibited. If you ever want to clear the cobwebs from your head and get away from it all, this is the way to go.

Many Forest Service campgrounds are quite remote and have no drinking water. You usually don't need to check in or make reservations, and sometimes, there is no fee. At many Forest Service campgrounds that provide drinking water, the camping fee is often only a few dollars, with payment made on the honor system. Because most of these campgrounds are in mountain areas, they are subject to winter closure due to snow or mud.

Dogs are permitted in national forests with no extra charge and no hassle. Leashes are required for all dogs in some places. Always carry documentation of current vaccinations.

National Forest Adventure Pass

Angeles, Cleveland, Los Padres, and San Bernardino National Forests require an Adventure Pass for each parked vehicle. Daily passes cost $5; annual passes are available for $30. You can buy Adventure Passes at national forest offices in Southern California and dozens of retail outlets and online vendors. The new charges are use fees, not entrance fees. Holders of Golden Age and Golden Access (not Golden Eagle) cards can buy the Adventure Pass at a 50 percent discount at national forest offices only, or at retail outlets for the retail price. A Golden Eagle passport is honored in lieu of an Adventure Pass.

When you buy an annual Adventure Pass, you can also buy an annual second-vehicle Adventure Pass for $5. Major credit cards are accepted at most retail and online outlets and at some forest service offices. You can buy Adventure Passes by telephone at 909/382-2622, -2623, -2621, or by mail at San Bernardino National Forest, Pass Program Headquarters, 602 S. Tippecanoe Avenue, San Bernardino,

CA 92408-2607. Checks should be made payable to USDA Forest Service.

You will not need an Adventure Pass while traveling through these forests, nor when you've paid other types of fees such as camping or ski pass fees. However, if you are camping in these forests and you leave the campground in your vehicle and park outside the campground for recreation, such as at a trailhead, day-use area, near a fishing stream, etc., you will need an Adventure Pass for your vehicle. You also need an Adventure Pass if camping at a no-fee campground. More information about the Adventure Pass program, including a listing of retail and online vendors, can be obtained at www.fsadventurepass.org.

National Forest Reservations

Reservations at some of the more popular campgrounds, and most of the group camps, are made by a reservation system. Reservations can be made up to 240 days in advance, and up to 360 days in advance for groups. To reserve a site, call 877/444-6777 or visit www.reserveusa.com. There is a reservation fee of $9 (usually) for a campsite in a national forest; major credit cards are accepted. Holders of Golden Age or Golden Access passports receive a 50 percent discount for campground fees, except for group sites.

National Forest Maps

National Forest maps are among the best you can get for the price. They detail all backcountry streams, lakes, hiking trails, and logging roads for access. They cost $7 or more, and they can be obtained in person at forest service offices or by contacting U.S. Forest Service, Attn: Map Sales, P.O. Box 8268, Missoula, MT 59807, 406/329-3024, or www.fs.fed.us/recreation/nationalforeststore. Major credit cards are accepted if ordering by telephone.

Forest Service Information

Forest Service personnel are most helpful for obtaining camping or hiking trail information. Unless you are buying a map or Adventure Pass, it is advisable to phone in advance to get the best service. For specific information on a national forest, contact the following offices:

USDA Forest Service
Pacific Southwest Region
1323 Club Drive
Vallejo, CA 94592
707/562-USFS (707/562-8737)
fax 707/562-9130
www.fs.fed.us/r5

Angeles National Forest
701 N. Santa Anita Avenue
Arcadia, CA 91006
626/574-1613
fax 626/574-5233
www.fs.fed.us/r5/angeles

Cleveland National Forest
10845 Rancho Bernardo Road, No. 200
San Diego, CA 92127-2107
858/673-6180
fax 858/673-6192
www.fs.fed.us/r5/cleveland

Eldorado National Forest
100 Forni Road
Placerville, CA 95667
530/622-5061
fax 530/621-5297
www.fs.fed.us/r5/eldorado

Humboldt-Toiyabe National Forest
1200 Franklin Way
Sparks, NV 89431
775/331-6444
fax 775/355-5399
www.fs.fed.us/r4/htnf

Inyo National Forest
351 Pacu Lane, Suite 200
Bishop, CA 93514
760/873-2400
fax 760/873-2458
www.fs.fed.us/r5/inyo

Klamath National Forest
1312 Fairlane Road
Yreka, CA 96097-9549
530/842-6131
fax 530/841-4571
www.fs.fed.us/r5/klamath

Lake Tahoe Basin Management Unit
35 College Drive
South Lake Tahoe, CA 96150
530/543-2600
fax 530/543-2693
www.fs.fed.us/r5/ltbmu

Lassen National Forest
2550 Riverside Drive
Susanville, CA 96130
530/257-2151
fax 530/252-6448
www.r5.fs.fed.us/r5/lassen

Los Padres National Forest
6755 Hollister Avenue, Suite 150
Goleta, CA 93117
805/968-6640
fax 805/961-5729
www.fs.fed.us/r5/lospadres

Mendocino National Forest
825 N. Humboldt Avenue
Willows, CA 95988
530/934-3316
fax 530/934-7384
www.fs.fed.us/r5/mendocino

Modoc National Forest
800 W. 12th Street
Alturas, CA 96101
530/233-5811
fax 530/233-8709
www.fs.fed.us/r5/modoc

Plumas National Forest
P.O. Box 11500
159 Lawrence Street
Quincy, CA 95971
530/283-2050
fax 530/283-7746
www.fs.fed.us/r5/plumas

San Bernardino National Forest
602 S. Tippecanoe Avenue
San Bernardino, CA 92408-2607
909/382-2600
fax 909/383-5770
www.fs.fed.us/r5/sanbernardino

Sequoia National Forest
Giant Sequoia National Monument
1839 S. Newcomb Street
Porterville, CA 93257
559/784-1500
fax 559/781-4744
www.fs.fed.us/r5/sequoia

Shasta-Trinity National Forest
3644 Avtech Parkway
Redding, CA 96002
530/226-2500
fax 530/226-2470
www.fs.fed.us/r5/shastatrinity

Sierra National Forest
1600 Tollhouse Road
Clovis, CA 93611
559/297-0706
fax 559/294-4809
www.fs.fed.us/r5/sierra

Six Rivers National Forest
1330 Bayshore Way
Eureka, CA 95501
707/442-1721
fax 707/442-9242
www.fs.fed.us/r5/sixrivers

Stanislaus National Forest
19777 Greenley Road
Sonora, CA 95370
209/532-3671
fax 209/533-1890
www.fs.fed.us/r5/stanislaus

Tahoe National Forest
631 Coyote Street
Nevada City, CA 95959
530/265-4531
fax 530/478-6109
www.fs.fed.us/r5/tahoe

STATE PARKS

The California State Parks system provides many popular camping spots in spectacular settings. These campgrounds include drive-in numbered sites, tent spaces, and picnic tables, with showers and bathrooms provided nearby. Reservations are often necessary during the summer. Although many parks are well known, there are still some little-known gems in the state parks system where campers can enjoy seclusion, even in the summer.

State park fees have increased significantly since 2008, but camping in a state park is still a good deal. Many of the campgrounds along the California coastline are particularly popular in summer and require planning to secure a campsite.

State Park Reservations

Most of the state park campgrounds are on a reservation system, and campsites can be booked up to seven months in advance at these parks. There are also hike-in/bike-in sites at many of the parks, and these are available on a first-come, first-served basis. Reservations can be made by telephone at 800/444-PARK (800/444-7275) or online at www.reserveamerica.com. A reservation fee of $7.50 is charged for a campsite. Major credit cards are accepted for reservations but are generally not accepted in person at the parks.

Camping discounts of 50 percent are available for holders of the Disabled Discount Pass, and free camping is allowed for holders of the Disabled Veteran/Prisoner of War Pass.

For general information about California State Parks, contact:

California Department of Parks and Recreation
Public Information Office
P.O. Box 942896
1416 9th Street
Sacramento, CA 94296
916/653-6995 or 800/777-0369
fax 916/653-6995
www.parks.ca.gov

NATIONAL PARKS

California's national parks are natural wonders, varying from the spectacular yet crowded Yosemite Valley to the remote and rugged Lava Beds National Monument. Reservations for campsites are available five months in advance for many of the national parks in California. In addition to campground fees, expect to pay a park entrance fee ranging from $10–20 per vehicle, or as low as $5 per person for hike-in/bike-in (you can buy an annual National Parks Pass that waives entrance fees). This entrance fee is valid for seven days. For an additional fee, a Golden Eagle sticker can be added to the National Parks Pass, thereby eliminating entrance fees at sites managed by the U.S. Fish and Wildlife Service, the U.S. Forest Service, and the Bureau of Land Management. Various discounts are available for holders of Golden Age and Golden Access passports, including a 50 percent reduction of camping fees (group camps not included) and a waiver of park entrance fees.

For Yosemite National Park reservations, call 800/436-PARK (800/436-7275) or visit http://reservations.nps.gov. Major credit cards are accepted.

For all other national parks, call 800/365-CAMP (800/365-2267) or visit http://reservations.nps.gov. Major credit cards are accepted.

National Park Service
Pacific West Region
One Jackson Center
1111 Jackson Street, Suite 700
Oakland, CA 94607
510/817-1304
www.nps.gov

Cabrillo National Monument
1800 Cabrillo Memorial Drive
San Diego, CA 92106-3601
619/557-5450
fax 619/226-6311
www.nps.gov/cabr

Channel Islands National Park
1901 Spinnaker Drive
Ventura, CA 93001
805/658-5730
fax 805/658-5799
www.nps.gov/chis

Death Valley National Park
P.O. Box 579
Death Valley, CA 92328-0579
760/786-3200
fax 760/786-3283
www.nps.gov/deva

Devils Postpile National Monument
P.O. Box 3999
Mammoth Lakes, CA 93546
760/934-2289 (summer only)
fax 760/934-8896 (summer only)
www.nps.gov/depo
For year-round information, contact Sequoia and Kings Canyon National Parks (see listing).

Golden Gate National Recreation Area
Fort Mason, Building 201
San Francisco, CA 94123-0022
415/561-4700
fax 415/561-4710
www.nps.gov/goga

Joshua Tree National Park
74485 National Park Drive
Twentynine Palms, CA 92277-3597
760/367-5500
fax 760/367-6392
www.nps.gov/jotr

Lassen Volcanic National Park
P.O. Box 100
Mineral, CA 96063-0100
530/595-4444
fax 530/595-3262
www.nps.gov/lavo

Lava Beds National Monument
1 Indian Well Headquarters
Tulelake, CA 96134
530/667-2282
fax 530/667-2737
www.nps.gov/labe

Mojave National Preserve
2701 Barstow Road
Barstow, CA 92311
760/733-4040 (information)
fax 760/252-6174
www.nps.gov/moja

Pinnacles National Monument
5000 Highway 146
Paicines, CA 95043
831/389-4485
fax 831/389-4489
www.nps.gov/pinn

Point Reyes National Seashore
Point Reyes Station, CA 94956-9799
415/464-5100
fax 415/464-5149
www.nps.gov/pore

Redwood National and State Parks
1111 2nd Street
Crescent City, CA 95531
707/464-6101
fax 707/464-1812
www.nps.gov/redw

**Santa Monica Mountains
National Recreation Area**
401 West Hillcrest Drive
Thousand Oaks, CA 91360
805/370-2301
fax 805/370-1850
www.nps.gov/samo

**Sequoia and Kings Canyon
National Parks**
47050 Generals Highway
Three Rivers, CA 93271-9651
559/565-3341
www.nps.gov/seki

Smith River National Recreation Area
P.O. Box 228
Gasquet, CA 95543
707/457-3131
fax 707/457-3794
www.fs.fed.us/r5/sixrivers

Whiskeytown National Recreation Area
P.O. Box 188
Whiskeytown, CA 96095
530/246-1225 or 530/242-3400
fax 530/246-5154
www.nps.gov/whis

Yosemite National Park
P.O. Box 577
Yosemite National Park, CA 95389
209/372-0200 for 24-hour recorded message
www.nps.gov/yose

U.S. ARMY CORPS OF ENGINEERS

Some of the family camps and most of the group camps operated by the U.S. Army Corps of Engineers are on a reservation system. Reservations can be made up to 240 days in advance, and up to 360 days in advance for groups. To reserve a site, call 877/444-6777 or visit www.reserveusa.com. The reservation fee is usually $9, and major credit cards are accepted. Holders of Golden Age or Golden Access passports receive a 50 percent discount for campground fees, except for group sites.

Los Angeles District
915 Wilshire Boulevard, Suite 980
Los Angeles, CA 90017-3401
213/452-3908
fax 213/452-4209
www.spl.usace.army.mil

Sacramento District
1325 "J" Street
Sacramento, CA 95814
916/557-5100
www.spk.usace.army.mil

South Pacific Division
333 Market Street
San Francisco, CA 94105
415/977-8272
fax 415/977-8316
www.spn.usace.army.mil

BUREAU OF LAND MANAGEMENT

Most of the Bureau of Land Management (BLM) campgrounds are primitive and in remote areas. Often, there is no fee charged for camping. Holders of Golden Age or Golden Access passports receive a 50 percent discount, except for group camps, at BLM fee campgrounds.

Bureau of Land Management
California State Office
2800 Cottage Way, Suite W-1834
Sacramento, CA 95825-1886
916/978-4400
fax 916/978-4416
www.blm.gov/ca

Alturas Field Office
708 W. 12th Street
Alturas, CA 96101
530/233-4666
fax 530/233-5696
www.blm.gov/ca/alturas

Arcata Field Office
1695 Heindon Road
Arcata, CA 95521-4573
707/825-2300
fax 707/825-2301
www.blm.gov/ca/arcata

Bakersfield Field Office
3801 Pegasus Drive
Bakersfield, CA 93308
661/391-6000
fax 661/391-6040
www.blm.gov/ca/bakersfield

Barstow Field Office
2601 Barstow Road
Barstow, CA 92311
760/252-6000
fax 760/252-6099
www.blm.gov/ca/barstow

Bishop Field Office
351 Pacu Lane, Suite 100
Bishop, CA 93514
760/872-5000
fax 760/872-5050
www.blm.gov/ca/bishop

California Desert District Office
22835 Calle San Juan de los Lagos
Moreno Valley, CA 92553
951/697-5200
fax 951/697-5299
www.blm.gov/ca/cdd

Eagle Lake Field Office
2950 Riverside Drive
Susanville, CA 96130
530/257-0456
fax 530/257-4831
www.blm.gov/ca/eaglelake

El Centro Field Office
1661 S. 4th Street
El Centro, CA 92243
760/337-4400
fax 760/337-4490
www.blm.gov/ca/elcentro

Folsom Field Office
63 Natoma Street
Folsom, CA 95630
916/985-4474
fax 916/985-3259
www.blm.gov/ca/folsom

Hollister Field Office
20 Hamilton Court
Hollister, CA 95023
831/630-5000
fax 831/630-5055
www.blm.gov/ca/hollister

Palm Springs/South Coast Field Office
P.O. Box 581260
North Palm Springs, CA 92258-1260
760/251-4800
fax 760/251-4899
www.blm.gov/ca/palmsprings

Redding Field Office
355 Hemsted Drive
Redding, CA 96002
530/224-2100
fax 530/224-2172
www.blm.gov/ca/redding

Ridgecrest Field Office
300 S. Richmond Road
Ridgecrest, CA 93555
760/384-5400
fax 760/384-5499
www.blm.gov/ca/ridgecrest

Ukiah Field Office
2550 N. State Street
Ukiah, CA 95482
707/468-4000
fax 707/468-4027
www.blm.gov/ca/ukiah

OTHER VALUABLE RESOURCES
State Forests
Jackson Demonstration State Forest
802 N. Main Street
Fort Bragg, CA 95437
707/964-5674
fax 707/964-0941

Mountain Home Demonstration State Forest
P.O. Box 517
Springville, CA 93265
559/539-2321 (summer)
559/539-2855 (winter)

County/Regional Park Departments
Del Norte County Parks
840 9th Street, Suite 11
Crescent City, CA 95531
707/464-7230
fax 707/464-5824
www.co.del-norte.ca.us

East Bay Regional Park District
P.O. Box 5381
Oakland, CA 94605-0381
510/562-PARK (510/562-7275) or
510/544-2200
fax 510/635-3478
www.ebparks.org

Humboldt County Parks
1106 2nd Street
Eureka, CA 95501
707/445-7651
fax 707/445-7409
www.co.humboldt.ca.us/

Marin Municipal Water District
220 Nellen Avenue
Corte Madera, CA 94925
415/945-1455
fax 415/927-4953
www.marinwater.org

Midpeninsula Regional Open Space District
330 Distel Circle
Los Altos, CA 94022-1404
650/691-1200
fax 650/691-0485
www.openspace.org

Pacific Gas and Electric Company
Corporate Real Estate/Recreation
5555 Florin-Perkins Road, Room 100
Sacramento, CA 95826
916/386-5164
fax 916/923-7044
www.pge.com/recreation

Sacramento County Regional Parks
3711 Branch Center Road
Sacramento, CA 95827
916/875-6961
fax 916/875-6050
www.sacparks.net

San Diego County
Parks and Recreation Department
2454 Heritage Park Row
San Diego, CA 92110
858/694-3049
fax 619/260-6492
www.co.san-diego.ca.us/parks

San Luis Obispo County
Parks Department
1087 Santa Rosa Street
San Luis Obispo, CA 93408
805/781-5930
fax 805/781-1102
www.slocountyparks.org

San Mateo County
Parks and Recreation Department
455 County Center, 4th Floor
Redwood City, CA 94063-1646
650/363-4020
fax 650/599-1721
www.eparks.net

Santa Barbara County
Parks and Recreation Department
610 Mission Canyon Road
Santa Barbara, CA 93105
805/568-2461
fax 805/568-2459
www.sbparks.com

Santa Clara County Parks Department
298 Garden Hill Drive
Los Gatos, CA 95032-7669
408/355-2200
fax 408/355-2290
www.parkhere.org

Sonoma County Regional Parks
2300 County Center Drive, Suite 120-A
Santa Rosa, CA 95404
707/565-2041
fax 707/579-8247
www.sonoma-county.org/parks

State and Federal Offices
California Department of
Boating and Waterways
2000 Evergreen Street, Suite 100
Sacramento, CA 95815-3888
916/263-1331 or 888/326-2822
www.dbw.ca.gov

California Department of Fish and Game
1416 9th Street, 12th Floor
Sacramento, CA 95814
916/445-0411
www.dfg.ca.gov

California Department of
Water Resources
1416 9th Street
P.O. Box 942836
Sacramento, CA 94236
916/653-6192
www.dwr.water.ca.gov

U.S. Fish and Wildlife Service
1849 C Street NW
Washington, DC 20240
800/344-WILD (800/344-9453)
or 202/208-4131
www.fws.gov

U.S. Geological Survey
Branch of Information Services
P.O. Box 25286, Bldg. 810,
MS 306, Federal Center
Denver, CO 80225
888/ASK-USGS (888/275-8747)
or 303/202-4700
www.usgs.gov

Information Services

Lake County Visitor Information Center
P.O. Box 1025
6110 East Highway 20
Lucerne, CA 95458
707/274-5652 or 800/525-3743
fax 707/274-5664
www.lakecounty.com

Mammoth Lakes Visitors Bureau
P.O. Box 48
437 Old Mammoth Road, Suite Y
Mammoth Lakes, CA 93546
888/GO-MAMMOTH (888/466-2666) or
760/934-2712
fax 760/934-7066
www.visitmammoth.com

Mount Shasta Visitors Bureau
300 Pine Street
Mount Shasta, CA 96067
530/926-4865 or 800/926-4865
fax 530/926-0976
www.mtshastachamber.com

The Nature Conservancy of California
201 Mission Street, 4th Floor
San Francisco, CA 94105-1832
415/777-0487
fax 415/777-0244
www.nature.org/california

Plumas County Visitors Bureau
550 Crescent Street
P.O. Box 4120
Quincy, CA 95971
530/283-6345 or 800/326-2247
fax 530/283-5465
www.plumascounty.org

Shasta Cascade Wonderland Association
1699 Highway 273
Anderson, CA 96007
530/365-7500 or 800/474-2782
fax 530/365-1258
www.shastacascade.com

Map Sources

Map Link
30 S. La Patera Lane, Unit 5
Goleta, CA 93117
805/692-6777 or 800/962-1394
fax 805/692-6787 or 800/627-7768
www.maplink.com

Olmsted and Bros. Map Company
P.O. Box 5351
Berkeley, CA 94705
tel./fax 510/658-6534

Tom Harrison Maps
2 Falmouth Cove
San Rafael, CA 94901-4465
tel./fax 415/456-7940 or 800/265-9090
www.tomharrisonmaps.com

U.S. Forest Service
Attn: Map Sales
P.O. Box 8268
Missoula, MT 59807
406/329-3024
fax 406/329-3030
www.fs.fed.us/recreation/nationalforeststore

U.S. Geological Survey
Branch of Information Services
P.O. Box 25286, Federal Center
Denver, CO 80225
303/202-4700 or
    888/ASK-USGS (888/275-8747)
fax 303/202-4693
www.usgs.gov

ANGLING RECORDS

FISH TALES: TOM STIENSTRA'S TOP CATCHES

species	weight	line
Sturgeon	400 lb.	30-lb. line
Shark	178 lb.	wire line
Sailfish	160 lb.	14-lb. test line
Tarpon	125 lb.	14-lb. line
Halibut	98 lb.	30-lb. line
Dorado	60 lb.	20-lb. line
Lake trout	42 lb.	8-lb. line
Yellowtail	38 lb.	20-lb. line
King salmon	32 lb.	20-lb. line
Striped bass	26 lb.	14-lb. line
Steelhead	17 lb.	8-lb. line
Atlantic bonito	15 lb. (nonregistered world record)	14-lb. line
Silver salmon	12 lb.	fly rod, 8-lb. tippet
Rainbow trout	11 lb.	fly rod, 6-lb. tippet
Catfish	11 lb.	8-lb. line
Largemouth bass	8 lb.	8-lb. line
Bonefish	7 lb.	fly rod, 8-lb. tippet
Brown trout	6 lb.	4-lb. line
Arctic grayling	3 lb. 8 oz.	4-lb. line
Cutthroat trout	3 lb. 8 oz.	6-lb. line

The Big Ones That Got Away...

You never dream about the fish you caught. But, damn, those ones that got away can haunt you: a 2,000-pound white shark; a tuna that spooled me in the Caribbean; a line-class world-record sturgeon (90-pounder on 8-pound line) after a long fight; and, of course, Jargo, the monstrous rainbow trout, by far my life-best, that spooled my fly reel on the Moraine River in Alaska. But it was a brown trout that realigned my senses that takes it all: a 24-pound brown trout at Lake Almanor, lost near the boat. Hal Janssen later caught, weighed, and released the same fish within 30 yards of the same spot.

CALIFORNIA ALL-TACKLE RECORDS
Freshwater

species	weight	location	angler	date
Bass, largemouth	22 lb. 0 oz.	Castaic Lake	Bob Crupi	March 15, 1991
Bass, smallmouth	9 lb. 13 oz.	Trinity Lake	Harold Hardin	July 3, 2007
Bass, spotted	10 lb. 4 oz.	Pine Flat Lake	Brian Shishido	May 3, 2001

Bass, striped	67 lb. 8 oz.	O'Neill Forebay	Hank Ferguson	May 7, 1992
Bass, white	5 lb. 5 oz.	Colorado River	Milton Mize	May 8, 1972
Bluegill	3 lb. 14 oz.	Rancho Murrieta Res.	Michael Holoubek	June 23, 2008
Brown bullhead	4 lb. 8 oz.	Trinity Lake	Garry Dittenbir	October 7, 1993
Carp	52 lb. 0 oz.	Lake Nacimiento	Lee Fryant	April 1968
Catfish, blue	113 lb. 5 oz.	San Vicente Res.	Steve Oudomsouk	July, 24, 2008
Catfish, channel	53 lb. 8 oz.	San Joaquin River	Randall Gilbert, Jr.	Sept. 22, 2008
Catfish, flathead	72 lb. 14 oz.	Colorado River	Billy Potter	April 22, 2003
Catfish, white	22 lb. 0 oz.	William Land Park Pond	James Robinson	March 21, 1994
Crappie, black	4 lb. 1 oz.	New Hogan Reservoir	Wilma Honey	March 29, 1975
Crappie, white	4 lb. 8 oz.	Clear Lake	Carol Carlton	April 26, 1971
Grayling, arctic	1 lb. 12 oz.	Lobdell Lake	Don Acton Jr.	August 27, 1974
Perch, Sacramento	3 lb. 10 oz.	Crowley Lake	Jack Johnson	May 22, 1979
Salmon, king	88 lb. 0 oz.	Sacramento River	Lindy Lindberg	November 21, 1979
Salmon, kokanee	4 lb. 13 oz.	Lake Tahoe	Dick Bournique	August 1, 1973
Salmon, silver	22 lb. 0 oz.	Lagunitas Creek	Milton Hain	January 3, 1959
Shad, American	7 lb. 5 oz.	Feather River	Craig Stillwell	May 9, 1985
Sturgeon	468 lb. 0 oz.	San Pablo Bay	Joey Pallotta	July 9, 1983
Sunfish, redear	5 lb. 3 oz.	Folsom South Canal	Anthony White Jr.	June 27, 1994
Trout, brook	9 lb. 12 oz.	Silver Lake	Texas Haynes	September 9, 1932
Trout, brown	26 lb. 8 oz.	Upper Twin Lake	Danny Stearman	April 30, 1987
Trout, cutthroat	31 lb. 8 oz.	Lake Tahoe	William Pomin	1911
Trout, golden	9 lb. 8 oz.	Virginia Lakes	O. A. Benefield	August 18, 1952
Trout, Mackinaw	37 lb. 6 oz.	Lake Tahoe	Robert Aronsen	June 21, 1974
Trout, steelhead	27 lb. 4 oz.	Smith River	Robert Halley	December 22, 1976
Trout, rainbow (inland lake)	23 lb. 0 oz.	Lake Natoma	Jeremy Brucklacher	January 17, 2000
Trout, rainbow (hatchery, lake)	28 lb. 5 oz.	Butte County pond	James Harrold	June 3, 2006

Saltwater

species	weight	location	angler	date
Albacore	90 lb. 0 oz.	Santa Cruz	Don Giberson	October 21, 1997
Barracuda	15 lb. 15 oz.	San Onofre	C. O. Taylor	August 24, 1957
Bass, barred sand	13 lb. 3 oz.	Huntington Flats	Robert Halal	August 29, 1988
Bass, kelp	14 lb. 7 oz.	San Clemente Island	C. O. Taylor	July 30, 1958
Bonito, Pacific	21 lb. 5 oz.	181 Spot	Kim Larson	October 19, 2003

Cabezon	23 lb. 4 oz.	Los Angeles	Bruce Kuhn	April 20, 1958
Dorado (dolphinfish)	66 lb. 0 oz.	209 Spot	Kim Carson	September 9, 1990
Flounder, starry	11 lb. 4 oz.	San Simeon	Steve Doshier	August 29, 1993
Halibut	67 lb. 4 oz.	Santa Rosa Island	Francisco Rivera	July 1, 2011
Lingcod	56 lb. 0 oz.	Crescent City/ Point St. George Reef	Carey Mitchell	July 12, 1992
Mackerel, jack	5 lb. 8 oz.	Huntington Beach	Joe Bairian	September 1, 1988
Marlin, blue	692 lb. 0 oz.	Balboa	A. Hamann	August 18, 1931
Marlin, striped	339 lb. 0 oz.	Catalina Island	Gary Jasper	July 4, 1985
Opaleye	6 lb. 4 oz.	Los Flores Creek	Leonard Itkoff	May 13, 1956
Ray, bat	181 lb. 0 oz.	Huntington Beach	Bradley Dew	July 24, 1978
Rockfish, black	9 lb. 2 oz.	San Francisco Mile Light/ Light Station	Trent Wilcox	September 3, 1988
Rockfish, bocaccio	17 lb. 8 oz.	Crescent City/ Point St. George Reef	Sam Strait	October 25, 1987
Rockfish, copper	8 lb. 5 oz.	Pigeon Point	Kenny Aab	August 18, 1985
Rockfish, yelloweye	18 lb. 3 oz.	Piedras Blancas	John Crossey	April 15, 1994
Salmon, king	65 lb. 4 oz.	Crescent City	Frank Cox	August 21, 2002
Seabass, white	78 lb. 0 oz.	Monterey	David Sternberg	April 4, 2002
Shark, blue	258 lb. 8 oz.	Channel Islands	Josh Ware Bollinger	August 29, 2008
Shark, mako	1,098 lb. 6 oz.	Anacapa Island	Sean Gizatullin	July 24, 2010
Shark, seven-gill	276 lb. 0 oz.	Humboldt Bay	Cliff Brewer	October 17, 1996
Shark, thresher	575 lb. 0 oz.	Carlsbad Canyon	Daniel Lara	May 26, 2007
Sheepshead, California	30 lb. 8 oz.	Newport Beach	Matt Freis	August 29, 2009
Surfperch, barred	4 lb. 2 oz.	Morro Bay	Artie J. Ferguson	November 8, 1995
Surfperch, barred (tie)	4 lb. 2 oz.	Oxnard	Fred Oakley	March 30, 1996
Swordfish	452 lb. 8 oz.	Catalina Island	David Denholm	September 30, 2003
Tuna, bigeye	240 lb. 0 oz.	Butterfly Bank	Steve Hutchinson	August 1, 1987
Tuna, bluefin	243 lb. 11 oz.	277 Spot	Karl Schmidbauer	September 8, 1990
Tuna, skipjack	26 lb. 0 oz.	San Diego	William Hall	August 28, 1970
Tuna, yellowfin	239 lb. 0 oz.	Catalina Island	Ronald Howarth	November 4, 1984
Whitefish	13 lb. 12 oz.	Cortes Bank	Bob Schwenk	April 23, 1988
Yellowtail	63 lb. 1 oz.	Santa Barbara Island	Kwang Nam Lee	June 18, 2000

IGFA ALL-TACKLE WORLD RECORDS

species	weight	location	angler	date
Albacore	88 lb. 2 oz.	Canary Island	Siegfried Dickemann	November 19, 1977
Barracuda, Pacific	26 lb. 8 oz.	Costa Rica	Doug Hettinger	January 3, 1999
Bass, kelp	14 lb. 7 oz.	Newport Beach, CA	Thomas Murphy	October 2, 1993
Bass, largemouth (tie)	22 lb. 4 oz.	Georgia	George Perry	June 2, 1932
Bass, largemouth (tie)	22 lb. 4 oz.	Japan	Kurita Manabu	July 2, 2009
Bass, smallmouth	11 lb. 15 oz.	Tennessee	David Hayes	July 9, 1955
Bass, spotted	10 lb. 4 oz.	Pine Flat Lake, CA	Bryan Shishido	April 21, 2001
Bass, striped (landlocked)	67 lb. 8 oz.	O'Neill Forebay, CA	Hank Ferguson	May 7, 1992
Bass, striped (nonlandlocked)	78 lb. 8 oz.	New Jersey	Al McReynolds	September 21, 1982
Bluegill	4 lb. 12 oz.	Alabama	T. S. Hudson	April 9, 1950
Bonito, Pacific	21 lb. 5 oz.	181 Spot, CA	Kim Larson	October 19, 2003
Catfish, channel	58 lb. 0 oz.	South Carolina	W. B. Whaley	July 7, 1964
Catfish, blue	143 lb. 0 oz.	Virginia	Richard Anderson	June 8, 2011
Crappie, black	5 lb. 0 oz.	Missouri	John Horstman	April 21, 2006
Crappie, white	5 lb. 3 oz.	Mississippi	Fred Bright	July 31, 1957
Halibut, California	58 lb. 9 oz.	Santa Rosa Island, CA	Roger Borrell	June 26, 1999
Halibut, Pacific	459 lb. 0 oz.	Alaska	Jack Tragis	June 11, 1996
Lingcod	82 lb. 9 oz.	Alaska	Robert Hammond	July 27, 2009
Marlin, Pacific blue	1,376 lb. 0 oz.	Hawaii	Jay deBeaubien	May 31, 1982
Marlin, striped	494 lb. 0 oz.	New Zealand	Bill Boniface	January 16, 1986
Perch, yellow	4 lb. 3 oz.	New Jersey	C. C. Abbot	May 1865
Sailfish, Pacific	221 lb. 0 oz.	Ecuador	C. W. Stewart	February 12, 1947
Salmon, king (chinook)	97 lb. 4 oz.	Alaska	Les Anderson	May 17, 1985
Salmon, sockeye	15 lb. 3 oz.	Alaska	Stan Roach	August 9, 1987
Salmon, silver (coho)	33 lb. 4 oz.	New York	Jerry Lifton	September 27, 1989
Sea bass, white	83 lb. 12 oz.	Mexico	L. C. Baumgardner	March 31, 1953
Shad, American	11 lb. 4 oz.	Massachusetts	Bob Thibodo	May 19, 1986
Shark, blue	528 lb. 0 oz.	New York	Joe Seidel	August 9, 2001
Shark, hammerhead	1,280 lb. 0 oz.	Florida	Bucky Dennis	May 23, 2006
Shark, white	2,664 lb. 0 oz.	Australia	Alfred Dean	April 21, 1959
Sturgeon	468 lb. 0 oz.	San Pablo Bay, CA	Joey Pallotta	July 9, 1983
Sunfish, redear	5 lb. 8 oz.	Lake Havasu, CA	Robert Lawler	May 2, 2011

Trout, brook	14 lb. 8 oz.	Canada	W. J. Cook	July 1916
Trout, brown	41 lb. 8 oz.	Wisconsin	Roger Hellen	July 16, 2010
Trout, cutthroat	41 lb. 0 oz.	Nevada	John Skimmerhorn	December 1925
Trout, golden	11 lb. 0 oz.	Wyoming	Charles Reed	August 5, 1948
Trout, Mackinaw (lake)	72 lb. 0 oz.	Canada	Lloyd Bull	August 19, 1995
Trout, rainbow	48 lb. 0 oz.	Canada	Sean Konrad	September 5, 2009
Tuna, bigeye (Pacific)	435 lb. 0 oz.	Peru	Russell Lee	April 17, 1957
Tuna, yellowfin	405 lb. 0 oz.	Mexico	Mike Livingston	January 30, 2010
Wahoo	184 lb. 0 oz.	Mexico	Sara Hayward	July 29, 2005
Yellowtail, California	109 lb. 2 oz.	Japan	Masakazu Taniwaki	October 24, 2009

For information about world records, contact the International Game Fish Association at www.IFGA.org. For information about California state records, contact the Department of Fish and Game at www.dfg.ca.gov.

Index

Acknowledgments

The fishing experts who contributed to this book are like a Fishing Hall of Fame. I am indebted to each for their great skills and abilities and for their willingness to share their expertise. The following were involved at some point and provided input for the book:

Senior research editor: Kathie Morgan

Field editor: Bob Simms

Tackle editors: Eric Naig, Jonah Li, Ed Rice, Kevin Jarnagin, John Beath

FRESHWATER

Bluegill, sunfish, and crappie: Tom Hedtke, Larry Green, Claude Davis, Clyde Gibbs, Bob Stienstra Sr.

Catfish: George Powers, Elvin Bishop, Michael Furniss

Fishing private ponds: Brian Riley, Jim Byrne, John Reginato, Ed Ow, Bob Simms, Tom Hedtke

Kokanee salmon: Bob Simms, Gary Coe, Gary Miralles

Largemouth bass: Jim Munk, Skeet Reese, Gary Dobyns, Jonah Li, Jack Neu, Sheldon Bright, Bob Simms, Larry Brower, Bob Robb, Terry Knight, Clancy Enlow

Mackinaw trout: Al Bruzza, Dan Hannum, Trevor Slaymaker, Mike Gaddis

Salmon: Al Vasconcellos, Chuck Harrison, Hank Mautz, Ray Beadle, Hal Janssen

Shad: Bill Adelman

Steelhead: Jim Csutoras, Michael Furniss, Ed Rice, Ed Moon, Dale Lackey, Albert Kutzkey, Tim Kutzkey, Jack Ellis

Sturgeon: Keith Fraser, Charlie Foster, Abe Cuanang, Hippo Lau, Armand Castagna, Dusty Baker

Trout: Ed Dunckel, Ed Rice, Jack Trout, Hal Janssen, Dave Lyons, Rambob Stienstra Jr., Ted Fay, Bob Simms, Dan Blanton, Gary Borger, Joe Kimsey, Gary Miralles, Dan Bacher, Guy Carl, Ray Rychnovsky, Rob Brown, Bill Sunderland, Don Vachini, Kathie Morgan

White bass: Wayne Smith, Ken Sauret

SALTWATER

Albacore and other tuna: Todd Magaline, Ron Gribble, Jonah Li, Roger Thomas, Jack Brown, Tom Rothery, Tom Coster

Bonito: Clyde Gibbs, Bob Robb, Rolla Williams, Jack Brown

Halibut: Cliff Anfinson, Ron Payden, Bill Dittman, Bill Beebe, Art Roby, Chuck Louie

Rockfish and lingcod: Frank Bodegraven, Craig Stone, Jonah Li, Bob Smith, Kurt Hochberg, Angelo Cuanang, Jim Klinger, Kathie Morgan, Jeremy Keyston, Kris Keyston, Mike Gaddis

Salmon: Dick Pool, Jacqueline Douglas, Roger Thomas, Craig Stone, Galen Onizuka, Jim McDaniel, Jim Klinger, Ed Migale, Doug Laughlin

Sharks: Jim Siegle, Dick Pool, Marc Cretarolo

Striped bass: Barry Canevaro, Chuck Louie, Cliff Anfinson, Abe Cuanang, Dick Walton, Bob Simms, Craig Hanson

Yellowtail: Scott Costa, Pat McDonell, Charlie Meyers, Randy Case, Bill Karr

Book overview: Kathie Morgan, Bob Simms, Ron Gribble, Al Bruzza, Rich Holland, Ed Dunckel, Dan Bacher, Pat McDonell, J. D. Richey, Robyn Schlueter, Janet Connaughton, Stephani Cruickshank, Bill Karr

Notes

Notes

Notes

Notes

Notes

Notes

www.moon.com

DESTINATIONS | ACTIVITIES | BLOGS | MAPS | BOOKS

MOON.COM is ready to help plan your next trip! Filled with fresh trip ideas and strategies, author interviews, informative travel blogs, a detailed map library, and descriptions of all the Moon guidebooks, Moon.com is all you need to get out and explore the world—or even places in your own backyard. While at Moon.com, sign up for our monthly e-newsletter for updates on new releases, travel tips, and expert advice from our on-the-go Moon authors. As always, when you travel with Moon, expect an experience that is uncommon and truly unique.

KEEP UP WITH MOON ON FACEBOOK AND TWITTER
JOIN THE MOON PHOTO GROUP ON FLICKR